Economics

Fourteenth Edition

Roger A. Arnold
California State University
San Marcos

Daniel R. Arnold
University of California, Berkeley

David H. Arnold
University of California, San Diego

Australia • Brazil • Canada • Mexico • Singapore • United Kingdom • United States

Economics, 14e
Roger A. Arnold, Daniel R. Arnold, David H. Arnold

SVP, Higher Education Product Management: Erin Joyner

VP, Product Management, Learning Experiences: Thais Alencar

Product Director: Joe Sabatino

Product Manager: Chris Rader

Product Assistant: Autumn Lala-Sonora

Learning Designer: Sarah Keeling

Senior Content Manager: Colleen A Farmer

Digital Delivery Quality Partner: Dan Swanson

Executive Product Marketing Manager: John Carey

IP Analyst: Ashley Maynard

IP Project Manager: Kumaresan Chandrakumar

Production Service: Straive

Designer: Chris Doughman

Cover Image Source: W. Phokin/Shutterstock.com and enviromantic/Getty Images

© 2023, 2019, 2016 Cengage Learning, Inc.

Unless otherwise noted, all content is Copyright © Cengage Learning, Inc.

ALL RIGHTS RESERVED. No part of this work covered by the copyright herein may be reproduced or distributed in any form or by any means, except as permitted by U.S. copyright law, without the prior written permission of the copyright owner.

For product information and technology assistance, contact us at
Cengage Customer & Sales Support, 1-800-354-9706
or support.cengage.com.

For permission to use material from this text or product, submit all requests online at **www.copyright.com**.

Library of Congress Control Number: 2021921067

ISBN: 978-0-357-72037-0

Cengage
200 Pier 4 Boulevard
Boston, MA 02210
USA

Cengage is a leading provider of customized learning solutions with employees residing in nearly 40 different countries and sales in more than 125 countries around the world. Find your local representative at **www.cengage.com**.

To learn more about Cengage platforms and services, register or access your online learning solution, or purchase materials for your course, visit **www.cengage.com**.

Printed in the United States of America
Print Number: 01   Print Year: 2022

Brief Contents

An Introduction to Economics

Part 1 — Economics: The Science of Scarcity
- Chapter 1 What Economics Is About 1
- Chapter 2 Production Possibilities Frontier Framework 40
- Chapter 3 Supply and Demand: Theory 58
- Chapter 4 Prices: Free, Controlled, and Relative 93
- Chapter 5 Supply, Demand, and Price: Applications 111

Macroeconomics

Part 2 — Macroeconomic Fundamentals
- Chapter 6 Macroeconomic Measurements, Part I: Prices and Unemployment 134
- Chapter 7 Macroeconomic Measurements, Part II: GDP and Real GDP 151

Part 3 — Macroeconimic Stability, Instability, and Fiscal Policy
- Chapter 8 Aggregate Demand and Aggregate Supply 174
- Chapter 9 Classical Macroeconomics and the Self-Regulating Economy 205
- Chapter 10 Keynesian Macroeconomics and Economic Instability: A Critique of the Self-Regulating Economy 229
- Chapter 11 Fiscal Policy and the Federal Budget 260

Part 4 — Money, the Economy, and Monetary Policy
- Chapter 12 Money, Banking, and the Financial System 284
- Chapter 13 The Federal Reserve System 299
- Chapter 14 Money and the Economy 318
- Chapter 15 Monetary Policy 348

Part 5 — Expectations and Growth
- Chapter 16 Expectations Theory and the Economy 374
- Chapter 17 Economic Growth: Resources, Technology, Ideas, and Institutions 400

Part 6 — Creative Destruction and Crony Capitalism
- Chapter 18 Creative Destruction and Crony Capitalism: Two Forces on the Economic Landscape Today 416

Microeconomics

Part 7 — Microeconomic Fundamentals
- Chapter 19 Elasticity 432
- Chapter 20 Consumer Choice: Maximizing Utility and Behavioral Economics 460
- Chapter 21 Production and Costs 488

Part 8 — Product Markets and Policies
- Chapter 22 Perfect Competition 521
- Chapter 23 Monopoly 549
- Chapter 24 Monopolistic Competition, Oligopoly, and Game Theory 572
- Chapter 25 Government and Product Markets: Antitrust and Regulation 593

Part 9 — Factor Markets and Related Issues
- Chapter 26 Factor Markets: With Emphasis on the Labor Market 611
- Chapter 27 Wages, Unions, and Labor 635
- Chapter 28 The Distribution of Income and Poverty 650
- Chapter 29 Interest, Rent, and Profit 667

Part 10 — Health Economics
- Chapter 30 Health Economics: Experiments, Disparities, and Prices 685

Part 11 — Market Failure, Public Choice, and Special-Interest Group Politics
- Chapter 31 Market Failure: Externalities, Public Goods, and Asymmetric Information 704
- Chapter 32 Public Choice and Special-Interest Group Politics 732

Part 12 — Economic Theories and Research
- Chapter 33 New Frontiers in Economic Research: Causal Inference and Machine Learning 752

The Global Economy

Part 13 — International Trade and Finance
- Chapter 34 International Trade 774
- Chapter 35 International Finance 791

Self-Test Appendix 809
Glossary 833
Index 845

*In memory of Craig Rader.
A staunch believer in and shining example
of the power of learning and education.*

Contents

Preface xxii

An Introduction to Economics

Part 1 Economics: The Science of Scarcity

Economics 24/7

Rationing Spots at Yale 5

When Is It Too Costly to Attend College? 8

Movie Studios Versus Netflix: Incentives Matter 11

Why Didn't I Think of That? The Case of Uber and Airbnb 14

 **Office Hours**

"I Don't Believe That Every Time a Person Does Something, He Compares the Marginal Benefits and Costs." 19

Chapter 1 What Economics Is About 1

Your Life, 2024–2034 1
A Definition of Economics 2
   Goods and Bads 2   Resources 2
   Scarcity and a Definition of Economics 2
Key Concepts in Economics 4
   Opportunity Cost 4   Opportunity Cost and Behavior 6   Benefits and Costs 7   Decisions Made at the Margin 7   Efficiency 9   Economics Is About Incentives 11   Unintended Effects 12   Exchange 13
***Ceteris Paribus* and Theory** 15
   Ceteris Paribus Thinking 15   What Is a Theory? 16
Economic Categories 18
   Positive Economics and Normative Economics 18   Microeconomics and Macroeconomics 19
Chapter Summary 20
Key Terms and Concepts 22
Questions and Problems 22

Appendix A Working with Diagrams 24

A-1 Slope of a Line 25
A-2 Slope of a Line is Constant 26
A-3 Slope of a Curve 26
A-4 The 45-Degree Line 26
A-5 Pie Charts 28
A-6 Bar Graphs 28
A-7 Line Graphs 30
Appendix Summary 31

Appendix B Should You Major in Economics? 33

B-1 Five Myths About Economics and Being an Economics Major 34
B-2 What Awaits You as an Economics Major? 36
B-3 What Do Economists Do? 37
B-4 Places to Find More Information 38
B-5 Concluding Remarks 39

Chapter 2 Production Possibilities Frontier Framework 40

The Production Possibilities Frontier 40
The Straight-Line PPF: Constant Opportunity Costs 40 The Bowed-Outward (Concave-Downward) PPF: Increasing Opportunity Costs 41 Law of Increasing Opportunity Costs 44 Economic Concepts in a Production Possibilities Frontier Framework 45

Specialization and Trade Can Move Us Beyond Our PPF 51
A Simple Two-Person PPF Model 51 On or Beyond the PPF? 52

Chapter Summary 55
Key Terms and Concepts 55
Questions and Problems 55

Chapter 3 Supply and Demand: Theory 58

What Is Demand? 58
The Law of Demand 59 Four Ways to Represent the Law of Demand 59 Why Does Quantity Demanded Go Down as Price Goes Up? 60 Individual Demand Curve and Market Demand Curve 61 A Change in Quantity Demanded Versus a Change in Demand 62 What Factors Cause the Demand Curve to Shift? 64 It Is Important to Know Why the Price Changed: Back to Substitutes and Complements 66 Movement Factors and Shift Factors 67

Supply 68
The Law of Supply 68 Why Most Supply Curves Are Upward Sloping 70 Changes in Supply Mean Shifts in Supply Curves 71 What Factors Cause the Supply Curve to Shift? 71 A Change in Supply Versus a Change in Quantity Supplied 73

The Market: Putting Supply and Demand Together 74
Supply and Demand at Work at an Auction 74 The Language of Supply and Demand: A Few Important Terms 75 Moving to Equilibrium: What Happens to Price When There Is a Surplus or a Shortage? 75 Speed of Moving to Equilibrium 77 Moving to Equilibrium: Maximum and Minimum Prices 78 The Connection Between Equilibrium and Predictions 79 Equilibrium in Terms of Consumers' and Producers' Surplus 80 What Can Change Equilibrium Price and Quantity? 83 Epilogue: Who Feeds Cleveland? 85

Chapter Summary 89
Key Terms and Concepts 89
Questions and Problems 90

Economics 24/7

The PPF and You 43

Deducing Where Sherlock Holmes Was on His Production Possibilities Frontier 45

The Covid-19 Pandemic and the PPF 48

Studying and Your PPF 50

 Office Hours

"What Purpose Does the PPF Serve?" 54

Economics 24/7

Higher Demand Causes Higher Prices and Higher Sales 77

Stoic Philosophy, Search Engines, and Consumers' Surplus 82

Shake Shack and Hamburger Prices 85

"Sorry, But This Flight Has Been Overbooked" 87

Office Hours

"I Thought Prices Equaled Costs Plus 10 Percent" 88

Contents

Economics 24/7

1973 and 1979 98

Does It Matter if the Demand Curve for Unskilled Labor Is Steep or Not? 101

What Does Price Have to Do with Being Late to Class? 104

Obesity and a Soda Tax 107

Office Hours

"I Thought Price Ceilings Were Good for Consumers" 108

Office Hours

"Doesn't High Demand Mean High Quantity Demanded?" 130

Chapter 4   Prices: Free, Controlled, and Relative 93

Price 93
　Price as a Rationing Device 93   Price as a Transmitter of Information 94

Price Controls 95
　Price Ceiling 95   Price Floor: Definition and Effects 99

Two Prices: Absolute and Relative 105
　Absolute (Money) Price and Relative Price 105   Taxes on Specific Goods and Relative Price Changes 106

Chapter Summary 109

Key Terms and Concepts 109

Questions and Problems 109

Chapter 5   Supply, Demand, and Price: Applications 111

Application 1: U-Haul Rates and Demand 111
Application 2: Subsidizing the Consumption of Anything Can Raise Its Price 112
Application 3: 10 A.M. Classes in College 114
Application 4: Why Do Colleges Use GPAs, ACTs, and SATs for Purposes of Admission? 116
Application 5: Why Is Medical Care So Expensive? 117
Application 6: Do You Pay for Good Weather? 119
Application 7: The Price of an Aisle Seat 121
Application 8: College Superathletes 122
Application 9: Easier-to-Obtain Loans and Higher Housing Prices 124
Application 10: Speculators, Price Variability, and Patterns 125
Application 11: Supply and Demand on a Freeway 126
Application 12: Are Renters Better Off? 128
Chapter Summary 131
Questions and Problems 132

Part 2   Macroeconomic Fundamentals

Economics 24/7

The Beatles at Shea Stadium 139

Houses for $30,000 and Gas at 35¢ a Gallon 139

Who Should Be Considered Unemployed? 144

Chapter 6   Macroeconomic Measurements, Part I: Prices and Unemployment 134

Measuring the Price Level 134
　Using the CPI to Compute the Price Level 134   Inflation and the CPI 136   The Personal Consumption Expenditure (PCE) Index 137   Converting Dollars from One Year to Another 138

Measuring Unemployment 140
　Who Are the Unemployed? 140   The Unemployment Rate and the Employment Rate 141   Common Misconceptions About the Unemployment and Employment Rates 142   Reasons for Unemployment 142   Discouraged Workers 142   Types of Unemployment 143   The Natural Unemployment Rate and Full Employment 144   Cyclical Unemployment 145

Office Hours

"Is There More Than One Reason the Unemployment Rate Will Fall?" 147

Gross Family Product 154

Money and Happiness 154

An Identity Is Not a Causal Theory 160

Office Hours

"Why Do We Use the Expenditure Approach to Measure Production?" 169

Chapter Summary 148
Key Terms and Concepts 149
Questions and Problems 149

Chapter 7 Macroeconomic Measurements, Part II: GDP and Real GDP 151

Gross Domestic Product 151
Calculating GDP 151 Final Goods and Intermediate Goods 152 What GDP Omits 152 GDP Is Not Adjusted for Bads Generated in the Production of Goods 153 Per-Capita GDP 153

The Expenditure Approach to Computing GDP for a Real-World Economy 156
Using the Expenditure Approach to Compute GDP 158 Why We Subtract *IM* From $C + I + G + EX$ 159 Common Misconceptions About Increases in GDP 159

The Income Approach to Computing GDP for a Real-World Economy 161
Computing National Income 161 From National Income to GDP: Making Some Adjustments 163 Other National Income Accounting Measurements 164 Net Domestic Product 164 Personal Income 165 Disposable Income 165

Real GDP 165
Why We Need Real GDP 165 Computing Real GDP 166 The General Equation for Real GDP 166 What Does It Mean if Real GDP Is Higher in One Year Than in Another? 167 Real GDP, Economic Growth, and Business Cycles 167

Chapter Summary 170
Key Terms and Concepts 171
Questions and Problems 171

Part 3 Macroeconomic Stability, Instability, and Fiscal Policy

When Would You Want to Be Paid in a Currency Other Than U.S. Dollars? 188

Your First Job After College May Depend on the *AD* and *SRAS* Curves 198

Office Hours

"What Purpose Does the AD–AS Framework Serve?" 200

Chapter 8 Aggregate Demand and Aggregate Supply 174

A Way to View the Economy 174

Aggregate Demand 175
Why Does the Aggregate Demand Curve Slope Downward? 176 An Important Word on the Three Effects 179 A Change in Quantity Demanded of Real GDP Versus a Change in Aggregate Demand 179 Changes in Aggregate Demand: Shifts in the *AD* Curve 180 How Spending Components Affect Aggregate Demand 181 Why Is There More Total Spending? 182 Factors That Can Change *C, I, G*, and *NX* (*EX – IM*) and Therefore Can Change *AD* (Shift the *AD* Curve) 182 Can a Change in the Money Supply Change Aggregate Demand? 186 If Consumption Rises, Does Some Other Spending Component Have to Decline? 187

Short-Run Aggregate Supply 189
Short-Run Aggregate Supply Curve: What It Is and Why It Is Upward Sloping 189 What Puts the "Short Run" in the *SRAS* Curve? 191 Changes in Short-Run Aggregate Supply: Shifts in the *SRAS* Curve 191 Something More to Come: People's Expectations 193

Putting *AD* and *SRAS* Together: Short-Run Equilibrium 193
How Short-Run Equilibrium in the Economy Is Achieved 193 Thinking in Terms of Short-Run Equilibrium Changes in the Economy 194 A Change in Real GDP and the Price Level Can Be Caused by a Change in *AD* or *SRAS*—And That "Or" Is Important to Remember 196 An Important Exhibit 197

Long-Run Aggregate Supply 197
 Going from the Short Run to the Long Run 197 Short-Run Equilibrium, Long-Run Equilibrium, and Disequilibrium 199

Chapter Summary 201
Key Terms and Concepts 202
Questions and Problems 202

Chapter 9 Classical Macroeconomics and the Self-Regulating Economy 205

The Classical View 205
 Classical Economists and Say's Law 205 Classical Economists and Interest Rate Flexibility 206 Classical Economists on Prices and Wages: Both Are Flexible 209

Three States of the Economy 210
 Real GDP and Natural Real GDP: Three Possibilities 210 The Labor Market and the Three States of the Economy 211 Common Misconceptions About the Unemployment Rate and the Natural Unemployment Rate 213

The Self-Regulating Economy 215
 What Happens if a Self-Regulating Economy Is in a Recessionary Gap? 216 What's the Connection Between a Slow Recovery and How Quickly or Slowly Wages Adjust? 216 What Happens if the Economy Is in an Inflationary Gap? 217 The Self-Regulating Economy: A Recap 218 Policy Implication of Believing That the Economy Is Self-Regulating 219 Changes in a Self-Regulating Economy: Short Run and Long Run 219 A Recap of Classical Macroeconomics and a Self-Regulating Economy 221 Does a Constant Price Level Mean the Economy Is Not Self-Regulating? 221 Business-Cycle Macroeconomics and Economic-Growth Macroeconomics 223

Chapter Summary 225
Key Terms and Concepts 226
Questions and Problems 226

Chapter 10 Keynesian Macroeconomics and Economic Instability: A Critique of the Self-Regulating Economy 229

Questioning the Classical Position and the Self-Regulating Economy 229
 Keynes's Criticism of Say's Law in a Money Economy 230 Keynes on Wage Rates 231 Different Markets, Different Rates of Adjustment 232 Keynes on Prices 235 Is It a Question of the Time It Takes for Wages and Prices to Adjust? 236

The Simple Keynesian Model 238
 Assumptions 238 The Consumption Function 239 Consumption and Saving 241 The Multiplier 241 The Multiplier and Reality 242

The Simple Keynesian Model in the AD–AS Framework 244
 Shifts in the Aggregate Demand Curve 244 The Keynesian Aggregate Supply Curve 244 The Economy in a Recessionary Gap 246 Government's Role in the Economy 247 The Theme of the Simple Keynesian Model 247

The Simple Keynesian Model in the TE–TP Framework 248
 Deriving a Total Expenditures (TE) Curve 248 Where the Consumption Curve and the Total Expenditures Curve Cut the Vertical Axis: More on Exhibit 11 250 What Will Shift the TE Curve? 251 Comparing Total Expenditures (TE) and Total Production (TP) 251 Moving from Disequilibrium to Equilibrium 251 The Economy in a Recessionary Gap and the Role of Government 254 Equilibrium in the Economy 254 The Theme of the Simple Keynesian Model 255

Economics 24/7

Does It Matter How Much People Save? 208

Births, Marriage, and the Savings Rate in China 209

Office Hours

"Do Economists Really Know What the Natural Unemployment Rate Equals?" 224

Economics 24/7

The Financial and Economic Crisis of 2007–2009: Can a Housing Bust Lead to an Imploding Economy? 234

Was Keynes a Revolutionary in Economics? 237

The Economics of Spring Break 243

Office Hours

"Does a Lot Depend on Whether Wages Are Flexible or Inflexible?" 256

Chapter Summary 257
Key Terms and Concepts 257
Questions and Problems 258

Chapter 11 Fiscal Policy and the Federal Budget 260

The Federal Budget 260
Government Expenditures 260 Government Tax Revenues 261 Income Tax Structures 261 What Different Income Groups Pay in Income Taxes 261 Budget Deficit, Surplus, or Balance 262 Structural and Cyclical Deficits 262 The Public Debt 263 2020: Things Change in a Big Way 263 Valued-Added Tax 263 Tax Deductions Versus Subsidies 265

Fiscal Policy 267
Some Relevant Fiscal Policy Terms 267 Two Important Notes 267

Demand-Side Fiscal Policy 268
Shifting the Aggregate Demand Curve 268 Fiscal Policy: Keynesian Perspective (Economy Is Not Self-Regulating) 268 Crowding Out: Questioning Expansionary Fiscal Policy 269 Lags and Fiscal Policy 271 Crowding Out, Lags, and the Effectiveness of Fiscal Policy 273 Democracy in Deficit 273

Supply-Side Fiscal Policy 276
Marginal Tax Rates and Aggregate Supply 276 The Laffer Curve: Tax Rates and Tax Revenues 277 Fiscal Policy and Expectations 279

Chapter Summary 281
Key Terms and Concepts 282
Questions and Problems 282

Economics 24/7

Do Voting Rules Matter to Taxing and Spending? 266

Does the Portion of the Laffer Curve the Economy Is On Matter? 279

Office Hours

What's the Top Marginal Tax Rate? 280

Part 4 Money, the Economy, and Monetary Policy

Chapter 12 Money, Banking, and the Financial System 284

Money: What Is It and How Did It Come to Be? 284
Money: A Definition 284 Three Functions of Money 285 From a Barter Economy to a Money Economy: The Origins of Money 285 Money, Leisure, and Output 287

Defining the Money Supply 287
M1 288 M2 288 Money Is More Than Currency 288 Where Do Credit Cards Fit In? 290

How Banking Developed 291
The Early Bankers 291

The Financial System 293
Direct and Indirect Finance 293 Adverse Selection Problems and Moral Hazard Problems 293 The Bank's Balance Sheet 294 A Bank's Business: Turning Liabilities Into Assets 295

Chapter Summary 297
Key Terms and Concepts 297
Questions and Problems 298

Economics 24/7

Why Hold Cash and How Would Things Be Different if There Were No Cash? 289

M-Pesa Instead of Cash in Kenya 290

Economics on the Yellow Brick Road 292

Office Hours

"Do We Really Need Financial Intermediaries?" 296

Economics 24/7

Central Bank Digital Currency (CBDC): What Does the Future Hold? 301

Negative Interest Rates (on Reserves) and the Fed 314

Office Hours

What is the Difference Between the Fed Setting Interest Rates and Influencing Interest Rates? 315

Economics 24/7

The California Gold Rush, or Really Expensive Apples 324

Grade Inflation: It's All Relative 333

Office Hours

"What Is the Current Expected Inflation Rate?" 344

Economics 24/7

Who Gets the Money First, and What Happens to Relative Prices? 361

A Change in the Money Supply and You 364

Chapter 13 The Federal Reserve System 299

The Structure and Functions of the Federal Reserve System (The Fed) 299
    The Structure of the Fed 299   Fed Tools and Monetary Policy: Past and Present 300

The Past: Open Market Operations, Discount Rate, and Required Reserve Ratio (Reserve Requirements) 302
    Reserves 302   The Money Supply Expansion Process: Open Market Operations 303   The Money Supply Contraction Process: Open Market Sale 306   The Required Reserve Ratio 308   The Discount Rate 308   More on the Federal Funds Rate 309   Summary of Monetary Policy in the Past (Before October 2008) 309

The Present: Interest on Reserves (IOR) 310
    Interest Rates 310   Interest on Reserves (IOR) Rate 310   The IOR Rate, the Federal Funds Rate, and Interest Rates on Loans 312   Summary of Monetary Policy in the Present (Since October 2008) 312

Chapter Summary 315
Key Terms and Concepts 316
Questions and Problems 316

Chapter 14 Money and the Economy 318

Money and the Price Level 318
    The Equation of Exchange 318   From the Equation of Exchange to the Simple Quantity Theory of Money 320   The Micro Underpinnings of the Macro Phenomenon: *M* leads to a change in *P* 321   The Simple Quantity Theory of Money in an *AD–AS* Framework 322   Dropping the Assumptions That *V* and *Q* Are Constant 325

Monetarism 326
    The Four Monetarist Positions 326   Monetarism and *AD–AS* 326   The Monetarist View of the Economy 329

Inflation 330
    One-Shot Inflation 330   Continued Inflation 334   Can You Get Rid of Inflation With Price Controls? 336

Money and Interest Rates 337
    Which Economic Variables Does a Change in the Money Supply Affect? 337   The Money Supply, the Loanable Funds Market, and Interest Rates 338   What Happens to the Interest Rate as the Money Supply Changes? 342   The Nominal and Real Interest Rates 343

Chapter Summary 344
Key Terms and Concepts 345
Questions and Problems 345

Chapter 15 Monetary Policy 348

Transmission Mechanisms 348
    The Money Market in the Keynesian Transmission Mechanism 348   The Keynesian Transmission Mechanism: Indirect 350   The Keynesian Mechanism May Get Blocked 351   The Monetarist Transmission Mechanism: Direct 354

Monetary Policy and the Problem of Inflationary and Recessionary Gaps 355
    A Different View of the Economy: Patterns of Sustainable Specialization and Trade (PSST) 357

Monetary Policy and the Activist–Nonactivist Debate 358
    The Case for Activist (or Discretionary) Monetary Policy 358   The Case for Nonactivist (or Rules-Based) Monetary Policy 359

Office Hours

"Does Monetary Policy Always Have the Same Effects?" 367

Nonactivist Monetary Proposals 361
    The Constant-Money-Growth-Rate Rule 362   The Predetermined-Money-Growth-Rate Rule 362   The Fed and the Taylor Rule 363   Average Inflation Targeting 363   Nominal GDP Targeting 363   A Gold Standard as Monetary Policy and the Value of the Dollar 365

Chapter Summary 368
Key Terms and Concepts 369
Questions and Problems 369

Appendix C   Bond Prices and the Interest Rate 371

Appendix Summary 373
Questions and Problems 373

Part 5   Expectations and Growth

Economics 24/7

Is the Downward-Sloping Phillips Curve Disappearing? 380

Rational Expectations in the College Classroom 385

The Money Supply, an Increase in Productivity, and What You Think 392

Office Hours

"Does New Classical Theory Call the Effects of Fiscal and Monetary Policy into Question?" 396

Economics 24/7

Technology Matters 405

Going Forward: Medical Costs, Economic Growth, and Tax Revenues 407

Economic Freedom and Growth Rates 412

Office Hours

"What Is the Difference Between Business Cycle Macroeconomics and Economic Growth Macroeconomics?" 413

Chapter 16   Expectations Theory and the Economy 374

Phillips Curve Analysis 374
    The Phillips Curve 374   Samuelson and Solow: The Americanization of the Phillips Curve 375

The Controversy Begins: Are There Really Two Phillips Curves? 376
    Things Aren't Always as We Think They Are 376   Friedman and the Natural Rate Theory 376   How Do People Form Their Expectations? 380

Rational Expectations and New Classical Theory 381
    Rational Expectations 382   Do People Really Anticipate Policy? 382   Price-Level Expectations and the *SRAS* Curve 383   Expected and Actual Price Levels 384   New Classical Economics and Four Different Cases 386   Comparing Exhibits 9 and 10 391   Rational Expectations and Changes in the Money Supply 391

New Keynesians and Rational Expectations 393
Looking at Things from the Supply Side: Real Business Cycle Theorists 394
Chapter Summary 397
Key Terms and Concepts 398
Questions and Problems 398

Chapter 17   Economic Growth: Resources, Technology, Ideas, and Institutions 400

A Few Basics About Economic Growth 400
    Do Economic Growth Rates Matter? 400

A Production Function and Economic Growth 402
    The Graphical Representation of the Production Function 402   From the Production Function to the *LRAS* Curve 404   Emphasis on Labor 406   Emphasis on Capital 408   Emphasis on Other Resources: Natural Resources and Human Capital 408   Emphasis on the Technology Coefficient and Ideas 408   Discovery and Ideas 409   Expanding Our Horizons 409   Institutions Matter 410

Chapter Summary 414
Key Terms and Concepts 414
Questions and Problems 415

Part 6 Creative Destruction and Crony Capitalism

Economics 24/7

The Future: Looking at Automation and Jobs 419

Bastiat and the Candlemaker's Petition 426

Does It Matter If There Is a Lot of Crony Capitalism in the Country? 429

Chapter 18 Creative Destruction and Crony Capitalism: Two Forces on the Economic Landscape Today 416

Creative Destruction 416
  Schumpeter, Creative Destruction, and Capitalism 416   Creative Destruction and Competition 417   How Do We Measure Creative Destruction? 417   Examples of Creative Destruction 418   Worries About Creative Destruction 418   Calls for Government Assistance 420   The Other Side of Creative Destruction 420

Crony Capitalism 421
  At the Heart of Crony Capitalism Is Rent Seeking 421   Two Things to Consider About Rent Seeking: The Transfer and the Wasted Resources 422   A Question for Tullock 423   Some Examples of Rent Seeking: Past and Present 423   Lobbyists and Rent Seeking 426   Why Would a Firm Want to Be a Rent Seeker? 428

Chapter Summary 429
Questions and Problems 431

Part 7 Microeconomic Fundamentals

Economics 24/7

Drug Busts and Crime 439

Elasticity and the Issue of "How Much" 441

When Is a Half-Packed Auditorium Better Than a Packed One? 442

Tuition Hikes at the College or University 445

House Prices and the Elasticity of Supply 451

 **Office Hours**

"What Is the Relationship Between Different Price Elasticities of Demand and Total Revenue?" 456

Chapter 19 Elasticity 432

Elasticity: Part 1 432
  Price Elasticity of Demand 432   Elasticity Is Not Slope 434   From Perfectly Elastic to Perfectly Inelastic Demand 434   Price Elasticity of Demand and Total Revenue (Total Expenditure) 437   Elastic Demand and Total Revenue 438

Elasticity: Part 2 443
  Price Elasticity of Demand Along a Straight-Line Demand Curve 443   Determinants of Price Elasticity of Demand 444

Other Elasticity Concepts 447
  Cross Elasticity of Demand 447   Income Elasticity of Demand 448   Price Elasticity of Supply 449   Price Elasticity of Supply and Time 449

The Relationship Between Taxes and Elasticity 452
  Who Pays the Tax? 452   Elasticity and the Tax 454   Degree of Elasticity and Tax Revenue 455

Chapter Summary 457
Key Terms and Concepts 458
Questions and Problems 458

Economics 24/7

The Gym and Diminishing Marginal Utility 464

How You Pay for Good Weather 468

$800 for Sure or $1,000 with a Probability of 85 Percent? An Experiment 470

Does It Matter to You... If You Are Subject to the Endowment Effect? 473

$40 and Two People: The Ultimatum Game 474

Office Hours

"Is There an Indirect Way of Proving the Law of Diminishing Marginal Utility?" 477

Economics 24/7

"He Never Showed Up" 490

Is Labor Being Misallocated Across U.S. Cities? 500

Social Media and Marginal Cost 508

Producing a Grade in a College Course 510

Office Hours

"What Is the Difference Between the Law of Diminishing Marginal Returns and Diseconomies of Scale?" 516

Chapter 20 Consumer Choice: Maximizing Utility and Behavioral Economics 460

Utility Theory 460
Utility: Total and Marginal 460   Law of Diminishing Marginal Utility 461   The Solution to the Diamond–Water Paradox 463

Consumer Equilibrium and Demand 465
Equating Marginal Utilities per Dollar 465   Maximizing Utility and the Law of Demand 466   Should the Government Provide the Necessities of Life for Free? 467

Behavioral Economics 469
Are People Willing to Reduce Others' Incomes? 469   Is One Dollar Always One Dollar? 470   Coffee Mugs and the Endowment Effect 471   Does the Endowment Effect Hold Only for New Traders? 472   Framing 474   Neuroeconomics 476

Chapter Summary 477
Key Terms and Concepts 478
Questions and Problems 478

Appendix D Budget Constraint and Indifference Curve Analysis 480

D-1 The Budget Constraint 480
D-1a Slope of the Budget Constraint 480
D-1b What Will Change the Budget Constraint? 480
D-2 Indifference Curves 481
D-3 Constructing an Indifference Curve 482
D-3a Characteristics of Indifference Curves 482
D-4 The Indifference Map and the Budget Constraint Come Together 485
D-5 From Indifference Curves to a Demand Curve 486
Appendix Summary 487
Key Terms and Concepts 487
Questions and Problems 487

Chapter 21 Production and Costs 488

Why Firms Exist 488
The Market and the Firm: Invisible Hand Versus Visible Hand 488   The Alchian-and-Demsetz Answer 489   Shirking on a Team 489   Ronald Coase on Why Firms Exist 490   Markets: Outside and Inside the Firm 491

Two Sides to Every Business Firm 491
More on Total Cost 492   Accounting Profit Versus Economic Profit 492   Zero Economic Profit Is Not as Bad as It Sounds 493

Production 494
Common Misconception About the Short Run and Long Run 495   Production in the Short Run 495   Whose Marginal Productivity Are We Talking About? 496   Marginal Physical Product and Marginal Cost 497   Average Productivity 499

Costs of Production: Total, Average, Marginal 501
The *AVC* and *ATC* Curves in Relation to the *MC* Curve 504   Tying Short-Run Production to Costs 507   Seeing How Things Came to Be 507   One More Cost Concept: Sunk Cost 508

Production and Costs in the Long Run 512
Long-Run Average Total Cost Curve 512   Economies of Scale, Diseconomies of Scale, and Constant Returns to Scale 513   Why Economies of Scale? 515   Why Diseconomies of Scale? 515   Minimum Efficient Scale and Number of Firms in an Industry 515

Contents   xv

Shifts in Cost Curves 515
Taxes 515   Input Prices 516   Technology 516
Chapter Summary 517
Key Terms and Concepts 518
Questions and Problems 518

Part 8 Product Markets and Policies

Economics 24/7

Restaurant Shut Downs and the Coronavirus 531

The Digital Revolution, Price, and Marginal Cost 534

How Is High-Quality Land Like a Genius Software Engineer? 543

Office Hours

"Do You Have to Know the MR = MC Condition in Order to Be Successful in Business?" 545

Chapter 22 Perfect Competition 521

The Theory of Perfect Competition 521
A Perfectly Competitive Firm Is a Price Taker 522   The Demand Curve for a Perfectly Competitive Firm Is Horizontal 522   Common Misconceptions About Demand Curves 523   The Marginal Revenue Curve of a Perfectly Competitive Firm Is the Same as Its Demand Curve 524   Theory and Real-World Markets 525

Perfect Competition in the Short Run 526
What Level of Output Does the Profit-Maximizing Firm Produce? 526   The Perfectly Competitive Firm and Resource Allocative Efficiency 526   To Produce or Not to Produce: That Is the Question 527   Common Misconceptions Over the Shutdown Decision 530   The Perfectly Competitive Firm's Short-Run Supply Curve 532   From Firm Supply Curve to Market (Industry) Supply Curve 533   Why Is the Market Supply Curve Upward Sloping? 535

Perfect Competition in the Long Run 535
The Conditions of Long-Run Competitive Equilibrium 535   The Perfectly Competitive Firm and Productive Efficiency 537   Industry Adjustment to an Increase in Demand 537   Profit from Two Perspectives 541   Industry Adjustment to a Decrease in Demand 541   Differences in Costs, Differences in Profits: Now You See It, Now You Don't 542   Profit and Discrimination 543

Topics for Analysis in the Theory of Perfect Competition 544
Do Higher Costs Mean Higher Prices? 544   Will the Perfectly Competitive Firm Advertise? 544   Supplier-Set Price Versus Market-Determined Price: Collusion or Competition? 545

Chapter Summary 546
Key Terms and Concepts 547
Questions and Problems 547

Economics 24/7

Monopoly and the Boston Tea Party 551

Google, Facebook, Monopoly, and Property Rights 558

Religion and Monopoly 562

One for $40 or Two for $70 565

Do Colleges and Universities Price-Discriminate? 566

Chapter 23 Monopoly 549

The Theory of Monopoly 549
Barriers to Entry: A Key to Understanding Monopoly 550   What Is the Difference Between a Government Monopoly and a Market Monopoly? 550

Monopoly Pricing and Output Decisions 551
The Monopolist's Demand and Marginal Revenue 552   The Monopolist's Demand Curve and Marginal Revenue Curve Are Not the Same 553   Price and Output for a Profit-Maximizing Monopolist 553   Comparing the Demand Curve in Perfect Competition with the Demand Curve in Monopoly 555   If a Firm Maximizes Revenue, Does It Automatically Maximize Profit Too? 555

Perfect Competition and Monopoly 556
Price, Marginal Revenue, and Marginal Cost 556   Monopoly, Perfect Competition, and Consumers' Surplus 556   Monopoly or Nothing? 557

The Case Against Monopoly 560
The Deadweight Loss of Monopoly 560   Does It Matter to You if There Is a Deadweight Loss Triangle? 561   Rent Seeking 561   X-Inefficiency 562

Office Hours

"Does the Single-Price Monopolist Lower Price Only on the Additional Unit?" 568

Economics 24/7

The People Wear Prada 576

How Is a New Year's Resolution Like a Cartel Agreement? 580

Office Hours

"Are Firms (as Sellers) Either Price Takers or Price Searchers?" 590

Economics 24/7

The DOJ, FTC, Google, and Facebook 595

Thomas Edison and Hollywood 598

High-Priced Ink Cartridges and Expensive Minibars 601

Office Hours

"What Is the Advantage of the Herfindahl Index?" 607

Price Discrimination 563
  Types of Price Discrimination 563 Why a Monopolist Wants to Price-Discriminate 564
  Conditions of Price Discrimination 564 Moving to $P = MC$ Through Price Discrimination 564 Coupons and Price Discrimination 567

Chapter Summary 569

Key Terms and Concepts 570

Questions and Problems 570

Chapter 24 Monopolistic Competition, Oligopoly, and Game Theory 572

The Theory of Monopolistic Competition 572
  The Monopolistic Competitor's Demand Curve 573 The Relationship Between Price and Marginal Revenue for a Monopolistic Competitor 573 Output, Price, and Marginal Cost for the Monopolistic Competitor 573 Will There Be Profits in the Long Run? 573 Excess Capacity: What Is It, and Is It "Good" or "Bad"? 574 The Monopolistic Competitor and Two Types of Efficiency 576

Oligopoly: Assumptions and Real-World Behavior 577
  The Concentration Ratio 577

Price and Output Under The Cartel Theory 578
  The Cartel Theory 578

Game Theory, Oligopoly, and Contestable Markets 581
  Prisoner's Dilemma 581 Oligopoly Firms' Cartels and the Prisoner's Dilemma 583
  Are Markets Contestable? 584 Necessary and Sufficient Conditions and Efficiency 585

A Review of Market Structures 586

Applications of Game Theory 587
  Grades and Partying 587 The Arms Race 588 Speed Limit Laws 589

Chapter Summary 590

Key Terms and Concepts 591

Questions and Problems 591

Chapter 25 Government and Product Markets: Antitrust and Regulation 593

Antitrust 593
  Antitrust Acts 594 Unsettled Points in Antitrust Policy 596 Antitrust and Mergers 599
  Common Misconceptions About Antitrust Policy 600 Network Monopolies 600

Regulation 602
  The Case of Natural Monopoly 602 Regulating the Natural Monopoly 604 Regulating Industries That Are Not Natural Monopolies 606 Theories of Regulation 606 The Costs and Benefits of Regulation 607

Chapter Summary 608

Key Terms and Concepts 609

Questions and Problems 609

Contents   xvii

Part 9   Factor Markets and Related Issues

Economics 24/7

Why Jobs Don't Always Move to a Low-Wage Country 619

Artificial Intelligence, Robotics, and the Future of Jobs and Wages 623

Who Pays the Social Security Tax? 629

Office Hours

"Why Do Economists Think in Twos?" 631

Economics 24/7

Technology, the Price of Competing Factors, and Displaced Workers 640

Unions, Profits, and Prices 646

Office Hours

"Don't Higher Wages Reduce Profits?" 647

Economics 24/7

Statistics Can Mislead if You Don't Know How They Are Made 654

Education and Income 655

Chapter 26   Factor Markets: With Emphasis on the Labor Market 611

Factor Markets 611
　The Demand for a Factor 611　Marginal Revenue Product: Two Ways to Calculate It 612　The *MRP* Curve Is the Firm's Factor Demand Curve 613　Value Marginal Product 613　An Important Question: Is *MRP* = *VMP*? 614　Marginal Factor Cost: The Firm's Factor Supply Curve 615　How Many Units of a Factor Should a Firm Buy? 616　When There Is More Than One Factor, How Much of Each Factor Should the Firm Buy? 616

The Labor Market 618
　Shifts in a Firm's *MRP*, or Factor Demand, Curve 618　Market Demand for Labor 620　The Elasticity of Demand for Labor 621　Market Supply of Labor 622　An Individual's Supply of Labor 622　Shifts in the Labor Supply Curve 624　Putting Supply and Demand Together 624　Why Do Wage Rates Differ? 625　Why Demand and Supply Differ Among Labor Markets 626　Why Did You Choose Your Major? 628　Marginal Productivity Theory 628

Labor Markets And Information 630
　Screening Potential Employees 630　Promoting from Within 630　Discrimination or an Information Problem? 631

Chapter Summary 632

Key Terms and Concepts 632

Questions and Problems 633

Chapter 27   Wages, Unions, and Labor 635

Objectives of Labor Unions 635
　Employment for All Members 635　Maximizing the Total Wage Bill 636　Maximizing Income for a Limited Number of Union Members 636　Wage–Employment Trade-Off 636

Practices of Labor Unions 637
　Affecting the Elasticity of Demand for Union Labor 638　Affecting the Demand for Union Labor 638　Affecting the Supply of Union Labor 639　Affecting Wages Directly: Collective Bargaining 639　Strikes 641

Effects of Labor Unions 641
　The Case of Monopsony 641　Unions' Effects on Wages 643　Unions' Effects on Prices 644　Unions' Effects on Productivity and Efficiency: Two Views 645

Chapter Summary 648

Key Terms and Concepts 648

Questions and Problems 648

Chapter 28   The Distribution of Income and Poverty 650

Some Facts About Income Distribution 650
　Who Are the Rich and How Rich Are They? 650　The Effect of Age on the Income Distribution 651　A Simple Equation 653

Measuring Income Equality 656
　The Lorenz Curve 656　The Gini Coefficient 657　A Limitation of the Gini Coefficient 658　Common Misconceptions about Income Inequality 658

Why Income Inequality Exists 659
　Factors Contributing to Income Inequality 659　Income Differences: Some Are Voluntary; Some Are Not 661

Office Hours

"Is the Number of Persons in Each Fifth the Same?" 664

Economics 24/7

Investment, Present Value, and Interest Rates 673

Is the Car Worth Buying? 673

Grain Prices and Land Rent 675

Office Hours

"How Is Present Value Used in the Courtroom?" 682

Poverty 662
What Is Poverty? 662 Limitations of the Official Poverty Income Statistics 663 Who Are the Poor? 663 What Is the Justification for Government Redistributing Income? 663

Chapter Summary 665

Key Terms and Concepts 666

Questions and Problems 666

Chapter 29 Interest, Rent, and Profit 667

Interest 667
Loanable Funds: Demand and Supply 667 The Price for Loanable Funds and the Return on Capital Goods Tend to Equality 669 Why Do Interest Rates Differ? 670 Nominal and Real Interest Rates 670 Present Value: What Is Something Tomorrow Worth Today? 671

Rent 674
David Ricardo, the Price of Grain, and Land Rent 674 The Supply Curve of Land Can Be Upward Sloping 676 Economic Rent and Other Factors of Production 676 Economic Rent and Baseball Players: Perspective Matters 677 Competing for Artificial and Real Rents 677

Profit 678
Theories of Profit 678 Profit and Loss as Signals 679

The Entrepreneur 679
A Market 679 How Can the Entrepreneur Increase Trade? 680 Turning Potential Trades into Actual Trades 680 A Necessary Condition: Turn Potential Trades Into Actual Trades in a Way Acceptable to Consumers 681 Can Increasing Trades in One Area Reduce Trades in Another? 681 Uncertainty and the Entrepreneur 681

Chapter Summary 682

Key Terms and Concepts 683

Questions and Problems 683

Part 10 Health Economics

Economics 24/7

COVID-19 and Health Disparities 694

Office Hours

"What's This Tax Exclusion for Employer-Sponsored Health Insurance That I've Been Hearing About?" 701

Chapter 30 Health Economics: Experiments, Disparities, and Prices 685

Why Health Economics? 685
What Makes Health Care Different? 686

The Demand for Health Care 687
The RAND Health Insurance Experiment 688

Social Determinants of Health 692
Health Disparities 693 Causes of Health Disparities 695

Health Care 697
Prices 697 Access 699 Insurance 699 Health Care Reform 700

Chapter Summary 702

Key Terms and Concepts 703

Questions and Problems 703

Contents

Part 11 Market Failure, Public Choice, and Special-Interest Group Politics

Economics 24/7

An Unintended Effect of Texting 708

Tribes, Transaction Costs, and Social Media 714

Will Nonexcludable Public Goods Be Provided by the Market Under a Certain Condition? 720

Culture as a Public Good 721

"They Paved Paradise and Put Up a Parking Lot" 722

Office Hours

"Doesn't It Seem Wrong to Let Some Business Firms Pay to Pollute?" 728

Economics 24/7

A Simple-Majority Voting Rule: The Case of the Statue in the Public Square 735

The Median Voter Model and the U.S. Supreme Court in 2018 736

Economic Illiteracy and Democracy 739

Chapter 31 Market Failure: Externalities, Public Goods, and Asymmetric Information 704

Externalities 704
  Costs and Benefits of Activities 704 Marginal Costs and Benefits of Activities 705 Social Optimality, or Efficiency, Conditions 706 Three Categories of Activities 706 Externalities in Consumption and in Production 706 Diagram of a Negative Externality 706 Diagram of a Positive Externality 709

Internalizing Externalities 710
  Persuasion 710 Taxes and Subsidies 711 Assigning Property Rights 711 Voluntary Agreements 712 Combining Property Rights Assignments and Voluntary Agreements 712 Beyond Internalizing: Setting Regulations 713

Environmental Policy 715
  Method 1: Government Regulation, or Command and Control 715 Method 2: Emission Taxes 716 Method 3: Tradable Pollution Permits (Cap and Trade) 716 Similarities and Differences Between Emission Taxes and Tradable Pollution Permits 717

Public Goods: Excludable and Nonexcludable 719
  Goods 719 The Free Rider 719 Nonexcludable Versus Nonrivalrous 721

Asymmetric Information 723
  Asymmetric Information in a Product Market 724 Asymmetric Information in a Factor Market 725 Is There Market Failure? 725 Adverse Selection 726 Moral Hazard 727

Chapter Summary 729

Key Terms and Concepts 730

Questions and Problems 730

Chapter 32 Public Choice and Special-Interest Group Politics 732

Public Choice Theory 732

The Political Market 733
  Moving Toward the Middle: The Median Voter Model 733 What Does the Theory Predict? 734

Voters and Rational Ignorance 737
  The Costs and Benefits of Voting 737 Rational Ignorance 738

More About Voting 740
  Example 1: Voting for a Nonexcludable Public Good 740 Example 2: Voting and Efficiency 741

Special-Interest Groups 742
  Information and Lobbying 743 Congressional Districts as Special-Interest Groups 743 Public-Interest Talk, Special-Interest Legislation 744 Rent Seeking 744 Bringing About Transfers 745 Information, Rational Ignorance, and Seeking Transfers 746

 **Office Hours**

"Doesn't Public Choice Paint a Bleak Picture of Politics and Government?" 748

Constitutional Economics 747
Chapter Summary 749
Key Terms and Concepts 750
Questions and Problems 750

Part 12 Economic Theories and Research

Economics

Spurious Correlations 754
Netflix and Big Data 767

 **Office Hours**

"I've Got a Question on Each of the Three Topics: Natural Experiments, Instrumental Variables, and Algorithms? 771

Chapter 33 New Frontiers in Economic Research: Causal Inference and Machine Learning 752

Causal Inference 752
  Correlation and Causation 753 Does the Minimum Wage Increase Unemployment? 754 Controlled Experiments 756 Natural Experiments 757 Natural Experiments in Macroeconomics 759

Lotteries: An Introduction to Instrumental Variables 761
  The Vietnam War Draft Lottery 761 School Lotteries 762 Judge Lotteries 762 Lotteries, Randomness, and Instrumental Variables 763 Regression Discontinuity Design 764 Summary of Causal Inference 766

Big Data and Machine Learning 766
  The Goal of Big Data and Machine Learning 766 Regularization 767 Cross-Validation 768 Machine Learning and Public Policy 768 Algorithmic Fears 769 Summary of Big Data and Machine Learning 770

The Importance of Data 770
Chapter Summary 772
Key Terms and Concepts 773
Questions and Problems 773

Part 13 International Trade and Finance

Economics

Offshore Outsourcing, or Offshoring 785

 **Office Hours**

"Should We Impose Tariffs If They Impose Tariffs?" 788

Chapter 34 International Trade 774

International Trade Theory 774
  How Countries Know What to Trade 775 A Common Misconception About How Much We Can Consume 777 How Countries Know When They Have a Comparative Advantage 777 Why Does the United States Both Export and Import Cars? Why Not Just One or the Other? 778

Trade Restrictions 779
  The Distributional Effects of International Trade 780 Consumers' and Producers' Surpluses 780 The Benefits and Costs of Trade Restrictions 780 Why Nations Sometimes Restrict Trade 784

Chapter Summary 788
Key Terms and Concepts 789
Questions and Problems 789

Economics 24/7

Does It Matter to You If the Dollar Depreciates? 794

The U.S. Dollar as the Primary Reserve Currency 797

Office Hours

"Why Is the Depreciation of One Currency Tied to the Appreciation of Another?" 805

Chapter 35 International Finance 791

The Foreign Exchange Market 791
    The Demand for Goods 792   The Demand for and Supply of Currencies 792

Flexible Exchange Rates 793
    The Equilibrium Exchange Rate 793   Changes in the Equilibrium Exchange Rate 794   Factors That Affect the Equilibrium Exchange Rate 795

Fixed Exchange Rates 798
    Fixed Exchange Rates and Overvalued or Undervalued Currency 799   What Is So Bad About an Overvalued Dollar? 800   Government Involvement in a Fixed Exchange Rate System 801   Options Under a Fixed Exchange Rate System 801

Fixed Exchange Rates versus Flexible Exchange Rates 803
    Promoting International Trade 803   Optimal Currency Areas 804

Chapter Summary 806

Key Terms and Concepts 807

Questions and Problems 807

Self-Test Appendix 809

Glossary 833

Index 845

Preface

This is the fourteenth edition of *Economics*. In it you will find three new chapters—chapters that will be particularly relevant to economic students in the early-to-mid 2020s. They are:

- Creative Destruction and Crony Capitalism: Two Forces on the Economic Landscape Today
- Health Economics: Experiments, Disparities, and Prices
- New Frontiers in Economic Research: Causal Inference and Machine Learning

With these three new chapters, students will learn what creative destruction is and how it plays out in today's world, what crony capitalism is and why it exists, what various health economic experiments tell us about how and why people buy health care and health insurance, how economists conduct research, how they infer causality, and how big data and machine learning are being used to make policy decisions. Creative destruction, crony capitalism, health care, research, data, and machine learning—this is much of the world today, and it is important for students to have the information, analytic tools, and ways of thinking to understand it.

This edition keeps much of what adopters have liked about previous editions. The content remains straightforward and accessible and comes with numerous boxed applications. We believe that economics has a lot to say these days and we want that communication between text and student to be as crystal clear, unambiguous, and accessible as possible. But to enrich the basic economic content, there need to be applications. Students need to see the basic economic tools of analysis being used to explain things, and here is where the applications come in. A hallmark of this text over various editions is the plentiful and relevant applications it features. This edition has 185 boxed applications that can be found under these four main titles: *Economics 24/7*, *Thinking Like an Economist*, *Finding Economics*, and *Office Hours*. A few of the many new ones to this edition include:

- Movie Studios vs Netflix: Incentives Matter
- The Future: Looking at Automation and Jobs
- Is Labor Being Misallocated Across U.S. Cities?
- Google, Facebook, Monopoly, and Property Rights
- Covid-19 and Health Disparities
- The Covid-19 Pandemic and the PPF
- Stoic Philosophy, Search Engines, and Consumers' Surplus
- Central Bank Digital Currency (CBDC): What Does the Future Hold?
- The Median Voter Model and the U.S. Supreme Court in 2018
- Netflix and Big Data
- The DOJ, FTC, Google, and Facebook
- Spurious Correlations
- Artificial Intelligence, Robotics, and the Future of Jobs

A major rewriting and reorganization of material covering money and banking and the Federal Reserve and monetary policy exists in this new edition. This rewriting and reorganization makes it clearer than ever how monetary policy was conducted before October 2008 and how it is conducted today.

This edition carries forward the video content, first started in earlier editions. There are two sets of instructional videos—*Economics in 5 Minutes* and *Video Lectures*; *What's Wrong with This Diagram?* videos; and *Problem Walk-Through* videos. The different types of videos are all instructional and designed to complement the chapter text material.

Supplements to the Text

A wide and helpful array of supplements is available with this edition to both students and instructors.

- An Instructor's Manual, written by Noreen Templin, Butler Community College, contains chapter summaries, chapter objectives, supplements, activities and assessments, and chapter outlines. It is available on the text website at http://www.cengage.com for instructors only.

- PowerPoint Slides, revised by Noreen Templin, Butler Community College, are available on the text website for use by instructor for enhancing their lectures. These fully accessible PowerPoint slides provide chapter-level presentations and highlight opportunities for increased peer-peer interactivity.

- A Test Bank, authored and revised for the fourteenth edition by Peggy Crane, Southwestern College, is delivered via Cognero, an online assessment system that supports the computerized Test Bank. Cognero allows instructors to create and assign tests, deliver tests through a secure online test center, and have the complete reporting and data dissemination at their fingertips.

In Appreciation

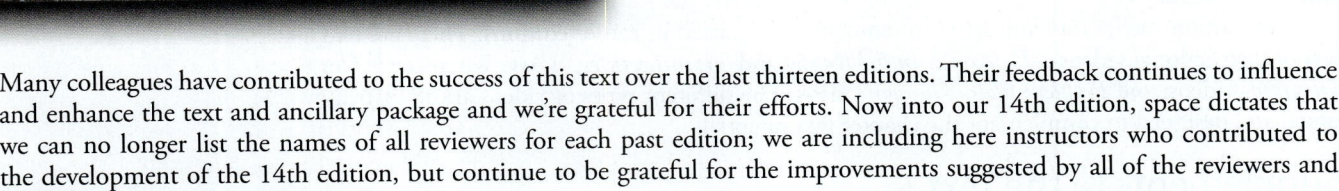

Many colleagues have contributed to the success of this text over the last thirteen editions. Their feedback continues to influence and enhance the text and ancillary package and we're grateful for their efforts. Now into our 14th edition, space dictates that we can no longer list the names of all reviewers for each past edition; we are including here instructors who contributed to the development of the 14th edition, but continue to be grateful for the improvements suggested by all of the reviewers and contributors to this product over the years.

Randy Barcus
Embry Riddle Aeronautical University - Daytona Beach Daytona Beach, FL

Yosef Bonaparte
University of British Columbia Kelowna, BC

Anthony Chan
Santa Monica College Los Angeles, CA

Amy Chataginer
Mississippi Gulf Coast Community College Biloxi, MS

Megan Cummins
Mt. San Jacinto College Long Beach, CA

Ribhi Daoud
Sinclair Community College Dayton, OH

Carol Decker
Tennessee Wesleyan College Niota, TN

Brittany Dobill
John A Logan College Carterville, IL

Tila Dorina
Embry Riddle Aeronautical University - Daytona Beach, FL

Matthew Dudman
California State University - Maritime Vallejo, CA

Harry Ellis
University of North Texas Denton, TX

Susan Emens
Kent State University - Trumbull Warren, OH

Fidel Ezeala-Harrison
Jackson State University Jackson, MS

John Finley
Columbus State University Columbus, GA

Lea Frances
Germanna Community College Orange, VA

John Gaughan
Penn State University Lehigh Valley Center Valley, PA

Sherry Grosso
University of South Carolina Sumter, SC

Travis Hayes
Dalton State College Dalton, GA

Aubrey Haynes
Southwest Texas Jr College Uvalde, TX

Dewey Heinsma
Mt. San Jacinto College Yucaipa, CA

Tony Hunnicutt
College of the Ouachitas Malvern, AR

Joe Hutlak
Union County College Cranford, NJ

Andres Jauregui
Columbus State University Columbus, GA

Deb Jones
Iowa Lakes Community College Emmetsburg, IA

Barry Kotlove
Edmonds Community College Lynnwood, WA

Katie Lotz
Lake Land College Mattoon, IL

Brian Lynch
Lake Land College Mattoon, IL

Michael Machiorlatti
Oklahoma City Community College Oklahoma City, OK

Mehrdad Madresehee
Lycoming College Williamsport, PA

Mike McGay
Wilmington University Newark, DE

Shah Mehrabi
Montgomery College Arlington, VA

José Mendez
John A Logan College Carterville, IL

Elizabeth Moorhouse
Lycoming College Williamsport, PA

Edward Murphy
Embry Riddle Aeronautical University - Daytona Beach Daytona Beach, FL

Charles Myrick
Oklahoma City Community College Warr Acres, OK

Charles Newton
Houston Community College Stafford, TX

In Appreciation

Ogbonnaya Nwoha
Grambling State University Ruston, LA

Charles Parker
Wayne State College Wayne, NE

Van Pham
Salem State University Salem, MA

John Pharr
Brookhaven College Garland, TX

Germain Pichop
Oklahoma City Community College Oklahoma City, OK

Craig Richardson
Winston-Salem State University Winston-Salem, NC

April Ruhmann
Southwest Texas Jr College Uvalde, TX

Sara Saderion
Houston Community College Houston, TX

Richard Sarkisian
Camden County College Blackwood, NJ

Daniel Saros
Valparaiso University Valparaiso, IN

Anthony Sawyer
Paris Junior College Paris, TX

Bill Schweizer
University of Mount Union Alliance, OH

Matt Shekels
North Arkansas College Harrison, AR

Kent Sickmeyer
Kaskaskia College Centralia, IL

Donald Sparks
The Citadel Charleston, SC

Boo Su
College of the Canyons Santa Clarita, CA

Omari Swinton
Howard University Upper Marlboro, MD

Krystal Thrailkill
Rich Mountain Community College Mena, AR

Kelly Whealan-George
Embry-Riddle Aeronautical University South Riding, VA

Beth Wilson
Humboldt State University Arcata, CA

Davin Winger
Oklahoma Panhandle State University Goodwell, OK

Peter Wui
University of Arkansas Pine Bluff Little Rock, AR

Mustafa Younis
Jackson State University Jackson, MS

Evaristo Zapata
Southwest Texas Jr College Eagle Pass, TX

We are indebted to all the outstanding and creative people we worked with on the 14th edition. Chris Rader, product manager; Colleen Farmer, senior content manager; Shannon Aucoin, subject matter expert; Eugenia Belova, subject matter expert; Sarah Keeling, senior learning designer; John Carey, executive marketing manager; and Peggy Crane of Southwestern College; and Noreen Templin of Butler Community College. There are a host of activities that go on behind the scenes when producing a book. The authors' names are on the book's cover, but really it is a team of people who end up tending to the 1,001 details that make the book what it is. It is hard to imagine a better team of creative, conscientious, and dedicated publishing professionals to work with anywhere.

Roger A. Arnold   Daniel R. Arnold   David H. Arnold

What Economics Is About

CHAPTER 1

Introduction

You are about to begin your study of economics. Before discussing particular topics in economics, we think it best to give you an overview of what economics is and of some of the key concepts. The key concepts can be compared to musical notes: Just as musical notes are repeated in any song (you hear the musical note G over and over again), the key concepts in economics are repeated too. Some of these concepts are scarcity, opportunity cost, efficiency, marginal decision making, incentives, and exchange.

1-1 Your Life, 2024–2034

What will your life be like during the years 2024–2034? What kind of work will you do after college? How much will you earn in that first job after college? Where will you be living, and who will be your friends? How many friends will you have? Will you buy a house in the next few years? If so, how much will you pay for the house? And, perhaps most importantly, will you be happy?

The specific answers to these questions and many more have to do with economics. For example, the salary you will earn has to do with the economic concept of *opportunity cost*. What you will do in your first job after college has to do with the *state of the economy* when you graduate. The price you pay for a house has to do with the state of the *housing market*. How many friends you have has to do with the economic concept of *scarcity*. Whether you are happy will depend on such things as the *net benefits* you receive in various activities, the *utility* you gain by doing certain things, and more.

In this chapter, we begin our study of economics. As you read the chapter (and those which follow), ask yourself how much of what you are reading is relevant to your life today and tomorrow. Ask: What does what I am reading have to do with *my* life? Our guess is that after answering this question a few dozen times, you will be convinced that economics explains much about your present and future.

1-2 A Definition of Economics

In this section, we discuss a few key economic concepts; then we incorporate knowledge of these concepts into a definition of economics.

1-2a Goods and Bads

Economists talk about *goods* and *bads*. A **good** is anything that gives a person **utility**, or satisfaction. Here is a partial list of some goods: a computer, a car, a watch, a television set, friendship, and love. You will notice from our list that a good can be either tangible or intangible. A computer is a tangible good; friendship is an intangible good. Simply put, for something to be a good (whether tangible or intangible), it only has to give someone utility or satisfaction.

A **bad** is something that gives a person **disutility** or dissatisfaction. If the flu gives you disutility or dissatisfaction, then it is a bad. If the constant nagging of an acquaintance is something that gives you disutility or dissatisfaction, then it is a bad.

People want goods, and they do not want bads. In fact, they will pay to get goods ("here is $1,000 for the computer"), and they will pay to get rid of bads ("I'd be willing to pay you, doctor, if you can prescribe something that will shorten the time I have the flu").

Can something be a *good* for one person and a *bad* for another person? Smoking cigarettes gives some people utility; it gives others disutility. We conclude that smoking cigarettes can be a *good* for some people and a *bad* for others. This must be why people tell their loved ones, "If you want to smoke, you should do it outside." In other words, "Get those *bads* away from me."

1-2b Resources

Goods do not just appear before us when we snap our fingers. It takes resources to produce goods. (Sometimes *resources* are referred to as *inputs* or *factors of production*.)

Generally, economists divide resources into four broad categories: *land, labor, capital,* and *entrepreneurship*.

- **Land** includes natural resources, such as minerals, forests, water, and unimproved land. For example, oil, wood, and animals fall into this category. (Sometimes economists refer to the category simply as *natural resources*.)
- **Labor** consists of the physical and mental talents that people contribute to the production process. For example, a person building a house is using his or her own labor.
- **Capital** consists of produced goods that can be used as inputs for further production. Factories, machinery, tools, computers, and buildings are examples of capital. One country might have more capital than another; that is, it has more factories, machinery, tools, and the like.
- **Entrepreneurship** refers to the talent that some people have for organizing the resources of land, labor, and capital to produce goods, seek new business opportunities, and develop new ways of doing things.

1-2c Scarcity and a Definition of Economics

We are now ready to define a key concept in economics: *scarcity*. **Scarcity** is the condition in which our wants (for goods) are greater than the limited resources (land, labor, capital, and entrepreneurship) available to satisfy those wants. In other words, we want goods, but not enough resources are available to provide us with all the goods we want.

Look at it this way: Our wants (for goods) are infinite, but our resources (which we need to produce the goods) are finite. Scarcity is the result of our infinite wants hitting up against finite resources.

Good
Anything from which individuals receive utility or satisfaction.

Utility
The satisfaction one receives from a good.

Bad
Anything from which individuals receive disutility or dissatisfaction.

Disutility
The dissatisfaction one receives from a bad.

Land
All natural resources, such as minerals, forests, water, and unimproved land.

Labor
The work brought about by the physical and mental talents that people contribute to the production process.

Capital
Produced goods—such as factories, machinery, tools, computers, and buildings—that can be used as inputs for further production.

Entrepreneurship
The talent that some people have for organizing the resources of land, labor, and capital to produce goods, seek new business opportunities, and develop new ways of doing things.

Scarcity
The condition in which our wants are greater than the limited resources available to satisfy those wants.

Chapter 1 What Economics Is About

Many economists say that if scarcity didn't exist, neither would economics. In other words, if our wants weren't greater than the limited resources available to satisfy them, there would be no field of study called economics. This is similar to saying that if matter and motion didn't exist, neither would physics or that if living things didn't exist, neither would biology. For this reason, we define **economics** in this text as the science of scarcity. More completely, *economics is the science of how individuals and societies deal with the fact that wants are greater than the limited resources available to satisfy those wants.*

> **Thinking Like an Economist**
>
> **Scarcity Affects Everyone** Everyone in the world—even a billionaire—has to face scarcity. Billionaires may be able to satisfy more of their wants for tangible goods (houses, cars) than most people, but they still may not have the resources to satisfy all their wants. Their wants might include more time with their children, more friendship, no disease in the world, peace, and a hundred other things that they don't have the resources to "produce."

Thinking in Terms of Scarcity's Effects Scarcity has effects, such as the need to make choices, the need for a rationing device, and competition.

Choices People have to make choices because of scarcity. Because our unlimited wants are greater than our limited resources, some wants must go unsatisfied. We must choose which wants we will satisfy and which we will not. Mia asks, "Do I go to Hawaii or do I pay off my car loan earlier?" Alex asks, "Do I buy the new sweater or two new shirts?"

Need for a Rationing Device A **rationing device** is a means of deciding who gets what of available resources and goods. Scarcity implies the need for a rationing device. If people have infinite wants for goods and if only limited resources are available to produce the goods, then a rationing device is needed to decide who gets the available quantity of goods. Dollar price is a rationing device. For instance, 100 cars are on the lot, and everyone wants a new car. How do we decide who gets what quantity of the new cars? The answer is to use the rationing device called *dollar price*. The people who pay the dollar price for a new car end up with one.

Scarcity and Competition Do you see competition in the world? Are people competing for jobs? Are states and cities competing for businesses? Are students competing for grades? The answer to all these questions is yes. The economist wants to know why this competition exists and what form it takes. First, the economist concludes, competition exists because of scarcity. If there were enough resources to satisfy all our seemingly unlimited wants, people would not have to compete for the available, but limited, resources.

Second, the economist sees that competition takes the form of people trying to get more of the rationing device. If dollar price is the rationing device, people compete to earn dollars. Look at your own case. You are a college student working toward a degree. One reason (but perhaps not the only reason) you are attending college is to earn a higher income after graduation. But why do you want a higher income? You want it because it will allow you to satisfy more of your wants.

Suppose muscular strength (measured by lifting weights), instead of dollar price, were the rationing device. Then people with more muscular strength would receive more resources and goods than people with less muscular strength. In that case, people would compete for muscular strength. (They would spend more time at the gym lifting weights.) The lesson is simple: *Whatever the rationing device is, people will compete for it.*

Economics
The science of scarcity; the science of how individuals and societies deal with the fact that wants are greater than the limited resources available to satisfy those wants.

Rationing Device
A means for deciding who gets what of available resources and goods.

> **Finding Economics**
>
> **At the Campus Bookstore** To learn economics well, you must practice what you learn. One of the ways to practice economics is to find it in everyday life. Consider the following scene: You are in the campus bookstore buying a book for your computer science course, and you are handing $85 to the cashier. Can you find the economics in this simple scene? Before you read on, think about it for a minute.
>
> Let's work backward to find the economics. You are currently handing the cashier $85. We know that dollar price is a rationing device. But let's now ask ourselves why we would need a rationing device to get the book. The answer is scarcity. In other words, scarcity is casting its long shadow there in the bookstore as you buy a book. We have found one of the key economic concepts—scarcity—in the campus bookstore. (If you also said that a book is a good, then you have found even more economics in the bookstore. Can you find more than scarcity and a good?)

(Answers to Self-Test questions are in Answers to Self-Test Questions at the back of the book.)

1. True or false? Scarcity is the condition of finite resources. Explain your answer.
2. How does competition arise out of scarcity?
3. How does choice arise out of scarcity?

1-3 Key Concepts in Economics

A number of key concepts in economics define the field. We discuss a few of these concepts next.

1-3a Opportunity Cost

So far, we have established that people must make choices because scarcity exists. In other words, because our seemingly unlimited wants push up against limited resources, some wants must go unsatisfied. We must therefore *choose* which wants we will satisfy and which we will not. The most highly valued opportunity or alternative forfeited when we make a choice is known as **opportunity cost**. Every time you make a choice, you incur an opportunity cost. For example, you have chosen to read this chapter. In making this choice, you denied yourself the benefits of doing something else. You could have watched television, sent text messages to a friend, taken a nap, eaten a few slices of pizza, read a novel, shopped for a new computer, and so on. Whatever you *would have chosen* to do is the opportunity cost of your reading this chapter. For instance, if you would have watched television instead of reading this chapter—if that was your next best alternative—then the opportunity cost of reading the chapter is watching television.

Opportunity Cost
The most highly valued opportunity or alternative forfeited when a choice is made.

There Is No Such Thing as a Free Lunch Economists are fond of saying that "there is no such thing as a free lunch." This catchy phrase expresses the idea that opportunity costs are incurred whenever choices are made. Perhaps this is an obvious point, but consider how often people mistakenly assume that there *is* a free lunch. For example, some parents think that education is free, because they do not pay tuition for their children to attend public elementary school. That's a misconception. "Free" implies no sacrifice and no opportunities forfeited, but an elementary school education requires resources that could be used for other things.

Chapter 1 What Economics Is About

Consider the people who speak about free medical care, free housing, free bridges ("there's no charge to cross it"), and free parks. Again, free medical care, free housing, free bridges, and free parks are misconceptions. The resources that have been used to provide medical care, housing, bridges, and parks could have been used in other ways.

Economics 24/7

Rationing Spots at Yale

Each year, Yale University receives more applications for admission to the freshman class than spots are available. In most years, for every 100 applications for admission that Yale receives, it can accept only seven applicants for admission. What Yale has to do, then, is ration its available admission spots.

How does it ration its available spots? One way is simply to use money as a rationing device. In other words, raise the dollar amount of attending Yale to a high enough level so that the number of spots equals the number of students willing and available to pay for admission. To illustrate, think of Yale as auctioning off spots in its freshman class. It calls out a price of $50,000 a year, and at this price, more people wish to be admitted to Yale than there are spots available. Yale keeps on raising the price until the number of students who are willing and able to pay the tuition is equal to the number of available spots. Maybe this price is, say, $200,000.

As we know, Yale does not ration its available spots this way. In fact, it uses numerous rationing devices in an attempt to whittle down the number of applicants to the number of available spots. For example, it might use the rationing device of high school grades. Anyone with a GPA in high school of less than, say, 3.50 is not going to be admitted. If, after doing this, Yale still has too many applicants, it might then make use of the rationing device of standardized test scores. Anyone with an SAT score of less than, say, 1300 is eliminated from the pool of applicants. If there are still too many applicants, then perhaps other rationing devices will be used, such as academic achievements, community service, degree of interest in attending Yale, and so on.

ISTOCKPHOTO/PETERSPIRO

Yale might also decide that it wants to admit certain students over others, even if the two categories of students have the same academic credentials. For example, suppose Yale wants at least one student from each state in the country, and only 10 students from Wyoming have applied to go to Yale whereas 500 students from California have applied. Then Yale could very well use the rationing device of state diversity to decide in favor of the student from Wyoming instead of the applicant from California.

In the first week of April each year, Yale sends out many more rejection letters than acceptance letters. There is no doubt some students who are rejected by Yale feel that some of the students who were accepted might not be as academically strong as they are. The student with a 4.00 GPA and a perfect SAT score of 1600 may feel he was slighted by Yale when he learns that a student in his high school with a 3.86 GPA and SAT score of 1350 was chosen over him. What did the 3.86–1350 student have that he didn't have? On what rationing device benchmark did the rejected student score lower?

In life, you will often hear people arguing over what the rationing device for certain things should be. Should high school grades and standardized test scores be the only two rationing devices for college admission? What role should money play as a rationing device when a high school graduate applies to college? What role should ethnic or racial diversity, or state diversity, or income diversity play in the application process? Our point is a simple one: With scarcity comes the need for a rationing device. More people want a spot at Yale than there are spots available. Yale has to use one or more rationing devices to decide who will be accepted and who will be rejected.

Thinking Like an Economist

Zero Price Doesn't Mean Zero Cost A friend gives you a ticket to an upcoming concert for zero price (i.e., you pay nothing). Does it follow that zero price means zero cost? No. There is still an opportunity cost of attending the concert. Whatever you would be doing if you don't go to the concert is the opportunity cost of attending. To illustrate, if you don't attend the concert, you would hang out with friends. The value you place on hanging out with friends is the opportunity cost of your attending the concert.

1-3b Opportunity Cost and Behavior

Economists believe that a change in opportunity cost can change a person's behavior. For example, Darnell, who is a sophomore at college, attends classes Monday through Thursday of every week. Every time he chooses to go to class, he gives up the opportunity to do something else, such as earn $15 an hour working at a job. The opportunity cost of Darnell's spending an hour in class is $15.

Now let's raise the opportunity cost of attending class. On Tuesday, we offer Darnell $70 to skip his economics class. He knows that if he attends his economics class, he will forfeit $70. What will Darnell do? An economist would predict that as the opportunity cost of attending class increases relative to the benefits of attending, Darnell is less likely to go to class.

This is how economists think about behavior: *The higher the opportunity cost of doing something, the less likely it is that it will be done.* This is part of the economic way of thinking.

Look at Exhibit 1, which summarizes some of the things about scarcity, choice, and opportunity cost up to this point.

EXHIBIT 1

Scarcity and Related Concepts

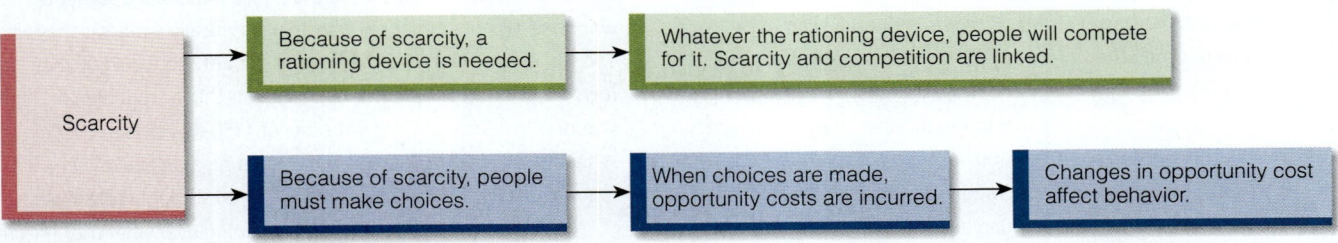

Finding Economics

In Being Late to Class Jordan is often a few minutes late to his biology class. The class starts at 10 a.m., but Jordan usually walks into the class at 10:03 a.m. The instructor has asked Jordan to be on time, but Jordan usually excuses his behavior by saying that the traffic getting to college was bad or that his alarm didn't go off at the right time or that something else happened to delay him. One thing the instructor observes, though, is that Jordan is never late when it comes to test day. He is usually in class a few minutes before the test begins. Where is the economics?

> We would expect behavior to change as opportunity cost changes. When a test is being given in class, the opportunity cost of being late to class is higher than when a test is not being given and the instructor is simply lecturing. If Jordan is late to class on test day, he then has fewer minutes to complete the test, and having less time can adversely affect his grade. In short, the higher the opportunity cost of being late to class, the less likely it is that Jordan will be late.

1-3c Benefits and Costs

If we could eliminate air pollution completely, should we do it? If your answer is yes, then you are probably focusing on the *benefits* of eliminating air pollution. For example, one benefit might be healthier individuals. Certainly, individuals who do not breathe polluted air have fewer lung disorders than people who do breathe polluted air.

But benefits rarely come without costs. The economist reminds us that, although eliminating pollution has its benefits, it has costs too. To illustrate, one way to eliminate all car pollution tomorrow is to pass a law stating that anyone caught driving a car will go to prison for 40 years. With such a draconian law in place and enforced, very few people would drive cars and all car pollution would be a thing of the past. Presto! Cleaner air! However, many people would think that the cost of obtaining that cleaner air is too high. Someone might say, "I want cleaner air, but not if I have to completely give up driving my car. How will I get to work?"

What distinguishes the economist from the noneconomist is that the economist thinks in terms of *both* costs *and* benefits. Often, the noneconomist thinks in terms of one or the other. Studying has its benefits, but it has costs too. Coming to class has benefits, but it has costs too. Getting up early each morning and exercising has its costs, but let's not forget that there are benefits too.

1-3d Decisions Made at the Margin

It is late at night, and you have already spent three hours studying for tomorrow's biology test. You look at the clock and wonder if you should study another hour. How would you summarize your thinking process? What question or questions would you ask yourself to decide whether to study another hour?

Perhaps without knowing it, you think in terms of the costs and benefits of further study. You probably realize that studying an additional hour has certain benefits (you may be able to raise your grade a few points), but it has costs too (you will get less sleep or have less time to watch television or talk on the phone with a friend). *That* you think in terms of costs and benefits, however, doesn't tell us *how* you think in terms of costs and benefits. For example, when deciding what to do, do you look at the *total costs* and *total benefits* of the proposed action, or do you look at something less than the total costs and benefits? According to economists, for most decisions, you think in terms of *additional,* or *marginal,* costs and benefits, not *total* costs and benefits. That's because most decisions deal with making a small, or additional, change.

To illustrate, suppose you just finished eating a hamburger and drinking a soda for lunch. You are still a little hungry and are considering whether to order another hamburger. An economist would say that, in deciding whether to order another hamburger, you compare the additional benefits of the second hamburger with its additional costs. In economics, the word *marginal* is a synonym for *additional.* So, we say that you compare the **marginal benefits (MB)** of the (next) hamburger to its **marginal costs (MC).** If the marginal benefits are greater than the marginal costs, you obviously expect a net benefit of ordering the next hamburger, and

Marginal Benefits (MB)
Additional benefits; the benefits connected with consuming an additional unit of a good or undertaking one more unit of an activity.

Marginal Costs (MC)
Additional costs; the costs connected with consuming an additional unit of a good or undertaking one more unit of an activity.

therefore, you order another. If, however, the marginal benefits are less than the marginal costs, you obviously expect a net cost of ordering the next hamburger, and therefore, you do not order another. Logically, the situation is as follows:

Condition	Action
MB of next hamburger > MC of next hamburger	Buy next hamburger
MB of next hamburger < MC of next hamburger	Do not buy next hamburger

What you don't consider when making this decision are the *total* benefits and *total* costs of hamburgers. That's because the benefits and costs connected with the first hamburger (the one you have already eaten) are no longer relevant to the current decision. You are not deciding between eating two hamburgers or eating no hamburgers; your decision is whether to eat a second hamburger after you have already eaten one.

According to economists, when individuals make decisions by comparing marginal benefits with marginal costs, they are making **decisions at the margin**. The employee makes a decision at the margin in deciding whether to work two hours overtime; the economics professor makes a decision at the margin in deciding whether to put an additional question on the final exam.

Decisions at the Margin
Decision making characterized by weighing the additional (marginal) benefits of a change against the additional (marginal) costs of a change with respect to current conditions.

Economics 24/7

When Is It Too Costly to Attend College?

Look around your class. Are there any big-name actors, sports stars, or comedians between the ages of 18 and 25 in your class? Probably not. The reason is that, for these people, the opportunity cost of attending college is much higher than it is for most 18-to-25-year-olds. Think of Chris Rock, a comedian, and Emma Stone and Ryan Gosling, both actors. These people and many more like them chose not to go to college. Why didn't they go? The fact is that they didn't go to college because it was too expensive for them to go to college. Not "too expensive" in the sense that the "tuition was too high," but expensive in terms of what they would have had to give up if they attended college—expensive in opportunity cost terms.

To understand this idea, think of what it's costing you to attend college. If you pay $7,000 tuition a semester for eight semesters, the full tuition amounts to $56,000. However, $56,000 is not the full cost of attending college, because if you were not a student, you could be earning income working at a job. For example, you could be working at a full-time job earning $42,000 annually. Certainly, this $42,000, or at least part of it if you are currently working part time, is forfeited because you are attending college. It is part of the total cost of your attending college.

The *tuition cost* may be the same for everyone who attends your college, but the *opportunity cost* is not. Some people have higher opportunity costs of attending college than others. It just so happens that Chris Rock, Emma Stone, and Ryan Gosling had extremely high opportunity costs of attending college. Each would have to give up hundreds of thousands of dollars if he or she were to attend college on a full-time basis.

Simply put, our story illustrates two related points we have made in this chapter. First, earlier we said that *the higher the opportunity cost of doing something, the less likely it will be done*. The opportunity cost of attending college is higher for some people than others, and that is why not everyone who can pay for college chooses to attend college.

Second, we said that economists believe that *individuals think and act in terms of costs and benefits and that they undertake actions only if they expect the benefits to outweigh the costs*. Thus, Chris Rock, Emma Stone, and Ryan Gosling saw certain benefits to attending college—just as you see certain benefits to attending college. But those benefits—although they may be the same for you and everyone else—are not enough to get everyone to attend college. That's because the benefits are not all that matters. The costs matter too. In the case of Chris Rock, Emma Stone, and Ryan Gosling, the costs of attending college were much higher than the benefits, so they chose not to attend college. In your case, the benefits are higher than the costs, so you have decided to attend college.

1-3e Efficiency

What is the right amount of time to study for a test? In economics, the *right amount* of anything is the *optimal* or *efficient* amount—the amount for which the marginal benefits equal the marginal costs. Stated differently, you have achieved **efficiency** when the marginal benefits equal the marginal costs.

Suppose you are studying for an economics test, and for the first hour of studying, the marginal benefits (*MB*) are greater than the marginal costs (*MC*):

Efficiency
Exists when marginal benefits equal marginal costs.

$$MB \text{ studying first hour} > MC \text{ studying first hour}$$

Given this condition, you will certainly study for the first hour, because it is worth it: The additional benefits are greater than the additional costs, so there is a net benefit to studying.

Suppose, for the second hour of studying, the marginal benefits are still greater than the marginal costs:

$$MB \text{ studying second hour} > MC \text{ studying second hour}$$

Then you will study for the second hour, because the additional benefits are still greater than the additional costs. In other words, studying the second hour is worthwhile. In fact, you will continue to study as long as the marginal benefits are greater than the marginal costs. Exhibit 2 illustrates this discussion graphically.

The *MB* curve of studying is downward sloping because we have assumed that the benefits of studying for the first hour are greater than the benefits of studying for the second hour and so on. The *MC* curve of studying is upward sloping because we have assumed that studying the second hour costs a person more (in terms of goods forfeited) than studying the first hour, studying the third hour costs more than studying the second, and so on. (If we assume that the additional costs of studying are constant over time, the *MC* curve is horizontal.)

In the exhibit, the marginal benefits of studying equal the marginal costs of studying at three hours. So, three hours is the *efficient* length of time to study in this situation. At less than three hours, the marginal benefits of studying are greater than the marginal costs; thus, at all these hours, studying has net benefits. At more than three hours, the marginal costs of studying are greater than the marginal benefits, so studying beyond three hours is not worthwhile.

EXHIBIT 2

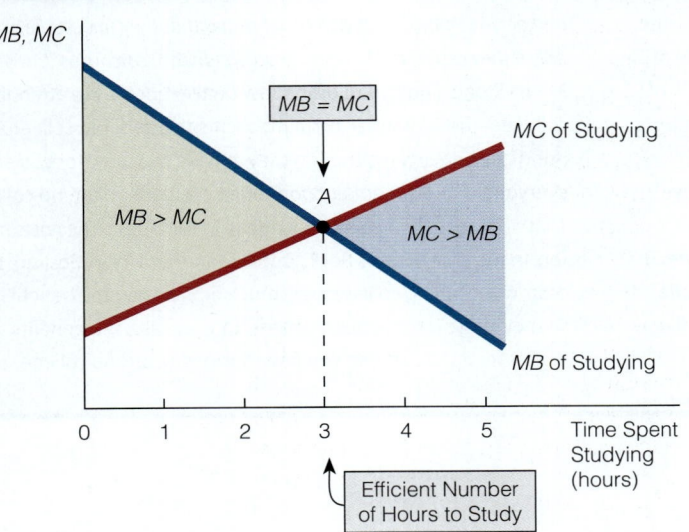

Efficiency

MB = marginal benefits and MC = marginal costs. In the exhibit, the MB curve of studying is downward sloping, and the MC curve of studying is upward sloping. As long as $MB > MC$, the person will study. The person stops studying when $MB = MC$. This point is where efficiency is achieved.

Maximizing Net Benefits Take another look at Exhibit 2. Suppose you had stopped studying after the first hour (or, equivalently, after the 60th minute). Would you have given up anything? Yes, you would have given up the *net benefits* of studying longer. To illustrate, notice that between the first and the second hour, the MB curve lies above the MC curve. This means that studying the second hour has net benefits. But if you hadn't studied that second hour—if you had stopped after the first hour—then you would have given up the opportunity to collect those net benefits. The same analysis holds for the third hour. We conclude that by studying three hours (but not one minute longer), you have maximized net benefits. In short, efficiency, which is consistent with $MB = MC$, is also consistent with maximizing net benefits.

Thinking Like an Economist

No $10 Bills on the Sidewalk An economist says that people try to maximize their net benefits. You ask for proof. The economist says, "You don't find any $10 bills on the sidewalk." What is the economist getting at by making this statement? Keep in mind that you don't find any $10 bills on the sidewalk because, if there were a $10 bill on the sidewalk, the first person to see it would pick it up; when you came along, it wouldn't be there. But why would the first person to find the $10 bill pick it up? The reason is that people don't pass by net benefits, and picking up the $10 bill comes with net benefits. The *benefits* of having an additional $10 are obvious; the *costs* of obtaining the additional $10 bill are simply what you give up during the time you are stooping down to pick it up. In short, the marginal benefits are likely to be greater than the marginal costs (giving us net benefits), and that is why the $10 bill is picked up. Saying that there are no $10 bills on the sidewalk is the same as saying that no one leaves net benefits on the sidewalk. In other words, people try to maximize net benefits.

1-3f Economics Is About Incentives

An **incentive** is something that encourages or motivates a person to undertake an action.

Often, what motivates a person to undertake an action is the belief that, by taking that action, she can make herself better off. For example, if we say that Piper has an incentive to study for the upcoming exam, we imply that, by studying, Piper can make herself better off, probably in terms of receiving a higher grade on the exam than if she didn't study.

Incentives are closely related to benefits and costs. Individuals have an incentive to undertake actions for which the benefits are greater than the costs or, stated differently, for which they expect to receive net benefits (benefits greater than costs).

Economists are interested in what motivates behavior. Why do people buy more of good X when its price falls? Why might people work longer hours when income tax rates decline? Why might people buy more of a particular good today if they expect the price of that good to go up next week? The general answer to many of these questions is that people do what they have an incentive to do. Economists then hunt for what the incentive is. For example, if people buy more of good X when its price goes down, what specifically is the incentive? How, specifically, do people make themselves better off by buying a good when its price declines. Do they get more utility or satisfaction? Or how do people make themselves better off if they buy a good today that they expect will go up in price next week?

Incentive
Something that encourages or motivates a person to undertake an action.

Economics 24/7

Movie Studios Versus Netflix: Incentives Matter

You go to a movie theater to see a movie, which is produced by, say, Universal Pictures. Is the movie theater in which you see the movie owned by Universal Pictures? Not these days. But this wasn't always the case. Back in the 1930s and 1940s, in what was considered the golden age of the movie business, movie studios owned their own movie theaters. But in 1948, based on an antitrust case brought by the U.S. Department of Justice, the Supreme Court ruled that movie studios could no longer own their own movie theaters.

Today, you might pay a $9–$15 ticket price to view a movie in a theater. The movie studio that made the movie and the theater owners share the revenue from that ticket price; it is not uncommon for the studio to earn around 60 percent of the ticket price and for the theater to earn 40 percent of it. But what is interesting is that the split between the studio and theater is not always the same in any given week of the movie's release. For example, the studio commonly gets a larger percentage of the first weekend's ticket gross, such as 90 percent. Then, in the second week, it might get 80 percent. At some point, the percentage turns in the favor of the theater in the later weeks of a movie's release.

Keep in mind that audiences are often the largest in the early weeks of a movie's release, so it makes financial sense for a movie studio to want its percentage of the split between it and the theaters to be the largest when audiences are the largest (and, in this case, when the ticket revenues are the largest).

Because the studio–theater split is largest for the studio in the early weeks of a movie's release, the studio now has an incentive to get as much ticket revenue for the movie as possible to be pushed up as close to the release date of the movie. To illustrate, if a movie runs for four weeks, and the studio has its most favorable split of 90/10 in the first week only, then it would be most beneficial for the studio if all the ticket revenue for the movie could be earned in the first week instead of being spread over four weeks. For example, it is better for the studio to earn 90 percent of a total ticket revenue of $100 million (which is $90 million) in the first week than to earn, say, 90 percent of $40 million (which is $36 million) in the first week, 80 percent of $30 million (which is $24 million) in the second week, 20 percent of $20 million (which is $4 million) in the third week, and 10 percent of $10 million (which is $1 million) in the fourth week. In other words, it is better to earn $90 million out of $100 million than to earn $65 million out of $100 million.

Given this, movie studios have an incentive to make movies that make a big initial bang at the box office. It is better to make a movie that comes out with a big bang and fizzles out later than to make a movie that starts slow and grows over time—so if there is a bang, it needs to come early. This incentivizes studios to make movies with a built-in demand—such as movies based on best-selling books or superhero, or event movies. An event movie is a movie whose release itself is considered a major event; it could be an anticipated sequel (almost all *Star Wars* movies were anticipated sequels or prequels), a big-budget movie with major stars, or a movie with state-of-the-art effects. That is to say, the types of movies that studios often make are related to the way they split the ticket revenue with theaters. In short, incentives matter. In this case, incentives influence what kinds of movies are most likely to get made by the studios.

Think about this. In recent years, Netflix has begun to produce some of its own content. Some of its content includes original series and movies. Netflix earns most of its revenue from subscription fees; there is no split, like what a movie studio has with a theater. Netflix, then, is much more inclined than a major movie studio to produce a movie or original series that it believes will grow *in time*, due to word of mouth. It is not as inclined to go for the big bang up front, close to the release date, like what a movie theater would do. For Netflix, the first week of an original movie's release is not as important as it is to a movie studio that is concerned with a declining split of the ticket revenue as weeks progress. The first week and the fourth week and the 10th week can all bring in new Netflix subscribers.

1-3g Unintended Effects

Economists think in terms of unintended effects. For instance, Andrés, 16 years old, currently works after school at a grocery store. He earns $9.50 an hour.

Suppose the state legislature passes a law specifying that the minimum dollar wage a person can be paid to do a job is $15 an hour. The legislators' intention in passing the law is to help people like Andrés earn more income.

Will the $15-an-hour legislation have the intended effect? Perhaps not. The manager of the grocery store may not find it worthwhile to continue employing Andrés if she has to pay him $15 an hour. In other words, Andrés may have a job at $9.50 an hour but not at $15 an hour. If the law specifies that no one may earn less than $15 an hour and the manager of the grocery store decides to fire Andrés rather than pay that amount, then an unintended effect of the legislation is Andrés losing his job.

As another example, let's analyze mandatory seat-belt laws to see whether they have any unintended effects. States have laws that require drivers to wear seat belts. The intended effect is to reduce the number of car-related fatalities by making it more likely that drivers will survive accidents.

Could these laws have an unintended effect? Some economists think so. They look at accident fatalities in terms of this equation:

$$\text{Total number of fatalities} = \text{Number of accidents} \times \text{Fatalities per accident}$$

For example, if there are 200,000 accidents and 0.10 fatality per accident, the total number of fatalities is 20,000.

The objective of a mandatory seat-belt program is to reduce the total number of fatalities by reducing the number of fatalities per accident (the fatality rate). Many studies have found that wearing seat belts does just that. If you are in an accident, you have a better chance of not being killed if you are wearing a seat belt.

Let's assume that, with seat belts, there is 0.08, instead of 0.10, fatality per accident. If there are still 200,000 accidents, then the total number of fatalities falls from 20,000 to 16,000. Thus, as the following table shows, the total number of fatalities drops if the number of fatalities per accident is reduced and the number of accidents is constant:

Number of Accidents	Fatalities per Accident	Total Number of Fatalities
200,000	0.10	20,000
200,000	0.08	16,000

However, some economists wonder whether the number of accidents stays constant. Specifically, they suggest that seat belts may have an unintended effect: *The number of accidents may increase* because wearing seat belts may make drivers feel safer. Feeling safer may cause them to take chances that they wouldn't ordinarily take, such as driving faster or more aggressively, or concentrating less on their driving and more on the music on the radio. For example, if the number of accidents rises to 250,000, then the total number of fatalities is again 20,000:

Number of Accidents	Fatalities per Accident	Total Number of Fatalities
200,000	0.10	20,000
250,000	0.08	20,000

We conclude the following: If a mandatory seat-belt law reduces the number of fatalities per accident (the intended effect) but increases the number of accidents (an unintended effect), then the law may not, contrary to popular belief, reduce the total number of fatalities. In fact, some economics studies show just that.

What does all this mean for you? You may be safer if you know that this unintended effect exists and you adjust accordingly. To be specific, when you wear your seat belt, your chances of getting hurt in a car accident are less than if you don't wear your seat belt. But if this added sense of protection causes you to drive less carefully than you would otherwise, then you could unintentionally offset the measure of protection your seat belt provides. To reduce the probability of hurting yourself and others in a car accident, *the best policy is to wear a seat belt and to drive as carefully as you would if you weren't wearing a seat belt.* Knowing about the unintended effect of wearing your seat belt could save your life.

1-3h Exchange

Exchange, or **trade**, is the giving up of one thing for something else. Economics is sometimes called the *science of exchange* because so much that is discussed in economics has to do with exchange.

We start with a basic question: Why do people enter into exchanges? The answer is that they do so to make themselves better off. When a person voluntarily trades $100 for a jacket,

Exchange (Trade)
The giving up of one thing for something else.

she is saying, "I prefer to have the jacket instead of the $100." And, of course, when the seller of the jacket voluntarily sells the jacket for $100, he is saying, "I prefer to have the $100 instead of the jacket." In short, through trade or exchange, each person gives up something he values less for something he values more.

You can think of trade in terms of utility or satisfaction. Imagine a utility scale that goes from 1 to 10, with 10 being the highest utility you can achieve. Now, suppose you currently have $40 in your wallet and you are at 7 on the utility scale. A few minutes later, you are in a store looking at some new shirts. The price of each is $20, and you end up buying two shirts for $40.

After you traded your $40 for the shirts, are you still at 7 on the utility scale? The likely answer is no. If you expected to have the same utility after the trade as you did before, you probably would not have traded your $40 for the shirts. The only reason you entered into the trade is that you *expected* to be better off after the trade than you were before it. In other words, you thought that trading your $40 for the shirts would move you up the utility scale from 7 to, say, 8.

Economics 24/7

Why Didn't I Think of That? The Case of Uber and Airbnb

Consider two companies, both headquartered in San Francisco. The first is Uber and the second is Airbnb. Uber is a company that operates a mobile-app-based transportation network. Here are how things work. One person needs transportation from home to the airport. Another person, with a car, who is in the vicinity of this first person, is willing and able to drive the person to the airport for a fee. Uber takes a percentage of the dollar transaction between driver and rider. In a way, you could say that Uber is a taxi company but owns no taxis.

Now consider Airbnb, which is essentially a website. Here are how things work at the website. One person wants to rent a room in a house, or an entire house, or, say, a couch in the living room of someone's house for a night, a week, or more. Another person, with a room or a house or a couch in the living room, is willing to accommodate this person. What Airbnb essentially does is put these two people in contact with each other and charge a fee. In a way, you could say that Airbnb is a hotel but owns no rooms.

Now what many people think when first learning about Uber and Airbnb is to ask themselves: Why didn't I think of that? How ingenious to start your own taxi business but not own any taxis, or to start your own hotel businesses but not own any rooms.

Now what must the founders of Uber and Airbnb have been thinking that others didn't? Whether they knew it or not, what they were thinking about was exchange or trade. As we stated earlier, exchange or trade is giving up one thing for something else. In the case of Uber, one person is giving up money for a ride to the airport. The other person is giving up time and a car to drive the first person to the airport for money. In the case of Airbnb, one person is giving up money for a week's stay in a house. The other person is giving up occupancy of the house for money.

Now what Uber and Airbnb essentially do is bring people together who want to trade with each other. Uber knows that there are people who want to be transported from one location to another and other people who want to do the transporting. Uber brings these two sets of people together. Airbnb knows that there are people who want to rent a room or a house in, say, Miami Beach for a day or a week and other people who want to rent out their room or a house in Miami for a day or a week. Airbnb brings these two sets of people together.

> So, how does one come up with the Uber or Airbnb ideas? Basically, both ideas have to do with trying to answer this question: *How do I bring together people who want to trade with each other but who are not currently trading with each other?* That is the question the founders of both Uber and Airbnb asked and answered, albeit the first with respect to transportation and the second with respect to lodging. Are there other instances where people who want to trade with each other are just waiting to be brought together?

1. Give an example to illustrate how a change in opportunity cost can affect behavior.
2. Studying has both costs and benefits. If you continue to study (e.g., for a test) for as long as the marginal benefits of studying are greater than the marginal costs, and you stop studying when the two are equal, will your action be consistent with having maximized the net benefits of studying? Explain your answer.
3. You stay up an additional hour to study for a test. The intended effect is to raise your test grade. What might be an unintended effect of staying up another hour to study?

1-4 *Ceteris Paribus* and Theory

We cover two important topics in this section: (1) *ceteris paribus* and (2) theory.

1-4a *Ceteris Paribus* Thinking

Dylan has eaten regular ice cream for years, and for years, his weight has been 190 pounds. One day, Dylan decides he wants to lose weight. With this objective in mind, he buys a new fat-free ice cream at the grocery store. The fat-free ice cream has half the calories of regular ice cream.

Dylan eats the fat-free ice cream for the next few months. He then weighs himself and finds that he has gained two pounds. Does this mean that fat-free ice cream causes people to gain weight and regular ice cream does not? The answer is no. Why did Dylan gain weight when he substituted fat-free ice cream for regular ice cream? Perhaps Dylan ate three times as much fat-free ice cream as regular ice cream. Or perhaps during the time he was eating fat-free ice cream, he wasn't exercising, and during the time he was eating regular ice cream, he was exercising. In other words, a number of factors—such as eating more ice cream or exercising less—may have offset the weight loss that Dylan would have experienced had these other factors not changed.

Now, suppose you want to make the point that Dylan would have lost weight by substituting fat-free ice cream for regular ice cream had these other factors not changed. What would you say? A scientist would say, "If Dylan has been eating regular ice cream and his weight has stabilized at 190 pounds, then substituting fat-free ice cream for regular ice cream will lead to a decline in weight, *ceteris paribus*."

The term **ceteris paribus** means *all other things constant* or *nothing else changes*. In our ice cream example, if nothing else changes—such as how much ice cream Dylan eats, how much exercise he gets, and so on—then switching to fat-free ice cream will result in weight loss. This expectation is based on the theory that a reduction in calorie consumption will result in weight loss and an increase in calorie consumption will result in weight gain.

Ceteris Paribus
A Latin term meaning *all other things constant* or *nothing else changes*.

Using the *ceteris paribus* assumption is important because, with it, we can clearly designate what we believe is the correct relationship between two variables. In the ice cream example, we can designate the correct relationship between calorie intake and weight gain.

Economists don't often talk about ice cream, but they will often make use of the *ceteris paribus* assumption. An economist might say, "If the price of a good decreases, the quantity of it consumed increases, *ceteris paribus*." For example, if the price of Pepsi decreases, people will buy more of it, assuming that nothing else changes.

But some people ask, "Why would economists want to assume that when the price of Pepsi falls, nothing else changes? Don't other things change in the real world? Why make assumptions that we know are not true?"

Of course, economists do not specify *ceteris paribus* because they want to say something false about the world. They specify it because they want to clearly define what they believe to be the real-world relationship between two variables. Look at it this way: If you drop a ball off the roof of a house, it will fall to the ground, unless someone catches it. This statement is true, and probably everyone would willingly accept it as true. But here is another true statement: If you drop a ball off the roof of a house, it will fall to the ground, *ceteris paribus*. In fact, the two statements are identical in meaning. This is because adding the phrase "unless someone catches it" in the first sentence is the same as saying "*ceteris paribus*" in the second sentence. If one statement is acceptable to us, the other should be too.

1-4b What Is a Theory?

Almost everyone, including you, builds and tests theories or models on a regular basis. (In this text, the words *theory* and *model* are used interchangeably.) Perhaps you thought that only scientists and others with high-level mathematics at their fingertips built and tested theories. However, theory building and testing is not the domain of only the highly educated and mathematically proficient. Almost everyone builds and test theories.

People build theories any time they do not know the answer to a question. Someone asks, "Why is the crime rate higher in the United States than in Belgium?" Or, "Why did Li Wei's girlfriend break up with him?" Or, "Why does Professor Avalos give easier final exams than Professor Shaw, even though they teach the same subject?" If you don't know the answer to a question, you are likely to build a theory so that you can provide an answer.

What exactly is a theory? To an economist, a **theory** is an abstract representation of the world. In this context, **abstract** means that you omit certain variables or factors when you try to explain or understand something. For example, suppose you were to draw a map for a friend, showing him how to get from his house to yours. Would you draw a map that showed every single thing your friend would see on the trip, or would you simply draw the main roads and one or two landmarks? If you'd do the latter, you would be abstracting from reality; you would be omitting certain things.

You would abstract for two reasons: First, to get your friend from his house to yours, you don't need to include everything on your map. Simply noting main roads may be enough. Second, if you did note everything on your map, your friend might get confused. Giving too much detail could be as bad as giving too little.

When economists build a theory or model, they do the same thing you do in drawing a map. They abstract from reality; they leave out certain things. They focus on the major factors or variables that they believe will explain the phenomenon they are trying to understand.

Suppose a criminologist's objective is to explain why some people turn to crime. Before actually building the theory, he considers a number of variables that may explain why some

Theory
An abstract representation of the real world designed with the intent to better understand it.

Abstract
The process (used in building a theory) of focusing on a limited number of variables to explain or predict an event.

people become criminals: (1) the ease of getting a gun, (2) child-rearing practices, (3) the neighborhood a person grew up in, (4) whether a person was abused as a child, (5) family education, (6) the type of friends a person has, (7) a person's IQ, (8) climate, and (9) a person's diet.

The criminologist may think that some of these variables greatly affect the chance that a person will become a criminal, some affect it only slightly, and others do not affect it at all. For example, a person's diet may have only a 0.0001 percent effect on the person becoming a criminal, whereas whether a person was abused as a child may have a 30 percent effect.

A theory emphasizes only the variables that the theorist believes are the main or critical ones that explain an activity or event. Thus, if the criminologist in our example thinks that parental child-rearing practices and family education are likely to explain much more about criminal behavior than the other variables are, then his (abstract) theory will focus on these two variables and ignore the others.

All theories are abstractions from reality. But it doesn't follow that (abstract) theories cannot explain reality. The objective in theory building is to ignore the variables that are essentially irrelevant to the case at hand, making it easier to isolate the important variables that the untrained observer would probably miss.

In the course of reading this text, you will come across numerous theories. Some of these theories are explained in words, and others are represented graphically. For example, Chapter 3 presents the theory of supply and demand. First, the parts of the theory are explained. Then the theory is represented graphically in terms of a supply curve and a demand curve.

What to Ask a Theorist Physicists, chemists, and economists aren't the only persons who build and test theories. Historians, sociologists, anthropologists, and many others build and test theories. In fact, as suggested earlier in this section, almost everyone builds theories (although not everyone tests theories).

Anytime you listen to someone expound on a theory, you should always ask a key question: "If your theory is correct, what do you predict we will see in the world?" To illustrate, let's consider a very simple example. Suppose your history professor comes to class each day clean shaven and dressed in slacks, shirt, and sports jacket. One day he comes to class unshaven and dressed in jeans and a somewhat wrinkled T-shirt. The difference in appearance is obvious. You turn to your friend who sits next to you in class and ask, "What do you think explains the difference in his appearance and dress?"

Notice that you have asked a question that does not have an obvious answer. Such questions are ripe for theory building. Your friend proposes an explanation. She says, "I think the professor forgot to set his alarm clock last night. He got up late this morning and didn't have time to shave or to dress the way he usually does. He just threw on the first clothes he found and rushed to class."

Your friend has advanced a theory of sorts. She has implicitly assumed that the professor wants to shave and dress in slacks, shirt, and sports jacket but that some unusual event prevented him from doing so today.

Somehow, you don't think your friend's theory is correct. Instead, you think your history professor has decided to make a life change of some sort. He has decided to look more casual, to take life a little easier, to be less formal. You tell your friend what you think explains your professor's new behavior.

You, like your friend, have advanced a theory of sorts. Whose theory, if either, is correct? Now is the time for you to ask your friend, and your friend to ask you, "If your theory is correct, what do you predict we will see in the world?"

Your friend's answer should be, "If *my* theory is correct, then the next time the professor comes to class, he will be clean shaven and dressed in his old way—slacks, shirt, and sports jacket." Your answer should be, "If *my* theory is correct, then the next time the professor comes to class, he will be unshaven and dressed as he is today—in jeans, T-shirt, and the like."

The question—If your theory is correct, what do you predict we will see in the world?—gives us a way to figure out who might be closer to the truth when people disagree. It minimizes talk and maximizes the chances of establishing who is correct and who is incorrect.

1. What is the purpose of building a theory?
2. How might a theory of the economy differ from a description of it?
3. Why is it important to test a theory? Why not simply accept a theory if it sounds right?
4. Your economics instructor says, "If the price of going to the movies goes down, people will go to the movies more often." A student in class says, "Not if the quality of the movies goes down." Who is right, the economics instructor or the student?

1-5 Economic Categories

Economics is sometimes broken down into different categories according to the type of questions asked. Four common economic categories are positive economics, normative economics, microeconomics, and macroeconomics.

1-5a Positive Economics and Normative Economics

Positive Economics
The study of *what is* in economics.

Normative Economics
The study of *what should be* in economics.

Positive economics attempts to determine *what is*. **Normative economics** addresses *what should be*. Essentially, positive economics deals with cause-effect relationships that can be tested. Normative economics deals with value judgments and opinions that cannot be tested.

Many topics in economics can be discussed in both a positive and a normative framework. Consider a proposed cut in federal income taxes. An economist practicing positive economics would want to know the *effect* of a cut in income taxes. For example, she may want to know how a tax cut will affect the unemployment rate, economic growth, inflation, and so on. An economist practicing normative economics would address issues that directly or indirectly relate to whether the federal income tax *should* be cut. For example, the economist may say that federal income taxes should be cut because the income tax burden on many taxpayers is currently high.

This book deals mainly with positive economics. For the most part, we discuss the economic world as it is, not the way someone might think it should be. Keep in mind, too, that no matter what your normative objectives are, positive economics can shed some light on how they might be accomplished. For example, suppose you believe that absolute poverty should be eliminated and that the unemployment rate should be lowered. No doubt you have ideas as to how these goals can be accomplished. But will your ideas work? For example, will a greater redistribution of income eliminate absolute poverty? Will lowering taxes lower the unemployment rate? There is no guarantee that the means you think will bring about certain ends will do so. This is where sound positive economics can help us see what is. As someone once said, "It is not enough to want to do good; it is important also to know how to do good."

1-5b Microeconomics and Macroeconomics

It has been said that the tools of microeconomics are microscopes and the tools of macroeconomics are telescopes. Macroeconomics stands back from the trees to see the forest. Microeconomics gets up close and examines the tree itself—its bark, its limbs, and its roots. **Microeconomics** is the branch of economics that deals with human behavior and choices as they relate to relatively small units: an individual, a firm, an industry, a single market. **Macroeconomics** is the branch of economics that deals with human behavior and choices as they relate to an entire economy. In microeconomics, economists discuss a single price; in macroeconomics, they discuss the price level. Microeconomics deals with the demand for a particular good or service; macroeconomics deals with aggregate, or total, demand for goods and services. Microeconomics examines how a tax change affects a single firm's output; macroeconomics looks at how a tax change affects an entire economy's output.

Microeconomists and macroeconomists ask different types of questions. A microeconomist might be interested in answering such questions as the following:

- How does a market work?
- What level of output does a firm produce?
- What price does a firm charge for the good it produces?
- How does a consumer determine how much of a good to buy?
- Can government policy affect business behavior?
- Can government policy affect consumer behavior?

A macroeconomist, by contrast, might be interested in answering such questions as these:

- How does the economy work?
- Why is the unemployment rate sometimes high and sometimes low?
- What causes inflation?
- Why do some national economies grow faster than others?
- What might cause interest rates to be low one year and high the next?
- How do changes in the money supply affect the economy?
- How do changes in government spending and taxes affect the economy?

Microeconomics
The branch of economics that deals with human behavior and choices as they relate to relatively small units: an individual, a firm, an industry, a single market.

Macroeconomics
The branch of economics that deals with human behavior and choices as they relate to highly aggregate markets (e.g., the market for goods and services) or the entire economy.

Office Hours

"I Don't Believe That Every Time a Person Does Something, He Compares the Marginal Benefits and Costs."

Student: In class yesterday, you said that individuals compare the marginal benefits (*MB*) of doing something (say, exercising) with the marginal costs (*MC*). If the marginal benefits are greater than the marginal costs, they exercise; if the marginal costs are greater than the marginal benefits, they don't. Here is what I am having a problem with: I don't believe that every time people do something, they compare the marginal benefits and costs. I think people do some things without thinking of benefits and costs; they do some things instinctively or because they have always done them.

Instructor: Can you give an example?

Student: I don't think of the benefits and costs of eating breakfast in the morning; I just eat breakfast. I don't think of the benefits and costs of doing my homework; I just do the homework before it is due. For me, many activities are automatic; I do them without thinking.

Instructor: It doesn't necessarily follow that you are not considering benefits and costs when you do something automatically. All you have to do is sense whether doing something comes with net benefits (benefits greater than costs) or net costs (costs greater than benefits). All you have to do is sense whether something is likely to make you better off or worse off. You eat breakfast in the morning because you have decided that it makes you better off. But making you better off is no different from saying that you receive net benefits from eating breakfast, which is no different from saying that the benefits of eating breakfast are greater than the costs. In other words, *better off* equals *net benefits* equals *benefits greater than costs*.

Student: I see what you're saying. But then how would you explain the fact that Caleb smokes cigarettes and Luis does not. If both Caleb and Luis consider the benefits and costs of smoking cigarettes, then it seems that either both would have to smoke or both would have to not smoke. The fact that different people do different things tells me that not everyone is considering the costs and benefits of their actions. If everyone did, they would all do the same thing.

Instructor: I disagree. Not everyone sees the costs and benefits of the same thing the same way. Caleb and Luis may not see the benefits or costs of smoking the same way. For Caleb, the benefits of smoking may be high, but for Luis, they may be low. It is no different from saying different people estimate the benefits of playing chess or eating a doughnut or riding a bicycle differently. The same holds for costs. Not everyone will estimate the costs of playing chess or eating a doughnut or riding a bicycle the same way. The costs of a person with diabetes eating a doughnut are much higher than the costs of a person without diabetes eating a doughnut.

Student: Let me see if I have this right. You are making two points. First, not everyone has the same benefits and costs of, say, running a mile. Second, everyone who does run a mile believes that the benefits are greater than the costs, and everyone who does not run a mile believes that the costs are greater than the benefits.

Instructor: Yes, that's it. All people are trying to make themselves better off (reap net benefits), but not all people will do *X* because not all people will be made better off by doing *X*.

Points to Remember

1. If you undertake those actions for which you expect to receive net benefits, then you are "thinking" in terms of costs and benefits. Specifically, you expect the marginal benefits to be greater than the marginal costs.
2. The costs and benefits of doing any activity are not necessarily the same for everybody. Caleb may expect higher benefits than Luis when it comes to doing *X*; Luis may expect higher costs than Caleb when it comes to doing *X*.

Chapter Summary

Goods, Bads, and Resources

- A good is anything that gives a person utility or satisfaction.
- A bad is anything that gives a person disutility or dissatisfaction.
- Economists divide resources into four categories: land, labor, capital, and entrepreneurship.
- Land includes natural resources, such as minerals, forests, water, and unimproved land.
- Labor is brought about by the physical and mental talents that people contribute to the production process.
- Capital consists of produced goods—such as machinery, tools, computers, trucks, buildings, and factories—that can be used as inputs for further production.
- Entrepreneurship is the talent that some people have for organizing the resources of land, labor, and capital to produce goods, seek new business opportunities, and develop new ways of doing things.

Chapter 1 What Economics Is About

Scarcity

- Scarcity is the condition in which our wants are greater than the limited resources available to satisfy them.
- Scarcity implies choice. In a world of limited resources, we must choose which wants will be satisfied and which will go unsatisfied.
- Because of scarcity, there is a need for a rationing device. A rationing device is a means of deciding who gets what quantities of the available resources and goods.
- Scarcity implies competition. If resources were ample to satisfy all our seemingly unlimited wants, people would not have to compete for the available, but limited, resources.

Opportunity Cost

- Every time a person makes a choice, he or she incurs an opportunity cost. Opportunity cost is the most highly valued opportunity or alternative forfeited when a choice is made. The higher the opportunity cost of doing something, the less likely it is that it will be done.

Costs and Benefits

- What distinguishes the economist from the noneconomist is that the economist thinks in terms of *both* costs and benefits. Asked what the benefits of taking a walk may be, an economist will also mention the related costs. Asked what the costs of studying are, an economist will also point out its benefits.

Decisions Made at the Margin

- Marginal benefits and costs are not the same as total benefits and costs. When deciding whether to talk on the phone one more minute, an individual would not consider the total benefits and total costs of speaking on the phone. Instead, the person would compare only the marginal benefits (additional benefits) of talking on the phone one more minute with the marginal costs (additional costs) of talking on the phone one more minute.

Incentives

- An incentive is something that encourages or motivates a person to undertake an action. Incentives are closely related to benefits and costs. Individuals have an incentive to undertake actions for which the benefits are greater than the costs or, stated differently, for which they expect to receive some net benefits (benefits greater than costs).

Efficiency

- As long as the marginal benefits of an activity are greater than its marginal costs, a person gains by continuing to do the activity—whether the activity is studying, running, eating, or watching television. The net benefits of an activity are maximized when the marginal benefits of the activity equal its marginal costs. Efficiency exists at this point.

Unintended Effects

- Economists often think in terms of causes and effects. Effects may be either intended or unintended. Economists want to denote both types of effects when speaking of effects in general.

Exchange

- Exchange, or trade, is the process of giving up one thing for something else. People enter into exchanges to make themselves better off.

Ceteris Paribus

- *Ceteris paribus* is a Latin term that means "all other things constant" or "nothing else changes." *Ceteris paribus* is used to designate what we believe is the correct relationship between two variables.

Theory

- Economists build theories to explain and predict real-world events. Theories are necessarily abstractions from, as opposed to descriptions of, the real world.
- All theories abstract from reality; they focus on the critical variables that the theorist believes explain and predict the phenomenon in question.

Economic Categories

- Positive economics attempts to determine what is; normative economics addresses what should be.
- Microeconomics deals with human behavior and choices as they relate to relatively small units: an individual, a firm, an industry, a single market. Macroeconomics deals with human behavior and choices as they relate to an entire economy.

Key Terms and Concepts

Good	Entrepreneurship	Decisions at the Margin	Positive Economics
Utility	Scarcity	Efficiency	Normative Economics
Bad	Economics	Incentive	Microeconomics
Disutility	Rationing Device	Exchange (Trade)	Macroeconomics
Land	Opportunity Cost	*Ceteris Paribus*	
Labor	Marginal Benefits	Theory	
Capital	Marginal Costs	Abstract	

Questions and Problems

1. The United States is considered a rich country because Americans can choose from an abundance of goods and services. How can there be scarcity in a land of abundance?
2. Give two examples for each of the following: (a) an intangible good, (b) a tangible good, (c) a bad.
3. Give an example of something that is a good for one person and a bad for someone else.
4. What is the difference between labor as a resource and entrepreneurship as a resource?
5. Can either scarcity or one of the effects of scarcity be found in a car dealership? Explain your answer.
6. Explain the link between scarcity and each of the following: (a) choice, (b) opportunity cost, (c) the need for a rationing device, and (d) competition.
7. Is it possible for a person to incur an opportunity cost without spending any money? Explain.
8. Discuss the opportunity costs of attending college for four years. Is college more or less costly than you thought it was? Explain.
9. Explain the relationship between changes in opportunity cost and changes in behavior.
10. Owen says that we should eliminate all pollution in the world. William disagrees. Who is more likely to be thinking like an economist, Owen or William? Explain your answer.
11. A friend pays for your lunch. Is this an example of a free lunch? Why or why not?
12. A noneconomist says that a proposed government project simply costs too much and therefore shouldn't be undertaken. How might an economist's evaluation be different?
13. Economists say that individuals make decisions at the margin. What does this mean?
14. How would an economist define the efficient amount of time spent playing tennis?
15. Ivan stops studying before the point at which his marginal benefits of studying equal his marginal costs. Is Ivan forfeiting any net benefits? Explain your answer.
16. What does an economist mean by saying that there are no $10 bills on the sidewalk?
17. A change in *X* will lead to a change in *Y*. The predicted change is desirable, so we should change *X*. Do you agree or disagree? Explain.
18. Why do people enter into exchanges?
19. When two individuals enter into an exchange, you can be sure that one person benefits and the other person loses. Do you agree or disagree with this statement? Explain your answer.
20. What is the difference between positive economics and normative economics? Between microeconomics and macroeconomics?
21. Would there be a need for a rationing device if scarcity did not exist? Explain your answer.
22. Jackie's alarm clock buzzes. She reaches over to the small table next to her bed and turns it off. As she pulls the covers back up, Jackie thinks about her 8:30 American History class. Should she go to the class today or sleep a little longer? She worked late last night and really hasn't had enough sleep. Besides, she's fairly sure her professor will be discussing a subject she already knows well. Maybe it would be okay to miss class today. Is Jackie more likely to miss some classes than she is to miss other classes? What determines which classes Jackie will attend and which classes she won't?
23. If you found $10 bills on the sidewalk regularly, we might conclude that individuals don't try to maximize net benefits. Do you agree or disagree with this statement. Explain your answer.

Chapter 1 What Economics Is About

24. The person who smokes cigarettes cannot possibly be thinking in terms of costs and benefits because it has been proven that cigarette smoking increases one's chances of getting lung cancer. Do you agree or disagree with the part of the statement that reads "the person who smokes cigarettes cannot possibly be thinking in terms of costs and benefits"? Explain your answer.

25. Tamara decides to go out on a date with Liam instead of Terrance. Do you think Tamara is using some kind of rationing device to decide whom she dates? If so, what might that rationing device be?

26. A theory is an abstraction from reality. What does this statement mean?

Working with Numbers and Graphs

1. Suppose the marginal costs of reading are constant and the marginal benefits of reading decline (over time). Initially, the marginal benefits of reading are greater than the marginal costs. Draw the *marginal-benefit (MB)* curve and *marginal-cost (MC)* curve of reading, and identify the efficient amount of reading. Next, explain why the efficient point is the point at which the net benefits of reading are maximized.

2. Using the diagram you drew in question 1, lower the marginal costs of reading, and identify the new efficient amount of reading. Also, identify the additional net benefits derived as a result of the lower marginal cost of reading.

3. Jim could undertake activity X, but chooses not to. Draw how the *marginal-benefit (MB)* and *marginal-cost (MC)* curves look for activity X from Jim's perspective.

Most of the diagrams in this book represent the relationship between two variables. Economists compare two variables to see how a change in one variable affects the other.

Suppose our two variables of interest are *consumption* and *income*. We want to show how consumption changes as income changes. We collect the data in Table 1. Simply by looking at the data in the first two columns, we can see that as income rises (column 1), consumption rises (column 2). If we wanted to show the relationship between income and consumption on a graph, we could place *income* on the horizontal axis, as in Exhibit 1, and *consumption* on the vertical axis. Point A represents income of $0 and consumption of $60, point B represents income of $100 and consumption of $120, and so on. If we draw a straight line through the points we have plotted, we have a picture of the relationship between income and consumption, based on the data we collected.

Notice that the line in Exhibit 1 slopes upward from left to right. As income rises, so does consumption. For example, as you move from point A to point B, income rises from $0 to $100, and consumption rises from $60 to $120. The line in Exhibit 1 also shows that as income falls, so does consumption. For example, as you move from point C to point B, income falls from $200 to $100, and consumption falls from $180 to $120. When two variables—such as consumption and income—change in the same way, they are said to be **directly related**.

Now let's take a look at the data in Table 2. Our two variables are the *price of T-shirts* and the *quantity demanded of T-shirts*. Just by looking at the data in the first two columns, we see that as price falls (column 1), quantity demanded rises (column 2). Suppose we want to plot these data. We could place *price of T-shirts* on the vertical axis, as in Exhibit 2, and *quantity demanded of T-shirts* on the horizontal axis. Point A represents a price of $20 and a quantity demanded

EXHIBIT 1

A Two-Variable Diagram Representing a Direct Relationship

The data in Table 1, plotted. Then points are connected with a straight line. The data represent a direct relationship: As one variable (say, income) rises, the other variable (consumption) rises too.

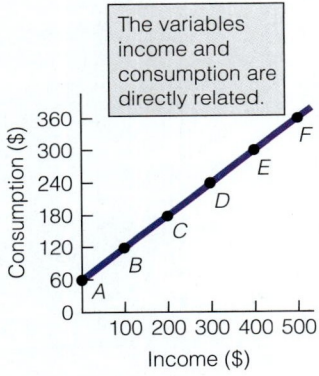

The variables income and consumption are directly related.

Directly Related
Two variables are directly related if they change in the same way.

Table 1

(1) When Income Is ($)	(2) Consumption Is ($)	(3) Point
0	60	A
100	120	B
200	180	C
300	240	D
400	300	E
500	360	F

Appendix A Working with Diagrams

Table 2

(1) When Price of T-shirts Is ($)	(2) Quantity Demanded of T-shirts Is	(3) Point
20	100	A
18	120	B
16	140	C
14	160	D
12	180	E

of 100, point B represents a price of $18 and a quantity demanded of 120, and so on. If we draw a straight line through the plotted points, we have a picture of the relationship between price and quantity demanded, based on the data in Table 2.

Notice the following:

- As price falls, the quantity demanded rises. For example, as price falls from $20 to $18, the quantity demanded rises from 100 to 120.

- As price rises, the quantity demanded falls. For example, when price rises from $12 to $14, quantity demanded falls from 180 to 160.

When two variables—such as price and quantity demanded—change in opposite ways, they are said to be **inversely related**.

As you have seen so far, variables may be directly related (when one increases, the other also increases) or inversely related (when one increases, the other decreases). Variables can also be **independent** of each other if, as one variable changes, the other does not.

EXHIBIT 2

A Two-Variable Diagram Representing an Inverse Relationship

The data in Table 2, plotted. The points are connected with a straight line. The data represent an inverse relationship: As one variable (price) falls, the other variable (quantity demanded) rises.

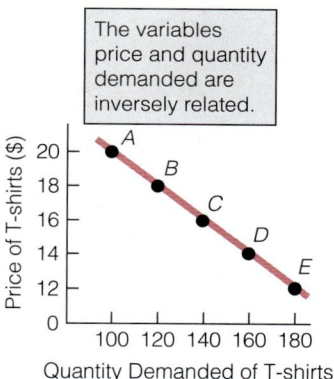

The variables price and quantity demanded are inversely related.

In Exhibit 3(a), as the X variable rises, the Y variable remains the same (at 20). Obviously, the X and Y variables are independent of each other: As one changes, the other does not.

In Exhibit 3(b), as the Y variable rises, the X variable remains the same (at 30). Again, we conclude that the X and Y variables are independent of each other: As one changes, the other does not.

A-1 Slope of a Line

In addition to knowing *how* two variables are related, we also often need to know *how much* one variable changes as the other changes. To find out, we need to only calculate the slope of the line. The **slope** is the ratio of the change in the variable on the vertical axis to the change in the variable on the horizontal axis. For example, if Y is on the vertical axis and X is on the horizontal axis, the slope is equal to $\Delta Y/\Delta X$. (The symbol "Δ" means "change in.")

$$\text{slope} = \frac{\Delta Y}{\Delta X}$$

Inversely Related
Two variables are inversely related if they change in opposite ways.

Independent
Two variables are independent if, as one changes, the other does not.

Slope
The ratio of the change in the variable on the vertical axis to the change in the variable on the horizontal axis.

EXHIBIT 3

Two Diagrams Representing Independence Between Two Variables

In parts (a) and (b), the variables X and Y are independent: As one changes, the other does not.

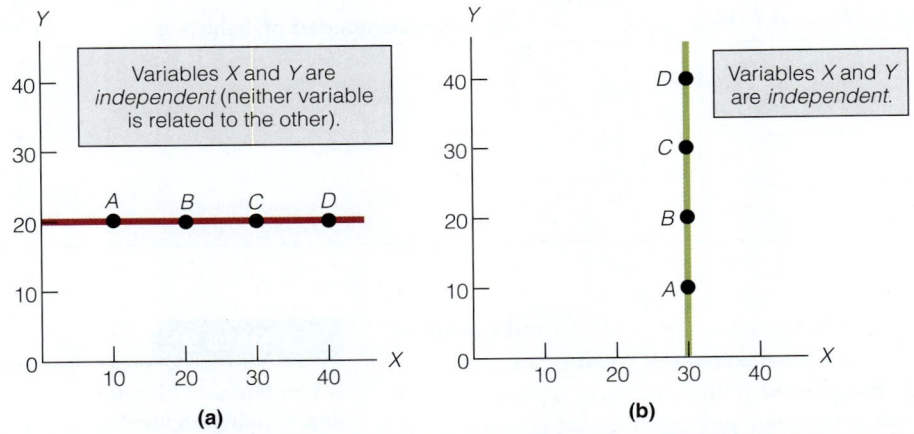

Exhibit 4 shows four lines. In each case, the slope is calculated. After studying parts (a)–(d), see if you understand why the slopes are negative, positive, zero, and infinite.

A-2 Slope of a Line is Constant

Look again at the line in Exhibit 4(a). The slope between points A and B is computed to be −1. If we had computed the slope between points B and C or between points C and D, would it still be −1? Let's compute the slope between points B and C. Moving from point B to point C, the change in Y is −10 and the change in X is +10. So, the slope is −1, as it was between points A and B. Now let's compute the slope between points A and D. Moving from point A to point D, the change in Y is −30 and the change in X is +30. Again, the slope is −1. Our conclusion is that the slope between any two points on a straight line is always the same as the slope between any other two points. To see this for yourself, compute the slope between points A and B and between points A and C using the line in Exhibit 4(b).

A-3 Slope of a Curve

In addition to straight lines, economics graphs use curves. The slope of a curve is not constant throughout, as it is for a straight line. The slope of a curve varies from one point to another. Calculating the slope of a curve at a given point requires two steps, as illustrated for point A in Exhibit 5. First, draw a line tangent to the curve at the point (a tangent line is one that just touches the curve but does not cross it). Second, pick any two points on the tangent line and determine the slope. In Exhibit 5, the slope of the line between points B and C is 0.67. The slope of the curve at point A (and only at point A) is therefore 0.67.

A-4 The 45-Degree Line

Economists sometimes use a *45-degree line* to represent data. This is a straight line that bisects the right angle formed by the intersection of the vertical and horizontal axes (see Exhibit 6). As a result, the 45-degree line divides the space enclosed by the two axes into *two equal parts*, as shown

Appendix A Working with Diagrams

EXHIBIT 4

Calculating Slopes

The slope of a line is the ratio of the change in the variable on the vertical axis to the change in the variable on the horizontal axis. In (a)–(d), we have calculated the slope.

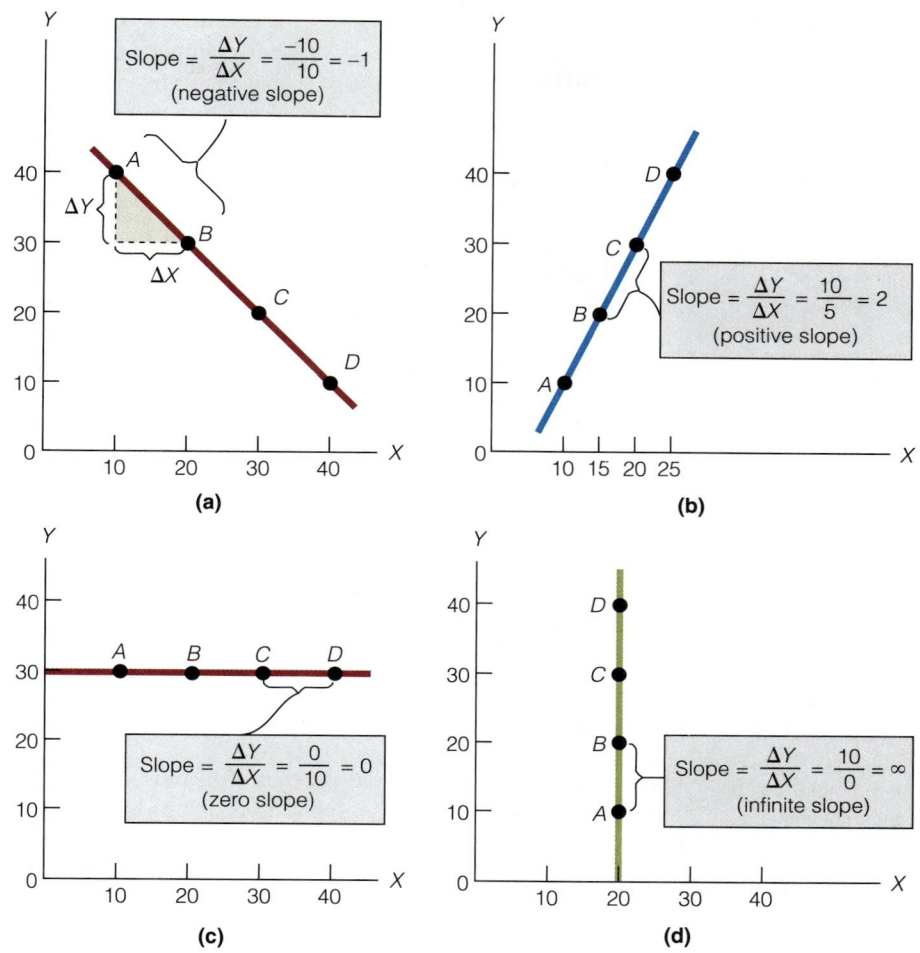

EXHIBIT 5

Calculating the Slope of a Curve at a Particular Point

The slope of the curve at point A is 0.67. This is calculated by drawing a line tangent to the curve at point A and then determining the slope of the line.

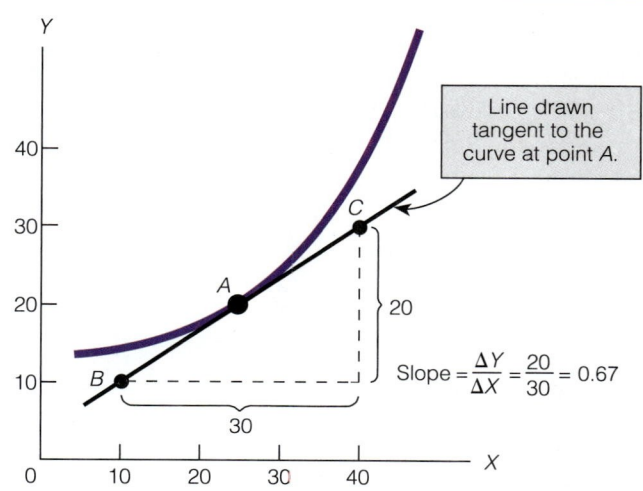

EXHIBIT 6

The 45-Degree Line

Any point on the 45-degree line is equidistant from each axis. For example, point A is the same distance from the vertical axis as it is from the horizontal axis.

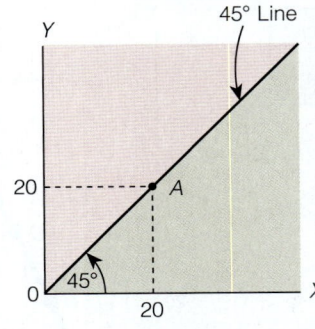

in the exhibit by the shading in different colors. The major characteristic of the 45-degree line is that any point on it is equidistant from both the horizontal and vertical axes. For example, point A is exactly as far from the horizontal axis as it is from the vertical axis. Thus, point A represents as much X as it does Y. Specifically, in the exhibit, point A represents 20 units of X and 20 units of Y.

A-5 Pie Charts

Pie charts appear in numerous places throughout this text. A pie chart is a convenient way to represent the different parts of something that when added together equal the whole. Let's consider a typical 24-hour weekday for Charles Myers. On a typical weekday, Charles spends 8 hours sleeping, 4 hours taking classes at the university, 4 hours working at his part-time job, 2 hours doing homework, 1 hour eating, 2 hours watching television, and 3 hours doing nothing in particular ("hanging around"). Exhibit 7 shows the breakdown of a typical weekday for Charles in pie chart form.

Pie charts send a quick visual message about rough percentage breakdowns and relative relationships. For example, Exhibit 7 clearly shows that Charles spends twice as much time working as doing homework.

A-6 Bar Graphs

Gross Domestic Product (GDP)
The value of the entire output produced annually within a country's borders.

The *bar graph* is another visual aid that economists use to convey relative relationships. Suppose we want to represent the gross domestic product for the United States in different years. The **gross domestic product (GDP)** is the value of the entire output produced annually within

EXHIBIT 7

A Pie Chart

The breakdown of activities for Charles Myers during a typical 24-hour weekday is represented in pie chart form.

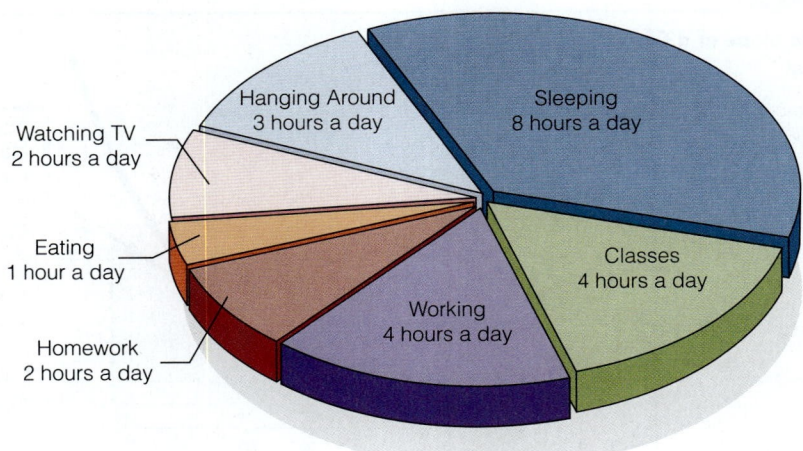

Appendix A Working with Diagrams

a country's borders. The bar graph in Exhibit 8 is a quick picture not only of the actual GDP for each year but also of the relative relationships between the GDP numbers for different years.

EXHIBIT 8

A Bar Graph

U.S. gross domestic product for different years is illustrated in bar graph form.

Source: Bureau of Economic Analysis.

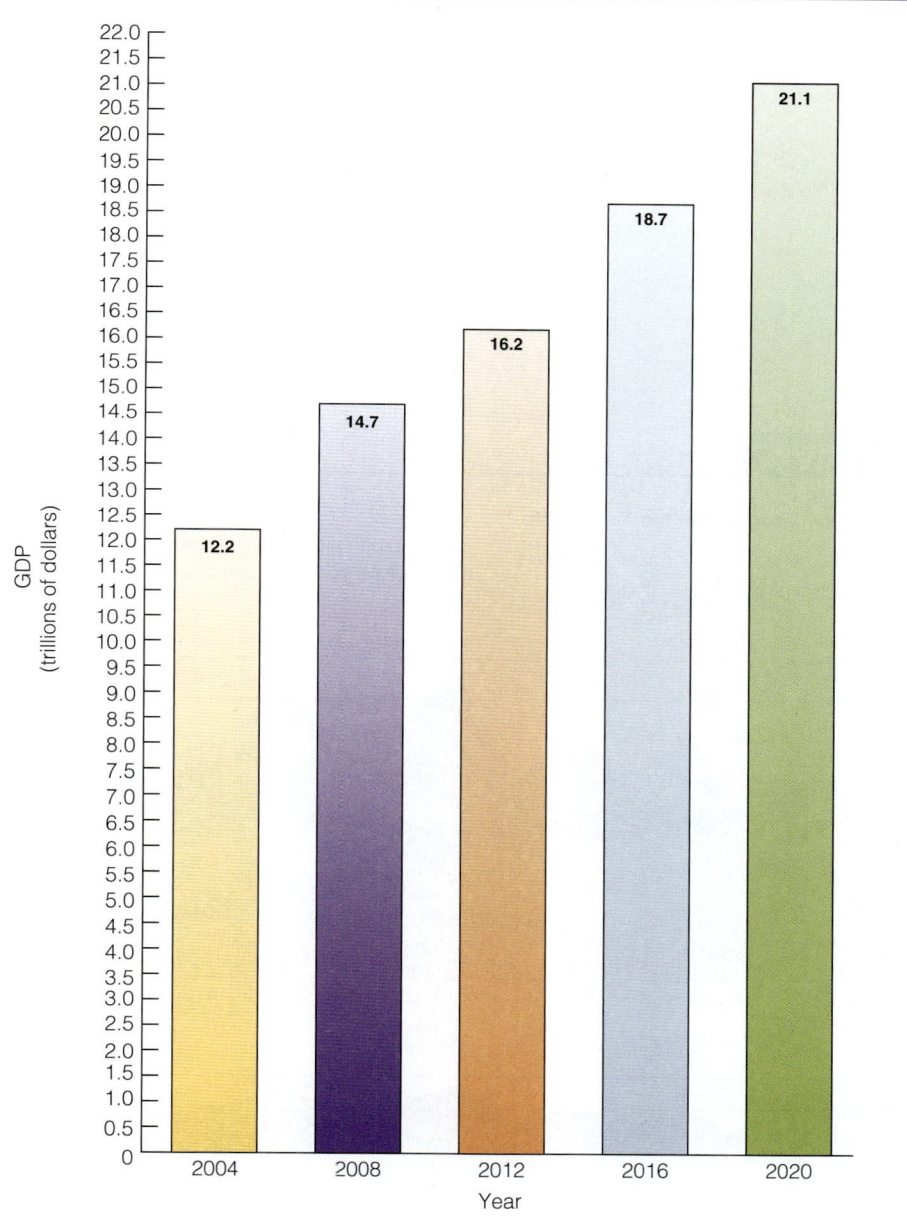

A-7 Line Graphs

Sometimes information is best and most easily displayed in a *line graph*, which is particularly useful for illustrating changes in a variable over a time period. Suppose we want to illustrate the variations in average points per game for a college basketball team over a number of years. The line graph in Exhibit 9(a) shows that the basketball team was on a roller coaster during the years 2008–2021. Perhaps the visual message is that the team's performance has not been consistent from one year to the next.

Suppose we plot the same data again, except this time using a different measurement scale on the vertical axis. As you can see in Exhibit 9(b), the variation in the team's performance appears much less pronounced than in part (a). In fact, we could choose a scale that, if we were to plot the data, would give us something close to a straight line. The point is simple: Data plotted in a line graph may convey different messages depending on the measurement scale used. Sometimes economists show two line graphs on the same axes. Usually, the purpose is to draw attention to either (1) the *relationship* between two variables or (2) the *difference* between them. In Exhibit 10, the line graphs show the variation and trend in (1) projected federal government expenditures and (2) projected tax receipts for the years 2022–2026, drawing attention to the "gap" between the two over the years.

EXHIBIT 9

The Two Line Graphs Plot the Same Data

(a) The average numbers of points per game for a college basketball team in different years are plotted. The variation between the years is pronounced. (b) The same data as in (a), but the variation in the performance of the team appears much less pronounced than in part (a).

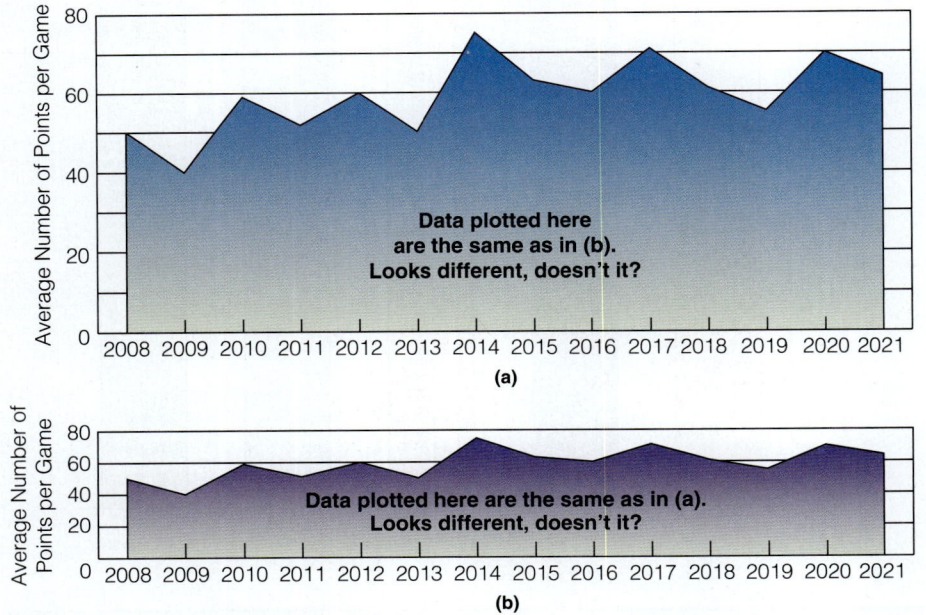

Year	Average Number of Points per Game
2008	50
2009	40
2010	59
2011	51
2012	60
2013	50
2014	75
2015	63
2016	60
2017	71
2018	61
2019	55
2020	70
2021	64

Appendix A Working with Diagrams

EXHIBIT 10

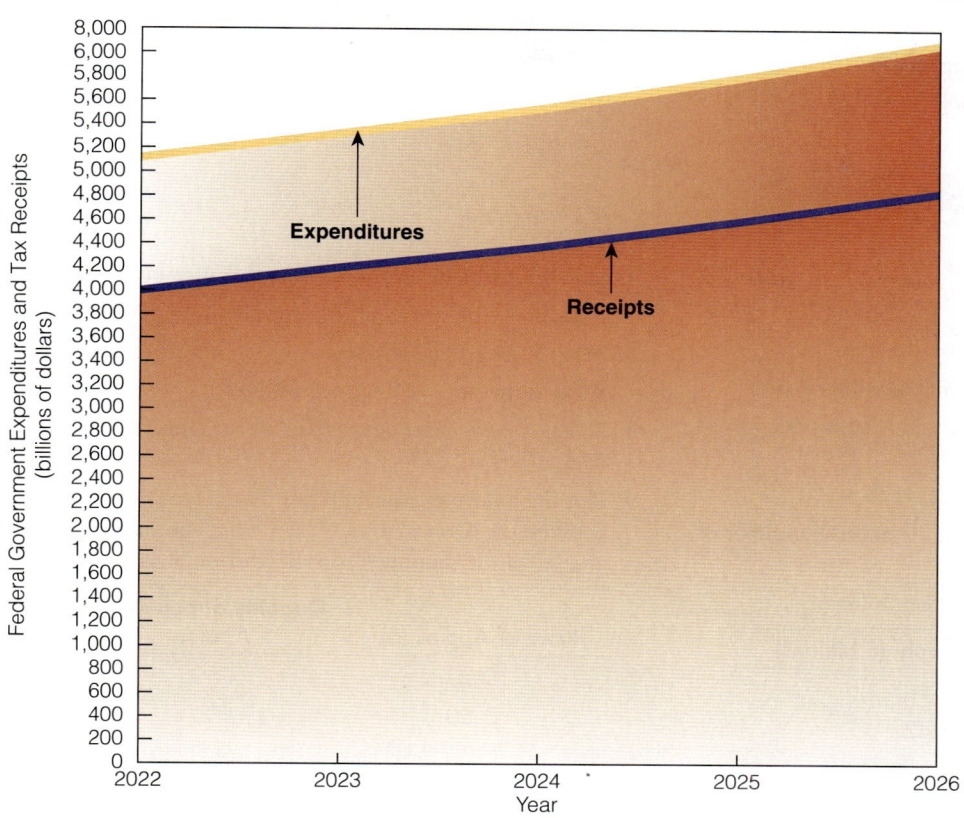

Projected Federal Government Expenditures and Tax Receipts, 2022–2026

Projected federal government expenditures and tax receipts are shown in line graph form for the period 2022–2026. Numbers are in billions of dollars.

Year	Expenditures	Receipts
2022	5,117	4,001
2023	5,325	4,206
2024	5,534	4,382
2025	5,877	4,562
2026	6,184	4,851

Source: Congressional Budget Office.

Appendix Summary

- Two variables are directly related if one variable rises as the other rises.
- An upward-sloping line (left to right) represents two variables that are directly related.
- Two variables are inversely related if one variable rises as the other falls.
- A downward-sloping line (left to right) represents two variables that are inversely related.
- Two variables are independent if one variable rises as the other remains constant.
- The slope of a line is the ratio of the change in the variable on the vertical axis to the change in the variable on the horizontal axis. The slope of a straight line is the same between any two points on the line.
- To determine the slope of a curve at a point, draw a line tangent to the curve at the point and then determine the slope of the tangent line.
- Any point on a 45-degree line is equidistant from the two axes.
- A pie chart is a convenient way to represent the different parts of something that when added together equal the whole. A pie chart visually shows rough percentage breakdowns and relative relationships.
- A bar graph is a convenient way to represent relative relationships.
- Line graphs are particularly useful for illustrating changes in one or more variables over time.

Key Terms and Concepts

Directly Related
Inversely Related
Independent
Slope
Gross Domestic Product (GDP)

Questions and Problems

1. What type of relationship would you expect between the following?
   a. Sales of hot dogs and sales of hot dog buns
   b. The price of winter coats and sales of winter coats
   c. The price of personal computers and the production of personal computers
   d. Sales of toothbrushes and sales of cat food
   e. The number of children in a family and the number of toys in a family

2. Represent the following data in bar graph form.

Year	U.S. Money Supply ($ billions)
2016	3,347
2017	3,642
2018	3,765
2019	3,952

3. Plot the following data, and specify the type of relationship between the two variables. (Place "Price" on the vertical axis and "Quantity Demanded" on the horizontal axis.)

Price of Apples ($)	Quantity Demanded of Apples
0.25	1,000
0.50	800
0.70	700
0.95	500
1.00	400
1.10	350

4. In Exhibit 4(a), determine the slope between points C and D.
5. In Exhibit 4(b), determine the slope between points A and D.
6. What is the special characteristic of a 45-degree line?
7. What is the slope of a 45-degree line?
8. When is a pie chart better than a bar graph for illustrating data?
9. Plot the following data, and specify the type of relationship between the two variables. (Place "Price" on the vertical axis and "Quantity Supplied" on the horizontal axis.)

Price of Apples ($)	Quantity Supplied of Apples
0.25	350
0.50	400
0.70	500
0.95	700
1.00	800
1.10	1,000

You are probably reading this textbook as part of your first college course in economics. You may be taking the course to satisfy a requirement in your major. Economics courses are sometimes required for students who plan to major in business, history, liberal studies, social science, or computer science.

Or you may be planning to major in economics. If you are like many college students, you may complain that not enough information is available about the various majors at your college or university. For example, students who major in business sometimes say that they are not quite certain what a business major is all about, but then they add that majoring in business is a safe bet. "After all," they assert, "you're pretty sure of getting a job if you have a business degree. That's not always the case with other degrees."

Many college students choose their majors on the basis of their high school courses. History majors, for example, might say that they decided to major in history because they "liked history in high school." Similarly, chemistry, biology, and math students say they chose their majors on the basis of their experiences in high school. If students found both math and economics easy and interesting in high school, then they are likely to major in math or economics. Conversely, if students had a hard time with chemistry in high school and found it boring, then they don't usually want to major in chemistry in college.

Students also often look to the dollars at the end of the college degree. Students may enjoy history and want to learn more of it in college, but they may tell themselves that they will earn a higher starting salary after graduation if they major in computer science or engineering. Thus, when choosing a major, students often consider (1) how much they enjoy studying a particular subject, (2) what they would like to see themselves doing in the future, and (3) what their income prospects are.

People may weight these three factors differently, but, regardless of the weighting, having more information is better than not having it, *ceteris paribus*. (We note "*ceteris paribus*" because having more information is not better if you have to pay more for it than it is worth. Who wants to pay $10 for information that provides only $1 in benefits? This appendix is therefore a low-cost way of providing you with more information about an economics major.)

We start by dispelling some of the misinformation about an economics major. Stated bluntly, some perceptions about an economics major and about a career in economics are just not true. For example, some people think that economics majors almost never study social relationships but, rather, only such things as inflation, interest rates, and unemployment. Not true. Economics majors study some of the same things that sociologists, historians, psychologists, and political scientists study.

In addition to busting myths, the appendix also provides you with information about economics as a major: what courses you study, how many courses you are likely to have to take, and more.

Finally, we tell you something about a career in economics. If you have opted to become an economics major, the day will come when you have your degree in hand. What's next? What is your starting salary likely to be? What will you be doing? Are you going to be happy doing what economists do? (If you never thought economics was about happiness, you already have some misinformation about the field. Contrary to what most noneconomists think, economics is not just about money. It is about happiness too.)

B-1 Five Myths About Economics and Being an Economics Major

Myth 1: Economics Is All Mathematics and Statistics. Some students choose not to major in economics because they think that economics is all mathematics and statistics. Math and statistics *are* used in economics, but certainly not overwhelmingly at the undergraduate degree level. Economics majors are usually required to take one statistics course and one math course (usually an introductory calculus course). Even students who say, "Math isn't my subject," are sometimes happy with the amount of math they need in economics. The fact is that, at the undergraduate level at many colleges and universities, economics is not a very math-intensive course of study. Economics uses many diagrams but not a large amount of math.

A proviso: The amount of math in the economics curriculum varies across colleges and universities. Some economics departments do not require their students to learn much math or statistics; others do. The majority of economics departments do not require much math or statistics at the undergraduate level. The graduate level is a different story.

If you are thinking of pursuing economics at the graduate level, you should enroll in numerous mathematics and statistics courses as an undergraduate.

Myth 2: Economics Is Only About Inflation, Interest Rates, Unemployment, and Other Such Things. If you study economics at college and then go on to become a practicing economist, no doubt people will ask you certain questions when they learn your chosen profession. Here are some:

- Do you think the economy is going to pick up?
- Do you think the economy is going to slow down?
- What stocks would you recommend?
- Do you think interest rates are going to fall?
- Do you think interest rates are going to rise?
- What do you think about buying bonds right now? Is it a good idea?

People ask these kinds of questions because most believe that economists study only stocks, bonds, interest rates, inflation, unemployment, and so on. Although economists do study these topics, they are only a tiny part of what economists study. It is not hard to find many economists today, both inside and outside academia, who spend most of their time studying anything but inflation, unemployment, stocks, bonds, and the like.

In fact, much of what economists study may surprise you. Some economists use their economic tools and methods to study crime, marriage, divorce, obesity, addiction, sports, voting behavior, bureaucracies, presidential elections, and much more. In short, today's economics is not your grandfather's economics. Many more topics are studied today in economics than were studied in years past.

Myth 3: People Become Economists Only If They Want to "Make Money." A while back we asked a few well-respected and well-known economists what got them interested in economics. Here is what some of them had to say:[1]

---

[1] See various interviews in Roger A. Arnold, *Economics*, 2nd ed. (St. Paul, MN: West Publishing Company, 1992).

Appendix B Should You Major in Economics?

Gary Becker, the 1992 winner of the Nobel Prize in Economics, said,

I got interested in economics when I was an undergraduate in college. I came into college with a strong interest in mathematics and at the same time with a strong commitment to do something to help society. I learned in the first economics course I took that economics could deal rigorously, à la mathematics, with social problems. That stimulated me because, in economics, I saw that I could combine both the mathematics and my desire to do something to help society.

Vernon Smith, the 2002 winner of the Nobel Prize in Economics, said,

My father's influence started me in science and engineering at Cal Tech, but my mother, who was active in socialist politics, probably accounts for the great interest I found in economics when I took my first introductory course.

Alice Rivlin, an economist and former member of the Federal Reserve Board, said,

My interest in economics grew out of concern for improving public policy, both domestic and international. I was a teenager in the tremendously idealistic period after World War II when it seemed terribly important to get nations working together to solve the world's problems peacefully.

Allan Meltzer, economist, said,

Economics is a social science. At its best it is concerned with ways (1) to improve well-being by allowing individuals the freedom to achieve their personal aims or goals and (2) to harmonize their individual interests. I find working on such issues challenging, and progress is personally rewarding.

Robert Solow, the 1987 winner of the Nobel Prize in Economics, said,

I grew up in the 1930s, and it was very hard not to be interested in economics. If you were a high school student in the 1930s, you were conscious of the fact that our economy was in deep trouble and no one knew what to do about it.

Charles Plosser, former president of the Federal Reserve Bank of Philadelphia and co-coiner of the term "real business cycle," said,

I was an engineer as an undergraduate with little knowledge of economics. I went to the University of Chicago Graduate School of Business to get an MBA and there became fascinated with economics. I was impressed with the seriousness with which economics was viewed as a way of organizing one's thoughts about the world to address interesting questions and problems.

Walter Williams, professor of economics at George Mason University and winner of numerous fellowships and awards, said,

I was a major in sociology in 1963 and I concluded that it was not very rigorous. Over the summer I was reading a book by W. E. B. DuBois, Black Reconstruction, and somewhere in the book it said something along the lines that blacks could not melt into the mainstream of American society until they understood economics, and that was something that got me interested in economics.

Murray Weidenbaum, former professor of economics at Washington University of St. Louis and former chairman of the Council of Economic Advisors, said,

A specific professor got me interested in economics. He was very prescient: He correctly noted that while lawyers dominated the policy-making process up until the 1940s, in the future economics would be an important tool for developing public policy. And he was right.

Irma Adelman, former professor of agricultural and resource economics at the University of California at Berkeley, said,

> I hesitate to say because it sounds arrogant. My reason [for getting into economics] was that I wanted to benefit humanity. And my perception at the time was that economic problems were the most important problems that humanity has to face. That is what got me into economics and into economic development.

Lester Thurow, economist and former dean of the MIT Sloan School of Management, said,

> [I got interested in economics because of] the belief—some would see it as naïve belief—that economics was a profession where it would be possible to help make the world better.

Myth 4: Economics Wasn't Very Interesting in High School, so It's Not Going to Be Very Interesting in College. A typical high school economics course emphasizes, and spends much time discussing, consumer economics. Students learn about credit cards, mortgage loans, budgets, buying insurance, renting an apartment, and other such things. These are important topics because not knowing their ins and outs can make your life much harder. Still, many students come away from high school thinking that economics is always and everywhere about consumer topics.

However, a high school economics course and a college economics course can be as different as day and night. Simply leaf through this book and look at the variety of topics covered, compared with those you might have covered in high school economics. Go on to look at texts used in other economics courses—ranging from law and economics, to the history of economic thought, to international economics, to sports economics—and you will see what we mean.

B-2 What Awaits You as an Economics Major?

If you become an economics major, what courses will you take? What are you going to study?

At the lower-division level, economics majors must take courses in the principles of macroeconomics and the principles of microeconomics. They usually also take a statistics course and a math course (usually calculus).

At the upper-division level, they must take intermediate microeconomics and intermediate macroeconomics, along with a certain number of electives. Some of the elective courses, among many others, are as follows:

- Money and banking
- Law and economics
- History of economic thought
- Behavioral economics
- Public finance
- Labor economics
- International economics
- Antitrust and regulation
- Health economics
- Economics of development

- Urban and regional economics
- Econometrics
- Mathematical economics
- Environmental economics
- Public choice
- Global managerial economics
- Sports economics
- Psychology and economics
- Economics of institutions
- Industrial organization
- Financial economics

Most economics majors take between 12 and 15 economics courses.

One of the attractive things about studying economics is that you will acquire many of the skills employers value highly. First, you will have the quantitative skills that are important in many business and government positions. Second, you will acquire the writing skills necessary in almost all lines of work. Third, and perhaps most importantly, you will develop the thinking skills that almost all employers agree are critical to success. According to the Law School Admissions Council, Economics majors had the sixth-highest Law School Admission Test (LSAT) scores out of 48 different majors. Math majors had the highest LSAT scores.

B-3 What Do Economists Do?

Today, economists work in many and varied fields. Here are some of the fields and some of the positions that economists hold in those fields:

Education
    College professor
    Researcher
    High school teacher

Journalism
    Researcher
    Industry analyst
    Economic analyst

Accounting
    Analyst
    Auditor
    Researcher
    Consultant

General Business
    Chief executive officer
    Business analyst

Marketing analyst
Business forecaster
Competitive analyst

Government
Researcher
Analyst
Speechwriter
Forecaster

Financial Services
Business journalist
International analyst
Newsletter editor
Broker
Investment banker

Banking
Credit analyst
Loan officer
Investment analyst
Financial manager

Other
Business consultant
Independent forecaster
Freelance analyst
Think tank analyst
Entrepreneur

Economists do a myriad of things, including the following:

- In business, economists often analyze economic conditions, make forecasts, offer strategic-planning initiatives, collect and analyze data, predict exchange rate movements, and review regulatory policies, among other things.

- In government, economists collect and analyze data, analyze international economic situations, research monetary conditions, advise on policy, and do much more.

- As private consultants, economists work with accountants, business executives, government officials, educators, financial firms, labor unions, state and local governments, and others.

B-4 Places to Find More Information

If you are interested in a major and perhaps a career in economics, here are some places you can go to and people you can speak with to acquire more information:

- To learn about the economics curriculum, speak with the economics professors at your college or university. Ask them what courses you would have to take as an economics

Appendix B Should You Major in Economics?

major and what elective courses are available. In addition, ask them why they chose to study economics: What is it about economics that interested them?

- For information about salaries and what economists do, you may want to visit the *Occupational Outlook Handbook* website (www.bls.gov/ooh/).

B-5 Concluding Remarks

Choosing a major is a big decision and therefore should not be made quickly and without much thought. This short appendix has provided you with some information about an economics major and a career in economics. Economics is not for everyone, but it may be right for you. A major in economics trains you in today's most marketable skills: good writing, quantitative analysis, and rigorous thinking. It is a major in which professors and students daily ask and answer some very interesting and relevant questions. It is a major that is highly regarded by employers. It may just be the right major for you.

CHAPTER 2
Production Possibilities Frontier Framework

Introduction
In the last chapter, you learned about various economic concepts, such as scarcity, choice, and opportunity cost. In this chapter, we develop a graphical framework of analysis for understanding these concepts and others. Specifically, we develop the production possibilities frontier.

2-1 The Production Possibilities Frontier

Think of yourself as being alone on an island. You can produce two goods and only two goods: coconuts and pineapples. Because your resources are limited, producing more of one good means producing less of the other. That type of thinking is the intuition behind the *production possibilities frontier*. Now keep that intuition in mind as we proceed.

2-1a The Straight-Line PPF: Constant Opportunity Costs

In Exhibit 1(a), we have identified five combinations of books and shirts that can be produced in an economy. For example, combination A is 4 books and 0 shirts, combination B is 3 books and 1 shirt, and so on. Next, we plotted these five combinations of books and shirts in Exhibit 1(b), with each combination representing a different point. For example, the combination of 4 books and 0 shirts is represented by point A. The line that connects points A–E is the production possibilities frontier. A **production possibilities frontier (PPF)** is the combination of two goods that can be produced in a certain span of time under the conditions of a given state of technology and fully employed resources.

Production Possibilities Frontier (PPF)
The possible combinations of two goods that can be produced during a certain span of time under the conditions of a given state of technology and fully employed resources.

Chapter 2 Production Possibilities Frontier Framework

Notice that the PPF is a straight line. This is because the opportunity cost of books and shirts (in our example) is constant:

Straight-line PPF = Constant opportunity costs

To illustrate what *constant opportunity costs* means, suppose the economy were to move from point *A* to point *B*. At point *A*, 4 books and 0 shirts are produced; at point *B*, 3 books and 1 shirt are produced:

- Point *A*: 4 books and 0 shirts
- Point *B*: 3 books and 1 shirt

What does the economy have to forfeit (in terms of books) to get 1 shirt? The answer is 1 book. We conclude that, in moving from point *A* to point *B*, the opportunity cost of 1 shirt is 1 book.

Now let's move from point *B* to point *C*. At point *B*, 3 books and 1 shirt are produced; at point *C*, 2 books and 2 shirts are produced:

- Point *B*: 3 books and 1 shirt
- Point *C*: 2 books and 2 shirts

So, how many books does the economy have to forfeit to get another shirt? The answer is 1 book. We conclude that, in moving from point *B* to *C*, the opportunity cost of 1 shirt is 1 book.

In fact, when we move from *C* to *D* or from *D* to *E*, we also notice that the opportunity cost of 1 shirt is 1 book. This is what we mean when we speak of constant opportunity costs: The opportunity cost of 1 shirt is *always* 1 book. And because opportunity costs are constant, the PPF in Exhibit 1(b) is a straight line. When opportunity costs are not constant, the PPF will not be a straight line, as you will see next.

2-1b The Bowed-Outward (Concave-Downward) PPF: Increasing Opportunity Costs

In Exhibit 2(a), we have identified five combinations of cell phones and coffee makers that can be produced in an economy. For example, combination *A* is 10 cell phones and 0 coffee makers, combination *B* is 9 cell phones and 1 coffee maker, and so on. We plotted these five combinations of cell phones and coffee makers in Exhibit 2(b), again with each combination representing a different point. The curved line that

EXHIBIT 1

Production Possibilities Frontier (Constant Opportunity Costs)

The economy can produce any of the five combinations of books and shirts in part (a). We have plotted these combinations in part (b). The PPF in part (b) is a straight line because the opportunity cost of producing either good is constant.

Combination	Books	Shirts	Point in Part (b)
A	4	0	A
B	3	1	B
C	2	2	C
D	1	3	D
E	0	4	E

(a)

(b)

EXHIBIT 2

Production Possibilities Frontier (Increasing Opportunity Costs)

The economy can produce any of the five combinations of cell phones and coffee makers in part (a). We have plotted these combinations in part (b). The PPF in part (b) is bowed outward because the opportunity cost of producing coffee makers increases as more coffee makers are produced.

Combination	Cell Phones	Coffee Makers	Point in Part (b)
A	10	0	A
B	9	1	B
C	7	2	C
D	4	3	D
E	0	4	E

(a)

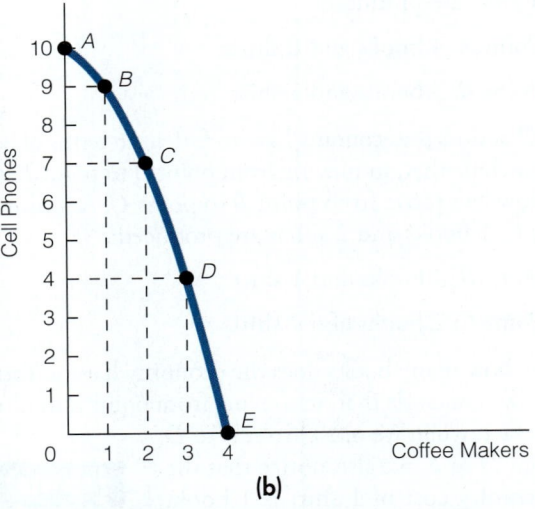

(b)

connects points *A–E* is the PPF. In this case, the production possibilities frontier is bowed outward (concave downward) because the opportunity cost of coffee makers increases as more coffee makers are produced:

Bowed-outward PPF = Increasing opportunity costs

To illustrate, let's start at point *A*, where the economy is producing 10 cell phones and 0 coffee makers, and move to point *B*, where the economy is producing 9 cell phones and 1 coffee makers:

- Point *A*: 10 cell phones and 0 coffee makers
- Point *B*: 9 cell phones and 1 coffee maker

What is the opportunity cost of a coffee maker in moving from point *A* to point *B*? Stated differently, what does the economy have to forfeit (in terms of cell phones) to get 1 coffee maker? The answer is 1 cell phone.

Now let's move from point *B* to point *C*. At point *B*, the economy is producing 9 cell phones and 1 coffee maker; at point *C*, the economy is producing 7 cell phones and 2 coffee makers:

- Point *B*: 9 cell phones and 1 coffee maker
- Point *C*: 7 cell phones and 2 coffee makers

Now how many cell phones does the economy have to forfeit to get 1 additional coffee maker? The answer this time is 2 cell phones. We conclude that, in moving from point *A* to point *B*, the opportunity cost of 1 coffee maker was 1 cell phone, but that, in moving from point *B* to point *C*, the opportunity cost of 1 (additional) coffee maker is 2 cell phones. If we were

Economics 24/7

The PPF and You

In Exhibit 3, we have shown a production possibilities frontier (PPF). On the horizontal axis, we have placed good X; on the vertical axis, good Y. On the PPF itself, we have identified three points, labeled points 1, 2, and 3. Does it matter to you if the economy is at one point instead of another? For example, does it matter to you if the economy is located at point 1 instead of point 3? To help us get at the answer, consider that at point 1 the economy is producing more of good Y and less of good X than at point 3. At point 3, the economy is producing more of good X and less of good Y than at point 1.

Consider the case in which there is no international trade. In this case, the point at which the economy is located on the PPF has a lot to say as to what people in the economy end up consuming. Specifically, an economy in which a lot of Y but very little X is produced is an economy in which people will most likely end up consuming much more Y than X.

In fact, it is more likely to be the case that because people want to consume more Y than X, firms end up producing more Y than X.

Consumption, to a large extent, directs production. If people want to consume numerous iPads and smartphones but very few V-neck sweaters, then it is likely that producers will end up producing what they think will sell—in this case, iPads and smartphones, and not so many V-neck sweaters.

We return to our original question: Does it matter to you if the economy is at one point of the PPF instead of another? To a large degree, it matters as to what you consume.

It also is likely to matter to your employment. You are more likely to end up working in an industry in which a lot of a particular good is produced than in an industry in which very little of some good is produced. In terms of our PPF diagram, if the economy is located at point 1 instead of point 3, you are more likely to work—as an accountant, attorney, factory worker, janitor, clerical worker, and so on—in the industry that produces good Y than in the industry that produces good X.

Now think about the following. Suppose that government decides that it wants to put more resources into a particular area, such as health care. Might this end up moving the economy from one point to another on the PPF, thus affecting your consumption and your employment? In other words, government raises taxes, then takes the increased tax revenue and directs them into health care. As a result, more health care is produced in the economy as it moves from one point to another point on the PPF—from a point that represents less health care to one that represents more health care. Could this affect you? It certainly could. After all, if more health care is produced, you now have a greater probability of working—once again, as an accountant, attorney, clerical worker, and so on—in the health care industry than if the government had not directed more resources into health care. In fact, directing more resources into the health care industry—thus moving the economy from one point to another on the PPF—can influence your decision about what work for which you train. For example, if the health care industry is expanding, you might end up training to be a nurse instead of an accountant or a lab technician or radiologist instead of a teacher.

EXHIBIT 3

A PPF and 3 points

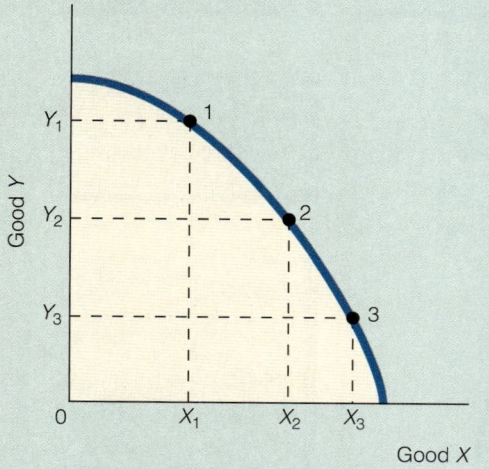

to continue producing additional coffee makers, we would see that we would have to give up increasingly more cell phones. You can see this easily if you consider the economy moving from point C to point D (where the opportunity cost of producing an additional coffee maker is 3 cell phones) or moving from point to D to point E (where the opportunity cost of producing an additional coffee maker is 4 cell phones). We end with a question: Why is the PPF in Exhibit 2(b) bowed outward? The reason is the increasing opportunity costs of producing coffee makers.

2-1c Law of Increasing Opportunity Costs

We know that the shape of the PPF depends on whether opportunity costs (1) are constant or (2) increase as more of a good is produced. In Exhibit 1(b), the PPF is a straight line; in Exhibit 2(b), it is bowed outward (curved). In the real world, most PPFs are bowed outward. In other words, for most goods, the opportunity costs *increase* as more of the good is produced. This relationship is referred to as the **law of increasing opportunity costs**.

The law of increasing opportunity costs holds for most goods because people have varying abilities. For example, some individuals are better suited to building houses than others are. When a construction company first starts building houses, it employs the people most skilled at doing so. The most skilled persons can build houses at lower opportunity costs than others can. But as the construction company builds more houses, it finds that it has already employed the most skilled builders, so it must employ those who are less skilled at building houses. The less skilled people build houses at higher opportunity costs: Whereas three skilled house builders could build a house in a month, as many as seven unskilled builders may be required to build one as fast. Exhibit 4 summarizes the points in this section.

Law of Increasing Opportunity Costs
As more of a good is produced, the opportunity costs of producing that good increase.

EXHIBIT 4

A Summary Statement About Increasing Opportunity Costs and a Production Possibilities Frontier That Is Bowed Outward (Concave Downward)

Many of the points about increasing opportunity costs and a PPF that is bowed outward are summarized here.

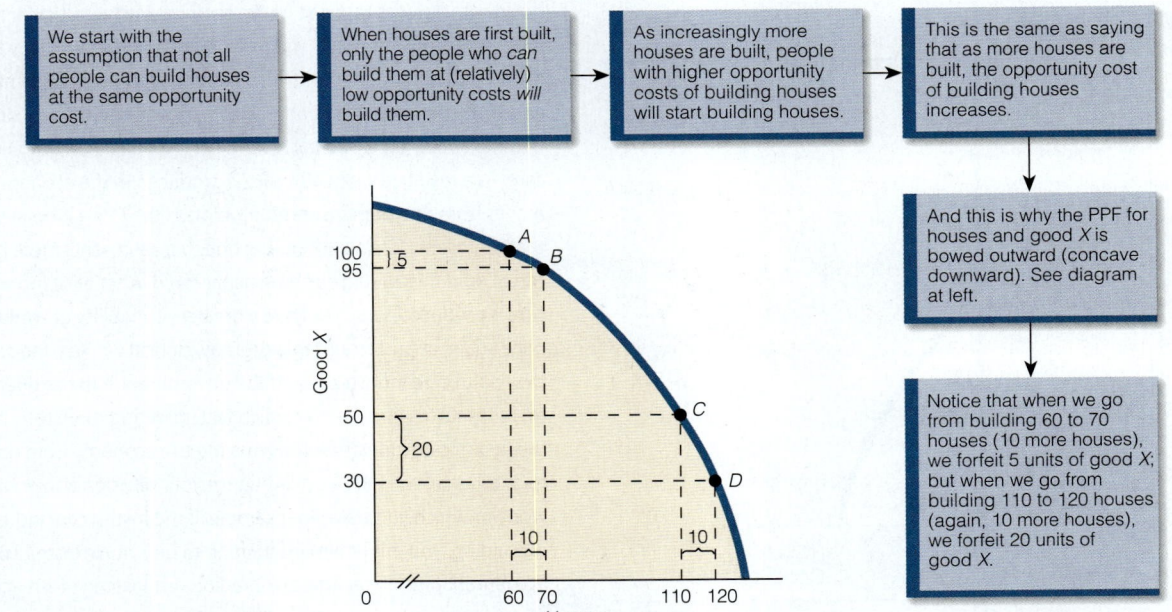

Economics 24/7

Deducing Where Sherlock Holmes Was on His Production Possibilities Frontier

Of Sherlock Holmes, it has been said that "his ignorance was as remarkable as his knowledge."[1] In fact, his companion, Dr. Watson, said, "Of contemporary literature, philosophy and politics he appeared to know next to nothing. . . . My surprise reached a climax, however, when I found incidentally that he was ignorant of the Copernican Theory and of the composition of the Solar System. That any civilized being in this nineteenth century should not be aware that the earth travelled round the sun appeared to be to me such an extraordinary fact that I could hardly realize it."[2]

When Dr. Watson expressed his surprise to Sherlock Holmes, Holmes told Watson that now that Watson had told him that the Earth revolves around the Sun, he would try his best to forget it. Holmes said, "You see, I consider that a man's brain originally is like a little empty attic, and you have to stock it with such furniture as you choose. A fool takes in all the lumber of every sort that he comes across, so that the knowledge which might be useful to him gets crowded out. . . . He will have nothing but the tools which may help him in doing his work. . . . Depend upon it there comes a time when for every addition of knowledge you forget something that you knew before."[3]

Holmes was interested in solving crimes, and he wanted his brain filled with only the things that would help him achieve his sole purpose. If he learned something that was irrelevant to this task, then something that was relevant to the purpose at hand would be discarded. In other words, he was on his PPF, and more of one thing necessarily meant less of something else.

Not only that, but Holmes wanted to stay at a particular point on his PPF. But which point? Well, let's deduce the answer together. Suppose that on the vertical axis there is "knowing more about things about the world, none of which is helpful in solving crime," and on the horizontal axis is "number of crimes solved." Now, if Holmes wants to solve as many crimes as possible, he obviously wants to be on his PPF at the point where it touches the horizontal axis. He wants to solve as many crimes as possible, given his resources (physical and mental). In other words, he wants to use all of his resources to do one thing and one thing only: solve crimes.

---

[1] Sir Arthur Conan Doyle, "A Study in Scarlet," *The Adventures of Sherlock Holmes,* Modern Library paperback edition (New York: Random House, 2003), chapter 2.
[2] Ibid.
[3] Ibid.

2-1d Economic Concepts in a Production Possibilities Frontier Framework

The PPF framework is useful for illustrating and working with economic concepts. This section discusses seven economic concepts in terms of the PPF framework. (See Exhibit 5.)

Scarcity Recall that scarcity is the condition in which the wants (for goods) are greater than the resources available to satisfy them. The finiteness of resources is graphically portrayed by the PPF in Exhibit 6. If the frontier could speak, it would tell us, "At this point in time, that's as far as you can go. You cannot go any farther. You are limited to choosing any combination of the two goods on the frontier or below it."

The PPF separates the production possibilities of an economy into two regions: (1) an attainable region, which consists of the points on the PPF itself and all points below it (this

EXHIBIT 5

The PPF Economic Framework

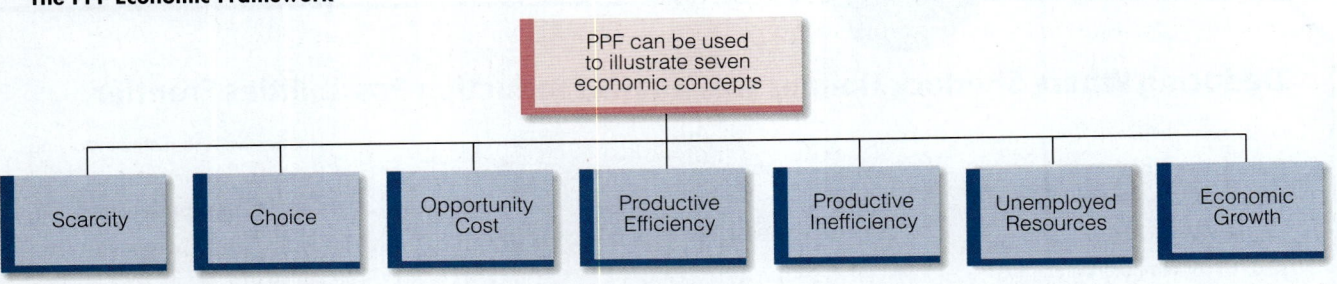

region includes points A–F), and (2) an unattainable region, which consists of the points above and beyond the PPF (such as point G). Recall that scarcity implies that some things are attainable and others are unattainable. Point A on the PPF is attainable, as is point F; point G is not.

Choice and opportunity cost are also shown in Exhibit 6. Note that, within the attainable region, individuals must choose the combination of the two goods they want to produce. Obviously, hundreds of combinations exist, but let's consider only two, represented by points A and B, respectively. Which of the two will individuals choose? They can't be at both points; they must make a choice.

Opportunity cost is illustrated as we move from one point to another on the PPF in Exhibit 6. Suppose we are at point A and choose to move to point B. At point A, we have 55,000 television sets and 5,000 cars; at point B, we have 50,000 television sets and 15,000

EXHIBIT 6

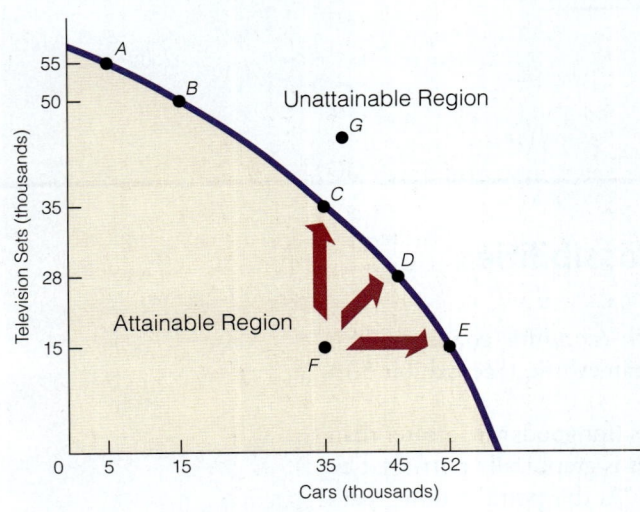

The PPF and Various Economic Concepts

The PPF can illustrate various economic concepts:

(1) Scarcity is illustrated by the frontier itself. Implicit in the concept of scarcity is the idea that we can have some things but not all things. The PPF separates an attainable region from an unattainable region.

(2) Choice is represented by our having to decide among the many attainable combinations of the two goods. For example, will we choose the combination of goods represented by point A or by point B?

(3) Opportunity cost is most easily seen as movement from one point to another, such as movement from point A to point B. More cars are available at point B than at point A, but fewer television sets are available. In short, the opportunity cost of more cars is fewer television sets.

(4) Productive efficiency is represented by the points *on* the PPF (such as A–E), while productive inefficiency is represented by any point *below* the PPF (such as F).

(5) Unemployment (in terms of resources being unemployed) exists at any productive-inefficient point (such as F), whereas resources are fully employed at any productive-efficient point (such as any point in the range A–E).

cars. What is the opportunity cost of a car? Because 10,000 *more* cars come at a cost of 5,000 *fewer* television sets, the opportunity cost of 1 car is 1/2 television set.

Productive Efficiency

Economists often say that an economy is **productive efficient** if it is producing the maximum output with the resources and technology that it has. In Exhibit 6, points A, B, C, D, and E are all productive-efficient points. Notice that all these points lie on the PPF. In other words, we are getting the most output from what we have of available resources and technology.

It follows that an economy is **productive inefficient** if it is producing less than the maximum output with the resources and technology that it has. In Exhibit 6, point F is a productive-inefficient point. It lies below the PPF; it is below the outer limit of what is possible. In other words, we can produce more goods with the available resources, or we can get more of one good without getting less of another.

To illustrate, suppose we move from inefficient point F to efficient point C. We produce more television sets and no fewer cars. What if we move from F to D? We produce more television sets and more cars. Finally, if we move from F to E, we produce more cars and no fewer television sets. Thus, moving from F can give us more of at least one good and no less of another good. In short, productive inefficiency implies that gains are possible in one area without losses in another.

Unemployed Resources

When the economy exhibits productive inefficiency, it is not producing the maximum output with the available resources and technology. One reason may be that the economy is not using all of its resources; that is, some of its resources are unemployed, as at point F in Exhibit 6.

When the economy exhibits productive efficiency, it is producing the maximum output with the available resources and technology. In other words, it is using all its resources to produce goods; its resources are fully employed, and none are unemployed. At the productive-efficient points A–E in Exhibit 6, no resources are unemployed.

Economic Growth

The term *economic growth* refers to the increased productive capabilities of an economy. Economic growth is illustrated by an outward shift in the PPF. Two major factors that produce economic growth are (1) an increase in the quantity of resources and (2) an advance in technology.

An increase in the quantity of resources (e.g., through a discovery of new resources) makes a greater quantity of output possible. In Exhibit 7(a), an increase in the quantity of resources makes it possible to produce both more military goods and more civilian goods. Thus, the PPF shifts outward from PPF_1 to PPF_2.

Technology refers to the body of skills and knowledge involved in the use of resources in production. An advance in technology commonly increases the ability to produce more output with a fixed quantity of resources or the ability to produce the same output with a smaller quantity of resources. For example, suppose an advance in technology allows the production of more of *both* military goods and civilian goods with the same quantity of resources. As a result, the PPF in Exhibit 7(a) shifts outward from PPF_1 to PPF_2. The outcome is the same as when the quantity of resources is increased.

If the advance in technology allows only more of *one good* (instead of both goods) to be produced with the same quantity of resources, then the PPF shifts outward, but not in the same way as shown in Exhibit 7(a). To illustrate, suppose an advance in technology allows only more civilian goods to be produced but not more military goods. Therefore, the maximum amount of military goods that can be produced does not change, but the maximum amount of civilian goods rises. This situation gives us the shift from PPF_1 to PPF_2 shown in Exhibit 7(b).

Productive Efficient
The condition in which the maximum output is produced with the given resources and technology.

Productive Inefficient
The condition in which less than the maximum output is produced with the given resources and technology. Productive inefficiency implies that more of one good can be produced without any less of another being produced.

Technology
The body of skills and knowledge involved in the use of resources in production. An advance in technology commonly increases the ability to produce more output with a fixed amount of resources or the ability to produce the same output with fewer resources.

EXHIBIT 7

Economic Growth Within a PPF Framework

An increase in resources or an advance in technology (that can lead to more of both goods being produced) can increase the production capabilities of an economy, leading to economic growth and a shift outward in the PPF, as shown in part (a). If the advance in technology leads to the greater production of only one good (such as civilian goods in this exhibit), then the PPF shifts outward, as shown in (b).

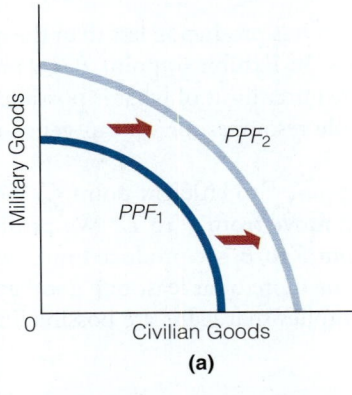
(a)

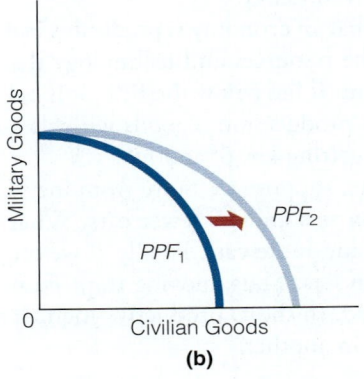
(b)

Economics 24/7

The Covid-19 Pandemic and the PPF

The economy is always producing some combination of goods and services, and the combination of goods and services it produces at one point in time might be very different than the combination of goods it produces at another point in time. Let's compare the combination of goods and services produced in, say, December 2019, and those produced in, say, April 2020. We have chosen those dates because December 2019 occurred prior to the COVID-19 pandemic, and April 2020 occurred during the pandemic. The earlier date occurred before the nationwide lockdowns (curfews, quarantines, stay-at-home orders, shutdowns), and the latter date occurred during the lockdowns. As you can imagine, the pandemic led to a change in the combination of goods and services produced.

Look at Exhibit 8. There you will see a production possibilities frontier. Protective masks and ventilators are on the horizontal axis, and all other goods are on the vertical axis. Suppose the economy was at point A on the PPF before the COVID-19 pandemic. Then the pandemic hit and the lockdowns went into effect. Restaurants, bars, retail stores, hair salons, and other businesses were closed. Clothing manufacturers did not produce as many clothes; furniture producers did not manufacture as much furniture; car manufacturers did not assemble as many cars.

Because of the pandemic, the economy moves toward producing more ventilators, protective masks, hand sanitizers, home food-delivery services, and so on. If all resources stay fully employed (which means the economy stays on the PPF), the economy will move from point A to, say, point B. At both point A and point B, some of the same goods and services are being produced, but less of "all other goods" are being produced during the pandemic than before it—fewer haircuts at salons and fewer meals in restaurants but more protective masks and ventilators.

Keep in mind that the economy only moves from point A to point B—both points being on the PPF—if all resources are fully employed. This wasn't the case during 2020. The pandemic brought with it layoffs, business closures, and job losses. The unemployment rate in the United States went from 3.8 percent in February 2020 to 13.0 percent in May 2020. Once the lockdowns commenced, the economy was no longer on its PPF; it was then below it, at a point like C. At point C, the economy is producing more things like protective masks and ventilators than it did at point A, even though there has been a reduction in *total* resources being employed in the economy.

Note that we said there has been a reduction in total resources being employed in the economy, not a reduction in the resources used to produce masks and ventilators. To discover the difference, suppose when resources were being fully employed and the economy was on its PPF, 100 units of resources were employed, and of these 100 units of resources, 90 went to produce "all other goods," and 10 went to produce masks and ventilators. But at point C, only 80 units of resources are being employed, 60 units of which are being used to produce "all other goods" and 20 units of which are being used to produce protective masks and ventilators.

What can a pandemic, like the COVID-19 pandemic, do to an economy? It can bring about a different combination of goods and services being produced (a different combination is produced at point C than at point A), raise the unemployment rate (the unemployment rate is higher at point C than at point A), and decrease the overall production of goods and services (less total output is produced at point C than at point A).

EXHIBIT 8

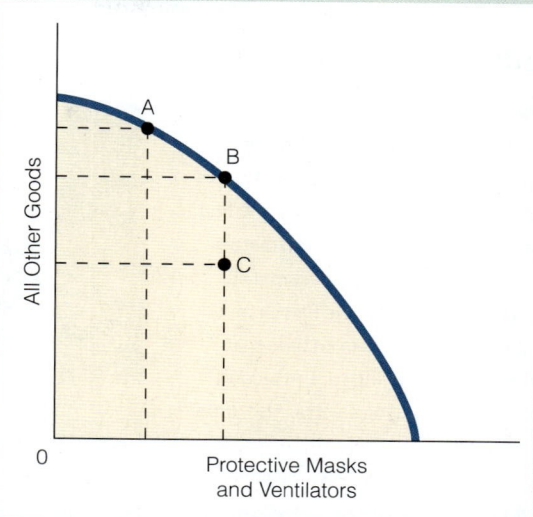

(Answers to Self-Test questions are in Answers to Self-Test Questions at the back of the book.)

1. What does a straight-line PPF represent? What does a bowed-outward PPF represent?
2. What does the law of increasing costs have to do with a bowed-outward PPF?
3. A politician says, "If you elect me, we can get more of everything we want." Under what condition is the politician telling the truth?
4. In an economy, only one combination of goods is productive efficient. True or false? Explain your answer.

Economics 24/7

Studying and Your PPF

You have your own PPF; you just may not know it. Suppose you are studying for two upcoming exams. You have only a total of six hours before you have to take the first exam, after which you will immediately proceed to take the second exam. Thus, time spent studying for the first exam (in economics) takes away from time that could be spent studying for the second exam (in math), and vice versa. Also, *time spent studying* is a resource in the production of a good grade: Less time spent studying for the economics exam and more time spent studying for the math exam means a higher grade in math and a lower grade in economics. For you, the situation may look as it does in Exhibit 9(a). We have identified four points (1–4) in the exhibit that correspond to the four combinations of two grades (one grade in economics and one grade in math).

Notice that each grade comes with a certain amount of time spent studying. This time is specified under the grade.

Given the resources you currently have (your labor and time), you can achieve any of the four combinations. For example, you can spend six hours studying for economics and get a *B* (point 1), but then you study math for zero hours and get an *F* in that course. Or you can spend four hours studying for economics and get a *C* (point 2), leaving you two hours to study for math, in which you get a *D*.

What do you need to get a higher grade in one course without getting a lower grade in the other course? You need more resources, which in this case is more time. If you have eight hours to study, your PPF shifts rightward, as in Exhibit 9(b). Now point 5 is possible (whereas it was not possible before you got more time). At point 5, you can get a *C* in economics and in math, an impossible combination of grades when you had less time (a PPF closer to the origin).

EXHIBIT 9

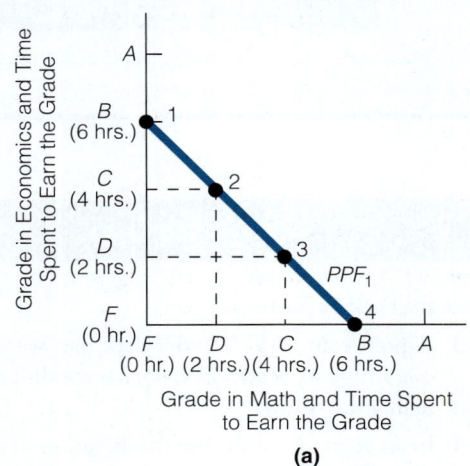

(a)

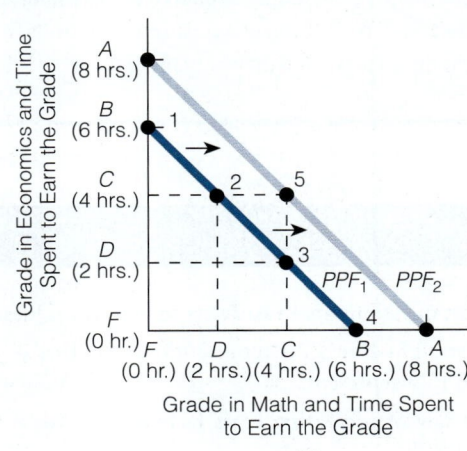

(b)

2-2 Specialization and Trade Can Move Us Beyond Our PPF

In this section, we explain how a country that specializes in the production of certain goods and then trades those goods to countries for other goods can make itself better off. In terms of its PPF, it can consume at a level *beyond* its PPF.

2-2a A Simple Two-Person PPF Model

Two individuals, Elizabeth and Brian, live near each other, and each engages in two activities: baking bread and growing apples. Let's suppose that, within a certain period, Elizabeth can produce 20 loaves of bread and no apples, or 10 loaves of bread and 10 apples, or no bread and 20 apples. (See Exhibit 10.) In other words, three points on Elizabeth's PPF correspond, respectively, to 20 loaves of bread and no apples, 10 loaves of bread and 10 apples, and no bread and 20 apples. As a consumer, Elizabeth likes to eat both bread and apples, so she decides to produce (and consume) 10 loaves of bread and 10 apples. This combination is represented by point B in Exhibit 10(a).

During the same period, Brian can produce 10 loaves of bread and no apples, or 5 loaves of bread and 15 apples, or no bread and 30 apples. In other words, these three combinations correspond, respectively, to three points on Brian's PPF. Brian, like Elizabeth, likes to eat both bread and apples, so he decides to produce and consume 5 loaves of bread and 15 apples. This combination is represented by point F in Exhibit 10(b).

Elizabeth thinks that both she and Brian may be better off if each specializes in producing only one of the two goods and trading it for the other. In other words, Elizabeth should produce either bread or apples but not both. Brian thinks that this may be a good idea but is not sure which good each person should specialize in producing.

An economist would advise each to produce the good that he or she can produce at a lower cost. In economics, a person who can produce a good at a lower cost than another person is said to have a **comparative advantage** in the production of the good.

Exhibit 10 shows that, for every 10 units of bread Elizabeth does not produce, she can produce 10 apples. In other words, the opportunity cost of producing 1 loaf of bread (B) is 1 apple (A):

$$\text{Opportunity costs for Elizabeth:} \quad 1B = 1A$$
$$1A = 1B$$

For every 5 loaves of bread that Brian does not produce, he can produce 15 apples. So, for every 1 loaf of bread he does not produce, he can produce 3 apples. Therefore, for every 1 apple he chooses to produce, he forfeits 1/3 loaf of bread:

$$\text{Opportunity costs for Brian:} \quad 1B = 3A$$
$$1A = 1/3B$$

Comparing opportunity costs, we see that Elizabeth can produce bread at a lower opportunity cost than Brian can. (Elizabeth forfeits 1 apple when she produces 1 loaf of bread, whereas Brian forfeits 3 apples for 1 loaf of bread.) By contrast, Brian can produce apples at a lower opportunity cost than Elizabeth can. We conclude that Elizabeth has a comparative advantage in the production of bread, and Brian has a comparative advantage in the production of apples.

Suppose both individuals specialize in the production of the good in which they have a comparative advantage. Then Elizabeth produces only bread and makes 20 loaves. Brian produces only apples and grows 30 of them.

Now suppose that Elizabeth and Brian decide to trade 8 loaves of bread for 12 apples. In other words, Elizabeth produces 20 loaves of bread and then trades 8 of them for 12 apples.

Comparative Advantage
The situation in which someone can produce a good at lower opportunity cost than someone else can.

EXHIBIT 10

Elizabeth's PPF, Brian's PPF

In (a), we show the combination of the two goods that Elizabeth can produce, first in terms of a table and then in terms of a PPF. Because Elizabeth wants to consume some of both goods, she chooses to produce the combination of the two goods represented by point B.

In (b), we show the combination of the two goods that Brian can produce, first in terms of a table and then in terms of a PPF. Because Brian wants to consume some of both goods, he chooses to produce the combination of the two goods represented by point F.

Elizabeth	
Bread	Apples
20	0
10	10
0	20

Brian	
Bread	Apples
10	0
5	15
0	30

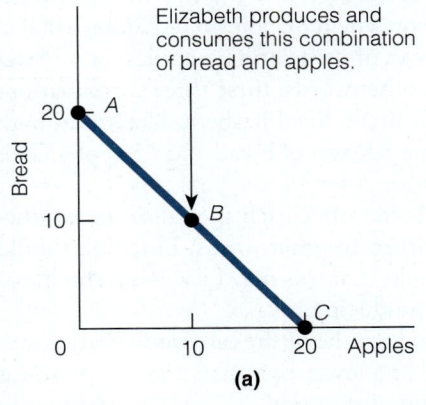

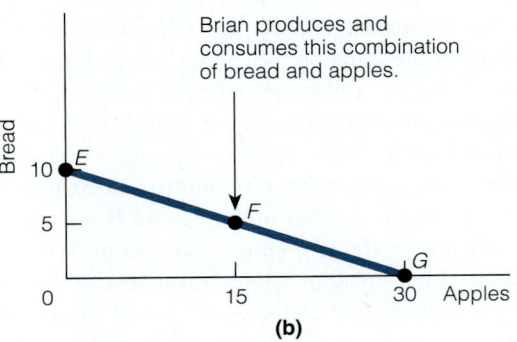

After the trade, Elizabeth consumes 12 loaves of bread and 12 apples. Compare this situation with what she consumed when she didn't specialize and didn't trade. In that situation, she consumed 10 loaves of bread and 10 apples. Clearly, Elizabeth is better off when she specializes and trades than when she does not.

But what about Brian? He produces 30 apples and trades 12 of them to Elizabeth for 8 loaves of bread. In other words, he consumes 8 loaves of bread and 18 apples. Compare this situation with what he consumed when he didn't specialize and didn't trade. In that situation, he consumed 5 loaves of bread and 15 apples. Thus, Brian is also better off when he specializes and trades than when he does not.

2-2b On or Beyond the PPF?

In Exhibit 11(a), we show the PPF for Elizabeth. When she was not specializing and not trading, she consumed the combination of bread and apples represented by point B (10 loaves of bread and 10 apples). When she did specialize and trade, her consumption of both goods increased, moving her to point D (12 loaves of bread and 12 apples). Here is the lesson learned: Through specialization and trade, Elizabeth's consumption moved beyond her PPF. It is easy to see the benefits of specialization and trade.

In Exhibit 11(b), we show the PPF for Brian. When he was not specializing and not trading, he consumed the combination of bread and apples represented by point F (5 loaves

EXHIBIT 11

Consumption for Elizabeth and Brian With and Without Specialization and Trade

A comparison of the consumption of bread and apples before and after specialization and trade shows that both Elizabeth and Brian benefit from producing the good in which each has a comparative advantage and trading for the other good.

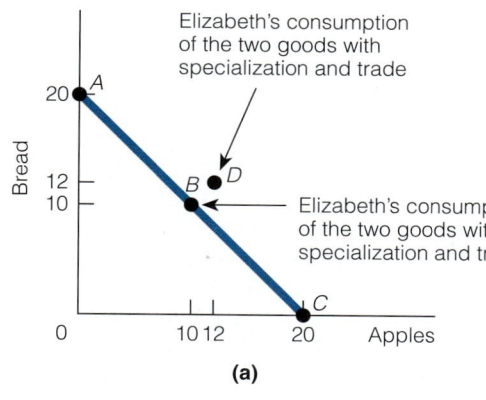
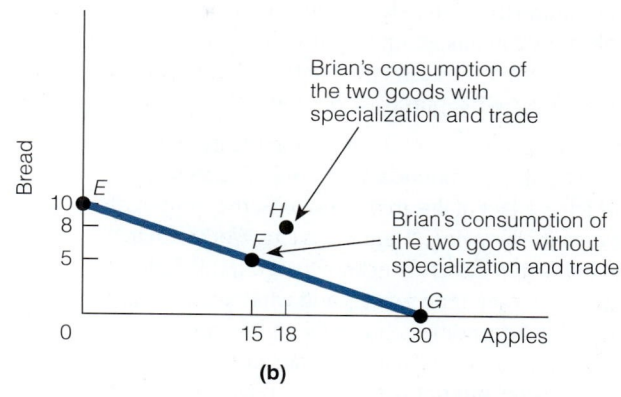

of bread and 15 apples). When he did specialize and trade, his consumption of both goods increased, moving him to point *H* (8 loaves of bread and 18 apples). Here is *this* lesson learned: Through specialization and trade, Brian's consumption moved beyond his PPF.

What holds for Elizabeth and Brian through specialization and trade holds for countries too. For example, if both Americans and Brazilians specialize in producing those goods for which they have a comparative advantage and then trade some of those goods for the other's goods, both Americans and Brazilians can consume more of both goods than if they don't specialize and don't trade.

A Benevolent and All-Knowing Dictator Versus the Invisible Hand
Suppose a benevolent dictator governs the country where Brian and Elizabeth live. We assume that this benevolent dictator knows everything about almost every economic activity in his country. In other words, he knows Elizabeth's and Brian's opportunity costs of producing bread and apples.

Because the dictator is benevolent and because he wants the best for the people who live in his country, he orders Elizabeth to produce only loaves of bread and Brian to produce only apples. Next, he tells Elizabeth and Brian to trade 8 loaves of bread for 12 apples.

Afterward, he shows Exhibit 11 to Elizabeth and Brian. They are both surprised that they are better off having done what the benevolent dictator told them to do.

Now in the original story of Elizabeth and Brian, there was no benevolent, all-knowing dictator. There were only two people who were guided by their self-interest to specialize and trade. In other words, self-interest did for Elizabeth and Brian what the benevolent dictator did for them.

Adam Smith, the eighteenth-century Scottish economist and founder of modern economics, spoke about the *invisible hand* that "guided" individuals' actions toward a positive outcome that they did not intend. That is what happened in the original story about Elizabeth and Brian. Neither intended to increase the overall output of society; each intended only to make himself or herself better off.

Office Hours
"What Purpose Does the PPF Serve?"

Student: Economists seem to have many uses for the PPF. For example, they can talk about scarcity, choice, opportunity costs, and many other topics in terms of the PPF. Beyond this capability, however, what purpose does the PPF serve?

Instructor: One purpose is to ground us in reality. For example, the frontier (or boundary) of the PPF represents scarcity, which is a fact of life. In other words, the frontier of the PPF is essentially saying, "Here is scarcity. Work with it." One of the important effects of acknowledging this fact is that we come to understand what *is* and what *is not* possible. For example, if the economy is currently on the frontier of its PPF, producing 100 units of X and 200 units of Y, then getting more of X is possible, but not without getting less of Y. In other words, the frontier of the PPF grounds us in reality: More of one thing means less of something else.

Student: But isn't this something we already knew?

Instructor: We understand that more of X means less of Y once someone makes this point, but think of how often we might act as if we didn't know it. John thinks he can work more hours at his job and get a good grade on his upcoming chemistry test. Well, he might be able to get a good grade (say, a 90), but this possibility ignores how much higher the grade could have been (say, five points higher) if he hadn't worked more hours at his job. The frontier of the PPF reminds us that there are trade-offs in life. That is an important reality to be aware of. We ignore it at our own peril.

Student: I've also heard that the PPF can show us what is necessary before the so-called average person in a country can become richer? Is this true? And how much richer do we mean here?

Instructor: We are talking about becoming richer in terms of having more goods and services. It's possible for the average person to become richer through economic growth. In other words, the average person in society becomes richer if the PPF shifts rightward by more than the population grows. To illustrate, suppose that a 100-person economy is currently producing 100 units of X and 200 units of Y. The average person can then have 1 unit of X and 2 units of Y.

Now suppose there is economic growth (shifting the PPF to the right), and the economy can produce more of both goods, X and Y. It produces 200 units of X and 400 units of Y. If the population has not changed (if it is still 100 people), then the average person can now have 2 units of X and 4 units of Y. The average person is richer in terms of both goods. If we change things and let the population grow from 100 persons to, say, 125 persons, it is still possible for the average person to have more through economic growth. With a population of 125 people, the average person now has 1.6 units of X and 3.2 units of good Y. In other words, as long as the productive capability of the economy grows by a greater percentage than the population, the average person can become richer (in terms of goods and services).

Student: Even if the economy is producing more of both goods (X and Y), the average person isn't necessarily better off in terms of goods and services, right? Can't all the extra output end up in the hands of only a few people instead of being evenly distributed across the entire population?

Instructor: That's correct. What we are assuming when we say that the average person can be better off is that, if we took the extra output and divided it evenly across the population, then the average person would be better off in terms of having more goods and services. By the way, this idea is exactly what economists mean when they say that the output (goods and services) per capita in a population has risen.

Points to Remember

1. The PPF grounds us in reality. It tells us what is and what is not possible in terms of producing various combinations of goods and services.
2. The PPF tells us that when we have efficiency (i.e., when we are at a point on the frontier itself), more of one thing means less of something else. In other words, the PPF tells us life has its trade-offs.
3. If the PPF shifts rightward and the population does not change, then output per capita rises.

Chapter Summary

An Economy's Production Possibilities Frontier

- An economy's PPF represents the possible combinations of two goods that the economy can produce in a certain span of time under the conditions of a given state of technology and fully employed resources.

Increasing and Constant Opportunity Costs

- A straight-line PPF represents constant opportunity costs: Increased production of a good comes at a constant opportunity cost.
- A bowed-outward (concave-downward) PPF represents the law of increasing opportunity costs: Increased production of a good comes at an increasing opportunity cost.

The Production Possibilities Frontier and Various Economic Concepts

- The PPF can be used to illustrate various economic concepts. Scarcity is illustrated by the frontier itself. Choice is illustrated by the fact that we have to find a point either on or below the frontier. In short, of the many attainable positions, one must be chosen. Opportunity cost is illustrated by a movement from one point to another on the PPF. Unemployed resources and productive inefficiency are illustrated by a point below the PPF. Productive efficiency and fully employed resources are illustrated by a point on the PPF. Economic growth is illustrated by a shift outward in the PPF.

Specialization, Trade, and the PPF

- Individuals can make themselves better off by specializing in the production of the good in which they have a comparative advantage and then trading some of that good for other goods. Someone who can produce the good at a lower opportunity cost than another person can have a comparative advantage in the production of the good.
- By specializing in the production of the good for which they have a comparative advantage and then trading it for other goods, people can move beyond their PPF.

Key Terms and Concepts

Production Possibilities Frontier (PPF)
Law of Increasing Opportunity Costs
Productive Efficient
Productive Inefficient
Technology
Comparative Advantage

Questions and Problems

1. Describe how each of the following would affect the U.S. PPF: (a) a war that takes place on U.S. soil, (b) the discovery of a new oil field, (c) a decrease in the unemployment rate, and (d) a law that requires individuals to enter lines of work for which they are not suited.
2. Explain how the following can be represented in a PPF framework: (a) the finiteness of resources implicit in the scarcity condition, (b) choice, (c) opportunity cost, (d) productive efficiency, and (e) unemployed resources.
3. What condition must hold for the PPF to be bowed outward (concave downward)? To be a straight line?
4. Look back at Exhibit 4 and notice that the slope between points A and B is flatter than it is between points C and D. What does the slope of a curve between two points have to do with the opportunity cost of producing additional units of a good?
5. Give an example to illustrate each of the following: (a) constant opportunity costs and (b) increasing opportunity costs.
6. Why are most PPFs for goods bowed outward (concave downward)?
7. Within a PPF framework, explain each of the following: (a) a disagreement between a person who favors more domestic welfare spending and one who favors more national defense spending, (b) an increase in the population, and (c) a technological change that makes resources less specialized.

8. Explain how to derive a PPF. For instance, how is the extreme point on the vertical axis identified? How is the extreme point on the horizontal axis identified?

9. If the slope of the PPF is the same between any two points, what does this relationship imply about costs? Explain your answer.

10. Suppose a nation's PPF shifts inward as its population grows. What happens, on average, to the material standard of living of the people? Explain your answer.

11. Can a technological advancement in sector X of the economy affect the number of people who work in sector Y of the economy? Explain your answer.

12. Use the PPF framework to explain something in your everyday life that was not mentioned in the chapter.

13. What exactly allows individuals to consume more if they specialize and trade than if they don't?

Working with Numbers and Graphs

1. Illustrate constant opportunity costs in a table similar to the one in Exhibit 1(a). Next, draw a PPF that is based on the data in the table.

2. Illustrate increasing opportunity costs (for one good) in a table similar to the one in Exhibit 2(a). Next, draw a PPF based on the data in the table.

3. Draw a PPF that represents the production possibilities for goods X and Y if there are constant opportunity costs. Next, represent an advance in technology that makes it possible to produce more of X but not more of Y. Finally, represent an advance in technology that makes it possible to produce more of Y but not more of X.

4. In the following figure, which graph depicts a technological breakthrough in the production of good X only?

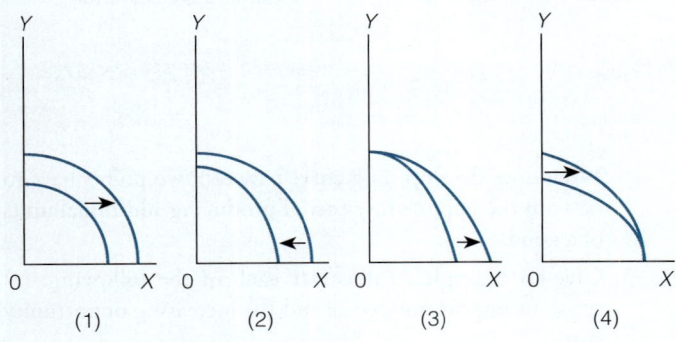

5. In the preceding figure, which graph depicts a change in the PPF that is a likely consequence of war?

6. If PPF_2 in the graph that follows is the relevant PPF, then which points are unattainable? Explain your answer.

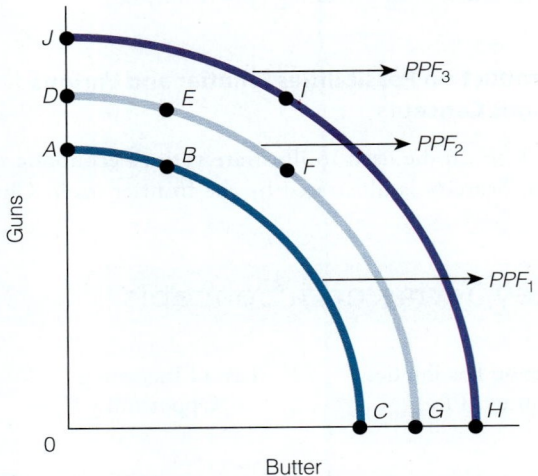

7. If PPF_1 in the preceding figure is the relevant PPF, then which point(s) represent productive efficiency? Explain your answer.

8. Nick can produce any of the following combinations of goods X and Y: (a) $100X$ and $0Y$, (b) $50X$ and $25Y$, and (c) $0X$ and $50Y$. Kamal can produce any of the following combinations of X and Y: (a) $50X$ and $0Y$, (b) $25X$ and $40Y$, and (c) $0X$ and $80Y$. Who has the comparative advantage in the production of good X? Of good Y? Explain your answer.

9. Using the data in problem 8, prove that both Nick and Kamal can be made better off through specialization and trade.
10. Suppose there is a PPF with two goods, X and Y. Suppose the economy is located at a point on the PPF. Does this point represent some of both goods or only one good and not the other?
11. The economy is producing $100X$ and $200Y$, but it could produce $200X$ and $300Y$ with the given resources and technology. Does it follow that when the economy is producing $100X$ and $200Y$, it is productive inefficient and that when it is producing $200X$ and $300Y$, it is productive efficient? Explain your answer.
12. A person can produce the following combinations of goods A and B: $20A$ and $0B$, $15A$ and $5B$, $10A$ and $10B$, $5A$ and $15B$, and $0A$ and $20B$. What is the opportunity cost of producing $1B$? Of producing $1A$?

CHAPTER 3
Supply and Demand: Theory

Introduction

Supply and demand have been called the "bread and butter" of economics. In this chapter, we discuss them, first separately and then together.

A **market** is any place people come together to trade. Economists often say that every market has *two* sides: a buying side and a selling side. The buying side of the market is usually referred to as the *demand* side; the selling side is usually referred to as the *supply* side. Let's begin with a discussion of *demand*.

Market
Any place people come together to trade.

Demand
The willingness and ability of buyers to purchase different quantities of a good at different prices during a specific period.

3-1 What Is Demand?

The word **demand** has a precise meaning in economics. It refers to:

1. the willingness and ability of buyers to purchase different quantities of a good,[1]
2. at different prices
3. during a specific period (per day, week, etc.).

For example, we can express part of Tyson's demand for magazines by saying that he is willing and able to buy 10 magazines a month at $4 per magazine and that he is willing and able to buy 15 magazines a month at $3 per magazine.

Remember this important point about demand: Unless both willingness and ability to buy are present, there is neither demand nor a buyer. For example, Josie may be willing to buy a computer but unable to pay the price; Tanya may be able to buy a computer but unwilling to do so. Neither Josie nor Tanya demands a computer, and neither is a buyer of a computer.

---

[1]. Demand takes into account services as well as goods. A few examples of goods are shirts, books, and TV sets. A few examples of services are dental care, medical care, and an economics lecture. To simplify the discussion, we refer only to goods.

3-1a The Law of Demand

Will people buy more units of a good at lower prices than at higher prices? For example, will people buy more shirts at $10 apiece than at $70 apiece? If your answer is yes, you instinctively understand the law of demand. The **law of demand** states that as the price of a good rises, the quantity demanded of the good falls, and as the price of a good falls, the quantity demanded of the good rises, *ceteris paribus*. Simply put, the law of demand states that the price of a good and the quantity demanded of it are inversely related, *ceteris paribus*. That is,

$$P \uparrow Q_d \downarrow$$
$$P \downarrow Q_d \uparrow, ceteris\ paribus$$

where P = price and Q_d = quantity demanded.

Quantity demanded is the number of units of a good that individuals are willing and able to buy at a particular price during a particular period. For example, suppose individuals are willing and able to buy 100 frozen dinners per week at a price of $4 per dinner. Therefore, 100 units is the quantity demanded of frozen dinners at $4 per dinner.

A warning: We know that the words "demand" and "quantity demanded" sound alike, but be aware that they do not describe the same thing. Demand is different from quantity demanded. Keep that in mind as you continue to read this chapter. For now, remind yourself that demand speaks to the willingness and ability of buyers to buy different quantities of a good at different prices. Quantity demanded speaks to the willingness and ability of buyers to buy a specific quantity (say, 100 units of a good) at a specific price (say, $10 per unit).

> **Law of Demand**
> As the price of a good rises, the quantity demanded of the good falls, and as the price of a good falls, the quantity demanded of the good rises, *ceteris paribus*.

3-1b Four Ways to Represent the Law of Demand

Here are four ways to represent the law of demand:

- *In Words*. We can represent the law of demand in words; we have done so already. Earlier we said that as the price of a good rises, quantity demanded falls, and as price falls, quantity demanded rises, *ceteris paribus*. That was the statement (in words) of the law of demand.

- *In Symbols*. We can also represent the law of demand in symbols, as we have also already done. In symbols, the law of demand is

$$P \uparrow Q_d \downarrow$$
$$P \downarrow Q_d \uparrow, ceteris\ paribus$$

- *In a Demand Schedule*. A **demand schedule** is the numerical representation of the law of demand. A demand schedule for good X is illustrated in Exhibit 1(a).

- *As a Demand Curve*. In Exhibit 1(b), the four price–quantity combinations in part (a) are plotted and the points connected, giving us a (downward-sloping) demand curve. A (downward-sloping) **demand curve** is the graphical representation of the inverse relationship between price and quantity demanded specified by the law of demand. In short, a demand curve is a picture of the law of demand.

> **Demand Schedule**
> The numerical tabulation of the quantity demanded of a good at different prices. A demand schedule is the numerical representation of the law of demand.
>
> **Demand Curve**
> The graphical representation of the law of demand.

EXHIBIT 1

Demand Schedule and Demand Curve

Part (a) shows a demand schedule for good X. Part (b) shows a demand curve, obtained by plotting the different price–quantity combinations in part (a) and connecting the points. On a demand curve, the price (in dollars) represents price per unit of the good. The quantity demanded, on the horizontal axis, is always relevant for a specific period (a week, a month, etc.).

Demand Schedule for Good X

Price (dollars)	Quantity Demanded	Point in Part (b)
4	10	A
3	20	B
2	30	C
1	40	D

(a)

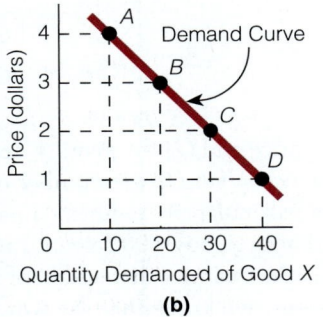

(b)

Finding Economics

In a Visit Home to See Mom A friend tells you that she flies home to see her mother only once a year. You ask why. She says, "Because the price of the ticket to fly home is $1,100." She then adds, "If the price were, say, $600 instead of $1,100, I'd fly home twice a year instead of once." Can you find any economics in what she is telling you? If you listen closely to what she says, she has identified two points on her demand curve for air travel home: One point corresponds to $1,100 and buying one ticket home, and the other point corresponds to $600 and buying two tickets home.

3-1c Why Does Quantity Demanded Go Down as Price Goes Up?

The law of demand states that price and quantity demanded are inversely related. This much you know. But do you know *why* quantity demanded moves in the direction opposite that of price? We identify two reasons.

The first reason is that *people substitute lower priced goods for higher priced goods*. Often, many goods serve the same purpose. Many different goods will satisfy hunger, and many different drinks will satisfy thirst. For example, both orange juice and grapefruit juice will satisfy thirst. On Monday, the price of orange juice equals the price of grapefruit juice, but on Tuesday, the price of orange juice rises. As a result, people will choose to buy less of the relatively higher priced orange juice and more of the relatively lower priced grapefruit juice. In other words, a rise in the price of orange juice will lead to a decrease in the quantity demanded of it.

The second reason for the inverse relationship between price and quantity demanded has to do with the **law of diminishing marginal utility**, which states that, over a given period, the marginal (or additional) utility or satisfaction gained by consuming equal successive units of a

Law of Diminishing Marginal Utility
Over a given period, the marginal (or additional) utility or satisfaction gained by consuming equal successive units of a good will decline as the amount consumed increases.

good will decline as the amount of the good consumed increases. For example, you may receive more utility, or satisfaction, from eating your first hamburger at lunch than from eating your second and, if you continue, more utility from your second hamburger than from your third.

What does marginal utility have to do with the law of demand? Economists state that the more utility you receive from a unit of a good, the higher the price you are willing to pay for it, and the less utility you receive from a unit of a good, the lower the price you are willing to pay for it. According to the law of diminishing marginal utility, individuals obtain less utility from additional units of a good. Therefore, they will buy larger quantities of a good only at lower prices, and their behavior reflects the law of demand.

3-1d Individual Demand Curve and Market Demand Curve

There is a difference between an individual demand curve and a market demand curve.

An individual demand curve represents the price–quantity combinations of a particular good for a *single buyer*. For example, an individual demand curve could show Ben's demand for T-shirts. By contrast, a market demand curve represents the price–quantity combinations of a good for *all buyers*. In this case, the demand curve would show all buyers' demand for T-shirts.

A market demand curve is derived by adding up individual demand curves, as shown in Exhibit 2. The demand schedules for Ben, Sophia, and other buyers are shown in part (a).

EXHIBIT 2

Deriving a Market Demand Schedule and a Market Demand Curve

Part (a) shows four demand schedules combined into one table. The market demand schedule is derived by adding the quantities demanded at each price. In (b), the data points from the demand schedule are plotted to show how a market demand curve is derived. Only two points on the market demand curve are noted.

Price	Ben	Sophia	Other Buyers	All Buyers
$15	1	2	20	23
14	2	3	45	50
13	3	4	70	77
12	4	5	100	109
11	5	6	130	141
10	6	7	160	173

(a)

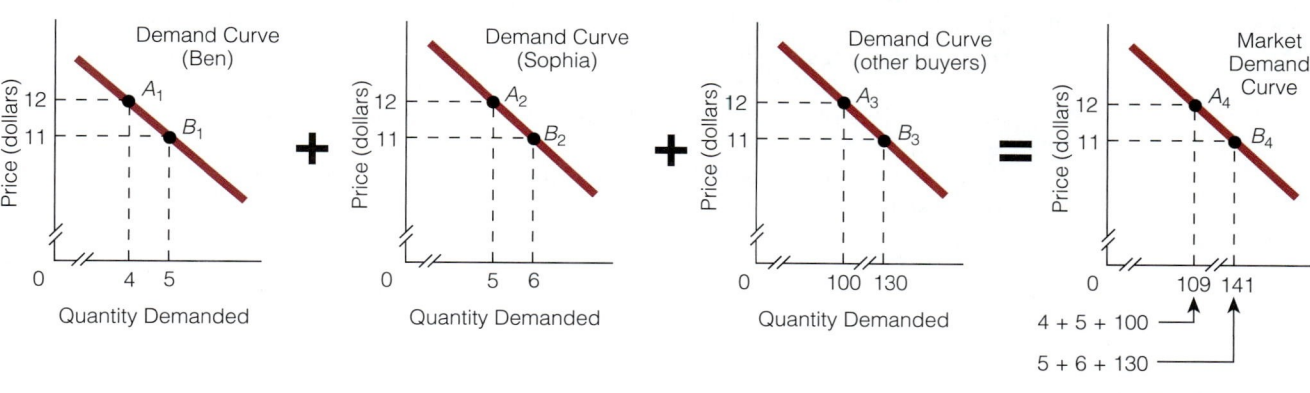

(b)

The market demand schedule is obtained by adding the quantities demanded at each price. For example, at $12, the quantities demanded are 4 units for Ben, 5 units for Sophia, and 100 units for other buyers. Thus, a total of 109 units are demanded at $12. In part (b), the data points for the demand schedules are plotted and added to produce a market demand curve. The market demand curve could also be drawn directly from the market demand schedule.

3-1e A Change in Quantity Demanded Versus a Change in Demand

Economists often talk about (1) a change in quantity demanded and (2) a change in demand. As stated earlier, although the phrase "quantity demanded" may sound like "demand," the two are not the same. In short, a change in quantity demanded *is not* the same as a change in demand. (Read the last sentence at least two more times.) We use Exhibit 1 to illustrate the difference between a change in quantity demanded and a change in demand.

A Change in Quantity Demanded Look at Exhibit 1. The horizontal axis is labeled "Quantity Demanded of Good X." Notice that quantity demanded is a *number*—such as 10, 20, 30, 40, and so on. More specifically, it is the number of units of a good that individuals are willing and able to buy at a particular price during some period. In Exhibit 1, if the price is $4, then the quantity demanded is 10 units of good X; if the price is $3, then the quantity demanded is 20 units of good X. In general,

> Quantity demanded = The number of units of a good that individuals are willing and able to buy at a particular price

Now, again looking at Exhibit 1, see if you can figure out what can change quantity demanded from 10 (which it is at point *A*) to 20 (which it is at point *B*), or what has to change before quantity demanded will change. The answer is on the vertical axis of Exhibit 1. The only thing that can change the quantity demanded of a good is its price:

> Change in quantity demanded = A movement from one point to another point on the same demand curve that is caused by a change in the price of the good

The price of a good is also called **own price**.

Own Price
The price of a good. For example, if the price of oranges is $1, this is its own price.

A Change in Demand Look again at Exhibit 1, this time focusing on the demand curve. Demand is represented by the *entire* curve. When talking about a change in demand, an economist is actually talking about a change—or shift—in the entire demand curve:

> Change in demand = Shift in demand curve

Demand can change in two ways: Demand can increase and demand can decrease. Let's look first at an *increase* in demand. Suppose we have the following demand schedule:

Demand Schedule A	
Price	Quantity Demanded
$20	500
$15	600
$10	700
$5	800

The demand curve for this demand schedule will look like the demand curve labeled D_A in Exhibit 3(a).

What does an increase in demand mean? It means that individuals are willing and able to buy more units of the good at each and every price. In other words, demand schedule A will change as follows:

Demand Schedule B (increase in demand)	
Price	Quantity Demanded
$20	~~500~~ 600
$15	~~600~~ 700
$10	~~700~~ 800
$5	~~800~~ 900

Whereas individuals were willing and able to buy 500 units of the good at $20, now they are willing and able to buy 600 units of the good at $20; whereas individuals were willing and able to buy 600 units of the good at $15, now they are willing and able to buy 700 units of the good at $15, and so on.

As shown in Exhibit 3(a), the demand curve that represents demand schedule B (D_B) lies to the right of the demand curve that represents demand schedule A (D_A). We conclude that *an increase in demand is represented by a rightward shift in the demand curve and means that individuals are willing and able to buy more of a good at each and every price:*

Increase in demand = Rightward shift in the demand curve

EXHIBIT 3

Shifts in the Demand Curve

In part (a), the demand curve shifts rightward from D_A to D_B. This shift represents an increase in demand. At each price, the quantity demanded is greater than it was before. For example, the quantity demanded at $20 increases from 500 units to 600 units. In part (b), the demand curve shifts leftward from D_A to D_C. This shift represents a decrease in demand. At each price, the quantity demanded is less. For example, the quantity demanded at $20 decreases from 500 units to 400 units.

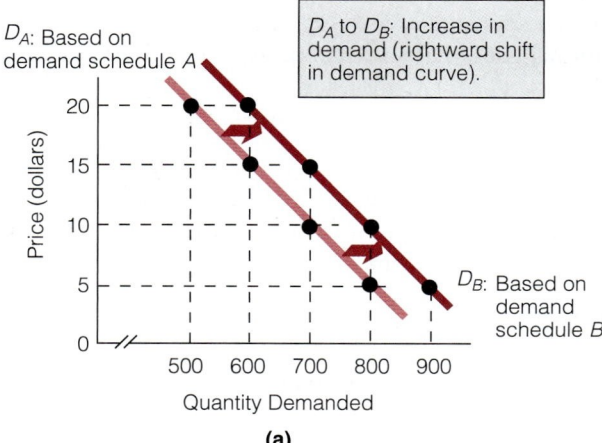

(a)

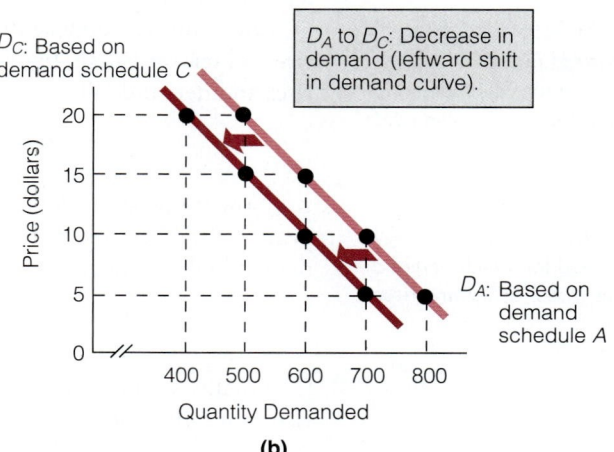

(b)

Now let's look at a decrease in demand. A decrease in demand means that individuals are willing and able to buy less of a good at each and every price. In this case, demand schedule *A* will change as follows:

Demand Schedule C (decrease in demand)	
Price	Quantity Demanded
$20	~~500~~ 400
$15	~~600~~ 500
$10	~~700~~ 600
$5	~~800~~ 700

As shown in Exhibit 3(b), the demand curve that represents demand schedule C (D_C) obviously lies to the left of the demand curve that represents demand schedule A (D_A). We conclude that a *decrease in demand is represented by a leftward shift in the demand curve and means that individuals are willing and able to buy less of a good at each and every price:*

Decrease in demand = Leftward shift in the demand curve

3-1f What Factors Cause the Demand Curve to Shift?

We know what an increase in demand and a decrease in demand mean: An increase in demand means that consumers are willing and able to buy *more* of a good at every price. A decrease in demand means that consumers are willing and able to buy *less* of a good at every price. We also know that an increase in demand is graphically portrayed as a rightward shift in a demand curve and that a decrease in demand is graphically portrayed as a leftward shift in a demand curve.

But what factors or variables can increase or decrease demand? What factors or variables can shift demand curves? They are (1) income, (2) preferences, (3) prices of related goods, (4) the number of buyers, and (5) expectations of future prices.

Income As a person's income changes (increases or decreases), that individual's demand for a particular good may rise, fall, or remain constant.

For example, suppose Ethan's income rises and, as a consequence, his demand for books rises. Then, for Ethan, books are a normal good. For a **normal good**, demand rises as income rises and demand falls as income falls:

X is a normal good: If income ↑, then D_X ↑. If income ↓, then D_X ↓

Normal Good
A good for which demand rises (falls) as income rises (falls).

Now suppose Marie's income rises and, as a consequence, her demand for canned baked beans falls. Then, for Marie, canned baked beans are an inferior good. For an **inferior good**, demand falls as income rises and demand rises as income falls:

Y is an inferior good: If income ↑, then D_Y ↓. If income ↓, then D_Y ↑

Inferior Good
A good for which demand falls (rises) as income rises (falls).

Finally, suppose that, when Morgan's income rises, his demand for toothpaste neither rises nor falls. Then, for Morgan, toothpaste is neither a normal good nor an inferior good.

Instead, it is a **neutral good**. For a neutral good, demand does not change as income rises or falls.

Neutral Good
A good for which demand does not change as income rises or falls.

Preferences People's preferences affect the amount of a good they are willing to buy at a particular price. A change in preferences in favor of a good shifts the demand curve rightward. A change in preferences away from the good shifts the demand curve leftward. For example, if people begin to favor Elmore Leonard novels to a greater degree than previously, the demand for his novels increases, and the demand curve shifts rightward.

Prices of Related Goods There are two types of related goods: substitutes and complements. Two goods are substitutes if they satisfy similar needs or desires. For many people, Coca-Cola and Pepsi are substitutes. If two goods are **substitutes**, then, as the price of one rises (falls), the demand for the other rises (falls). For instance, higher Coca-Cola prices will increase the demand for Pepsi as people substitute Pepsi for the higher-priced Coke. [See Exhibit 4(a).] Other examples of substitutes are coffee and tea, corn chips and potato chips, different brands of margarine, and foreign and domestic cars. Generalizing, we obtain

Substitutes
Two goods that satisfy similar needs or desires.

$$X \text{ and } Y \text{ are substitutes: If } P_X \uparrow, \text{ then } D_Y \uparrow. \text{ If } P_X \downarrow, \text{ then } D_Y \downarrow$$

Two goods are **complements** if they are consumed jointly. For example, tennis rackets and tennis balls are used together to play tennis. If two goods are complements, then, as the price of one rises (falls), the demand for the other falls (rises). For example, higher tennis racket prices will decrease the demand for tennis balls, as Exhibit 4(b) shows. Other examples of complements are cars and tires, lightbulbs and lamps, and golf clubs and golf balls. Generalizing yields the following relationship:

Complements
Two goods that are used jointly in consumption.

$$X \text{ and } Y \text{ are complements: If } P_X \uparrow, \text{ then } D_Y \downarrow. \text{ If } P_X \downarrow, \text{ then } D_Y \uparrow$$

Number of Buyers The demand for a good in a particular market area is related to the number of buyers in the area: more buyers means higher demand; fewer buyers means lower demand. The number of buyers may increase owing to a heightened birthrate, rising immigration, the migration of people from one region of the country to another, and so on. The number of buyers may decrease owing to an increased death rate, war, the migration of people from one region of the country to another, and so on.

Expectations of Future Price Buyers who expect the price of a good to be higher next month may buy it now, thus increasing the current (or present) demand for the good. Buyers who expect the price of a good to be lower next month may wait until next month to buy it, thus decreasing the current (or present) demand for the good.

For example, suppose you are planning to buy a house. One day, you hear that house prices are expected to go down in a few months. Consequently, you decide to delay your purchase for a while. Alternatively, if you hear that prices are expected to rise in a few months, you might go ahead and make your purchase now.

EXHIBIT 4

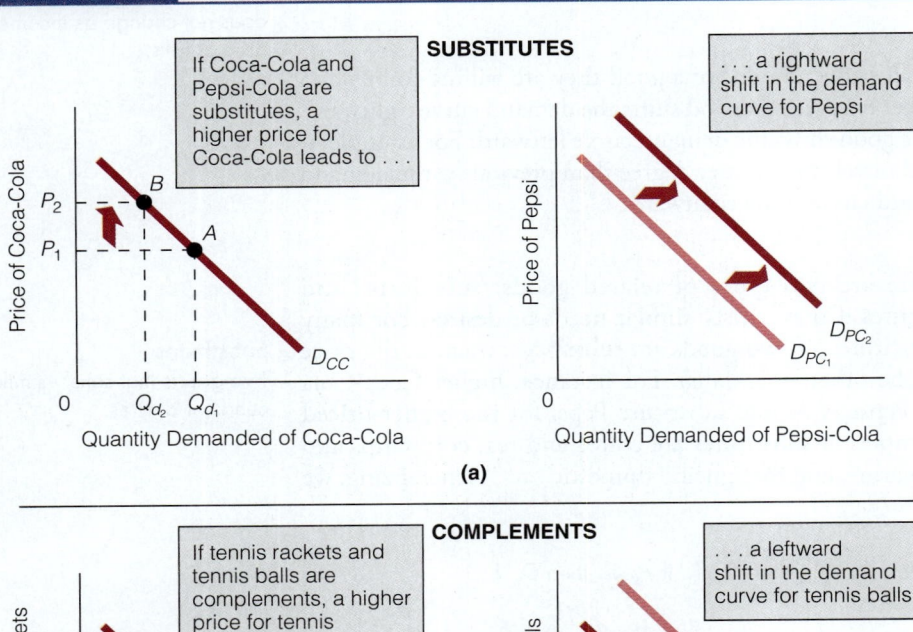
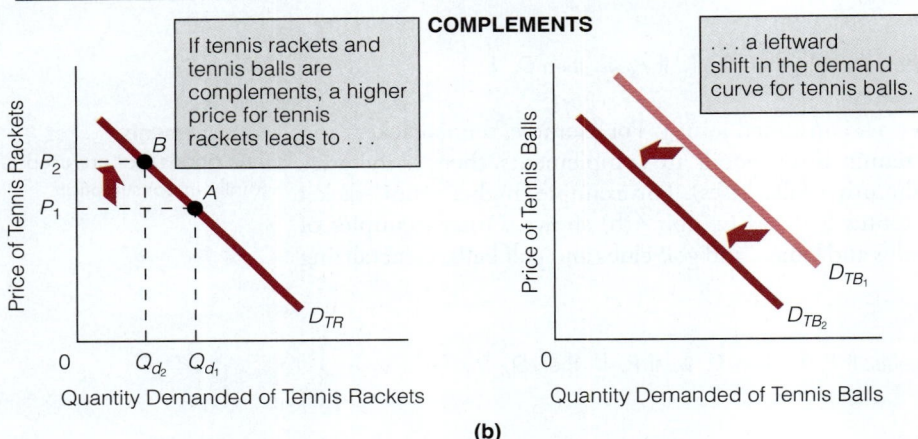

Substitutes and Complements

(a) Coca-Cola and Pepsi are substitutes: The price of one and the demand for the other are directly related. As the price of Coca-Cola rises, the demand for Pepsi increases. (b) Tennis rackets and tennis balls are complements: The price of one and the demand for the other are inversely related. As the price of tennis rackets rises, the demand for tennis balls decreases.

3-1g It Is Important to Know Why the Price Changed: Back to Substitutes and Complements

According to our earlier discussion of substitutes, two goods are substitutes if, as the price of one rises (falls), the demand for the other rises (falls). For example, consider the substitutes coffee and tea: As the price of coffee rises, it makes sense to think that people will cut back on buying as much coffee (the quantity demanded of coffee declines) and increase their demand for tea.

But will a higher price of coffee always cause this set of events? The answer depends on *why* the price of coffee increases. Is it because the supply of coffee decreases or because the demand for coffee increases?

If the supply of coffee decreases, the price of coffee will rise. This will cause people to cut back on buying coffee (the quantity demanded of coffee declines) and increase their demand for tea.

Now suppose the demand for coffee rises—say, because peoples' preference for coffee becomes stronger. The price of coffee will rise. This time, however, the higher price of coffee *will not* cause people to increase their demand for tea. If coffee becomes more expensive because the demand for coffee increases, it seems peculiar to think that the demand for tea also increases. (If pears become more expensive because the demand for pears increases, does the demand for apples have to increase too? No. If pens become more expensive because the demand for pens increases, does the demand for pencils have to increase too? No.)

So, when it's said that two goods are substitutes if as the price of one rises (falls), the demand for the other rises (falls), is this correct? It is, as long as the initial price rise or fall is due to a change in supply and not a change in demand.

Now let's turn to complements. According to our earlier discussion of complements, two goods are complements if, as the price of one rises (falls), the demand for the other falls (rises). For example, consider the complements, pasta and pasta sauce: As the price of pasta rises, it makes sense to think that people will cut back on buying as much pasta (the quantity demanded of pasta declines) and therefore decrease their demand for pasta sauce.

But will a higher price of pasta always cause this set of events? The answer depends on *why* the price of pasta increases? Is it because the supply of pasta decreases or because the demand for pasta increases?

If the supply of pasta decreases, the price of pasta will rise. This will cause people to cut back on buying as much pasta (quantity demanded of pasta falls) and decrease their demand for pasta sauce.

Now suppose the demand for pasta rises—say, because peoples' preferences for pasta becomes stronger. The price of pasta will rise. This time, though, the higher price of pasta will not cause people to decrease their demand for pasta sauce. If anything, they will want to buy more pasta sauce to go with the increased pasta they have purchased.

So when it's said that two goods are complements if as the price of one rises (falls), the demand for the other falls (rises), is this correct? It is, as long as the initial price rise or fall is due to a change in supply and not a change in demand.

There is an important lesson to be learned from our discussion of price, substitutes, and complements. It is that we should never "reason from" or "start an economic explanation with" a price change. ("Price changed and then the following happened . . ."). Instead, we should start an economic explanation one step before the price changed. We should start it with *why* the price changed. (Demand increased and then price increased or supply decreased and then price increased). That's because, as we have seen here, *why* price changes matters.

3-1h Movement Factors and Shift Factors

Economists often distinguish between (1) factors that can bring about movement along curves and (2) factors that can shift curves.

The factors that cause movement along curves are sometimes called *movement* factors. In many economic diagrams, such as the demand curve in Exhibit 1, the movement factor (price) is on the vertical axis.

The factors that actually shift the curves are sometimes called *shift* factors. The shift factors for the demand curve are income, preferences, the price of related goods, and so on. Often, shift factors do not appear in the economic diagrams. For example, although in Exhibit 1 the movement factor—price—is on the vertical axis, the shift factors do not appear anywhere in the diagram. We just know what they are and that they can shift the demand curve.

When you see a curve in this book, first ask which factor will move us along the curve. In other words, what is the movement factor? Second, ask which factors will shift the curve. In other words, what are the shift factors? Exhibit 5 summarizes the shift factors that can change demand and the movement factors that can change quantity demanded.

EXHIBIT 5

A Change in Demand Versus a Change in Quantity Demanded

(a) A change in demand refers to a shift in the demand curve. A change in demand can be brought about by a number of factors. (See the exhibit and the text.)

(b) A change in quantity demanded refers to a movement along a given demand curve. A change in quantity demanded is brought about only by a change in (a good's) own price.

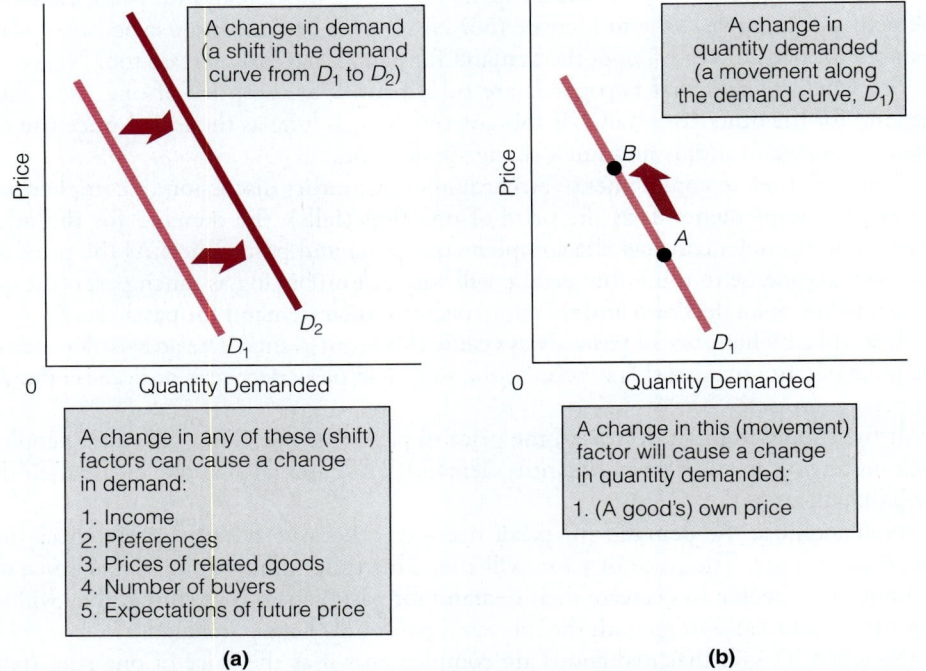

A change in any of these (shift) factors can cause a change in demand:
1. Income
2. Preferences
3. Prices of related goods
4. Number of buyers
5. Expectations of future price

(a)

A change in this (movement) factor will cause a change in quantity demanded:
1. (A good's) own price

(b)

(Answers to Self-Test questions are in Answers to Self-Test Questions at the back of the book.)

1. As Sandi's income rises, her demand for popcorn rises. As Mark's income falls, his demand for prepaid telephone cards rises. What kinds of goods are popcorn for Sandi and telephone cards for Mark?
2. Why are demand curves downward sloping?
3. Give an example that illustrates how to derive a market demand curve.
4. What factors can change demand? What factors can change quantity demanded?

3-2 Supply

Supply
The willingness and ability of sellers to produce and offer to sell different quantities of a good at different prices during a specific period.

Just as the word "demand" has a specific meaning in economics, so does the word "supply." **Supply** refers to

1. the willingness and ability of sellers to produce and offer to sell different quantities of a good
2. at different prices
3. during a specific period (per day, week, etc.).

3-2a The Law of Supply

Law of Supply
As the price of a good rises, the quantity supplied of the good rises, and as the price of a good falls, the quantity supplied of the good falls, *ceteris paribus*.

The **law of supply** states that as the price of a good rises, the quantity supplied of the good rises, and as the price of a good falls, the quantity supplied of the good falls, *ceteris paribus*. Simply put, the price of a good and the quantity supplied of the good are directly related, *ceteris paribus*. (The quantity supplied is the number of units that sellers are willing and able to produce and offer to sell at a particular price.) The **(upward-sloping) supply curve** is the graphical representation of the law of supply. (see Exhibit 6.) The law of supply can be summarized as

$$P \uparrow Q_s \uparrow$$
$$P \downarrow Q_s \downarrow, \text{ceteris paribus}$$

where P = price and Q_s = quantity supplied.

(Upward-Sloping) Supply Curve
The graphical representation of the law of supply.

The law of supply holds for the production of most goods. It does not hold when there is no time to produce more units of a good. For example, suppose a theater in Atlanta is sold out for tonight's play. Then, even if ticket prices increased from $100 to $140, the theater would have no additional seats and no time to produce more. The supply curve for theater seats is illustrated in Exhibit 7(a). It is fixed at the number of seats in the theater, 500.[2]

The law of supply also does not hold for goods that cannot be produced over any period. For example, the violin maker Antonio Stradivari died in 1737, so, because he cannot produce

EXHIBIT 6

A Supply Curve

The upward-sloping supply curve is the graphical representation of the law of supply, which states that price and quantity supplied are directly related, *ceteris paribus*. On a supply curve, the price (in dollars) represents the price per unit of the good. The quantity supplied, on the horizontal axis, is always relevant for a specific period (a week, a month, etc.).

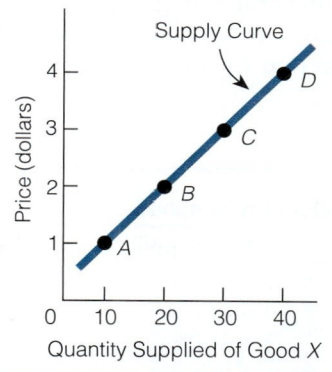

EXHIBIT 7

Supply Curves When There Is No Time to Produce More or When No More Can Be Produced

The supply curve is not upward sloping when there is no time to produce additional units or when additional units cannot be produced. In those cases, the supply curve is vertical.

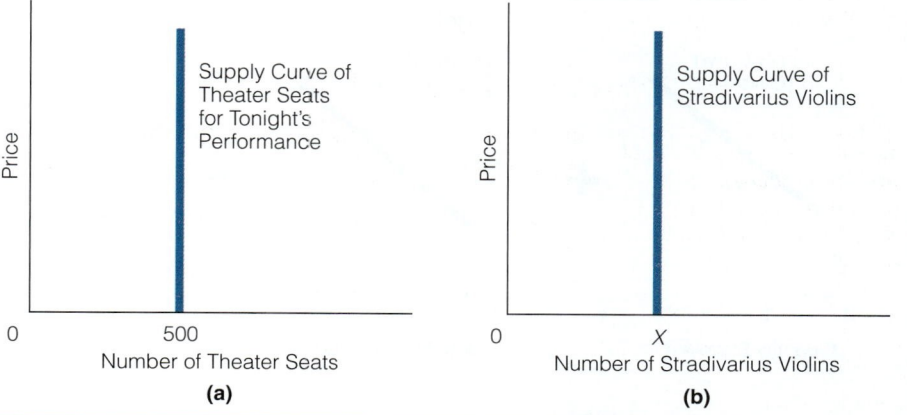

---

[2]. The vertical supply curve is said to be perfectly inelastic.

any violins anymore, a rise in the price of Stradivarius violins does not affect the number of Stradivarius violins supplied, as Exhibit 7(b) illustrates.

3-2b Why Most Supply Curves Are Upward Sloping

Most supply curves are upward sloping. The fundamental reason for this behavior involves the *law of diminishing marginal returns*, discussed in a later chapter. Here, suffice it to say that an upward-sloping supply curve reflects the fact that, under certain conditions, a higher price is an incentive to producers to produce more of the good. The incentive comes in the form of higher profits. For example, suppose the price of good X rises, and nothing else (such as the per-unit costs of producing good X) changes. In that case, the producers of good X will earn higher profits per unit and are thus encouraged to increase the quantity of good X that they supply to the market.

Generally, though, producing more of a good does not come with constant per-unit costs. As we learned in Chapter 2, the law of increasing opportunity costs is usually at work. In other words, the increased production of a good comes at increased opportunity costs. An upward-sloping supply curve simply reflects the fact that costs rise when more units of a good are produced.

Supply Schedule
The numerical tabulation of the quantity supplied of a good at different prices. A supply schedule is the numerical representation of the law of supply.

The Market Supply Curve An individual supply curve represents the price–quantity combinations for a single seller. The market supply curve represents the price–quantity combinations for all sellers of a particular good. Exhibit 8 shows how a market supply curve can be derived by adding individual supply curves. In part (a), a **supply schedule**, the

EXHIBIT 8

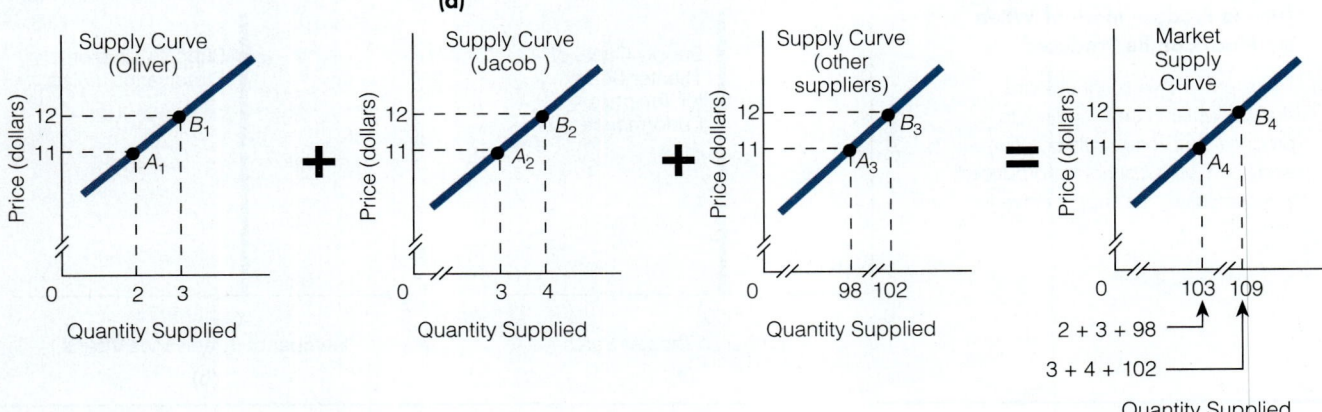

Deriving a Market Supply Schedule and a Market Supply Curve

Part (a) shows four supply schedules combined into one table. The market supply schedule is derived by adding the quantities supplied at each price. In (b), the data points from the supply schedules are plotted to show how a market supply curve is derived. Only two points on the market supply curve are noted.

numerical tabulation of the quantity supplied of a good at different prices, is given for Oliver, Jacob, and other suppliers. The market supply schedule is obtained by adding the quantities supplied at each price, *ceteris paribus*. For example, at $11, the quantities supplied are 2 units for Oliver, 3 units for Jacob, and 98 units for the other suppliers. Thus, 103 units are supplied at $11. In part (b), the data points for the supply schedules are plotted and added to produce a market supply curve (which could also be drawn directly from the market supply schedule).

3-2c Changes in Supply Mean Shifts in Supply Curves

Just as demand can change, so can supply. The supply of a good can rise or fall. An increase in the supply of a good means that suppliers are willing and able to produce, and offer to sell more of, the good at all prices. For example, suppose that, in January, sellers are willing and able to produce and offer for sale 600 shirts at $25 each and that, in February, they are willing and able to produce and sell 900 shirts at $25 each. Then an increase in supply shifts the entire supply curve to the right, as shown in Exhibit 9(a).

The supply of a good decreases if sellers are willing and able to produce and offer to sell less of the good at all prices. For example, suppose that, in January, sellers are willing and able to produce and offer for sale 600 shirts at $25 each and that, in February, they are willing and able to produce and sell only 300 shirts at $25 each. Then a decrease in supply shifts the entire supply curve to the left, as shown in Exhibit 9(b).

3-2d What Factors Cause the Supply Curve to Shift?

We know that the supply of any good can change, but what causes supply to change? What causes supply curves to shift? The factors that can change supply include (1) the prices of relevant resources, (2) technology, (3) the prices of related goods, (4) the number of sellers, (5) expectations of future price, (6) taxes and subsidies, and (7) government restrictions.

EXHIBIT 9

Shifts in the Supply Curve

(a) The supply curve shifts rightward from S_1 to S_2. This shift represents an increase in the supply of shirts: At each price, the quantity supplied of shirts is greater. For example, the quantity supplied at $25 increases from 600 shirts to 900 shirts. (b) The supply curve shifts leftward from S_1 to S_2. This shift represents a decrease in the supply of shirts: At each price, the quantity supplied of shirts is less. For example, the quantity supplied at $25 decreases from 600 shirts to 300 shirts.

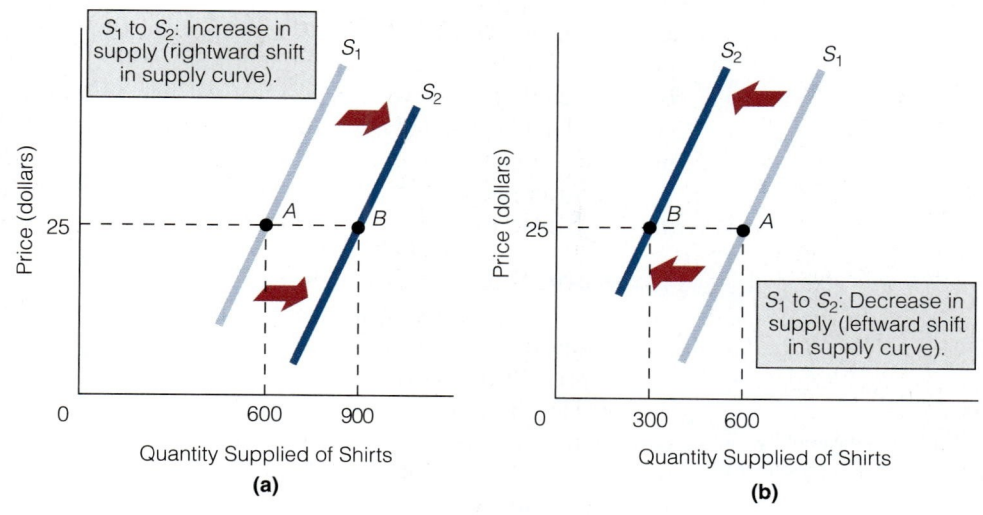

Prices of Relevant Resources Resources are needed to produce goods. For example, wood is needed to produce doors. If the price of wood falls, producing doors becomes less costly. How will door producers respond? Will they produce more doors, the same number, or fewer? With lower costs and prices unchanged, the profit from producing and selling doors has increased; as a result, the (monetary) incentive to produce doors is increased, so door producers will produce and offer to sell more doors at each and every price. Thus, the supply of doors will increase, and the supply curve of doors will shift rightward. If the price of wood rises, producing doors becomes more costly. Consequently, the supply of doors will decrease, and the supply curve of doors will shift leftward.

Technology In Chapter 2, technology was defined as the body of skills and knowledge involved in the use of resources in production. Also, an advance in technology was said to refer to the ability to produce more output with a fixed amount of resources, reducing per-unit production costs. To illustrate, suppose it takes $100 to produce 40 units of a good. Then the per-unit cost is $2.50. If an advance in technology makes it possible to produce 50 units at a cost of $100, then the per-unit cost falls to $2.00.

We expect that if the per-unit production costs of a good decline, then the quantity supplied of the good at each price will increase. Why? Lower per-unit costs increase profitability and therefore provide producers with an incentive to produce more. For example, if corn growers develop a way to grow more corn by using the same amount of water and other resources, then per-unit production costs will fall, profitability will increase, and growers will want to grow and sell more corn at each price. The supply curve of corn will shift rightward.

Prices of Other Goods Think of a farmer who is producing wheat. Suddenly, the price of something he is not producing (say, corn) rises relative to the price of wheat. The farmer might then shift his farming away from wheat to corn. In other words, as the price of corn rises relative to wheat, the farmer switches from wheat production to corn production. We conclude that a change in the price of one good can lead to a change in the supply of another good.

Number of Sellers If more sellers begin producing a good, perhaps because of high profits, the supply curve will shift rightward. If some sellers stop producing a good, perhaps because of losses, the supply curve will shift leftward.

Expectations of Future Price If the price of a good is expected to be higher in the future, producers may hold back some of the product today (if possible—perishables cannot be held back). Then they will have more to sell at the higher future price. Therefore, the *current* supply curve will shift leftward. For example, if oil producers expect the price of oil to be higher next year, some may hold oil off the market this year to be able to sell it next year. Similarly, if they expect the price of oil to be lower next year, they might pump more oil this year than previously planned.

Taxes and Subsidies Some taxes increase per-unit costs. Suppose a shoe manufacturer must pay a $2 tax per pair of shoes produced. This tax leads to a leftward shift in the supply curve, indicating that the manufacturer wants to produce and offer to sell fewer pairs of shoes at each price. If the tax is eliminated, the supply curve shifts rightward.

Subsidies have the opposite effect. Suppose the government subsidizes the production of corn by paying corn farmers $2 for every bushel of corn they produce. Then, because of the subsidy, the quantity supplied of corn is greater at each price and the supply curve of corn shifts rightward. The removal of the subsidy shifts the supply curve of corn leftward. A rough rule of thumb is that we get more of what we subsidize and less of what we tax.

Subsidies
A monetary payment by government to a producer of a good or service.

Chapter 3 Supply and Demand: Theory

Government Restrictions Sometimes government acts to reduce supply. Consider a U.S. import quota—a quantitative restriction on foreign goods—on South Korean television sets. The quota reduces the supply of South Korean television sets in the United States. It thus shifts the supply curve leftward. The elimination of the import quota allows the supply of South Korean television sets in the United States to shift rightward.

Licensure has a similar effect. With licensure, individuals must meet certain requirements before they can legally carry out a task. For example, owner–operators of day-care centers must meet certain requirements before they are allowed to sell their services. No doubt this requirement reduces the number of day-care centers and shifts the supply curve of day-care centers leftward.

3-2e A Change in Supply Versus a Change in Quantity Supplied

A change in *supply* is not the same as a change in *quantity supplied*. A change in supply is a shift in the supply curve, as illustrated in Exhibit 10(a). For example, saying that the supply of oranges has increased is the same as saying that the supply curve for oranges has shifted rightward. The factors that can change supply (i.e., shift the supply curve) are prices of relevant resources, technology, prices of other goods, the number of sellers, expectations of future prices, taxes and subsidies, and government restrictions.

A change in quantity supplied refers to a movement along a supply curve, as in Exhibit 10(b). The only factor that can directly cause a change in the quantity supplied of a good is a change in the price of the good.

EXHIBIT 10

A Change in Supply Versus a Change in Quantity Supplied

(a) A change in supply refers to a shift in the supply curve. A change in supply can be brought about by several factors. (See the exhibit and the text.)

(b) A change in quantity supplied refers to a movement along a given supply curve. A change in quantity supplied is brought about only by a change in (a good's) own price.

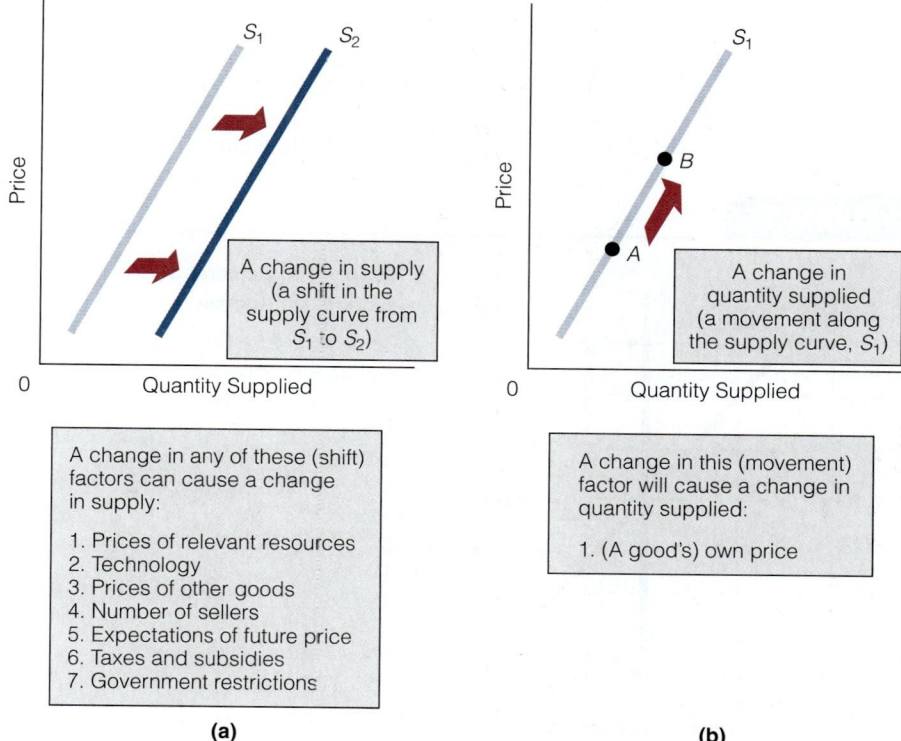

A change in supply (a shift in the supply curve from S_1 to S_2)

A change in any of these (shift) factors can cause a change in supply:
1. Prices of relevant resources
2. Technology
3. Prices of other goods
4. Number of sellers
5. Expectations of future price
6. Taxes and subsidies
7. Government restrictions

A change in quantity supplied (a movement along the supply curve, S_1)

A change in this (movement) factor will cause a change in quantity supplied:
1. (A good's) own price

(a)   (b)

1. What would the supply curve for houses (in a given city) look like for a period of (a) the next 10 hours and (b) the next three months?
2. What happens to the supply curve if each of the following occurs?
   a. The number of sellers decreases.
   b. A per-unit tax is placed on the production of a good.
   c. The price of a relevant resource falls.
3. "If the price of apples rises, the supply of apples will rise." True or false? Explain your answer.

3-3 The Market: Putting Supply and Demand Together

In this section, we put supply and demand together and discuss the market. The purpose of the discussion is to gain some understanding about how prices are determined.

3-3a Supply and Demand at Work at an Auction

In Exhibit 11, the supply curve of corn is vertical. It intersects the horizontal axis at 40,000 bushels; that is, the quantity supplied is 40,000 bushels. The demand curve for corn is downward sloping.

Now, suppose you are at a computerized auction where bushels of corn are bought and sold. At this auction, the auctioneer will adjust the corn price to sell all the corn offered for sale. Each potential buyer of corn is sitting in front of a computer and can immediately input the number of bushels he or she wants to buy. For example, if Nancy wants to buy 5,000 bushels of corn, she simply keys "5,000" into her computer. The total number of bushels that all potential buyers are willing and able to buy appears on the auctioneer's computer screen.

The auction begins. Follow along in Exhibit 11 as it develops. The auctioneer announces the price on the computer screens:

- *$9.00!* The potential buyers think for a second and then register the numbers of bushels they are willing and able to buy at that price. On the auctioneer's screen, the total is 10,000 bushels, which is the quantity demanded of corn at $9.00. The auctioneer, realizing that 30,000 bushels of corn (40,000 − 10,000 = 30,000) will go unsold at this price, decides to lower the price per bushel.

- *$8.00!* The quantity demanded increases to 20,000 bushels, but the quantity supplied of corn at this price is still greater than the quantity demanded. The auctioneer tries again.

EXHIBIT 11

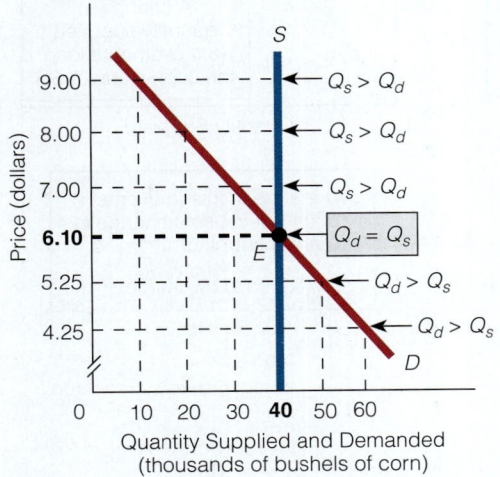

Supply and Demand at Work at an Auction

Let Q_d = quantity demanded and Q_s = quantity supplied. The auctioneer calls out different prices, and buyers record how much they are willing and able to buy. At prices of $9.00, $8.00, and $7.00, $Q_s > Q_d$. At prices of $4.25 and $5.25, $Q_d > Q_s$. At a price of $6.10, $Q_d = Q_s$.

- **$7.00!** The quantity demanded increases to 30,000 bushels, but the quantity supplied at $7.00 is still greater than the quantity demanded. The auctioneer drops the price further.
- **$4.25!** At this price, the quantity demanded jumps to 60,000 bushels, but that is 20,000 bushels more than the quantity supplied. The auctioneer calls out a higher price.
- **$5.25!** The quantity demanded drops to 50,000 bushels, but buyers still want to buy more corn at this price than there is corn to be sold. The auctioneer calls out one more time.
- **$6.10!** At this price, the quantity demanded of corn is 40,000 bushels, and the quantity supplied of corn is 40,000 bushels. The auction stops. Sold! The 40,000 bushels of corn are bought and sold at $6.10 per bushel.

3-3b The Language of Supply and Demand: A Few Important Terms

If the quantity supplied is greater than the quantity demanded, a **surplus**, or **excess supply**, exists. If the quantity demanded is greater than the quantity supplied, a **shortage**, or **excess demand**, exists. In Exhibit 11, a surplus exists at $9.00, $8.00, and $7.00. A shortage exists at $4.25 and $5.25. The price at which the quantity demanded equals the quantity supplied is the **equilibrium price**, or **market-clearing price**. In our example, $6.10 is the equilibrium price. The quantity that corresponds to the equilibrium price is the **equilibrium quantity**. In our example, it is 40,000 bushels of corn. Any price at which quantity demanded is not equal to quantity supplied is a **disequilibrium price**.

A market that exhibits either a surplus ($Q_s > Q_d$) or a shortage ($Q_d > Q_s$) is said to be in **disequilibrium**. A market in which the quantity demanded equals the quantity supplied ($Q_d = Q_s$) is said to be in **equilibrium** (point E in Exhibit 11).

3-3c Moving to Equilibrium: What Happens to Price When There Is a Surplus or a Shortage?

What did the auctioneer do when the price was $9.00 and there was a surplus of corn? He lowered the price. What did the auctioneer do when the price was $5.25 and there was a shortage of corn? He raised the price. The behavior of the auctioneer can be summarized in this way: If a surplus exists, lower the price; if a shortage exists, raise the price. That is how the auctioneer moved the corn market into equilibrium.

Not all markets have auctioneers. (When was the last time you saw an auctioneer in the grocery store?) But many markets act *as if* an auctioneer were calling out higher and lower prices until the equilibrium price is reached. In many real-world, auctioneerless markets, prices fall when there is a surplus and rise when there is a shortage. Why?

Why Does Price Fall When There Is a Surplus? In Exhibit 12, there is a surplus at a price of $15: The quantity supplied (150 units) is greater than the quantity demanded (50 units). At $15, suppliers will not be able to sell all they had hoped to sell. As a result, their inventories will grow beyond the level they hold in preparation for changes in demand. Sellers will then want to reduce their inventories. Some will lower prices to do so, some will cut back on production, and others will do a little of both. As shown in the exhibit, price and output tend to fall until equilibrium is achieved.

Why Does Price Rise When There Is a Shortage In Exhibit 12, there is a shortage at a price of $5: The quantity demanded (150 units) is greater than the quantity supplied

---

Surplus (Excess Supply)
A condition in which the quantity supplied is greater than the quantity demanded. Surpluses occur only at prices above the equilibrium price.

Shortage (Excess Demand)
A condition in which the quantity demanded is greater than the quantity supplied. Shortages occur only at prices below the equilibrium price.

Equilibrium Price (Market-Clearing Price)
The price at which the quantity demanded of a good equals the quantity supplied.

Equilibrium Quantity
The quantity that corresponds to the equilibrium price. The quantity at which the amount of the good that buyers are willing and able to buy equals the amount that sellers are willing and able to sell, and both equal the amount actually bought and sold.

Disequilibrium Price
A price other than the equilibrium price. A price at which the quantity demanded does not equal the quantity supplied.

Disequilibrium
A state of either surplus or shortage in a market.

Equilibrium
Equilibrium means "at rest." Equilibrium in a market is the price–quantity combination from which buyers or sellers do not tend to move away. Graphically, equilibrium is the intersection point of the supply and demand curves.

(50 units). At $5, buyers will not be able to buy all they had hoped to buy. Some buyers will then bid up the price to get sellers to sell to them instead of to other buyers. Some sellers, seeing buyers clamor for the goods, will realize that they can raise the price of the goods they have for sale. Higher prices will also call forth added output. Thus, price and output tend to rise until equilibrium is achieved.

Exhibit 13 brings together much of what we have discussed about supply and demand.

EXHIBIT 12

Moving to Equilibrium

If there is a surplus, sellers' inventories rise above the level the sellers hold in preparation for changes in demand. Sellers will want to reduce their inventories. As a result, price and output fall until equilibrium is achieved. If there is a shortage, some buyers will bid up the price of a good to get sellers to sell to them instead of to other buyers. Some sellers will realize that they can raise the price of the goods they have for sale. Higher prices will call forth added output. Price and output rise until equilibrium is achieved. (*Note:* Recall that price, on the vertical axis, is price per unit of the good, and quantity, on the horizontal axis, is for a specific period. In this text, we do not specify those qualifications on the axes themselves, but consider them to be understood.)

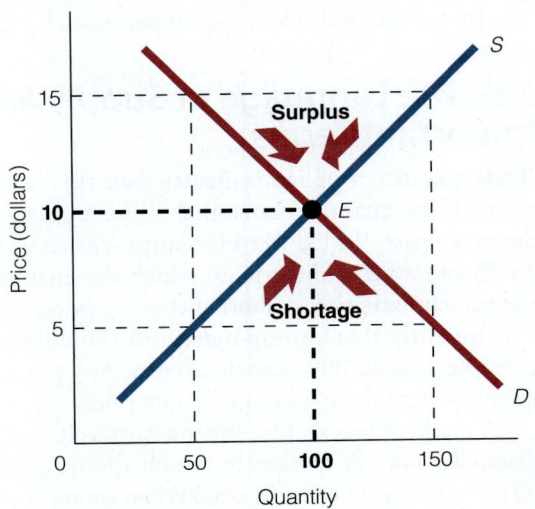

Price	Q_s	Q_d	Condition
$15	150	50	Surplus
10	100	100	Equilibrium
5	50	150	Shortage

EXHIBIT 13

A Summary Exhibit of a Market (Supply and Demand)

This exhibit ties together the topics discussed so far in the chapter. A market is composed of both supply and demand. Also shown are the factors that affect supply and demand and therefore indirectly affect the equilibrium price and quantity of a good.

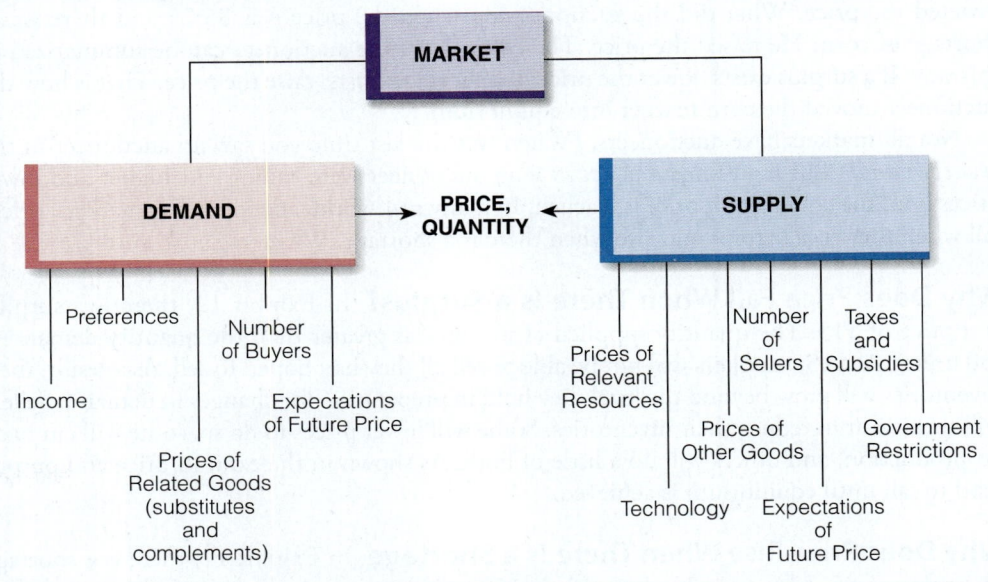

3-3d Speed of Moving to Equilibrium

On June 4, 2021, at 11:30 a.m. (Eastern time), the price of a share of Apple stock was $125.28. A minute later, the price had fallen to $125.14. Obviously, the stock market equilibrates quickly. If demand falls, then initially there is a surplus of the stock at the current equilibrium price. The price then falls, and there is no longer a surplus. All this happens in seconds.

Now consider a house offered for sale in any city in the United States. The sale price of a house may remain the same even though the house does not sell for months. For example, a person offers to sell her house for $400,000. One month passes, no sale; two months pass, no sale; three months pass, no sale; and so on. Ten months later, the house is still not sold, and the price is still $400,000.

Is $400,000 the equilibrium price of the house? Obviously not. At the equilibrium price, there would be a buyer for the house and a seller of the house: The quantity demanded would equal the quantity supplied. At a price of $400,000, there is a seller but no buyer. The $400,000 price is above the equilibrium price. At $400,000, the housing market has a surplus; equilibrium has not been achieved.

Some people may be tempted to argue that supply and demand are at work in the stock market but not in the housing market. A better explanation, though, is that *not all markets equilibrate at the same speed*. Although the stock market may take only seconds to go from surplus or shortage to equilibrium, the housing market may take months to do so.

Economics 24/7

Higher Demand Causes Higher Prices and Higher Sales

Suppose you hear someone say the following: "There are plenty of examples of the price of a good rising and people buying more of the good. For example, during the period 2000–2006, house prices were rising (sometimes quite rapidly) in the United States, and all you heard about back then was how house sales were up. In other words, prices were up and house sales were up. That seems to me to contradict the law of demand, which states that if prices rise, sales will go down."

This person is making a very fundamental mistake. He thinks that the higher price is what causes people to buy more, when it is people who want to buy more that causes the higher price.

Think of a downward sloping demand curve, like the one shown in Exhibit 14(a). At a price of $10, the quantity demanded is 100, and at the higher price of $12, the quantity demanded is 80. This illustrates the law of demand: A higher price brings about a lower quantity demanded.

Now look at Exhibit 14(b). When the demand curve is D_1 and the equilibrium price is $10, the quantity demanded is 100. Now suppose demand rises, and the demand curve shifts rightward from D_1 to D_2. First, what happens to the equilibrium price of the

(Continued)

EXHIBIT 14

Higher Prices

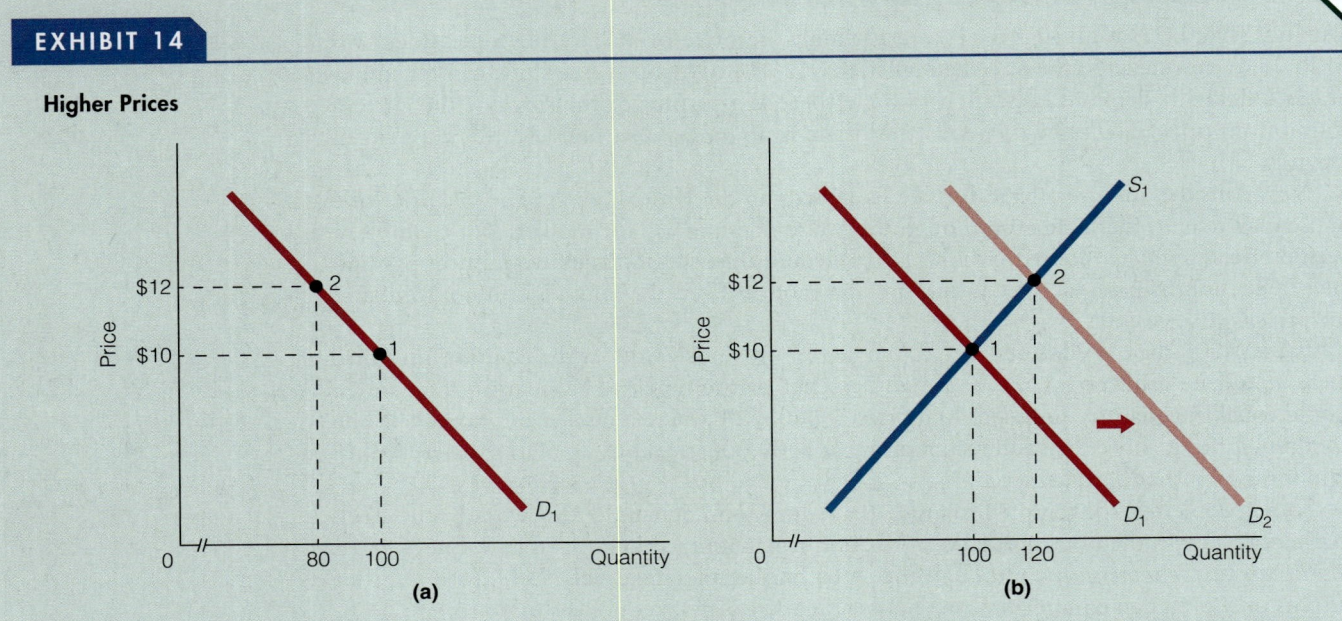

good? It rises from $10 to $12. Now ask yourself what the quantity demanded is at $12, given that the demand curve has shifted rightward. The answer is that it is 120. In other words, we see that the quantity demanded is higher at $12 than it was at $10—but this is because the demand curve shifted rightward; it is not because of the higher price alone.

Let's now think about what was happening in the period 2000–2006 when house prices were rising and house sales were rising too. Was it the higher house prices that caused the greater house sales? No. Instead, it was the increased demand for houses that caused both the higher house prices and the higher house sales.

3-3e Moving to Equilibrium: Maximum and Minimum Prices

There is another way to demonstrate how a market moves to equilibrium. Exhibit 15 shows the market for good X. Look at the first unit of good X. What is the *maximum price buyers are willing to pay* for it? The answer is $70. Just follow the dotted line up from the first unit of the good to the demand curve. What is the *minimum price sellers need to receive before they are willing to sell* this unit of good X? It is $10. Follow the dotted line up from the first unit to the supply curve. Because the maximum buying price is greater than the minimum selling price, the first unit of good X will be exchanged.

What about the second unit? For the second unit, buyers are willing to pay a maximum price of $60, and sellers need to receive a minimum price of $20. Thus, the second unit of good X will be exchanged. In fact, exchange will occur as long as the maximum buying price is greater than the minimum selling price. The exhibit shows that a total of four units of good X will be exchanged. The fifth unit will not be exchanged, because the maximum buying price ($30) is less than the minimum selling price ($50).

EXHIBIT 15

Moving to Equilibrium in Terms of Maximum and Minimum Prices

As long as the maximum buying price of a good is greater than the minimum selling price, an exchange will occur. This condition is met for units 1–4. The market converges on equilibrium through a process of mutually beneficial exchanges.

Units of Good X	Maximum Buying Price	Minimum Selling Price	Result
1st	$70	$10	Exchange
2nd	60	20	Exchange
3rd	50	30	Exchange
4th	40	40	Exchange
5th	30	50	No exchange

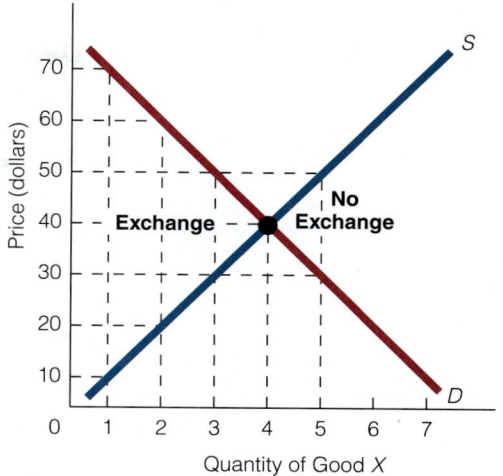

In this process, buyers and sellers trade money for goods as long as both benefit from the trade. The market converges on a quantity of 4 units of good X and a price of $40 per unit. This point is the equilibrium point. In other words, mutually beneficial trade drives the market to equilibrium.

3-3f The Connection Between Equilibrium and Predictions

In a market setting, both equilibrium and disequilibrium are real-world states. A market is in disequilibrium if there is either a shortage or a surplus in the market. In other words, if quantity demanded is not equal to quantity supplied, the market is in disequilibrium. In contrast, if quantity demanded equals quantity supplied, the market is in equilibrium.

Besides being real-world states, equilibrium and disequilibrium are mental constructs that economists use to think about things. As a mental construct, equilibrium represents a balance of forces from which there is no tendency to move. Disequilibrium represents an imbalance, from which there is a tendency to move. To illustrate, when a market is in disequilibrium, such as when quantity demanded is greater than quantity supplied, price will *move up*. When quantity supplied is greater than quantity demanded, price will *move down*. In other words, disequilibrium, as a mental construct, means that something is going to happen. What exists now won't continue to exist for long. The last page of the book has yet to be read.

Seen in this light, the concepts of equilibrium and disequilibrium are used by economists to "foreshadow" what is about to happen. Hence, both concepts are related to the predictions that economists make.

To see this relationship explicitly, consider again a market in disequilibrium: The quantity demanded of a good is greater than the quantity supplied. For economists, this state of affairs is temporary. The market, currently in disequilibrium, will soon edge its way over to equilibrium. Economists, then, know where the market is headed. Knowing where it is headed—to equilibrium—they then make a prediction that might sound something like this:

The market is currently in disequilibrium, with quantity demanded being greater than quantity supplied. A state of equilibrium exists when quantity demanded equals quantity supplied.

So disequilibrium will soon turn into equilibrium. [Notice here that the economists are making a prediction: Disequilibrium will turn into equilibrium.] It follows that things will soon change. How will they change, you ask? Well, quantity demanded will need to go down, and quantity supplied will need to rise, so that they equal each other. [Again, the economists are making a prediction of what is to come.] And how will this state of affairs come about? By price rising (again, another prediction).

We conclude that the economists' concept of equilibrium is related to the economists' predictions. It is a two-step process:

1. *The economists compare "what is" with what exists in equilibrium. For example, the market shortage is compared with market equilibrium.*

2. *If "what is" is not what exists in equilibrium, then the economists predict the path the market will take to get from "what is" to equilibrium. For example, price will rise until quantity demanded and quantity supplied are equal.*

In short, the economists use the concepts of disequilibrium and equilibrium in much the same way that a person uses a map. We are at point X and we want to go to point Y. The shortest route is this way. The economists say the market is in disequilibrium, and soon it will be in equilibrium. Here is the "path" (we predict) that the market will follow to get from disequilibrium to equilibrium.

3-3g Equilibrium in Terms of Consumers' and Producers' Surplus

Equilibrium can be viewed in terms of two important economic concepts: consumers' surplus and producers' (or sellers') surplus. **Consumers' surplus (CS)** is the difference between the maximum buying price and the price paid by the buyer:

Consumers' surplus = Maximum buying price − Price paid

For example, if the highest price you would pay to see a movie is $10 and you pay $7 to see it, then you have received a $3 consumers' surplus. Obviously, the more consumers' surplus that consumers receive, the better off they are. Wouldn't you have preferred to pay, say, $4 to see the movie instead of $7? If you had paid only $4, your consumers' surplus would have been $6 instead of $3.

Producers' (or sellers') surplus (PS) is the difference between the price received by the producer or seller and the minimum selling price:

Producers' (sellers') surplus = Price received − Minimum selling price

Suppose the minimum price the owner of the movie theater would have accepted for admission is $5 but sells admission for $7, not $5. The producers' or sellers' surplus is therefore $2. A seller prefers a large producers' surplus to a small one. The theater owner would have preferred to sell admission to the movie for $8 instead of $7 because then producers' surplus would be $3.

Total surplus (TS) is the sum of consumers' surplus and producers' surplus:

Total surplus = Consumers' surplus + Producers' surplus

In Exhibit 16(a), consumers' surplus is represented by the shaded triangle. This triangle includes the area under the demand curve and above the equilibrium price. According to the definition, consumers' surplus is the highest price that buyers are willing to pay (the maximum

---

Consumers' Surplus (CS)
The difference between the maximum price a buyer is willing and able to pay for a good or service and the price actually paid.
(CS = Maximum buying price − Price paid.)

Producers' (Sellers') Surplus (PS)
The difference between the price sellers receive for a good and the minimum or lowest price for which they would have sold the good.
(PS = Price received − Minimum selling price.)

Total Surplus (TS)
The sum of consumers' surplus and producers' surplus. (TS = CS + PS.)

EXHIBIT 16

Consumers' and Producers' Surplus

(a) *Consumers' surplus.* As the shaded area indicates, the difference between the maximum, or highest, amount that buyers would be willing to pay for a good and the price that they actually pay is consumers' surplus. (b) *Producers' surplus.* As the shaded area indicates, the difference between the price that sellers receive for a good and the minimum or lowest price they would be willing to sell the good for is producers' surplus.

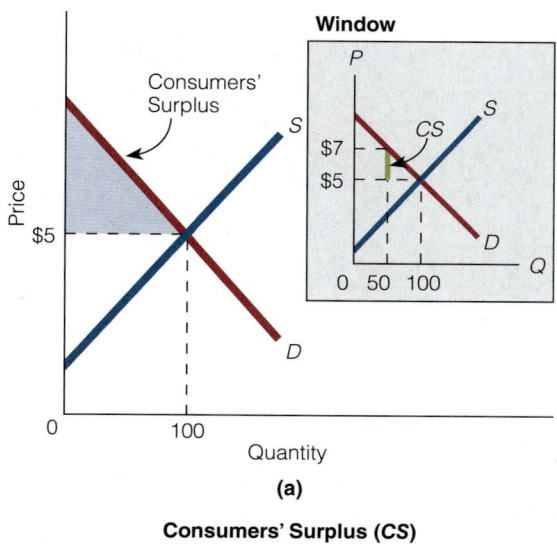

(a) Consumers' Surplus (CS)

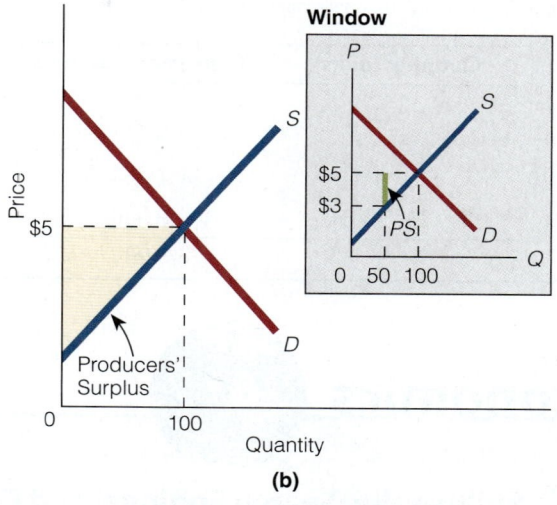

(b) Producers' Surplus (PS)

buying price) minus the price they pay. For example, the window in part (a) shows that buyers are willing to pay as high as $7 for the 50th unit, but they pay only $5. Thus, the consumers' surplus on the 50th unit of the good is $2. If we add the consumers' surplus on each unit of the good between the first and the 100th unit, inclusive (the equilibrium quantity), we obtain the shaded consumers' surplus triangle.

In Exhibit 16(b), producers' surplus is also represented by a shaded triangle. This triangle includes the area above the supply curve and under the equilibrium price. Keep in mind the definition of producers' surplus: the price received by the seller minus the lowest price the seller would accept for the good. The window in part (b) shows that sellers would have sold the 50th unit for as low as $3 but actually sold it for $5. Thus, the producers' surplus on the 50th unit of the good is $2. If we add the producers' surplus on each unit of the good between the first and the 100th unit, inclusive, we obtain the shaded producers' surplus triangle.

Now consider consumers' surplus and producers' surplus at the equilibrium quantity. Exhibit 17 shows that the consumers' surplus at equilibrium is equal to areas $A + B + C + D$ and the producers' surplus at equilibrium is equal to areas $E + F + G + H$. At any other exchangeable quantity—such as 25, 50, or 75 units—both consumers' surplus and producers' surplus are less. For example, at 25 units, consumers' surplus is equal to area A, and producers' surplus is equal to area E. At 50 units, consumers' surplus is equal to areas $A + B$, and producers' surplus is equal to areas $E + F$.

Equilibrium has a special property: At equilibrium, both consumers' surplus and producers' surplus are maximized. In short, total surplus is maximized.

EXHIBIT 17

Equilibrium, Consumers' Surplus, and Producers' Surplus

Consumers' surplus is greater at the equilibrium quantity (100 units) than at any other exchangeable quantity. Producers' surplus is greater at the equilibrium quantity than at any other exchangeable quantity. For example, consumers' surplus is areas $A + B + C$ at 75 units, but areas $A + B + C + D$ at 100 units. Producers' surplus is areas $E + F + G$ at 75 units, but areas $E + F + G + H$ at 100 units.

Quantity (units)	Consumers' Surplus	Producers' Surplus
25	A	E
50	A + B	E + F
75	A + B + C	E + F + G
100 (equilibrium)	A + B + C + D	E + F + G + H

(a)

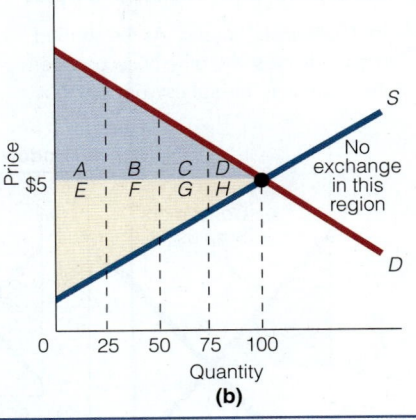

(b)

Economics 24/7

Stoic Philosophy, Search Engines, and Consumers' Surplus[1]

"Do not indulge in dreams of having what you have not, but reckon up the chief of the blessings you do possess, and then thankfully remember how you would crave for them if they were not yours."

— Marcus Aurelius, *Meditations*

Consider some of things we do on a daily basis. We check email on our smartphones, use Google maps to find our way from our home to a restaurant we want to go to for dinner, check our Facebook page, and, of course, use Google Search to learn about Pierre de Fermat's contributions to mathematics.

Now suppose someone asks the person what each of these products—email, Google Maps, Facebook, and Google Search—are worth to us? At first, we aren't sure what to say, so the question is asked a slightly different way: How much would you have to be paid to do without email? How much would you have to be paid to do without Google Search? We say we would have to be paid $50 a month to give up email, $100 a month to give up Google Search, $20 a month to give up Facebook, and $25 a month to give up Google Maps. The dollar amount we choose is a good measure of what each of these products is worth to us—a good measure of the benefits, expressed in dollar terms, of each of the products. And because each product came with zero price, the dollar amount is a good measure of the consumers' surplus we receive for each product. In other words, we receives $50 a month in consumers' surplus for email and $100 a month in consumers' surplus for Google Search.

Economists Erik Brynjolfsson, Felix Eggers, and Avinash Gannamaneni tried to measure what certain digital goods were worth to people. In their words, "We explore the potential of massive online choice experiments to measure consumers' surplus to accept compensation for losing access to various digital goods and thereby estimate the consumer surplus generated from these goods."[2] Their research concluded that the typical person would need to be paid about $17,700 a year to do without search engines,

---

[1] This feature is based on "Using Massive Online Choice Experiments to Measure Changes in Well-Being," NBER Working Paper No. 24514 (issued in April 2018) by Erik Brynjolfsson, Felix Eggers, Avinash Gannamaneni and "How Much Would I Have to Pay You to Quit Facebook?" by Tim Harford, *Financial Times*, April 27, 2018.

[2] "Using Massive Online Choice Experiments to Measure Changes in Well-Being," by Erik Brynjolfsson, Felix Eggers, Avinash Gannamaneni," NBER Working Paper No. 24514 (issued in April 2018).

$8,500 a year to give up email, more than $1,150 a year to give up Netflix and YouTube, and slightly more than $300 to give up social media. (As an aside, the economists learned that indoor toilets were valued more highly than internet service.)

How does this relate to Stoic philosophers, like Marcus Aurelius, quoted earlier. The Stoic philosophers such as Zeno (c. 334–262 BC), Epictetus (c. 55–135 AD), Marcus Aurelius (c. 121–180 AD), and Seneca (c. 4 BC–65 AD) had a way of finding a sense of how much something was worth to them—by practicing what is called *negative visualization*. In negative visualization, you imagine having lost those things that you value. Imagine what it would be like if you lost your best friend, or the apartment you live in, or being able to eat a pizza, or your college education. By doing this—imagining what it would be like to do without something that you currently have—you get a sense of what that something is worth to you. Put another way, through negative visualization, you get a sense of the consumers' surplus you receive from those things you currently have. We are not typically aware of the consumers' surplus we receive from certain things until we practice negative visualization or are asked how much we would need to be reimbursed to give up certain things. Whereas the Stoic philosophers determined consumers' surplus through negative visualization, modern-day economists find it by asking people various questions and conducting surveys and experiments.

3-3h What Can Change Equilibrium Price and Quantity?

Equilibrium price and quantity are determined by supply and demand. Whenever demand changes or supply changes or both change, equilibrium price and quantity change. Exhibit 18 illustrates eight different cases where this scenario occurs. Cases (a)–(d) illustrate the four basic changes in supply and demand: Either supply changes or demand changes. Cases (e)–(h) illustrate changes in both supply and demand.

- *Case (a):* Demand rises (the demand curve shifts rightward from D_1 to D_2), and supply is constant (the supply curve does not move). As a result of demand rising and supply remaining constant, the equilibrium price rises from P_1 to P_2, and the equilibrium quantity rises from 10 units to 12 units. Now, let's see if you can identify what has happened to quantity supplied (not supply) as price has risen from P_1 to P_2. (Remember, quantity supplied changes if *price* changes.) As price rises from P_1 to P_2, quantity supplied rises from 10 units to 12 units. We see this situation as a movement up the supply curve from point 1 to point 2, corresponding (on the horizontal axis) to a change from 10 units to 12 units.

- *Case (b):* Demand falls (the demand curve shifts leftward from D_1 to D_2), and supply is constant. As a result, the equilibrium price falls from P_1 to P_2, and the equilibrium quantity falls from 10 to 8 units. Now ask, has the quantity supplied (not supply) changed? Yes, it has. As a result of price falling from P_1 to P_2, we move down the supply curve from point 1 to point 2, and the quantity supplied falls from 10 units to 8 units.

- *Case (c):* Supply rises (the supply curve shifts rightward from S_1 to S_2), and demand is constant. As a result, the equilibrium price falls from P_1 to P_2, and the equilibrium quantity rises from 10 units to 12 units. Now ask: Has the quantity demanded (not demand) changed? Yes, it has. As a result of price falling from P_1 to P_2, we move down the demand curve from point 1 to point 2, and the quantity demanded rises from 10 units to 12 units.

- *Case (d):* Supply falls (the supply curve shifts leftward from S_1 to S_2), and demand is constant. As a result, the equilibrium price rises from P_1 to P_2, and the equilibrium quantity falls from 10 to 8 units. One last time: Has quantity demanded (not demand) changed? Yes, it has. As a result of price rising from P_1 to P_2, we move up the demand curve from point 1 to point 2, and quantity demanded falls from 10 units to 8 units.

EXHIBIT 18

Equilibrium Price and Quantity Effects of Supply Curve Shifts and Demand Curve Shifts

The exhibit illustrates the effects on equilibrium price and quantity of a change in demand, a change in supply, and a change in both. Below each diagram, the condition leading to the effects is noted, using the following symbols: (1) a bar over a letter means *constant* (thus, $\bar{S}$ means that supply is constant); (2) a downward-pointing arrow ($\downarrow$) indicates a fall; and (3) an upward-pointing arrow ($\uparrow$) indicates a rise. A rise (fall) in demand is the same as a rightward (leftward) shift in the demand curve. A rise (fall) in supply is the same as a rightward (leftward) shift in the supply curve.

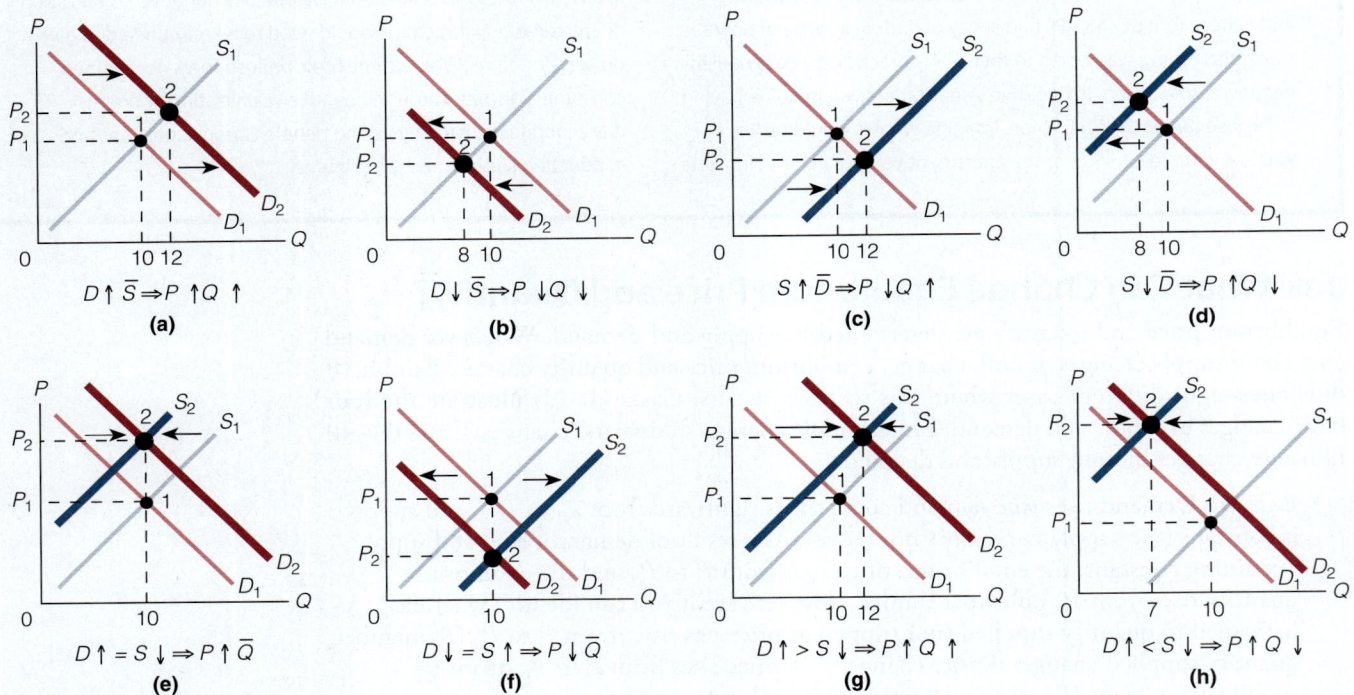

- *Case (e):* Demand rises (the demand curve shifts from D_1 to D_2), and supply falls (the supply curve shifts leftward from S_1 to S_2) by an equal amount. As a result, the equilibrium price rises from P_1 to P_2, and the equilibrium quantity remains constant at 10 units.

- *Case (f):* Demand falls (the demand curve shifts leftward from D_1 to D_2), and supply rises (the supply curve shifts rightward from S_1 to S_2) by an equal amount. As a result, the equilibrium price falls from P_1 to P_2, and the equilibrium quantity is constant at 10 units.

- *Case (g):* Demand rises (the demand curve shifts rightward from D_1 to D_2) by a greater amount than supply falls (the supply curve shifts leftward from S_1 to S_2). As a result, the equilibrium price rises from P_1 to P_2, and the equilibrium quantity rises from 10 units to 12 units.

- *Case (h):* Demand rises (the demand curve shifts rightward from D_1 to D_2) by a smaller amount than supply falls (the supply curve shifts leftward from S_1 to S_2). As a result, the equilibrium price rises from P_1 to P_2, and the equilibrium quantity falls from 10 units to 7 units.

Economics 24/7

Shake Shack and Hamburger Prices

Have you ever been to a restaurant with a long line of people in front of it waiting to be seated? This long line is evidence of a shortage. So why doesn't the restaurant raise prices?

Before answering that question, let's consider what happens in the wheat and stock markets when a shortage occurs. Almost immediately, the price rises. In the wheat market, the price can change daily. The same holds for the stock market. In fact, in the stock market, the price of a stock can change within a matter of seconds. In both the wheat and stock markets, price reacts quickly to shortages and surpluses. Price in these markets is flexible and adjusts almost instantly to any surplus or shortage in the market.

In contrast, consider what happens in the Shake Shack market. Shake Shack is a fast-casual restaurant chain that serves hot dogs, hamburgers, fries, and milkshakes. Around lunch time, you often will see a long line of customers waiting to get into a Shake Shack to place their orders, which is evidence of a shortage, so why doesn't Shake Shack raise its prices to eliminate the shortage?

There is evidence to support firms' opting to maintain stable prices because their customers prefer stable (and therefore predictable)

prices to prices that change weekly, daily, or even hourly, in response to market conditions. For example, the Shake Shack customer who buys a hamburger at lunchtime might resent it if Shack Shack charges a higher price for a hamburger at noon than it charges another customer at 3:30 pm. The resentment may generate bad feelings directed at Shake Shack and therefore adversely affect its overall business.

3-3i Epilogue: Who Feeds Cleveland?

Here is a question to think about: Who feeds Cleveland? If you have a hard time answering the question, or even making sense of the question, then that is probably for one of two reasons. First, asking "who" feeds Cleveland is an odd question. No one person feeds Cleveland. We can't point to the president of the United States, or to the CEO of a large company, or to a specific farmer, and say, "He feeds Cleveland." That's why the "who feeds" question may initially draw a blank stare.

But more importantly, the question is hard to answer because we have been born into a world where food always has existed for people in Cleveland. We never hear of any stories of mass starvation in Cleveland. We never hear that the people in Cleveland are hungry. We have just taken it for granted—and never really given it much thought—that people in Cleveland eat, just as people in New York, Los Angeles, or Topeka, Kansas, eat.

But still, the question nags at us. Obviously, there must be some reason that the people in Cleveland always seem to have food to eat. Who or what is it that makes this possible? Is there a government agency called the Department of Food located in Washington, D.C., that gives orders to people to send food to Cleveland? We know there isn't. Well, then, how does Cleveland get all the food that it consumes? Who or what does feed Cleveland?

The answer is "the market." The market feeds Cleveland. It also feeds every other city in the country. Here is how the market works: The people in Cleveland want to eat. They want to eat all kinds of things: steaks, potato chips, chicken, tomatoes, carrots, bananas, and bread. There are other people who produce these items. They produce these items for one single reason: because they want to sell them for money, which they can then use to buy themselves things they want.

The producers and sellers of these food items send these items to Cleveland. Some of these people even build stores and restaurants in Cleveland where this food can be purchased or eaten. The people who build these stores and restaurants in Cleveland do what they do for the same reason that the producers of the food items did what they did because they want to sell what they have to sell for money, which they can then use to buy themselves things they want.

Now let's enter a grocery store in Cleveland. The manager of the store is walking down the snacks aisle when she notices that Oreo cookies are leaving the shelves more quickly than before. She thinks to herself that people must really want to buy Oreo cookies. So she places an order for Oreo cookies that is larger than the order she placed last week. If the same thing is happening in other grocery stores—if Oreo cookies are flying off the shelves—then other managers are doing the same thing too: placing larger orders for Oreo cookies. The manufacturers of Oreo cookies end up producing more Oreo cookies and sending them out to grocery stores to be sold. If Oreo cookies have been flying off the shelves faster than ever because the demand for Oreo cookies has increased, Oreo cookies might go up in price.

The higher price of Oreo cookies might then prompt other cookie manufacturers to come out with a cookie that is similar to an Oreo cookie. After all, almost nothing is copied as often as success.

Now leave the grocery store and go to a restaurant. On the menu at the restaurant are numerous items. Some of those items sell better than other items. If an item sells well, the restaurant keeps the item on the menu. If an item sells poorly, it removes the item from the menu. For example, if, for some reason, peoples' preferences for food changes from Mexican cuisine to Italian cuisine, then the Mexican restaurants either convert to Italian restaurants or go out of business.

So, we now know that "the market" feeds Cleveland, and we have some idea of exactly how it feeds Cleveland, namely, sellers of food get together with buyers of food and then trade their food for money. Also, as the demand for a food item changes, the producers or sellers of food respond in a way that the buyers of food want them to respond. When the buyers want more cookies, the suppliers of cookies give them more cookies; when the buyers want more Italian food and less Mexican food, the restaurateurs deliver.

Now, if "the market" were an invention, much the way a car or TV or personal computer were invented, we'd have to say that it is quite some invention. It would be a more significant invention than almost anything you can think of because "the market" does something as important as feed Cleveland. It is also "the thing" within which other inventions appear. If there were no market, would there be any reason to invent cars, computers, cell telephones, and so on?

So, if "the market" were an invention, it would be a most important invention, if not the most important invention of all time. But, alas, no one invented the market. The market is simply the very quiet and invisible manifestation of the actions of millions of people simply trying to make themselves better off.

The market—that "thing" that ends up feeding Cleveland, making more Oreo cookies, changing the menu when restaurant goers want a change in the menu, and so on—is a **spontaneous order**. It is something that emerged as an unintended effect of peoples' actions directed at trying to make themselves better off.

Spontaneous Order
The spontaneous and unintended emergence of order out of the self-interested actions of individuals; an unintended consequence of human action, with emphasis placed on the word "unintended."

Economics 24/7

"Sorry, But This Flight Has Been Overbooked"

Airlines often overbook flights; that is, they accept more reservations than they have seats available on a flight. Airlines know that a certain (usually small) percentage of individuals with reservations will not show up. An empty seat means that the airline's cost per actual passenger on board is higher than it would be if the seat were occupied by a paying passenger. So, airlines try to make sure to have few empty seats. One way to reduce the number of empty seats is to overbook.

In the past, when more people with reservations showed up for a flight than there were seats available, the airline simply "bumped" passengers. In other words, the airline would tell some passengers that they could not fly on that flight. Understandably, the bumped passengers were disappointed and angry.

One day while shaving, economist Julian Simon (1932–1998) came up with a better way to deal with overbooking. He argued that the airline should enter into a market transaction with the ticket holders who had reserved seats for an overbooked flight. Instead of bumping people randomly, an airline should ask passengers to sell their seats back to the airline. Passengers who absolutely had to get from one city to another would not sell their seats, but passengers who did not have to fly right away might be willing to sell their tickets for, say, first class on a later flight or some other compensation.

Simon wrote the executives of various airlines and outlined the details of his plan. He even told them that the first airline which enacted the plan would likely reap larger sales. The airline could, after all, guarantee its passengers that they would not get bumped. Most airline executives wrote back and told him that his idea was a reasonably good one but was unworkable.

Simon then contacted various economists and asked them to support his idea publicly. Some did; some didn't. For years, Simon pushed his idea with airline executives and government officials.

Then Alfred Kahn, an economist, was appointed chairman of the Civil Aeronautics Board. Simon contacted Kahn with his plan, and Kahn liked it. According to Simon, "Kahn announced something like the scheme in his first press conference. He also had the great persuasive skill to repackage it as a 'voluntary' bumping plan, and at the same time to increase the penalties that airlines must pay to involuntary bumpees, a nice carrot-and-stick combination."

The rest, as people say, is history. Simon's plan has been in operation since 1978. Simon wrote, "The volunteer system for handling airline oversales exemplifies how markets can improve life for all concerned parties. In case of an oversale, the airline agent proceeds from lowest bidder upwards until the required number of bumpees is achieved. Low bidders take the next flight, happy about it. All other passengers fly as scheduled, also happy. The airlines can overbook more, making them happy too."

1. When a person goes to the grocery store to buy food, there is no auctioneer calling out prices for bread, milk, and other items. Therefore, supply and demand cannot be operative. Do you agree or disagree? Explain your answer.

2. The price of a personal computer of a given quality is lower today than it was five years ago. Is this necessarily the result of a lower demand for computers? Explain your answer.

3. What is the effect on equilibrium price and quantity of the following?
   a. A decrease in demand that is greater than the increase in supply
   b. An increase in supply
   c. A decrease in supply that is greater than the increase in demand
   d. A decrease in demand

4. At equilibrium quantity, what is the relationship between the maximum buying price and the minimum selling price?

5. If the price paid for a certain item is $40 and the consumers' surplus is $4, then what is the maximum buying price for that item? If the minimum selling price is $30 and the producers' surplus is $4, then what is the price received by the seller?

Office Hours

"I Thought Prices Equaled Costs Plus 10 Percent"

Student: My uncle produces and sells lamps. I asked him once how he determines the price he sells his lamps for. He said he takes his costs and adds 10 percent. In other words, if it cost him $200 to make a lamp, he sells it for a price of $220. If all sellers do the same thing, then prices aren't being determined by supply and demand, are they?

Instructor: Supply and demand could still be at work, even given what your uncle said. For example, the $220 could be the equilibrium price (determined by supply and demand) for the type of lamps your uncle is producing and selling. Look at it this way: If your uncle could sell the lamps for, say, $250 each, then he would have told you that he takes his cost (of $200) and adds on 25 percent ($50) to get "his price" of $250.

Student: Is the point that what looks like *cost plus 10 percent* to me could really be supply and demand?

Instructor: Yes, that's the point. But we can add something else to make the point stronger. Think of the housing market for a minute. Are the prices of houses determined by *cost plus 10 percent* or by supply and demand? Let's see if we can think through an example together. Suppose you buy a house for $400,000 in one year and then decide to sell it 10 years later. What price do you charge for the house? Do you charge the (market) equilibrium price for that house, or do you charge what you paid for the house ($400,000) plus 10 percent ($40,000), for a total of $440,000?

Student: Oh, I think I see what you mean. You mean that if the equilibrium price for the house happened to be $650,000, I wouldn't charge only $440,000.

Instructor: Exactly. In other words, the price determined by supply and demand would take precedence over the cost-plus-10-percent price. Now, going back to your uncle, we see that he might have just thought that he was charging a price of cost plus 10 percent because the equilibrium price for the good he produced and sold happened to be 10 percent higher than his cost. But, as stated before, if that equilibrium price had been 25 percent higher, your uncle would have told you that his price was determined by his taking his costs and adding 25 percent. The equilibrium price was determining the percentage that your uncle said he added to costs; he didn't just pick a percentage out of thin air.

Points to Remember

1. What looks like cost plus 10 percent (cost plus some markup) could instead be supply and demand at work.
2. Supply and demand are obviously determining prices at, say, an auction. A single good (say, a painting) is for sale, and numerous buyers bid on it. The bidding stops when only one buyer is left. At the price the last bidder bid, the quantity demanded (of the painting) equals the quantity supplied, and both equal 1. Even if you do not see supply and demand at work in nonauction settings, supply and demand are still at work determining prices.

Chapter Summary

Demand

- The law of demand states that as the price of a good rises, the quantity demanded of it falls, and as the price of a good falls, the quantity demanded of it rises, *ceteris paribus*. The law of demand holds that price and quantity demanded are inversely related.
- Quantity demanded is the total number of units of a good that buyers are willing and able to buy at a particular price.
- A (downward-sloping) demand curve is the graphical representation of the law of demand.
- Factors that can change demand and cause the demand curve to shift are income, preferences, the prices of related goods (substitutes and complements), the number of buyers, and expectations of future price.
- The only factor that can directly cause a change in the quantity demanded of a good is a change in the good's own price.

Supply

- The law of supply states that as the price of a good rises, the quantity supplied of the good rises, and as the price of a good falls, the quantity supplied of the good falls, *ceteris paribus*. The law of supply asserts that price and quantity supplied are directly related.
- The law of supply does not hold when there is no time to produce more units of a good during a given period or when goods cannot be produced at all over that period.
- An upward-sloping supply curve is the graphical representation of the law of supply. More generally, a supply curve (no matter how it slopes) represents the relationship between the price and quantity supplied.
- Factors that can change supply and cause the supply curve to shift are the prices of relevant resources, technology, the prices of other goods, expectations of future price, taxes and subsidies, and government restrictions.
- The only factor that can directly cause a change in the quantity supplied of a good is a change in the good's own price.

The Market

- Demand and supply together establish the equilibrium price and equilibrium quantity.
- A surplus exists in a market if, at some price, the quantity supplied is greater than the quantity demanded. A shortage exists if, at some price, the quantity demanded is greater than the quantity supplied.
- Mutually beneficial trade between buyers and sellers drives the market to equilibrium.

Consumers' Surplus, Producers' Surplus, and Total Surplus

- Consumers' surplus is the difference between the maximum buying price and the price paid by the buyer:

    Consumers' surplus = Maximum buying price − Price paid

- Producers' (or sellers') surplus is the difference between the price the seller receives and the minimum selling price:

    Producers' surplus = Price received − Minimum selling price

- The more consumers' surplus that buyers receive, the better off they are. The more producers' surplus that sellers receive, the better off they are. Total surplus is the sum of consumers' surplus and producers' surplus.
- Total surplus (the sum of consumers' surplus and producers' surplus) is maximized at equilibrium.

Key Terms and Concepts

Market
Demand
Law of Demand
Demand Schedule
Demand Curve
Law of Diminishing Marginal Utility
Own Price
Normal Good
Inferior Good
Neutral Good
Substitutes
Complements
Supply
Law of Supply
Upward-Sloping Supply Curve
Supply Schedule
Subsidy
Surplus (Excess Supply)
Shortage (Excess Demand)
Equilibrium Price (Market-Clearing Price)
Equilibrium Quantity
Disequilibrium Price
Disequilibrium
Equilibrium
Consumers' Surplus (CS)
Producers' (Sellers') Surplus (PS)
Total Surplus (TS)
Spontaneous Order

Questions and Problems

1. What is wrong with the following statement? Demand refers to the willingness of buyers to purchase different quantities of a good at different prices during a specific period.
2. What is the difference between *demand* and *quantity demanded*?
3. True or false? As the price of oranges rises, the demand for oranges falls, *ceteris paribus*. Explain your answer.
4. "The price of a bushel of wheat, which was $3.00 last month, is $3.70 today. The demand curve for wheat must have shifted rightward between last month and today." Discuss.
5. Some goods are bought largely because they have "snob appeal." For example, the residents of Beverly Hills gain prestige by buying expensive items. In fact, they won't buy some items unless they are expensive. The law of demand, which holds that people buy more at lower prices than higher prices, obviously doesn't hold for the residents of Beverly Hills. The following rules apply in Beverly Hills: high prices, buy; low prices, don't buy. Discuss.
6. "The price of T-shirts keeps rising and rising, and people keep buying more and more. T-shirts must have an upward-sloping demand curve." Identify the error.
7. With respect to each of the following changes, identify whether the demand curve will shift rightward or leftward:
   a. An increase in income (the good under consideration is a normal good)
   b. A rise in the price of a substitute good (caused by a decline in supply)
   c. A rise in expected future price
   d. A fall in the number of buyers
8. What does a sale on shirts have to do with the law of demand (as applied to shirts)?
9. What is wrong with this statement: As the price of a good falls, the supply of that good falls, *ceteris paribus*.
10. In the previous chapter, you learned about the law of increasing opportunity costs. What does this law have to do with an upward-sloping supply curve?
11. How might the price of corn affect the supply of wheat?
12. What is the difference between supply and quantity supplied?
13. What is the difference between a movement factor and a shift factor?
14. Compare the ratings for television shows with prices for goods. How are ratings like prices? How are ratings different from prices? (*Hint:* How does rising demand for a particular television show manifest itself?)
15. At equilibrium in a market, the maximum price that buyers would be willing to pay for the good is equal to the minimum price that sellers need to receive before they are willing to sell the good. Do you agree or disagree with this statement? Explain your answer.
16. Must consumers' surplus equal producers' surplus at the equilibrium price? Explain your answer.
17. Many movie theaters charge a lower admission price for the first show on weekday afternoons than they do for a weeknight or weekend show. Explain why.
18. A Dell computer is a substitute for an HP® computer. What happens to the demand for HP computers and the quantity demanded of Dell computers as the price of a Dell falls (as a result of a change in supply)?
19. Describe how each of the following will affect the demand for personal computers:
    a. A rise in income (assuming that computers are a normal good)
    b. A lower expected price for computers
    c. Cheaper software
    d. Computers that are simpler to operate
20. Describe how each of the following will affect the supply of personal computers:
    a. A rise in wage rates
    b. An increase in the number of sellers of computers
    c. A tax placed on the production of computers
    d. A subsidy for the production of computers
21. The price of good *X* is higher in year 2 than in year 1 and people are buying more of good *X* in year 2 than year 1. Obviously, the law of demand does not hold. Do you agree or disagree? Explain your answer.
22. Use the law of diminishing marginal utility to explain why demand curves slope downward.
23. Explain how the market moves to equilibrium in terms of shortages and surpluses and in terms of maximum buying prices and minimum selling prices.
24. Identify what happens to equilibrium price and quantity in each of the following cases:
    a. Demand rises and supply is constant.
    b. Demand falls and supply is constant.
    c. Supply rises and demand is constant.
    d. Supply falls and demand is constant.
    e. Demand rises by the same amount that supply falls.

Chapter 3 Supply and Demand: Theory

f. Demand falls by the same amount that supply rises.
g. Demand falls less than supply rises.
h. Demand rises more than supply rises.
i. Demand rises less than supply rises.
j. Demand falls more than supply falls.
k. Demand falls less than supply falls.

25. Suppose the demand curve for a good is downward sloping and the supply curve is upward sloping. Now suppose demand rises. Will producers' surplus rise or fall? Explain your answers.

26. When speeding tickets were $100, usually 500 speeders were on the roads each month in a given city; when ticket prices were raised to $250, usually 215 speeders were on the roads in the city each month. Can you find any economics in this observation?

27. What does it mean to say that "the market" feeds Cleveland, Austin, Atlanta, or Indianapolis?

Working with Numbers and Graphs

1. Suppose the price is $10, the quantity supplied is 50 units, and the quantity demanded is 100 units. For every $1 rise in price, the quantity supplied rises by 5 units and the quantity demanded falls by 5 units. What is the equilibrium price and quantity?

2. Using numbers, explain how a market demand curve is derived from two individual demand curves.

3. Draw a diagram that shows a larger increase in demand than the decrease in supply.

4. Draw a diagram that shows a smaller increase in supply than the increase in demand.

5. At equilibrium in the following figure, what area(s) represent consumers' surplus? producers' surplus?

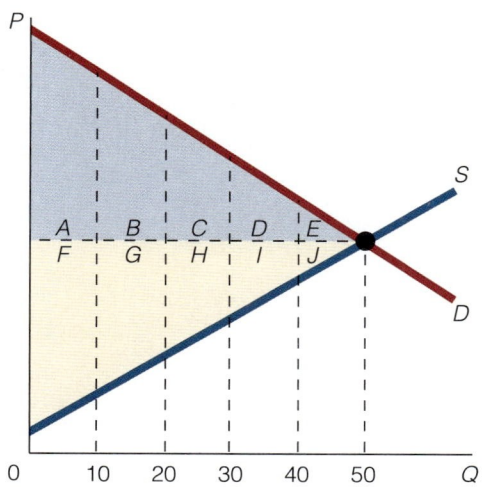

6. At what quantity in the preceding figure is the maximum buying price equal to the minimum selling price?

7. In the figure that follows, can the movement from point 1 to point 2 be explained by a combination of an increase in the price of a substitute and a decrease in the price of nonlabor resources? Explain your answer.

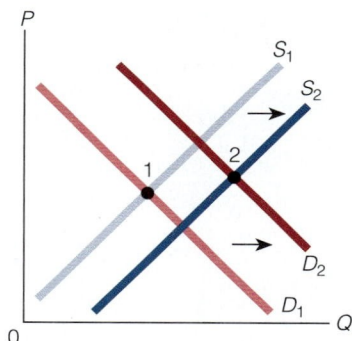

8. Suppose the demand curve is downward sloping, the supply curve is upward sloping, and the equilibrium quantity is 50 units. Show on a graph that the difference between the maximum buying price and minimum selling price is greater at 25 units than at 33 units.

9. Fill in the blanks in the following table.

This Happens ...	Does Equilibrium Price Rise, Fall, or Remain Unchanged?	Does Equilibrium Quantity Rise, Fall, or Remain Unchanged?
Demand rises and supply remains constant	A	B
Supply declines more than demand rises	C	D
Demand rises more than supply rises	E	F
Demand rises by the same amount as supply rises	G	H
Supply falls and demand remains constant	I	J
Demand falls more than supply falls	K	L

Prices: Free, Controlled, and Relative

CHAPTER 4

Introduction

In the last chapter, we discussed supply and demand. Mainly, we saw how supply and demand work together to determine prices. In this chapter, we discuss prices at greater length. First, we discuss two of the key "jobs" that price performs: (1) rationing resources and goods and (2) transmitting information. Second, we discuss government controls that can be imposed on prices. Specifically, we discuss both price ceilings and price floors. Third, we discuss two types of price: absolute (or money) price and relative price.

4-1 Price

To most people, price is a number with a dollar sign in front of it, such as $10. But price is much more. Price performs two major jobs: It acts (1) as a rationing device and (2) as a transmitter of information.

4-1a Price as a Rationing Device

In Chapter 1, we said that wants (for goods) are unlimited and resources are limited, so scarcity exists. As a result of scarcity, a rationing device is needed to determine who gets what of the available limited resources and goods. (Because resources are limited, goods are limited also, given that the production of goods requires resources.) Price serves as that rationing device. It rations resources to the producers who pay the price for the resources. It rations goods to those buyers who pay the price for the goods. The process is as simple as this: Pay the price, and the resources or goods are yours. Don't pay the price, and they aren't.

Is dollar price a fair rationing device? Doesn't it discriminate against the poor? After all, the poor have fewer dollars than the rich, so the rich can get more of what they want than can the poor. True, dollar price does discriminate against the poor. But then, as economists know, every rationing device discriminates against someone. To illustrate, suppose for some reason that tomorrow dollar price could not be used as a rationing device. Some rationing device would still be necessary, because scarcity would still exist. How would we ration gas at the gasoline station, food in the grocery store, or tickets for the Super Bowl? Let's consider some alternatives to dollar price as a rationing device.

Suppose *first come, first served* is the rationing device. For example, suppose only 40,000 Super Bowl tickets are available. If you are one of the first 40,000 in line for a Super Bowl ticket, you get a ticket. If you are person number 40,001 in line, you don't. Such a method discriminates against those who can't get in line quickly enough. What about slow walkers or people with disabilities? What about people without cars who can't drive to where the tickets are distributed?

Or suppose *brute force* is the rationing device. For example, of the 40,000 Super Bowl tickets, you get one as long as you can take it away from someone else. Against whom does this rationing method discriminate? Obviously, it discriminates against the weak and nonaggressive.

Or suppose *beauty* is the rationing device. The more beautiful you are, the better your chances are of getting a Super Bowl ticket. Again, the rationing device discriminates against someone.

These and many other alternatives to dollar price could be used as rationing devices. However, each discriminates against someone, and none is clearly superior to dollar price.

In addition, if first come, first served; brute force; beauty; or another alternative to dollar price is the rationing device, what incentive would the producer of a good have to produce the good? With dollar price as a rationing device, a person produces computers and sells them for money. He then takes the money and buys what he wants. But if the rationing device were, say, brute force, he would not have an incentive to produce. Why produce anything when someone will end up taking it away from you? In short, in a world where dollar price isn't the rationing device, people are likely to produce much less than in a world where dollar price is the rationing device.

4-1b Price as a Transmitter of Information

Rationing isn't the only job that price performs. Although it may sound odd, price also *transmits information*. Consider the following story: On Saturday, Aiko walks into a local grocery store and purchases a half gallon of orange juice for $2.50. On Sunday, unknown to her, a cold spell hits Florida and wipes out half the orange crop. The cold spell ends up shifting the supply curve of oranges leftward, which drives up the price of oranges. Because oranges are a resource in the production of orange juice, the supply curve of orange juice shifts leftward, and the price of orange juice rises.

Aiko returns to the grocery store in a week. She notices that the half gallon of orange juice she bought last week for $2.50 has now risen to $3.50. Because Aiko has a downward-sloping demand curve for orange juice, she ends up buying less orange juice. She buys only a quart of orange juice instead of a half gallon.

What role did price play in Aiko's decision to cut back on the consumption of orange juice? It played a major role. If the price hadn't risen, Aiko probably wouldn't have reduced her purchases and consumption of orange juice. Aiko reacted to the price rise, but what the price rise was "saying"—if we had ears to hear it—is this: "The relative scarcity of a good has risen because of a cold spell in Florida. In other words, the gap between people's wants for orange juice and the amount of orange juice available to satisfy those wants has widened."

Now, we know that Aiko might not have "heard" price saying this. But if you understand economics, that is just what price *is* saying. In other words, price is a transmitter of information that often relates to the relative scarcity of a good. A market system, oddly enough, is powerful enough to have people respond in appropriate ways to the information that price is transmitting, even if the people do not fully hear or understand that information. In the case of Aiko, her cutting back on the consumption of orange juice conserves orange juice in the face of an act of nature that ended up making orange juice relatively scarcer.

Think of how this reaction is similar to what people who tell you to conserve water want. For example, in California in the summer of 2015, public messages on television asked people to cut back on their consumption of water because water in the state was in short supply. The appropriate behavior to take was to cut back on the consumption of water, because it had become relatively scarcer. You were being civic minded if you did so. Well, movements in price can get you to be civic minded too. When the price of orange juice rises because of a cold spell in Florida, you might automatically cut back on your consumption, thus conserving on the consumption of a good that has become relatively scarcer.

(Answers to Self-Test questions are in Answers to Self-Test Questions at the back of the book.)

1. Why is there a need for a rationing device, whether it is price or something else?
2. If price is not the rationing device used, then individuals won't have as sharp an incentive to produce. Explain.
3. What kind of information does price often transmit?

4-2 Price Controls

A rationing device—such as dollar price—is needed because scarcity exists. But price is not always allowed to be a rationing device. Sometimes price is controlled. There are two types of price controls: price ceilings and price floors. In the discussion of price controls, the word "price" is used in the generic sense. It refers to the price of an apple, for example; the price of labor (a wage); the price of credit (the interest rate); and so on.

4-2a Price Ceiling

Definition and Effects A **price ceiling** is a government-mandated maximum price above which legal trades cannot be made. For example, suppose the government mandates that the maximum price at which good X can be bought and sold is $8. Therefore, $8 is a price ceiling. If $8 is below the equilibrium price of good X, as in Exhibit 1, any or all of the following effects may arise:[1] shortages, fewer exchanges, nonprice-rationing devices, buying and selling at prohibited prices, and tie-in sales.

Price Ceiling
A government-mandated maximum price above which legal trades cannot be made.

---

[1] If the price ceiling is above the equilibrium price (e.g., $8 is the price ceiling and $4 is the equilibrium price), the ceiling has no effect. Usually, however, a price ceiling is below the equilibrium price.

EXHIBIT 1

A Price Ceiling

The price ceiling is $8, and the equilibrium price is $12. At $12, quantity demanded = quantity supplied. At $8, quantity demanded > quantity supplied. (Recall that price, on the vertical axis, always represents price per unit. Quantity, on the horizontal axis, always holds for a specific period.)

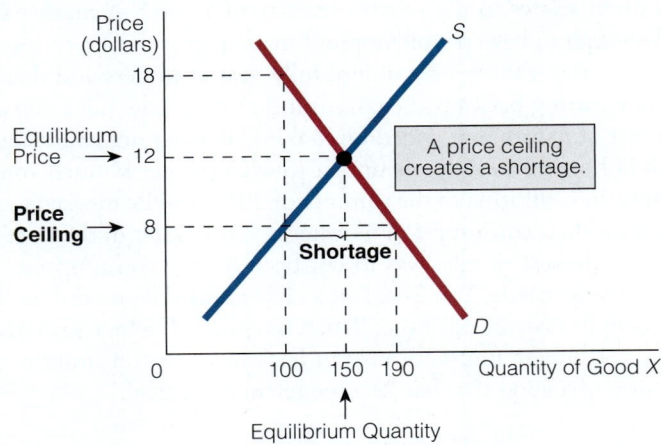

Shortages At the $12 equilibrium price in Exhibit 1, the quantity demanded of good X (150) is equal to the quantity supplied (150). At the $8 price ceiling, a shortage exists: The quantity demanded (190) is greater than the quantity supplied (100). When a shortage exists, price and output tend to rise to equilibrium. But when a price ceiling exists, they cannot rise to equilibrium because it is unlawful to trade at the equilibrium price.

Fewer Exchanges At the equilibrium price of $12 in Exhibit 1, 150 units of good X are bought and sold. At the price ceiling of $8, 100 units of good X are bought and sold. (Buyers would prefer to buy 190 units, but only 100 are supplied.) We conclude that price ceilings cause fewer exchanges to be made.

Notice in Exhibit 1 that the demand curve is above the supply curve for all quantities less than 150 units. (At 150 units, the demand curve and the supply curve intersect and thus share the same point in the two-dimensional space.) Thus, the maximum buying price is greater than the minimum selling price for all units less than 150. In particular, the maximum buying price is greater than the minimum selling price for units 101–149. For example, buyers might be willing to pay $17 for the 110th unit, and sellers might be willing to sell the 110th unit for $10. But no unit after the 100th unit (not the 110th unit, not the 114th unit, not the 130th unit) will be produced and sold because of the price ceiling. In short, the price ceiling prevents mutually advantageous trades from being realized.

Nonprice-Rationing Devices If the equilibrium price of $12 fully rations good X before the price ceiling is imposed, then a lower price of $8 only partly rations this good. In short, price ceilings prevent price from rising to the level sufficient to ration goods fully. But if price is responsible for only part of the rationing, what accounts for the rest?

The answer is that some other (nonprice) rationing device, such as first come, first served. In Exhibit 1, 100 units of good X will be sold at $8, although buyers are willing to buy 190 units at this price. What happens? Possibly, good X will be sold on a first-come, first-served basis for $8 per unit. In other words, to buy good X, a person must not only pay $8 per unit but also be one of the first people in line.

Buying and Selling at a Prohibited Price Buyers and sellers may regularly circumvent a price ceiling by making their exchanges under the table. For example, some buyers may offer some sellers more than $8 per unit for good X. No doubt, some sellers will accept the offers. But why would some buyers offer more than $8 per unit when they can buy good X for $8? Because not all buyers can buy the amount of good X they want at $8. As Exhibit 1 shows, there is a shortage. Buyers are willing to buy 190 units at $8, but sellers are willing to sell only 100 units. In short, 90 fewer units will be sold than buyers would like to buy. Some buyers will go unsatisfied. How, then, does any one buyer make it more likely that sellers will sell to him or her instead of to someone else? The answer is by offering to pay a higher price. However, because it is illegal to pay a higher price, the transaction must be made under the table.

Tie-In Sales In Exhibit 1, the maximum price buyers would be willing and able to pay per unit for 100 units of good X is $18. (This is the price on the demand curve at a quantity of 100 units.) The maximum legal price, however, is $8. The difference between the two prices often prompts a **tie-in sale**, a sale whereby one good can be purchased only if another good is also purchased. For example, if Ralph's Gas Station sells gasoline to customers only if they buy a car wash, the two goods are linked in a tie-in sale.

Suppose that the sellers of good X in Exhibit 1 also sell good Y. Then they might offer to sell buyers good X at $8 only if the buyers agree to buy good Y at, say, $10. We choose $10 as the price for good Y because $10 is the difference between the maximum per-unit price buyers are willing and able to pay for 100 units of good X ($18) and the maximum legal price ($8).

In New York City and other communities with rent-control laws, tie-in sales sometimes result from rent ceilings on apartments. Occasionally, to rent an apartment, an individual must agree to buy the furniture in the apartment.

Tie-in Sale
A sale whereby one good can be purchased only if another good is also purchased.

Buyers and Higher and Lower Prices Do buyers prefer lower to higher prices? "Of course," you might say, "buyers prefer lower prices to higher prices. What buyer would want to pay a higher price for anything?" And yet, even though price ceilings are often lower than equilibrium prices, does it follow that buyers prefer price ceilings to equilibrium prices? Not necessarily. Price ceilings have effects that equilibrium prices do not: shortages; the use of first come, first served as a rationing device; tie-in sales, and so on. A buyer could prefer to pay a higher price (an equilibrium price) than pay a lower price and have to deal with the effects of a price ceiling. All we can say for certain is that buyers prefer lower prices to higher prices, *ceteris paribus*. As in many cases, the *ceteris paribus* condition makes all the difference.

Price Ceilings and False Information Let's go back to the orange juice example from the first section of this chapter. In that example, a cold spell destroys part of the orange crop, leading to a higher price for oranges and orange juice. The market price of orange juice then rises from $2.50 to $3.50 a half gallon.

Now let's change things. Suppose that, instead of letting the new, lower supply of orange juice and demand for orange juice determine the market price of orange juice at $3.50 a half gallon, government imposes a price ceiling on orange juice at $2.50 a half gallon. Think about what the price ceiling does to prevent price from transmitting information. Specifically, the price ceiling prevents the correct information about the increased relative scarcity of orange juice (due to the cold spell) from getting through to consumers. It's as if price is a radio signal, and the price ceiling jams the signal. Because of the jammed price signal, consumers mistakenly believe that nothing has changed. As far as they are concerned, they can continue buying orange juice at the same rate of consumption they did earlier. But, of course, they can't: There are fewer oranges and less orange juice in the world. One way or another, some people are going to have to curtail their consumption of orange juice.

The lesson is simple: Price ceilings (that are below the equilibrium price) distort the flow of accurate information to buyers. Buyers get a false view of reality; they then base their buying behavior on incorrect information. Problems follow, and the unintended, unexpected, and undesirable effects of price ceilings soon occur.

> **Thinking Like An Economist**
>
> **Look for the Unintended Effects** Economists think in terms of unintended effects. For example, a price ceiling policy intended to lower prices for the poor may cause shortages, the use of nonprice rationing devices, illegal market transactions, and tie-in sales. When we consider both the price ceiling and its effects, whether the poor have been helped is not so clear. The economist knows that wanting to do good (for others) is not sufficient: Knowing how to do good is important too.

Economics 24/7

1973 and 1979

In 1973, there were gas lines in the United States. Drivers in their cars waited in long lines to buy gas. Sometimes they waited a couple of hours or more. In some states, a person couldn't buy gas on just any day of the week. Those who had a license plate number that ended with an odd number (such as TBN-347) could buy gas on odd-numbered days of the month, while those who had a license plate number that ended with an even number (such as BNR-874) could buy gas on even-numbered days of the month. In 1979, it was much the same: long lines of drivers waiting to buy gas.

In 1965, there were no long lines of drivers waiting to buy gas, nor was this the case in, say, 1987, 1995, or 2016. What was so different about 1973 and 1979? In those two years, the federal government imposed price ceilings on gasoline. The price ceilings made all the difference, because, as we have pointed out in this chapter, price ceilings lead to shortages and shortages lead to rationing devices other than only money price being used to ration goods. One common nonprice-rationing device is first come, first served, which leads to long lines.

As you might expect, sometimes those long lines produced certain problems, as when someone tried to cut in front of drivers waiting in line. In one case, an attendant at the gas station tried to prevent someone from cutting into line and was almost run over by the driver of the car. In many cases, fights broke out among drivers waiting in line.

McDonald's ran a television ad in 1979 based on gas lines. In fact, the ad was titled "Gas Line." The scene is a gas station with a long line of drivers in cars waiting to buy gas. One man says to another right behind him in line, "Excuse me, would you watch my place in line, I'm just going to run over to McDonald's." The second man responds, "Yeah," and then asks the first man if he could bring

him back a Big Mac. On his way to McDonald's, other drivers in cars ask for a variety of McDonald's products: fries, a Coke, a strawberry shake, and so on. The last scene shows everyone eating their McDonald's products and having a good time but still waiting in the gas line. If you would like to see the actual ad, it can be found on YouTube at http://www.youtube.com/watch?v=tjXhwevOVAE.

4-2b Price Floor: Definition and Effects

A **price floor** is a government-mandated minimum price below which legal trades cannot be made. For example, suppose the government mandates that the minimum price at which good X can be sold is $20. Then the $20 minimum is a price floor. (See Exhibit 2.)

Price Floor
A government-mandated minimum price below which legal trades cannot be made.

Effects of a Price Floor If the price floor is above the equilibrium price, the following two effects arise:[2] surpluses and fewer exchanges.

Surpluses At the $15 equilibrium price in Exhibit 2, the quantity demanded of good X (130) is equal to the quantity supplied (130). At the $20 price floor, a surplus exists.

The quantity supplied (180) is greater than the quantity demanded (90). Usually, a surplus is temporary. When a surplus exists, price and output tend to fall to equilibrium. But when a price floor exists, they cannot fall to equilibrium because it is unlawful to trade at the equilibrium price.

Fewer Exchanges At the equilibrium price in Exhibit 2, 130 units of good X are bought and sold. At the price floor, 90 units are bought and sold. (Sellers want to sell 180 units, but buyers buy only 90.) Thus, price floors cause fewer exchanges to be made.

EXHIBIT 2

A Price Floor

The price floor is $20 and the equilibrium price is $15. At $15, quantity demanded = quantity supplied. At $20, quantity supplied > quantity demanded.

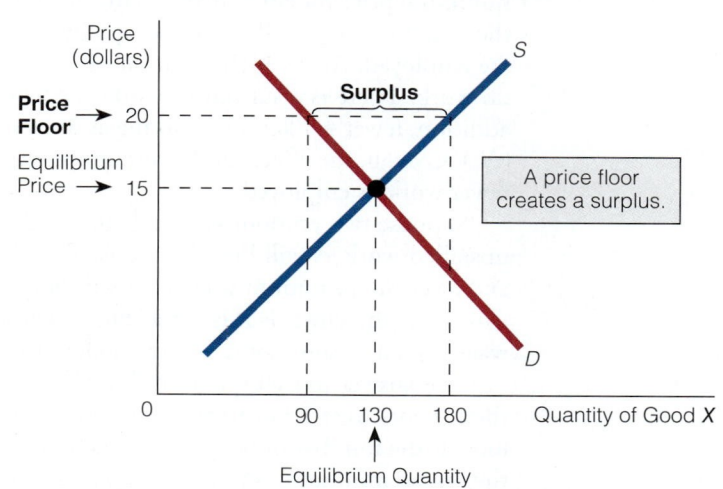

---

[2] If the price floor is below the equilibrium price (e.g., $20 is the price floor and $25 is the equilibrium price), then the price floor has no effects. Usually, however, a price floor is above the equilibrium price.

EXHIBIT 3

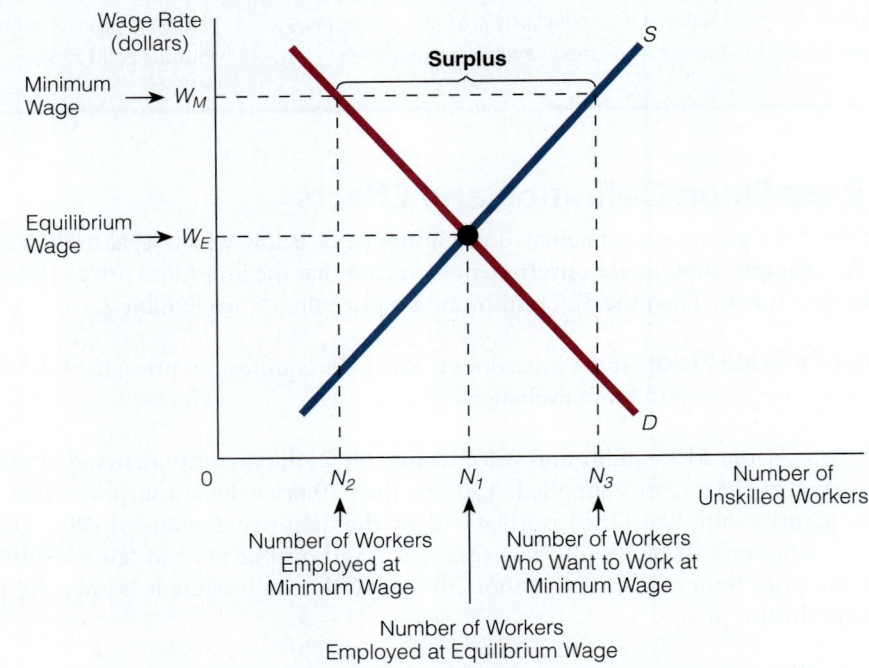

Effects of the Minimum Wage

At a minimum wage of W_M an hour, there is a surplus of workers and fewer workers are employed than would be employed at the equilibrium wage W_E.

The Minimum Wage If a price floor is a legislated minimum price below which trades cannot legally be made, then the *minimum wage* is a price floor—a government-mandated minimum price for labor. It affects the market for unskilled labor. In Exhibit 3, we assume that the minimum wage is W_M and the equilibrium wage is W_E. At the equilibrium wage, N_1 workers are employed. At the higher minimum wage, N_3 workers want to work, but only N_2 actually do work. There is a surplus of workers equal to $N_3 - N_2$ in this unskilled labor market. In addition, fewer workers are working at the minimum wage (N_2) than at the equilibrium wage (N_1). Overall, the effects of the minimum wage are (1) a surplus of unskilled workers and (2) fewer workers employed.

Suppose two economists decide to test the theory that, as the minimum wage rises, some unskilled workers will lose their jobs. They look at the number of unskilled workers before and after the minimum wage is raised. Surprisingly, they find that the number of unskilled workers is the same. Is this sufficient evidence to conclude that an increase in the minimum wage does not cause some workers to lose their jobs?

The answer to that question depends on whether the economists have adequately tested their theory. Instead of focusing on the number of people who lose their jobs, suppose they look at the number of people who keep their jobs but have their hours reduced as a result of the higher minimum wage. Let's look at an example. Suppose a local hardware store currently employs Michael and Kayla to work after school cleaning up and stocking shelves. The owner of the store pays each of them the minimum wage of, say, $7.25 an hour. Then the minimum wage is raised to $10.75 an hour. Will either Michael or Kayla lose their jobs as a result? Not necessarily. Instead, the owner of the store could reduce the number of hours he employs the two workers. For example, instead of having each of them work 20 hours a week, he might ask each to work only 14 hours a week.

Now let's consider our original question again: Has the higher minimum wage eliminated jobs? In a way, no. It has, however, reduced the number of hours a person works in a job. (Of course, if we define a job as including both a particular task and a certain number of hours taken to complete that task, then the minimum wage increase has eliminated "part" of the job.) This discussion argues for changing the label on the horizontal axis in Exhibit 3 from "Number of Unskilled Workers" to "Number of Unskilled Labor Hours."

Thinking Like an Economist

Direction Versus Magnitude In economics, some questions relate to direction and some to magnitude. For example, suppose someone asks, "If the demand for labor is downward sloping and the labor market is competitive, how will a minimum wage that is above the equilibrium wage affect employment?" This person is asking a question that relates to the direction of the change in employment. Usually, these types of questions can be answered by applying a theory. Applying the theory of demand, an economist might say, "At higher wages, the quantity demanded of labor, or the employment level, will be lower than at lower wages." The word "lower" speaks to the *directional change* in employment.

Now suppose someone asks, "How much will employment decline?" This question relates to *magnitude*. Usually, questions that deal with magnitude can be answered only through some kind of empirical (data collection and analysis) work. In other words, we would have to collect employment figures at the equilibrium wage and at the minimum wage and then find the difference.

Economics 24/7

Does It Matter if the Demand Curve for Unskilled Labor Is Steep or Not?

Suppose the U.S. Congress is considering raising the federal minimum wage by $5. Some people say that the $5 higher minimum wage will lead to a higher unemployment rate among unskilled laborers in the country. Others argue that there will be almost no increase in the unemployment rate among the unskilled. You are not quite sure what to think. Whether a $5 raise in the federal minimum wage will lead to a higher unemployment or not depends upon how steep the demand curve for unskilled labor is.

Take a look at the two demand curves for unskilled labor in Exhibit 4. Demand curve D_1 is steeper than demand curve D_2. Now suppose the supply of unskilled labor intersects both demand

EXHIBIT 4

A Higher Wage and the Steepness of the Demand Curve for Unskilled Labor

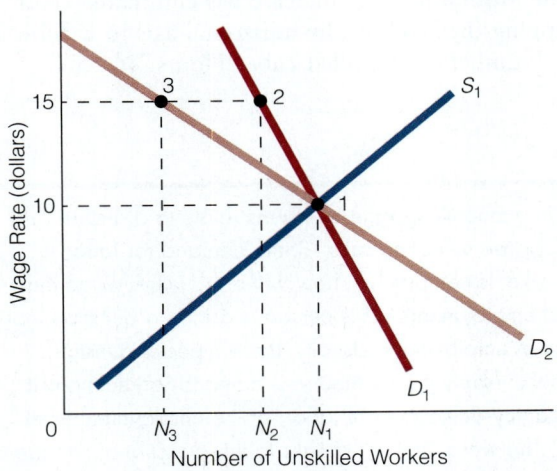

curves at point 1, and the equilibrium wage rate—no matter which demand curve represents the buying side of the labor market—is $10. At this wage rate, we see that the number of people who will have jobs in this market is N_1. Let's also assume that $10 is the current minimum wage.

If the U.S. Congress raises the minimum wage by $5, the new minimum wage becomes $15. With either D_1 or D_2, there is going to be a cutback in the number of people with jobs, but with D_1, the cutback is smaller (N_1 to N_2) than with D_2 (N_1 to N_3). In other words, the steeper the demand curve for unskilled labor, the smaller the cutback in the number of people with jobs.

Put yourself in the position of an unskilled worker. Would the higher minimum wage matter to you? If you keep your job at the higher minimum wage, you are now earning $5 more an hour than you did before. But you may not keep your job at the higher minimum wage. After all, some people are not going to have the job at $15 an hour that they had at $10 an hour. Obviously, if you are one of these people, the minimum wage has hurt you by pricing you out of the unskilled labor market.

But let's not leave it there. Let's think of how the higher minimum wage, and the degree of steepness of the demand curve for unskilled labor, can affect what you see in a restaurant you regularly attend. Perhaps you have noticed that, in some restaurants today, there are tablets at restaurant tables that one can use to order food. That is, instead of having a server come to a table and take your order, it is now possible in some food establishments to sit down at a table and place your order via a tablet. Just tap on the items you want to purchase—a hamburger with lettuce, tomato, and mayonnaise, with a small order of fries, and a large soft drink. Once your order is submitted, it takes just a short while before someone delivers your order to your table.

With tablets for ordering, the restaurant does not need to hire as many servers. With tablets, possibly three servers can now do what it took six servers to do previously. What does this have to do with the minimum wage and the degree of steepness of the demand curve for unskilled labor? Quite a bit. The higher the minimum wage above the equilibrium wage, and the less steep the demand curve for labor, the greater the cutback in the number of servers (who are often paid the minimum wage) a restaurant is likely to hire, or keep employed, and the greater the likelihood the restaurant will "employ" tablets to replace the servers. In the end, an uptick in the minimum wage, the steepness of the demand curve for unskilled labor, and tablets at your restaurant table are linked.

Price Floors, Changes in Consumers' and Producers' Surplus, and Deadweight Losses

We now turn to a discussion of consumers' surplus, producers' surplus, and price floors in terms of a specific example: a price floor on an agricultural foodstuff.

Exhibit 5 shows the demand for and supply of an agricultural foodstuff (corn, wheat, soybeans, etc.). If the market is allowed to move to equilibrium, the equilibrium price will be P_1, and the equilibrium quantity will be Q_1. Consumers' surplus will equal the area under the demand curve and above the equilibrium price: areas $1 + 2 + 3$. Producers' surplus will equal the area under the equilibrium price and above the supply curve: areas $4 + 5$. Total surplus, of course, is the sum of consumers' surplus and producers' surplus: areas $1 + 2 + 3 + 4 + 5$.

EXHIBIT 5

Agricultural Price Floors

The demand for and supply of an agricultural foodstuff are shown in this exhibit. The equilibrium price is P_1; consumers' surplus (CS) is areas $1 + 2 + 3$; producers' surplus is areas $4 + 5$. A price floor of P_F effectively transfers some of the consumers' surplus to producers in the form of a gain in producers' surplus. Specifically, at P_F, consumers' surplus is area 1, and producers' surplus is areas $2 + 4$. Consumers are net losers because consumers' surplus has decreased by areas $2 + 3$. Producers are net gainers because producers' surplus has increased from areas $4 + 5$ to areas $2 + 4$, and area 2 is larger than area 5. Overall, the economic pie of CS + PS has decreased from areas $1 + 2 + 3 + 4 + 5$ to areas $1 + 2 + 4$.

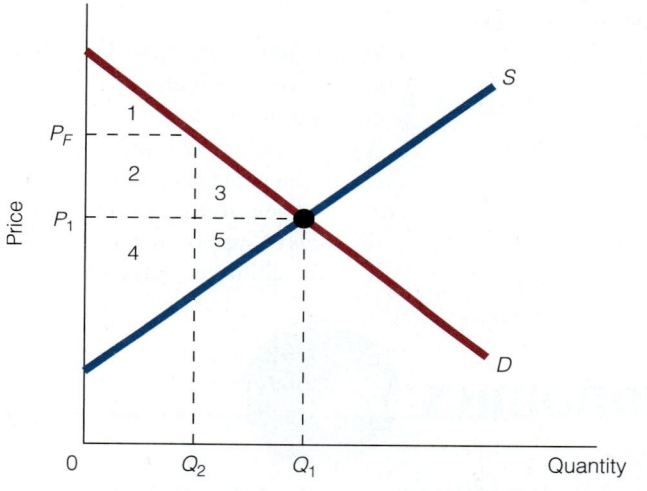

Now, suppose that the suppliers of the foodstuff argue for (and receive) a price floor P_F. At this higher price, consumers do not buy as much as they once did. They now buy Q_2, whereas they used to buy Q_1. In addition, consumers' surplus is now only area 1, and producers' surplus is areas $2 + 4$.

Obviously, consumers have been hurt by the increased (government-mandated) price P_F; specifically, they have lost consumers' surplus equal to areas $2 + 3$.

How have suppliers fared? Whereas their producers' surplus was equal to areas $4 + 5$ at P_1, it is now equal to areas $2 + 4$. (Area 2, which used to be part of consumers' surplus, has been transferred to producers and is now part of producers' surplus.) Whether producers are better off depends on whether area 2 (what they gain from P_F) is larger than area 5 (what they lose from P_F). Visually, we can tell that area 2 is larger than area 5, so producers are better off.

What is the overall effect of the price floor? Have producers gained more than consumers have lost, or have consumers lost more than producers have gained? To answer this question, we note that consumers lose areas 2 and 3 in consumers' surplus, and producers gain area 2 in producers' surplus and lose area 5 in producers' surplus. So the gains and losses are as follows:

Losses to consumers:	areas $2 + 3$
Gains to producers:	area 2
Losses to producers:	area 5

Part of the loss to consumers is offset by the gain to producers (area 2), so net losses amount to areas 3 + 5. In other words, the total surplus—the sum of consumers' surplus and producers' surplus—is lower than it was. Whereas it used to be areas 1 + 2 + 3 + 4 + 5, it now is areas 1 + 2 + 4. The total surplus lost is in areas 3 + 5. In short, (1) consumers lose, (2) producers gain, and (3) society (which is the sum of consumers and producers) loses.

You can think of this example in terms of a pie. Initially, the pie was made up of areas 1 + 2 + 3 + 4 + 5. This rather large pie registered all the gains of consumers and producers. After the price floor P_F was imposed, the pie shrank to areas 1 + 2 + 4; in other words, the pie was smaller by areas 3 + 5.

A loss in total surplus—in our example, areas 3 + 5—is sometimes called a **deadweight loss**. This is the loss to society of not producing the competitive, or supply-and-demand-determined, level of output. In terms of Exhibit 5, it is the loss to society of producing Q_2 instead of producing Q_1.

Deadweight Loss
The loss to society of not producing the competitive, or supply-and-demand-determined, level of output.

What Some People Get Wrong In sum, some persons argue that a price floor creates a situation in which (1) someone wins and someone loses and (2) the gains for the winner are equal to the losses for the loser (e.g., one person loses $5, and another person wins $5). A quick look at Exhibit 5 tells us that (2) is not true. The losses (for consumers) are not offset by the gains (for producers). A price floor ends with a *net loss*, or *deadweight loss*, of areas 3 + 5. Now think of how hard it would have been to identify this deadweight loss without the tools of supply, demand, consumers' surplus, and producers' surplus. Economic tools often have the ability to make what is invisible visible.

Economics 24/7

What Does Price Have to Do with Being Late to Class?

Class starts at 10 o'clock in the morning. At 10:09, Pam Ferrario walks in late. She apologizes to the instructor, saying, "I've been on campus 20 minutes, but I couldn't find a parking spot." Her classmates nod, knowing full well what she is talking about. Here at the university, especially between the hours of 9 a.m. and 2 p.m., parking spots are hard to come by.

This scene is replayed every day at many universities and colleges across the country. Students are late for class because on many days there isn't a parking space to be found.

Think of the ways in which parking spaces can be rationed at a college campus. One way is on a first-come, first-served basis. In

other words, students are not charged a fee to park; they just park where spaces are available. At zero price for parking, the quantity demanded of spaces is likely to be greater than the quantity supplied, and a shortage of parking spaces will result at certain times of the day. To deal with this shortage, students will likely try to be "first in line" for a parking spot, causing them to leave for the campus earlier than they would otherwise. Instead of leaving home at 9:40 a.m. for a 10 o'clock class, one leaves at 9:30 a.m. Now, who pays for the first-come, first-served parking scheme? Of course, the students do, not in money, but in time.

Naturally, if the student doesn't leave home early enough to get a parking spot, then perhaps he or she will end up going up and down the parking aisles, looking for an open spot. This way, the student ends up paying for a parking spot by being late to class.

So, if parking spaces are allocated on a first-come, first-served basis, it is likely that the student will end up paying in terms of time or in terms of being late to class.

The alternative is to pay in terms of money price. The university could, say, install parking meters and adjust the parking fee in such a way as to have the quantity demanded of parking spaces equal the quantity supplied of parking spaces at various times of the day.

Of course, if, by chance, the university sets the parking fee at a level below the equilibrium price, then the student will end up paying for the parking scheme in terms of both money price and first come, first served, because a parking fee below equilibrium will generate a shortage of parking spaces, and thus, spaces will be rationed on a first-come, first-served basis.

You may often hear people say that price is a bad way to ration parking spaces at a college campus. But, then, what is the alternative? If price does not ration parking spots, something else will. In short, students who want to park on campus are going to have to pay for parking; it is just a question of *how* they pay. Do they pay in terms of their time, in being late to class, or in money price?

1. Do buyers prefer lower prices to higher prices?
2. "When there are long-lasting shortages, there are long lines of people waiting to buy goods. It follows that the shortages cause the long lines." Do you agree or disagree? Explain your answer.
3. Who might argue for a price ceiling? A price floor?

4-3 Two Prices: Absolute and Relative

In everyday language, we often use the word "price" without specifying the kind of price. Economists often distinguish the *absolute*, or *money*, *price* of a good from the *relative price* of a good.

4-3a Absolute (Money) Price and Relative Price

The **absolute (money) price** is the price of the good in money terms. For example, the absolute price of a car might be $30,000. The **relative price** is the price of the good *in terms of another good*. To illustrate, suppose the absolute price of a car is $30,000 and the absolute price of a computer is $2,000. Then the relative price of the car—that is, the price of the car *in terms of computers*—is 15 computers. A person gives up the opportunity to buy 15 computers when buying a car:

Absolute (money) Price
The price of a good in money terms.

Relative Price
The price of a good in terms of another good.

$$\text{Relative price of a car (in terms of computer)} = \frac{\text{Absolute price of a car}}{\text{Absolute price of a computer}}$$
$$= \frac{\$30,000}{\$2,000}$$
$$= 15$$

Now let's compute the relative price of a computer—that is, the price of a computer in terms of a car:

$$\text{Relative price of a computer (in terms of car)} = \frac{\text{Absolute price of a computer}}{\text{Absolute price of a car}}$$

$$= \frac{\$2{,}000}{\$30{,}000}$$

$$= \frac{1}{15}$$

Thus, the relative price of a computer in this example is 1/15 of a car. A person gives up the opportunity to buy 1/15 of a car when buying a computer.

Now consider this question: What happens to the relative price of a good if its absolute price rises and nothing else changes? For example, if the absolute price of a car rises from $30,000 to $40,000, what happens to its relative price? Obviously, the relative price rises from 15 computers to 20 computers. In short, if the absolute price of a good rises and nothing else changes, then its relative price rises too.

Thinking Like an Economist

Higher Absolute Price Can Sometimes Mean Lower Relative Price Economists know that a good can go up in price at the same time that it becomes relatively cheaper. How can this happen? Suppose the absolute price of a pen is $1 and the absolute price of a pencil is 10¢. The relative price of 1 pen, then, is 10 pencils.

Now let the absolute price of a pen rise to $1.20 at the same time that the absolute price of a pencil rises to 20¢. As a result, the relative price of 1 pen falls to 6 pencils. In other words, the absolute price of pens rises (from $1 to $1.20) at the same time that pens become relatively cheaper (in terms of how many pencils you have to give up to buy a pen).

How does this phenomenon happen? Well, the absolute price of a pen went up by 20 percent (from $1 to $1.20) at the same time that the absolute price of a pencil doubled (from 10¢ to 20¢). Because the absolute price of a pen went up by a smaller percentage than the absolute price of a pencil increased, the relative price of a pen fell.

4-3b Taxes on Specific Goods and Relative Price Changes

Suppose that the equilibrium price of good X is $10 and that the equilibrium price of good Y is $20. The relative price of good X is therefore ½ unit of good Y, and the relative price of good Y is 2 units of good X:

$$1X = \tfrac{1}{2}Y$$

$$1Y = 2X$$

Given these relative prices of X and Y, consumers will buy some combination of the two goods. For example, a given consumer might end up buying 10 units of X each week and 12 units of Y.

Now suppose that the government imposes a tax only on the purchase of good X. Then the tax effectively raises the price the consumer pays for the good from $10 to $15. Because no tax is placed on good Y, its price remains at $20.

Chapter 4 Prices: Free, Controlled, and Relative

The tax thus changes the relative prices of the two goods. The after-tax relative prices are

$$1X = ¾Y$$
$$1Y = 1.33X$$

Comparing the new relative prices with the old relative prices, we recognize that the tax makes X relatively more expensive (going from $½Y$ to $¾Y$) and makes Y relatively cheaper (going from $2X$ to $1.33X$). In other words, a tax placed only on X ends up making X relatively more expensive and Y relatively cheaper. As a result, we would expect consumers to buy relatively less X and relatively more Y. Think in terms of two familiar goods: Coke and Pepsi. A tax placed on Coke, but not on Pepsi, will induce consumers to buy relatively less Coke and relatively more Pepsi.

Economics 24/7

Obesity and a Soda Tax

The percentage of the U.S. population that is deemed obese today is higher than it was 20 years ago. Obesity is a health problem, so we often hear proposals directed at trying to reduce the obesity rate in the country. One proposal is to place a tax on high-fat, high-calorie, so-called junk food. A similar proposal is to place a tax on soda.

We now know that a tax placed on one good (but not on another) will change the relative prices of the two goods. Placing a tax on good X, but not on good Y, will make good X relatively more expensive and Y relatively cheaper, prompting consumers to purchase relatively less X and relatively more Y.

Consider a tax placed on soda. We would expect the absolute (money) price of soda to rise. And if the tax is placed only on soda, its relative price will rise too. As soda becomes relatively more expensive, we would expect fewer sodas to be consumed and obesity to decline. Right? Well, fewer sodas might be purchased and consumed, but whether obesity will decline is not so clear. Consider soda and sugared iced tea. Both soda and sugared iced tea are sweet drinks. They might even be substitutes. With this idea in mind, suppose the absolute price of a soda is $1 and the absolute price of an iced tea (with sugar) is 50¢. It follows that the relative prices are

1 soda = 2 sugared iced teas
1 sugared iced tea = ½ soda

Now let's place a tax on soda that drives its price up to $2. The new relative prices for soda and iced tea are

1 soda = 4 sugared iced teas
1 sugared iced tea = ¼ soda

As a result of the tax on soda, its relative price has risen, but the relative price of sugared iced tea has fallen. We would thus expect people to consume relatively less soda and relatively more sugared iced tea.

Obesity is lessened by ingesting fewer calories, not the same number or more calories. Simply put, the soda tax might reduce the consumption of sodas, but it doesn't necessarily reduce obesity. Although the soda tax makes soda relatively more expensive, it makes soda substitutes (such as sugared iced tea) relatively less expensive and thus makes a rise in the consumption of sugared iced tea more likely.

1. If the absolute (or money) price of good A is $40 and the absolute price of good B is $60, what is the relative price of each good?

2. Someone says, "The price of good X has risen, so good X is more expensive than it used to be." In what sense is this statement correct? In what sense is this statement either incorrect or misleading?

Office Hours
"I Thought Price Ceilings Were Good for Consumers"

Student: I still don't quite understand how a price ceiling can hurt consumers. After all, a price ceiling is usually set below the equilibrium price of a good, and everyone knows that consumers prefer lower prices to higher prices.

Instructor: The problem is that when a price ceiling is imposed on a good, certain things happen that don't benefit consumers. Look at it this way: Consumers like the lower price that goes along with the price ceiling, but what they don't like are some of the effects of the price ceiling.

Student: But it seems to me that if you picked 100 consumers at random and asked them whether they preferred the price of bread to be $1 a loaf as opposed to $2, all 100 consumers would say they prefer the lower price. Because a price ceiling is usually lower than the equilibrium price, doesn't this example prove that consumers benefit from price ceilings? After all, why would they say they prefer paying $1 than $2 for a loaf of bread if they didn't see it benefiting them?

Instructor: A couple of things could be going on here. First, consumers might intuitively take the question to be asking whether they prefer the *$1 price determined by supply and demand to the $2 price determined by supply and demand*. If this is how they understand the question, then it certainly seems reasonable for them to say they prefer the lower price to the higher price. You might not get the same response from consumers, though, if you asked them this question:

Which of the following two options do you prefer?

Option A:

$2 (equilibrium) price of bread

Option B:

$1 (price ceiling) price of bread + shortages of bread + lines of people waiting to buy bread, and so on

Student: In other words, your point is that consumers prefer lower to higher prices, assuming that nothing else changes but the price of the good. But if lower prices, as the result of price ceilings, come with shortages and long lines of people waiting to buy bread, then they may not prefer lower to higher prices.

Instructor: Yes, that is the point.

Student: A slightly different question: Do you think that all consumers know the adverse effects of price ceilings?

Instructor: Probably not. In fact, even after government imposes a price ceiling and certain adverse effects (shortages, long lines, etc.) set in, consumers may fail to relate the cause to the effects of the price ceiling. In other words, X causes Y, but individuals either don't understand how (they don't connect the two) or believe that something else—Z—causes Y.

Points to Remember

1. Consumers may prefer a lower to higher price, *ceteris paribus*, but not necessarily a lower price with shortages to a higher price without shortages.
2. X may cause Y, but it doesn't necessarily follow that everyone will understand that X causes Y.

Chapter Summary

Price

- As a result of scarcity, a rationing device is needed to determine who gets what of the available limited resources and goods. Price serves as a rationing device.
- Price acts as a transmitter of information relating to the change in the relative scarcity of a good.

Price Ceilings

- A price ceiling is a government-mandated maximum price. If a price ceiling is below the equilibrium price, some or all of the following effects arise: shortages, fewer exchanges, nonprice-rationing devices, buying and selling at prohibited prices, and tie-in sales.
- Consumers do not necessarily prefer (lower) price ceilings to (higher) equilibrium prices. They may prefer higher prices and none of the effects of price ceilings to lower prices and some of the effects of price ceilings. All we can say for sure is that consumers prefer lower prices to higher prices, *ceteris paribus*.

Price Floors

- A price floor is a government-mandated minimum price. If a price floor is above the equilibrium price, the following effects arise: surpluses and fewer exchanges.

Absolute Price and Relative Price

- The absolute price of a good is the price of the good in terms of money.
- The relative price of a good is the price of the good in terms of another good.

Key Terms and Concepts

Tie-in Sale
Price Ceiling
Price Floor
Deadweight Loss
Absolute (Money) Price
Relative Price

Questions and Problems

1. "If price were outlawed as the rationing device used in markets, there would be no need for another rationing device to take its place. We would have reached utopia." Discuss.
2. What kind of information does price transmit?
3. Should grades in an economics class be "rationed" according to dollar price instead of how well a student does on exams? If they were and prospective employers learned of it, what effect might this have on the value of your college degree?
4. Think of ticket scalpers at a rock concert, a baseball game, or an opera. Might they exist because the tickets to these events were originally sold for less than the equilibrium price? Why or why not? In what way is a ticket scalper like and unlike your retail grocer, who buys food from a wholesaler and then sells it to you?
5. Many of the proponents of price ceilings argue that government-mandated maximum prices simply reduce producers' profits and do not affect the quantity supplied of a good on the market. What must the supply curve look like if the price ceiling does not affect the quantity supplied?
6. James lives in a rent-controlled apartment and for the past few weeks has been trying to get the supervisor to fix his shower. What does waiting to get one's shower fixed have to do with a rent-controlled apartment?
7. Explain why fewer exchanges are made when a disequilibrium price (below the equilibrium price) exists than when the equilibrium price exists.
8. Buyers always prefer lower prices to higher prices. Do you agree or disagree with this statement? Explain your answer.

9. What is the difference between a price ceiling and a price floor? What effect is the same for both a price ceiling and a price floor?

10. If the absolute price of good X is $10 and the absolute price of good Y is $14, then what is (a) the relative price of good X in terms of good Y and (b) the relative price of good Y in terms of good X?

11. Give a numerical example that illustrates how a tax placed on the purchase of good X can change the relative price of good X in terms of good Y.

Working With Numbers and Graphs

1. In the diagram, what areas represent the deadweight loss due to the price ceiling (P_C)?

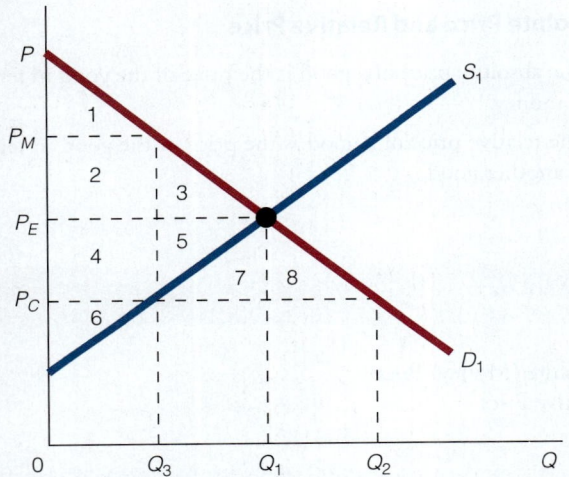

2. In the preceding diagram, what areas represent consumers' surplus at the equilibrium price of P_E? At P_C? (Keep in mind that, at P_C, the equilibrium quantity is neither produced nor sold.)

3. Using Exhibit 1 in the chapter, suppose the price ceiling is $13 instead of $8. Would the consequences of the price ceiling we identified in the text (such as a shortage, fewer exchanges) arise? Why or why not?

4. Draw a market that is in equilibrium, and identify the area of consumers' surplus and producers' surplus. Now place a price ceiling in the market, and identify the rise and fall in consumers' surplus. Finally, identify the decline in producers' surplus.

5. The absolute prices of goods X, Y, and Z are $23, $42, and $56, respectively. What is the relative price of X in terms of Y? What is the relative price of Y in terms of Z? What is the relative price of Z in terms of X?

6. There are two goods: X and Y. The absolute price of X rises, and the absolute price of Y does not change. Prove that the relative price of X rises in terms of Y.

Supply, Demand, and Price: Applications

CHAPTER 5

Introduction

In the previous two chapters, we discussed supply, demand, and price. In this chapter, we *work with* supply, demand, and price. The theory of supply and demand is not very useful to you unless you can use it to explain some of the things you see around you in everyday life. In this chapter, we discuss medical care, changing house prices, college classes at 10 a.m., driving on a freeway, standardized tests (such as the SAT), college athletes, and more—all in the general framework of supply and demand.

5-1 Application 1: U-Haul Rates and Demand[1]

Suppose you want to rent a 10-foot U-Haul truck to move from Los Angeles, California, to Phoenix, Arizona. Will that truck cost you the same dollar amount as it would if you want to move from Phoenix to Los Angeles? The answer is no. Here are the rates:

Los Angeles to Phoenix: $939
Phoenix to Los Angeles: $189

Why is it more expensive to rent a U-Haul truck going from Los Angeles to Phoenix than from Phoenix to Los Angeles?

---

[1]. The idea for this feature came from Mark Perry's discussion of U-Haul rates at his blog, AEI/Carpe Diem at http://www.aei.org/publication/blog/carpe-diem/.

Before we answer that question, consider the U-Haul rates for the following combinations of cities:[2]

>New York City to Austin, Texas: $2,448
>Austin, Texas, to New York City: $938
>Chicago, Illinois, to Raleigh, North Carolina: $1,547
>Raleigh, North Carolina, to Chicago, Illinois: $524
>Baltimore, Maryland, to Nashville, Tennessee: $906
>Nashville, Tennessee, to Baltimore, Maryland: $416

Now what you will notice in the four combinations of cities that we have cited is that it is more expensive to rent a truck that goes in one direction than it is to rent a truck that goes in the reverse direction. It is more expensive to go from New York City to Austin than from Austin to New York City; it is more expensive to go from Los Angeles to Phoenix than from Phoenix to Los Angeles.

Why is this? The answer has to do with the demand of going from point 1 to 2 relative to the demand of going from point 2 to 1. We can say that the demand to move from, say, New York City to Austin is higher than the demand to move from Austin to New York City. Given the higher demand to move to some cities than others, the demand for U-Haul trucks to move to these cities is higher than the demand to move to many other cities. Higher demand translates into higher U-Haul rental rates.

(Answers to Self-Test questions are in Answers to Self-Test Questions at the back of the book.)

1. If more people want to move from California to Texas than want to move from Texas to California, might U-Haul rates reflect this difference? Explain your answer.

2. Why might median house prices be higher in one city than in another?

5-2 Application 2: Subsidizing the Consumption of Anything Can Raise Its Price

Any point on a demand curve represents the highest price (maximum buying price) buyers will pay per unit for a specific quantity of a good. With this in mind, look at Exhibit 1(a). Focus first on the demand curve, D_1. The highest price that buyers will pay for the first unit of the good here is $10.

Now ask yourself what will happen to the demand curve D_1 if government were to subsidize the purchases of the good. Suppose government were to give $1 to each person

---

[2] All U-Haul rates in this feature are based on the one-way rental of a 10-foot truck on October 30, 2020.

EXHIBIT 1

Subsidies and Demand

In (a), we show that the highest price buyers will pay for the first unit of the good is $10 if D_1 holds. If government offers a $1 subsidy for each unit of the good the buyer purchases, then the highest price buyers will pay for the first unit of the good is $11. D_2 is the demand curve with the subsidy of $1. In (b), we show the demand for the good with and without the subsidy. Notice that price ends up higher ($5.50) when a subsidy (for the purchase of the good) exists than when it does not exist ($5.00).

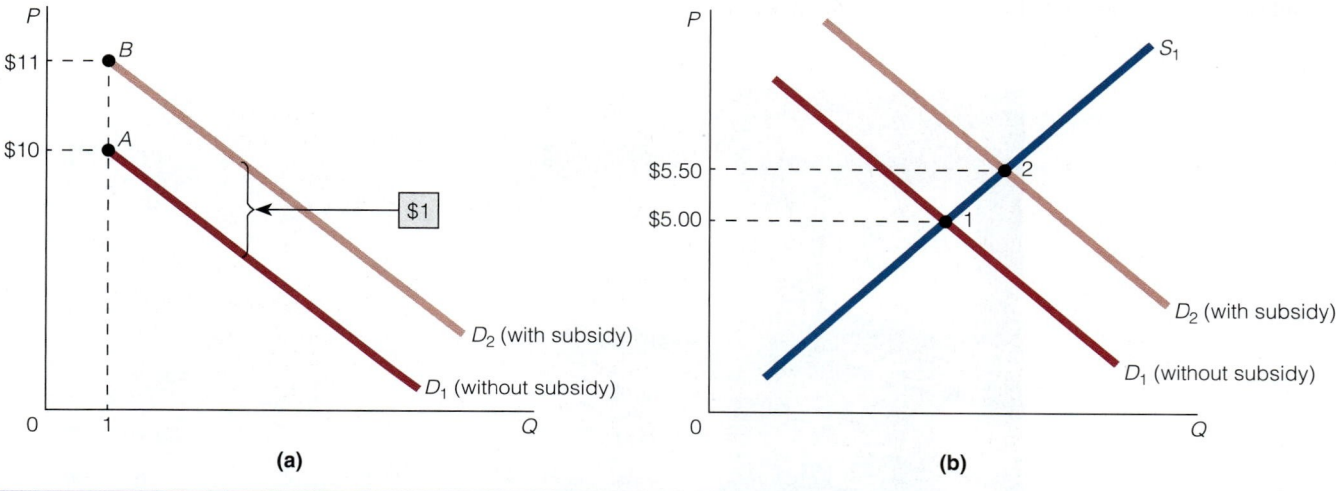

who purchased a unit of the good. Now the highest price that buyers would be willing to pay for the first unit of the good would be $11 instead of $10. That's because paying $11 and getting $1 from the government is the same as paying $10 and not getting anything from the government.

As a result of the subsidy, (for purchasing the good), the demand curve for the good now moves upward from D_1 to D_2. At each quantity (on the horizontal axis), the new demand curve, D_2 (which is the demand curve with the subsidy) lies $1 higher than the old demand curve, D_1 (which is the demand curve without the subsidy).

Now in Exhibit 1(b), we put both D_1 and D_2 together with the supply curve for the good. Notice that when the purchases of the good are not subsidized—when D_1 holds—the equilibrium price for the good is lower ($5.00) than when the purchases of the good are subsidized ($5.50)—that is, when D_2 holds. We conclude that a government subsidy that is applied to the purchases (and consumption) of a good ends up raising the price of the good.

Now consider the following. Someone argues that both health care and higher education are expensive for many people. He argues that the government should subsidize buyers of both health care and higher education. For example, tell college students that for every $100 they pay for college, the government will give them $40. Or tell people that are buying health care that for every $100 they pay for health care, the government will give them $30. What is likely to happen as a consequence? Both the demand for health care and for education will rise and, along with higher demand, will come higher prices for both health care and higher education.

1. If a subsidy is provided for the consumption of good X, and the subsidy is different for different units of good X (e.g., $40 subsidy on the first unit of good X and $32 on the second unit of good X, etc.), would the demand curve without a subsidy be parallel to the demand curve with a subsidy, as is the case in Exhibit 1? Explain your answer.

2. Suppose a subsidy is provided to the buyers of solar panels. What is likely to happen to the price of solar panels? Explain your answer.

5-3 Application 3: 10 A.M. Classes in College

Suppose an economics class is offered in the same classroom twice in a day: at 10 a.m. and at 8 p.m. Most students would prefer the 10 a.m. class to the 8 p.m. class. So, in Exhibit 2, the supply of seats in the class is the same at each time, but the demand to occupy those seats is not. Because the demand is greater for the 10 a.m. class than for the 8 p.m. class, the equilibrium price for the morning class is higher than the equilibrium price for the evening class.

But the university or college charges the same tuition no matter what time students choose to take the class. The university doesn't charge students a higher tuition if they enroll in 10 a.m. classes than if they enroll in 8 p.m. classes.

Suppose that tuition T_1 is charged for all classes and that T_1 is the equilibrium tuition for 8 p.m. classes. (See Exhibit 2.) T_1 is therefore below the equilibrium tuition for 10 a.m. classes: At T_1, the quantity demanded of seats for the morning classes will be greater than the quantity supplied; more students will want the earlier class than there is space available.

EXHIBIT 2

The Supply of and Demand for College Classes at Different Times

A given class is offered at two times, 10 a.m. and 8 p.m. The supply of seats in the classroom is the same at both times; however, student demand for the 10 a.m. class is higher than that for the 8 p.m. class. The university charges the same tuition, T_1, regardless of which class a student takes. At this tuition level, there is a shortage of seats for the 10 a.m. class. Seats are likely to be rationed on a first-come, first-served (first to register) basis or on seniority (seniors take precedence over juniors, juniors over sophomores, etc.).

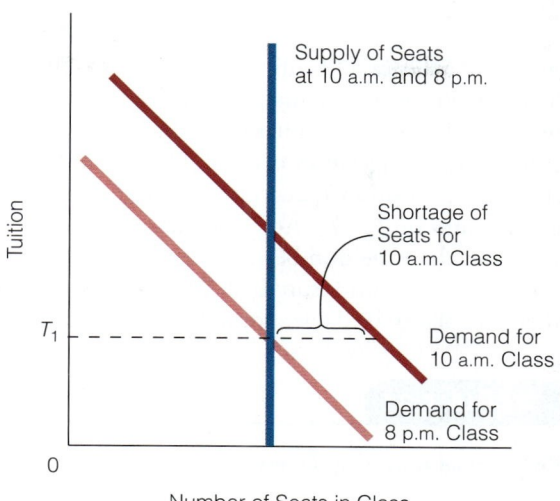

How will the university allocate the available seats? It may do so on a first-come, first-served basis. Students who are first to register get the 10 a.m. class; the latecomers have to take the 8 p.m. class. Or the university could ration the high-demand classes by giving their upper-class students (seniors) first priority.

Thinking Like an Economist

Remembering Price Upon seeing students clamoring to get 10 a.m. classes, noneconomists conclude that the demand is high for mid-morning classes. They then wonder why the university doesn't schedule more 10 a.m. classes. The economist knows that what noneconomists see is as much an effect of price as of demand. The demand for 10 a.m. classes may be high, but the quantity demanded may not be if the price is high enough. In fact, even though the demand for classes at certain times may vary, some set of prices will make the quantity demanded of each class the same.

1. Suppose college students are given two options. With option A, the price a student pays for a class is always the equilibrium price. For example, if the equilibrium price to take Economics 101 is $600 at 10 a.m. and $400 at 4 p.m., then students pay more for the early class than they do for the later class. With option B, the price a student pays for a class is the same regardless of the time the class is taken. Given the choice between options A and B, many students would say that they prefer option B to option A. Is this the case for you? If so, why would that be your choice?

2. How is the analysis of the 10 a.m. class similar to the analysis of a price ceiling in a market?

5-4 Application 4: Why Do Colleges Use GPAs, ACTs, and SATs for Purposes of Admission?

At many colleges and universities, students pay part of the price of their education (in the form of tuition payments), and taxpayers and private donors pay part (by way of tax payments and charitable donations, respectively). Thus, the tuition that students pay to attend colleges and universities is usually less than the equilibrium tuition. To illustrate, suppose a student pays tuition T_1 at a given college or university. As shown in Exhibit 3, T_1 is below the equilibrium tuition T_E. At T_1, the number of students who want to attend the university (N_1) is greater than the number of openings at the university (N_2); that is, quantity demanded is greater than quantity supplied. The university receives more applications for admission than there are places available. Something has to be done. But what?

EXHIBIT 3

College and University Admissions

If the college or university charges tuition T_1, and if T_E is the equilibrium tuition, then a shortage will be generated. The college or university will then use some nonprice-rationing device—such as GPAs, ACTs, and SATs—as an admission criterion.

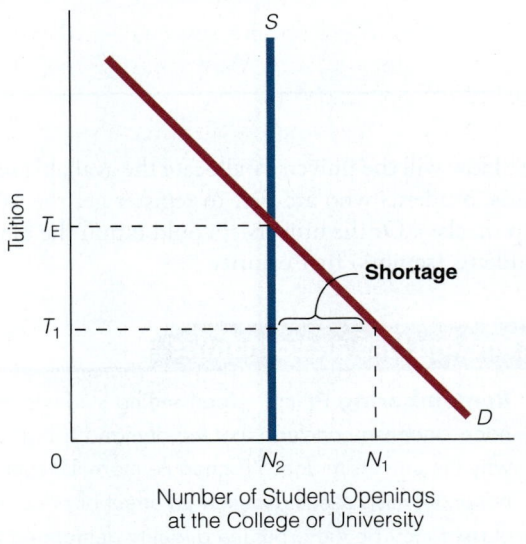

The college or university is likely to ration its available space by a combination of money price and some nonprice-rationing devices. The student must then pay the tuition T_1 *and* meet the standards of the nonprice-rationing devices. Colleges and universities typically use such things as GPAs (grade point averages), ACT scores, and SAT scores as rationing devices.

Thinking Like an Economist

Identifying Rationing Devices The noneconomist sees a GPA of 3.8 and an SAT score of 1300 or better as requirements for admission. Economists see them as rationing devices. Economists then go on to ask why these particular nonprice-rationing devices are used. They reason that nonprice-rationing devices *would not* be needed if the (dollar) price were fully rationing the good or service.

1. The demand rises for admission to a university, but both the tuition and the number of openings in the entering class remain the same. Will this change affect the admission standards of the university? Explain your answer.
2. Administrators and faculty at state colleges and universities often say that their standards of admission are independent of whether there is a shortage or surplus of openings at the university. Do you think that this statement is true? Do you think that faculty and administrators ignore surpluses and shortages of openings when setting admission standards? Explain your answer.

5-5 Application 5: Why Is Medical Care So Expensive?

Think of how you buy groceries. You go to the store, place certain products in your basket, and then pay for them at the cash register.

Now think of how you buy medical care. You go to the doctor or hospital, give the doctor's office or hospital your health insurance card, perhaps make a co-payment of $10 or $20, and then receive medical care. Your doctor or the hospital then bills your insurance company for the bulk of your expenses.

What is the difference between how you buy groceries and how you buy medical care? In the grocery store, only two parties are involved in the transaction: you (the buyer) and the grocery store (the seller). In the medical care example, three parties are involved: you, the doctor or hospital, and the insurance company. The insurance company is often referred to as the "third party." So no third party is involved in the grocery store transaction, but one is involved in purchasing medical care.

The existence of a third party separates the buying of something from the paying for something. In the grocery store, the person who buys the groceries and the person who pays for them are the same (you). In the medical care example, the person who buys and receives the medical care (you) is different from the person or entity that pays for the medical care (the insurance company).

"Wait a minute," you say. "You indirectly pay for your medical care by paying monthly insurance premiums to the medical insurance company." That is partly true, but what happens is like being at a buffet. You pay a set dollar price for the buffet, and then you can eat all you want. Our guess is that at a buffet you eat more than you would if you had to pay for each plateful.

The same often happens with medical care. You pay a set premium to the insurance company (let's say, $250 a month), and then you enter the health care buffet line. Might you end up buying more health care than you would if each doctor visit and lab test at the health care buffet were priced separately?

Before we continue, let's consider two objections to this analogy.

First, you might say, "But I don't buy medical care as I buy food in the food buffet line. I like shrimp, steak, salads, and desserts, but who likes being X-rayed, being prodded and poked by doctors, and taking medicine? No one buys MRIs as if they were shrimp cocktails."

That objection is true, of course, but it begs the point: Once you get sick and go to the doctor or hospital, the existence of a third party (who pays for your medical care) makes it easier for your doctor or the hospital to opt for more medical examinations or procedures and care than you need. For example, a conversation in your doctor's office may go like this:

Doctor: I think you have condition X, but just to be sure, let's order some blood tests and get an MRI too.

You: Whatever you think is best.

Now ask yourself how you might respond if you had to pay—out of pocket—for the blood test and MRI. The dialogue might change:

Doctor: I think you have condition X, but just to be sure, let's order some blood tests and get an MRI too.

You: How much is this going to cost me, doctor? And is all this really necessary?

The point is simple: Once you have paid your insurance premium, the price you pay for medical care amounts only to your co-payment (which is usually minimal). For all practical purposes, the dollar amount you pay for medical care, out of pocket, is close to zero—a fairly low price for health care. We can expect that the quantity demanded of medical care would be greater at zero than at some positive dollar amount.

Second, let's link the *quantity demanded* for medical care in general (which is high if the price of medical care is zero) with the *demand for specific items* that make up medical care. (In our food buffet example, we would link the *quantity demanded* of food with the *demand* for specific food items—shrimp, chocolate ice cream, a Caesar salad, and the like.)

If the quantity demanded of medical care is higher at a zero price than at some positive price, then we would expect the demand for the *specific items* that make up medical care to be higher than it would be if the quantity demanded of medical care were lower. This situation is shown diagrammatically in Exhibit 4. In Exhibit 4(a), the demand for medical care is downward sloping. If the price is zero for health care, then the quantity demanded of medical care is 100 units. But if the price is some positive dollar amount (such as P_1), then the quantity demanded of medical care is 50 units.

Exhibit 4(b) does not show the demand for medical care in general, just the demand for a specific item of medical care: X-rays. Of the two demand curves in panel (b), the first (D_1) is the demand that exists for X-rays if the *quantity demanded of medical care* is 50 units in

EXHIBIT 4

The Price of Medical Care and the Demand for X-rays

(a) If the price of medical care is low (e.g., zero), the quantity demanded of medical care is 100 units. If the price of medical care for you is P_1, the quantity demanded of medical care for you is 50 units. (b) The lower the price of medical care and the higher the quantity demanded of medical care in panel (a), the higher is the demand curve for X-rays in (b). (c) The higher the demand for X-rays, the higher the price of X-rays is.

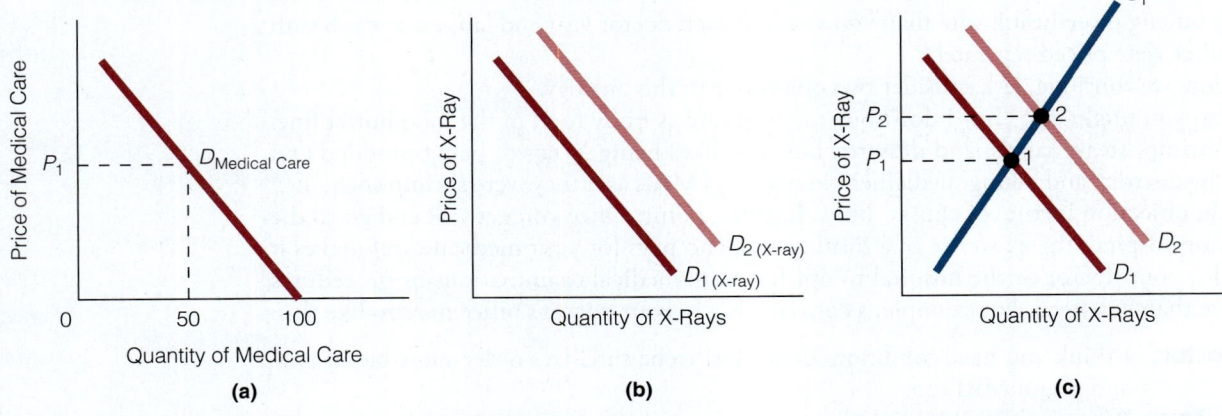

panel (a); it is the demand for X-rays if the price for medical care (shown in panel a) is P_1. The second demand curve (D_2) is the demand curve for X-rays if the *quantity demanded of medical care* is 100 units in panel (a); it is the demand for X-rays if the price for medical care (shown in panel a) is zero.

Here is the point in a nutshell:

1. The *lower* the price of medical care, the higher the quantity demanded of medical care and the demand for X-rays will be. That is,

$$\text{Price of medical care is low} \rightarrow \text{Quantity demanded of medical care is high} \rightarrow$$
$$\text{Demand for X-rays is high}$$

2. The *higher* the price of medical care, the lower the quantity demanded of medical care and the demand for X-rays will be. That is,

$$\text{Price of medical care is high} \rightarrow \text{Quantity demanded of medical care is low} \rightarrow$$
$$\text{Demand for X-rays is low}$$

Now, the question is, what does a high demand for X-rays do to the price of an X-ray? Obviously, it pushes the price upward. [See Exhibit 4(c).]

As a result, the health insurance company finds itself paying more for the X-rays you receive. Can you see what will happen next? The health insurance company makes the argument that, with rising medical costs, the premiums for your coverage need to rise too.

Why is health insurance as expensive as it is? You now have a large part of the answer. Think of the buffet.

1. Suppose food insurance exists. You pay the food insurance company a certain dollar amount each month, and then you purchase all the food you want from your local grocery store. The grocery store sends the bill to your food insurance company. What will happen to the price of food and to the premium you pay for food insurance?

2. In Exhibit 4(a), suppose that the price a person has to pay for medical care is between P_1 and zero. Where would the demand for X-rays in panel (b) be in relationship to D_1 and D_2?

5-6 Application 6: Do You Pay for Good Weather?

Some places in the country are considered to have better weather than others. For example, most people would say the weather in San Diego, California, is better than the weather in Fargo, North Dakota. Often, a person in San Diego will say, "You can't beat the weather today. And the good thing about it is that you don't have to pay a thing for it. It's free."

In one sense, the San Diegan is correct: There is no weather market. Specifically, no one comes around each day and asks San Diegans to pay a certain dollar amount for the weather.

But in another sense, the San Diegan is incorrect: San Diegans do pay for their good weather—albeit indirectly. How do they pay? To enjoy the weather in San Diego on a regular basis, you have to live there; you need to have housing. There is a demand for housing in San Diego, just as there is a demand for housing in other places. Is the demand for housing in San Diego higher than it would be if the weather were not so good? Without the good weather, living in San Diego would not be as pleasurable, and therefore, the demand to live there would be lower. (See Exhibit 5.)

In short, the demand for housing in San Diego is higher because the city enjoys good weather. It follows that the price of housing is higher too (P_2, as opposed to P_1, in Exhibit 5). Thus, San Diegans indirectly pay for their good weather because they pay higher housing prices than they would if the area had bad weather.

Was our representative San Diegan right when he said that the good weather was free?

EXHIBIT 5

Good Weather and the Price of Housing

We show two demand curves, D_1 and D_2. D_1 represents the demand for housing in San Diego if the weather were not so good. The higher demand curve D_2 shows the demand for housing in San Diego given that the weather is good. Notice that the price of housing in San Diego is higher because the weather there is good. Lesson learned: You pay for good weather (in San Diego) in terms of higher house prices.

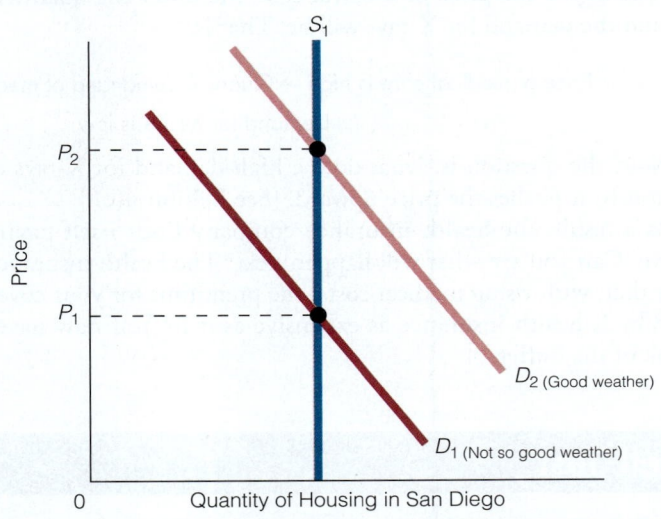

Finding Economics

Good Schools and House Prices Suppose there are two neighborhoods, A and B. The kids who live in neighborhood A go to school A, and the kids who live in neighborhood B go to school B. Currently, school A has a much better academic reputation than school B. Can you find the economics?

This case is really no more than a disguised version of our good-weather example. If school A is better than school B, then the equilibrium price of houses in neighborhood A is likely to be higher than the equilibrium price of similar houses in neighborhood B. Just as we pay for good weather in terms of house prices, we pay for good schools in terms of house prices too.

1. Give an example to illustrate that someone may "pay" for clean air in much the same way that she "pays" for good weather.

2. If people pay for good weather, who ultimately receives the "good-weather payment"?

5-7 Application 7: The Price of an Aisle Seat

Most airlines will reserve an assigned seat for you when you buy a ticket. For example, if you want to buy an airline ticket from American Airlines, you can go online, purchase the ticket, and then look at a graphic that shows unreserved seats. If seat 13A is the one you want and no one has chosen it, then it is yours if you click it in the graphic.

Southwest Airlines does things differently. You do not reserve a seat when you book a flight. You choose a seat when you board the plane. If you are one of the first to board, you have your pick of many seats; if you are one of the last, you have your pick of very few seats.

Keep in mind that aisle seats are more popular than middle seats. Usually, for every aisle seat, there is a middle seat (assuming that the row of seats on each side of the plane consists of 3 seats: window, middle, and aisle). So, if the plane has 50 aisle seats, it also has 50 middle seats. In other words, the supply of middle seats equals the supply of aisle seats.

However, the demand for aisle seats is higher than the demand for middle seats. If price were to equilibrate the middle seats market and the aisle seats market, we would expect the price of an aisle seat to be higher than that of a middle seat. (See Exhibit 6.)

EXHIBIT 6

The Market for Middle and Aisle Seats on Airline Flights

We have assumed that the supply of aisle seats is equal to the supply of middle seats. Because the demand for aisle seats is higher than the demand for middle seats, we conclude that the equilibrium price for an aisle seat is higher than the equilibrium price for a middle seat. In the diagram, P_2 is the equilibrium price for an aisle seat, and P_1 is the equilibrium price for a middle seat.

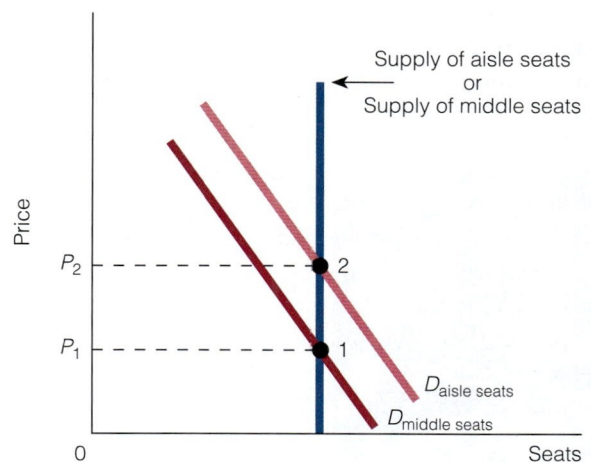

Does Southwest charge more for an aisle seat than a middle seat? Perhaps if you asked the airline this question, its answer would be no. But Southwest does charge more for priority boarding. If you want to board before others, you must choose the Business Select option when purchasing a ticket. If you board before others, you obviously have a larger selection of seats to choose from than later boarders do. Because most people prefer aisle to middle seats, those who board the plane first will probably choose the aisle seats.

So does Business Select come with an additional charge? Yes. On the day we checked, the added charge was $28. In effect, Southwest was charging $28 more for an aisle seat than a middle seat, as we would expect, because the demand for aisle seats is higher than the demand for middle seats whereas the supply of each is the same.

1. If the equilibrium price is $400 for an aisle seat and $350 for a middle seat but an airlines company charges $350 for each seat, we would expect a shortage to appear in the aisle seat market. (More people will want aisle seats than there are aisle seats available.) How will the airlines decide who gets an aisle seat?

2. Suppose the supply of aisle, middle, and window seats is each 100 seats but the demand for aisle seats is greater than the demand for window seats, which, in turn, is greater than the demand for middle seats. If the equilibrium price of an aisle seat is $300, where do the equilibrium prices of middle and window seats stand in relation to this price?

5-8 Application 8: College Superathletes

Suppose a young man, 17 years old, is one of the best high school football players in the country. As a superathlete, the young man will be recruited by football coaches at many colleges and universities. Every one of those schools will likely want its coach to be successful at signing up the young athlete; after all, at many universities, athletics is a moneymaker.

Suppose our superathlete decides to attend college A, where he receives a "full ride"—a full scholarship. How should this full scholarship be viewed? One way is to say that the superathlete is charged zero tuition to attend the college. (In other words, whereas some students pay a price of $30,000 a year to attend, the superathlete pays nothing.)

Another way to view the full scholarship is as a two-step process. First, the college pays the superathlete a dollar amount equal to the full tuition. Second, it charges the superathlete the full tuition. (In other words, the college gives the athlete $30,000 with one hand and then collects it with the other.)

Either way we view the scholarship, the effect is the same for the athlete. For purposes of our analysis, let's view it the second way: as a payment to the athlete, combined with full price being charged. This view leads to two important questions:

1. Can the college pay the athlete more than the full tuition? In other words, if the full tuition is $30,000 a year, can the college pay the athlete, say, $35,000 a year?

2. Is the superathlete being paid what he is worth?

Because of National Collegiate Athletic Association (NCAA) rules, the answer to the first question is essentially no. The NCAA states that a college or university cannot pay a student to attend, and for all practical purposes, the NCAA views payment as anything more than a full scholarship. The NCAA position is that college athletes are amateurs, and amateurs cannot be paid to play their sport.

How does the NCAA rule affect the second question? What if the athlete's worth to the college or university is greater than the dollar amount of the full tuition? For example, suppose the athlete will increase the revenues of the college by $100,000 a year and the full tuition is $30,000 a year. In this case, the NCAA rule is actually a price ceiling (a below-equilibrium imposed price) on what the college may pay an athlete.

What is the effect of this price ceiling? Let's consider the demand (on the part of various colleges) for a single superathlete and the supply of this single superathlete. (See Exhibit 7.) We assume that the supply curve for athletic services is vertical at 1. Then, if the representative college charges $30,000 in tuition because of the NCAA rule, that dollar amount is the effective price ceiling (or wage ceiling). If the single athlete's market equilibrium wage is $35,000 and the NCAA rule did not exist, the athlete's wage would rise to $35,000. This dollar amount is equal to areas $B + C$ in Exhibit 7. The consumers' surplus for the college that buys the athlete's services for $35,000 is obviously equal to area A.

However, the NCAA rule stipulates that the college cannot pay the athlete more than $30,000 (full tuition). So the athlete's payment falls from $35,000 to $30,000, or from areas $B + C$ to simply area C. The college's consumers' surplus then increases to areas $A + B$. Essentially, the NCAA rule transfers part of the athlete's income—area B—to the college in the form of greater consumers' surplus.

Update: Things Have Changed As this book was about to be published, the U.S. Supreme Court on June 21, 2021, in a unanimous decision, sided with college athletes against the NCAA. At issue in the case were the NCAA rules that limited benefits for college players as part of their scholarships. In other words, the athletes were effectively arguing that they were worth more than simply the full-tuition scholarship they received and that they should be "paid" accordingly. The U.S. Supreme Court agreed. The Court decision essentially makes it possible for a university or conference to offer college athletes benefits that cannot be capped by the NCAA. The proviso: The benefits have to be tied to the athlete's education. Exactly what this will entail hasn't yet been fully decided– but there is no doubt that the price ceiling (we discussed in this application) is going to be raised, if not eliminated.

EXHIBIT 7

The College Athlete

The exhibit shows the demand for and supply of a college athlete. If the market wage for the college athlete is $35,000, then the buyer of the athlete—in this case, the college—receives consumers' surplus equal to area A. If the wage can be held down to the tuition cost of attending the college—$30,000 in this example—then the college receives consumers' surplus of areas A + B.

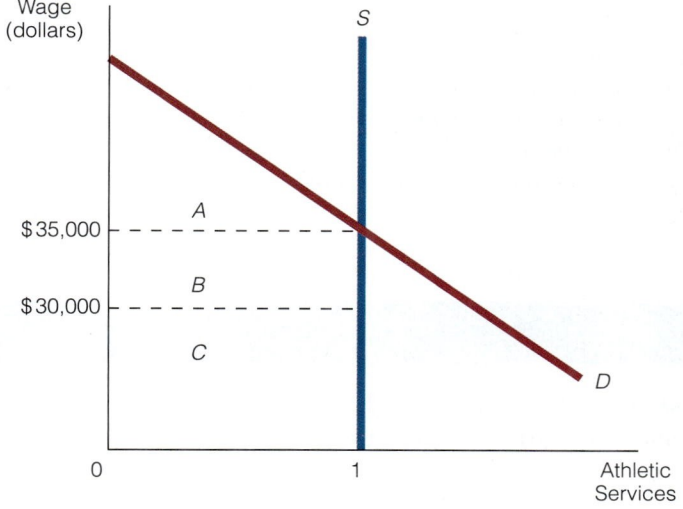

5-9 Application 9: Easier-to-Obtain Loans and Higher Housing Prices

If the federal government wants to make it easier for people to buy houses, one thing it can do is push for lowered lending standards. For example, suppose that lenders require individuals who want a mortgage loan to buy a house to make a down payment of 20 percent of the sale price. Now suppose that the government passes a law stating that no lender can require more than a 5 percent down payment before granting a loan. Will this law make it easier for individuals to buy homes? Not necessarily. The interest rate on a mortgage loan that requires only a 5 percent down payment might be higher than the rate on one that requires a 20 percent down payment.

Can government do *anything* now? Well, it could undertake specific monetary actions that have the effect of lowering interest rates. (We will discuss these actions in detail in a later chapter.)

Then what happens? The government seems to have met its objective of making it easier for individuals to buy houses. After all, prospective buyers now have to come up with only a 5 percent down payment (instead of 20 percent), and they end up paying lower interest rates for the loans they receive. So are home buyers necessarily better off with this kind of government assistance? Not exactly.

By making mortgage loans easier to get, the government has indirectly increased the demand for houses. As the demand for houses rises, so do house prices. In short, making it easier to get home mortgage loans (as described) results in rising home prices, which make buying a house harder:

Lower down payments + Lower interest rates → Easier-to-obtain loans →

Higher demand for houses → Higher house prices

The main point is simply this: Government set out to make buying a home easier for more people by passing laws that forced lenders to accept lower down payments and by undertaking actions to put downward pressure on interest rates. But making it easier for individuals to get loans had the effect of raising the demand for, and the prices of, houses. Higher house prices made it harder for people to buy homes.

Continuing on with the story, suppose government now states that individuals need even more help to get a home because housing prices have risen. So, in its attempt to help people buy a house, government pushes for even lower lending standards (maybe requiring only a 1 percent down payment) and lower interest rates. Will that do the trick? Not likely: The lower lending standards and interest rates will probably stimulate greater demand for housing, leading to even higher housing prices.

1. If lowering lending standards can indirectly raise housing prices, can increasing lending standards lower housing prices? Explain.

2. Suppose anyone who buys a house in a certain year gets to pay $1,000 less in income taxes (assuming that the tax owed is greater than $1,000). Would the tax credit affect house prices? Explain your answer.

5-10 Application 10: Speculators, Price Variability, and Patterns

Think of an abstract good, say, X. Let's suppose that the price of good X initially varies over a month. Sometimes it is $10, other times it is $13, and at other times it is $12. Usually, when prices fluctuate, speculators will enter the market. That's because, when prices fluctuate, there is profit to be earned by buying low and selling high. In terms of our example so far, there is profit to be earned by buying at $10 and selling at $13.

The common view of speculators is that they somehow hurt others by trying to make themselves better off. Well, they certainly might be trying to make themselves better off, but it doesn't necessarily follow that, because they are doing what is in their best interest, others will be made worse off.

To understand why, suppose that on Monday through Wednesday of every week, the price of good X is $10, and on Thursday of every week, the price of good X rises to $14. Clearly, then, there is price variability over part of the week. How will speculators respond to this variability? Obviously, they will buy good X on Monday through Wednesday and sell it on Thursday.

But their buying good X on Monday through Wednesday will drive up the price of good X on those days, and their selling good X on Thursday will drive down the price. In other words, speculators will end up changing the Monday-through-Thursday pattern of the price of good X. No longer will the pattern be $10 on Monday through Wednesday and $14 on Thursday. The price will be higher than $10 on Monday through Wednesday and lower than $14 on Thursday. In fact, speculators will continue to buy and sell good X until the price of good X is the same every day. For example, the price of good X may end up being $11 every day of the week.

Essentially, the speculators have done three things: (1) bought low and sold high; (2) changed the pattern of price from $10 on three days and $14 on one day to $11 for each of four days; and (3) moved some of the supply of good X from certain days to other days.

Now, with this example in mind, let's think of a possible real-world scenario. Suppose that unusually bad weather for growing crops threatens the Midwest of the United States. High prices for food are expected as a result. Are speculators likely to respond to the news of impending bad weather? Most likely, they will translate bad weather into higher food prices. Given their objective to buy low and sell high, they will likely buy certain (food) crops today (before the bad weather hits) and sell those crops later (after the bad weather has hit). Speculators' actions will end up making food a little more expensive today and a little less expensive later. In other words, instead of a loaf of bread being $2 today and $5 later, a loaf of bread may end up being $3.50 both today and later.

What speculators essentially do, then, as a byproduct of buying low and selling high, is "spread out" the pain of bad weather (on food prices) over a longer time. Instead of taking all the "hurt" of high prices after the bad weather has hit, speculators move some of the "hurt" to before the bad weather hits. As a result, there will be less "hurt" after the bad weather hits.

Now, to see even more dramatically what happens as a result of speculators "buying low and selling high," suppose we change our example and have the bad weather result in no crops and thus no food. Under these dire circumstances, wouldn't the activities of the speculators—reallocating the current supply of food away from today to later and thereby changing the pattern of prices—be truly lifesaving?

1. Speculators can benefit themselves and others at the same time. Do you agree or disagree with this statement? Explain your answer with an example.

2. The price of a given good is likely to be less variable with than without speculators. Explain.

5-11 Application 11: Supply and Demand on a Freeway

What does a traffic jam on a busy freeway in any large city have to do with supply and demand? Actually, it has quite a bit to do with supply and demand. Look at the question this way: There is a demand for driving on the freeway and a supply of freeway space. The supply of freeway space is fixed. (Roadways do not expand and contract over a day, week, or month.) The demand, however, fluctuates: It is higher at some times than at others. For example, we would expect the demand for driving on the freeway to be higher at 8 a.m. (rush hour) than at 11 p.m. But even though the demand may vary, the money price for driving on the freeway is always the same: zero. A zero money price means that motorists do not pay tolls to drive on the freeway.

Exhibit 8 shows two demand curves for driving on the freeway: $D_{8\text{a.m.}}$ and $D_{11\text{p.m.}}$. We have assumed the demand at 8 a.m. to be greater than at 11 p.m. We have also assumed that, at $D_{11\text{p.m.}}$ and zero money price, the freeway market clears: The quantity demanded of freeway space equals the quantity supplied. At the higher demand, $D_{8\text{a.m.}}$, this is not the case. At zero money price, a shortage of freeway space exists: The quantity demanded of freeway space is greater than the quantity supplied. The shortage appears as freeway congestion and

EXHIBIT 8

Freeway Congestion, and Supply and Demand

The demand for driving on the freeway is higher at 8 a.m. than at 11 p.m. At zero money price and $D_{11\text{p.m.}}$, the freeway market clears. At zero money price and $D_{8\text{a.m.}}$, there is a shortage of freeway space, which shows up as freeway congestion. At a price (toll) of 70¢, the shortage is eliminated and freeway congestion disappears.

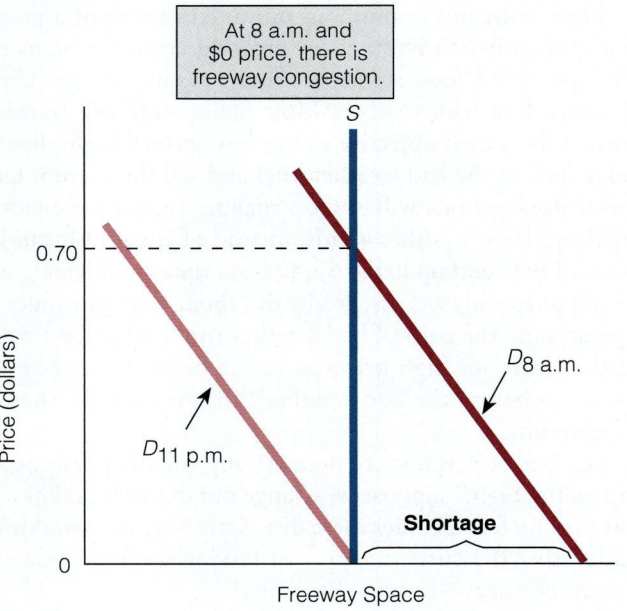

bumper-to-bumper traffic. One way to eliminate the shortage is through an increase in the money price of driving on the freeway at 8 a.m. For example, as Exhibit 8 shows, a toll of 70¢ would clear the freeway market at 8 a.m.

If charging different prices (tolls) on freeways, depending on the time of day, sounds like an unusual idea, consider how Miami Beach hotels price their rooms. They charge different prices for their rooms, depending on the time of year. During the winter months, when the demand for vacationing in Miami Beach is high, the hotels charge higher prices than when the demand is (relatively) low. If different prices were charged for freeway space, depending on the time of day, freeway space would be rationed the same way Miami Beach hotel rooms are rationed.

Finally, consider three alternatives usually proposed to counter freeway congestion:

- *Tolls:* Tolls deal with the congestion problem by adjusting price to its equilibrium level, as shown in Exhibit 8.

- *Building more freeways:* Building more freeways deals with the problem by increasing supply. In Exhibit 8, the supply curve of freeway space would have to be shifted to the right so that there is no longer any shortage of space at 8 a.m.

- *Encouraging carpooling:* More carpooling deals with the problem by decreasing demand. Two people in one car take up less space on a freeway than two people in two cars. In Exhibit 8, if, through carpooling, the demand at 8 a.m. begins to look like the demand at 11 p.m., then there is no longer a shortage of freeway space at 8 a.m.

A final note: A fee to drive in the Central London area was introduced in 2003. Anyone going into or out of the Central London area between 7:00 a.m. and 10:00 p.m. must pay a fee of approximately $20. (Not everyone has to pay the fee. For example, taxi drivers, ambulance drivers, drivers of police vehicles, motorcycle drivers, and bicyclists are exempt. The residents who live in the area receive a 90 percent discount.) Many people have claimed the fee a success because it has cut down on traffic and travel times and reduced pollution in the area.

As of this writing, by 2023, New York City will implement a fee program to drive. Drivers entering Manhattan below 60th Street could pay $10 to $15 a day for cars and possibly double for trucks.

Thinking Like an Economist

It's One of Three The economist knows that when there are buyers and sellers of anything (bread, cars, or freeway space), only three conditions are possible: equilibrium, shortage, or surplus. When the economist sees traffic congestion, the first thing that comes to mind is the shortage of road space. But why is there a shortage? The economist knows that shortages occur at prices below the equilibrium price. In other words, the price of driving on the road is too low.

1. In Exhibit 8, at what price is there a surplus of freeway space at 8 a.m.?

2. If the driving population increases in an area and the supply of freeway space remains constant, what will happen to freeway congestion? Explain your answer.

5-12 Application 12: Are Renters Better Off?

We begin with an analysis of two laws related to the eviction of a renter:

- Under law 1, a renter has 30 days to vacate an apartment after being served with an eviction notice.
- Under law 2, the renter has 90 days to vacate.

Landlords will find it less expensive to rent apartments under law 1 than under law 2. Under law 1, the most money a landlord can lose after serving an eviction notice is 30 days' rent. Under law 2, a landlord can lose up to 90 days' rent. Obviously, losing 90 days' rent is more costly than losing 30 days' rent.

A different supply curve of apartments exists under each law. The supply curve under law 1 (S_1 in Exhibit 9) lies to the right of the supply curve under law 2 (S_2). It is less expensive to supply apartments under law 1 than under law 2.

If the supply curve is different under the two laws, the equilibrium rent will be different too. As shown in Exhibit 9, the equilibrium rent will be lower under law 1 (R_1) than under law 2 (R_2).

So,

- Under law 1, a renter pays lower rent (good) and has fewer days to vacate the apartment (bad).
- Under law 2, a renter pays a higher rent (bad) and has more days to vacate the apartment (good).

Who pays for the additional days to vacate the apartment under law 2? The renter pays for them by paying a higher rent.

EXHIBIT 9

Apartment Rent and the Law

Under law 1, a renter has 30 days to leave an apartment after receiving an eviction notice from his or her landlord. Under law 2, a renter has 90 days to leave an apartment after receiving an eviction notice. The cost to the landlord of renting an apartment is higher under law 2 than law 1, so the supply curve of apartments under law 1 lies to the right of the supply curve of apartments under law 2. Different supply curves mean different rents. Apartment rent is higher under law 2 (R_2) than under law 1 (R_1).

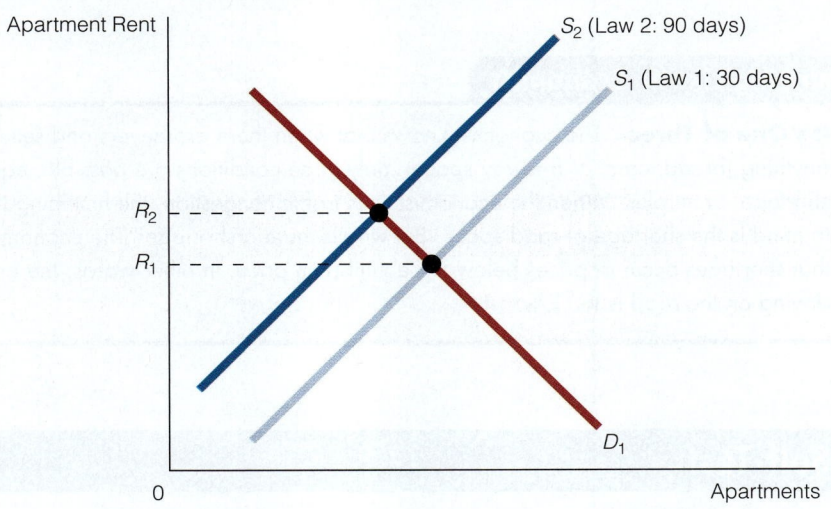

Finding Economics

In an HMO You may frequently hear people complain about their health maintenance organizations (HMOs). Of the diverse and wide-ranging complaints, a common one is that patients usually cannot sue their HMOs in state courts for denial of benefits and poor-quality care. Some people argue that patients should have the right to sue their HMOs.

Let's consider two settings: one in which patients cannot sue their HMOs and one in which they can. If patients cannot sue, an HMO's liability cost is lower than if patients can sue. A difference in liability costs is then reflected in different supply curves.

To illustrate, recall that any single point on a supply curve is the minimum price sellers need to receive for them to be willing and able to sell that unit of a good. Suppose that, when patients cannot sue, an HMO is willing and able to provide health care to John for $300 a month. If patients can sue, is the HMO still willing and able to provide the service for $300 a month? Not likely. Because of the higher liability cost due to patients' ability to sue, the HMO is still willing and able to provide health care to John, but for, say, $350 month, not $300.

Saying that a seller's minimum price for providing a good or service rises is the same as saying that the seller's supply curve has shifted upward and to the left. In other words, the supply curve of HMO-provided health care will shift upward and to the left if patients have the right to sue. This is how the supply curve of apartments moved in Exhibit 8. So, will a difference in supply curves affect the price patients pay for their HMO-provided health care coverage? Yes. One effect of moving from a setting in which patients do not have the right to sue to one in which they do is that patients will have to pay more for their HMO-provided health care coverage.

Economists don't determine whether a patient having the right to sue is good or bad or right or wrong. Economists use their tools (in this instance, supply and demand) to point out that the things people want, such as the right to sue their HMOs, often come with price tags. Individuals must decide whether the price they pay is worth what they receive in return.

1. Economists often say, "There is no such thing as a free lunch." How is this saying related to patients moving from a system in which they cannot sue their HMOs to one in which they can?

2. A professor tells her students that they can have an extra week to complete their research papers. Under what condition are the students better off with the extra week? Can you think of a case where the students would actually be worse off with the extra week?

Office Hours

"Doesn't High Demand Mean High Quantity Demanded?"

Student: The other day in class, you said, "The demand for 10 a.m. classes may be high, but the quantity demanded may not be if the price is high enough." In other words, you were saying that high demand doesn't necessarily mean high quantity demanded. But I thought it did. Could you explain?

Instructor: Let me explain what's going on by first showing you the demand schedule for two goods, A and B:

Good A Demand Schedule		Good B Demand Schedule	
Price	Quantity Demanded	Price	Quantity Demanded
$6	100	$6	200
7	80	7	150
8	60	8	125
9	40	9	90

As you can see from the two schedules, the demand for good B is greater than the demand for good A. In other words, if we were to derive a demand curve for each good (based on its demand schedule), the demand curve for good B would lie farther to the right than the demand curve for good A.

Now, suppose we look at quantity demanded for each good at the price of $6. The quantity demanded of good A (the low-demand good) is 100 units, and the quantity demanded of good B (the high-demand good) is 200 units. What can we conclude? At the same price for each good ($6), the quantity demanded is higher when demand is higher.

But now let's consider quantity demanded for each good when the price of good A is $6 and the price of good B is $9. The quantity demanded of good A (the low-demand good) is 100 units, and the quantity demanded of good B (the high-demand good) is 90 units. In other words, if the price is high enough for good B (the high-demand good), then the quantity demanded of good B may be lower than the quantity demanded of good A (the low-demand good).

Now let's go back and repeat the statement I made in class: "The demand for 10 a.m. classes may be high, but the quantity demanded may not be if the price is high enough." Now do you understand what I was saying?

Student: Yes, I think I do. You were saying that high demand doesn't necessarily mean high quantity demanded if we are dealing with different prices.

Instructor: Yes, that's it.

Points to Remember

1. High demand means high quantity demanded, but only if the prices for the high-demand good and the low-demand good are the same. From our example, at a price of $6, the quantity demanded for the high-demand good B is greater than quantity demanded for the low-demand good A.

2. The quantity demanded for the low-demand good can be higher than the quantity demanded for the high-demand good if the prices for the two goods are not the same and the price for the high-demand good is high enough. From our example, at a price of $9 for good B (the high-demand good), the quantity demanded is lower than the quantity demanded for good A (the low-demand good) at a price of $6.

Chapter Summary

U-Haul Rates and Demand

- We might think that the U-Haul rate to go from location X to location Y would be the same as to go from Y to X, but this isn't always so. If the demand to go from X to Y is greater than the demand to go from Y to X, then the U-Haul rate is likely to be higher going from X to Y than from Y to X.

Subsidizing the Consumption of Anything Can Raise Its Price

- A subsidy placed on the purchase of a good will raise the demand curve for that good by the amount of the subsidy.
- Subsidizing the consumption of a good will often lead to a higher equilibrium price for the good.

10 A.M. Classes in College

- Colleges usually charge the same tuition for a class no matter when it is taken. The supply of seats in the class may be the same for each time slot, but the demand for the class may be different. At least for some classes, the quantity demanded of seats will be greater than the quantity supplied. Thus, some nonprice-rationing device will have to be used to achieve equilibrium.

Why Do Colleges Use GPAs, ACTs, and SATs for Purposes of Admission?

- Colleges and universities charging students less than the equilibrium tuition for admission create a shortage of spaces at their schools. Consequently, colleges and universities have to impose some nonprice-rationing device, such as GPAs or ACT or SAT scores.

Why Is Medical Care So Expensive?

- When it comes to medical care, often three parties are involved: the person who sells medical care, the person who buys medical care, and the person who (directly) pays for the medical care (the third party).
- Once people have paid their medical insurance premium, the price paid thereafter for medical care may amount to no more than a co-payment (usually minimal). For all practical purposes, then, the dollar amount they have to pay out of pocket to get medical care is zero. We thus expect the quantity demanded of medical care to be greater than it would be at some positive dollar amount.

Do You Pay for Good Weather?

- If good weather gives people utility, then the demand for and the price of housing will be higher in a city with good weather than in a city with bad weather, *ceteris paribus*. Thus, people who buy houses in good-weather locations indirectly pay for the good weather.

The Price of an Aisle Seat

- If the supply of aisle and middle seats is the same, but the demand for aisle seats is greater, then the equilibrium price for aisle seats will be greater than the equilibrium price of middle seats.

College Superathletes

- A college superathlete may receive a full scholarship to play a sport at a university, but the full scholarship may be less than the equilibrium wage for the superathlete (because of a mandate that the athlete cannot be paid the difference between his higher equilibrium wage and the dollar amount of his full scholarship). In such a case, the university gains at the expense of the athlete.

Government, Loans, and Housing Prices

- Lower lending standards and lower interest rates make it easier to get a mortgage loan. But as getting a mortgage loan becomes easier, the demand for housing rises. As the demand for housing rises, house prices rise.

Speculators, Price Variability, and Patterns

- Speculators try to make themselves better off by buying a product at a low price and then selling it (later) at a high price. In pursuit of profit, they often reallocate a good from a period where it is in greater supply to a period where it is in lesser supply. As a result of reallocating supply, price patterns are changed too. As an example, suppose unusually bad weather for growing crops threatens the Midwest of the United States. High prices for food are expected as a result. Given their objective to buy low and sell high, speculators will likely buy certain (food) crops today (before the bad weather hits) and sell those crops later (after the bad weather has hit). Speculators' actions will end up making food a little more expensive today and a little less expensive later. Instead of taking all the "hurt" of high prices after the bad weather has hit, speculators move some of the "hurt" to before the bad weather hits. As a result, there will be less "hurt" after the bad weather hits.

Supply and Demand on a Freeway

- The effect of a disequilibrium price (below the equilibrium price) for driving on a freeway is a traffic jam. If the price to drive on a freeway is $0 and, at this price, the quantity demanded of freeway space is greater than the quantity supplied, then a shortage of freeway space will result, in the form of freeway congestion.

Are We Really Making Renters Better Off?

- If renters have 90 days instead of 30 days to vacate an apartment, the supply curve of apartments will shift upward and to the left. As a result, renters will pay higher rents when they have 90 days to vacate an apartment.

Questions and Problems

1. Explain how lower lending standards and lower interest rates can lead to higher house prices.
2. If there were no third parties in medical care, medical care prices would be lower. Do you agree or disagree? Explain your answer.
3. Three prestigious universities all charge relatively high tuition. Still, each uses ACT and SAT scores as admission criteria. Is charging a relatively high tuition and using standardized test scores as admission criteria inconsistent? Explain your answer.
4. What do the applications about freeway congestion and 10 a.m. classes have in common?
5. Economics has been called the "dismal science" because it sometimes "tells us" that things are true when we would prefer them to be false. For example, although there are no free lunches, might we prefer that there were? Was there anything in this chapter that you learned was true that you would have preferred to be false? If so, identify it. Then explain why you would have preferred it to be false.
6. In the discussion of health care and the right to sue your HMO, we state, "Saying that a seller's minimum price for providing a good or service rises is the same as saying that the seller's supply curve has shifted upward and to the left." Does it follow that, if a seller's minimum price falls, the supply curve shifts downward and to the right? Explain your answer.
7. Application 6 explains that even though no one directly and explicitly pays for good weather ("here is $100 for the good weather"), you may pay for good weather indirectly, such as through housing prices. Identify three other things (besides good weather) that you believe people pay for indirectly.
8. Suppose there exists a costless way to charge drivers on the freeway. Under this costless system, tolls on the freeway would be adjusted according to traffic conditions. For example, when traffic is usually heavy, as it is from 6:30 a.m. to 9:00 a.m. on a weekday, the toll to drive on the freeway would be higher than when traffic is light. In other words, freeway tolls would be used to equate the demand for freeway space with its supply. Would you be in favor of such a system to replace our current (largely zero price) system? Explain your answer.
9. Wilson walks into his economics class 10 minutes late because he couldn't find a place to park. Because of his tardiness, he doesn't hear the professor tell the class that there will be a quiz at the next session. Consequently, Wilson is unprepared for the quiz and ends up failing it. Might Wilson's failing the quiz have anything to do with the price of parking?
10. University A charges more for a class for which there is high demand than for a class for which there is low demand. University B charges the same for all classes. All other things being equal between the two universities, which university would you prefer to attend? Explain your answer.
11. Suppose the equilibrium wage for a college athlete is $40,000, but the university can offer only $22,000 (full tuition). How might the university administrators, coaches, or university alumni lure the college athlete to choose their school over others?
12. Consider the theater in which a Broadway play is performed. If tickets for all seats are the same price (say, $200), what economic effect might arise?

Chapter 5 Supply, Demand, and Price: Applications

13. What is the relationship between the probability of a person being admitted to the college of his choice and the tuition the college charges?
14. Aliyah is flying from Albuquerque, New Mexico, to Dallas, Texas, on a commercial airliner. She asks for an aisle seat, but only middle seats are left. Why aren't any aisle seats left? (*Hint:* The airline charges the same price for an aisle seat as a middle seat.)
15. Speculation (on prices) leads to gains for the speculator and losses for others. Do you agree or disagree? Explain your answer.
16. Explain why subsidizing the purchase of good X could end up raising the price of good X.

Working with Numbers and Graphs

1. Diagrammatically show and explain why there is a shortage of classroom space for some college classes and a surplus for others.
2. Jacob has been trying to sell his house for six months, but so far he has had no buyers. Draw the market for Jacob's house.
3. Think of two types of books, A and B. Book A can be purchased new by someone and resold as a used book. Book B can only be purchased new by someone. (It cannot be resold as a used book.) All other things being equal between the two books, draw the demand curve for each book.
4. As price declines, quantity demanded rises but quantity supplied does not change. Draw the supply and demand curves that represent this state of affairs.
5. As price declines, quantity demanded rises and quantity supplied falls. Draw the supply and demand curves that represent this state of affairs.
6. Explain diagrammatically why a good whose consumption is subsidized is likely to sell for a higher price than a good whose consumption is not subsidized.

Introduction

Government economists often collect and analyze the latest economic data. Their analyses include computing important economic measurements such as the inflation rate and the unemployment rate. Our elected representatives and certain government officials then use these measurements in formulating economic policy. The structure and timing of that economic policy often affect you in your roles as buyer, seller, taxpayer, and employee.

6-1 Measuring the Price Level

There is a difference between *price* and the *price level*. The word price refers to a single price, such as the price of apples or the price of oranges. The **price level** is a weighted average of all the prices of all the goods and services in the economy. The key phrase in that definition is "a weighted average of all the prices." Here is a rough way of thinking about a price level. Suppose an economy consists of three goods: apples, oranges, and pears. Suppose also that the prices of apples, oranges, and pears are 50¢, 60¢, and 80¢ cents, respectively. Then the average price of these three goods is 63¢. That is also the price level.

6-1a Using the CPI to Compute the Price Level

Economists measure the price level by constructing a **price index**. One major price index is the **Consumer Price Index (CPI)**.[1] The CPI is based on a representative group of goods and services, called the *market basket*, purchased by a typical household. The market basket includes

Price Level
A weighted average of the prices of all goods and services.

Price Index
A measure of the price level.

Consumer Price Index (CPI)
The weighted average of prices of a specific set of goods and services purchased by a typical household; a widely cited index number for the price level.

---

[1] Although changes in the CPI are often used to compute the change in the so-called cost of living, one's cost of living usually involves more than what is measured by the CPI. For example, the CPI does not include income taxes, yet income taxes are a part of the cost of living for most people.

Chapter 6 Macroeconomic Measurements, Part I: Prices and Unemployment

eight major categories of goods and services: (1) food and beverages, (2) housing, (3) apparel, (4) transportation, (5) medical care, (6) recreation, (7) education and communication, and (8) other goods and services.

To simplify our discussion, we assume that the market basket includes only three goods instead of the many goods it actually contains. Our market basket consists of 10 pens, 5 shirts, and 3 pairs of shoes.

To calculate the CPI, first calculate the total dollar expenditure on the market basket in two years: the current year and the base year. The **base year** is a benchmark year that serves as a basis of comparison for prices in other years.

In Exhibit 1, we multiply the quantity of each good in the market basket (column 1) by its current-year price (column 2) to compute the current-year expenditure on each good (column 3). By adding the dollar amounts in column 3, we obtain the total dollar expenditure on the market basket in the current year. This amount is $167.

To find the total expenditure on the market basket in the base year, we multiply the quantity of each good in the market basket (column 1A) by its base-year price (column 2A) and then add all these products (column 3A). This gives us $67.

To find the CPI, we use the formula

$$\text{CPI} = \left(\frac{\text{Total dollar expenditure on market basket in current year}}{\text{Total dollar expenditure on market basket in base year}} \right) \times 100$$

As shown in Exhibit 1, the current-year CPI for our tiny economy is 249.

Base Year
The year chosen as a point of reference or basis of comparison for prices in other years; a benchmark year.

EXHIBIT 1

Computing the Consumer Price Index

This exhibit uses hypothetical data to show how the CPI is computed. To find the total dollar expenditure on market basket in current year, we multiply the quantities of goods in the market basket by their current-year prices and add all the products. This gives us $167. To find the total dollar expenditure on market basket in base year, we multiply the quantities of goods in the market basket by their base-year prices and add all the products. This gives us $67. We then divide $167 by $67 and multiply the quotient by 100.

(1) Market Basket		(2) Current-Year Prices (Per Item)		(3) Current-Year Expenditures	(1A) Market Basket		(2A) Base-Year Prices (Per Item)		(3A) Base-Year Expenditures
10 pens	×	$0.70	=	$ 7.00	10 pens	×	$ 0.20	=	$ 2.00
5 shirts	×	14.00	=	70.00	5 shirts	×	7.00	=	35.00
3 pairs of shoes	×	30.00	=	90.00	3 pairs of shoes	×	10.00	=	30.00
				$167.00					**$67.00**

↗ Total dollar expenditure on market basket in current year

↗ Total dollar expenditure on market basket in base year

$$\text{CPI} = \left(\frac{\text{Total dollar expenditure on market basket in current year}}{\text{Total dollar expenditure on market basket in base year}} \right) \times 100$$

$$= \left(\frac{\$167}{\$67} \right) \times 100$$

$$= 249$$

EXHIBIT 2

CPI, 1982–2021

Year	CPI	Year	CPI
1982	96.5	2002	179.9
1983	99.6	2003	184.0
1984	103.9	2004	188.9
1985	107.6	2005	195.3
1986	109.6	2006	201.6
1987	113.6	2007	207.342
1988	118.3	2008	215.303
1989	124.0	2009	214.537
1990	130.7	2010	218.056
1991	136.2	2011	224.939
1992	140.3	2012	229.594
1993	144.5	2013	232.957
1994	148.2	2014	236.736
1995	152.4	2015	237.017
1996	156.9	2016	240.007
1997	160.5	2017	245.120
1998	163.0	2018	251.107
1999	166.6	2019	255.657
2000	172.2	2020	258.811
2001	177.1	2021	269.195

Source: The data were reported at the website of the U.S. Bureau of Labor Statistics. Beginning in 2007, the Bureau of Labor Statistics began reporting the CPI to three decimal points. The CPI identified in the exhibit for 2021 is for May 2021.

The CPI for the United States for the years 1982 to 2021 is shown in Exhibit 2.

More About the Base Year Recall that the base year is a benchmark year that serves as a basis of comparison for prices in other years. The CPI in the base year is 100. How do we know this? Look again at the formula for calculating the CPI: The numerator is *Total dollar expenditure on market basket in current year*, and the denominator is *Total dollar expenditure on market basket in base year*. In the base year, the current year *is* the base year, so the numerator and denominator are the same. The ratio is 1, and $1 \times 100 = 100$.

Notice, however, that in Exhibit 2, there is no year in which the CPI is 100. This does not mean that there is no base year. Instead, the base year has been defined by the government to be the period 1982–1984. Look at the CPI in each of the years 1982, 1983, and 1984. If we add the CPIs for the three years and divide by 3, we get 100: $(96.5 + 99.6 + 103.9) / 3 = 100$.

When We Know the CPI for Various Years, We Can Compute the Percentage Change in Prices To find the percentage change in prices between any two years, use the formula

$$\text{Percentage change in prices} = \left(\frac{\text{CPI}_{\text{later year}} - \text{CPI}_{\text{earlier year}}}{\text{CPI}_{\text{earlier year}}} \right) \times 100$$

For example, Exhibit 2 shows that the CPI in 1990 was 130.7 and the CPI in 2005 was 195.3. The percentage change in prices over this period was therefore 49.43 percent:

$$\text{Percentage change} = \left(\frac{195.3 - 130.7}{130.7} \right) \times 100 = 49.43$$

This means that prices increased 49.43 percent from 1990 to 2005. You can think of the percentage change in prices in this way: What cost $1 in 1990 cost approximately $1.49 in 2005.

6-1b Inflation and the CPI

Inflation
An increase in the price level.

Real Income
Nominal income adjusted for price changes.

Nominal Income
The current dollar amount of a person's income.

Inflation is an increase in the price level and is usually measured on an annual basis. The *inflation rate* is the positive percentage change in the price level on an annual basis. When you know the inflation rate, you can find out whether your income is (1) keeping up with, (2) not keeping up with, or (3) more than keeping up with inflation. How you are doing depends on whether your income is rising by (1) the same percentage as, (2) a smaller percentage than, or (3) a greater percentage than the inflation rate. When you make this computation and comparison, you are determining your real income for different years. **Real income** is a person's **nominal income** (or current dollar amount of income) adjusted for any change in prices. Real income is computed as follows:

$$\text{Real income} = \left(\frac{\text{Nominal income}}{\text{CPI}} \right) \times 100$$

Case 1. Keeping Up With Inflation: Real Income Stays Constant Jim earns $50,000 in year 1 and $55,000 in year 2. The CPI is 100 in year 1 and 110 in year 2, so the inflation rate is 10 percent: $[(110 - 100)/100] \times 100 = 10$. Jim's income has risen by 10 percent: $[(\$55,000 - \$50,000)/\$50,000] \times 100 = 10$. Jim's income has risen by the same percentage as the inflation rate, so he has kept up with inflation. This is evident when we see that Jim's real income is the same in both years. In year 1, it is $50,000, and in year 2, it is $50,000 too:

$$\text{Real income year 1} = \left(\frac{\$50,000}{100}\right) \times 100 = \$50,000$$

$$\text{Real income year 2} = \left(\frac{\$55,000}{110}\right) \times 100 = \$50,000$$

Case 2. Not Keeping Up With Inflation: Real Income Falls Madison earns $50,000 in year 1 and $52,000 in year 2. The CPI is 100 in year 1 and 110 in year 2. Madison's income has risen by 4 percent, and the inflation rate is 10 percent. Her income has risen by a smaller percentage than the inflation rate, so she has not kept up with inflation. Madison's real income has fallen from $50,000 in year 1 to $47,273 in year 2:

$$\text{Real income year 1} = \left(\frac{\$50,000}{100}\right) \times 100 = \$50,000$$

$$\text{Real income year 2} = \left(\frac{\$52,000}{110}\right) \times 100 = \$47,273$$

Case 3. More Than Keeping Up With Inflation: Real Income Rises Kolb earns $50,000 in year 1 and $60,000 in year 2. The CPI is 100 in year 1 and 110 in year 2. Kolb's income has risen by 20 percent, and the inflation rate is 10 percent. His income has risen by a greater percentage than the inflation rate, so he has more than kept up with inflation. Kolb's real income has risen from $50,000 in year 1 to $54,545 in year 2:

$$\text{Real income year 1} = \left(\frac{\$50,000}{100}\right) \times 100 = \$50,000$$

$$\text{Real income year 2} = \left(\frac{\$60,000}{110}\right) \times 100 = \$54,545$$

6-1c The Personal Consumption Expenditure (PCE) Index

The CPI, as we stated earlier, is based on a representative group of goods and services called the market basket. This market basket is assumed to be fixed—for example, a fixed (unchanging) number of units of good X in the basket, a fixed number of units of Y, and so on.

Now, if the number of units of the different goods and services is fixed and then if the price of one good rises (say, the price of good X), it is assumed that consumers just buy the same number of units of that good at the higher price. For example, they used to buy 10 units of good X at $1 each, but now they buy 10 units of good X at $1.25 each. In reality, though, what often happens is that as the price of one good rises, consumers might buy less of that good and more of another. In other words, they may make substitutions. As the price of steak rises, they may buy less steak and more chicken. The CPI, however, does not account for these substitutions.

One price index that does account for substitutions is the personal consumption expenditure (PCE) index. The PCE index not only takes into account the change in prices of goods, but also the change in the quantity of goods purchased. In other words, the quantities of the goods and services in the PCE basket are continually updated to reflect changes in spending patterns. In the United States, the PCE index is the preferred price index of monetary policymakers.

> **Finding Economics**
>
> **In Your Paycheck** Ella comments to a friend that she recently received a $5-an-hour raise at work. Her friend congratulates her and then goes on to talk about how prices have been rising lately. Where is the economics?
>
> Obviously, if Ella's nominal (or money) income has risen, and prices have risen too, then Ella's real income might have changed. Has her real income risen, fallen, or stayed the same? The answer depends on how much her nominal income has risen relative to how much prices have gone up. Let's say her nominal income has risen by 5 percent and prices have increased by 2 percent. In that case, Ella's real income has gone up.

6-1d Converting Dollars from One Year to Another

Suppose someone says, "Back in 1960, I had an annual salary of $10,000 a year. That sure isn't much these days." Of course, the person is right in one sense: An annual salary of $10,000 doesn't buy much these days, but was it a good salary back in 1960? It certainly could have been, because prices in 1960 weren't as high as they are today. For example, the CPI was 29.6 in 1960 and 269.195 in 2021. In other words, one of the things that make a salary good or not so good is what the salary can buy.

Now, suppose someone tells you that a $10,000 salary in 1960 is the same as an $90,944 salary today. Would you then be better able to say whether the $10,000 salary was good or not so good? Of course, because you understand what it means to earn $90,944 today. Economists convert a past salary into today's salary by using this formula:

$$\text{Salary in today's (current) dollars} = \text{Salary}_{\text{earlier year}} \times \left(\frac{\text{CPI}_{\text{current year}}}{\text{CPI}_{\text{earlier year}}}\right)$$

Assume that the CPI today is the same as the most recent CPI in Exhibit 2 (the CPI for 2021). Using the formula, we get

$$\text{Salary in 2021 dollars} = \$10{,}000 \times \left(\frac{269.195}{29.6}\right) = \$90{,}944$$

> **Finding Economics**
>
> **In What Grandfather Says** Lauren, who is 25, told her grandfather that she just got a job that pays $75,000 a year. Her grandfather said, "That's a lot of money. When I got my first real job I earned only $18,000 a year. You're earning a whole lot more than I did." Where is the economics?
>
> Income earned in one period cannot always be adequately compared to income earned in another period. To make the proper comparison, we need to convert the dollars earned in one period into dollars earned in the other period. Lauren is earning $75,000 today, but her grandfather earned $18,000 (in his first job) many years ago. Obviously, earning $18,000 many years ago is not the same as earning $18,000 today, so Lauren's grandfather's statement that she is earning a whole lot more than he did might not be accurate.

Economics 24/7

The Beatles at Shea Stadium

What I remember most about the concert was that we were so far away from the audience. And screaming had become the thing to do. Everybody screamed.

—Ringo Starr

It was Sunday, August 15, 1965. The Beatles—John, Paul, George, and Ringo—took a Wells Fargo armored truck to Shea Stadium, home of the New York Mets baseball team from 1964 to 2008 and to the New York Jets football team from 1964 to 1983. Awaiting them were 55,600 screaming fans. Two thousand security personnel were at the stadium to handle the crowd.

It was the first stop on the Beatles U.S. tour, which ran from August 15 to August 31, 1965. It was the first concert to be held at a major stadium. The set listed such Beatles' favorites as the following:

"Twist and Shout"
"She's a Woman"
"Ticket to Ride"
"Help!"
"Can't Buy Me Love"
"Hard Day's Night"

Most tickets were priced between $4.10 and $5.65. Many tickets were priced at $5.10. That sounds like a pretty cheap ticket price nowadays. But what was a $5.10 ticket to see the Beatles in 1965 comparable to in 2021? We use the following formula to find out:

$$\text{Ticket in 2021 dollars} = \$5.10 \times \left(\frac{269.195}{31.5}\right) = \$43.58$$

Buying a $5.10 ticket to see the Beatles at Shea Stadium in 1965 was the same as buying a $43.58 ticket in 2021. Who knew that you could see the Beatles at such a historic event for so little?

Economics 24/7

Houses for $30,000 and Gas at 35¢ a Gallon

Suppose a house back in 1961 sold for $30,000. Sounds cheap, doesn't it? But if we don't adjust those past dollars in terms of today's dollars, we get a false impression of how "cheap" things were. A house that sold for $30,000 in 1961 is equivalent to a house selling for $270,000 in 2021. In other words, $30,000 in 1961 is equal to $270,000 in 2021.

What people often forget is that dollars in the past are not the same as dollars in the present if prices have changed between the past and the present. Back when John Kennedy was president of the United States, he earned a salary of $100,000 a year. That would be equivalent to earning slightly more than $900,000 today. But the current president of the United States earns $400,000 a year. In other words, the president of the United States in 1961 earned more than the current president of the United States earns. That is an odd sentence to read, and hard concept to get across, unless you understand that dollars in 1961 aren't the same dollars as the

(Continued)

dollars today. That is why it is so important to take dollars in the past and convert them into dollars today so that a meaningful comparison can be made.

Sometimes you hear from people who lived during the late 1950s and early 1960s how "cheap" gas was. They might say, "I remember when gas was 35¢ a gallon." That sounds cheap today, but 35¢ in 1961 is not the same as 35¢ today. In 2021, it was the same as $3.15, which is what gas was selling for in some parts of the United States in 2021. It's hard for many people to believe that when they were buying gas in 2021 for $3.15 that was like paying 35¢ a gallon back in 1961.

1. Explain how the CPI is calculated.
2. What is a base year?
3. In year 1, your annual income is $45,000 and the CPI is 143.6; in year 2, your annual income is $51,232 and the CPI is 150.7. Has your real income risen, fallen, or remained constant? Explain your answer.

6-2 Measuring Unemployment

Every month, the government surveys thousands of households to gather information about labor market activities. It uses the information from the survey to derive the number of Americans who are unemployed.

6-2a Who Are the Unemployed?

The total population of the United States can be divided into two broad groups (see Exhibit 3). One group consists of persons who are (1) under 16 years of age, (2) in the armed forces, or (3) institutionalized (in a prison, mental institution, or home for the aged). The second group, which consists of all others in the total population, is called the *civilian noninstitutional population*.

The civilian noninstitutional population, in turn, can be divided into two groups: persons *not in the labor force* and persons in the *civilian labor force*. (Economists often refer to the latter group as, simply, the labor force instead of the civilian labor force.) Thus,

Civilian noninstitutional population = Persons not in the labor force + Civilian labor force

- Persons not in the labor force are neither working nor looking for work. In this category are, for example, people who are retired, who are engaged in housework in their own home, or who choose not to work.

EXHIBIT 3

Breakdown of the U.S. Population and the Labor Force

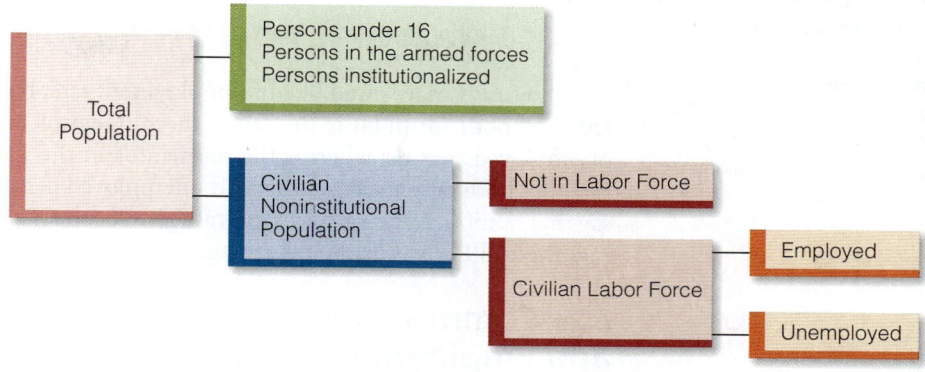

- Persons in the civilian labor force fall into one of two categories: *employed* or *unemployed*. That is,

    Civilian labor force = Employed persons + Unemployed persons

According to the Bureau of Labor Statistics (BLS), employed persons consist of the following groups:

- All persons who did any work for pay or profit during the survey reference week. (The survey used to measure employment and unemployment is the Current Population Survey, a monthly survey conducted for the BLS by the U.S. Census Bureau.)
- All persons who did at least 15 hours of unpaid work in a family-operated enterprise.
- All persons who were temporarily absent from their regular jobs because of illness, vacation, bad weather, industrial dispute, or various personal reasons.

According to the BLS, unemployed persons consist of the following groups:

- All persons who did not have jobs, who made specific active efforts to find a job during the prior four weeks, and who were available for work.
- All persons who were not working and who were waiting to be called back to a job from which they had been temporarily laid off.

6-2b The Unemployment Rate and the Employment Rate

The **unemployment rate** is the percentage of the civilian labor force that is unemployed. It is equal to the number of unemployed persons divided by the civilian labor force:

$$\text{Unemployment rate (U)} = \frac{\text{Number of unemployed persons}}{\text{Civilian labor force}}$$

The **employment rate** (sometimes referred to as the *employment–population ratio*) is the percentage of the civilian noninstitutional population that is employed. It is equal to the number of employed persons divided by the civilian noninstitutional population:

$$\text{Employment rate (E)} = \frac{\text{Number of employed persons}}{\text{Civilian noninstitutional population}}$$

Unemployment Rate
The percentage of the civilian force that is unemployed: Unemployment rate = Number of unemployed persons ÷ Civilian labor force

Employment Rate
The percentage of the civilian noninstitutional population that is employed: Employment rate = Number of employed persons ÷ Civilian noninstitutional population.

Labor Force Participation Rate (LFPR)
The percentage of the civilian noninstitutional population that is in the civilian labor force: Labor force participation rate = Civilian labor force ÷ Civilian noninstitutional population.

Finally, the **labor force participation rate (LFPR)** is the percentage of the civilian noninstitutional population that is in the civilian labor force:

$$\text{Labor force participation rate (LFPR)} = \frac{\text{Civilian labor force}}{\text{Civilian noninstitutional population}}$$

The LFPR may sound like the employment rate, but it is different. Although the denominator in both formulas is the same, the numerator in the employment rate is the number of employed persons whereas the numerator in the LFPR is the civilian labor force (which includes both employed persons and unemployed persons). For this reason, some economists say that, although the employment rate gives us the percentage of the population that is working, the LFPR gives us the percentage of the population that is *willing to work*.

6-2c Common Misconceptions About the Unemployment and Employment Rates

Many people mistakenly think that if the unemployment rate is 7 percent, the employment rate must be 93 percent. Their assumption is that the unemployment rate plus the employment rate must equal 100 percent. But the unemployment and employment rates do not add up to 100 percent because the denominator of the unemployment rate is not the same as the denominator of the employment rate. The unemployment rate is a *percentage of the civilian labor force*. The employment rate is a *percentage of the civilian noninstitutional population*, which is a larger number than the civilian labor force.

6-2d Reasons for Unemployment

Usually, we think of an unemployed person as someone who has been fired or laid off from his or her job. Certainly, some unemployed persons fit this description, but not all of them do. According to the BLS, an unemployed person may fall into one of four categories:

1. *Job loser.* This person was employed in the civilian labor force and was either fired or laid off. Most unemployed persons fall into this category.
2. *Job leaver.* This person was employed in the civilian labor force and quit the job. For example, if Jim quit his job with company *X* and is looking for a better job, he is a job leaver.
3. *Reentrant.* This person was previously employed, hasn't worked for some time and is currently reentering the labor force.
4. *New entrant.* This person has never held a full-time job for two weeks or longer and is now in the civilian labor force looking for a job.

In sum,

$$\text{Unemployed persons} = \text{Job losers} + \text{Job leavers} + \text{Reentrants} + \text{New entrants}$$

6-2e Discouraged Workers

Suppose Zachary is fired from his job at company *A* in September, and he looks for a job for about six months. During this time, he is considered an unemployed person and is counted in the calculation of the unemployment rate. At the end of the sixth month, Zachary is discouraged; he doesn't think he will ever find a job, and he stops looking. A month passes, and he still is not looking for a job. Is Zachary considered an unemployed person? The answer is no. To be an unemployed person, you have to meet certain conditions, one of which is that you have to be actively looking for work. But Zachary isn't actively looking for work, and he isn't waiting to be called back to a job or to report to a job. So Zachary isn't unemployed, and for that reason he does not get counted in the calculation of the unemployment rate.

The Bureau of Labor Statistics (BLS) considers Zachary a *discouraged worker*. According to the BLS, discouraged workers are "persons not in the labor force who want and are available for a job and who have looked for work sometime in the past 12 months (or since the end of their last job if they held one within the past 12 months), but who are not currently looking because they believe there are no jobs available or there are none for which they would qualify."[2] You may think that, for all practical purposes, a discouraged worker is the same as an unemployed person, because neither has a job. But they aren't the same for calculating the unemployment rate. The unemployed person gets counted, but the discouraged worker does not.

Some economists think that, because discouraged workers are not considered unemployed, the unemployment rate is biased downward. Consequently, it doesn't really give us a good fix on the "real" unemployment problem in society.

6-2f Types of Unemployment

There are several different types of unemployment.

Frictional Unemployment Every day, demand conditions change in some markets, causing qualified individuals with transferable skills to leave some jobs and move to others. To illustrate, suppose there are two computer firms, A and B. For some reason, the demand falls for firm A's computers and rises for firm B's computers. Consequently, firm A produces fewer computers. With fewer computers being produced, firm A doesn't need as many employees, so it fires some employees. By contrast, firm B is producing more computers. With more computers being produced, firm B hires additional employees. The employees fired from firm A have skills that they can transfer to firm B; after all, both firms produce computers. However, it takes time for people to make the transfer. During this time, they are said to be frictionally unemployed.

Frictional unemployment is unemployment that is due to the natural so-called frictions in the economy and that is caused by changing market conditions and represented by qualified individuals with transferable skills who change jobs. The frictional unemployment rate (U_F) is the percentage of the labor force that is frictionally unemployed:

$$U_F = \frac{\text{Number of frictionally unemployed persons}}{\text{Civilian labor force}}$$

A dynamic, changing economy like that of the United States always has frictional unemployment. Many economists believe that the basic cause of frictional unemployment is imperfect or incomplete information, which prevents individuals from leaving one job and finding another instantly. For example, imagine an economy with 1,000 job vacancies and 1,000 persons qualified to fill the jobs. Some unemployment is likely because not every one of the 1,000 job seekers will know where the available jobs are. Nor will all employers give the job to the first applicant who knocks on the door. Employers don't know whether better applicants are around the corner. Matching qualified workers with the available jobs takes time.

Structural Unemployment Unemployment due to structural changes in the economy that eliminate some jobs and create others for which the unemployed are unqualified is called structural unemployment. Most economists argue that structural unemployment is largely the consequence of automation (labor-saving devices) and long-lasting shifts in demand.

Frictional Unemployment
Unemployment that is due to the natural so-called frictions in the economy and that is caused by changing market conditions and represented by qualified individuals with transferable skills who change jobs.

Structural Unemployment
Unemployment due to structural changes in the economy that eliminate some jobs and create others for which the unemployed are unqualified.

---

[2] See *BLS Information* (U.S. Bureau of Labor Statistics, February 28, 2008).

The structurally unemployed differ from the frictionally unemployed mainly in that they do not have transferable skills. Their choice is between prolonged unemployment and retraining. For example, suppose automobile workers are being laid off and the demand for computer analysts is rising. If the automobile workers do not currently have the skills needed to become computer analysts, they are structurally unemployed. The structural unemployment rate (U_S) is the percentage of the labor force that is structurally unemployed:

$$U_S = \frac{\text{Number of structurally unemployed persons}}{\text{Civilian labor force}}$$

Natural Unemployment Adding the frictional unemployment rate and the structural unemployment rate gives the natural unemployment rate (or natural rate of unemployment, U_N):

Natural unemployment rate (U_N) = Frictional unemployment rate (U_F) + Structural unemployment rate (U_S)

Currently, most economists estimate the natural unemployment rate at between 4.0 and 5.0 percent.

Natural Unemployment
Unemployment caused by frictional and structural factors in the economy: Natural unemployment rate = Frictional unemployment rate + Structural unemployment rate.

6-2g The Natural Unemployment Rate and Full Employment

What do you think of when you hear the term "full employment"? Most people think *full employment* means that the actual or reported unemployment rate is zero. But a dynamic, changing economy can never have full employment of this type because of the frictional and structural changes that continually occur. In fact, it is natural for some unemployment to exist—some natural unemployment, that is. For this reason, economists *do not* equate full employment with a zero unemployment rate. Instead, **full employment** exists *when the economy is operating at its natural unemployment rate*. For example, if the natural unemployment rate is 5 percent, then full employment exists when the unemployment rate (in the economy) is 5 percent. In other words, the economy can be operating at full employment and some people will still be unemployed.

Full Employment
The condition that exists when the unemployment rate is equal to the natural unemployment rate.

Economics 24/7

Who Should Be Considered Unemployed?

Start with the official unemployment rate. In October 2020, the official unemployment rate was 6.9 percent.

Some economists argue that this 6.9 percent unemployment rate is not the most nearly accurate measurement of the degree of labor utilization in the economy. For example, because discouraged workers are not counted as officially unemployed, obviously, some people want to work but are not working. Thus, labor is not fully being utilized; it is being *underutilized*.

Discouraged workers are a subset of a larger group called *marginally attached workers*. According to the Bureau of Labor Statistics, marginally attached workers are persons not in the labor force who want and are available for work, and who have looked for a job sometime in the prior 12 months (or since the end of their last job if they held one within the past 12 months), but were not counted as unemployed because they had not searched for work in the four weeks preceding the survey. When asked why they didn't search for work, they might say "for family or transportation reasons."

As we stated earlier in this chapter, discouraged workers, according to the BLS, are persons not in the labor force who want and are available for a job and who have looked for work sometime in the past 12 months (or since the end of their last job if they held one within the past 12 months), but who are not currently looking because they believe that there are no jobs available or there are none for which they would qualify. When asked why they didn't search for work, they usually state some job-related reason, such as "there are no jobs to be had, or there are no jobs for which I qualify."

If we count all marginally attached workers (not just discouraged workers) as unemployed, the unemployment rate in October 2020 rises to 8.0 percent. Some argue that this number is a better measure of labor underutilization in the economy than the official unemployment rate (or the unemployment rate with discouraged workers only and not all marginally attached workers).

Finally, if we add in those persons who have had to settle for part-time work, but want and are available for full-time work, the unemployment rate rises to 11.6 percent in October 2020.

Now think of two persons running for the same national political office. The incumbent argues that the official unemployment rate has come down recently and that it is now, say, 6.9 percent. "We're making progress on the economic front," he says.

The challenger argues that the official unemployment rate is not really the most nearly representative measurement of the degree to which labor is being underutilized in the economy. She says that the "true" or "most nearly accurate" unemployment rate—by which she means the one that takes into account all marginally attached workers and people who want to work full time but have taken part-time work for economic reasons—is 11.6 percent. That's a big difference, and often the public is left wondering who is right and who is wrong; who is telling the truth and who isn't.

The fact is both persons can be telling the truth; it's just that one is choosing to shine the light on the official unemployment rate, and the other shines the light on the unemployment rate that takes into account additional groups of people (such as the marginally attached workers).

6-2h Cyclical Unemployment

The unemployment rate in the economy is not always the natural rate. The difference between the existing unemployment rate and the natural unemployment rate is the **cyclical unemployment rate** (U_C):

Cyclical unemployment rate (U_C) = Unemployment rate (U) − Natural unemployment rate (U_N)

Cyclical Unemployment Rate
The difference between the unemployment rate and the natural unemployment rate.

When the existing unemployment rate (U) is greater than the natural unemployment rate (U_N), the cyclical unemployment rate (U_C) is positive. For example, if $U = 8$ percent and $U_N = 5$ percent, then $U_C = 3$ percent. When the unemployment rate is less than the natural unemployment rate, the cyclical unemployment rate is negative. For example, if $U = 4$ percent and $U_N = 5$ percent, then $U_C = -1$ percent.

Various unemployment rates are summarized in Exhibit 4. Unemployment rates according to education, race, and ethnicity are shown in Exhibit 5.

EXHIBIT 4

Various Unemployment Rates

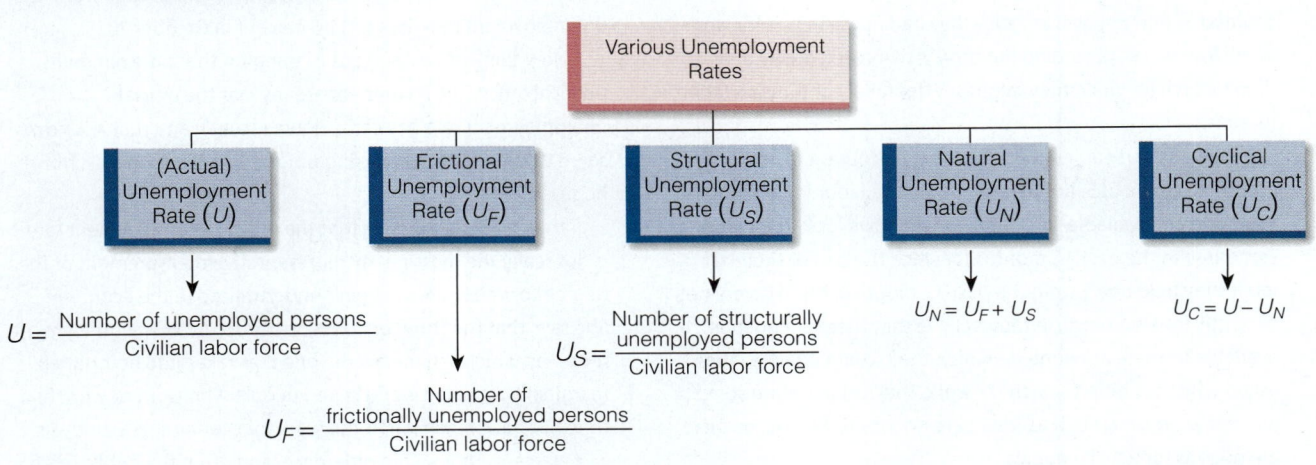

EXHIBIT 5

Unemployment Rates According to Education, Race, and Ethnicity

In (a), we show the U.S. unemployment rate according to education. Notice that college graduates tend to have the lowest unemployment rate of all the education groups. (b) Unemployment rate according to race and ethnicity.

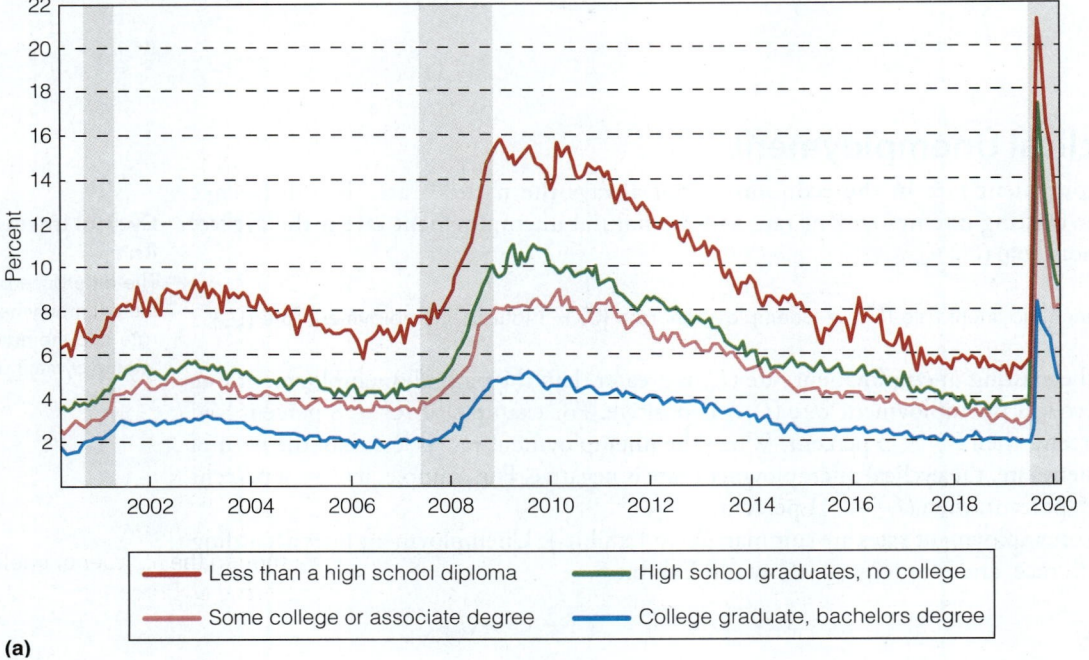

(a)

(Continued)

EXHIBIT 5 (Continued)

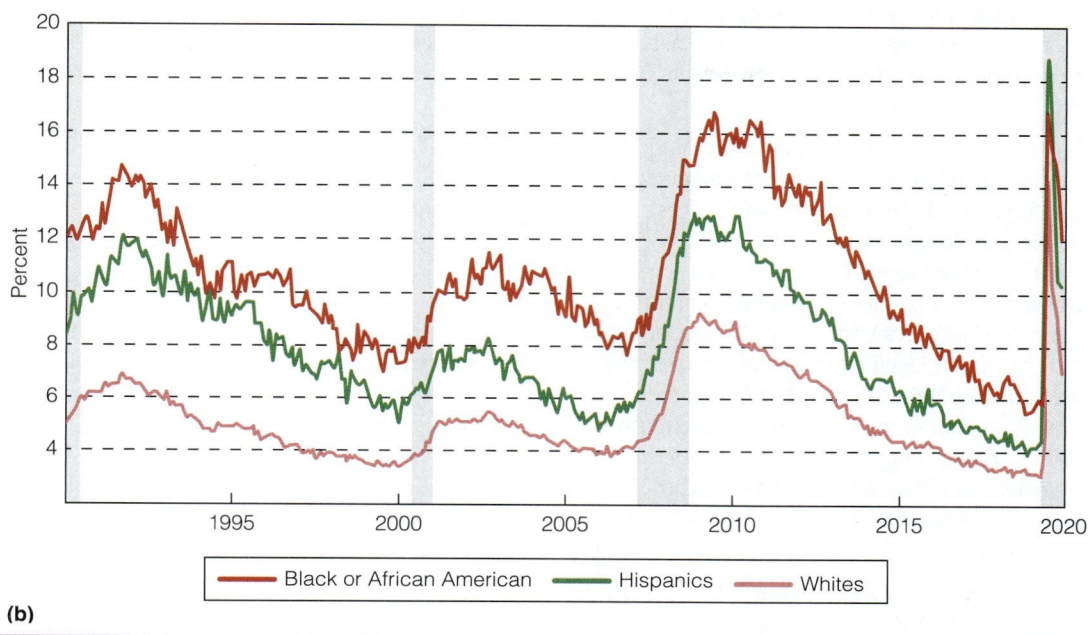

(b)

Source: Bureau of Labor Statistics

---

1. What is the major difference between a person who is frictionally unemployed and one who is structurally unemployed?

2. What does a positive cyclical unemployment rate imply?

Office Hours

"Is There More Than One Reason the Unemployment Rate Will Fall?"

Student: If the unemployment rate drops, does it follow that some of the people who were once unemployed are now employed?

Instructor: Not always. To see why, recall that the unemployment rate is equal to the number of unemployed persons divided by the civilian labor force:

$$\text{Unemployment rate} = \frac{\text{Number of unemployed persons}}{\text{Civilian labor force}}$$

Now, let's say that there are 100 unemployed persons and the civilian labor force consists of 1,000 persons. Then the unemployment rate is 10 percent. Suppose the number of unemployed persons rises to 105 (a 5 percent increase) at the same time that the civilian labor force rises to 1,120 (a 12 percent increase). Then the new unemployment rate is 9.4 percent, even though the number of unemployed persons has not decreased. In fact, it has increased from 100 to 105.

Student: In other words, if the number of unemployed persons rises by a smaller percentage than the civilian labor force rises, the unemployment rate will decline—even though the number of unemployed persons has risen.

Instructor: Yes, that's correct. Now consider something else. Suppose again that there are 100 unemployed persons in a civilian labor force of 1,000 persons. As before, these numbers give us an unemployment rate of 10 percent. Now suppose that 10 of the unemployed persons become discouraged workers and stop looking for work. Then the number of unemployed falls to 90, and the civilian labor force (which consists of employed plus unemployed persons) falls to 990. The unemployment rate now is 9.09 percent. The unemployment rate has dropped, but not for the reason most people think. It hasn't dropped because some of the unemployed persons found jobs; it has dropped because some of the unemployed became so discouraged that they stopped looking for jobs.

Student: In other words, we might think that the unemployment rate has dropped because 10 of the 100 unemployed persons found work, but in reality, those 10 persons did not find work. They just became so discouraged that they left the civilian labor force.

Instructor: Yes, that's correct.

Student: Does the government do anything to take these discouraged workers into account?

Instructor: The Bureau of Labor Statistics computes an alternative unemployment rate that includes discouraged workers in the ranks of both the unemployed and the civilian labor force. In short, it computes what it calls "total unemployed plus discouraged workers, as a percent of the civilian labor force plus discouraged workers":[3]

$$\text{Alternative unemployment rate} = \frac{\text{Number of unemployed persons} + \text{Discouraged workers}}{\text{Civilian labor force} + \text{Discouraged workers}}$$

This alternative unemployment rate tells us what the unemployment rate would look like if we included discouraged workers in our calculation.

Points to Remember

1. The unemployment rate can decline even if the number of unemployed persons has not declined. For example, if the number of unemployed persons rises by a smaller percentage than that of the civilian labor force, the unemployment rate will decline (even though more, not fewer, persons are unemployed).

2. An alternative unemployment rate is defined as

$$\text{Alternative unemployment rate} = \frac{\text{Number of unemployed persons} + \text{Discouraged workers}}{\text{Civilian labor force} + \text{Discouraged workers}}$$

---

[3] See alternative unemployment measure U-4 in, for example, "Alternative Measures of Labor Underutilization for States, Second Quarter of 2013 through First Quarter of 2014 Averages," *Local Area Unemployment Statistics* (U.S. Bureau of Labor Statistics, April 25, 2014), http://www.bls.gov/lau/stalt.htm.

Chapter Summary

Measuring Prices

- One major price index is the consumer price index (CPI).
- Inflation is an increase in the price level or price index.
- A given dollar amount in an earlier year does not have the same purchasing power in a later year (or current year) if prices are different in the two years. To convert a dollar amount of an earlier year into today's (or current) dollars, we use the following formula:

$$\text{Dollar amount in today's (current) dollars} = \text{Dollar amount}_{\text{earlier year}} \times \left(\frac{CPI_{\text{current year}}}{CPI_{\text{earlier year}}} \right)$$

Unemployment and Employment

- An unemployed person may be a job loser, a job leaver, a reentrant, or a new entrant.
- The unemployment rate may be biased downward because discouraged workers are not considered unemployed.
- Frictional unemployment, due to the natural so-called frictions of the economy, is caused by changing market conditions and is represented by qualified individuals with transferable skills who change jobs.
- Structural unemployment is due to structural changes in the economy that eliminate some jobs and create others for which the unemployed are unqualified.
- Natural unemployment is caused by frictional and structural factors in the economy. The natural unemployment rate equals the sum of the frictional unemployment rate and the structural unemployment rate.
- Full employment exists when the unemployment rate is equal to the natural unemployment rate.
- The cyclical unemployment rate is the difference between the existing unemployment rate and the natural unemployment rate.

Key Terms and Concepts

Price Level
Price Index
Consumer Price Index (CPI)
Base Year
Inflation
Real Income
Nominal Income
Unemployment Rate
Employment Rate
Labor Force Participation Rate
Frictional Unemployment
Structural Unemployment
Natural Unemployment
Full Employment
Cyclical Unemployment Rate

Questions and Problems

1. What does the CPI in the base year equal? Explain your answer.
2. Show that, if the percentage rise in prices is equal to the percentage rise in nominal income, then one's real income does not change.
3. When is the total dollar expenditure on the market basket in the base year the same as in the current year?
4. How does structural unemployment differ from frictional unemployment?
5. What does it mean to say that the country is operating at full employment?
6. What is "natural" about natural unemployment?
7. What is the difference between the employment rate and the labor force participation rate?
8. If the unemployment rate is 4 percent, it does not follow that the employment rate is 96 percent. Explain why.
9. What criteria must be met for a person to be characterized as unemployed?
10. What is the difference between a job leaver and a reentrant?
11. How is a discouraged worker different from an unemployed worker?
12. If the price of, say, oranges has risen, does it follow that the price level has risen too? Explain your answer.
13. What is the relationship between your nominal income and the inflation rate if you are more than keeping up with inflation?
14. Explain how the CPI is computed.

Working with Numbers and Graphs

1. Suppose 60 million people are employed, 10 million are unemployed, and 30 million are not in the labor force. What does the civilian noninstitutional population equal?

2. Suppose 100 million people are in the civilian labor force and 90 million people are employed. How many people are unemployed? What is the unemployment rate?

3. Change the current-year prices in Exhibit 1 to $1 for pens, $28 for shirts, and $32 for a pair of shoes. Based on these prices, what is the CPI for the current year?

4. Regina earned an annual salary of $45,000 in 1986. What is this salary equivalent to in 2020 dollars? (Use Exhibit 2 to find the CPI in the years mentioned.)

5. A house cost $80,000 in 1986. What is this price equivalent to in 2019 dollars? (Use Exhibit 2 to find the CPI in the years mentioned.)

6. Using the following data, compute (a) the unemployment rate, (b) the employment rate, and (c) the labor force participation rate:

Civilian noninstitutional population	200 million
Number of employed persons	126 million
Number of unemployed persons	8 million

7. Based on the following data, compute (a) the unemployment rate, (b) the structural unemployment rate, and (c) the cyclical unemployment rate:

Frictional unemployment rate	2 percent
Natural unemployment rate	5 percent
Civilian labor force	100 million
Number of employed persons	82 million

8. Using Exhibit 2, compute the percentage change in prices between (a) 1987 and 1992, (b) 1998 and 2009, and (c) 2005 and 2017.

9. Assume that the market basket contains 10X, 20Y, and 45Z. The current-year prices for goods X, Y, and Z are $1, $4, and $6, respectively. The base-year prices are $1, $3, and $5, respectively. What is the CPI in the current year?

10. If the CPI is 150 and nominal income is $100,000, what does real income equal?

Macroeconomic Measurements, Part II: GDP and Real GDP

CHAPTER 7

Introduction

Each day in the United States, many thousands of goods and services are produced. How do we measure all this economic activity? One of the principal ways is to compute GDP, or gross domestic product. GDP is one of the most important economic measurements used by economists. In this chapter, we explain what GDP is and discuss how to compute it. We then turn to a discussion of Real GDP and how to compute it.

7-1 Gross Domestic Product

In any given year, people in the United States produce goods and services—television sets, books, pencil sharpeners, attorney services, haircuts, and much more. Have you ever wondered what the total dollar value is for all those goods and services? In 2019, it was $21.43 trillion. In other words, in 2019, people living and working in the United States produced $21.43 trillion worth of goods and services. That dollar amount is what economists call the gross domestic product. Simply put, **gross domestic product (GDP)** is *the total market value of all final goods and services produced annually within a country's borders.*

Gross Domestic Product (GDP)
The total market value of all final goods and services produced annually within a country's borders.

7-1a Calculating GDP

To show how GDP is computed, suppose the following data represent the prices and quantities of three goods produced in a tiny economy this year:

Goods	Quantity Produced of Each Good	Price of Each Good
A	10	$2
B	20	$3
C	30	$5

151

What is the GDP of this tiny economy? GDP is the total market value of all final goods and services produced annually within a country's borders. GDP, then, is the sum (Σ) of the products of the prices (P) of all goods and the quantities (Q) of those goods produced:

$$GDP = \Sigma(PQ)$$

In the case of our hypothetical economy,

$$GDP = (\$2 \times 10 \text{ units}) + (\$3 \times 20 \text{ units}) + (\$5 \times 30 \text{ units}) = \$230$$

7-1b Final Goods and Intermediate Goods

In our definition of GDP, reference was made to "final goods and services." If GDP is the total market value of these goods and services, why do we need to specify them as *final*? The reason is that there is a difference between a final good and an intermediate good. A **final good** (or service) is a good in the hands of the final user, the ultimate consumer. It is the orange juice that the consumer buys in the store.

So, then, what are the oranges that go to make the orange juice? The oranges are an *intermediate good*. An **intermediate good** is an input to the production of a final good. In other words, the oranges were used to produce orange juice (the final good).

Only expenditures on final goods are counted when computing GDP, in order to avoid the *double counting* that would occur if we counted expenditures on both final and intermediate goods. **Double counting** refers to counting a good more than once when computing GDP. To illustrate, if we count the oranges and the orange juice, then we count the oranges twice because they are in the orange juice.

Final Good
A good in the hands of its final user.

Intermediate Good
A good that is an input to the production of a final good.

Double Counting
Counting a good more than once when computing GDP.

Finding Economics

In a Factory, Restaurant, and Law Office James works in a car factory in Detroit. Where is the economics? Obviously, cars are being produced in the factory. The production of these cars will add to the GDP for the current year.

Emma works as a cook in a coffeehouse. Sam has just ordered an egg salad sandwich on rye (toasted) with coleslaw and a root beer. Where is the economics? Emma will make the sandwich and coleslaw. These two items plus the root beer are part of the GDP for the current year.

Blake is in his attorney's office talking about his upcoming court case. Where is the economics? The service the attorney is providing to Blake is part of the GDP for the current year.

7-1c What GDP Omits

Some exchanges that take place in an economy are not included in GDP. These trades range from sales of used cars to illegal drug deals.

Certain Nonmarket Goods and Services If a family hires a person to cook and clean, the service is counted in GDP. If family members perform the same tasks, however, their services are not counted in GDP. In the first case, a service is bought and sold for a price in a market setting. In the second case, it is not; no transaction takes place.

Underground Activities, Both Legal and Illegal The underground economy consists of unreported exchanges that take place outside the normal recorded markets. Some underground activities involve illegal goods (e.g., cocaine), and others involve legal goods and tax evasion. Illegal goods and services are not counted in GDP because no record exists of the transactions. There are no written records of illegal drug sales, illegal gambling, and illegal prostitution. Nor are there written records of some legal activities that individuals want to keep from government notice. For example, a gardener might agree to do gardening work only on the condition that he is paid in cash. Obviously, a person may legally buy or sell gardening services, but the transaction might not be recorded if one or both parties do not want it to be. Why might the gardener want to be paid in cash? Perhaps he doesn't want to pay taxes on the income received—an objective more easily accomplished if no written record of the income is generated.

Sales of Used Goods GDP measures *current production* (i.e., production occurring during the current year). A used-car sale, for example, does not enter into the current-year statistics because the car was counted when it was originally produced.

Financial Transactions The trading of stocks and bonds is not counted in GDP because it does not represent the production of new assets. It is simply the trading of existing assets (the exchange of stocks or bonds for money).

Government Transfer Payments A **transfer payment** is a payment to a person that is not made in return for goods and services currently supplied. Government transfer payments, such as Social Security benefits and veterans' benefits, are not counted in GDP because they are not payments to individuals for *current production*.

> **Transfer Payment**
> A payment to a person that is not made in return for goods and services currently supplied.

Leisure The length of the workweek has fallen in the United States since the beginning of the twentieth century, and the leisure time individuals have for consumption has increased. Leisure is a good in much the same way that cars, houses, and shoes are goods. But leisure is not counted in GDP because it is too difficult to quantify.

7-1d GDP Is Not Adjusted for Bads Generated in the Production of Goods

Economic growth often comes with certain bads (anything from which individuals receive disutility or dissatisfaction). For example, producing cars, furniture, and steel often generates air and water pollution, which most people consider as bads. GDP counts the goods and services, but it does not deduct the air and water pollution. Thus, argue some economists, GDP overstates our overall economic welfare.

7-1e Per-Capita GDP

If we divide a country's GDP by the population in the country, we get *per-capita GDP*. For example, if a country has a GDP of $5 trillion and its population is 200 million, per-capita GDP is $25,000 ($5 trillion ÷ 200 million people). In 2019, the per-capita GDP in the United States was $65,281.

Economics 24/7

Gross Family Product

One of the ways to understand GDP is to think of what it would be comparable to in a family. Instead of talking about what a country produces in a year, let's talk about what a family produces. Let's call the total market value of what the family produces gross family product (GFP).

Just as not every country has the same GDP, not every family has the same GFP. One family can have a higher or lower GFP than another. The difference in GFP might be because more people are producing in one family than in another. For example, suppose family A is composed of five individuals, and family B is composed of eight. More family members (more resources) can produce more output.

The same holds for countries. China might have a higher GDP than, say, France because China has a larger population. The national Chinese "family" is larger than the French "family."

Of course, one family might have a higher GFP than another for other reasons. For example, even with the same number of people in two families, one family might have a higher GFP. Perhaps the members of family A work more hours than those of family B. All other things equal, more work can result in more output.

The same holds for countries. The GDP of one country might be higher than the GDP of another because the workers in one country work more hours a week than those in the other country.

Finally, consider that, even when the size of two families is the same and when the number of hours worked each week by the two families is the same, one family could still have a higher GFP than another. To understand why, keep in mind that GFP measures the total market value of the family output. Note the phrase "total market value," computed by multiplying the price of each unit of output by the number of units produced. If a family is producing chairs, then its GFP will be equal to the price of each chair multiplied by the number of chairs produced. One hundred dollars ($100) per chair multiplied by, say, 100 chairs equals a GFP of $10,000. If another family produces 100 shirts at a price of $25, its GPF will be lower. Thus, one family's GFP might be higher than another's GFP because the per-unit price of what it produces is higher.

Economics 24/7

Money and Happiness

The Easterlin paradox (named after the economist Richard Easterlin) is a key concept in happiness economics, or the economics of happiness. The paradox is obvious once we identify two important points made by Easterlin. In his research, he found that (i) rich people in a country were often happier than poor people in the same country. In other words, as you get richer in a country, your happiness level increases. But then Easterlin also found that (ii) people in richer countries were really not happier than people in poorer countries. Now, (i) and (ii) seem at odds with each other, in the following sense: If richer people in a country are happier than poorer people in a country, then shouldn't it follow that people in rich countries should be happier than people in poor countries, at least within poorer countries that meet basic needs (such as food, clothing, and shelter). But according to Easterlin's findings, they aren't. This at least seeming paradox has led many researchers to conclude that, once a society has met certain basic needs, greater income doesn't bring greater happiness.

Economists Betsey Stevenson and Justin Wolfers have questioned the Easterlin paradox. Their finding: Not only do richer people in a country experience greater subjective well-being (greater happiness or contentment) than poor people within a country, but also, people in rich countries experience greater subjective well-being than people in poor countries. Moreover, there doesn't seem to be any satiation point. In other words, people keep experiencing greater subjective well-being with greater income, even after they have met their basic needs. Here is how Stevenson and Wolfers put it:

> Many scholars have argued that once "basic needs" have been met, higher income is no longer associated with higher subjective well-being. We assess the validity of this claim in comparisons of both rich and poor countries, and also of rich and poor people within a country. Analyzing multiple datasets, multiple definitions of "basic needs" and multiple questions about well-being, we find no support for this claim. The relationship between well-being and income is roughly linear-log and does not diminish as income rises. If there is a satiation point [a point at which higher income does not bring greater subjective well-being] we are yet to reach it."[1]

Part of the data Stevenson and Wolfers used came from the polling organization Gallup. Gallup asked about a half a million people in different countries (over time) to consider a "satisfaction ladder," on which there were 10 rungs. The top rung represents the best-possible life for them, the bottom rung the worst-possible life. They were then asked to identify themselves on the ladder from 0 to 10. Stevenson and Wolfers results are shown in Exhibit 1(a). Notice that, for each country, subjective well-being rises as self-reported

---
[1] Betsey Stevenson and Justin Wolfers, "Subjective Well-Being and Income: Is There Any Evidence of Satiation?" NBER Working Paper 18992 (Cambridge, MA: National Bureau of Economic Research, April 2013).

EXHIBIT 1

Income and Subjective Well-Being

In (a), we notice that, for each country, subjective well-being rises as household income rises. In (b), we see that people in rich countries experience greater subjective well-being than people in poor countries.

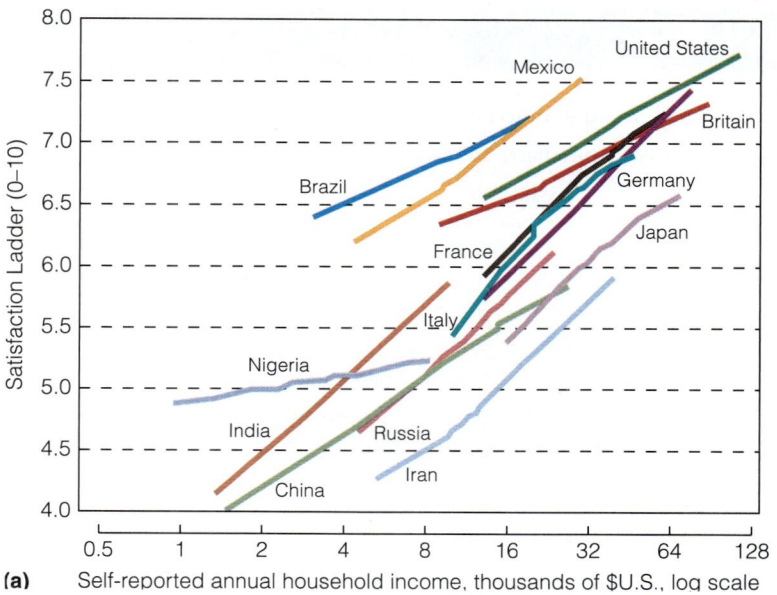

annual household income rises. In other words, all lines move upward from left to right.

Now look at Exhibit 1(b). Each dot represents a country, giving us a fix on its per-capita GDP (in thousands of U.S. dollars) and subjective well-being. Notice that the line that is fitted to the data (the dots) slopes upward from left to right, telling us that people who live in richer countries experience greater subjective well-being than those who live in poor countries. Notice also that there doesn't seem to be a point at which the upward-sloping line flattens out.

One of the questions that has yet to be answered is what it is exactly that drives the relationship between subjective well-being and income. In other words, if, as income rises, subjective well-being rises, too, why is that? Stevenson, in an interview, commented on this question, observing that people often say that when they have more income, they are treated with more respect and that they have more choices over how they will spend their time. In other words, with more income may come more respect and more choices, and these two factors may be the driving forces behind greater subjective well-being.

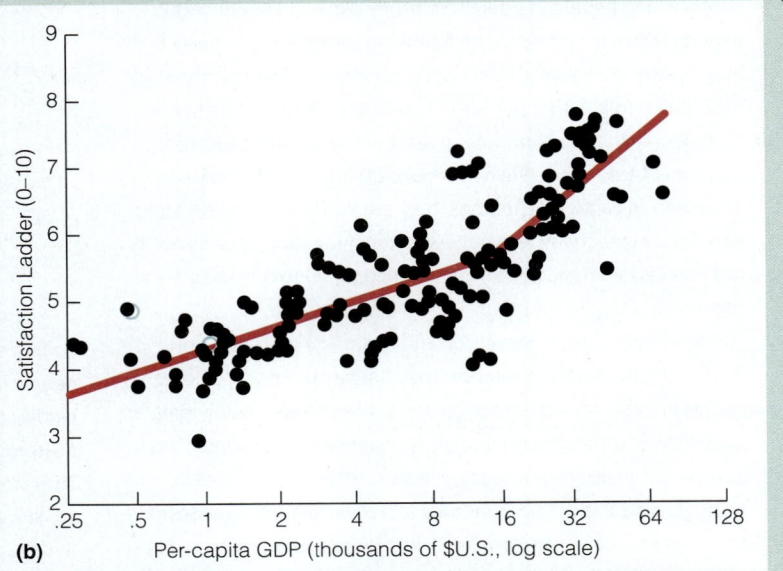
(b)

(Answers to Self-Test questions are in Answers to Self-Test Questions at the back of the book.)

1. Why aren't stock purchases and sales counted in GDP?
2. Suppose the GDP for a country is $0. Does this mean that there was no productive activity in the country? Explain your answer.

7-2 The Expenditure Approach to Computing GDP for a Real-World Economy

In a tiny economy, we can compute GDP simply by multiplying the price of each good produced by the quantity of the good produced:

$$\text{GDP} = \Sigma PQ$$

The U.S. economy is anything but tiny. Economists cannot simply multiply the price of each good produced by the quantity of it. In a large economy, GDP can be measured in a number of different ways. A principal way is called the *expenditure approach* to measuring

GDP. In this approach, economists sum the spending (on final goods and services) in four sectors of the economy: (1) household, (2) business, (3) government, and (4) foreign.

In each of these four sectors, economic actors buy goods and services; in other words, they spend. By sector, the expenditures are called, respectively, (1) *consumption*; (2) gross private domestic investment, or simply *investment*; (3) government consumption expenditures and gross investment, or simply *government purchases*; and (4) *net exports*:

Sectors of the Economy	Spending Called ...
Household	Consumption
Business	Investment
Government	Government purchases
Foreign	Net exports

Before we see how economists add up the expenditures of these sectors, let's discuss the components of each of the expenditures.

Consumption
Consumption (C) includes spending on

- **Durable goods.** Durable goods are goods that are expected to last for more than three years, such as refrigerators, ovens, or cars.
- **Nondurable goods.** Nondurable goods are goods that are not expected to last for more than three years, such as food.
- **Services.** Services are intangible items, such as lawn care, car repair, and entertainment.

Consumption expenditures in the United States usually account for 70 percent of GDP. In short, consumption is the largest spending component of GDP.

Investment
Investment (I) is the sum of

- Purchases of newly produced capital goods.
- Changes in business inventories, sometimes referred to as **inventory investment**.
- Purchases of new residential housing.[2]

The sum of the purchases of newly produced capital goods and the purchases of new residential housing is often referred to as **fixed Investment**. In other words,

Investment = Fixed investment + Inventory investment.

Fixed investment is the larger of the two components.

Government Purchases
Government Purchases (G) include federal, state, and local government purchases of goods and services and gross investment in highways, bridges, and so on. Not included in government purchases are **government transfer payments**, which are payments to people that are not made in return for currently supplied goods and services. Social Security benefits and welfare payments are two examples of transfer payments; neither is a payment for current productive efforts.

Consumption
The sum of spending on durable goods, nondurable goods, and services.

Investment
The sum of all purchases of newly produced capital goods, changes in business inventories, and purchases of new residential housing.

Inventory Investment
Changes in the stock of unsold goods.

Fixed Investment
Business purchases of capital goods, such as machinery and factories, and purchases of new residential housing.

Government Purchases
Federal, state, and local government purchases of goods and services, and gross investment in highways, bridges, and so on.

Government Transfer Payments
Payments to persons that are not made in return for currently supplied goods and services.

---

[2] For purposes of computing GDP, the purchases of new residential housing (although undertaken by members of the household sector) are considered investment.

Net Exports People, firms, and governments in the United States sometimes purchase foreign-produced goods. These purchases are referred to as **imports** (*IM*). Foreign residents, firms, and governments sometimes purchase U.S.-produced goods. These purchases are referred to as **exports** (*EX*). If imports are subtracted from exports, we are left with **net exports** (*NX*):

$$NX = EX - IM$$

Obviously, net exports can be positive or negative. If exports are greater than imports, then *NX* is positive; if imports are greater than exports, then *NX* is negative.

Imports
Total domestic (U.S.) spending on foreign goods.

Exports
Total foreign spending on domestic (U.S.) goods.

Net Exports
Exports minus imports.

7-2a Using the Expenditure Approach to Compute GDP

The expenditure approach to measuring or computing GDP calls for totaling the purchases of final goods and services made in the four sectors of the economy. (See Exhibit 2.) This statement may give you reason to pause, because our earlier definition of GDP did not mention *purchases* of final goods and services. Rather, we defined GDP as the total market value of all final goods and services *produced* annually within a nation's borders.

EXHIBIT 2

The Expenditure Approach to Computing GDP

The expenditure components of GDP are consumption, investment, government purchases, and net exports. The exhibit shows what is included in each of these components.

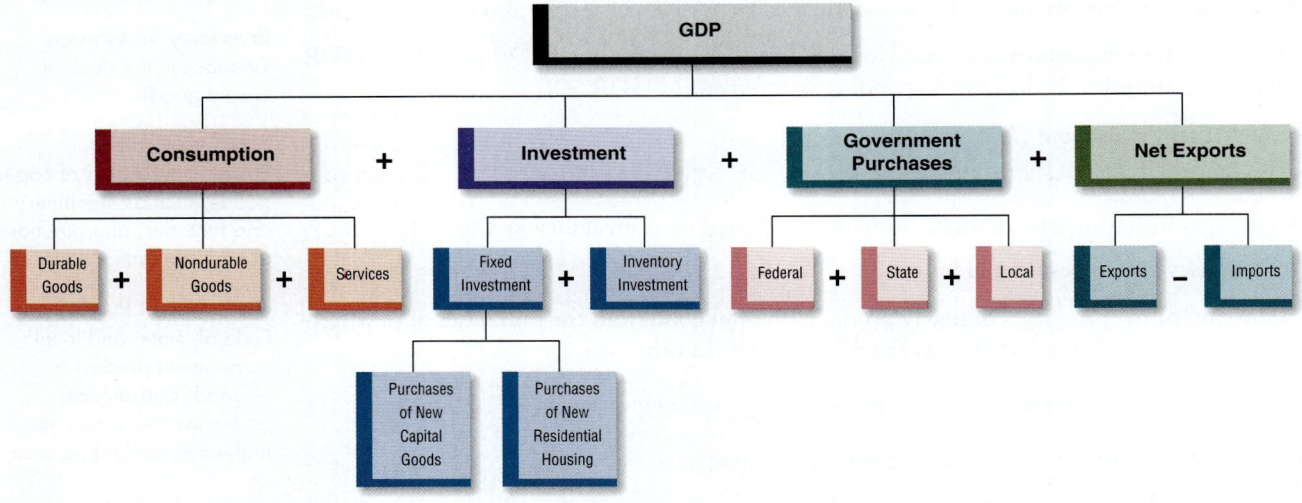

The discrepancy is cleared up quickly when we note that national income accountants (government economists who compute GDP) assume that anything produced but not sold to consumers is "bought" by the firm that produced it. In other words, if a car is produced but not sold, it goes into business inventory and is consider "purchased" by the automaker firm that produced it. Thus, we can compute GDP by summing the purchases made by the four sectors of the economy. GDP equals consumption (*C*), plus investment (*I*), plus government purchases (*G*), plus net exports (*EX – IM*):

$$GDP = C + I + G + (EX - IM)$$

Exhibit 3 shows the dollar amounts of the four components of GDP for the United States in 2019.

EXHIBIT 3

Components of GDP (Expenditure Approach)

The expenditure approach to computing GDP sums the purchases made by final users of goods and services. The expenditure components include consumption, investment, government purchases, and net exports. The data are for 2019.

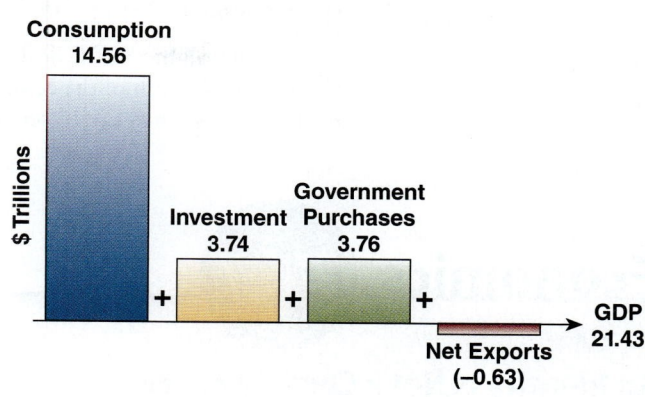

7-2b Why We Subtract *IM* From *C + I + G + EX*

If you get on a scale holding a 10-pound rock, and the scale reads 180 pounds, do you weigh 180 pounds, or do you weigh 170 pounds? Obviously, you weigh 170 pounds. Now if your consumption spending for the year is $15,000 and $9,000 of that total was spent on goods produced in the United States, which dollar figure—$15,000 or $9,000—should be used to reflect goods produced in the United States? Of course, the $9,000. With this in mind, consider the accounting identity:

$$GDP = C + I + G + (EX - IM)$$

When national income accounts measure the consumption spending in the economy (*C*), it consists of (1) spending on goods produced in the United States and (2) spending on goods produced in other countries—in other words, spending on imports. To illustrate, suppose $C = \$400$ billion. This $400 billion is made up of (1) $300 billion spent on goods produced in the United States and (2) $100 billion spent on goods produced in other countries (imports). To find an accurate measure of what is produced in the United States, we subtract the spending on goods produced in other countries. That is why *IM* is subtracted from *C + I + G + EX* in the accounting identity identified earlier.

7-2c Common Misconceptions About Increases in GDP

Are all increases in GDP good for the economy? To answer this question, consider that if investment rises and no other component of GDP declines, GDP will rise. Recall that investment can rise for one of three reasons: (1) Firms may purchase more newly produced capital goods (firms buy more factories and machinery); (2) individuals may purchase new residential housing (someone buys a new home); or (3) firms' inventory investment rises. Further, firms' inventory investment can rise in two ways:

- *Planned inventory investment.* Firms may deliberately produce more units of a good and add them to inventory.
- *Unplanned inventory investment.* Consumers don't buy as many units of output as firms have produced, and unsold units are added to inventory.

Now compare two settings:

- *Setting 1.* Firms purchase more newly produced capital goods (more factories and machinery). As a result, investment rises and so does GDP, all other things remaining constant.

- **Setting 2.** Buyers don't buy as many units of output as firms have produced. The unsold units find their way into (unplanned) inventory investment. As a result, investment rises and so does GDP, all other things remaining constant.

Are the higher GDP dollars in settings 1 and 2 equivalent? We think not. As far as the health and strength of the economy are concerned, the increase in GDP in setting 1 is superior to the increase in GDP in setting 2.

Economics 24/7

An Identity Is Not a Causal Theory

Using the expenditure approach to measuring GDP, we see that

$$GDP = C + I + G + (EX - IM)$$

This equation is referred to as the *national income identity*. An identity is an equality that must be true regardless of its variables. In other words, no matter what dollar amounts we record for C, I, G, and $EX - IM$, the sum of those amounts will be GDP.

Now suppose someone says the following: "The way to raise the country's GDP is to reduce imports (IM). So we should place tariffs on imports, which will result in people buying fewer imported goods; if import spending declines too, then GDP will rise. This has to be right, because if $IM = \$300$ billion, and then it declines to $\$200$ billion, GDP will rise by $\$100$ billion."

If you only considered the national income identity, what the person has said would seem to be right. But remember that $GDP = C + I + G + (EX - IM)$ is an identity, not a causal theory. In other words, it doesn't mean that a decline in import spending will *cause* a rise in GDP.

When someone says that a decline in import spending will raise GDP (basing their argument on the national income identity), what they are doing is assuming that, as import spending declines, all other components of GDP remain unchanged, but this isn't likely to be true. To illustrate, suppose the United States made it illegal to import oil, thus lowering import spending. Oil in the United States would likely become more expensive, and gasoline at the pump would likely rise in price. If consumers bought the higher-priced gasoline without cutting back their purchases, then they would end up spending more dollars on gasoline consumption, which would leave them with fewer dollars to spend on non-gasoline goods. Higher-priced gasoline could increase the costs to businesses, which could negatively affect business spending (I).

Now consider the following scenario: The president of the United States is sitting in the Oval Office of the White House with a few advisors. The president wonders out loud how we can get GDP up in the country. One of the president's advisors says that back when he took economics in college, he learned that $GDP = C + I + G + (EX - IM)$. So it is obvious that if we want the GDP to rise, we must try to lower import spending. The advisor goes on to suggest placing tariffs or quotas on imports, based on the expectation that tariffs will reduce import spending, which will raise GDP. In this argument, the advisor made a mistake (by assuming that an identity is a causal theory) that could end up causing a lot of economic strife.

1. Describe the expenditure approach to computing GDP in a real-world economy.
2. Will GDP be smaller than the sum of consumption, investment, and government purchases if net exports are negative? Explain your answer.
3. If GDP is $400 billion and the country's population is 100 million, does it follow that each individual in the country has $40,000 worth of goods and services?

7-3 The Income Approach to Computing GDP for a Real-World Economy

A second way to compute GDP, the income approach, should give us the same dollar amount of GDP as the expenditure approach. Let's look at an example. Suppose that, in a given economy, 10 units of good A are produced and 20 units of good B are produced. Suppose further that the price of good A is \$1 and the price of good B is \$2. Then, if buyers purchase all the units of each of the two goods, they will have spent \$50 on these two goods: (\$1 × 10 units) + (\$2 × 20 units) = \$50. In other words, the expenditure approach to measuring GDP gives us \$50 of GDP in this little economy.

However, money spent by one person is money earned by another. The person who sells 10 units of good A at \$1 per unit receives an income of \$10. The \$10 spent by the buyer is \$10 earned by the seller.

Exhibit 4 shows a circular flow diagram of the economy. This diagram illustrates that, in a simple economy, GDP computed by summing the purchases of the four sectors of the economy is equal to GDP computed by summing the income earned by the different resources. In other words, dollar purchases (or dollar expenditures) equal dollar income. More specifically, money spent to buy goods and services ends up flowing to the resources that produce them. (Again, think in terms of a tiny economy in which one person buys 10 oranges for \$1 each. His expenditure equals \$10. But the \$10 also represents income for the person who sold the buyer the oranges. The expenditure for one person is the income for another.)

Two steps are involved in computing GDP with the income approach. First, compute national income. Second, adjust national income for certain things. The end result is GDP.

7-3a Computing National Income

National income is the sum of five components: (1) compensation of employees, (2) proprietors' income, (3) corporate profits, (4) rental income of persons, and (5) net interest.

Compensation of Employees The compensation of employees is equal to the total of (1) wages and salaries paid to employees; (2) employers' contributions to Social Security and employee benefit plans; and (3) the monetary value of fringe benefits, tips, and paid vacations. The compensation of employees is the largest component of national income.

Proprietors' Income Proprietors' income includes all forms of income earned by self-employed individuals and the owners of unincorporated businesses, including unincorporated farmers. Included in farm income is an estimate of the value of the food grown and consumed on farms.

Corporate Profits Corporate profits include all the income earned by the stockholders of corporations. Some of the profits are paid to stockholders in the form of dividends, some are kept within the firm to finance investments (these are called *undistributed profits* or *retained earnings*), and some are used to pay taxes on corporate profits. (The portion of corporate profits used to pay these taxes is counted as income "earned" by households even though households do not receive the income.)

Rental Income (of Persons) Rental income is the income received by individuals for the use of their nonmonetary assets (e.g., land, houses, offices). It also includes returns to individuals who hold copyrights and patents. Finally, it includes an imputed value for

---

National Income
Total income earned by U.S. citizens and businesses, no matter where they reside or are located. National income is the sum of the payments to resources (land, labor, capital, and entrepreneurship): National income = Compensation of employees + Proprietors' income + Corporate profits + Rental income of persons + Net interest.

EXHIBIT 4

The Circular Flow: Total Purchases (Expenditures) Equal Total Income in a Simple Economy

The exhibit shows an economy with four sectors: households, business firms, government, and foreign economies. Each sector purchases goods and services. The sum of these purchases is GDP [GDP = C + I + G + (EX − IM)].

The purchases (expenditures) made in product markets flow to business firms, which then use these monies to buy resources in resource markets. In other words, the monies flow to the owners (suppliers) of land, labor, capital, and entrepreneurship. The sum of these resource payments is total income, which flows to households. In this simple economy, where some things have been ignored, total purchases (expenditures) equal total income. Because total purchases (expenditures) equal GDP and total purchases equal total income, it follows that GDP equals total income.

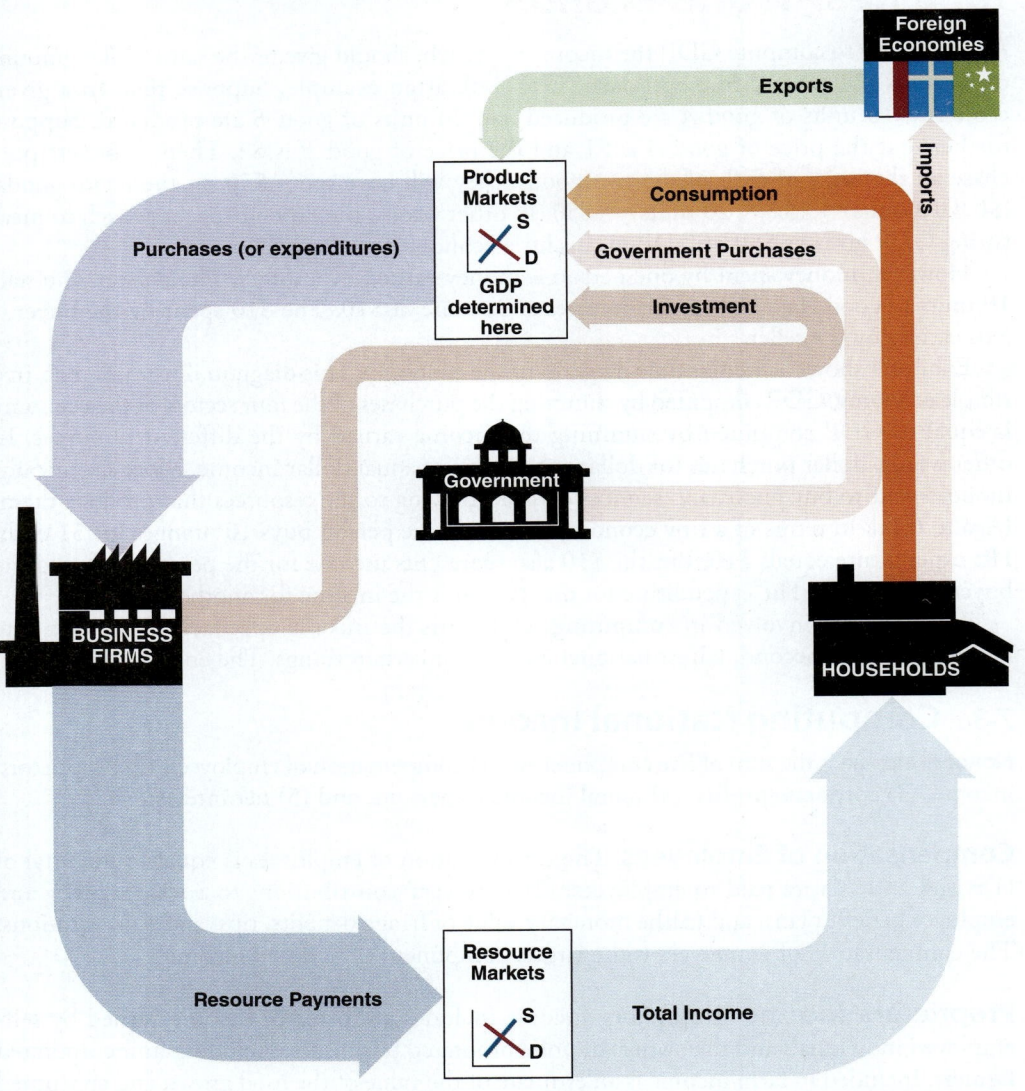

owner-occupied houses. For example, people may own the house they live in and therefore not pay any rent, but for purposes of national income accounting, a rental value is imputed. In short, home ownership is viewed as a business that produces a service that is sold to the owner of the business.

Net Interest Net interest is the interest income received by U.S. households and government, minus the interest they paid out.

National Income We can summarize national income and its components as follows:

National income = Compensation of employees
+ Proprietors' income
+ Corporate profits
+ Rental income
+ Net interest

7-3b From National Income to GDP: Making Some Adjustments

After computing national income, we might think that there is nothing else to do—that national income should equal GDP. We naturally think that every dollar spent is someone's income. But when we check the actual figures for national income and GDP, we find that they are not equal. In other words, not every dollar spent is someone else's income. For example, if Maria spends $10 to buy a book, $9.50 of the $10 might end up in the seller's pocket as income, but the remaining 50¢ might go for taxes.

With this idea in mind, the income approach to computing GDP requires us to add certain things to national income and to subtract certain things from it. The following equation and Exhibit 5 show what must be added to and subtracted from national income to compute GDP (keep the equation and exhibit in mind as you continue to read):

GDP = National income
− Income earned from the rest of the world
+ Income earned by the rest of the world
+ Indirect business taxes
+ Capital consumption allowance
+ Statistical discrepancy

EXHIBIT 5

The Income Approach to Computing GDP

The exhibit identifies the components of national income and the adjustments necessary to compute GDP according to the income approach.

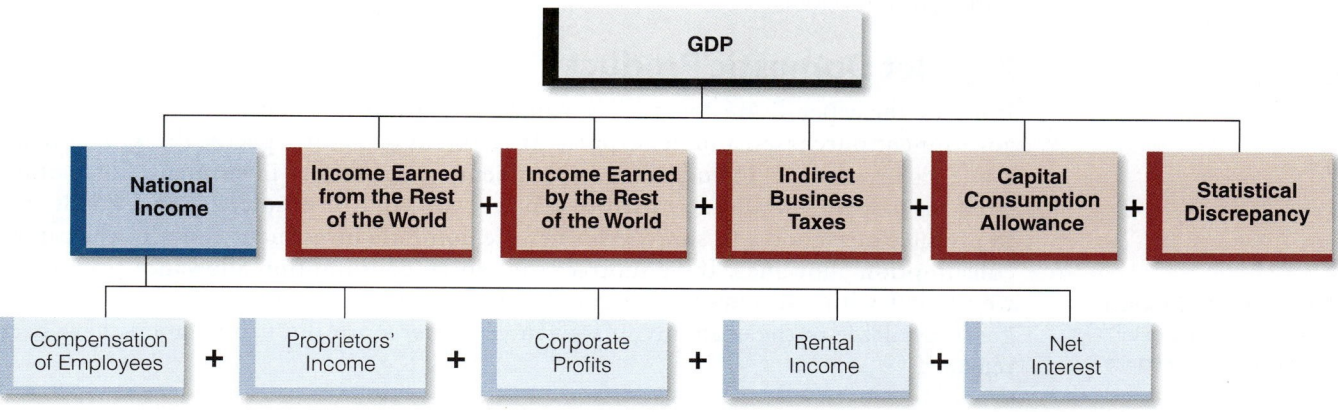

Income Earned from the Rest of the World, Income Earned by the Rest of the World In computing national income, we include the income earned by U.S. citizens who work and live in other countries, but we do not include the income earned by foreigners who work and live in the United States. If we want to compute GDP, we have to adjust for both these incomes. We do so by (1) subtracting from national income the income earned from the rest of the world (i.e., income that U.S. citizens living abroad earned by producing and selling goods) and (2) adding to national income the income earned by the rest of the world (this is income that non-U.S. citizens earned by producing and selling goods in the United States).

Indirect Business Taxes Indirect business taxes are made up mainly of excise taxes, sales taxes, and property taxes. These taxes are not part of national income because they are not considered a payment to any resource (land, labor, etc.). Think of them as monies collected by government, not payments to land, labor, capital, or entrepreneurship.

Indirect taxes are included in the purchases of goods and services (you pay a sales tax when you buy most goods) and so are included when the expenditure approach is used to compute GDP. Therefore, we must add indirect business taxes to national income.

Capital Consumption Allowance Some capital goods are used up in the production process through natural wear, obsolescence, or accidental destruction (e.g., the machinery that breaks down and cannot be repaired). The cost to replace these capital goods is called the **capital consumption allowance**, or **depreciation**. It is added to national income because we want a measure of all the income earned in the economy. National income, by itself, doesn't include the income payments implicit in the capital consumption allowance.

> **Capital Consumption Allowance (Depreciation)**
> The estimated amount of capital goods used up in production through natural wear, obsolescence, and accidental destruction.

Statistical Discrepancy GDP and national income are computed with the use of different sets of data. Hence, statistical discrepancies, or pure computational errors, often occur and must be accounted for in the national income accounts.

7-3c Other National Income Accounting Measurements

Besides GDP and national income, three other national income accounting measurements are important: net domestic product, personal income, and disposable income. All five measurements—GDP, national income, net domestic product, personal income, and disposable income—are often used interchangeably to measure the output produced and income earned in an economy.

7-3d Net Domestic Product

If we use the expenditure approach to compute GDP, we add consumption, investment, government purchases, and net exports. Investment (or, more specifically, gross private domestic investment) includes fixed investment and inventory investment. Some of the fixed investment, however, is used to replace worn-out or obsolete capital goods, not to produce new goods. In short, gross private domestic investment contains the capital consumption allowance. If we subtract the capital consumption allowance from GDP, we are left with **net domestic product** (NDP). NDP measures the total value of new goods available in the economy in a given year after worn-out capital goods have been replaced:

> **Net Domestic Product**
> GDP minus the capital consumption allowance.

Net domestic product (NDP) = GDP − Capital consumption allowance

7-3e Personal Income

Not all income earned is received, and not all income received is earned. An example of income earned but not received is undistributed profits, which stockholders earn but do not receive. Instead, the corporation usually reinvests the undistributed profits. An example of income received but not earned is Social Security benefits.

Personal income is the amount of income that individuals actually receive. It is equal to national income minus such major earned but not received items as undistributed corporate profits, social insurance taxes (Social Security contributions), and taxes on corporate profits, plus transfer payments (which are received but not earned):

$$\begin{aligned}
\text{Personal income} = &\text{ National income} \\
&- \text{ Undistributed corporate profits} \\
&- \text{ Social insurance taxes} \\
&- \text{ Corporate profits taxes} \\
&+ \text{ Transfer payments}
\end{aligned}$$

> **Personal Income**
> The amount of income that individuals actually receive. It is equal to national income minus undistributed corporate profits, social insurance taxes, and corporate profits taxes, plus transfer payments.

7-3f Disposable Income

The portion of personal income that can be used for consumption or saving is referred to as disposable personal income, or simply **disposable income**. It is equal to personal income minus personal taxes (especially income taxes):

$$\text{Disposable income} = \text{Personal income} - \text{Personal taxes}$$

Sometimes disposable income is referred as spendable income, take-home pay, or after-tax income.

> **Disposable Income**
> The portion of personal income that can be used for consumption or saving. It is equal to personal income minus personal taxes (especially income taxes).

7-4 Real GDP

This section defines Real GDP, shows how to compute it, and then explains how it is used to measure economic growth.

7-4a Why We Need Real GDP

In 2011, U.S. GDP was $15.84 trillion. One year later, in 2012, GDP was $16.19 trillion. Although you know that GDP was higher in 2012 than in 2011, do you know *why*?

As you think about your answer, look at GDP in a one-good economy. Suppose 10 units of good X are produced and each unit is sold for $10; then GDP in that economy is $100:

$$\text{GDP} = \$10 \times 10 \text{ units} = \$100$$

Now suppose GDP rises from $100 to $250. Why? It could rise because the price of the one good increased from $10 to $25:

$$\text{GDP} = \$\mathbf{25} \times 10 \text{ units} = \$250$$

Or it could rise because the quantity of output produced increased from 10 units to 25 units:

$$\text{GDP} = \$10 \times \mathbf{25 \text{ units}} = \$250$$

Part 2 Macroeconomic Fundamentals

Or it could rise because the price of the good increased to $12.50 and the quantity increased to 20 units:

$$\text{GDP} = \$12.50 \times 20 \text{ units} = \$250$$

To gauge the health of the economy, economists want to know why GDP increased. If GDP increased simply because price increased, then the economy is not growing. For an economy to grow, more output must be produced.

Because an increase in GDP can be due in part simply to an increase in price, a more meaningful measure is Real GDP. **Real GDP** is GDP adjusted for price changes.

Real GDP
The value of the entire output produced annually within a country's borders, adjusted for price changes.

7-4b Computing Real GDP

One way to compute Real GDP is to find the value of the output for the different years in terms of the same prices—that is, the base-year prices. Consider the following data for our one-good economy:

Year	Price of Good X	Quantity Produced of Good X (units)	GDP
1	$10	100	$10 × 100 = **$1,000**
2	$12	120	$12 × 120 = **$1,440**
3	$14	140	$14 × 140 = **$1,960**

The data show why GDP is higher in years 2 and 3: Both price and quantity have increased. However, we want to separate the part of GDP that is higher because of an increase in quantity from the part that is higher because of an increase in price. We want the Real GDP: the part of GDP that is higher because the quantity of output is higher.

To compute Real GDP for any year, multiply the quantity of the good produced in a given year by the price of the good in the base year. Thus, if year 1 is the base year, then, to find Real GDP in year 2, we multiply the quantity of the good produced in year 2 by the price of the good in year 1. Similarly, to find Real GDP in year 3, we multiply the quantity of the good produced in year 3 by the price of the good in year 1. The following table calculates Real GDP in years 1, 2, and 3:

Year	Price of Good X	Quantity Produced of Good X (units)	GDP	Real GDP
1 (base year)	$10	100	$10 × 100 = **$1,000**	$10 × 100 = **$1,000**
2	$12	120	$12 × 120 = **$1,440**	$10 × 120 = **$1,200**
3	$14	140	$14 × 140 = **$1,960**	$10 × 140 = **$1,400**

7-4c The General Equation for Real GDP

The real world has more than one good and more than one price. The general equation used to compute Real GDP is

$$\text{Real GDP} = \Sigma(\text{Base-year prices} \times \text{Current-year quantities})$$

Σ, the Greek capital letter sigma, stands for summation. Thus, Real GDP is the sum of the products of the current-year quantities and their base-year prices. In 2019, Real GDP in the United States was $19.07 trillion.

7-4d What Does It Mean if Real GDP Is Higher in One Year Than in Another?

If GDP is, say, $9 trillion in year 1 and $9.5 trillion in year 2, we cannot be sure why it has increased from one year to the next. (1) Did prices rise while output remained constant? (2) Did output rise while prices remained constant? (3) Or did prices and output both rise?

However, if Real GDP is, say, $8 trillion in year 1 and $8.3 trillion in year 2, we know why it has increased. Real GDP rises only if output rises. In other words, Real GDP rises only if more goods and services are produced.

7-4e Real GDP, Economic Growth, and Business Cycles

Suppose you have to choose between two countries. In country *A*, Real GDP grows by 3 percent each year. In country *B*, Real GDP is the same each year; if Real GDP was $500 billion last year, it is $500 billion in the current year, and it will be $500 billion next year. In which of the two countries would you prefer to live, *ceteris paribus*?

Or make a choice between countries *C* and *D*. In country *C*, Real GDP takes a roller coaster ride, alternating between rising and falling. It rises for some months, then falls, then rises again, then falls, and so on. In country *D*, Real GDP simply rises year after year. In which of the two countries would you prefer to live, *ceteris paribus*?

If you chose one country over the other in each of these two cases, then you are implicitly saying that Real GDP matters to you. One of the reasons economists study Real GDP is that it matters to you and others. In other words, because Real GDP is important to you, it is important to economists.

Economists study two major macroeconomic topics that have to do with Real GDP: *economic growth* and *business cycles*.

Economic Growth Annual **economic growth** has occurred if Real GDP in one year is higher than Real GDP in the previous year. For example, if Real GDP is $8.1 trillion in one year and $8.3 trillion in the next, the economy has undergone economic growth. The growth rate is equal to the (positive) percentage change in Real GDP and is computed as follows:

Economic Growth
Increases in Real GDP.

$$\text{Percentage change in Real GDP} = \left(\frac{\text{Real GDP}_{\text{later year}} - \text{Real GDP}_{\text{earlier year}}}{\text{Real GDP}_{\text{earlier year}}} \right) \times 100$$

The Ups and Downs in the Economy: The Business Cycle If Real GDP is on a roller coaster—rising and falling and rising and falling—the economy is said to be going through a **business cycle**. Economists usually talk about four or five phases of the business cycle. We identify five in Exhibit 6 and in the following list:

Business Cycle
Recurrent swings (up and down) in Real GDP.

1. **Peak.** At the *peak* of the business cycle, Real GDP is at a temporary high. In Exhibit 6, Real GDP is at a temporary high at Q_1.

2. **Contraction.** The *contraction* phase represents a decline in Real GDP. According to the standard definition of *recession*, two consecutive quarterly declines in Real GDP constitute a recession.

EXHIBIT 6

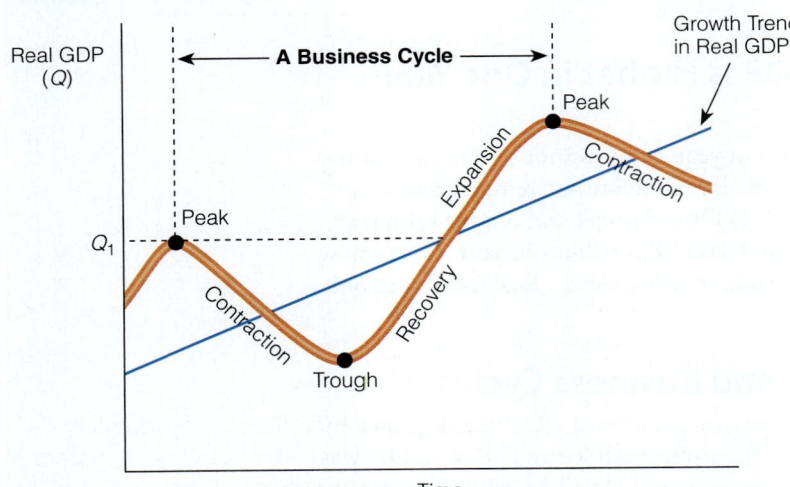

The Phases of the Business Cycle

The phases of a business cycle include the peak, contraction, trough, recovery, and expansion. A business cycle is measured from peak to peak.

3. *Trough*. The low point in Real GDP, just before it begins to turn up, is called the *trough* of the business cycle.
4. *Recovery*. The *recovery* is the period when Real GDP is rising. It begins at the trough and ends at the initial peak. The recovery in Exhibit 6 extends from the trough until Real GDP is again at Q_1.
5. *Expansion*. The *expansion* phase refers to increases in Real GDP beyond the recovery. In Exhibit 6, it refers to increases in Real GDP above Q_1.

An entire business cycle is measured from peak to peak. The typical business cycle is approximately four to five years, although a few have been shorter and some have been longer.

National Bureau of Economic Research (NBER) and Recessions The standard definition of a recession is two consecutive quarterly declines in Real GDP, but this is not the only definition of a recession. The National Bureau of Economic Research has this to say about a recession:

> *A recession is a period between a peak and a trough.... During a recession, a significant decline in economic activity spreads across the economy and can last from a few months to more than a year.*

The NBER definition is therefore different from the standard definition of a recession. According to the quote just cited, "a recession is a significant decline in economic activity [that] spreads across the economy."

1. Suppose GDP is $6 trillion in year 1 and $6.2 trillion in year 2. What has caused the rise in GDP?
2. Suppose Real GDP is $5.2 trillion in year 1 and $5.3 trillion in year 2. What has caused the rise in Real GDP?
3. Can an economy be faced with endless business cycles and still see its Real GDP grow over time? Explain your answer.

Office Hours

"Why Do We Use the Expenditure Approach to Measure Production?"

Student: When GDP was first defined, emphasis was placed on goods and services being *produced*. The definition of GDP was "the total market value of all final goods and services *produced* annually within a country's borders."

Instructor: Yes, that is correct.

Student: But when we computed GDP, we simply summed the *expenditures* made by each of the four sectors of the economy. In other words, we added consumption, investment, government purchases, and net exports.

Now, here is my problem. When we define GDP, we speak about production: final goods and services *produced*. But when we compute GDP, production doesn't seem to come up. Instead, we sum *expenditures* made by the four sectors of the economy.

My point is simple: A good can be produced that is not purchased. So, if we add up only expenditures (or purchases), aren't we underestimating production?

Instructor: I see your point. What you are perhaps saying is this. Suppose 100 chairs are produced in the year, but only 75 of them are purchased. In that case, counting only purchases (or expenditures) underestimates production. And production is what we really want to get at because GDP is defined as the total market value of all final goods and services produced.

Student: Yes, that's right. That's what I am getting at.

Instructor: Well, remember one important category of expenditures: investment. Investment consists of the expenditures of the business sector. We know that investment is the sum of fixed investment and inventory investment, but let's focus on inventory investment for a minute. Think of how goods might get into inventory. One way is for the firm to deliberately produce goods and put some into inventory. In other words, a company produces 1,000 chairs, sends 900 of them to different retailers, and then puts 100 into inventory in case there is an unexpected increase in demand for chairs. We'll call these 100 chairs *planned inventory*.

Now think of another way that chairs can be added to inventory. Suppose that, when the firm sends those 900 chairs to different retailers, not all of the chairs sell. Only 700 of them sell. What will retailers do with the remaining 200 chairs? One thing they might do is return them to the producer. So what does the firm do with those 200 returned chairs? For now, they put them into inventory. We'll call these 200 chairs *unplanned inventory*.

Here is the important point: The 300 chairs in inventory (100 chairs in planned inventory and 200 chairs in unplanned inventory) are part of overall investment. In other words, if investment for the year equals $2.1 trillion for the economy, then the market value of the 300 chairs in inventory is part of that $2.1 trillion.

When computing GDP, we count those 300 chairs in the same way we count the 700 that were produced and purchased. In short, everything produced in the economy is purchased by someone. In our example, the 300 chairs were "purchased" by the firm that produced them.

Student: Let me see if I have this right. If a firm produces a good and it is bought by, say, a consumer, that good is counted in GDP. But if the good is not bought by a consumer, then it is considered to be purchased by the firm that produced it. In other words, the chair company produces 1,000 chairs, sells 700 to consumers, and "sells" 300 to itself. It "buys" 300 of its own chairs. Is that right?

Instructor: That's right.

Student: But isn't that cheating somehow? After all, the 300 chairs weren't actually sold to anyone. They certainly weren't sold in the way we usually think of something being sold.

Instructor: That's true. But remember what we are trying to get at with GDP: the total market value of all final goods and services produced. Those 300 chairs were certainly produced. Looking at the 300 chairs as being purchased by the firm that produced them is simply a way of counting them. And counting those 300 chairs is what we want to do when we are trying to measure GDP.

Student: Yes, I see that now.

Points to Remember

1. GDP is the total market value of all final goods and services *produced* annually within a country's borders.

2. We can use the expenditure approach to measure production as long as all goods and services produced but not sold to end consumers are considered to be "purchased" by the firm that produced them.

Chapter Summary

Gross Domestic Product

- Gross domestic product (GDP) is the total market value of all final goods and services produced annually within a country's borders.
- Either the expenditure approach or the income approach can be used to compute GDP.
- To avoid the problem of double counting, only final goods and services are included in GDP.
- GDP omits certain nonmarket goods and services, both legal and illegal underground activities, the sale of used goods, financial transactions, transfer payments, and leisure (even though leisure is a good). Finally, GDP is not adjusted for the bads (e.g., pollution) that sometimes accompany production.

Expenditures

- Expenditures on U.S. goods and services include consumption, gross private domestic investment (investment), government consumption expenditures and gross investment (government purchases), and net exports (exports minus imports).
- Consumption includes spending on durable goods, nondurable goods, and services.
- Investment includes purchases of newly produced capital goods (fixed investment), changes in business inventories (inventory investment), and purchases of new residential housing (also fixed investment).
- Government purchases include federal, state, and local government purchases of goods and services, and gross investment in highways, bridges, and so on. Government purchases do not include transfer payments.
- Net exports equals the total foreign spending on domestic goods (exports) minus the total domestic spending on foreign goods (imports).

Computing GDP

- According to the expenditure approach, $GDP = C + I + G + (EX - IM)$. In other words, GDP equals consumption, plus investment, plus government purchases, plus net exports.

Measurements Other Than GDP

- Net domestic product (NDP) equals gross domestic product (GDP) minus the capital consumption allowance:

$$NDP = GDP - \text{Capital consumption allowance}$$

- National income equals the sum of resource, or factor, payments:

$$\begin{aligned} \text{National income} = &\text{ Compensation of employees} \\ &+ \text{Proprietors, income} \\ &+ \text{Corporate profits} \\ &+ \text{Rental income} \\ &+ \text{Net interest} \end{aligned}$$

- Personal income equals national income minus undistributed corporate profits; social insurance taxes; and taxes on corporate profits, taxes, plus transfer payments:

$$\begin{aligned} \text{Personal Income} = &\text{ National income} \\ &- \text{Undistributed corporate profits} \\ &- \text{Social insurance taxes} \\ &- \text{Corporate profits taxes} \\ &+ \text{Transfer payments} \end{aligned}$$

- Disposable income = Personal income − Personal taxes

Real GDP

- Real GDP is GDP adjusted for price changes. It is GDP in base-year dollars.

Economic Growth and Business Cycles

- Annual economic growth has occurred if Real GDP in one year is higher than Real GDP in the previous year.
- The business cycle has five phases: peak, contraction, trough, recovery, and expansion. A complete business cycle is measured from peak to peak.

Key Terms and Concepts

Gross Domestic Product (GDP)
Final Good
Intermediate Good
Double Counting
Transfer Payment
Consumption
Investment
Inventory Investment
Fixed Investment
Government Purchases
Government Transfer Payments
Imports
Exports
Net Exports
National Income
Capital Consumption Allowance (Depreciation)
Net Domestic Product (NDP)
Personal Income
Disposable Income
Real GDP
Economic Growth
Business Cycle

Questions and Problems

1. "I just heard on the news that GDP is higher this year than it was last year. This means that we're better off this year than last year." Comment.
2. Which of the following are included in the calculation of this year's GDP? (a) 12-year-old Logan mowing his family's lawn; (b) Adil Naser buying a used car; (c) Kate Sabitini buying a bond issued by General Motors; (d) Ed Ferguson's receipt of a Social Security payment; and (e) the illegal drug transaction at the corner of Elm and Fifth.
3. Discuss the problems you see in comparing the GDPs of two countries, say, the United States and the People's Republic of China.
4. The manuscript for this book was keyed by the author. Had he hired someone to do the keying, GDP would have been higher than it was. What other activities would increase GDP if they were done differently? What activities would decrease GDP if they were done differently?
5. Why does GDP omit the sales of used goods? Of financial transactions? Of government transfer payments?
6. A business firm produces a good this year that it doesn't sell. As a result, the good is added to the firm's inventory. How does this inventory good find its way into GDP?
7. What are the five components of national income?
8. Is it true that net domestic product plus the capital consumption allowance is equal to GDP? Explain your answer.
9. What is the capital consumption allowance?
10. Economists prefer to compare Real GDP figures for different years instead of comparing GDP figures. Why?
11. What is the difference between a recovery and an expansion?
12. Define each of the following terms:
    a. Contraction
    b. Business cycle
    c. Trough
    d. Disposable income
    e. Net domestic product
13. Does the expenditure approach to computing GDP measure U.S. spending on all goods, U.S. spending on only U.S. goods, or U.S. and foreign spending on only U.S. goods? Explain your answer.
14. In the first quarter of the year, Real GDP was $400 billion; in the second quarter, it was $398 billion; in the third quarter, it was $399 billion; and in the fourth quarter, it was $395 billion. Has there been a recession? Explain your answer.

Working with Numbers and Graphs

1. Net exports are −$114 billion and exports are $857 billion. What are imports?
2. Consumption spending is $3.708 trillion, spending on nondurable goods is $1.215 trillion, and spending on services is $2.041 trillion. What does spending on durable goods equal?
3. Inventory investment is $62 billion, and total investment is $1.122 trillion. What does fixed investment equal?
4. In year 1, the prices of goods X, Y, and Z are $2, $4, and $6 per unit, respectively. In year 2, the prices of goods X, Y, and Z are $3, $4, and $7, respectively. In year 2, twice as many units of each good are produced as in year 1. In year 1, 20 units of X, 40 units of Y, and 60 units of Z are produced. If year 1 is the base year, what does Real GDP equal in year 2?
5. Nondurable goods spending = $400 million, durable goods spending = $300 million, new residential housing spending = $200 million, and spending on services = $500 million. What does consumption equal?
6. According to the circular flow diagram in Exhibit 4, consumption spending flows into U.S. product markets, but import spending does not. But U.S. households buy imported goods in U.S. markets, don't they? Explain.
7. If personal taxes are $400 billion and disposable income is $4,000 billion, then what does personal income equal?
8. If national income is $5,000 billion, compensation of employees is $2,105 billion, proprietors' income is $1,520 billion, corporate profits are $490 billion, and net interest is $128 billion, then what does rental income equal?
9. Use the table to answer the following questions:

Item	Dollar Amount (in $ billions)
Durable goods	200
Nondurable goods	400
Services	700
Fixed investment	120
Inventory investment	20
Government Purchases	500
Exports	100
Imports	150
Capital consumption allowance	20
Compensation of employees	700
Proprietors' income	480
Corporate profits	200
Rental income	200
Income earned from the rest of the world	40
Income earned by the rest of the world	200
Indirect business taxes	80
Statistical discrepancy	30
Undistributed corporate profits	20
Social insurance taxes	80
Corporate profits taxes	30
Transfer payments	50
Personal taxes	100
Net interest	20

   a. What does GDP equal?
   b. What does NDP equal?
   c. What does national income equal?
   d. What does personal income equal?
   e. What does disposable income equal?
   f. If purchases of new capital goods are $90 billion, then what does purchases of new residential housing equal?
   g. What do net exports equal?

10. If Real GDP is $487 billion in year 1 and $498 billion in year 2, what is the economic growth rate?

11. The figure that follows shows a business cycle. Identify each of the following as a phase of the business cycle:

    a. Point *A*
    b. Between points *A* and *B*
    c. Point *B*
    d. Between points *B* and *C*
    e. Point *D*

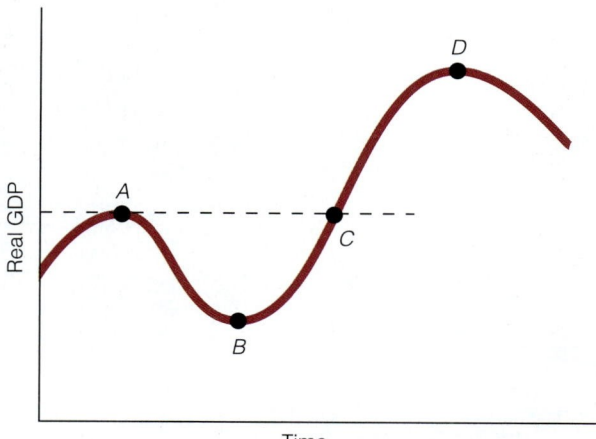

CHAPTER 8
Aggregate Demand and Aggregate Supply

Introduction

Businesses make decisions based on what is happening in the economy today and what they expect will happen in the economy in the future. For example, their profitability is based in part on the wages they must pay their employees, the prices of their nonlabor inputs, the productivity of their workers, and business taxes. If businesses want to expand in the future, they must consider all these things and try to predict their future sales. If they trade overseas, they must worry about exchange rates and foreign real national income. We discuss all such things and more in this chapter.

8-1 A Way to View the Economy

This chapter begins our theoretical discussion of an economy. We can think of an economy as consisting of two major activities: buying and producing (see Exhibit 1). Specifically, goods and services are produced, and goods and services are bought. When economists speak about aggregate demand (*AD*), they are speaking about the buying side of the economy. When economists speak about aggregate supply (*AS*), they are speaking about the producing side of the economy. Thus,

Buying side of the economy = Aggregate demand
Producing side of the economy = Aggregate supply

With respect to production, two periods are relevant: production in the short run and production in the long run. When referring to short-run aggregate supply (*SRAS*), economists are speaking about production in the short run. When referring to long-run aggregate supply (*LRAS*), they are speaking about production in the long run.

Production in the short run = Short-run aggregate supply
Production in the long run = Long-run aggregate supply

EXHIBIT 1

An Economy

There are two sides to an economy: a buying side and a producing side. There are two periods that relate to the producing side: production in the short run and production in the long run. Buying side = Aggregate demand (AD); Production in the short run = Short-run aggregate supply (SRAS); Production in the long run = Long-run aggregate supply (LRAS).

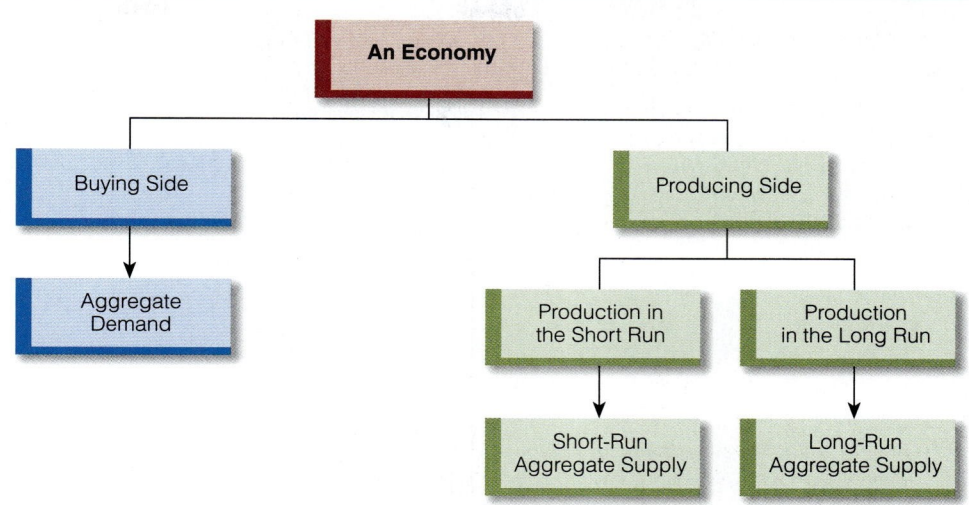

The framework of analysis we use is called aggregate demand–aggregate supply (*AD–AS*). That framework of analysis has three parts:

1. Aggregate demand (*AD*)
2. Short-run aggregate supply (*SRAS*)
3. Long-run aggregate supply (*LRAS*)

8-2 Aggregate Demand

Recall from the last chapter that people, firms, and governments buy U.S. goods and services. **Aggregate demand** is the quantity demanded of these U.S. goods and services, or the quantity demanded of U.S. Real GDP, at various price levels, *ceteris paribus*. For example, the following whole set of data represents aggregate demand:

Aggregate Demand

Price Index	Quantity Demanded of Goods and Services (Quantity Demanded of Real GDP)
100	$1,200 billion worth of goods and services
110	$1,000 billion worth of goods and services
120	$800 billion worth of goods and services

Aggregate Demand
The quantity demanded of all goods and services (Real GDP) at different price levels, *ceteris paribus*.

An **aggregate demand (AD) curve** is the graphical representation of aggregate demand. An *AD* curve is shown in Exhibit 2. Notice that it is downward sloping, indicating an inverse relationship between the price level (*P*) and the quantity demanded of Real GDP (*Q*): As the price level rises, the quantity demanded of Real GDP falls; as the price level falls, the quantity demanded of Real GDP rises, *ceteris paribus*.

Aggregate Demand (AD) Curve
A curve that shows the quantity demanded of all goods and services (Real GDP) at different price levels, *ceteris paribus*.

EXHIBIT 2

The Aggregate Demand Curve

The aggregate demand curve is downward sloping, specifying an inverse relationship between the price level and the quantity demanded of Real GDP.

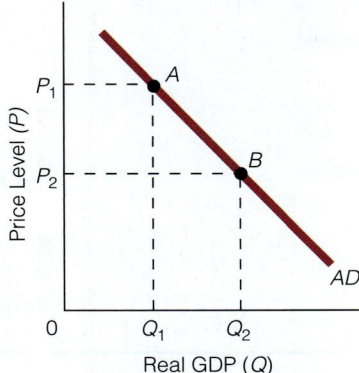

Aggregate Demand Curve The price level and quantity demanded of Real GDP are inversely related.

Real Balance Effect
The change in the purchasing power of dollar-denominated assets that results from a change in the price level.

Monetary Wealth
The value of a person's monetary assets. Wealth, as distinguished from monetary wealth, refers to the value of all assets owned, both monetary and nonmonetary. In short, a person's wealth equals his or her monetary wealth (e.g., $1,000 cash) plus nonmonetary wealth (e.g., a car or a house).

Purchasing Power
The quantity of goods and services that can be purchased with a unit of money. Purchasing power and the price level are inversely related: As the price level goes up (down), purchasing power goes down (up).

8-2a Why Does the Aggregate Demand Curve Slope Downward?

Asking why the *AD* curve slopes downward is the same as asking why the relationship between the price level and the quantity demanded of Real GDP is inverse. This inverse relationship and the resulting downward slope of the *AD* curve are explained by (1) the real balance effect, (2) the interest rate effect, and (3) the international trade effect.

Real Balance Effect (Due to a Change in the Price Level) The **real balance effect** states that the inverse relationship between the price level and the quantity demanded of Real GDP is established through changes in the value of **monetary wealth**, or the value of a person's monetary assets. Changes in monetary wealth usually take the form of increased or decreased **purchasing power**—that is, the quantity of goods and services that can be purchased with a unit of money.

To illustrate, consider a person who has $50,000 in cash. Suppose the price level falls. As this happens, the purchasing power of the person's $50,000 rises. The $50,000, which once could buy 100 television sets at $500 each, can now buy 125 sets at $400 each. Saying that an increase in the purchasing power of the person's $50,000 is identical to saying that his monetary wealth has increased. (Isn't the $50,000 more valuable when it can buy more than when it can buy less?) And, as he becomes wealthier, he buys more goods.

So a fall in the price level causes purchasing power to rise, increasing a person's monetary wealth. As people become wealthier, the quantity demanded of Real GDP rises.

Now suppose the price level rises. In this event, the purchasing power of the $50,000 falls. The $50,000, which once could buy 100 television sets at $500 each, can now buy 80 sets at $625 each. Saying that a decrease in the purchasing power of the person's $50,000 is identical to saying that his monetary wealth has decreased. And as he becomes less wealthy, he buys fewer goods.

Chapter 8 Aggregate Demand and Aggregate Supply

In sum, a rise in the price level causes purchasing power to fall, decreasing a person's monetary wealth. As people become less wealthy, the quantity demanded of Real GDP falls.

Interest Rate Effect (Due to a Change in the Price Level)

The **interest rate effect** states that the inverse relationship between the price level and the quantity demanded of Real GDP is established through changes in the part of household and business spending that is sensitive to changes in interest rates.

Suppose a person buys a fixed bundle of goods (food, clothing, and shelter) each week. Then the price level falls, increasing the purchasing power of the person's money. With more purchasing power (per dollar), she can purchase her fixed bundle of goods with less money. What does she do with part of this increase in her monetary wealth? She saves it. In terms of simple supply-and-demand analysis, the supply of credit increases. Subsequently, the price of credit (the interest rate) drops. As the interest rate drops, households and businesses borrow more, so they end up buying more goods. Thus, the quantity demanded of Real GDP rises.

Now suppose the price level rises, decreasing the purchasing power of the person's money. With less purchasing power (per dollar), she cannot purchase her fixed bundle of goods with the same amount of money. If she wants to continue to buy the goods, she needs to acquire more money. To do that, she goes to a bank and requests a loan. In terms of simple supply-and-demand analysis, the demand for credit increases. Consequently, the interest rate rises. As the interest rate rises, households borrow less to finance, say, automobile purchases, and firms borrow less to finance new capital goods spending. Thus, the quantity demanded of Real GDP falls.

> **Interest Rate Effect**
> The changes in household and business buying as the interest rate changes (in turn, a reflection of a change in the demand for or supply of credit brought on by price level changes).

International Trade Effect (Due to a Change in the Price Level)

The **international trade effect** is the change in foreign sector spending as the price level changes. The inverse relationship between the price level and the quantity demanded of Real GDP is established through foreign sector spending, which includes U.S. spending on foreign goods (imports) and foreign spending on U.S. goods (exports).

Suppose the price level in the United States falls. As this happens, U.S. goods become relatively cheaper than foreign goods. As a result, both Americans and foreigners buy more U.S. goods. The quantity demanded of U.S. Real GDP rises.

Now suppose the price level in the United States rises. In that event, U.S. goods become relatively more expensive than foreign goods. As a result, both Americans and foreigners buy fewer U.S. goods. The quantity demanded of U.S. Real GDP falls.

For a review of the three effects—real balance, interest rate, and international trade—see Exhibit 3.

> **International Trade Effect**
> The change in foreign sector spending as the price level changes.

Finding Economics

In a Store, Buying a Watch Jim is in a store, buying a watch imported from Switzerland. What does this purchase have to do with a downward-sloping aggregate demand curve? When we ask Jim why he's buying a Swiss watch, he tells us that the Swiss watch is cheaper than the American watch. The reason could very well be that the U.S. price level has recently risen relative to the Swiss price level. In other words, when Jim buys the Swiss watch instead of the American watch, we could be seeing the international trade effect in action.

EXHIBIT 3

Why the Aggregate Demand Curve Is Downward Sloping

This exhibit outlines the three effects that explain why the *AD* curve is downward sloping. Each effect relates to a change in the price level (*P*) leading to a change in the quantity demanded of Real GDP (*Q*).

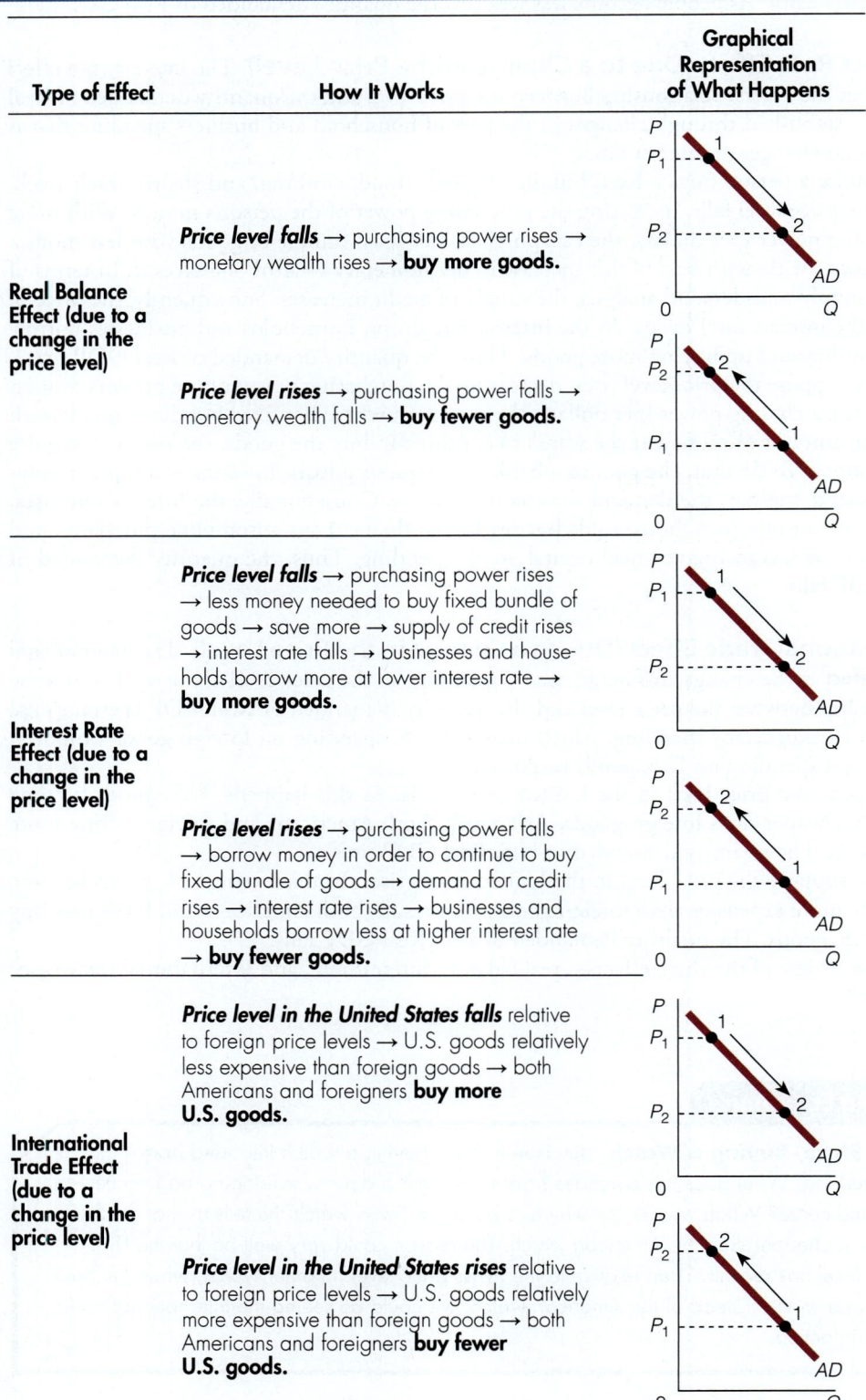

Type of Effect	How It Works
Real Balance Effect (due to a change in the price level)	**Price level falls** → purchasing power rises → monetary wealth rises → **buy more goods.**
	Price level rises → purchasing power falls → monetary wealth falls → **buy fewer goods.**
Interest Rate Effect (due to a change in the price level)	**Price level falls** → purchasing power rises → less money needed to buy fixed bundle of goods → save more → supply of credit rises → interest rate falls → businesses and households borrow more at lower interest rate → **buy more goods.**
	Price level rises → purchasing power falls → borrow money in order to continue to buy fixed bundle of goods → demand for credit rises → interest rate rises → businesses and households borrow less at higher interest rate → **buy fewer goods.**
International Trade Effect (due to a change in the price level)	**Price level in the United States falls** relative to foreign price levels → U.S. goods relatively less expensive than foreign goods → both Americans and foreigners **buy more U.S. goods.**
	Price level in the United States rises relative to foreign price levels → U.S. goods relatively more expensive than foreign goods → both Americans and foreigners **buy fewer U.S. goods.**

8-2b An Important Word on the Three Effects

As explained, the aggregate demand curve is downward sloping because of the real balance, interest rate, and international trade effects. However, keep in mind that what caused these three effects is a change in the price level. In other words, when discussing, say, the interest rate effect, we are talking about the interest rate effect of *a change in the price level*:

Price level changes → Interest rate effect

Why is this point important? Because the interest rate can change as a result of things *other than the price level changing*, and not everything that changes the interest rate leads to a movement from one point to another point on the *AD* curve. Other things that change the interest rate can lead to a shift in the *AD* curve instead. We will have more to say about this point later. For now, though, simply keep in mind the cause of each of the three effects: a change in the price level—the variable on the vertical axis in Exhibit 2.

8-2c A Change in Quantity Demanded of Real GDP Versus a Change in Aggregate Demand

A change in the price level brings about a change in the quantity demanded of Real GDP. As the price level falls, the quantity demanded of Real GDP rises, *ceteris paribus*. In Exhibit 4(a), a change in the quantity demanded of Real GDP is represented as a *movement* from one point (*A*) on AD_1 to another point (*B*) on AD_1.

EXHIBIT 4

A Change in the Quantity Demanded of Real GDP Versus a Change in Aggregate Demand

(a) A change in the quantity demanded of Real GDP is graphically represented as a *movement* from one point, *A*, on AD_1 to another point, *B*, on AD_1. A change in the quantity demanded of Real GDP is the result of a change in the price level. (b) A change in aggregate demand is graphically represented as a *shift* in the aggregate demand curve from AD_1 to AD_2.

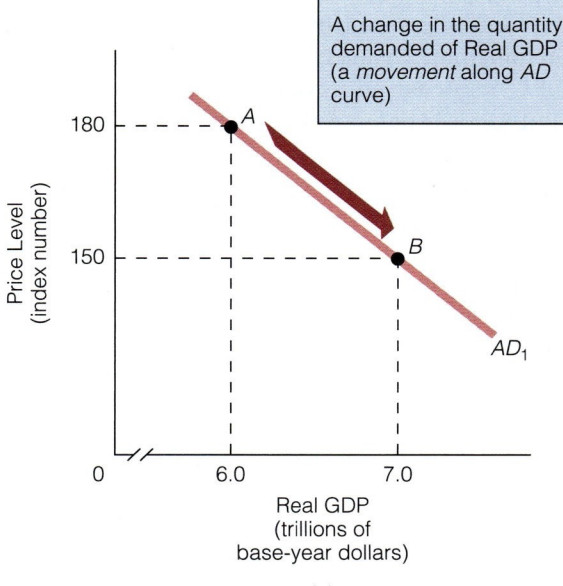
(a)

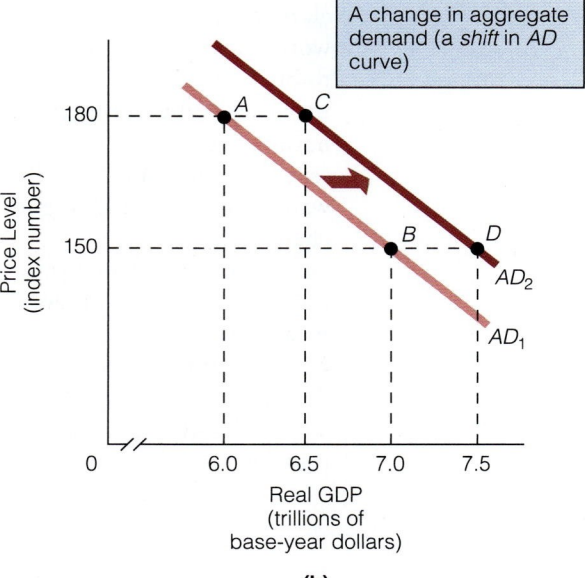
(b)

A change in aggregate demand is represented in Exhibit 4(b) as a *shift* in the aggregate demand curve from AD_1 to AD_2. When the aggregate demand curve shifts, the quantity demanded of Real GDP changes even though the price level remains constant. For example, at a price level (index number) of 180, the quantity demanded of Real GDP on AD_1 in Exhibit 4(b) is $6.0 trillion. But at the same price level (180), the quantity demanded of Real GDP on AD_2 is $6.5 trillion.

> **Thinking Like an Economist**
>
> **Shift Factors Versus Movement Factors, Once Again** To the economist, not all factors are alike. For some factors, the change is from one point to another on the same curve. These are *movement factors*. The price level is a movement factor. Raise it, and we move up on the *AD* curve; lower it, and we move down.
>
> Other factors, if they change, shift curves. These are *shift factors*. We turn now to discuss shift factors with respect to the *AD* curve.

8-2d Changes in Aggregate Demand: Shifts in the *AD* Curve

What can change aggregate demand? What can cause aggregate demand to rise, and what can cause it to fall?

The simple answer is that aggregate demand changes when spending on U.S. goods and services changes. If spending increases at a given price level, aggregate demand rises; if spending decreases at a given price level, aggregate demand falls. That is,

Spending increases at a given price level → AD rises

Spending decreases at a given price level → AD falls

Suppose the price level in the economy is represented by the Consumer Price Index (CPI), and the index is currently 150. At this price level, U.S. residents, firms, and governments—along with foreigners, foreign firms, and foreign governments—want to buy, say, $7.0 trillion worth of U.S. goods and services. Then something changes, and all of a sudden, they all want to buy a total of $7.5 trillion worth of U.S. goods and services. Now, before you conclude that they want to buy more goods and services because the prices of goods and services have fallen, keep in mind that the price level has not changed. The price level—still represented by the CPI—is still 150. In other words, all these people, firms, and governments want to buy more U.S. goods even though the prices of the goods and services have not changed.

When individuals, firms, and governments want to buy more U.S. goods and services even though the prices of the goods have not changed, we say that aggregate demand has increased. As a result, the *AD* curve *shifts* to the right. Of course, when individuals, firms, and governments want to buy fewer U.S. goods and services at a given price level, we say that aggregate demand has decreased. As a result, the *AD* curve *shifts* to the left.

Exhibit 4(b) shows a change in aggregate demand (a shift in the *AD* curve). At point *B*, the price level is 150, and total expenditures on U.S. goods and services are $7.0 trillion. At point *D*, the price level is still 150, but total expenditures on U.S. goods and services have increased to $7.5 trillion. Why has aggregate demand moved from point B to point D; that is, what has caused the increase in total expenditures? To find out, we have to look at the components of total expenditures.

8-2e How Spending Components Affect Aggregate Demand

The last chapter identified four major spending components: consumption (C), investment (I), government purchases (G), and net exports (NX). Recall, in addition, that net exports equals exports (EX) minus imports (IM). Let's keep the numbers simple: $C = \$100$, $I = \$100$, $G = \$100$, $EX = \$50$, and $IM = \$15$. If $EX = \$50$ and $IM = \$15$, then net exports = $35.

Using these dollar figures, we calculate that $335 is spent on U.S. goods and services. We get this dollar amount by finding the sum of consumption, investment, government purchases, and net exports:

$$\text{Total expenditures on U.S. goods and services} = C + I + G + NX$$

Obviously, this dollar amount will go up if (1) C rises, (2) I rises, (3) G rises, or (4) NX rises (or any combination of them rises). In other words, a rise in consumption, investment, government purchases, or net exports will raise spending on U.S. goods and services:

$$C\uparrow, I\uparrow, G\uparrow, NX\uparrow \rightarrow \text{Total expenditures on U.S. goods and services} \uparrow$$

Now, what will cause spending on U.S. goods and services to go down? Obviously, such spending will decline if (1) C falls, (2) I falls, (3) G falls, or (4) NX falls (or any combination of them falls):

$$C\downarrow, I\downarrow, G\downarrow, NX\downarrow \rightarrow \text{Total expenditures on U.S. goods or services} \downarrow$$

Because we now know what causes total expenditures on U.S. goods and services to change, we can relate the components of spending to (U.S.) aggregate demand. If, *at a given price level*,

- Consumption, investment, government purchases, or net exports *rise*, aggregate demand will rise, and the AD curve will shift to the right.

- Consumption, investment, government purchases, or net exports *fall*, aggregate demand will fall, and the AD curve will shift to the left.

We can write these relationships as

$$\text{If, at a given price level, } C\uparrow, I\uparrow, G\uparrow, NX\uparrow, \text{ then } AD\uparrow$$
$$\text{If, at a given price level, } C\downarrow, I\downarrow, G\downarrow, NX\downarrow, \text{ then } AD\downarrow$$

The flowcharts in Exhibit 5 show how changes in spending components affect aggregate demand.

EXHIBIT 5

Changes in Aggregate Demand

The flowcharts show how aggregate demand changes with changes in various spending components.

C = consumption,
I = investment,
G = government purchases,
NX = net exports,
EX = exports,
IM = imports.
Keep in mind that NX = EX − IM.

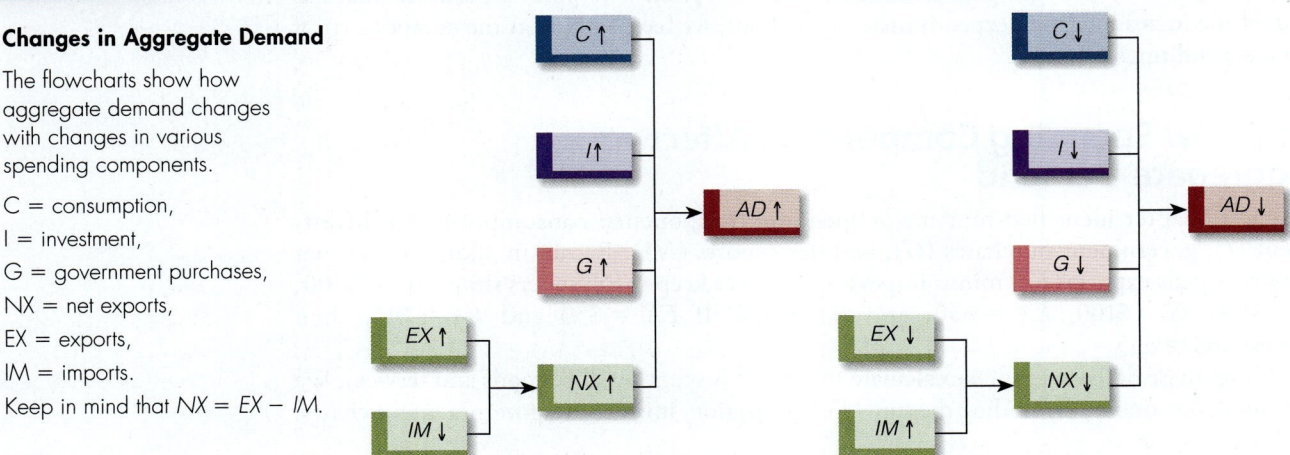

(a)   (b)

8-2f Why Is There More Total Spending?

Here is a question that an economics professor might place on an exam:

> *True or false? The price level falls and total spending rises. As a result of total spending rising, aggregate demand in the economy rises and the AD curve shifts rightward.*

You may think that the answer is true—perhaps because you are accustomed to thinking that, if total spending rises, aggregate demand rises. But aggregate demand rises only if total spending rises at *a given price level*.

To illustrate the difference between (1) total spending rising at a falling price level and (2) total spending rising at a given price level, consider the following two examples:

- *Example 1.* The price level falls, and goods and services become cheaper. As a result of lower prices, individuals start to buy more goods and services. Consequently, total spending rises.

- *Example 2.* The price level does not change. Still, something in the economy changes, so people start buying more goods and services. As a result of their buying more goods and services, total spending in the economy rises.

In both cases, total spending rises. But in example 1, total spending rises because prices have fallen. The result is a *movement* down a given *AD* curve. In example 2, total spending rises even when prices remain unchanged. The result is a *shift* rightward in the *AD* curve.

Lesson learned: Total spending can rise for one of two reasons. The first deals with a decline in prices and leads to a *movement* along a given *AD* curve. The second deals with a change in some factor other than prices and leads to a *shift* in the *AD* curve.

8-2g Factors That Can Change C, I, G, and NX (EX − IM) and Therefore Can Change AD (Shift the AD Curve)

What can change aggregate demand in the economy? The answer is a change in any or all of consumption, investment, government purchases, and net exports (exports minus imports). So, if, for example, someone asks you why *AD* increased, you might say "because consumption increased."

Chapter 8 Aggregate Demand and Aggregate Supply

But suppose the person then asks, "What caused consumption to increase?" Your answer to one question simply leads to another question. If a change in consumption changes aggregate demand, what changes consumption? The same question can be asked about changes in investment, government purchases, and net exports (i.e., exports minus imports). For example, if aggregate demand increased because investment increased, then what caused investment to increase?

This section looks at some of the many factors that can change consumption, investment, and net exports. A later chapter considers the factors that can change government purchases.

Consumption Four factors can affect consumption: wealth, expectations about future prices and income, the interest rate, and income taxes.

1. *Wealth*. Individuals consume not only on the basis of their present income but also on the basis of their **wealth**. Suppose each of two individuals has an income of $80,000 a year. One has $75,000 in the bank, and the other has no assets at all. We would expect the person with $75,000 in the bank to spend more of her income on consumption goods this year. Greater wealth makes individuals feel financially more secure and thus more willing to spend:

    Wealth
    The value of all assets owned, both monetary and nonmonetary.

    - Increases in wealth lead to increases in consumption. If consumption increases, aggregate demand rises and the *AD* curve shifts to the right.
    - Decreases in wealth lead to declines in consumption, which lead to a fall in aggregate demand. Consequently, the *AD* curve shifts to the left.

    $$\text{Wealth}\uparrow \rightarrow C\uparrow \rightarrow AD\uparrow$$
    $$\text{Wealth}\downarrow \rightarrow C\downarrow \rightarrow AD\downarrow$$

2. *Expectations About Future Prices and Income*. Individuals' expectations of future prices can increase or decrease aggregate demand:

    - If individuals expect *higher* prices in the future, they increase their current consumption expenditures to buy goods at the lower current prices. The increase in consumption leads to an increase in aggregate demand.
    - If individuals expect *lower* prices in the future, they decrease current consumption expenditures. The reduction in consumption leads to a decrease in aggregate demand.

    $$\text{Expect higher future prices} \rightarrow C\uparrow \rightarrow AD\uparrow$$
    $$\text{Expect lower future prices} \rightarrow C\downarrow \rightarrow AD\downarrow$$

    Similarly, expectations regarding income can affect aggregate demand:

    - Expectations of a *higher* future income increase consumption, leading to an increase in aggregate demand.
    - Expectations of a *lower* future income decrease consumption, leading to a decrease in aggregate demand.

    $$\text{Expect higher future income} \rightarrow C\uparrow \rightarrow AD\uparrow$$
    $$\text{Expect lower future income} \rightarrow C\downarrow \rightarrow AD\downarrow$$

3. *Interest Rate*. Current empirical work shows that spending on consumer durables is sensitive to the interest rate:

    - Buyers often pay for these items by borrowing, so an *increase* in the interest rate increases the monthly payment amounts linked to the purchase of durables and thereby reduces their consumption. The reduction in consumption leads to a decline in aggregate demand.

- Alternatively, a *decrease* in the interest rate reduces monthly payment amounts and thereby increases the consumption of durables. The increase in consumption leads to an increase in aggregate demand.

$$\text{Interest rate}\uparrow \rightarrow C\downarrow \rightarrow AD\downarrow$$
$$\text{Interest rate}\downarrow \rightarrow C\uparrow \rightarrow AD\uparrow$$

4. *Income Taxes.* Let's consider personal income taxes—that is, the taxes a person pays on earned income:
    - As income taxes *rise*, disposable income decreases. When people have less take-home pay to spend, consumption falls. Consequently, aggregate demand decreases.
    - A *decrease* in income taxes has the opposite effect: It raises disposable income. When people have more take-home pay to spend, consumption rises and aggregate demand increases.

$$\text{Income taxes}\uparrow \rightarrow C\downarrow \rightarrow AD\downarrow$$
$$\text{Income taxes}\downarrow \rightarrow C\uparrow \rightarrow AD\uparrow$$

Investment Three factors can change investment: the interest rate, expectations about future sales, and business taxes.

1. *Interest Rate.* Changes in interest rates affect business decisions:
    - As the interest rate *rises*, the cost of an investment project rises, and businesses invest less. As investment decreases, aggregate demand decreases.
    - As the interest rate *falls*, the cost of an investment project falls, and businesses invest more. Consequently, aggregate demand increases.

$$\text{Interest rate}\uparrow \rightarrow I\downarrow \rightarrow AD\downarrow$$
$$\text{Interest rate}\downarrow \rightarrow I\uparrow \rightarrow AD\uparrow$$

2. *Expectations About Future Sales.* Businesses invest because they expect to sell the goods they produce:
    - If businesses become *optimistic* about future sales, investment spending grows, and aggregate demand increases.
    - If businesses become *pessimistic* about future sales, investment spending contracts, and aggregate demand decreases.

$$\text{Businesses become optimistic about future sales} \rightarrow I\uparrow \rightarrow AD\uparrow$$
$$\text{Businesses become pessimistic about future sales} \rightarrow I\downarrow \rightarrow AD\downarrow$$

3. *Business Taxes.* Businesses naturally consider expected after-tax profits when they make their investment decisions:
    - An *increase* in business taxes lowers expected profitability. With less profit expected, businesses invest less. As investment spending declines, so does aggregate demand.
    - A *decrease* in business taxes raises expected profitability and investment spending, increasing aggregate demand.

$$\text{Business taxes}\uparrow \rightarrow I\downarrow \rightarrow AD\downarrow$$
$$\text{Business taxes}\downarrow \rightarrow I\uparrow \rightarrow AD\uparrow$$

Net Exports Two factors can change net exports: foreign real national income and the exchange rate.

1. *Foreign Real National Income.* Just as Americans earn a national income, so do people in other countries. The earnings of those people constitute foreign national income. By adjusting this foreign national income for price changes, we obtain foreign real national income:

   - As foreign real national income *rises*, foreigners buy more U.S. goods and services. Thus, U.S. exports (*EX*) rise. As exports rise, net exports rise, *ceteris paribus*. As net exports rise, aggregate demand increases.

   - The process also works in reverse: As foreign real national income *falls*, foreigners buy fewer U.S. goods, and exports fall. The fall in exports lowers net exports, reducing aggregate demand.

   Foreign real national income ↑ → U.S. exports ↑ → U.S. net exports ↑ → AD ↑

   Foreign real national income ↓ → U.S. exports ↓ → U.S. net exports ↓ → AD ↓

2. *Exchange Rate.* The **exchange rate** is the price of one currency in terms of another currency; for example, $1.25 may be exchanged for €1 (1 euro). A currency has **appreciated** in value if more of a foreign currency is needed to buy it. A currency has **depreciated** in value if more of it is needed to buy a foreign currency. For example, a change in the exchange rate from $1.25 = €1 to $1.50 = €1 means that more dollars are needed to buy 1 euro; the euro has appreciated. And because more dollars are needed to buy €1, the dollar has depreciated.

   - *Depreciation* in a nation's currency makes foreign goods more expensive. Consider an Irish coat that is priced at €200 when the exchange rate is $1.25 = €1. To buy the Irish coat for €200, an American has to pay $250 ($1.25 for each of €200, for a total of $250). Now suppose the dollar depreciates to $1.50 = €1. The American now has to pay $300 for the coat.

   - The process just described is symmetrical. An *appreciation* in a nation's currency makes foreign goods cheaper. For example, if the exchange rate goes from $1.25 = €1 to $1 = €1, the Irish coat will cost the American only $200.

   The depreciation and appreciation of the U.S. dollar affect net exports:

   - As the dollar *depreciates*, foreign goods become more expensive, Americans cut back on imported goods, and foreigners (whose currency has appreciated) increase their purchases of U.S. exported goods. If exports rise and imports fall, net exports increase, and aggregate demand increases.

   - As the dollar *appreciates*, foreign goods become cheaper, Americans increase their purchases of imported goods, and foreigners (whose currency has depreciated) cut back on their purchases of U.S. exported goods. If exports fall and imports rise, net exports decrease, thus lowering aggregate demand.

   Dollar depreciates → U.S. exports ↑ and U.S. imports ↓ → U.S. net exports ↑ → AD ↑

   Dollar appreciates → U.S. exports ↓ and U.S. imports ↑ → U.S. net imports ↓ → AD ↓

(See Exhibit 6 for a summary of the factors that change aggregate demand.)

> **Exchange Rate**
> The price of one currency in terms of another currency.
>
> **Appreciated**
> An increase in the value of one currency relative to other currencies.
>
> **Depreciated**
> A decrease in the value of one currency relative to other currencies.

EXHIBIT 6

Factors That Change Aggregate Demand

Aggregate demand (AD) changes whenever consumption (C), investment (I), government purchases (G), or net exports (EX − IM) change. The factors that can affect C, I, and EX − IM, and thereby indirectly affect aggregate demand, are listed.

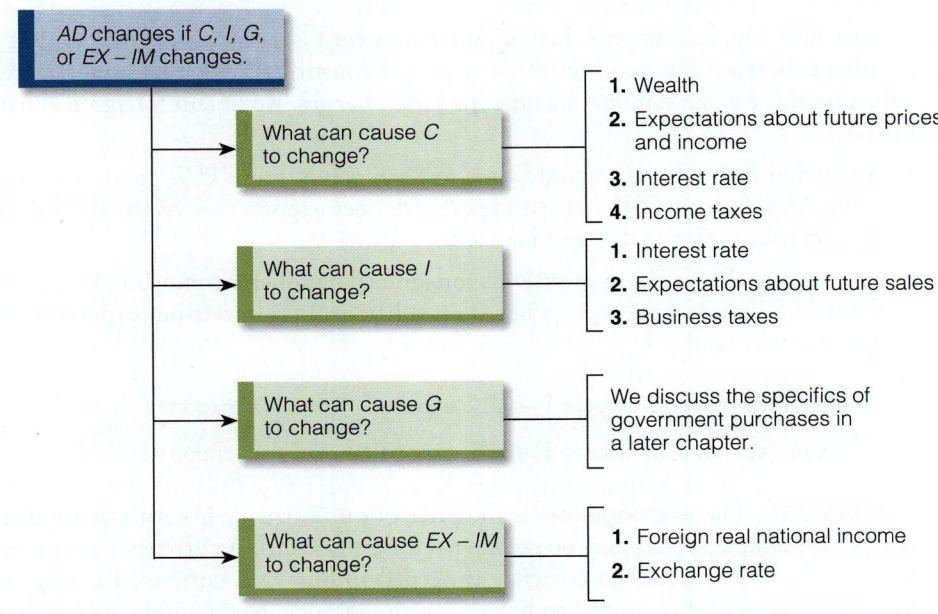

Thinking Like an Economist

The W–X–Y–Z Explanation In the previous discussion, we said, for example, that if the dollar depreciates, U.S. exports will rise and U.S. imports will fall, in turn causing U.S. net exports to rise, in turn causing aggregate demand to rise. A summarization of this type of argument might go like this: A change in W leads to a change in X, which leads to a change in Y, which leads to change in Z. Let's call this kind of explanation the W–X–Y–Z explanation.

Economists often think in terms of one thing changing something else, in turn changing still something else, and so on. Some people find this kind of thinking curious. They ask, "Why not simply say that W leads to Z instead of saying that W leads to X, which leads to Y, which leads to Z?"

Saying that W leads to Z might make things easier (there would be less to remember), but what the shortcut gains in ease, it loses in completeness. It is best to explain just how one thing eventually leads to something else happening.

8-2h Can a Change in the Money Supply Change Aggregate Demand?

Changes in such factors as interest rates, business taxes, exchange rates, and the like can change aggregate demand (indirectly) by directly changing consumption, investment, and net exports. What about the money supply? Can a change in the money supply lead to a change in aggregate demand?

Let's see. Suppose the money supply rises from, say, $1,400 billion to $1,500 billion. Will this change in the money supply result in an increase in aggregate demand? Most economists would say that it does, but they differ on how. One way to explain the effect (in the context of our discussion) is as follows: (1) A change in the money supply affects interest rates, (2) a change in interest rates changes consumption and investment, and (3) a change in consumption and investment affects aggregate demand. Therefore, a change in the money supply is a catalyst in a process that ends with a change in aggregate demand. (We will have much more to say about the money supply and interest rates in later chapters.)

8-2i If Consumption Rises, Does Some Other Spending Component Have to Decline?

Suppose $C = \$100$, $I = \$100$, $G = \$100$, and $NX = \$100$. Then total expenditures equal $400. Now suppose C rises by $50, to a level of $150. Must one or more other spending components decline by $50? In other words, if one spending component rises, does another spending component have to decline? To answer that question, we need to talk about two factors: the money supply and velocity.

Let's say that the money supply in the economy is $1 and that $1 is currently in the hands of Joe. Joe takes the $1 and buys good X from Amaia. Later, Amaia takes the $1 (that she received earlier from Joe) and buys good Y from Eduardo. Still later, Educardo takes the $1 (that he received earlier from Amaia) and buys good Z from Fatima.

Here is what we know: We started with a money supply of just $1, and that dollar changed hands three times. The number of times a dollar changes hands (or is spent) to buy final goods and services is what economists call **velocity**. (If we were dealing with a money supply of more than just $1, we would define velocity not as "the number of times, etc." but as the *average number* of times a dollar is spent to buy final goods and services in a year.) In our simple example, velocity is 3.

Velocity
The average number of times a dollar is spent to buy final goods and services in a year.

The product of our money supply ($1) and velocity (3) is $3, which represents the total amount of spending in the economy. From our example, two things are obvious: First, total spending in the economy can be a greater dollar amount than the money supply. Proof: In our example, the money supply was $1, but total spending equaled $3. Second, total spending depends on the money supply and velocity. Proof: Total spending in our example was the money supply *times* velocity.

Let's return to the original question: If consumption rises, must some other spending component decline? The answer is yes, if neither the money supply nor the velocity changes. But the answer is no if either the money supply or the velocity rises.

To illustrate how the answer can be yes, suppose again that the money supply is $1 and velocity is 3 and that total spending is therefore $3. Let's break up our total of $3 spending in this way: $1 goes for consumption, $1 goes for investment, and $1 goes for government purchases. Consumption rises to $2, and the money supply and velocity remain at $1 and 3, respectively. So total spending is still $3, and, therefore, a $1 increase in consumption necessitates a decline in some other spending component by $1. After all, total spending is locked in at $3; if one spending component rises by a certain amount, one or more other spending components must decline by the same amount.

But total spending isn't locked in if either the money supply or the velocity changes. Again, suppose that consumption rises from $1 to $2 but that velocity or the money supply increases. Then no other spending component needs to change. To see why, suppose the money supply has risen to $1.40 and velocity is still 3. Total spending now is $4.20 instead of $3, so consumption could have risen to $2 without any decline in investment or government purchases. In other words, C can equal $2, I can still equal $1, and G can still equal $1 (or even more, $1.20).

Economics 24/7

When Would You Want to Be Paid in a Currency Other Than U.S. Dollars?

Most people who work in the United States are paid in dollars, but when would you *want* to be paid in another currency? In thinking about the question, consider the exchange rate between the dollar and the euro. Suppose the exchange rate is $1 = €1, and the exchange rate is expected to stay constant. Your employer owes you $10,000. Does it matter if the employer pays you in dollars or euros? At the current exchange rate, $10,000 is the same as €10,000, so whether you are paid in euros or dollars does not matter.

Now suppose that you expect the exchange rate to change to $2 = €1 and that you expect the dollar to depreciate and the euro to appreciate. Does the currency in which you are paid matter? Yes, it does. Being paid in euros is preferable because the euro is expected to appreciate in value.

To see why payment in euros is preferable, ask yourself what happens if you are paid $10,000 instead of €10,000. If the exchange rate is $2 = €1, then after you are paid $10,000, the $10,000 is all you have. But if you are paid €10,000 euros, you could have $20,000, because €10,000 can be exchanged for $20,000 at the new rate.

So let's refine the original question: If you are usually paid in dollars, when would you prefer not to be paid in dollars? The answer is "when you think that the value of the dollar is going to fall relative to the value of other currencies."

Here's the problem, though: Most of us who work for U.S. employers don't have the option of getting paid in the currency of our choice. Most of us cannot go to our employer and say, "This month, could you please pay me in euros instead of dollars?"

However, you can always convert the currency in which we are paid into another currency. Suppose that you are always paid in dollars but think that the value of the dollar is going to decline relative to the value of the euro. Your employer pays you $10,000 when the exchange rate is $1 = €1, and you think that the dollar is going to depreciate in value relative to the euro. You immediately take the $10,000 your employer paid you and exchange the dollars for €10,000. Then you wait. If the exchange rate actually does change to, say, $2 for €1, you then exchange your €10,000 for $20,000. In short, if you want to be paid in euros or yen or pesos, your employer may not comply with your wishes, but you have the option of acting on your own wishes.

The same is true if the money supply remains constant at $1 and velocity increases from 3 to 4. At velocity of 4, total spending is $4. Again, consumption can rise to $2 without requiring a decline in any other spending component.

We recap:

- If both the money supply and velocity are constant, a rise in one spending component (such as consumption) necessitates a decline in one or more other spending components.
- If either the money supply or the velocity rises, one spending component can rise without requiring any other spending component to decline.

(Answers to Self-Test questions are in Answers to Self-Test Questions at the back of the book.)

1. Explain the real balance effect.
2. Explain what happens to the *AD* curve if the dollar appreciates relative to other currencies.
3. The money supply has risen, but total spending has declined. Is this state of affairs possible? Explain your answer.

8-3 Short-Run Aggregate Supply

Aggregate demand is one side of the economy; aggregate supply is the other. **Aggregate supply** is the quantity supplied of all goods and services (Real GDP) at various price levels, *ceteris paribus*. Aggregate supply includes both short-run aggregate supply (*SRAS*) and long-run aggregate supply (*LRAS*). Short-run aggregate supply is discussed in this section.

Aggregate Supply
The quantity supplied of all goods and services (Real GDP) at different price levels, *ceteris paribus*.

8-3a Short-Run Aggregate Supply Curve: What It Is and Why It Is Upward Sloping

A **Short-run aggregate supply (SRAS) curve** (see Exhibit 7) shows the quantity supplied of all goods and services (Real GDP, or output) at different price levels, *ceteris paribus*. Notice that the *SRAS* curve is upward sloping: As the price level rises, firms increase the quantity supplied of goods and services; as the price level drops, firms decrease the quantity supplied of goods and services. Why is the *SRAS* curve upward sloping? Economists have put forth a few explanations; we discuss two of them.

Short-Run Aggregate Supply (SRAS) Curve
A curve that shows the quantity supplied of all goods and services (Real GDP) at different price levels, *ceteris paribus*.

Sticky Wages Some economists believe that wages are "sticky," or inflexible. This may be because wages are locked in for a few years because of labor contracts that workers and management enter into. For example, management and labor may agree to lock in wages for the next one to three years. Both labor and management may see this move as in their best interest: Management then has some idea of what its labor costs will be for the duration of the contract, and workers may have a sense of security knowing that their wages can't be lowered. Wages may also be sticky because of certain social conventions or perceived notions of fairness. Whatever the specific reason for sticky wages, let's see how they provide an explanation of an upward-sloping *SRAS* curve.

Firms pay *nominal wages* (e.g., $30 an hour), but they often decide how many workers to hire on the basis of real wages. *Real wages* are nominal wages divided by the price level:

$$\text{Real wages} = \frac{\text{Nominal Wages}}{\text{Price level}}$$

EXHIBIT 7

The Short-Run Aggregate Supply Curve

The short-run aggregate supply curve is upward sloping, specifying a direct relationship between the price level and the quantity supplied of Real GDP.

Short-Run Aggregate Supply Curve
The price level and quantity supplied of Real GDP are directly related.

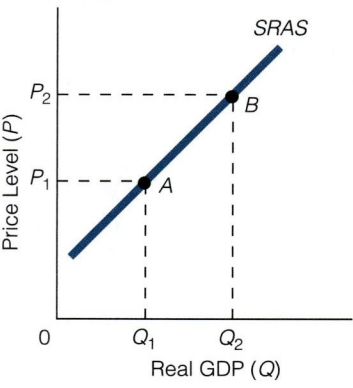

For example, suppose that the nominal wage is $30 an hour and that the price level, as measured by a price index, is 1.50.[1] Then the real wage is $20. Note, in general, that

- The quantity supplied of labor is *directly related* to the real wage: As the real wage rises, the quantity supplied of labor rises; as the real wage falls, the quantity supplied of labor falls:

$$\text{Real wage} \uparrow \rightarrow \text{Quantity supplied of labor} \uparrow$$
$$\text{Real wage} \downarrow \rightarrow \text{Quantity supplied of labor} \downarrow$$

In short, more individuals are willing to work, and current workers are willing to work more, at higher real wages than at lower real wages:

- The quantity demanded of labor is *inversely related* to the real wage: As the real wage rises, the quantity demanded of labor falls; as the real wage falls, the quantity demanded of labor rises:

$$\text{Real wage} \uparrow \rightarrow \text{Quantity demanded of labor} \downarrow$$
$$\text{Real wage} \downarrow \rightarrow \text{Quantity demanded of labor} \uparrow$$

In short, firms will employ more workers the cheaper it is to hire them.

So, suppose that a firm has agreed to pay its workers $30 an hour for the next three years and that it has hired 1,000 workers. When it agreed to that nominal wage, it thought that the price index would remain at 1.50 and that the real wage would stay at $20.

Now suppose the price index *falls* to 1.25. In that event, the real wage rises to $24 ($30 ÷ 1.25), which is higher than the firm expected when it agreed to lock in nominal wages at $30 an hour. If the firm had known that the real wage would turn out to be $24 (and not remain at $20), it would never have hired 1,000 workers. It would have hired, say, 800 workers instead.

So what does the firm do? As we stated, there is an inverse relationship between the real wage and the quantity demanded of labor (the number of workers that firms want to hire). Now that the real wage has risen (from $20 to $24), the firm cuts back on its labor (say, from 1,000 to 800 workers). With fewer workers working, less output is produced.

So, if nominal wages are sticky, a decrease in the price level (which pushes real wages up) will result in a decrease in output. This is what an upward-sloping *SRAS* curve represents: As the price level falls, the quantity supplied of goods and services declines. That is,

$$\text{Decline in price level and constant nominal wage} \rightarrow \text{Real wage} \uparrow \rightarrow$$
$$\text{Firms hire fewer workers} \rightarrow \text{Decline in quantity supplied of Real GDP}$$

Worker Misperceptions Another explanation for the upward-sloping *SRAS* curve holds that workers may misperceive changes in the real wage. To illustrate, if the nominal wage is $30 an hour and the price level, as measured by a price index, is 1.50, then the real wage is $20. Now, suppose the nominal wage falls to $25 and the price level falls to 1.25. Then the real wage is still $20 ($25 ÷ 1.25 = $20), *but workers may not know this.* They know that their nominal wage has fallen (i.e., they are earning $25 an hour instead of $30). They also may know that the price level is lower, but they initially may not know *how much* lower the price

---

[1] Alternatively, you can view the price index as 1.50 times 100, or 150. In this case, the formula for the real wage would change to Real wages = (Nominal wage ÷ Price level) × 100

Chapter 8 Aggregate Demand and Aggregate Supply

level is. For example, suppose they mistakenly believe that the price level has fallen from 1.50 to 1.39. They will then think that their real wage has actually fallen from $20 ($30 ÷ 1.50) to $17.98 ($25 ÷ 1.39). In response to the misperceived falling real wage, workers may reduce the quantity of labor they are willing to supply. With fewer workers (resources), firms produce less.

So, if workers misperceive changes in the real wage, then a fall in the price level will bring about a decline in output, a situation that is illustrative of an upward-sloping *SRAS* curve:

Nominal wages and *price level decline* by equal percentage →
Real wage remains constant → But workers mistakenly think real wage has fallen →
Workers reduce quantity supplied of labor → *Less output is produced*

8-3b What Puts the "Short Run" in the *SRAS* Curve?

According to most macroeconomists, the SRAS curve slopes upward because of sticky wages or worker misperceptions. No matter what the explanation, though, things are likely to change over time. Wages will not be sticky forever (labor contracts will expire), and workers will figure out that they misperceived changes in the real wage. Only for a certain period—identified as the short run—are these issues likely to be relevant.

8-3c Changes in Short-Run Aggregate Supply: Shifts in the *SRAS* Curve

A change in the quantity supplied of Real GDP is brought about by a change in the price level and is shown as a *movement* along the *SRAS* curve. But what can change short-run aggregate supply? What can *shift* the *SRAS* curve? The factors that can shift the *SRAS* curve are wage rates, prices of nonlabor inputs, productivity, and supply shocks.

Wage Rates Changes in wage rates have a major impact on the position of the *SRAS* curve because wage costs are usually a firm's major cost item. The impact of a rise or fall in equilibrium wage rates can be understood in terms of the following equation:

Profit per unit = Price per unit − Cost per unit

Higher wage rates mean higher costs and, at constant prices, translate into lower profits and a reduction in the number of units (of a given good) that firms will want to produce. Lower wage rates mean lower costs and, at constant prices, translate into higher profits and an increase in the number of units (of a given good) firms will decide to produce.

The impact of higher and lower equilibrium wages is shown in Exhibit 8. At the given price level, P_1 on $SRAS_1$, the quantity supplied of Real GDP is Q_1. When wage rates become higher, a firm's profits at a given price level decrease. Consequently, the firm reduces production. In the diagram, this change corresponds to moving from Q_1 to Q_2, which, at the given price level, is point *B* on a new aggregate supply curve ($SRAS_2$). Thus, a rise in equilibrium wage rates leads to a leftward shift in the aggregate supply curve. For a fall in equilibrium wage rates, the steps are simply reversed.

Prices of Nonlabor Inputs There are other inputs to the production process besides labor. Changes in the prices of nonlabor inputs affect the *SRAS* curve in the same way that changes in wage rates do: An increase in the price of a nonlabor input (e.g., oil) shifts the *SRAS* curve leftward; a decrease in its price shifts the *SRAS* curve rightward.

EXHIBIT 8

Wage Rates and a Shift in the Short-Run Aggregate Supply Curve

A rise in wage rates shifts the short-run aggregate supply curve leftward. A fall in wage rates shifts the short-run aggregate supply curve rightward.

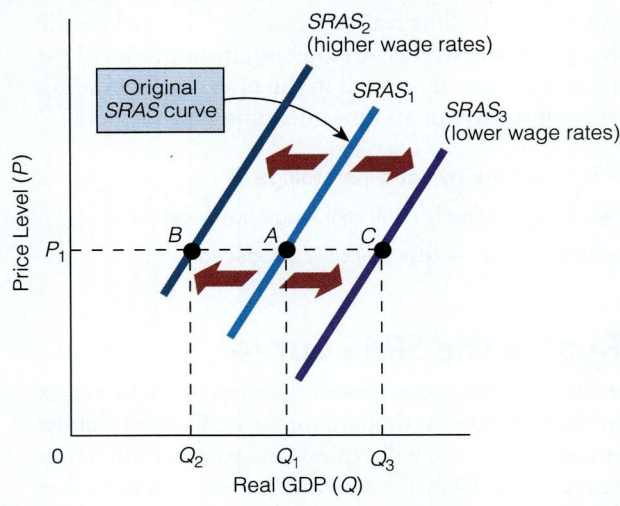

Productivity *Productivity* is the output produced per unit of input employed over some length of time. Although various inputs can become more productive, let's consider the labor input. An increase in labor productivity means that businesses will produce more output with the same amount of labor, causing the *SRAS* curve to shift rightward. A decrease in labor productivity means that businesses will produce less output with the same amount of labor, causing the *SRAS* curve to shift leftward. A host of factors lead to increased labor productivity, including a more educated labor force, a larger stock of capital goods, and technological advancements.

Supply Shocks Major natural or institutional changes that affect aggregate supply are referred to as *supply shocks*. Supply shocks are of two varieties. *Adverse supply shocks* shift the *SRAS* curve leftward. Bad weather that wipes out a large part of the Midwestern wheat crop would be an adverse supply shock. *Beneficial supply shocks* shift the *SRAS* curve rightward; for example, a major oil discovery or unusually good weather leading to increased production of a food staple would be a beneficial supply shock. Both kinds of supply shock are reflected in resource or input prices.

Exhibit 9 summarizes the factors that affect short-run aggregate supply.

EXHIBIT 9

Changes in Short-Run Aggregate Supply

The flowcharts show how short-run aggregate supply changes with changes in several factors.

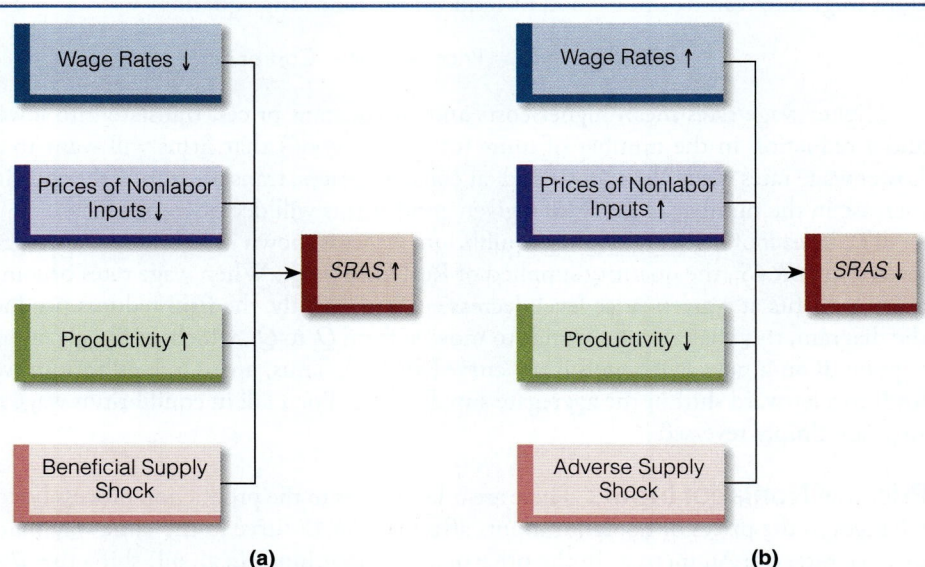

(a)   (b)

8-3d Something More to Come: People's Expectations

So far in this chapter, we have said that several factors are capable of shifting the *SRAS* curve: wage rates, prices of nonlabor inputs, productivity, and supply shocks. In a later chapter (Chapter 16), we will begin to discuss how people's expectations (of certain key economic variables) can affect the price level and Real GDP. At that point, we will add another factor that can shift the *SRAS* curve: the *expected price level*.

---

1. Explain what happens to the short-run aggregate supply (*SRAS*) curve if wage rates decline.
2. Give an example of an increase in labor productivity.
3. Discuss the details of the worker misperceptions explanation for the upward-sloping *SRAS* curve.

8-4 Putting *AD* and *SRAS* Together: Short-Run Equilibrium

In this section, we put aggregate demand and short-run aggregate supply together to show how short-run equilibrium in the economy is achieved. Aggregate demand and short-run aggregate supply determine the price level and Real GDP in the short run.

8-4a How Short-Run Equilibrium in the Economy Is Achieved

Exhibit 10 shows an aggregate demand (*AD*) curve and a short-run aggregate supply (*SRAS*) curve. The quantity demanded of Real GDP and the quantity supplied of Real GDP are illustrated at three different price levels: P_1, P_2, and P_E.

At P_1, the quantity supplied of Real GDP (Q_2) is greater than the quantity demanded (Q_1). In other words, there is a surplus of goods. As a result, the price level drops, firms decrease output, and consumers increase consumption. Why do consumers increase consumption as the price level drops? (*Hint*: Think of the real balance, interest rate, and international trade effects.)

EXHIBIT 10

Short-Run Equilibrium

At P_1, the quantity supplied of Real GDP is greater than the quantity demanded. As a result, the price level falls, and firms decrease output. At P_2, the quantity demanded of Real GDP is greater than the quantity supplied. As a result, the price level rises, and firms increase output. Short-run equilibrium occurs at point *E*, where the quantity demanded of Real GDP equals the (short-run) quantity supplied. This point is the intersection of the aggregate demand (*AD*) curve and the short-run aggregate supply (*SRAS*) curve. (*Note*: Although real-world *AD* and *SRAS* curves can, and likely do, have some curvature to them, we have drawn both as straight lines. This depiction does not affect the analysis. Whenever the analysis is not disturbed, we follow suit throughout this text.)

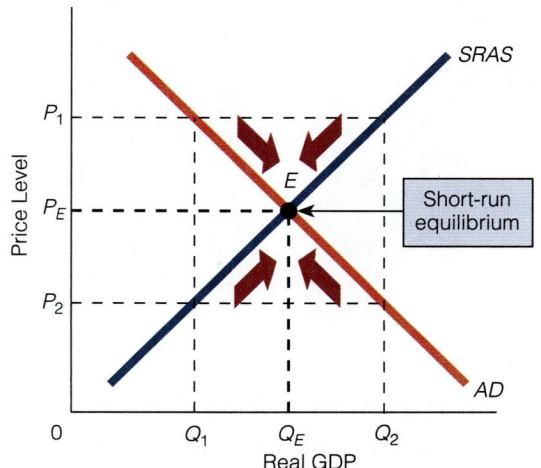

At P_2, the quantity supplied of Real GDP (Q_1) is less than the quantity demanded (Q_2). In other words, there is a shortage of goods. As a result, the price level rises, firms increase output, and consumers decrease consumption.

In instances of both surplus and shortage, economic forces are moving the economy toward E, where the quantity demanded of Real GDP equals the (short-run) quantity supplied of Real GDP. E is the point of **short-run equilibrium**, P_E is the short-run equilibrium price level, and Q_E is the short-run equilibrium Real GDP.

A change in aggregate demand, in short-run aggregate supply, or in both will obviously affect the price level and/or Real GDP. For example, an increase in aggregate demand raises the equilibrium price level and, in the short run, Real GDP [Exhibit 11(a)]. An increase in short-run aggregate supply lowers the equilibrium price level and raises Real GDP [Exhibit 11(b)]. A decrease in short-run aggregate supply raises the equilibrium price level and lowers Real GDP [Exhibit 11(c)].

> **Short-Run Equilibrium**
> The condition in the economy when the quantity demanded of Real GDP equals the (short-run) quantity supplied of Real GDP. This condition is met where the aggregate demand curve intersects the short-run aggregate supply curve.

8-4b Thinking in Terms of Short-Run Equilibrium Changes in the Economy

We know that certain factors can lead to a change in aggregate demand or in short-run aggregate supply. In addition, we know that if either aggregate demand or short-run aggregate supply changes, the price level and Real GDP will also change in the short run.

Exhibit 12 shows us how changes in AD or $SRAS$ can affect the economy and change P and Q. (Refer to Exhibit 12 as we continue our discussion.) For example, when a factor changes, we ask ourselves a series of questions:

- Does the factor affect the AD curve or the $SRAS$ curve? If the answer is neither, then there will be no change in either curve.
- If the answer is the AD curve, then does it shift to the right or to the left?
- If the answer is the $SRAS$ curve, does it shift to the right or to the left?

EXHIBIT 11

Changes in Short-Run Equilibrium in the Economy

(a) An increase in aggregate demand increases the price level and Real GDP.
(b) An increase in short-run aggregate supply decreases the price level and increases Real GDP.
(c) A decrease in short-run aggregate supply increases the price level and decreases Real GDP.

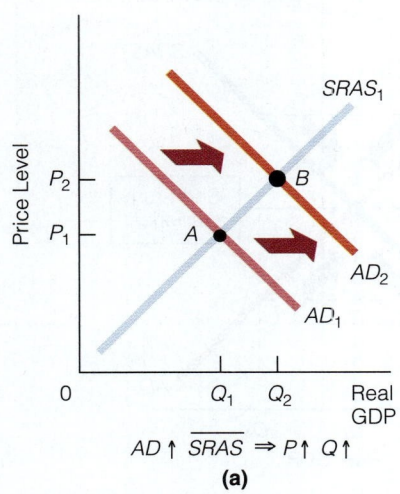
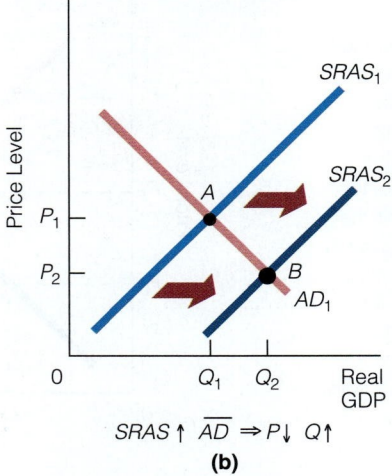
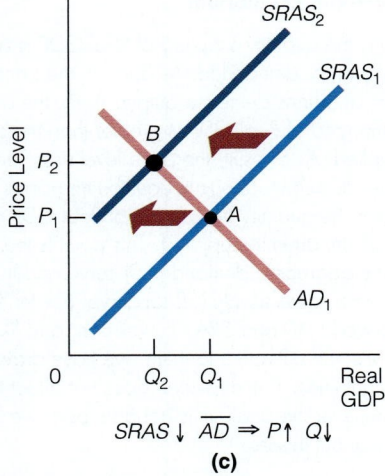

EXHIBIT 12

How a Factor Affects the Price Level and Real GDP in the Short Run

In the exhibit, P = Price level and Q = Real GDP.

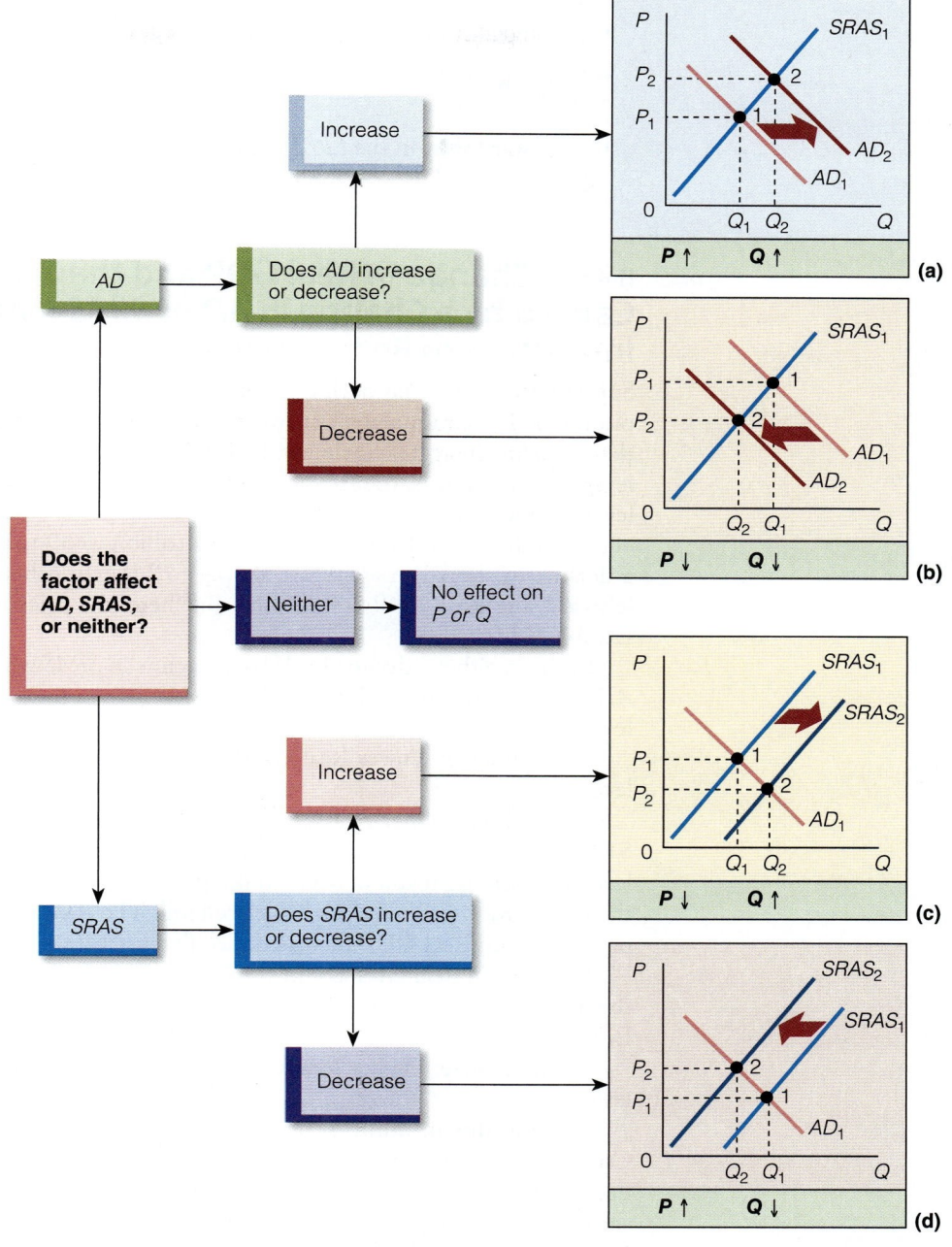

After observing a shift in one or more curves, we identify the new equilibrium and what has happened to both the price level and Real GDP in the short run.

To illustrate, suppose there is an adverse supply shock in the economy:

- The shock shifts the *SRAS* curve leftward.
- Nothing has changed on the demand side of the economy, so the *AD* curve remains stable.
- A leftward shift in the *SRAS* curve in the face of an unchanged *AD* curve increases the price level and decreases Real GDP.

8-4c A Change in Real GDP and the Price Level Can Be Caused by a Change in *AD* or *SRAS*—And That "Or" Is Important to Remember

Suppose Real GDP has declined from $10 trillion to $9 trillion. What has happened to the price level? If your immediate answer is that the price level has fallen, then you may be thinking that a decline in aggregate demand (*AD*) is the cause of the lower Real GDP and lower price level. In other words, the *AD* curve shifted leftward, and both the price level and Real GDP level declined. See Exhibit 12(b).

But a decline in Real GDP from $10 trillion to $9 trillion could also be consistent with a decline in short-run aggregate supply (*SRAS*). In other words, if the SRAS curve shifts leftward, the Real GDP will decline. But here, the price level rises instead of declines. See Exhibit 12(d).

In short, either a decline in *AD* or a decline in *SRAS* will lower Real GDP, but a decline in *AD* will also lead to a lower price level, whereas a decline in *SRAS* will lead to a higher price level.

To summarize: Lower Real GDP is consistent with a lower price level or a higher price level.

What about higher Real GDP? Suppose Real GDP has increased from $10 trillion to $11 trillion. What has happened to the price level? If your immediate answer is that the price level has risen, then you may be thinking that a rise in aggregate demand (*AD*) is the cause of the higher Real GDP and higher price level. The *AD* curve shifted rightward, and both the price level and Real GDP increased. See Exhibit 12(a).

But a rise in Real GDP could also be consistent with a lower price level. If *SRAS* increases, the *SRAS* curve shifts rightward. This will lead to higher Real GDP and lower price level. See Exhibit 12(c).

To summarize: Higher Real GDP is consistent with a higher price level or a lower price level.

Keeping this in mind, suppose one day you are watching TV news and a member of Congress is talking about the economy. She says that Real GDP in the economy has been declining, and the unemployment rate has been rising. "The cause of the decline in Real GDP," she says, "is that aggregate demand in the economy has declined. We've got to do something to stimulate aggregate demand in the economy." Is she right that the declining aggregate demand is the cause of the declining Real GDP? Maybe, but not necessarily. The first thing we have to determine is why Real GDP declined. Is it because *AD* declined (as our member of Congress says), or is it because *SRAS* declined? The economist realizes that declining *AD* is not the only possible cause of declining Real GDP. In fact, aggregate demand may not have declined at all; it could have been *SRAS* that declined.

8-4d An Important Exhibit

Exhibit 13 summarizes the material discussed so far in this chapter. Specifically, much of our discussion has been about the economy in the short run, about changes in the price level (P), and about changes in Real GDP (Q) in the short run.

Exhibit 13 tells us that changes in AD and $SRAS$ will change the price level and Real GDP in the short run. Then it shows which factors actually change AD and which change $SRAS$.

While referring to Exhibit 13, consider what a fall in the interest rate will do to P and Q in the short run. If the interest rate falls, both consumption (C) and investment (I) will rise. If both C and I rise, then AD will rise or the AD curve will shift rightward. If the AD curve shifts rightward, the price level (P) will rise, and so will Real GDP (Q).

8-5 Long-Run Aggregate Supply

In this section, we discuss long-run aggregate supply and draw a long-run aggregate supply ($LRAS$) curve. We also discuss long-run equilibrium and explain how it differs from short-run equilibrium.

8-5a Going from the Short Run to the Long Run

Graphically, short-run equilibrium is at the intersection of the AD curve and the (upward-sloping) $SRAS$ curve. As explained earlier, economists give different reasons for an upward-sloping $SRAS$ curve, which have to do with sticky wages or worker misperceptions. So, when either of these two conditions holds, short-run equilibrium identifies the Real GDP that the economy produces. In time, though, wages become unstuck, and misperceptions turn into

EXHIBIT 13

A Summary Exhibit of AD and SRAS

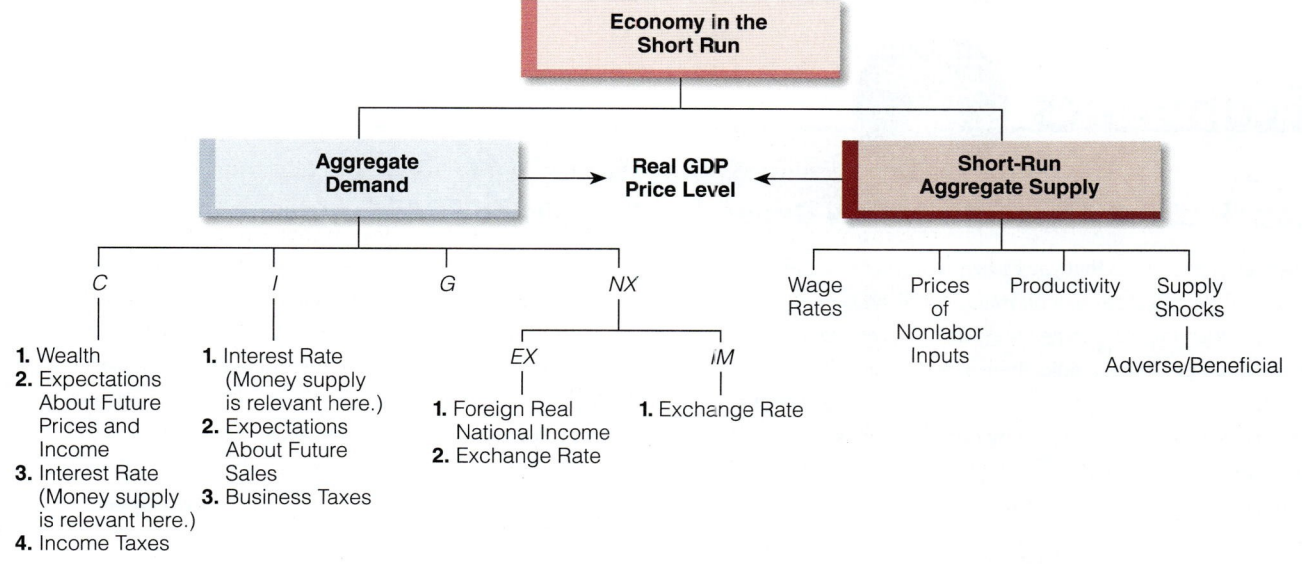

Natural Real GDP
The Real GDP that is produced at the natural unemployment rate. Also, the Real GDP that is produced when the economy is in long-run equilibrium.

Long-Run Aggregate Supply (LRAS) Curve
A curve that represents the output the economy produces when wages and prices have adjusted to their final equilibrium levels and when workers do not have any relevant misperceptions. The LRAS curve is a vertical line at the level of Natural Real GDP.

Long-Run Equilibrium
The condition that exists in the economy when wages and prices have adjusted to their (final) equilibrium levels and when workers do not have any relevant misperceptions. Graphically, long-run equilibrium occurs at the intersection of the AD and LRAS curves.

accurate perceptions. In that event, the economy is said to be in the *long run*. In other words, the two conditions do not hold in the long run.

An important macroeconomic question is, "Will the level of Real GDP that the economy produces in the long run be the same as in the short run?" Most economists say that it will not. They argue that, in the long run, the economy produces the full-employment Real GDP, or the **Natural Real GDP** (Q_N). The aggregate supply curve that identifies the output the economy produces in the long run, the **long-run aggregate supply (LRAS) curve**, is portrayed as the vertical line in Exhibit 14.

Long-run equilibrium identifies the level of Real GDP the economy produces when wages and prices have adjusted to their final equilibrium levels and when workers have no relevant misperceptions. Graphically, this point occurs at the intersection of the *AD* and *LRAS* curves. Further, the level of Real GDP that the economy produces in long-run equilibrium is the Natural Real GDP.

EXHIBIT 14

Long-Run Aggregate Supply (LRAS) Curve

The LRAS curve represents the output the economy produces when all economy-wide adjustments have taken place and workers do not have any relevant misperceptions. It is a vertical line at the level of Natural Real GDP.

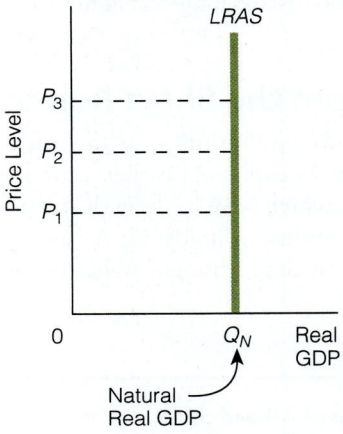

Economics 24/7

Your First Job After College May Depend on the *AD* and *SRAS* Curves

There are some things that you can see with your physical eyes. For example, you can see a car with your physical eyes.

And then there are some things that you can see only with your mind's eye. For example, there actually is an *AD* curve in an economy, but we have never seen a real *AD* curve with our physical eyes. We can't walk into our backyard, look up into the sky, and see the country's *AD* curve. We can see *AD* curves only with our mind's eye. We then draw those *AD* curves on paper or a board.

Now, although we cannot see the real *AD* curve in the economy, we know that it exists, and we also know that its position on a two-dimensional diagram affects your job prospects after college. Put it this way: You might have thought that learning what the *AD* curve looks like and what makes it shift right or left has nothing to do with you. But that's incorrect. To see why, suppose that you will be graduating from college in, say, two years. In two years, there will be an *AD* curve in the economy just as there is an *AD* curve in the economy right now.

to shift the AD curve to the left. Will that matter to you? Well, think of what lower AD means in the economy, all other things remaining constant. It means that less Real GDP will be produced. Fewer houses will be built, fewer cars will be produced, and fewer attorney services will be demanded, among other things. Now ask again, will that matter to you? It certainly will matter to you if, two years from now, when you graduate from college, you are looking for a job. Lower aggregate demand, which translates into less Real GDP, will translate into fewer employers visiting colleges to hire college graduates. It will translate into fewer employers reading your résumé and getting back to you for a job interview. Our point is a simple one: In a textbook or on a classroom board, the AD curve may look like something that is unrelated to you and your everyday life. But that isn't true at all. That AD curve may have much to do with how hard or easy it is for you to get your first job after college.

But where will that AD curve in two years be positioned relative to the AD curve that exists right now? Let's suppose that, between now and then, something happens in the economy

8-5b Short-Run Equilibrium, Long-Run Equilibrium, and Disequilibrium

The two equilibrium states in an economy—short-run and long-run—are shown graphically in Exhibit 15. In Exhibit 15(a), the economy is at point 1, producing amount Q_1 of Real GDP. At point 1, the quantity supplied of Real GDP (in the short run) is equal to the quantity demanded of Real GDP, and both are Q_1. The economy is in short-run equilibrium. In Exhibit 15(b), the economy is at point 1, producing Q_N. In other words, it is producing Natural Real GDP. The economy is in long-run equilibrium when it produces Q_N.

EXHIBIT 15

Equilibrium States of the Economy

There are two equilibrium states in the economy: short-run equilibrium, shown in part (a), and long-run equilibrium, shown in part (b). During the time an economy moves from one equilibrium state to another, it is said to be in disequilibrium.

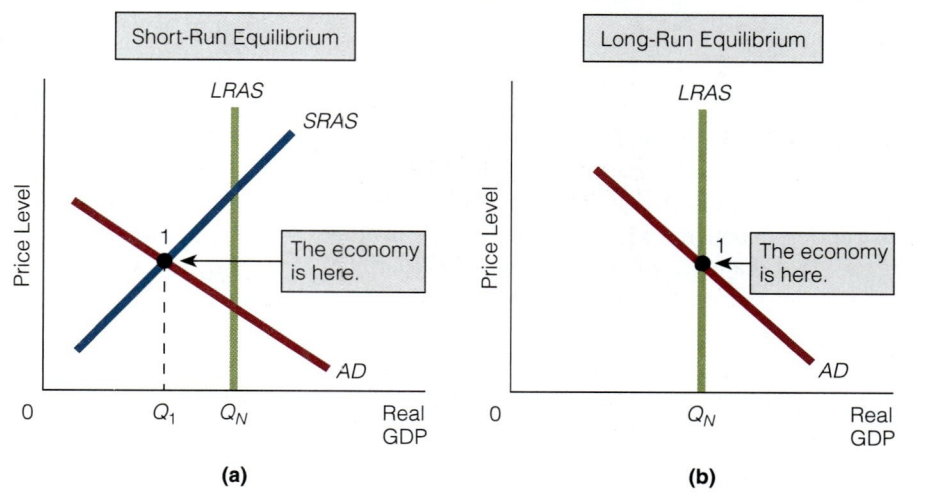

In both short-run and long-run equilibrium, the quantity supplied of Real GDP equals the quantity demanded. So, what is the difference between short-run equilibrium and long-run equilibrium? In long-run equilibrium, the quantities supplied and demanded of Real GDP equal Natural Real GDP [Exhibit 15(b)]; in short-run equilibrium, the quantities supplied and demanded of Real GDP are either more than or less than Natural Real GDP.

Let's illustrate that difference with numbers. Suppose Q_N = $9.0 trillion. In long-run equilibrium, the quantity supplied of Real GDP equals the quantity demanded: $9.0 trillion. In short-run equilibrium, the quantity supplied of Real GDP equals the quantity demanded, but neither equals $9.0 trillion. For example, the quantity supplied of Real GDP could equal the quantity demanded of Real GDP if each equals $8.5 trillion.

When the economy is in neither short-run nor long-run equilibrium, it is said to be in *disequilibrium*. Essentially, disequilibrium is the state of the economy as it moves from one short-run equilibrium to another or from short-run equilibrium to long-run equilibrium. In disequilibrium, the quantity supplied and the quantity demanded of Real GDP are not equal.

Self-Test

1. What is the difference between short-run equilibrium and long-run equilibrium?

2. Diagrammatically represent an economy that is in neither short-run nor long-run equilibrium.

Office Hours

"What Purpose Does the AD–AS Framework Serve?"

Student: What purpose does the *AD–AS* framework serve?

Instructor: One purpose is to link some variables to other variables.

Student: How so?

Instructor: Well, consider a rise in income taxes. We learned in this chapter that a rise in income taxes will lead to a decline in consumption. And we know that a decline in consumption will lead to a decline in aggregate demand. Finally, we know that a decline in aggregate demand will lead to a decline in both the price level and Real GDP. In other words, the *AD–AS* framework helps us to link a rise in *income taxes* to a decline in both the *price level* and *Real GDP*.

Student: Oh, I see. It's sort of like the *AD–AS* framework is a road. We start at one point on the road (where income taxes are being raised), and then we follow the road until we come to the end (where the price level and Real GDP have declined).

Instructor: That's a good way of putting it. Let's now start at another point along the road. Let's start with a decline in wage rates.

Student: If wage rates decline, short-run aggregate supply increases (the *SRAS* curve shifts to the right). As a result, the price level declines, and Real GDP rises.

Instructor: That's correct. Now let's go back to your original question: What purpose does the *AD–AS* framework serve? What would your answer be now?

Student: I think I would say what you said: "It links some variables to other variables." But I'd add that it provides an explanation for changes in the price level and in Real GDP too.

Instructor: Explain what you mean by that.

Student: Well, suppose someone were to ask me what might cause Real GDP to decline. Using the *AD–AS* framework, I would say that a decline in either *AD* or *SRAS* would lead to a decline in Real GDP. Then, if the person wanted more specificity, I could say that such things as an adverse supply shock, a decline in productivity, the U.S. dollar appreciating, and so on, could lead to a decline in Real GDP.

Instructor: You make a good point.

Points to Remember
1. The *AD–AS* framework serves to link some variables to others. For example, a change in income taxes can ultimately be linked to a change in the price level and in Real GDP.
2. The *AD–AS* framework helps us to understand changes in both the price level and the Real GDP.

Chapter Summary

Aggregate Demand

- Aggregate demand is the quantity demanded of all goods and services (Real GDP) at different price levels, *ceteris paribus*.
- The aggregate demand (*AD*) curve slopes downward, indicating an inverse relationship between the price level and the quantity demanded of Real GDP.
- The *AD* curve slopes downward because of the real balance effect, the interest rate effect, and the international trade effect.
- The real balance effect states that the inverse relationship between the price level and the quantity demanded of Real GDP is established through changes in the value of a person's monetary wealth, or money holdings. Specifically, a fall in the price level causes purchasing power to rise, increasing a person's monetary wealth. As people become wealthier, they buy more goods. By contrast, a rise in the price level causes purchasing power to fall, reducing a person's monetary wealth. As people become less wealthy, they buy fewer goods.
- The interest rate effect states that the inverse relationship between the price level and the quantity demanded of Real GDP is established through changes in the part of household and business spending that is sensitive to changes in interest rates. If the price level rises, a person needs more money to buy a fixed bundle of goods. In an effort to acquire more money, the person's demand for credit rises, as does the interest rate. As the interest rate rises, businesses and households borrow less and buy fewer goods. Thus, the quantity demanded of Real GDP falls. By contrast, if the price level falls, a person needs less money to buy a fixed bundle of goods. Part of the increase in a person's monetary wealth is saved, so the supply of credit rises and the interest rate falls. As the interest rate falls, businesses and households borrow more and buy more goods. Thus, the quantity demanded of Real GDP rises.
- The international trade effect states that the inverse relationship between the price level and the quantity demanded of Real GDP is established through foreign sector spending. Specifically, as the price level in the United States rises, U.S. goods become relatively more expensive than foreign goods, and both Americans and foreigners buy fewer U.S. goods. The quantity demanded of U.S. Real GDP then falls. By contrast, as the price level in the United States falls, U.S. goods become relatively less expensive than foreign goods, and both Americans and foreigners buy more U.S. goods. The quantity demanded of U.S. Real GDP then rises.
- At a given price level, a rise in consumption, investment, government purchases, or net exports will increase aggregate demand and shift the *AD* curve to the right. At a given price level, a fall in consumption, investment, government purchases, or net exports will decrease aggregate demand and shift the *AD* curve to the left.

Factors That Can Change C, I, and NX (EX − IM) and Therefore Change AD

- The following factors can change consumption: wealth, expectations about future prices and income, the interest rate, and income taxes. The following factors can change investment: the interest rate, expectations about future sales, and business taxes. The following factors can change net exports (exports less imports): foreign real national income and the exchange rate. A change in the money supply can affect one or more spending components (e.g., consumption) and therefore affect aggregate demand.

Money Supply and Velocity

- Velocity is the average number of times a dollar is spent to buy final goods and services in a year.
- If the money supply and velocity are constant, a rise in one spending component (such as consumption) entails a decline in one or more other components. If either the money supply or the velocity rises, a rise in one component does not entail a decline in the others.

Short-Run Aggregate Supply

- Aggregate supply is the quantity supplied of all goods and services (Real GDP) at different price levels, *ceteris paribus*.
- The short-run aggregate supply (SRAS) curve is upward sloping, indicating a direct relationship between the price level and the quantity supplied of Real GDP.
- A decrease in wage rates, a decrease in the price of nonlabor inputs, an increase in productivity, and beneficial supply shocks all shift the *SRAS* curve to the right. An increase in wage rates, an increase in the price of nonlabor inputs, a decrease in productivity, and adverse supply shocks all shift the *SRAS* curve to the left.

Short-Run Equilibrium

- Graphically, short-run equilibrium exists at the intersection of the *AD* and *SRAS* curves. A shift in either or both of these curves can change the price level and, hence, Real GDP. For example, an increase in aggregate demand increases the price level and Real GDP, *ceteris paribus*.

Long-Run Aggregate Supply and Long-Run Equilibrium

- The long-run aggregate supply (*LRAS*) curve is vertical at the Natural Real GDP level.
- Graphically, long-run equilibrium exists at the intersection of the *AD* and *LRAS* curves. It is the condition that exists in the economy when all economy-wide adjustments have taken place and workers do not hold any (relevant) misperceptions. In long-run equilibrium, the quantity demanded of Real GDP equals the quantity supplied of Real GDP, which in turn equals Natural Real GDP.

Three States of an Economy

- An economy can be in short-run equilibrium, long-run equilibrium, or disequilibrium.

Key Terms and Concepts

Aggregate Demand
Aggregate Demand (*AD*) Curve
Real Balance Effect
Monetary Wealth
Purchasing Power
Interest Rate Effect
International Trade Effect
Wealth
Exchange Rate
Appreciation
Depreciation
Velocity
Aggregate Supply
Short-Run Aggregate Supply (*SRAS*) Curve
Short-Run Equilibrium
Natural Real GDP
Long-Run Aggregate Supply (*LRAS*) Curve
Long-Run Equilibrium

Questions and Problems

1. Is aggregate demand a specific dollar amount? For example, is it correct to say that aggregate demand is $9 trillion this year?
2. Explain each of the following: (a) real balance effect, (b) interest rate effect, and (c) international trade effect.
3. Graphically portray (a) a change in the quantity demanded of Real GDP and (b) a change in aggregate demand.
4. There is a difference between a change in the interest rate that is brought about by a change in the price level and a change in the interest rate that is brought about by a change in some factor other than the price level. The first will change the quantity demanded of Real GDP, and the second will change the *AD* curve. Do you agree or disagree with this statement? Explain your answer.
5. The amount of Real GDP (real output) that households are willing and able to buy may change if there is a change in either (a) the price level or (b) some nonprice factor, such as wealth, interest rates, and the like. Do you agree or disagree? Explain your answer.

Chapter 8 Aggregate Demand and Aggregate Supply

6. Explain what happens to aggregate demand in each of the following cases:
   a. The interest rate rises.
   b. Wealth falls.
   c. The dollar depreciates relative to foreign currencies.
   d. Households expect lower prices in the future.
   e. Business taxes rise.
7. Explain what is likely to happen to U.S. export and import spending as a result of the dollar depreciating in value.
8. Explain how expectations about future prices and income will affect consumption.
9. Explain how expectations about future sales will affect investment.
10. How will an increase in the money supply affect aggregate demand?
11. Can there be an increase in total spending in the economy without there first being an increase in the money supply?
12. Under what conditions can consumption rise without some other spending component declining?
13. Can total spending be a greater dollar amount than the money supply? Explain your answer.
14. Will a direct increase in the price of U.S. goods relative to foreign goods lead to a change in the quantity demanded of Real GDP or to a change in aggregate demand? Will a change in the exchange rate that subsequently increases the price of U.S. goods relative to foreign goods lead to a change in the quantity demanded of Real GDP or to a change in aggregate demand? Explain your answers.
15. Explain how each of the following will affect short-run aggregate supply:
    a. An increase in wage rates
    b. A beneficial supply shock
    c. An increase in the productivity of labor
    d. A decrease in the price of a nonlabor resource (e.g., oil)
16. What is the difference between a change in the quantity supplied of Real GDP and a change in short-run aggregate supply?
17. A change in the price level affects which of the following?
    a. The quantity demanded of Real GDP
    b. Aggregate demand
    c. Short-run aggregate supply
    d. The quantity supplied of Real GDP
18. In the short run, what is the impact on the price level and Real GDP of each of the following?
    a. An increase in consumption brought about by a decrease in interest rates
    b. A decrease in exports brought about by the dollar appreciating
    c. A rise in wage rates
    d. A beneficial supply shock
    e. An adverse supply shock
    f. A decline in productivity
19. Identify the details of each of the following explanations for an upward-sloping *SRAS* curve:
    a. Sticky-wage explanation
    b. Worker-misperception explanation
20. What is the difference between short-run equilibrium and long-run equilibrium?
21. An economist is sitting in the Oval Office of the White House, across the desk from the president of the United States. The president asks, "How does the unemployment rate look for the next quarter?" The economist answers, "It's not good. I don't think Real GDP is going to be as high as we initially thought. The problem seems to be foreign income; it's just not growing at the rate we thought it was going to grow." How can foreign income affect U.S. Real GDP?

Working with Numbers and Graphs

1. Suppose that, at a price index of 154, the quantity demanded of U.S. Real GDP is $10.0 trillion worth of goods. Do these data represent aggregate demand or a point on an aggregate demand curve? Explain your answer.
2. Diagrammatically represent the short-run effect of each of the following on the price level and on Real GDP:
   a. An increase in wealth
   b. An increase in wage rates
   c. An increase in labor productivity

3. Diagrammatically represent each of the following, and identify its short-run effect on Real GDP and the price level:
   a. An increase in *SRAS* that is greater than the increase in *AD*
   b. A decrease in *AD* that is greater than the increase in *SRAS*
   c. An increase in *SRAS* that is less than the increase in *AD*

4. In the following figure, which part is representative of each of the following?
   a. A decrease in wage rates
   b. An increase in the price level
   c. A beneficial supply shock
   d. An increase in the price of nonlabor inputs

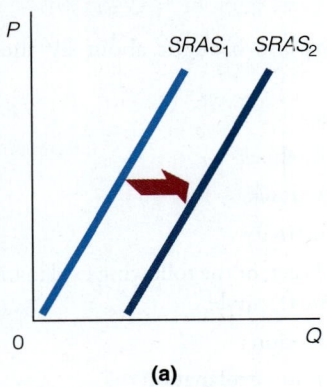
(a)

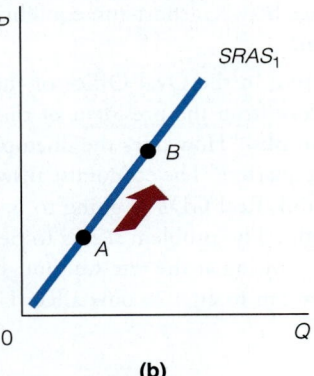
(b)

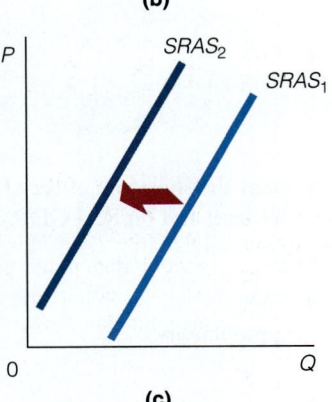
(c)

5. Fill in the blank spaces (A–Z) in the table that follows.

Factor and change	Shifts AD or SRAS curve?	Curve shifts right or left?
Wealth rises	A	B
Business taxes fall	C	D
Dollar depreciates	E	F
Wage rate falls	G	H
Adverse supply shock	I	J
Government purchases rise	K	L
Interest rate rises	M	N
Foreign real national income falls	O	P
Income taxes decline	Q	R
Velocity rises	S	T
Money supply falls	U	V
Productivity declines	W	X
Prices of nonlabor inputs rise	Y	Z

6. Fill in the blank spaces (A–BB) in the table that follows.

Factor and change	Shifts the AD or SRAS curve?	Curve shifts right or left?	Change in price level: up or down?	Change in Real GDP: up or down?
Velocity falls	A	B	C	D
Expected future income rises	E	F	G	H
Wage rates rise	I	J	K	L
Business taxes fall	M	N	O	P
Beneficial supply shock	Q	R	S	T
Prices of nonlabor inputs decline	U	V	W	X
Money supply rises	Y	Z	AA	BB

Classical Macroeconomics and the Self-Regulating Economy

CHAPTER 9

Introduction

For hundreds of years, scientists have tried to understand humankind and their surroundings. Biologists have observed and conducted experiments to understand human and animal behavior. Ecologists have developed models to try to understand the relationships between the plants and animals in forests and oceans. Astronomers have constructed increasingly powerful telescopes to try to understand phenomena in space. And economists have built and tested theories to try to understand the economy. This chapter presents one view about how the economy works.

9-1 The Classical View

The term *classical economics* is often used to refer to an era in the history of economic thought that stretched from about 1750 to the early 1900s. Although classical economists lived and wrote many years ago, their ideas are often employed by some modern-day economists.

9-1a Classical Economists and Say's Law

You know from your study of supply and demand that markets can experience temporary shortages and surpluses, such as a surplus in the apple market. But can the economy have a general surplus—that is, a general glut of goods and services? The classical economists thought not, largely because they believed in Say's law (named after Jean-Baptiste Say). In its simplest version, **Say's law** states that supply creates its own demand.

The law is most easily understood in terms of a barter economy. Consider a person baking bread in such an economy; the baker is a supplier of bread. According to Say, the baker works at his trade because he plans to demand other goods. As he is baking bread, the baker is thinking of the goods and services he will obtain in exchange for the bread. Thus, his act of supplying bread is linked to his demand for other goods. Supply creates its own demand.

Say's Law
Supply creates its own demand. Production creates enough demand to purchase all the goods and services the economy produces.

If supplying some goods leads to a simultaneous demand for other goods, then Say's law implies that there cannot be either (1) a general overproduction of goods (a time during which supply in the economy is greater than demand) or (2) a general underproduction of goods (a time during which demand in the economy is greater than supply).

But what if the baker is baking bread in a money economy? Does Say's law hold? Over a certain period, the baker earns an income as a result of supplying bread, but what does he do with the income? One use of the money is to buy goods and services. However, his demand for goods and services does not necessarily match the income that he generates by supplying bread. The baker may spend less than his full income, putting some away as savings. So we might think that Say's law does not hold in a money economy because the act of supplying goods and services—thus earning income—need not create an equal amount of demand.

But the classical economists disagreed. They argued that, even in a money economy, in which individuals sometimes spend less than their full incomes, Say's law still holds. Their argument was partly based on the assumption of interest rate flexibility.

9-1b Classical Economists and Interest Rate Flexibility

For Say's law to hold in a money economy, the funds saved must give rise to an equal amount of funds invested; that is, what leaves the spending stream through one door must enter it through another door. If not, then some of the income earned from supplying goods may not be used to demand goods (good-bye, Say's law). As a result, goods will be overproduced.

The classical economists argued that saving is matched by an equal amount of investment because of interest rate flexibility in the credit market. In Exhibit 1, I represents investment and S represents saving. I_1 is downward sloping, indicating an inverse relationship between the amount of funds firms invest and the interest rate (i). The reason for the downward slope is straightforward: The interest rate is the cost of borrowing funds. The higher the interest rate is, the fewer funds firms borrow and invest; the lower the interest rate, the more funds firms borrow and invest.

EXHIBIT 1

The Classical View of the Credit Market

In classical theory, the interest rate is flexible and adjusts so that saving equals investment. Thus, if saving increases and the saving curve shifts rightward from S_1 to S_2 (arrow 1), the increase in saving eventually puts pressure on the interest rate and moves it downward from i_1 to i_2 (arrow 2). A new equilibrium is established at E_2 (arrow 3), where once again the amount households save equals the amount firms invest.

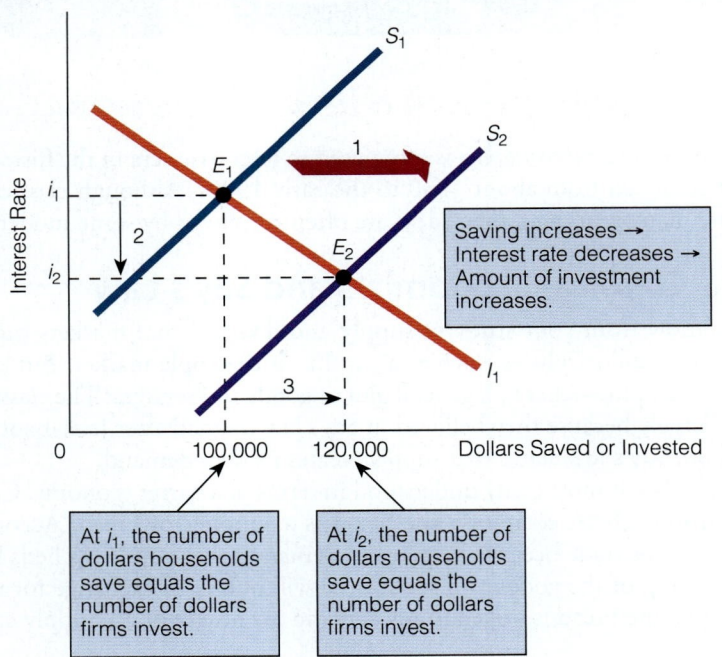

Saving increases → Interest rate decreases → Amount of investment increases.

At i_1, the number of dollars households save equals the number of dollars firms invest.

At i_2, the number of dollars households save equals the number of dollars firms invest.

S_1 is upward sloping, indicating a direct relationship between the amount of funds that households save and the interest rate. The reason is that the higher the interest rate is, the higher the reward is for saving (or the higher the opportunity cost of consuming). So fewer funds are consumed, and more funds are saved. Market-equilibrating forces move the credit market to interest rate i_1 and the equilibrium point to E_1. At E_1, the number of dollars households save ($100,000) equals the number of dollars firms invest ($100,000).

Suppose now that saving increases at each interest rate level. In Exhibit 1, the saving increase is represented by a rightward shift in the saving curve from S_1 to S_2. The classical economists believed that an increase in saving puts downward pressure on the interest rate; accordingly, it would move to i_2, thereby increasing the number of dollars firms invest. Ultimately, the number of dollars households save ($120,000) once again equals the number of dollars firms invest ($120,000). Again, interest rate flexibility ensures that saving equals investment. (What goes out one door comes in the other.) In short, changes in the interest rate uphold Say's law in a money economy in which there is saving.

Let's use a few numbers to illustrate what classical economists were saying. Suppose that, at a given price level, total expenditures (TE) in a very tiny economy are $5,000. Total expenditures (total spending on domestic goods and services) equal the sum of consumption (C), investment (I), government purchases (G), and net exports ($EX-IM$). Thus, if $C = \$3,000$, $I = \$600$, $G = \$1,200$, and $EX - IM = \$200$, then

$$TE + C + I + G + (EX - IM)$$
$$\$5,000 = \$3,000 + \$600 + \$1,200 + \$200$$

The $5,000 worth of goods and services that the four sectors of the economy want to purchase also happens to be the exact dollar amount of goods and services that suppliers want to sell.

What happens when saving is increased in the economy? Saving (S) is equal to the amount of a person's disposable income (Y_d) minus consumption (C):

$$\text{Savings } (S) = \text{Disposable income } (Y_d) - \text{Consumption } (C)$$

For example, if Harriet earns a disposable income of $40,000 a year and spends $38,000, she saves $2,000.

For saving to increase, consumption must decrease (see Exhibit 2). If saving increases by $100, then consumption must fall from $3,000 to $2,900. At first glance, this statement seems to imply that total expenditures will fall to $4,900. But classical economists disagreed. Their ideas implied that investment will increase by $100, going from $600 to $700. Total expenditures will remain constant at $5,000 and will be equal to the dollar amount of the goods and services that suppliers want to sell. Thus, we have

$$TE = C + I + G + (EX - IM)$$
$$\$5,000 = \$2,900 + \$700 + \$1,200 + \$200$$

According to the classical view of the economy, then, Say's law holds both in a barter economy and in a money economy. In a money economy, according to classical economists, interest rates will adjust to equate saving and investment. Therefore, any fall in consumption (and consequent rise in saving) will be matched by an equal rise in investment. In essence, at a given price level, total expenditures will not decrease as a result of an increase in saving.

What does an increase in saving imply for aggregate demand (AD)? An earlier chapter explains that aggregate demand changes only if total spending in the economy changes at a given price level. Therefore, because total spending does not change as a result of an increase in saving, aggregate demand does not change.

EXHIBIT 2

The Classical View of Say's Law in a Money Economy

According to classical economists, a decrease in consumption and subsequent increase in saving will be matched by an equal increase in investment. Thus, there is no change in total expenditures.

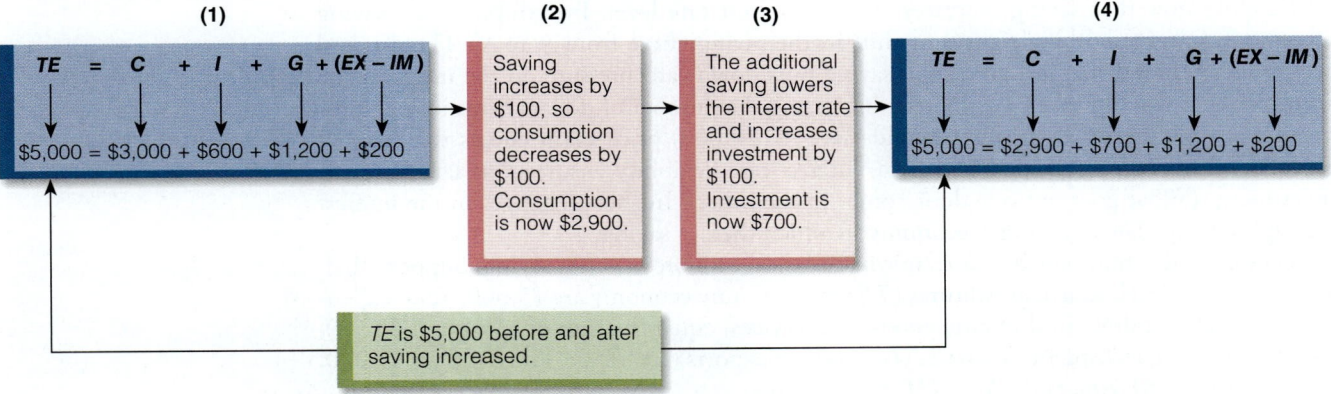

Economics 24/7

Does It Matter How Much People Save?

Suppose that one day you read that the savings rate has increased; that is, individuals are saving more of their incomes than they have in previous periods. Does it matter to you how much of their incomes people save? For example, does it matter if people save 10¢ out of every dollar they earn as opposed to 6¢ out of every dollar?

We know that if people increase their saving, the savings curve (in the classical view of the credit market) shifts rightward. As a result of this, there is initially a surplus of funds in the credit market, which puts downward pressure on the interest rate.

As the interest rate drops, investment increases. Now ask yourself, what does investment consist of? In an earlier chapter, we said that investment is the sum of all purchases of newly produced capital goods, changes in business inventories, and purchases of new residential housing. Let's emphasize the part of investment that has to do with the purchases of newly produced capital goods. As a result of the interest rate declining, there is likely to be more purchases of newly produced capital goods, and some of those purchases of newly produced capital goods will be for a higher-quality capital than might have existed previously.

Now let's ask ourselves how more capital goods might impact the productivity of labor. Economists often point out that more capital often increases the productivity of labor. A person working with a tractor is more productive at farming than a person working with a hoe. As a result of more and higher-quality capital goods being utilized, labor is more productive, and the more productive labor is, the greater the demand for labor. Following through with our analysis, the greater the demand for labor is, the greater the equilibrium wage rate will be.

Does it matter to you how much people save? It can very well matter in regards to what wage rate you and others are paid.

9-1c Classical Economists on Prices and Wages: Both Are Flexible

Classical economists believed that most, if not all, markets are competitive; that is, supply and demand operate in all markets. If, for example, the labor market has a surplus, the surplus will be temporary. Soon the wage rate will decline, and the quantity supplied of labor will equal the quantity demanded of it. Similarly, given a shortage in the labor market, the wage rate will rise, and the quantity supplied will equal the quantity demanded.

What holds for wages in the labor market holds for prices in the goods-and-services market. Prices will adjust quickly to any surpluses or shortages, and equilibrium will be quickly reestablished. In short, the classical view is that prices and wages are flexible: They rise and decline in response to shortages and surpluses.

Economics 24/7

Births, Marriage, and the Savings Rate in China

The household savings rate—that is, the percentage of disposable income (after-tax income) that households save—often varies across countries and over time. For example, the savings rate in China is much higher than in the United States. To illustrate, the savings rate in China today is approximately 30 percent; in the United States, it is about 6 percent. To see changes over time, consider that China's saving rate was 16 percent in 1990, and the U.S. savings rate in the early part of the first decade of the 2000s was about 3 percent.

The high savings rate in China, as compared to almost all countries in the world, has not gone unnoticed by economists. They have wondered why the savings rate is so high. Does it have to do with the rising costs of health care, uncertainty over old-age pensions, financial development in the country, or something else? Two economists, Shang-Jin Wei and Xiaobo Zhang, have argued that the cause of the high savings rate in China has to do with the former one-child policy in China, which resulted in approximately 122 boys being born in the country for every 100 girls.[1] (China ended the one-child policy in 2015.) The one-child, or family planning, policy in China mandated that, with some exceptions, couples were only allowed to have one child. This policy, combined with a preference of Chinese parents to prefer having sons over daughters, produced a strong imbalance in the sex ratio of births in China. Shang-Jin Wei notes that "the availability of ultrasound makes it easy for parents to detect the gender of a fetus and abort the child that's not the 'right' sex for them."[2]

What did this family planning practice in China, combined with a preference for sons, have to do with the high savings rate in China? According to Wei and Zhang, the imbalance in the births of boys as compared to girls in China affected the marriage market in China. The fact that there were approximately 122 boys born for every 100 girls meant that about one in five boys born in China would be cut out of the marriage market in China when they grew up. According to Wei, "The resulting pressure on the marriage market in China might induce men, and parents with sons, to do things to make themselves more competitive. Wealth helps to increase a man's competitive edge in the marriage market."[3] In other words, a high savings rate translates into greater competitiveness in the marriage market.

When Wei and Zhang looked at savings data across various regions of China, they found that households with sons saved more than households with daughters on average. They also found that the savings rate for households with sons tended to rise when they lived in a region with an even bigger imbalance of boy-to-girl births.

[1]. See Shang-Jin Wei and Xiabo Zhang, "The Competitive Saving Motive: Evidence from Rising Sex Ratios and Savings Rates in China," NBER Working Paper 15093 (2009).
[2]. See "Why Do the Chinese Save So Much" by Sang-Jin Wei in *Forbes*, February 2, 2010.
[3]. Ibid.

(Answers to Self-Test questions are in Answers to Self-Test Questions at the back of the book.)

1. Explain Say's law in terms of a barter economy.
2. According to classical economists, if saving rises and consumption spending falls, will total spending in the economy decrease? Explain your answer.
3. What is the classical position on prices and wages?

9-2 Three States of the Economy

The background information in this section will enable you to understand the views of economists who believe that the economy is self-regulating. Specifically, we discuss three states of the economy, the correspondence between the labor market and the three states of the economy, and more.

9-2a Real GDP and Natural Real GDP: Three Possibilities

In the last chapter, Natural Real GDP was defined as the Real GDP produced at the natural unemployment rate. Real GDP at that rate is produced when the economy is in long-run equilibrium.

Economists often refer to three possible states of an economy when they consider the relationship between Real GDP and Natural Real GDP:

- Real GDP is less than Natural Real GDP.
- Real GDP is greater than Natural Real GDP.
- Real GDP is equal to Natural Real GDP.

Let's now graphically portray each of these three possible states of the economy.

Real GDP Is Less Than Natural Real GDP (Recessionary Gap) Exhibit 3(a) shows an *AD* curve, an *SRAS* curve, and the *LRAS* curve. It also shows that Natural Real GDP (Q_N) is produced in the long run.

Short-run equilibrium is at the intersection of the *AD* and *SRAS* curves, so, in Exhibit 3(a), short-run equilibrium is at point 1. The Real GDP level that the economy is producing at point 1 is designated by Q_1.

Now, compare Q_1 with Q_N. Obviously, Q_1 is less than Q_N. In other words, the economy is currently producing a level of Real GDP in the short run that is less than its Natural Real GDP level. When the Real GDP that the economy is producing is less than its Natural Real GDP, the economy is said to be in a **recessionary gap**.

Recessionary Gap
The condition in which the Real GDP that the economy is producing is less than the Natural Real GDP and the unemployment rate is greater than the natural unemployment rate.

Inflationary Gap
The condition in which the Real GDP that the economy is producing is greater than the Natural Real GDP and the unemployment rate is less than the natural unemployment rate.

Real GDP Is Greater Than Natural Real GDP (Inflationary Gap) In Exhibit 3(b), the *AD* and *SRAS* curves intersect at point 1, so short-run equilibrium is at point 1. The Real GDP level that the economy is producing at point 1 is designated by Q_1. Again, compare Q_1 with Q_N. Obviously, Q_1 is greater than Q_N. In other words, the economy is currently producing a level of Real GDP in the short run that is greater than its Natural Real GDP level, or potential output. When the Real GDP that the economy is producing is greater than its Natural Real GDP, the economy is said to be in an **inflationary gap**.

EXHIBIT 3

Real GDP and Natural Real GDP: Three Possibilities

In (a), the economy is in short-run equilibrium at a Real GDP level of Q_1. Q_N is Natural Real GDP, or the potential output of the economy. Notice that $Q_1 < Q_N$. When this condition ($Q_1 < Q_N$) exists, the economy is said to be in a recessionary gap. In (b), the economy is in short-run equilibrium at a Real GDP level of Q_1. Q_N is Natural Real GDP, or the potential output of the economy. Notice that $Q_1 > Q_N$. When this condition ($Q_1 > Q_N$) exists, the economy is said to be in an inflationary gap. In (c), the economy is operating at a Real GDP level of Q_1 which is equal to Q_N. In other words, the economy is producing its Natural Real GDP, or potential output. When this condition $Q_1 = Q_N$ exists, the economy is said to be in long-run equilibrium.

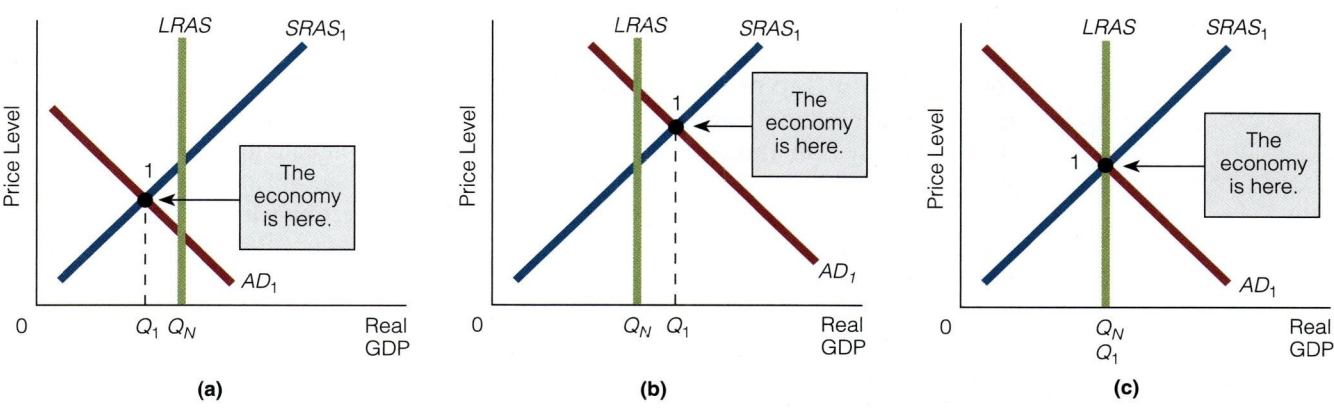

Real GDP Is Equal to Natural Real GDP (Long-Run Equilibrium) In Exhibit 3(c), the *AD* and *SRAS* curves indicate that short-run equilibrium is at point 1. The Real GDP level that the economy is producing at point 1 is designated by Q_1.

Once more, compare Q_1 and Q_N. This time, Q_1 is equal to Q_N. In other words, the economy is currently producing a level of Real GDP that is equal to its Natural Real GDP, or potential output. When the Real GDP that the economy is producing is equal to its Natural Real GDP, the economy is in *long-run equilibrium*.

Thinking Like an Economist

Thinking in Threes The economist often thinks in threes. For the economist, a market (1) has a shortage, (2) has a surplus, or (3) is in equilibrium. Similarly, for the economist, an economy is in
- either a recessionary gap, producing a level of Real GDP lower than Natural Real GDP,
- or an inflationary gap, producing a level of Real GDP higher than Natural Real GDP,
- or long-run equilibrium, producing a level of Real GDP equal to Natural Real GDP.

9-2b The Labor Market and the Three States of the Economy

If the economy can be in three possible states, so can the labor market. In what follows, we identify the three possible states of the labor market and then tie each to a possible state of the economy.

We know that the labor market consists of the demand for, and the supply of, labor. Like a goods market, the labor market can manifest (1) equilibrium, (2) a shortage, or (3) a surplus. So the three possible states of the labor market are as follows:

- *Equilibrium.* When the labor market is in equilibrium, the quantity demanded of labor is equal to the quantity supplied.

- *Shortage.* When the labor market has a shortage, the quantity demanded of labor is greater than the quantity supplied.

- *Surplus.* When the labor market has a surplus, the quantity supplied of labor is greater than the quantity demanded.

Recessionary Gap and the Labor Market The unemployment rate that exists when the economy produces Natural Real GDP is, of course, the natural unemployment rate. So if the economy is in a recessionary gap, is the labor market in equilibrium or does it have a shortage or a surplus?

To answer this question, suppose the economy is in a recessionary gap, producing Real GDP of $9 trillion (worth of goods and services) when Natural Real GDP—or potential output—is $10 trillion. Then, is the existing unemployment rate, producing $9 trillion worth of goods and services, greater or less than the natural unemployment rate that exists when the economy is producing $10 trillion worth of goods and services? In fact, the unemployment rate is greater than the natural unemployment rate, because fewer workers are needed to produce a Real GDP of $9 trillion than are needed to produce a Real GDP of $10 trillion. *Ceteris paribus*, the unemployment rate will be higher at a Real GDP level of $9 trillion than it is at a level of $10 trillion.

So, when the economy is in a recessionary gap, the unemployment rate is *higher* than the natural unemployment rate. This conclusion implies a surplus in the labor market: The quantity supplied of labor is greater than the quantity demanded; that is, more people want to work than there are jobs available. In sum,

If the economy is in a recessionary gap, the unemployment rate is higher than the natural unemployment rate, and a surplus exists in the labor market.

Inflationary Gap and the Labor Market Now suppose the economy is in an inflationary gap, producing a Real GDP level of $11 trillion (worth of goods and services) when Natural Real GDP, or potential output, is $10 trillion.

Again, the unemployment rate that exists when the economy produces Natural Real GDP is the natural unemployment rate. Is the unemployment rate that exists when the economy is producing $11 trillion worth of goods and services greater or less than the natural unemployment rate when the economy is producing $10 trillion worth? The unemployment rate is less than the natural unemployment rate because more workers are needed to produce a Real GDP of $11 trillion than are needed to produce a Real GDP of $10 trillion. *Ceteris paribus*, the unemployment rate will be lower at a Real GDP level of $11 trillion than it is at $10 trillion.

So, when the economy is in an inflationary gap, the unemployment rate is *lower* than the natural unemployment rate. This conclusion implies a shortage in the labor market: The quantity demanded of labor is greater than the quantity supplied; that is, more jobs are available than there are people who want to work. In sum,

If the economy is in an inflationary gap, the unemployment rate is less than the natural unemployment rate, and a shortage exists in the labor market.

Long-Run Equilibrium and the Labor Market Finally, suppose the economy is in long-run equilibrium. That is, it is producing a Real GDP level equal to Natural Real GDP. In this state, the unemployment rate in the economy is the same as the natural unemployment rate. This conclusion implies that the labor market has neither a shortage nor a surplus but is in equilibrium. In sum,

If the economy is in long-run equilibrium, the unemployment rate equals the natural unemployment rate, and the labor market is in equilibrium.

The following table summarizes three possible states of the economy and the related states of the labor market:

State of the Economy	What Do We Call It?	Relationship Between Unemployment Rate and Natural Unemployment Rate	State of the Labor Market
Real GDP < Natural Real GDP	Recessionary gap	Unemployment rate > natural unemployment rate	Surplus exists
Real GDP > Natural Real GDP	Inflationary gap	Unemployment rate < natural unemployment rate	Shortage exists
Real GDP = Natural Real GDP	Long-run equilibrium	Unemployment rate = natural unemployment rate	Equilibrium exists

9-2c Common Misconceptions About the Unemployment Rate and the Natural Unemployment Rate

Some people mistakenly think that the economy's unemployment rate *cannot* be lower than the natural unemployment rate (as it is in an inflationary gap). In other words, if the natural unemployment rate is 5 percent, then the unemployment rate can never be 4 percent. But that assumption is a myth.

To explain why, we need to look at two production possibilities frontiers (PPFs). In Exhibit 4, the two such frontiers are the physical PPF (purple curve) and the institutional PPF (blue curve). The physical PPF illustrates different combinations of goods that the economy can produce given the physical constraints of (1) finite resources and (2) the current state of technology. The institutional PPF illustrates different combinations of goods that the economy can produce given the two physical constraints of (1) finite resources and (2) the current state of technology, plus (3) any institutional constraints. Broadly defined, an institutional constraint is anything that prevents economic agents from producing the maximum Real GDP that is physically possible.

For example, the minimum-wage law, which is an institutional constraint, specifies that workers must be paid at least the legislated minimum wage. One effect of this law is that unskilled people whose value to employers falls below the legislated minimum wage will not be hired. Having fewer workers means less output, *ceteris paribus*. (This is why the institutional PPF lies closer to the origin than the physical PPF does.)

Within the confines of society's physical and institutional constraints is a natural unemployment rate. This situation is represented by any point on the institutional PPF. In the exhibit, points *A*, *B*, and *C* are all such points.

EXHIBIT 4

The Physical and Institutional PPFs

A society has both a physical PPF and an institutional PPF. The physical PPF illustrates different combinations of goods the economy can produce given the physical constraints of (1) finite resources and (2) the current state of technology. The institutional PPF illustrates different combinations of goods the economy can produce given the physical constraints of (1) finite resources, (2) the current state of technology, and (3) any institutional constraints. The economy is at the natural unemployment rate if it is located on its institutional PPF, such as at points A, B, or C. An economy can never operate beyond its physical PPF, but it is possible for it to operate beyond its institutional PPF because institutional constraints are not always equally effective. If the economy does operate beyond its institutional PPF, such as at point D, then the unemployment rate in the economy is lower than the natural unemployment rate.

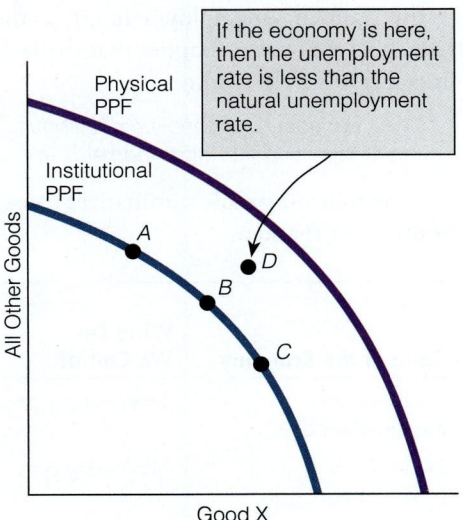

An economy can never operate beyond its physical PPF, but it can operate beyond its institutional PPF. For example, suppose inflation reduces the purchasing power of the minimum wage, thus reducing or eliminating the constraining influence of the minimum-wage law on the unskilled labor market.[4] This change would make one of society's institutional constraints ineffective, allowing the economy to temporarily move beyond the institutional constraint. Consider, for example, point D in Exhibit 4. At point D, the unemployment rate that exists in the economy is less than the natural unemployment rate.

Three States of the Economy and Two PPF Curves So an economy can operate beyond its institutional PPF but below its physical PPF. Now, let's tie the three states of an economy to the institutional and physical PPF curves.

Exhibit 5 shows the institutional PPF and the physical PPF, along with three points: A, B, and C. Point A, below the institutional PPF, represents an economy in a recessionary gap, producing less than Natural Real GDP, Q_N. Point B, on the institutional PPF, represents an economy in long-run equilibrium, producing Natural Real GDP. Finally, point C, beyond the institutional PPF but below the physical PPF, represents an economy in an inflationary gap, producing more than Natural Real GDP. Thus, each of the three states of the economy—recessionary gap, inflationary gap, and long-run equilibrium—can be identified as a point in relation to both the institutional PPF and the physical PPF.

---

[4] Inflation reduces the real (inflation-adjusted) minimum wage. If the minimum wage is $15 and the price level is $1, then the real minimum wage is $15. If the price level rises to $2.00, then the real minimum wage falls to $7.50. The lower the real minimum wage is, the greater the number of unskilled workers whom employers will hire, because the demand curve for unskilled workers is downward sloping.

EXHIBIT 5

Three States of the Economy and Two PPFs

In this exhibit, we show three states of the economy in terms of the institutional PPF and the physical PPF. Point A, which is below the institutional PPF, represents an economy in a recessionary gap. Point B, on the institutional PPF, represents an economy in long-run equilibrium. Point C, beyond the institutional PPF but below the physical PPF, represents an economy in an inflationary gap.

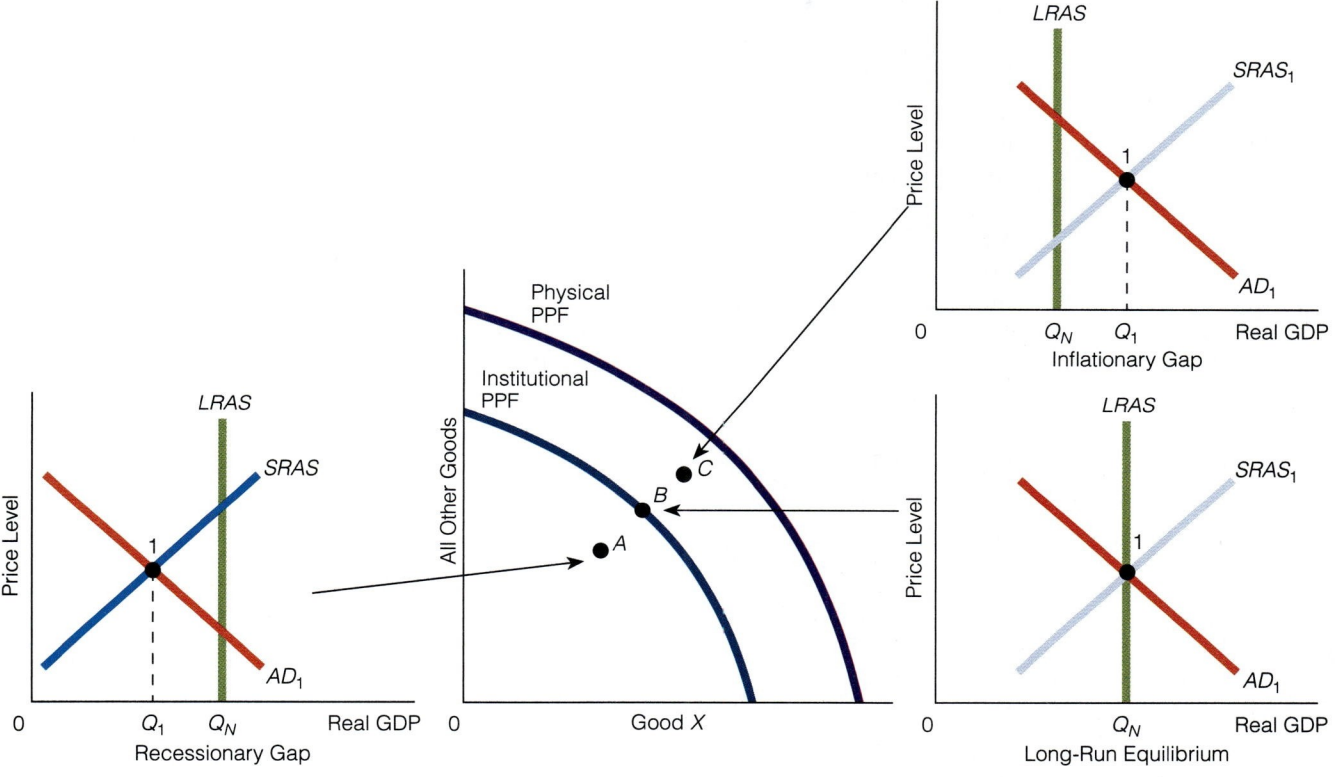

1. What is a recessionary gap? An inflationary gap?
2. What is the state of the labor market when the economy is in a recessionary gap? In an inflationary gap?
3. Suppose the economy is in an inflationary gap. Locate the position of the economy in relation to the two PPFs discussed in this section.

9-3 The Self-Regulating Economy

Some economists believe that the economy is self-regulating. In other words, if the economy is not at the natural unemployment rate (or full employment)—that is, it is not producing Natural Real GDP—then it can move on its own to this position. The notion of a self-regulating economy is quite classical, but it is also a view held by some modern-day economists. This section describes how a self-regulating economy works.

9-3a What Happens if a Self-Regulating Economy Is in a Recessionary Gap?

If the economy is in a recessionary gap, then

1. it is producing a Real GDP level that is less than Natural Real GDP,
2. the unemployment rate is greater than the natural unemployment rate, and
3. a surplus exists in the labor market.

Exhibit 6(a) illustrates this case for a Real GDP of $9 trillion and a Natural Real GDP of $10 trillion. What, if anything, happens in the economy? According to economists who believe that the economy is self-regulating, the surplus in the labor market begins to exert downward pressure on wages.[5] In other words, as old wage contracts expire, business firms negotiate contracts that pay workers lower wage rates.

Then, as wage rates fall, the *SRAS* curve begins to shift to the right, ultimately moving from $SRAS_1$ to $SRAS_2$, as in Exhibit 6(b). As a result of the increase in short-run aggregate supply, the price level falls. As the price level falls, the quantity demanded of Real GDP rises because of the real balance, interest rate, and international trade effects (all discussed in the last chapter). As the price level falls, the economy moves from one point on the *AD* curve to a point farther down on the same curve. In Exhibit 6(b), this is a move from point 1 to point 2.

As long as the economy's Real GDP is less than its Natural Real GDP, the price level continues to fall. Ultimately, the economy moves to long-run equilibrium at point 2, corresponding to P_2 and a Natural Real GDP of $10 trillion. The process may be depicted as follows:

Recessionary gap →

Unemployment rate > Natural unemployment rate →

Surplus in labor market → Wages fall → *SRAS* curve shifts to the right →

Economy moves into long-run equilibrium

9-3b What's the Connection Between a Slow Recovery and How Quickly or Slowly Wages Adjust?

We know from an earlier chapter that the recovery phase of the business cycle is evidenced by Real GDP rising from a trough to the point at which Real GDP was at an earlier peak. For example, if the previous peak was at a Real GDP level of $800 billion, and the trough was at a Real GDP level of $724 billion, then the recovery phase of the business cycle would be when Real GDP rises from $724 billion to $800 billion.

Now, if it takes a long time (many months or years) for Real GDP to rise from $724 billion to $800 billion, many economists would say that the economy is recovering slowly. However, if it takes only a short time (a matter of a few months) for Real GDP to rise from the lower to the higher level, this is consistent with a fast recovery.

What are the causes for a slow recovery? Suppose the economy is in a recessionary gap, as it is in panel (a) of Exhibit 6. Real GDP at point 1 in the exhibit is $9 trillion. Suppose that $9 trillion is the trough. Now, if the economy is self-regulating, we know that when the economy is in a recessionary gap, the labor market is in surplus, which means that wages are likely to decline. How slow or fast wages decline will have a lot to do with how long it will

---

[5] In this discussion of how the self-regulating economy eliminates a recessionary gap, we have emphasized wages (in the labor market) adjusting downward. Resource prices other than wages may fall as well.

EXHIBIT 6

The Self-Regulating Economy: Removing a Recessionary Gap

(a) The economy is at P_1 and a Real GDP of $9 trillion. Because Real GDP is less than Natural Real GDP ($10 trillion), the economy is in a recessionary gap, and the unemployment rate is higher than the natural unemployment rate. (b) Wage rates fall, and the short-run aggregate supply curve shifts from $SRAS_1$ to $SRAS_2$. As the price level falls, the real balance, interest rate, and international trade effects increase the quantity demanded of Real GDP. Ultimately, the economy moves into long-run equilibrium at point 2.

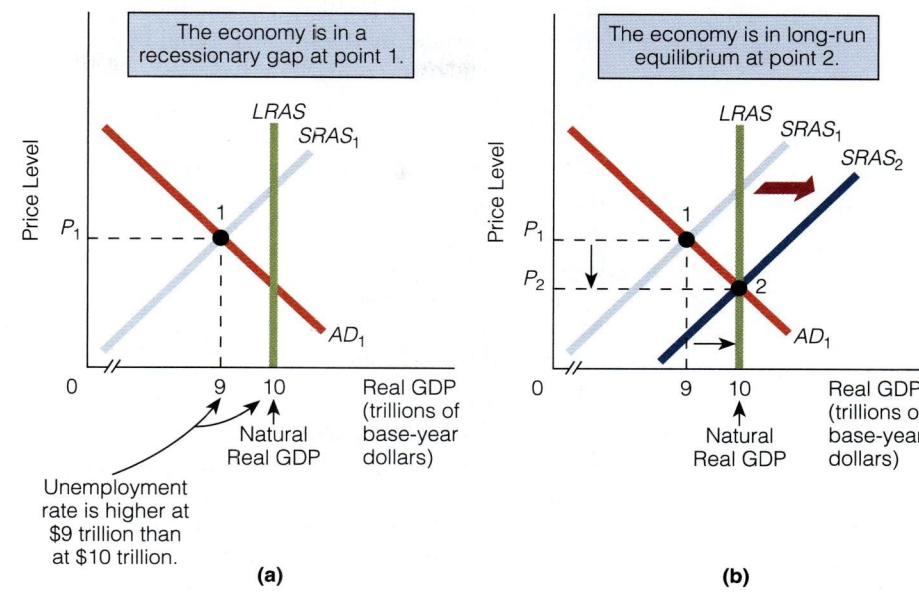

take Real GDP to rise above $9 trillion (on its way toward $10 trillion in the exhibit). The longer it takes for wages to fall, the longer it will be before the SRAS curve in the exhibit shifts rightward—as shown in panel (b) of the exhibit—and the longer it will be before Real GDP rises above its trough level of $9 trillion.

To illustrate our point in an extreme way, suppose that in panel (a), when the economy is at point 1, wages were to fall sharply and quickly so that the SRAS curve shifted to the right (as shown in panel b) in three weeks. How long did it take Real GDP to start rising to a level above the trough level of $9 trillion? The answer is not long; in fact, in a matter of three weeks, it went from $9 trillion to $10 trillion. This is consistent with an economy recovering fairly fast.

It is easier to understand that the longer it takes wages to fall, and the longer it takes for the SRAS curve to shift rightward, the longer it will be before Real GDP starts rising above its trough level, and the slower the recovery will be.

What is the connection between a slow recovery and the speed at which wages adjust during a recessionary gap? The connection is quite tight: The longer it takes wages to adjust, the slower the recovery will be.

9-3c What Happens if the Economy Is in an Inflationary Gap?

If the economy is in an inflationary gap,

1. it is producing a Real GDP level that is greater than Natural Real GDP,
2. the unemployment rate is less than the natural unemployment rate, and
3. a shortage exists in the labor market.

Exhibit 7(a) illustrates this case for a Real GDP of $11 trillion and a Natural Real GDP of $10 trillion. What happens in the economy in this situation? According to economists who believe the economy is self-regulating, the shortage in the labor market begins to exert upward pressure on wages. In other words, as old wage contracts expire, business firms negotiate contracts that pay workers higher wage rates.

Then, as wage rates rise, the SRAS curve begins to shift to the left, ultimately moving from $SRAS_1$ to $SRAS_2$ in Exhibit 7(b). As a result of the decrease in short-run aggregate supply, the price level rises. As the price level rises, the quantity demanded of Real GDP falls because of the real balance, interest rate, and international trade effects. The economy moves from one point on the AD curve to a point farther up on the same curve. In Exhibit 7(b), this is a move from point 1 to point 2.

As long as the economy's Real GDP is greater than its Natural Real GDP, the price level will continue to rise. Ultimately, the economy moves to long-run equilibrium at point 2, corresponding to P_2 and a Natural Real GDP of $10 trillion. The process may be depicted as follows:

Inflationary gap →

Unemployment rate < Natural unemployment rate →

Shortage in labor market → Wages rise → SRAS curve shifts to the left →

Economy moves into long-run equilibrium

9-3d The Self-Regulating Economy: A Recap

We have seen that if the economy is in a recessionary gap, wage rates fall (along with other resource prices), the SRAS curve shifts to the right, the price level falls, and the economy moves down the AD curve. The economy moves in the direction of long-run equilibrium, ultimately achieving the Natural Real GDP level.

EXHIBIT 7

The Self-Regulating Economy: Removing an Inflationary Gap

(a) The economy is at P_1 and a Real GDP of $11 trillion. Because Real GDP is greater than Natural Real GDP ($10 trillion), the economy is in an inflationary gap, and the unemployment rate is lower than the natural unemployment rate. (b) Wage rates rise, and the short-run aggregate supply curve shifts from $SRAS_1$ to $SRAS_2$. As the price level rises, the real balance, interest rate, and international trade effects decrease the quantity demanded of Real GDP. Ultimately, the economy moves into long-run equilibrium at point 2.

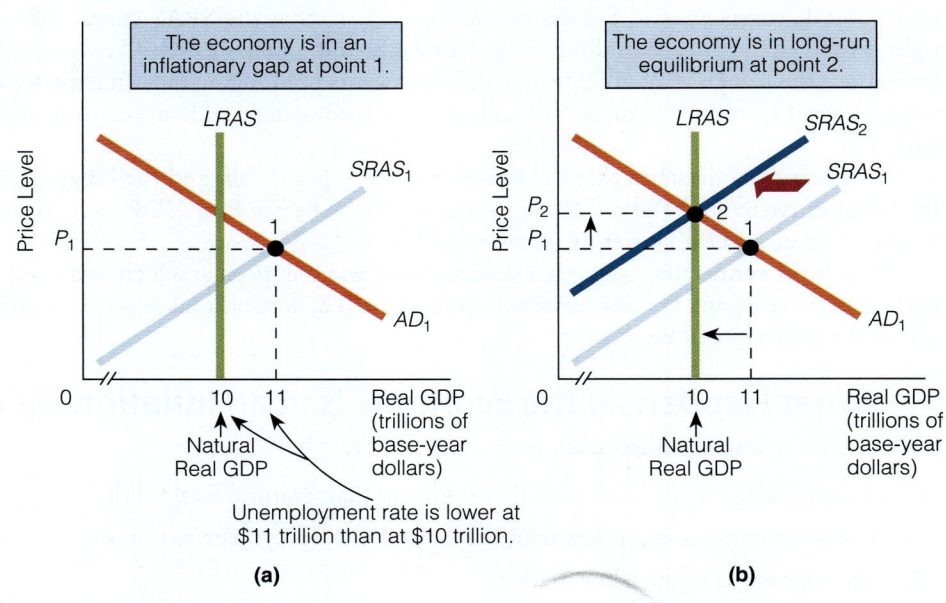

If the economy is in an inflationary gap, wage rates rise (along with other resource prices), and the SRAS curve shifts to the left. At the same time, the price level rises, and the economy moves up the AD curve. The economy moves in the direction of long-run equilibrium, ultimately achieving the Natural Real GDP level.

Flexible wage rates (and other resource prices) play a critical role in the self-regulating economy. For example, suppose wage rates are not *flexible* and do not fall in a recessionary gap. Then the SRAS curve does not shift to the right, the price level does not fall, and the economy doesn't move down the AD curve toward long-run equilibrium. Similarly, if wage rates are not flexible and do not rise in an inflationary gap, then the economy won't move up the AD curve toward long-run equilibrium.

The economists who say the economy is self-regulating believe that wage rates and other resource prices are *flexible* and that they move up and down in response to market conditions. These economists believe that *wage rates will fall* when there is a *surplus of labor* and that *wage rates will rise* when there is a *shortage of labor*. You will see in the next chapter that this flexible wages and prices position has not gone unchallenged.

The following table summarizes how a self-regulating economy works for the three possible states of the economy:

State of the Economy	What Happens if the Economy Is Self-Regulating?
Recessionary gap (Real GDP < Natural Real GDP)	Wages fall and SRAS curve shifts to the right until Real GDP = Natural Real GDP.
Inflationary gap (Real GDP > Natural Real GDP)	Wages rise and SRAS curve shifts to the left until Real GDP = Natural Real GDP.
Long-run equilibrium (Real GDP = Natural Real GDP)	No change in wages and no change in SRAS.

9-3e Policy Implication of Believing That the Economy Is Self-Regulating

For economists who believe in a self-regulating economy, full employment is the norm: *The economy always moves back to its Natural Real GDP level.* Stated differently, if the economy contracts an "illness"—in the form of a recessionary or an inflationary gap—it is capable of healing itself through changes in wages and prices. This position on how the economy works has led these economists to advocate a macroeconomic policy of **laissez-faire**, or noninterference. In these economists' view, government has no economic management role to play.

Laissez-Faire
A public policy of not interfering with market activities in the economy.

9-3f Changes in a Self-Regulating Economy: Short Run and Long Run

If the economy is self-regulating, how does a change in aggregate demand affect the economy in the short run and the long run? In Exhibit 8(a), the economy is initially in long-run equilibrium at point 1. An increase in aggregate demand is then brought about by, say, an increase in government purchases (a possibility discussed in the last chapter). The AD curve shifts right from AD_1 to AD_2, and in the short run, the economy moves to point 2, with both Real GDP and the price level higher than at point 1. Now, at point 2, the economy is in an inflationary gap. If the economy is self-regulating, wages will soon rise, and the SRAS curve will shift to the left—ultimately from $SRAS_1$ to $SRAS_2$. The economy will end up at point 3 in long-run equilibrium.

Let's examine the changes in the short run and the long run. As a result of an increase in aggregate demand, Real GDP rises, and the price level rises in the short run. In addition, because Real GDP rises, the unemployment rate falls. In the long run, when the economy is at point 3, it is producing exactly the same level of Real GDP that it was producing originally (Q_N), but at a higher price level.

Conclusion: If the economy is self-regulating, an increase in aggregate demand can raise the price level and Real GDP in the short run, but in the long run, the only effect is a rise in the price level. In other words, in the long run, we have only higher prices to show for an increase in aggregate demand.

Now let's consider what happens if aggregate demand falls. In Exhibit 8(b), the economy is initially in long-run equilibrium at point 1 when aggregate demand decreases. The AD curve then shifts left from AD_1 to AD_2, and in the short run, the economy moves to point 2, with both Real GDP and the price level lower than at point 1.

Now, at point 2, the economy is in a recessionary gap. If the economy is self-regulating, wages will soon fall and the $SRAS$ curve will shift to the right—ultimately from $SRAS_1$ to $SRAS_2$. The economy winds up at point 3 in long-run equilibrium.

Again, let's examine the changes in the short run and the long run. As a result of a decrease in aggregate demand, Real GDP falls in the short run, as does the price level. In addition, because Real GDP falls, the unemployment rate rises. In the long run, when the economy is at point 3, it is producing exactly the same level of Real GDP that it was producing originally (Q_N), but at a lower price level.

EXHIBIT 8

Changes in a Self-Regulating Economy: Short Run and Long Run

In (a), the economy is initially at point 1 in long-run equilibrium. Aggregate demand rises, and the AD curve shifts right from AD_1 to AD_2. The economy is at point 2 in the short run, with a higher Real GDP and a higher price level than at point 1. The economy is also in an inflationary gap at point 2. If the economy is self-regulating, wages will soon rise, the $SRAS$ curve will shift leftward from $SRAS_1$ to $SRAS_2$, and the economy will be in long-run equilibrium at point 3. At point 3, the economy is producing the same Real GDP that it did at point 1. In other words, in the long run, an increase in aggregate demand only raises the price level. In (b), the economy is initially at point 1 in long-run equilibrium. Aggregate demand falls, and the AD curve shifts leftward from AD_1 to AD_2. The economy is at point 2 in the short run, with a lower Real GDP and a lower price level than at point 1. The economy is also in a recessionary gap. If the economy is self-regulating, wages will soon fall, the $SRAS$ curve will shift rightward from $SRAS_1$ to $SRAS_2$, and the economy will be in long-run equilibrium at point 3. At point 3, the economy is producing the same Real GDP that it did at point 1. In other words, in the long run, a decrease in aggregate demand only lowers the price level.

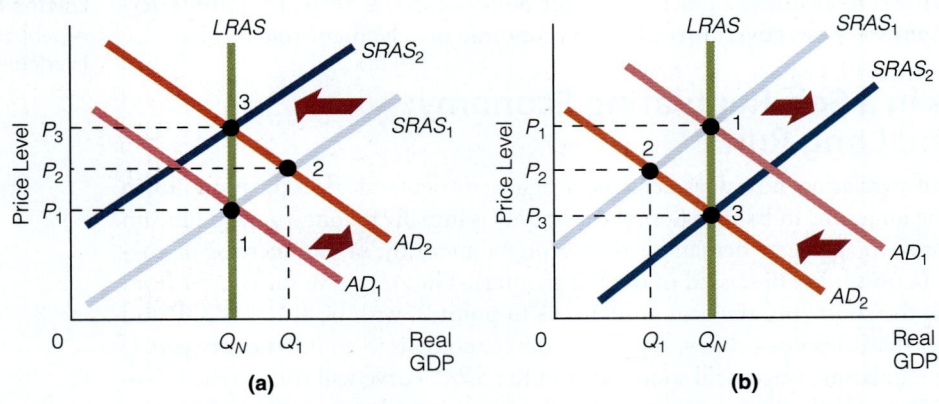

Conclusion: If the economy is self-regulating, a decrease in aggregate demand can lower the price level and Real GDP in the short run, but in the long run, the only effect is a lower price level. The following table illustrates the short- and long-run effects of a change in aggregated demand:

Change in AD	In the Short Run	In the Long Run
AD ↑	P ↑, Q ↑	P ↑, Q does not change
AD ↓	P ↓, Q ↓	P ↓, Q does not change

Let's return to Exhibit 8(a) to clarify a point about long-run equilibrium. In the exhibit, the economy starts at point 1 in long-run equilibrium and then moves to point 2. At point 2, both the price level and Real GDP are higher than they were at point 1. In other words, if AD rises, both the price level and Real GDP rise in the short run. If the economy is self-regulating, it does not remain at point 2 but rather moves to point 3, where it is again in long-run equilibrium. At point 3, the price level is higher than it was at point 2, but Real GDP is lower. Why, then, don't we say that Real GDP is lower in the long run than it is in the short run instead of saying that Real GDP does not change in the long run? The answer is that the long run is measured from one long-run equilibrium point to another long-run equilibrium point. In Exhibit 8(a), we look at the long run by comparing points 1 and 3. When we make this comparison, we notice two things: The price level is higher at point 3 than at point 1, and Real GDP is the same.

9-3g A Recap of Classical Macroeconomics and a Self-Regulating Economy

According to classical macroeconomics, in a self-regulating economy,

1. Say's law holds.
2. Interest rates change such that savings equals investment.
3. The economy is self-regulating, making full employment and an economy that produces Natural Real GDP the norm.
4. Prices and wages are flexible. In other words, if the economy is in a recessionary gap, wages fall, and the economy soon moves itself toward producing Natural Real GDP (at a lower price level than in the recessionary gap). If the economy is in an inflationary gap, wages rise, and the economy soon moves itself toward producing Natural Real GDP (at a higher price level than in the inflationary gap).
5. Because the economy is self-regulating, laissez-faire is the policy prescription.

9-3h Does a Constant Price Level Mean the Economy Is Not Self-Regulating?

Suppose that, in year 1, the economy is in a recessionary gap, it is self-regulating, and it is beginning to remove itself from the recessionary gap. In other words, wages are beginning to fall, and the SRAS curve is beginning to shift rightward. As a result, the price level is beginning to decline. Pictorially,

Recessionary gap → Wages begin to fall → SRAS begins to shift rightward → Price level begins to decline

Now suppose that, in year 2, the economy is no longer in a recessionary gap. It is in long-run equilibrium, producing Natural Real GDP (Q_N). But here is the problem: The price level hasn't declined. This development is odd, because if the economy was in a recessionary gap and the economy is self-regulating, we would expect the price level to be lower once the economy removes itself from the recessionary gap. For example, look back at Exhibit 6(b) to see that the price level is lower at point 2 (once the economy has removed itself from a recessionary gap) than at point 1 (when it was in a recessionary gap).

Does a constant price level mean that the economy is not self-regulating? Not at all. While the economy was self-regulating (and the *SRAS* curve was shifting to the right), aggregate demand in the economy might have risen. Moreover, the rise in aggregate demand could be totally unrelated to the change occurring on the supply side of the economy (as evidenced by the *SRAS* curve's shift to the right).

Think of it this way: The *SRAS* curve is the right hand, and it is moving. The *AD* curve is the left hand; it is moving too, and its movement is unrelated to what the right hand (the *SRAS* curve) is doing. In the end, both hands (the *SRAS* curve and the *AD* curve) determine what happens to the price level.

In Exhibit 9, the economy is initially at point 1, in a recessionary gap. The self-regulating properties of the economy are in force: wages are falling, and the *SRAS* curve is shifting rightward from $SRAS_1$ to $SRAS_2$. At the same time, something has occurred to increase aggregate demand (e.g., government purchases or the money supply might have increased), and the *AD* curve shifts rightward from AD_1 to AD_2. In the end, the two new curves—$SRAS_2$ and AD_2—intersect at point 2 in the exhibit. The economy is no longer in a recessionary gap, and the price level has remained constant.

Here's what we should take away from this discussion: Two (or more) things can happen at the same time in an economy, and unless we understand this fact, we may assume that something is false when it is actually true. If the economy is removing itself from a recessionary gap, we expect the price level to decline, but it doesn't. So is the economy not self-regulating? No. Something else could have been happening at the same time the economy was removing itself from a recessionary gap, and this "something else" (in our example, a rise in aggregate demand) could offset the falling price level.

EXHIBIT 9

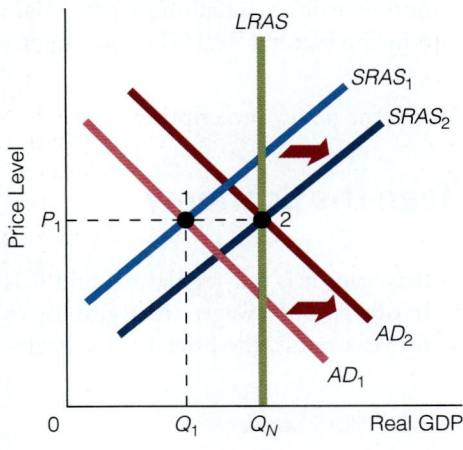

A Self-Regulating Economy with Aggregate Demand Increasing

The economy is initially in a recessionary gap at point 1. Because the economy is self-regulating, the *SRAS* curve shifts to the right, whereupon something unrelated to the self-regulating properties of the economy occurs. Specifically, aggregate demand rises, and the *AD* curve shifts rightward. The economy ends up at point 2, out of the recessionary gap but with no change in the price level.

9-3i Business-Cycle Macroeconomics and Economic-Growth Macroeconomics

In Chapter 8, we introduced the *AD–AS* model, involving the aggregate demand (*AD*) curve, the short-run aggregate supply (*SRAS*) curve, and the long-run aggregate supply (*LRAS*) curve. In this chapter, working mainly with two of those three curves (the *AD* and *SRAS* curves), we did two things. First, we showed what would happen if a self-regulating economy were in either a recessionary or an inflationary gap (see Exhibits 6 and 7, respectively). In both cases, the *SRAS* curve would shift so that the economy moved into long-run equilibrium. Second, we started from a point of long-run equilibrium and introduced a change in aggregate demand (see Exhibit 8). We explained what happens in the economy (specifically to the price level and Real GDP) in both the short run and the long run.

You have enough background now to understand the difference between business-cycle macroeconomics and economic-growth macroeconomics. Both can be explained with respect to Real GDP and a few curves. In some upcoming chapters, we will deal with business-cycle macroeconomics—that is, with changes in the *AD* and *SRAS* curves around a *fixed LRAS* curve. But in other chapters, we will be dealing with economic-growth macroeconomics—that is, with *rightward-shifting* changes in the *LRAS* curve. Business-cycle and economic-growth macroeconomics essentially make up two categories of macroeconomics. Keep these two categories in mind as you continue your study of macroeconomics.

Business-Cycle Macroeconomics In this chapter, we have been looking at the *business cycle*: the recurrent ups and downs in Real GDP. To understand the business cycle, let us again examine Exhibit 8(a). The economy starts off in long-run equilibrium at point 1. Next, the aggregate demand curve shifts to the right. In the short run, Real GDP rises from Q_N to Q_1. Eventually, though, the *SRAS* curve shifts to the left, the economy is back in long-run equilibrium at point 3, and Real GDP returns to its natural level at Q_N.

We could describe what happened this way: Real GDP initially rose and then fell with respect to a *fixed LRAS* curve. This is what business-cycle macroeconomics deals with: (up and down) changes in Real GDP around a *fixed LRAS* curve.

In many upcoming chapters, we will delve into business-cycle macroeconomics: What shifts the *AD* curve? Why might Real GDP initially rise and then fall? Macroeconomists often have to ask and then try to answer such questions relating to business-cycle macroeconomics.

Economic-Growth Macroeconomics If business-cycle macroeconomics can be described as changes in Real GDP with respect to a *fixed LRAS* curve, then economic-growth macroeconomics can be described as *increases* in Real GDP due to a *rightward-shifting LRAS* curve. In Exhibit 10, we start with AD_1 and $LRAS_1$. Long-run equilibrium is at point 1, and Natural Real GDP is Q_{N1}. Now, suppose the *LRAS* curve shifts rightward, first to $LRAS_2$ and then to $LRAS_3$. At the same time, Real GDP rises, first to Q_{N2} and then to Q_{N3}. These rightward shifts in *LRAS* curve illustrate economic growth. Our study of economic-growth macroeconomics deals with the factors that can lead to a rightward shift in the *LRAS* curve.

EXHIBIT 10

Economic-Growth Macroeconomics

Economic-growth macroeconomics deals with rightward shifts in the long-run aggregate supply curve (LRAS).

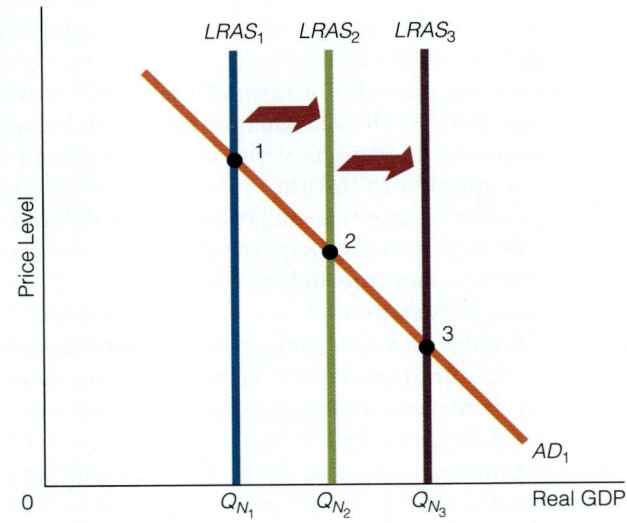

---

1. If the economy is self-regulating, what happens if it is in a recessionary gap?
2. If the economy is self-regulating, what happens if it is in an inflationary gap?
3. If the economy is self-regulating, how do changes in aggregate demand affect the economy in the long run?

Office Hours

"Do Economists Really Know What the Natural Unemployment Rate Equals?"

Student: Do economists know what the natural unemployment rate equals at any given moment?

Instructor: They estimate it but can't be absolutely sure that their estimate of the natural unemployment rate is the same as the actual rate. After all, not all economists arrive at the same estimate for the natural unemployment rate. One economist might estimate it at 4.3 percent, whereas another estimates it at 4.6 percent.

Student: Well, if that's true, then not every economist would agree that the economy is in, say, a recessionary gap if the unemployment rate is, say, 4.5 percent. Am I correct?

Instructor: You are correct. For example, the economist who thinks that the natural unemployment rate is 4.3 percent will think that the economy is in a recessionary gap if the actual unemployment rate is 4.5 percent, but the economist who thinks that the natural unemployment rate is 4.6 percent will not. Here's an analogy: A thinks that B's normal body temperature is 98.9 degrees, and C thinks that it is only 98.6 degrees. If B's body temperature today is 98.9 degrees, C will think that B is running a low-grade fever, but A will not.

Student: Does making a too-high or too-low estimate of the natural unemployment rate matter to the economy? In other words, do the incorrect estimates (that economists sometimes make) matter?

Instructor: Actually, the answer is yes and no. The answer is no if the economy is self-regulating and government doesn't try to move the economy out of either a recessionary or an inflationary gap by implementing economic policies. As in the example of misestimating B's normal body temperature, if no one gives B any medicine, then misestimating his body temperature probably doesn't matter.

But in later chapters, you are going to read about the government implementing economic policies to try to remove the economy from either a recessionary or an inflationary gap. Then misestimating the natural unemployment rate does matter.

To illustrate, suppose the natural unemployment rate has fallen from 5.0 percent to 4.7 percent but economists and government economic policymakers have not figured that out yet. In other words, they still believe that the natural unemployment rate is 5.0 percent. Now, if the actual unemployment rate is 4.7 percent, then the economy is in long-run equilibrium. Economists and government economic policymakers, however, mistakenly believe that the economy is in an inflationary gap (with the actual unemployment rate of 4.7 percent lower than their too-high estimate of 5.0 percent). Thinking that the economy is in an inflationary gap, economists expect prices to rise in the future. To offset the higher prices in the future, they propose a reduction in the growth rate of the money supply in the hopes of reducing aggregate demand (shifting the AD curve to the left). The Federal Reserve (the monetary authority, also called the Fed) follows suit and reduces the growth rate of the money supply, whereupon the AD curve shifts leftward. But notice the effect of the Fed's action in terms of our AD–AS model: A reduction in aggregate demand throws the economy into a recessionary gap. (Remember, the economy was actually in long-run equilibrium when the monetary policy action was carried out.)

Our conclusion is simple: A misestimate of the natural unemployment rate, if acted on, can move an economy from long-run equilibrium into a recessionary gap.

Back to the original question: Does getting a too-high or too-low estimate of the natural unemployment rate matter to the economy? The answer is yes; it certainly can matter to the economy.

Points to Remember

1. Economists can misestimate the natural unemployment rate.
2. Acting on a misestimated natural unemployment rate can affect the economy (sometimes adversely)—for example, by influencing economic policy actions.

Chapter Summary

Say's Law

- Say's law states that supply creates its own demand. All economists believe that Say's law holds in a barter economy, where there can be no general overproduction or underproduction of goods. Classical economists believed that Say's law also holds in a money economy. In their view, even if consumption drops and saving rises, economic forces are at work producing an equal increase in investment. According to classical economists, interest rates are flexible, and they move to a level where the amount of saving and the amount of investment in an economy are equal.

Classical Economists on Markets, Wages, and Prices

- Classical economists believed that most, if not all, markets are competitive and that wages and prices are flexible.

Three States of the Economy

- Natural Real GDP is the level of Real GDP produced when the economy is operating at the natural unemployment rate.
- The economy can be producing a Real GDP level that (1) is equal to Natural Real GDP, (2) is greater than Natural Real

GDP, or (3) is less than Natural Real GDP. In other words, the economy can be in (1) long-run equilibrium, (2) an inflationary gap, or (3) a recessionary gap, respectively.

- In long-run equilibrium, the Real GDP that the economy is producing is equal to Natural Real GDP. The unemployment rate in the economy is equal to the natural unemployment rate, and the labor market is in equilibrium.
- In a recessionary gap, the Real GDP that the economy is producing is less than Natural Real GDP. The unemployment rate in the economy is greater than the natural unemployment rate, and a surplus exists in the labor market.
- In an inflationary gap, the Real GDP that the economy is producing is greater than Natural Real GDP. The unemployment rate in the economy is less than the natural unemployment rate, and a shortage exists in the labor market.

The Institutional and Physical Production Possibilities Frontiers

- The physical PPF illustrates different combinations of goods that the economy can produce given the physical constraints of (1) finite resources and (2) the current state of technology. The institutional PPF illustrates different combinations of goods that the economy can produce given the physical constraints of (1) finite resources and (2) the current state of technology, plus (3) any institutional constraints.
- If an economy is operating on its institutional PPF, it is operating at the natural unemployment rate. If it is operating at a point beyond the institutional PPF but below the physical PPF, it is operating at an unemployment rate less than the natural unemployment rate. If it is operating at a point below the institutional PPF, it is operating at an unemployment rate above the natural unemployment rate.

The Self-Regulating Economy

- Some economists contend that the economy can eliminate both recessionary and inflationary gaps smoothly and quickly by itself.
- If the economy is self-regulating and in a recessionary gap, then the unemployment rate in the economy is greater than the natural unemployment rate and a surplus exists in the labor market. As wage contracts expire, wage rates fall. As a result, the *SRAS* curve shifts to the right, and the price level falls. As the price level falls, the quantity demanded of Real GDP rises. Ultimately, the economy moves into long-run equilibrium, where it produces Natural Real GDP.
- If the economy is self-regulating and in an inflationary gap, then the unemployment rate in the economy is less than the natural unemployment rate, and a shortage exists in the labor market. As wage contracts expire, wage rates rise. As a result, the *SRAS* curve shifts to the left, and the price level rises. As the price level rises, the quantity demanded of Real GDP falls. Ultimately, the economy moves into long-run equilibrium, where it produces Natural Real GDP.

Business-Cycle Macroeconomics and Economic-Growth Macroeconomics

- This text presents both business-cycle macroeconomics and economic-growth macroeconomics. Business-cycle macroeconomics deals with changes in Real GDP around a fixed *LRAS* curve. Economic-growth macroeconomics deals with *increases* in Real GDP due to a rightward-shifting *LRAS* curve.

Key Terms and Concepts

Say's Law   Recessionary Gap   Inflationary Gap   Laissez-faire

Questions and Problems

1. What is the classical economics position on (a) wages, (b) prices, and (c) interest rates?
2. According to classical economists, does Say's law hold in a money economy? Explain your answer.
3. How do you explain why investment falls as the interest rate rises?
4. Explain why saving rises as the interest rate rises.
5. According to classical economists, does an increase in saving shift the *AD* curve to the left? Explain your answer.
6. What does it mean to say that the economy is in a recessionary gap? In an inflationary gap? In long-run equilibrium?

7. What is the state of the labor market in (a) a recessionary gap, (b) an inflationary gap, and (c) long-run equilibrium?

8. Describe the relationship of the (actual) unemployment rate to the natural unemployment rate in each of the following economic states: (a) a recessionary gap, (b) an inflationary gap, and (c) long-run equilibrium.

9. Diagrammatically represent an economy in (a) an inflationary gap, (b) a recessionary gap, and (c) long-run equilibrium.

10. Explain how an economy can operate beyond its institutional PPF but not beyond its physical PPF.

11. According to economists who believe in a self-regulating economy, what happens—step-by-step—when the economy is in a recessionary gap? What happens when the economy is in an inflationary gap?

12. If wage rates are not flexible, can the economy be self-regulating? Explain your answer.

13. Explain the importance of the real balance, interest rate, and international trade effects to long-run (equilibrium) adjustment in the economy.

14. Suppose that the economy is self-regulating, that the price level is 132, that the quantity demanded of Real GDP is $4 trillion, that the quantity supplied of Real GDP in the short run is $3.9 trillion, and that the quantity supplied of Real GDP in the long run is $4.3 trillion. Is the economy in short-run equilibrium? Will the price level in long-run equilibrium be greater than, less than, or equal to 132? Explain your answers.

15. Suppose that the economy is self-regulating, that the price level is 110, that the quantity demanded of Real GDP is $4 trillion, that the quantity supplied of Real GDP in the short run is $4.9 trillion, and that the quantity supplied of Real GDP in the long run is $4.1 trillion. Is the economy in short-run equilibrium? Will the price level in long-run equilibrium be greater than, less than, or equal to 110? Explain your answers.

16. Ava is telling her friend Harper that wages are rising and so is the unemployment rate. She tells Harper that she (Ava) may be the next person to be fired at her company and that she may have to move back in with her parents. What does the economy have to do with Ava's possibly having to move back in with her parents?

17. Leo says, "I think it's a little like when you have a cold or the flu. You don't need to see a doctor. In time, your body heals itself. That's sort of the way the economy works too. We don't really need government coming to our rescue every time the economy gets a cold." According to Leo, how does the economy work?

18. Beginning with long-run equilibrium, explain what happens to the price level and Real GDP in the short run and in the long run as a result of (a) a decline in AD, (b) a rise in AD, (c) a decline in SRAS, and (d) a rise in SRAS.

Working with Numbers and Graphs

1. In the following figure, which point is representative of
    a. the economy on its *LRAS* curve?
    b. the economy in a recessionary gap?
    c. the economy in an inflationary gap?

2. Which of the following figures, (a)–(c), is consistent with or representative of
    a. the economy operating at the natural unemployment rate?
    b. a surplus in the labor market?
    c. a recessionary gap?
    d. a cyclical unemployment rate of zero?

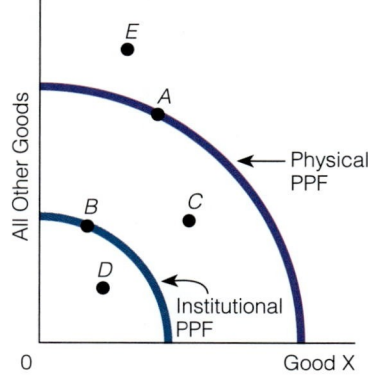

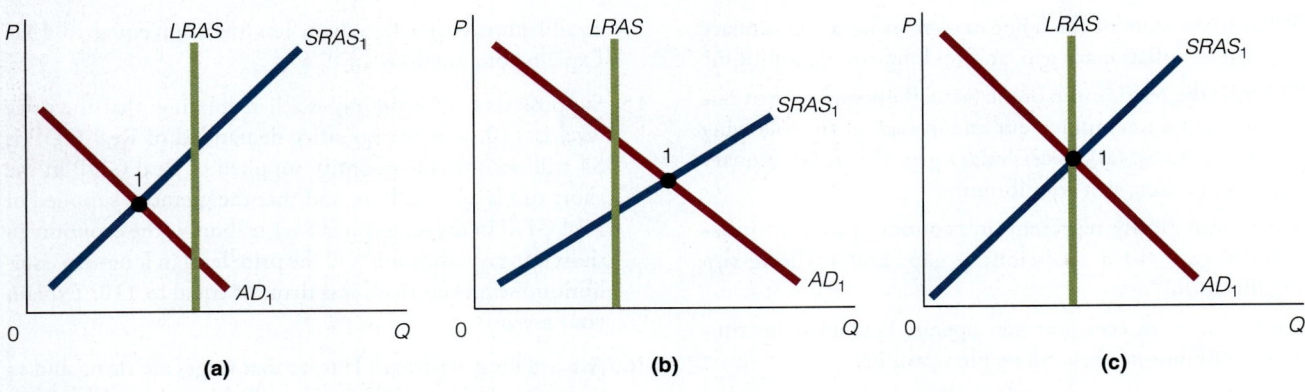

3. Represent the following situations diagrammatically:
   a. An economy in which AD increases as the economy is self-regulating out of a recessionary gap
   b. An economy in which AD decreases as the economy is self-regulating out of an inflationary gap
4. Economist Jones believes that there is always sufficient (aggregate) demand in the economy to buy all the goods and services supplied at full employment. Diagrammatically represent what the economy looks like for Jones.
5. Diagrammatically show what happens when the institutional constraints in the economy become less effective.
6. Diagrammatically represent an economy in a recessionary gap. Next, identify where the economy in a recessionary gap lies in terms of both the institutional PPF and the physical PPF.
7. Fill in the blank spaces (A–O) in the table that follows. In the table, Q = Real GDP and Q_N = Natural Real GDP.

State of the Economy	Is the Economy in a Recessionary Gap, Inflationary Gap, or Long-Run Equilibrium?	Does Equilibrium, a Shortage, or a Surplus Exist in the Labor Market?	Will Wages Fall, Rise, or Remain Unchanged?	Will the SRAS Curve Shift Right, Left, or Remain Unchanged?	Is the Economy Above, Below, or on Its Institutional PPF?
$Q < Q_N$	A	B	C	D	E
$Q > Q_N$	F	G	H	I	J
$Q = Q_N$	K	L	M	N	O

Introduction

In the last chapter, we discussed the economy as a self-regulating mechanism. For example, we learned that an economy can remove itself from a recessionary gap. In this chapter, we challenge that assertion and discuss the views of economists who believe that the economy may not be able to self-regulate and get to Natural Real GDP. In other words, the economy may not be able to move itself out of a recessionary gap. The ideas in this chapter are mostly those of one man, John Maynard Keynes, who taught economics at Cambridge University in England during the first half of

10-1 Questioning the Classical Position and the Self-Regulating Economy

John Maynard Keynes, an English economist, changed how many economists viewed the economy. Keynes's major work, *The General Theory of Employment, Interest and Money*, was published in 1936.[1] Just prior to publication of the book, the Great Depression had plagued many countries of the world. Looking around at the world during that time, one had to wonder whether the classical view of the economy could be right. Unemployment was sky high in many countries, and many economies had been contracting.

Where was Say's law, with its promise that there would be no general gluts? When was the self-regulating economy going to heal itself of its depression illness? Where was full employment? And, given the depressed state of the economy, could anyone believe any longer that laissez-faire was the right policy? With the Great Depression as recent history, Keynes and the Keynesians thought that, although their theory might not be right in every detail, they certainly had enough evidence to say that the classical view of the economy was wrong.

---

[1] John Maynard Keynes, *The General Theory of Employment, Interest and Money* (New York: Harcourt, Brace, 1936).

Keynes challenged all four of the following classical position beliefs: (1) Say's law holds so that insufficient demand in the economy is unlikely. (2) Wages, prices, and interest rates are flexible. (3) The economy is self-regulating. (4) Laissez-faire is the right and sensible economic policy.

10-1a Keynes's Criticism of Say's Law in a Money Economy

According to classical economists and Say's law, if consumption spending falls because saving increases, then total spending will not fall, because the added saving will simply bring about more investment spending. Such spending will happen through changes in the interest rate: The added saving will put downward pressure on the interest rate, and at a lower interest rate, businesses will borrow and invest more. Through changes in the interest rate, the amount of saving will always equal the amount invested.

Keynes disagreed. He didn't think that added saving would necessarily stimulate an equal amount of added investment spending. Exhibit 1 illustrates Keynes's point of view. Let consumption equal $3,000, investment equal $600, government purchases equal $1,200, and net exports equal $200. Then saving increases by $100, lowering consumption to $2,900. According to the classical economists, investment will rise by $100 at the same time, going from $600 to $700. Keynes asked, what is the guarantee that an increase in investment will equally match an increase in saving? What if saving rises by $100 (and consumption goes down by $100), but investment rises by, say, only $40 (instead of $100)? Then the original equation for total expenditures, $TE = C + I + G + (EX - IM)$, changes from

$$TE = \$3{,}000 + \$600 + \$1{,}200 + \$200 = \$5{,}000$$

to

$$TE = \$2{,}900 + \$640 + \$1{,}200 + \$200 = \$4{,}940$$

not to

$$TE = \$2{,}900 + \$700 + \$1{,}200 + \$200 = \$5{,}000$$

Thus, total expenditures decrease from $5,000 to $4,940, and if, at a given price level, total spending falls, so will aggregate demand. In other words, according to Keynes, aggregate demand could fall if saving increases.

Of course, a classical economist would retort that, as a result of a $100 increase in saving, interest rates will fall enough to guarantee that investment will increase by $100. Keynes countered by saying that individuals save and invest for a host of reasons and that no single factor, such as the interest rate, links these activities.

Furthermore, whereas the classical economists believed that saving and investment depend on the interest rate, Keynes believed that both saving and investment depend on a number of factors that may be far more influential than the interest rate. Keynes held that saving is more responsive to changes in income than to changes in the interest rate and that investment is more responsive to technological changes, business expectations, and innovations than to changes in the interest rate.

EXHIBIT 1

Keynes's View of Say's Law in a Money Economy

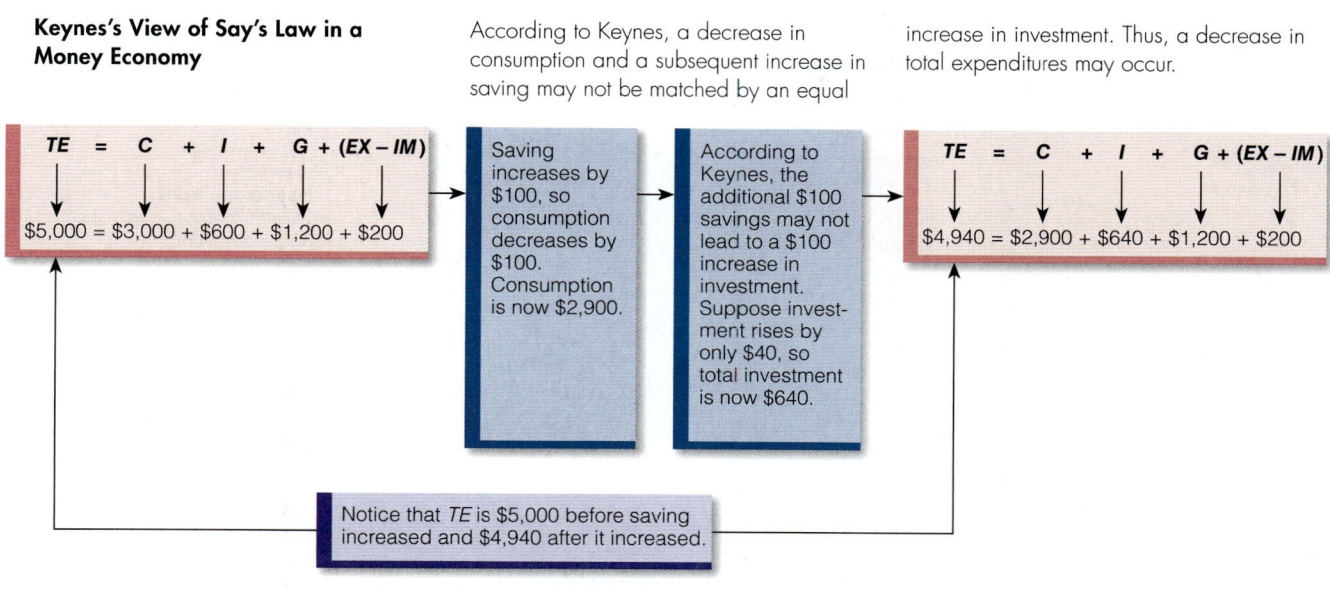

Consider the difference between Keynes and the classical economists on saving:

- The classical economists held that saving is directly related to the interest rate: As the interest rate goes up, saving rises, and as the interest rate goes down, saving falls, *ceteris paribus*.

- Keynes thought that this assumption might not always be true. To see why, suppose that individuals are saving for a certain goal—say, a retirement fund of $100,000. Then they might save less per period at an interest rate of 10 percent than at an interest rate of 5 percent because a higher interest rate means that they can save less per period and still meet their goal by the time they are ready to retire. For example, if the interest rate is 5 percent, they need $50,000 in savings to earn $2,500 in interest income per year. If the interest rate is 10 percent, they need only $25,000 in savings to earn $2,500 in interest annually.

As for investment, Keynes believed that the interest rate is important in determining the level of investment but not as important as other variables, such as the expected rate of profit on investment. Keynes argued that if business expectations are pessimistic, then much investment is unlikely, regardless of how low the interest rate is.

10-1b Keynes on Wage Rates

As explained in the last chapter, if the unemployment rate in the economy is greater than the natural unemployment rate, a surplus exists in the labor market: The number of job seekers is high relative to the number of jobs available. Consequently, according to classical economists, wage rates will fall.

Keynes didn't see the adjustment as so simple. Instead, he asserted, employees will naturally resist an employer's efforts to cut wages, and labor unions may resist wage cuts. In short, wage rates may be inflexible in a downward direction.

EXHIBIT 2

The Economy Gets Stuck in a Recessionary Gap

According to Keynes's view, if the economy is in a recessionary gap at point 1, wage rates may not fall. The economy may be stuck in the recessionary gap.

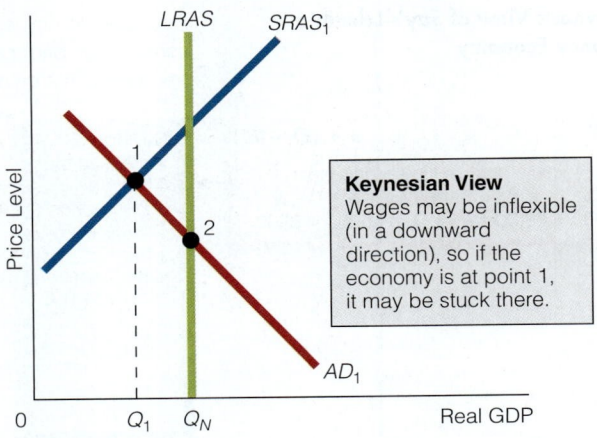

Keynesian View
Wages may be inflexible (in a downward direction), so if the economy is at point 1, it may be stuck there.

If wage rates will not fall, is the economy then unable to get itself out of a recessionary gap? The Keynesian answer is yes. If employee and labor union resistance prevents wage rates from falling, then the *SRAS* curve will not shift to the right. If it does not shift to the right, the price level won't come down. If the price level does not come down, buyers will not purchase more goods and services and move the economy out of a recessionary gap. As Exhibit 2 shows, the economy is stuck at point 1. It cannot get to point 2.

Keynes believed that the economy is inherently unstable and that it may not automatically cure itself of a recessionary gap. In other words, *the economy may not be self-regulating.*

10-1c Different Markets, Different Rates of Adjustment

Keynes's notion that wages may not fall to their equilibrium level brings up the issue of various markets and the adjustment path in each. Let's first look at a market in which prices equilibrate very quickly: the stock market. Consider the market for stock *A*. There is a demand for this stock and a supply of it. If the demand rises, the price of the stock will rise. If the demand falls, the price of the stock will fall. Stock prices are flexible (upward and downward), and they move quickly to their equilibrium value. For example, the demand for stock *A* might rise at 10 o'clock in the morning, and one minute later, at 10:01, the new higher equilibrium price of stock *A* is reached.

Now, not all markets adjust to their equilibrium values as quickly as the stock market. Many economists argue that the labor market might be very different from the stock market. They say that, in the labor market, wages may adjust very slowly to their new equilibrium values. For a certain period, wages may not adjust at all, especially when there is a surplus of labor and we would expect wages to decline.

Exhibit 3 shows the demand for, and supply of, labor. Currently, the labor market is in equilibrium at W_1. At this wage, the quantity demanded of labor equals the quantity supplied of labor, and both are 100 workers. Now let's suppose the demand for goods and services declines in the economy; that is, the aggregate demand (*AD*) curve shifts

EXHIBIT 3

The Labor Market and Inflexible Wages Downward

We start with D_1 and S_1 and the labor market in equilibrium at point 1. The equilibrium wage rate is W_1. The demand for labor declines, and the new equilibrium wage rate is W_2. Will employers end up paying W_2? "Not necessarily," say economists who believe that the wage rate (in the labor market) is inflexible downward. The reasons they offer include long-term labor contracts, fear of declining productivity resulting from lower wages, and avoiding having disgruntled workers in the workplace.

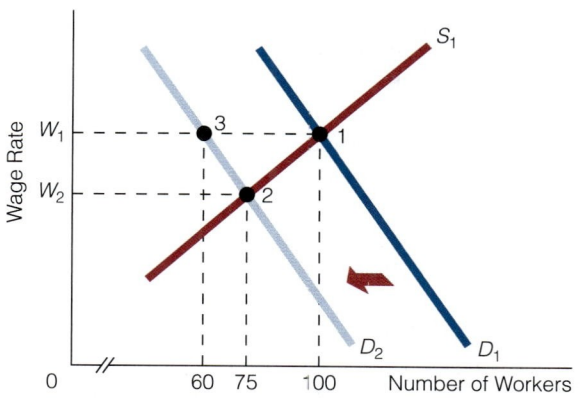

---

leftward. As a result of lower AD in the economy, firms are producing and selling fewer goods and services. Therefore, their demand for labor decreases; in Exhibit 3, the demand-for-labor curve shifts leftward from D_1 to D_2. If the labor market were like the stock market and equilibrated quickly to its new equilibrium wage rate (W_2), the labor market would move to point 2. Fewer people would be working at point 2 than at point 1, and the people who were working would be earning less (W_2 instead of W_1). Also, 25 people would have been fired.

Keynesian economists often argue that the labor market does not adjust in the same way or as quickly as the stock market does. In other words, wage rates aren't likely to fall simply because the demand for labor has declined (from D_1 to D_2). The wage rate W_1 is likely to be inflexible downward; that is, it isn't likely to *decline*—at least for some time.

Why is the wage rate inflexible downward? One explanation has to do with long-term labor contracts. To illustrate, suppose management and workers enter into a three-year contract that specifies a wage rate of $20 an hour for the duration of the contract. Management might want to enter into such a contract for two reasons: fewer labor negotiations and fewer worker strikes, both of which effectively diminish or disappear while the contract is in force. Workers also want to enter into such a contract for two reasons: wage security and fewer strikes (strikes are costly for workers too).

There may also be solid microeconomic reasons for inflexible wages downward. Some economists argue that, at times, firms find it in their best interest to pay wage rates above equilibrium levels. For example, according to **efficiency wage models**, labor productivity depends on the wage rate that the firm pays its employees. Specifically, a cut in wages can cause a decline in labor productivity, in turn raising the firm's costs. (Basically, these models say that workers are more productive when they are paid a higher wage than when they are paid a lower one.) By paying an above-equilibrium wage, firms provide an incentive to workers to be productive and to do less shirking, among other things. If shirking declines, so do the monitoring (management) costs of the firm.

Efficiency Wage Models
These models hold that it is sometimes in the best interest of business firms to pay their employees wage rates that are higher than the equilibrium wage rate.

Look again at Exhibit 3, and think of how things look from the perspective of the employer, the person hiring workers. The demand for labor has declined, and the new equilibrium wage rate is W_2. If the employer decides to go with the new equilibrium wage rate, two things will happen: The employer has to (1) fire 25 workers and (2) pay the 75 remaining workers a lower wage rate than they were previously receiving. But then the employer is likely to have to face 75 disgruntled workers every day. Now, disgruntled workers (who may not understand *why* the employer has decided to pay them less) are not likely to be the same as when they were paid more. They may be less productive, shirk more, and perhaps even steal from the employer.

Will things be much different if the employer continues to pay W_1 and keeps 60 workers instead of 75 workers (in other words, fire 40 workers instead of 25)? Some economists argue that paying W_1 might be better for the employer than paying the lower wage W_2. At W_2, the employer has 75 workers who are angry because they are being paid a lower wage—and the employer has to work with these 75 disgruntled workers every day. But if the employer pays W_1 instead of W_2 and fires 40 workers, they will all be disgruntled, but they won't be disgruntled *at work*. They are disgruntled *at home*, away from the employer. The remaining 60 workers are not disgruntled because they haven't had their wage rate lowered and they haven't been fired. In fact, they may appreciate their employer all the more for not cutting their wage rates and for not firing them.

To recap, Keynesian economists often argue that the labor market is not the same as the stock market. The stock market equilibrates quickly to changes in demand and supply. The labor market may adjust slowly. In particular, a lowered demand for labor may not be met with a declining wage rate. Wage rates might be inflexible downward (at least for

Economics 24/7

The Financial and Economic Crisis of 2007–2009: Can a Housing Bust Lead to an Imploding Economy?

In the last chapter, we discussed a self-regulating economy: When the economy is in a recessionary gap, it regulates itself back to long-run equilibrium. In this chapter, we have stated that an economy could get stuck in a recessionary gap if wages are inflexible downward. Some economists use the model in this chapter to explain the events of the financial and economic crisis of 2007–2009.

Suppose an economy in long-run equilibrium undergoes a shock, such as the bursting of the housing bubble, with the prices of houses dropping. In the United States, housing prices started declining in mid-2006. Because the value of a house is a part of a person's overall wealth, a decline in house prices leads to a decline in a person's wealth. As a result of a decline in wealth, the person is

poorer (or less rich) and consequently cuts back on consumption. A decline in consumption leads to a decline in aggregate demand, so the aggregate demand curve shifts leftward, as in Exhibit 4(a), and the economy is now in a recessionary gap.

If the economy were self-regulating, it could get itself out of the recessionary gap. But if wages are inflexible downward, the economy is stuck in the recessionary gap.

Now look at the labor market in Exhibit 4(b). The labor market is initially in equilibrium at point 1. As a result of aggregate demand falling in the economy [see Exhibit 4(a)], firms are selling less output. So they do not need as much labor, and the demand for labor shifts leftward in Exhibit 4(b). Because the wage rate is inflexible downward, the number of workers hired in the labor market falls from 10 million to 8 million. In other words, 2 million workers are fired. As workers are fired, their incomes fall; as a result of lower incomes, individuals cut back on consumption. So aggregate demand shifts leftward again and the economy falls into a deeper recessionary gap [see Exhibit 4(c)].

What does this exposition tell us? A housing bust (declining house prices) can be the catalyst for an economy that falls into a recessionary gap. Further, if the economy is not self-regulating, a cascade of events can cause the economy to "implode" upon itself. A decline in aggregate demand leads to a recessionary gap that, if wages are inflexible downward, leads to some workers being fired, leading in turn to lower incomes and another decline in aggregate demand. Thus, the recessionary gap deepens. Graphically, in Exhibit 4, instead of being between Q_1 and Q_2, the recessionary gap is between Q_1 and Q_3.

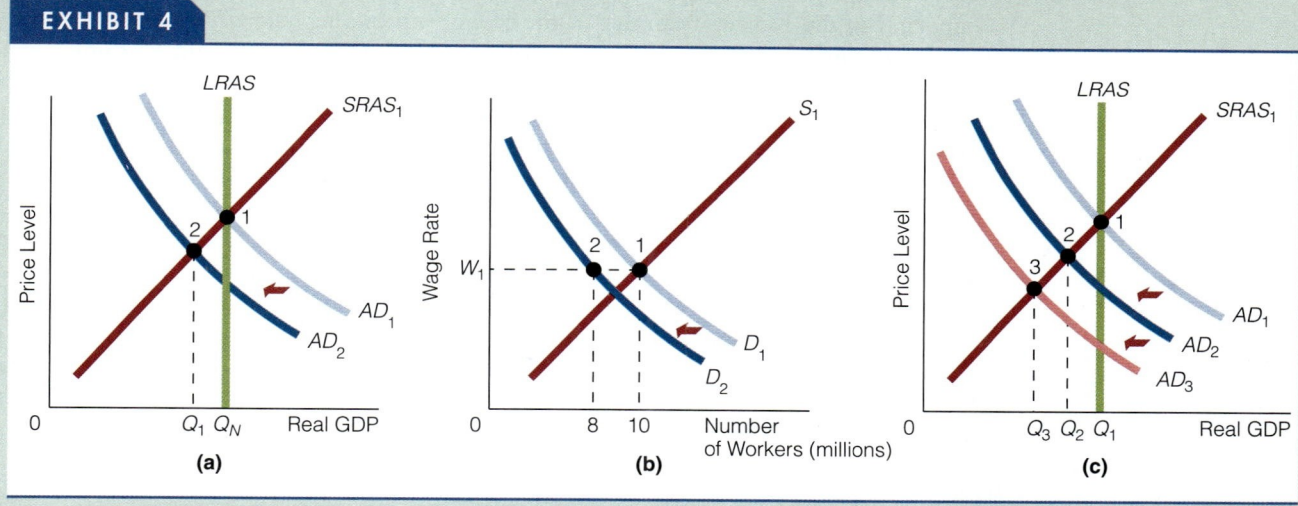

EXHIBIT 4

some time). If wage rates are inflexible downward, then the self-regulating properties of an economy (discussed in Chapter 9) are in question. Specifically, an economy might get stuck in a recessionary gap, represented by point 1 in Exhibit 2.

10-1d Keynes on Prices

Recall again what classical economists (among others) believe occurs when a recessionary gap exists: Wage rates fall, the *SRAS* curve shifts to the right, and the price level begins to decrease—stop right there! The phrase "the price level begins to decrease" tells us that classical economists believe that prices in the economy are flexible: They move up and down in response to market forces.

Keynes said that the internal structure of an economy is not always competitive enough to allow prices to fall. Recall from Chapter 3 how the forces of supply and demand operate when price is above equilibrium. A surplus is generated, and price falls until the quantity supplied of the good equals the quantity demanded. Keynes suggested that anticompetitive or monopolistic elements in the economy sometimes prevent price from falling.

10-1e Is It a Question of the Time It Takes for Wages and Prices to Adjust?

Classical economists believed that both wages and prices are flexible and adjust downward in a recessionary gap. Keynes, however, suggested that wages and prices are not flexible in a downward direction and may not adjust downward in a recessionary gap.

Many economists today take a position somewhere between Keynes's and that of the classical economists. For them, the question is not whether wages and prices are flexible downward, but *how long it takes for them to adjust downward.*

Exhibit 5 shows the economy in a recessionary gap at point 1. The relevant short-run aggregate supply curve is $SRAS_1$; the wage rate is $10 per hour, and the price level is P_1. Classical economists expect the wage rate and price level to fall, whereas Keynes said that might not happen. But did Keynes mean that, if the economy is in a recessionary gap, *the wage rate will never fall, and the price level will never adjust downward?* Most economists think not. The question is *how long* the wage rate and price level will take to fall. Will they fall in a few weeks? In a few months? In five years? The question is relevant because the answer determines how long an economy will be in a recessionary gap and thus how long the economy takes to self-regulate.

Look at the question this way: If it takes only a few weeks or months for wage rates to fall (say, to $8 an hour), for the short-run aggregate supply curve to shift from $SRAS_1$ to $SRAS_2$, and for the price level to fall from P_1 to P_2, then, for all practical purposes, the economy is almost instantaneously self-regulating. But if all this takes years to happen, the economy can hardly be considered self-regulating over any reasonable amount of time.

The classical position is that the time required for wages and prices to adjust downward is short enough to call the economy self-regulating. The Keynesian position is that the time is long enough to say that the economy is not self-regulating. Instead, the Keynesians believe that the economy is inherently unstable and that it can remain in a recessionary gap for a long time.

EXHIBIT 5

A Question of How Long It Takes for Wage Rates and Prices to Fall

Suppose the economy is in a recessionary gap at point 1. Wage rates are $10 per hour, and the price level is P_1. The issue may not be whether wage rates and the price level fall, but how long they take to reach long-run levels. If they take a short time, then classical economists are right: The economy is self-regulating. If they take a long time—perhaps years—then Keynes is right: The economy is not self-regulating over any reasonable length of time.

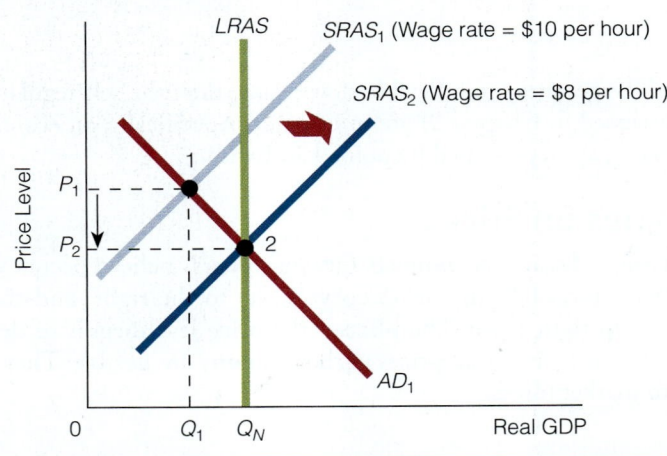

The following chart is a quick review of some of the differences in the views of the classical economists and Keynes:

	Classical Economists	**Keynes**
Say's law	Holds in a money economy. In other words, all output produced will be demanded.	May not hold in a money economy. In other words, more output may be produced than will be demanded.
Savings	Amount saved and interest rate are directly related. Savers save more at higher interest rates and save less at lower interest rates.	Savers may not save more at higher interest rates or save less at lower interest rates. If savers have a savings goal in mind, then a higher interest rate means that savers can save less and still reach their goal.
Investment	Amount invested is inversely related to interest rate. Businesses invest more at lower interest rates and invest less at higher interest rates.	If expectations are pessimistic, a lower interest rate may not stimulate additional business investment.
Prices	Flexible	May be inflexible downward.
Wages	Flexible	May be inflexible downward.

Economics 24/7

Was Keynes a Revolutionary in Economics?

John Maynard Keynes was born in Cambridge, England, on June 5, 1883, and died at Tilton (in Sussex) on April 21, 1946. His father was John Neville Keynes, an eminent economist and author of *The Scope and Method of Political Economy*.[2] Keynes's mother was one of the first female students to attend Cambridge University and presided as mayor of the city of Cambridge for a time.

John Maynard Keynes was educated at Eton and at King's College, Cambridge, where he received a degree in mathematics in 1905. At Cambridge, he studied under the well-known and widely respected economist Alfred Marshall. In 1925, Keynes married Russian ballerina Lydia Lopokova. He was prominent in British social and intellectual circles and enjoyed art, theater, opera, debate, and collecting rare books.

TIM GIDAL/PICTURE POST/GETTY IMAGES

Many economists rank Keynes's *The General Theory of Employment, Interest and Money* (published on February 4, 1936) alongside Adam Smith's *Wealth of Nations* (published on March 9, 1776) and Karl Marx's *Das Kapital* (full title, *Kritik der politischen Ökonomie* (English, *Capital: Critique of Political Economy*, published in three volumes from 1867 to 1894) as the most influential economic treatises ever written.

Before the publication of *The General Theory*, Keynes presented the ideas contained in the work in a series of university lectures that he gave between October 10, 1932, and December 2, 1935. Ten days after his last lecture, he sent off to the publisher the manuscript for what was to become *The General Theory*.

[2] John Neville Keynes, *The Scope and Method of Political Economy* (London and New York: Macmillan, 1891).

(Continued)

Keynes's lectures were said to be both shocking (he was pointing out the errors of the classical school) and exciting (he was proposing something new). One of the students at these lectures was Lorie Tarshis, who later wrote the first Keynesian introductory textbook, *The Elements of Economics*.[3] In another venue, Tarshis wrote about the Keynes lectures and specifically about why Keynes's ideas were revolutionary:

> I attended that first lecture, naturally awed but bothered. As the weeks passed, only a stone would not have responded to the growing excitement these lectures generated. So I missed only two over the four years—two out of the thirty lectures. And like others, I would feel the urgency of the task. No wonder! These were the years when everything came loose; when sober dons and excitable students seriously discussed such issues as: Was capitalism not doomed? Should Britain not take the path of Russia or Germany to create jobs? Keynes obviously believed his analysis led to a third means to prosperity far less threatening to the values he prized, but until he had developed the theory and offered it in print, he knew that he could not sway government. So he saw his task as supremely urgent. I was also a bit surprised by his concern over too low a level of output. I had been assured by all I had read that the economy would bob to the surface, like a cork held under water—and output would rise, of its own accord, to an acceptable level. But Keynes proposed something far more shocking: that the economy could reach an equilibrium position with output far below capacity. That was an exciting challenge, sharply at variance with the views of Pigou and Marshall who represented "The Classical [Orthodox] School" in Cambridge, and elsewhere.[4]

[3.] Lorie Tarshis, *The Elements of Economics, an Introduction to the Theory of Price and Employment* (Boston: Houghton Mifflin, 1947).

[4.] Lorie Tarshis, "Keynesian Revolution," in John Eatwell, Murray Milgate, and Peter Newman, eds., *The New Palgrave: A Dictionary of Economics* (Boston: vol. 3 (London: Macmillan Press, 1987), p. 48.

(Answers to Self-Test questions are in Answers to Self-Test Questions at the back of the book.)

1. What do Keynesians mean when they say that the economy is inherently unstable?
2. "What matters is not whether the economy is self-regulating, but whether prices and wages are flexible and adjust quickly." Comment.
3. According to Keynes, why might aggregate demand be too low?

10-2 The Simple Keynesian Model

Economists build models and theories to better understand the economic world. Of the many such models, we have already discussed a few: the theory of supply and demand and the classical theory of interest rates. In this section, we identify and discuss a few of the key components and themes of another prominent macroeconomics model: *the simple Keynesian model*.

10-2a Assumptions

In the simple Keynesian model, certain simplifying assumptions hold:

- First, the price level is assumed to be constant until the economy reaches its full-employment, or Natural Real GDP, level.
- Second, there is no foreign sector: The model represents a *closed economy*, not an *open economy*. So total spending in the economy is the sum of consumption, investment, and government purchases.
- Third, the monetary side of the economy is excluded.

10-2b The Consumption Function

Although Keynes was interested in the level of total spending in general, he was particularly concerned about consumption, which was a major concern because it is by far the largest slice of the total spending pie.

Keynes made three basic points about consumption:

1. Consumption depends on disposable income (income minus taxes).
2. Consumption and disposable income move in the same direction.
3. When disposable income changes, consumption changes by less.

These three points make a specific statement about the relationship between consumption and disposable income: the **consumption function**, which can written as

$$C = C_0 + (MPC)(Y_d)$$

where you already know that C is consumption, and where we use Y_d to specify disposable income. Let's look, then, at MPC and C_0. Think of consumption (as specified by the consumption function) as made up of two parts:

- *Autonomous consumption* (C_0) is independent of disposable income.
- *Induced consumption* [$MPC(Y_d)$] depends on disposable income.

MPC stands for **marginal propensity to consume**, which is the ratio of the change in consumption to the change in disposable income:

$$\text{Marginal propensity to consume} = \frac{\text{Change in consumption}}{\text{Change in disposable income}}$$

$$MPC = \frac{\Delta C}{\Delta Y_d}$$

The Greek symbol delta (Δ) stands for "change in." Thus, the MPC is equal to the change in consumption divided by the change in disposable income. To illustrate, suppose consumption rises from $800 to $900 as disposable income rises from $1,000 to $1,200. If we divide the change in consumption ($100) by the change in disposable income ($200), we see that the MPC equals 0.50. (Notice that the MPC is always a positive number between 0 and 1 because of Keynes's points 2 and 3.)

C_0 is **autonomous consumption**, which changes *not* as disposable income changes but, rather, because of other factors.

The difference between autonomous and *induced* consumption can be illustrated with an example. Suppose your taxes are lowered and your disposable income consequently rises. With more disposable income, you buy more goods and services (e.g., entertainment, books, DVDs). The increase in disposable income has *induced* you to consume more—hence the name *induced consumption*. Next, suppose that, even though your disposable income has not changed, for some reason, you are consuming more. You might be consuming more medication because you have recently become ill, or you might be consuming more car maintenance services because your car just broke down. Whatever the reason, you are consuming more of various goods and services even though your disposable income has not changed at all. This type of consumption is autonomous (i.e., independent) of disposable income—hence the name *autonomous consumption*.

Consumption Function
The relationship between consumption and disposable income. In the consumption function used in this text, consumption is directly related to disposable income and is positive even at zero disposable income: $C = C_0 + (MPC)(Y_d)$.

Marginal Propensity to Consume
The ratio of the change in consumption to the change in disposable income: $MPC = \Delta C/\Delta Y_d$

Autonomous Consumption
The part of consumption that is independent of disposable income.

Look again at the consumption function:

Consumption = Autonomous consumption
+ (Marginal propensity to consume × Disposable income)

$$C = C_0 + (MPC \times Y_d)$$

Suppose C_0 is $800, MPC is 0.80, and Y_d is $1,500, and we insert these numbers into the consumption function:

$$C = \$800 + (0.80 \times \$1{,}500) = \$800 + \$1{,}200 = \$2{,}000$$

So what will cause an increase in consumption? Consumption, C, will increase if any of the variables C_0, MPC, and Y_d increases. Thus, C can be increased in three ways:

1. *Raise autonomous consumption.* Suppose in our example that autonomous consumption, C_0, goes from $800 to $1,000. This change will raise consumption to $2,200: $C = \$1{,}000 + (0.80 \times \$1{,}500) = \$2{,}200$

2. *Raise disposable income.* Suppose disposable income, Y_d, goes from $1,500 to $1,800. This change will raise consumption to $2,240: $C = \$800 + (0.80 \times \$1{,}800) = \$2{,}240$. The increase in consumption from $2,000 to $2,240 is due to an increase of $240 in induced consumption, a dollar amount that the increase in disposable income induced.

3. *Raise the MPC.* Suppose the MPC rises to 0.90. This change will raise consumption to $2,150: $C = \$800 + (0.90 \times \$1{,}500) = \$2{,}150$.

In Exhibit 6, C_0 is assumed to be equal to $200 billion and the MPC to 0.80; thus, $C = \$200$ billion $+ (0.8)(Y_d)$. We then calculated different levels of consumption (column 3) for different levels of disposable income (column 1).

EXHIBIT 6

Consumption and Saving at Different Levels of Disposable Income (in billions)

Our consumption function is $C = C_0 + (MPC)(Y_d)$, where C_0 has been set at $200 billion and $MPC = 0.80$.

Saving is the difference between Y_d and $C: S = Y_d - [C_0 = (MPC)(Y_d)]$. All dollar amounts are in billions.

(1) Disposable Income, Y_d	(2) Change in Disposable Income, ΔY_d	(3) Consumption $C = C_0 + (MPC)(Y_d)$	(4) Change in Consumption	(5) Saving $S = Y_d - [C_0 + (MPC)(Y_d)]$	(6) Change in Saving
$ 800	$__	$ 840	$__	− $40	$__
1,000	200	1,000	160	0	40
1,200	200	1,160	160	40	40
1,400	200	1,320	160	80	40
1,600	200	1,480	160	120	40
1,800	200	1,640	160	160	40

10-2c Consumption and Saving

In Exhibit 6, we also calculated the saving levels (column 5) at the different levels of disposable income. How did we calculate these levels? Well, we know that $C = C_0 + (MPC)(Y_d)$ and that households can only consume or save. So it follows that saving, S, is the difference between disposable income and consumption:

$$\begin{aligned} \text{Saving} &= \text{Disposable income} - \text{Consumption} \\ &= \text{Disposable income} - [\text{Autonomous consumption} \\ &\quad + (\text{Marginal propensity to consume} \times \text{Disposable income})] \\ S &= Y_d - [C_0 - (MPC \times Y_d)] \end{aligned}$$

The **marginal propensity to save (MPS)** is the ratio of the change in saving to the change in disposable income:

$$\text{Marginal propensity to save} = \frac{\text{Change in saving}}{\text{Change in disposable income}}$$

$$MPS = \frac{\Delta S}{\Delta Y_d}$$

> **Marginal Propensity to Save (MPS)**
> The ratio of the change in saving to the change in disposable income: $MPS = \Delta S/\Delta Y_d$

Disposable income can be used only for consumption or saving; that is, $C + S = Y_d$. So any change to disposable income can change only consumption or saving. Therefore, the marginal *MPC* plus the *MPS* must equal 1.

$$\text{Marginal propensity to consume} + \text{Marginal propensity to save} = 1$$
$$MPC + MPS = 1$$

In Exhibit 6, the *MPC* is 0.80; so the *MPS* is 0.20.

10-2d The Multiplier

We know from the consumption function that a rise in autonomous consumption (C_0) will raise consumption (C) and, in turn, raise total spending. But *how much* will total spending rise? If C_0 rises by $40 billion, will total spending rise by $40 billion? According to Keynes, total spending would not rise by only $40 billion. The rise in C_0 will act as a catalyst to additional spending, and total spending will rise, in this case, by *more than* $40 billion.

For example, suppose an economy consists of 10 people, represented by the letters A–J. Suppose also that person A increases his autonomous consumption by buying $40 more of additional goods from person B. Now person B has witnessed an increase of $40 in her income. According to Keynes, person B will spend some fraction of this additional income, and how much she spends depends on her marginal propensity to consume (*MPC*). If her *MPC* is 0.80, then she will spend 80 percent of $40, or $32. If she spends this additional $32 on purchasing goods from person C, then person C's income rises by $32, and now he will spend some percentage of that additional income. Again, how much he will spend depends on his *MPC*. If we again assume that the *MPC* is 0.80, then person C spends $25.60. So

Person A increases his *autonomous consumption* by $40 →
This increase generates $40 *additional income* for person B →
Person B increases her *consumption* by $32 →
This increase generates $32 *additional income* for person C →
Person C increases his *consumption* by $25.60 →
And so on and so on.

All this economic activity represents the *multiplier process*: An initial rise in one (the first) person's autonomous consumption leads to a rise in income for another (the second) person, which then leads to additional consumption by the second person, which generates additional income for a third person, and so on and so on.

Suppose we now sum the initial rise in autonomous spending ($40) and all the additional spending it generates through the multiplier process. How much additional spending will have been generated? In other words, by how much will total expenditures rise?

The answer depends on the value of the multiplier. The **multiplier** (m) is equal to 1 divided by $1-MPC$:

$$\text{Multiplier } (m) = \frac{1}{1 - MPC}$$

For example, if the $MPC = 0.80$ (in each round of spending), then the multiplier equals 5:

$$\begin{aligned}\text{Multiplier } (m) &= \frac{1}{1 - MPC} \\ &= \frac{1}{1 - 0.80} \\ &= \frac{1}{0.20} \\ &= 5\end{aligned}$$

Multiplier
The number that is multiplied by the change in autonomous spending to obtain the change in total spending. The multiplier (m) is equal to $1 \div (1 - MPC)$. If the economy is operating below Natural Real GDP, then the multiplier is the number that is multiplied by the change in autonomous spending to obtain the change in Real GDP.

Our original increase in autonomous consumption ($40), multiplied by the multiplier (5), equals $200. So in our example, a $40 increase in autonomous consumption would increase total spending by $200.

Just as consumption has an autonomous spending component, so do investment and government purchases. The multiplier process holds for these spending components too.

The process also holds for a decrease in autonomous spending by one of these sectors of total spending. So, in general,

Change in total spending = Multiplier × Change in autonomous spending

To illustrate, suppose business owners become optimistic about the future of the economy. They believe that members of the household and government sectors will soon start buying more goods and services. In the expectation of better times, businesses buy more factories and capital goods, so investment spending rises. In this case, investment spending has risen even without any change in income or Real GDP; hence, the rise is in autonomous investment spending. According to the multiplier analysis, this additional autonomous investment spending will change total spending by some multiple. For example, if the multiplier is 5, then a $1 increase in autonomous investment will raise total spending by $5.

10-2e The Multiplier and Reality

So, in simple terms, a change in autonomous spending leads to a *greater change* in total spending. Also, in the simple Keynesian model, the change in total spending *is equal* to the change in Real GDP (assuming that the economy is operating below Natural Real GDP). The reason is that, in the model, prices are assumed to be constant until Natural Real GDP is reached, so any change in nominal total spending is equal to the change in *real* total spending.

However, two reality checks are necessary. First, the multiplier takes time to have an effect. In a textbook, going from an initial increase in autonomous spending to a multiple increase

Economics 24/7

The Economics of Spring Break

During the weeklong spring break, many college students put away their books; pack their shorts, swimsuits, and tanning oil; jump into their cars; and head for the beaches. As they are driving to Fort Lauderdale, Galveston, Myrtle Beach, Daytona Beach, San Diego, and other coastal cities, the multiplier is getting ready to go to work.

Look at it this way: When college students from around the country head for, say, Daytona Beach, they have dollars in their pockets. They will spend many of these dollars in Daytona Beach on food and drink, motel rooms, dance clubs, and so on. As far as Daytona Beach is concerned, the dollars represent autonomous spending. More important, the dollars can raise the total income of Daytona Beach by some multiple. College students buy pizzas, beer, and sodas. The people who sell these items find their incomes rising. They, in turn, spend some fraction of their increase in income, generating additional income for still others, who spend some fraction of their increase in income, and so on and so on.

For example, suppose college students spend $7 million in Daytona Beach during spring break. If the *MPC* is, say, 0.60 in Daytona Beach and if all the added income generated is spent in Daytona Beach, then college students will increase nominal income in that town by $17.5 million:

$$\frac{1}{1 - MPC} \times \$7 \text{ million}$$
$$= \frac{1}{0.40} \times \$7 \text{ million}$$
$$= 2.5 \times \$7 \text{ million}$$
$$= \$17.5 \text{ million}$$

Do the people who live in Daytona Beach want college students to visit their city during spring break? Many of them do because it means extra dollars in their pockets. College students from out of town, together with the multiplier, often make for robust economic times!

in either total spending or Real GDP takes only seconds. In the real world, this process takes many months.

Second, for the multiplier to increase Real GDP, *idle resources must exist at each spending round*. After all, if Real GDP is increasing (i.e., output is increasing) at each spending round, *idle resources must be available to be brought into production*. If they are not available, then increased spending will simply result in higher prices without an increase in Real GDP. Simply put, GDP will increase, but Real GDP won't.

1. How is autonomous consumption different from consumption?
2. If the *MPC* is 0.70, what does the multiplier equal?
3. What happens to the multiplier as the *MPC* falls?

10-3 The Simple Keynesian Model in the *AD–AS* Framework

The first section of this chapter presented a few of Keynes's criticisms of the self-regulating economy, or classical position. The second section identified and discussed some of the key components of the simple Keynesian model, particularly the consumption function and the multiplier. In this section, we analyze the simple Keynesian model in terms of the aggregate demand and aggregate supply (*AD–AS*) framework. In the next section, we discuss the simple Keynesian model in terms of the total expenditures and total production (*TE–TP*) framework.[5]

10-3a Shifts in the Aggregate Demand Curve

Because there is no foreign sector in the simple Keynesian model, total spending consists of consumption (*C*), investment (*I*), and government purchases (*G*). Because the economy has no monetary side, changes in any of these variables can shift the *AD* curve. For example, a rise in consumption will shift the *AD* curve to the right; a decrease in investment will shift it to the left.

Let's consider aggregate demand in terms of what we know about the consumption function and the multiplier. A rise in autonomous consumption (C_0) will raise consumption (*C*) and therefore shift the *AD* curve to the right. How much the *AD* curve will shift depends on the multiplier. In our earlier example, autonomous consumption C_0 increases by $40, and the multiplier (*m*) is 5.

$$\begin{aligned} \text{Change in total spending} &= \text{Multiplier} \times \text{Change in autonomous spending} \\ &= m \times \Delta C_0 \\ &= 5 \times \$40 \\ &= \$200 \end{aligned}$$

Exhibit 7 illustrates how the *AD* curve shifts in this situation. The original aggregate demand curve is AD_1. Autonomous consumption (C_0) rises by $40, shifting the curve to AD_2, but the *AD* curve does not stay there. Because of the multiplier, the initial autonomous consumption spending generates more spending, eventually pushing the *AD* curve to AD_3. In other words, at the end of the process, the *AD* curve has shifted from AD_1 to AD_3. Part of this shift ($40) is due to the initial rise in autonomous consumption, and part ($160) is due to the multiplier.

10-3b The Keynesian Aggregate Supply Curve

As noted earlier, in the simple Keynesian model, the price level is assumed to be constant until it reaches its full-employment, or Natural Real GDP, level. What does this assumption say about the Keynesian aggregate supply curve?

Think back to the discussions of aggregate demand and aggregate supply in the last two chapters and in the first section of this chapter. The *AD* curve is downward sloping, and the *SRAS* curve is upward sloping. Therefore, any shift in the *AD* curve (rightward or leftward) will automatically change (raise or lower) the price level. If the price level is assumed to be constant, then the Keynesian aggregate supply curve must have a horizontal section.

---

[5] Some instructors may choose to assign only one of these two sections. It is clear at the end of the chapter which questions and problems go with which sections.

EXHIBIT 7

The Multiplier and Aggregate Demand

An initial increase in autonomous consumption raises total spending and shifts the aggregate demand curve from AD_1 to AD_2. The curve does not end here, however. Because of the multiplier, the increase in autonomous spending generates additional income and additional spending, shifting the aggregate demand curve to AD_3.

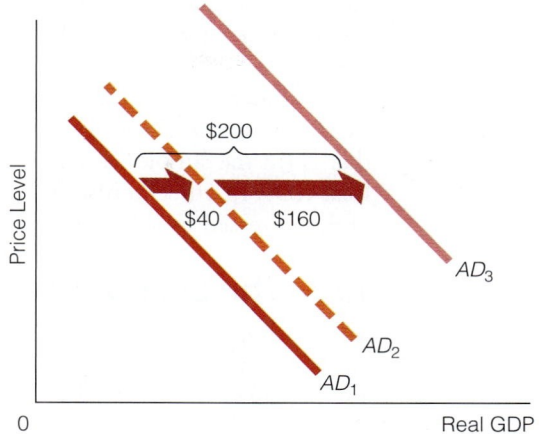

As shown in Exhibit 8, the Keynesian aggregate supply (*AS*) curve has both a horizontal section and a vertical section. The *AS* curve is horizontal until Q_N, or Natural Real GDP, is reached because the simple Keynesian model assumes that the price level is constant until Q_N is reached. Given this *AS* curve, what happens in the economy when the *AD* curve shifts? On the one hand, an increase in aggregate demand from AD_1 to AD_2 raises Real GDP from Q_1 to Q_2 but does not change the price level. (The price level remains at P_1.) On the other hand, once the economy has reached Q_N, any increases in aggregate demand change the price level. For example, an increase in aggregate demand from AD_3 to AD_4 raises the price level from P_2 to P_3.

EXHIBIT 8

The AS Curve in the Simple Keynesian Model

The *AS* curve in the simple Keynesian model is horizontal until Q_N (Natural Real GDP) and vertical at Q_N. It follows that any changes in aggregate demand in the horizontal section do not change the price level, but any changes in aggregate demand in the vertical section do change the price level.

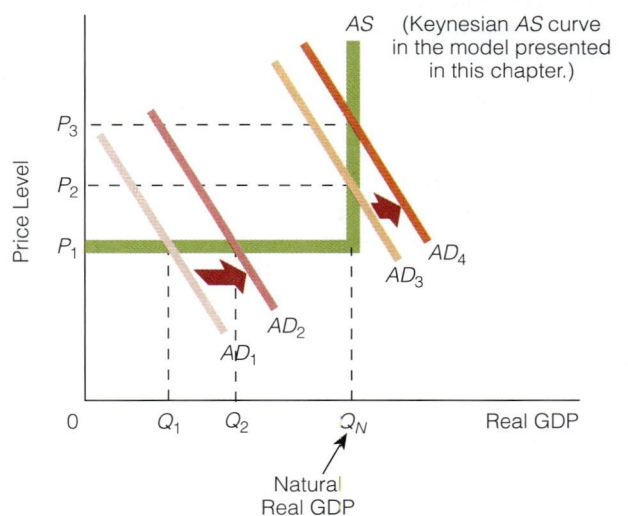

According to Keynes, a change in autonomous spending (e.g., a change in autonomous consumption) will stimulate additional spending in the economy. In our example, a rise in autonomous consumption of $40 generated an additional $160 worth of spending, so total spending increased by $200. (The multiplier was 5 because we assumed that the *MPC* was 0.80.)

Consider this question: Under what condition will a $200 *increase in total spending* lead to a $200 *increase in Real* GDP? That happens when the aggregate supply curve is horizontal—that is (in the simple Keynesian model), when the economy is producing less than Natural Real GDP. In other words, the *AD* curve in the economy must be shifting rightward (because of the increased spending) but must be within the *horizontal section* of the Keynesian *AS* curve.

10-3c The Economy in a Recessionary Gap

If, according to classical economists, the economy is self-regulating, then a recessionary gap or an inflationary gap is only temporary. In time, the economy moves into long-run equilibrium and produces Natural Real GDP (Q_N).

Keynes did not accept the idea that the economy always works this way, believing rather that the economy could get stuck in a recessionary gap. As shown in Exhibit 9, the economy could therefore be stuck at Q_1 (its equilibrium position) and be unable to get to Q_N on its own. In other words, the economy is at point *A*, and it is not able to get to point *B*. Keynes believed that the private sector—consisting of the household and business sectors—might not be able to move the economy from point *A* to point *B*. Stated differently, neither consumption nor investment will rise enough to shift the aggregate demand curve from its current position (AD_1).

But suppose the interest rate in the economy falls. Won't this be enough to get businesses to invest more, and, thus, won't the *AD* curve begin to shift rightward, headed for point *B*? Not necessarily, said Keynes, who didn't believe that investment spending was always responsive to changes in interest rates. For example, suppose businesses are pessimistic about future sales,

EXHIBIT 9

Can the Private Sector Remove the Economy from a Recessionary Gap?

The economy is at point A, producing Q_1. Q_1 is less than Q_N, so the economy is in a recessionary gap. The question is whether the private sector (consisting of consumption and investment spending) can remove the economy from the recessionary gap by increasing spending enough to shift the aggregate demand curve rightward to go through point B. Keynes believed that sometimes it could not. No matter how low interest rates fell, investment spending would not rise because of pessimistic business expectations with respect to future sales.

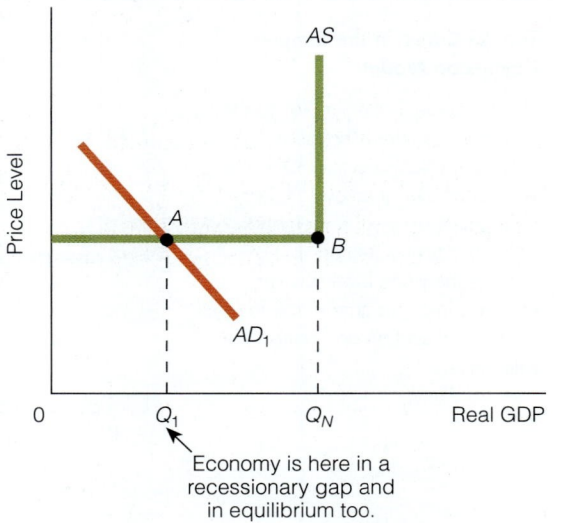

and the interest rate drops. Are businesses going to invest more just because interest rates have dropped, or might they feel so pessimistic that they choose not to invest, despite the lower interest rate? Keynes believed that the latter scenario could be the case.

10-3d Government's Role in the Economy

In the self-regulating economy of the classical economists, government does not have a management role to play. The private sector (households and businesses) is capable of self-regulating the economy at its Natural Real GDP level. By contrast, Keynes believed that the economy is not self-regulating and that economic instability is a possibility. In other words, the economy could get stuck in a recessionary gap.

Economic instability opens the door to government's playing a role in the economy. According to Keynes and to many Keynesians, if the private sector cannot self-regulate the economy at its Natural Real GDP level, then maybe the government must help. In terms of Exhibit 9, maybe the government has a role to play in shifting the *AD* curve rightward so that it goes through point *B*. We discuss the role government might play in the economy in the next chapter.

> **Thinking Like an Economist**
>
> **From How the Economy Works to One's Policy Positions** An economist's view of the economy (how the economy works) and policy suggestions are often linked. For example, classical economists and their modern-day counterparts, who view the economy as self-regulating or inherently stable, believe in a laissez-faire policy: Government should keep its hands off the economy. Keynesians, however, who view the economy as inherently unstable, suggest that government has an economic role to play. In short, policy suggestions are sometimes a consequence of how one views the internal, or inherent, workings of an economy.

10-3e The Theme of the Simple Keynesian Model

In terms of *AD* and *AS*, the essence of the simple Keynesian model can be summarized in five statements:

1. The price level remains constant until Natural Real GDP is reached.
2. The *AD* curve shifts if there is a change in *C*, *I*, or *G*.
3. According to Keynes, the economy could be in equilibrium and in a recessionary gap too. In other words, the economy can be at point *A* in Exhibit 9.
4. The private sector may not be able to get the economy out of a recessionary gap. In other words, the private sector (households and businesses) may not be able to increase *C* or *I* enough to get the *AD* curve in Exhibit 9 to intersect the *AS* curve at point *B*.
5. The government may have a management role to play in the economy. According to Keynes, government may have to raise aggregate demand enough to stimulate the economy to move it out of the recessionary gap and to its Natural Real GDP level.
6. We show the simple Keynesian model in the *AD–AS* framework in Exhibit 10 in both (a) flowchart form and (b) diagrammatic form.

EXHIBIT 10

The Simple Keynesian Model in the AD–AS Framework

The purpose of the simple Keynesian model is to explain changes in Real GDP. In (a), the model is presented as a flowchart. Real GDP is determined by aggregate demand and aggregate supply. Aggregate demand depends on C, consumption; I, investment; and G, government purchases. In (b), we show a diagrammatic exposition of the model in the AD–AS framework.

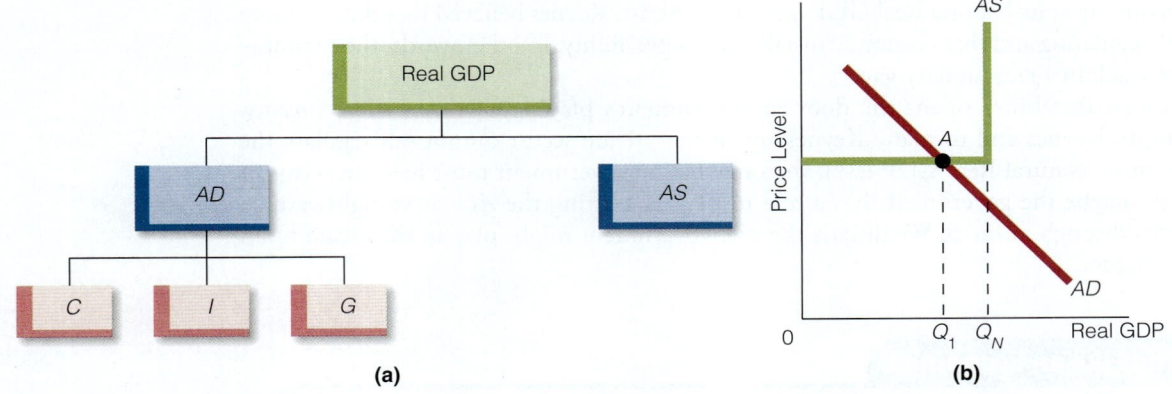

1. What was Keynes's position on the self-regulating properties of an economy?
2. What will happen to Real GDP if autonomous spending rises and the economy is operating in the horizontal section of the Keynesian AS curve? Explain your answer.
3. An economist who believes that the economy is self-regulating is more likely to advocate laissez-faire than one who believes that the economy is inherently unstable. Do you agree or disagree? Explain your answer.

10-4 The Simple Keynesian Model in the *TE–TP* Framework

Just as a story can be told in different languages, an economic model can be presented in various frameworks. The last section presented the simple Keynesian model in terms of the familiar (diagrammatic) *AD–AS* framework of analysis. But (historically) the simple Keynesian model was first presented not in terms of *AD–AS* but in terms of the *TE–TP* framework. This framework has been known by different names, three of which are the Keynesian cross, income expenditure, and total expenditure–total production. In our discussion, we will refer to it as total expenditure—total production, or simply the *TE–TP* framework.

10-4a Deriving a Total Expenditures (*TE*) Curve

Just as we derived *AD* and *AS* curves in the *AD–AS* framework, we want to derive a total expenditures (*TE*) curve in the *TE–TP* framework. Total expenditures are the sum of its parts: consumption, investment, and government purchases. To derive a *TE* curve, first derive

EXHIBIT 11

The Derivation of the Total Expenditures (TE) Curve

At different levels of Real GDP, we sum (a) consumption, (b) investment, and (c) government purchases to derive the TE curve (d).

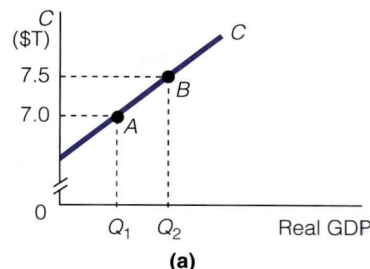

(a)

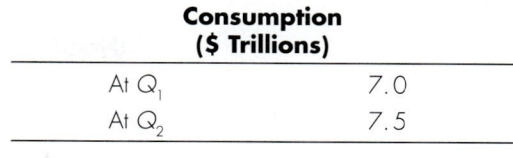

Consumption ($ Trillions)	
At Q_1	7.0
At Q_2	7.5

$+$

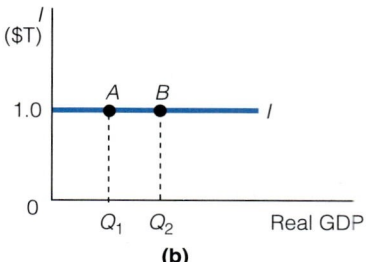

(b)

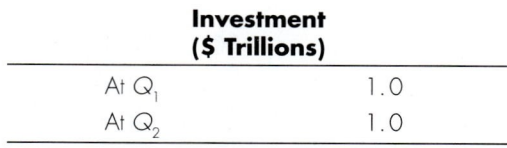

Investment ($ Trillions)	
At Q_1	1.0
At Q_2	1.0

$+$

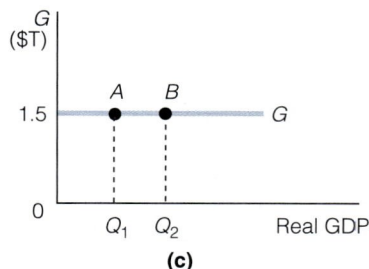

(c)

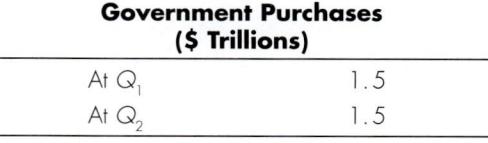

Government Purchases ($ Trillions)	
At Q_1	1.5
At Q_2	1.5

$=$

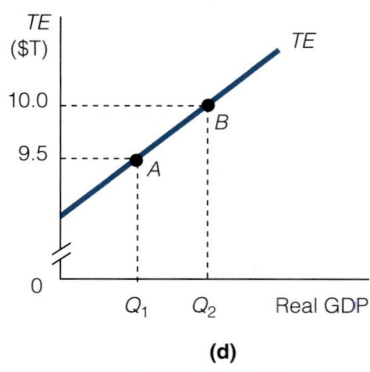

(d)

Total Expenditures ($ Trillions)	
At Q_1	9.5
At Q_2	10.0

a diagrammatic representation of consumption, investment, and government purchases, as shown in Exhibit 11.

1. *Consumption.* As disposable income rises, so does consumption, as shown arithmetically in columns (1) and (3) of Exhibit 6. Because the *MPC* is less than 1, consumption rises by less than disposable income rises. Consumption also rises as Real GDP rises, but again

by a smaller percentage. For example, if Real GDP rises by $100, consumption may rise by $80. Exhibit 11(a) shows consumption as an upward-sloping curve. Notice that, as Real GDP rises from Q_1 to Q_2, consumption rises from $7 trillion to $7.5 trillion.

2. *Investment.* To simplify things in deriving *TE*, the investment curve in Exhibit 11(b) is shown to be constant at $1 trillion, whether Real GDP is Q_1 or Q_2.

3. *Government purchases.* We simplify the government spending curve too. In Exhibit 11(c), government purchases are constant at $1.5 trillion, regardless of the amount of Real GDP.

Exhibit 11(d) shows a *TE* curve. We simply added the components of total expenditures at the two Real GDP levels (Q_1 and Q_2), plotted the relevant points, and then drew a line through the points. At Q_1, total expenditures are $9.5 trillion, and at Q_2, they are $10.0 trillion. The *TE* curve is upward sloping.

10-4b Where the Consumption Curve and the Total Expenditures Curve Cut the Vertical Axis: More on Exhibit 11

Look back at panels (a) and (d) of Exhibit 11. Notice that in panel (a) the consumption curve (*C*) cuts the vertical axis at some positive dollar amount when either disposable income or Real GDP is zero. A question arises: How can consumption be some positive dollar amount when, say, disposable income is zero? To answer the question, let's return to the consumption equation:

$$C = C_0 + (MPC)(Y_d)$$

Now notice that autonomous consumption, C_0, is independent of disposable income, Y_d. In other words, when disposable income is zero, autonomous consumption can be some positive dollar amount. For example, suppose we set autonomous consumption equal to $800. We can then rewrite the consumption function as

$$C = \$800 + (MPC)(Y_d)$$

This means that overall consumption (*C*) will be $800 even if disposable income is zero dollars. (If we set Y_d in the equation, then $C = C_0 = \$800$.)

Now let's return to panel (a) of Exhibit 11. Ask yourself what the distance from the origin up to the point where the curve cuts the vertical axis equals? The answer is that it equals autonomous consumption.

Now turn to panel (d) in Exhibit 11. Notice that the total expenditures curve (*TE*) cuts the vertical axis when Real GDP is zero dollars. So, then, what does the distance from the origin up to the point where the curve cuts the vertical axis equal? It equals autonomous consumption (C_0), plus investment, plus government purchases. To see why, keep in mind that total expenditures equals $C + I + G$. That is,

$$TE = C + I + G$$

Now, because $C = C_0 + (MPC)(Y_d)$,

$$TE = [C_0 + (MPC)(Y_d)] + I + G$$

Now set disposable income equal to zero dollars. Then total expenditures equals

$$TE = [C_0 + (MPC)(\$0)] + I + G$$

In other words, $TE = C_0 + I + G$ when disposable income equals zero.

10-4c What Will Shift the *TE* Curve?

The *TE* curve in the *TE–TP* framework plays the same role as the *AD* curve in the *AD–AS* framework. Both the *AD* curve and the *TE* curve shift with a change in *C*, *I*, or *G*. For example, a rise in *C* will shift the *TE* curve upward; a decline in *I* will shift the *TE* curve downward.

10-4d Comparing Total Expenditures (*TE*) and Total Production (*TP*)

Businesses produce the goods and services that are bought in the three sectors of the economy (household, business, and government). Sometimes, though, businesses produce too much or too little in comparison to what the three sectors buy. For example, suppose businesses produce $10 trillion worth of goods and services, but the three sectors buy only $9.5 trillion worth. In this case, businesses have produced too much relative to what the three sectors of the economy buy.

Alternatively, businesses might produce $10 trillion worth of goods and services, but the three sectors of the economy buy $10.5 trillion worth. In this case, businesses have produced too little relative to what the three sectors of the economy buy. (If you are wondering how the three sectors of the economy can buy more than businesses produce, the answer has to do with the goods that businesses hold in inventory. We will soon explain the process.)

Finally, businesses could produce $10 trillion worth of goods and services, and the three sectors of the economy could buy exactly $10 trillion worth. In this case, businesses have produced exactly the right amount of goods and services.

Thus, the economy may be in one of three possible states in the *TE–TP* framework: The total expenditures (*TE*) of the three sectors of the economy can be less than, greater than, or equal to the dollar value of total production (*TP*). In other words, one of the following relations generally holds:

$$TE < TP$$
$$TE > TP$$
$$TE = TP$$

According to many economists, if the economy is currently operating where $TE < TP$ or $TE > TP$ (both states are described as disequilibrium), it will eventually move to where $TE = TP$ (where the economy is in equilibrium). The next section explains how this happens.

10-4e Moving from Disequilibrium to Equilibrium

Business firms hold an inventory of their goods to guard against unexpected changes in the demand for their product. For example, General Motors may hold an inventory of a certain type of car in case the demand for it unexpectedly and suddenly increases.

Although we know why business firms hold an inventory of their goods, we don't know *how much* inventory they will hold. For example, we do not know whether General Motors will hold an inventory of 1,000 cars, 2,000 cars, or 10,000 cars. (Inventories are usually held in terms of, say, a 45- or 60-day supply, but we have simplified things.) We do know that General Motors and all other business firms have some *optimum inventory*, which is "just the right amount" of inventory—not too much and not too little. With this concept in mind, consider two cases that illustrate how business inventory levels play an important role in the economy's adjustment from disequilibrium to equilibrium in the *TE–TP* framework.

Case 1: TE < TP Assume that business firms hold an optimum inventory level of $300 billion worth of goods, that the firms produce $11 trillion worth of goods, and that the three sectors of the economy buy $10.8 trillion worth of goods. In this case, producers produce more than individuals buy ($TE < TP$). The difference is added to inventories, and inventory levels rise unexpectedly to $500 billion, which is $200 billion more than the $300 billion that firms see as optimal.

This unexpected rise in inventories signals to firms that they have *overproduced*. Consequently, they cut back on the quantity of goods they are producing. The cutback in production causes Real GDP to fall, bringing Real GDP closer to the (lower) output level that the three sectors of the economy are willing and able to buy. Ultimately, *TP* will equal *TE*.

Case 2: TE > TP Assume that business firms hold their optimum inventory level ($300 billion worth of goods), that they produce $10.4 trillion worth of goods, and that members of the three sectors buy $10.6 trillion worth of goods. How can individuals buy more than businesses produce? Firms make up the difference out of inventory. In our example, inventory levels fall from $300 billion to $100 billion because individuals purchase $200 billion more of goods than firms produced (to be sold). In fact, that is why firms maintain inventories in the first place: to be able to meet an unexpected increase in sales.

The unexpected fall in inventories signals to firms that they have *underproduced*. Consequently, they increase the quantity of goods they produce. The rise in production causes Real GDP to rise, bringing Real GDP closer to the (higher) real output level that the three sectors are willing and able to buy. Ultimately, *TP* will equal *TE*.

The Graphical Representation of the Three States of the Economy in the *TE–TP* Framework The three states of the economy are represented in Exhibit 12. The exhibit shows a *TE* curve, which we derived earlier, and a *TP* curve, which is simply a 45-degree line (45 degrees because it bisects the 90-degree angle at the origin). Notice that, at any point on the *TP* curve, total production is equal to Real GDP (*TP* = Real GDP).[6] The reason is that *TP* and Real GDP are different names for the same thing. Real GDP, remember, is simply the total market value of all final goods and services produced annually within a country's borders, adjusted for price changes.

Look at the three Real GDP levels in the exhibit. At Q_1, Real GDP is $11 trillion. At that Real GDP level, *TE* is $10.8 trillion, and *TP* is $11 trillion. This configuration illustrates Case 1, in which producers produce more than individuals buy ($TE < TP$), with the difference added to inventories. The unexpected rise in inventories signals to firms that they have overproduced, and consequently, they cut back on the quantity of goods they produce. The cutback in production causes Real GDP to fall, ultimately bringing Real GDP down to Q_E ($10.7 trillion in the exhibit).

Now look at Q_2, where Real GDP is $10.4 trillion. At this Real GDP level, *TE* equals $10.6 trillion, and *TP* equals $10.4 trillion. This configuration illustrates Case 2, in which

---

[6.] Earlier, we said that the *TE* curve plays the role in the *TE–TP* framework that the *AD* curve plays in the *AD–AS* framework. In other words, roughly speaking, the *AD* curve is the *TE* curve. Similarly, the *TP* curve plays the role in the *TE–TP* framework that the *AS* curve plays in the *AD–AS* framework. In other words, roughly speaking, the *TP* curve is the *AS* curve. In the *AD–AS* framework, equilibrium is at the intersection of the *AD* and *AS* curves. As you will soon learn, in the *TE–TP* framework, equilibrium is at the intersection of the *TE* and *TP* curves.

EXHIBIT 12

The Three States of the Economy in the TE–TP Framework

At Q_E, $TE = TP$ and the economy is in equilibrium. At Q_1, $TE < TP$ resulting in an unexpected increase in inventories, signaling firms that they have overproduced, in turn leading the firms to cut back production. The cutback in production reduces Real GDP, and the economy tends to move from Q_1 to Q_E. At Q_2, $TE > TP$, resulting in an unexpected decrease in inventories, signaling firms that they have underproduced, in turn leading the firms to raise production. The increased production raises Real GDP, and the economy tends to move from Q_2 to Q_E.

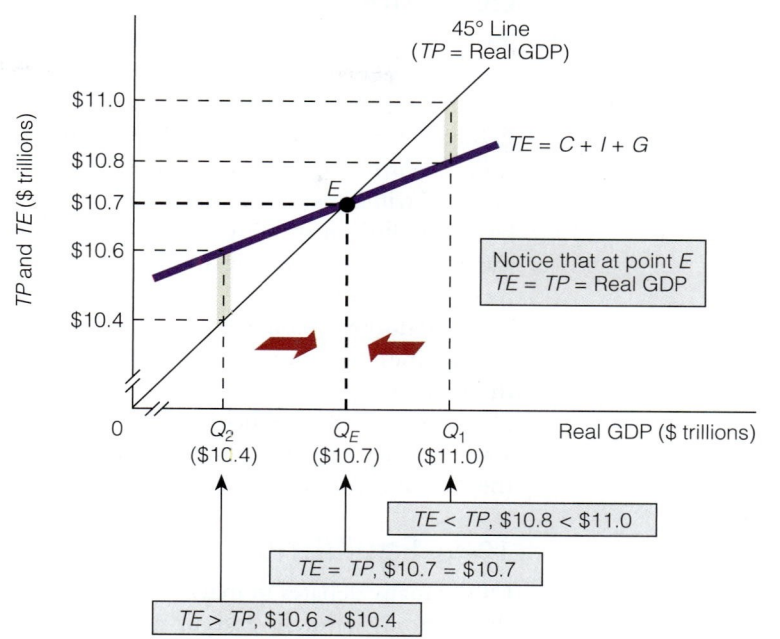

Notice that at point E
$TE = TP = $ Real GDP

$TE < TP$, $\$10.8 < \$11.0$

$TE = TP$, $\$10.7 = \$10.7$

$TE > TP$, $\$10.6 > \$10.4$

---

the three sectors of the economy buy more goods than business firms have produced ($TE > TP$). Business firms then draw from inventories to make up the difference between what they have produced and what the three sectors of the economy buy. Subsequently, inventories fall below optimum levels, and consequently, businesses increase the quantity of goods they produce. The rise in production causes Real GDP to rise, ultimately moving Real GDP up to Q_E (again, $10.7 trillion).

When the economy is producing Q_E, or $10.7 trillion worth of goods and services, it is in equilibrium. At this Real GDP level, TP and TE are the same, at $10.7 trillion. The following table summarizes some key points about the state of the economy in the TE–TP framework:

State of the Economy	What Happens to Inventories?	What Do Firms Do?
$TE < TP$: Individuals are buying less output than firms produce.	Inventories rise above optimum levels.	Firms cut back production to reduce inventories to their optimum levels.
$TE > TP$: Individuals are buying more output than firms produce.	Inventories fall below optimum levels.	Firms increase production to raise inventories to their optimum levels.
$TE = TP$: Individuals are buying whatever output firms produce, and no more than that.	Inventories are at their optimum levels.	Firms neither increase nor decrease production.

10-4f The Economy in a Recessionary Gap and the Role of Government

Recall that, according to Keynes, the economy can be in equilibrium and in a recessionary gap too, as explained in the section on the simple Keynesian model in the *AD–AS* framework [see Exhibit 10(b)]. The same situation can exist in the *TE–TP* framework. For example, in Exhibit 12, the economy equilibrates at point *E* and thus produces a Real GDP level of $10.7 trillion worth of goods and services. However, there is no guarantee that the Real GDP level of $10.7 trillion is the Natural Real GDP level. As shown in Exhibit 13, the economy could be in equilibrium at point *A*, producing Q_E, when the Natural Real GDP level is Q_N. Because the economy is producing at a Real GDP level that is less than Natural Real GDP, it is in a recessionary gap.

How does the economy get out of the recessionary gap? Will the private sector (households and businesses) be capable of pushing the *TE* curve in Exhibit 13 upward so that it goes through point *B*, at which Q_N is produced? According to Keynes, the economy is not necessarily going to do so. Keynes believed that government may be necessary to get the economy out of a recessionary gap. For example, government may have to raise its purchases (raise *G*) so that the *TE* curve shifts upward and goes through point *B*.

10-4g Equilibrium in the Economy

Of the many debates in macroeconomics, one concerns equilibrium in the economy: where the economy naturally ends up after all adjustments have been made. As explained in the last chapter, some economists believe that the economy is self-regulating and that an economy naturally ends up in the long run producing Natural Real GDP. In this chapter, we have talked about economists who believe that the economy can be inherently unstable and that

EXHIBIT 13

The Economy: In Equilibrium and in a Recessionary Gap Too

Using the *TE–TP* framework, we see that the economy is in equilibrium at point *A*, producing Q_E. Natural Real GDP, however, is greater than Q_E, so the economy is in a recessionary gap as well as being in equilibrium.

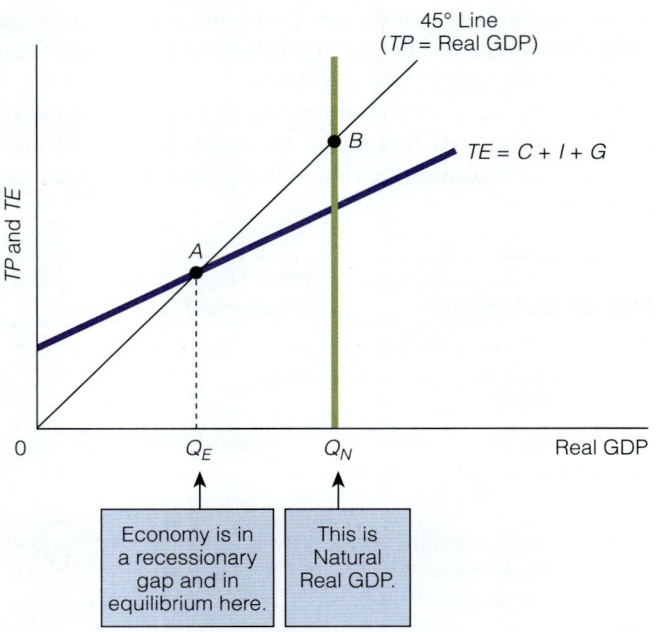

it can naturally end up producing a level of Real GDP less than Natural Real GDP. To the first group of economists, equilibrium is a desirable state of affairs; to the second group, equilibrium may not be if Real GDP is less than Natural Real GDP.

10-4h The Theme of the Simple Keynesian Model

In terms of *TE* and *TP*, the essence of the simple Keynesian model can be summed up in five statements:

1. The price level is constant until Natural Real GDP is reached.
2. The *TE* curve shifts if there is a change in any of *C, I,* and *G*.
3. According to Keynes, the economy could be in equilibrium and in a recessionary gap too. In other words, the economy can be at point *A* in Exhibit 13.
4. The private sector may not be able to get the economy out of a recessionary gap. In other words, the private sector (households and businesses) may not be able to increase *C* or *I* enough to get the *TE* curve in Exhibit 13 to rise and pass through point *B*.
5. The government may have a management role to play in the economy. According to Keynes, government may have to raise *TE* enough to stimulate the economy to move it out of the recessionary gap and to its Natural Real GDP level.

We show the simple Keynesian model in the *TE–TP* framework in Exhibit 14 in both (a) flowchart form and (b) diagrammatic form.

EXHIBIT 14

The Simple Keynesian Model in the TE–TP Framework

The purpose of the simple Keynesian model is to explain changes in Real GDP. In (a), the model is presented as a flowchart. Real GDP is determined by total expenditures (*TE*) and total product (*TP*). Total expenditures (*TE*) depend on C, consumption; I, investment; and G, government purchases. In (b) is a diagrammatic exposition of the model in the *TE–TP* framework.

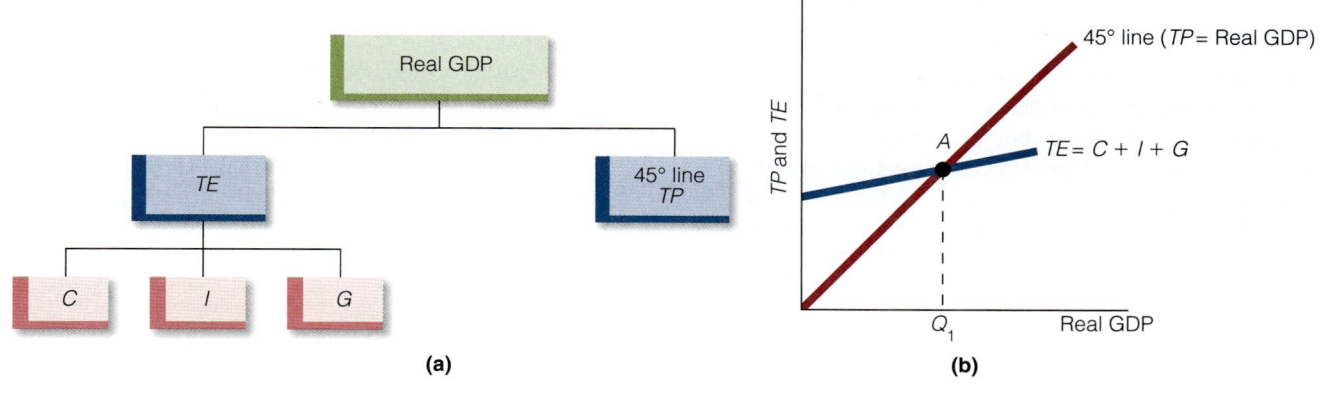

1. What happens in the economy if total production (*TP*) is greater than total expenditures (*TE*)?

2. What happens in the economy if total expenditures (*TE*) are greater than total production (*TP*)?

Office Hours

"Does a Lot Depend on Whether Wages Are Flexible or Inflexible?"

Student: Can what we learned in this chapter be seen as a criticism of what we learned in the last chapter?

Instructor: Much of it can be viewed as a criticism. Specifically, in the last chapter, you learned the views of economists who believe that the economy is self-regulating. In this chapter, you learned the views of economists who believe that the economy is not always self-regulating.

Student: What is at the heart of the disagreement between these two groups of economists?

Instructor: That's a good question. One thing at the heart of the disagreement is whether wages are flexible or inflexible. To illustrate, look back at Exhibit 2. There you see an economy in a recessionary gap. Now, if wages are flexible (as stated in the last chapter), then they will soon fall, and the SRAS curve in Exhibit 2 will shift to the right. In time, the economy will remove itself from the recessionary gap, to point 2 in the exhibit. However, if wages are inflexible downward (as stated in this chapter), then wages will not fall, the SRAS will not shift to the right, and the economy will remain stuck—at point 1 in the exhibit—in the recessionary gap.

Student: Suppose the economists who say that the economy can get stuck in a recessionary gap are right. What then? Does the economy just stay stuck forever?

Instructor: What these economists usually propose is a government response. Specifically, they advocate fiscal or monetary policy to get the economy unstuck. We haven't discussed either fiscal or monetary policy yet, but we plan to in the next chapter.

Student: It seems to me that a lot depends on whether wages are flexible or inflexible. On the one hand, if wages are flexible, the economy self-regulates, removes itself from a recessionary gap, and thus requires no government response. On the other hand, if wages are inflexible (downward), the economy can get stuck in a recessionary gap, and a government response may be needed.

Instructor: That's right. And because much depends on whether wages are flexible or inflexible, economists research such things as wages in various industries. For example, trying to find out whether wages in industries X and Y are flexible or inflexible may seem abstruse and esoteric to many people—who cares?—but, as you have just pointed out, a lot can depend on having the right answers.

Points to Remember

1. Not all economists agree on how the economy works. In the last chapter, you learned the views of economists who believe that the economy is self-regulating. In this chapter, you learned the views of economists who believe that the economy is not always self-regulating.

2. Often, much depends on what may appear to be a small issue. An economist tells you that she is researching the degree of flexibility of wages in industry X. You may think, "What a small issue to research. Who cares about the degree of flexibility of wages? After all, wages are what they are." However, as we have shown, sometimes these so-called small issues can make a big difference, such as whether government becomes involved in the economy.

Chapter Summary

Keynes on Wage Rates and Prices

- Keynes believed that wage rates and prices may be inflexible downward. He said that employees and labor unions will resist employer's wage cuts and that, because of anticompetitive or monopolistic elements in the economy, prices will not fall.

Keynes on Say's Law

- Keynes did not agree that Say's law would necessarily hold in a money economy. He thought that it was possible for consumption to fall (for saving to increase) by more than investment increased. Consequently, a decrease in consumption (or an increase in saving) could lower total expenditures and aggregate demand in the economy.

Consumption Function

- Keynes made three points about consumption and disposable income: (1) Consumption depends on disposable income. (2) Consumption and disposable income move in the same direction. (3) As disposable income changes, consumption changes by less. These three ideas are incorporated into the consumption function, $C = C_0 + (MPC \times Y_d)$, where C_0 is autonomous consumption, MPC is the marginal propensity to consume, and Y_d is disposable income.

The Multiplier

- A change in autonomous spending will bring about a multiple change in total spending. The overall change in spending is equal to the multiplier $[1/(1 - MPC)]$ times the change in autonomous spending.

The Simple Keynesian Model in the *AD–AS* Framework

- Changes in consumption, investment, and government purchases will change aggregate demand.
- A rise in C, I, or G will shift the AD curve to the right.
- A decrease in C, I, or G will shift the AD curve to the left.
- The aggregate supply curve in the simple Keynesian model has both a horizontal section and a vertical section. The kink between the two sections is at the Natural Real GDP level. If aggregate demand changes in the horizontal section of the curve (when the economy is operating below Natural Real GDP), Real GDP changes, but the price level does not. If aggregate demand changes in the vertical section of the curve (when the economy is operating at Natural Real GDP), the price level changes, but Real GDP does not.

The Simple Keynesian Model in the *TE–TP* Framework

- Changes in consumption, investment, and government purchases will change total expenditures.
- A rise in C, I, or G will shift the TE curve upward.
- A decrease in C, I, or G will shift the TE curve downward.
- If total expenditures (TE) equals total production (TP), the economy is in equilibrium. If $TE < TP$, the economy is in disequilibrium, and inventories will unexpectedly rise, signaling firms to cut back production. If $TE > TP$, the economy is in disequilibrium, and inventories will unexpectedly fall, signaling firms to increase production.
- Equilibrium occurs where $TE = TP$. The equilibrium level of Real GDP may be less than the Natural Real GDP level, and the economy may be stuck at this lower level of Real GDP.

A Keynesian Theme

- Keynes proposed that the economy could reach its equilibrium position even if Real GDP is below Natural Real GDP; that is, the economy could be in equilibrium and in a recessionary gap too. Furthermore, he argued that the economy may not be able to get out of a recessionary gap by itself: Government may need to play a management role in the economy.

Key Terms and Concepts

Efficiency Wage Models
Consumption Function
Multiplier

Marginal Propensity to Consume (*MPC*)

Autonomous Consumption

Marginal Propensity to Save (*MPS*)

Questions and Problems

Questions 1–5 are based on the first section of the chapter, questions 6–12 are based on the second section, questions 13–20 are based on the third section, and questions 21–25 are based on the fourth section.

1. How is Keynes's position different from the classical position with respect to wages, prices, and Say's law?
2. Classical economists assumed that wage rates, prices, and interest rates are flexible and will adjust quickly. Consider an extreme case: Suppose classical economists believed that wage rates, prices, and interest rates would adjust instantaneously. What would the classical aggregate supply (AS) curve look like? Explain your answer.
3. Give two reasons explaining why wage rates may not fall.
4. How was Keynes's position different from the classical position with respect to saving and investment?
5. According to some economists, why might business firms pay wage rates above market-clearing levels?
6. Given the Keynesian consumption function, how would a cut in income tax rates affect consumption? Explain your answer.
7. Look at the Keynesian consumption function: $C = C_0 + (MPC \times Y_d)$. What part of it relates to autonomous consumption? What part of it relates to induced consumption? Define autonomous consumption and induced consumption.
8. Using the Keynesian consumption function, prove numerically that, as the MPC rises, saving declines.
9. Explain the multiplier process.
10. What is the relationship between the MPC and the multiplier?
11. Explain how a rise in autonomous spending can increase total spending by some multiple.
12. In which factors will a change lead to a change in consumption?
13. According to Keynes, can an increase in saving shift the AD curve to the left? Explain your answer.
14. What factors will shift the AD curve in the simple Keynesian model?
15. According to Keynes, an increase in saving and a decrease in consumption may lower total spending in the economy. But how could that happen if the increased saving lowers interest rates (as shown in the last chapter)? Wouldn't a decrease in interest rates increase investment spending, thus counteracting the decrease in consumption spending?
16. Can a person believe that wages are inflexible downward for, say, one year and also believe in a self-regulating economy? Explain your answer.
17. According to Keynes, can the private sector always remove the economy from a recessionary gap? Explain your answer.
18. What does the aggregate supply curve look like in the simple Keynesian model?
19. "In the simple Keynesian model, increases in AD that occur below Natural Real GDP will have no effect on the price level." Do you agree or disagree with this statement? Explain your answer.
20. Suppose consumption rises while investment and government purchases remain constant. How will the AD curve shift in the simple Keynesian model? Under what condition will the rise in Real GDP be equal to the rise in total spending?
21. Explain how to derive a total expenditures (TE) curve.
22. What role do inventories play in the equilibrating process in the simple Keynesian model (as described in the TE–TP framework)?
23. Identify the three states of the economy in terms of TE and TP.
24. If Real GDP is $10.4 trillion in Exhibit 12, what is the state of business inventories?
25. How will a rise in government purchases change the TE curve in Exhibit 12?

Working with Numbers and Graphs

Questions 1 and 2 are based on the second section of the chapter, questions 3 and 4 are based on the third section, and questions 5–8 are based on the fourth section.

1. Compute the multiplier in each of the following cases:
   a. $MPC = 0.60$
   b. $MPC = 0.80$
   c. $MPC = 0.50$

2. Write an investment function (equation) that specifies two components:
   a. Autonomous investment spending
   b. Induced investment spending

3. Economist A believes that changes in aggregate demand affect only the price level, and economist B believes that changes in aggregate demand affect only Real GDP. What do the AD and AS curves look like for each economist?

4. Use the accompanying figure to explain the following two statements:

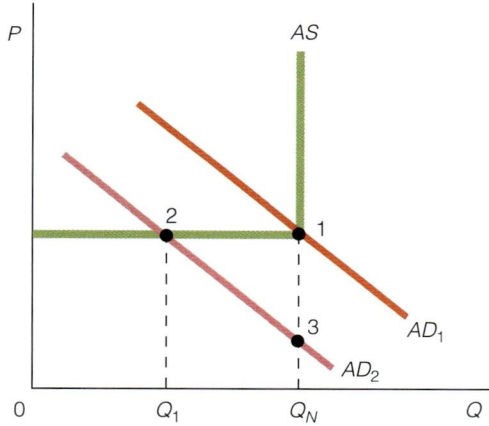

   a. According to Keynes, aggregate demand may be insufficient to bring about the full-employment output level (or Natural Real GDP).
   b. A decrease in consumption (due to increased saving) is not matched by an increase in investment spending.

5. The TE curve in Exhibit 11(d) is upward sloping because the consumption function is upward sloping. Explain.

6. In Exhibit 11(d), what does the vertical distance between the origin and the point at which the TE curve cuts the vertical axis represent?

7. In the accompanying figure, explain what happens if
   a. The economy is at Q_1
   b. The economy is at Q_2

8. In the accompanying figure, if Natural Real GDP is Q_2, in what state is the economy at point A?

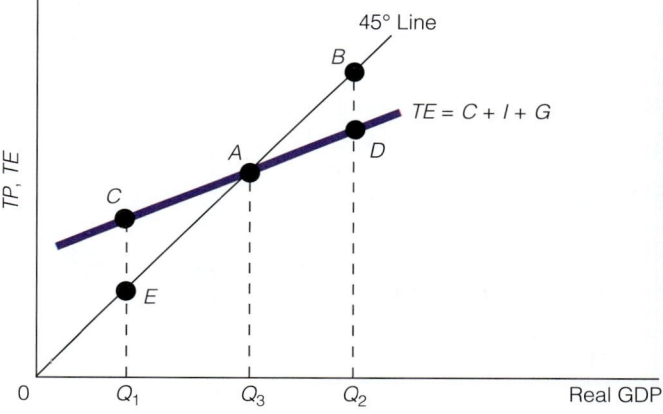

Introduction

Fiscal policy consists of changes in government expenditures and/or taxes to achieve economic goals, such as low unemployment, stable prices, and economic growth. In the United States, the Congress and the president together fashion fiscal policy. We begin our discussion with some facts and figures about government expenditures and taxation, and then we go on to discuss the effect of fiscal policy on the economy.

11-1 The Federal Budget

The federal budget has two, not necessarily equal, parts: government expenditures and tax revenues. You are familiar with the term *government purchases* from earlier chapters. Government expenditures—sometimes simply called government spending—are not the same as government purchases. Government expenditures are the sum of government purchases and government transfer payments.[1]

11-1a Government Expenditures

In 2019, the federal government spent $4.446 trillion, which was 20.09 percent of GDP for that year.

The bulk of the $4.446 trillion in government spending in 2019 was spent on four programs: national defense, Social Security, Medicare, and Income Security. These four programs together accounted for about 64 percent of all government spending that year.

[1.] Remember from an earlier chapter that government purchases are the purchases of goods and services by government at all levels. Transfer payments are payments to persons, such as Social Security payments, that are not made in return for goods and services currently supplied. In this chapter, the terms *government expenditures, government spending, government purchases,* and *transfer payments* all refer to the *federal* government.

11-1b Government Tax Revenues

The federal government imposes taxes and fees that generate revenue. In 2019, government revenues totaled $3.462 trillion, which was 16.3 percent of GDP for that year.

The bulk of government tax revenues comes from three taxes: the individual income tax, the corporate income tax, and payroll taxes (which include Social Security and Medicare taxes). In 2019, these three taxes accounted for 92 percent of total government tax revenues; the income tax by itself accounted for 49.6 percent of total government revenues.

11-1c Income Tax Structures

An income tax structure can be progressive, proportional, or regressive. Under a **progressive income tax**, the tax rate increases as a person's taxable income level rises. To illustrate, suppose Russell pays taxes at the rate of 15 percent on a taxable income of $20,000. When his (taxable) income rises to, say, $30,000, he pays at a rate of 28 percent. And when his income rises to, say, $55,000, he pays at a rate of 31 percent. A progressive income tax is usually capped. Currently, the U.S. income tax structure is progressive.

Under a **proportional income tax**, the same tax rate is used for all income levels. A proportional income tax is sometimes referred to as a *flat tax*. For example, Lidia pays taxes at a rate of 10 percent whether her taxable income is $10,000 or $100,000.

Under a **regressive income tax**, the tax rate decreases as a person's taxable income level rises. For example, Breanna's tax rate is 10 percent when her taxable income is $10,000 and 8 percent when her taxable income rises to $20,000.

Exhibit 1 shows and briefly explains the preceding three income tax structures.

Progressive Income Tax
An income tax system in which one's tax rate rises as taxable income rises (up to some point).

Proportional Income Tax
An income tax system in which a person's tax rate is the same regardless of taxable income.

Regressive Income Tax
An income tax system in which a person's tax rate declines as his or her taxable income rises.

EXHIBIT 1

Three Income Tax Structures

The three income tax structures outlined are the progressive, proportional, and regressive structures.

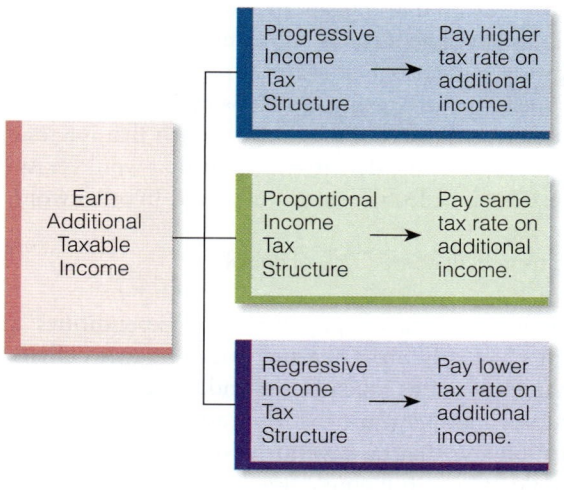

11-1d What Different Income Groups Pay in Income Taxes

Economists often look at the tax situations of different income groups. For example, in 2017, the top 1 percent of income earners in the United States earned 21.04 percent of the total income earned that year and paid 38.47 percent of the total federal income taxes collected. The table that follows shows the income and taxes for various income groups in 2017. The column labeled "Income Split Point" identifies the dollar amount you would have had to earn in 2017 to be in the income group in that row. For example, to be in the top 1 percent of income earners in 2017, you would have had to earn more than $515,371.

Income Group	Group's Percentage of Total Income	Group's Percentage of Federal Income Taxes	Income Split Point
Top 1%	21.04	38.47	Greater than $515,371
Top 5%	36.53	59.14	Greater than $208,053
Top 10%	47.74	70.08	Greater than $145,135
Top 25%	69.14	86.10	Greater than $83,682
Top 50%	88.75	96.89	Greater than $41,740
Bottom 50%	11.25	3.11	Less than $41,740

11-1e Budget Deficit, Surplus, or Balance

The government budget can be in one of three states:

- If government expenditures are greater than tax revenues, the federal government runs a **budget deficit**.
- If tax revenues are greater than government expenditures, the federal government runs a **budget surplus**.
- If government expenditures equal tax revenues, the federal government runs a **balanced budget**.

Budget Deficit
Government expenditures greater than tax revenues.

Budget Surplus
Tax revenues greater than government expenditures.

Balanced Budget
Government expenditures equal to tax revenues.

In 2019, the budget deficit was $984 billion. In the years ahead, budget deficits are projected in the trillions.

If the government spends more than its tax revenue and thus runs a budget deficit, where does it get the money to finance the deficit? For example, if the government spends $100 and receives only $70 in taxes, where does it get the $30 difference? The federal government—actually the U.S. Treasury—borrows the $30; that is, it finances the budget deficit with borrowed funds.

11-1f Structural and Cyclical Deficits

Suppose the budget is currently balanced and then Real GDP in the economy drops. As Real GDP drops, the tax base of the economy falls, and if tax rates are held constant, tax revenues will fall. Another result of the decline in Real GDP is that transfer payments (e.g., unemployment compensation) will rise. Thus, government expenditures will rise as tax revenues fall. Consequently, a balanced budget turns into a budget deficit—a result of the downturn in economic activity, not because of current spending and taxing decisions by the government. Economists use the term **cyclical deficit** to describe the part of the budget deficit that is a result of a downturn in economic activity. The remainder of the deficit—the part that would exist if the economy was operating at full employment—is called the **structural deficit**. In other words,

Cyclical Deficit
The part of the budget deficit that is a result of a downturn in economic activity.

Structural Deficit
The part of the budget deficit that would exist even if the economy was operating at full employment.

Total budget deficit = Structural deficit + Cyclical deficit

To illustrate, suppose the economy is in a recessionary gap, government expenditures are currently $3.3 trillion, and tax revenues are $3.0 trillion. Then the (total) budget deficit is $300 billion. Economists estimate that what government expenditures and tax revenues would be if the economy was operating at full employment. Assume that they estimate that government expenditures would be only $3.2 trillion and that tax revenues would be $3.1 trillion. The structural deficit—the deficit that would exist at full employment—would therefore be $100 billion. The cyclical deficit—the part of the budget deficit that is a result of economic downturn—would be $200 billion.

11-1g The Public Debt

A budget deficit occurs when government expenditures are greater than tax revenues for a *single year*. The **public debt**, sometimes called the "federal debt" or "national debt," is the *total* amount the federal government owes its creditors. Some of this debt is held by agencies of the U.S. government; that is, one entity in the government owes it to another. The remainder of the debt is held by the public and is referred to either as *public debt held by the public* or as *net public debt*. In June 2021, the public debt was $28.295 trillion, and the public debt held by the public was $22.173 trillion. The lowest recorded public debt was $33,733.05, on January 1, 1835.

Public Debt
The total amount that the federal government owes its creditors.

11-1h 2020: Things Change in a Big Way

Here are how things looked in 2019 and 2020:

Year	Government Expenditures (billions of dollars)	Budget Deficit (billions of dollars)	Budget Deficit as a Percentage of GDP	Public Debt Held by the Public (trillions of dollars)	Public Debt Held by the Public as a Percentage of GDP
2019	4,447	984	4.6	17.17	79.2
2020	6,682	3,215	14.9	21.35	101.2

Notice the rather dramatic increases in all items between 2019 and 2020. In actuality, increases in three items were not expected. The Congressional Budget Office (CBO)—back in January 2020—had projected government expenditures in 2020 to be $4,647 billion. Instead, it was 6,682 billion. Also, the CBO projected the budget deficit in 2020 to be $1,105 billion. Instead, it was $3,215 billion. As to the public debt held by the public, the CBO projected it would be $17.85 trillion, but instead it turned out to be $21.35 trillion.

The CBO projections usually are not off as much as they were in 2020, so what happened? When the CBO made its projections in January 2020, the coronavirus pandemic (COVID-19) had not yet hit the United States. The lockdowns, masks, social distancing, a sharp uptick in unemployment, businesses shutting down, and other effects of the pandemic hadn't happened yet. That was a month or so away. In reaction to the economic contraction that started in February 2020, there were certain fiscal policy responses that included targeted relief for certain businesses and individuals, as well as a more traditional fiscal policy response in terms of expansionary fiscal policy (more on this later in the chapter). As of this writing, the federal government had enacted four laws that were designed to reduce the economic impact of the pandemic, costing trillions of dollars. This largely explains why things look so different between 2019 and 2020 and why the CBO projections for government expenditures, the budget deficit, and the public debt made in January 2020 turned out to be so wrong.

11-1i Valued-Added Tax

Some persons have proposed higher taxes or new taxes to deal with the enlarged budget deficits and growing public debt. One tax that has been suggested is the value-added tax (VAT). Some have proposed VAT as a supplementary revenue source, others as a substitute for current taxes.

There are two things to understand about a value-added tax: the value-added part and the tax part.

The Value-Added Part *Value added* is the difference between what a producer sells a final good for and what it pays for an intermediate good. For example, suppose a farmer finds a seed and plants it. In time, wheat appears. The farmer harvests the wheat and sells it to a baker for $1. The value added is $1.00. The sequence of events is as follows:

- The farmer sells the wheat to the baker for $1.00.
- The farmer doesn't buy any intermediate goods (so intermediate goods "purchased" = $0.00).
- Value added = $1.00 − $0.00 = $1.00.
- Dollar amount kept by farmer = $1.00.

Now the baker, who has purchased the wheat, turns it into a loaf of bread, which he sells to a final consumer for $1.40. The value added is $0.40. The sequence of events is as follows:

- The baker sells the loaf of bread to a consumer for $1.40.
- The baker bought the wheat (the intermediate good) from the farmer for $1.00.
- Value added = $1.40 − $1.00 = $0.40.
- Dollar amount kept by baker = $0.40.

Notice two things:

- The sum of the values added ($1.00 + $0.40) is equal to the price paid by the final consumer for the loaf of bread ($1.40):

$$\text{Sum of values added } (\$1.00 + \$0.40) = \text{Price of the loaf of bread purchased by consumer } (\$1.40)$$

The value added at each stage of production is equal to the dollar amount kept by the seller of the good. For instance, the valued added by the farmer was $1.00, and this is the amount he kept.

The Tax Part VAT is a *tax* applied to the *value added* at *each stage of production*. Suppose the VAT rate is 10 percent. A VAT rate of 10 percent applied to the $1.00 value added by the farmer is $0.10. A VAT tax rate of 10 percent applied to the $0.40 value added by the baker is $0.04. The total VAT ends up being $0.14.

Value added by farmer	$1.00
VAT rate of 10% applied to value added by farmer	$0.10
Value added by baker	$0.40
VAT rate of 10% applied to valued added by baker	$0.04
Total VAT = $0.10 + $0.04	$0.14

To see how the $0.14 ends up with government, we need to revisit our farmer–baker example, but this time with a VAT applied. Before, the farmer charges the baker $1.00 for wheat. This time, with a VAT tax rate of 10 percent, he charges the baker 10 percent more, or $1.10, for the wheat. Here is how things now look for the farmer:

- The farmer sells the wheat to the baker for $1.10.
- The farmer turns over 10¢ to the government (the VAT at the farmer's stage of production).
- The farmer keeps $1.00, which is the amount he kept when there was no VAT.

Whereas the baker sold a loaf of bread to the consumer for $1.40 before, this time, with a VAT rate of 10 percent, he charges 10 percent more, or $1.54, for a loaf of bread. Here is how things now look for the baker:

- The baker sells the loaf of bread to the consumer for $1.54.
- The baker paid $1.10 for the wheat.
- The baker turns over $0.04 to government (the VAT at the baker's stage of production).
- The baker keeps $1.54, *minus* $1.10 (what he paid to the farmer), *minus* $0.04 (what he turned over to government), or $0.40, which is what he kept when there was no VAT.

Finally, here are how things look for the consumer and government:

- Without the VAT, the customer paid $1.40 for a loaf of broad. With the VAT, she pays $1.54.
- Without the VAT, government collected no VAT revenues. With the VAT, government collects $0.14 in VAT revenue.

So, the VAT (1) generates tax revenue and (2) raises prices.

VAT Compared with a Sales Tax The VAT is nothing more than a less visible sales tax. To illustrate, in the example of the farmer and baker, this time we impose, instead of a VAT, a sales tax of 10 percent at the point of final purchase. In other words, our consumer buys a loaf of bread for a price of $1.40 plus a 10 percent sales tax of $0.14: Price + Tax = $1.54.

Notice two things: (1) The consumer pays $1.54 for the bread when a VAT is applied and when a sales tax is applied. (2) The sales tax of $0.14 is exactly equal to the VAT. In other words, government has two ways to generate $0.14 in tax revenue: Impose a VAT or charge a sales tax. Either way, the customer ends up paying $1.54 for a loaf of bread, and government generates $0.14 in tax revenue.

Finally, in comparing a VAT with a sales tax, critics often stress the point that a VAT is less visible than a sales tax. If a sales tax is raised from, say, 5 to 6 percent, almost everyone who buys something is aware of the tax increase. Indeed, the sales receipt plainly identifies the new, higher sales tax. But if the VAT rate is raised by the same amount, not everyone will know that the VAT has been raised. People may simply think that sellers are charging higher prices because the VAT is not itemized separately from what sellers charge other sellers. In the farmer–baker example, with a VAT, the farmer simply charged the baker $1.10 for wheat instead of $1.00, and the baker simply charged the consumer $1.54 for a loaf of bread instead of $1.40. With a VAT, consumers find it hard to distinguish between the seller's charging a higher price because the VAT rate has been raised and the seller's charging a higher price even without the VAT rate being raised. The VAT critics add the following: When a sales tax is raised, people look to government and say, "*Government* raised my taxes." When VAT is raised, people say, "*Sellers* raised the prices I pay."

11-1j Tax Deductions Versus Subsidies

In the popular press, you will often hear someone say that some company or group is getting a subsidy (from the federal government) of so many dollars. It could be that the company or group is receiving a subsidy—but this is not always the case. Often, some people will talk

Economics 24/7

Do Voting Rules Matter to Taxing and Spending?

Earlier in the chapter, we identified the budget deficit in 2019 as $984 billion. Are budget deficits what they are no matter what voting rule is used to pass tax and spending bills?

To illustrate, consider two voting rules: a simple-majority rule (51 percent is needed for passage of a bill) and a supermajority rule (say, 66 percent is needed for passage).

Consider both rules in the U.S. Senate, where there are 100 senators. Now, suppose a Senate bill proposes that government spending be raised by $200 billion. Under which voting rule—simple majority or supermajority—is the bill more likely to be passed and spending increased by $200 billion? The answer is the simple-majority voting rule, because it is harder to get 66 senators than 51 senators to agree on the spending increase. In short, the closer the voting rule for the bill moves to unanimity (100 out of 100 must agree before a bill is passed), the less likely it will be to pass the bill. We conclude, then, that if the objective is to limit government spending, a supermajority voting rule is more effective at doing that than a simple-majority voting rule.

What about raising taxes? Suppose a Senate bill proposes to raise income tax rates across the board. Is the bill more likely to be passed with a supermajority voting rule or a simple-majority voting rule? The answer is again a simple-majority voting rule. So, if the objective is to increase the probability of tax increases being passed, a simple-majority voting rule is more effective than a supermajority voting rule.

Now consider cutting both taxes and spending. If this is the objective, then, once more, a simple majority is more likely to get both done than a supermajority: It is easier to get 51 senators to agree on cutting taxes and spending than to get 66 to agree.

Finally, suppose one's objective is to increase government spending and decrease taxes. What voting rule is most likely to be effective? To get more government spending, you want the voting rule that makes this easier to do, which is simple majority. To decrease taxes, again you want the voting rule that makes *that* easier to do, which, once more, is simple majority. But keep this in mind too: If you want spending to increase and taxes to decrease, you want to make the opposite of each (decrease government spending and increase taxes) hard to do. So, for a bill that proposes a cut in government spending, you would opt for a supermajority, and for a bill that proposes an increase in taxes, you would want a supermajority too.

So does the voting rule matter to whether government spending and taxes are raised or lowered? Yes. In short, government spending, taxing, and budget deficits are not simply a matter of being what they are. They are what they are, to a large degree, because of the voting rules used. Use a different set of voting rules, and it's likely that things would be different. To put it starkly, just ask yourself how likely government spending and taxes would increase or decrease with a unanimity voting rule.

---

about subsidies when they should be talking about tax deductions. The fact is there is a difference between a subsidy and a tax deduction. With a subsidy, money goes from one person to another. Money comes from Chris and goes to Jolie. With a tax deduction, it doesn't. To illustrate, if company X is being subsidized, this means that government is essentially taking money from taxpayers and handing it over to company X. But with a tax deduction, that is not happening. Instead, government is saying that if the company does something—such as keep its factories in the United States—then it can reduce the taxes that it pays by some dollar amount. In other words, instead of paying $10 million in taxes, it now pays, say, $8 million in taxes.

Self-Test

(Answers to Self-Test questions are in Answers to Self-Test Questions at the back of the book.)

1. Explain the differences among progressive, proportional, and regressive income tax structures.
2. What percentage of all income taxes was paid by the top 5 percent of income earners in 2017? What percentage of total income did this income group receive in 2017?
3. What four taxes account for the bulk of federal tax revenues?
4. Explain the cyclical budget deficit.

11-2 Fiscal Policy

As described in the previous chapter, some economists believe that the economy is inherently unstable. They argue that government should play a role in managing the economy because the economy can get stuck in a recessionary gap. They believe that government should try to move the economy out of the recessionary gap and toward Natural Real GDP.

A major way government can influence the economy is through *fiscal policy*. **Fiscal policy** consists of changes in government expenditures and/or taxes to achieve economic goals, such as low unemployment, price stability, and economic growth.

11-2a Some Relevant Fiscal Policy Terms

Expansionary fiscal policy calls for increases in government expenditures and/or decreases in taxes in order to achieve macroeconomic goals. **Contractionary fiscal policy** is implemented through decreases in government expenditures and/or increases in taxes to achieve macroeconomic goals. In sum, we have

- *Expansionary fiscal policy:* Government expenditures are up and/or taxes are down.
- *Contractionary fiscal policy:* Government expenditures are down and/or taxes are up.

When deliberate government actions bring about changes in its expenditures and taxes, fiscal policy is said to be *discretionary*. For example, a decision by Congress to increase government spending by, say, $10 billion in an attempt to lower the unemployment rate is an act of **discretionary fiscal policy**. In contrast, a change in either government expenditures or taxes that occurs automatically in response to economic events is referred to as an act of **automatic fiscal policy**. To illustrate, suppose Real GDP in the economy turns downward, causing more people to become unemployed and, as a result, to automatically receive unemployment benefits. These added unemployment benefits automatically boost government spending.

11-2b Two Important Notes

In your study of this chapter, keep in mind the following two important points:

1. We deal only with *discretionary fiscal policy*—that is, deliberate actions on the part of policymakers to affect the economy through changes in government spending and/or taxes.
2. We assume that any change in government spending is due to a change in government purchases, not to a change in transfer payments. In other words, we assume that transfer payments are constant and therefore that changes in government spending are a reflection only of changes in government purchases.

Fiscal Policy
Changes in government expenditures and/or taxes aimed at achieving economic goals, such as low unemployment, stable prices, and economic growth.

Expansionary Fiscal Policy
Increases in government expenditures and/or decreases in taxes in order to achieve particular economic goals.

Contractionary Fiscal Policy
Decreases in government expenditures and/or increases in taxes in order to achieve economic goals.

Discretionary Fiscal Policy
Deliberate changes in government expenditures and/or taxes in order to achieve economic goals.

Automatic Fiscal Policy
Changes in government expenditures and/or taxes that occur automatically without (additional) congressional action.

11-3 Demand-Side Fiscal Policy

This section focuses on how government spending and taxes—fiscal policy—can affect the demand side of the economy—that is, aggregate demand.

11-3a Shifting the Aggregate Demand Curve

How do changes in government purchases (G) and taxes (T) affect aggregate demand? Recall that a change in consumption, investment, government purchases, or net exports can change aggregate demand and therefore shift the AD curve. For example, an increase in government purchases (G) increases aggregate demand and shifts the AD curve to the right. A decrease in G decreases aggregate demand and shifts the AD curve to the left.[2]

A change in taxes (T) can affect consumption, investment, or both and therefore can affect aggregate demand. For example, a decrease in income taxes increases disposable (after-tax) income, permitting individuals to increase their consumption. As consumption rises, the AD curve shifts to the right. An increase in taxes decreases disposable income, lowers consumption, and shifts the AD curve to the left.

11-3b Fiscal Policy: Keynesian Perspective (Economy Is Not Self-Regulating)

The model of the economy in Exhibit 2(a) shows a downward-sloping AD curve and an upward-sloping $SRAS$ curve. As you can see, the economy is initially in a recessionary gap at point 1. Aggregate demand is too low to move the economy to equilibrium at the Natural Real

EXHIBIT 2

Fiscal Policy in Keynesian Theory: Ridding the Economy of Recessionary and Inflationary Gaps

(a) In Keynesian theory, expansionary fiscal policy eliminates a recessionary gap. Increased government purchases, decreased taxes, or both lead to a rightward shift in the aggregate demand curve from AD_1 to AD_2, restoring the economy to the natural level of Real GDP, Q_N. (b) Contractionary fiscal policy is used to eliminate an inflationary gap. Decreased government purchases, increased taxes, or both lead to a leftward shift in the aggregate demand curve from AD_1 to AD_2, restoring the economy to the natural level of Real GDP, Q_N.

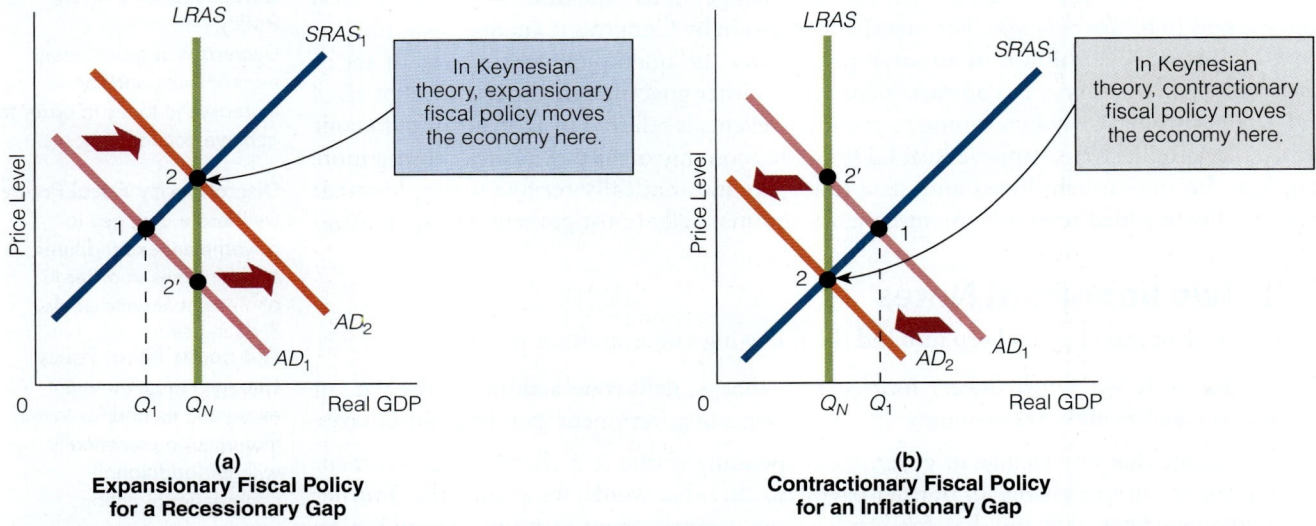

(a) Expansionary Fiscal Policy for a Recessionary Gap

(b) Contractionary Fiscal Policy for an Inflationary Gap

---

[2] Later in this chapter, when we discuss crowding out, we question the effect of an increase in government purchases on aggregate demand.

GDP level. The Keynesian *perspective* of the economy is that the economy is not self-regulating. So the Keynesian *prescription* is to enact expansionary fiscal policy measures (an increase in government purchases or a decrease in taxes) to shift the aggregate demand curve rightward from AD_1 to AD_2 and to move the economy to the Natural Real GDP level at point 2.

Why not simply wait for the short-run aggregate supply curve to shift rightward and intersect the aggregate demand curve at point 2′ (2 prime)? Again, the Keynesians usually respond that the economy is not self-regulating, making one of two arguments: (1) The economy is stuck at point 1 and won't move naturally to point 2′, perhaps because wage rates won't fall. (2) The short-run aggregate supply curve takes too long to shift rightward, and in the interim, we must deal with the high cost of unemployment and a lower level of Real GDP. In Exhibit 2(b), the economy is initially in an inflationary gap at point 1. In this situation, Keynesians are likely to propose a contractionary fiscal measure (a decrease in government purchases or an increase in taxes) to shift the aggregate demand curve leftward from AD_1 to AD_2 and move the economy to point 2.

In Exhibit 2, fiscal policy has worked as intended. In panel (a), the economy was in a recessionary gap, and expansionary fiscal policy eliminated the gap. In panel (b), the economy was in an inflationary gap, and contractionary fiscal policy eliminated it. In (a) and (b), fiscal policy is at its best and working as intended.

11-3c Crowding Out: Questioning Expansionary Fiscal Policy

Not all economists believe that fiscal policy works as just described. Some economists bring up the subject of *crowding out*. **Crowding out** is a decrease in private expenditures (consumption, investment, etc.) as a consequence of increased government spending or the need to finance a budget deficit.

Crowding out can be direct or indirect, as described in these two examples:

1. *Direct effect.* The government spends more on public libraries, and individuals buy fewer books at bookstores.[3]

2. *Indirect effect.* The government spends more on social programs and defense without increasing taxes; as a result, the size of the budget deficit increases. Consequently, the government must borrow more funds to finance the larger deficit. The increase in borrowing causes the demand for credit (i.e., the demand for loanable funds) to rise, in turn causing the interest rate to rise. As a result, investment drops. Thus, more government spending indirectly leads to less investment spending.

Types of Crowding Out In the first example, the government spends more on public libraries. Let's say that the government spends $2 billion more on public libraries and that consumers choose to spend not $1 less on books at bookstores. Then, obviously, there is no crowding out, or *zero crowding out*.

Now suppose that, after the government has spent $2 billion more on public libraries, consumers choose to spend $2 billion less at bookstores. Obviously, crowding out exists, and the degree of crowding out is dollar for dollar. When $1 of government spending offsets $1 of private spending, **complete crowding out** is said to exist.

Finally, suppose that, after the government has spent $2 billion more on public libraries, consumers spend $1.2 billion less on books at bookstores. Again, crowding out occurs, but it

Crowding Out
The decrease in private expenditures that occurs as a consequence of increased government spending or the need to finance a budget deficit.

Complete Crowding Out
A decrease in one or more components of private spending that completely offsets the increase in government spending.

[3.] We are not saying that, for example, if the government spends more on public libraries, individuals will necessarily buy fewer books at bookstores; rather, if they do, that would be an example of crowding out. The same holds for example 2.

Incomplete Crowding Out
A decrease in one or more components of private spending that only partially offsets the increase in government spending.

is not dollar for dollar, not complete crowding out. **Incomplete crowding out** occurs when the decrease in one or more components of private spending only partially offsets the increase in government spending.

The following table summarizes the different types of crowding out:

Type of Crowding Out	Example
Zero crowding out (sometimes called "no crowding out")	Government spends $2 billion more, and private sector spending stays constant.
Complete crowding out	Government spends $2 billion more, and the private sector spends $2 billion less.
Incomplete crowding out	Government spends $2 billion more, and the private sector spends, say, $1.2 billion less.

Graphical Representation of Crowding Out In the event that *complete* or *incomplete crowding out* occurs, expansionary fiscal policy will have less impact on aggregate demand and Real GDP than Keynesian theory predicts. Let's look at the graphical representation of crowding out. Exhibit 3 illustrates the consequences of complete and incomplete crowding out and, for comparison, includes zero crowding. As shown, here are the three possibilities for crowding out:

- *Zero crowding out (no crowding out)*. In Exhibit 3, the economy is initially at point 1, with Real GDP at Q_1. Expansionary fiscal policy then shifts the aggregate demand curve to AD_2 and moves the economy to point 2. Among other things, the implicit

EXHIBIT 3

Zero (No), Incomplete, and Complete Crowding Out

The exhibit shows the effects of zero, incomplete, and complete crowding out in the AD–AS framework. Starting at point 1, expansionary fiscal policy shifts the aggregate demand curve to AD_2 and moves the economy to point 2 and Q_N. The Keynesian theory that predicts this outcome assumes zero, or no, crowding out; an increase in, say, government spending does not reduce private expenditures. With incomplete crowding out, an increase in government spending causes private expenditures to decrease by less than the increase in government spending. The net result is a shift in the aggregate demand curve to AD'_2. The economy moves to point 2' and Q'_2. With complete crowding out, an increase in government spending is completely offset by a decrease in private expenditures, and the net result is that aggregate demand does not increase at all. The economy remains at point 1 and Q_1.

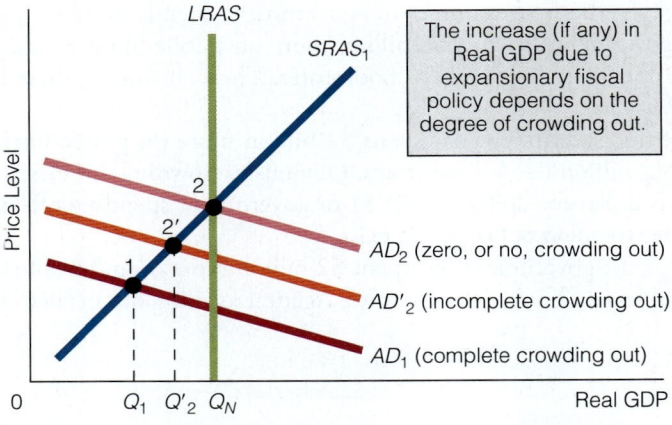

The increase (if any) in Real GDP due to expansionary fiscal policy depends on the degree of crowding out.

assumption is that there is zero (no) crowding out. Real GDP has increased from Q_1 to Q_N. Therefore, the unemployment rate will fall from its level at Q_1 to a lower level at Q_N. So, if there is no crowding out, expansionary fiscal policy increases Real GDP and lowers the unemployment rate.

- *Incomplete crowding out.* The aggregate demand curve shifts (on net) only to AD'_2 because a fall in private expenditures *partially offsets* the initial stimulus in aggregate demand that was due to increased government spending. The economy moves to point 2′, and Real GDP increases from Q_1 to Q'_2. Therefore, the unemployment rate will fall from what it was at Q_1 to what it is at Q'_2. Also, the changes in both Real GDP and the unemployment rate are smaller with incomplete crowding out than with zero crowding out. So, given incomplete crowding out, expansionary fiscal policy increases Real GDP and lowers the unemployment rate, but not as much as with zero crowding out.

- *Complete crowding out.* A fall in private expenditures *completely offsets* the initial stimulus in aggregate demand that was due to increased government spending, and the aggregate demand curve does not move (on net) at all. Real GDP does not change, and neither does the unemployment rate. So, with complete crowding out, expansionary fiscal policy has no effect on the economy. The economy remains at point 1.

See Exhibit 4 for a summary flowchart of the different types of crowding out.

EXHIBIT 4

Expansionary Fiscal Policy (Government Spending Increases), Crowding Out, and Changes in Real GDP and the Unemployment Rate

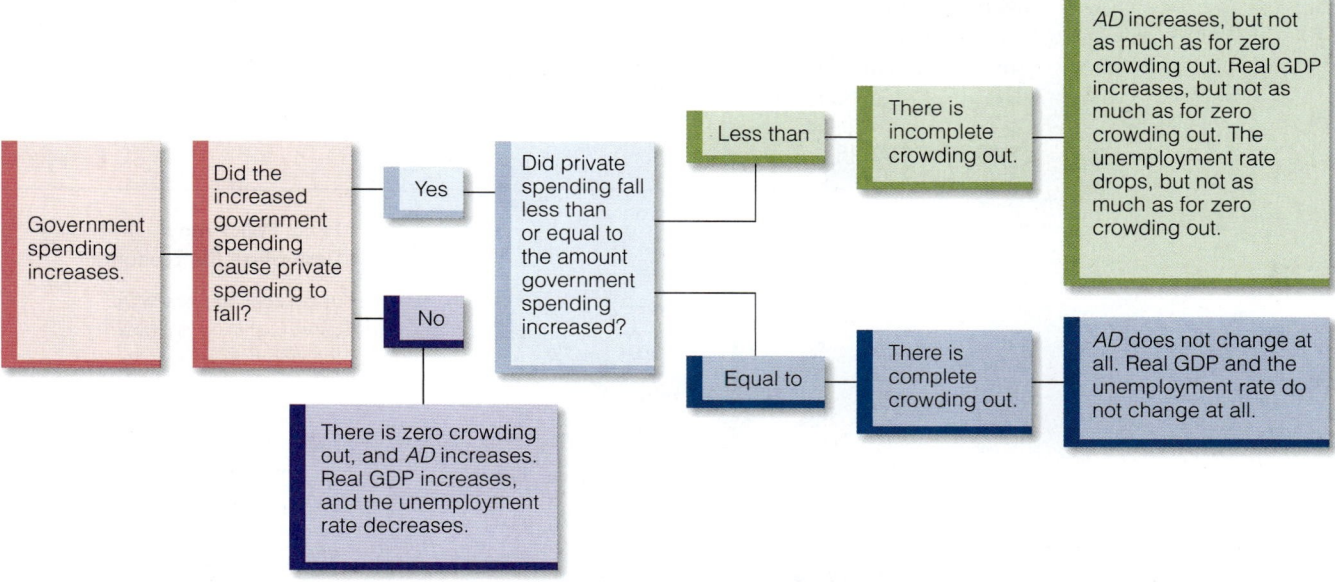

11-3d Lags and Fiscal Policy

Even if we prove beyond a shadow of a doubt that there is no (in other words, there is zero) crowding out, should fiscal policy be used to solve the problems of inflationary and recessionary gaps? Many economists would answer not necessarily, because of *lags*. There are five types of lags:

1. *The data lag.* Policymakers are not aware of changes in the economy as soon as they happen. For example, if the economy turns downward in January, the decline may not be apparent for two to three months.

2. *The wait-and-see lag.* When policymakers become aware of a downturn in economic activity, they rarely enact counteractive measures immediately. Instead, they usually adopt a relatively cautious wait-and-see attitude to be sure that the observed events are not just short-run phenomena.

3. *The legislative lag.* After policymakers decide that some type of fiscal policy measure is required, Congress or the president has to propose the measure, build political support for it, and get it passed. The legislative lag can take many months.

4. *The transmission lag.* Once enacted, a fiscal policy measure takes time to go into effect. For example, a discretionary expansionary fiscal policy measure mandating increased spending for public works projects requires construction companies to submit bids for the work, prepare designs, negotiate contracts, and so on.

5. *The effectiveness lag.* After being implemented, a policy measure takes time to affect the economy. If government spending is increased on Monday, the aggregate demand curve does not shift rightward on Tuesday.

Given the cumulative effect of these five lags, some economists argue that discretionary fiscal policy is not likely to have its intended impact on the economy. By the time the full impact of the policy is felt, the economic problem it was designed to solve (1) may no longer exist, (2) may not exist to the degree it once did, or (3) may have changed altogether.

Exhibit 5 illustrates the effect of lags. As shown, the economy is currently in a recessionary gap at point 1. The recession is under way before government officials recognize it. After it is recognized, however, Congress and the president consider enacting expansionary fiscal policy in the hope of shifting the AD curve from AD_1 to AD_2 so that it will intersect the $SRAS$ curve at point 1′, at Natural Real GDP.

EXHIBIT 5

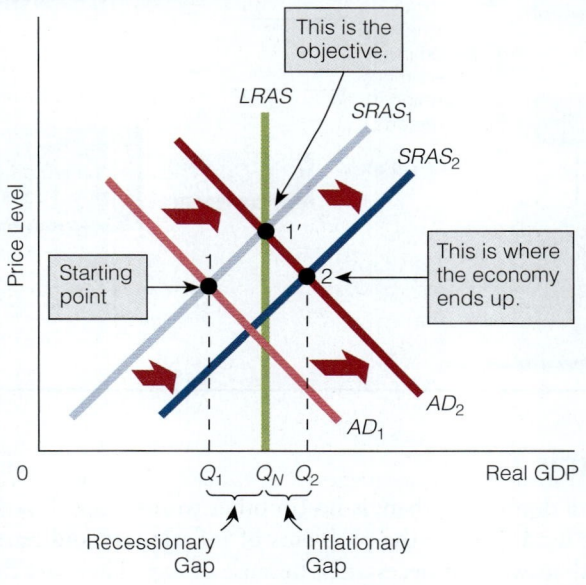

Fiscal Policy May Destabilize the Economy

In this scenario, the $SRAS$ curve is shifting rightward (healing the economy of its recessionary gap), but this information is unknown to policymakers. Policymakers implement expansionary fiscal policy, and the AD curve ends up intersecting $SRAS_2$ at point 2 instead of intersecting $SRAS_1$ at point 1′. Policymakers thereby move the economy into an inflationary gap, thus destabilizing the economy.

In the interim, unknown to everybody, the economy is "healing," or regulating, itself: The *SRAS* curve is already shifting to the right. However, government officials don't see this change because collecting and analyzing data about the economy takes time.

Thinking that the economy is not healing itself or not healing itself quickly enough, the government enacts expansionary fiscal policy. In time, the *AD* curve shifts rightward. But by the time the increased demand is felt in the goods-and-services market, the *AD* curve intersects the *SRAS* curve at point 2. In effect, the government has moved the economy from point 1 to point 2, not, as it had intended, from point 1 to point 1′. The government has moved the economy into an inflationary gap. Instead of stabilizing and moderating the ups and downs in economic activity (the business cycle), the government has intensified the fluctuations.

11-3e Crowding Out, Lags, and the Effectiveness of Fiscal Policy

Economists who believe that crowding out is always zero and that lags are insignificant conclude that fiscal policy is effective at moving the economy out of a recessionary gap. Economists who believe that crowding out is always complete and/or that lags are significant conclude that fiscal policy is ineffective in that respect.

11-3f Democracy in Deficit

We live in a world of continuing budget deficits and climbing national debt. How did this situation come to be? If we go back in time, we see that deficits and debt were not the rule. Yes, there were years of budget deficits, but they were often offset by years of budget surpluses. This was how it was supposed to be, some argue. The government, like the family, wasn't supposed to live beyond its means—it wasn't supposed to spend more than tax revenues—except when there was an emergency. And the emergency was usually defined as war. In other words, if the country was engaged in war, that was enough of an emergency to live beyond its means and spend more than tax revenues. Deficits and the piling up of debt were accepted during wartime. But then, when the war was over, it was time to run budget surpluses and to pay down the debt.

This view of how things were supposed to be contained within it an implicit view of government. Government did not have a management role to play in the economy. It was not supposed to try to stabilize the economy—to stimulate the economy during recessionary times and to dampen down the economy during inflationary times. There was no need to stabilize the economy because, it was thought, the economy did that itself. The economy contained its own self-regulating properties.

Here is how it worked: When the economy was in a recessionary gap, with the actual unemployment rate above the natural unemployment rate, there was a surplus in the labor market. Eventually, the surplus would lead to lowered wages. As wages fell, the short-run aggregate supply curve in the economy shifted rightward, and eventually the economy would move into long-run equilibrium, producing Natural Real GDP.

Of course, when the problem was an inflationary instead of a recessionary gap, things would work differently. When the economy was in an inflationary gap, the actual unemployment rate was below the natural unemployment rate, and there was a shortage in the labor market. Eventually, the shortage would lead to higher wages. As wages rose, the short-run aggregate supply curve in the economy shifted leftward, and the economy eventually would move into long-run equilibrium, producing Natural Real GDP.

In other words, no matter in what state the economy was—a recessionary or an inflationary gap—it would soon move out of that state and into long-run equilibrium, at which it would produce the Natural Real GDP level at full employment. The economy could self-regulate. Thus, there was no need for government to manage the economy; it did very well on its own (thank you very much).

With no economic management role for government to play, what was government supposed to do and how was it supposed to do it? It was supposed to provide roads, national defense, and police and fire protection; operate the court system; enforce contracts; and so on; and it was supposed to do this through a combination of spending and taxing. But—as was mentioned earlier—except in wartime, it was supposed to do it under the direction of an unwritten, but not unobserved, rule of running a balanced budget.

According to economists James Buchanan and Richard Wagner, in their work *Democracy in Deficit*,[4] the unwritten balanced budget rule was largely cast aside with the advent of the Keynesian Revolution in economics. John Maynard Keynes saw an economic management role for government to play. His view evolved out of his belief that the economy was not always inherently self-regulating. For example, the economy may not be able to remove itself from a recessionary gap. When it couldn't, government had a role to play. If wages wouldn't drop, and the short-run aggregate supply curve wouldn't shift rightward to move the economy into long-run equilibrium, then perhaps government should try to get the aggregate demand curve to shift rightward and eliminate the recessionary gap. How? Through expansionary fiscal policy. That is, by either cutting taxes or raising government spending.

Or consider when the economy might slip over into an inflationary gap. If the economy was self-regulating, wages would soon rise, and the short-run aggregate supply curve would shift leftward, removing the economy from the inflationary gap. But if that didn't happen, perhaps government should enact contractionary fiscal policy and shift the aggregate demand curve leftward, thus pushing the economy out of the inflationary gap.

The Keynesian Revolution therefore brought forth a policy prescription that read, "If the economy gets stuck in either a recessionary or an inflationary gap and can't move itself into long-run equilibrium to produce Natural Real GDP, then the government should regulate the economy into long-run equilibrium. Doing so calls for expansionary fiscal policy (lower taxes and/or higher government spending) to remove the economy from the recessionary gap and contractionary fiscal policy (higher taxes and/or lower government spending) to remove the economy from the inflationary gap.

Now, let's assume that Keynes and the Keynesians are right—that the economy is not self-regulating, that it can get stuck in either a recessionary or an inflationary gap. And let's also assume that the Keynesian prescription of expansionary fiscal policy for a recessionary gap and contractionary fiscal policy for an inflationary gap is correct. In other words, expansionary fiscal policy will eliminate a recessionary gap, and contractionary fiscal policy will eliminate an inflationary gap. Would all then be well with the economy? To try to answer that question, we need first ask ourselves how easy or hard it would be for elected officials (Congress and a president) to enact both sides of the fiscal policy coin. One side of that coin—the expansionary fiscal policy side—is likely to be much more politically popular than the other side of the coin—the contractionary fiscal policy side.

---

[4]. James M. Buchanan and Richard E. Wagner, *Democracy in Deficit: The Political Legacy of Lord Keynes* (New York: Academic Press, 1977).

The expansionary fiscal policy side consists of government spending more and/or taxing less. In other words, politicians will go to the voters and tell them that they want to give them greater money benefits (more spending) and/or they want to cut their taxes. This approach is likely to be met with applause from the voters. But the specifics of contractionary fiscal policy, consisting of cuts in government spending and/or higher taxes, are not so likely. In short, the Keynesian policy prescription consists of two sides of the fiscal coin: more spending and lower taxes when the economy is in a recessionary gap, and less spending and higher taxes when the economy is in an inflationary gap.

But given the reality of modern-day politics, one side of that fiscal coin is going to be much more popular with the voters and thus with the politicians running for office or reelection. Think of it this way: The Keynesian prescription says to offer candy (more spending and lower taxes) to the voters when there is a recessionary gap but take that candy away (less spending and higher taxes) when there is an inflationary gap. Now, if the voters do not understand that less spending and higher taxes are "what is needed" to remove the economy from an inflationary gap, you can see how that policy prescription might be hard to sell when voters are being sought. There is a political bias, then, toward expansionary fiscal policy: more spending and lower taxes. But what does more spending and lower taxes lead to? It leads to budget deficits. And continued budget deficits lead to ever greater national debt.

So what went wrong? According to Buchanan and Wagner, the problem is that Keynes and the Keynesians proposed changes in the state of the budget in order to stabilize the economy yet all the while assumed that those changes would be brought about by a government that is not subject to the pull and push of everyday, democratic politics. To explain, Buchanan and Wagner argue that Keynes, in particular, believed in a benevolent despot theory of government. Such a government is one that does what is right for the people, given the circumstances at hand, and ignores politics.

To illustrate, suppose that the economy is in an inflationary gap and requires contractionary fiscal policy: a decline in government spending or a rise in taxes. But suppose also that the political environment at the time is one in which people do not want their government to cut spending benefits or raise their taxes. What will a benevolent despot do? The despot will do what is needed at the time, irrespective of what people may or may not want. If the economy is in an inflationary gap, he will cut spending and raise taxes, so that the inflationary gap will be eliminated and the economy will stabilize in long-run equilibrium. The situation would be similar to that of doctors who, worried about patients, gives them some horrible-tasting medicine because the doctors know that it will make the patients get well.

But representative governments do not behave as benevolent despots, argue Buchanan and Wagner. And to assume that they do—as, they argue, Keynes did—will only lead to unintended and unexpected effects.

Buchanan and Wagner are not arguing that Keynes's view of how the economy works is wrong. They argue instead that, if we assume that Keynes's view of how the economy works is correct and that his call for expansionary fiscal policy in a recessionary gap and for contractionary fiscal policy in an inflationary gap is correct, too, then there is still a political dimension to achieving certain economic policies that needs to be addressed. And that dimension is, no matter what the economic situation—inflationary gap or recessionary gap—expansionary fiscal policy (more spending and lower taxes) always seems to politically trump contractionary fiscal policy (less spending and higher taxes). In other words, although Keynesian economics might argue for contractionary fiscal policy during an inflationary gap, everyday politics is going to push for expansionary fiscal policy, and in the end, politics often trumps economics.

To conclude, Keynesian fiscal policy prescriptions may be all right if government acts like a benevolent despot who is not swayed by political considerations. But prescribed in a political environment in which politicians and elected representatives seek votes, those same fiscal policy prescriptions are altogether different. With a benevolent despot, we get higher taxes sometimes and lower taxes at other times; we get more spending sometimes and less spending at other times. But with real-world, democratic politics, we usually get more spending and lower taxes, no matter the economic ill. In other words, to use the title of the Buchanan and Wagner book on the subject, we get a "democracy in deficit." We get big deficits and big debt.

1. How does crowding out create questions about the effectiveness of expansionary demand-side fiscal policy? Give an example.
2. How might lags reduce the effectiveness of fiscal policy?
3. Give an example of an indirect effect of crowding out.

11-4 Supply-Side Fiscal Policy

Fiscal policy effects may be felt on the supply side as well as on the demand side of the economy. For example, a reduction in tax rates may alter an individual's incentive to work and produce, thus altering aggregate supply.

11-4a Marginal Tax Rates and Aggregate Supply

When fiscal policy measures affect tax rates, they may affect both aggregate supply and aggregate demand. Consider a reduction in an individual's marginal tax rate. The **marginal (income) tax rate** is equal to the change in a person's tax payment divided by the change in the person's taxable income:

Marginal (Income) Tax Rate
The change in a person's tax payment divided by the change in taxable income: ΔTax payment $\div$ ΔTaxable income.

$$\text{Marginal tax rate} = \frac{\Delta \text{ Tax payment}}{\Delta \text{ Taxable income}}$$

For example, if Serena's taxable income increases by $1 and her tax payment increases by $0.28, then her marginal tax rate is 28 percent. If her taxable income increases by $1 and her tax payment increases by $0.35, then her marginal tax rate is 35 percent.

All other things held constant, lower marginal tax rates increase the incentive to engage in productive activities (work) relative to leisure and tax-avoidance activities.[5] As resources shift from leisure to work, short-run aggregate supply increases. Most economists predict that, when the lower marginal tax rates are permanent (not a one-shot phenomenon), not only the short-run aggregate supply curve but also the long-run aggregate supply curve will shift rightward. Exhibit 6 illustrates the predicted effect of a permanent marginal tax rate cut on aggregate supply.

---

[5] When marginal tax rates are lowered, two things happen: (1) individuals will have more disposable income, and (2) the amount of money that individuals can earn (and keep) by working increases. As a result of the first effect, individuals will choose to work less. As a result of the second effect, individuals will choose to work more. Whether an individual works less or more on net depends on whether effect 1 is stronger than or weaker than effect 2. We have assumed that effect 2 is stronger than effect 1; so, as marginal tax rates decline, the net effect is that individuals work more.

EXHIBIT 6

The Predicted Effect of a Permanent Marginal Tax Rate Cut on Aggregate Supply

A cut in marginal tax rates increases the attractiveness of productive activity relative to leisure and tax-avoidance activities and shifts resources from the latter to the former, thus shifting rightward both the short-run and the long-run aggregate supply curves.

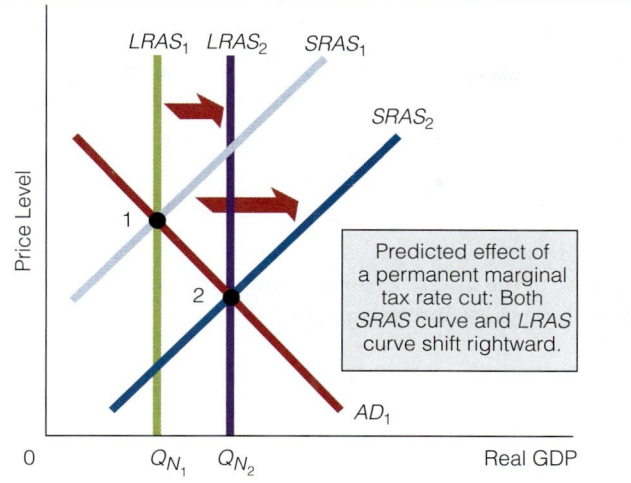

11-4b The Laffer Curve: Tax Rates and Tax Revenues

High tax rates are followed by attempts of ingenious men to beat them as surely as snow is followed by little boys on sleds.

—Arthur Okun, economist (1928–1980)

If (marginal) income tax rates are reduced, will income tax revenues increase or decrease? Most people think that the answer is obvious: Lower tax rates mean lower tax revenues. However, economist Arthur Laffer explained why this may not be the case. As the story goes, Laffer, while dining with a journalist at a restaurant in Washington, D.C., drew the curve shown in Exhibit 7 on a napkin. The curve came to be known as the **Laffer curve**. Laffer's objective was to explain the possible relationships between tax rates and tax revenues. In the exhibit, tax revenues are on the vertical axis, and tax rates are on the horizontal axis. Laffer made three major points about the curve:

Laffer Curve
The curve, named after economist Arthur Laffer, that shows the relationship between tax rates and tax revenues. According to the Laffer curve, as tax rates rise from zero, tax revenues rise, reach a maximum at some point, and then fall with further increases in tax rates.

EXHIBIT 7

The Laffer Curve

When the tax rate is either 0 or 100 percent, tax revenues are zero. Starting from a zero tax rate, increases in tax rates first increase tax revenues (from point A to point B) and then decrease tax revenues (from point B to point C). Starting from a 100 percent tax rate, decreases in tax rates first increase tax revenues (from point C to point B) and then decrease tax revenues (from point B to point A). The curve suggests that there is some tax rate that maximizes tax revenues.

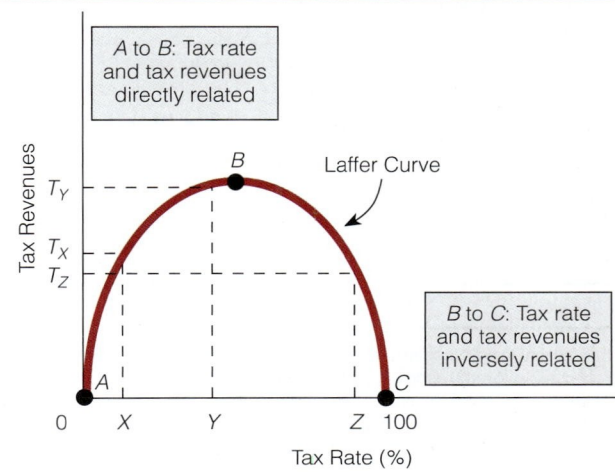

1. Zero tax revenues will be collected at two (marginal) tax rates: 0 and 100 percent. Obviously, no tax revenues will be raised if the tax rate is zero, and if the tax rate is 100 percent, no one will work and earn income because the entire amount would be taxed away.

2. An increase in tax rates could cause tax revenues to increase. For example, an increase in tax rates from X to Y percent will increase tax revenues from T_X to T_Y.

3. A decrease in tax rates could cause tax revenues to increase. For example, a decrease in tax rates from Z to Y percent will increase tax revenues from T_Z to T_Y. This point brought public attention to the Laffer curve.

Both an *increase* and a *decrease* in tax rates at different times can increase tax revenues because of the interrelationships among tax rates, the **tax base**, and tax revenues. The equation describing those interrelationships is[6]

$$\text{Tax revenues} = \text{Tax base} \times \text{(average) Tax rate}$$

Tax Base
In terms of income taxes, the total amount of taxable income. Tax revenues = Tax base × (average) Tax rate

For example, a tax rate of 20 percent multiplied by a tax base of $100 billion generates $20 billion of tax revenues.

Obviously, tax revenues are a function of two variables: (1) the tax rate and (2) the tax base. Whether tax revenues increase or decrease when the average tax rate is lowered depends on whether the tax base expands by a greater or lesser percentage than the percentage reduction in the tax rate. Exhibit 8 illustrates the point. The tax rate starts at 20 percent, with a tax base of $100 billion and tax revenues of $20 billion. As the tax rate is reduced, the tax base expands: The rationale is that individuals work more, invest more, enter into more trades, and shelter less income from taxes at lower tax rates.

However, the real question is *how much* does the tax base expand following the tax rate reduction? Suppose the tax rate in Exhibit 8 is reduced to 15 percent. In case 1, the reduction increases the tax base to $120 billion: A 25 percent decrease in the tax rate (from 20 to 15 percent) causes a 20 percent increase in the tax base (from $100 billion to $120 billion).

EXHIBIT 8

Tax Rates, the Tax Base, and Tax Revenues

Tax revenues equal the tax base times the (average) tax rate. If the percentage reduction in the tax rate is greater than the percentage increase in the tax base, tax revenues decrease (case 1). If the percentage reduction in the tax rate is less than the percentage increase in the tax base, tax revenues increase (case 2). All dollar amounts are in billions of dollars.

	(1) Tax Rate	(2) Tax Base	(3) Tax Revenues (1) × (2)	Summary
Start with:	20%	$100	$20	—
Case 1:	15	120	18	↓ Tax rate ↓ Tax revenues
Case 2:	15	150	22.5	↓ Tax rate ↑ Tax revenues

---

[6] Note that the average tax rate is equal to an individual's tax payment divided by taxable income (tax payment ÷ taxable income). Second, a lower average tax rate requires a lower marginal tax rate. This relationship follows from the average-marginal rule, which states that if the marginal magnitude is below the average magnitude, then the average is pulled down, and if the marginal magnitude is above the average magnitude, then the average is pulled up. Simply put, if an individual pays less tax on an additional taxable dollar (constituting evidence of a marginal tax rate reduction), then his or her average tax naturally falls.

Economics 24/7

Does the Portion of the Laffer Curve the Economy Is On Matter?

Take a look at the Laffer curve in Exhibit 7. Notice that there are two portions to the curve. There is the upward-sloping portion of the curve that goes between points *A* and *B* and the downward-sloping portion of the curve that goes between points *B* and *C*. If tax rates are raised in the upward-sloping part of the curve, tax revenues rise. But if tax rates are raised in the downward-sloping part of the curve, tax revenues decline.

Now, let's connect a change in tax revenues to the budget deficit. We know that a budget deficit exists when government expenditures are greater than tax revenues, thus a change in tax revenues will change the size of the budget deficit. Let's assume that the economy is in the upward-sloping portion of the Laffer curve, and tax rates are raised. We know that tax revenues will rise, and, consequently, the budget deficit will decline. With a smaller budget deficit, the government will now need to borrow less to finance the deficit. The decreased

need to borrow will cause the demand for loanable funds (or the demand for credit) to decline. As the demand for loanable funds (or credit) declines, the interest rate will drop.

Will a declining interest rate affect you? Suppose you are thinking of buying a new car and you need to take out a car loan to do so. Will the lower interest rate for the car loan matter to you?

Now suppose there is an increase in tax rates, but this time the economy is in the downward-sloping portion of the Laffer curve. As tax rates rise, tax revenue falls, and as tax revenue declines, *ceteris paribus*, the deficit gets larger. In order to finance the larger budget deficit, the government's demand for credit will rise, causing the interest rate to rise. Will this higher interest rate affect you? It certainly could: If you go ahead and get the car loan, you will have to pay a higher interest rate.

Tax revenues then drop to $18 billion. In case 2, the tax base expands by 50 percent, to $150 billion. Because the tax base increases by a greater percentage than the percentage decrease in the tax rate, tax revenues increase (to $22.5 billion).

Of course, either case is possible. According to the Laffer curve, tax revenues increase if a tax rate reduction is made on the downward-sloping portion of the curve (between points *B* and *C* in Exhibit 7), and tax revenues decrease following a tax rate reduction on the upward-sloping portion of the curve (between points *A* and *B*).

11-4c Fiscal Policy and Expectations

Even if, when tax rates are lowered, people do not work more and produce more, it cannot unequivocally be said that lower tax rates do not stimulate work and production. To explain, consider two different settings, one in which income tax rates are lowered in year 1 with no further cuts expected in future years and the other in which income tax rates are lowered in year 1 with further cuts expected in future years (years 2, 3, 4, and so on).

In the first setting (tax rate cuts in year 1, none expected in the future), suppose individuals do not respond by working and producing more. We can then conclude that, all other things being equal, tax rate cuts do not stimulate more work and production.

In the second setting (tax rate cuts in year 1, additional cuts expected in future years), suppose individuals do not respond by working and producing more. This time we cannot conclude that tax rate cuts do not stimulate more work and production, because individuals may simply be waiting to work and produce more when tax rates are even lower in future years. Look at it this way: Even though tax rates are lower in year 1 than in year 0, they are higher than they will be in year 2.

Now look at the opposite condition: raising tax rates. Raising tax rates should lead to individuals' cutting back on work and production, but this effect may not come to pass if tax rates are expected to rise more in future years. In fact, raising the tax rate in year 1, with an expected tax rate hike to follow in year 2, could actually get people to work and produce more in year 1. In relative terms, the tax rate is lower in year 1 than it will be in year 2.

1. Give an arithmetic example to illustrate the difference between the marginal and average tax rates.

2. If income tax rates rise, will income tax revenues rise too?

Office Hours

What's the Top Marginal Tax Rate?

Student: Is the U.S. income tax structure a progressive tax structure?

Instructor: Yes. There are currently seven marginal tax rates. These percentage rates are 10, 12, 22, 24, 32, 35, and 37.

Student: At what taxable income does the highest marginal tax rate start?

Instructor: For a single person in 2020, it started at $518,400.

Student: What would that person have paid in income taxes that year?

Instructor: $156,235. If we divide $156,235 in taxes paid by a taxable income of $518,400, it follows that this person would have paid 30.13 percent of his or her taxable income in income taxes. Stated differently, the person has an average income tax rate of 30.13 percent.

Student: Individuals' marginal tax rate can be different than their average tax rate, correct?

Instructor: That's correct.

Student: I've read that the top marginal tax rate in 1952–53 was 92 percent. Is this correct? Did it apply to many taxpayers?

Instructor: It is correct, and it applied to about 10,000 households in the United States. That top rate kicked in at an income of $200,000, which is equivalent to $2 million today.

Student: I'm interested in knowing how many people file income tax returns in the United States. Is there data on this?

Instructor: In 2017, there were 143.3 million federal income tax returns filed in the United States. The taxable income of these returns was about $10.9 trillion.

Student: How many tax returns were filed by the top 1 percent of income earners, and what was the taxable income of this group?

Instructor: The top 1 percent filed 1.4 million tax returns, and the taxable income of this group was $2.3 trillion. On this dollar amount, they paid $615 billion in federal income taxes.

Student: How much did the bottom 50 percent and the top 50 percent each pay in federal income taxes?

Instructor: The bottom 50 percent paid $49 billion; the top 50 percent paid $1.5 trillion.

Points to Remember

1. There is a difference between the marginal tax rate a person pays and the average tax rate. For instance, a person could pay a marginal tax rate of 37 percent and pay an average tax rate of 26 percent.
2. If individuals are in the top tax bracket, it doesn't follow that they pay the top marginal tax rate on all of their taxable income. For example, if the top marginal tax rate of, say, 40 percent starts at a taxable income of $450,000, then the person with a taxable income of $450,001 ($450,000 + $1) pays the top rate on only $1.

Chapter Summary

Government Spending

- In 2019, the federal government spent $4.446 trillion, 20.9 percent of the country's GDP. About 64 percent of the money went to Social Security, Medicare, Income Security, and national defense.
- With a proportional income tax, everyone pays taxes at the same rate, regardless of income level. With a progressive income tax, a person pays taxes at a higher rate (up to some top rate) as his or her income level rises. With a regressive income tax, a person pays taxes at a lower rate as the person's income level rises.
- The federal income tax is a progressive income tax.

Taxes

- In 2019, the federal government took in $3.462 trillion in tax revenues. Most of this amount came from three taxes: the individual income tax, the corporate income tax, and payroll taxes.

Deficits, Surpluses, and the Public Debt

- If government expenditures are greater than tax revenues, a budget deficit results; if government expenditures are less than tax revenues, a budget surplus results. If government expenditures equal tax revenues, the budget is balanced. Budget deficits are predicted for the near future.
- A cyclical deficit is the part of the budget deficit that is a result of a downturn in economic activity.
- A structural deficit is the part of the deficit that would exist if the economy were operating at full employment.
- Total budget deficit = Structural deficit + Cyclical deficit.
- The public debt is the total amount that the federal government owes its creditors.

Fiscal Policy: General Remarks

- Fiscal policy consists of changes in government expenditures and/or taxes to achieve economic goals. Expansionary fiscal policy entails increases in government expenditures and/or decreases in taxes. Contractionary fiscal policy entails decreases in government expenditures and/or increases in taxes.

Demand-Side Fiscal Policy: A Keynesian Perspective

- In Keynesian theory, demand-side fiscal policy can be used to rid the economy of a recessionary gap or an inflationary gap. A recessionary gap calls for expansionary fiscal policy, and an inflationary gap calls for contractionary fiscal policy. Ideally, fiscal policy changes aggregate demand sufficiently to rid the economy of either a recessionary gap or an inflationary gap.

Crowding Out

- Crowding out is the decrease in private expenditures that occurs as a consequence of increased government spending and/or the greater need to finance a budget deficit. The crowding-out effect suggests that expansionary fiscal policy does not work to the degree that Keynesian theory predicts.

- Complete (incomplete) crowding out occurs when the decrease in one or more components of private spending completely (partially) offsets the increase in government spending.

Why Demand-Side Fiscal Policy May be Ineffective

- Demand-side fiscal policy may be ineffective at achieving certain macroeconomic goals because of (1) crowding out and (2) lags.

Supply-Side Fiscal Policy

- When fiscal policy measures affect tax rates, they may affect both aggregate supply and aggregate demand. It is generally accepted that a marginal tax rate reduction increases the attractiveness of work relative to leisure and tax-avoidance activities and thus leads to an increase in aggregate supply.
- Tax revenues equal the tax base multiplied by the (average) tax rate. Whether tax revenues decrease or increase as a result of a tax rate reduction depends on whether the percentage increase in the tax base is greater or less than the percentage reduction in the tax rate. If the percentage increase in the tax base is greater than the percentage reduction in the tax rate, then tax revenues will increase. If the percentage increase in the tax base is less than the percentage reduction in the tax rate, then tax revenues will decrease.

Key Terms and Concepts

Progressive Income Tax
Proportional Income Tax
Regressive Income Tax
Budget Deficit
Budget Surplus
Balanced Budget
Cyclical Deficit
Structural Deficit
Public Debt
Fiscal Policy
Expansionary Fiscal Policy
Contractionary Fiscal Policy
Discretionary Fiscal Policy
Automatic Fiscal Policy
Crowding Out
Complete Crowding Out
Incomplete Crowding Out
Marginal (Income) Tax Rate
Laffer Curve
Tax Base

Questions and Problems

1. What is the difference between government expenditures and government purchases?
2. How much were government expenditures in 2019? How much were government tax revenues in 2019?
3. The bulk of federal government expenditures go to four programs. What are they?
4. What percentage of total income did the top 10 percent of income earners earn in 2017? What percentage of federal income taxes did this group pay in 2017?
5. Is it true that, under a proportional income tax structure, a person who earns a high income will pay more in taxes than a person who earns a low income? Explain your answer.
6. A progressive income tax always raises more revenue than a proportional income tax does. Do you agree or disagree? Explain your answer.
7. Yuri favors progressive taxation and equal after-tax pay for equal work. Comment.
8. What is the difference between a structural deficit and a cyclical deficit?
9. What is the difference between discretionary fiscal policy and automatic fiscal policy?
10. According to Buchanan and Wagner, why is there a political bias toward expansionary fiscal policy and not contractionary fiscal policy?
11. Explain two ways crowding out may occur.
12. Why is crowding out an important issue in the debate over the use of fiscal policy?
13. Some economists argue for the use of fiscal policy to solve economic problems; others argue against it. What are some of the arguments on both sides?
14. Give a numerical example to illustrate the difference between complete crowding out and incomplete crowding out.
15. The debate over using government spending and taxing powers to stabilize the economy involves more than technical economic issues. Do you agree or disagree? Explain your answer.

16. Is crowding out equally likely under all economic conditions? Explain your answer.
17. Tax cuts will likely affect aggregate demand and aggregate supply. Does it matter which is affected more? Explain in terms of the *AD–AS* framework.
18. Explain how, under certain conditions, expansionary fiscal policy can destabilize the economy.
19. Identify and explain the five lags associated with fiscal policy.
20. Suppose the economy is in a recessionary gap, and both Smith and Jones advocate expansionary fiscal policy. Does it follow that both Smith and Jones favor so-called big government?
21. Will tax cuts that the public perceives to be temporary affect the *SRAS* and *LRAS* curves differently than tax cuts that are perceived to be permanent? Explain your answer.
22. What is the difference between a marginal tax rate and an average tax rate?
23. Will tax revenue necessarily rise if tax rates are lowered? Explain your answer.
24. Gabrielle is sitting with a friend at a coffee shop, and they are talking about the new tax bill. Gabrielle thinks that cutting tax rates at this time would be wrong: "Lower tax rates," she says, "will lead to a larger budget deficit, and the budget deficit is already plenty big." Do lower tax rates mean a larger deficit? Why or why not?

Working with Numbers and Graphs

Use the following table to answer questions 1–4:

Taxable Income	Income Taxes
$1,000–$5,000	10% of taxable income
$5,001–$10,000	$500 + 12% of everything over $5,000
$10,001–$15,000	$1,100 + 15% of everything over $10,000

1. If a person's income is $6,000, how much does he pay in taxes?
2. If a person's income is $14,000, how much does she pay in taxes?
3. What is the marginal tax rate on the 10,001st dollar? What is the marginal tax rate on the 10,000th dollar?
4. What is the average tax rate of someone with a taxable income of $13,766?
5. A hypothetical society has three income earners, and all three must pay income taxes. The taxable income of Ciara is $40,000, the taxable income of Isabella is $100,000, and the taxable income of Justin is $200,000.
    a. How much tax revenue is raised under a proportional income tax when the tax rate is 10 percent? How much is raised if the tax rate is 15 percent?
    b. A progressive tax system is installed with a rate of 5 percent on income of $0–$40,000, a rate of 8 percent on income from $40,001 to $100,000, and a rate of 15 percent on all income over $100,000. Will this system raise more or less tax revenue than a proportional tax rate of 10 percent? Explain your answer.
6. Show graphically how fiscal policy works in the ideal case.
7. Illustrate graphically how government can use supply-side fiscal policy to get an economy out of a recessionary gap.
8. Illustrate the following graphically:
    a. Fiscal policy destabilizes the economy.
    b. Fiscal policy eliminates an inflationary gap.
    c. Fiscal policy only partly eliminates a recessionary gap.

CHAPTER 12

Money, Banking, and the Financial System

Introduction

This chapter is about money: how it emerged out of a barter economy and the functions it serves. It is also about banking: how it came to exist and how it looks today. Finally, it is about the financial system in the United States: what it is and what it does.

12-1 Money: What Is It and How Did It Come to Be?

The story of money starts with a definition and a history lesson. This section discusses what money is and isn't (the definition) and how money came to be (the history lesson).

12-1a Money: A Definition

To the noneconomist, the words "income," "credit," and "wealth" are synonyms for "money." In each of the next three sentences, the word "money" is used incorrectly; the word in parentheses is the word an economist would use.

1. How much money (income) did you earn last year?
2. Most of her money (wealth) is tied up in real estate.
3. It sure is difficult to get money (credit) in today's tight mortgage market.

In economics, the words "money," "income," "credit," and "wealth" are not synonyms. The most general definition of **money** is any good that is widely accepted for purposes of exchange (payment for goods and services) and the repayment of debt.

Money
Any good that is widely accepted for purposes of exchange and the repayment of debt.

12-1b Three Functions of Money

Money has three major functions; it is a

1. Medium of exchange.
2. Unit of account.
3. Store of value.

Money as a Medium of Exchange If money did not exist, goods would have to be exchanged by **barter**—that is, the exchange of goods and services for other goods and services, without the use of money. If you wanted a shirt, you would have to trade some good in your possession, say, a jackknife, for it. But first, you would have to locate a person who has a shirt and who wants to trade it for a knife. In a money economy, searching for a seller is not necessary. You can either (1) exchange money for a shirt or (2) exchange the knife for money and then the money for the shirt. The buyer of the knife and the seller of the shirt do not have to be the same person. Money is the medium through which the exchange occurs; it acts as a **medium of exchange**. As such, money reduces the *transaction costs* of exchanges. Exchange is easier and less time consuming in a money economy than in a barter economy.

Money as a Unit of Account A **unit of account** is a common measure in which values are expressed. In a barter economy, the value of every good is expressed in terms of all other goods; there is no common unit of measure. For example, 1 horse might equal 100 bushels of wheat, or 200 bushels of apples, or 20 pairs of shoes, or 10 suits, or 55 loaves of bread, and so on. In a money economy, a person doesn't have to know the price of an apple in terms of oranges, pizzas, chickens, or potato chips, as in a barter economy. A person needs only to know the price in terms of money. And because all goods are denominated in money, determining relative prices is easy and quick. For example, if 1 apple is $1 and 1 orange is 50¢, then 1 apple is worth 2 oranges.

Money as a Store of Value The function we call a **store of value** is related to a good's ability to maintain its value over time. This is the least exclusive function of money, because other goods—for example, paintings, houses, and stamps—can store value too. At times, money has not maintained its value well, such as during periods of high inflation. For the most part, though, money has served as a satisfactory store of value. This function allows us to accept payment in money for our productive efforts and to keep that money until we decide how we want to spend it.

Barter
Exchanging goods and services for other goods and services without the use of money.

Medium of Exchange
Anything that is generally acceptable in exchange for goods and services; a function of money.

Unit of Account
A common measure in which relative values are expressed; a function of money.

Store of Value
The ability of an item to hold value over time; a function of money.

12-1c From a Barter Economy to a Money Economy: The Origins of Money

The thing that differentiates man and animals is money.

—Gertrude Stein

At one time, there was trade but no money. Instead, people bartered. They traded one apple for two eggs, a banana for a peach.

Today we live in a money economy, but how did we move from a barter to a money economy? Did a king or queen issue an edict: "Let there be money"? Actually, money evolved in a much more natural, market-oriented manner.

Making exchanges takes longer (on average) in a barter economy than in a money economy because the *transaction costs* are higher in a barter economy. In other words, the time and effort incurred to consummate an exchange are greater in a barter economy than in a money economy.

Suppose *A* wants to trade apples for oranges in a barter economy. He locates *B*, who has oranges. *A* offers to trade apples for oranges, but *B* tells *A* that she does not like apples and would rather have peaches. Then *A* must either (1) find someone who has oranges and who wants to trade oranges for apples or (2) find someone who has peaches and who wants to trade peaches for apples, after which he must return to *B* and trade peaches for oranges. Suppose *A* continues to search and finds *C*, who has oranges and wants to trade oranges for (*A*'s) apples. In economics terminology, *A* and *C* are said to have a **double coincidence of wants**. Two people have a double coincidence of wants if what the first person wants is what the second person has and what the second person wants is what the first person has. A double coincidence of wants is a necessary condition for a trade to take place.

In a barter economy, some goods are more readily accepted than others in an exchange. This characteristic may originally be the result of chance, but when traders notice the difference in marketability, their behavior tends to reinforce the effect. To see why, suppose that, of 10 goods *A–J*, good *G* is the most marketable (the most acceptable). On average, good *G* is accepted 5 of every 10 times it is offered in an exchange, whereas the remaining goods are accepted, on average, only 2 of every 10 times. Given this difference, some individuals accept good *G* simply because of its relatively greater acceptability, even though they have no plans to consume it. They accept good *G* because they know that they can easily trade it for most other goods at a later time (unlike the item originally in their possession). Thus, the marketability of good *G* snowballs. The more people accept good *G* for its relatively greater acceptability, the greater its relative acceptability becomes, in turn causing more people to accept it.

This is how money evolved. When good *G*'s acceptance evolves to the point that it is widely accepted for purposes of exchange, good *G* is money. Historically, goods that have evolved into money include gold, silver, copper, cattle, salt, cocoa beans, and shells.

Double Coincidence of Wants
In a barter economy, a requirement that must be met before a trade can be made. The term specifies that a trader must find another trader who at the same time is willing to trade what the first trader wants and wants what the first trader has.

Finding Economics

In a POW Camp You wouldn't think you could find money in a prisoner-of-war (POW) camp, but you can. During World War II, an American, R. A. Radford, was captured and imprisoned in a POW camp. While in the camp, he made some observations about economic developments, which he later described in the journal *Economica*. He noted that the Red Cross would periodically distribute packages to the prisoners that contained such goods as cigarettes, toiletries, chocolate, cheese, jam, margarine, and tinned beef. Not all the prisoners had the same preferences for the goods. For example, some liked chocolate more than others; some smoked cigarettes, and others did not. Because of their preferences, the prisoners began to trade, say, a chocolate bar for cheese, and a barter system emerged. After a short while, money appeared in the camp, but not U.S. dollars or any other government currency. The good that emerged as money—the good that was widely accepted for purposes of exchange—was cigarettes. As Radford noted, "The cigarette became the standard of value. In the permanent camp people started by wandering through the bungalows calling their offers—'cheese for seven [cigarettes].'"

12-1d Money, Leisure, and Output

Exchanges take less time in a money economy than in a barter economy because a double coincidence of wants (when it comes to goods) is unnecessary: Everyone is willing to trade for money. The movement from a barter to a money economy therefore frees up some of the transaction time, which people can use in other ways.

To illustrate, suppose making trades takes 10 hours a week in a barter economy, but only 1 hour in a money economy. In a money economy, then, each week has 9 hours that don't have to be spent making exchanges and that people can use for other purposes. Some will use them to work, others will use them for leisure, and still others will divide the 9 hours between work and leisure. Thus, a money economy is likely to have both more output (because of the increased production) and more leisure time than a barter economy. In other words, a money economy is likely to be richer in both goods and leisure than a barter economy.

A person's standard of living depends, to a degree, on the number and quality of goods the person consumes and on the amount of leisure he or she consumes. We would thus expect the average person's standard of living to be higher in a money economy than in a barter economy.

Finding Economics

With William Shakespeare in London It is the early 1590s, and William Shakespeare is sitting at a desk writing the prologue to *Romeo and Juliet*. Where is the economics?

More specifically, what is the connection between Shakespeare's writing a play and the emergence of money out of a barter economy? In a money economy, individuals usually specialize in the production of one good or service because they can do so. In a barter economy, specializing is extremely costly. For Shakespeare, living in a barter economy would mean writing plays all day and then going out and trying to trade what he had written that day for apples, oranges, chickens, and bread. Would the baker trade two loaves of bread for two pages of *Romeo and Juliet*? Had Shakespeare lived in a barter economy, he would have soon learned that he did not have a double coincidence of wants with many people and that, if he were going to eat and be housed, he would need to spend time baking bread, raising chickens, and building a shelter instead of thinking about *Romeo and Juliet*.

In a barter economy, trade is difficult, so people produce for themselves. In a money economy, trade is easy, so individuals produce one thing, sell it for money, and then buy what they want with the money. A William Shakespeare who lived in a barter economy would no doubt spend his days very differently from the William Shakespeare who lived in England in the sixteenth century. Put bluntly, without money, the world might never have enjoyed *Romeo and Juliet*.

12-2 Defining the Money Supply

If money is any good that is widely accepted for purposes of exchange, is a $10 bill money? Is a dime money? Is a checking account or a savings account money? What constitutes money? In other words, what is included in the money supply? Two frequently used definitions of the money supply are M1 and M2.

Federal Reserve System (the Fed)
The central bank of the United States.

Currency
Coins and paper money.

Savings Deposit
An interest-earning account at a commercial bank or thrift institution.

Money Market Deposit Account (MMDA)
An interest-earning account at a bank or thrift institution, for which a minimum balance is usually required and most of which offer limited check-writing privileges.

Time Deposit
An interest-earning deposit with *a specified maturity date*. Time deposits are subject to penalties for early withdrawal—that is, withdrawal before the maturity date. Small-denomination time deposits are deposits of less than $100,000.

Money Market Mutual Fund (MMMF)
An interest-earning account at a mutual fund company, for which a minimum balance is usually required and most of which offer limited check-writing privileges.

12-2a M1

Beginning in May 2020, the **Federal Reserve System (the Fed)**, which is the central bank of the United States, defined the M1 money supply as consisting of (1) **currency** held outside banks, (2) demand deposits, and (3) other liquid deposits.

Demand deposits are non-interest-earning deposits with banks that are available "on demand" at any time without any restrictions. Other liquid deposits consist of *other checkable deposits* and **savings deposits** (including **money market deposit accounts**). Other checkable accounts (which do pay interest) include such items as NOW balances (negotiable order of withdrawal) at depository institutions and share draft accounts at credit unions.

Now let's simplify things. M1 is sometimes referred to as the *narrow definition of the money supply* or as *transactions money*; it consists of the most liquid forms of money. These are items that can easily and readily be used to make everyday transactions. For this reason, a simpler way to define the M1 money supply is to say it is equal to (a) currency plus transaction deposits or (b) currency plus checkable deposits. We choose the latter – currency plus checkable deposits. So think of things this way: we are lumping together items (2) and (3) in the Fed definition of the M1 money supply under *checkable deposits*. So, we say that M1 money supply is equal to currency held outside banks plus checkable deposits. This is clearly consistent with the Fed, when it states that:

> Physical currency and checkable bank deposits constitute money. And, indeed, these objects make up the definition of what economists label as the M1 money supply.[1]

12-2b M2

Now let's turn to M2, which is sometimes referred to as the *broad measure of the money supply*. This consists of more components than M1. First, M2 includes M1. In other words, everything that is in M1 – such as currency and checkable deposits – is in M2 too. Specifically, beginning in May 2020, the Fed defined M2 as consisting of (1) M1, (2) small-denomination time deposits and (3) retail money market mutual funds.

A **time deposit** is an interest-earning deposit with a specified maturity date and is subject to penalties for early withdrawal – that is before the maturity date. (Small-denomination time deposits are time deposits of less than $100,000). A **money market mutual fund** is an interest-earning account at a mutual fund company for which a minimum balance is usually required.

In May 2020, M1 was $16,275 billion and M2 was $17,893 billion. In April 2021, M1 had risen to $18,935 billion and M2 had risen to $20,108 billion. As an aside, we mention a historical note here. Prior to May 2020, there was a larger dollar difference between M1 and M2 than there is today. That's because M1 didn't include some items that it does today. To give you some idea of the difference in M1 and M2 before May 2020, consider that in November 2019 M1 was $3,845 billion and M2 was $15,304 billion.

12-2c Money Is More Than Currency

Most noneconomists hear the word "money" and think of currency—paper money (dollar bills) and coins. For example, if a thief stops you on a dark street at night and demands, "Your money or your life," you can be sure the thief wants your currency. People often

---

[1] *What's behind the recent surge in the M1 money supply?* The FRED Blog, January 11, 2021.

equate money and currency. To an economist, though, money is more than just currency. According to the M1 definition, money is currency and checkable deposits. (However, if robbed by a thief, economists would be unlikely to hand over their currency and then write a check too.)

Economics 24/7

Why Hold Cash and How Would Things Be Different if There Were No Cash?

Here is a way to "make money": Let's say that you have $10,000 cash. You can take the cash and purchase a risk-free government bond with it that pays, say, 2 percent interest and turn $10,000 into $10,200. Easy!

Now suppose the dollar amounts are greater. Suppose you have $10 million cash. You can take the cash and again purchase a risk-free government bond that pays a 2 percent interest rate. This time you would have turned $10 million into $10.2 million.

If we have found such an easy way to turn every dollar bill into more than one-dollar bill, why does anyone hold cash? Why keep an asset in cash form instead of in risk-free government-bond form? The answer is that while the government bond provides something that cash does not—interest—cash also provides something that the government bond does not—convenience. We can say that there is a *convenience yield* to holding cash. There is an obvious convenience to holding cash in that it can easily and quickly be used to make purchases that you want to make.

Cash also has the ability to hide transactions. To illustrate, suppose someone wants to evade paying taxes. If A pays B $100 cash for a service performed, there is no record of that $100 being earned by B, and therefore, if B does not report that $100 as income, B does not pay taxes on that $100 income.

Cash can also hide illegal transactions. This time, A wants to bribe B, and B wants to accept the bribe. Is the bribe less likely to be caught if A writes a check to B or pays him in cash?

Cash, of course. Or suppose A wants to buy illegal drugs from B. Check or cash? Cash again. Like it or not, part of the convenience yield of cash comes from its ability to hide certain transactions.

Recently, some advocate for becoming a cashless society in order to reduce illegal and tax-evasion transactions. Without cash, without physical paper money, people couldn't engage in tax evasion (certainly not as easily) and illegal drug transactions would be curtailed. And, of course, without cash, it would make it much harder to be mugged for your money.

But there may be some unintended effects of banning cash. Perhaps there would be far fewer children standing in front of their houses selling lemonade on a hot summer day. And without cash, there would be a record of almost all transactions. A cashless society is one in which every transaction must be passed through banks, credit card companies, phone providers (think of mobile money, an electronic wallet service—which allows individuals to store, send, and receive money using their mobile phone), and payment apps. The proponents of keeping cash argue that in a cashless society, a degree of personal purchasing privacy is lost.

In Sweden, only about 3 percent of transactions are made with cash. It is the country that comes closest today to being a cashless society. You can see a YouTube video on Sweden and its largely cashless society at https://www.youtube.com/watch?v=LoZ3Yk1I_2o.

12-2d Where Do Credit Cards Fit In?

A credit card is commonly referred to as plastic money, but it is not money. A credit card is an instrument or a document that makes it easier for the holder to obtain a loan. When Jaslyn hands the department store clerk her MasterCard or Visa, she is, in effect, spending someone else's money (which already existed). The department store submits the claim to the bank, the bank pays the department store, and then the bank bills the holder of its credit card. By using her credit card, Jaslyn spends someone else's money, and she ultimately must repay her credit card debt with money. These transactions shift around the existing quantity of money among individuals and firms, but they do not change the total.

(Answers to Self-Test questions are in Answers to Self-Test Questions at the back of the book.)

1. Why (not how) did money evolve out of a barter economy?
2. If individuals remove funds from their demand deposits and transfer them to their money market deposit accounts, will M1 fall? Explain your answer.
3. How does money reduce the transaction costs of making trades?

Economics 24/7

M-Pesa Instead of Cash in Kenya

In the United States, if you have cash that you would like to deposit into a checking account, it is fairly easy to do so. You can easily open up a checking account with one of the thousands of commercial banks in the country. No doubt, there is one near where you live. In Africa, if you have cash that you would like to deposit into a checking account, you may not be able to do so as easily as in the United States. Why? Because you may live in a place where there are no banks nearby. For many people in Africa, this means that they will go without a bank account. For these people, it means that they have to buy all their goods with cash, and if they want to send money to relatives who live far away from them, they would have to send cash through the mail or wire the funds (which often comes with expensive fees that need to be paid).

M-Pesa is a mobile phone–based money transfer service. The M in M-Pesa stands for mobile and pesa is the Swahili word for money. M-Pesa was launched in 2007 by Vodafone. Initially, it operated in Keyna and Tanzania, but today it operates in more countries, such as Afghanistan, South Africa, India, Egypt, and others. Here is how people—say, living in Kenya—would get started using M-Pesa.

First, they purchase a SIM card from a telecommunications company called Safaricom. A SIM card is a microchip in a cell phone that connects to a particular phone network.

Second, they activate M-Pesa on their cell phone.

Third, they take the cash that they have and go to a M-Pesa booth or kiosk that can be found in a supermarket, pharmacy, or

> phone shop. They tell the person at the booth, kiosk, or phone shop their cell phone number and hand them the cash. At this point, the person working at the M-Pesa booth confirms their customers' identity using their phone. Their phone number effectively becomes their bank account number. Next, they will receive a text message that their balance in their M-Pesa account has a balance of so many Kenyan shillings (the currency of Kenya).
>
> Fourth, now they can send money to someone, withdraw cash, get a microloan, and more. Let's say they want to send money to a friend. They would go to the main menu on the M-Pesa app, enter the phone number of the person they want to send money to (if this person has M-Pesa too, then the person's phone number is his or her account number), identify the amount of money they want to transfer, and then enter their M-Pesa PIN (personal identification number). If they want to buy something from a retailer, they would input the retailer's specific M-Pesa number, state the amount to transfer to the retailer, and then enter their PIN.

12-3 How Banking Developed

Just as money evolved, so did banking. This section discusses the origins of banking and sheds some light on, and aids in understanding, modern banking.

12-3a The Early Bankers

Our money today is easy to carry and transport, but it was not always so portable. For example, when money consisted principally of gold coins, carrying it about was neither easy nor safe. First, gold is heavy. Second, gold was not only inconvenient for customers to carry, but it was also inconvenient for merchants to accept. Third, a person transporting thousands of gold coins can easily draw the attention of thieves. Yet storing gold at home can also be risky. Most individuals therefore turned to their local goldsmiths for help because they had safe storage facilities. Goldsmiths were thus the first bankers. They took in other people's gold and stored it for them. To acknowledge that they held deposited gold, goldsmiths issued receipts, called *warehouse receipts*, to their customers.

Once people's confidence in the receipts was established, they used the receipts to make payments instead of using the gold itself. In time, the paper warehouse receipts circulated as money. For instance, if Antonio wanted to buy something from Christine that was priced at 10 gold pieces, he could simply give his warehouse receipt to Christine instead of going to the goldsmith, obtaining the gold, and then delivering it to Christine. For both Antonio and Christine, using the receipts was easier than exchanging the actual gold.

At this stage of banking, warehouse receipts were fully backed by gold; they simply represented gold in storage. Goldsmiths later began to recognize that, on an average day, few people redeemed their receipts for gold. Many individuals traded the receipts for goods and seldom requested the gold itself. In short, the receipts had become money, widely accepted for purposes of exchange.

Sensing opportunity, goldsmiths began to lend some of the stored gold, realizing that they could earn interest on the loans without defaulting on their pledge to redeem the warehouse receipts when presented. In most cases, however, the gold borrowers also preferred warehouse receipts to the actual gold. Thus, the warehouse receipts came to represent a greater amount of gold than was actually on deposit. Consequently, the money supply increased, now measured in terms of gold and the paper warehouse receipts issued by the goldsmith–bankers.

Thus, **fractional reserve banking** had begun. In a fractional reserve system, banks create money by holding on reserve only a fraction of the money deposited with them and lending the remainder.

Fractional Reserve Banking
A banking arrangement that allows banks to hold reserves equal to only a fraction of their deposit liabilities.

Economics 24/7

Economics on the Yellow Brick Road

I'll get you, my pretty.

—Wicked Witch of the West in *The Wizard of Oz*

In 1893, the United States fell into economic depression. The stock market crashed, banks failed, workers were laid off, and many farmers lost their farms. Some people blamed the depression on the gold standard. They proposed that, instead of having only gold backing U.S. currency, the monetary standard should be bimetallic; that is, both gold and silver should back the currency. This change, they said, would lead to an increase in the money supply. Many people thought that, with more money in circulation, economic hard times would soon be a thing of the past.

One of the champions of silver was William Jennings Bryan, the Democratic candidate for the U.S. presidency in 1896. Bryan had established himself as a friend to the many Americans who had been hurt by the depression, especially farmers and industrial workers. Bryan's views were shared by L. Frank Baum, the author of *The Wonderful Wizard of Oz*, the book that was the basis for the 1939 movie *The Wizard of Oz*.

Baum blamed the gold standard for the hardships faced by farmers and workers during the depression. Baum saw the farmer and the worker as the so-called average person, and he saw William Jennings Bryan as the best-possible hope for the average person in this country.

Many people believe that Baum's most famous work, *The Wonderful Wizard of Oz*, is an allegory for the presidential election of 1896.[2] Some say that Dorothy, in the book and the movie, represents Bryan. Both Dorothy and Bryan were young. (Bryan was a 36-year-old presidential candidate.) Like the cyclone in the movie that transported Dorothy to the Land of Oz, the delegates at the 1896 Democratic National Convention lifted Bryan into a new political world, the world of presidential politics.

As Dorothy begins her travels to the Emerald City (Washington, D.C.) with Toto (the Democratic Party) to meet the Wizard of Oz, she travels down a yellow brick road (the gold standard). On her way, she meets the scarecrow (the farmer), the tin man (the industrial worker), and the cowardly lion, who some believe represents the Populist Party of the time. (The Populist Party was sometimes depicted as a lion in the political cartoons of the time. It was a cowardly lion in that, as some say, it did not have the courage to fight an independent campaign for the presidency in 1896.) The message is clear: Bryan, with the help of the Democratic and Populist parties and with the votes of the farmers and the industrial workers, will travel to Washington.

But then, when Dorothy and the others reach the Emerald City, they are denied their wishes, just as Bryan is denied the presidency. He loses the election to William McKinley.

But the story is not over. There is still the battle with the Wicked Witch of the West, who wears a golden cap (the gold standard). When the Wicked Witch sees Dorothy's silver shoes—they were changed to ruby in the movie—she desperately wants them for their magical quality. But she is not to get her way. Dorothy kills the Wicked Witch of the West. She then clicks her silver shoes together, and they take her back home, where all is right with the world.

[2.] This interpretation is based on "William Jennings Bryan on the Yellow Brick Road," by John Geer and Thomas Rochon, *Journal of American Culture* (Winter 1993), pp. 59–63, and "The Wizard of Oz: Parable on Populism," by Henry Littlefield, *American Quarterly* (Spring 1964), pp. 47–58.

1. How exactly were goldsmiths the first bankers?

2. What is a fractional reserve banking system?

12-4 The Financial System

A financial system is essentially a means of getting people with surplus funds together with people who have a shortage of funds. Stated differently, it is a means of getting lenders (i.e., savers) and borrowers together.

Why is getting lenders and borrowers together important? The short answer is that getting them together is a way to put good ideas into action. Suppose you have saved funds that you want to lend. Elsewhere, someone has a shortage of funds but an idea for a new business venture. That person doesn't have the necessary funds to launch his new business venture. He needs to find people like you—people with funds to lend—who wouldn't mind trading him your funds now in return for his making interest payments to you later.

Thus, an economy that can get saved funds to borrowers can benefit not only the lenders but the borrowers too. And it can also benefit others. If the borrower really does have a good idea for a new business venture, future customers will benefit when the business is up and running. Maybe the firm will produce something that many thousands of others want to buy.

12-4a Direct and Indirect Finance

Lenders can get together with borrowers directly or indirectly; that is, there are two types of finance: direct and indirect. In **direct finance**, the lenders and borrowers come together in a market setting, such as the bond market, in which people who want to borrow funds issue bonds. For example, company A might issue a bond that promises to pay an interest rate of 10 percent annually for the next 10 years. A person with funds to lend might then buy that bond for a particular price. The buying and selling in a bond market are simply lending and borrowing. The buyer of the bond is the lender, and the seller of the bond is the borrower.

In **indirect finance**, lenders and borrowers go through a **financial intermediary**, which takes in funds from people who want to save and then lend the funds to people who want to borrow. For example, a commercial bank is a financial intermediary, doing business with both savers and borrowers. Through one door come the savers, looking for a place to deposit their funds and earn regular interest payments. Through another door come the borrowers, seeking loans on which they will pay interest. The bank, or the financial intermediary, ends up channeling the saved funds to borrowers.

12-4b Adverse Selection Problems and Moral Hazard Problems

When it comes to lending and borrowing, adverse selection or moral hazards can arise. Both are the result of **asymmetric information**, a situation in which one party to a transaction has information that the other party does not have. For example, suppose Ursula is going to sell her house. As the seller of the house, she has more information about it than potential buyers have. Ursula knows whether the house has plumbing problems, cracks in the foundation, and so on. Potential buyers do not.

The effect of asymmetric information can be either an adverse selection problem or a moral hazard problem. The adverse selection problem occurs *before* the loan is made, and the moral hazard problem occurs *afterward*.

Direct Finance
A method of transferring money whereby borrowers and lenders come together in a market setting, such as the bond market.

Indirect Finance
A method of transferring money whereby funds are loaned and borrowed through a financial intermediary.

Financial Intermediary
An institution that transfers funds from those who want to lend funds to those who want to borrow them.

Asymmetric Information
A situation in which an economic agent on one side of a transaction has information that an economic agent on the other side of the transaction does not have.

Adverse Selection
A phenomenon that occurs when parties on one side of the market who have information not known to others self-select in a way that adversely affects parties on the other side of the market.

Before the Loan Is Made An **adverse selection** problem occurs when parties on one side of the market have information not known to others and self-select on the basis of that information in a way that adversely affects parties on the other side of the market. Think of it this way: Two people want a loan. One person is a good credit risk, and the other is a bad credit risk. The person who is the bad credit risk is the person more likely to ask for the loan, and that situation is an instance of adverse selection.

Suppose two people, Steven and Shannel, want to borrow $10,000, and Jason has $10,000 to lend. Shannel wants to borrow the $10,000 to buy a piece of equipment for her small business. She plans to pay back the loan, and she takes her loan commitments seriously. Steven wants to borrow the $10,000 so that he can go to Las Vegas and play roulette. He will pay back the loan only if he scores big in Las Vegas. He is not the type of person who takes his loan commitments seriously. Who is more likely to ask Jason for the loan, Steven or Shannel? Steven is, because he knows that he will pay back the loan only if he wins big in Las Vegas; he sees a loan as essentially "free money." Heads, Steven wins; tails, Jason loses.

Now, if Jason gives a little thought to his lending activities, he may realize that there are borrowers like Steven in the world. Ideally, Jason wants to lend only to the Shannels of the world, but Jason can't always tell who is a Shannel and who is a Steven. On the one hand, Shannel will tell Jason the truth about what she wants to do with the loan, and she is likely to pay back the loan. On the other hand, Steven may lie to Jason about what he plans to do with the loan, and he is not as likely to pay back the loan as Shannel is.

If Jason can't tell the Shannels from the Stevens, what can he do? He might just decide not to give a loan to anyone. In other words, his inability to solve the adverse selection problem (i.e., to tell the good risks from the bad risks) may be enough for him to decide not to lend to anyone.

At this point, a financial intermediary can help. A financial intermediary, such as a bank, does not require Jason to worry about who will and who will not pay back a loan. Jason needs simply to turn over his saved funds to the bank, in return for the bank's promise to pay him a 5 percent interest rate per year. Then the bank takes on the responsibility of trying to separate the Shannels from the Stevens. The bank will run a credit check on everyone (the Shannels and Stevens alike); the bank will collect information on who has a job and who doesn't; the bank will ask the borrower to put up some collateral on the loan; and so on. In other words, the bank's job is to solve the adverse selection problem.

Moral Hazard
A condition that exists when one party to a transaction changes his or her behavior in a way that is hidden from, and costly to, the other party.

After the Loan Is Made A **moral hazard** problem occurs when one party to a transaction changes his or her behavior in a way that is hidden from, and is costly to, the other party. Suppose you want to lend some saved funds. You give Tracy a $5,000 loan because she promised you that she was going to use the funds to help her get through college. Instead, once Tracy receives the $5,000, she decides to use the funds to buy some clothes and take a vacation to St. Thomas in the Caribbean.

Because of such potential moral hazard problems, you might decide to cut back on granting loans. You want to protect yourself from borrowers who do things that are costly to you. Again, a financial intermediary has a role to play. A financial intermediary, such as a bank, might try to solve the moral hazard problem by specifying that a loan can be used only for a particular purpose (e.g., paying for college). It might require the borrower to provide regular information on, and evidence of, how the borrowed funds are being used; to accept the loan in installments ($1,000 this month, $1,000 next month); and so on.

Balance Sheet
A record of the assets and liabilities of a bank.

Asset
Anything of value that is owned or that one has claim to.

Liability
Anything that is owed to someone else.

12-4c The Bank's Balance Sheet

We can learn a lot about banks by looking at a bank's **balance sheet**, which lists the bank's assets and liabilities. An **asset** is anything of value that the bank owns or has claim to. A **liability** is anything that the bank owes to someone else. A few examples of a bank's assets are the *reserves*

EXHIBIT 1

A Bank's Balance Sheet

Here we show a bank's balance sheet. On the left-hand side are assets (what others owe to the bank): reserves (equal to bank deposits at the Fed, plus vault cash), any loans the bank has made to others (e.g., a car loan the bank gave to someone), and any securities the bank owns. On the right-hand side are liabilities (what the bank owes to others): checkable deposits (held for the bank's customers), nontransaction deposits (e.g., small-denomination time deposits), and borrowings (i.e., any loans the banks may have taken out). Also, it is customary to show bank capital (or net worth)—the difference between assets and liabilities—on the right-hand side of the balance sheet. In the balance sheet shown, assets are $110 million and liabilities are $100 million, so bank capital (or net worth) is $10 million.

Assets ($ millions)		Liabilities ($ millions)	
Reserves	10	Checkable deposits	50
Loans	90	Nontransaction deposits (e.g., small-denomination time deposits)	50
Securities	10	Borrowings	0
		Bank capital (net worth)	10

the bank holds, any loans the bank has made to borrowers, and any securities the bank might own. A few examples of a bank's liabilities are the checkable deposits it holds for its customers, any nontransaction deposits (such as small-denomination time deposits), and any loans the bank has taken out (e.g., a loan the bank might have received from the Fed). Exhibit 1 shows a simplified, but typical, balance sheet for a bank.

12-4d A Bank's Business: Turning Liabilities Into Assets

A bank's business is to turn its liabilities into assets. Suppose you open up a checkable deposit account with bank A and deposit $10,000 into the account. Your checkable deposit is a liability for the bank. The balance in the checkable deposit account is what the bank *owes* you. The bank then turns the bulk of the funds in your checkable deposit account into an asset. Specifically, the bank might use the bulk of those funds to grant a loan to someone. So a bank wants liabilities because liabilities are its sources of funds—the seeds, if you will—for growing its assets.

The difference between a bank's assets and liabilities constitutes the bank's capital, or its net worth:

$$\text{Bank capital (or net worth)} = \text{Assets} - \text{Liabilities}$$

For example, if a bank has $120 million in assets and $112 million in liabilities, its net worth (or the bank's capital) is equal to $8 million. Typically, a bank's capital is recorded on the right-hand side of its balance sheet, as shown in Exhibit 1.

The bank's capital can be viewed as a cushion against **insolvency**, which exists when a bank's liabilities are greater than its assets:

$$\text{Insolvency} \rightarrow \text{Liabilities} > \text{Assets}$$

An insolvent bank has failed and can be shut down.

Insolvency
A condition in which one's liabilities are greater than one's assets.

1. Esteban promises Ana that he will pay for any expenses she has on her trip beyond $1,000. Does Esteban's promise create an adverse selection problem or a moral hazard problem? Explain your answer.
2. Bank A finds that many of the loans it extended to individuals are not being paid back. How do the defaults affect bank A's capital, or net worth?
3. What do financial intermediaries do?

Office Hours
"Do We Really Need Financial Intermediaries?"

Student: I've heard that financial intermediaries are simply "middlemen." They don't really provide any service other than shuffling money between two groups of people. In other words, they take the money that the lender wants to lend and simply hand it over to the borrower who wants to borrow.

Instructor: Ask yourself, if financial intermediaries did not exist, how would life be different? Would there be as much lending and borrowing activity in the world? Remember, adverse selection problems and moral hazard problems reduce the amount of lending (and therefore borrowing), and because financial intermediaries help to solve these two problems, there would be more lending and borrowing in a world with financial intermediaries than in one without them.

Student: I am assuming that would be bad?

Instructor: Well, recall that lending and borrowing channel funds to those who can use those funds to start businesses, to come up with new products, to establish new and better production techniques, and to do other beneficial things. So lending and borrowing are beneficial not only to the lender and the borrower, but to others too. Your current material standard of living would probably not be as high as it is had you not lived in a country with substantial borrowing and lending.

Besides serving the function of providing financing for new businesses and the production of new products, and so on, lending and borrowing allow people to consume earlier in life than they would otherwise be able to. To illustrate, suppose Maria is 26 years old and wants to buy a condominium. Condos in her area sell for about $300,000, but Maria does not have $300,000; she has only $20,000. Without lending and borrowing, Maria would have to do without the condo until she can save $300,000. But with borrowing and lending, Maria can make a $20,000 down payment on the condo and borrow the remaining $280,000. She can begin living in the condo many years earlier than would otherwise be possible.

In conclusion, lending and borrowing not only provide the financing for new businesses and the production of new products, production techniques, and so on, but they also permit individuals to enjoy the benefits of certain goods and services for a greater number of years than would be possible without lending and borrowing. Because someone will lend her $280,000, Maria gets to enjoy the benefits of her condo for many additional years.

Points to Remember
1. Financial intermediaries often solve adverse selection and moral hazard problems (when it comes to lending and borrowing activity).
2. Financial intermediaries provide financing for new businesses and the production of new products and often allow people to consume earlier in life than they would otherwise be able to.

Chapter Summary

What Money Is

- Money is any good that is widely accepted for purposes of exchange and in the repayment of debts.
- Money serves as a medium of exchange, a unit of account, and a store of value.
- Money evolved out of a barter economy as traders attempted to make exchange easier. A few goods that have been used as money are gold, silver, copper, cattle, rocks, and shells.
- Our money today has value because of its general acceptability.

The Money Supply

- The Fed defines M1 as consisting of currency held outside banks, demand deposits and other liquid deposits. We have simplified things by lumping demand deposits and other liquid deposits together in the category of *checkable deposits*. So, M1 equals currency held outside banks and checkable deposits.
- M2 consists of M1, small-denomination time deposits, and retail money market mutual funds.
- Credit cards are not money. When a credit card is used to make a purchase, a liability is incurred. That is not the case when money is used to make a purchase.

The Financial System

- A financial system is a means of getting people with surplus funds (with funds to lend) together with people who have a shortage of funds (who want to borrow funds).

- Asymmetric information is a situation in which one party to a transaction has information that the other party does not. The two types of asymmetric information problems are adverse selection and moral hazard.
- Adverse selection is a phenomenon in which parties on one side of the market have information not known to others and self-select on the basis of that information in a way that adversely affects parties on the other side of the market.
- Moral hazard is the condition that exists when one party to a transaction changes his or her behavior in a way that is hidden from, and costly to, the other party.

A Bank's Balance Sheet

- A bank's balance sheet records the bank's assets and liabilities.
- A bank's business is to turn its liabilities into assets.
- Bank capital, or net worth, is the difference between a bank's assets and its liabilities. Bank capital (net worth) = Assets − Liabilities.
- A bank is insolvent if its liabilities are greater than its assets.

Key Terms and Concepts

Money
Barter
Medium of Exchange
Unit of Account
Store of Value
Double Coincidence of Wants
Currency
Savings Deposit
Time Deposit
Money Market Deposit Account (MMDA)
Money Market Mutual Fund (MMMF)
Fractional Reserve Banking
Direct Finance
Indirect Finance
Financial Intermediary
Asymmetric Information
Adverse Selection
Moral Hazard
Balance Sheet
Asset
Liability
Insolvency

Questions and Problems

1. "How much money did you make last year?" What is wrong with that statement?
2. Suppose the value of the dollar declines relative to other currencies. How does the decline affect the three functions of money?
3. Does inflation, which is an increase in the price level, affect the three functions of money? If so, how?
4. "People in a barter economy came up with the idea of money because they wanted to do something to make society better off." Do you agree or disagree with this statement? Explain your answer.
5. "A barter economy would have very few comedians." Do you agree or disagree with this statement? Explain your answer.
6. Money makes trade easier. Would having a money supply twice as large as it currently is make trade twice as easy? Would having a money supply half its current size make trade half as easy?
7. Explain why gold backing is not necessary to give paper money value.
8. "Money is a means of lowering the transaction costs of making exchanges." Do you agree or disagree? Explain your answer.
9. If you were on an island with 10 other people and there were no money, do you think that money would emerge on the scene? Why or why not?
10. If the component currency rises, does this affect both M1 and M2 or just M1? Explain your answer.
11. Why isn't a credit card money?
12. Define the following:
    a. Time deposit
    b. Money market mutual fund
    c. Money market deposit account
    d. Fractional reserve banking
13. Explain the process by which goldsmiths could increase the money supply.
14. What is a financial system, and why would a country with a well-developed and fully functionally financial system be better off than a country without it?
15. Identify each of the following as either an adverse selection problem or a moral hazard problem:
    a. Poor drivers apply for car insurance more than good drivers do.
    b. The federal government promises to help banks that get into financial problems.
    c. The federal government insures checkable deposits (promises to repay the holder of the checkable deposit if the bank fails).
16. Explain how financial intermediaries help to solve adverse selection problems and moral hazard problems when it comes to lending and borrowing.
17. Explain the difference between a bank's loans and its borrowings.

Working with Numbers and Graphs

1. A bank's assets are $90 million, and its liabilities are $71 million. Its assets increase by 10 percent, and its liabilities increase by 6 percent. What is the *percentage change* in the bank's capital, or net worth?
2. A bank's assets are $100 million and its liabilities are $80 million. What is the bank's net worth?
3. Suppose M1 is $2,000 billion, small-denomination time deposits are $4,000 billion, and retail money market mutual funds are $3,000 billion. How much does M2 equal?
4. Currency held outside banks is $100 billion, checkable deposits are $1,000 billion, small-denomination time deposits are $300 billion and money market mutual funds are $400 billion. What does M1 equal?

CHAPTER 13

The Federal Reserve System

Introduction

Tourists in Washington, D.C., usually visit the White House, the Capitol, and the Supreme Court, where major decisions are made that affect peoples' lives. Such decisions affecting peoples' lives are also made in another building in Washington, D.C., but tourists rarely visit it: The Federal Reserve. In this building, the Board of Governors of the Federal Reserve System and the members of the Federal Open Market Committee determine U.S. monetary policy. This chapter discusses many of the details of the Federal Reserve System.

13-1 The Structure and Functions of the Federal Reserve System (The Fed)

The **Federal Reserve System (the Fed)** is the central bank of the United States. Other nations have central banks, such as the Bank of Sweden, the Bank of England, the Banque de France, the Bank of Japan, the Deutsche Bundesbank, and the like.

Federal Reserve System (the Fed)
The central bank of the United States.

13-1a The Structure of the Fed

The Federal Reserve System came into existence with the Federal Reserve Act of 1913 and began operations in November 1914. The act divided the country into Federal Reserve Districts. As Exhibit 1 shows, there are 12 districts, each with a Federal Reserve Bank and its own president.

Within the Fed, a seven-member **Board of Governors** coordinates and controls the activities of the Federal Reserve System. The board members serve 14-year terms and are appointed by the president with U.S. Senate approval. To limit political influence on Fed policy, the terms of the governors are staggered—with one new appointment every other year—so that a president cannot "pack" the board. The president also designates one member as chairman of the board for a four-year term.

Board of Governors
The governing body of the Federal Reserve System.

EXHIBIT 1

Federal Reserve Districts and Federal Reserve Bank Locations

The boundaries of the Federal Reserve Districts, the cities in which a Federal Reserve Bank is located, and the location of the Board of Governors (Washington, D.C.) are all noted on the map.

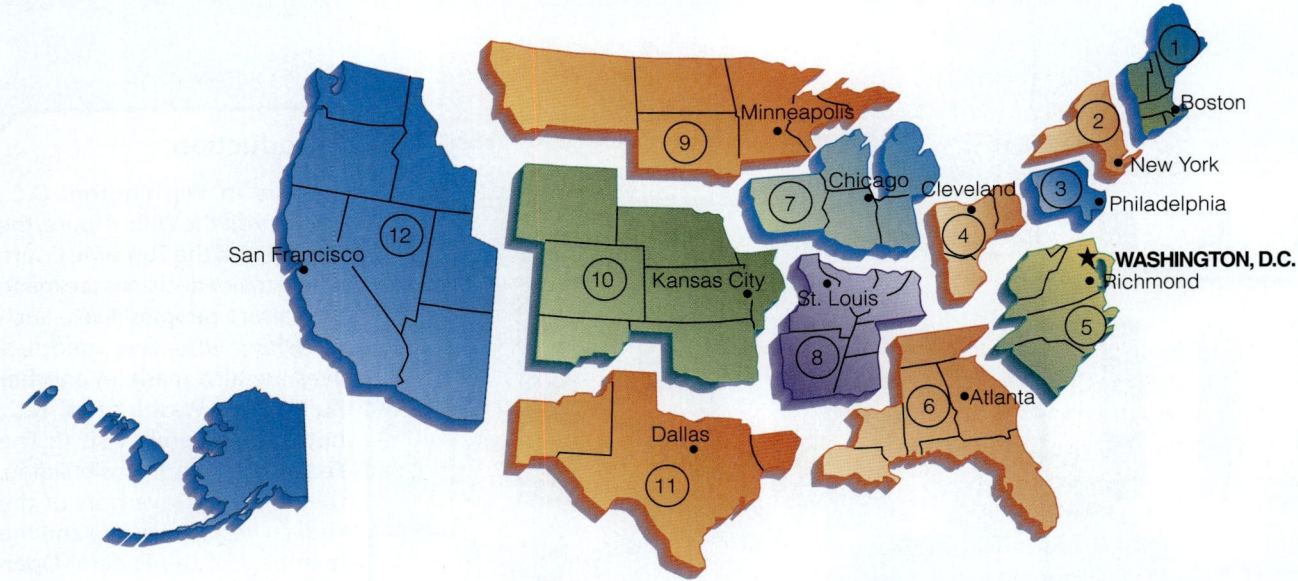

Federal Open Market Committee (FOMC)
The Fed's 12-member policymaking group that reviews economic and financial conditions and determines the appropriate stance of monetary policy.

Monetary Policy
Changes in the money supply and interest rates by the Fed in order to meet certain goals such as maximum employment and stable prices.

The major policymaking group in the Fed is the **Federal Open Market Committee (FOMC)**. The FOMC reviews economic and financial conditions and determines the appropriate stance of monetary policy. **Monetary policy** consists of changes in the money supply and interest rates by the Fed in order to meet certain macroeconomic goals such as maximum employment and stable prices.

13-1b Fed Tools and Monetary Policy: Past and Present

If you were to go to the Federal Reserve website, you would find that the Fed makes this statement: "The Federal Reserve has a variety of policy tools that it uses in order to implement monetary policy." Included in the list of tools are four that we focus on in this text:

1. Open market operations
2. Discount Rate
3. Required Reserve Ratio (Reserve Requirements)
4. Interest on Reserves (IOR) rate and Overnight Reverse Repurchase (ON-RRP) rate

We define all of these policy tools later. For now, we simply acquaint you with the four key policy tools the Fed either has used in the past or currently does use to conduct monetary policy.

Economics 24/7

Central Bank Digital Currency (CBDC): What Does the Future Hold?

On May 20, 2021, the chair of the Federal Reserve, Jerome Powell, made a major announcement. He said that the Fed would, in the summer of 2021, issue a discussion paper outlining current thinking on digital payments—with a particular focus on the benefits and risks associated with CBDC (Central Bank Digital Currency) in the U.S. context.

With this announcement, the Fed indicated that it was open to creating CBDC in the future. But what exactly is CBDC? Simply put, it is a digital form of currency that is backed by a Central Bank and has legal tender status. The "legal tender status" means that a CBDC is recognized by law as a means to settle a public or private debt or meet a financial obligations—such as tax payments, contracts, and legal fines or damages. In other words, a creditor is legally obligated to accept legal tender as payment for a debt. For example, Federal Reserve Notes (dollar bills) and coins are legal tender. Creditors are required to accept them as payment. (As an aside, someone might ask what is an essential difference between, say, bitcoin and CBDC? The answer is that bitcoin is not legal tender, CBDC would be.)

So, how is CBDC different from currency today? Currency, as we learned in the last chapter, consists of paper money and coins. A $10 bill is currency, as is a quarter and a dime. CBDC is similar to the $10 bill and the quarter and dime, except it is a digital representation of the value of that currency. Think of it this way: With a CBDC you might have an account with the Fed (in much the same way that you have a checking account with a bank today). In that account, you would simply have the dollar value of all the physical cash you could instead have. It would be as if someone came to you and asked, "How much cash do you have?" Your answer is $1,200 cash. The person then says, "Would you prefer to keep this cash on you, and use it to buy this and that, or would you prefer to have a Fed account with a $1,200 value?" Keep in mind, too, that you could use the funds in that account to buy goods as easily as you do today with physical cash. You might simply use a mobile app (the Fed might offer its own mobile app) to transfer funds from your Fed account into someone else's.

If a CBDC existed, many people might choose to hold their funds in a Fed account instead of having a checking account with a bank. Of course, one consequence of a significant number of a bank's customers deciding to hold CBDC instead of their bank checking account is that banks couldn't create as many loans. (As you will learn later in the chapter, if you deposit $100 in a bank, much of that $100 can be used to create a loan for someone else.)

There are numerous issues of interest related to CBDC. The issues deal with privacy, counterfeiting, hacking, negative interest rates, monetary policy and more. You can be sure that in the next few years you will continue to hear more about CBDC.

You will notice that we used both the present and past tense when we mentioned the policy tools: tools that the Fed *has used* (in the past) or currently does *use* (in the present). Did we mean to imply that the Fed conducted monetary policy differently in the past than it does today? Indeed, we did.

To provide you with a complete understanding of the Fed's history, we will discuss the Fed's conduct of monetary policy in both the past (in Section 13-2) and present (in Section 13-3).

13-2 The Past: Open Market Operations, Discount Rate, and Required Reserve Ratio (Reserve Requirements)

When it comes to monetary policy, we can talk about the past and the present in three different ways. The first way is in terms of time periods. The past is the period *before* October 2008 and the present is the period *since* October 2008. Why is the date October 2008 so important here? Because October 2008 is when the Fed *first began* to pay interest on reserves, which leads us to the delineation of our second way.

The second way is to say the past is that period during which the Fed did not pay interest on reserves. (We will define *reserves* shortly). The present is that period during which the Fed pays interest on reserves.

The third way is to say the past is the period during which the entire banking system held limited (very low) reserves—for example, reserves of $1 billion. The present is that period during which the banking system holds ample (plentiful) reserves—for example, reserves of $3 trillion or more. (Note: The dramatic increase in reserves in the banking system was largely because the Fed responded to the financial crisis of 2007–2009 and its aftermath with a series of monetary policy measures that greatly increased the supply of reserves.)

Here, in summary form, are the defining characteristics of both the past and the present of the Fed's monetary policy history.

The Past

- Before October 2008
- The Fed did not pay interest on reserves
- The banking system held limited (low) reserves

The Present

- Since October 2008
- The Fed pays interest on reserves
- The banking system holds ample (plentiful) reserves

Before we discuss how monetary policy was conducted in the past, we take some time to define some very important terms.

13-2a Reserves

Many banks have an account with the Fed. This account is similar to a checking account that an individual has with a commercial bank. Economists refer to such an account with the Fed as either a *reserve account* or a *bank deposit at the Fed*. Banks also have currency, or cash, in their vaults—called vault cash—on the bank premises. The sum of (1) bank deposits at the Fed and (2) the bank's vault cash is known as **reserves**:

Reserves
The sum of bank deposits at the Fed and vault cash.

Reserves = Bank deposits at the Fed + Vault cash

Chapter 13 The Federal Reserve System

The Required Reserve Ratio and Required Reserves In the past, the Fed mandated that member commercial banks must hold a certain fraction of their checkable deposits in *reserve form*. In other words, that fraction of checkable deposits had to be in the form of bank deposits at the Fed and/or vault cash because the sum of these two accounts equals reserves.

The fraction of checkable deposits that banks must hold in reserve form is called the **required reserve ratio (r)**. The dollar amount of those deposits is called **required reserves**, and the rule specifying the amount of reserves that a bank must hold to back up deposits is the **reserve requirement**. To find the required reserves for a given bank, multiply the required reserve ratio by checkable deposits (in the bank):

$$\text{Required reserves} = r \times \text{Checkable deposits}$$

For example, assume that customers have deposited $40 million in a neighborhood bank and that the Fed has set the required reserve ratio at 1/10, or 10 percent. Required reserves for the bank then equals $4 million (0.10 × $40 million = $4 million)

Excess Reserves The difference between a bank's (total) reserves and its required reserves is its **excess reserves**:

$$\text{Excess reserves} = \text{Reserves} - \text{Required reserves}$$

For example, if the bank's (total) reserves are $5 million and its required reserves are $4 million, then it holds excess reserves of $1 million.

Note: Banks can use excess reserves to make loans. Before October 2008, the Fed did not pay interest on any reserves (required or excess), so banks had a monetary incentive to create loans with their excess reserves. That incentive was lessened when the Fed began paying interest on reserves in October 2008.

13-2b The Money Supply Expansion Process: Open Market Operations

In an earlier chapter we defined the M1 money supply as currency held outside banks plus checkable deposits. Now let's suppose that checkable deposits are $10,000 and currency is $0. It follows that the money supply is $10,000:

$$\text{Money supply} = \$10,000$$

For now, we are going to assume that the entire $10,000 in checkable deposits is held in one bank: Bank *A*. We will also assume that the required reserve ratio is 10 percent and that Bank *A* is currently holding $1,000 in required reserves and no excess reserves. Here is the relevant part of the balance sheet for Bank *A*:

Bank A			
Assets		**Liabilities**	
Reserves	$1,000	Checkable Deposits	$10,000
Loans	$9,000		

Required Reserve Ratio (r)
A percentage of each dollar deposited that must be held in reserve form (specifically, as bank deposits at the Fed or vault cash).

Required Reserves
The minimum dollar amount of reserves a bank must hold against its checkable deposits, as mandated by the Fed.

Reserve Requirement
The Fed rule that specifies the amount of reserves a bank must hold to back up deposits.

Excess Reserves
Any reserves held beyond the required amount; the difference between (total) reserves and required reserves.

Open Market Purchase
The buying of government securities by the Fed.

Open Market Operation
Consists of open market purchases and open market sales. Open market purchases consist of the buying of government securities by the Fed. Open market sales consist of the selling of government securities by the Fed.

The Fed Conducts an Open Market Purchase The Fed conducts an **open market purchase**, which is a type of **open market operation**; specifically, it buys government securities from a bank. In this example, the Fed buys $500 worth of government securities from Bank A. (Although government securities are assets for banks, we have not shown these assets on Bank A's balance sheet in order that we may focus only on reserves, loans, and checkable deposits.) Bank A turns over the government securities to the Fed, and, in return, the Fed must pay Bank A $500.

Where does the Fed get the $500 to pay Bank A? The answer is *out of thin air*. Bank A currently has a reserve account (bank deposits at the Fed) of $1,000. The Fed simply changes the balance in that account (with a stroke of a computer key) from $1,000 to $1,500. Here is what the balance sheet now looks like for Bank A:

Bank A			
Assets		**Liabilities**	
Reserves	$1,500	Checkable Deposits	$10,000
Loans	$9,000		

The Situation for Bank A The balance sheet for Bank A shows $1,500 in reserves and $10,000 in checkable deposits. If the required reserve ratio is 10 percent, Bank A is required to hold only $1,000 in reserves. So, Bank A has $500 in *excess reserves*.

Suppose Bank A takes the entire $500 in excess reserves and creates a loan for Jill. Specifically, it grants Jill a $500 loan in the form of a new checkable deposit with a balance of $500. In other words, instead of giving Jill $500 in currency, Bank A simply tells Jill that she now has a checkable deposit (a checking account) with the bank and that the balance in the account is $500.

What Is the Money Supply Now? Checkable deposits started off at $10,000 in Bank A but are now $10,500. The extra $500 checkable deposit is the *new deposit* that the bank created for Jill. The money supply is now $10,500:

$$\text{Money supply} = \$10,500$$

Here is what happened to increase the money supply:

Open market purchase → More reserves for Bank A
→ Bank A created more loans in the form of *new checkable deposits*
→ Money supply increased

The Process Continues Jill now takes the $500 loan from Bank A (in the form of a new checkable deposit) and spends it. Specifically, she writes a check for $500 to Adrian for the materials she buys from him. Adrian then takes the $500 (he received from Jill) and deposits the full amount into his checking account at Bank B. The situation for Bank B looks like this:

Bank B			
Assets		**Liabilities**	
Reserves	$500	Checkable Deposits (Adrian's account)	$500

Where did $500 in reserves in Bank B come from? When the check that Jill wrote to Adrian clears, Bank A has to turn over $500 to Bank B. To make this happen, Bank A instructs the Fed to move $500 out of its reserve account and deposit the amount into Bank B's reserve account.

Bank B's balance sheet shows $500 in reserves and $500 in checkable deposits. But if the required reserve ratio is 10 percent, Bank B is required to hold only $50 in reserves. Bank B has $450 in excess reserves.

Bank B uses the entire $450 in excess reserves to create a loan of $450 for Todd in the form of a checkable deposit. In other words, Bank B creates a new checkable deposit of $450.

What Is the Money Supply Now? The money supply of $10,000 went up to $10,500 because Bank A extended a loan (created a new checkable deposit) for Jill. Bank B then extended a loan (created a new checkable deposit) of $450, so the money supply is now $10,950:

$$\text{Money supply} = \$10{,}950$$

Some people might think that, because Jill's checkable deposit balance went from $500 to $0 when her check cleared, the money supply should now be $10,450, not $10,950. But this point ignores the fact that, when Jill pays off her $500 loan to Bank A, the bank can lend the $500 to someone else. Thus, Bank A can create a new checkable deposit of $500 to take the place of Jill's old one of $500.

The Effects of No Cash Leakage and Zero Excess Reserves Held by Banks Up to this point, we have assumed two things.

First, we assumed that both Banks A and B always used *all their excess reserves* to create loans (new checkable deposits); that is, the two banks did not hold any excess reserves. If they had held some positive amount of excess reserves, the money supply would have been affected. Specifically, suppose that, when Bank A had $500 in excess reserves, it created only a $200 loan (instead of a $500 loan) and held $300 in excess reserves. In that case, the money supply would have increased from $10,000, but only to $10,200, not $10,500. In other words, the more excess reserves banks hold, the smaller the increase will be in the money supply.

Second, when Jill paid $500 to Adrian, Adrian deposited the entire $500 into Bank B, but, of course, Adrian didn't have to do that. Instead, he could have deposited only $200 of the $500 into Bank B and asked for $300 in currency. In this case, there would have been a **cash leakage** of $300. Bank B's reserves would have increased by only $200, not $500, and the bank could not have created a new loan (a new checkable deposit) of $450.

Given no cash leakage and zero excess reserves held by banks, how much does the money supply increase? The money supply story is ongoing. As we move from Bank B to Bank C to Bank D, and so on, each new bank creates some new loans (new checkable deposits), but each time the amount created is smaller than the amount that the previous bank created. Whereas Bank A created $500 and Bank B created $450, Bank C might create $405, and so on (see Exhibit 2). In total, all the banks (together) create $5,000 in new checkable deposits. Here is the equation we use to calculate this amount:

$$\Delta \text{Checkable deposits (or money supply)} = \frac{1}{r} \times \Delta R$$

where r = the required reserve ratio and ΔR = the change in reserves resulting from the initial injection of funds. In our example, r = 10 percent and ΔR = $500. In the equation, the

Cash Leakage
Occurs when funds are held as currency instead of deposited into a checking account.

EXHIBIT 2

The Fed, Banks, and an Increase in Checkable Deposits or the Money Supply

We assume that $r = 10$ percent, there is no cash leakage, banks hold zero excess reserves, and the Fed ends up increasing the reserves in Bank A's reserve account by $500 through an open market purchase. As a result of the Fed's open market purchase, Bank A finds itself with $500 in excess reserves that it uses to create a new loan or new checkable deposit. This action starts a process that ends with all relevant banks together creating $5,000 in new checkable deposits (or money).

Creation of new checkable deposits, given that

(i) $r = 10\%$

(ii) There is no cash leakage.

(iii) Banks hold zero excess reserves.

(iv) There is a $500 increase in reserves for Bank A as a result of the Fed's open market purchase.

Bank	Increase in Checkable Deposits	New Required Reserves	New Checkable Deposits Created by Extending New Loans
A	$ 0	$ 0	$ 500
B	500	50	450
C	450	45	405
D	405	40.50	364.50
⋮	⋮	⋮	⋮
Total			$ 5,000

Simple Deposit Multiplier
The reciprocal of the required reserve ratio r: $1/r$.

reciprocal of the required reserve ratio $(1/r)$ is known as the **simple deposit multiplier**. The arithmetic for the example is

$$\Delta \text{Checkable deposits (or money supply)} = \frac{1}{0.10} \times \$500$$
$$= 10 \times \$500$$
$$= \$5,000^1$$

The change in checkable deposits (or the money supply) is $5,000; thus, the Fed's open market purchase resulted in the money supply *rising* from $10,000 to $15,000.

13-2c The Money Supply Contraction Process: Open Market Sale

Let's again start with Bank *A* and its balance sheet:

Bank A			
Assets		**Liabilities**	
Reserves	$1,000	Checkable Deposits	$10,000
Loans	$9,000		

---

[1] In the equation, we are looking at the change in checkable deposits or the money supply. Because checkable deposits are the only component of the money supply that is changing, any change in checkable deposits is equal to the change in the money supply.

We will also assume that the initial money supply is $10,000:

$$\text{Money supply} = \$10,000$$

This time, the Fed undertakes an **open market sale**; that is, it sells government securities. Let's say the Fed sells $400 worth of government securities to Bank A.

The Fed turns the securities over to Bank A and then subtracts $400 from Bank A's reserve account. Just as the Fed can create money *out of thin air*, it can make it disappear *into thin air*. Here is what Bank A's balance sheet now looks like (as before, we do not show the securities on the balance sheet so that we can focus on reserves, loans, and checkable deposits):

Open Market Sale
The selling of government securities by the Fed.

Bank A			
Assets		Liabilities	
Reserves	$600	Checkable Deposits	$10,000
Loans	$9,000		

Reserves for Bank A have gone from $1,000 to $600. Given that checkable deposits are $10,000, Bank A is **reserve deficient**. If the required reserve ratio is 10 percent, Bank A is required to hold $1,000 in reserves ($10,000 × 0.10). But after the open market sale, Bank A is holding only $600 in reserves, so it is reserve deficient by $400.

Reserve Deficient
The situation that exists when a bank holds fewer reserves than specified by the required reserve ratio.

When a bank is reserve deficient, it can do a number of things: It can (1) try to get a loan from another bank, (2) try to get a loan from the Fed, or (3) apply some of its loan repayments to the reserve deficiency position. In our example, suppose the bank chooses option 3. Now, suppose also that, on the day Bank A becomes reserve deficient, Nira walks into the bank and pays back the $400 loan she took out months ago.

If Bank A weren't reserve deficient, it would probably create a $400 loan (new checkable deposit) for someone else with the $400 it received from Nira. In that case, although Nira's checkable deposit balance would go to zero, someone else's checkable deposit balance would rise by $400. The creation of the loan by the bank would keep the money supply constant.

But because the bank is reserve deficient, it keeps the $400 as reserves. As a result, checkable deposits *decline* by $400; consequently, the money supply declines by $400, to $9,600:

$$\text{Money supply} = \$9,600$$

The contraction of the money supply does not stop with Bank A. It moves on to Banks B, C, D, and others. To illustrate, suppose the loan repayment that Nira made to Bank A was written on a check issued by Bank B. Then, when the check clears, the reserves of Bank B decline, and Bank B finds itself reserve deficient. It then applies loan repayments to its reserve deficiency position. The effect continues with Banks C, D, and so on.

To find out how much checkable deposits (the money supply) will decline, apply the equation used earlier:

$$\triangle\text{Checkable deposits (or money supply)} = \frac{1}{r} \times \triangle R$$

Recall that r = the required reserve ratio and $\triangle R$ = the change in reserves resulting from the initial removal of funds. In our example, $r = 10$ percent and $\triangle R = -\$400$. The arithmetic is

$$\triangle\text{Checkable deposits (or money supply)} = \frac{1}{0.10} \times -\$400$$
$$= 10 \times -\$400$$
$$= -\$4,000$$

13-2d The Required Reserve Ratio

Look again at the equation for computing the change in the money supply:

$$\triangle \text{Checkable deposits (or money supply)} = \frac{1}{r} \times \triangle R$$

Notice the role that the required reserve ratio plays in the equation. If $r = 10$ percent, then the simple deposit multiplier $(1 \div r)$ is 10. Accordingly, for a $1 change in reserves, the change in checkable deposits (money supply) is $10. If the Fed lowers the required reserve ratio to, say, 5 percent, then the simple deposit multiplier is 20 $(1 \div 0.05 = 20)$. Now a $1 rise in reserves will lead to a $20 increase in the money supply. If instead the required reserve ratio is raised to 20 percent, the simple deposit multiplier $(1 \div r)$ is 5 $(1 \div 0.20 = 5)$, so a $1 rise in reserves will lead to a $5 increase in the money supply.

In sum,

- Lowering the required reserve ratio will increase the money supply.
- Raising the required reserve ratio will decrease the money supply.[2]

$$r \downarrow \rightarrow \frac{1}{r} \uparrow \rightarrow \text{Money supply} \uparrow$$

$$r \uparrow \rightarrow \frac{1}{r} \downarrow \rightarrow \text{Money supply} \downarrow$$

13-2e The Discount Rate

Discount Loan
A loan the Fed makes to a commercial bank.

Discount Rate
The interest rate the Fed charges depository institutions that borrow reserves from it; the interest rate charged on a discount loan.

Federal Funds Market
A market in which banks lend reserves to one another, usually for short periods.

Federal Funds Rate
The interest rate in the federal funds market; the interest rate banks charge one another to borrow reserves.

If Bank A wants a $1 million loan, it can go to the Fed or another bank (say, Bank B) for it. The loan the bank gets from the Fed is called a **discount loan**, and the interest rate the bank pays for a discount loan is called the **discount rate**. The discount rate is set by the Fed.

The loan that Bank A might get from another bank is usually called an *overnight loan* (because it is typically a loan of short duration, such as overnight). The market in which banks lend reserves to one another, usually for short periods, is called *the market for reserves* or the **federal funds market**. The interest rate that Bank A pays for an overnight loan is called the **federal funds rate**, which is determined in the federal funds market. Specifically, the demand for and the supply of reserves determines the federal funds rate, in much the same way that the demand for and supply of apples determines the price of apples.

The discount rate is another tool that the Fed can use to regulate the money supply. If the Fed wants to increase the money supply, it can lower the discount rate below the federal funds rate. To illustrate, suppose the federal funds rate is 5 percent. All the Fed has to do is to set the discount rate at, say, 3 percent. Now Bank A has an incentive to go to the Fed instead of to another bank for the $1 million it wants. The Fed gives the bank the $1 million discount loan by increasing the balance in the bank's reserve account by $1 million. With more reserves, the bank can create more loans (more checkable deposits), and, as a result, the money supply rises.

In sum,

Fed sets discount rate below federal funds rate → Banks borrow from Fed →
Banks have more reserves → Banks may make more loans and
checkable deposits → Money supply rises

Alternatively, if the Fed wants to contract the money supply, it can set the discount rate above the federal funds rate. Now banks will *not* go to the Fed for loans, and as the banks

---

[2] Keep in mind here that we are discussing how changes in the required reserve ratio led to changes in the money supply in the past. On March 26, 2020, the Fed lowered reserve requirements to zero.

repay discount loans taken out in the past, reserves in the banking system decline. (When a bank repays a discount loan, the Fed *subtracts* the repayment from the bank's reserve account.) In sum,

> Fed sets discount rate above federal funds rate → Banks do not borrow from the Fed, and as banks repay past discount loans → Banks have fewer reserves → Money supply declines

13-2f More on the Federal Funds Rate

We have, so far, discussed three Fed tools for changing the money supply in the past (or *before* 2008)—open market operations, the required reserve ratio, and the discount rate. One of those three tools—open market operations—was often used by the Fed in the past to change the federal funds rate. As you remember, the federal funds rate is the interest rate that banks charge each other for reserves. We now turn to an explanation of how the Fed changed the federal funds rate in the past (before 2008).

Essentially, the Fed changed the federal funds rate by doing two things: First, it would set a **federal funds rate target**, and then (2) it would conduct open market operations to change the market determined federal funds rate so as to "hit" the target.

Federal Funds Rate Target The interest rate that the Fed wants the federal funds rate to be.

As stated earlier, the federal funds rate is determined in the federal funds market—where there is a demand for reserves and a supply of reserves. Suppose the market-determined federal funds rate is 4 percent, and the Fed wanted to lower it to 3 percent. How did it do this? It would first set a federal funds rate target of 3 percent, and then it would conduct an open market purchase—which, as we know, has the effect of injecting reserves into the banking system. As a result of the open market purchase, the *supply of reserves* in the market for reserves rises. As the supply of reserves rises, the price of those reserves—which is the federal funds rate—falls. The Fed continues these transactions until the federal funds rate falls from 4 percent to 3 percent—that is, until the federal funds rate matches the federal funds rate target.

Of course, if the Fed wanted to raise the federal funds rate, it would do the opposite. This time, suppose the federal funds rate is 3 percent, and the Fed wanted to raise it to 4 percent. It would then set the federal funds rate target at 4 percent, conduct open market sales—which, as we know, lower the supply of reserves in the banking system and federal funds market. As a result, the price of those reserves—the federal funds rate—rises.

13-2g Summary of Monetary Policy in the Past (Before October 2008)

1. The Fed conducted monetary policy in the past (before 2008) using the policy tools of open market operations, the required reserve ratio, and the discount rate.
2. The Fed indirectly changed the federal funds rate through open market operations. If it wanted to raise the federal funds rate, it would conduct an open market sale. If it wanted to decrease the federal funds rate, it would conduct an open market purchase.

---

1. How does the money supply change as a result of (a) an increase in the discount rate, (b) an open market purchase, (c) an increase in the required reserve ratio?
2. What is the difference between the federal funds rate and the discount rate?
3. If Bank A borrows $10 million from Bank B, what happens to the reserves in Bank A? What happens in the banking system?
4. If Bank A borrows $10 million from the Fed, what happens to the reserves in Bank A? What happens in the banking system?

13-3 The Present: Interest on Reserves (IOR)

In the last section, we discussed those policy tools the Fed used in the past to conduct monetary policy. In this section, we discuss the policy tool the Fed uses to conduct monetary policy in the present (or *since* October 2008).

13-3a Interest Rates

The Federal Reserve conducts the nation's monetary policy by managing the level of short-term interest rates and influencing the overall availability and cost of credit in the economy. Monetary policy directly affects short-term interest rates; it indirectly affects longer-term interest rates, currency exchange rates, and prices of equities and other assets and thus wealth. Through these channels, monetary policy influences household spending, business investment, production, employment, and inflation in the United States.

Board of Governors of the Federal Reserve System
https://www.fedreservegov.org/monetarypolicy.php

Notice three important points in the statement made by the Board of Governors of the Federal Reserve System:

1. Today, the Fed conducts monetary policy by managing the level of short-term interest rates.
2. The Fed indirectly affects long-term interest rates.
3. By affecting interest rates, monetary policy influences household spending (consumption), business investment, employment, and inflation.

Now, if the Fed affects interest rates in order to influence consumption, investment, and so on, then the question is: *How does it influence interest rates?* The answer is that it does so by indirectly changing the federal funds rate.

This leads us to another question: *How does the Fed indirectly change the federal funds rate?* The answer is that it changes two administered interest rates: the IOR rate and the ON-RRP rate. We define these two administered rates and explain the process next.

Fed changes the IOR rate and the ON-RRP rate → Which leads to a change in the federal funds rate → Which changes interest rates → Which influences consumption, investment, employment, and inflation

13-3b Interest on Reserves (IOR) Rate

As stated previously, before October 2008, the Fed did not pay interest on the reserves a bank held. For instance, if a bank held, say, $10 million in required reserves and $90 million in excess reserves, it didn't receive any interest on those reserves. Today, the Fed pays an interest rate on those reserves; it is called the **interest on reserves (IOR) rate**. The IOR rate is the *primary tool* the Fed presently uses to conduct monetary policy; it is the primary tool the Fed uses to indirectly change the federal funds rate.

What Does the Fed Do if It Wants to Change the Federal Funds Rate? Suppose the federal funds rate is 2 percent, and the Fed wants to raise it. To do this, it sets the IOR rate at a level above 2 percent—say, 2.5 percent.

IOR rate > Federal funds rate

Interest on Reserves Rate (IOR rate)
The interest rate the Fed pays on reserves. Today, it is the primary tool the Fed uses to indirectly change the federal funds rate and conduct monetary policy.

Chapter 13 The Federal Reserve System

What will happen now? Banks will borrow reserves in the federal funds market at 2 percent and place those reserves on deposit with the Fed to earn 2.5 percent. As a result, reserves in the federal funds market decline, pushing up the federal funds rate.

Now suppose the Fed wants to lower the federal funds rate to less than 2 percent. This time it sets the IOR rate at a level below 2 percent—say, 1.5 percent.

$$\text{IOR rate} < \text{Federal funds rate}$$

This time, banks will remove some of the reserves they hold with the Fed that earn 1.5 percent and lend out those reserves in the federal funds market to earn 2 percent. In the process, reserves in the federal funds market increase, pushing down the federal funds rate.

Notice that in both of our examples, the federal funds rate gravitated toward the IOR rate. When the IOR rate was 2.5 percent and the federal funds rate was 2 percent, the federal funds rate increased; when the IOR rate was 1.5 percent and the federal funds rate was 2 percent, the federal funds rate decreased.

Initially, the IOR rate looks like the lower boundary below which banks will not lend. Why lend at an interest rate of 1 percent if the IOR rate, paid by the Fed on reserves, is 2 percent? In short, no bank will lend at an interest rate lower than the IOR rate.

But a complication arises. Banks aren't the only entities that can operate in the federal funds market. Some nonbank financial institutions do too—and these institutions do not earn the IOR rate. So, not being able to earn the safe return of the IOR rate, these nonbank financial institutions might lend at a federal funds rate that is lower than the IOR rate. The Fed deals with this issue by paying these nonbank financial institutions an interest rate called the *ON-RRP rate*. While the IOR rate is the primary tool the Fed uses today to conduct monetary policy, the ON-RPP rate is the secondary tool.

ON-RRP stands for **O**ver**N**ight **R**everse **R**e**P**urchase. When the Fed conducts an overnight RRP agreement, it sells a security to a nonbank financial institution while agreeing to buy back the security the next day at a higher price. The financial institution now earns interest on the transaction, which is equal to the difference between the lower and higher price. On a percentage basis, it earns the **ON-RRP rate**. For example, suppose a security is sold for $1,000 and bought back for $1,013. The ON-RRP rate would be 1.3 percent ($13/$1,000 × 100 = 1.3 percent).

ON-RRP Rate
The interest rate a nonbank financial institution earns on an overnight RRP.

Once the institution knows it can receive the ON-RRP rate, it will not lend in the federal funds market (or any other market) at an interest rate that is lower. For example, if the ON-RRP rate is 1.3 percent, it won't lend at less than 1.3 percent.

The Fed normally sets the ON-RRP rate a bit below what it sets the IOR rate. For example, it might set the IOR rate at 2 percent and the ON-RRP rate at 1.75 percent. It follows that banks won't lend at less than 2 percent, and nonbank financial institutions (which do not have access to the IOR rate) will not lend at less than 1.75 percent. Because the federal funds rate will tend to settle somewhere between the IOR rate and the ON-RRP rate, the federal funds rate target is often expressed as a range. For example, the Fed may announce its *federal funds rate target range* as 1.00 to 1.25 percent, choosing to set the ON-RRP rate at the bottom of the range and the IOR rate at the top of the range. It follows that the ON-RRP rate is the actual (interest rate) floor below which the federal funds rate will not fall.

13-3c The IOR Rate, the Federal Funds Rate, and Interest Rates on Loans

There is a close link between the federal funds rate and interest rates (especially short-term interest rates). To illustrate, suppose the interest rate on loans is 3 percent and the federal funds rate is 3 percent. Now, the Fed decides to lower the federal funds rate to somewhere between 1.75 and 2.00 percent.

The first thing the Fed does is set the federal funds rate target range as 1.75 to 2.00 percent, with the ON-RRP rate at the bottom of the range and the IOR rate at the top. We explained earlier the complete process by which the federal funds rate falls to somewhere within the range.

Let's say the federal funds rate falls to 1.80 percent. What happens next? Interest rates will start to decline too. To understand why, keep in mind that banks can do one of three things with their reserves:

1. Hold the reserves with the Fed and earn the IOR rate
2. Lend out the reserves in the federal funds market and earn the federal funds rate
3. Create loans with the reserves and earn the interest rate on those loans

Now suppose again that the IOR rate is 2.00 percent, the federal funds rate has fallen to 1.80 percent, and the interest rate on a loan is 3.00 percent. Given this scenario, what will banks do? Banks will hold fewer reserves with the Fed earning an IOR rate of 2.00 percent (or lend in the federal funds market earning 1.80 percent) and instead move some of those reserves into creating loans that earn 3.00 percent. As a result of an increase in the supply of loans, the price of those loans—the interest rate on those loans—declines.

In conclusion, changes in the federal funds rate can lead to changes in interest rates—which, as we noted earlier, can lead to changes in consumption and investment spending.

13-3d Summary of Monetary Policy in the Present (Since October 2008) [3]

1. The Fed conducts monetary policy today by influencing interest rates.
2. It influences interest rates by indirectly raising or lowering the federal funds rate.
3. The Fed can move the federal funds rate within a certain range by administering two rates—the IOR rate and the ON-RRP rate. The IOR rate is the primary tool the Fed uses to conduct monetary policy, and the ON-RRP rate is a supplementary tool.

For a review of the policy tools the Fed used in the past and present to conduct monetary policy, see Exhibit 3.

---

[3]. For an excellent discussion of the way Fed conducts monetary policy today, see "The Fed's New Monetary Policy Tools," by Jane Ihrig and Scott A. Wolla. *Page One Economics*, a publication of the Federal Reserve Bank of St. Louis, August 2020.

EXHIBIT 3

The Past and Present: Fed Tools and Monetary Policy

In this exhibit we show the tools the Fed used in the past and in the present to conduct monetary policy. The past is that period before October 2008. It is a period in which the Fed did not pay interest on reserves and there were limited (low) reserves in the banking system. The present is that period since October 2008. It is a period in which the Fed pays interest on reserves and there are ample (plentiful) reserves in the banking system.

The Past (Before October 2008)

Policy Tool	Fed Action	Effect in Terms of Money Supply and/or Federal Funds Rate
Open Market Operations	Open Market Purchase	Money Supply Rises/Federal Funds Rate Falls
	Open Market Sale	Money Supply Falls/Federal Funds Rate Rises
Required Reserve Ratio	Lower Required Reserves Ratio	Money Supply Rises
	Raise Required Reserve Ratio	Money Supply Falls
Discount Rate	Lower Discount Rate (Below Federal Funds Rate)	Money Supply Rises
	Raise Discount Rate (Above Federal Funds Rate)	Money Supply Falls

The Present (Since October 2008)

Policy Tool	Fed Action	Effect in Terms of Federal Funds Rate
IOR Rate and ON-RRP Rate	Objective: Lower Federal Funds Rate	
	Action: Set *federal funds rate target range* below the federal funds rate with the IOR rate at the top of the range and the ON-RRP rate at the bottom.	Federal Funds Rate Falls
	Objective: Raise Federal Funds Rate	
	Action: Set *federal funds rate target range* above the federal funds rate with the IOR rate at the top of the range and the ON-RRP rate at the bottom.	Federal Funds Rate Rises

1. Does the Fed use open market operations to change the federal funds rate today?
2. Suppose the Fed wants to lower the federal funds rate. How does it proceed to do this today?
3. Identify and define both the primary and secondary tools the Fed uses to conduct monetary policy today.

Economics 24/7

Negative Interest Rates (on Reserves) and the Fed

Several central banks, including the Bank of Japan and the European Central Bank, have implemented negative interest rates. In practice this means that, instead of receiving interest on the reserves they hold with the central bank, banks are charged a fee on reserves above a threshold. . . . *By putting downward pressure on the interest rates most relevant to borrowing and spending decisions, the introduction of negative interest rates should work through the same channels as more standard monetary policies.*[4]

—Ben Bernanke, former chair of the Federal Reserve

We know from our discussion in this chapter that banks hold reserves with their central banks. In the United States, for example, Bank *A* might hold $100 million in reserves with the Fed. These are funds that Bank *A* is not using for anything else. The Fed pays Bank *A* an interest rate on the $100 million in reserves. That interest rate, we recall, is the interest on reserves (IOR) rate.

Now consider that, in 2012, the central bank of Denmark was the first central bank to go below zero on the interest rate it paid to banks that held reserves with it. In 2014, several of Europe's central banks followed, as did the Bank of Japan in 2016.

Why would a central bank go below zero? Why might the Fed, for example, pay a negative IOR? To answer this question, let's ask what else a bank can do with reserves other than receive interest from the Fed. It can lend out those reserves to other banks or to individuals and firms. As for the latter (lending to individuals and firms), suppose that instead of holding, say, $100 million in reserves with the Fed, earning, say, 1 percent, a bank could instead create new loans of $100 million for individuals and firms on which the banks would receive some market interest rate return. In other words, a bank will consider the IOR rate and the market interest rate on loans to individuals and firms when deciding what to do with its reserves.

Now suppose the following situation exists. (1) The interest rate that a bank receives from the Fed on reserves is 1 percent, IOR = 1 percent. (2) Because market interest rates are so low at the time, banks seem content to receive the 1 percent interest rate instead of using the reserves to create loans. But (3) the Fed would prefer that banks use the reserves to create loans, thus stimulating spending in the economy. What could the Fed do? It could charge the banks a fee to hold reserves beyond a certain level. In other words, it could charge banks a negative IOR. Suppose that negative interest rate is a −0.5 percent. This means that commercial banks would actually have to pay the Fed to hold its reserves. What will banks do now? Will they pay a fee to the Fed for holding reserves, or will they decide instead to use those reserves to create loans? The expectation is that with a negative IOR, banks would prefer to use their reserves to give out loans and therefore stimulating spending.

---

[4] "What Tools Does the Fed Have Left? Part 1: Negative Interest Rates, March 18, 2016, at https://www.brookings.edu/blog/ben-bernanke/2016/03/18/what-tools-does-the-fed-have-left-part-1-negative-interest-rates/.

Office Hours

What is the Difference Between the Fed Setting Interest Rates and Influencing Interest Rates?

Student: In this chapter, we have discussed numerous different interest rates: discount rate, federal funds rate, interest rate on loans, and so on. Sometimes the Fed is setting interest rates, and sometimes it is influencing, affecting, or indirectly changing interest rates. What is the difference here?

Instructor: In this chapter, we have discussed three rates that the Fed sets directly. These are called administered rates—rates that the Fed administers and can set at any level it chooses. These are the discount rate, the IOR rate, and the ON-RRP rate. In other words, if the Fed wants to set the IOR rate at 2 percent, then that will be done. The same holds for the discount rate and the ON-RRP rate.

Student: What about the federal funds rate?

Instructor: That interest rate is determined in a market setting: the federal funds market or the market for reserves. In that market, there is a demand for reserves and a supply of reserves. To change the federal funds rate, the Fed can't simply say the federal funds rate will be X percent for it to be done. That is not how things work. As we have discussed in this chapter, the Fed has to set up a federal funds rate target range. It then has to set the IOR rate at the top of the range and the ON-RRP rate at the bottom. By doing this, the Fed sets up a process that leads to a change in the federal funds rate. That's why we often remind ourselves that the Fed *indirectly* changes the federal funds rate. It *directly* changes the discount rate, IOR rate, and the ON-RRP rate though.

Student: What about interest rates that banks charge for loans? Suppose I walk into a bank and ask for a loan. I would pay some interest rate for that loan. Is the Fed setting that interest rate or just influencing it—that is, indirectly changing it?

Instructor: That interest rate you pay for the loan is not an administered rate set by the Fed. That interest rate is determined in a market setting, where there is a demand for loans and a supply of loans. The Fed—by being able to set the IOR rate and ON-RRP rate and therefore indirectly change the federal funds rate—can indirectly change, influence, or affect that interest rate you pay for a loan.

Student: So let me recap to see if I have this straight now. The discount rate, IOR rate, and the ON-RRP rate are administered rates. They are set by the Fed; they are not determined in a market setting. But the federal funds rate and the interest rate that I might pay on a bank loan are determined in a market setting, and while the Fed cannot set these rates, it can influence them.

Instructor: That is correct.

Chapter Summary

The Federal Reserve System

- There are 12 Federal Reserve Districts. The Board of Governors controls and coordinates the activities of the Federal Reserve System. The Board is made up of seven members, each appointed to a 14-year term. The major policymaking group in the Fed is the Federal Open Market Committee (FOMC), a 12-member group.

Reserves, Required and Excess

- Reserves equal bank deposits and the Fed plus vault cash. The dollar amount of reserves a bank must hold is equal to the required reserve ratio times the bank's checkable deposits. Required reserves = $r \times$ Checkable deposits where r = required reserve ratio. Excess reserve is the difference between total reserves and required reserves. Excess reserves = Total reserves − Required reserves

Fed Tools and Monetary Policy in the Past (Before October 2008)

- When it comes to monetary policy, we define the past as the period before October 2008. It is that period during which the Fed did not pay interest on reserves and the banking system held limited (low) reserves.
- In the past, the Fed conducted monetary policy using open market operations, the discount rate, and the required reserve ratio (reserve requirements).
- An open market purchase by the Fed increased the money supply.
- An open market sale by the Fed decreased the money supply.
- An increase in the required reserve ratio led to a decrease in the money supply.
- A decrease in the required reserve ratio led to an increase in the money supply.
- If the Fed wanted to increase the money supply, it could lower the discount rate below the federal funds rate.
- If the Fed wanted to decrease the money supply, it could raise the discount rate above the federal funds rate.
- If the Fed wanted to lower the federal funds rate in the past, it would conduct an open market purchase.
- If the Fed wanted to raise the federal funds rate in the past, it would conduct an open market sale.

Fed Tools and Monetary Policy in the Present (Since October 2008)

- When it comes to monetary policy, we define the present as the period since October 2008. It is that period during which the Fed does pay interest on reserves and the banking system holds ample (plentiful) reserves.
- The primary tool the Fed uses in the present is the interest on reserves (IOR) rate. The IOR rate is the interest rate that the Fed pays on reserves. A secondary tool of the Fed is the ON-RRP rate.
- The Fed uses the IOR rate and ON-RRP rate to indirectly change the federal funds rate.
- If the Fed wants to lower the federal funds rate, it sets a federal funds rate target range that is below the current federal funds rate. If the Fed wants to raise the federal funds rate, it sets the federal funds rate target range above the current federal funds rate.
- By indirectly changing the federal funds rate, the Fed can influence interest rates and spending (consumption and investment).

Key Terms and Concepts

The Federal Reserve System (The Fed)
Board of Governors
Federal Open Market Committee (FOMC)
Monetary Policy
Reserves
Required Reserves Ratio (r)
Excess Reserves
Open Market Purchase
Cash Leakage
Simple Deposit Multiplier
Open Market Sale
Reserve Deficient
Reserve Requirement
Discount Loan
Discount Rate
Federal Funds Market
Federal Funds Rate
Federal Funds Rate Target
Interest on Reserves (IOR) Rate
Overnight Reverse Repurchase (ON-RRP) Rate

Questions and Problems

1. What is monetary policy?
2. What are reserves, required reserves, and excess reserves?

Questions 3–8 relate to Fed policy tools and monetary policy in the past (before October 2008).

3. Explain how an open market purchase increases the money supply.
4. Explain how an open market sale decreases the money supply.
5. Suppose the Fed raises the required reserve ratio, a move that is normally thought to reduce the money supply. However, banks find themselves with a reserve deficiency after the required reserve ratio is increased and are likely to react by requesting a loan from the Fed. Does this action prevent

the money supply from contracting as predicted? Explain your answer.

6. Suppose Bank A borrows reserves from Bank B. Now that Bank A has more reserves than previously, will the money supply increase? Explain your answer.

7. Explain how a decrease in the required reserve ratio increases the money supply.

8. In the past, how did the Fed change the federal funds rate?

Questions 9–13 relate to Fed policy tools and monetary policy in the present (since October 2008).

9. What is the IOR rate? What is the ON-RRP rate?

10. According to a statement made by the Board of Governors of the Federal Reserve System, the "Federal Reserve conducts the nation's monetary policy by managing the level of short-term interest rates." To what end? What is the Fed trying to do by managing the level of short-term interest rates?

11. Suppose the Fed wants to raise the federal funds rate. How would it use the IOR rate and ON-RRP rate to do this?

12. Suppose the Fed wants to lower the federal funds rate. How would it use the IOR rate and the ON-RRP rate to do this?

13. There are three things that a bank can do with its reserves. What are they?

CHAPTER 14
Money and the Economy

Introduction
Does the money supply matter to the economy? Does a rise or fall in the money supply make a difference? In this chapter, we talk about the money supply and its effects on the economy. We discuss changes in the money supply and in the price level, changes in the money supply and in Real GDP, and changes in the money supply and interest rates.

14-1 Money and the Price Level

Classical economists believed that changes in the money supply affect the price level in the economy. Their position was based on the equation of exchange and on the simple quantity theory of money.

14-1a The Equation of Exchange

The **equation of exchange** is an identity stating that the money supply (M) multiplied by velocity (V) must be equal to the price level (P) times Real GDP (Q). That is,

$$MV \equiv PQ$$

where $\equiv$ means "must be equal to." This is an identity, and an identity is valid for all values of the variables.

Equation of Exchange
An identity stating that the money supply (M) times velocity (V) must be equal to the price level (P) times Real GDP (Q): $MV \equiv PQ$.

As we learned in an earlier chapter, *velocity* is the average number of times a dollar is spent to buy final goods and services in a year. For example, suppose an economy has only five $1 bills. In January, the first of the $1 bills moves from *A*'s hands to *B*'s hands to buy good *X*. Then, in June, it goes from *B*'s hands to *C*'s hands to buy good *Y*. And in December, it goes from *C*'s hands to *D*'s hands to buy good *Z*. Over the course of the year, this dollar bill has changed hands three times.

The other dollar bills also change hands during the year. Suppose the second dollar bill changes hands five times; the third, six times; the fourth, two times; and the fifth, seven times. Given this information, we can calculate the average number of times a dollar changes hands in purchases. In this case, the number is 4.6, which is the **velocity**.

In a large economy such as ours, counting how many times each dollar changes hands is impossible, so calculating velocity as we just did is impossible. For a large economy, we use a different method:

- First, we calculate GDP.
- Next, we calculate the average money supply (M).
- Finally, we divide GDP by the average money supply to obtain velocity (V):

$$V = \frac{GDP}{M}$$

Velocity
The average number of times a dollar is spent to buy final goods and services in a year.

For example, if $4,800 billion worth of transactions occur in a year (*GDP*) and the average money supply during the year is $800 billion (*M*), then a dollar must have been used an average of six times during the year to purchase goods and services:

$$V = \frac{\$4{,}800 \text{ billion}}{\$800 \text{ billion}}$$

Because GDP is equal to $P \times Q$, this identity can be written

$$V = \frac{P \times Q}{M}$$

Multiplying both sides by *M*, we get

$$MV \equiv PQ$$

which is the equation of exchange. Thus, the equation of exchange is derived from the definition of velocity.

The equation of exchange can be interpreted in different ways:

1. The money supply multiplied by velocity must equal the price level times Real GDP: $M \times V \equiv P \times Q$.

2. The money supply multiplied by velocity must equal GDP: $M \times V \equiv GDP$ (because $P \times Q \equiv GDP$).

3. Total spending or expenditures (measured by *MV*) must equal the total sales revenues of business firms (measured by *PQ*): $MV \equiv PQ$.

The third way of interpreting the equation of exchange is perhaps the most intuitively easy to understand: The total expenditures (of buyers) must equal the total sales (of sellers). Consider a simple economy with only one buyer and one seller. If the buyer buys a book for $20, then the seller receives $20. Stated differently, the money supply in the example ($20) times velocity (1) is equal to the price of the book ($20) times the quantity of the book (1).

14-1b From the Equation of Exchange to the Simple Quantity Theory of Money

The equation of exchange is an identity, not an economic theory. To turn it into a theory, we make some assumptions about the variables in the equation. Many eighteenth-century classical economists, as well as American economist Irving Fisher (1867–1947) and English economist Alfred Marshall (1842–1924), made the following assumptions:

1. Changes in velocity are so small that, for all practical purposes, velocity can be assumed to be constant (especially over short periods).
2. Real GDP, or Q, is fixed in the short run.

Hence, the classical theorists turned the equation of exchange, which is simply true by definition, into a theory by assuming that both V and Q are fixed, or constant. With these two assumptions, we have the **simple quantity theory of money**: If V and Q are constant, then changes in M will bring about *strictly proportional* changes in P. In other words, the simple quantity theory of money predicts that changes in the money supply will bring about strictly proportional changes in the price level.

Exhibit 1 shows the assumptions and predictions of the simple quantity theory. On the left side of the exhibit are noted the key assumptions of the theory: V and Q are constant, as indicated by the bars over them. Also, $M \times \overline{V} = P \times \overline{Q}$ is noted. We use the equals sign (=) instead of the identity sign (≡) because we are speaking about the empirical simple quantity theory, not the analytical equation of exchange. (The equals sign can be read as "is predicted to be equal"; that is, given our assumptions, $M \times V$, or MV, is predicted to be equal to $P \times Q$, or PQ.)

Starting with the first row, the money supply is $500; velocity is 4; the price level, or price index, is $2; and Real GDP ($Q$) is 1,000 units.[1] Therefore, GDP equals $2,000. In the second row, the money supply increases by 100 percent, from $500 to $1,000, and both V and Q are constant, at 4 and 1,000, respectively. The price level moves from $2 to $4. On the right side of the exhibit, we see that a 100 percent increase in M predicts a 100 percent increase in P. That is, changes in P are predicted to be strictly proportional to changes in M. In the third row, M increases by 50 percent, and P is predicted to increase by 50 percent. In the fourth row, M decreases by 20 percent, and P is predicted to decrease by 20 percent.

Simple Quantity Theory of Money
The theory which assumes that velocity (V) and Real GDP (Q) are constant and predicts that changes in the money supply (M) lead to strictly proportional changes in the price level (P).

EXHIBIT 1

Assumptions and Predictions of the Simple Quantity Theory of Money

The simple quantity theory of money assumes that both V and Q are constant. (A bar over each indicates this in the exhibit.) The theory predicts that changes in M lead to strictly proportional changes in P. (*Note*: For purposes of this example, think of Q as "so many units of goods" and of P as the "average price paid per unit of these goods.")

	Assumptions of Simple Quantity Theory			Predictions of Simple Quantity Theory			
M	× $\overline{V}$	=	P	× $\overline{Q}$		% Change in M	% Change in P
$500	4		$2	1,000			
1,000	4		4	1,000		+100%	+100%
1,500	4		6	1,000		+50	+50
1,200	4		4.80	1,000		−20	−20

[1] You are used to seeing Real GDP expressed as a dollar figure and a price index as a number without a dollar sign in front of it. We have switched things for purposes of this example because it is easier to think of Q as "so many units of goods" and P as "the average price paid per unit of those goods."

So the simple quantity theory assumes that both V and Q are constant in the short run and therefore predicts that changes in M lead to strictly proportional changes in P.

How good are the predictions of the simple quantity theory of money? Do changes in the money supply actually lead to *strictly proportional* changes in the price level? For example, if the money supply goes up by 7 percent, does the price level go up by 7 percent? If the money supply goes down by 4 percent, does the price level go down by 4 percent? The answer is that the strict proportionality between changes in the money supply and changes in the price level does not show up in the data (at least not very often).

Generally, though, the evidence supports the spirit (or essence) of the simple quantity theory of money: the higher the growth rate in the money supply, the greater is the growth rate in the price level. To illustrate, we would expect that a growth rate in the money supply of, say, 40 percent would generate a greater increase in the price level than, say, a growth rate in the money supply of 4 percent. And this effect is pretty much what we see. For example, countries with more rapid increases in their money supplies often witness more rapid increases in their price levels than do countries that witness less rapid increases in their money supplies.

14-1c The Micro Underpinnings of the Macro Phenomenon: *M* leads to a change in *P*

In macroeconomics, there is often a discussion of economic aggregates. You can think of an aggregate as a collective sum. For example, aggregate demand is a macroeconomic aggregate. It is not the demand for a particular good or services but, instead, the demand for all goods and services. Consumption spending is a macroeconomic aggregate too. It is not the household spending on a particular good or service but the household spending on all goods and services.

If we look at the equation of exchange, $MV = PQ$, we have here four aggregates. M, the money supply, is an aggregate, as are velocity (V), the price level (P), and Q (Real GDP). When we say that a change in M (one aggregate) can lead to a change in P (another aggregate), we sometimes leave our reader with the impression that one aggregate acts upon another aggregate, in much the same way that perhaps the Sun acts upon the Earth.

What is sometimes missing when we say that a change in M can lead to a change in P is a full explanation of just how this happens. In other words, what happens at a micro level—or at the level of the individual—that explains how a change in M can lead to a change in P?

Let's go through the microeconomic underpinnings. We start by differentiating between a person's actual money balances and desired money balances. A person's actual money balances consist of the amount of money that the person actually holds (and therefore does not spend). This is the money that a person has in cash and in a checking account. Let's say this amount is $4,000. A person's desired money balances consist of the amount of money that the person desires or wants to hold. Let's say this amount is $4,000 too. When a person's actual and desired money balances are equal, we can say that the person is in a personal monetary equilibrium.

Now suppose the Fed increases the money supply, and, as a result, individuals find themselves holding more money than they desire to hold. In other words, their actual money balances are greater than their desired money balances. Let's say actual money balances for a particular person are $5,000, and desired money balances are still $4,000. In other words, the person is actually holding (in cash or in his checking account) $1,000 more than he actually wants to hold. What will he do with that $1,000? He certainly is not going to burn it—no one burns money. He is going to spend it; he is going to trade his excess money of $1,000 for goods and services. He is going to trade his excess $1,000 for a computer, or more clothes, or a short trip somewhere. By doing this, he is increasing the demand for goods and services, and as the demand for goods and services rise, so do prices.

Let's return to $MV = PQ$ and our earlier statement that a change in one aggregate (M) can lead to a change in another aggregate P. Do you see how this happens now? Do you see the micro underpinnings of the macro phenomenon of a change in M leading to a change in P? It happens at the individual level in terms of a person's desired and actual money balances. Upsetting the initial equality between these two money balances leads to an adjustment process on the part of individuals that gives us the change in M bringing about a changing in P.

14-1d The Simple Quantity Theory of Money in an *AD–AS* Framework

What does the simple quantity theory of money look like in the *AD–AS* framework?

The *AD* Curve in the Simple Quantity Theory of Money The simple quantity theory of money builds on the equation of exchange. Recall that one way of interpreting the equation of exchange is that the total expenditures of buyers (MV) must equal the total sales of sellers (PQ). Thus, MV is the total expenditures of buyers, and PQ is the total sales of sellers. Let's take the total expenditures of buyers a few steps further:

$$MV = \text{Total expenditures}$$

Now, total expenditures (TE) is defined as the sum of the expenditures made by the four sectors of the economy (consumption, investment, government purchases, and net exports):

$$TE = C + I + G + (EX - IM)$$

So, because $MV = TE$,

$$MV = C + I + G + (EX - IM)$$

At a given price level, anything that changes C, I, G, EX, or IM changes aggregate demand and thus shifts the aggregate demand (*AD*) curve. Hence, if MV equals $C + I + G + (EX - IM)$, then *a change in the money supply* (M) *or a change in velocity* (V) *will change aggregate demand and therefore lead to a shift in the AD curve*. In other words, aggregate demand depends on *both* the money supply and velocity:

- An increase in the money supply will increase aggregate demand and shift the *AD* curve to the right.
- A decrease in the money supply will decrease aggregate demand and shift the *AD* curve to the left.
- An increase in velocity will increase aggregate demand and shift the *AD* curve to the right.
- A decrease in velocity will decrease aggregate demand and shift the *AD* curve to the left.

But *in the simple quantity theory of money, velocity is assumed to be constant*. Thus, only changes in the money supply can shift the *AD* curve.

The AD curve for the simple quantity theory of money is shown in Exhibit 2(a). The $(M, \overline{V})$ next to the curve is a reminder of which factors can shift the AD curve. Again, the bar over the V indicates that velocity is assumed to be constant.

The AS Curve in the Simple Quantity Theory of Money
In the simple quantity theory of money, the level of Real GDP is assumed to be constant in the short run. Exhibit 2(b) shows Real GDP fixed at Q_1. The AS curve is vertical at this level of Real GDP.

AD and AS in the Simple Quantity Theory of Money
Exhibit 2(c) shows both the AD and AS curves in the simple quantity theory of money. Suppose AD_1 is initially operative. In the exhibit, AD_1 is based on a money supply of $800 billion and a velocity of 2. The price level is P_1.

Now, suppose we increase the money supply to $820 billion, and velocity remains constant at 2. Then, according to the simple quantity theory of money, the price level will increase, and it does. The increase in the money supply shifts the AD curve from AD_1 to AD_2 and pushes up the price level from P_1 to P_2.

EXHIBIT 2

The Simple Quantity Theory of Money in the AD–AS Framework

(a) In the simple quantity theory of money, the AD curve is downward sloping. Velocity is assumed to be constant, so changes in the money supply will change aggregate demand. (b) In the simple quantity theory of money, Real GDP is fixed in the short run. Thus, the AS curve is vertical. (c) In the simple quantity theory of money, an increase in the money supply will shift the AD curve rightward and increase the price level. A decrease in the money supply will shift the AD curve leftward and decrease the price level.

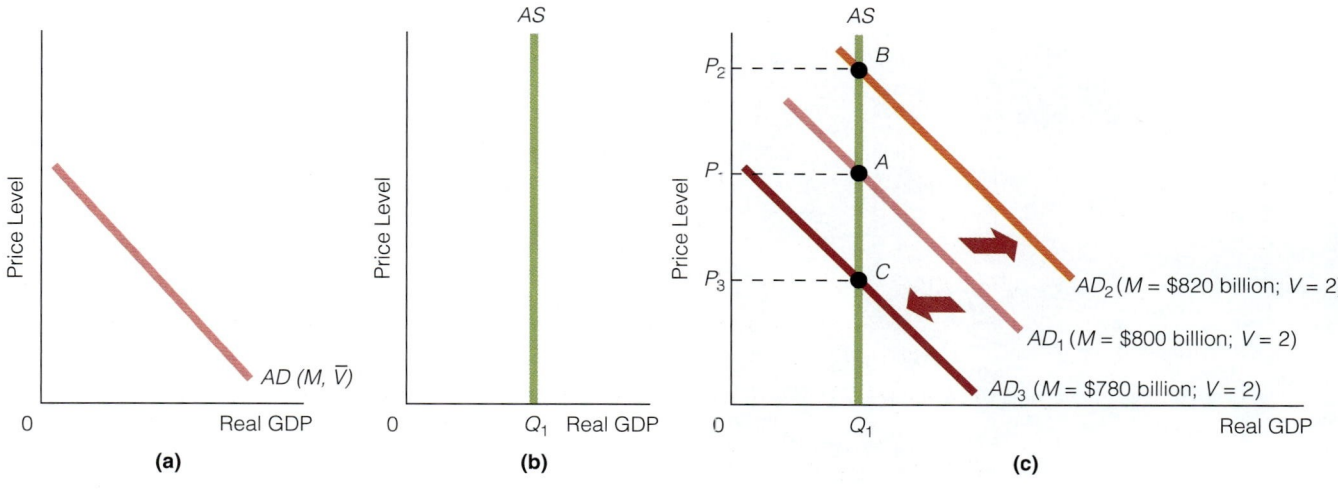

Suppose that instead of increasing the money supply, we decrease it to $780 billion, again with velocity remaining constant at 2. Then, according to the simple quantity theory of money, the price level will decrease, and it does. The decrease in the money supply shifts the AD curve from AD_1 to AD_3 and pushes the price level down from P_1 to P_3.

Economics 24/7

The California Gold Rush, or Really Expensive Apples

Soon there was too much money in California and too little of everything else.

—J. S. Holiday, The World Rushed In

The only peacetime rise [in prices] comparable in total magnitude [to the 40 to 50 percent rise in prices from 1897 to 1914] followed the California gold discoveries in the early 1850s.

—Milton Friedman and Anna Schwartz, A Monetary History of the United States, 1867–1960

John Sutter was a Swiss immigrant who arrived in California in 1839. On the chilly morning of January 24, 1848, James Marshall, a carpenter, was busy at work building a sawmill for Sutter. Then something glistening caught his eye, and he reached down and picked it up. Marshall said to the workers he had hired, "Boys, by God I believe I have found a gold mine." Marshall later wrote, "I reached my hand down and picked it up; it made my heart thump, for I was certain it was gold. The piece was about half the size and shape of a pea. Then I saw another."

In time, Marshall and his workers came across more gold, and before long, people from all across the United States and from many other countries headed to California. The California gold rush had begun.

The California gold rush resulted in an increase in the amount of money in circulation and illustrates how such a fairly dramatic increase can affect prices. As more gold was mined and the supply of money went up, prices began to rise. Although prices rose generally across the country, the earliest and most dramatic price rises occurred in and near the areas where gold was discovered. Near the gold mines, the prices of food and clothing shot up. For example, whereas a loaf of bread sold for 4¢ in New York (equivalent to 84¢ today), near the mines the price was 75¢ (the equivalent of $15.67 today). Eggs sold for about $2 each ($41 today), apples for $4 ($83.59), a butcher's knife for $30 ($626), and boots went for $100 a pair ($2,089).

In San Francisco, land prices soared dramatically because of the city's relative closeness to the mines. In 18 months, real estate that cost $16 (the equivalent of $334 today) before gold was discovered jumped to $45,000 ($940,000 today).

A sharp rise in prices similar to that created by the California gold discoveries followed other gold discoveries too. For example, the gold stock of the world is estimated to have doubled from 1890 to 1914, through both discoveries (in South Africa, Alaska, and Colorado) and improved methods of mining and refining gold. During this period, world prices increased as well.

14-1e Dropping the Assumptions That V and Q Are Constant

If we drop the assumptions that velocity (V) and Real GDP (Q) are constant, we have a more general theory of the factors that cause changes in the price level. In this theory, changes in the price level depend on three variables:

1. Money supply
2. Velocity
3. Real GDP

Let's again start with the equation of exchange:

$$M \times V \equiv P \times Q$$

If the equation of exchange holds, then

$$P \equiv \frac{M \times V}{Q}$$

This equation shows that the money supply, velocity, and Real GDP determine the price level. In other words, the price level depends on the money supply, velocity, and Real GDP.

What kinds of changes in M, V, and Q will bring about inflation (an increase in the price level), *ceteris paribus*? Obviously, an increase in M or V or a decrease in Q will cause the price level to rise, so an increase in M or V or a decrease in Q is inflationary:

Inflationary tendencies: $M\uparrow$, $V\uparrow$, $Q\downarrow$

What will bring about deflation (a decrease in the price level), *ceteris paribus*? Obviously, a decrease in M or V or an increase in Q will cause the price level to fall, so a decrease in M or V or an increase in Q is deflationary:

Deflationary tendencies: $M\downarrow$, $V\downarrow$, $Q\uparrow$

(Answers to Self-Test questions are in Answers to Self-Test Questions at the back of the book.)

1. If $M \times V$ increases, why does $P \times Q$ have to rise?
2. What is the difference between the equation of exchange and the simple quantity theory of money?
3. Predict what will happen to the AD curve as a result of each of the following:
   a. The money supply rises.
   b. Velocity falls.
   c. The money supply rises by a greater percentage than velocity falls.
   d. The money supply falls.

14-2 Monetarism

Economists who call themselves *monetarists* have not been content to rely on the simple quantity theory of money. They do *not* hold that velocity is constant, nor do they hold that output is constant.

14-2a The Four Monetarist Positions

We begin with a brief explanation of the four positions held by monetarists. Then we discuss how, on the basis of these positions, monetarists view the economy.

Velocity Changes in a Predictable Way In the simple quantity theory of money, velocity is assumed to be constant; therefore, only changes in the money supply bring about changes in aggregate demand. Monetarists assume not that velocity is constant but, rather, that it can and does change. However, they believe that velocity changes in a predictable and therefore understandable way, not randomly. Monetarists hold that velocity is a function of certain variables—the interest rate, the expected inflation rate, the frequency with which employees receive paychecks, and more—and that changes in velocity can be predicted.

Aggregate Demand Depends on the Money Supply and on Velocity Earlier, we showed that TE (total expenditures in the economy) equals MV. To better understand the economy, some economists—such as Keynesians—focus on the spending components of TE (C, I, G, EX, and IM). Other economists—such as monetarists—focus on the money supply (M) and velocity (V). For example, Keynesians often argue that changes in C, I, G, EX, or IM can change aggregate demand, whereas monetarists often argue that changes in M and V can change aggregate demand.

The *SRAS* Curve Is Upward Sloping In the simple quantity theory of money, the level of Real GDP (Q) is assumed to be constant in the short run, so the aggregate supply curve is vertical, as shown in Exhibit 2. According to monetarists, Real GDP may change in the short run, and, therefore, the *SRAS* curve is upward sloping.

The Economy Is Self-Regulating (Prices and Wages Are Flexible) Monetarists believe that prices and wages are flexible. Monetarists therefore believe that the economy is self-regulating; thus, it can move itself out of a recessionary or inflationary gap and into long-run equilibrium, producing Natural Real GDP.

14-2b Monetarism and *AD–AS*

If monetarists tend to stress velocity and the money supply when discussing how the economy works, what effect does this view have in the *AD–AS* framework? Exhibit 3 helps to explain some of the highlights of monetarism. We consider each of the four parts (a)–(d) separately.

Part (a) We start with the economy in long-run equilibrium, producing Natural Real GDP (Q_N) at price level P_1. Monetarists believe that changes in the money supply will change aggregate demand. For example, suppose the money supply rises from $800 billion to $820 billion. If velocity is constant, the AD curve shifts to the right, from AD_1 to AD_2 in the exhibit. As a result, Real GDP rises to Q_1, and the price level rises to P_2. And, of course, if Real GDP rises, the unemployment rate falls, *ceteris paribus*.

EXHIBIT 3

Monetarism in an AD–AS Framework

According to monetarists, changes in the money supply and in velocity can change aggregate demand. In (a), an increase in the money supply shifts the AD curve to the right and raises Real GDP and the price level. Monetarists believe that the economy is self-regulating: In time, it moves back to its Natural Real GDP level at a higher price level. The same self-regulating properties are present in (b)–(d).

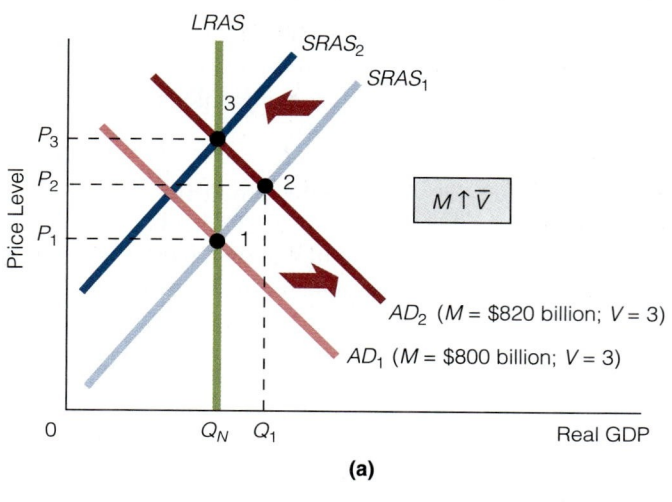
(a)

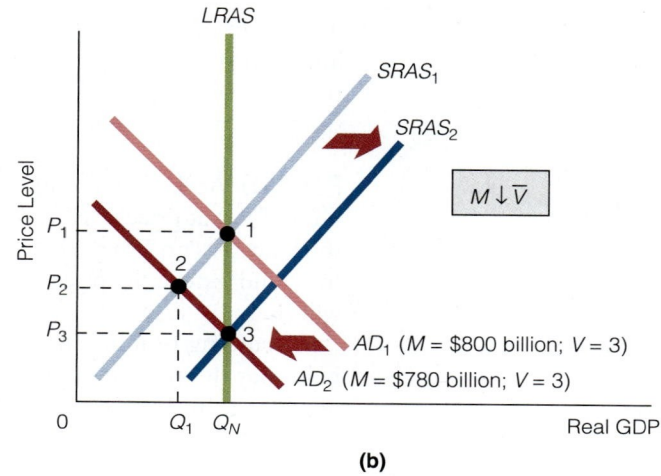
(b)

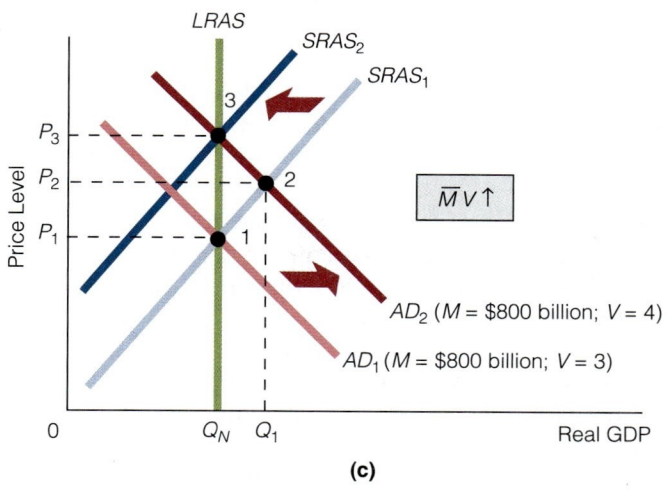
(c)

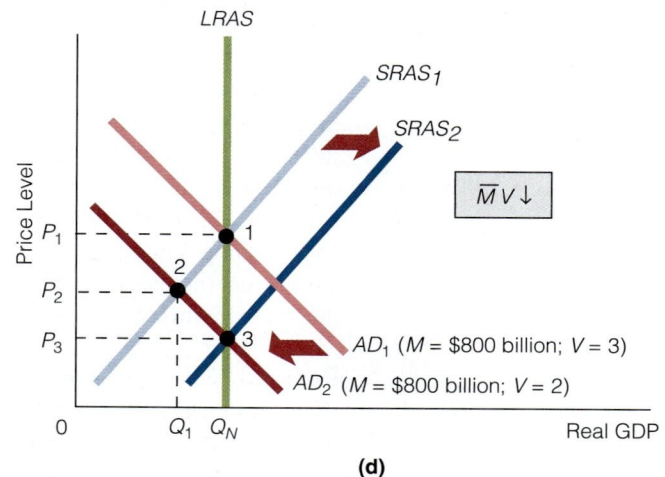
(d)

According to monetarists, the economy is in an inflationary gap at Q_1. However, given the monetarist belief in a self-regulating economy, soon wages will be bid up because the unemployment rate in an inflationary gap is less than the natural unemployment rate. The increase in wages will cause the SRAS curve to shift leftward from $SRAS_1$ to $SRAS_2$. The economy will then return to long-run equilibrium, producing the same level of Real GDP as it did originally (Q_N), but at a higher price level.

What monetarists predict will happen to the economy in the short run because of an increase in the money supply is slightly different from what they predict will happen in the long run. In the short run, Real GDP will rise, and the unemployment rate will fall. In the long run, Real GDP will return to its natural level, as will the unemployment rate, and the price level will be higher.

Part (b) Again, the economy is initially in long-run equilibrium, producing Natural Real GDP (Q_N) at price level P_1. A decrease in the money supply, with velocity held constant, will shift the AD curve to the left from AD_1 to AD_2. This leftward shift will then reduce Real GDP to Q_1 and reduce the price level to P_2. Because Real GDP has fallen, the unemployment rate will rise.

According to monetarists, the economy in part (b) is in a recessionary gap. Monetarists hold that the economy can get itself out of a recessionary gap because the economy is self-regulating. In time, wages will fall, the SRAS curve will shift to the right, and the economy will be back in long-run equilibrium producing Q_N, albeit at a lower price level.

Here, too, the short- and long-run effects of a decrease in the money supply differ, according to monetarists. In the short run, Real GDP will fall, and the unemployment rate will rise. In the long run, Real GDP will return to its natural level, as will the unemployment rate, and the price level will be lower.

Part (c) Once more, we start with the economy in long-run equilibrium. Instead of the money supply changing, velocity changes. An increase in velocity causes the AD curve to shift to the right from AD_1 to AD_2. As a result, Real GDP rises, as does the price level. The unemployment rate falls as Real GDP rises.

According to monetarists, the economy is in an inflationary gap, but, in time, it will move back to long-run equilibrium. So, in the short run, an increase in velocity raises Real GDP and lowers the unemployment rate. In the long run, Real GDP returns to its natural level, as does the unemployment rate, and the price level is higher.

Part (d) We begin again with the economy in long-run equilibrium. A decrease in velocity then causes the AD curve to shift to the left from AD_1 to AD_2. As a result, Real GDP falls, as does the price level. The unemployment rate rises as Real GDP falls.

According to monetarists, the economy is in a recessionary gap, but in time, it will move back to long-run equilibrium. So, in the short run, a decrease in velocity lowers Real GDP and increases the unemployment rate. In the long run, Real GDP returns to its natural level, as does the unemployment rate, and the price level is lower.

14-2c The Monetarist View of the Economy

The diagrammatic exposition of monetarism in Exhibit 3 reveals that monetarists believe that

- The economy is self-regulating.
- Changes in velocity and the money supply can change aggregate demand.
- Changes in velocity and the money supply will change the price level and Real GDP in the short run but only the price level in the long run.

We need to make one other important point with respect to monetarists. Consider this question: Can a change in velocity offset a change in the money supply? Suppose velocity falls and the money supply rises. By itself, a decrease in velocity will shift the *AD* curve to the left. And, by itself, an increase in the money supply will shift the *AD* curve to the right. The decline in velocity could shift the *AD* curve to the left by the same amount as the increase in the money supply shifts the *AD* curve to the right. If so, then a change in the money supply would have no effect on Real GDP, on the short-run price level, and on the long-run price level. In other words, changes in monetary policy may be ineffective at changing Real GDP and the price level.

Monetarists think that this condition—a change in velocity completely offsetting a change in the money supply—does not occur often. They believe (1) that velocity does not change very much from one period to the next (i.e., it is relatively stable) and (2) that changes in velocity are predictable (as mentioned earlier).

So, in the monetarist view of the economy, changes in velocity are not likely to offset changes in the money supply. Therefore, *changes in the money supply will largely determine changes in aggregate demand and thus changes in Real GDP and the price level.* For all practical purposes, an increase in the money supply will raise aggregate demand, increase both Real GDP and the price level in the short run, and increase only the price level in the long run. A decrease in the money supply will lower aggregate demand, decrease both Real GDP and the price level in the short run, and decrease only the price level in the long run.

---

1. What do monetarists predict will happen in the short run and in the long run as a result of each of the following (in each case, assume that the economy is in long-run equilibrium)?
    a. Velocity rises.
    b. Velocity falls.
    c. The money supply rises.
    d. The money supply falls.
2. Can a change in velocity offset a change in the money supply (and thus leave no effect on aggregate demand)? Explain your answer.

14-3 Inflation

In everyday usage, the word "inflation" refers to any increase in the price level. Economists, though, like to differentiate between two types of increases in the price level: a one-shot increase and a continued increase.

14-3a One-Shot Inflation

One-shot inflation is exactly what it sounds like: a one-shot, or one-time, increase in the price level. Suppose the CPI for years 1–5 is as follows:

Year	CPI
1	100
2	110
3	110
4	110
5	110

> **One-Shot Inflation**
> A one-time increase in the price level; an increase in the price level that does not continue.

Notice that the price level is higher in year 2 than in year 1 but that after year 2 it does not change. In other words, it takes a one-shot jump in year 2 and then stabilizes. This is an example of one-shot inflation, which can originate on either the demand side or the supply side of the economy.

One-Shot Inflation: Demand-Side Induced In Exhibit 4(a), the economy is initially in long-run equilibrium at point 1. Suppose the aggregate demand curve shifts rightward from AD_1 to AD_2. As this happens, the economy moves to point 2, where the price level is P_2. At point 2 in Exhibit 4(b), the Real GDP that the economy is producing (Q_2) is greater than Natural Real GDP, so the unemployment rate in the economy is lower than the natural unemployment rate. Consequently, as old wage contracts expire, workers are paid higher wage rates because unemployment is relatively low. As wage rates rise, the $SRAS$ curve shifts leftward from $SRAS_1$ to $SRAS_2$. The long-run equilibrium position is now at point 3. The price level and Real GDP at each of the three points are as follows:

Point	Price Level	Real GDP
1 (start)	P_1	$Q_1 = Q_N$
2	P_2	Q_2
3 (end)	P_3	$Q_1 = Q_N$

Notice that at point 3 the economy is at a higher price level than at point 1 but at the same Real GDP level.

Price levels that go from P_1 to P_2 to P_3 may seem like more than a one-shot increase. But because the price level stabilizes (at P_3), we cannot characterize it as continually rising. So the change in the price level is representative of one-shot inflation.

EXHIBIT 4

One-Shot Inflation: Demand-Side Induced

(a) The aggregate demand curve shifts rightward from AD_1 to AD_2. As a result, the price level increases from P_1 to P_2; the economy moves from point 1 to point 2. (b) Because the Real GDP that the economy produces (Q_2) is greater than Natural Real GDP, the unemployment rate that exists is less than the natural unemployment rate. Wage rates therefore rise, and the short-run aggregate supply curve shifts leftward from $SRAS_1$ to $SRAS_2$. Long-run equilibrium is at point 3.

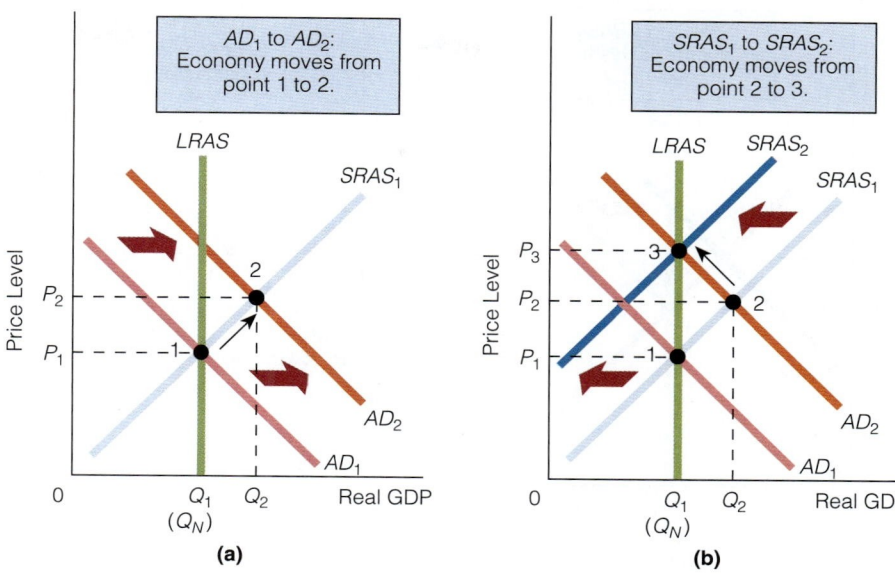

One-Shot Inflation: Supply-Side Induced In Exhibit 5(a), the economy is initially in long-run equilibrium at point 1. Suppose the short-run aggregate supply curve shifts leftward from $SRAS_1$ to $SRAS_2$ because, say, oil prices increase. As the curve shifts, the economy moves to point 2, where the price level is P_2.

At point 2 in Exhibit 5(b), the Real GDP that the economy is producing (Q_2) is less than Natural Real GDP, so the unemployment rate in the economy is greater than the natural unemployment rate. Consequently, as old wage contracts expire, workers are paid lower wage rates because unemployment is relatively high. As wage rates fall, the short-run aggregate supply curve shifts rightward from $SRAS_2$ to $SRAS_1$. The long-run equilibrium position is at point 1 again. (If wage rates are somewhat inflexible, moving from point 2 back to point 1 may take some time.) The price level and Real GDP at each of the three points are as follows:

Point	Price Level	Real GDP
1 (start)	P_1	$Q_1 = Q_N$
2	P_2	Q_2
1 (end)	P_1	$Q_1 = Q_N$

Because the price level initially increased from P_1 to P_2, this case is descriptive of one-shot inflation.

EXHIBIT 5

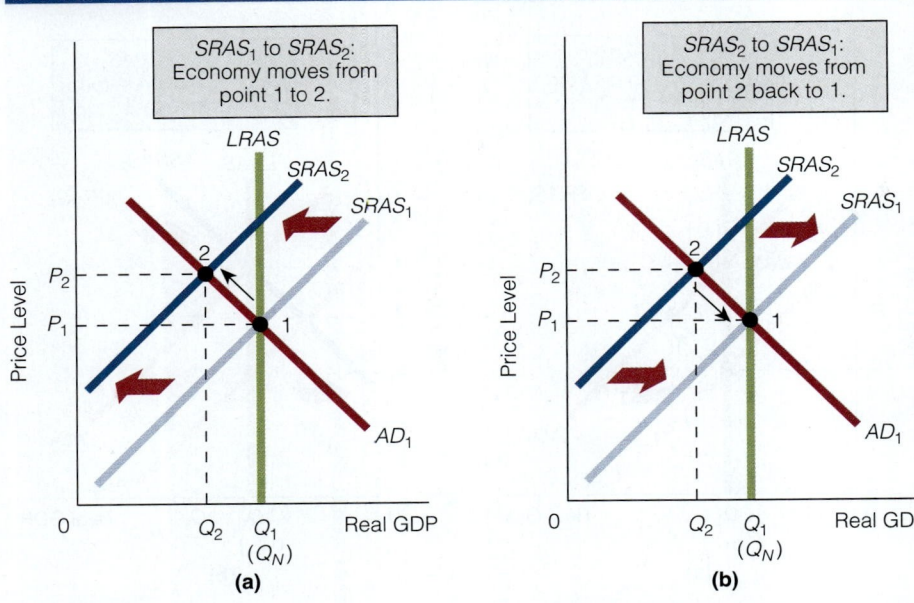

One-Shot Inflation: Supply-Side Induced

(a) The short-run aggregate supply curve shifts leftward from $SRAS_1$ to $SRAS_2$. As a result, the price level increases from P_1 to P_2; the economy moves from point 1 to point 2.
(b) Because the Real GDP that the economy produces (Q_2) is less than Natural Real GDP, the unemployment rate that exists is greater than the natural unemployment rate. Some economists argue that when this happens, wage rates will fall, and the short-run aggregate supply curve will shift rightward from $SRAS_2$ (back to $SRAS_1$). Long-run equilibrium is at point 1.

Confusing Demand-Induced and Supply-Induced One-Shot Inflation

Demand-induced and supply-induced one-shot inflation are easy to confuse.[2] To illustrate, suppose the Federal Reserve System increases the money supply. With more money in the economy, there can be greater total spending at any given price level. Consequently, the *AD* curve shifts rightward.

Next, prices begin to rise, and, soon afterward, wage rates begin to rise (because the economy is in an inflationary gap). Many employers, perhaps unaware that the money supply has increased, certainly are aware that they are paying their employees higher wages. Thus, employers may think that the higher price level is due to higher wage rates, not to the increased money supply that preceded the higher wage rates. But they would be wrong. What may look like a supply-induced rise in the price level is really demand-induced.

We can tell this same story in terms of the diagrams in Exhibit 4. In (a), the *AD* curve shifts rightward because, as explained, the money supply increases. Employers, however, are unaware of what has happened in part (a). What they see is part (b), in which they end up paying higher wage rates to their employees, and the *SRAS* curve shifts leftward. Unaware that the *AD* curve shifted rightward in (a), but aware that the *SRAS* curve shifted leftward in (b), employers mistakenly conclude that the rise in the price level originated with a supply-side factor (higher wage rates), not with a demand-side factor (an increase in the money supply).

---

[2] Sometimes the terms "demand-side inflation" and "supply-side inflation" are used.

Thinking Like an Economist

Your Eyes Can Deceive You People tend to believe that what they see with their own eyes or what they experience directly in their daily lives causes the effects they notice. In our last example, employers mistakenly believed that the stimulus for the rise in the price level was a rise in wage rates (which they had experienced firsthand), not an increase in the money supply (which they probably did not know had occurred). But the economist knows that the cause of a phenomenon may be far removed from our personal orbit. This awareness is part of the economic way of thinking.

Economics 24/7

Grade Inflation: It's All Relative

Inflation can sometimes be deceptive. Suppose Jones produces and sells motorcycles. The average price for one of his motorcycles is $10,000. Unknown to Jones, the Fed increases the money supply. Months pass, and then one day Jones notices that the demand for his motorcycles has increased. Jones raises the prices of his motorcycles and earns a higher dollar income.

Jones is excited about earning more income, but soon he realizes that the prices of many of the things he buys have increased too. Food, clothing, and housing prices have all gone up. Jones is earning a higher dollar income, but he is also paying higher prices. In relative terms, Jones's financial position may be the same as, or even worse than, it was before the price of motorcycles increased.

Now let's consider grade inflation. Beginning in the 1960s, the average GPA at most colleges and universities across the country began to rise. Whereas professors once gave out the full range of grades—A, B, C, D, and F—today many professors give only As and Bs and a few Cs. The so-called Gentleman's C, once a mainstay on many college campuses, is said to have been replaced by the "Gentleperson's B."

Grade inflation can deceive you, just as general price inflation deceived Jones. To illustrate, suppose you get higher grades (without studying more or working harder). Your average grade goes from, say, C+ to B, and you believe that you have an advantage over other college and university students. You reason that, with higher grades, you will have a better chance of getting a good job or of getting into graduate school.

But you do only if your grades go up *and no one else's do*. In other words, your relative position must improve. Grade inflation at thousands of colleges and universities across the country prevents you from gaining that advantage. You get higher grades, but so does everyone else. Your GPA increases from, say, 2.90 to 3.60, but other students' GPAs increase similarly.

So, as long as other students are getting higher grades too, better grades for you do not necessarily make it easier for you to compete with others for a job or for admission to graduate school. In essence, grade inflation, like general price inflation, is deceptive. With price inflation, you may initially think that your financial position has improved because you are earning more for what you sell, but then you realize that you have to pay more for the things you buy. With grade inflation, you may initially think that you have an advantage over other students because you are receiving higher grades, but then you learn that everyone else is getting higher grades too. Your relative position may be the same as it was before grade inflation boosted your GPA.

14-3b Continued Inflation

Suppose the CPI for years 1 to 5 is as follows:

Year	CPI
1	100
2	110
3	120
4	130
5	140

Notice that the CPI goes from 100 to 110, then from 110 to 120, and so on. Each year, the CPI is higher than the year before. This continued increase in the price level is an example of **continued inflation**.

Continued Inflation
A continued increase in the price level.

From One-Shot Inflation to Continued Inflation Continued increases in aggregate demand can turn one-shot inflation into continued inflation. (Later in this chapter, we describe what leads to continued increases in aggregate demand.) The process is illustrated in Exhibit 6. (The diagram looks scary, but not when you take it one step at a time.)

EXHIBIT 6

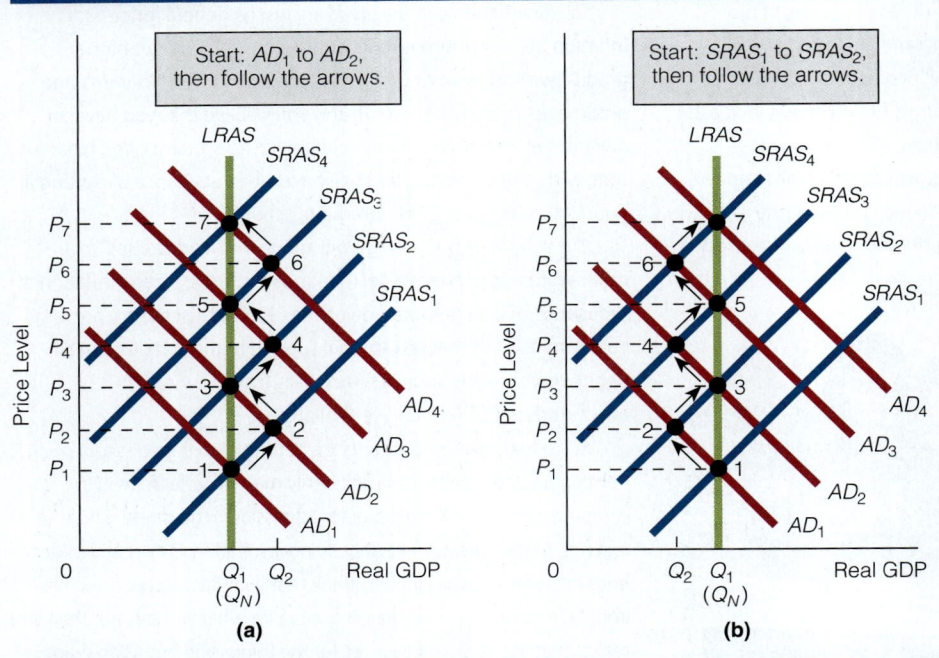

Changing One-Shot Inflation into Continued Inflation

(a) The aggregate demand curve shifts rightward from AD_1 to AD_2. The economy initially moves from point 1 to point 2 and finally to point 3. Continued increases in the price level are brought about through continued increases in aggregate demand. (b) The short-run aggregate supply curve shifts leftward from $SRAS_1$ to $SRAS_2$. The economy initially moves from point 1 to point 2. The economy will return to point 1 unless there is an increase in aggregate demand. We see here, as in (a), that continued increases in the price level are brought about through continued increases in aggregate demand.

Beginning at point 1 in Exhibit 6(a), the aggregate demand curve shifts rightward from AD_1 to AD_2. The economy moves from point 1 to point 2. At point 2, the unemployment rate in the economy is less than the natural unemployment rate. As a result, wage rates rise and cause the short-run aggregate supply curve to shift leftward from $SRAS_1$ to $SRAS_2$. The economy moves from point 2 to point 3. At point 3, the economy is in long-run equilibrium.

Suppose that at point 3 the economy experiences *another* rightward shift in the aggregate demand curve (to AD_3). The process keeps repeating itself, and the economy moves from point 3 to point 4 and to point 5. Still *another* rightward shift in the aggregate demand curve moves the economy from point 5 to point 6 and to point 7. The exhibit stops at point 7, but it could have continued. The result of this process is a *continually rising price level*—from P_1 to P_7 and beyond. Continued increases in aggregate demand cause continued inflation.

Continued inflation from the supply side of the economy is illustrated in Exhibit 6(b). Beginning at point 1, the short-run aggregate supply curve shifts leftward from $SRAS_1$ to $SRAS_2$. The economy moves from point 1 to point 2. At point 2, the unemployment rate in the economy is greater than the natural unemployment rate. According to some economists, the natural tendency is for wage rates to fall and for the $SRAS$ curve to shift rightward, moving the economy back to point 1.

This natural tendency of the economy to return to point 1 will be offset, however, if the aggregate demand curve shifts rightward. Then, instead of moving from point 2 back to point 1, the economy moves from point 2 to point 3. At point 3, the economy is in long-run equilibrium, and the price level is higher than at point 2.

Suppose the economy now experiences another leftward shift in the aggregate supply curve (to $SRAS_3$). Then the economy moves from point 3 to point 4 and would naturally return to point 3 unless the aggregate demand curve shifts rightward. If it does, the economy moves to point 5. The same process moves the economy from point 5 to point 6 and to point 7, where the exhibit stops. This process results in a continually rising price level—from P_1 to P_7 and beyond. Again, *continued increases in aggregate demand cause continued inflation.*

The Effect of Continued Declines in SRAS Can continued declines in $SRAS$ cause continued inflation? For example, suppose a labor union continually asks for and receives higher wages. As wages continually increase, the $SRAS$ curve will continually shift leftward, leading to a continually rising price level. This scenario could happen but isn't likely. Every time workers ask for and receive higher wages—shifting the $SRAS$ curve leftward—Real GDP declines. Because not as many workers are needed to produce a lower Real GDP as are needed to produce a higher Real GDP, some of the workers will lose their jobs. Labor unions are not likely to adopt a policy that would put more and more of their members out of work.

There is another argument against declines in $SRAS$ causing continued inflation. The CPI and the Real GDP level for, say, 1960 indicate that today both are higher than they were in 1960. The higher price level means that, since 1960, we have experienced continued inflation in the United States but that this continued inflation has accompanied a (generally) rising Real GDP. If the continued inflation of the past few decades had been caused by continued declines in $SRAS$, Real GDP would not have been rising. Instead, it would have been falling. (As $SRAS$ declines, the price level rises, and Real GDP falls.) In short, the continued inflation in the United States had to be caused by continued increases in AD, not by continued decreases in $SRAS$.

The Big Question If continued increases in aggregate demand cause continued inflation, what causes continued increases in aggregate demand? At a given price level, anything that increases total expenditures increases aggregate demand and shifts the AD curve to the right.

With this idea in mind, consider an increase in the money supply. With more money in the economy, total expenditures can be greater at a given price level. Consequently, aggregate demand increases, and the *AD* curve shifts rightward.

Economists widely agree that the only factor that can change *continually* in such a way as to bring about continued increases in aggregate demand is the money supply. Specifically, continued increases in the money supply lead to continued increases in aggregate demand, which generate continued inflation:

Continued increases in the money supply → Continued increases

in aggregate demand → Continued inflation

The money supply is the *only* factor that can continually increase without causing a reduction in one of the four components of total expenditures (consumption, investment, government purchases, and net exports). This point is important because someone might ask, "Can't government purchases continually increase and so cause continued inflation?" That is unlikely, for two reasons:

- Government purchases cannot go beyond either real or political limits. The real upper limit is 100 percent of GDP. No one knows what the political upper limit is, but it is likely to be less than 100 percent of GDP. In either case, once government purchases reach their limit, they can no longer increase.

- Some economists argue that government purchases that are not financed with new money may crowd out one of the other expenditure components (see Chapter 11). Thus, increases in government purchases are not guaranteed to raise total expenditures because, if government purchases rise, consumption may fall to the degree that government purchases have increased. For example, for every additional dollar government spends on public education, households may spend $1 less on private education.

The emphasis on the money supply as the only factor that can continue to increase and thus cause continued inflation has led most economists to agree with Nobel Laureate Milton Friedman that "inflation is always and everywhere a monetary phenomenon."

14-3c Can You Get Rid of Inflation With Price Controls?

Suppose that in country A the government regularly imposes price ceilings on goods and services. For example, while the market price of good X is, say, $10, the price ceiling for that good is set at $8; while the market price of good Y is, say, $4, the price ceiling for that good is set at $3.

Now, suppose the central bank in country A increases the money supply dramatically. Then we would predict that prices in the country would soon follow upward. In other words, inflation would soon occur. But can inflation occur if the government maintains its price ceilings? For example, if the market price of good X rises from $10 to $12 and the market price of good Y rises from $4 to $7, won't these goods still sell at the price of their ceilings: $8 and $3, respectively. And if this is the case—if goods X and Y still sell at $8 and $3, respectively—hasn't the government been able to "legislate" inflation away?

Well, not exactly. As we discussed in an earlier chapter, there are consequences of price ceilings (set below the equilibrium price). One of those consequences is that nonmoney rationing devices will be used—one of which is first come, first served, which results in long lines of people waiting to buy goods. Look at it this way: If the market price of good X is $10 and the price ceiling for the good is set at $8, there is a shortage of the good and people will line up to buy good X. Let's say that the average length of the line is 25 people. Now, if the market price of good X rises to $12 and the price ceiling for the good remains set at $8, people will continue to line up to buy the good, but now the lines will be longer. The average length of the line may rise to, say, 50 people.

So how is inflation felt in a country that imposes and maintains price ceilings? The answer is in the length of the lines of people. The longer the lines, the higher is the inflation rate.

1. The prices of houses, cars, and television sets have increased. Has there been inflation?
2. Is continued inflation likely to be supply-side induced? Explain your answer.
3. What type of inflation is Milton Friedman referring to when he says that "inflation is always and everywhere a monetary phenomenon?"

14-4 Money and Interest Rates

Let's review how changes in the money supply affect different economic variables.

14-4a Which Economic Variables Does a Change in the Money Supply Affect?

The money supply can affect interest rates, but to understand how, we need to review how the money supply affects different economic variables:

1. *Money and the supply of loans.* Chapter 13 explained the actions of the Fed that change the money supply. For example, if the Fed were to lower the interest it pays on reserves, banks might be prompted to hold fewer reserves with the Fed and instead use those reserves to create new loans thus indirectly increasing the supply of loans. Also, since the new loans are created in the form of new checkable deposits, the money supply rises.

2. *Money and Real GDP.* The current chapter shows how a change in the money supply can change aggregate demand and thereby change the price level and Real GDP in the short run. For example, look back at Exhibit 3(a). The economy starts at point 1, producing Q_N. An increase in the money supply then shifts the AD curve rightward, from AD_1 to AD_2. In the short run, the economy moves to point 2 and produces a higher level of Real GDP (Q_1). Similarly, in the short run, a decrease in the money supply produces a lower level of Real GDP. [see Exhibit 3(b)].

3. *Money and the price level.* The current chapter also shows how a change in the money supply can change the price level. Again, look back at Exhibit 3(a). Initially, at point 1, the price level is P_1. An increase in the money supply then shifts the AD curve rightward

from AD_1 to AD_2. In the short run, the price level in the economy moves from P_1 to P_2. In the long run, the economy is at point 3, and the price level is P_3. Exhibit 3(b) shows how a decrease in the money supply affects the price level.

So changes in the money supply affect (1) the supply of loans, (2) Real GDP, and (3) the price level.

Can the money supply affect anything else? Many economists say that, because the money supply affects the price level, it also affects the *expected inflation rate*. As an example, your expected inflation rate—the inflation rate you expect will be realized over the next year—may be 5 percent, 6 percent, or some other rate. Changes in the money supply affect the expected inflation rate either directly or indirectly. The equation of exchange indicates that the greater the increase in the money supply is, the greater the rise in the price level will be. And we would expect that the greater the rise in the price level is, the higher the expected inflation rate will be, *ceteris paribus*. For example, we would predict that a money supply growth rate of, say, 10 percent a year generates a greater actual inflation rate and a larger expected inflation rate than a money supply growth rate of 2 percent a year.

In sum, changes in the money supply (or changes in the rate of growth of the money supply) can affect the following:

1. The supply of loans
2. Real GDP
3. The price level
4. The expected inflation rate

14-4b The Money Supply, the Loanable Funds Market, and Interest Rates

Exhibit 7(a) shows the loanable funds market. The demand for loanable funds (D_{LF}) is downward sloping, indicating that borrowers will borrow more funds as the interest rate declines. The supply of loanable funds (S_{LF}) is upward sloping, indicating that lenders will lend more funds as the interest rate rises. The equilibrium interest rate (i_1 percent) is determined through the forces of supply and demand. If there is a surplus of loanable funds, the interest rate falls; if there is a shortage of loanable funds, the interest rate rises.

Anything that affects either the supply of or the demand for loanable funds will obviously affect the interest rate. All four of the factors that are affected by changes in the money supply—the supply of loans, Real GDP, the price level, and the expected inflation rate—affect either the supply of or demand for loanable funds.

The Supply of Loans A Fed action causes banks to use more of their reserves to create new loans and therefore increases the supply of loanable funds. As a result, the interest rate declines [see Exhibit 7(b)]. This change in the interest rate due to a change in the supply of loanable funds is called the **liquidity effect**.

Liquidity Effect
The change in the interest rate due to a change in the supply of loanable funds.

Real GDP A change in Real GDP affects both the supply of and the demand for loanable funds.

First, how does Real GDP affect the supply of loanable funds? When Real GDP rises, people's wealth is greater. (Real GDP consists of goods, and goods are a component of wealth.) When people become wealthier, they often demand more bonds (in much the same way that they may demand more houses, cars, and jewelry). Demanding more bonds (buying more bonds), however, is nothing more than lending more money to others. When you buy a bond issued by company A, you are essentially giving the company a loan. The company says, "Do you want to buy this bond for $10,000?" You say yes. When you buy the bond from the company for $10,000, you essentially give the company a $10,000 loan, which it is obligated to repay with interest. When the company pays off the bond to you, it returns the $10,000 plus interest. So, as Real GDP rises, individuals become wealthier, and they tend to buy more bonds—that is, extend more loans. The supply of loanable funds thus increases.

Second, how does Real GDP affect the demand for loanable funds? When Real GDP rises, profitable business opportunities usually abound, and businesses issue or supply more bonds to take advantage of those opportunities. But supplying more bonds is nothing more than demanding more loanable funds. So, when Real GDP rises, corporations issue or supply more bonds, thereby demanding more loanable funds.

In sum, when Real GDP increases, both the supply of and the demand for loanable funds increase. Usually, the overall effect on the interest rate is that the demand for loanable funds increases by more than the supply, so the interest rate rises. The change in the interest rate due to a change in Real GDP is called the **income effect** [see Exhibit 7(c)].

Income Effect
The change in the interest rate due to a change in Real GDP.

The Price Level A downward-sloping AD curve is explained by (1) the real balance effect, (2) the interest rate effect, and (3) the international trade effect (see Chapter 8). With respect to the interest rate effect, when the price level rises, the purchasing power of money falls. People may therefore increase their demand for credit or for loanable funds to borrow the funds necessary to buy a fixed bundle of goods. This change in the interest rate due to a change in the price level is called the **price-level effect** [see Exhibit 7(d)].

Price-Level Effect
The change in the interest rate due to a change in the price level.

The Expected Inflation Rate A change in the expected inflation rate affects both the supply of and demand for loanable funds. Suppose the expected inflation rate is zero and that, when the expected inflation rate is zero, the equilibrium interest rate is 6 percent, as in Exhibit 7(e). Now suppose the expected inflation rate rises from 0 percent to 4 percent. What will this rise in the expected inflation rate do to the demand for and supply of loanable funds? Borrowers (demanders of loanable funds) will be willing to pay 4 percent more interest for their loans because they expect to be paying back the loans with dollars that have 4 percent less buying power than the dollars they are borrowing. If they wait to buy goods they want, the prices will have risen by 4 percent. To beat the price rise, consumers are willing to pay up to 4 percent more to borrow money to purchase the goods now. In effect, the demand-for-loanable-funds curve shifts rightward so that at Q_1 borrowers are willing to pay a 4 percent higher interest rate.

On the other side of the loanable funds market, the lenders (the suppliers of loanable funds) require a 4 percent higher interest rate to compensate them for the 4 percent less valuable dollars with which the loan will be repaid. In effect, the supply-of-loanable-funds curve shifts leftward [see Exhibit 7(e)].

EXHIBIT 7

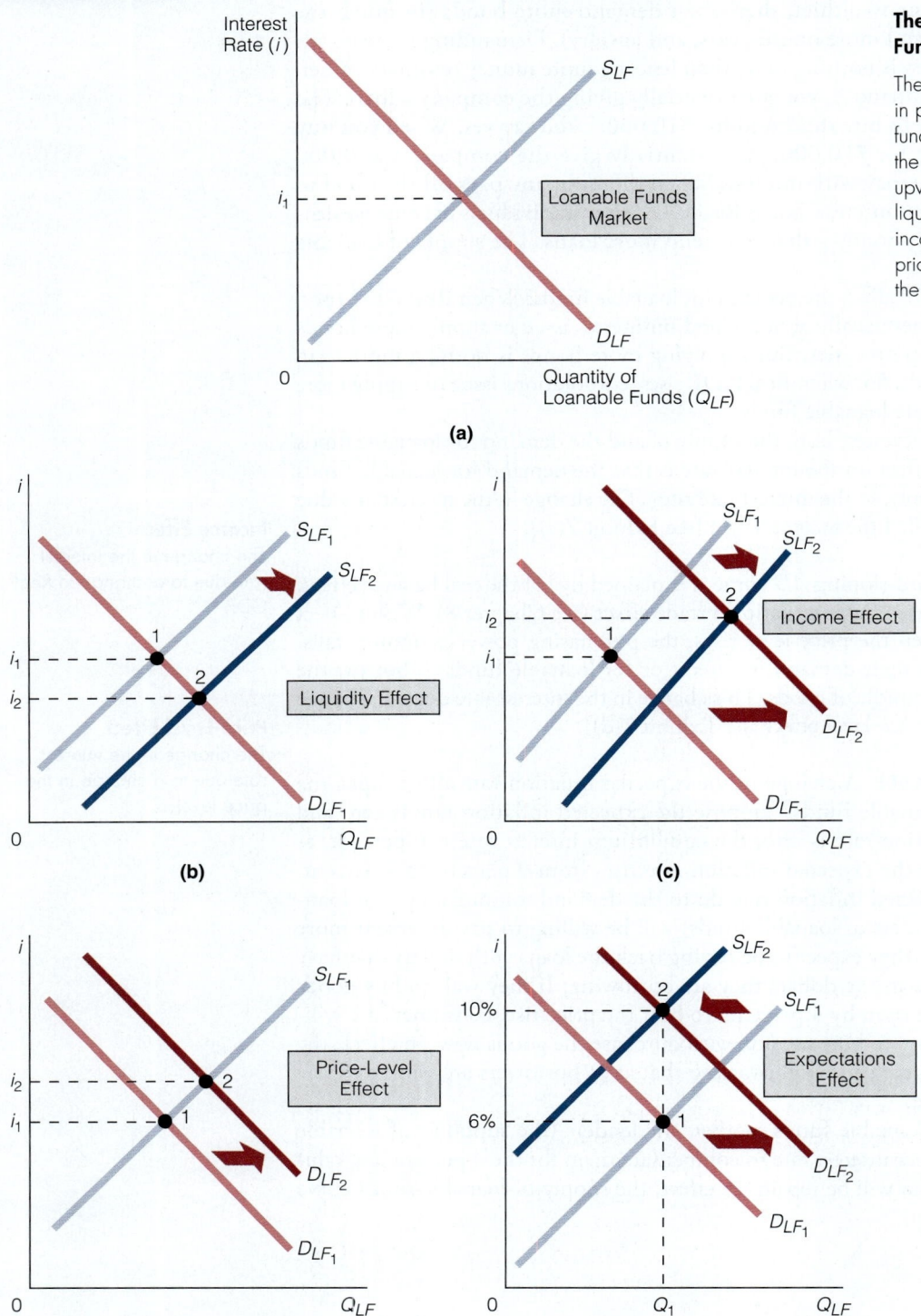

The Interest Rate and the Loanable Funds Market

The loanable funds market is shown in part (a). The demand for loanable funds (D_{LF}) is downward sloping; the supply of loanable funds (S_{LF}) is upward sloping. Part (b) shows the liquidity effect, part (c) shows the income effect, part (d) shows the price-level effect, and part (e) shows the expectations effect.

Thus, an expected inflation rate of 4 percent increases the demand for loanable funds and decreases the supply of loanable funds. So the interest rate is 4 percent higher than it was when the expected inflation rate was zero. A change in the interest rate due to a change in the expected inflation rate is referred to as the **expectations effect** (or *Fisher effect*, after U.S. economist Irving Fisher).

Exhibit 8 summarizes how a change in the money supply directly and indirectly affects the interest rate.

Expectations Effect
The change in the interest rate due to a change in the expected inflation rate.

EXHIBIT 8

How the Fed Affects the Interest Rate

This exhibit summarizes the way the Fed affects the interest rate through its monetary policy. For example, if the Fed were to lower the interest it pays on reserves, banks might be prompted to hold fewer reserves with the Fed and instead use those reserves to create new loans (new checkable deposits), thus increasing the money supply. An action such as this would not only affect the supply of loans, but Real GDP, the price level and the expected inflation rate too.

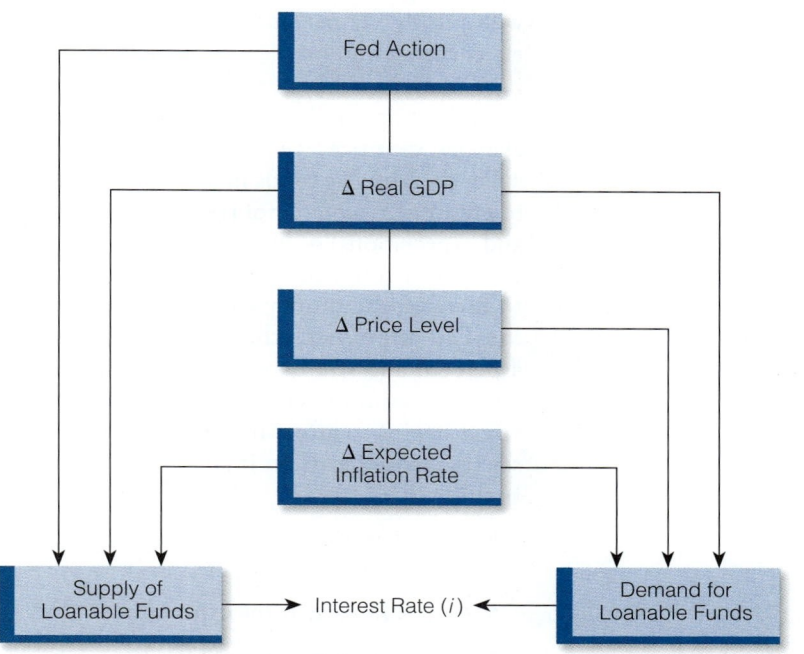

The Difference Between the Price-Level Effect and the Expectations Effect To many people, the price-level effect sounds the same as the expectations effect. After all, both have something to do with the price level.

But they are different. Consider a one-shot change in the money supply that ultimately moves the price level from a price index of 120 to a price index of 135. The price-level effect is the change in the interest rate that is related to the actual rise in price level. The demand for loanable funds creeps up steadily as the price index rises from 120 to 121, to 122, to 123, and so on, to 135. Once the price index hits 135, though, there is no further reason for the demand for loanable funds to rise because the price level isn't rising anymore.

As the price level is rising, people's expected inflation rate is rising. They may feel that they know where the price level is headed (from 120 to 135) and adjust accordingly. Once the price level hits 135 (and given that the change in the money supply is a one-shot change), the expected inflation rate falls to zero. Any change in the interest rate due to a rise in the expected inflation rate is now over, and, therefore, the expected inflation rate no longer has an effect on the interest rate. But certainly, the price level still has an effect, because the price level is higher than it was originally. In the end, the effect on the interest rate due to a rise in the price level remains, and the effect on the interest rate due to a rise in the expected inflation rate disappears.

14-4c What Happens to the Interest Rate as the Money Supply Changes?

Suppose the Fed takes action to raise the rate of growth of the money supply from, say, 3 percent to 5 percent a year. What effect does this action have on the interest rate? Some people will quickly say that it will lower the interest rate, thinking perhaps that only the liquidity effect comes into play.

That would be the right answer if all an increase in the money supply growth rate did was affect the supply of loanable funds, but, as explained, this isn't the only effect. Real GDP changes, the price level changes, and the expected inflation rate changes, and all these changes affect the loanable funds market, just as the Fed action did. Figuring out what happens to the interest rate is a matter of trying to figure out when each effect (liquidity, income, price level, and expectations) occurs and how strong each is.

To illustrate, suppose that, on December 31, everyone expects the Fed to continue to increase the money supply at a growth rate of 2 percent a year. Then, on January 1, the Fed announces that it will increase the rate of growth of the money supply to 4 percent and will begin to take actions to effect this outcome immediately. One second after the announcement, people's expected inflation rate may rise. The expectations effect begins to affect interest rates immediately. Consequently, on January 2, the interest rate is higher than it was one day earlier. The sequence of events may be described as follows:

- *Point 1 in time:* The Fed says that it will increase the growth rate of the money supply.
- *Point 2 in time:* If the expectations effect kicks in immediately, then …
- *Point 3 in time:* Interest rates rise.

At point 3 in time, a natural conclusion to draw is that an increase in the rate of growth in the money supply *raises* the interest rate. The problem with this conclusion, though, is that *not all the effects (liquidity, income, etc.) have occurred yet*. In time, the liquidity effect puts downward pressure on the interest rate. Suppose the liquidity effect goes to work on January 15, and the interest rate begins to fall from what it was on January 2. Then, on January 15, someone could say, "Obviously, an increase in the rate of growth of the money supply *lowers* interest rates."

- *Point 4 in time:* The liquidity effect kicks in.
- *Point 5 in time:* As a result of what happened at point 4, the interest rate drops. The interest rate is now lower than it was at point 3.

14-4d The Nominal and Real Interest Rates

If you were to call a bank and ask what it charges for, say, a car loan, the bank would quote an interest rate. The quoted interest rate is the rate we have been discussing, the interest rate that comes about through the interaction of the demand for and supply of loanable funds. Sometimes, this interest rate is called the **nominal interest rate**, or market interest rate.

The nominal interest rate may not be the true cost of borrowing, because part of the nominal interest rate is a reflection of the expected inflation rate. Suppose the nominal interest rate is 9 percent and the expected inflation rate is 2 percent. Then, if you take out a loan for $10,000 at 9 percent, you will have to pay back the loan amount ($10,000) plus $900 in interest at the end of the year. In other words, for a $10,000 loan, you have to repay $10,900.

Now suppose the expected inflation rate turns out to be the actual inflation rate. As an example, people expect the inflation rate to be 2 percent, and it turns out to be 2 percent. In this case, the dollars you pay back will be worth less—by 2 percent—than the dollars you borrowed. In other words, you borrowed dollars that were worth 2 percent more in purchasing power than the dollars you repaid.

This fact should be taken into account in determining your real cost of borrowing. Economists would say that the real cost of borrowing was not 9 percent, but 7 percent. The real cost of borrowing is sometimes called the **real interest rate**, which is equal to the nominal interest rate minus the expected inflation rate:[3]

$$\text{Real interest rate} = \text{Nominal interest rate} - \text{Expected inflation rate}$$

Given this equation, the nominal interest rate is therefore equal to the real interest rate plus the expected inflation rate:

$$\text{Nominal interest rate} = \text{Real interest rate} + \text{Expected inflation rate}$$

Nominal Interest Rate
The interest rate actually charged (or paid) in the market; the market interest rate: Nominal interest rate = Real interest rate + Expected inflation rate.

Real Interest Rate
The nominal interest rate minus the expected inflation rate. When the expected inflation rate is zero, the real interest rate equals the nominal interest rate.

---

1. If the expected inflation rate is 4 percent and the nominal interest rate is 7 percent, what is the real interest rate?
2. Is it possible for the nominal interest rate to rise immediately following an increase in the money supply? Explain your answer.
3. The Fed affects only the interest rate via the liquidity effect. Do you agree or disagree? Explain your answer.

---

[3] A broader definition is Real interest rate = Nominal interest rate − Expected rate of change in the price level. This definition is useful because we will not always be dealing with an expected inflation rate; we could be dealing with an expected deflation rate.

Office Hours

"What Is the Current Expected Inflation Rate?"

Student: Is there some way to figure out the expected inflation rate at any given time?

Instructor: One way to find out the expected inflation rate is to look at the spread—the difference—between the yield on conventional bonds and the yield on indexed bonds with the same maturity.

Student: What's a conventional bond? What's an inflation-indexed bond?

Instructor: An inflation-indexed bond guarantees the purchaser a certain real rate of return; a conventional, or non-indexed, bond does not. For example, suppose you purchase an *inflation-indexed*, 10-year, $1,000 bond that pays 4 percent interest. Then, if there is no inflation, the annual interest payment is $40. But if the inflation rate is 3 percent, the bond issuer marks up the value of your security by 3 percent—from $1,000 to $1,030. Your annual interest payment is then 4 percent of this new higher amount—that is, 4 percent of $1,030, or $41.20.

Now, investors are willing to accept a lower yield on inflation-indexed bonds because they get something that they don't get with conventional bonds: protection against inflation. So, although a conventional bond may yield, say, 6 percent, an inflation-indexed bond may yield 4 percent. The spread is the difference between the two rates.

Student: And how does the spread or difference relate to the expected inflation rate?

Instructor: Well, the spread is a measure of the inflation rate that investors expect will exist over the life of the bond. To illustrate with real numbers, let's say that we go to www.bloomberg.com/ and learn that an *inflation-indexed* 10-year Treasury bond has an interest rate of 1.72 percent and that a conventional 10-year Treasury bond has an interest rate of 4.02 percent. The difference, or spread, is therefore 2.3 percent. In other words, on this day, investors (or the market) expect that the inflation rate is going to be 2.3 percent.

So, by checking the spread between interest rates on conventional and inflation-indexed bonds with the *same maturity* (i.e., both mature in the same number of months or years), you can see what the market expects that the inflation rate will be. As the spread widens, the market expects a higher inflation rate; as it narrows, the market expects a lower inflation rate.

Points to Remember

1. We discussed two types of bonds: inflation-indexed and conventional. Each type of bonds pays an interest rate.
2. The spread, or difference, between the interest rates on a conventional and an inflation-indexed bond is the market's expected inflation rate. The larger the spread, the higher is the expected inflation rate (the inflation rate the market expects in the future). The smaller the spread, the lower is the expected inflation rate (the lower the inflation rate the market expects in the future).

Chapter Summary

The Equation of Exchange

- The equation of exchange is an identity: $MV \equiv PQ$. The equation of exchange can be interpreted in different ways: (1) The money supply multiplied by velocity must equal the price level times Real GDP: $M \times V \equiv P \times Q$. (2) The money supply multiplied by velocity must equal GDP: $M \times V \equiv GDP$. (3) Total expenditures (measured by MV) must equal the total sales revenues of business firms (measured by PQ): $MV \equiv PQ$.

- The equation of exchange is not a theory of the economy. However, the equation of exchange can be turned into a theory by making assumptions about some of the variables. For example, if we assume that both V and Q are constant, then we have the simple quantity theory of money, which predicts that changes in the money supply cause *strictly proportional* changes in the price level.

- A change in the money supply or a change in velocity will change aggregate demand and therefore lead to a shift in the AD curve. Specifically, either an increase in the money supply or an increase in velocity will increase aggregate demand and therefore shift the AD curve to the right. A decrease in the money supply or a decrease in velocity will decrease aggregate demand and therefore shift the AD curve to the left.
- In the simple quantity theory of money, Real GDP is assumed to be constant in the short run. This assumption means that the AS curve is vertical. Also, velocity is assumed to be constant, so only a change in money supply can change aggregate demand. In the face of a vertical AS curve, any change in the money supply shifts the AD curve and changes only the price level, not Real GDP.

Monetarism

- According to monetarists, if the economy is initially in long-run equilibrium, then (1) an increase in the money supply will raise the price level and Real GDP in the short run and will raise only the price level in the long run; (2) a decrease in the money supply will lower the price level and Real GDP in the short run and will lower only the price level in the long run; (3) an increase in velocity will raise the price level and Real GDP in the short run and will raise only the price level in the long run; (4) a decrease in velocity will lower the price level and Real GDP in the short run and will lower only the price level in the long run.

One-Shot Inflation and Continued Inflation

- One-shot inflation can result from an increase in aggregate demand or a decrease in short-run aggregate supply.
- For one-shot inflation to change to continued inflation, a continued increase in aggregate demand is necessary and sufficient. Continued increases in the money supply cause continued increases in aggregate demand and continued inflation.

The Money Supply and Interest Rates

- Changes in the money supply can affect the interest rate by means of the liquidity, income, price level, and expectations effects.
- The change in the interest rate due to a change in the supply of loanable funds is called the liquidity effect. The change in the interest rate due to a change in Real GDP is called the income effect. The change in the interest rate due to a change in the price level is called the price-level effect. The change in the interest rate due to a change in the expected inflation rate is called the expectations effect (or Fisher effect).

Nominal and Real Interest Rates

- Real interest rate = Nominal interest rate − Expected inflation rate
- Nominal interest rate = Real interest rate + Expected inflation rate

Key Terms and Concepts

Equation of Exchange
Velocity
Simple Quantity Theory of Money
One-Shot Inflation
Continued Inflation
Liquidity Effect
Income Effect
Price-Level Effect
Expectations Effect
Nominal Interest Rate
Real Interest Rate

Questions and Problems

1. What are the assumptions and predictions of the simple quantity theory of money? Does the simple quantity theory of money predict well?
2. Can the money supply support a GDP level greater than itself? Explain your answer.
3. In the simple quantity theory of money, the AS curve is vertical. Explain why.
4. In the simple quantity theory of money, what will lead to an increase in aggregate demand? In monetarism, what will lead to an increase in aggregate demand?

5. According to the simple quantity theory of money, what will happen to Real GDP and the price level as the money supply rises? Explain your answer.

6. In monetarism, how will each of the following affect the price level in the short run?
   a. An increase in velocity
   b. A decrease in velocity
   c. An increase in the money supply
   d. A decrease in the money supply

7. According to monetarism, an increase in the money supply will lead to a rise in Real GDP in the long run. Do you agree or disagree with this statement? Explain your answer.

8. Suppose the objective of the Fed is to increase Real GDP. To this end, it increases the money supply. Can anything offset the increase in the money supply so that Real GDP does not rise? Explain your answer.

9. What is the difference in the long run between a one-shot increase in aggregate demand and a one-shot decrease in short-run aggregate supply?

10. "One-shot inflation may be a demand-side (of the economy) or a supply-side phenomenon, but continued inflation is likely to be a demand-side phenomenon." Do you agree or disagree with this statement? Explain your answer.

11. Explain how demand-induced, one-shot inflation may seem like supply-induced, one-shot inflation.

12. In recent years, economists have argued about the true value of the real interest rate at any one time and over time. Given that Nominal interest rate = Real interest rate + Expected inflation rate, it follows that Real interest rate = Nominal interest rate − Expected inflation rate. Why do you think that there is so much disagreement over the true value of the real interest rate?

13. With respect to the interest rate,
    a. what is the liquidity effect?
    b. what is the price-level effect?
    c. what is the expectations effect?

14. Suppose the money supply rises. Is the interest rate guaranteed to decline initially? Why or why not?

15. To a potential borrower, which would be more important, the nominal interest rate or the real interest rate? Explain your answer.

16. Suppose the money supply rises on Tuesday and by Thursday the interest rate has risen also. Is the rise in the interest rate more likely the result of the income effect or of the expectations effect? Explain your answer.

17. Suppose the money supply increased 30 days ago. Whether the nominal interest rate is higher, lower, or the same today as it was 30 days ago depends on what? Explain your answer.

18. What does inflation look like in a country that imposes and maintains price ceilings on goods and services?

19. In an equation-of-exchange framework, the price level is dependent upon the money supply, velocity, and Real GDP. Do you agree or disagree? Explain your answer.

Working with Numbers and Graphs

1. How will things change in the AD–AS framework if a change in the money supply is completely offset by a change in velocity?

2. Graphically show each of the following:
   a. Continued inflation due to supply-side factors
   b. One-shot, demand-induced inflation
   c. One shot, supply-induced inflation

3. Use the accompanying figure to answer questions a and b.
   a. Suppose the economy is self-regulating and is at point A when there is a one-shot, demand-induced inflation. If there are no other changes in the economy, at what point will the economy settle?

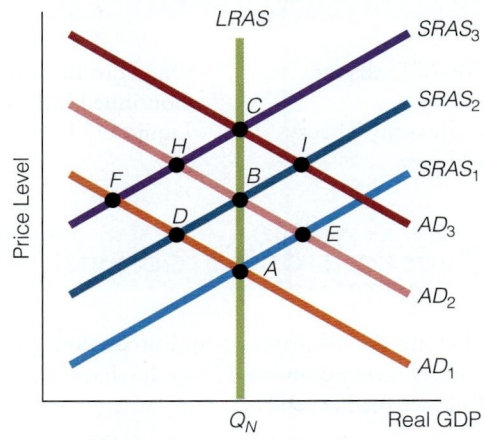

b. Suppose the economy is at point A when it is faced with two adverse supply shocks. The Fed tries to counter these shocks by increasing aggregate demand. What path will the economy follow?

4. Starting with a position of long-run equilibrium, use the monetarist model to graphically portray what happens to the price level and Real GDP in the short run and in the long run as a result of (a) a rise in the money supply and (b) a decline in velocity.

5. What does the real interest rate equal, given the following?
   a. Nominal interest rate = 8 percent; expected inflation rate = 2 percent
   b. Nominal interest rate = 4 percent; expected inflation rate = −4 percent
   c. Nominal interest rate = 4 percent; expected inflation rate = 1 percent

6. What does the nominal interest rate equal, given the following?
   a. Real interest rate = 3 percent; expected inflation rate = 1 percent
   b. Real interest rate = 5 percent; expected inflation rate = −3 percent

7. Can total expenditures ever be greater than the money supply? Explain your answer.

8. Take a look at Exhibit 6(a). If the economy starts at point 1 and then moves to point 2 as a result of an increase in aggregate demand, then how and why does the economy move from point 2 to point 3?

Introduction

When it comes to monetary policy, most economists agree that the goals are to stabilize the price level, to achieve low unemployment, and to promote economic growth, among other things. What they sometimes disagree about is the degree to which, and under what conditions, monetary policy achieves these goals. In this chapter, we discuss monetary policy, beginning with the details of the money market. Then, we discuss how changes in the money market—brought about by changes in the money supply—can affect the economy.

15-1 Transmission Mechanisms

Transmission Mechanism
The routes, or channels, traveled by the ripple effects that the money market creates and that affect the goods-and-services market. (The goods-and-services market is represented by the aggregate demand and aggregate supply curves in the AD–AS framework.)

Demand for Money (Balances)
The inverse relationship between the quantity demanded of money (balances) and the price of holding money (balances).

Changes in one market can often ripple outward to affect other markets. The routes, or channels, that these ripple effects travel are known as the **transmission mechanism**. In this section, we discuss two transmission mechanisms: the Keynesian and the monetarist.

15-1a The Money Market in the Keynesian Transmission Mechanism

Like all markets, the money market has two sides: a demand side and a supply side.[1]

The Demand for Money As an illustration of the **demand for money (balances)**, the price of holding money balances is on the vertical axis and the quantity of money is on the horizontal axis. The price of holding money balances—specifically, the opportunity cost of holding money—is the interest rate. By holding money, individuals forfeit the opportunity to hold

---

[1] In everyday language, the term "money market" is often used to refer to the market for short-term securities, where there is a demand for and a supply of short-term securities. This is not the money market discussed here. In this money market, there is a demand for and a supply of *money*.

that portion of their wealth in other forms. For instance, the person who holds $1,000 in cash gives up the opportunity to purchase a $1,000 asset that yields interest (e.g., a bond). Thus, the interest rate is the opportunity cost of holding money. A person can be described as "paying the price" of forfeited interest by holding money.

Exhibit 1(a) illustrates the demand for money (balances). As the interest rate increases, the opportunity cost of holding money increases, and individuals choose to hold less money. As the interest rate decreases, the opportunity cost of holding money decreases, and individuals choose to hold more money.

The Supply of Money Exhibit 1(b) shows the supply of money as a vertical line at the quantity of money that is determined largely by the Fed. The reason the money supply is largely, but not exclusively, determined by the Fed is that both banks and the public also are important players in the money supply process (as explained in earlier chapters).

Equilibrium in the Money Market The money market is in equilibrium when the quantity demanded of money equals the quantity supplied. In Exhibit 2, equilibrium exists at the interest rate i_1. At a higher interest rate, i_2, the quantity supplied of money is greater than the quantity demanded, and there is an excess supply of money ("too much" money). At a lower interest rate, i_3, the quantity demanded of money is greater than the quantity supplied, and there is an excess demand for money ("too little" money). Only at i_1 are the quantity demanded and the quantity supplied of money equal. At i_1, there are no shortages or surpluses of money and no excess demands or excess supplies. Individuals are holding the amounts of money they want to hold.

EXHIBIT 1

The Demand for and Supply of Money

(a) The demand curve for money is downward sloping. (b) The supply curve of money is a vertical line at the quantity of money that is largely, but not exclusively, determined by the Fed.

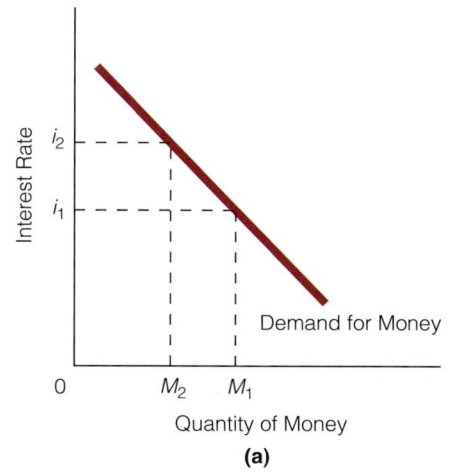
(a)

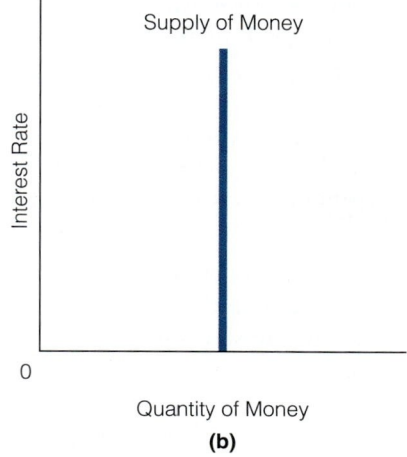
(b)

EXHIBIT 2

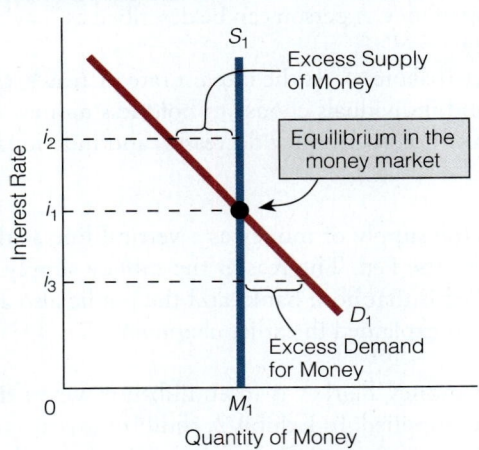

Equilibrium in the Money Market

At an interest rate of i_1, the money market is in equilibrium: There is neither an excess supply of money nor an excess demand for money.

15-1b The Keynesian Transmission Mechanism: Indirect

The Keynesian route between the money market and the goods-and-services market is an indirect one. Exhibit 3 is a market-by-market depiction of the Keynesian transmission mechanism.

- *The money market.* Suppose the money market is in equilibrium at interest rate i_1 in part (a). Then, the Fed undertakes an action that results in banks creating more loans (creating more checkable deposits) and therefore increasing the money supply. Accordingly, the money supply curve shifts rightward from S_1 to S_2. A greater supply of loans puts downward pressure on the interest rate, as reflected in the movement from i_1 to i_2.

- *The investment goods market.* A fall in the interest rate stimulates investment. In the investment goods market in part (b), investment rises from I_1 to I_2.

- *The goods-and-services market (AD–AS framework).* Recall that the Keynesian model has a horizontal aggregate supply curve in the goods-and-services market until full employment or Natural Real GDP is reached (see Chapter 10). The decline in the interest rate has brought about an increase in investment, as shown in part (b). Rising investment increases total spending in the economy and shifts the *AD* curve to the right [part (c)]. As a result, Real GDP rises from Q_1 to Q_2, and the price level does not change.

In sum, when the money supply increases, the Keynesian transmission mechanism works as follows: An increase in the money supply lowers the interest rate, causing investment to rise and the *AD* curve to shift rightward. Real GDP then increases. The process works in reverse for a decrease in the money supply. Symbolically,

$$\text{Money supply} \uparrow \rightarrow i \downarrow \rightarrow I \uparrow \rightarrow AD \uparrow \rightarrow Q \uparrow, \bar{P}$$
$$\text{Money supply} \downarrow \rightarrow i \uparrow \rightarrow I \downarrow \rightarrow AD \downarrow \rightarrow Q \downarrow, \bar{P}$$

EXHIBIT 3

The Keynesian Transmission Mechanism

The exhibit shows how the Keynesian transmission mechanism operates, given an increase in the money supply. (a) An increase in the money supply brings on a lower interest rate. (b) As a result, investment increases. (c) As investment increases, total expenditures rise and the aggregate demand curve shifts rightward. Real GDP rises from Q_1 to Q_2.

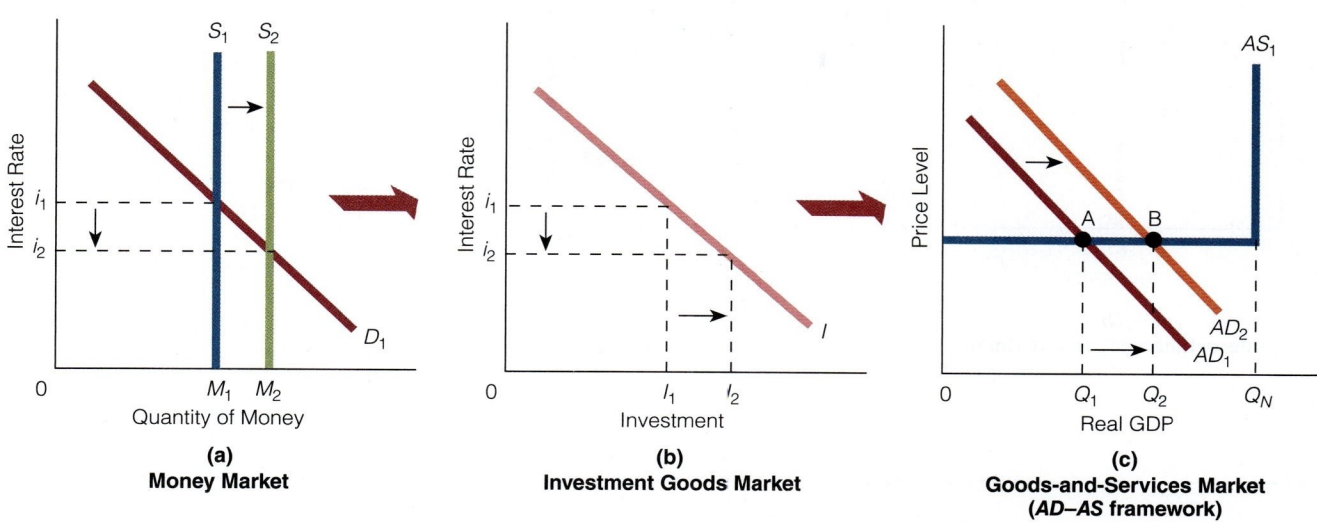

15-1c The Keynesian Mechanism May Get Blocked

The Keynesian transmission mechanism is *indirect*. Changes in the money market *do not directly affect* the goods-and-services market (and thus Real GDP) because the investment goods market stands between the two markets. Possibly (although not likely), the link between the money market and the goods-and-services market could be broken in the investment goods market. Here's how.

Interest-Insensitive Investment Some Keynesian economists believe that investment is not always responsive to interest rates. For example, when business firms are pessimistic about future economic activity, a decrease in interest rates will do little, if anything, to increase investment. When investment is completely insensitive to changes in interest rates, the investment demand curve is vertical, as in Exhibit 4(a).

Interest-insensitive investment has an effect on the Keynesian transmission mechanism described in Exhibit 3. If the investment demand curve is vertical (instead of downward sloping), a fall in interest rates will not increase investment, and if investment does not increase, neither will aggregate demand or Real GDP. Thus, the Keynesian transmission mechanism would be short-circuited in the investment goods market, severing the link between the money market in part (a) of Exhibit 3 and the goods-and-services market in part (c):

$$\text{Money supply} \uparrow \rightarrow i \downarrow$$
$$\text{Investment insensitive to changes in } i \rightarrow \overline{I} \rightarrow \overline{AD} \rightarrow \overline{Q}, \overline{P}$$

EXHIBIT 4

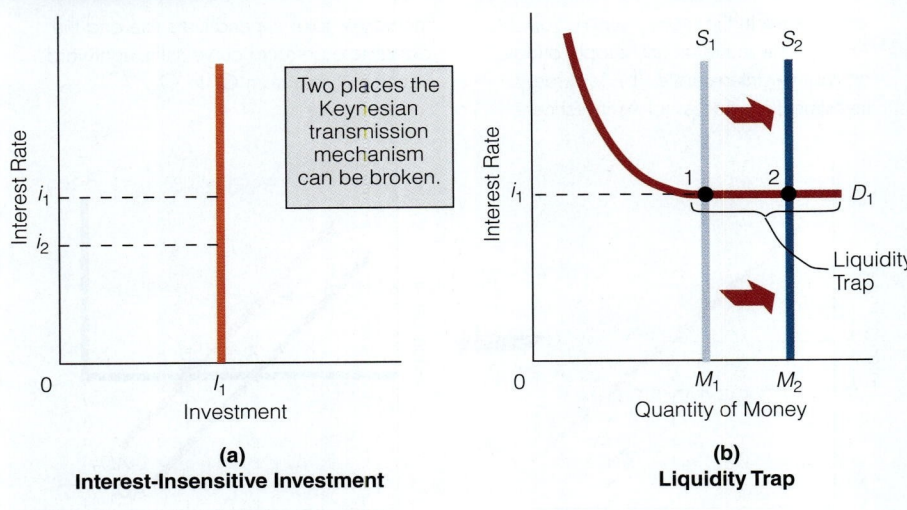

Breaking the Link Between the Money Market and the Goods-and-Services Market: Interest-Insensitive Investment and the Liquidity Trap

The Keynesian transmission mechanism allows the link between the money market and the goods-and-services market to be broken in two places. (a) If investment is totally interest insensitive, a change in the interest rate will not change investment; therefore, aggregate demand and Real GDP will not change. (b) If the money market is in the liquidity trap, an increase in the money supply will not lower the interest rate. It follows that there will be no change in investment, aggregate demand, or Real GDP.

The Liquidity Trap Keynesians have sometimes argued that the demand curve for money could become horizontal at some low interest rate. In Exhibit 4(b), the demand curve for money becomes horizontal at i_1. This horizontal section of the curve is referred to as the **liquidity trap**.

Liquidity Trap
The horizontal portion of the demand curve for money.

If the money supply is increased (e.g., from S_1 to S_2) when the money market is in the liquidity trap, the money market moves from point 1 to point 2, and individuals are willing to hold all the additional money supply at the given interest rate. Once again, this condition breaks the Keynesian transmission mechanism illustrated in Exhibit 3. Obviously, if an increase in the money supply does *not* lower the interest rate, then investment, aggregate demand, and Real GDP do not change. The liquidity trap can thus break the link between the money market and the goods-and-services market:

$$\text{Money supply} \uparrow$$
$$\text{Liquidity trap} \rightarrow \bar{i} \rightarrow \bar{I} \rightarrow \overline{AD} \rightarrow \overline{Q}, \overline{P}$$

Because the Keynesian transmission mechanism is indirect, both *interest-insensitive investment demand* and the *liquidity trap* may occur. Therefore, Keynesians conclude that, at times, monetary policy will be unable to increase Real GDP and decrease unemployment. Viewing the money supply as a string, some economists have argued that you cannot push on a string. In other words, you cannot always force Real GDP up by increasing (pushing up) the money supply.

Exhibit 5 presents a review of the Keynesian transmission mechanism and how it may get blocked.

EXHIBIT 5

The Keynesian View of Monetary Policy

According to the Keynesian transmission mechanism, if the Fed raises the money supply, the interest rate will drop, stimulating investment and aggregate demand. Consequently, Real GDP will rise. However, things may not work out this way if there is a liquidity trap or if investment is insensitive to changes in the interest rate.

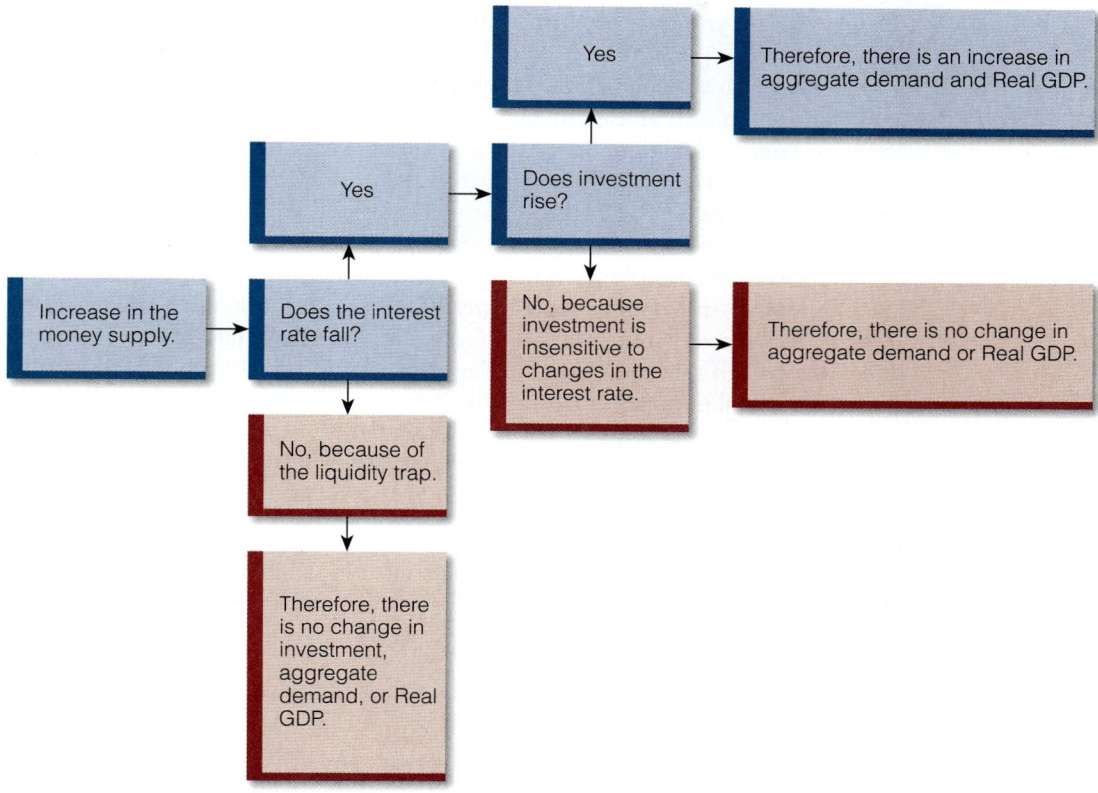

Bond Prices, Interest Rates, and the Liquidity Trap The liquidity trap, or the horizontal section of the demand curve for money, seems to come out of the clear blue sky. Why might the demand curve for money become horizontal at some low interest rate? To understand the explanation, you must first understand the relationship between bond prices and interest rates.

Consider Ellie, who buys good X for $100 today and sells it one year later for $110. Her actual rate of return is 10 percent; that is, the difference between the selling price and the buying price ($10), divided by the buying price ($100), is 10 percent. Now, suppose good X is a bond. Ellie buys the bond for $100 and sells it one year later for $110. Her actual interest rate return is the same: 10 percent. If, however, Ellie buys the bond for $90 instead of $100 but still sells it for $110, her interest rate return is 22 percent: $20 ÷ $90 = 22 percent. The point is simple: *As the price of a bond decreases, the actual interest rate return, or the interest rate, increases.*

So bond prices and interest rates are inversely related. For example, last year, Juan bought a bond for $1,000 that promises to pay him $100 a year in interest. Thus, the annual interest rate return is 10 percent: $100 ÷ $1,000 = 10 percent. Suppose, however, the market, or nominal, interest rate is higher now than it was last year when Juan bought his bond. Now bond suppliers have to promise to pay $120 a year to someone who buys a $1,000 bond.

The change in rate has an effect on the price Juan can get in the market for the $1,000 bond he bought last year, assuming that he wants to sell it. If a purchaser can buy a new $1,000 bond that pays $120 a year, why pay Juan $1,000 for an (old) bond that pays only $100? Accordingly, Juan has to lower the price of his bond below $1,000, but the question is by how much? The price has to be far enough below $1,000 so that the interest rate return on his old bond will be competitive with (i.e., at least equal to) the interest rate return on new bonds.

Juan's bond will sell for $833. At that price, a buyer of his bond will receive $100 a year and an interest rate of 12 percent—the same interest rate offered by a new $1,000 bond paying $120 a year. In other words, $100 is the same percentage of $833 as $120 is of $1,000: 12 percent. Therefore, *the market interest rate is inversely related to the price of old, or existing, bonds.*

This inverse relationship can help you understand how a liquidity trap comes to be. At a low interest rate, the money supply increases but does not result in an excess supply of money. Interest rates are very low, so bond prices are very high. Would-be buyers believe that bond prices are so high that they have no place to go but down, so individuals would rather hold all the additional money supply than use it to buy bonds.

15-1d The Monetarist Transmission Mechanism: Direct

Monetarist theory proposes a direct link between the money market and the goods-and-services market. The monetarist transmission mechanism is short: Changes in the money market have a direct impact on aggregate demand, as illustrated in Exhibit 6. An increase in the money supply from S_1 to S_2 in part (a) leaves individuals with an excess supply of money. As a result, they

EXHIBIT 6

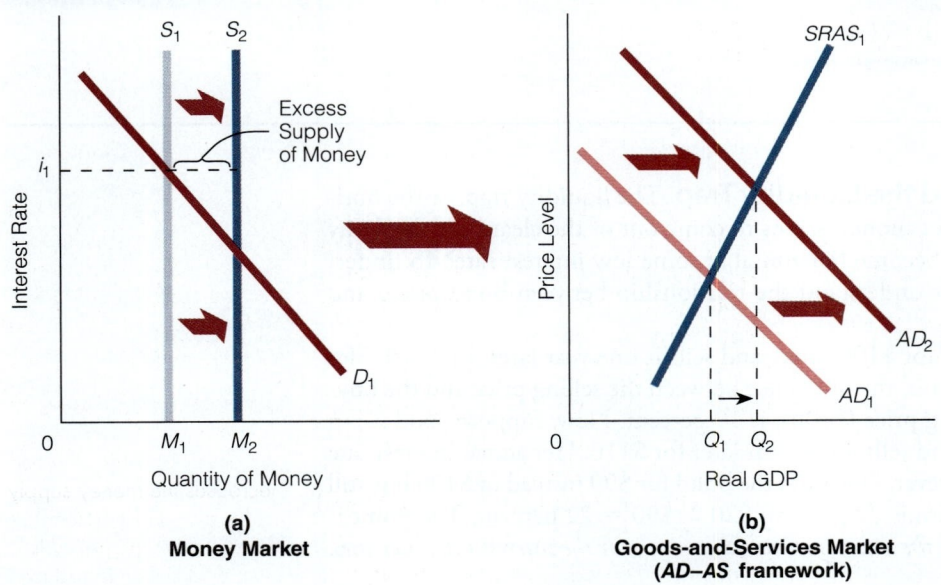

(a) Money Market

(b) Goods-and-Services Market (*AD–AS* framework)

The Monetarist Transmission Mechanism

The monetarist transmission mechanism is short and direct. Changes in the money market directly affect aggregate demand in the goods-and-services market. For example, an increase in the money supply leaves individuals with an excess supply of money that they spend on a wide variety of goods.

increase their spending on a wide variety of goods. Households buy more refrigerators, personal computers, television sets, clothes, and vacations. Businesses purchase additional machinery. The aggregate demand curve in part (b) is directly affected. In the short run, Real GDP rises from Q_1 to Q_2. The process works in reverse for a decrease in the money supply. Symbolically,

$$\text{Money supply} \uparrow \rightarrow AD \uparrow \rightarrow Q \uparrow, P \uparrow$$
$$\text{Money supply} \downarrow \rightarrow AD \downarrow \rightarrow Q \downarrow, P \downarrow$$

In sum, the Keynesian transmission mechanism from the money market to the goods-and-services market is indirect; the monetarist transmission mechanism is direct.

(Answers to Self-Test questions are in Answers to Self-Test Questions at the back of the book.)

1. Explain the inverse relationship between bond prices and interest rates.
2. "According to the Keynesian transmission mechanism, as the money supply rises, there is a direct impact on the goods-and-services market." Do you agree or disagree with this statement? Explain your answer.
3. Explain how the monetarist transmission mechanism works when the money supply rises.

15-2 Monetary Policy and the Problem of Inflationary and Recessionary Gaps

In Chapter 11, we explained how expansionary and contractionary fiscal policies might be used to move the economy out of recessionary and inflationary gaps, respectively, and questioned the effectiveness of fiscal policy. In this section, we discuss how monetary policy might be used to *eliminate* both recessionary and inflationary gaps.

In Exhibit 7(a), the economy is in a recessionary gap at point 1; aggregate demand is too low to bring the economy into equilibrium at Natural Real GDP.

- Economist *A* argues that, in time, the short-run aggregate supply curve will shift rightward to point 2 [see Exhibit 7(b)], so it is best to leave things alone.
- Economist *B* says that the economy will take too long to get to point 2 on its own and that, in the interim, the economy is suffering the high cost of unemployment and a lower level of output.
- Economist *C* maintains that the economy is stuck in the recessionary gap.

Economists *B* and *C* propose **expansionary monetary policy** to move the economy to its Natural Real GDP level. An appropriate increase in the money supply will shift the aggregate demand curve rightward to AD_2, and the economy will be in long-run equilibrium at point 2' [see Exhibit 7(c)]. The recessionary gap is eliminated through the use of expansionary monetary policy.

In Exhibit 8(a), the economy is in an inflationary gap at point 1.

- Economist *A* argues that, in time, the economy will move to point 2 [see Exhibit 8(b)], so it is best to leave things alone.
- Economist *B* argues that it would be better to decrease the money supply (**contractionary monetary policy**); aggregate demand will then shift leftward to AD_2, and the economy will move to point 2' [see Exhibit 8(c)].
- Economist *C* agrees with economist *B* but points out that the price level is lower at point 2' than at point 2, although Real GDP is the same at both points.

Expansionary Monetary Policy
The policy by which the Fed increases the money supply and decreases (short-term) interest rates; the policy is often undertaken to increase aggregate demand.

Contractionary Monetary Policy
The policy by which the Fed decreases the money supply and increases (short-term) interest rates; the policy is often undertaken to reduce aggregate demand.

EXHIBIT 7

Monetary Policy and a Recessionary Gap

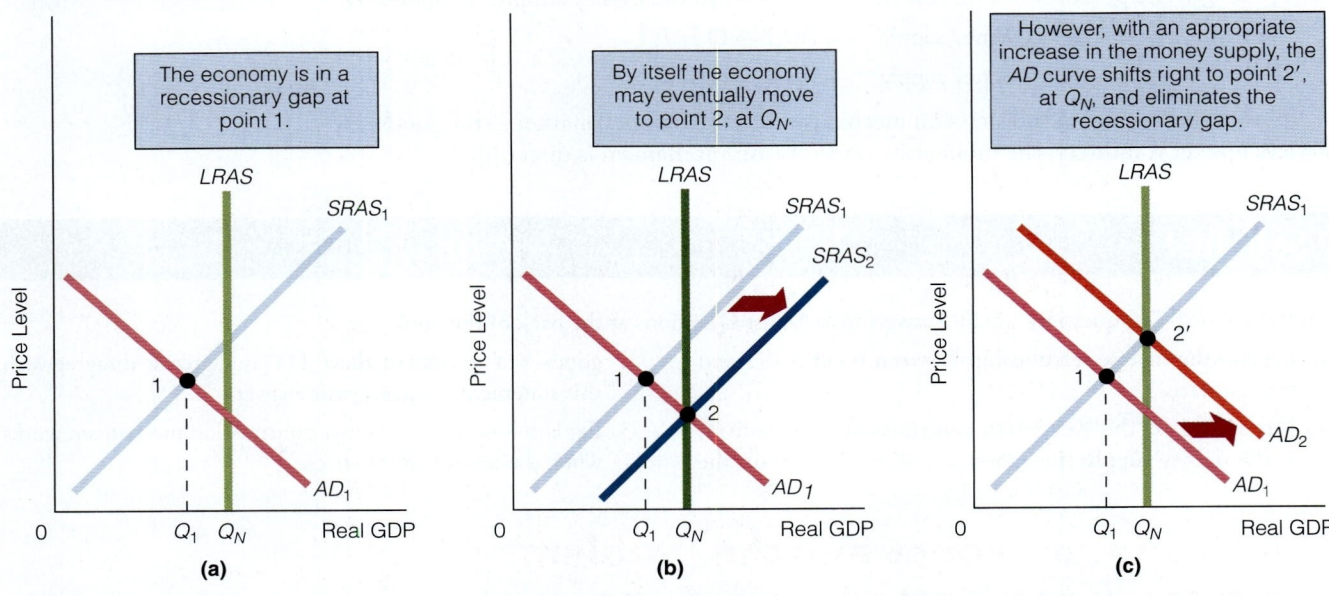

EXHIBIT 8

Monetary Policy and an Inflationary Gap

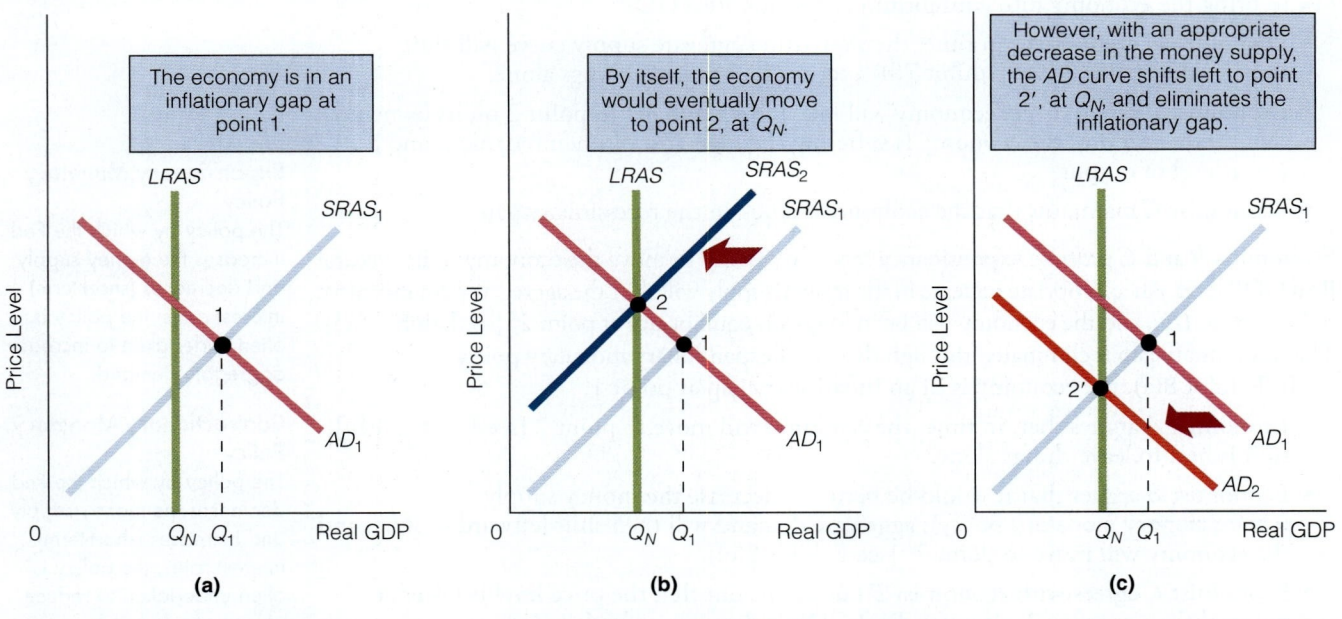

Most Keynesians believe that the natural forces of the market economy work much faster and more assuredly in eliminating an inflationary gap than in eliminating a recessionary gap. In terms of Exhibits 7 and 8, they argue that the short-run aggregate supply curve in Exhibit 8(b) is much more likely to shift leftward to point 2, eliminating the inflationary gap, than the short-run aggregate supply curve in Exhibit 7(b) to shift rightward to point 2, eliminating the recessionary gap. The reason is that wages and prices rise more quickly than they fall. (Of course, many Keynesians believe that wages are inflexible in a downward direction.) Consequently, Keynesians are more likely to advocate expansionary monetary policy to eliminate a stubborn recessionary gap than they are to recommend contractionary monetary policy to eliminate a not-so-stubborn inflationary gap.

15-2a A Different View of the Economy: Patterns of Sustainable Specialization and Trade (PSST)

Arnold Kling is an economist who has proposed a new perspective on the economy.[2] It is called *patterns of sustainable specialization and trade*, or PSST. It is a very different perspective than has been expressed in the *AD–AS* model that we have discussed widely in this textbook. Many of the models and theories we have discussed put emphasis on aggregate demand. Specifically, consider an economy that is initially in long-run equilibrium, producing Natural Real GDP. Then, something in the economy changes in such a way as to lower aggregate demand. The *AD* curve shifts leftward, and the economy falls into a recessionary gap. Stated differently, economic activity decreases because of a drop in aggregate demand.

Now, according to Arnold Kling, the decline in economic activity may have nothing to do with a decline in aggregate demand. In fact, a decline in economic activity can occur even if aggregate demand remains constant. To understand how this can happen, Kling argues, economic activity should not be viewed solely as stemming from spending in the economy. Instead, economic activity is best viewed by focusing on specialization and trade.

At any given point in time, certain specializations are needed to sustain the pattern of trade dictated by buying preferences. For example, buyers may want to buy goods *X*, *Y*, and *Z* in large quantities, and specializations *X′*, *Y′*, and *Z′* are necessary to produce these goods. Now, if business firms are not producing goods *X*, *Y*, and *Z*, or if labor is not skilled in specializations *X′*, *Y′*, and *Z′*, then what buyers want to buy is out of synchrony with what business and labor are producing and have to sell. As a result, sales decline, not necessarily because aggregate demand in the economy has dropped, but because, as we stated, *businesses and labor are out of synchrony with what buyers want to buy*. In short, the current pattern of specialization and trade is *unsustainable*. To illustrate, a person who was taking applications for subprime mortgages in 2006 had to find a different line of work by 2009, and someone who operated a large bookstore in a mall 10 years ago might find that business unsustainable today.

In Kling's perspective on the economy, it is the job of the entrepreneur to reconfigure specializations and trade so that both are sustainable—that is, so that both are consistent with what buyers want to buy. Is this reconfiguration easy to do? Not usually: Entrepreneurs may have to experiment before they figure out what configuration of specializations and trade is in synchrony with what buyers want to buy.

Now, such reconfigurations certainly go on all the time in a dynamic economy, but, Kling argues, there can be times when they are harder to either figure out or adjust to. For example,

---

[2] To read about this perspective in detail, see two of Kling's articles: "Patterns of Sustainable Specialization and Trade: A Smith–Ricardo Theory of Macroeconomics," http://www.adamsmith.org/sites/default/files/research/files/PSST.pdf; and "PSST: Patterns of Sustainable Specialization and Trade," *Capitalism and Society*, vol. 6, no. 2 (2011), http://arnoldkling.com/essays/papers/PSSTCap.pdf.

if there are large-scale shifts in demand or periods when major changes in technology are occurring, it might take more "trial and error" before the reconfiguration of capital and labor occurs and is consistent with a pattern of sustainable specialization and trade.

In addition, sometimes reconfigurations of capital and labor face impediments that are unrelated to purely economic issues. For example, suppose reconfigurations of capital and labor are now necessary in a field such as health care or education. Then, entrepreneurs may be willing and able to direct the reconfigurations into a sustainable pattern of specialization and trade but may not be permitted to do so because of licensing or credential requirements currently necessary to enter the field.

One conclusion reached from the PSST perspective of the economy is that sometimes a fiscal or monetary stimulus designed to boost aggregate demand will not work at reviving the economy. After all, if the recession is due to buyers and sellers being out of synchrony with each other, greater aggregate demand isn't the solution. And not only is a boost in aggregate demand not the solution, it could make matters worse. If the stimulus is directed at propping up unsustainable specializations and trade, then it sends the wrong signal to some workers. Specifically, it falsely tells some workers that their current specializations (the jobs they are currently capable of doing) will continue to be in demand when, in fact, they may not be.

15-3 Monetary Policy and the Activist–Nonactivist Debate

Recall that some economists argue that fiscal policy either is ineffective (owing to crowding out) or works in unintended and undesirable ways (owing to lags). Other economists, notably Keynesians, believe that neither is the case and that fiscal policy not only can, but should, be used to smooth out the business cycle. This point of contention is part of the activist–nonactivist debate, which encompasses both fiscal and monetary policy. This section addresses the *monetary policy* component of the debate.

Activists argue that monetary policy should be deliberately used to smooth out the business cycle. They are in favor of economic **fine-tuning**, which is the (usually frequent) use of monetary policy to counteract even small undesirable movements in economic activity. Sometimes, the monetary policy they advocate is called either *activist monetary policy* or *discretionary monetary policy*.

Nonactivists argue *against* the use of activist or discretionary monetary policy. Instead, they propose a *rules-based monetary policy* (also called a *nonactivist monetary policy*). An example of a rules-based monetary policy is a policy based on a predetermined steady growth rate in the money supply, such as allowing the money supply to grow 3 percent a year no matter what is happening in the economy.

15-3a The Case for Activist (or Discretionary) Monetary Policy

The case for activist (or discretionary) monetary policy rests on three major claims:

1. *The economy does not always equilibrate quickly enough at Natural Real GDP.* Consider the economy at point 1 in Exhibit 7(a). Some economists maintain that, left on its own, the economy will eventually move to point 2 in part (b). Activists argue that the economy takes too long to move from point 1 to point 2 and that, in the interim, too much output is lost, and too high an unemployment rate must be tolerated. They believe that an activist monetary policy speeds things along so that higher output and a lower unemployment rate can be achieved more quickly.

Activists
Persons who argue that monetary and fiscal policies should be deliberately used to smooth out the business cycle.

Fine-Tuning
The (usually frequent) use of monetary and fiscal policies to counteract even small undesirable movements in economic activity.

Nonactivists
Persons who argue against the deliberate use of discretionary fiscal and monetary policies to smooth out the business cycle. They believe in a permanent, stable, rule-oriented monetary and fiscal framework.

2. *Activist monetary policy works; it is effective at smoothing out the business cycle.* Activists are quick to point to the undesirable consequences of the constant monetary policy of the mid-1970s. In 1973, 1974, and 1975, the money supply growth rates were 5.5 percent, 4.3 percent, and 4.7 percent, respectively. These percentages represent a nearly constant growth rate in the money supply. The economy, however, went through a recession during that time, with Real GDP falling between 1973 and 1974 and between 1974 and 1975. Activists argue that an activist and flexible monetary policy would have reduced the high cost the economy had to pay in terms of lost output and high unemployment.

3. *Activist monetary policy is flexible; nonactivist (rules-based) monetary policy is not.* Activists argue that flexibility is a desirable quality in monetary policy; inflexibility is not. Implicitly, activists maintain that the more closely monetary policy can be designed to meet the particulars of a given economic environment, the better. For example, at certain times, the economy requires a sharp increase in the money supply, and at other times, it needs a sharp decrease; at still other times, only a slight increase or decrease is needed. Activists argue that activist (discretionary) monetary policy can change as the monetary needs of the economy change; nonactivist, rules-based, or "the-same-for-all-seasons" monetary policy cannot.

15-3b The Case for Nonactivist (or Rules-Based) Monetary Policy

The case for nonactivist (or rules-based) monetary policy also rests on three major claims:

1. *In modern economies, wages and prices are sufficiently flexible to allow the economy to equilibrate at reasonable speed at Natural Real GDP.* For example, nonactivists point to the sharp drop in union wages in 1982 in response to high unemployment. In addition, they argue that government policies largely determine the flexibility of wages and prices. For example, when government decides to cushion people's unemployment (e.g., through unemployment compensation), wages will not fall as quickly as when government does nothing. Nonactivists believe that a laissez-faire, hands-off approach by government promotes speedy wage and price adjustments and thus a quick return to Natural Real GDP.

2. *Activist monetary policies may not work.* Some economists argue that there are really two types of monetary policy: (1) monetary policy that is anticipated by the public and (2) monetary policy that is not. Anticipated monetary policy may not be effective at changing Real GDP or the unemployment rate. We discuss this subject in detail in the next chapter, but here is a brief explanation: Suppose the public correctly anticipates that the Fed will soon increase the money supply by 10 percent. Consequently, the public reasons that aggregate demand will increase from AD_1 to AD_2, as shown in Exhibit 9, and that prices will rise.

Now, in this scenario, workers are concerned particularly about the expected higher price level because they know that higher prices decrease

EXHIBIT 9

Expansionary Monetary Policy and No Change in Real GDP

If expansionary monetary policy (and thus a higher price level) is anticipated, workers may bargain for and receive higher wage rates. It is then possible that the SRAS curve will shift leftward to the same degree that expansionary monetary policy shifts the AD curve rightward. Result: No change in Real GDP.

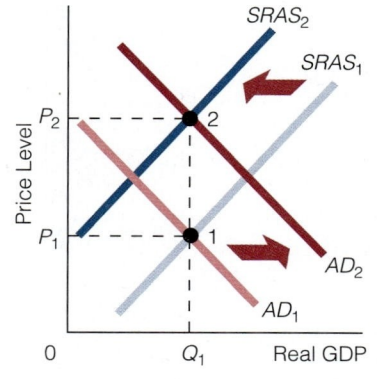

the buying power of their wages. So, in an attempt to maintain their real wages, workers bargain for and receive higher money wage rates, thereby shifting the short-run aggregate supply curve from $SRAS_1$ to $SRAS_2$ in Exhibit 9.

Now, if the $SRAS$ curve shifts leftward (owing to higher wage rates) to the same degree as the AD curve shifts rightward (owing to the increased money supply), Real GDP does not change but stays constant at Q_1. Thus, *a correctly anticipated increase in the money supply will be ineffective at raising Real GDP.*

3. *Activist monetary policies are likely to be destabilizing rather than stabilizing; they are likely to make matters worse, not better.* Nonactivists point to *lags* as the main reason that activist (or discretionary) monetary policies are likely to be destabilizing. (The total lag consists of the data, wait-and-see, legislative, transmission, and effectiveness lags discussed in Chapter 11.) Nonactivists argue that a long lag (e.g., 12 to 20 months) makes it almost impossible to conduct effective activist monetary policy: By the time the Fed's monetary stimulus arrives on the scene, the economy may not need any stimulus, and, thus, the policy measures will likely destabilize the economy. In this instance, the stimulus makes things worse rather than better.

Exhibit 10 illustrates the last point. Suppose the economy is currently in a recessionary gap at point 1. The recession is under way before Fed officials recognize it. Once they become aware of the recession, however, the officials consider expanding the money supply in the hopes of shifting the AD curve from AD_1 to AD_2 so that it will intersect the $SRAS$ curve at point 1', at Natural Real GDP.

In the interim, however, unknown to everybody, the economy is regulating itself: The $SRAS$ curve is shifting to the right. But because collecting and analyzing data about the economy takes time, Fed officials don't realize that this shift is occurring. Thinking that the economy is not regulating itself, or not regulating itself quickly enough, Fed officials implement expansionary monetary policy, and the AD curve shifts rightward. By the time the increased money

EXHIBIT 10

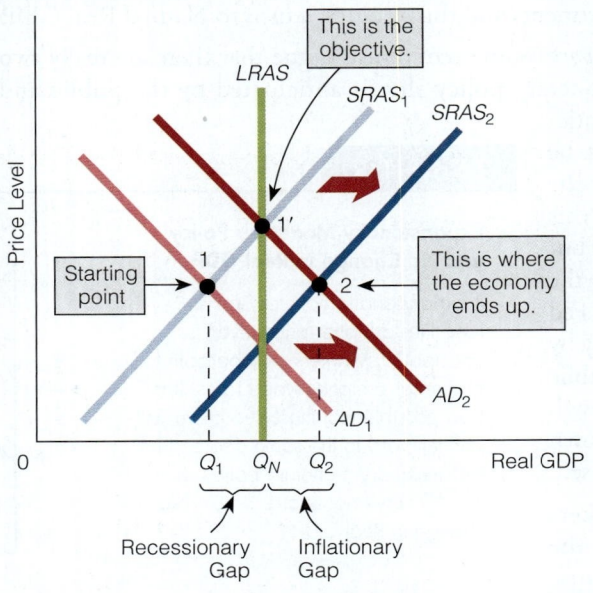

Monetary Policy May Destabilize the Economy

In this scenario, the $SRAS$ curve is shifting rightward (ridding the economy of its recessionary gap), but Fed officials do not realize that this is happening. They implement expansionary monetary policy, and the AD curve ends up intersecting $SRAS_2$ at point 2 instead of intersecting $SRAS_1$ at point 1'. Fed officials end up moving the economy into an inflationary gap and, thus, destabilizing the economy.

supply is felt in the goods-and-services market, the *AD* curve intersects the *SRAS* curve at point 2. In short, the Fed has moved the economy from point 1 to point 2—not, as it had hoped, from point 1 to point 1′. The Fed has moved the economy into an inflationary gap. Instead of stabilizing and moderating the business cycle, the Fed has intensified it.

Economics 24/7

Who Gets the Money First, and What Happens to Relative Prices?

Besides expansionary and contractionary monetary policies and their effects on Real GDP and the price level, other effects have to be considered:

- The distribution of the increase in the money supply (in the case of expansionary monetary policy)
- How a change in the money supply might affect relative prices (as opposed to the price level)

SORBIS/SHUTTERSTOCK.COM

Let's look at how these two effects interact. When the money supply expands by, say, $100 billion, not every member of the public gets some of the new money. To illustrate, suppose the Fed undertakes an action that results in banks giving out more loans, thus creating more checkable deposits and, therefore, raising the money supply.

Now, let's say that one of the first people to get a new loan is Andrea, who spends the money from her new loan to buy good *X* from Yoshi. If Andrea would not have purchased good *X* without the loan, then the demand for good *X* presumably rises because of the loan. Therefore, if the demand for good *X* rises, so will its absolute (or money) price. If the absolute price of good *X* rises, so will its relative price, *ceteris paribus*. Conclusion: An increase in the money supply can change not only the price level, but relative prices too.

Of course, an increase in the money supply changes relative prices because not everyone gets the new money at the same time. Andrea gets the new money before the seller of good *X* (Yoshi) gets it, and so on. When the money supply is increased, some people get the new money before others, so the goods and services these people buy rise in price relative to the prices of the goods and services they do not buy. If the Andreas of the world (who get the new money first) buy good *X* and not good *Y*, and the non-Andreas of the world (who get the new money later) buy good *Y* and not good *X*, we can expect that, initially, the price of good *X* will rise relative to the price of good *Y*.

15-4 Nonactivist Monetary Proposals

The five nonactivist (or rules-based) monetary proposals are as follows:

1. The constant-money-growth-rate rule
2. The predetermined-money-growth-rate rule
3. The Taylor rule
4. Average inflation targeting
5. (Nominal) GDP targeting

15-4a The Constant-Money-Growth-Rate Rule

Many nonactivists argue that the sole objective of monetary policy is to stabilize the price level. To this end, they propose a *constant-money-growth-rate rule*. One version of the rule is as follows:

> The annual money supply growth rate will be constant at the average annual growth rate of Real GDP.

For example, if the average annual Real GDP growth rate is approximately 3.3 percent, the money supply should be put on automatic pilot and be permitted to grow at an annual rate of 3.3 percent. The money supply will grow at this rate regardless of the state of the economy.

Some economists predict that a constant-money-growth-rate rule will bring about a stable price level over time because of the equation of exchange ($MV \equiv PQ$). If the average annual growth rate in Real GDP (Q) is 3.3 percent and the money supply (M) grows at 3.3 percent, the price level should remain stable over time. Advocates of this rule argue that in some years the growth rate in Real GDP will be below its average rate, causing an increase in the price level, and that in other years the growth rate in Real GDP will be above its average rate, causing a fall in the price level, but over time, the price level will be stable.

15-4b The Predetermined-Money-Growth-Rate Rule

Critics of the constant-money-growth-rate rule point out that it makes two assumptions: (1) Velocity is constant; (2) the money supply is defined correctly. Critics argue that velocity has not been constant in some periods. Also, which definition of the money supply is the proper one and, therefore, which money supply growth rate should be fixed—M1, M2, or some broader monetary measure—are not yet clear.

Largely in response to the charge that velocity is not always constant, some nonactivists prefer the following rule:

> The annual growth rate in the money supply will be equal to the average annual growth rate in Real GDP minus the growth rate in velocity.

In other words,

$$\%\Delta M = \%\Delta Q - \%\Delta V$$

With this rule, the growth rate of the money supply is not fixed. It can vary from year to year, but it is predetermined in that it is dependent on the growth rates of Real GDP and velocity. For this reason, we call the rule the *predetermined-money-growth-rate rule*. To illustrate its workings, consider the following extended version of the equation of exchange:

$$\%\Delta M + \%\Delta V = \%\Delta P + \%\Delta Q$$

Suppose $\%\Delta Q$ is 3 percent and $\%\Delta V$ is 1 percent. The rule specifies that the growth rate in the money supply should be 2 percent. This growth rate would keep the price level stable; there would be a 0 percent change in P:

$$\%\Delta M + \%\Delta V = \%\Delta P + \Delta Q$$
$$2\% + 1\% = 0\% + 3\%$$

15-4c The Fed and the Taylor Rule

Economist John Taylor has argued for a middle ground of sorts between activist and nonactivist monetary policy. He has proposed that monetary authorities use a rule to guide them in making their discretionary decisions.

His rule has come to be known as the *Taylor rule*, which specifies how policymakers should set the federal funds rate target. (Recall from an earlier chapter that the federal funds rate is the interest rate that banks charge one another for reserves.) The economic thinking behind the Taylor rule is that there is some federal funds rate target that is consistent with (1) stabilizing inflation around a rather low inflation rate and (2) stabilizing Real GDP around its full-employment level. The aim is to find this target and then to use the Fed's tools to hit it.

Taylor defines the particulars of the rule as follows: The federal funds rate target

should be one-and-a-half times the inflation rate plus one-half times the GDP gap plus one.[3]

Algebraically, the Taylor rule says,

Federal funds rate target = 1.5 (inflation rate) + 0.5 (GDP gap) + 1

In this equation, the GDP gap measures the percentage deviation of Real GDP from its potential level. Let's use the rule to find the federal funds rate target that Taylor recommends to the Fed. Suppose the inflation rate is 5 percent and the GDP gap is 3 percent. Putting these percentages in our equation, we get

Federal funds rate target = 1.5 (5 percent) + 0.5 (3 percent) + 1
= 7.5 + 1.5 + 1
= 10 percent

15-4d Average Inflation Targeting

The Fed has recently chosen **average inflation targeting** as its preferred monetary policy framework. This policy aims to keep the average inflation rate at 2 percent over a specific time period. For example, it might attempt to keep the inflation rate at an average of 2 percent over a four- to five-year period. To illustrate, suppose the interest rate is 2 percent in year 1 and 3 percent in year 2. The average over two years is therefore 2.5 percent. But if the inflation target as set by the Fed is 2 percent, then the Fed will act in such a way as to bring the inflation rate down in year 3. For example, if it could move the inflation rate down to 1 percent, then over a three-year period, the average inflation rate is 2 percent—which is the inflation target. It could instead try to lower the inflation rate down to 2 percent in year 3 and to 1 percent in year 4, so that over the four-year period, the average inflation rate is 2 percent.

Now let's see what the Fed does if the average inflation rate is below the target rate. Suppose that the inflation rate is 2 percent in year 1 and 1 percent in year 2. The average is 1.5 percent. Now the Fed would try to raise the inflation rate in year 3 to 3 percent so that the average over the three-year period is 2 percent, the inflation target. Or it could try to hit its target rate over a four-year period by attempting to raise the inflation rate to 2 percent in year 3 and 3 percent in year 4. This gives us an average inflation rate of 2 percent over a four-year period.

Average Inflation Targeting
The policy of trying to keep the average inflation rate over a specific time period at a certain target rate (say, 2 percent).

15-4e Nominal GDP Targeting

A new economic school arose late in the first decade of the 2000s: *market monetarism*.[4] It originated not in the academic journals or in a particular economics department in any country but in the blogosphere. What was the event that prompted the birth of market monetarism? It was

---

[3] See John Taylor, *Getting Off Track* (Stanford, CA: Hoover Institution Press, 2009), p. 67.
[4] The term "market monetarism" was coined by Danish economist Lars Christensen in August 2011.

the Great Recession, the recession that began in December 2007 and took a sharp downward movement in September 2008. At the time, many economists argued that the Great Recession was caused by the financial crisis that was occurring as well. In other words, they argued that problems in the banking and financial sectors of the economy were the cause of the recession. The economists that came to be known as market monetarists disagreed. They argued that the recession was caused by monetary policy that was "too tight" or "too contractionary" (relative to what was necessary to stabilize the economy). Among these economists was Scott Sumner, who strongly advocated market monetarist ideas in his blog *TheMoneyIllusion*. Sumner, like other market monetarists, argues that the optimal monetary policy is for the Fed to set a Nominal GDP target—such as a rise of 5 to 6 percent a year in Nominal GDP—and then adjust the growth of the money supply in such a way as to hit the target.

We can understand the market monetarists' policy prescription in terms of the equation of exchange, which we first discussed in an earlier chapter. Remember that the equation of exchange states that the money supply times velocity must equal (Nominal) GDP: $M \times V \equiv GDP$. Now, suppose there is a financial crisis and, as a result, people try to hold more money (spend less). The lesser spending is likely to reduce velocity, and if the Fed doesn't offset the decline in velocity sufficiently, GDP will decline. For example, suppose

Economics 24/7

A Change in the Money Supply and You

Does it matter to you if the money supply rises by 4 percent or 10 percent, or if it declines by 5 percent or 2 percent? Does it even matter to you if the money supply rises, falls, or remains constant?

For many people, changes in the money supply are far removed from their daily lives. While driving to work, paying the bills, talking with friends, or completing a paper for school, what does it matter what happens to the money supply?

To try to get an answer to this question, consider that the extended version of the exchange equation states that

$$\%\Delta M + \%\Delta V = \%\Delta P + \%\Delta Q$$

Now, if we subtract the %ΔQ from both sides of the equation, we are left with

$$\%\Delta P = \%\Delta M + \%\Delta V - \%\Delta Q$$

Suppose that the %ΔV = 1 percent and %ΔQ = 2 percent. Now if the %ΔM = 3 percent, it follows that the %ΔP = 2 percent. But if the %ΔM = 9 percent, then the %ΔP = 8 percent. In short, the percentage rise in the money supply impacts the percentage increase in the prices that you end up paying.

Now suppose the money supply were to decline by 4 percent. Does it matter? If the %ΔM = −4 percent, then the %ΔP = −5 percent. Now the prices you pay will have decreased by 5 percent.

Our point is a simple one: Directional changes in the money supply (up or down) and the magnitude of changes in the money supply (up by 5 percent as opposed to 10 percent) impact prices. And prices, specifically the prices you pay to buy the goods and services you want or need, impact you.

velocity declines by 8 percent and the money supply rises by 6 percent; then GDP will *decline* by 2 percent. If the objective is to raise Nominal GDP by 5 percent, an 8 percent decline in velocity would obligate the Fed to increase the money supply by 13 percent. Anything less prompts market monetarists to argue that monetary policy is "too tight."

If monetary policy leads to a decline in Nominal GDP, nominal income declines (because Nominal GDP and nominal income are two sides of the same coin). As a result of a decline in nominal incomes, individuals will have a hard time paying off their debts (that were contracted at an earlier time and were based on nominal incomes that were not expected to decline or to decline as much as they have). Take a representative case: A person has an income of $100,000 a year and incurs a debt that she has to pay off monthly for five years. Each month for five years, she must pay $2,000. Then, Nominal GDP (nominal income) declines. Consequently, the income of our debtor falls, and she finds it harder to pay off her monthly debt of $2,000. As a result, she contracts her spending in the economy and her demand for goods and services declines. If there are enough debtors pulling back their spending, aggregate demand in the economy declines, firms lose sales and issue layoffs, the unemployment rate rises, and so on.

15-4f A Gold Standard as Monetary Policy and the Value of the Dollar

The type of monetary policy we have discussed so far is implemented by the Fed. It is largely the Fed that either increases or decreases the money supply. Moreover, the Fed has the ability to increase or decrease the money supply by as much or as little as it believes is appropriate to bring about desirable economic consequences (such as low inflation and low unemployment).

Some economists argue that Fed-directed monetary policy has, over time, led to a decline in the value of the dollar. In other words, a dollar today doesn't buy as much as it once did. This, of course, is simply the other side of the inflation coin. One side of the inflation coin reads, "The price level is rising." The other side of the coin reads, "Because the price level is rising, the dollar doesn't buy as many goods and services as it once did."

So have prices increased? Has the value of the dollar declined? Well, let's go back to 1950 and check the Consumer Price Index (which measures the price level). In 1950, the index was 24.1. By February 2021, it had risen to 263.014. To find the percentage change in prices during the period 1950–2021, we simply subtract 24.1 from 263.014 and divide by 24.1. The result is 991 percent, meaning that something which cost $20 in 1950 would cost $218.20 in February 2021.

If you would like to see how much prices have changed over the years, go to the website http://www.usinflationcalculator.com/. There, you will find an inflation calculator. You can simply choose any year from 1913 to the current year, key in a dollar amount (such as $20 or $200), and then see what that dollar item would cost in a different year (say, the current year). For example, if one keys in 1945 and $100, one finds that the $100 item in 1945 would cost $1,461 in 2021.

Now, some economists argue that one of the reasons the value of the dollar has declined so much over the years is because of the monetary policy of the Fed. The Fed-directed, discretionary monetary policy has caused a lot of inflation over the years, leading to a continuing decline in the value of the dollar. They then argue that a way to combat this decline is to take monetary policy out of the hands of the Fed. But what would take its place? Some advocate a monetary rule, some of which we have already discussed.

Others advocate a gold standard. The advocates of a gold standard often argue that, when the United States was on a gold standard, the price level in the nation was fairly stable, and there was very little inflation. According to economist Michael Bordo,

The great virtue of the gold standard was that it assured long-term price stability. Compare the aforementioned average annual inflation rate of 0.1 percent between 1880 and 1914 with the average of 4.1 percent between 1946 and 2003.[5]

How does a gold standard work? To illustrate, suppose the monetary authority states that it is willing to buy and sell gold for a set price of $1,000 an ounce and that this monetary policy will be the only one that it implements. Then, the $1,000 price of gold is the *official price of gold*.

Now suppose the *market price of gold*, which is the price of gold determined in the gold market, rises above $1,000 an ounce—say, to $1,100 an ounce. What will members of the public do? They will go to the monetary authority and buy gold at the official price of $1,000 an ounce. Then, they will turn around and sell that ounce of gold in the gold market for $1,100. But, of course, as people buy gold from the monetary authority and sell it in the gold market, the supply of gold in the gold market will be rising, so we can expect the market price of gold to fall. The market price of gold will keep falling until no one has any incentive to go to the monetary authority and buy gold anymore. In other words, it will keep falling until the market price of gold is $1,000, which is equal to the official price of gold.

Now, as the price of gold is falling, what will be happening to the general price level (as measured, say, by the Consumer Price Index)? It should be falling too, and here is why: When the public buys gold from the monetary authority, it buys that gold with money. That money leaves the economy. (Think of the public turning over ten $100 bills for every ounce of gold it buys from the monetary authority.) Now, the monetary authority doesn't spend that money; it simply removes it from circulation, so the result is a reduction in the money supply in the economy, and, according to the exchange equation, if nothing else changes, the price level declines. In other words, the price of gold and the general price level move down together. The sequence of events is as follows:

Market price of gold > Official price of gold → Public buys gold from monetary authority → Public exchanges money for gold → Money supply declines → Price level declines

Now let's reverse things. Suppose the market price of gold falls to $900. What will people do now? They will go to the monetary authority and sell their gold for $1,000. After all, the monetary authority said that it would buy gold for $1,000, and it is better to sell gold for $1,000 to the monetary authority than to sell it to someone else for $900. But selling gold to the monetary authority takes gold out of the market (the supply of gold in the market declines), and, thus, the market price of gold will start to rise. When will it stop rising? Answer: When there is no longer any monetary incentive to sell gold to the monetary authority instead of to others—that is, when the market price of gold rises to the official price of gold at $1,000.

Now, as the market price of gold rises from $900 to $1,000, what is happening to the general price level? Well, as people sell their gold to the monetary authority, they get money from the monetary authority in return. (Think of the monetary authority turning over ten $100 bills for every ounce of gold it buys.) As a result, the money supply in the economy rises, and, according to the exchange equation, as we raise the money supply, if nothing else changes, the price level rises. We conclude that both the price of gold and the general price level rise together. The sequence of events is as follows:

Market price of gold < Official price of gold → Public sells gold to monetary authority → Public receives money for gold → Money supply rises → Price level rises

---

[5] Michael D. Bordo, "The Gold Standard," in *The Concise Encyclopedia of Economics*.

So far, then, we have seen that, if the monetary authority agrees to buy gold from and sell gold to the public at an official price of, say, $1,000, then it will stabilize the market price of gold at $1,000 an ounce. Again, that's because, if the market price rises above or falls below the official price of $1,000 an ounce, forces are at work to move the market price of gold back to the official price. Also, as we have seen, by stabilizing the price of gold, it is possible to stabilize the general price level as well because, as we have explained, the general price level moves up and down with the price of gold. This is the reason that some economists argue that a gold standard stabilizes the price level, thus preventing a decline in the value of the dollar.

1. Would a rules-based monetary policy produce price stability?
2. Suppose the inflation rate is 4 percent and the GDP gap is 5 percent. What is the Taylor rule recommendation for the federal funds rate target?
3. What is the monetary policy prescription of the market monetarists?

Office Hours

"Does Monetary Policy Always Have the Same Effects?"

Student: Does monetary policy always have the same effects?

Instructor: Instead of my giving you the answer, think back to the Keynesian transmission mechanism, and try to answer your question.

Student: In the Keynesian transmission mechanism, an increase in the money supply lowers the interest rate. The lower interest rate then increases investment, and the increased investment raises aggregate demand.

Instructor: Ask yourself whether the lower interest rate always raises investment.

Student: No, it doesn't always raise investment. If investment is interest insensitive, the lower interest rate will leave investment unchanged.

Instructor: There is something else too. Suppose investment is responsive to changes in the interest rate. In other words, if the interest rate falls, investment will rise. But the question is whether investment always rises by the same amount. For example, if in year 1 the interest rate falls from 6 percent to 5 percent and investment rises from $300 billion to $400 billion, does it follow that every time the interest rate falls from 6 percent to 5 percent, investment will rise by $100 billion?

Student: I see your point. You're saying that, although investment might always rise as the interest rate falls, it doesn't necessarily rise by the same amount every time. If it doesn't rise by the same amount every time, then there is no guarantee that aggregate demand will rise by the same amount every time (because increases in investment lead to increases in aggregate demand).

Instructor: That's correct. We'd then have to conclude that expansionary monetary policy won't always increase aggregate demand by the same amount. In other words, a money supply expansion of $30 billion might raise aggregate demand more at one time than at some other time.

Student: So one answer to my question—whether monetary policy always has the same effects—is no, monetary policy doesn't always change aggregate demand by the same amount.

Instructor: That's correct. This discussion also helps us to understand why economists—even those of the same school of thought—might disagree with each other. For example, suppose economists A and B believe that monetary policy affects the economy through the Keynesian transmission mechanism. Then, just because both accept the Keynesian transmission mechanism doesn't necessarily mean that they both think that a given increase in the money supply is going to affect aggregate demand to the same degree. Although they might agree that an expansion in the money supply will increase aggregate demand, they might disagree as to how much aggregate demand will increase. Economist A might think that aggregate demand will rise only a little because investment will not rise much when the interest rate drops. Economist B might think that aggregate demand will rise a lot because investment will rise a lot when the interest rate drops.

Points to Remember

1. Monetary policy doesn't always have the same effects. With reference to the Keynesian transmission mechanism, expansionary monetary policy might lead to a large change in investment at some times (when investment is highly responsive to changes in the interest rate) and only a small change in investment at other times (when investment is somewhat insensitive to changes in the interest rate). Expansionary monetary policy therefore might not always change aggregate demand to the same degree.

2. Even economists of the same school of thought can disagree with each other at times. For example, although two economists might agree that a rise in the money supply will change investment (or aggregate demand), they might disagree as to how much investment (or aggregate demand) will change.

Chapter Summary

The Keynesian Transmission Mechanism

- The Keynesian route between the money market and the goods-and-services market is indirect. Changes in the money market must affect the investment goods market before the goods-and-services market is affected. Under the assumptions that no liquidity trap exists and investment is not interest insensitive, the transmission mechanism works as follows for an increase in the money supply: An increase in the money supply lowers the interest rate and increases investment, thereby increasing aggregate demand and shifting the *AD* curve rightward. Consequently, Real GDP rises. Under the same assumptions, the transmission mechanism works as follows for a *decrease* in the money supply: A decrease in the money supply raises the interest rate and decreases investment, thereby decreasing aggregate demand and shifting the *AD* curve leftward. As a result, Real GDP falls.

- The Keynesian transmission mechanism may be short-circuited either by the liquidity trap or by interest-insensitive investment. Both are Keynesian notions. Keynesians predict that, if either is present, expansionary monetary policy will be unable to change Real GDP.

The Monetarist Transmission Mechanism

- The monetarist route between the money market and the goods-and-services market is direct. Changes in the money supply affect aggregate demand. An increase in the money supply causes individuals to increase their spending on a wide variety of goods.

Bond Prices and Interest Rates

- Interest rates and the prices of old, or existing, bonds are inversely related.

The Activist–Nonactivist Debate

- Activists argue that monetary policy should be deliberately used to smooth out the business cycle; they favor using activist, or discretionary, monetary policy to fine-tune the economy. Nonactivists argue against the use of discretionary monetary policy; they propose nonactivist, or rules-based, monetary policy.

- The case for discretionary monetary policy rests on three major claims: (1) The economy does not always equilibrate quickly enough at Natural Real GDP. (2) Activist monetary

policy works. (3) Activist monetary policy is flexible, and flexibility is a desirable quality in monetary policy.
- The case for nonactivist monetary policy rests on three major claims: (1) There is sufficient flexibility in wages and prices in modern economies to allow them to equilibrate at reasonable speed at Natural Real GDP. (2) Activist monetary policies may not work. (3) Activist monetary policies are likely to make matters worse rather than better.

Nonactivist (Or Rules-Based) Monetary Proposals

- The constant-money-growth-rate rule states that the annual money supply growth rate will be constant at the average annual growth rate of Real GDP.
- The predetermined-money-growth-rate rule states that the annual growth rate in the money supply will be equal to the average annual growth rate in Real GDP minus the growth rate in velocity.
- The Taylor rule specifies the following equation:

   Federal funds rate target = 1.5 (inflation rate) + 0.5 (GDP gap) + 1.

- Average inflation targeting is a policy of trying to keep the average inflation rate over a specific time period at a certain target rate (say, 2 percent).
- Market monetarists advocate a monetary policy that targets Nominal GDP growth.

Key Terms and Concepts

Transmission Mechanism
Demand for Money (Balances)
Liquidity Trap
Expansionary Monetary Policy
Contractionary Monetary Policy
Activists
Fine-tuning
Nonactivists
Average Inflation Targeting

Questions and Problems

1. Consider the following: Two researchers, A and B, are trying to determine whether eating fatty foods leads to heart attacks. The researchers proceed differently. Researcher A builds a model in which fatty foods may first affect X in one's body, and if X is affected, then Y may be affected, and if Y is affected, then Z may be affected. Finally, if Z is affected, the heart is affected, and the individual has an increased probability of suffering a heart attack. Researcher B doesn't proceed in this step-by-step fashion. She conducts an experiment to see whether people who eat many fatty foods have more, fewer, or the same number of heart attacks as people who eat few fatty foods. Which researcher's methods have more in common with the research methodology implicit in the Keynesian transmission mechanism? Which researcher's methods have more in common with the research methodology implicit in the monetarist transmission mechanism? Explain your answer.
2. If bond prices fall, will individuals want to hold more or less money? Explain your answer.
3. Why is the demand curve for money downward sloping?
4. Explain how it is possible to have too much money.
5. Explain how the Keynesian transmission mechanism works.
6. Explain how the monetarist transmission mechanism works.
7. It has been suggested that nonactivists are not concerned with the level of Real GDP and unemployment because most (if not all) nonactivist monetary proposals set stabilization of the price level as their immediate objective. Discuss.
8. Suppose the combination of more accurate data and better forecasting techniques would make it easy for the Fed to predict a recession 10 to 16 months in advance. Would this state of affairs strengthen the case for activism or nonactivism? Explain your answer.
9. According to the theory of patterns of specialization and sustainable trade (PSST), economic activity can decline in the face of unchanged aggregate demand. How so?
10. Suppose it were proved that liquidity traps do not occur and that investment is not interest insensitive. Would this be enough to disprove the claim that expansionary monetary policy is not always effective at changing Real GDP? Why or why not?
11. Both activists and nonactivists make good points for their respective positions. Do you think activists could say anything to nonactivists to convince them to accept the activist position, and vice versa? If so, what is it that they would say? If not, why not?

12. The discussion of supply and demand in Chapter 3 noted that, if two goods are substitutes for each other, the price of one and the demand for the other are directly related. For example, if Pepsi and Coca-Cola are substitutes, an increase in the price of Pepsi will increase the demand for Coca-Cola. Suppose that bonds and stocks are substitutes for each other. We know that interest rates and bond prices are inversely related. What do you predict is the relationship between stock prices and interest rates? Explain your answer.

13. Argue the case for and against a monetary rule.

14. How does average inflation targeting work?

15. Monetary policy can affect relative prices. Do you agree or disagree with this statement? Explain your answer.

16. According to market monetarists, what problems might arise from a sharp decline in Nominal GDP?

17. Does the monetary policy of market monetarists take into account changes in velocity? Explain your answer.

18. Explain how a gold standard, as monetary policy, would work.

Working with Numbers and Graphs

1. Last year, Manuel bought a bond for $10,000 that promises to pay him $900 a year. This year, he can buy a bond for $10,000 that promises to pay $1,000 a year. If Manuel wants to sell his old bond, what is its price likely to be?

2. Last year, Charu bought a bond for $10,000 that promises to pay her $1,000 a year. This year, investors can buy a bond for $10,000 that promises to pay $800 a year. If Charu wants to sell her old bond, what is its price likely to be?

3. The annual average percentage change in Real GDP is 2.3 percent, and the annual average percentage change in velocity is 1.1 percent. Using the monetary rule discussed in the text, what percentage change in the money supply will keep prices stable (on average)?

4. Show graphically that the more interest insensitive the investment demand curve is, the less likely it is that monetary policy will be effective at changing Real GDP.

5. In each of parts (a)–(d), which panel in the accompanying figure best describes the situation?
    a. Expansionary monetary policy that removes the economy from a recessionary gap
    b. Expansionary monetary policy that is destabilizing
    c. Contractionary monetary policy that removes the economy from an inflationary gap
    d. Monetary policy that is ineffective at changing Real GDP

6. Graphically portray the Keynesian transmission mechanism under the following conditions:
    a. A decrease in the money supply
    b. No liquidity trap
    c. Downward-sloping investment demand

7. Graphically portray the monetarist transmission mechanism when the money supply declines.

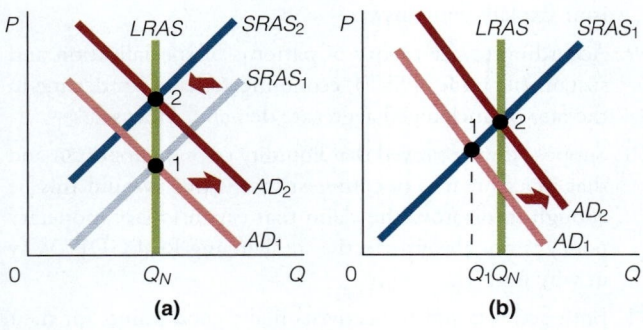
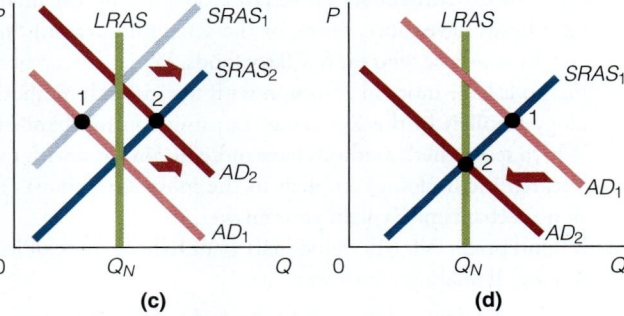

Bond prices and the interest rate are inversely related: as the price of bonds rises, the interest rate falls; as the price of bonds falls, the interest rate rises. In this appendix, we explain this relationship by looking closely at the money market and the bond market. The money market is shown in equilibrium in Exhibit 1(a). The equilibrium interest rate is 5 percent. The bond market is shown in equilibrium in Exhibit 1(b). The equilibrium bond price is P_{B1}.

Suppose people have only two ways to hold their wealth: in money or in bonds. In other words, a person must always decide, "How much of my wealth do I hold in money, and how much do I hold in bonds?" If someone's wealth is currently equal to $100,000, does this person hold $50,000 (of that wealth) in money and $50,000 in bonds, or $25,000 in money and $75,000 in bonds, and so on?

In this scenario, because wealth can be held only in the form of money and bonds, if someone thinks that she is holding *too much* money, she also must be thinking that she is holding too few bonds. In other words, a surplus of money necessarily implies a shortage of bonds. To illustrate, let's say the person is currently holding $25,000 in money and $75,000 in bonds. Let's also say that she thinks that she is holding too much of her wealth in money. Then she must also think that she is holding too little of her wealth in bonds. Consequently, she might want to take $5,000 of her money and buy $5,000 worth of bonds so that she has $20,000 in money and $80,000 in bonds. So, if a surplus of money signifies a shortage of bonds, then, in market terms, a surplus in the money market implies a shortage in the bond market.

EXHIBIT 1

The Money Market and the Bond Market

(a) The money market in equilibrium at an interest rate of 5 percent.

(b) The bond market is in equilibrium at a bond price of P_{B1}. When one of these markets is in equilibrium, the other is too.

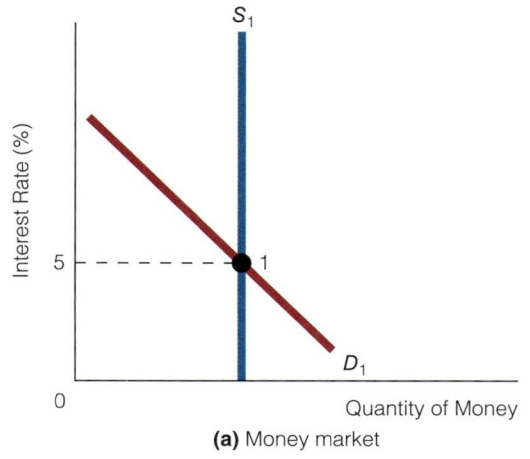

(a) Money market

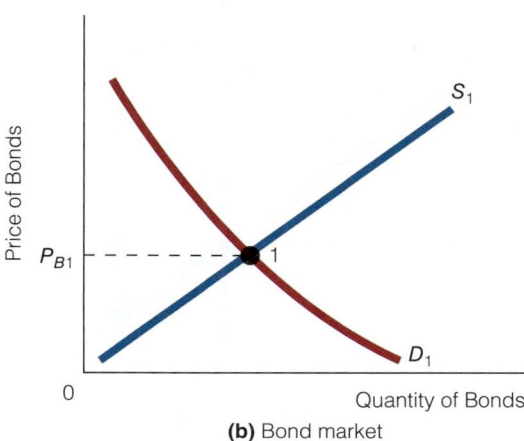

(b) Bond market

Now suppose our person believes that she is holding *too little* money. Instead of holding $25,000 in money, she would prefer to hold $30,000 in money. But, of course, holding too little money implies that our person is holding too much of her wealth in bonds. In other words, a shortage of money implies a surplus of bonds. Thus, a shortage in the money market implies a surplus in the bond market.

Let's recap:

Holding too much of one's wealth in money → Holding too little of one's wealth in bonds

or

Surplus in the money market → Shortage in the bond market

and

Holding too little of one's wealth in money → Holding too much of one's wealth in bonds

or

Shortage in the money market → Surplus in the bond market

Now let's look at Exhibit 2. At point 1 in each graph, the respective market is in equilibrium: People are holding just the right amount of money and just the right amount of bonds. Suppose the Fed undertakes an action that increases the money supply. Then the money supply curve in Exhibit 2(a) shifts rightward from S_1 to S_2. At the initial interest rate of 5 percent, the money market now has a surplus of money. But, as we recall, a surplus of money in the money market must mean a shortage of bonds in the bond market.

EXHIBIT 2

Changes in the Money Market Affect the Bond Market

(a) The money market is initially in equilibrium at point 1; the equilibrium interest rate is 5 percent. (b) The bond market is initially in equilibrium at point 1; the equilibrium bond price is P_{B1}. The Fed increases the money supply. In the money market [shown in (a)], the supply-of-money curve shifts rightward from S_1 to S_2. At the interest rate of 5 percent, there is now a surplus of money. With their surplus of money, individuals start to buy more bonds, so the demand-for-bonds curve in panel (b) shifts rightward from D_1 to D_2. The result is a shortage of bonds in the bond market at the price of P_{B1}. Both markets are now in disequilibrium. The equilibrating process in the bond market pushes bond prices up. As bond prices rise, the interest rate falls, and that happens in the money market [shown in (a)]. Eventually, both markets are back in equilibrium, with the equilibrium interest rate now 4 percent and the price of bonds now P_{B2}.

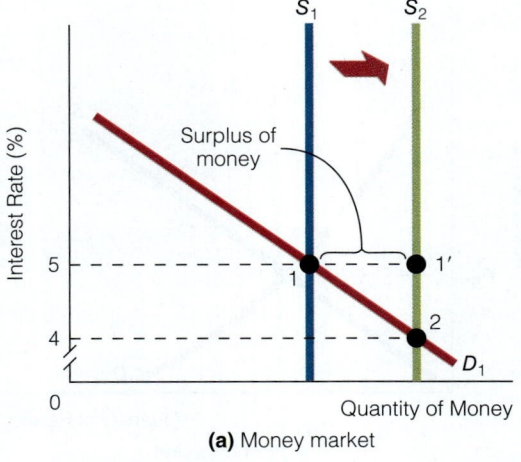
(a) Money market

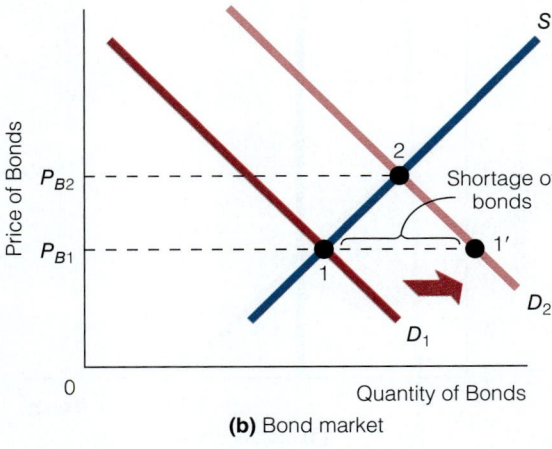
(b) Bond market

Appendix C Bond Prices and the Interest Rate

How does this shortage manifest itself? As a result of the surplus in the money market, individuals take their "surplus money" and start to buy bonds. The demand for bonds in the bond market then shifts rightward from D_1 to D_2 [Exhibit 2(b)]. So, now there is a surplus of money in the money market at 5 percent and a shortage of bonds in the bond market at P_{B1}. Both markets are in disequilibrium at the specified interest rate and bond price.

The markets will begin to equilibrate. In the bond market, the price of bonds will begin to rise toward P_{B2}. As the price of bonds rises, the interest rate in the money market starts to fall, moving toward its equilibrium level of 4 percent. Finally, both markets are in equilibrium: The money market is at 4 percent, and the bond market is at P_{B2}.

Appendix Summary

- Suppose that an individual can hold his wealth only as money or bonds. Then, if a person believes that he is holding too much of his wealth in money, he also believes that he is holding too little of it in bonds. Similarly, if he believes that he is holding too little of his wealth in money, he also believes that he is holding too much of it in bonds.

- A surplus in the money market implies a shortage in the bond market. A shortage in the money market implies a surplus in the bond market.

Questions and Problems

1. Draw both the money market and bond market in equilibrium. Next, explain, and show diagrammatically, what happens to the interest rate and the price of bonds as a result of the Fed's increasing the money supply.

2. Draw both the money market and bond market in equilibrium. Next, explain, and show diagrammatically, what happens to the interest rate and the price of bonds as a result of the Fed's decreasing the money supply.

3. Identify the state of the bond market (equilibrium, shortage, and surplus), given each of the following:
   a. Shortage in the money market
   b. Surplus in the money market
   c. Equilibrium in the money market

4. Fed actions affect the money market but not the bond market. Do you agree or disagree with this statement? Explain your answer.

CHAPTER 16
Expectations Theory and the Economy

Introduction

In this chapter, we discuss two expectations theories: adaptive and rational. We begin our discussion of expectations theory and the economy with a debate that raged within the economics profession years ago over the shape of the Phillips curve.

16-1 Phillips Curve Analysis

Phillips Curve
A curve that originally showed the relationship between wage inflation and unemployment and that now more often shows the relationship between price inflation and unemployment.

The **Phillips curve** is used to analyze the relationship between inflation and unemployment. We begin the discussion of the Phillips curve by focusing on the work of three economists: A. W. Phillips, Paul Samuelson, and Robert Solow.

16-1a The Phillips Curve

In 1958, A. W. Phillips of the London School of Economics published a paper in the economics journal *Economica*: "The Relation Between Unemployment and the Rate of Change of Money Wages in the United Kingdom, 1861–1957." As the title suggests, Phillips collected data about the rate of change of money wages, sometimes referred to as *wage inflation*, and about *unemployment rates* in the United Kingdom over almost a century. He then plotted the rate of change in money wages against the unemployment rate for each year. Finally, he fit a curve to the data points (Exhibit 1).

EXHIBIT 1

The Original Phillips Curve

This curve was constructed by A. W. Phillips, using data for the United Kingdom from 1861 to 1913. (The relationship here is also representative of the experience of the United Kingdom through 1957.) The original Phillips curve suggests an inverse relationship between wage inflation and unemployment—a wage inflation–unemployment trade-off. (Note: Each dot represents a single year.)

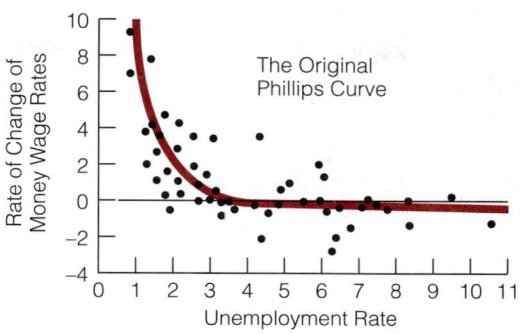

An Inverse Relationship The curve, which came to be known as the Phillips curve, is downward sloping, suggesting that the rate of change of money wages (wage inflation) and unemployment rates are *inversely related*.[1] This inverse relationship, in turn, suggests a trade-off between wage inflation and unemployment. Higher wage inflation means lower unemployment; lower wage inflation means higher unemployment.

Policymakers concluded from the Phillips curve that simultaneously lowering wage inflation and unemployment was impossible; they could do only one or the other. So the combination of low wage inflation and low unemployment was unlikely. This was the bad news.

The good news was that rising unemployment and rising wage inflation did not go together either. Thus, the combination of high unemployment and high wage inflation was also unlikely.

Stagflation
The simultaneous occurrence of high rates of inflation and unemployment.

16-1b Samuelson and Solow: The Americanization of the Phillips Curve

In 1960, two American economists, Paul Samuelson and Robert Solow, published an article in the *American Economic Review* in which they fit a Phillips curve to the U.S. economy from 1935 to 1959. In addition to using U.S. data instead of British data, they measured *price inflation rates* (instead of wage inflation rates) against unemployment rates. They found an inverse relationship between (price) inflation and unemployment (see Exhibit 2).[2]

Economists concluded from the Phillips curve that **stagflation**, or high inflation together with high unemployment, was extremely unlikely. The economy could register (1) high unemployment and low inflation or (2) low unemployment and high inflation. Also,

EXHIBIT 2

The Phillips Curve and a Menu of Choices

Samuelson and Solow's early work using American data showed that the Phillips curve was downward sloping. Economists reasoned that stagflation was extremely unlikely and that the Phillips curve presented policymakers with a menu of choices—points A, B, C, and D.

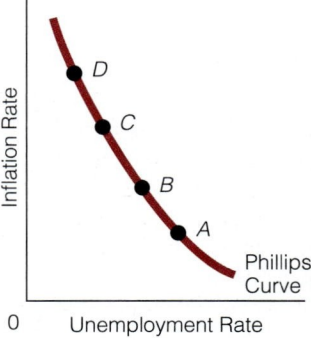

---

[1]. Early explanations for the inverse relationship between wage inflation and unemployment focused on the state of the labor market, given changes in aggregate demand. When aggregate demand is increasing, businesses expand production and hire more employees. As the unemployment rate falls, the labor market becomes tighter, and employers find it increasingly difficult to hire workers at old wages. Businesses must then offer higher wages in order to obtain additional workers. Unemployment and money wages move in opposite directions.

[2]. Today, when economists speak of the Phillips curve, they are usually referring to the relationship between price inflation rates and unemployment rates instead of the relationship between wage inflation rates and unemployment rates.

economists noticed that the Phillips curve presented policymakers with a *menu of choices*. For example, policymakers could choose to move the economy to any of the points on the Phillips curve shown in Exhibit 2. If they decided that, say, point A, with high unemployment and low inflation, was preferable to point D, with low unemployment and high inflation, then so be it. Getting the economy to the desired point was simply a matter of reaching the right level of aggregate demand. To Keynesian economists, who were gaining a reputation for advocating fine-tuning the economy (i.e., using small-scale measures to counterbalance undesirable economic trends), this conclusion seemed consistent with their theories and policy proposals.

16-2 The Controversy Begins: Are There Really Two Phillips Curves?

This section discusses the work of Milton Friedman and the hypothesis that there are two Phillips curves, not one.

16-2a Things Aren't Always as We Think They Are

In the 1970s and early 1980s, economists began to question many of the conclusions about the Phillips curve—questions prompted largely by events that happened after 1969. Exhibit 3 shows the U.S. inflation and unemployment rates for the years 1961–2003. The 1961–1969 period, which is shaded, depicts the original Phillips curve trade-off between inflation and unemployment. The remaining period, 1970–2003, as a whole does not, although some subperiods, such as 1976–1979, do.

Note that, in the period 1970–2003, stagflation—high unemployment and high inflation—is possible. For example, 1975, 1981, and 1982 are definitely years of stagflation. The existence of stagflation implies that a trade-off between inflation and unemployment may not always exist.

16-2b Friedman and the Natural Rate Theory

In his presidential address to the American Economic Association in 1967 (published in the *American Economic Review*), Milton Friedman attacked the idea of a *permanent* downward-sloping Phillips curve. Friedman's key point was that there are two Phillips curves, not one: a short-run Phillips curve and a long-run Phillips curve. Friedman said, "There is always a temporary tradeoff between inflation and unemployment; there is no permanent tradeoff." Specifically, *there is a trade-off in the short run but not in the long run*. Friedman's discussion not only introduced two types of Phillips curves but also opened the macroeconomics door wide, once and for all, to expectations theory: the idea that people's expectations about economic events affect economic outcomes.

Exhibit 4 illustrates both the short- and long-run Phillips curves. In window 1, the economy is in long-run equilibrium, operating at Q_1, which is equal to Q_N. In the main diagram, the economy is at point 1 at the natural rate of unemployment, U_N. Further and most important, *we assume that the expected inflation rate and the actual inflation rate are the same* at 2 percent.

Now suppose government *unexpectedly* increases aggregate demand from AD_1 to AD_2, as shown in window 2. As a result, the *actual* inflation rate increases (say, to 4 percent), but in the short run (immediately after the increase in aggregate demand), individual decision makers do not know this. Consequently, the *expected* inflation rate remains at 2 percent. In short, aggregate demand increases at the same time that people's expected inflation rate remains constant.

EXHIBIT 3

The Diagram That Raises Questions: Inflation and Unemployment, 1961–2003

The period 1961–1969 clearly depicts the original Phillips curve trade-off between inflation and unemployment. The later period, 1970–2003, as a whole, does not. However, some subperiods do, such as 1976–1979. The diagram presents empirical evidence that stagflation may exist; an inflation–unemployment trade-off may not always hold.

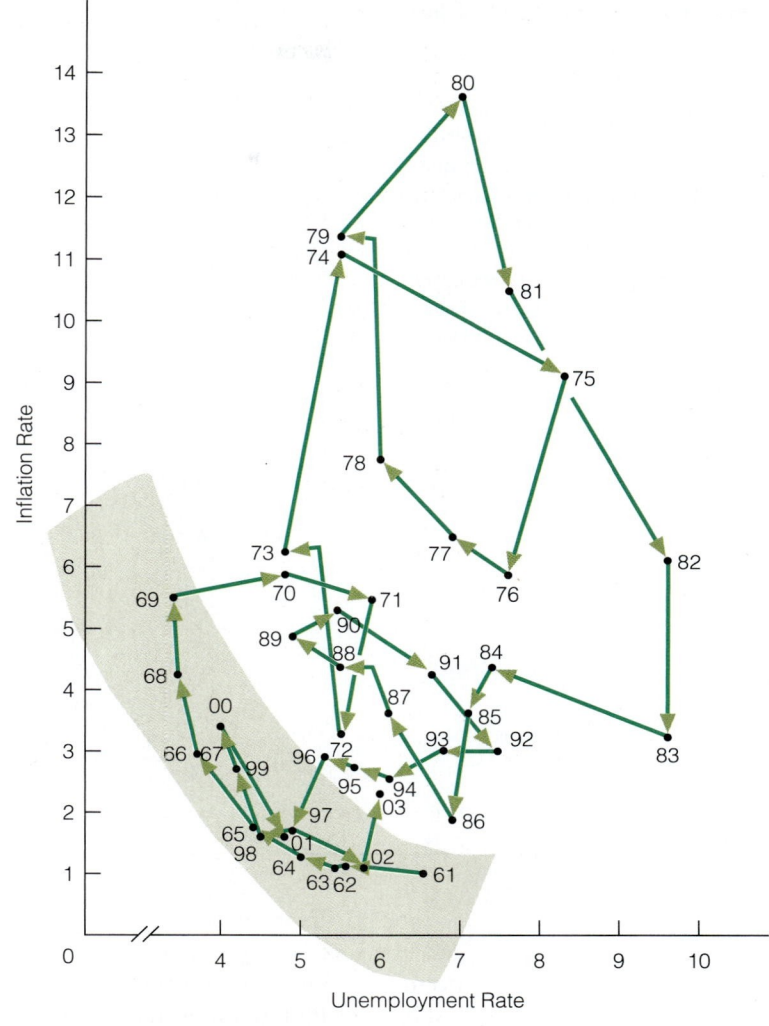

Because of this combination of events, certain consequences unfold. The higher aggregate demand causes temporary shortages and higher prices. Businesses then respond to the higher prices and subsequent higher profits by increasing output. Higher output requires more employees, so businesses start hiring more workers. As hiring increases, many currently unemployed individuals find work. Furthermore, many of the newly employed persons accept the prevailing wage rate because they think the wages will have greater purchasing power (because they expect the inflation rate to be 2 percent) than, in fact, the wages will turn out to have.

So far, the results of an increase in aggregate demand with no change in the expected inflation rate are (1) an increase in Real GDP from Q_1 to Q_2 (see window 2) and (2) a corresponding decrease in the unemployment rate from U_1 to U_2 (in the main diagram).

The question is whether point 2 is a stable equilibrium. Friedman answered that it is not. He argued that, *as long as the expected inflation rate is not equal to the actual inflation rate, the economy is not in long-run equilibrium.*

EXHIBIT 4

Short-Run and Long-Run Phillips Curves

Starting at point 1 in the main diagram, and under the assumption that the expected inflation rate stays constant as aggregate demand increases, the economy moves to point 2. As the expected inflation rate changes and comes to equal the actual inflation rate, the economy moves to point 3. Points 1 and 2 lie on a short-run Phillips curve. Points 1 and 3 lie on a long-run Phillips curve. (*Note:* The percentages in parentheses, which follow the *SRAS* curves in the windows, refer to the expected inflation rates.)

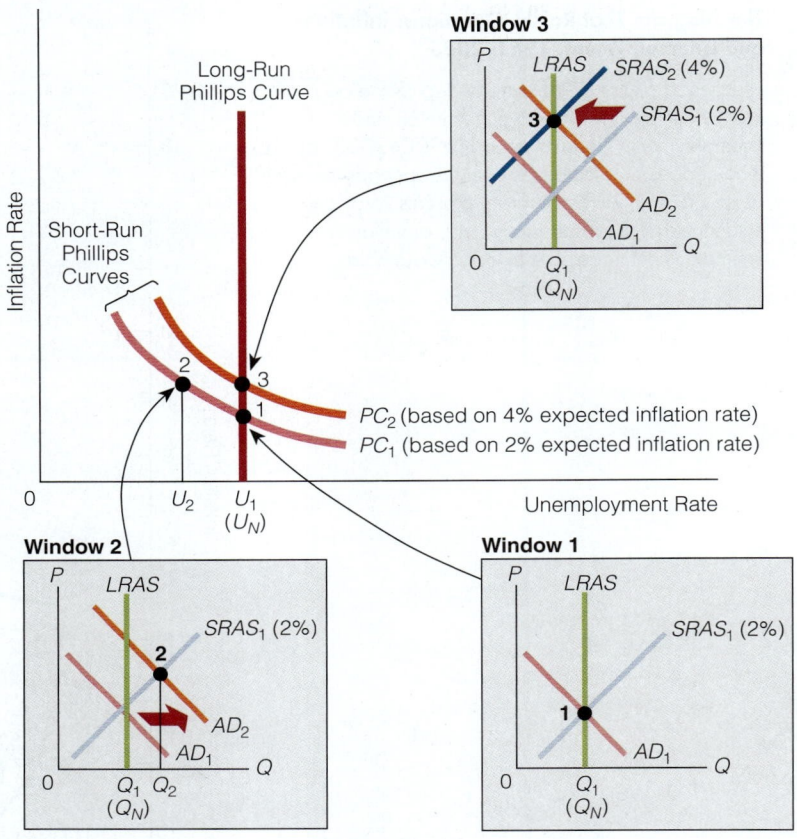

Friedman Natural Rate Theory
Within the Phillips curve framework, the idea that, in the long run, unemployment is at its natural rate and that there is a long-run Phillips curve, which is vertical at the natural rate of unemployment.

For Friedman, as for most economists today, the movement from point 1 to point 2 on PC_1 is a short-run movement. Economists refer to PC_1, along which short-run movements occur, as a *short-run Phillips curve*.

In time, inflation expectations begin to change. As prices continue to climb, wage earners realize that their real (i.e., inflation-adjusted) wages are lower than they thought. In hindsight, they realize that they accepted nominal (money) wages based on an expected inflation rate (2 percent) that was too low. So they revise their inflation expectations upward.

At the same time, some wage earners quit their jobs because they choose not to continue working at such low *real wages*. Eventually, the combination of some workers quitting their jobs and most (if not all) workers revising their inflation expectations upward causes wage rates to move upward.

Higher wage rates then shift the short-run aggregate supply curve from $SRAS_1$ to $SRAS_2$ (see window 3), ultimately moving the economy back to Natural Real GDP and to the natural rate of unemployment at point 3 (see the main diagram). The curve that connects point 1, where the economy started, and point 3, where it ended, is called the *long-run Phillips curve*.

Thus, the short-run Phillips curve exhibits a trade-off between inflation and unemployment, whereas the long-run Phillips curve does not. This idea is implicit in what has come to be called the **Friedman natural rate theory** (or the *Friedman fooling theory*). According to this

EXHIBIT 5

Mechanics of the Friedman Natural Rate Theory

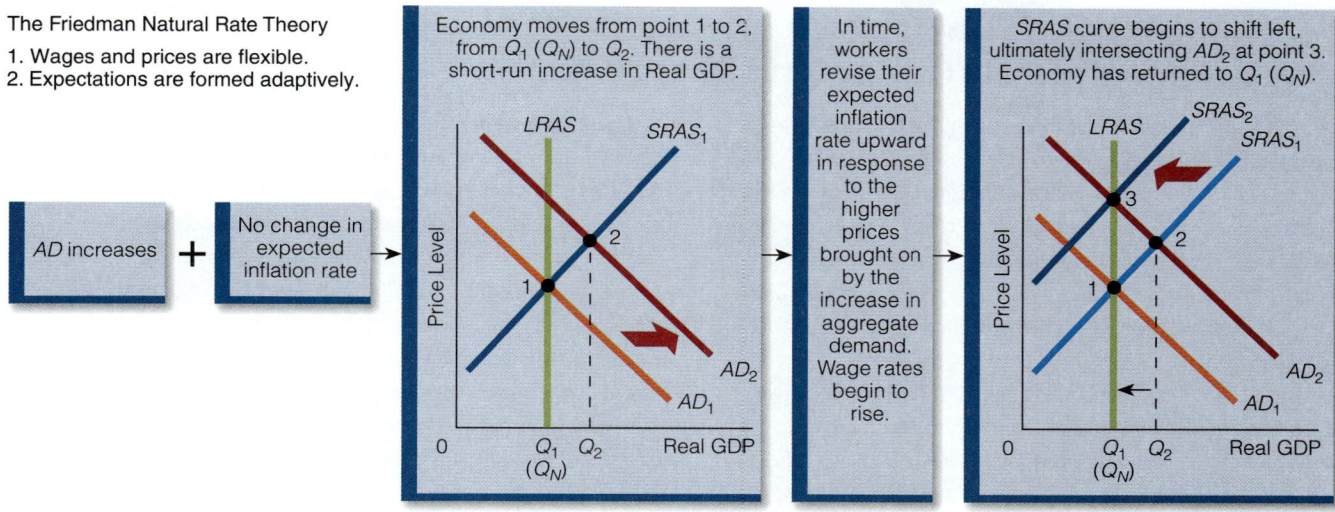

theory (Exhibit 5), in the long run, the economy returns to its natural rate of unemployment, and it moved away from the natural unemployment rate in the first place only because workers were fooled (in the short run) into thinking the inflation rate was lower than it was.

How, specifically, do people's expectations relate to the discussion of the short- and long-run Phillips curves? In Exhibit 4, the economy starts out at point 1 in the main diagram, and then something happens: Aggregate demand increases. This increase raises the inflation rate, *but workers don't become aware of the change in the inflation rate for a while.* In the interim, their expected inflation rate is too low, and as a result, they are willing to work at jobs (and produce output) that they wouldn't work at if they perceived the inflation rate realistically.

In time, workers perceive the inflation rate realistically. Their expected inflation rate is no longer too low; it has risen to equal the actual inflation rate. The response, as predicted, is that the unemployment rate rises and output falls.

So, because workers' expectations (of inflation) are, in the short run, inconsistent with reality, workers produce more output than they would produce if their expectations were consistent with reality. This is how people's expectations can affect such real economic variables as Real GDP and the unemployment rate.

Thinking Like an Economist

Perceptions of Reality Matter People say they base their actions on reality. When it rains, they pull out an umbrella; when they have a hard time seeing, they get their eyes checked. People also base their actions on their *perceptions* of reality, as workers do in the Friedman natural rate theory. Although the inflation rate has actually increased, workers don't perceive the change. Thus, in the short run (during the period in which they misperceive reality), workers base their actions not on reality but on their perception of it.

Economics 24/7

Is the Downward-Sloping Phillips Curve Disappearing?

In this text, we have drawn the short-run Phillips Curve downward sloping, which illustrates an inverse relationship between the inflation rate (on the vertical axis) and the unemployment rate (on the horizontal axis). A downward-sloping Phillips Curve is indicative of a trade-off between inflation and unemployment: When the unemployment rate is low, the inflation rate is relatively high, and when the unemployment rate is high, the inflation rate is relatively low.

If we fit the inflation-unemployment data for 1975–1984, we have a downward-sloping Phillips Curve. The same thing holds, but to a lesser degree, for the years 1985–1994. But then for the years 1995–2018, the Phillips Curve seems much less downward sloping. In fact, for the years 2015–2018, it seems nearly flat. In other words, the trade-off between inflation and unemployment (visible in a Phillips Curve that is downward sloping) seems to have disappeared. For example, in May 2018, the unemployment rate was a low 3.8 percent, and the inflation rate was a low 2.04 percent.

Now, if you were an economist in the period 2015–2018 used to predicting inflation based on a downward-sloping Phillips Curve framework, you would have said something like this: "It looks like the unemployment rate is fairly low, so we can expect that inflation is going to rise soon. That's because there is a trade-off between unemployment and inflation."

In other words, you were used to seeing the inverse relationship between inflation and unemployment manifest itself, and you thought it would continue to do so. It is almost like saying that you haven't eaten for 10 hours, so you can expect to get hungry anytime now. But, then, for some reason unknown to you, you don't get hungry. It was the same for the economist who predicted inflation would be rising because unemployment was low. But then inflation didn't rise.

Now, if the inflation rate is pretty much the same—say, 2 percent—no matter what the unemployment rate is, we have a flat Phillips Curve, not a downward-sloping one. The theory behind the downward-sloping Phillips curve—the theoretical reason we expect the inflation rate to rise when the unemployment rate is low goes like this: When the unemployment rate is low, labor markets are likely to be "tight," or witnessing a shortage. Accordingly, wages are expected to rise. But, then, if firms do not want to give up their "markup" (price above cost by, say, 8 percent), they will raise prices. In summary, low unemployment indicates tight labor markets, which means wages will rise, and soon afterward, prices will follow. Except, as we said earlier, in more recent years, things didn't follow this path, and so the downward-sloping Phillips curve couldn't be found in the data.

What could have happened to explain a disappearing downward-sloping Phillips curve? Some have suggested that labor union power has diminished in recent decades, making it much less likely that labor can easily bargain for higher wages. Others have suggested that inflation expectations have a lot to do with the disappearing downward-sloping Phillips curve. Inflation expectations can affect workers' demand for wage increases. If you expect inflation to stay around 2 percent, then you are much less likely to bargain for significantly higher wages than if you expect inflation to rise to 10 percent. Maybe, some argue, the Fed has, through monetary policy, done such a good job at keeping the inflation rate at a low 2 percent rate that workers simply don't expect that the inflation rate is going to rise much above 2 percent, and this affects their demand for wage increases. The economic research continues in its attempt to find the definitive reason or reasons for the flattening out of the downward-sloping Phillips curve.

16-2c How Do People Form Their Expectations?

Implicit in the Friedman natural rate theory is an assumption about how individuals form their expectations. Essentially, the theory holds that individuals form their expected inflation rate by looking at *past inflation rates*. Suppose someone were to ask you your expected inflation rate for the upcoming year. Would your response be closer to 50 percent or to 2 percent? If you use **adaptive expectations** to arrive at your expected inflation rate, the answer is closer to 2 percent than to 50 percent, because you haven't seen recent past inflation rates of 50 percent. But you have seen recent past inflation rates near 2 percent.

Notice that, with adaptive expectations, individuals look to the past—they look over their shoulders to see what *has happened*—in formulating their best guess as to what *will happen*. This is what individuals do in the Friedman natural rate theory, which assumes that people have adaptive expectations.

Some economists have argued the point. They believe that people form their expected inflation rate not by using adaptive expectations but by means of *rational expectations*. We discuss this view in the next section.

Adaptive Expectations
Expectations that individuals form from past experience and modify slowly as the present and the future become the past (i.e., as time passes).

Finding Economics

At the Bargaining Table Suppose you read the following report in the newspaper: "Recent wage negotiations between management and labor unions in the city have come to a halt. The two sides in the negotiations are unable so far to come to an agreement on annual wage rate increases for the duration of the four-year contract." Where is the economics?

First, if the two sides are negotiating an annual wage rate increase, then each is probably basing the increase on an expected inflation rate. Management might be saying, "We believe that the average annual inflation rate over the next four years will be 2 percent, so we are willing to agree to an annual wage rate increase of 2 percent each year for the next four years. The labor unions might be saying, "Because we expect the average annual inflation rate over the next four years to be 3.5 percent, we believe that 3.5 percent is the right annual wage rate increase for us."

(Answers to Self-Test questions are in Answers to Self-Test Questions at the back of the book.)

1. What condition must exist for the Phillips curve to present policymakers with a permanent menu of choices (between inflation and unemployment)?
2. Is there a trade-off between inflation and unemployment? Explain your answer.
3. The Friedman natural rate theory is sometimes called the fooling theory. Who is being fooled, and what are they being fooled about?

16-3 Rational Expectations and New Classical Theory

Rational expectations have played a major role in the Phillips curve controversy. We discuss rational expectations and new classical theory next.

16-3a Rational Expectations

In the early 1970s, a few economists, including Robert Lucas of the University of Chicago (winner of the 1995 Nobel Prize in Economics), began to question the short-run trade-off between inflation and unemployment. Essentially, Lucas combined the natural rate theory with rational expectations.[3]

Rational Expectations
Expectations that individuals form on the basis of past experience and their predictions about the effects of present and future policy actions and events.

The theory of **rational expectations** holds that individuals form the expected inflation rate not only on the basis of their past experience with inflation (looking over their shoulders) but also on their predictions about the effects of present and future policy actions and events (looking around and ahead). In short, the expected inflation rate is formed by looking at the past, present, and future. To illustrate, suppose the inflation rate has been 2 percent for the past seven years. Then, the chairman of the Fed's Board of Governors speaks about "sharply stimulating the economy." Proponents of rational expectations argue that the expected inflation rate might immediately jump upward on the basis of the current announcement by the chairman.

A major difference between adaptive and rational expectations is the *speed* at which the expected inflation rate changes. If the expected inflation rate is formed adaptively, then it is slow to change. Because it is based only on the past, individuals wait until the present becomes the past before changing their expectations. If the expected inflation rate is formed rationally, it changes quickly because it is based on the past, present, and future.

16-3b Do People Really Anticipate Policy?

One assumption of rational expectations is that people anticipate policy. Suppose you chose people at random on the street and asked them, "What do you think the Fed will do in the next few months?" Do you think you would be more likely to receive an intelligent answer or the response, "What's the Fed?" Most readers of this text would probably expect the second answer. In fact, the general feeling is that the person on the street knows little about economics or economic institutions. So, no, people don't really anticipate policy. But suppose you chose people at random in the Wall Street area of Manhattan and asked the same question. In this case, the answer is likely to be well thought out; at least *these* people anticipate policy.

However, not all persons need to anticipate policy. *As long as some do*, the consequences may be the same *as if* all persons do. For example, Juanita is anticipating policy if she decides to buy 100 shares of SKA because her best friend, Tammy, heard from her friend Pahal that his broker, Mika, told him that SKA's stock is expected to go up. Juanita is anticipating policy because it is likely that Mika obtained her information from a researcher in the brokerage firm who makes it his business to watch the Fed and to anticipate its next move.

Of course, policy is anticipated not just for the purpose of buying and selling securities. Labor unions hire professional forecasters (Fed watchers) to predict future inflation rates—important information to have during wage contract negotiations. Banks hire forecasters to predict inflation rates, which they incorporate into the interest rates they charge. Export businesses hire forecasters to predict the future exchange-rate value of the dollar. The average investor may subscribe to a business or investment newsletter for information in order to predict interest rates, the price of gold, or next year's inflation rate more accurately. The person thinking of refinancing a mortgage watches one of the many financial news shows on television to find out about the government's most recent move and how it will affect interest rates in, say, the next three months.

---

[3] Rational expectations appeared on the economic scene in 1961, when John Muth published "Rational Expectations and the Theory of Price Movements" in *Econometrica*. For about 10 years, the article received little attention from the economics profession. Then, in the early 1970s, with the work of Robert Lucas, Thomas Sargent, Neil Wallace, Robert Barro, and others, the article began to be noticed.

> **Finding Economics**
>
> **While Playing a Game of Chess** Where is the economics in a game of chess? Chess players often anticipate each other's moves. Player 1 might be thinking that if she moves from e4 to e5, player 2 will move from b5 to c6. But then the first player asks herself, "What comes next? Will my opponent then be likely to move from c6 to d6?"
>
> What people do in a game of chess and what they do when predicting government policy actions might not be all that different. In a game of chess, you are playing to win, and whether you win depends on how well you can anticipate your opponent's moves. Anticipating policy actions is not much different, as you will shortly see. How well you do in the economy also has a lot to do with how well you anticipate government policy actions.

16-3c Price-Level Expectations and the *SRAS* Curve

We know that various factors can shift the *SRAS* curve: wage rates, the price of nonlabor inputs, supply shocks, and so on. In this chapter, we show how a change in expectations can lead to a shift in the *SRAS* curve.

Real Wage The real (inflation-adjusted) wage is equal to the nominal wage divided by the price level:

$$\text{Real Wage} = \frac{\text{Nominal Wage}}{\text{Price Level}} \times 100$$

Suppose that the nominal wage is $40 and that the price level, as represented by a price index, is 110. The real wage is therefore $36.36: [($40 ÷ 110) × 100]. Obviously, a person's real wage will rise if either the nominal wage rises or the price level declines, or if both occur. For example, suppose the price level falls from 110 to 95. Then the real wage rises to $42.10, and under certain conditions, as one's real wage rises, one chooses to work more. Conversely, as one's real wage falls, one chooses to work less. Thus,

Price level falls → Real wage rises → Work more

Price level rises → Real wage falls → Work less

Working More or Less and Shifts in the *SRAS* Curve Labor is an input into the production process, so more labor (in terms of either individuals or labor hours) means more output. When people work more, more output is produced, so the *SRAS* curve shifts rightward. When people work less, less output is produced, so the *SRAS* curve shifts leftward.

Now we can connect the expected price level to the *SRAS* curve:

- *Example 1.* Suppose individuals expect the price level to decline. Then they expect their real wages to rise and will work more. Working more produces more output, so the *SRAS* curve shifts rightward. These logical relationships can be summed up as follows:

Expect price level to fall → Expect real wage to rise → Work more → Produce more output → *SRAS* curve shifts rightward

- *Example 2.* Suppose individuals expect the price level to rise. Then they expect their real wage to decline and will work less. Working less produces less output, so the *SRAS* curve shifts leftward.

Expect price level to rise → Expect real wage to fall → Work less → Produce less output → *SRAS* curve shifts leftward

Exhibit 6 shows three *SRAS* curves. After each curve is the expected price level in parentheses. The higher the expected price level is, the closer the *SRAS* curve lies to the vertical axis and the origin. The lower the expected price level is, the farther away from the vertical axis and the origin the *SRAS* lies. Therefore, a rise in the expected price level will shift the *SRAS* curve to the left; a fall in the expected price level will shift the *SRAS* curve to the right.

16-3d Expected and Actual Price Levels

The difference between an actual price level and an expected price level is fairly clear:

- The *actual price level* is exactly what it sounds like: the price level that actually exists. For example, someone might say that the price level today is 140. This, then, is the actual price level. We will use P_A to represent the actual price level.

- The *expected price level* is what you expect the price level will be sometime in the future. For example, you might expect that the price level in, say, one year will be 150. This is your expected price level. We will use P_{EX} to represent the expected price level.

Obviously, individuals' expectations (P_{EX}) can have one of three relationships to the actual price level (P_A):

$$P_{EX} = P_A$$
$$P_{EX} > P_A$$
$$P_{EX} < P_A$$

EXHIBIT 6

The Expected Price Level and the *SRAS* Curve

Every *SRAS* curve is based on some expected price level. For example, $SRAS_1$ in the exhibit is based on an *expected price level* of 150. As the expected price level rises, the *SRAS* curve shifts leftward; as the expected price level falls, the *SRAS* curve shifts rightward.

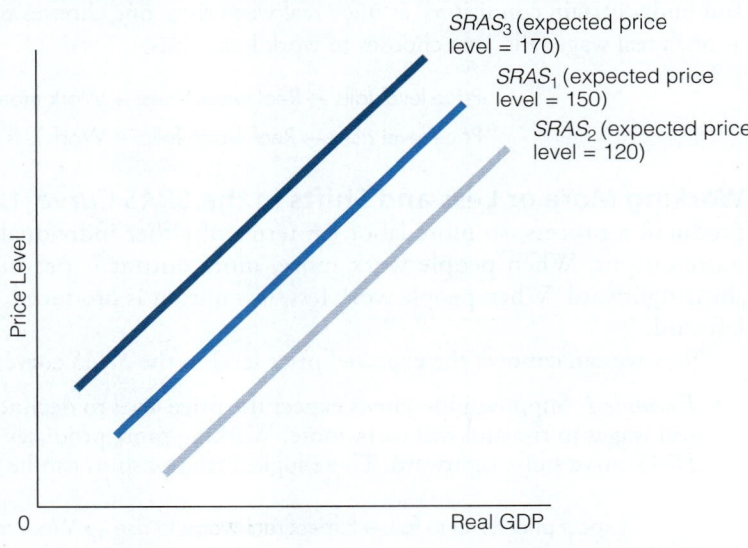

Economics 24/7

Rational Expectations in the College Classroom

If people hold rational expectations, then the outcome of a policy will be different if the policy is unanticipated than if it is anticipated. Specifically, unanticipated policy changes can move the economy away from the natural unemployment rate, but correctly anticipated policy changes cannot. Does something similar happen in a college classroom?

Suppose Raimy's history class starts at 9:00 a.m., and he "naturally" arrives 1 minute before class starts. In other words, his so-called natural waiting time is 1 minute.

The first day of class, Raimy arrives at 8:59, his instructor arrives at 8:59:30, and he starts class promptly at 9:00 a.m.

The second day of class, Raimy arrives at 8:59, his instructor arrives at 9:01:30, and he starts class at 9:02 a.m. On this day, Raimy has waited 3 minutes, which is more than his natural waiting time of 1 minute.

The timing of the start of class on the third, fourth, and fifth days is the same as on the second, so, for the second through fifth days, Raimy is operating at more than his natural waiting time.

The theory of rational expectations holds that people will not continue to make the same mistake. In this case, Raimy will take his professor's recent arrival time into account and adjust his timing accordingly. Thus, on the sixth day of class, instead of arriving at 8:59, Raimy arrives at 9:01. This day, the instructor again arrives at 9:01:30 and begins class at 9:02 a.m., and Raimy has moved back to his natural waiting time of 1 minute.

So far, Raimy's natural waiting time was met on the first day of class. On the second through fifth days of class, the professor obviously changed his policy as to his arrival time. Raimy didn't

anticipate this change of policy, so he was fooled into waiting more than his natural waiting time. But Raimy did not continue to make the same mistake: He adjusted to his professor's policy change and went back to his 1-minute natural waiting time.

Now let's change the scenario. At the end of the first day of class, the professor announces, "I know I arrived at class at 8:59:30 today, but I won't do that again. From now on, I will arrive at 9:01:30."

In this situation, the professor has announced his policy change. Raimy hears the announcement and correctly anticipates the professor's arrival time from now on. With that information, he adjusts his behavior: Instead of arriving at class at 8:59, he arrives at 9:01. Thus, Raimy has correctly anticipated his professor's policy change, and he will remain at his natural waiting time. (He will not move from it, even temporarily.)

To illustrate, suppose the Fed increases the money supply, and the *AD* curve shifts rightward. Then, if the *SRAS* curve is upward sloping, there will be a short-run and a long-run effect on the price level. Suppose that, when the economy is back in long-run equilibrium, the actual price level (P_A) will be 155. But when the Fed increases the money supply, you expect that the price level in the future will be 165. In other words, your expected price level is greater than the actual price level: $P_{EX} > P_A$. Obviously, you made a mistake: You overestimated what the price level would be. You "guessed" too high. In the new classical theoretical framework, using rational expectations, "guessing" too high, too low, or just right can have an effect on the economy. In the following section, we demonstrate the technique.

16-3e New Classical Economics and Four Different Cases

New classical theory holds that individuals have rational expectations and that prices and wages are flexible. With these two points in mind, we apply new classical theory to four different cases (or settings):

- Case 1: Policy Correctly Anticipated
- Case 2: Policy Incorrectly Anticipated (Bias Upward)
- Case 3: Policy Incorrectly Anticipated (Bias Downward)
- Case 4: Policy Unanticipated

Each setting relates to a different perspective individuals have with respect to economic policy. We discuss monetary policy, but everything we say with respect to monetary policy in the upcoming discussion also holds for demand-side fiscal policy.

Case 1: Policy Correctly Anticipated Suppose an economy is in long-run equilibrium, as shown at point 1 in Exhibit 7. The actual price level is 100, and $SRAS_1$ is based on the expected price level of 100. In other words, in long-run equilibrium, the actual price level (P_A) and the expected price level (P_{EX}) are the same.

$$\text{Starting point: } P_A = P_{EX}$$

Now the Fed increases the money supply, and this Fed policy action is *correctly anticipated* by the public. What "correctly anticipated" means here is that individuals know not only that the Fed is increasing the money supply but also how much the money supply is increasing and

EXHIBIT 7

Policy Correctly Anticipated

We assume that rational expectations hold, that wages and prices are flexible, that any policy action is anticipated correctly, and that the economy is in long-run equilibrium. The actual price level is 100, and the expected price level (on which the $SRAS_1$ curve is based) is also 100. The Fed increases the money supply, and the AD curve shifts rightward. Because policy is anticipated correctly, individuals know that the new long-run equilibrium price level will be 110. Knowing this, they change their expected price level to 110. As a result, the SRAS curve shifts leftward from $SRAS_1$ to $SRAS_2$. Keep in mind that AD and SRAS change at the same time. In other words, the AD curve shifts rightward at the same time that the SRAS curve shifts leftward. The result is that the Fed's action leads to a higher price level but does not change Real GDP. The action is ineffective at changing Real GDP; thus, we have the policy ineffectiveness proposition (PIP) holding.

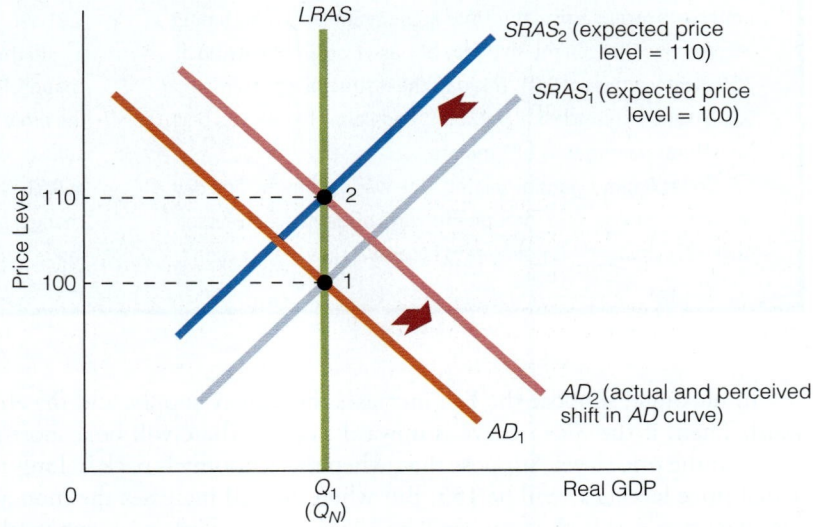

what the actual price level will be when the economy reaches its new long-run equilibrium position. The exhibit shows that the actual price level *will be* 110 when the economy reaches its new long-run equilibrium at point 2.

So, how does the fact that individuals are correctly anticipating policy (and the consequences of that policy) affect the *expected price level*? If individuals know where the actual price level is headed (i.e., to 110), they will immediately change their expected price level to 110. Look at it this way: Reality is changing in the economy; the price level is going to rise from 100 to 110 because of the Fed's action. Correctly anticipating the new price level is like having a crystal ball and knowing exactly what is going to happen. Consequently, individuals immediately change their expectations of the future on the basis of their correctly viewed perception of what is really going to happen.

Now, if the expected price level changes to 110, the SRAS curve in the exhibit will shift leftward from $SRAS_1$ to $SRAS_2$. However, the SRAS curve shifts leftward at essentially the same time that the AD curve shifts rightward. The economy therefore moves from point 1 (its starting point) to point 2 (or ending point).

Exhibit 7 shows that, even though the Fed increases the money supply (and the AD curve shifts rightward), Real GDP does not change. We started at Q_1 (or Q_N) and ended up at Q_1 (or Q_N). Therefore, if policy is correctly anticipated and if rational expectations hold, the only thing an increase in the money supply does in the economy is raise the price level. It does not change Real GDP. In other words, the Fed policy action was ineffective at changing Real GDP. This scenario represents what economists call the **policy ineffectiveness proposition (PIP)**.

Case 2: Policy Incorrectly Anticipated (Bias Upward) Again, an economy starts at long-run equilibrium, shown as point 1 in Exhibit 8. The two operative (i.e., true) curves are AD_1 and $SRAS_1$. $SRAS_1$ is based on an expected price level (P_{EX}) of 100, which is the same as the actual price level (P_A).

$$\text{Starting point: } P_A = P_{EX}$$

Once again, the Fed increases the money supply, and the AD curve shifts rightward from AD_1 to AD_2. This time, however, individuals mistakenly believe that the AD curve has shifted rightward by more than it actually has. In other words, they mistakenly think that the AD curve has shifted from AD_1 to AD_3. Individuals have thus *incorrectly anticipated policy with an upward bias*.

Obviously, individuals have made a mistake, and this mistake is going to have consequences. Specifically, because individuals mistakenly believe that the AD curve in the economy is AD_3 now, they think that the new long-run equilibrium price level (the point at which AD_3 intersects LRAS) will be 118; that is, their expected price level is 118. But the actual price level is never going to be 118. The actual price level in the future is going to be 110, the point at which AD_2 intersects L. So the expected price level is higher than what the actual price will be:

$$P_{EX} > P_A$$

Now, as a result of individuals changing their expected price level from 100 to 118, the SRAS curve shifts leftward from $SRAS_1$ to $SRAS_2$. So far, then, the AD curve has actually shifted from AD_1 to AD_2, and the SRAS curve has shifted from $SRAS_1$ to $SRAS_2$. So, in the short run, the economy ends up at the intersection of AD_2 and $SRAS_2$—that is, at point 2 in the exhibit. This is an odd result, because we are accustomed to believing that an increase in the money

Policy Ineffectiveness Proposition (PIP)
If (1) a policy change is correctly anticipated, (2) individuals form their expectations rationally, and (3) wages and prices are flexible, then neither fiscal policy nor monetary policy is effective at meeting macroeconomic goals.

EXHIBIT 8

Policy Incorrectly Anticipated—Bias Upward

(1) The economy starts in long-run equilibrium at point 1 and $P_A = P_{EX}$. (2) The Fed increases the money supply, and the AD curve actually shifts rightward from AD_1 to AD_2. (3) Individuals have incorrectly anticipated the Fed's action: They believe that the Fed has increased the money supply more than it actually has, so they believe that the AD curve has shifted from AD_1 to AD_3. This is a mistake. (4) Mistakenly assuming that the AD curve has shifted rightward from AD_1 to AD_3, individuals think that the new actual price level will end up being 118, the value at which the AD_3 curve intersects the LRAS curve. Accordingly, they change their expected price level to 118, and the SRAS curve shifts leftward from $SRAS_1$ to $SRAS_2$. (5) The short-run equilibrium for the economy turns out to be at point 2. (6) Eventually, individuals figure out that they made a mistake—that the real AD curve is AD_2, not AD_3. So the new long-run equilibrium will be 110, not 118 (as earlier believed). As a result, individuals now readjust their expected price level down from 118 to 110. Accordingly, the SRAS curve shifts rightward from $SRAS_2$ to $SRAS_3$. The economy is now in long-run equilibrium at point 3, and the expected price level is equal to the actual price level.

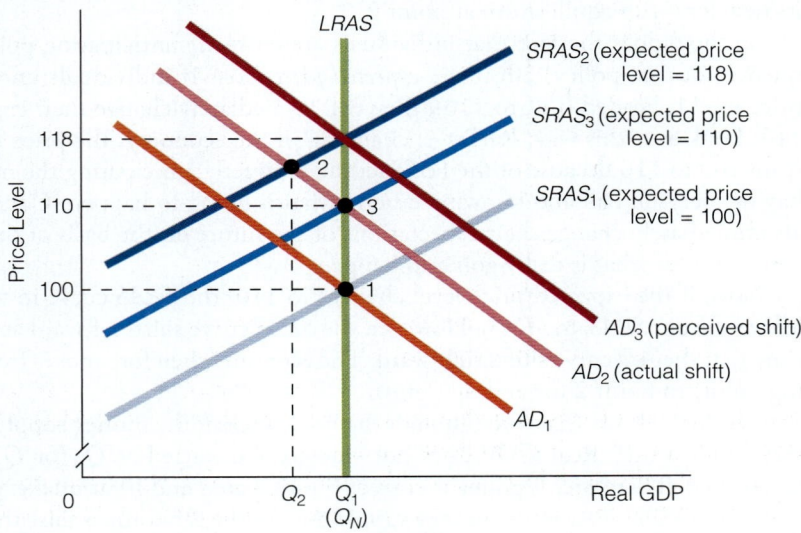

supply leads to higher, not lower, Real GDP in the short run, but that is not what we see in Exhibit 8. Instead, Real GDP has fallen from Q_1 to Q_2. In other words, expansionary monetary policy has actually led to a decline in Real GDP. But why? It happened because of the mistake people made: They anticipated the Fed action incorrectly—with a bias upward.

The time will come when individuals realize that they made a mistake. In time, they will realize that the price level never actually increased to 118 and that AD_3 in the exhibit never really existed. They only perceived all that. In time, they will realize that the operative AD curve in the economy is AD_2 and that the long-run equilibrium price level consistent with this aggregate demand curve is 110. Accordingly, they will adjust their expected price level downward from 118 to 110. As they do, the SRAS curve shifts rightward from $SRAS_2$ to $SRAS_3$, and the economy moves into long-run equilibrium at point 3, where $P_A = P_{EX}$.

Let's recap: (1) The economy starts in long-run equilibrium at point 1, and $P_A = P_{EX}$. (2) The Fed increases the money supply, and the AD curve actually shifts rightward from AD_1 to AD_2. (3) Individuals have incorrectly anticipated the Fed's action. They believe that the Fed has increased the money supply more than it actually did, so they also believe that the AD curve has shifted from AD_1 to AD_3. This is a mistake. (4) Mistakenly assuming that the AD curve has shifted rightward from AD_1 to AD_3, individuals think that the new actual price level will end up being 118, which is where the AD_3 curve intersects the LRAS curve. Accordingly, they change their expected price level to 118, and the SRAS curve shifts leftward from $SRAS_1$ to $SRAS_2$. (5) The short-run equilibrium for the economy turns out to be at point 2. Interestingly, because individuals have incorrectly anticipated policy with a bias upward, an increase in the money supply actually leads to a decline in Real GDP in the short run. (6) Eventually, individuals figure out that they made a mistake—that the real AD curve is AD_2, not AD_3. So the new long-run equilibrium will be 110, not 118 (as earlier believed). As a result, individuals now adjust their expected price level down from 118 to 110. Accordingly, the SRAS curve shifts rightward from $SRAS_2$ to $SRAS_3$. The economy is now in long-run equilibrium at point 3, and the expected price level is equal to the actual price level.

Case 3: Policy Incorrectly Anticipated (Bias Downward) Just as individuals can incorrectly anticipate policy with a bias upward, they can also incorrectly anticipate policy with a bias downward. In Exhibit 9, an economy starts in long-run equilibrium at point 1. The Fed then increases the money supply, and the AD curve shifts from AD_1 to AD_2. Individuals mistakenly think that the AD curve has shifted from AD_1 to AD_3. In other words, they believe that the Fed has increased the money supply by less than it actually has. They have incorrectly anticipated policy with a bias downward.

Because individuals have incorrectly anticipated policy with a bias downward, they mistakenly believe that the new actual long-run equilibrium price level will be 110. So they change their expected price level from 100 to 110, and the SRAS curve shifts leftward from $SRAS_1$ to $SRAS_2$. Short-run equilibrium for the economy now comes at the intersection of AD_2 and $SRAS_2$—that is, at point 2. In the short run, an increase in the money supply has increased Real GDP from Q_1 to Q_2.

EXHIBIT 9

Policy Incorrectly Anticipated—Bias Downward

An economy starts in long-run equilibrium at point 1. The expected price level is equal to the actual price level. The Fed increases the money supply, and the AD curve shifts rightward from AD_1 to AD_2. However, individuals mistakenly believe that the AD curve has shifted rightward by less, from AD_1 to AD_3. As a result of this misunderstanding, individuals mistakenly believe that the new long-run equilibrium price level will be 110. They then change their expected price level to 110, and the SRAS curve shifts leftward from $SRAS_1$ to $SRAS_2$.
The short-run equilibrium in the economy comes at point 2. Eventually, individuals realize their mistake. They come to understand that AD_2 is the only operative AD curve in the economy and that the long-run equilibrium price level consistent with AD_2 is 115. Accordingly, they revise their expected price level from 110 to 115, and the SRAS curve shifts leftward from $SRAS_2$ to $SRAS_3$. The economy moves into long-run equilibrium at point 3.

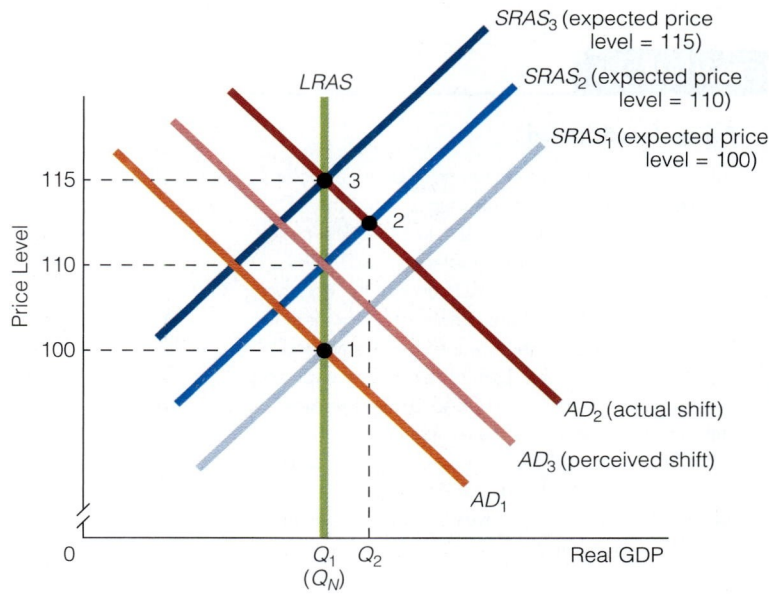

Eventually, individuals realize that they have made a mistake. Eventually, they realize that AD_3 does not exist and that AD_2 is the only operative AD curve in the economy. So the new long-run equilibrium price level will be 115. Realizing that the long-run equilibrium level will be 115, individuals revise their expected price level from 110 to 115, and the $SRAS$ curve shifts from $SRAS_2$ to $SRAS_3$. The economy is now in long-run equilibrium at point 3, and the expected price level equals the actual price level.

Case 4: Policy Unanticipated Besides correctly anticipating the new price level and incorrectly anticipating it with an upward or a downward bias, the only possibility left is not anticipating it at all.

In Exhibit 10, an economy starts in long-run equilibrium at point 1. Here, the actual price level equals the expected price level. Then the Fed increases the money supply, and the AD curve shifts rightward from AD_1 to AD_2. In this case, individuals do not anticipate the Fed's policy action; it is unanticipated. What this means is that individuals do not notice that the AD curve in the economy has shifted. They mistakenly believe that AD_1 (not AD_2) is the operative AD curve in the economy. Because they do not know that the AD curve has shifted, they do not expect any change in the price level. They expect it to remain at 100. Individuals therefore have no reason to revise their expected price level, and it stays at 100.

In the short run, the economy moves to point 2. So a rising money supply leads to a rise in Real GDP in the short run. In time, individuals will realize that things have changed and that the Fed's action has shifted the AD curve rightward. In short, they will come to realize that the operative AD curve in the economy is AD_2, not AD_1. Individuals will then realize that the long-run equilibrium price level consistent with AD_2 is 115. Accordingly, they will revise their expected price level upward to 115, and the $SRAS$ curve will shift leftward from $SRAS_1$ to $SRAS_2$. The economy will move into long-run equilibrium at point 3, and the expected price level will be equal to the actual price level.

EXHIBIT 10

Policy Unanticipated

An economy starts in long-run equilibrium at point 1. The Fed increases the money supply, and the AD curve shifts rightward from AD_1 to AD_2. The policy action by the Fed is unanticipated, so individuals mistakenly believe that the AD curve in the economy has not shifted. Thus, there is no reason for them to believe that the price level will soon change and therefore no reason for them to revise their expected price level. As a result, the $SRAS$ curve does not shift and in the short run the economy moves to point 2. In time, individuals revise their expected price level upward and the $SRAS$ curve shifts leftward. The economy moves back into long-run equilibrium at point 3.

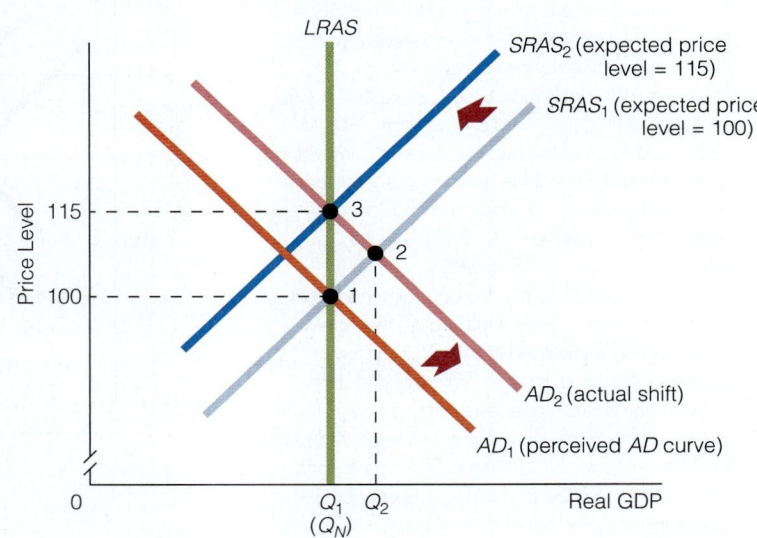

16-3f Comparing Exhibit 9 and 10

The short-run equilibrium positions in Exhibits 9 and 10 led to the same conclusion: An increase in the money supply could increase Real GDP in the short run. In Exhibit 10, the policy was unanticipated; in Exhibit 9, we assumed that the policy was incorrectly anticipated—biased downward. So how could two very different assumptions lead to the same short-run outcome? The answer is that Q_2 in Exhibit 10 represents a higher Real GDP level than Q_2 in Exhibit 9. For example, if Q_2 in Exhibit 10 is $12 trillion, then Q_2 in Exhibit 9 is less—say, $11 trillion. If we assumed that the policy was unanticipated in Exhibit 9, the short-run equilibrium point would be not at point 2 but at the intersection of the AD_2 and $SRAS_1$ curves. This point is not identified in Exhibit 9, but it is to the "southeast" of point 2. If we viewed the Real GDP level that corresponds to this point, it would be greater than Q_2 in the exhibit.

Thinking Like an Economist

What People Think Can Matter to Outcomes Think of how economics might differ from chemistry. In chemistry, if you add two molecules of hydrogen to one molecule of oxygen, you always get water. What is often frustrating to economists is that sometimes the noneconomist thinks that economics works like chemistry: X plus Y should always give us Z. Sadly, that is not how economics works. If you add expansionary monetary policy to an economy, you don't always get a rise in short-run Real GDP. Sometimes you get a rise (when policy is unanticipated), sometimes no change (when policy is correctly anticipated), and other times a decline (when policy is incorrectly anticipated by being biased upward).

The factor affecting economics that is not at work in chemistry is the human factor. What new classical economists teach us about human beings is that their perceptions of things (vis-à-vis reality) have a large part to play in determining outcomes.

16-3g Rational Expectations and Changes in the Money Supply

The question *Does it matter to you if the money supply rises or falls?* is a question that we could have asked in earlier chapters, as well as in this one.

If we had asked it in earlier chapters—say, before we introduced rational expectations to our macroeconomics discussion—perhaps your answer would have gone something like this:

> *Of course it matters if the money supply rises or falls. If the money supply rises, then aggregate demand in the economy increases and the AD curve (in the AD–AS framework) shifts rightward, and as a result, Real GDP rises in the short run. A rising Real GDP could make it easier for me to get a job: More produced output means that more resources will be hired. Since I am the resource labor, there is a better chance I will be hired.*
>
> *Following this line of thought, if the money supply falls, then aggregate demand in the economy decreases, and the AD curve shifts leftward, and, as a result, Real GDP declines in the short run. A declining Real GDP could make it harder for me to get a job.*

After reading about rational expectations in this chapter, is your answer to the rising–falling money supply question likely to be the same? It is not likely to be the same if both a rising and a declining money supply can have the *same* short-run effect on Real GDP.

To illustrate, suppose the money supply declines, and monetary policy is unanticipated. As a result of a decline in the money supply, the AD curve shifts leftward, and since policy is unanticipated, there is no change in the *SRAS* curve in the short run. What is the effect in the short run on Real GDP if the *AD* curve shifts leftward and the *SRAS* curve remains unchanged? Real GDP declines.

Now suppose that instead of the money supply declining, it increases, and, furthermore, the monetary policy is anticipated incorrectly with a bias upward. As a result of the rising money supply, the *AD* curve shifts rightward. And since the monetary policy is anticipated incorrectly with a bias upward, the *SRAS* curve shifts leftward more than the *AD* curve shifts rightward (see Exhibit 8). The result is that, in the short run, Real GDP declines, just as it did when the money supply decreased and policy was unanticipated.

Economics 24/7

The Money Supply, an Increase in Productivity, and What You Think

Think about your study of macroeconomics in earlier chapters. You learned that changes in such things as taxes, government purchases, interest rates, the money supply, and more could change Real GDP, the price level, and the unemployment rate. For example, starting with the economy in long-run equilibrium, a rise in the money supply will raise Real GDP in the short run and raise the price level in the long run. Or consider that an increase in productivity can shift the *SRAS* curve to the right and thus bring about a change in Real GDP and the price level. In short, most of this text discusses how changes in real variables can affect the economy.

With the introduction of expectations theory, we move to a different level of analysis. Now we learn that what people think can also affect the economy. In other words, not only can a change in the world's oil supply affect the economy—almost everyone would expect that—but so can whether or not someone believes that the Fed will increase the money supply.

Think back to our discussion of rational expectations and incorrectly anticipated policy (e.g., bias upward). Suppose the economy is in long-run equilibrium when the Fed undertakes an expansionary monetary policy move. The Fed expects to increase the money supply by, say, $30 billion, but somehow economic agents believe that the increase in the money supply will be closer to $70 billion. In other words, economic agents think that the

money supply will rise by more than it will actually rise. Does it matter that their thoughts are wrong? Expectations theory says it does. As we showed in Exhibit 8, incorrect thoughts can lead to lower Real GDP and higher prices—just as a cutback in the world's oil supply can lead to lower Real GDP and higher prices. In other words, "what's in people's heads" and "a cutback in the world's oil supply" can have the same effects. In other words, what we think can affect what happens in the economy. Who would have thought it?

1. Does the PIP always hold?
2. When policy is unanticipated, what difference is there between the natural rate theory built on adaptive expectations and the natural rate theory built on rational expectations?
3. Identify the changes in the price level and Real GDP in both the short run and the long run as a result of the Fed's increasing the money supply. Assume that the Fed's action is incorrectly anticipated (by being biased upward), that wages and prices are flexible, and that individuals hold rational expectations.

16-4 New Keynesians and Rational Expectations

The new classical theory assumes that wages and prices are flexible. In this theory, an increase in the expected price level results in an immediate and equal rise in wages and prices, and the aggregate supply curve immediately shifts to the long-run equilibrium position.

In response to the new classical assumption of flexible wages and prices, a few economists developed what has come to be known as the *new Keynesian rational expectations theory*. This theory assumes that rational expectations are a reasonable characterization of how expectations are formed, but it drops the new classical assumption of complete wage and price flexibility. According to the theory, long-term labor contracts often prevent wages and prices from fully adjusting to changes in the expected price level. (In other words, prices and wages are somewhat sticky, are rigid, or are inflexible.)

Consider the possible situation at the end of the first year of a three-year wage contract. Workers realize that the actual price level is higher than they expected when they negotiated the contract, but they are unable to do much about it because their wages are locked in for the next two years. Price rigidity might also come into play because firms often engage in fixed-price contracts with their suppliers. As discussed in Chapter 10, Keynesian economists today assert that, for microeconomic-based reasons, long-term labor contracts and above-market wages are sometimes in the best interest of both employers and employees (the efficiency wage theory).

To see what the theory predicts, look at Exhibit 11. The economy is initially in long-run equilibrium at point 1. The public correctly anticipates an increase in aggregate demand from AD_1 to AD_2, and as a result, the expected price level changes. Because of some wage and price rigidities, however, the short-run aggregate supply curve does not shift all the way from $SRAS_1$ to $SRAS_2$, and the economy does not move from point 1 to point 2 (as in new classical theory). Instead, the short-run aggregate supply curve shifts to $SRAS'_2$ because rigidities prevent complete wage and price adjustments. In the short run, the economy moves from point 1 to point 2' (2 prime), from Q_N to Q_A. Had the policy been unanticipated, Real GDP would have increased from Q_N to Q_{UA} in the short run.

EXHIBIT 11

The Short-Run Response to Aggregate Demand–Increasing Policy (in the New Keynesian Theory)

Starting with the economy at point 1, an increase in aggregate demand is correctly anticipated. As a result, the short-run aggregate supply curve shifts leftward, but not all the way to $SRAS_2$ (as would be the case in the new classical theory). Instead, it shifts only to $SRAS'_2$ because of some wage and price rigidities; the economy moves to point 2' (in the short run), and Real GDP increases from Q_N to Q_A. If the policy had been unanticipated, Real GDP would have increased from Q_N to Q_{UA}.

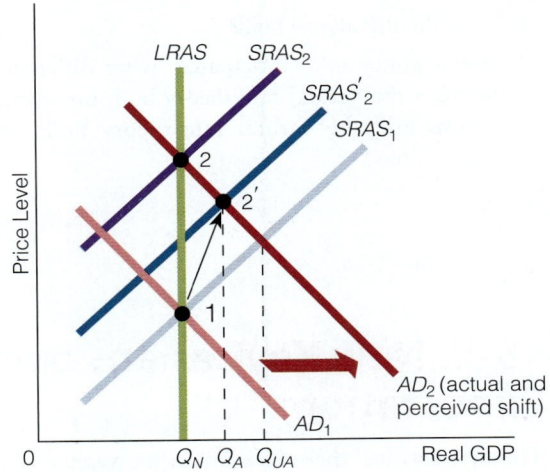

16-5 Looking at Things from the Supply Side: Real Business Cycle Theorists

Throughout this chapter, changes in Real GDP have originated on the demand side of the economy. When discussing the Friedman natural rate theory, the new classical theory, and the new Keynesian theory, we began our analysis by shifting the AD curve to the right. Then we explained what happens in the economy as a result. The presentation so far in this chapter seems to assume that all changes in Real GDP originate on the demand side of the economy. In fact, some economists believe this assumption to be true.

Other economists do not. One group of such economists, called *real business cycle theorists*, believe that changes on the supply side of the economy can lead to changes in both Real GDP and unemployment. Real business cycle theorists argue that a decrease in Real GDP (which refers to the contractionary part of a business cycle) can be brought about by a major supply-side change that reduces the capacity of the economy to produce. Moreover, they argue that what looks like a contraction in Real GDP originating on the demand side of the economy can be, in essence, the effect of what has happened on the supply side.

In Exhibit 12, an adverse supply shock reduces the capacity of the economy to produce. This effect is represented by a shift inward in the economy's production possibilities frontier, or a leftward shift in the long-run aggregate supply curve from $LRAS_1$ to $LRAS_2$. The shift moves the economy from point A to point B. As shown in the exhibit, a leftward shift in the long-run aggregate supply curve means that Natural Real GDP has fallen.

EXHIBIT 12

Real Business Cycle Theory

We start with a supply-side change capable of reducing the capacity of the economy to produce. The change is manifested by a leftward shift of the long-run aggregate supply curve from $LRAS_1$ to $LRAS_2$ and a fall in the Natural Real GDP level from Q_{N1} to Q_{N2}. A reduction in the productive capacity of the economy filters to the demand side and, in our example, reduces consumption, investment, and the money supply. The aggregate demand curve shifts leftward from AD_1 to AD_2.

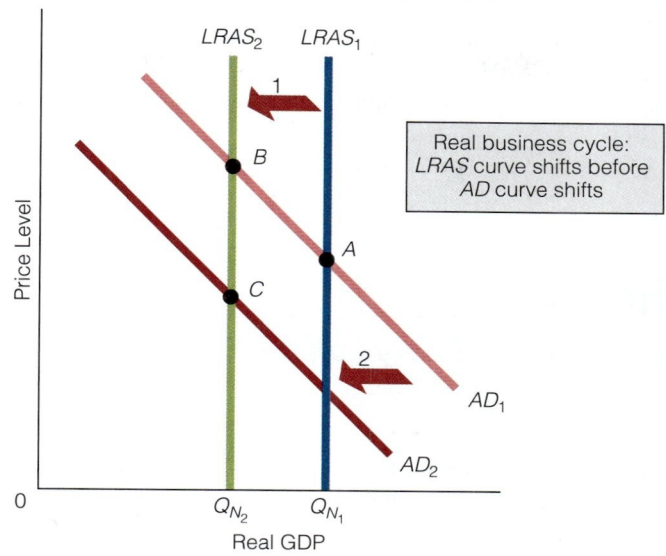

As a result of the leftward shift in the *LRAS* curve and the decline in Real GDP, firms reduce their demand for labor and scale back employment. Then, because of the lower demand for labor (putting downward pressure on money wages) and the higher price level, real wages fall. As real wages fall, workers choose to work less and unemployed persons choose to extend the length of their unemployment. As a result, workers have less income and their lower incomes soon lead them to reduce consumption.

Either because consumption has fallen or because businesses have become pessimistic (prompted by the decline in the productive potential of the economy), or for both reasons, businesses have less incentive to invest. As a result, firms borrow less from banks, the volume of outstanding loans falls, and thus the money supply falls. A decrease in the money supply causes the aggregate demand curve to shift leftward, from AD_1 to AD_2 in Exhibit 12, and the economy moves to point *C*.

Real business cycle theorists sometimes point out how easily a demand-induced decline in Real GDP can be confused with a supply-induced decline. In our example, both the aggregate supply side and the aggregate demand side of the economy change, but the aggregate supply side changes first. If the change in aggregate supply is overlooked, and only the changes in aggregate demand (or, specifically, a change in one of the variables that can change aggregate demand, such as the money supply) are observed, then the contraction in Real GDP will appear to be demand induced. In terms of Exhibit 12, the leftward shift in the *LRAS* curve would be overlooked, but the leftward shift in the *AD* curve would be observed, giving the impression that the contraction is demand induced.

If real business cycle theorists are correct, the cause–effect analysis of a contraction in Real GDP would be turned upside down. As just one example, changes in the money supply may be an *effect* of a contraction in Real GDP (originating on the supply side of the economy), not its *cause*.

1. It is reported that the money supply has recently declined. Is the decline consistent with a demand-induced business cycle, with a supply-induced business cycle, or with both? Explain your answer.

2. How are new Keynesians, who believe that people hold rational expectations, different from new classical economists, who also believe that people hold rational expectations?

Office Hours

"Does New Classical Theory Call the Effects of Fiscal and Monetary Policy into Question?"

Student: When I started this course in macroeconomics, I was hoping to learn the unequivocal answers to some simple questions, such as, "What effect does fiscal policy have on the economy?" and "What effect does monetary policy have on the economy?" I don't think I am getting the answers. For example, fiscal and monetary policies seem to have different effects on Real GDP in the short run, depending on whether the policies are unanticipated, incorrectly anticipated, or correctly anticipated. Am I right about this?

Instructor: You're right. A given policy action (such as expansionary monetary policy) can have different effects on Real GDP (in the short run), depending on whether the policy is unanticipated, correctly anticipated, and so on.

Student: What am I supposed to learn from this?

Instructor: The obvious point, which you've identified, is that policies have different effects, depending on the degree to which individuals correctly anticipate the policies. The not-so-obvious point is that it might not be wise to use government policy actions to stabilize the economy.

Student: How do you come to that point? What are the details?

Instructor: Let's say that the economy is currently in a recessionary gap and Real GDP is $11 trillion. Policymakers want to raise the Real GDP level to Natural Real GDP at, say, $11.2 trillion. To achieve this goal, either expansionary fiscal or monetary policy is implemented. Are we guaranteed that Real GDP will rise from $11 trillion to $11.2 trillion?

Student: No.

Instructor: Why is that?

Student: Well, according to the new classical economists, it's because individuals may incorrectly anticipate the policy in such a way as to reduce Real GDP instead of raising it.

Instructor: That's right. Suppose, for example, the Fed plans to raise the money supply by $100 billion, but the public mistakenly believes that the Fed will raise the money supply by, say, $180 billion. Then, in the short run, the *AD* curve will shift to the right, and the *SRAS* curve will shift to the left, but the *SRAS* curve will shift left by more than the *AD* curve will shift to the right. (That is what was shown in Exhibit 8.) And the result will be a decline, not an increase, in Real GDP—at least in the short run.

Student: So the monetary policy action can end up doing the very opposite of what it was intended to do. It was intended to raise Real GDP, but it lowered it instead.

Instructor: That's correct. What the new classical economists are really pointing out is that we can't always be sure of a discretionary policy action's effect on Real GDP. In turn, the uncertainty should make economists less sure, or a little more humble, when it comes to advocating certain economic policy actions for government to implement.

Points to Remember

1. According to the new classical economists, economic policy actions may not always have the intended effect on Real GDP in the short run.
2. Economic policy actions may accomplish the opposite of what they were intended to accomplish.

Chapter Summary

The Phillips Curve

- In 1958, A. W. Phillips plotted a curve to a set of data points. The curve exhibited an inverse relationship between wage inflation and unemployment, and came to be known as the Phillips curve. From the Phillips curve, economists concluded that neither the combination of low inflation and low unemployment nor the combination of high inflation and high unemployment was likely.
- Economists Paul Samuelson and Robert Solow fit a Phillips curve to the U.S. economy. Instead of measuring wage inflation against unemployment rates (as Phillips did), they measured price inflation against unemployment rates and found an inverse relationship between the two variables.
- On the basis of the findings of Phillips and of Samuelson and Solow, economists concluded that (1) stagflation, or high inflation and high unemployment, is extremely unlikely, and (2) the Phillips curve presents policymakers with a menu of different combinations of inflation and unemployment rates.

Friedman Natural Rate Theory

- Milton Friedman pointed out that there are two types of Phillips curves: a short-run and a long-run Phillips curve. The short-run Phillips curve exhibits the inflation–unemployment trade-off; the long-run Phillips curve does not. Consideration of both short- and long-run Phillips curves opened macroeconomics to expectations theory.
- The Friedman natural rate theory holds that, in the short run, a decrease (increase) in inflation is linked to an increase (decrease) in unemployment, but in the long run, the economy returns to its natural rate of unemployment. In other words, there is a trade-off between inflation and unemployment in the short run, but not in the long run.
- The Friedman natural rate theory was expressed in terms of adaptive expectations, according to which individuals formed their inflation expectations by considering past inflation rates. Later, some economists expressed the theory in terms of rational expectations. Rational expectations theory holds that individuals form their expected inflation rate by considering present and past inflation rates, as well as all other available and relevant information—in particular, the effects of present and future policy actions.

New Classical Theory

- Implicit in the new classical theory are two assumptions: (1) Individuals form their expectations rationally, and (2) wages and prices are completely flexible.
- In the new classical theory, policy has different effects (1) when it is unanticipated; (2) when it is incorrectly anticipated, bias upward; (3) when it is incorrectly anticipated, bias downward; and (4) when it is correctly anticipated. To illustrate, consider two cases: (A) when policy is incorrectly anticipated, bias upward, and (B) when policy is correctly anticipated. Assume that, in both cases, a demand-side policy increases aggregate demand in the economy. Then, in case A, the *AD* curve will shift rightward by less than the *SRAS* initially shifts leftward, bringing about a decline in Real GDP in the short run. In case B, the *AD* curve will shift rightward to the same degree and at the same time as, but in the opposite direction of, the *SRAS* curve. In this case, Real GDP does not change.

New Keynesian Theory

- Implicit in the new Keynesian theory are two assumptions: (1) Individuals form their expectations rationally, and (2) wages and prices are not completely flexible in the short run.
- The economic effects predicted by the new classical theory and the new Keynesian theory if policy is correctly anticipated are not the same in the short run. Because the new Keynesian theory assumes that wages and prices are not completely flexible in the short run, given an anticipated change in aggregate demand, the short-run aggregate supply curve cannot immediately shift to its long-run equilibrium position. The new Keynesian theory predicts a short-run trade-off between inflation and unemployment (in the Phillips curve framework).

Real Business Cycle Theory

- According to real business cycle theory, real business cycle contractions (in Real GDP) originate on the supply side of the economy. A contraction in Real GDP might follow this pattern: (1) An adverse supply shock reduces the economy's ability to produce. (2) The *LRAS* curve shifts leftward. (3) As a result, Real GDP declines, and the price level rises. (4) The number of persons employed falls, as do real wages, owing to a decrease in the demand for labor (lowering money wages) and a higher price level. (5) Incomes decline. (6) Consumption and investment decline. (7) The volume of outstanding loans declines. (8) The money supply falls. (9) The *AD* curve shifts leftward.

Key Terms and Concepts

Phillips Curve
Stagflation

Friedman Natural Rate Theory

Adaptive Expectations
Rational Expectations

Policy Ineffectiveness Proposition (PIP)

Questions and Problems

1. What does it mean to say that the Phillips curve presents policymakers with a menu of choices?
2. According to Friedman, how do we know when the economy is in long-run equilibrium?
3. What is a major difference between adaptive and rational expectations? Give an example of each.
4. "The policy ineffectiveness proposition (connected with new classical theory) does not eliminate policymakers' ability to reduce unemployment through aggregate demand–increasing policies, because they can always increase aggregate demand by more than the public expects." What might be the weak point in this argument?
5. Why is the new classical theory associated with the word "classical?" Why has it been said that classical theory failed where new classical theory succeeds—because the former could not explain the business cycle (the ups and downs of the economy), but the latter can?
6. Suppose a permanent downward-sloping Phillips curve existed and offered a menu of choices of different combinations of inflation and unemployment rates to policymakers. How do you think society would go about deciding which point on the Phillips curve it wanted to occupy?
7. Assume a current short-run trade-off between inflation and unemployment, as well as a change in technology that permits the wider dispersion of economic policy news. How would the change affect the trade-off? Explain your answer.
8. New Keynesian theory holds that wages are not completely flexible because of such things as long-term labor contracts. New classical economists often respond that experience teaches labor leaders to develop and bargain for contracts that allow for wage adjustments. Do you think that the new classical economists have a good point? Why or why not?
9. What evidence can you point to that suggests individuals form their expectations adaptively? What evidence can you point to that suggests individuals form their expectations rationally?
10. Suppose the government undertakes an expansionary fiscal policy measure that raises aggregate demand, but individuals incorrectly anticipate the measure, bias upward. What will the short- and long-run changes be in the price level and Real GDP?
11. Explain both the short- and long-run movements of the Friedman natural rate theory, assuming that expectations are formed adaptively.
12. Explain both the short- and long-run movements of the new classical theory, assuming that expectations are formed rationally and policy is unanticipated.
13. "Even if some people do not form their expectations rationally, the new classical theory is not necessarily of no value." Discuss this statement.
14. In real business cycle theory, why can't the change in the money supply prompted by a series of events catalyzed by an adverse supply shock be considered the cause of the business cycle?
15. The expected inflation rate is 5 percent, and the actual inflation rate is 7 percent. According to Friedman, is the economy in long-run equilibrium? Explain your answer.

Working with Numbers and Graphs

1. Illustrate graphically what would happen in the short run and in the long run to the price level and Real GDP level if individuals hold rational expectations, prices and wages are flexible, and individuals underestimate the decrease in aggregate demand (bias downward).

2. Illustrate graphically what would happen in the short run and in the long run to the price level and Real GDP if individuals hold rational expectations, prices and wages are flexible, and individuals overestimate the rise in aggregate demand (bias upward).

3. Illustrate graphically what would happen to the price level and Real GDP level if individuals hold rational expectations, prices and wages are flexible, and individuals correctly anticipate a rise in aggregate demand.

4. In each of the figures (a–d) that follow, the starting point is 1. Which part (a, b, c, or d) illustrates each of the following?
   a. Friedman natural rate theory (short run)
   b. New classical theory (unanticipated policy, short run)
   c. Real business cycle theory
   d. New classical theory (incorrectly anticipated policy, overestimating increase in aggregate demand, short run)
   e. Policy ineffectiveness proposition (PIP)

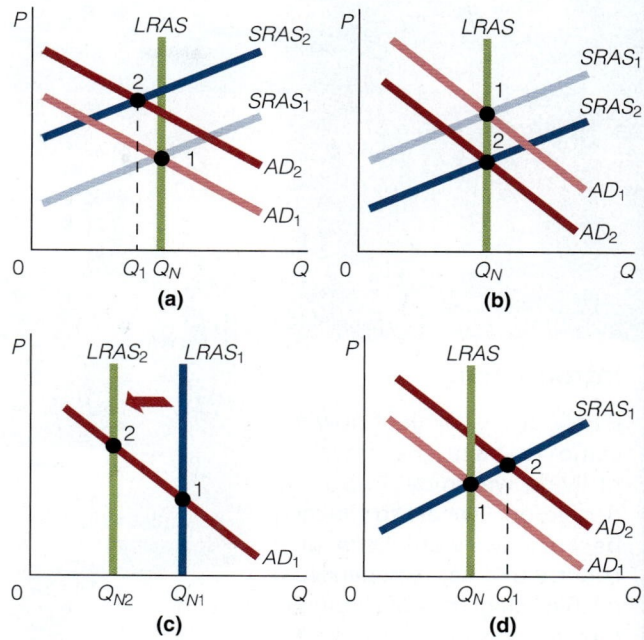

5. Illustrate graphically what would happen in the short run and in the long run if individuals hold adaptive expectations, prices and wages are flexible, and aggregate demand decreases.

CHAPTER 17

Economic Growth: Resources, Technology, Ideas, and Institutions

Introduction

Rarely do we think of how we came to have the standard of living we enjoy. To a large degree, our lives are so enriched because we were born in a country that has experienced a relatively high rate of economic growth. How might your life be different if the U.S. economy had had a lower growth rate over, say, the last century? To answer this question, you need to know the causes of economic growth.

17-1 A Few Basics About Economic Growth

The term "economic growth" refers either to absolute real economic growth or to per-capita real economic growth. **Absolute real economic growth** is an increase in Real GDP from one period to the next. Exhibit 1 shows absolute real economic growth (the percentage change in Real GDP) for the United States for the period 2010–2019.

Per-capita real economic growth is an increase from one period to the next in per-capita Real GDP, which is Real GDP divided by population:

$$\text{Per-capita Real GDP} = \frac{\text{Real GDP}}{\text{Population}}$$

17-1a Do Economic Growth Rates Matter?

Suppose the (absolute) real economic growth rate is 4 percent in one country and 3 percent in another. The difference in growth rates may not seem very significant, but if the growth rates are sustained over a long time, the people who live in each country will see a real difference

Absolute Real Economic Growth
An increase in Real GDP from one period to the next.

Per-Capita Real Economic Growth
An increase from one period to the next in per-capita Real GDP, which is Real GDP divided by population.

EXHIBIT 1

Absolute Real Economic Growth Rates for the United States, 2010–2019

This exhibit shows the absolute real economic growth rates (or percentage change in Real GDP) in the United States for the period 2010–2019.

Source: *Economic Report of the President, 2021.*

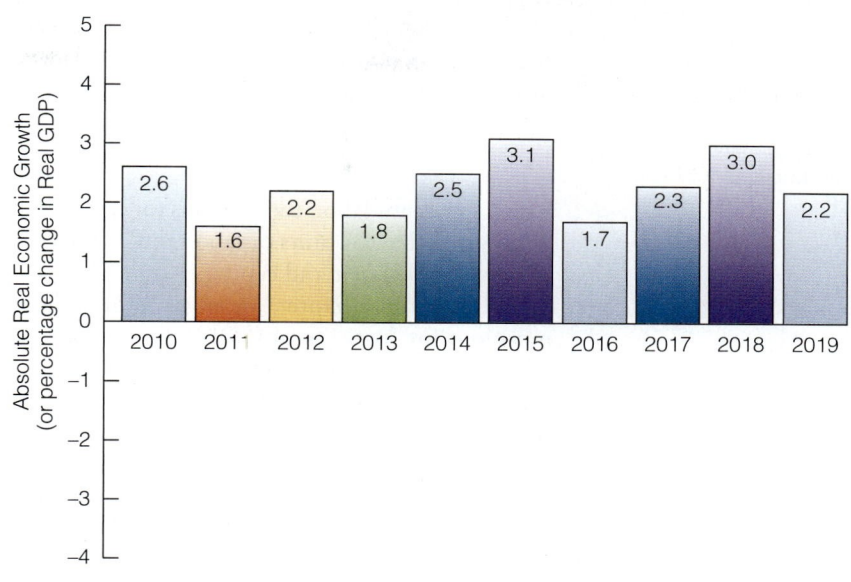

in their standard of living. For example, if a country's economic growth rate is 5 percent each year, its Real GDP will double in 14 years. By contrast, if a country has a 2 percent annual growth rate, its Real GDP will double in 35 years. In other words, a country with a 5 percent growth rate can double its Real GDP in 21 fewer years than a country with a 2 percent growth rate. (To calculate the time required for any variable to double, simply divide its percentage growth rate into 70. This is called the *rule of 70.*)

Thinking Like an Economist

Economic Growth Matters Economic growth has been a major topic of discussion for economists for over two centuries. Adam Smith, the founder of modern economics, wrote a book on the subject that was published in 1776: *An Inquiry into the Nature and Causes of the Wealth of Nations.* In the book, Smith set out to answer the question of why some countries are rich and others are poor. Today, we'd ask, "Why do some countries have a high per-capita Real GDP and others have a low per-capita Real GDP?" For economists, getting the right answer to this question is of major importance to the lives of billions of people.

17-2 A Production Function and Economic Growth

Production Function
A function that specifies the relation between technology and the quantity of factor inputs to output, or Real GDP.

A **production function** specifies the relation between technology and the quantity of factor inputs to output, or Real GDP. For example, look at this production function:

$$\text{Real GDP} = T(L, K)$$

The L stands for labor, the K stands for capital, and the T stands for the technology coefficient. Suppose we have 4 units of labor and 2 units of capital. Then, in all, we have 6 units of our two resources, labor and capital.

In an earlier chapter, an advance in technology was defined as the ability to produce more output (more Real GDP) with a given level of resources, such as labor and capital. The T, or technology coefficient, in our production function captures this idea. Suppose we set our T equal to 0.40. Then, given that L equals 4 and K equals 2, our production function now reads

$$\text{Real GDP} = 0.4\,(4 + 2)$$
$$\text{Real GDP} = 0.4\,(6)$$
$$\text{Real GDP} = 2.4 \text{ units of output}$$

In other words, we have taken particular amounts of labor and capital, added them together at a certain level of technology—evidenced in a technology coefficient of 0.4—and ended up with 2.4 units of output, or Real GDP.

Obviously, our production function—which focuses on the three factors of T, L, and K—implies that an increase in any one of these factors will lead to a rise in Real GDP. For example, if we increase labor from 4 to 8 units, Real GDP will rise to 4 units of output. Alternatively, if we raise T from 0.4 to 0.5, holding labor at 4 units and capital at 2 units, Real GDP will rise from 2.4 units to 3.0 units.

17-2a The Graphical Representation of the Production Function

Exhibit 2(a) represents the production function graphically. Real GDP (Q) is on the vertical axis, and labor (L) is on the horizontal axis. The curve in the two-dimensional space is the graphical representation of the production function. At a given level of labor, L_1, we get Q_1 amount of Real GDP. A change in labor—say, from L_1 to L_2—will give us more Real GDP, as shown in Exhibit 2(b).

Now, a change in either K or T will shift the production function up or down. For example, Exhibit 2(c) shows what happens to the production function if K rises. Initially, $K = 1$, and this, combined with L_1 and a given technology coefficient, produces Q_1 Real GDP. If K rises to 2, and this higher K is combined with the same amount of labor and the same technology coefficient, Real GDP rises to Q_2.

Exhibit 2(d) shows what happens if the technology coefficient rises. Initially, $T = 0.4$. Combining this with a given amount of labor and capital produces a Real GDP level of Q_1. If T rises to 0.5 and nothing else changes, then Real GDP rises to Q_2.

So our production function specifies that output or Real GDP depends on labor, capital, and the technology coefficient (which captures the essence of advances in technology).

EXHIBIT 2

The Production Function

(a) The production function specifies the relation among labor (L), capital (K), and technology (technology coefficient, T).
(b) Changes in L lead to changes in Real GDP (Q). (c) A rise in capital (K) leads to an upward shift in the production function and to more Real GDP (for a given level of L and a given technology coefficient, T). (d) A rise in the technology coefficient (T) leads to an upward shift in the production function and to more Real GDP (for a given level of L and K).

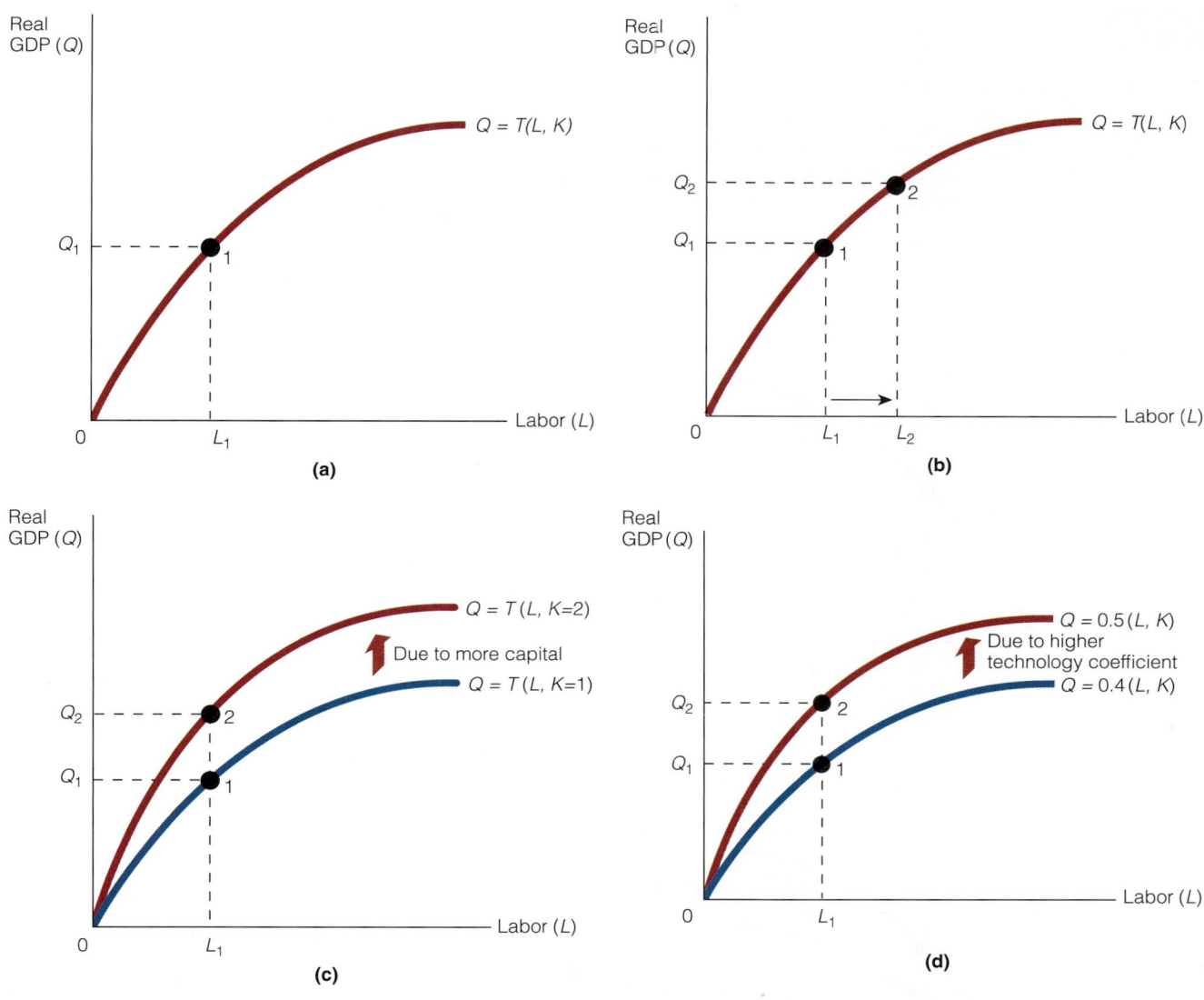

Specifically, a rise in labor will move us from one point to another on the same production function, ending with more Real GDP. A rise in capital or a rise in the technology coefficient will lead to a shift upward in the production function, also ending with more Real GDP.

17-2b From the Production Function to the *LRAS* Curve

The changes in, and the movements along, the production function can be linked to shifts in the *LRAS* curve. In Exhibit 3(a), we start with L_1, which gives us Real GDP of Q_1. We then take Q_1 from panel (a) and move it to panel (b). Q_1 is the Real GDP that the economy is producing when it is at the natural unemployment rate; in other words, Q_1 is Natural Real GDP. This level of Real GDP is consistent with $LRAS_1$ in the exhibit.

EXHIBIT 3

The Production Function and the *LRAS* Curve

(a) More labor (*L*) leads to more Real GDP (shown in terms of the production function). (b) More *L* shifts the *LRAS* curve to the right. (c) A higher technology coefficient (*T*) shifts the production function up and brings about more Real GDP, *Q*. (d) A heightened technology coefficient (*T*) leads to a rightward shift in the *LRAS* curve. (Although not shown in this exhibit, a rise in *K* would do the same thing as a rise in *T* in terms of shifting the production function upward and shifting the *LRAS* curve to the right.)

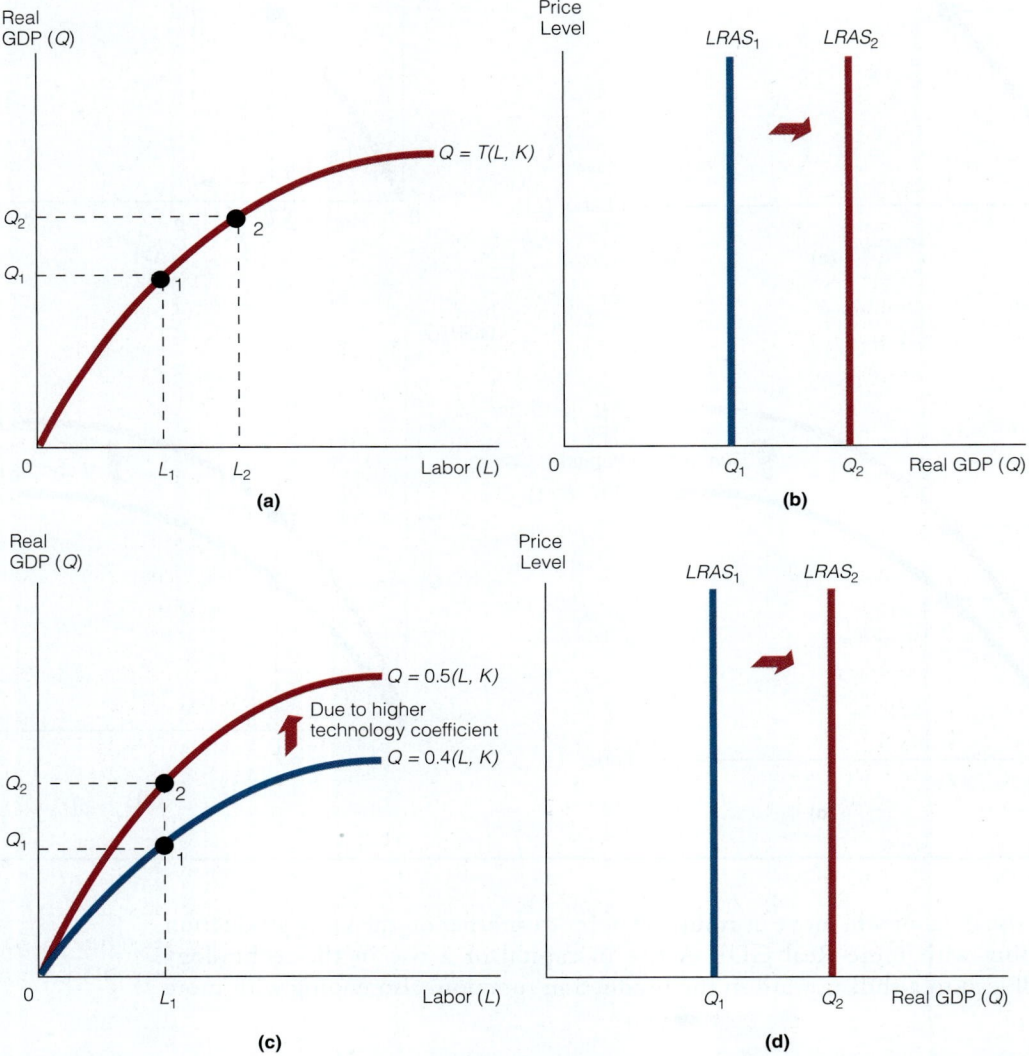

Suppose now that we raise the level of labor in panel (a) to L_2. This change in labor moves us along our production function, from point 1 to point 2 at a higher Real GDP level, Q_2. In panel (b), this new, higher Real GDP is consistent with $LRAS_2$.

Therefore, a rise in the level of labor moves us along the given production function and shifts the $LRAS$ curve to the right. If you were to now superimpose an AD curve on panel (b), you would see that a shift rightward in the $LRAS$ curve brings about a lower price level and a higher Real GDP level. With a heightened Real GDP level, we have economic growth.

In panel (c), we again start with L_1, which gives us Q_1 Real GDP. If the technology coefficient then rises from 0.4 to 0.5, the production function shifts upward. Hence, at a given level of labor and capital, we have more Real GDP, Q_2. Carrying over the changes in Real GDP from panel (c) to panel (d), we see that a rise in the technology coefficient shifts the $LRAS$ curve to the right. Again, we have economic growth.

Economics 24/7

Technology Matters

Most people will tell you that their material standard of living matters to them. In short, the number and quality of the goods and services they are able to consume matters. Now, if one's material standard of living matters, then economic growth must as well because, all other things being held equal, the more economic growth there is, the higher one's standard of living. Finally, if economic growth matters to one's standard of living, does the rate of economic growth matter too? Consider that if the economic growth rate is 2 percent, it will take 35 years for Real GDP to double, but if the growth rate is 3 percent, it will take 23.3 years for Real GDP to double. In other words, a 1 percent increase in the growth rate reduces the time it takes Real GDP to double by 11.7 years. Therefore, if one's standard of living matters, it follows that economic growth matters, which means that the economic growth rate matters too.

What might the economic growth rate depend upon? What might cause the economic growth rate to be 4 percent instead of 1 percent? With this question in mind, consider technology. We know that the production function specified in this chapter, Real GDP = $T(L, K)$, holds that Real GDP depends upon technology, labor, and capital. In Exhibit 2(d), we see that an advancement in technology, shown in terms of a rise in the technology coefficient from 0.4 to 0.5, leads to an upward shift in the production function, and, when the production function shifts upward, there is an increase in Real GDP (shown in the exhibit as an increase from Q_1 to Q_2).

ISTOCKPHOTO/JASONDOIY

Now suppose that there was a higher rate of technological advancement; instead of the technology coefficient (T) rising from 0.4 to 0.5, it rose from 0.4 to 0.6. Would this have mattered to the growth rate in Real GDP and to one's material standard of living? It certainly would have because the higher the rate of technological advancement, the greater the upward shift in the production function, and the greater the increase in Real GDP, which means the greater the economic growth rate. And, as we specified earlier, the greater the economic growth rate, the fewer years it takes for Real GDP to double and the quicker one's material standard of living increases.

17-2c Emphasis on Labor

Exhibit 3 showed that a rise in labor would lead to a rightward shift in the *LRAS* curve. In other words, a rise in labor would result in economic growth. Then what, in turn, might lead to a rise in labor? Put differently, if X and Y lead to a rise in labor, then X and Y are factors that promote economic growth.

One such factor that is often mentioned is taxes. Specifically, some economists propose promoting economic growth by cutting taxes on such activities as working. The idea is that, if the marginal income tax rate is cut, workers will work more, and as they work more, output will rise. Think of this idea in terms of the labor market. Exhibit 4(a) shows a labor

EXHIBIT 4

The Labor Market, the Production Function, and the *LRAS* Curve

(a) Lower taxes on income shifts the labor supply curve rightward from S_{L1} to S_{L2}. As a result of the lower taxes and the rightward shift in the labor supply curve, the equilibrium amount of labor rises from L_1 to L_2. (b) More labor leads to more Real GDP in terms of the production function. (c) More Real GDP corresponds to a rightward shift in the *LRAS* curve.

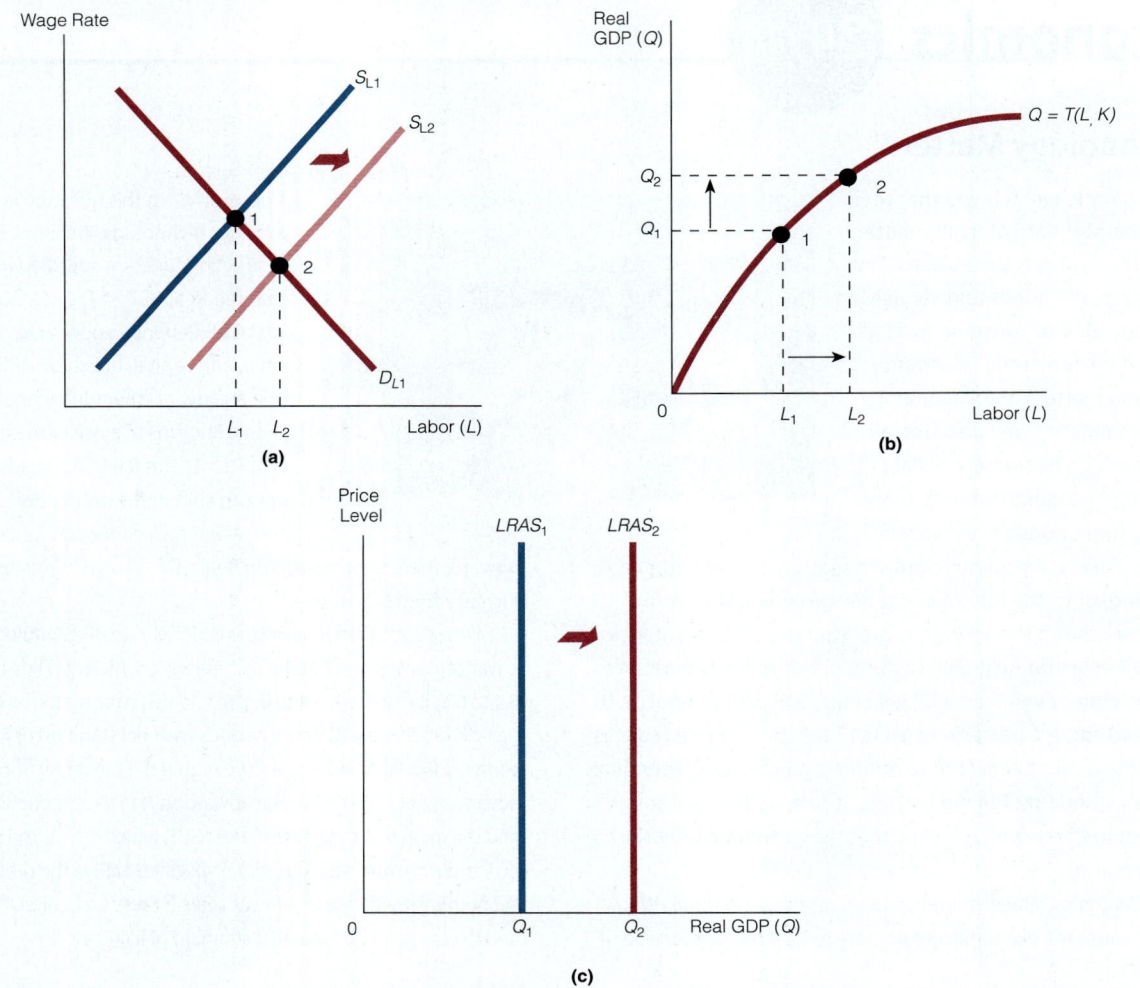

market that is in equilibrium at point 1. The equilibrium quantity of labor in this market is L_1. If L_1 is put into our production function, as shown in panel (b), it gives us Q_1 amount of Real GDP. Finally, if Q_1 from panel (b) is placed in panel (c), Q_1 is consistent with the $LRAS_1$ curve.

Now suppose we lower taxes on income. As a result, the labor supply curve in panel (a) shifts rightward. In other words, as the overall return on working increases because of a drop in income taxes, more people decide to go to work, and many of those already working decide to work more. The new equilibrium quantity of labor, L_2, is shown in panel (a). If we carry over the greater quantity of labor to panel (b), showing our production function, more labor produces the higher level of Real GDP, Q_2. Then, in panel (c), the new higher level of Real GDP corresponds to a new $LRAS$ curve, $LRAS_2$.

Therefore, lower income taxes shift the labor supply to the right, raising the equilibrium quantity of labor, which produces more Real GDP or shifts the $LRAS$ curve to the right. Again, we have witnessed economic growth.

Economics 24/7

Going Forward: Medical Costs, Economic Growth, and Tax Revenues

The economic growth rate of the country impacts how hard or easy it is to finance public expenditures, such as health care. A low growth rate acts as a tight rope around public expenditures; a high growth rate acts as a loose one. In the field of medicine, innovations are increasingly common. These innovations are, in some cases, lifesaving, but they are often expensive. To the degree that government finances a large percentage of the health care expenditures in the country (think Medicare, Medicaid, and various health care subsidies), a government that is constrained by falling, constant, or slowly rising tax revenues—all reflective of the degree of economic growth in the country—will have a hard time financing the rising expenditures brought on by medical innovations.

Changes in tax revenues are closely related to economic growth. Generally, high economic growth rates generate greater increases in tax revenues than low economic growth rates, as the following example illustrates: If the average income tax rate is 10 percent and Real GDP in the country is $100 billion, tax revenues are the product of the two, or $10 billion. If economic growth causes Real GDP to rise by 2 percent to $102 billion, tax revenues rise to $10.2 billion; but if Real GDP rises by 3 percent to $103 billion, tax revenues to $10.3 billion.

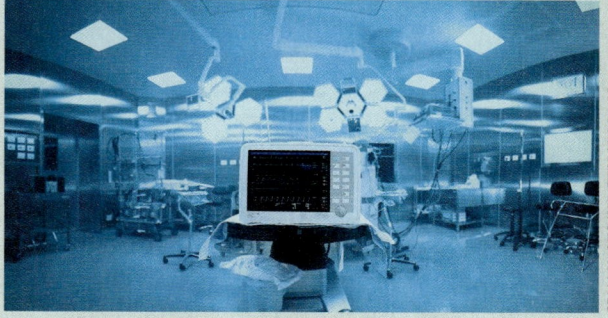

No one can know for sure the degree to which medical innovations will advance in coming years. However, with advances in medical technology, medical knowledge, and genomics, it is likely that medical innovations in the next 30 years will come at a faster pace than the last 30 years. Consequently, we can expect costlier medical treatments. If these costlier medical treatments are met with slow or no economic growth, then tax revenues will likely be insufficient to finance the rising costs and government will be forced to either raise taxes or deny payment for the new medical treatments reflective of medical innovation.

17-2d Emphasis on Capital

So more labor can lead to economic growth, but so can more capital. How much capital is available depends on such things as the tax treatment of capital returns and interest rates. Consider two settings. In the first, taxes on the returns to capital are high; in the second, taxes on the returns to capital are low. Which setting offers a stronger incentive to employ capital in the production process? When taxes on the returns to capital are low, we predict the following: As taxes decline on the returns from capital, more capital is utilized in the production process, shifting the production function upward and thereby shifting the *LRAS* curve to the right.

The interest rate can also affect the amount of capital employed, because firms often borrow the funds to buy the capital goods used in production. In short, the process can work like this: A decline in interest rates prompts firms to borrow more. The firms use the borrowed funds to purchase capital goods. As they purchase and utilize more capital (in the production process), the production function shifts upward, and the *LRAS* curve shifts rightward.

17-2e Emphasis on Other Resources: Natural Resources and Human Capital

Our production function so far has included only two resources—labor and capital—and technology. When building economic growth models, economists often specify a production function of this sort.

However, for reasons of completeness, a more fully specified production function would also include natural resources (*NR*) and human capital (*H*). For example, producing goods—such as chairs, desks, and paper—often takes natural resources—such as wood. In fact, economists often speak in terms of four resources (Chapter 1): land, labor, capital, and entrepreneurship. "Land" is simply another name for natural resources.

Producing many goods also takes human capital, which is different from the kind of capital we represented as *K*. The capital referred to earlier is *physical capital*—such things as machines, computers, and factories. **Human capital** is what you acquire by attending college, plus the skills and knowledge you pick up through education, training, and experience. You enroll in a number of courses, learn certain material, and acquire certain thinking skills; these are all components of human capital.

> **Human Capital**
> The knowledge and skills a person acquires through education, training, and experience.

Adding human capital and natural resources to our production function leads us to specify that function this way:

$$\text{Real GDP} = T\,(L,\ K,\ NR,\ H)$$

17-2f Emphasis on the Technology Coefficient and Ideas

Beginning in the 1980s, economists began discussing economic growth differently than they did in previous decades. They began placing more attention on technology, ideas, institutions, and education. The discussion often took place under the rubric of *new growth theory*.

The name "new growth theory" implies that a theory of economic growth came before it, and, indeed, neoclassical growth theory preceded new growth theory. A number of economists believe that new growth theory came about to answer some of the questions that neoclassical growth theory could not, in much the same way that a new medical theory may arise to answer questions that an old medical theory cannot answer.

Neoclassical growth theory emphasized two resources: labor and physical capital. Technology was discussed, but only tangentially. Technology was said to be exogenous; that is, it came from outside the economic system. It fell out of the sky; it was outside our control. We simply accepted this assumption as a given.

New growth theory holds that technology is endogenous; it is a central part of the economic system. More important, the amount and quality of technology that is developed depend on the amount of resources we devote to it: The more resources that go into developing technology, the more and better technology is developed.

Economist Paul Romer, whose name is synonymous with new growth theory, asks us to think about technology as we would about prospecting for gold. For one individual, the chances of finding gold are so small that if someone did find gold, the strike would simply be viewed as good luck. However, if 10,000 individuals are looking for gold across a wide geographical area, the chances of finding it would greatly improve. As with gold prospecting, so it is with technological advances. If one person is trying to advance technology, his or her chances of success are much smaller than if hundreds or thousands of persons are trying.

New growth theory also emphasizes the process of discovering and formulating ideas as they relate to technological advances. The emphasis is on ideas rather than on objects, which are material, tangible things, such as natural resources and capital goods. Some countries are poor because they lack objects (natural resources and capital goods). Yet some countries have had very few objects and have been able to grow economically. For example, in the 1950s, Japan had few natural resources and capital goods, but it still grew economically. Some economists believe that Japan grew because it had access to ideas or knowledge.

17-2g Discovery and Ideas

If discovering ideas is important to technological advances and therefore to economic growth, then we need to figure out ways to promote the discovery process. One way is for business firms not to get locked into doing things in one way and one way only. They must let their employees—from the inventor in the lab to the worker on the assembly line—try new ways of getting the job done. Some might carry this idea further: Businesses need to create an environment that is receptive to new ideas; they need to encourage their employees to try new ways of doing things.

Employee flexibility, which is a part of the discovery process, is becoming a larger part of the U.S. economy. To some degree, the discovery process is seen in the amount of time and effort firms devote to discovery in contrast to the amount of time they devote to actually manufacturing goods. Consider the computer software business. Millions of dollars and hundreds of thousands of work hours are devoted to coming up with new and useful software, whereas only a tiny fraction of the work effort and hours go into making, copying, and shipping the disks that contain the software.

17-2h Expanding Our Horizons

According to Romer, "economic growth occurs whenever people take resources and rearrange them in ways that are more valuable." Let's focus on the word "rearrange." We can think of rearranging as in rearranging the pieces of a puzzle, as in changing the ingredients in a recipe, or as in rearranging the way workers go about their daily work. When we rearrange anything, we do that thing differently. Sometimes differently is better, and sometimes it is worse.

Think of how you study for a test. Perhaps you read the book first, go back and underline, study the book, and then finally study your lecture notes. Would it be better to study differently? You won't know until you try.

As with studying for a test, so it is with producing a car, computer software, or a shopping mall. We do not find better ways of doing things unless we experiment. And with repeated experiments, we often discover new and better ideas, ideas that ultimately lead to economic growth. The research and development of new medicines makes for a good example. Sometimes, what makes a mildly effective medicine into a very effective one is a change in one or two molecules of a certain chemical. A small change—a change perhaps no one would ever think would matter—can make a large difference.

A policy prescription follows from that mind-set: We should think of ways to make the process of discovering ideas, experimenting with different ways of doing things, and developing new technology more likely. Without this kind of effort, we are likely to diminish our growth potential. If we believe that ideas are important to economic growth, then we need to have ideas about how to generate more ideas. Romer calls these second-level ideas *meta-ideas*: ideas about how to support the production and transmission of other ideas.

Some ways have been proposed. Perhaps we need to invest more funds in education or in research and development. Or perhaps we need to find better ways to protect people's ideas. (Few people will invest the time, money, and effort to discover new ideas if the ideas can easily be stolen.)

In the twenty-first century, countries with the most natural resources and capital goods aren't likely to be the ones that grow the fastest. If new growth theory is correct, the successful ones will be those that have discovered how to encourage and develop the most and best ideas.

17-2i Institutions Matter

Crops don't grow equally well in all soils. Some soils are more conducive to the growing than others. Similarly, many economists argue that some environments are more conducive to economic growth than others.

One of the ways economists differentiate one environment from another is by their institutions. But what are institutions in this context? Douglass North, a well-respected economist in the area of institutional research, defines an **institution** as "the rules of the game in a society or, more formally, the humanly devised constraints that shape human interaction." Specifically, institutions consist of a country's rules and regulations, laws, customs, and business practices. Consider two countries, A and B, each with different institutions. In country A, the rule of law operates (no one is above the law), contracts are enforced, private property rights are protected, and free international trade is permitted. In country B, the rule of law does not hold, contracts are not always enforced, private property is not protected (and is often seized), and high tariffs and quotas are placed on imported goods. In North's terminology, the "rules of the game" are different in these two countries.

Here are a few of the institutions that most economists agree are conducive to economic growth:

- Property rights structure
- The legal system
- Growth-promoting policies versus transfer-promoting policies
- Other institutions

Property Rights Structure Think of two property rights structures, X and Y. Under X, a person is allowed to own property (a piece of land, a business, a store, an invention, etc.); that is, private property is permitted. Under Y, a person is not allowed to own property; private property is not permitted. The incentive to produce goods and services is hardly the same in each of the

Institution
The rules of the game in a society or, more formally, the humanly devised constraints that shape human interaction; the rules and regulations, laws, customs, and business practices of a country.

two property rights structures. Undoubtedly, the incentive to produce is greater under property rights structure *X* than *Y*. Why produce anything under *Y* if what you produce does not belong to you? In short, different property rights structures come with different incentives to produce. All other things equal, the property rights structures that permit individuals to own property will be more conducive to production and economic growth than those that do not.

Now consider two other property rights structures, *A* and *B*. Under both, individuals are allowed to own property. But in *A*, a person's private property rights are not as well protected as in *B*. For example, in *A*, the government sometimes confiscates a person's private property; in *B*, that never happens. Again, the incentive to produce is not the same under *A* and *B*. The more secure the private property rights are, the greater the incentive is to produce. Why produce if what you produce might be taken away from you?

Therefore, not only do private property rights matter to production and economic growth; so does the security of those private property rights.

The Legal System In country *A*, the legal system is dependable, honest, and dedicated to enforcing legitimate contracts and to protecting private property. In country *B*, the legal system is the polar opposite. In which country, *A* or *B*, are individuals more likely to have a greater incentive to start businesses, lend and borrow funds, invest, produce goods, and innovate—all important to the process of economic growth? Most economists would say in country *A*, where the legal system is dependable, honest, and sound. That conclusion becomes quickly obvious once you think of what is involved with starting a business, lending and borrowing, investing, innovating, and producing: dealing with other people. If you start a business, you will often need to deal with other people to finance the business, to hire workers, to buy from suppliers, and so on. In your dealings with other people, you need to be assured that your agreements (or contracts) with them are upheld and enforced and that others cannot steal from you and get away with it. This is why the legal system is important to economic growth. A legal system that is dependable, honest, and dedicated to enforcing legitimate contracts and protecting private property reduces the transaction costs of dealing with others, thus providing individuals with a greater incentive to engage in activities conducive to economic growth.

Growth-Promoting Policies Versus Transfer-Promoting Policies Consider two types of economic policies: growth-promoting policies and transfer-promoting policies. A growth-promoting policy increases Real GDP; it enlarges the size of the economic pie. A transfer-promoting policy leaves the size of the economic pie unchanged, but it increases the size of the slice that one group gets relative to another.

For example, suppose group *A*, a special-interest group, currently gets 1/1,000 of the economic pie, and the economic pie is $1,000. Then, the group gets a $1 slice. But group *A* wants to get more than a $1 slice, and it can do so in one of two ways. The first is to lobby for a policy that increases the size of its slice of the economic pie. In other words, group *A* gets a larger slice (say, a $2 slice) at the expense of someone else's getting a smaller slice. Alternatively, group *A* can lobby for a policy that increases the size of the pie—say, from $1,000 to $1,500. In this case, group *A* gets not the full increase of $500, but 1/1,000 of the increase, or 50¢. So group *A* has to decide whether it is better to lobby for a growth-promoting policy (in which it gets 1/1,000 of any increase in Real GDP) or for a transfer-promoting policy (in which it gets 100 percent of any transfer).

According to Mancur Olson, in *The Rise and Decline of Nations*, special-interest groups are more likely to argue for transfer-promoting policies than growth-promoting policies and the cost–benefit calculation of each policy is the reason.[1] This behavior affects economic growth in

---

[1] Mancur Olson, *The Rise and Decline of Nations* (New Haven, CT, and London: Yale University Press, 1982).

Economics 24/7

Economic Freedom and Growth Rates

Does economic freedom matter to a country's economic growth rate? There is some evidence that it does. Consider the time in which there were two Germanys: an East Germany and a West Germany. The two Germanys were much the same in terms of culture, people, climate, language, and so on, except that West Germans enjoyed more economic freedom than East Germans. Did this major difference between the two Germanys matter to economic growth? Most economists answer yes: Between 1950 and 1991, the average annual growth rate in East Germany was 1.3 percent; in West Germany, it was 4.4 percent.

The same sort of difference holds between North Korea and South Korea. South Korea permits much more economic freedom than North Korea. Does this difference affect economic growth rates? During the second half of the twentieth century, the average annual growth rate in South Korea was more than three times higher than in North Korea.

The evidence from the two Koreas and two Germanys tells us that economic freedom does matter to economic growth, especially when other factors (that matter to growth) are much the same between the countries.

But when the other factors are not the same, problems arise. Suppose country A has less economic freedom than country B. Will country A grow less than country B during the next 5 or 10 years? Not necessarily. The economic growth rate in a country could depend on the economic base from which the growth emanates.

Suppose that country A has a Real GDP of $10 billion, that country B has a Real GDP of $100 billion, and that Real GDP grows by $2 billion in both countries. Then, the economic growth rate in country A (the country with less economic freedom) is 20 percent, but the economic growth rate in country B (the country with more economic freedom) is only 2 percent. Does it follow that economic freedom is a hindrance to economic growth? Not at all. It may simply look that way because something different between the two countries—namely, the economic base from which growth emanates—isn't being considered.

that the more special-interest groups there are in a country, the more likely it is that transfer-promoting policies will be lobbied for instead of growth-promoting policies. Individuals will try to get a larger slice of a constant-size economic pie rather than trying to increase the size of the pie. In short, numerous and politically strong special-interest groups are detrimental to economic growth.

Other Institutions Some other institutions are often mentioned as conducive to economic growth: open and competitive markets, free (international) trade, policies that promote economic freedom, a stable monetary system, taxes and regulations that are not burdensome, and a strong and effective educational system.

(Answers to self-test questions are in Answers to Self-Test Questions at the back of the book.)

1. Explain how a decline in taxes that affects the labor market can end up shifting the *LRAS* curve to the right.
2. What is the difference between physical and human capital?
3. What is the difference between neoclassical growth theory and new growth theory with respect to technology?
4. In the production function specified in Exhibit 2(a), what variable(s) are movement factors (which will move us along the production function)? What variable(s) are shift factors (which will shift the production function)?

Office Hours

"What Is the Difference Between Business Cycle Macroeconomics and Economic Growth Macroeconomics?"

Student: I am searching for a way to put the macroeconomics presented in this chapter in perspective with the macroeconomics presented in the other chapters. Can you help?

Instructor: In most of the previous chapters, the *LRAS* curve did not move. It was fixed at some Natural Real GDP level. In this chapter, we discussed the factors that can shift the *LRAS* curve: We discussed how the economy can move from one Real GDP level to a higher Real GDP level. This shift was obvious in all the exhibits.

Let me add some economic terminology to the discussion. In previous chapters, we discussed mainly business cycle macroeconomics. In this chapter, we have discussed economic growth macroeconomics.

Student: Specifically, what does business cycle macroeconomics deal with?

Instructor: It deals with two things: (1) differences between Real GDP and Natural Real GDP and (2) ways of moving the economy to its Natural Real GDP level. Suppose Natural Real GDP is $11 trillion, and the current Real GDP in the economy is $10 trillion. Obviously, because Real GDP is less than Natural Real GDP, the economy is in a recessionary gap. If the economy is self-regulating, it will eventually move to its Natural Real GDP level. If it is not self-regulating, then perhaps monetary or fiscal policy can be used to move the economy to its Natural Real GDP level.

Student: How does business cycle macroeconomics differ from what was discussed in this chapter?

Instructor: In this chapter, we discussed mainly economic growth. This topic deals with the economy moving from one Natural Real GDP level to a higher one—specifically, how the economy might move from a Natural Real GDP level of, say, $11 trillion to a higher Natural Real GDP level of, say, $11.7 trillion.

Student: Does it follow that, when we're discussing how the economy moves from one Natural Real GDP level to a higher one, we are simultaneously discussing rightward shifts in the *LRAS* curve?

Instructor: Yes, that's correct. In fact, let's define both business cycle macroeconomics and economic growth macroeconomics with respect to the *LRAS* curve. Business cycle macroeconomics deals with economic activity occurring around a single *LRAS* curve. Economic growth macroeconomics (starting from an efficient level of production) deals with rightward shifts in the *LRAS* curve.

Points to Remember

1. Business cycle macroeconomics deals with economic activity occurring around a single *LRAS* curve (or around a specific Natural Real GDP level).
2. Economic growth macroeconomics (starting from an efficient level of production) deals with rightward shifts in the *LRAS* curve (or moving from a lower to a higher level of Natural Real GDP).

Chapter Summary

Economic Growth

- Absolute real economic growth refers to an increase in Real GDP from one period to the next.
- Per-capita real economic growth refers to an increase from one period to the next in per-capita Real GDP, which is Real GDP divided by population.

The Production Function

- A production function specifies the relation between technology and the quantity of factor inputs to output or Real GDP.
- Real GDP = $T(L, K)$. This production function specifies that Real GDP, or output, is a function of technology—as evidenced in the technology coefficient (T)—labor (L), and (physical) capital (K). Another production function is Real GDP = $T(L, K, NR, H)$. This production function specifies that Real GDP, or output, is a function of technology—as evidenced in the technology coefficient (T)—labor (L), (physical) capital (K), natural resources (NR), and human capital (H).

The Production Function and Economic Growth

- Using the production function Real GDP = $T(L, K)$, we know that increases in T, L, and K will raise Real GDP and that decreases in T, L, and K will decrease Real GDP. Also, changes in Real GDP will lead to shifts in the $LRAS$ curve as a result of changes in T, L, and K. For example, a rise in K will raise Real GDP, leading to a rightward shift in the $LRAS$ curve.

- A change in taxes affects the labor supply curve, thus leading to a change in the amount of labor employed in the labor market. In turn, this change in the amount of labor employed leads to a change in Real GDP and to a shift in the $LRAS$ curve (see Exhibit 4).
- How much capital is employed in the production process depends on such things as the tax treatment of capital returns and interest rates.

New Growth Theory

- New growth theory holds that technology is endogenous; neoclassical growth theory holds that technology is exogenous. When something is endogenous, it is part of the economic system, under our control or influence. When something is exogenous, it is not part of the system; instead, it is assumed to be given to us, often mysteriously through a process that we do not understand.
- According to Paul Romer, discovering and implementing new ideas is what causes economic growth.
- Certain institutions can promote the discovery of new ideas and therefore promote economic growth.

Economic Growth and Special-Interest Groups

- According to Mancur Olson, the more special-interest groups a country has, the more likely it is that transfer-promoting policies will be lobbied for instead of growth-promoting policies. Individuals will try to get a larger slice of a constant-size economic pie rather than trying to increase the size of the pie.

Key Terms and Concepts

Absolute Real Economic Growth

Per-Capita Real Economic Growth

Production Function
Human Capital

Institution

Questions and Problems

1. Why might per-capita real economic growth be a more useful measurement than absolute real economic growth?
2. Identify how changes in L, K, and T can lead to changes in output, or Real GDP.
3. What does it mean to say that "a change in labor moves us along a given production function?"
4. What do interest rates and the tax treatment of returns to capital have to do with economic growth?
5. What is *new* about new growth theory?
6. How does discovering and implementing new ideas cause economic growth?
7. What is the difference between business cycle macroeconomics and economic growth macroeconomics?
8. What is an institution? Why might institutions matter to how much economic growth a country experiences?
9. Some property rights structures provide more and stronger incentives to produce goods and services than other such structures do. Do you agree or disagree with this statement? Explain your answer.
10. Why might special-interest groups favor transfer-promoting policies over growth-promoting policies?

Working with Numbers and Graphs

1. The economy of country X is currently growing at 2 percent a year. How many years will it take to double the Real GDP of country X?
2. Explain numerically how an advance in technology can lead to more output, or Real GDP.
3. A rise in physical capital can raise Real GDP and lead to a rightward shift in the *LRAS* curve. Show this relationship diagrammatically.
4. A change in the labor market can change the equilibrium amount of labor employed, thus leading to a change in Real GDP and to a shift in the *LRAS* curve. Show this sequence of events diagrammatically.
5. Let labor be the variable shown on the horizontal axis and Real GDP on the vertical axis. Suppose there is a rise in labor. Does the rise lead to a *movement along* the production function or to a *shift in* the production function? Explain your answer. Next, draw the change in the LRAS curve that results from a rise in labor.
6. Again, let labor be the variable shown on the horizontal axis and Real GDP on the vertical axis. Suppose there is an increase in physical capital. Does the increase lead to a *movement along* the production function or to a *shift in* the production function? Explain your answer. Next, draw the change in the *LRAS* curve that results from an increase in physical capital.

CHAPTER 18
Creative Destruction and Crony Capitalism: Two Forces on the Economic Landscape Today

Introduction

Creative destruction and crony capitalism, the topics of this chapter, explain much of what we see in the economic landscape today. In this chapter, we define creative destruction and crony capitalism, give current and past examples of each, and explain why they exist.

18-1 Creative Destruction

Creative destruction is a process whereby something is being created and something is being destroyed. New technologies, new kinds of products, and new methods of production are being created while old technologies, old kinds of products, and old methods of production are being destroyed or are becoming obsolete. According to Joseph Schumpeter, the economist who first described creative destruction, it is a "process of industrial mutation that incessantly revolutionizes the economic structure from within, incessantly destroying the old one, incessantly creating a new one."[1]

18-1a Schumpeter, Creative Destruction, and Capitalism

Joseph Schumpeter was born in what is today the Czech Republic, on February 8, 1883. He graduated from the University of Vienna in 1904, began teaching at the University of Czernowitz in 1909, and later moved on to the University of Graz in Austria and the University of Bonn. He was at Harvard University for the years 1932–1950. He died on January 8, 1950,

---

[1]. Joseph A. Schumpeter, Capitalism, Socialism and Democracy. London: Routledge, p. 82, 1942.

at the age of 66. His most influential work was *Capitalism, Socialism, and Democracy*, which was published in 1942. In that major work, Schumpeter argued that creative destruction was an essential fact of capitalism. It is, according to Schumpeter, "at the heart of capitalism." He goes on to state:

> *Capitalism, then, is by nature a form or method of economic change and not only never is but never can be stationary …. The fundamental impulse that sets and keeps the capitalist engine in motion comes from the new consumers' goods, the new methods of production or transportation, the new markets, the new forms of industrial organization that capitalist enterprise creates … incessantly revolutionizes the economic structure from within, incessantly destroying the old one, incessantly creating a new one. This process of Creative Destruction is the essential fact about capitalism.*

There are a few things from this quotation that warrant emphasis. First, Schumpeter says that capitalism is a method of change. He talks of a "capitalist engine" that is always in motion, but what is it exactly that keeps the capitalist engine always moving? It is new consumers' goods, new methods of production or transportation, new markets, and new forms of industrial organization. Schumpeter emphasizes the *new*, which, in turn, destroys the old or renders it obsolete and, in doing so, replaces it.

It is the entrepreneur, according to Schumpeter, who plays the major role in the process of creative destruction, comes up with new methods of production and new consumer goods, and sometimes creates new markets in the process. For Schumpeter, it was the entrepreneur who played a starring role in the capitalist economic system and who was the face of creative destruction.

18-1b Creative Destruction and Competition

According to Schumpeter, competition is a rivalrous process in which the old is replaced by the new. Schumpeter wrote:

> *Economists are at long last emerging from the stage in which price competition was all they saw …. In capitalist reality as distinguished from its textbook picture, it is not that kind of competition which counts but the competition from a new commodity, the new technology, the new source of supply, the new type of organization—competition which commands a decisive cost or quality advantage and which strikes not at the margins of profits and the outputs of existing firms but at their foundations and their very lives.*

For Schumpeter, competition is an activity whereby a seller comes up with a new good, a new production process, or a new technology. It is a disruptive force, more than simply competing on price ("You lower your price by $1, and I will lower my price by $1); akin to coming up with a new product that would put the seller of an old product out of business.

18-1c How Do We Measure Creative Destruction?

One key measure of creative destruction is job flows, as evidenced in job creation and destruction from one period to the next. To use a historical example, consider that the introduction of the automobile led to an increase in employment in the automobile industry (no one was employed in this industry before it came into existence) and a decrease in employment in the buggy-making industry. Or consider that the introduction of the incandescent bulb led to an increase in employment in the incandescent bulb industry and a decrease of employment in the kerosene lamp industry.

Another measure of creative destruction is the change in certain key indices. For example, when the first Standard and Poor's (S&P) index of 90 major U.S. companies was created in the 1920s, the companies on that original list stayed there for an average of 65 years. Illustrating the sharp increase in creative destruction, by 1998, the average anticipated tenure on the S&P index had fallen to just 10 years. Similarly, take a look at the most valuable corporations today in terms of market value, where we can see both the phenomenon and intensity of creative destruction that has occurred in recent years. The five most valuable corporations were all founded in 1975 or later, and three of the five were founded during the years since 1994: Apple (1976), Amazon (1994), Alphabet (2015; Google founded in 1998), Microsoft (1975), and Facebook (2004).

18-1d Examples of Creative Destruction

To cement our understanding of creative destruction, it is time to provide some examples of it at work. Let's start with early eighteenth-century British industries, which were generally relatively unsophisticated. Textile production at the time was done in small workshops or in the homes of spinners, weavers, and dyers. It was a "cottage industry" that involved thousands of individuals. In 1769, Robert Arkwright patented his water frame, or spinning frame—the first textile machine powered by water. Following the water frame was James Hargreaves's spinning jenny, which revolutionized the process of cotton spinning. Then came Edmund Cartwright's power loom, which enabled the production of inexpensive cloth. These innovations changed the economic landscape of the time and gave way to worker unrest. English textile workers and weavers began to destroy weaving machinery as a form of protest. They feared that their craft skills were being replaced by machines.

Another example of creative destruction can be found in the transportation industry. As railroads spread across the United States, freight rates fell dramatically, causing the old canal and turnpike system essentially to go extinct. Reaching back further, before railroads, the steamship displaced canoes and sailboats.

Other examples of creative destruction—innovations, products, or processes that gave way to both creation and destruction, changed employment patterns, and created new markets—include the moving assembly line, the telegraph and telephone, plastics, engines of all sorts, the incandescent bulb, filmmaking, the automobile, and more.

More recent examples include the personal computer, the internet, the microprocessor, lasers, fiber optics, satellite technologies, smartphones, robotics, 3-D printing, information technology, online streaming, artificial intelligence (AI), driverless cars, cloud computing, genetic engineering, and more. Companies such as Netflix, Uber, Airbnb, Amazon, Facebook, Google, and others are just part of a long list of companies that can be considered entities that make up a large part of the creative destruction landscape today. Netflix and online streaming have essentially forced Blockbuster (a provider of home movie and video game rental services that once employed more than 80,000 people across the globe) to close all its stores. Amazon has caused many retail stores to close its doors. Uber has hurt the taxi business, and Airbnb has hurt the hotel and motel industry. Software and the internet have caused the loss of jobs for bookkeepers, tax preparers, and travel agents, to name only a few categories of workers.

Will creative destruction continue to play out on the economic road ahead? It is very likely. Innovations pouring forth in such fields as education, nanotechnology, genetic engineering, biotechnology, machine learning, and artificial intelligence, among others, will very likely continue the pace of creative destruction that has been witnessed in the past 20 to 30 years.

18-1e Worries About Creative Destruction

It is the "destruction" part of creative destruction that causes worry. The fear of losing one's job that causes anxiety and a sense of foreboding as to what awaits in a future shaped by creative destruction. Consider that, in 1990, the Big Three automakers—General Motors,

Ford, and Chrysler—brought in $36 billion in revenue (which was equivalent to $73 billion in 2021) and employed more than a million workers. In 2019, a different "Big Three"—Apple, Facebook, and Google—generated a revenue of $542 billion and employed 266,000 workers.

The workers of Eastman Kodak saw their jobs of printing pictures and producing cameras disappear largely as a result of the introduction of the smartphone that contained cameras. Tax preparers have lost jobs to software (TurboTax), travel agents to software and the internet, typewriter repairmen to computers and software, department store clerks to Amazon, and so on.

Not only does creative destruction call into question the permanency of certain jobs; it also calls into question the continuing usefulness of certain skills and training. Which jobs will creative destruction create, and which ones will it destroy? Which skills and training will it reward, and which skills and training will it devalue? Going forward, will individuals who study data science at college, but not those who study history, be able to get jobs? For today's college student, creative destruction—especially at the pace at which it is moving today—is a concern. It signals to the student that tomorrow's job market is likely to look a lot different than today's, but we can't be sure exactly what it will look like, so we can't be sure what the right thing is to study to be ready for tomorrow.

Economics 24/7

The Future: Looking at Automation and Jobs

I argue that the interplay between machine and human comparative advantage allows computers to substitute for workers in performing routine, codifiable tasks while amplifying the comparative advantage of workers in supplying problem-solving skills, adaptability, and creativity.

—David Autor, economist, MIT [2]

Automation is a process by which machines replace tasks previously performed by humans.[3] With this in mind, consider that Carl Frey and Michael Osborne, both at Oxford University, have said that, based on their research, 47 percent of total U.S. employment is at risk of automation over the next 10 to 20 years.[4] Automation often brings increases in labor productivity and economic growth, which are seen as positive, but also more job losses and income disparity, which are seen as negative.

Automation is at the forefront of our lives today, and so the debate over and fear of what benefits and costs automation will bring is often front and center of both economic and public debates. But hopes and fears over automation are not new: During the Industrial Revolution, handloom weavers worried about what new machines would mean for their livelihoods. Would textile workers lose their jobs? If so, would they be able to find new jobs?

---

[2] See *Why Are There Still So Many Jobs?* In *Journal of Economic Perspectives*. Volume 29, Number 3. Summer 2015, page 5.
[3] See *Modeling Automation* by Daron Acemoglu and Pascual Restrepo in NBER Working Paper No. 24321 (Issued in February 2018).
[4] *The Future of Employment: How Susceptive Are Jobs to Computerization?* by Carl Benedikt Frey and Michael A. Osborne, September 17, 2013, page 44, at www.oxfordmartin.ox.ac.uk/downloads/academic/The_Future_of_Employment.pdf.

Automation has often been seen as a substitute for labor: The machine replaces the labor. Of course, machines can replace labor—think of a tractor replacing workers with hoes. But machines can complement labor, too, and this leads to more jobs. The classic case is that of automatic teller machines (ATMs) being introduced in the 1970s.[5] (Actually, the first ATM was introduced in the United States on September 2, 1969, by Chemical Bank at its branch in Rockville Centre, New York.) One would think that ATMs would replace bank tellers, but they didn't. The average bank branch required about 21 bank tellers, and that number was cut to 13 bank tellers with the introduction of the ATM. But because of the use of the ATM, banks found it cheaper to operate a branch, and so they began to increase the number of bank branch offices, which subsequently increased the demand for bank tellers. Overall, the increase in demand for bank tellers due to the opening of more branch offices was greater than the decrease in the demand for bank tellers due to the introduction of the ATM.

The ATM also began to change what a bank teller did. According to economist David Autor,

> *As the routine cash-handling tasks of bank tellers receded, information technology also enabled a broader range of bank personnel to become involved in "relationship banking." Increasingly, banks recognized the value of tellers enabled by information technology, not primarily as checkout clerks, but as salespersons, forging relationships with customers and introducing them to additional bank services like credit cards, loans, and investment products.[6]*

Keep in mind that while many people think that automation will lead to a massive loss of jobs, automation has increased at the same time that the unemployment rate was low. For example, during the period 2016–2019, the unemployment rate averaged 4.2 percent. (The unemployment rate increased dramatically in 2020, but this was largely due to the COVID-19 pandemic).

Might the automation that is coming in the future lead to large job losses without new job opportunities opening up? We can't know for sure. Maybe, as some experts say, "this time will be different" because while, in the past, automation was mainly concerned with doing routine tasks (counting, boxing, moving things from one point to another), this time, the automation might be smarter and more capable of completing complex tasks—tasks that human labor has, so far, had a comparative advantage in doing relative to capital goods.

[5.] See *Learning by Doing: The Real Connection between Innovation, Wages, and Wealth*, by James Bessen, Yale University Press, 2015.
[6.] See "Why Are There Still So Many Jobs?" In *Journal of Economic Perspectives*, Volume 29, Number 3, Summer 2015, page 7.

18-1f Calls for Government Assistance

Creative destruction does not occur in a political vacuum. Often, job losses, education uncertainty, and changing market conditions bring forth certain proposals, many of which have government playing a role. Such proposals include retraining services for workers who lose their jobs to automation, a universal basic income, or regulations and taxes to stifle or slow down the process of creative destruction.

18-1g The Other Side of Creative Destruction

There are two parts to creative destruction: the destruction part and the creation part. Jobs, industries, companies, products, and production processes are what is being destroyed. And what is being created? The same things that are being destroyed: jobs, industries, companies, products, and production processes. Much of the world we inhabit today is full with the creative part of creative destruction. In fact, creative destruction is the reason that today people in the most fiscally poor countries carry more computer power in their cell phones than many people in the wealthiest countries had access to in the 1970s. To a large degree, it explains why, worldwide, people whose incomes are below the poverty threshold often have a much higher quality of life than Europe's monarchs had in the Middle Ages.

Creative destruction comes with a displacement effect, but it also comes with countervailing forces to the displacement effect, too.[7] The *displacement effect* occurs when workers lose jobs because of the automation that often is a part of creative destruction: in the past, farm workers being displaced by harvesters and plows; today, travel agents and tax preparers being displaced by software; perhaps in the future, truck drivers being displaced by driverless trucks. One countervailing force to the displacement effect is the *productivity effect*, which occurs when the cost of producing automated tasks declines, causing the economy to expand and increase the demand for labor in non-automated tasks. For example, when labor becomes too expensive relative to capital, firms substitute capital for labor to reduce costs. These lower costs in producing goods and services can lead to lower prices, thus increasing the purchasing power and monetary wealth of consumers. Consumers with more wealth will likely increase their demand for goods and services (and some of those goods may not be produced with AI and robotics). Higher demand for goods and services leads to a higher demand for labor, causing wages to rise. A historical example can be found in agriculture, where machinery led to lower costs of production, reduced prices, and consumers who increased their demand for many nonagricultural goods, thereby indirectly increasing the demand for the labor that produced those goods.

Another force offsetting the displacement effect is the *reinstatement effect*, which occurs when the creation of new tasks creates new jobs. Think of new job tasks and titles that exist today but did not exist until recently, such as virtual assistant, well-being coach, social media manager, app developer, web analyst, data scientist, and so on. In the past, new technologies (steam, electricity, the internet) all led to new kinds of jobs. It is likely to be no different with advancing AI and robotics.

(Answers to Self-Test questions are in Answers to Self-Test Questions at the back of the book.)

1. What does creative destruction create and what does it destroy?
2. What is the productivity effect?
3. What is the displacement effect?

18-2 Crony Capitalism

Crony capitalism is "a system in which government, big business, and powerful interest groups work together to further their joint interests. Government protects and subsidizes powerful corporations and in (implicit) exchange, the government uses those businesses to carry out government policies outside of the ordinary processes of government."[8]

18-2a At the Heart of Crony Capitalism Is Rent Seeking

The engine of crony capitalism is the process known as rent-seeking.

Todd Zywicki[9]

[7.] See "Artificial Intelligence, Automation and Work," by Daron Acemoglu and Pascual Restrepo in *Economics of Artificial Intelligence: An Agenda*, edited by Ajay Agrawal, Avi Goldfarb and Joshua Gans. The paper can be found at www.nber.org/chapters/c14027.pdf.
[8.] See "Rent-Seeking, Crony Capitalism, and the Crony Constitution" by Todd Zywicki. *Supreme Court Economic Review*, Volume 23, Number 1, 2015.
[9.] See Todd Zywicki, "Rent-Seeking, Crony Capitalism, and the Crony Constitution," George Mason University Legal Studies Research Paper Series, LS 15-08.

Rent seeking consists of the actions of individuals and groups that spend resources to influence public policy in the hope of redistributing, or transferring, income to themselves from others. Simply put, rent seeking describes the process by which well-organized interests seek favors from government. The term "rent," used in the context we have used it here, often confuses people because in in most contexts, "rent" refers to the payment for an apartment or house. In economics, rent or, more formally, *economic rent* is a payment in excess of opportunity cost.

When any entity seeks rents (that is, when it is rent seeking), it is spending resources to gain some government privilege or favor. To illustrate, suppose there are 10 firms in an industry, A–J. One day, firm A hires a group of lobbyists to lobby Congress on its behalf. Specifically, it seeks a change in the law such that firm A will be given a monopoly privilege. Firm A wants to eliminate its competition by having Congress pass a law that makes it the sole producer and seller of the good that all 10 firms currently produce and sell. We would then say that firm A is rent seeking; it is using resources (hiring lobbyists) to seek a government favor or privilege that will, if granted, eliminate competition and raise prices, thus making firm A better off at the expense of consumers and other producers.

Rent seeking is not unique to capitalism or any one particular economic system. Rent seeking is something that can occur in all economic systems—socialism, communism, and mixed economic systems.

18-2b Two Things to Consider About Rent Seeking: The Transfer and the Wasted Resources

Suppose there are 10 U.S. firms (in an industry) that all produce good X. Currently, these firms are selling good X in the U.S. market, along with five foreign firms that are also selling good X in the U.S. market. The 10 U.S. firms determine that they would be better off if they could somehow eliminate or at least hamper their foreign competition. They decide that one way they can do this is to try to get the U.S. government to impose tariffs on foreign imports of good X. The 10 U.S. firms get together and hire research teams, lobbyists, and others to try to influence the U.S. government to impose tariffs on the foreign producers of good X. In time, the U.S. government does impose tariffs on foreign producers of good X. As a result of the tariff, the price of good X in the United States rises. U.S. consumers end up paying higher prices for good X, the U.S. firms that supply good X end up selling more units of good X at higher prices, and the U.S. government collects some tariff revenue.

This is an act of rent seeking on the part of the 10 U.S. firms. They have sought and received a special privilege from the U.S. government—the imposition of tariffs on their foreign (producer) competitors. As a result of this successful rent seeking on their parts, two things have happened. First, there has been a transfer from U.S. consumers to U.S. producers. Because of the higher prices U.S. consumers pay, some of the **consumers' surplus** they received (when they paid lower prices) is transferred from them to U.S. producers, in the form of greater **producers' surplus** received by these producers. In other words, part of consumers' surplus is transferred to producers in the form of greater producers' surplus. Just to put a dollar figure on this transfer, let's say that $1 billion of consumers' surplus is transferred to producers in the form producers' surplus. Rent seeking leads to a *transfer*, and the transfer is what is lost by some and won by others.

Keep in mind that rent seeking (seeking special favors or privileges through government) has been around for a very long time. It is not an activity that started 10, 20, or even 100 years ago; it has been around for centuries. But it was economist Gordon Tullock who developed the theory of rent seeking and the idea that rent seeking leads to inefficiency and wastes resources. Tullock's basic insight was that, in the process of seeking rents, the rent seekers make expenditures (in our example, hire research teams, hire lobbyists, etc.) that not only reduce

Consumers' Surplus (CS)
The difference between the maximum price a buyer is willing and able to pay for a good or service and the price actually paid.

Producers' (Sellers') Surplus (PS)
The difference between the price sellers receive for a good and the minimum or lowest price for which they would have sold the good.

some of the gains to the beneficiaries of rent seeking but also waste resources. After all, if the U.S. firms in our example spend, say, $10 million to lobby government to get the tariffs, that's $10 million that cannot be used to produce goods. Instead of spending $10 million to produce more goods, the firms spend $10 million to bring about a transfer.

To see exactly how wasteful rent seeking can be, consider the following example. At time period 1, there are 100 people in a tiny society, and all of the 100 people spend their days producing goods and services for others. The GDP at the end of the year turns out to be, say, $5 million. At time period 2, all 100 people decide that they will not be producers any more, but instead, they will spend their time, energy, and resources seeking rents: They will try to bring about transfers from others to themselves. With everyone seeking rents, many fewer goods and services are produced and GDP dramatically declines.

As stated earlier, rent seeking leads to a transfer. With a transfer, what one person gains, another person loses. In our tariff example, what the U.S. consumers lost, the U.S. producers gained. So someone could argue that, on net, nothing much has really changed except that one group of persons (consumers) have less, and another group of persons (producers) have more. In other words, transfers are zero sum: The winnings equal the losses, so when we add the (positive) winnings to the (negative) losses, they sum to zero.

But there are the wasted resources for which we need to account. The wasted resources that go to bring about a transfer and not to produce goods are a loss to society as a whole: Fewer resources being used to produce means fewer goods and services produced. Rent seeking, then, leads to a decline in the size of the economic pie.

18-2c A Question for Tullock

Gordon Tullock was once asked,[10]

> How might things be changed so that there is less rent seeking in the world and thus less waste?

Here is his answer:

This is a difficult question. It is easy to think of ways to remedy particular situations, but the general issue is very difficult. In fact, most governments throughout history have been dominated by rent-seeking activity. For some time in the nineteenth century, most of northwestern Europe was not—but this is an exceptional period. I think we ought to look for explanations of why that period was the way it was, instead of explanations of why we have returned to the normal, yet less desirable, state of affairs.

Anyway, all I can recommend is that economists talk about the social wastefulness of rent seeking and try to convince people that it is undesirable. Some economists have said that economic education does pay off. It seems to me that nineteenth-century northwestern Europe is an example of a place and a time where it did, and with some pressure it may do so again. In any case, David Ricardo [the British political economist, 1772–1823] and his friends were successful, and I see no reason why we can't be, too.

18-2d Some Examples of Rent Seeking: Past and Present

During Queen Elizabeth's [the First] very long reign she oftentimes found herself in need of more money than Parliament had appropriated for her to use. As a result, she sometimes tried to supplement her subsidy from Parliament by selling royal monopolies.

Steven G. Calabresi and Larissa Price
Monopolies and the Constitution: A History of Crony Capitalism

---

[10.] See Interview: Gordon Tullock in *Economics* by Roger A. Arnold, 559–560. St Paul: West Publishing Company, 1989.

- **English Kings and Queens.** The original meaning of the word "monopoly" was the granting of a special privilege, by government, to someone or some group of persons to work in a particular trade or produce and sell a specific good. Often, the grant of special privilege was in the form of a license or patent. The English kings and queens of the late sixteenth and early seventeenth centuries regularly made such grants of privileges to favored persons—allowing them, in many cases, to be the sole suppliers of certain goods (such as sweet wines, starch, salt, etc.). The grant of special privilege to be the sole provider of a good essentially eliminated competition: Now no one but the person or the company that received the grant of privilege could produce and trade the good.

- **The Ferry Boat Company.** In 1927, the State of Washington gave a ferry boat company the exclusive right to operate a ferry at the northern end of Washington's Lake Chelan. Today, the small community of Stehekin, which is located at the northern end of Lake Chelan, is only accessible by boat or plane. Not long ago, two brothers, Jim and Cliff Courtney, wanted to compete with the ferry boat company that held the exclusive right to service Stehekin by providing a ferry boat service themselves. The State of Washington denied their plan to do so. In 2011, the Institute for Justice joined with the Courtneys and filed a federal civil rights lawsuit to challenge the State of Washington. In 2013, the 9th U.S. Circuit Court of Appeals concluded that the Courtneys could not operate a ferry on Lake Chelan.

- **The British East India Company.** In 1773, the British East Company was in financial trouble, and it sought a monopoly grant from Parliament to export tea to the American colonies. Parliament passed the Tea Act, giving them that monopoly grant.

- **Taxi Medallions.** In 2013, a taxi medallion in New York City sold for $1.3 million. Every cab in New York City has to have a medallion, and the city limits the number of medallions to a little more than 13,000. By limiting the number of taxi medallions, New York City limits taxicab competition and keeps taxi rates higher than they would be if it permitted free entry into the taxicab industry. The fairly recent entry of ride-share companies such as Uber and Lyft have provided the taxicab industry with competition and have led to a dramatic decline in the price of a taxi medallion.

- **Cargo Preference Laws.** Cargo preference laws require that a percentage of U.S. government cargo, including international food aid, must be transported on U.S. flag vessels. Because foreign-flag vessels cannot compete here, the rates government must pay to carry its cargo on U.S. flag vessels is higher than it would be if other cargo vessels could compete. The chief beneficiaries here are the companies that own the U.S. flagged ships that carry the U.S. food aid.

- **Export–Import Bank of the United States.** The Export–Import Bank is an export credit agency of the U.S. federal government. It essentially makes it easier for domestic firms to export their goods by helping overseas customers arrange financing for the U.S. goods. For example, when an overseas customer can't find a private-sector lender to extend credit, the Export–Import bank steps in with loans and loan guarantees. In the past, a large percentage of the bank's activities have benefited just a few large U.S. corporations.

- **Sugar.** The U.S. government protects the domestic sugar industry through import quotas and a loan program that effectively serves as an effective price floor on sugar. As a result, the price of U.S. sugar is almost double the world price. In other words, U.S. consumers and business have had to pay for the protection the U.S. government has afforded the U.S. sugar industry.

- **Trucking.** From 1935 to the mid-1970s, interstate trucking was regulated by the Interstate Commerce Commission (ICC). The Motor Carrier Act of 1935 required that new trucking companies must have a "certificate of public convenience and necessity" from the ICC. Trucking companies who operated in 1935 automatically received certificates under certain conditions. However, new trucking companies found it difficult to get certificates. The Motor Carrier Act essentially limited the competition in the trucking industry, causing trucking rates to be higher than they would have been if competition had been permitted.

- **Certificate of Need (CON) Laws.** CON laws are state laws that require health care providers to prove that their services are "needed" before they are allowed to offer services to customers. For example, suppose there are two hospitals located in a particular city. Along comes a company that wants to open up another hospital in the city so that there would now be three. Can the company that wants to open up the new hospital do so? Can it easily enter the hospital market in the city? Not always. In 35 states and in Washington, D.C., government permission is required to open up or expand a health care facility, such as a hospital. The permission comes in the form of a CON. The beneficiaries of the CON system are the already existing hospitals in the area. Essentially, what the CON system does is to restrict competition for the existing hospitals.

- **Government Bailouts.** A government bailout consists of government providing emergency funding to a failing entity (such as a corporation) so as to avoid it shutting down. Bailouts can come in different forms—such as loans, loan guarantees, stock, bonds, and cash. In August 1971, the U.S. Congress passed the Emergency Loan Guarantee Act. This act provided funds to any major business enterprise that was in financial crisis. The first recipient was Lockheed Aircraft Corporation. The bailout took the form of $250 million emergency loan guarantees. Essentially, a loan guarantee is a promise made by one party (the guarantor—in this case, the U.S. government) to assume the debt obligation of a borrower (in this case, Lockheed) if the borrower defaults. Some of the companies that have received a bailout include Penn Central Railroad (1970), Franklin National Bank (1974), Chrysler (1980), Continental Illinois National Bank and Trust Company (1984), various savings and loan associations (1989), the airline industry (2001), Bear Stearns (2008), Fannie Mae and Freddie Mac (2008), and American International Group (2008). The Troubled Asset Relief Program (TARP), signed into law in 2008, was a $700 billion bailout that gave hundreds of financial firms and auto companies emergency government assistance. During the COVID-19 pandemic, loans, direct grants, and loan guarantees became fairly common.

- **Subsidies.** The agricultural industry is a large beneficiary of direct subsidies. In the last 10 years, it has received nearly $200 billion in subsidies. In fact, about 39 percent of the nation's 2.1 million farms receive direct subsidies. In fact, in 2008, the average household income of farms that received $30,000 or more in subsidies was $210,000.[11] Another industry, the energy industry, received more than $14 billion in direct subsidies in 2010.

- **Tariffs and Quotas.** Placing tariffs and quotas on foreign imports essentially benefits domestic producers at the expense of domestic consumers. For instance, placing a tariff on foreign-produced steel makes that steel more expensive and less able to compete with domestically-produced steel.

- **Rent Seeking Exists Where [Fill in the Blank] Exists.** There are many hundreds of specific examples of rent-seeking activity going on in the United States and around the world today. We find rent seeking where we find tax incentives, special government financing, bailouts, regulatory preferences such as monopolies or mandates, tariffs, quotas, government subsidies, tax privileges, taxpayer-financed economic development funds, and government loan guarantees or forgiveness, and more. Essentially, wherever special preferences, protections, and subsidies exist, rent seeking exists.

---

[11] See *The Pathology of Privilege: The Economic Consequences of Government Favoritism*, by Matthew Mitchell, Mercatus Center, George Mason University; and U.S. Energy Information Administration, *Direct Federal Financial Interventions and Subsidies in Fiscal Year 2010*.

Economics 24/7

Bastiat and the Candlemaker's Petition

Frédéric Bastiat (1801–1850) was a French economist and economic journalist. This keen observer of the political economic scene would often, in a style all his own, criticize and mock those who sought government privileges to aid themselves at the same time as stifling their competition. In a famous essay, "The Candlemaker's Petition," originally published in 1845, he wrote a tongue-in-cheek account of candle manufacturers petitioning the French Parliament to aid them by stifling their competition. But who (or what) exactly is their competition? Read a short excerpt from the petition and see for yourself:

COURTESY OF RIJKSMUSEUM

> Gentlemen:
>
> We [candle manufacturers] are suffering from the ruinous competition of a rival who apparently works under conditions so far superior to our own for the production of light that he is flooding the domestic market with it at an incredibly low price; for the moment he appears, our sales cease, all the consumers turn to him, and a branch of French industry whose ramifications are innumerable is all at once reduced to complete stagnation. This rival, which is none other than the sun, is waging war on us....
>
> We ask you to be so good as to pass a law requiring the close of all windows, dormers, skylights, inside and outside shutters, curtains, casements, bull's-eyes, deadlights, and blinds – in short, all openings, holes, chinks, and fissures through which the light of the sun is wont to enter houses, to the detriment of the fair industries with which, we are proud to say, we have endowed the country, a country that cannot, without betraying ingratitude, abandon us today to so unequal a combat.[12]

Bastiat goes on to say that if Parliament bans the sun, great things will happen for France. By creating a need for artificial light, various industries will be encouraged. No sun means more candles are needed. More candles mean more tallow (which is used to make candles) has to be obtained. And since tallow is a hard fat that comes from cattle and sheep, cattle and sheep have to be raised, which means that more fields have to be cleared, and so on and so on. In the end, assisting the candlemakers—by passing a law requiring the closing of all windows and curtains and so on—will benefit the country.

The candlemaker's petition ends by reminding the French Parliament that it has already done for the coal, iron, wheat, and textiles industries what the candlemaker is asking of it now. Bastiat ends the petition with these words:

> Make your choice [Gentlemen of the Parliament], but be logical; for as long as you ban, as you do, foreign coal, iron, wheat, and textiles, in proportion as their price approaches zero, how inconsistent it would be to admit the light of the sun, whose price is zero all day long!

[12] See http://bastiat.org/en/petition.html.

18-2e Lobbyists and Rent Seeking

The dictionary definition of lobbyist is "one who conducts activities aimed at influencing or swaying public officials and especially members of a legislative body on legislation."[13] Each of the 50 states of the United States also define lobbyist or lobbying, sometimes in slightly different ways, but most states' definitions of lobbying have a common theme, which can be found in this, Alabama's definition of lobbying: "The practice of promoting, opposing, or in any manner influencing or attempting to influence the introduction, defeat, or enactment of legislation

[13] See Merriam-Webster Dictionary.

before any legislative body."[14] At the federal level, according the National Conference of State Legislatures, a lobbyist is "any individual who is employed or retained by a client for financial or other compensation for services that include more than one lobbying contract."[15] A lobbying contract is defined as "any oral or written communication to a covered executive branch official or a covered legislative branch official that is made on behalf of a client with regard to (i) the formulation, modification, or adoption of Federal legislation (including legislative proposals); (ii) the formulation, modification, or adoption of a Federal rule, regulation, Executive order, or any other program, policy, or position of the U.S. Government."[16]

It is clear from the definitions that lobbyists are hired to influence public policy. Not all lobbyists are seeking special privileges for the clients they work for, and not all lobbyists are seeking rents, but a significant number of them are. This would be expected, and in an environment where rent-seeking lobbying is often rewarded (by means of receiving a bailout, monopoly privilege, tariff, subsidy, and so on), rent seeking will exist. If government is even slightly open to rent-seeking efforts, the rent seekers will come.

To get some idea of just how much lobbying (if not always rent-seeking lobbying) goes on in the United States at the federal government level, here is only a partial list of different federal government departments, bureaus, and agencies (and alongside each the number of lobbyists) that engaged in lobbying that particular department, bureau, or agency in 2020.

- Department of Health and Human Services: 2,691
- Department of the Treasury: 2,846
- Centers for Medicare and Medicaid Services: 1,583
- Department of Agriculture: 1,702
- Department of Defense: 1,646
- Environmental Protection Agency: 1,600
- Department of Labor: 1,555
- Department of Education: 830

Here is a list of some of the top lobbyist groups in 2020 and the dollar amounts they spent on lobbying that year:

U.S. Chamber of Commerce	$59,300,000
National Association of Realtors	$58,896,779
Pharmaceutical Research & Manufacturers of America	$20,707,000
American Hospital Association	$18,266,173
Blue Cross/Blue Shield	$16,274,480
American Medical Association	$15,245,000
Facebook Inc.	$14,990,000
Amazon.com	$13,755,000

Each year, the members of Congress introduce thousands of bills, but only a handful come to a vote. Lobbyists will often track these bills to see if a particular bill might affect their clients. Lobbyists must disclose which particular issues or bills they worked on a given year. In what follows, we identify the number of lobbyists that were interested in and worked on specific

---

[14.] See the National Conference of State Legislatures at www.ncsl.org/research/ethics/50-state-chart-lobby-definitions.aspx.
[15.] See Lobbying Disclosure Act, Office of the Clerk, U.S. House of Representatives at https://lobbyingdisclosure.house.gov/lda.html.
[16.] Ibid.

House and Senate bills in 2020. In the list, H.R. stands for House of Representatives, and S. stands for Senate; thus, bill H.R. 748 originated in the House of Representatives. (Bill H.R. 748 was titled the CARES ACT; it was a bill written and passed into law that dealt with the economic fallout from the COVID-19 pandemic in the United States). In the following list, we identify five bills that originated in 2020 by bill number, title, and the number of lobbyists that worked on each bill.

H.R. 748	CARES Act	1,989
H.R. 6800	The Heroes Act	1,601
S. 3548	CARES Act	763
S. 1895	Lower Health Care Costs Act	279
S. 2302	America's Transportation Infrastructure Act	189

18-2f Why Would a Firm Want to Be a Rent Seeker?

Why would a firm want to be a rent seeker instead of just going about its business and producing its goods and services and offering them up for sale in the market? To illustrate, suppose there is a steel company that has two options: (1) It can produce and sell steel and not ask for any favors from government; or (2) it can produce and sell steel and engage in rent seeking, specifically incurring the rent-seeking costs to lobby government for tariffs on imported steel. Pursuing (2) could give the steel company a competitive edge in the domestic steel market since tariffs on imported steel will disadvantage foreign steel producers at the expense of domestic steel producers. But, of course, this comes at a cost for the company: It has to incur the costs of lobbying for and getting the tariffs.

The firm is likely to look at the expected net return for each option and then make its decision. If the expected net return is higher for (1) than (2), it is likely to choose (1); if the expected net return is higher for (2) than (1), it is likely to choose (2).

Part of making the decision will depend upon how the firm views its chances of getting the tariff that it lobbies for. Has the government been responsive to granting special privileges to firms in the past or not? For example, a government that opens its doors to lobbyists asking for special privileges is likely to have more special interests knocking at its door than one that does not.

How the special privilege a firm asks for can be "sold" to the public at large can also play a role in how it is received by the government. Does the steel company say, "We are searching for a special privilege—in particular, a tariff—that will be placed on imported steel. Such a tariff will help us—the domestic steel company—but, of course, the steel consumers will end up having to pay more for steel as a result. We win; others lose." Probably not. Instead, the steel company—and its lobbyists—are likely going to try couch their special-interest privilege in general-interest talk. They might argue, "The domestic steel companies need tariffs to be placed on foreign steel. This will help the workers in the domestic steel industry and provide the tax revenue for the cities in which the steel companies are located. It is a matter of saving jobs and guaranteeing stable tax revenues for the community."

1. What is rent seeking?
2. What was Tullock's basic insight into rent seeking?
3. Give an example of how rent seeking can waste resources.

Economics 24/7

Does It Matter If There Is a Lot of Crony Capitalism in the Country?

Consider two countries, A and B. In country A, there is almost no crony capitalism. Laws forbid government from giving out special preferences, protections, and subsidies. If a company in this country asks for a tariff to be placed on foreign goods that it competes with, the answer is no; it is not allowed.

In country B, in contrast, there are no laws that forbid government from giving out special preferences, protections, and subsidies. As a result, many such special preferences, protections, and subsidies are given out.

Now consider a business in each of the two countries. In country A, the business knows that there is only one way it can succeed: It has to produce a product or service that consumers want to buy, and it has to be able to meet its competition head on.

In country B, the business has an option available to it that it does not have in country A. Not only can it succeed by producing a product that consumers want to buy by meeting its competition head on, but it can also go to government and ask for a special privilege, protection, or subsidy. It can ask for a tariff that stifles its foreign competitors, it can ask for a monopoly privilege that advantages it to the detriment to its competition, and so on. Stated differently, in country A, the business cannot seek rents, so it does not engage in any rent-seeking activity; instead, all its time, energy, and resources have to be invested in productive activity. But in country B, the business can devote time, energy, and resources both to productive activity and to rent seeking.

Keep in mind that rent seeking wastes resources, which cannot be used to produce goods and services or to promote the growth of economic output—such as the production of more cars, houses, and computers. In other words, between the two countries, there are likely to be more resources wasted in B than in A. In the end, rent seeking and crony capitalism waste resources. The production of goods and services is likely to be greater in country A than in country B, all other things being equal. The country that wastes resources is likely to have less growth than the country that does not.

Does economic growth matter to you? Economic growth is closely related to how many goods and services you have available to you, how many jobs are created, how much you end up paying for the goods and services you buy (greater supply, lower prices), and more.

Chapter Summary

Schumpeter, Creative Destruction, and Capitalism

- Joseph Schumpeter described creative destruction as a "process of industrial mutation that incessantly revolutionizes the economic structure from within, incessantly destroying the old one, incessantly creating a new one."

- According to Schumpeter, the entrepreneur plays the major role in the process of creative destruction, develops new methods of production and new consumer goods, and sometimes creates new markets in the process.

- Schumpeter argued that creative destruction is an essential fact of capitalism. In his words, it is "at the heart of capitalism."

Measure of Creative Destruction

- One key measure of creative destruction is job flows, as evidenced in job creation and destruction from one period to the next. For example, the introduction of the automobile led to an increase in the employment in the automobile industry and a decrease in the employment in the buggy-making industry.
- Another measure consists of identifying changes in certain key indices. For example, the first Standard and Poor's index of 90 major U.S. companies was created in the 1920s. The companies on that original list stayed there for an average of 65 years. By 1998, however, the average anticipated tenure on the S&P index had fallen to 10 years.

Some Examples of Creative Destruction

- Examples of creative destruction include railroads, the moving assembly line, telegraph and telephone, plastics, the automobile, personal computers, the internet, lasers, information technology, online streaming, artificial intelligence, and more.

Worries About Creative Destruction

- It is the "destruction" part of creative destruction that often comes with worries and calls into question the permanency or impermanency of certain jobs, skills, and training. Which jobs will creative destruction destroy, and which skills and training will it devalue?

Creative Destruction and Three Effects

- Creative destruction comes with the displacement effect, the productivity effect, and the reinstatement effect. The displacement effect occurs when workers lose jobs because of creative destruction—think of farm workers being displaced by harvesters and plows. The productivity effect occurs when the cost of automating tasks falls, leading to an expanding economy and an increase in the demand for non-automated tasks—think of the introduction of machinery in agriculture leading to lower costs of production, reduced prices (for agricultural goods), and wealthier consumers who then increase their demand for nonagricultural goods and indirectly increase the demand for the labor that produces the nonagricultural goods. The reinstatement effect occurs with the creation of new jobs—think of past new technologies—such as steam, electricity, and the internet—leading to new jobs.

Crony Capitalism and Rent Seeking

- Crony capitalism is "a system in which government, big business, and powerful interest groups (especially labor unions) work together to further their joint interests. Government protects and subsidizes powerful corporations and in (implicit) exchange, the government uses those businesses to carry out government policies outside of the ordinary processes of government."[17]
- At the heart of crony capitalism is rent seeking, which consists of the actions of individuals and groups that spend resources to influence public policy in the hope of redistributing (transferring) income to themselves from others.
- Rent seeking comes with both a transfer and wasted resources. The resources that go to bring about a transfer, instead of producing goods, are wasted and therefore bring about a loss to society as a whole.

Some Examples of Rent Seeking: Past and Present

- The English kings and queens of the late sixteenth and early seventeenth centuries regularly granted monopoly privileges to favored persons.
- In 1927, the State of Washington gave a ferry boat company the exclusive right to operate a ferry at the northern end of Lake Chelan.
- The British Parliament gave a monopoly grant to the British East India Company.
- Every cab in New York City has to have a medallion, and the city limits the number of medallions to a little more than 13,000.
- Cargo preference laws required that a percentage of U.S. government cargo, including international food aid, must be transported on U.S.-flag vessels.
- The Export-Import Bank is an export credit agency of the U.S. federal government that assists domestic firms in exporting their goods to overseas customers by arranging loans and loan guarantees for overseas customers.
- The U.S. government protects the domestic sugar industry through import quotas and a loan program that effectively serves as an effective price floor on sugar.
- The Motor Carrier Act essentially limited the competition in the trucking industry, causing trucking rates to be higher than they would have been if competition had been permitted.
- As a general rule, rent seeking exists wherever special preferences, protections, and subsidies exist.

---

[17] See "Rent-Seeking, Crony Capitalism, and the Crony Constitution" by Todd Zywicki. *Supreme Court Economic Review*, Volume 23, Number 1, 2015.

Questions and Problems

1. According to Joseph Schumpeter, where does the fundamental impulse that sets and keeps the capitalist engine in motion come from?
2. What is creative destruction?
3. According to Schumpeter, who plays the major role in the process of creative destruction?
4. Is the competition within creative destruction that Schumpeter talked about and perfect competition the same? Explain your answer.
5. One key measure of creative destruction is job flows. Explain.
6. Give eight examples of products, technologies, or modes of transportation that can be considered part of the process of creative destruction.
7. How does education uncertainty relate to creative destruction?
8. What is the displacement effect? Give an example of it.
9. What are the productivity effect and the reinstatement effect?
10. What is crony capitalism?
11. What is rent seeking?
12. Identify the two parts of rent seeking, and explain each.
13. Give an example that illustrates the wasted resources in rent seeking.
14. What is the original meaning of the word "monopoly"?
15. In this chapter, past and present examples of rent seeking were given. What was the effect of rent seeking on consumers in the ferry boat company example, the taxi medallion example, and the sugar example?
16. What are cargo preference laws, and who are the chief beneficiaries of them?
17. What does rent seeking have to do with lobbyists?

CHAPTER 19

Elasticity

Introduction

Suppose that, in New York City, a Broadway play is performed in a theater with 1,500 seats. Will the play take in more revenue if the average ticket price for a performance is $100 or if it is $200? If you said $200, consider some other questions: Will the play take in more revenue if the average price is $200 or $280? Will it take in more revenue if the average price is $280 or $320? Are you beginning to get suspicious? Perhaps the highest ticket price won't generate the greatest amount of revenue, but which ticket price will? The answer may surprise you.

19-1 Elasticity: Part 1

The law of demand states that price and quantity demanded are inversely related, *ceteris paribus*. But it doesn't tell us by what percentage the quantity demanded changes as price changes. Suppose price rises by 10 percent. As a result, quantity demanded falls, but by what percentage does it fall? The notion of price elasticity of demand can help answer this question. The general concept of elasticity provides a technique for estimating the response of one variable to changes in another. It has numerous applications in economics.

19-1a Price Elasticity of Demand

The law of demand states that there is a *directional relationship* between price and quantity demanded: Price and quantity demanded are inversely related. But the law of demand does *not* tell us *how much* quantity demanded declines as price rises. The *magnitudinal relationship* between price and quantity demanded brings us to a discussion of **price elasticity of demand**, which is a measure of the responsiveness of quantity demanded to changes in price. More specifically, it addresses the percentage change in quantity demanded for a given percentage change in price. (Keep in mind "percentage change," not just "change.")

Price Elasticity of Demand
A measure of the responsiveness of quantity demanded to changes in price.

Let's say that a seller of a good—a computer—raises the price by 10 percent, and as a result, the quantity demanded for the computer falls by 20 percent. The percentage change in quantity demanded (Q_d)—20 percent—divided by the percentage change in price (P)—10 percent—is called the *coefficient of price elasticity of demand* (E_d):

$$E_d = \frac{\text{Percentage change in quantity demanded}}{\text{Percentage change in price}} = \frac{\%\Delta Q_d}{\%\Delta P}$$

In the formula, E_d = coefficient of price elasticity of demand, or simply elasticity coefficient; % = percentage; and Δ stands for "change in."

If we apply the calculation to our simple example—in which quantity demanded changes by 20 percent and price changes by 10 percent—we get 2. An economist would say either, "The coefficient of price elasticity of demand is 2" or, more simply, "Price elasticity of demand is 2." Either expression means that the percentage change in quantity demanded will be two times any percentage change in price.[1] If price changes by 5 percent, the quantity demanded will change by 10 percent; if price changes by 10 percent, the quantity demanded will change by 20 percent.

Where Is the Missing Minus Sign? Price and quantity demanded move in opposite directions: When price rises, quantity demanded falls; when price falls, quantity demanded rises. In our example, when price rises by 10 percent, quantity demanded falls by 20 percent. When you divide a *negative 20 percent* by a *positive 10 percent*, you don't get 2; you get –2. Instead of saying that the price elasticity of demand is 2, you might think that price elasticity of demand is –2. However, by convention, economists usually simplify things by using the absolute value of the price elasticity of demand; thus, they drop the minus sign.

Formula for Calculating Price Elasticity of Demand Using percentage changes to calculate price elasticity of demand can lead to conflicting results, depending on whether price rises or falls. Therefore, economists use the following formula to calculate price elasticity of demand:[2]

$$E_d = \frac{\frac{\Delta Q_d}{Q_{d\ average}}}{\frac{\Delta P}{P_{average}}}$$

In the formula, ΔQ_d stands for the absolute change in Q_d. For example, if Q_d changes from 50 units to 100 units, then ΔQ_d is 50 units. ΔP stands for the absolute change in price. For example, if price changes from $12 to $10, then ΔP is $2. $Q_{d\ average}$ stands for the average of the two quantities demanded, and $P_{average}$ stands for the average of the two prices.

For the data on price and quantity demanded in Exhibit 1, the calculation is

$$E_d = \frac{\frac{50}{75}}{\frac{2}{11}} = 3.67$$

Because we use the average price and average quantity demanded in the equation for price elasticity of demand, 3.67 may be considered the price elasticity of demand at a point *midway*

---

[1]. This statement assumes that we are changing price from its current level.
[2]. This formula is sometimes called the *midpoint formula for calculating price elasticity of demand*.

EXHIBIT 1

Calculating Price Elasticity of Demand

We identify two points on a demand curve. At point A, price is $12, and quantity demanded is 50 units. At point B, price is $10, and quantity demanded is 100 units. When calculating price elasticity of demand, we use the *average* of the two prices and the *average* of the two quantities demanded. The formula for price elasticity of demand is

$$E_d = \frac{\frac{\Delta Q_d}{Q_{d\ average}}}{\frac{\Delta P}{P_{average}}}$$

For example, the calculation is

$$E_d = \frac{\frac{50}{75}}{\frac{2}{11}} = 3.67$$

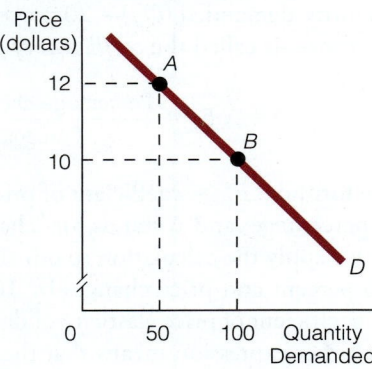

---

between the two points identified on the demand curve. For example, in Exhibit 1, 3.67 is the price elasticity of demand between points A and B on the demand curve.

19-1b Elasticity Is Not Slope

Some people think that slope and price elasticity of demand are the same, but they are not. Suppose we identify a third point on the demand curve in Exhibit 1. The following table shows the price and quantity demanded for our three points.

Point	Price	Quantity Demanded
A	$12	50
B	10	100
C	8	150

To calculate the *price elasticity of demand* between points A and B, we divide the percentage change in quantity demanded (between the two points) by the percentage change in price (between the two points). Using the formula for price elasticity of demand, we get 3.67.

The *slope of the demand curve* between points A and B is the ratio of the change in the variable on the vertical axis to the change in the variable on the horizontal axis. Thus, the slope of the demand curve reflects the *level* of change, not the *percentage* change:

$$\text{Slope} = \frac{\Delta \text{Variable on vertical axis}}{\Delta \text{Variable on horizontal axis}} = \frac{-2}{50} = -0.04$$

Now, let's calculate the price elasticity of demand and the slope between points B and C. The price elasticity of demand is 1.80; the slope is still -0.04.

19-1c From Perfectly Elastic to Perfectly Inelastic Demand

Look back at the equation for the elasticity coefficient and think of it as

$$E_d = \frac{\text{Percentage change in quantity demanded}}{\text{Percentage change in price}} = \frac{\text{Numerator}}{\text{Denominator}}$$

EXHIBIT 2

Price Elasticity of Demand — Demand may be elastic, inelastic, unit elastic, perfectly elastic, or perfectly inelastic.

Elasticity Coefficient	Responsiveness of Quantity Demanded to a Change in Price	Terminology
$E_d > 1$	Quantity demanded changes proportionately more than price changes: $\%\Delta Q_d > \%\Delta P$.	Elastic
$E_d < 1$	Quantity demanded changes proportionately less than price changes: $\%\Delta Q_d < \%\Delta P$.	Inelastic
$E_d = 1$	Quantity demanded changes proportionately to price change: $\%\Delta Q_d = \%\Delta P$.	Unit elastic
$E_d = \infty$	Quantity demanded is extremely responsive to even very small changes in price.	Perfectly elastic
$E_d = 0$	Quantity demanded does not change as price changes.	Perfectly inelastic

Focusing on the numerator and denominator, we realize that the numerator can be (1) greater than, (2) less than, or (3) equal to the denominator. These three cases, along with two peripherally related cases, are discussed in the paragraphs that follow. Exhibits 2 and 3 provide summaries of the discussion.

Elastic Demand ($E_d > 1$) If the numerator (percentage change in quantity demanded) is greater than the denominator (percentage change in price), then the elasticity coefficient is greater than 1, and demand is elastic [see Exhibit 3(a)]:

Percentage change in quantity demanded > Percentage change in price →

$E_d > 1 \rightarrow$ Demand is elastic

Thus, $E_d > 1$ represents **elastic demand**; that is, the quantity demanded changes proportionately more than price changes. A 10 percent increase in price causes, say, a 20 percent reduction in quantity demanded ($E_d = 2$).

Inelastic Demand ($E_d < 1$) If the numerator (percentage change in quantity demanded) is less than the denominator (percentage change in price), then the elasticity coefficient is less than 1, and demand is inelastic [see Exhibit 3(b)]:

Percentage change in quantity demanded < Percentage change in price →

$E_d < 1 \rightarrow$ Demand is inelastic

Thus, $E_d < 1$ represents **inelastic demand**; that is, the quantity demanded changes proportionately less than price changes. A 10 percent increase in price causes, say, a 4 percent reduction in the quantity demanded ($E_d = 0.4$).

Unit Elastic Demand ($E_d = 1$) If the numerator (percentage change in quantity demanded) equals the denominator (percentage change in price), then the elasticity coefficient is 1, and we have unit elasticity of demand [see Exhibit 3(c)]:

Percentage change in quantity demanded = Percentage change in price →

$E_d = 1 \rightarrow$ Demand is unit elastic

Thus, $E_d = 1$ represents **unit elastic demand**; that is, the quantity demanded changes proportionately with price changes. For example, a 10 percent increase in price causes a 10 percent decrease in quantity demanded ($E_d = 1$).

Elastic Demand
The demand that occurs when the percentage change in quantity demanded is greater than the percentage change in price. Quantity demanded changes proportionately more than price changes.

Inelastic Demand
The demand that occurs when the percentage change in quantity demanded is less than the percentage change in price. Quantity demanded changes proportionately less than price changes.

Unit Elastic Demand
The demand that occurs when the percentage change in quantity demanded is equal to the percentage change in price. Quantity demanded changes proportionately to price changes.

EXHIBIT 3

Graphical Representation of Price Elasticity of Demand

(a) The percentage change in quantity demanded is greater than the percentage change in price: $E_d > 1$, and demand is elastic. (b) The percentage change in quantity demanded is less than the percentage change in price: $E_d < 1$, and demand is inelastic. (c) The percentage change in quantity demanded is equal to percentage change in price: $E_d = 1$, and demand is unit elastic. (d) A small change in price reduces quantity demanded to zero: $E_d = \infty$, and demand is perfectly elastic. (e) A change in price does not change quantity demanded: $E_d = 0$, and demand is perfectly inelastic.

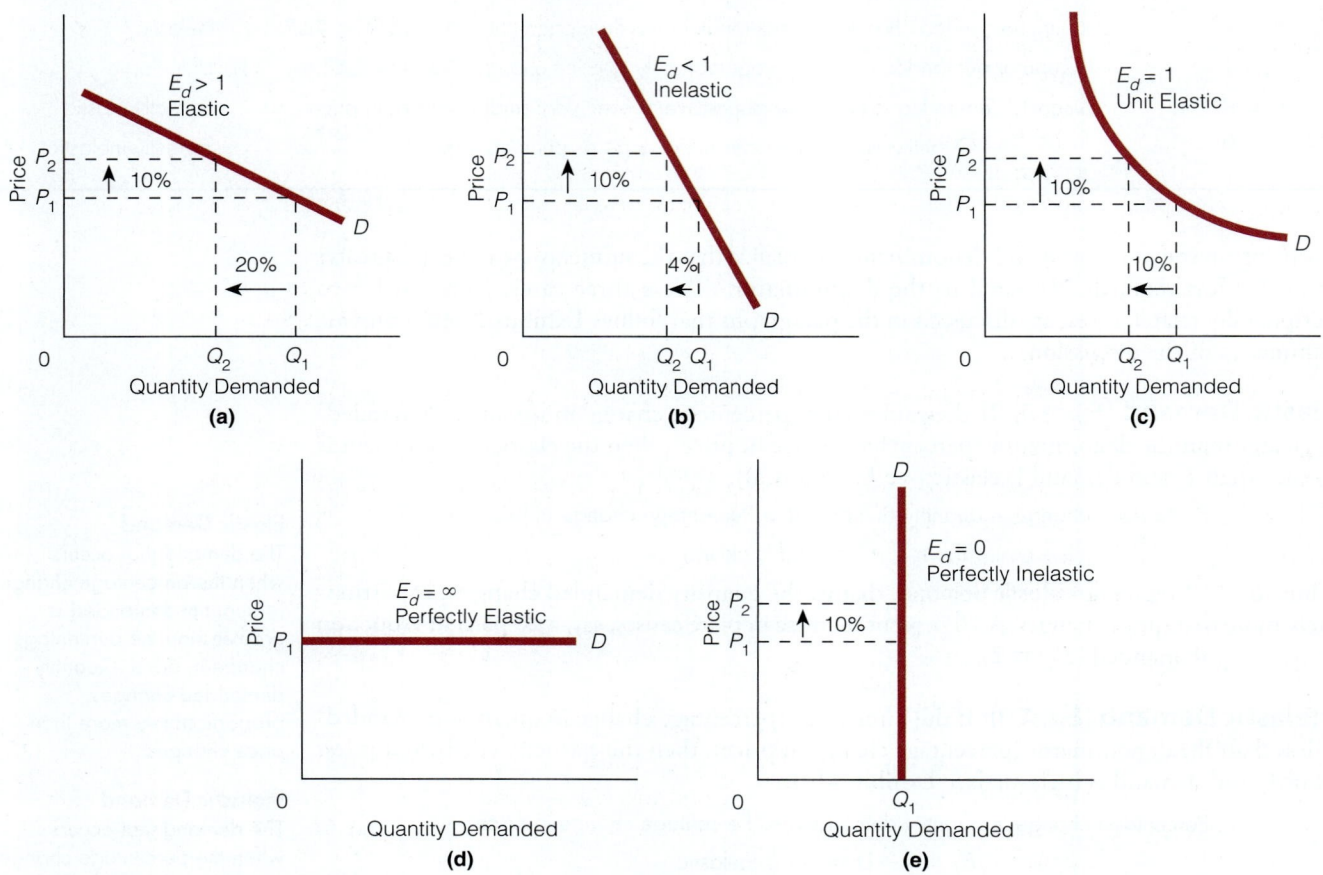

Perfectly Elastic Demand
The demand that exists when a small percentage change in price causes an extremely large percentage change in quantity demanded (from buying all to buying nothing).

Perfectly Inelastic Demand
The demand that exists when quantity demanded does not change as price changes.

Perfectly Elastic Demand ($E_d = \infty$) If quantity demanded is extremely responsive to changes in price, the result is **perfectly elastic demand** [see Exhibit 3(d)]. For example, suppose buyers are willing to buy all units of a seller's good at $5 per unit but nothing at $5.10. In other words, a small percentage change in price causes an extremely large percentage change in quantity demanded (from buying all to buying nothing). The percentage is so large, in fact, that economists say it is infinitely large.

Perfectly Inelastic Demand ($E_d = 0$) If quantity demanded is completely unresponsive to changes in price, the result is **perfectly inelastic demand** [see Exhibit 3(e)]. For example, suppose the price of Dogs Love It dog food rises 10 percent (from $2 to $2.20), and Jeremy doesn't buy any less of it per week for his dog. Then, a change in price causes no change in quantity demanded, and Jeremy's demand for Dogs Love It dog food is perfectly inelastic between a price of $2 and a price of $2.20.

Perfectly Elastic and Perfectly Inelastic Demand Curves Even though you are used to seeing a downward-sloping demand curve, Exhibit 3 shows two demand curves that are not downward sloping. But aren't *all* demand curves supposed to be downward sloping because, according to the law of demand, an inverse relationship exists between price and quantity demanded? In the real world, no demand curve is perfectly elastic (horizontal) or perfectly inelastic (vertical) at all prices. Thus, the perfectly elastic and perfectly inelastic demand curves in Exhibit 3 should be viewed as representations of the extreme limits between which all real-world demand curves fall.

However, a few real-world demand curves do *approximate* the perfectly elastic and inelastic demand curves in Exhibits 3(d) and (e); that is, they come very close. For example, the demand for a particular farmer's wheat approximates the perfectly elastic demand curve in Exhibit 3(d). A later chapter discusses the perfectly elastic demand curve for firms in perfectly competitive markets.

> **Finding Economics**
>
> **At the Local Coffee Bar** Suppose you buy 7 coffees at the local coffee bar each week when the price of a cup of coffee is $2, and you buy 5 coffees a week when the price is $2.50. Where is the economics?
>
> Actually, economics appears in two places. First, the law of demand is visible because you buy *fewer* cups of coffee at the higher price. Second, calculating your price elasticity of coffee between the lower and higher prices is easy. It is 1.5, which means that your demand for coffee is *elastic*.

19-1d Price Elasticity of Demand and Total Revenue (Total Expenditure)

The **total revenue (TR)** of a seller equals the price of a good times the quantity of the good sold.[3] For example, if the hamburger stand down the street sells 100 hamburgers today at $1.50 each, its total revenue is $150.

Suppose the hamburger vendor raises the price of a hamburger to $2. What do you predict will happen to total revenue? Most people, in the widespread belief that higher prices bring higher total revenue, say that total revenue will increase. However, total revenue may increase, decrease, or remain constant. To see how, suppose price rises to $2 but, because of the higher price, the quantity of hamburgers sold falls to 50. Then total revenue is now $100 (whereas it was $150). Whether total revenue rises, falls, or remains constant after a price change depends on whether the percentage change in the quantity demanded is, respectively, less than, greater than, or equal to the percentage change in price. Thus, price elasticity of demand influences total revenue.

Total Revenue (TR)
Price times quantity sold.

---

[3] In this discussion, "total revenue" and "total expenditure" are equivalent terms. *Total revenue* equals price times quantity sold. *Total expenditure* equals price times quantity purchased. If something is sold, it must be purchased, making total revenue equal to total expenditure. The term "total revenue" is used when one is looking at things from the point of view of the sellers in a market. The term "total expenditure" is used when one is looking at things from the point of view of the buyers in a market. Buyers make expenditures; sellers receive revenues.

19-1e Elastic Demand and Total Revenue

If demand is elastic, the percentage change in quantity demanded is greater than the percentage change in price. Given a price rise of, say, 5 percent, the quantity demanded falls by more than 5 percent—say, 8 percent—having an effect on total revenue. Because quantity demanded falls, or sales fall off, by a greater percentage than the percentage rise in price, total revenue decreases. In short, if demand is elastic, a price rise decreases total revenue:

$$\text{Demand is elastic: } P \uparrow \rightarrow TR \downarrow$$

If demand is elastic and price falls, the quantity demanded rises (price and quantity demanded are inversely related) by a greater percentage than the percentage drop in price, causing total revenue to increase. In short, if demand is elastic, a price decline increases total revenue:

$$\text{Demand is elastic: } P \downarrow \rightarrow TR \uparrow$$

Exhibit 4(a) shows the relationship between a change in price and total revenue if demand is elastic. Between points A and B on the demand curve, demand is elastic. At point A, price is P_1 and quantity demanded is Q_1. Total revenue is equal to the rectangle $0P_1AQ_1$. Now, suppose we lower price to P_2. After the price decline, total revenue is now the rectangle $0P_2BQ_2$—which, as you can see, is larger than rectangle $0P_1AQ_1$. In other words, if demand is elastic and price declines, then total revenue will rise.

Of course, when price moves in the opposite direction, rising from P_2 to P_1, then the total-revenue rectangle becomes smaller. In other words, if demand is elastic and price rises, then total revenue will fall.

EXHIBIT 4

Price Elasticity of Demand and Total Revenue

In (a), demand is elastic between points A and B. Thus, a drop in price from P_1 to P_2 will increase the size of the total revenue rectangle from $0P_1AQ_1$ to $0P_2BQ_2$. A rise in price from P_2 to P_1 will decrease the size of the total revenue rectangle from $0P_2BQ_2$ to $0P_1AQ_1$. In other words, when demand is elastic, price and total revenue are inversely related. In (b), demand is inelastic between points A and B. Therefore, a drop in price from P_1 to P_2 will decrease the size of the total revenue rectangle from $0P_1AQ_1$ to $0P_2BQ_2$. A rise in price from P_2 to P_1 will increase the size of the total revenue rectangle from $0P_2BQ_2$ to $0P_1AQ_1$. In other words, when demand is inelastic, price and total revenue are directly related.

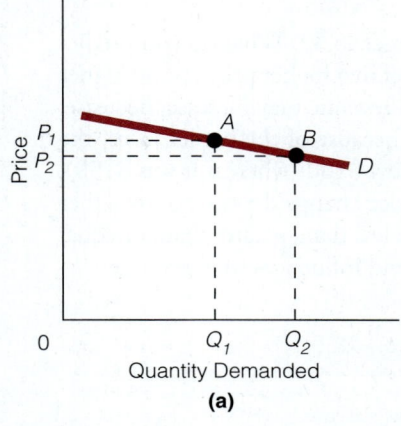
(a)

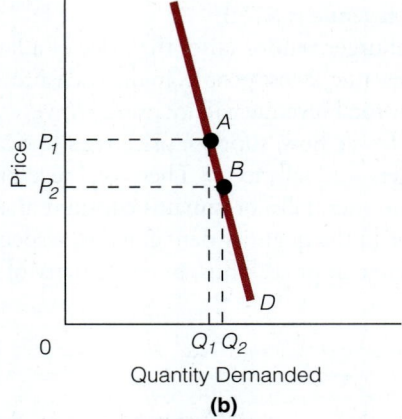
(b)

Economics 24/7

Drug Busts and Crime

Most people agree that the sale or possession of drugs such as cocaine and heroin should be illegal, but sometimes laws may have unintended effects. Do drug laws have unintended effects? Let's analyze the enforcement of drug laws in terms of supply, demand, and price elasticity of demand.

Suppose that, for every $100 of illegal drug sales, 60 percent of the $100 paid is obtained by illegal means. That is, buyers of $100 worth of illegal drugs obtain $60 of the purchase price from criminal activities such as burglaries, muggings, and similar illegal acts.

In Exhibit 5, the demand for and supply of cocaine in a particular city are represented by D_1 and S_1, respectively. The equilibrium price of $50 an ounce and the equilibrium quantity of 1,000 ounces give cocaine dealers a total revenue of $50,000. If 60 percent of this total revenue is obtained by the criminal activities of cocaine buyers, then $30,000 worth of crime has been committed to purchase the $50,000 worth of cocaine.

Now, suppose that a drug bust in the city reduces the supply of cocaine. Then, the supply curve shifts leftward from S_1 to S_2, the equilibrium price rises to $120 an ounce, and the equilibrium quantity falls to 600 ounces. The demand for cocaine is inelastic between the two prices, at 0.607. When demand is inelastic, an increase in price will raise total revenue, so the total revenue

received by cocaine dealers is now $72,000. If we again assume that 60 percent of the total revenue paid comes from criminal activity, then $43,200 worth of crime has been committed to purchase the $72,000 worth of cocaine.

Therefore, if the demand for cocaine is inelastic and people commit crimes to buy drugs, then a drug bust can actually increase the amount of drug-related crime. Obviously, this is an unintended effect of the enforcement of drug laws.

EXHIBIT 5

Drug Busts and Drug-Related Crime

In the exhibit, P = price of cocaine, Q = quantity of cocaine, and TR = total revenue from selling cocaine. At a price of $50 for an ounce of cocaine, the equilibrium quantity is 1,000 ounces, and total revenue is $50,000. If $60 of every $100 cocaine purchase is obtained through crime, then $30,000 worth of crime is committed to purchase $50,000 worth of cocaine. As a result of a drug bust, the supply of cocaine shifts leftward; the price rises and the quantity falls. Because we have assumed that the demand for cocaine is inelastic, total revenue rises to $72,000. As the accompanying table shows, 60 percent of this dollar amount, or $43,200, comes from criminal activities.

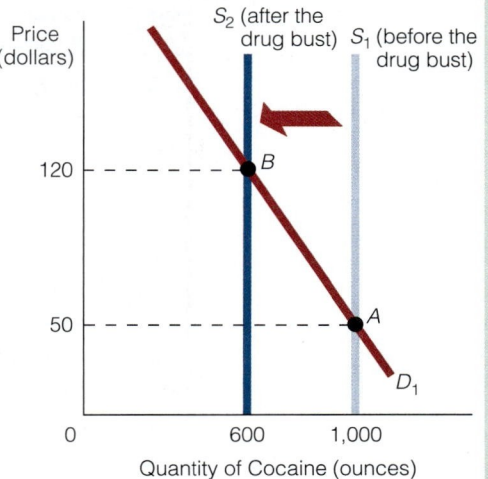

	P	Q	TR	Dollar Amount of TR Obtained Through Crime
Before Drug Bust	$50	1,000	$50,000	$30,000
After Drug Bust	120	600	72,000	43,200

Inelastic Demand and Total Revenue If demand is inelastic, the percentage change in quantity demanded is less than the percentage change in price. That is, if price rises, then quantity demanded falls, but by a smaller percentage than the percentage rise in price. As a result, total revenue increases. So, if demand is inelastic, a price rise increases total revenue. However, if price falls, then quantity demanded rises by a smaller percentage than the percentage fall in price, and total revenue decreases. In other words, if demand is inelastic, then a price decline decreases total revenue. In sum, price and total revenue are directly related:

$$\text{Demand is inelastic: } P \uparrow \rightarrow TR \uparrow$$

$$\text{Demand is inelastic: } P \downarrow \rightarrow TR \downarrow$$

You can see the relationship between inelastic demand and total revenue in Exhibit 4(b), where demand is inelastic between points A and B on the demand curve. If we start at P_1 and lower price to P_2, then the total-revenue rectangle goes from $0P_1AQ_1$ to the smaller rectangle $0P_2BQ_2$. In other words, if demand is inelastic and price falls, then total revenue will fall.

Moving from the lower price, P_2, to the higher price, P_1, does just the opposite: If demand is inelastic and price rises, then the total revenue rectangle becomes larger; that is, total revenue rises.

Unit Elastic Demand and Total Revenue If demand is unit elastic, the percentage change in quantity demanded equals the percentage change in price. That is, if price rises, then quantity demanded falls by the same percentage as the percentage rise in price. Total revenue does not change. If price falls, then quantity demanded rises by the same percentage as the percentage drop in price. Again, total revenue does not change. If demand is unit elastic, a rise or fall in price leaves total revenue unchanged. (For a review of the relationship between price elasticity of demand and total revenue, see Exhibit 6.)

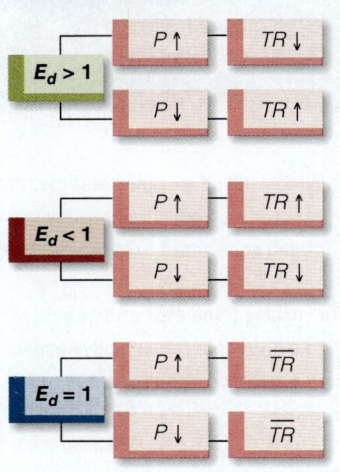

EXHIBIT 6

Elasticities, Price Changes, and Total Revenue

If demand is elastic, a price rise leads to a decrease in total revenue (TR), and a price decline leads to an increase in total revenue. If demand is inelastic, a price rise leads to an increase in total revenue, and a price decline leads to a decrease in total revenue. If demand is unit elastic, a rise or fall in price does not change total revenue.

Finding Economics

In an Earthquake Suppose an earthquake in Los Angeles destroys 10 percent of the apartment stock. Where is the economics?

As a result of the earthquake, we can expect the average rent for an apartment in the city to rise. Some people go further and argue that, because of the earthquake, landlords will take in more total revenue than they did before the earthquake, but that is not necessarily true. To see why, suppose the rent before the earthquake is $2,000, and 100,000 apartments are rented. Then the monthly total revenue is $200 million. Now, suppose the earthquake reduces the number of apartments to 90,000. Then, as a result of a lower supply of apartments, the average rent rises to, say, $2,100 a month. At this higher rent per month, the monthly total revenue from apartments is $189 million. Total revenue is lower because the demand for apartments between the lower rent and the higher rent is elastic. If demand is elastic and price rises, then total revenue falls.

Economics 24/7

Elasticity and the Issue of "How Much"

Elasticity is a measurement of how much one thing changes given how much something else changes. Price elasticity of demand is the percentage change in quantity demanded given some percentage change in price. Income elasticity of demand is the percentage change in the quantity demanded of a good given some percentage change in income. Price elasticity of supply is the percentage change in the quantity supplied of a good given some percentage change in price.

Elasticity—of demand, income, or supply, or even some other type of elasticity—is often the right concept to consider in discussing various topics. Let's illustrate. Suppose someone says, "If we raise income tax rates, people will work much less. After all, who will work as much when she has to pay 60 cents out of every dollar earned as when she has to pay 30 cents out of every dollar earned? Well, it could be true that higher income tax rates will dampen the incentive to earn income through work, but *how much* it dampens the incentive to work depends on an elasticity concept—specifically, how much work declines as taxes rise. For example, if tax rates rise by 10 percent, do people end up working 10 percent less, more than 10 percent less, or less than 10 percent less. And might the answer depend upon whether we're raising, say, the highest marginal tax rate from 30 percent to 33 percent or from 20 percent to 22 percent?

Or consider someone who argues that if the minimum wage rate is raised by, say, $2, then the number of people hired (at the new, higher) minimum wage will fall. If the demand for labor is downward sloping, then certainly, fewer people will be hired at a higher than a lower wage, but *what percentage fewer* will be hired depends upon an elasticity concept. In other words, as wage rate rises by, say, 5 percent, what is the percentage decline in the quantity demanded of labor—more than 5 percent, less than 5 percent, or exactly 5 percent?

Or, finally, suppose someone says that, if we tax cigarettes at a higher rate than we do now, teenagers are less likely to start smoking or to continue smoking, and therefore, the higher tax will end up saving a generation from starting and developing the habit of cigarette smoking. No doubt, a tax on cigarettes will make cigarettes more expensive to purchase, likely leading to a cutback in the purchases of cigarettes. But *how much* of a cutback will there be? Will there be a large cutback (because the demand for cigarettes is highly elastic), a small cutback (because the demand for cigarettes is highly inelastic), or no cutback at all (because the demand for cigarettes is perfectly inelastic)?

As you can tell from our examples, the concept of elasticity is relevant to the question of how much or what percentage something will change as a result of something else changing. And sometimes, knowing the answer to that question is extremely important to the issue at hand. For example, if higher taxes on cigarettes really don't reduce cigarette consumption very much, then perhaps there is a better way than taxes to reduce the consumption of cigarettes among the young, should that be the objective.

Economics 24/7

When Is a Half-Packed Auditorium Better Than a Packed One?

Suppose you are the manager of a famous rock group that will soon go on a tour of 30 U.S. cities. In each of the 30 cities, the group will play in an auditorium. Let's say the auditorium in St. Louis, Missouri, seats 20,000 people. Is it better to sell all 20,000 tickets for the rock group's performance or to sell less than 20,000 tickets—maybe 10,000 tickets?

Most people will say that it is better to sell 20,000 tickets than 10,000 tickets. But is it necessarily better? To sell 20,000 tickets, the price per ticket will have to be lower than the price per ticket to sell 10,000 tickets. For example, suppose that to sell all 20,000 tickets, the ticket price must be $50. In that case, the total revenue will be $1 million. However, suppose that at $120 per ticket, 10,000 tickets (and no more) can be sold. In that case, the total revenue will be $1.2 million. In other words, a $50 ticket price fills the auditorium to capacity and generates $1 million. A $120 ticket price fills only half the auditorium but generates $1.2 million.

Of course, our analysis here implicitly assumes that only one ticket price, either $50 or $120, can be charged. If more than one price can be charged, then the 10,000 good seats in the auditorium might be sold for $120 each and the remaining 10,000 not-so-good seats might be sold for $50 each. The total revenue would be $1.7 million. In short, if only one price can be charged, then a half-packed auditorium may, under certain conditions, generate more revenue than a packed auditorium. But if two prices can be charged, then a packed auditorium is preferable to a half-packed auditorium. In fact, charging a higher price for good seats and a lower price for not-so-good seats actually happens at rock concerts, plays, basketball games, and more. Now we know why.

(Answers to Self-Test questions are in Answers to Self-Test Questions at the back of the book.)

1. On Tuesday, the price and quantity demanded are $7 and 120 units, respectively. Ten days later, the price and quantity demanded are $6 and 150 units, respectively. What is the price elasticity of demand between the $7 and $6 prices?

2. What does a price elasticity of demand of 0.39 mean?

3. Identify what happens to total revenue as a result of each of the following:

    a. Price rises and demand is elastic.
    b. Price falls and demand is inelastic.
    c. Price rises and demand is unit elastic.
    d. Price rises and demand is inelastic.
    e. Price falls and demand is elastic.

4. Alexi says, "When a seller raises his price, his total revenue rises." What is Alexi implicitly assuming?

19-2 Elasticity: Part 2

This section discusses the elasticity ranges of a straight-line downward-sloping demand curve and the determinants of price elasticity of demand.

19-2a Price Elasticity of Demand Along a Straight-Line Demand Curve

The price elasticity of demand for a straight-line downward-sloping demand curve varies from highly elastic to highly inelastic. Consider the price elasticity of demand at the upper range of the demand curve in Exhibit 7(a). Whether the price falls from $9 to $8 or rises from $8 to $9, using the formula for price elasticity of demand, we calculate the price elasticity of demand as 5.66.[4]

Now, consider the price elasticity of demand at the lower range of the demand curve in Exhibit 7(a). Whether the price falls from $3 to $2 or rises from $2 to $3, we calculate the price elasticity of demand as 0.33.

In other words, along the range of the demand curve identified, price elasticity goes from being greater than 1 (5.66) to being less than 1 (0.33). Obviously, on its way from being greater than 1 to being less than 1, price elasticity of demand must be equal to 1 somewhere on the curve. In Exhibit 7(a), we have identified the price elasticity of demand as equal to 1 at the *midpoint* of the demand curve.[5]

The elastic and inelastic ranges along the straight-line downward-sloping demand curve can be related to a total revenue curve [see Exhibit 7(b)]. If we start in the elastic range of the demand curve in Exhibit 7(a) and lower price, then total revenue rises, as shown in Exhibit 7(b). That is, as price is coming down within the elastic range of the demand curve in part (a), total revenue is rising in part (b).

When price has fallen enough that we move into the inelastic range of the demand curve in part (a), further price declines simply lower total revenue, as shown in part (b). Therefore, total revenue is at its highest—its peak—when price elasticity of demand equals 1.

EXHIBIT 7

Price Elasticity of Demand Along a Straight-Line Demand Curve

In (a), the price elasticity of demand varies along the straight-line downward-sloping demand curve. The curve has an elastic range (where $E_d > 1$) and an inelastic range (where $E_d < 1$). At the midpoint of any straight-line downward-sloping demand curve, price elasticity of demand is equal to 1 ($E_d = 1$).

Part (b) shows that, in the elastic range of the demand curve, total revenue rises as price is lowered. In the inelastic range of the demand curve, further price declines result in declining total revenue. Total revenue reaches its peak when price elasticity of demand equals 1.

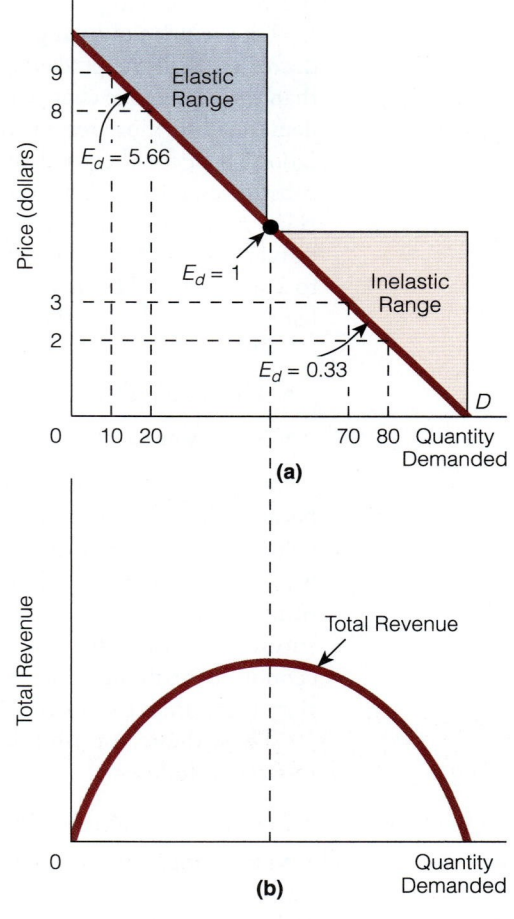

[4.] Keep in mind that our formula uses the average of the two prices and the average of the two quantities demanded. You may want to look back at the formula to refresh your memory.

[5.] For any straight-line downward-sloping demand curve, price elasticity of demand equals 1 at the midpoint of the curve.

19-2b Determinants of Price Elasticity of Demand

Four factors are relevant to the determination of price elasticity of demand:

1. Number of substitutes
2. Necessities versus luxuries
3. Percentage of one's budget spent on the good
4. Time

Because all four factors interact, we hold all other things constant as we discuss each factor.

Number of Substitutes Suppose good A has 2 substitutes and good B has 15 substitutes. Assume that each of the 2 substitutes for good A is as good a substitute (or a good enough substitute) for that good as each of the 15 substitutes is for good B.

Let the price of each good rise by 10 percent. Then, the quantity demanded of each good decreases. Will the percentage change in the quantity demanded of good A be greater or less than the percentage change in quantity demanded of good B? In other words, will the quantity demanded be more responsive to the 10 percent price rise for the good that has 2 substitutes (good A) or for the good that has 15 substitutes (good B)? The answer is the good with 15 substitutes, good B. The reason is that the greater the opportunities are for substitution (good B has more substitutes than good A has), the greater the cutback in the quantity of the good purchased will be as its price rises. When the price of good A rises 10 percent, people can turn to 2 substitutes. The quantity demanded of good A falls, but not by as much as if 15 substitutes had been available, as there are for good B.

The relationship between the availability of substitutes and price elasticity is clear:

- The more substitutes a good has, the higher the price elasticity of demand will be.
- The fewer substitutes a good has, the lower the price elasticity of demand will be.

For example, the price elasticity of demand for Chevrolets is higher than that for all cars because there are more substitutes for Chevrolets than there are for cars. To understand this relationship, note that everything that is a substitute for a car (taking a bus, getting on a train, walking, bicycling, etc.) is also a substitute for a specific type of car, such as a Chevrolet, but some substitutes for a Chevrolet (Ford, Toyota, Chrysler, Mercedes-Benz, etc.) are not substitutes for a car. They are simply types of cars. Similarly, there are more substitutes for this economics textbook than there are for textbooks, and there are more substitutes for Coca-Cola than there are for soft drinks.

Thus, the relationship between the availability of substitutes and price elasticity can be restated as follows:

- The more broadly defined the good, the fewer substitutes it will have.
- The more narrowly defined the good, the more substitutes it will have.

Necessities Versus Luxuries Generally, the more that a good is considered a luxury (a good that we can do without) rather than a necessity (a good that we cannot do without), the higher the price elasticity of demand will be. For example, consider two goods: jewelry and a medicine for controlling high blood pressure. If the price of jewelry rises, cutting back on purchases is easy: No one really needs jewelry to live. However, if the price of the medicine for controlling one's high blood pressure rises, cutting back is not so easy. We expect the price elasticity of demand for jewelry to be higher than that for high blood pressure medicine.

Percentage of One's Budget Spent on the Good Julieta has a monthly budget of $3,000. Of this monthly budget, she spends $3 per month on pens and $400 per month on dinners at restaurants. In terms of percentages, she spends 0.1 percent of her monthly budget on pens and 13 percent of her monthly budget on dinners at restaurants. Suppose both the price of pens and the price of dinners at restaurants double. Julieta is likely to be more responsive to the change in the price of restaurant dinners than to the change in the price of pens. She feels the pinch of a doubling in the price of a good on which she spends 0.1 percent of her budget a lot less than a doubling in price of a good on which she spends 13 percent. So Julieta is more likely to ignore the increased price of pens than she is to ignore the heightened price of restaurant dinners. Julieta's behavior illustrates the idea that buyers are (and thus the quantity demanded is) more responsive to price as the percentage of their budget that goes for the purchase of the good increases. In general,

- The greater the percentage of one's budget that goes to purchase a good, the higher the price elasticity of demand will be.
- The smaller the percentage of one's budget that goes to purchase a good, the lower the price elasticity of demand will be.

Time As time passes, buyers have greater opportunities to be responsive to a price change. For example, if the price of electricity went up today and you knew about it, you probably would not change your consumption of electricity today as much as you would three months from today. As time passes, you have more chances to change your consumption by finding substitutes (natural gas), changing your lifestyle (buying more blankets and turning down the thermostat at night), and so on. Thus,

- The more time that passes (since the price change), the higher the price elasticity of demand for the good will be.
- The less time that passes, the lower the price elasticity of demand for the good will be.

In other words, the price elasticity of demand for a good is higher in the long run than in the short run.

Economics 24/7

Tuition Hikes at the College or University

Suppose you are the seller of some good. You have many customers who buy your good, and each customer has his or her own demand for your good. Let's suppose that some of your customers currently have elastic demand for your good, others inelastic demand, and still others unit elastic demand. What does this then mean for you? It means that if you raise the price of your good, everyone will cut back on buying your good, but some will cut back by a larger percentage than the percentage increase in price (these are the ones who have elastic demand), others will cut back by a smaller percentage than the percentage increase in price (there are the ones who have inelastic demand), and still others will cut back by the same percentage as the percentage increase in price (these are the ones with unit elastic demand). In other words, your customers will all cut back on buying your good if you raise your price, but not everyone will cut back by the same percentage.

(Continued)

Now, is a price increase a good idea? Well, for those customers who have inelastic demand, a price increase will result in greater total revenue for you. For those customers who have elastic demand, a price increase will result in lower total revenue for you. And for those customers who have unit elastic demand, a price increase will result in the same revenue for you. In all, for two of the three groups (the inelastic and unit elastic demand groups), a price increase either helps you or leaves you the same. But for the one of the three groups, the elastic demand group, a price increase lowers your total revenue.

What to do? Ideally, what you might want to do is raise the price to the inelastic demand group (and possibly the unit elastic demand group too), but leave the price unchanged for the elastic demand group. In other words, charge two groups the higher price, but leave the price unchanged for the other group.

But often this is hard to do because you post a single price to everyone. Think of this in terms of a restaurant owner. On the menu, a shrimp dinner has one price, not one price for people with inelastic demand and another price for people with elastic demand.

Now, one way to get around being locked into one price is to post one but not actually charge one price. In other words, tell everyone the price is being raised from, say, $15 to $20, but then give some people a discount on price depending on their elasticity of demand for the good.

One institution that often does this is the college or university. The college or university raises tuition, but then gives some students a "discount" in the form of more financial aid. (Both universities and the federal government can and do give financial aid. The university can then raise tuition for some and not for others by "increasing" the tuition for all, knowing full well that students receiving financial aid may have their financial aid package increased by the federal government.) The students it gives a discount to in the form of more financial aid tend to be students whose income (or parent's income) makes paying for education a larger percentage of their budget than others. Recall from our earlier discussion *that the larger the percentage of one's budget spent on a good, the higher the price elasticity of demand will be*. In other words, the college or university figures out a way to raise the tuition for those whose demand for the education being sold is likely to be inelastic and keep it the same (or nearly the same) for those whose demand for the education is likely to be elastic. Financial aid has a lot more to do with total revenue and price elasticity of demand than you may have originally thought.

1. If good *X* has 7 substitutes and demand is inelastic, then if there are 9 substitutes for good *X*, will demand be elastic? Explain your answer.

2. Price elasticity of demand is predicted to be higher for which good of the following combinations of goods?
   a. Dell computers or computers
   b. Heinz ketchup or ketchup
   c. Perrier water or water

   Explain your answer.

19-3 Other Elasticity Concepts

This section looks at three other elasticities:

- Cross elasticity of demand
- Income elasticity of demand
- Price elasticity of supply

19-3a Cross Elasticity of Demand

Cross elasticity of demand measures the responsiveness in the quantity demanded of one good to changes in the price of another good. It is calculated by dividing the percentage change in the quantity demanded of one good by the percentage change in the price of another. That is,

$$E_c = \frac{\text{Percentage change in quantity demanded of one good}}{\text{Percentage change in price of another good}}$$

Cross Elasticity of Demand
A measure of the responsiveness in quantity demanded of one good to changes in the price of another good.

where E_c stands for the coefficient of cross elasticity of demand, or the elasticity coefficient.

This concept is often used to determine whether two goods are substitutes for or complements to each other and the degree to which one good is a substitute for or a complement to the other. Consider, for example, Skippy peanut butter and Jif peanut butter. Suppose that when the price of Jif increases by 10 percent, the quantity demanded of Skippy increases by 45 percent. Then, the cross elasticity of demand for Skippy with respect to the price of Jif is

$$E_c = \frac{\text{Percentage change in quantity demanded of Skippy}}{\text{Percentage change in price of Jif}}$$

$$E_c = \frac{45}{10} = 4.5$$

In this case, the cross elasticity of demand is a positive 4.5. When the cross elasticity of demand is positive, the percentage change in the quantity demanded of one good (the good mentioned in the numerator) moves in the same direction as the percentage change in the price of the other good (the good mentioned in the denominator). A positive cross elasticity of demand is a characteristic of goods that are substitutes. As the price of Jif rises, the demand curve for Skippy shifts rightward, causing the quantity demanded of Skippy to increase at every price. So, if $E_c > 0$, the two goods are substitutes:

$$E_c > 0 \rightarrow \text{Goods are substitutes}$$

If the elasticity coefficient is negative ($E_c < 0$), then the two goods are complements:

$$E_c < 0 \rightarrow \text{Goods are complements}$$

A negative cross elasticity of demand occurs when the percentage change in the quantity demanded of one good (the good mentioned in the numerator) and the percentage change in the price of another good (the good mentioned in the denominator) move in opposite directions. For example, suppose the price of cars increases by 5 percent and the quantity demanded of car tires decreases by 10 percent. Calculating the cross elasticity of demand, we have -10 percent $\div 5$ percent $= -2$. Thus, cars and car tires are complements.

The concept of cross elasticity of demand can be very useful. For instance, a company that sells cheese might ask what goods are substitutes for cheese. The answer would help the company identify its competitors. The company could identify substitutes for cheese by calculating the cross elasticity of demand between cheese and other goods. A positive cross elasticity of demand would indicate that the two goods were substitutes, and the higher the cross elasticity of demand is, the greater the degree of substitution will be.

19-3b Income Elasticity of Demand

Income elasticity of demand measures the responsiveness of quantity demanded to changes in income. It is calculated by dividing the percentage change in quantity demanded of a good by the percentage change in income. That is,

$$E_y = \frac{\text{Percentage change in quantity demanded}}{\text{Percentage change in income}}$$

where E_y denotes the coefficient of income elasticity of demand, or the elasticity coefficient.

Income elasticity of demand is positive ($E_y > 0$) for a *normal good*. Recall that a normal good is a good whose demand, and thus whose quantity demanded, increases, given an increase in income. Hence, for a normal good, the variables in the numerator and denominator in the formula for the income elasticity of demand move in the same direction:

$$E_y > 0 \rightarrow \text{Normal good}$$

In contrast to a normal good, the demand for an *inferior good* decreases as income increases. Income elasticity of demand for an inferior good is negative ($E_y < 0$):

$$E_y < 0 \rightarrow \text{Inferior good}$$

We calculate the income elasticity of demand for a good by using the same approach we used to calculate price elasticity of demand, namely,

$$E_y = \frac{\frac{\Delta Q_d}{Q_{d\ average}}}{\frac{\Delta Y}{Y_{average}}}$$

where $Q_{d\ average}$ is the average quantity demanded of the good and $Y_{average}$ is the purchaser's average income.

Now, suppose a person's income increases from $500 to $600 per month and, as a result, the quantity demanded of good X increases from 20 units to 30 units per month. Then we have income elasticity of 2.2, as shown here:

$$E_y = \frac{\frac{10}{25}}{\frac{100}{550}} = 2.2$$

Since E_y is a positive number, good X is a normal good. Also,

- Because $E_y > 1$, demand for good X is said to be **income elastic**. In other words, the percentage change in quantity demanded of the good is greater than the percentage change in the purchaser's income.
- If $E_y < 1$, the demand for the good is said to be **income inelastic**.
- If $E_y = 1$, then the demand for the good is **income unit elastic**.

Income Elasticity of Demand
A measure of the responsiveness of quantity demanded to changes in income.

Income Elastic
The condition that exists when the percentage change in quantity demanded of a good is greater than the percentage change in income.

Income Inelastic
The condition that exists when the percentage change in quantity demanded of a good is less than the percentage change in income.

Income Unit Elastic
The condition that exists when the percentage change in quantity demanded of a good is equal to the percentage change in income.

19-3c Price Elasticity of Supply

Price elasticity of supply measures the responsiveness of quantity supplied to changes in price. It is calculated by dividing the percentage change in the quantity supplied of a good by the percentage change in the price of the good. Mathematically,

$$E_s = \frac{\text{Percentage change in quantity supplied}}{\text{Percentage change in price}}$$

where E_s stands for the coefficient of price elasticity of supply, or the elasticity coefficient. We use the same approach to calculate the price elasticity of supply that we used to calculate the price elasticity of demand.

In addition, supply can be classified as elastic, inelastic, unit elastic, perfectly elastic, or perfectly inelastic:

- Elastic supply ($E_s > 1$) refers to a percentage change in quantity supplied that is greater than the percentage change in price of the good [see Exhibit 8(a)]:

  Percentage change in quantity supplied > Percentage change in price →

  $E_s > 1 \rightarrow$ Elastic supply

- Inelastic supply ($E_s < 1$) refers to a percentage change in quantity supplied that is less than the percentage change in price of the good [see Exhibit 8(b)]:

  Percentage change in quantity supplied < Percentage change in price →

  $E_s < 1 \rightarrow$ Inelastic supply

- Unit elastic supply ($E_s = 1$) refers to a percentage change in quantity supplied that is equal to the percentage change in price of the good [see Exhibit 8(c)]:

  Percentage change in quantity supplied = Percentage change in price →

  $E_s = 1 \rightarrow$ Unit elastic supply

- In the case of perfectly elastic supply ($E_s = \infty$), a small change in price changes the quantity supplied by an infinitely large amount (and, thus, the supply curve, or a portion of the overall supply curve, is horizontal) [see Exhibit 8(d)].

- In the case of perfectly inelastic supply ($E_s = 0$), a change in price brings no change in quantity supplied (and, thus, the supply curve, or a portion of the overall supply curve, is vertical) [see Exhibit 8(e)].

(See Exhibit 9 for a summary of concepts related to elasticity.)

> **Price Elasticity of Supply**
> A measure of the responsiveness of quantity supplied to changes in price.

19-3d Price Elasticity of Supply and Time

For goods whose quantity supplied can increase with time—a characteristic of most goods (but not, e.g., original Picasso paintings)—the longer the period of adjustment is to a change in price, the higher the price elasticity of supply will be. The obvious reason is that additional production takes time or may be impossible.

For instance, suppose that the demand for new housing increases in your city and that the increase occurs all at once on Tuesday, placing upward pressure on the price of housing. Then the number of houses supplied will not be much different on Saturday than it was on Tuesday.

EXHIBIT 8

Price Elasticity of Supply

(a) The percentage change in quantity supplied is greater than the percentage change in price: $E_s > 1$, and supply is elastic. (b) The percentage change in quantity supplied is less than the percentage change in price: $E_s < 1$, and supply is inelastic. (c) The percentage change in quantity supplied is equal to the percentage change in price: $E_s = 1$, and supply is unit elastic. (d) A small change in price changes quantity supplied by an infinite amount: $E_s = \infty$, and supply is perfectly elastic. (e) A change in price does not change quantity supplied: $E_s = 0$, and supply is perfectly inelastic.

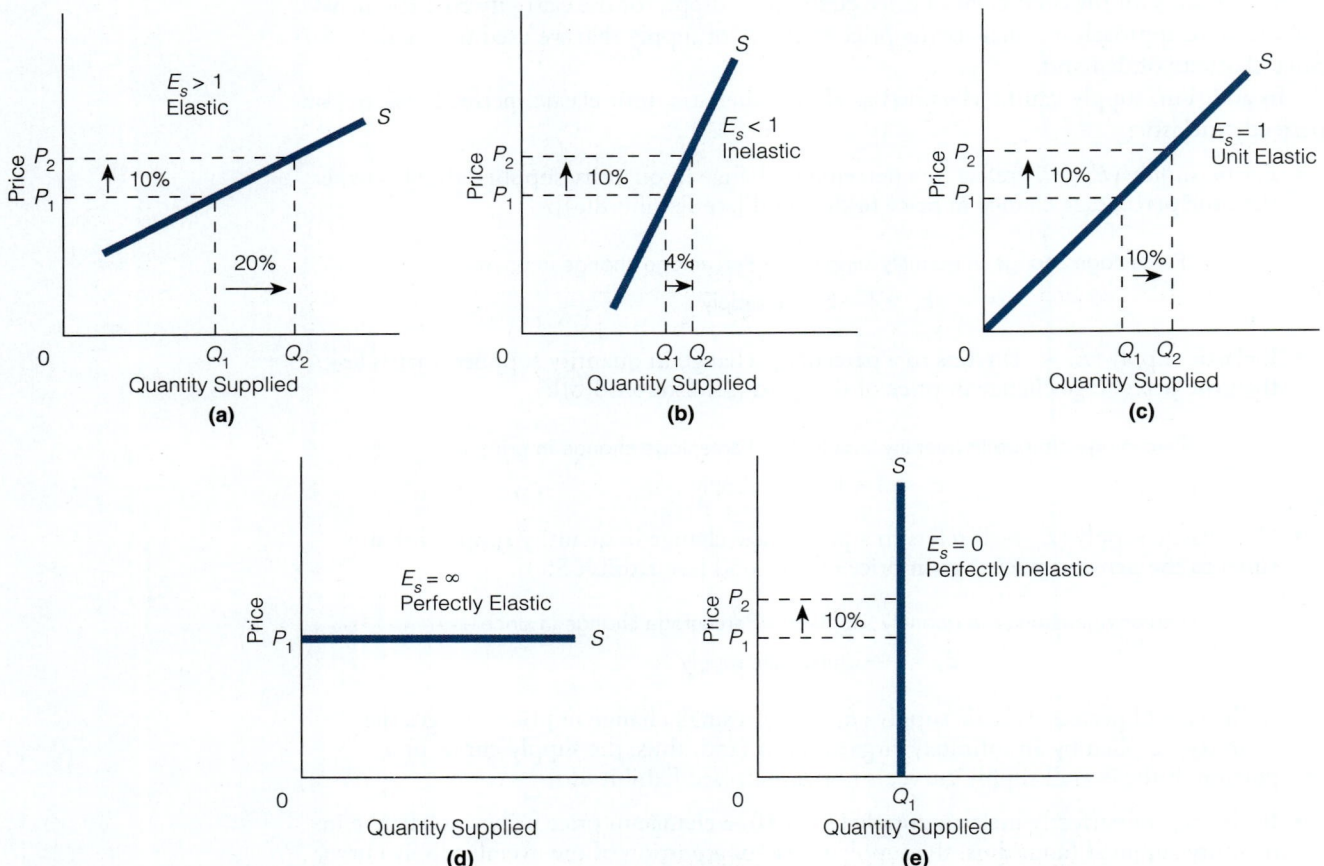

It will take time for suppliers to determine whether the increase in demand is permanent. If they decide that it is temporary, not much will change. If, however, they decide that the increase in demand is permanent, they need time to move resources from the production of other things into the production of new housing. Simply put, the change in quantity supplied of housing is likely to be different in the long run than in the short run, given a change in price. This effect translates into a higher price elasticity of supply in the long run than in the short run.

EXHIBIT 9

Summary of the Four Elasticity Concepts

Type	Calculation	Possibilities	Terminology
Price elasticity of demand	$\dfrac{\text{Percentage change in quantity demanded}}{\text{Percentage change in price}}$	$E_d > 1$	Elastic
		$E_d < 1$	Inelastic
		$E_d = 1$	Unit elastic
		$E_d = \infty$	Perfectly elastic
		$E_d = 0$	Perfectly inelastic
Cross elasticity of demand	$\dfrac{\text{Percentage change in quantity demanded of one good}}{\text{Percentage change in price of another good}}$	$E_c < 0$	Complements
		$E_c > 0$	Substitutes
Income elasticity of demand	$\dfrac{\text{Percentage change in quantity demanded}}{\text{Percentage change in income}}$	$E_y > 0$	Normal good
		$E_y < 0$	Inferior good
		$E_y > 1$	Income elastic
		$E_y < 1$	Income inelastic
		$E_y = 1$	Income unit elastic
Price elasticity of supply	$\dfrac{\text{Percentage change in quantity supplied}}{\text{Percentage change in price}}$	$E_s > 1$	Elastic
		$E_s < 1$	Inelastic
		$E_s = 1$	Unit elastic
		$E_s = \infty$	Perfectly elastic
		$E_s = 0$	Perfectly inelastic

Economics 24/7

House Prices and the Elasticity of Supply

House prices increased in the United States during the years 1998 through mid-2006. House prices did not rise by the same percentage in all cities and states, however. For example, house prices increased more in Los Angeles than in Houston. House prices increased more in Florida than in Idaho. Why didn't house prices rise by the same percentage in every location? Why did they rise more in some places than in others?

One reason could be that demand didn't increase by the same amount in all locations. The demand for houses in, say, San Francisco could have risen by more than the demand for houses in Topeka, Kansas. No doubt, this differential increase in demand is part of the explanation.

But another part of the explanation has to do with supply. As the price of a good rises, we expect the quantity supplied of the good to rise too. In other words, the supply curve of the good is upward sloping. But, although the supply curve of housing is upward sloping, not all supply curves have the same elasticity of supply.

For example, Exhibit 10 shows two supply curves, S_1 and S_2. S_1 has lower elasticity of supply than S_2. Now, suppose that

(Continued)

S_1 represents the supply curve of housing in city 1 and that S_2 represents the supply curve of housing in city 2. Suppose also that the demand for housing in each city rises from D_1 to D_2, as in Exhibit 10. As a result, the price of houses rises in both cities, but it rises by more in city 1 than in city 2. In other words, the lower the elasticity of supply is, the greater the increase in price will be.

But why would the elasticity of supply be lower for housing in city 1 than in city 2? The answer could have to do with land use regulations. Suppose that each city has 1,000 vacant areas and that house developers are able to put houses up on only 10 percent of vacant land in city 1 but 70 percent of vacant land in city 2. Then, for a given rise in price, the developers in city 2 can put up more houses (of a given size of house and plot) than developers in city 1 can put up. As a result, if the demand for houses rises by the same amount in city 1 and city 2, more houses will be built in city 2 than in city 1, so the price of houses will rise by less in city 2 than in city 1.

EXHIBIT 10

House Prices and Elasticity of Supply

S_1 represents the supply of housing in city 1, and S_2 represents the supply of housing in city 2. S_1 has lower elasticity of supply than S_2. Suppose the demand for housing in each city rises from D_1 to D_2. As a result, the price of houses rises in both cities but it rises by more in city 1 than city 2. In other words, the lower the elasticity of supply, the greater is the increase in price.

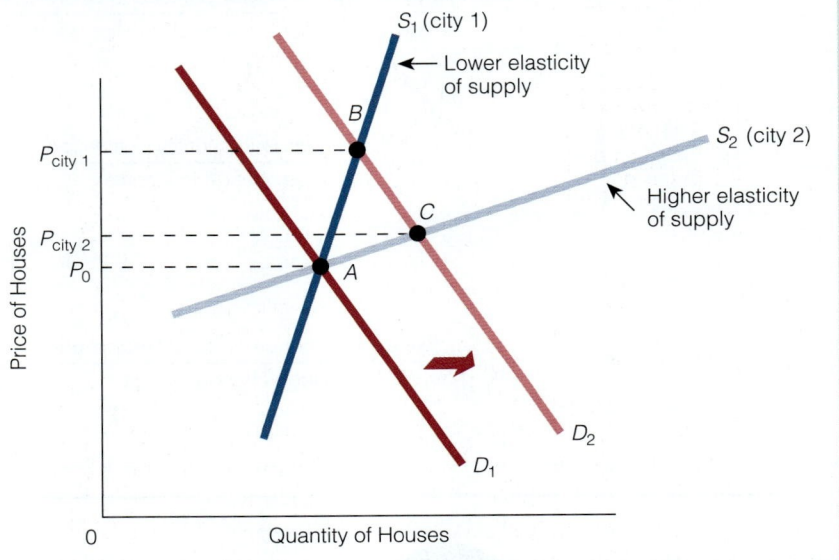

19-4 The Relationship Between Taxes and Elasticity

Before explaining how elasticity affects taxes and tax revenues, we explore how supply and demand determine who pays a tax.

19-4a Who Pays the Tax?

Many people think that if government places a tax on the seller of a good, the seller actually pays the tax. However, the *placement* of a tax is not the same as its *payment*, and placement does not guarantee payment. To see why, suppose the government imposes a tax on sellers of books. Then sellers are taxed $1 for every book they sell: sell a book, send $1 to the government. The government action changes the equilibrium in the book market. In Exhibit 11, before the tax is imposed, the equilibrium price and the quantity of books are $15 and Q_1, respectively. The tax per book shifts the supply curve leftward from S_1 to S_2. The vertical

EXHIBIT 11

Who Pays the Tax?

A tax placed on the sellers of books shifts the supply curve from S_1 to S_2 and raises the equilibrium price from $15.00 to $15.50. Part of the tax is paid by buyers through a higher price paid ($15.50 instead of $15.00), and part of the tax is paid by sellers through a lower price kept ($14.50 instead of $15.00).

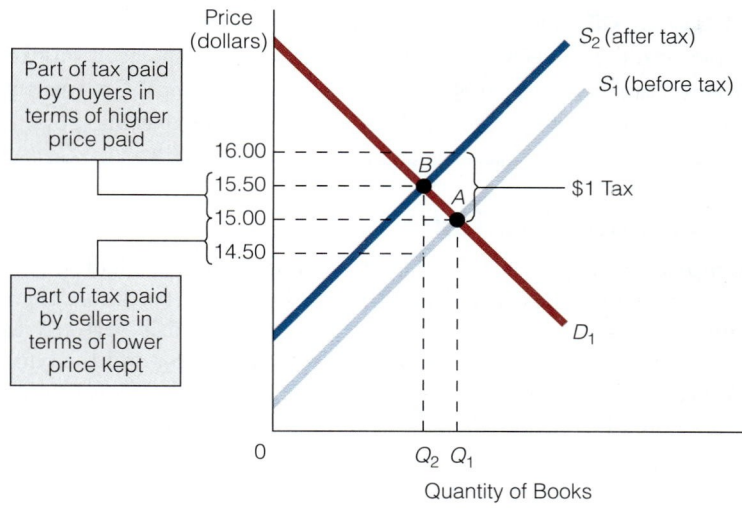

distance between the two supply curves represents the $1-per-book tax, because what matters to sellers is how much they keep for each book sold, not how much buyers pay. For example, if sellers are keeping $15 per book for Q_1 books before the tax is imposed, then they will want to keep as much after the tax is imposed. But if the tax is $1, the only way they can keep $15 per book for Q_1 books is to receive $16 per book. They receive $16 per book from buyers, turn over $1 to the government, and keep $15. In other words, each quantity on the new supply curve, S_2, corresponds to a $1 higher price than it did on the old supply curve, S_1.

However, the new equilibrium price will not necessarily be $1 higher than the old equilibrium price. In this case, the new equilibrium happens to be at a price of $15.50 and a quantity Q_2. Buyers pay $15.50 per book after the tax is imposed, as opposed to $15.00 before the tax was imposed. The difference between the new and old prices is the amount of the $1.00 tax that buyers pay per book. In this example, buyers pay 50¢, or one-half of the $1.00 tax per book:

Before the tax, buyers pay $15.00.
After the tax, buyers pay $15.50.

The sellers receive $15.50 per book from buyers after the tax is imposed, as opposed to $15.00 per book before the tax was imposed, but they do not get to keep $15.50 per book. One dollar has to be turned over to the government, leaving the sellers with $14.50. Before the tax was imposed, however, sellers received and kept $15.00 per book. In this example, the difference between $15.00 and $14.50—50¢—is the amount of the tax per book that sellers pay:

Before the tax, sellers receive $15.00 and keep $15.00.
After the tax, sellers receive $15.50 and keep $14.50.

So, although the full tax was *placed* on the sellers, they *paid* only one-half of it; although none of the tax was placed on buyers, they paid one-half of it too. The lesson is that government can place a tax on whomever it wants, but the laws of supply and demand determine who actually ends up paying it.

> **Thinking Like an Economist**
>
> **Placement Can Be Different from Payment** According to a layperson, if the government places a tax on entity A, then entity A pays the tax. The economist knows that the placement and the payment of a tax are two different things. Government may determine the placement of a tax, but supply and demand determine who pays.

19-4b Elasticity and the Tax

In our tax example, buyers paid half of the $1 tax and sellers paid half, but that is not the outcome in every situation. In some situations, the buyer can pay more than half the tax. In fact, the buyer can pay the full tax if demand for the good is perfectly inelastic, as in Exhibit 12(a). Here, the tax shifts the supply curve from S_1 to S_2, and the equilibrium price rises from $15.00 to $16.00. In other words, if demand is perfectly inelastic and a tax is placed on the sellers of a good, buyers pay the full tax as part of a higher price.

EXHIBIT 12

Different Elasticities and Who Pays the Tax

Four extreme cases are illustrated here. If demand is perfectly inelastic (a) or if supply is perfectly elastic (c), then buyers pay the full tax even though the tax may be placed entirely on sellers. If demand is perfectly elastic (b) or if supply is perfectly inelastic (d), then the full tax is paid by the sellers.

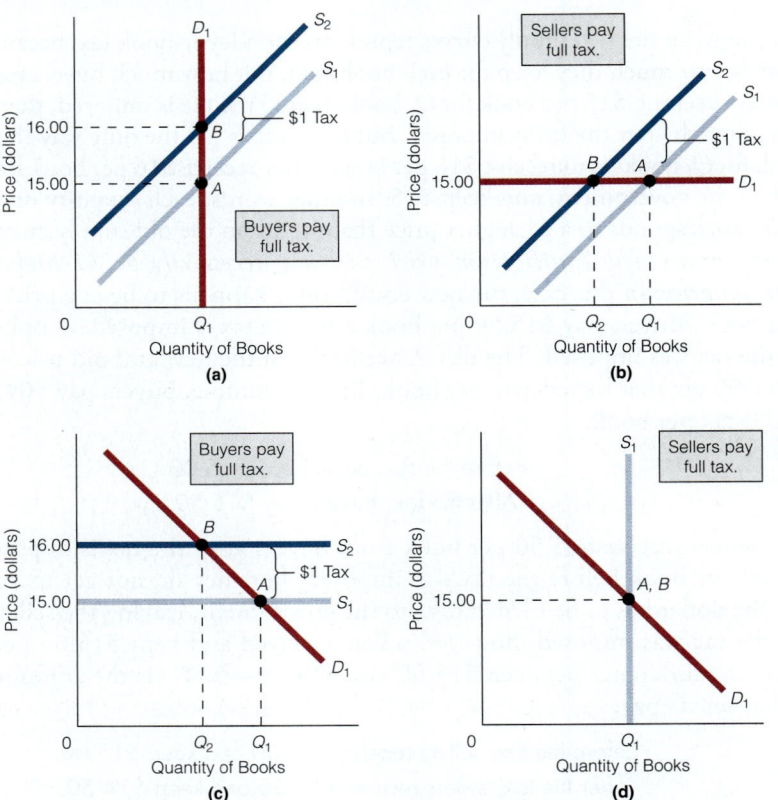

Parts (b)–(d) of Exhibit 12 show other cases. In part (b), demand is perfectly elastic. The tax shifts the supply curve from S_1 to S_2, but the equilibrium price does not change. Sellers must therefore pay the full tax if demand is perfectly elastic. In part (c), supply is perfectly elastic, and buyers pay the full tax. In part (d), a change in price causes no change in quantity supplied. If sellers try to charge a higher price than $15 for their good (and thus try to get buyers to pay some of the tax), a surplus will result, driving the price back down to $15. In this case, sellers pay the full tax. Although the exhibit does not show it, sellers would receive $15, turn over $1 to the government, and keep $14 for each unit sold.

19-4c Degree of Elasticity and Tax Revenue

Suppose that, of two sellers, seller A faces a perfectly inelastic demand for her product and is currently selling 10,000 units a month. Suppose also that seller B faces an elastic demand for his product and is currently selling 10,000 units a month. Government is thinking about placing a $1 tax per unit of product sold on one of the two sellers. If government's objective is to maximize tax revenues, it should tax seller A, because that seller is facing the inelastic demand curve.

In Exhibit 13, the demand curve facing seller A is D_1, and the demand curve facing seller B is D_2. S_1 represents the supply curve for both firms. Currently, both firms are at equilibrium at point A, selling 10,000 units. If government places a $1 tax per unit sold on seller A, then the supply curve shifts to S_2, and the equilibrium is now at point C. Because demand is perfectly inelastic, seller A still sells 10,000 units and the government's tax revenue from seller A equals the tax ($1) times 10,000 units, or $10,000. If government places the $1 tax per unit sold on seller B, then tax revenue will be only $8,000 Because, when the tax shifts the supply curve to S_2, the equilibrium moves to point B, at which only 8,000 units are sold.

The lesson is that, given the $1 tax per unit sold, tax revenues are maximized by placing the tax on the seller who faces the more inelastic (less elastic) demand curve.

EXHIBIT 13

Maximizing Tax Revenues

Two sellers, A and B, are each currently selling 10,000 units of their good. Seller A faces the demand curve D_1, and seller B faces D_2. If the objective is to maximize tax revenues with a $1 tax per unit of product sold and if only one seller can be taxed, then taxing seller A will maximize tax revenues, and taxing seller B will not. Note that, after the tax has been placed, the supply curve shifts from S_1 to S_2. Seller A is in equilibrium at point C, selling 10,000 units, and seller B is in equilibrium at point B, selling 8,000 units. Because tax revenues equal the tax per unit times the quantity of output sold, taxing seller A raises $10,000 in tax revenues whereas taxing B raises $8,000.

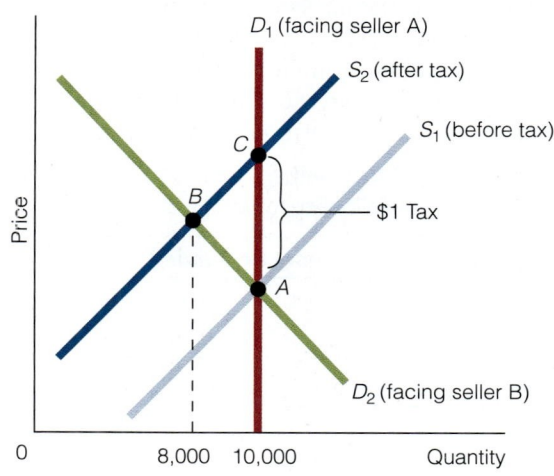

1. What does an income elasticity of demand of 1.33 mean?
2. What does perfectly inelastic supply signify?
3. Why will government raise more tax revenue if it applies a tax to a good with inelastic demand than if it applies the tax to a good with elastic demand?
4. Under what condition would a per-unit tax placed on the sellers of computers be fully paid by the buyers of computers?

Office Hours

"What Is the Relationship Between Different Price Elasticities of Demand and Total Revenue?"

Student: I'm still not sure I understand the relationship between price elasticity of demand and total revenue.

Instructor: Let's use some numbers to illustrate the relationship. Here we have identified two points on a demand curve:

Price	Quantity Demanded
$10	110
$12	100

The price elasticity of demand between these two points is 0.52, so demand is inelastic. Now let's find the total revenue at each price. If we assume that the economy is in equilibrium (at which quantity demanded is equal to quantity supplied), then total revenue at $10 is $1,100. (We get this amount by multiplying $10 by 110.) When price is $12, total revenue is $1,200. We conclude that if price elasticity of demand is less than 1 (demand is inelastic), then a rise in price will raise total revenue. Therefore, if we lower the price (from $12 to $10), total revenue will decline.

Now let's change one of the numbers in the table—from 100 to 80. Then we have the following table:

Price	Quantity Demanded
$10	110
$12	80

If we compute the new price elasticity of demand, we get 1.73, meaning that demand is elastic. Now let's compute total revenue at each price. At $10, that's $1,100. At the higher price of $12, total revenue is $960. So, if price elasticity is greater than 1 (demand is elastic) and if price rises, total revenue falls. And, of course, if price falls (from $12 to $10), total revenue will rise.

Student: So, in the first example, when demand was inelastic, we raised price, and total revenue increased. But in the second example, when demand was elastic and we raised price, total revenue decreased.

Instructor: Yes, that's correct. When demand is inelastic, the directional change in price brings about the same directional change in total revenue: When price rises, total revenue rises; when price falls, total revenue falls. But when demand is elastic, the directional change in price brings about an opposite directional change in total revenue: When price rises, total revenue falls; when price falls, total revenue rises.

Points to Remember

1. When demand is inelastic, price and total revenue move in the same direction.
2. When demand is elastic, price and total revenue move in opposite directions.

Chapter Summary

Price Elasticity of Demand

- Price elasticity of demand is a measure of the responsiveness of quantity demanded to changes in price.
- If the percentage change in quantity demanded is greater than the percentage change in price, demand is elastic.
- If the percentage change in quantity demanded is less than the percentage change in price, demand is inelastic.
- If the percentage change in quantity demanded is equal to the percentage change in price, demand is unit elastic.
- If a small change in price causes an infinitely large change in quantity demanded, demand is perfectly elastic.
- If a change in price causes no change in quantity demanded, demand is perfectly inelastic.
- The coefficient of price elasticity of demand (E_d) is negative, signifying the inverse relationship between price and quantity demanded. For convenience, however, the absolute value of the elasticity coefficient is used.

Total Revenue and Price Elasticity of Demand

- If demand is elastic, price and total revenue are inversely related: as price rises (falls), total revenue falls (rises).
- If demand is inelastic, price and total revenue are directly related: as price rises (falls), total revenue rises (falls).
- If demand is unit elastic, total revenue is independent of price: as price rises (falls), total revenue remains constant.

Determinants of Price Elasticity of Demand

- The more substitutes a good has, the higher the price elasticity of demand for the good is; the fewer substitutes a good has, the lower the price elasticity of demand is.
- The more that a good is considered a luxury instead of a necessity, the higher the price elasticity of demand will be.
- The greater the percentage of one's budget that goes to purchase a good, the higher the price elasticity of demand will be; the smaller the percentage of one's budget that goes to purchase a good, the lower the price elasticity of demand will be.
- The more time that passes (since a price change), the higher the price elasticity of demand will be; the less time that passes, the lower the price elasticity of demand.

Cross Elasticity of Demand

- Cross elasticity of demand measures the responsiveness in the quantity demanded of one good to changes in the price of another good.
- If $E_c > 0$, two goods are substitutes for each other. If $E_c < 0$, two goods are complements to each other.

Income Elasticity of Demand

- Income elasticity of demand measures the responsiveness of quantity demanded to changes in income.
- If $E_y > 0$, the good is a normal good. If $E_y < 0$, the good is an inferior good.
- If $E_y > 1$, demand is income elastic. If $E_y < 1$, demand is income inelastic. If $E_y = 1$, demand is income unit elastic.

Price Elasticity of Supply

- Price elasticity of supply measures the responsiveness of quantity supplied to changes in price.
- If the percentage change in quantity supplied is greater than the percentage change in price, then supply is elastic.
- If the percentage change in quantity supplied is less than the percentage change in price, then supply is inelastic.
- If the percentage change in quantity supplied is equal to the percentage change in price, then supply is unit elastic.
- Price elasticity of supply is higher in the long run than in the short run.

Taxes and Elasticity

- The placement of a tax is different from its payment. For example, a tax may be placed on the seller of a good, and both the seller and buyer end up paying the tax.
- In this chapter, we discuss a per-unit tax that was placed on the seller of a specific good (books). This tax shifted the supply curve of books leftward. The vertical distance between the old supply curve (before the tax) and the new supply curve (after the tax) was equal to the per-unit tax.
- If a per-unit tax is placed on the seller of a good, both the buyer and the seller will pay part of the tax if the demand curve is downward sloping and the supply curve is upward sloping.

- The more inelastic the demand, the larger the percentage of the tax that the buyer will pay.
- The more elastic the demand, the smaller the percentage of the tax that the buyer will pay.
- When demand is perfectly inelastic or supply is perfectly elastic, buyers pay the full tax.
- When demand is perfectly elastic or supply is perfectly inelastic, sellers pay the full tax.

Key Terms and Concepts

Price Elasticity of Demand
Elastic Demand
Inelastic Demand
Unit Elastic Demand
Perfectly Elastic Demand
Perfectly Inelastic Demand
Total Revenue (*TR*)
Cross Elasticity of Demand
Income Elasticity of Demand
Income Elastic
Income Inelastic
Income Unit Elastic
Price Elasticity of Supply

Questions And Problems

1. Explain how a seller can determine whether the demand for his or her good is inelastic, elastic, or unit elastic between two prices.
2. For each of the following, identify where demand is elastic, inelastic, perfectly elastic, perfectly inelastic, or unit elastic:
    a. Price rises by 10 percent, and quantity demanded falls by 2 percent.
    b. Price falls by 5 percent, and quantity demanded rises by 4 percent.
    c. Price falls by 6 percent, and quantity demanded does not change.
    d. Price rises by 2 percent, and quantity demanded falls by 1 percent.
3. Prove that price elasticity of demand is not the same as the slope of a demand curve.
4. Suppose the current price of gasoline at the pump is $4 per gallon and that 1 million gallons are sold per day. Politicians propose to add a $1 tax to the price of a gallon of gasoline. They say that the tax will generate $1 million in tax revenues per day. What assumption are they making?
5. For each of the following, identify whether total revenue rises, falls, or remains constant:
    a. Demand is inelastic and price falls.
    b. Demand is elastic and price rises.
    c. Demand is unit elastic and price rises.
    d. Demand is inelastic and price rises.
    e. Demand is elastic and price falls.
6. Suppose a straight-line downward-sloping demand curve shifts rightward. Is the price elasticity of demand higher, lower, or the same between any two prices on the new (higher) demand curve than on the old (lower) demand curve?
7. Suppose a city is hit by a tornado that destroys 25 percent of the housing in the area. Would you expect the total expenditure on housing after the tornado to be greater than, less than, or equal to what it was before the tornado? Explain your answer.
8. For each of the following pairs of goods, which has the higher price elasticity of demand?
    a. Airline travel in the short run or airline travel in the long run
    b. Television sets or Sony television sets
    c. Cars or Fords
    d. Cell phones or Samsung cell phones
    e. Popcorn or Orville Redenbacher's popcorn
9. How might you determine whether toothpaste manufacturers and mouthwash manufacturers are competitors?
10. Suppose that the demand for product *A* is perfectly inelastic and that the buyers of *A* get the funds to pay for it by stealing.
    a. If the supply of *A* decreases, what happens to its price?
    b. What happens to the amount of crime committed by the buyers of *A*?
11. Suppose you learned that the price elasticity of demand for wheat is 0.7 between the current price for wheat and a price $2 higher per bushel. Do you think that farmers collectively would try to reduce the supply of wheat and drive the price

up $2 higher per bushel? Explain your answer. Assuming that they would try to reduce supply, what problems might they have in actually doing so?

12. In 1947, the U.S. Department of Justice brought a suit against the DuPont Company (which, at the time, sold 75 percent of all the cellophane in the United States) for monopolizing the production and sale of cellophane. In court, DuPont tried to show that cellophane was only one of several goods in the market in which it was sold. The company argued that its market was not the cellophane market but the flexible-packaging materials market, which included (besides cellophane) waxed paper, aluminum foil, and other such products. DuPont pointed out that it had only 20 percent of all sales in this more broadly defined market. Using this information, discuss how the concept of cross elasticity of demand would help establish whether DuPont should have been viewed as a firm in the cellophane market or as a firm in the flexible-packaging materials market.

13. "If government wishes to tax certain goods, it should tax goods that have inelastic rather than elastic demand." What is the rationale for this statement?

14. A tax is placed on the sellers of a good. What happens to the percentage of this tax that buyers pay as the price elasticity of demand for the good decreases? Explain your answer.

Working with Numbers and Graphs

1. A college raises its annual tuition from $23,000 to $24,000, and its student enrollment falls from 4,877 to 4,705. Compute the price elasticity of demand. Is demand for the college elastic or inelastic?

2. As the price of good X rises from $10 to $12, the quantity demanded of good Y rises from 100 units to 114 units. Are X and Y substitutes or complements? What is the cross elasticity of demand?

3. The quantity demanded of good X rises from 130 to 145 units as income rises from $2,000 to $2,500 a month. What is the income elasticity of demand for good X?

4. The quantity supplied of a good rises from 120 to 140 as price rises from $4 to $5.50. What is the price elasticity of supply of the good?

5. In the accompanying figure, what is the price elasticity of demand between the two prices on D_1? On D_2?

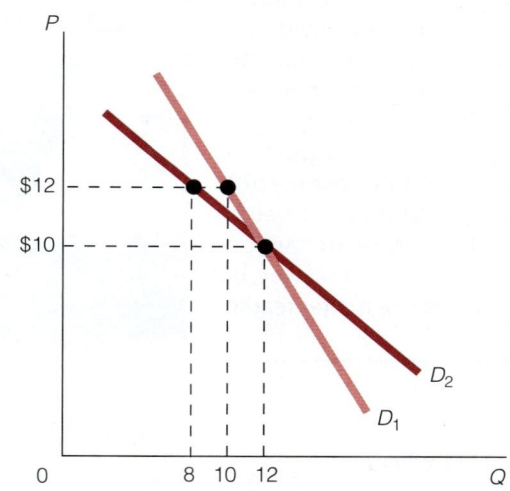

CHAPTER 20
Consumer Choice: Maximizing Utility and Behavioral Economics

Introduction

Just before purchasing a computer, a book, or an iPad, what do you think about? Do you say, "Do I want this or not?" Many people would give this answer. Economists have put this response under the microscope and rephrased it: "The marginal utility of this item divided by its price is greater than the marginal utility of other items divided by their prices, so I am going to make this purchase because it will increase my overall utility." You may not believe now that you—or anyone else—would think that way, but you may believe it after reading this chapter.

20-1 Utility Theory

Water is cheap, and diamonds are expensive. But water is necessary to life, and diamonds are not. Isn't it odd—even paradoxical—that what is necessary to life is cheap and what is not necessary is expensive? Eighteenth-century economist Adam Smith wondered about this question. He observed that things with the greatest value in use (or that are the most useful) often have a relatively low price and things with little or no value in use have a high price. Smith's observation came to be known as the **diamond–water paradox**, or the paradox of value. The paradox challenged economists, and they sought a solution to it. This section begins to develop parts of the solution they found.

Diamond–Water Paradox
The observation that things with the greatest value in use sometimes have little value in exchange, and things with little value in use sometimes have the greatest value in exchange.

Utility
A measure of the satisfaction, happiness, or benefit that results from the consumption of a good.

Utils
An artificial construct used to measure utility.

20-1a Utility: Total and Marginal

Saying that a good gives you **utility** is the same as saying that it has the power to satisfy your wants or that it gives you satisfaction. For example, suppose you buy your first unit of good X, and you get a certain amount of utility, say, 10 **utils** from it. (Utils are an artificial construct used to measure utility; we realize that you have never seen a util—no one has.) You buy a second unit of good X, and, once again, you get a certain amount of utility from this second unit, say, 8 utils. You purchase a third unit and receive 7 utils. The sum of the number of utils (the amount of utility) you obtain from each of the 3 units is the total utility you receive from purchasing good X: 25 utils. Total utility is the total satisfaction one receives from consuming a particular quantity of a good (in this example, 3 units of good X).

Total utility is different from marginal utility. Marginal utility is the *additional* utility gained from consuming an additional unit of good X. **Marginal utility** (*MU*) is the change in total utility (ΔTU) divided by the change in the quantity (ΔQ) consumed of a good:

$$MU = \frac{\Delta TU}{\Delta Q}$$

The change in the quantity consumed of a good is usually stipulated to be equal to 1 unit.

To illustrate, suppose you receive 10 utils of total utility from consuming 1 apple and 19 utils of total utility from consuming 2 apples. Then the marginal utility of the second apple (the additional utility of consuming an additional apple) is 9 utils. As a person consumes more apples, total utility rises, but marginal utility (additional utility received from the additional apple) falls. In other words, total utility rises as marginal utility falls.

Total Utility
The total satisfaction a person receives from consuming a particular quantity of a good.

Marginal Utility
The additional utility a person receives from consuming an additional unit of a good.

> **Thinking Like an Economist**
>
> **Total Utility and Marginal Utility Can Move in Opposite Directions** The economist knows that marginal utility and total utility can move in opposite directions. So a rise in total utility doesn't mean that marginal utility is rising too. To illustrate, look at the following table:
>
> | (1) Number of Apples Consumed | (2) Total Utility (utils) | (3) Marginal Utility (utils) |
> |---|---|---|
> | 1 | 10 | 10 |
> | 2 | 19 | 9 |
> | 3 | 27 | 8 |
>
> Clearly, in moving from one, to two, to three apples, total utility rises, but marginal utility falls.

20-1b Law of Diminishing Marginal Utility

Do you think that the marginal utility of the second unit is greater than, less than, or equal to the marginal utility of the first unit? To begin to answer this question, consider the difference in marginal utility between the third unit and the second unit and between the fifth unit and the fourth unit (had we extended the number of units consumed). In general, the question is whether the marginal utility of the unit that follows a given unit is greater than, less than, or equal to that of the unit that precedes the given unit.

Economists have generally answered "less than." The **law of diminishing marginal utility** states that, over a given period, the marginal utility gained by consuming equal successive units of a good declines as the amount consumed increases. In other words, the number of utils gained by consuming the first unit of a good is greater than the number of utils gained by consuming the second unit (which is greater than the number gained by the third, which is greater than the number gained by the fourth, and so on).

The law of diminishing marginal utility is illustrated in Exhibit 1. The table in part (a) shows both the total utility of consuming a certain number of units of a good and the marginal utility of consuming additional units. The graph in part (b) shows the total utility curve for

Law of Diminishing Marginal Utility
The marginal utility gained by consuming equal successive units of a good will decline as the amount consumed increases.

EXHIBIT 1

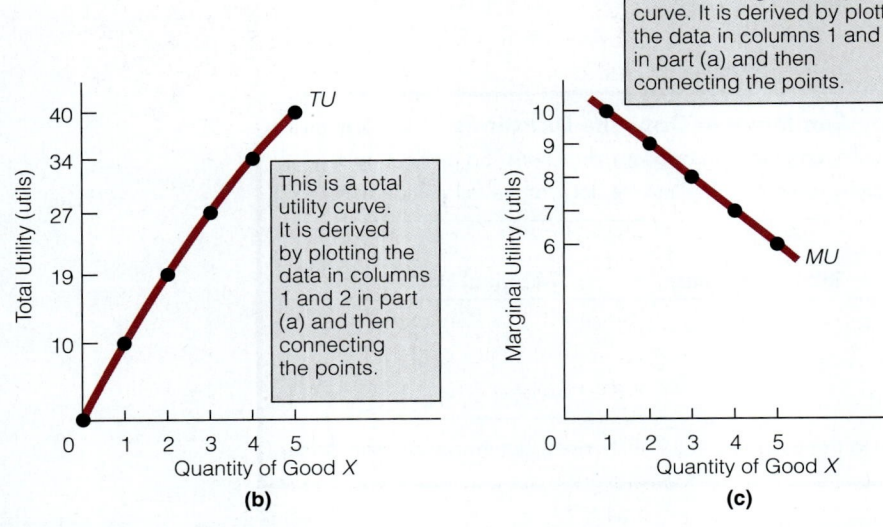

Total Utility, Marginal Utility, and the Law of Diminishing Marginal Utility

TU = total utility and MU = marginal utility. (a) Both total utility and marginal utility are expressed in utils. Marginal utility is the change in total utility divided by the change in the quantity consumed of the good: $MU = \Delta TU/\Delta Q$. (b) Total utility curve. (c) Marginal utility curve. Together, (b) and (c) demonstrate that total utility can increase (b) as marginal utility decreases (c).

the data in part (a), and the graph in part (c) shows the marginal utility curve for the data in part (a). The graphs in parts (b) and (c) show that total utility can increase as marginal utility decreases. This relationship between total utility and marginal utility is important in unraveling the diamond–water paradox.

The law of diminishing marginal utility is based on the idea that, if a good has a variety of uses but only 1 unit of the good is available, then the consumer will use the first unit to satisfy his or her most urgent want. If 2 units are available, the consumer will use the second unit to satisfy a less urgent want. Suppose that good X can be used to satisfy wants A through E, with A being the most urgent and E being the least. Also, B is more urgent than C, C is more urgent than D, and D is more urgent than E. We can chart the wants as follows:

Suppose the first unit of good *X* can satisfy any one—but only one—of wants A through E. An individual will choose to satisfy the most urgent want, A, instead of B, C, D, or E, because people ordinarily satisfy their most urgent want before satisfying all others. If you were dying of thirst in a desert (having gone without water for, say, three days) and came across a quart of water, you would drink, not wash your hands; that is, you would satisfy your most urgent want first. Washing your hands in the water would give you less utility than drinking it.

The Millionaire and the Pauper: What the Law Says and Doesn't Say Who gets more utility from one more dollar, a poor man or a millionaire? Most people would say that a poor man gets more utility from one more dollar because the poor man has far fewer dollars than the millionaire. To a millionaire, one more dollar is nothing. A millionaire has so many dollars, one more doesn't mean a thing.

Some people think that the law of diminishing marginal utility substantiates the claim that a millionaire gets less utility from one more dollar than a poor man does. Unfortunately, though, this interpretation is a misreading of the law. The law says that, for the millionaire or the poor man, an additional dollar is worth less than the dollar that preceded it. Let's say the millionaire has $2 million and the poor man has $1,000. We now give each of them one more dollar. The law of diminishing marginal utility says that (1) the additional dollar is worth less to the millionaire than her two-millionth dollar and (2) the additional dollar is worth less to the poor man than his one-thousandth dollar. That is all the law says. We do not, and cannot, know whether the additional dollar is worth more or less to the millionaire than it is to the poor man. In sum, the law says something about the millionaire and about the poor man (both persons value the last dollar less than the next-to-last dollar), but it does not say anything about the millionaire's utility compared to the poor man's utility.

To compare the utility the millionaire gets from the additional dollar with the utility the poor man gets from it is to fall into the trap of making an **interpersonal utility comparison**. The utility that one person gets cannot be scientifically or objectively compared with the utility that another person gets from the same thing because utility is subjective. Who knows for certain how much satisfaction (utility) the millionaire gets from the additional dollar, compared with that of the poor man? On the one hand, the poor man may care little for money; he may shun it, consider the love of it the root of all evil, and prefer to consume the things in life that do not require money. On the other hand, the millionaire may be interested only in amassing more money. We must not guess at the utility that someone obtains from consuming a certain item, compare it with our guess about the utility that another person obtains from consuming the same item, and then call our guesses scientific facts.

Interpersonal Utility Comparison
Comparing the utility one person receives from a good, service, or activity with the utility another person receives from the same good, service, or activity.

20-1c The Solution to the Diamond–Water Paradox

Goods have both total utility and marginal utility. Water, for example, is extremely useful: We cannot live without it. Thus, we would expect its total utility (its total usefulness) to be high, but its marginal utility to be low because water is relatively plentiful. As the law of diminishing marginal utility states, the utility of successive units of a good diminishes as consumption of the good increases. In short, water is immensely useful, but there is so much of it that individuals place relatively little value on another unit of it.

In contrast, diamonds are not as useful as water. Hence, we would expect the total utility of diamonds to be lower than that of water, but their marginal utility to be high because there are relatively few diamonds in the world. In other words, the consumption of diamonds (in contrast to that of water) takes place at relatively high marginal utility. Diamonds, which are rare, are used only for their few valuable uses. Water, which is plentiful, gets used for its many valuable uses as well as for its not-so-valuable uses (e.g., spraying the car with the hose for 2 more minutes even though you are 99 percent sure that the soap is fully rinsed off).

So the total utility of water is high because water is extremely useful. The total utility of diamonds is comparatively low because diamonds are not as useful as water. The marginal utility of water is low because water is so plentiful that people consume it at low marginal utility. The marginal utility of diamonds is high because diamonds are so scarce that people consume them at high marginal utility.

Prices therefore reflect marginal utility, not total utility.

(Answers to Self-Test questions are in Answers to Self-Test Questions at the back of the book.)

1. State and solve the diamond–water paradox.
2. What does falling total utility imply for marginal utility? Give an arithmetical example to illustrate your answer.
3. When would a good's total utility and marginal utility be the same?

Economics 24/7

The Gym and Diminishing Marginal Utility

Many people buy a gym membership but do not use it regularly. This is usually how things go: A person visits a gym. He sees people working out; he sees all the different exercise machines. A gym employee tells him that a membership is a great deal, only $1 a day. He signs up for a membership. He visits the gym every other day for the first week of his membership. Then weeks go by without his visiting. He begins to feel guilty about not using his membership, so he drags himself to the gym. A few more weeks pass, and then he drags himself to the gym one more time. Finally, three months pass without his going at all. One day he gets on the phone and cancels his gym membership. He doesn't even want to add up how much he has spent for a gym membership he rarely used. He sits down, has a bowl of ice cream, and watches television.

What has happened is that our gym member has underestimated the law of diminishing marginal utility applied to exercising at a gym. When he first visits the gym and looks at all the people working out, he might feel that here is a place where utility can be gained. But that utility might simply be the utility he expects to receive on his *first visit* to the gym, times the number of planned visits to the gym. In other words, he expects to receive, say, 100 utils on his first visit, and he plans to visit the gym 90 days a year. That is a total of 9,000 utils.

What our gym member overlooks is that the utility he receives on his second visit might be less than the utility he receives on his first visit. In other words, the law of diminishing marginal utility might apply to exercising at the gym. For all we know, there could be a dramatic drop-off in marginal utility with, say, the third or fourth visit. His marginal utility per visit might go something like this: first visit, 100 utils; second visit, 80 utils; third visit, 20 utils; fourth visit, 5 utils.

In short, our gym member's decision to join the gym might have been made on the basis of his thinking that he wouldn't experience diminishing marginal utility when, in fact, that is exactly what he does experience.

Now let's return to the gym employee who told our prospective gym member that the gym membership was a great deal: only $1 a day. That $1 a day might have been a great deal for the first day (the first visit to the gym), because our gym member received more than one dollar's worth of utility on the first visit. But then diminishing marginal utility kicked in, and by the time he got to the fifth visit, he no longer was receiving more than one dollar's worth of utility.

20-2 Consumer Equilibrium and Demand

This section identifies the condition necessary for consumer equilibrium and then discusses the relationship between equilibrium and the law of demand. The analysis is based on the assumption that individuals seek to maximize utility.

20-2a Equating Marginal Utilities per Dollar

Suppose there are only two goods in the world: apples and oranges. At present, a consumer is spending his entire income consuming 10 apples and 10 oranges a week. For a particular week, the marginal utility (MU) and price (P) of each are as follows:[1]

$$MU_{oranges} = 30 \text{ utils}$$
$$MU_{apples} = 20 \text{ utils}$$
$$P_{oranges} = \$1$$
$$P_{apples} = \$1$$

So the consumer's marginal (last) dollar spent on apples returns 20 utils per dollar, and his marginal (last) dollar spent on oranges returns 30 utils per dollar. The ratio MU_O/P_O (O = oranges) is greater than the ratio MU_A/P_A (A = apples):

$$\frac{MU_O}{P_O} > \frac{MU_A}{P_A}$$

If the consumer recognizes this fact one week, he might redirect his purchases of apples and oranges the next week: "If I buy an orange, I receive more utility [30 utils] than if I buy an apple [20 utils]. It's better to buy 1 more orange with $1 and 1 less apple. I gain 30 utils from buying the orange, which is 10 utils more than if I buy the apple."

As the consumer buys 1 more orange and 1 less apple, however, the marginal utility of oranges falls (recall what the law of diminishing marginal utility says about consuming

---

[1] You may wonder where we get these marginal utility figures. They are points on hypothetical marginal utility curves, such as the one in Exhibit 1. What is important is that one number is greater than the other. We could easily have picked other numbers, such as 300 and 200.

additional units of a good), and the marginal utility of apples rises (the consumer is consuming fewer apples). Because the consumer has bought 1 more orange and 1 less apple, he now has 11 oranges and 9 apples. At this new combination of goods,

$$MU_O = 25 \text{ utils}$$
$$MU_A = 25 \text{ utils}$$
$$P_O = \$1$$
$$P_A = \$1$$

Now the ratio MU_O/P_O equals the ratio MU_A/P_A. The consumer is getting exactly the same amount of utility (25 utils) per dollar from each of the two goods. There is no way for the consumer to redirect his purchases (i.e., buy more of one good and less of another good) and have more utility. Thus, the consumer is in equilibrium; that is, he derives the same marginal utility per dollar for all goods. The condition for **consumer equilibrium** is

$$\frac{MU_A}{P_A} = \frac{MU_B}{P_B} = \frac{MU_C}{P_C} = \ldots = \frac{MU_Z}{P_Z}$$

where the letters A–Z represent all the goods a person buys.[2]

A person in consumer equilibrium has *maximized total utility*. By spending his or her dollars on goods that give the greatest marginal utility and, in the process, bringing about the consumer equilibrium condition, the consumer is adding as much to total utility as is possible.

Consumer Equilibrium
The equilibrium that occurs when the consumer has spent all of his or her income and the marginal utilities per dollar spent on each good purchased *are* equal: $MU_A/P_A = MU_B/P_B = \ldots = MU_Z/P_Z$, where the letters A–Z represent all the goods a person buys.

20-2b Maximizing Utility and the Law of Demand

Suppose a consumer of oranges and apples is currently in equilibrium; that is,

$$\frac{MU_O}{P_O} = \frac{MU_A}{P_A}$$

When in equilibrium, the consumer is maximizing utility. Now, suppose the price of oranges falls. Then the situation becomes

$$\frac{MU_O}{P_O} > \frac{MU_A}{P_A}$$

The consumer will attempt to restore equilibrium by buying more oranges. This behavior—buying more oranges when their price falls—is consistent with the law of demand.

Therefore, the consumer's attempt to reach equilibrium—which is another way of saying that the consumer is seeking to maximize utility—is consistent with the law of demand. In other words, maximization of utility is consistent with the law of demand. The next time people say that they don't maximize utility, ask them if they buy more units of a good when the price is lowered—that is, whether their behavior is consistent with the law of demand. If they say yes, then you can be sure they maximize utility, because maximization of utility is consistent with the law of demand.

---

[2] We are assuming that the consumer exhausts his or her income and that saving is treated as a good.

20-2c Should the Government Provide the Necessities of Life for Free?

Some people argue that because food and water are necessities of life and no one can live without them, charging for them is wrong. The government should provide them to everyone for free. Similarly, others argue that medical care is a necessity for those who are sick. Without proper care, sick people will either die or experience an extremely low quality of life. Making people pay for medical care is wrong: The government should provide it for free to those who need it. Each argument labels something as a necessity of life (food, water, medical care) and then makes the policy proposal that government should provide the necessity for free.

Suppose government did give food, water, and medical care to everyone for free—at zero price (although not at zero taxes). At zero price, people would want to consume these goods up to the point of zero marginal utility for each good. If the marginal utility of the good (expressed in dollars) is greater than its price, people can derive more utility from purchasing the good than they lose in parting with the dollar price of the good. For example, if the price of a good is $5, an individual will continue consuming the good as long as the marginal utility derived from it is greater than $5. If the price is $0, the person will continue to consume the good as long as the marginal utility derived from it is greater than $0.

Resources must be used to produce every unit of a good consumed. If the government uses scarce resources to provide goods with low marginal utility (which food, water, and medical care would have at zero price), then fewer resources are available to produce other goods. The resources could then be redirected to producing goods with a higher marginal utility, thereby raising total utility.

The people who argue that certain goods should be provided free implicitly assume that the not-so-valuable uses of food, water, and medical care are valuable enough to warrant a system of taxes to pay for the complete provision of them at zero price. It is questionable, however, whether the least valuable uses of food, water, and health care are worth the sacrifices of other goods that would necessarily be forfeited if more of these goods were produced.

Think about the question this way: Currently, water is relatively cheap, and people use it for its valuable purposes and its not-so-valuable purposes. But if water were cheaper than it is—if its price were zero—would it be used to satisfy its more valuable uses, its not-so-valuable uses, and its absolutely least valuable use? If food had a zero price, would it be used to satisfy its more valuable uses, its not-so-valuable uses, and its absolutely least valuable use (food fights perhaps)?

Thinking Like an Economist

Yes, There Can Be Too Much of a Good Thing. As odd as it may sound to say so, there is such a thing as too much health care. The right amount of health care is the amount at which the marginal benefit or marginal utility (of an additional unit of health care) equals the marginal cost. Let's say that the marginal cost of health care is $40 but that, under a system of free health care for everyone, no one directly pays even one cent for personal health care. All health care bills are paid by the federal government with tax monies. In such a case, an individual is likely to continue consuming health care until his marginal utility equals zero. In other words, a person will consume, say, the one-hundredth unit of health care, even though the one-hundredth unit comes with only $0.0000001 worth of benefits to him and a cost of $40 to society at large. Economists say that if individuals are getting not even a penny's worth of benefits from care that costs $40 to provide, then that is too much health care.

Economics 24/7

How You Pay for Good Weather

Suppose two cities are alike in every way except one: the weather. One city is called Good-Weather City (*GWC*) and the other Bad-Weather City (*BWC*). In *GWC*, temperatures are moderate all year, and the sky is always blue. In *BWC*, the winter brings snow and freezing rain, and the summer brings high humidity and high temperatures. *BWC* has all the forms of weather that people dislike.

We assume that people get more utility from living in good weather than from living in bad weather and that the median price (*P*) of a home in the two cities is the same: $200,000. In terms of marginal utility and housing prices,

$$\frac{MU_{GWC}}{P_{H,GWC}} > \frac{MU_{BWC}}{P_{H,BWC}}$$

That is, the marginal utility of living in *GWC* (MU_{GWC}), divided by the price of a house in *GWC* ($P_{H,GWC}$), is greater than the marginal utility of living in *BWC* (MU_{BWC}), divided by the price of a house in *BWC* ($P_{H,BWC}$). *GWC* offers greater utility per dollar than does *BWC*.

At least some people will move from *BWC* to *GWC*. The people in *BWC* who want to move will put their houses up for sale, increasing the supply of houses for sale and lowering the price. As these people move to *GWC*, they increase the demand for houses there, and house prices in *GWC* begin to rise.

This process will continue until the price of a house in *GWC* has risen high enough, and the price of a house in *BWC* has fallen low enough, so that the *MU/P* ratios in the two cities are the same. In other words, the process continues until

$$\frac{MU_{GWC}}{P_{H,GWC}} = \frac{MU_{BWC}}{P_{H,BWC}}$$

At this point, a consumer receives the same utility per dollar in the two cities; the two cities are the same as regards the utility of a dollar.

Now, consider a young couple choosing which city to live in. The couple will not necessarily choose *GWC* because it has a better climate. *GWC* has a better climate than *BWC*, but *BWC*

has lower housing prices. One partner says, "Let's live in *GWC*. Think of all that great weather we'll enjoy. We can go outside every day." The other partner says, "But if we live in *BWC*, we can have either a much bigger and better house for the money or more money to spend on things other than housing. Think of the better cars and clothes we'll be able to buy or the vacations we'll be able to take because we won't have to spend as much money to buy a house."

What has happened is that the initial greater satisfaction of living in *GWC* (the higher utility per dollar) has been eroded by people moving there, thereby raising housing prices. On the one hand, *GWC* doesn't look as good as it once did. On the other hand, *BWC* doesn't look as bad as it once did. It still doesn't have the good climate that *GWC* has, but it now has lower housing prices. The utility per dollar of living in *BWC* has risen as a consequence of lowered housing prices.

As long as one city is better (in some way) than another, people will move to it. In the process, they will change things just enough so that it is no longer relatively better. In the end, you have to pay for paradise.

1. Alessandro purchases two goods, X and Y, and the utility gained for the last unit purchased of each is 16 utils and 23 utils, respectively. The prices of X and Y are $1 and $1.75, respectively. Is Alessandro in consumer equilibrium? Explain your answer.

2. In a two-good world (goods A and B), what does it mean to be in consumer disequilibrium?

20-3 Behavioral Economics

Economists are interested in how people behave with respect to marginal utility. Economic theory predicts that when the MU/P ratio for one good is greater than it is for another, individuals will buy more of the good with the higher MU/P ratio and less of the good with the lower MU/P ratio. Seeking to maximize their utility, individuals will buy more of one good and less of another until the MU/P ratios for all goods are the same.

In traditional economic theories and models, individuals are assumed to be rational, self-interested, and consistent. For about the last 30 years, however, behavioral economists have challenged the traditional economic models. Behavioral economists argue that some human behavior does not fit neatly—at a minimum, easily—into the traditional economic framework. In this section, we describe some of the findings of behavioral economists.

20-3a Are People Willing to Reduce Others' Incomes?

Two economists, Daniel Zizzo and Andrew Oswald, set up a series of experiments with four groups, each with four people. Each person was given the same amount of money and was asked to gamble with it. At the end of each act of gambling, two of the four persons in each group had won some money, and two had lost some. Then each of the four people in each group was given the opportunity to pay (or forfeit) some amount of money (to a bank) to reduce the take of the others in the group. To illustrate, in the group consisting of Smith, Matsui, Brown, and Rivera, Smith and Rivera had more money after gambling, and Matsui and Brown had less. All four were given the opportunity to reduce the amount of money held by the others in the group. For example, Brown could pay to reduce Smith's money, Matsui could pay to reduce Rivera's, and so on.

A reasonable expectation is that no one will spend money to hurt someone else if doing so means leaving himself poorer. However, Zizzo and Oswald found that 62 percent of the participants did just that: They made themselves worse off to make someone else worse off.

Possibly, people behave this way because they are more concerned with relative rank and status than with absolute well-being. Thus, the poorer of the two individuals doesn't mind paying, say, 25¢ to reduce the richer person's take by, say, $1. After the poorer person pays 25¢, the gap between him and the richer person is smaller.

Some economists argue that such behavior is irrational and inconsistent with utility maximization. Other economists say it is no such thing. They argue that if people get utility from relative rank, then, in effect, they are buying a move up the relative rank ladder by reducing the size of the gap between themselves and others.

Economics 24/7

$800 for Sure or $1,000 with a Probability of 85 Percent? An Experiment

Here is an experiment in which individuals are presented with two options:

- Option A: Receive $800
- Option B: Receive $1,000 with a probability of 85 percent and receive nothing with a probability of 15 percent.

In this experiment, there is a sure thing (option A) and an option that is a gamble (option B). The expected payoff for the two options is not the same. The expected payoff for option A is, of course, $800. In other words, a person is guaranteed (has a probability of 100 percent) of receiving $800. Under option B, one has an 85 percent chance of $1,000 and a 15 percent chance of receiving nothing. Here is the expected payoff:

$$0.85(\$1,000) + 0.15(\$0) = \$850$$

In conclusion, then, the expected payoff of option A is $800, and the expected payoff of option B is $850. Standard economics, built on persons who seek to maximize their expected utility or net benefits, says that, given a choice between options A and B, individuals would choose option B over A. But is that what the experiment found? Not at all: The overwhelming number of people chose option A, with the expected payoff of $800, instead of option B, with the expected payoff of $850. In other words, they opted for the sure thing instead of the gamble.

One criticism here is that the experiment itself has been called into question. To illustrate, in the experiment, individuals were offered the option of a sure thing with an expected payoff of $800 and the option of a gamble with an expected payoff of $850. Most people chose the sure thing, even though the expected payoff was $50 less than the expected payoff of the gamble. But would the experimental results be different if the expected payoff were larger than $50? Suppose the sure thing's expected payoff was $800 and the gamble's expected payoff was $1,000. Would people still go with the sure thing over the gamble if the gamble's expected payoff were $200 more, instead of $50 more, than the sure thing's payoff? Would people still go with the sure thing over the gamble if the gamble's expected payoff were $10,000 more, instead of $50 more, than the sure thing's payoff? In other words, the difference between the two expected payoffs (sure thing and gamble) may make all the difference as to how people decide.

20-3b Is One Dollar Always One Dollar?

Do people treat money differently depending on where it comes from? Traditional economics argues that they should not; after all, a dollar is a dollar is a dollar. Specifically, a dollar that someone gives you as a gift is no different from a dollar you earn or a dollar you find on the street. When people treat some dollars differently from other dollars, they are *compartmentalizing*: They are saying that dollars in some compartments (of their minds) are valued differently from dollars in other compartments.

Suppose you plan to see a Broadway play, the ticket for which costs $100. You buy the $100 ticket on Monday to see the play on Friday night. When Friday night arrives, you realize you have lost the ticket. Do you spend another $100 to buy another ticket (given that another ticket can be purchased)?[4]

Now let's change the circumstances slightly. Instead of buying the ticket on Monday, you plan to buy the ticket at the ticket window on Friday night. At the ticket window on Friday night, you realize you have lost $100 somewhere between home and the theater. Given that you still have enough money to buy a $100 ticket to the play, do you buy it?

---

[4]. This example comes from Gary Belsky and Thomas Gilovich, *Why Smart People Make Big Money Mistakes and How to Correct Them* (New York:Simon & Schuster, 1999).

Regardless of how you answer each question, some economists argue that your answers should be consistent. If you say no to the first question, you should say no to the second. If you say yes to the first, you should say yes to the second. The two questions, based on two slightly different settings, present you with essentially the same choice.

However, when asked the two questions, many people say that they will not pay an additional $100 to buy a second ticket (having lost the first one) but will spend an additional $100 to buy a first ticket (having lost $100 in cash between home and the theater). Some people argue that spending an additional $100 on an additional ticket is the same as paying $200 to see the play—and that is just too much to pay. However, they don't see themselves as spending $200 to see the play when they lose $100 and pay $100 for a ticket. In either case, though, $200 is gone. Behavioral economists argue that people who answer the two questions differently (yes to one and no to the other) are compartmentalizing. They are treating two $100 amounts in two different ways, as if they come from two different compartments. For example, if people will not buy a second $100 ticket (having lost the first $100 ticket) but will buy a first ticket (having lost $100 cash), their behavior is effectively indicating that $100 lost on a ticket is different from $100 lost in cash.

Consider another situation. Suppose you earn $1,000 by working hard at a job and also win $1,000 at the roulette table in Las Vegas. Would you feel freer to spend the $1,000 you won than to spend the $1,000 you earned? If the answer is yes, then you are treating money differently, depending on where it came from and on what you had to do to get it. Nothing is necessarily wrong or immoral about that, but it is interesting because $1,000 is $1,000 is $1,000—no matter where it came from and no matter what you had to do to get it.

Finally, consider an experiment conducted by two marketing professors. Drazen Prelec and Duncan Simester once organized a sealed-bid auction for tickets to a Boston Celtics basketball game. Half the participants in the auction were told that, if they had the winning bid, they had to pay in cash. The other half of the participants were told that, if they had the winning bid, they had to pay with a credit card.

Under the assumption that the two groups were divided randomly and that neither group showed a stronger or weaker preference for seeing the Celtics game, the average bid from the people who had to pay cash should have been the same as the average bid from the people who had to pay with a credit card. But that didn't happen; instead, the average bid of the people who had to pay with a credit card was higher than the average bid of the people who had to pay with cash. Using a credit card somehow caused people to bid higher dollar amounts than they would have bid if they had to pay cash. Money from the credit card compartment seemed to be more quickly or easily spent than money from the cash compartment.

20-3c Coffee Mugs and the Endowment Effect

In an economics experiment, coffee mugs were allocated randomly to half the people in a group. Each person with a mug was asked to state a price at which he would be willing to sell his mug. Each person without a mug was asked to state a price at which he would be willing to buy a mug.

Even though the mugs were allocated randomly (in other words, the people who received mugs did not necessarily value them more than those who did not receive them), the lowest price at which the owner would sell the mug was, on average, higher than the highest price at which a buyer would pay to buy a mug. For example, the sellers wouldn't sell the mugs for less than $15, and the buyers wouldn't pay more than $10.

This outcome—called the *endowment effect*—is odd. Even though we have no reason to believe that the people who received the mugs valued them more than the people who didn't receive them, people seem to place a high value on something (such as a mug) simply because they own it. In other words, they seem to show an inclination to hold on to what they have.

If this tendency applies to you, think of what it means. When you go into a store to buy a sweater, you might determine that a sweater is worth no more to you than, say, $40 and that you are not willing to pay more than $40 for it. But if someone gave you the sweater as a gift and you were asked to sell it, you wouldn't be willing to sell it for less than, say, $50. Owning the sweater makes it more valuable to you.

Economist David Friedman says that such behavior is not limited to humans.[5] He points out that some species of animals exhibit territorial behavior; that is, they are more likely to fight to keep what they have than to fight to get what they do not have. As Friedman notes, "It is a familiar observation that a dog will fight harder to keep his own bone than to take another dog's bone."

Friedman argues that this type of behavior in humans makes perfect sense in a hunter–gatherer society. Here is what Friedman has to say:

> Now consider the same logic [found in the fact that a dog will fight harder to keep the bone he has than to take a bone from another dog] in a hunter–gatherer society—in which there are no external institutions to enforce property rights. Imagine that each individual considers every object in sight, decides how much each is worth to him, and then tries to appropriate it, with the outcome of the resulting Hobbesian struggle determined by some combination of how much each wants things and how strong each individual is. It does not look like a formula for a successful society, even on the scale of a hunter–gatherer band.
>
> There is an alternative solution, assuming that humans are at least as smart as dogs, robins, and fish. Some method, possibly as simple as physical possession, is used to define what "belongs to" whom. Each individual then commits himself to fight very hard to protect his "property"—much harder than he would be willing to fight in order to appropriate a similar object from someone else's possession—with the commitment made via some psychological mechanism presumably hardwired into humans. The result is both a considerably lower level of (risky) violence and a considerably more prosperous society.
>
> The fact that the result is attractive does not, of course, guarantee that it will occur—evolution selects for the reproductive interest of the individual, not the group. But in this case they are the same. To see that, imagine a population in which some individuals have adopted the commitment strategy [outlined above—that is, fighting for what you physically possess], and some have adopted different commitment strategies—for example, a strategy of fighting to the death for whatever they see as valuable. It should be fairly easy to see that individuals in the first group will, on average, do better for themselves—hence have (among other things) greater reproductive success—than those in the second group.
>
> How do I commit myself to fight very hard for something? One obvious way is some psychological quirk that makes that something appear very valuable to me. Hence the same behavior pattern that shows up as territorial behavior in fish and ferocious defense of bones in dogs shows up in Cornell students [who were given the coffee mugs] as an endowment effect. Just as in the earlier cases, behavior that was functional in the environment in which we evolved continues to be observed, even in an environment in which its function has largely disappeared.[6]

20-3d Does the Endowment Effect Hold Only for New Traders?

The endowment effect has not gone untested. John List, an economist at the University of Chicago, wanted to know whether new traders were more likely than experienced traders to experience the endowment effect. He went to a sports card exchange where people trade regularly. In one

---

[5]. See his "Economics and Evolutionary Psychology" at his website, http://www.daviddfriedman.com/Academic/econ_and_evol_psych/economics_and_evol_psych.html.
[6]. Ibid., p. 10.

experiment, he took aside a group of card fans and gave them such things as sports autographs and sports badges. He then gave them the opportunity to trade. He observed that the more experience traders had (at trading such items), the less prone they were to the endowment effect.

One criticism of this experiment was that new traders were less likely to trade than experienced traders because novices were not sure of the value of the sports autographs. To meet this criticism, List conducted another experiment with chocolate and coffee mugs, where he was sure everyone did know the values of the items. Once again, he observed some endowment effect, but it was not as evident as in the sports memorabilia case, and—more important—only newer traders demonstrated the effect. In other words, experience as a trader seems to make one less prone to the endowment effect.

We value X more highly if we have it than if we do not have it because such behavior at one point in our evolution made possible a system of property rights in a world where the alternative was the Hobbesian jungle.

Economics 24/7

Does It Matter to You . . . If You Are Subject to the Endowment Effect?

Consider Isaac, who is currently getting ready to sell the house that he has owned and lived in for 20 years. He has decided that he will not sell his house for less than $600,000. His realtor tells him that comparable houses in the neighborhood are selling for $550,000 and that he has probably overpriced his house by $50,000. However, Isaac says that he believes his house is "worth" $600,000, and that he won't sell his house for any less. Isaac's realtor asks him how much he would be willing to pay for the house if he were buying it today. And he says that he would be willing to pay $550,000.

This is a case of the endowment effect: Isaac is placing a higher dollar value on the house he has owned for 20 years than he would place on the house if he didn't own it.

Does it matter if Isaac is subject to the endowment effect? It could very well matter. To illustrate just how, consider the following scenario. Isaac goes ahead and lists his house for $600,000. He has had people looking at his house, but so far, everyone who has looked at his house has offered $550,000 for it, which is the price he would likely offer if he were buying the house today. Isaac turns down every offer, continuing to believe that his house is "worth" $600,000.

Over time, Isaac begins to wonder if, perhaps, he should sell his house for $550,000. The reality of not receiving an offer of $600,000 for some time makes him believe that buyers may simply be unwilling to pay $600,000 for his house. Finally, he decides to lower the price of his house. But now, the market price of the house no longer appears to be $550,000. Demand for houses in his neighborhood has fallen recently, and now the market equilibrium price for his house appears to be $520,000. In the end, Isaac ends up selling his house for $520,000.

Does it matter to Isaac that he was subject to the endowment effect? It mattered $30,000, which is the difference between what he could have sold his house for when he first placed it on the market and what he ended up selling it for.

Economics 24/7

$40 and Two People: The Ultimatum Game[7]

The ultimatum game involves two people and one pot of money. One person divides the money between himself and the other person. The other person, who knows how much money has been allotted to him, can either accept his portion of the money or reject it. If he rejects it, then neither person gets any money. To illustrate, suppose Jack is going to divide $40 between himself and Mateo. Jack gives himself $35, and he gives Mateo $5. At this point, Mateo can either accept or reject the $5 that Jack has apportioned to him. If he accepts it, then he gets the $5, and Jack gets the $35. But if he rejects it, neither he nor Jack gets any money.

In Mateo's position, would you accept the $5 or reject it? Often, your strategy may depend on whether this is a one-time deal or there are other rounds of play. If there are other rounds of play, you might reject the initial offer of $5 so that you send a message to Jack: Either divide the money more nearly equal (closer to $20 each), or I will make sure you get nothing. Over several rounds of play, this strategy may give you the most money overall.

But if it is a one-round game, which is the way the ultimatum game is often played, does rejecting the deal make sense, no matter how Jack divides the money? If Jack gives himself $35 and you $5 and if you reject the deal, you do not get the $5. If you accept the deal, you get at least the $5. When economists have experimented with the one-round ultimatum game, they find that many participants reject the money offer if it is not close to half the money. In other words, they are likely to reject an offer of $35–$5 (where they receive the $5) or an offer of $30–$10, whereas they are likely to accept an offer of $20–$20.

Some economists reason that this tendency to reject uneven splits of the money shows that people are more concerned with their relative income position than with their absolute income position. In other words, how much income one has does not seem to matter as much as how much income one has relative to others.

In one experiment, performed by economist Terence Burnham of Harvard University, the results showed that men with higher testosterone levels were more likely to reject unequal offers of money than those with lower testosterone levels. Five of seven men with the highest testosterone levels in the group rejected an unequal offer, whereas only one of 19 men with lower testosterone levels rejected an unequal offer. Because high testosterone is highly correlated with social dominance (in many societies), one conclusion might be that the higher a man's testosterone level is, the more relative position (as opposed to absolute position) seems to matter.

Another way of looking at the results of the ultimatum game is to say that sometimes people are irrational. In other words, turning down a $35–$5 offer is irrational because having $5 is better than not having $5. Of course, another perspective is that rejecting such an offer is not irrational at all for someone who is trying to maximize his or her relative position in society, not the number of dollars the person has. In such a case, rejecting offers that lower one's relative position *is* rational.

[7] This feature is based on "Money Isn't Everything" in *The Economist*, July 5, 2007.

20-3e Framing

In economics, the term *framing* refers to how a problem is presented. To illustrate, we draw on the work of Amos Tversky and Daniel Kahneman, who have shown that framing can influence the choices one makes. In fact, how a problem is framed can lead to a reversal of preferences.

Before getting to how problems are framed, consider the following two options, a sure thing and a gamble:

- *Sure Thing*. You are guaranteed a payment of $50.
- *Gamble*. A coin is tossed. If heads comes up, you win nothing; if tails comes up, you win $100.

The *expected payoff* of the sure thing is $50 ($50 × 100 percent = $50). The expected payoff of the gamble is $50 ($0 × ½ + $100 × ½ = $50). Notice that, in this example, the expected payoffs of the sure thing and the gamble are the same: $50. Three terms can be used to describe a person's attitude toward risk. Given a sure thing and a gamble that have the same expected payoff:

- A person who prefers the sure thing over the gamble is called *risk averse*.
- A person who prefers the gamble over the sure thing is *risk loving*.
- A person who is indifferent between the two options is *risk neutral*.

Tversky and Kahneman proposed an Asian disease problem: Suppose the United States is preparing for an outbreak of an unusual Asian disease, which could kill 600 people. A group of individuals is asked to choose between two options (programs) that have been proposed to combat the disease. The choice is framed as follows:

- *Option A (a sure thing).* Two hundred people will be saved.
- *Option B (a gamble).* There is a one-third probability that 600 people will be saved and a two-thirds probability that no one will be saved.

Notice that the expected payoff for each option is the same. In option A (the sure thing), 200 people will be saved, and 400 people will die. In option B (the gamble), one-third of 600 people are expected to be saved, for an expected payoff of 200 lives saved and 400 lives lost. When Tversky and Kahneman surveyed people as to their preference between the two options, 72 percent of the people chose option A (the sure thing), and 28 percent chose option B (the gamble). Because options A and B have the same expected payoff and the majority of people chose the sure thing over the gamble, we conclude that people are generally risk averse.

In a second survey, a group of individuals was confronted with another two options, framed in the following way:

- *Option C (the sure thing).* Four hundred people will die.
- *Option D (the gamble).* There is a one-third probability that nobody will die and a two-thirds probability that 600 people will die.

The expected payoff in option C (the sure thing) is that 400 people will die and 200 people will be saved. The expected payoff in option D (the gamble) is that 400 people will die and 200 people will be saved (600 × 2/3 = 400 die; 600 × 1/3 = 200 saved). Once again, the expected payoffs of the two options are the same. More importantly, the expected payoffs of options C and D are the same as the expected payoffs of options A and B from the previous survey. It is therefore reasonable to think that the results of the second survey would be similar to the results of the first survey.

As it turns out, the results were completely different: Only 22 percent of the persons surveyed chose the sure thing (as opposed to 72 percent in the first survey), and 78 percent chose the gamble (as opposed to 28 percent in the first survey). People were now overwhelmingly choosing the gamble over the sure thing. The conclusion from the second survey is that people are generally risk loving.

What made the difference in choosing between options A and B and between options C and D? The answer is that the options were framed differently. Options A and B were phrased in terms of *people saved*; options *C* and *D* were phrased in terms of *people dying*. When the options were phrased in terms of lives saved, the majority of people chose the sure thing and were risk averse. But when the options were phrased in terms of people dying, the majority of people chose the gamble and therefore were risk loving. Conclusion: *Even when the expected payoffs are the same, how the options are framed (people saved or people dying) can affect the choices people make.* In our example, framing caused risk-averse choosers to become risk-loving choosers.

20-3f Neuroeconomics

Neuroeconomics is a branch of behavioral economics. In neuroeconomics, the brain is studied with tools such as magnetic resonance imaging (MRI) to see what is happening when people make choices, have certain thoughts, try to solve certain problems, and so on. For a concrete example of an issue that might interest a neuroeconomist, consider choices that human beings make that involve two time references: the present and the future.

There are two key subsystems of the brain. One deals with how we feel emotionally, how we respond to people, and how we respond to what we consider fair and unfair. This is the limbic system. The other subsystem of the brain deals with calculating, conscious, future-oriented thinking. This is the analytic system.

Using magnetic resonance imaging, researchers find that both systems of the brain show activity when faced with some choices. For example, when individuals are asked to choose between receiving $20 now and receiving $23 in a month, both the limbic and analytic systems show activity. Notice that the choice here has to do with a present–future trade-off: Get something now, or get more of that something in the future.

When faced with present–future choices, the limbic system (which weights the present heavily) seems to win out over the analytic system: Individuals choose the present (receive $20 now) over the future (receive $23 in a month). Stated differently, temptation wins out over waiting. Brain researchers think that, when faced with a present–future trade-off, the brain might weight the present high and future low because responding quickly and definitively to present rewards might have come with an evolutionary advantage, since future rewards in an environment in which human evolution took place were so uncertain. Grab what you can now, for tomorrow may not come.

But what does the brain do when an individual is faced with *two future-oriented choices*, such as receiving $20 in two weeks (the future) or receiving $23 in a month (a slightly more distant future). In that case, researchers have found activity in the analytic system but not in the limbic system. It is as if the limbic system has dropped out of its tug-of-war with the analytic system. As a result, individuals often choose the later future-oriented choice: $23 in a month instead of $20 in two weeks.

1. Bijan's grandmother is very cautious about spending money. Yesterday, she gave Bijan a gift of $100 for his birthday. Bijan also received a gift of $100 from his father, who isn't nearly as cautious about spending money as Bijan's grandmother is. Bijan believes that buying frivolous things with his grandmother's gift would be wrong, but not with his father's gift. Is Bijan compartmentalizing? Explain your answer.

2. Summarize David Friedman's explanation of the endowment effect.

Office Hours

"Is There an Indirect Way of Proving the Law of Diminishing Marginal Utility?"

Student: In class, you proved that the law of demand is consistent with utility maximization. This was an important proof for me because I had always accepted the law of demand as true, but I never really felt easy with the idea that individuals seek to maximize utility. Your proof that the law of demand is consistent with utility maximization helps put this earlier uneasiness of mine to rest.

Having said that, I want to know if there is any similar proof of the law of diminishing marginal utility? The law of diminishing marginal utility sounds true, but can it be proven so?

Instructor: Yes, there is. To illustrate, let's start with something that we know is true because it is so obvious: People trade. Now, it's not likely that they would trade if the law of diminishing marginal utility did not hold.

Student: In other words, you're saying that the law of diminishing marginal utility is consistent with the fact that people trade.

Instructor: Yes. Consider two people, Smith and Jones. Smith has 100 apples and Jones has 100 oranges. As Smith consumes her apples, her marginal utility declines. Her 10th apple doesn't give her as much utility as her ninth, and so on. The same is true for Jones with respect to oranges. In other words, as Smith and Jones consume successive units of what they have, their respective marginal utilities fall.

At some point, Smith's marginal utility of consuming another apple is likely less than her marginal utility of consuming something different—such as an orange. And at some point, Jones's marginal utility of consuming another orange is likely less than his marginal utility of consuming something different—say, an apple. When this point comes, Smith and Jones will trade. For Smith, the marginal utility of consuming an apple will be less than the marginal utility of consuming an orange, and she will gladly trade an apple for an orange. For Jones, the marginal utility of consuming an orange will be less than the marginal utility of consuming an apple, and he will gladly trade an orange for an apple.

Now, suppose the law of diminishing marginal utility did not exist. Then Smith would have the same marginal utility when she consumed her first and her 100th apple, and this marginal utility would always be greater than her marginal utility of consuming an orange. The situation would be reversed for Jones: He would have the same marginal utility when he consumed his first and his 100th orange, and that marginal utility would always be greater than his marginal utility of consuming an apple. Thus, Smith and Jones would never trade with each other. The law of diminishing marginal utility, at work on both apples and oranges, eventually gets Smith and Jones to trade.

Points to Remember

1. The law of demand is consistent with utility maximization.
2. The law of diminishing marginal utility is consistent with the fact that individuals trade.

Chapter Summary

The Law of Diminishing Marginal Utility

- The law of diminishing marginal utility holds that, as the amount of a good consumed increases, the marginal utility of the good decreases.
- The law of diminishing marginal utility should not be used to make interpersonal utility comparisons. For example, the law does not say that a millionaire receives less (or more) utility from an additional dollar than a poor man does. All it says is that, for both the millionaire and the poor man, the last dollar has less value than the next-to-last dollar has.

The Diamond–Water Paradox

- The diamond–water paradox states that what has great value in use sometimes has little value in exchange and that what has little value in use sometimes has great value in exchange. A knowledge of the difference between total utility and marginal utility is necessary to unravel the paradox.

- A good can have high total utility and low marginal utility. For example, water's total utility is high, but because water is so plentiful, its marginal utility is low. In short, water is immensely useful, but it is so plentiful that individuals place relatively low value on another unit of it. In contrast, diamonds are not as useful as water, but because there are few diamonds in the world, the marginal utility of diamonds is high. In sum, on the one hand, a good can be extremely useful and have a low price if the good is in plentiful supply (high value in use, low value in exchange); on the other hand, a good can be of little use and have a high price if the good is in short supply (low value in use, high value in exchange).

Consumer Equilibrium

- Individuals seek to equate marginal utilities per dollar. For example, if a person receives more utility per dollar spent on good A than on good B, she will reorder her purchases and buy more A and less B. The tendency is to move away from the condition $MU_A/P_A > MU_B/P_B$ and toward the condition $MU_A/P_A = MU_B/P_B$. The latter condition represents consumer equilibrium (in a two-good world).

Marginal Utility Analysis and the Law of Demand

- Marginal utility analysis can be used to illustrate the law of demand, which states that price and quantity demanded are inversely related, *ceteris paribus*. Starting from consumer equilibrium in a world containing only two goods, A and B, a decline in the price of A will cause MU_A/P_A to be greater than MU_B/P_B. As a result, the consumer will purchase more of good A in order to restore herself to equilibrium.

Behavioral Economics

- Behavioral economists argue that some human behavior does not fit neatly—at a minimum, easily—into the traditional economic framework.
- Behavioral economists believe that they have identified human behaviors that are inconsistent with the model of persons as rational, self-interested, and consistent: (1) Individuals are willing to spend some money to lower the incomes of others, even if doing so lowers their own incomes. (2) Individuals don't always treat one dollar as one dollar: Some dollars seem to be treated differently than others. (3) Individuals sometimes value X more if it is theirs than if it isn't theirs and they are seeking to acquire it. (4) The way a set of options is framed (presented) can matter to the choices individuals make.

Key Terms and Concepts

Diamond–Water Paradox
Utility
Util
Total Utility
Marginal Utility
Law of Diminishing
Interpersonal Utility Comparison
Consumer Equilibrium

Questions and Problems

1. Give a numerical example that illustrates total utility rising as marginal utility declines.
2. The law of diminishing marginal utility is consistent with the fact that people trade. Do you agree or disagree? Explain your answer.
3. "If we take $1 away from a rich person and give it to a poor person, the rich person loses less utility than the poor person gains." Comment.
4. Is it possible to get so much of a good that it turns into a bad? If so, give an example.
5. If a person consumes fewer units of a good, will marginal utility of the good increase as total utility decreases? Why or why not?
6. The marginal utility of good A is 4 utils, and its price is $2. The marginal utility of good B is 6 utils, and its price is $1. Is the individual consumer maximizing (total) utility if she spends a total of $3 by buying one unit of each good? If not, how can more utility be obtained?
7. Individuals who buy second homes usually spend less for them than they do for their first homes. Why is this the case?
8. Describe five everyday examples of you or someone else making an interpersonal utility comparison.

Chapter 20 Consumer Choice: Maximizing Utility and Behavioral Economics

9. Is there a logical link between the law of demand and the assumption that individuals seek to maximize utility? (*Hint:* Think of how the condition for consumer equilibrium can be used to express the inverse relationship between price and quantity demanded.)
10. List five sets of two goods each (i.e., each set is composed of two goods; for example, diamonds and water make up one set) such that the good with the greater value in use has a lower value in exchange than does the good with the lower value in use.
11. Do you think that people with high IQs are in consumer equilibrium (equating marginal utilities per dollar) more often than people with low IQs? Why or why not?
12. What is the endowment effect?
13. After each toss of a coin, one person has more money and one person has less. If the person with less money cares about relative rank and status, will he be willing to pay, say, $1 to reduce the other person's winnings by, say, 50¢? Will he be willing to pay 25¢ to reduce the other person's winnings by $1? Explain your answers.
14. How is buying a house in a good school district like sending children to a private school?
15. Of two similar houses on a street, one faces the ocean and the other does not. How might we determine the price of an ocean view? Explain your answer.
16. What is framing, and what effect can it have on the choices that individuals make?

Working With Numbers and Graphs

1. The marginal utility for the third unit of X is 60 utils, and the marginal utility for the fourth unit of X is 45 utils. If the law of diminishing marginal utility holds, what is the minimum total utility of X?
2. Fill in blanks A–D in the following table.

Units of Good Consumed	Total Utility (utils)	Marginal Utility (utils)
1	10	10
2	19	A
3	B	8
4	33	C
5	35	D

3. The total utilities of the first 5 units of good X are 10, 19, 26, 33, and 40 utils, respectively. In other words, the total utility of 1 unit is 10 utils, the total utility of 2 units is 19 utils, and so on. What is the marginal utility of the third unit?

Use the following table to answer Questions 4 and 5:

Units of Good X	Total Utility of Good X (utils)	Units of Good Y	Total Utility of Good Y (utils)
1	20	1	19
2	35	2	32
3	48	3	40
4	58	4	45
5	66	5	49

4. If Sam spends $5 (total) a week on good X and good Y, and if the price of each good is $1 per unit, then how many units of each good does he purchase to maximize utility?
5. Given the number of units of each good that Sam purchases in Question 4, what is his total utility?
6. Draw the marginal utility curve for a good that has constant marginal utility.
7. The marginal utility curve for units 3–5 of good X is below the horizontal axis. Draw the corresponding part of the total utility curve for good X.

Budget Constraints
All the combinations, or bundles, of two goods a person can purchase, given a certain money income and prices for the two goods.

D-1 The Budget Constraint

Societies have production possibilities frontiers, and individuals have **budget constraints**. A budget constraint is built on three components: two prices and the individual's income. To illustrate, suppose O'Brien has a monthly income of $1,200. Then, in a world of two goods, X and Y, O'Brien can spend his total income on X, he can spend his total income on Y, or he can spend part of his income on X and part on Y. Suppose the price of X is $100 and the price of Y is $80. Then, if O'Brien spends his total income on X, he can purchase a maximum of 12 units; if he spends his total income on Y, he can purchase a maximum of 15 units. Locating these two points on a two-dimensional diagram and then drawing a line between them, as shown in Exhibit 1, gives us O'Brien's budget constraint. Any point on the budget constraint, as well as any point in the triangular area between it and the origin, represents a possible combination (or bundle) of the two goods available to O'Brien.

EXHIBIT 1

The Budget Constraint

An individual's budget constraint gives us a picture of the different combinations (bundles) of two goods available to the individual. (We assume a two-good world; for a many-good world, we could put one good on one axis and all other goods on the other axis.) The budget constraint is derived by finding the two points representing the maximum amount of each good that an individual can consume (given his or her income and the prices of the two goods) and connecting those points.

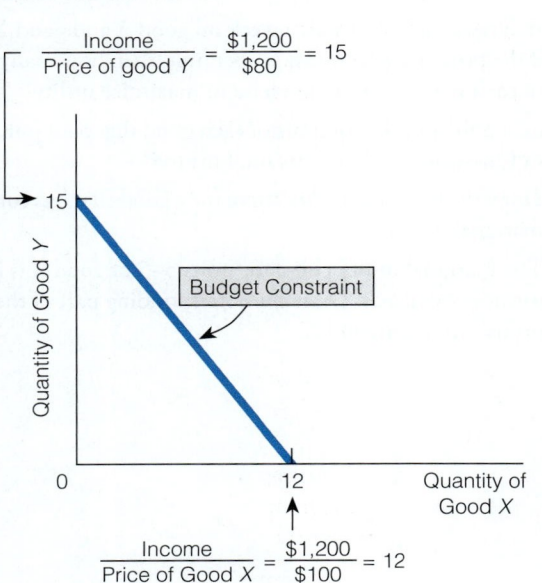

D-1a Slope of the Budget Constraint

The slope of the budget constraint has special significance. The absolute value of the slope represents the relative prices of the two goods X and Y. In Exhibit 1, the slope, or P_X / P_Y, is equal to 1.25, indicating that the relative price of 1 unit of X is 1.25 units of Y.

D-1b What Will Change the Budget Constraint?

If any of the three variables—the two prices and the individual's income—changes, then the budget constraint changes. Not all changes are alike, however. Consider a fall in the price of good X from $100 to $60. With this change, the

EXHIBIT 2

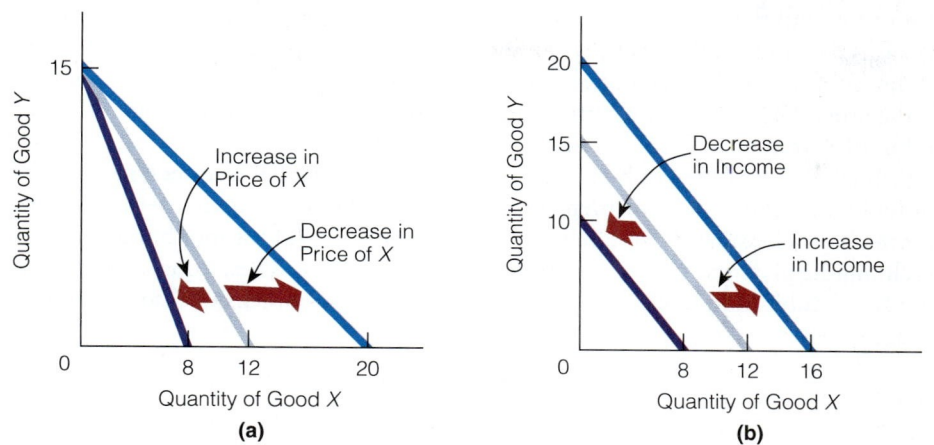

Changes in the Budget Constraint

(a) A change in the price of good X or good Y will change the slope of the budget constraint. (b) A change in income will change the position of the budget constraint while the slope remains constant. Whenever a budget constraint changes, the number of combinations (bundles) of the two goods available to the individual changes too.

---

maximum number of units of good X purchasable with an income of $1,200 rises from 12 to 20. As a result, the budget constraint revolves away from the origin, as shown in Exhibit 2(a). The number of O'Brien's possible combinations of the two goods increases: More bundles of the two goods are available after the price decrease than before.

Now consider what happens to the budget constraint if the price of good X rises. If it goes from $100 to, say, $150, then the maximum number of units of good X falls from 12 to 8. In this case, the budget constraint revolves *toward* the origin and the number of bundles available to O'Brien decreases. In sum, a change in the price of either good changes the slope of the budget constraint, with the result that relative prices and the number of bundles available to the individual also change.

We turn now to a change in income. If O'Brien's income rises to $1,600, the maximum number of purchasable units of X rises to 16, and the maximum number of purchasable units of Y rises to 20. The budget constraint then shifts rightward (away from the origin) and is parallel to the old budget constraint. As a consequence, the number of bundles available to O'Brien increases [Exhibit 2(b)]. If, by contrast, O'Brien's income falls from $1,200 to $800, the extreme endpoints on the budget constraint become $X = 8$ and $Y = 10$. Now the budget constraint shifts leftward (toward the origin) and is parallel to the old budget constraint. As a consequence, the number of bundles available to O'Brien falls.

D-2 Indifference Curves

An individual can, of course, choose any bundle of the two goods on the budget constraint or in the triangular area between it and the origin. If she spends her total income and therefore chooses a point on the budget constraint, this action raises two important questions: (1) Which bundle of the many bundles of the two goods does the individual choose? (2) How does the individual's chosen combination of goods change, given a change in prices or income? Both questions can be answered by combining the budget constraint with the graphical expression of the individual's preferences in an indifference curve.

D-3 Constructing an Indifference Curve

A person can be indifferent between two bundles of goods. Suppose that bundle *A* consists of 2 pairs of shoes and 6 shirts and that bundle *B* consists of 3 pairs of shoes and 4 shirts. A person who is indifferent between these two bundles is implicitly saying that one bundle is as good as the other. She is likely to say this, though, only if she receives equal total utility from the two bundles. If not, she would prefer one bundle to the other.

If we tabulate all the different bundles from which the individual receives equal utility, we have an **indifference set**. We can then plot the data in the indifference set and draw an **indifference curve**. Consider the indifference set in Exhibit 3(a). Of the four bundles of goods, *A–D*, each bundle gives the same total utility as every other one. These equal-utility bundles are plotted in Exhibit 3(b). Connecting these bundles in a two-dimensional space gives us an indifference curve.

Indifference Set
A group of bundles of two goods that give an individual equal total utility.

Indifference Curve
The curve that represents an indifference set and that shows all the bundles of two goods giving an individual equal total utility.

D-3a Characteristics of Indifference Curves

Indifference curves for goods have certain characteristics that are consistent with reasonable assumptions about consumer behavior:

1. *Indifference curves are downward sloping (from left to right).* The assumption that consumers always prefer more of a good to less requires that indifference curves slope downward from left to right. Consider the alternatives to downward sloping: vertical, horizontal, and upward sloping (from left to right). A horizontal or vertical curve would combine bundles of goods, some of which had more of one good and no less of another good than other bundles had [Exhibit 4(a–b)]. (If bundle *B* contains more of one good and no less of another good than bundle *A* does, an individual would not be indifferent between them. Remember, individuals prefer more to less.) An upward-sloping curve would combine bundles of goods, some of which had more of both goods than other bundles had [Exhibit 4(c)]. More simply, indifference curves are downward sloping because a person has to get more of one good in order to maintain the same level of satisfaction (utility) when giving up some of another good.

EXHIBIT 3

An Indifference Set

Bundle	Milk (units)	Orange Juice (units)
A	8	3
B	5	4
C	3	5
D	2	6

(a)

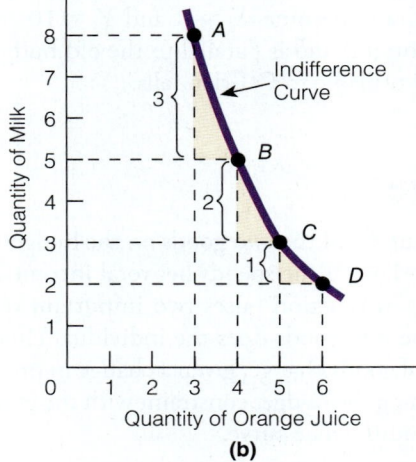

(b)

An Indifference Set and an Indifference Curve

An indifference set is a number of bundles of two goods such that each bundle yields the same total utility. An indifference curve represents an indifference set. In this exhibit, data from the indifference set (a) are used to derive an indifference curve (b).

Appendix D Budget Constraint and Indifference Curve Analysis

EXHIBIT 4

Indifference Curves for Goods Do Not Look Like This

(a) Bundle B has more milk and no less orange juice than bundle A, so an individual would prefer B to A and not be indifferent between them. (b) Bundle B has more orange juice and no less milk than bundle A, so an individual would prefer B to A and not be indifferent between them. (c) Bundle B has more milk and more orange juice than bundle A, so an individual would prefer B to A and not be indifferent between them.

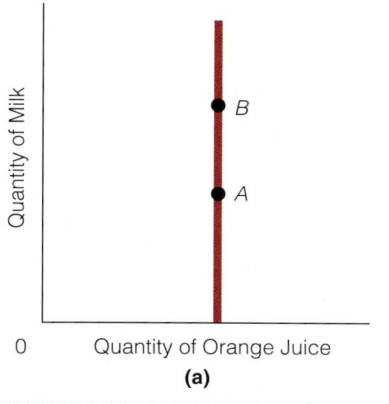
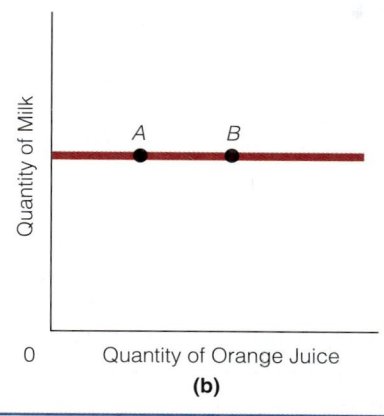
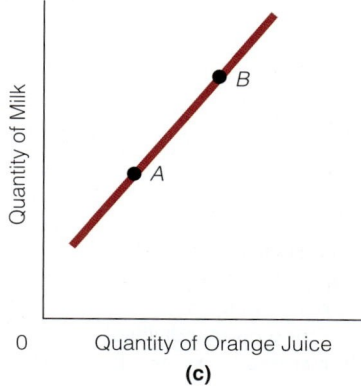

2. *Indifference curves are convex to the origin.* As we move down and to the right along the indifference curve, it becomes flatter. For example, at 8 units of milk [point *A* in Exhibit 3(b)], the individual is willing to give up 3 units of milk to get an additional unit of orange juice (and thus move to point *B*). At point *B*, where she has 5 units of milk, she is willing to give up only 2 units of milk to get an additional unit of orange juice (and thus move to point *C*). Finally, at point *C*, with 3 units of milk, she is now willing to give up only 1 unit of milk to get an additional unit of orange juice. Therefore, the more of one good that an individual has, the more units she will give up to get an additional unit of another good; the less of one good that an individual has, the fewer units she will give up to get an additional unit of another good.

What we have just described is reasonable: our observation is a reflection of diminishing marginal utility at work. As the quantity of a good consumed increases, the marginal utility of that good decreases; therefore, the more of one good an individual has, the more units he can (and will) sacrifice to get an additional unit of another good and still maintain total utility. Stated differently, if the law of diminishing marginal utility did not exist, saying that indifference curves of goods are convex to the origin would not make sense.

Another important point about marginal utilities is that *the absolute value of the slope of the indifference curve*—the **marginal rate of substitution**—*represents the ratio of the marginal utility of the good on the horizontal axis to the marginal utility of the good on the vertical axis*:

$$\frac{MU_{\text{good on horizontal axis}}}{MU_{\text{good on vertical axis}}}$$

Marginal Rate of Substitution
The amount of one good that an individual is willing to give up to obtain an additional unit of another good and maintain equal total utility.

Let's look carefully at the preceding assertion. First, the absolute value of the slope of the indifference curve is the marginal rate of substitution (*MRS*). The *MRS* is the amount of one good an individual is willing to give up to obtain an additional unit of another good and maintain equal total utility. For example, in Exhibit 3(b), we see that moving from point A to point B, the individual is willing to give up 3 units of milk to get an additional unit of orange juice, with total utility between the two points remaining constant. The marginal rate of substitution is therefore 3 units of milk for 1 unit of orange juice in the area between points A and B. Further, the absolute value of the slope of the indifference curve (the MRS) is equal to the ratio of the MU of the good on the horizontal axis to the MU of the good on the vertical axis. How can this be? Well, if an individual giving up 3 units of milk and receiving 1 unit of orange juice maintains her total utility, then (in the area under consideration) the marginal utility of orange juice is approximately three times the marginal utility of milk. In general,

Absolute value of the slope of the indifference curve = Marginal rate of substitution

$$= \frac{MU_{\text{good on horizontal axis}}}{MU_{\text{good on vertical axis}}}$$

Indifference Curve Map
A map that represents a number of indifference curves for a given individual with reference to two goods.

Transitivity
The principle whereby, if A is preferred to B and B is preferred to C, then A is preferred to C.

3. *Indifference curves that are farther from the origin are preferable to those that are nearer to the origin because they represent larger bundles of goods.* Exhibit 3(b) shows only one indifference curve. However, different bundles of the two goods exist and have indifference curves passing through them. These bundles have less of both goods or more of both goods than those in Exhibit 3(b). Plotting a number of indifference curves on the same diagram gives us an **indifference curve map**, which represents a number of indifference curves for a given individual with reference to two goods (see Exhibit 5).

In Exhibit 5, although only five indifference curves have been drawn, many more could have been added. For example, many indifference curves lie between I_1 and I_2. Also, the farther away from the origin an indifference curve lies, the higher the total utility is that it represents. To see why, compare point A on I_1 and point B on I_2. At point B, there is the same amount of orange juice as at point A but more milk. Point B is therefore preferable to point A, and, because B is on I_2 and A is on I_1, I_2 is preferable to I_1. The reason is simple: An individual receives more utility at any point on I_2 (because more goods are available) than at any point on I_1.

4. *Indifference curves do not cross (intersect).* Indifference curves do not cross because individuals' preferences exhibit **transitivity**, the logical principle whereby, if A is preferred to B and B is preferred to C, then A is preferred to C. For example, if Kristin prefers Coca-Cola to Pepsi and she also prefers Pepsi to root beer, then she must prefer Coca-Cola to root beer. If she said she preferred root beer to Coca-Cola, she would be contradicting her earlier preferences. To say that an individual has transitive preferences means that she maintains a logical order of preferences over a given period.

EXHIBIT 5

An Indifference Map

A few of the many possible indifference curves are shown. Any point in the two-dimensional space is on an indifference curve. Indifference curves farther away from the origin represent greater total utility than those closer to the origin.

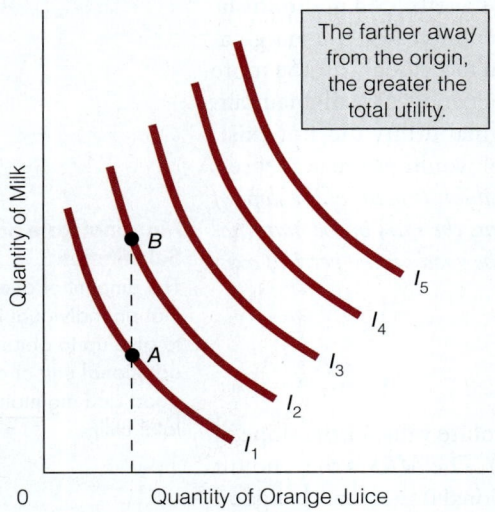

The farther away from the origin, the greater the total utility.

Consider what intersecting indifference curves would represent. In Exhibit 6, indifference curves I_1 and I_2 intersect at point A, which lies on both I_1 and I_2. Now, an individual must be indifferent between A and B, because they lie on the same indifference curve. The same holds for A and C. But if the individual is indifferent between A and B and between A and C, then she must be indifferent between B and C. But C has more of both goods than B, and, thus, the individual will *not* be indifferent between B and C; rather, she will prefer C to B. Thus, we cannot have transitive preferences and make sense of intersecting indifference curves. We can, however, have transitive preferences and make sense of *nonintersecting* indifference curves. Therefore, we go with the latter.

D-4 The Indifference Map and the Budget Constraint Come Together

Together, the indifference map and the budget constraint illustrate consumer equilibrium. We have the following facts:

- The individual has a budget constraint.
- The absolute value of the slope of the budget constraint equals the relative prices of the two goods under consideration, say, P_X / P_Y.
- The individual has an indifference map.
- The absolute value of the slope of the indifference curve at any point is the marginal rate of substitution, which is equal to the marginal utility of one good divided by the marginal utility of another good, or MU_X / MU_Y.

The necessary condition for consumer equilibrium is obviously that the individual will try to reach a point on the highest indifference curve possible. This point is where the slope of the budget constraint is equal to the slope of an indifference curve (or where the budget constraint is tangent to an indifference curve). At that point, consumer equilibrium is established, and the following condition holds:

$$\frac{P_X}{P_Y} = \frac{MU_X}{MU_Y}$$

EXHIBIT 6

Intersecting Indifference Curves Are Inconsistent With Transitive Preferences

Point A lies on both indifference curves I_1 and I_2. This means that the individual is indifferent between A and B and between A and C, a pair of conditions that (supposedly) results in her being indifferent between B and C. But individuals prefer more to less (when it comes to goods) and thus would prefer C to B. We cannot have transitive preferences and make sense of intersecting indifference curves.

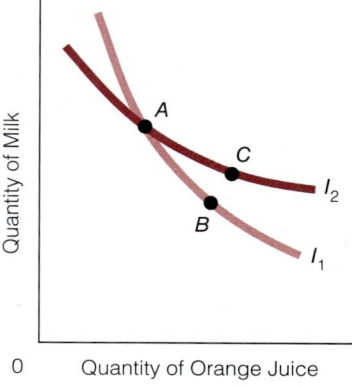

EXHIBIT 7

Consumer Equilibrium

Consumer equilibrium exists at the point where the slope of the budget constraint is equal to the slope of an indifference curve or where the budget constraint is tangent to an indifference curve. In the exhibit, this point is E. Here, $P_X / P_Y = MU_X / MU_Y$; or, rearranging, we have $MU_X / P_X = MU_Y / P_Y$.

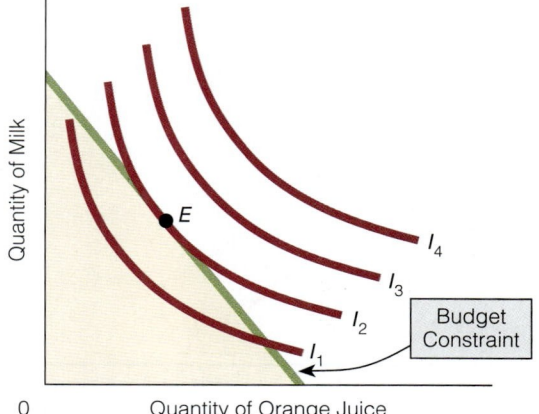

In Exhibit 7, the preceding condition is met at point E. Note that the condition looks similar to that for consumer equilibrium described in this chapter. By rearranging the terms in the condition, we get[1]

$$\frac{MU_X}{P_X} = \frac{MU_Y}{P_Y}$$

D-5 From Indifference Curves to a Demand Curve

We can now derive a demand curve within a budget constraint–indifference curve framework. Exhibit 8(a) shows two budget constraints, one reflecting a $10 price for good X and the other reflecting a $5 price for good X. As the price of X falls, the consumer moves from point A to point B. At B, 35 units of X are consumed; at A, 30 units of X are consumed. So a lower price for X results in greater consumption of X. By plotting the relevant price and quantity data, we derive a demand curve for good X in Exhibit 8(b).

EXHIBIT 8

From Indifference Curves to a Demand Curve

(a) At a price of $10 for good X, consumer equilibrium is at point A, with the individual consuming 30 units of X. As the price falls to $5, the budget constraint moves outward (away from the origin) and the consumer moves to point B and consumes 35 units of X. Plotting the price–quantity data for X gives a demand curve for X in (b).

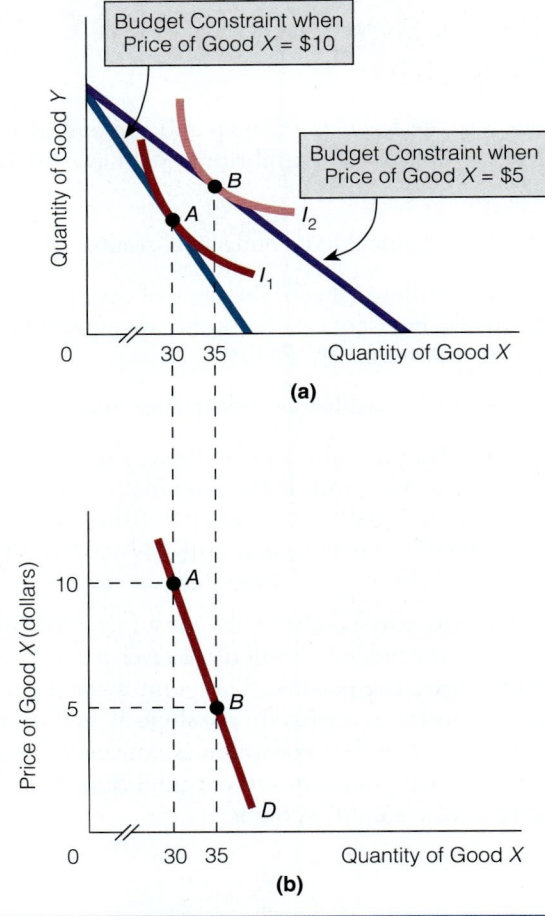

---

[1] Start with $P_X/P_Y = MU_X/MU_Y$ and cross multiply. This gives $P_X MU_Y = P_Y MU_X$. Next, divide both sides by P_X. This gives $MU_Y = P_Y MU_X/P_X$. Finally, divide both sides by P_Y. This gives $MU_Y/P_Y = MU_X/P_X$.

Appendix Summary

- A budget constraint represents all combinations of bundles of two goods that a person can purchase, given a certain money income and prices for the two goods.
- An indifference curve shows all the combinations or bundles of two goods that give an individual equal total utility. Indifference curves are downward sloping, they are convex to the origin, and they do not cross. The farther away from the origin an indifference curve is, the greater total utility it represents for the individual.
- Consumer equilibrium is at the point where the slope of the budget constraint equals the slope of the indifference curve.
- A demand curve can be derived within a budget constraint–indifference curve framework.

Key Terms and Concepts

Budget Constraint
Indifference Set
Indifference Curve
Indifference Curve Map
Marginal Rate of Substitution
Transitivity

Questions and Problems

1. Diagram the following budget constraints:
   a. Income = $4,000; P_X = $50; P_Y = $100
   b. Income = $3,000; P_X = $25; P_Y = $200
   c. Income = $2,000; P_X = $40; P_Y = $150
2. Explain why indifference curves
   a. are downward sloping.
   b. are convex to the origin.
   c. do not cross.
3. Explain why consumer equilibrium is the same under marginal utility analysis or indifference curve analysis.
4. Use indifference curve analysis to derive a demand curve.

Introduction

Everyone deals with business firms on a daily basis. People buy goods from firms: cars, clothes, food, books, entertainment, and other products. And people work for firms as accountants, truck drivers, vice presidents, and editors. Our lives are constantly intermingled with business firms, as buyers of goods and as sellers of our labor services. Even though we deal with business firms daily, most of us probably know little about them. Why do they exist? What do they try to maximize? How do they go about producing the goods they produce? What concepts must firms concern themselves with? In this chapter, we answer many of these questions.

21-1 Why Firms Exist

A **business firm** is an entity that employs resources, or factors of production, to produce goods and services to be sold to consumers, other firms, or the government. To understand why firms exist, we must explain worker behavior, markets, and the questions a firm must answer.

Business Firm
An entity that employs factors of production (resources) to produce goods and services to be sold to consumers, other firms, or the government.

21-1a The Market and the Firm: Invisible Hand Versus Visible Hand

Through the forces of supply and demand, the market guides and coordinates individuals' actions, and it does so in an impersonal manner. No one orders buyers to reduce quantity demanded when price increases; they just do it. No one orders sellers to increase quantity supplied when price increases; they just do it. No one orders more resources to be moved into the production of personal computers when the demand and price for personal computers increase. The market guides individuals from the production of one good into the production of another. It coordinates individuals' actions so that suppliers and demanders find mutual satisfaction at equilibrium. As economist Adam Smith observed, individuals in a market setting are "led by an invisible hand to promote an end which was no part of their intention."

Now, contrast the invisible hand of the market with the visible hand of a manager in a firm. The manager tells the employee on the assembly line to make more computer chips. The manager tells the employee to design a new engine, to paint the lamps green, to put steak and lobster on the menu. Thus, both the invisible hand of the market and the visible hand of the firm's manager guide and coordinate individuals' actions. There is, in other words, both **market coordination** and **managerial coordination**.

If the market is capable of guiding and coordinating individuals' actions, why did firms (and managers) arise in the first place? Why do firms exist?

21-1b The Alchian-and-Demsetz Answer

Economists Armen Alchian and Harold Demsetz suggest that firms are formed when benefits can be obtained from individuals working as a team.[1] Sometimes, the sum of what individuals can produce as a team is greater than the sum of what they can produce alone:

Sum of team production > Sum of individual production

Consider 11 individuals, all making shoe boxes. Each working alone produces 10 shoe boxes per day, for a total daily output of 110 shoe boxes. If they work as a team, however, the same 11 individuals can produce 140 shoe boxes. The added output (30 shoe boxes) may be reason enough for them to work together as a team and to create a firm.

21-1c Shirking on a Team

Although forming a firm can increase output, team production can have problems that do not occur in individual production. One problem of team production is **shirking**, which occurs when workers put forth less than the agreed-to effort. The amount of shirking increases on teams because the costs of shirking to individual team members are lower than when they work alone.

Consider five individuals—Felipe, Delaney, Jonas, Savva, and Rachel—who form a team to produce lightbulbs because they realize that the sum of their team production will be more than the sum of their individual production. They agree to team-produce the lightbulbs, sell them, and split the proceeds five equal ways. On an average day, they produce 140 bulbs and sell each one for $2. Total revenue per day is $280, with each of the five team members receiving $56. Then Jonas begins to shirk. Owing to his shirking, production falls to 135 lightbulbs per day and total revenue falls to $270 per day. Each person now receives $54. Notice that while Jonas did all the shirking, his reduction in pay was only $2, one-fifth of the $10 drop in total revenue.

Economists predict that, in situations (such as team production) where one person receives all the benefits from shirking and pays only a part of the costs, there will be more shirking than when the person who shirks bears the full cost of shirking.

The Monitor (Manager): Taking Care of Shirking
The **monitor** (or manager) plays an important role in the firm. The monitor reduces the amount of shirking by firing shirkers and rewarding the productive members of the firm. In carrying out this task, the monitor can preserve the benefits (increased output) that often come with team production and reduce, if not eliminate, the costs (increased shirking) associated with team production. But then the question is, who or what monitors the monitor? How can the monitor be kept from shirking?

Market Coordination
The process in which individuals perform tasks, such as producing certain quantities of goods, on the basis of changes in market forces, such as supply, demand, and price.

Managerial Coordination
The process in which managers direct employees to perform certain tasks.

Shirking
The behavior of a worker who is putting forth less than the agreed-to effort.

Monitor
A person in a business firm who coordinates team production and reduces shirking.

---

[1] Armen Alchian and Harold Demsetz, "Production, Information Costs, and Economic Organization," *American Economic Review 62* (December 1972): 777–795.

Economics 24/7

"He Never Showed Up"

College professors sometimes assign group projects to their students. They ask students to form groups of, say, five students each, and then they give each group a topic to research, write about, and present to the class. Moreover, the professors often assign the grade the group earns to each individual member of the group. In other words, if the group gets a "B" for its work, then each member of the group is assigned a "B."

Typically, at the beginning of the project, the group meets, assigns different members different tasks, and then arranges to meet later to put all their separate parts of the project together. Let's look at the group project from the perspective of one of the five members. He could very well think, "My grade is largely dependent on what others do, because I contribute only one-fifth of the work to the project. If I don't work very hard on the project, my grade will be a little lower. Therefore, there are certain costs to me of not doing my part, but there are certain benefits too.

In other words, there are both costs and benefits to my shirking. I have a lot of other things to do right now, so the benefits of shirking outweigh the costs. Consequently, I won't spend much time on the project."

In a group project, the costs of shirking are spread over five people and the benefits are received by one person. In an individual project, both the full costs and the full benefits accrue to the same person. The difference in the two projects will affect behavior. We would predict that there will be more shirking in a group project than in an individual project because the costs of shirking are relatively lower in the group project. Often, the professor will hear about this shirking. A member of the group, who does not shirk or shirks very little compared with others, says to the professor, "We were supposed to work on this project together, but Benny hasn't really been doing his part. In fact, we were supposed to meet at the library last night around seven, and he never showed up."

Residual Claimant
Persons who share in the profits of a business firm.

One possibility is to give the monitor an incentive not to shirk. This is often done by making the monitor a **residual claimant** of the firm. A residual claimant receives the excess of revenues over costs (profits) as income. If the monitor shirks, then profits are likely to be lower (or even zero or negative), and the monitor will receive less income.

21-1d Ronald Coase on Why Firms Exist

Ronald Coase, winner of the 1991 Nobel Prize in Economics, argued that "the main reason why it is profitable to establish a firm would seem to be that there is a cost of using the price mechanism."[2] Stated differently, firms exist either to economize on buying and selling everything or to reduce transaction costs.

For example, suppose it takes 20 different operations to produce good X. One way to produce good X, then, is to enter into a separate contract with everyone necessary to complete the 20 different operations. If we assume that one person completes one and only one operation, then we have 20 different contracts. Obviously, costs are associated with preparing and monitoring all these contracts. A firm is a recipe for reducing these costs, effectively replacing many contracts with one.

---
[2] Ronald Coase, "The Nature of the Firm," *Economica*, November 1937.

Here is what Coase had to say:

> *The costs of negotiating and concluding a separate contract for each exchange transaction which takes place on a market must also be taken into account.... It is true that contracts are not eliminated when there is a firm, but they are greatly reduced. A factor of production (or the owner thereof) does not have to make a series of contracts as would be necessary, of course, if this cooperation were a direct result of the working of the price mechanism. For this series of contracts is substituted one. At this state, it is important to note the character of the contract into which a factor enters that is employed within a firm. The contract is one whereby the factor [the employee], for a certain remuneration (which may be fixed or fluctuating), agrees to obey the directions of an entrepreneur within certain limits.*[3]

21-1e Markets: Outside and Inside the Firm

When we put the firm under the microeconomic microscope, what we see is a market of sorts at work. Economics is largely about trades or exchanges; it is about market transactions. In supply-and-demand analysis, the exchanges are between the buyers of goods and services and the sellers of goods and services. In the theory of the firm, the exchanges take place at two levels: (1) at the level of individuals coming together to form a team and (2) at the level of workers choosing a monitor.

Let's look at the theory of the firm in the context of exchange. Individuals initially come together because they realize that the sum of what they can produce as a team is greater than the sum of what they can produce as individuals. In essence, each individual trades working alone for working on a team. Later, after the team has been formed, the team members learn that shirking reduces the amount of the added output they came together to capture in the first place. Now the team members enter into another trade or market transaction: They trade some control over their daily behavior—specifically, they trade an environment in which the cost of shirking is low (teamwork without a monitor) for an environment in which the cost of shirking is high (teamwork with a monitor)—in order to receive a larger absolute amount of the potential benefits that drew them together. In effect, some individuals buy the monitoring services that other individuals sell.

As you continue your study of microeconomics, look for the markets that appear at different levels of analysis.

21-2 Two Sides to Every Business Firm

There are two sides to every market: a buying side (demand) and a selling side (supply). Similarly, there are two sides to every business firm: a revenue side and a cost side. We can see both sides of a firm by focusing on profit. The firm's objective is to maximize **profit**—the difference between total revenue and total cost:

Profit = Total revenue − Total cost

Profit
The difference between total revenue and total cost.

Looking at this profit equation, we can easily understand what any firm would like: its total revenue to be as high as possible and its total cost to be as low as possible. That way, its profit is as high as possible.

Total revenue is equal to the price of a good multiplied by the quantity of the good sold. For example, if a business firm sells 100 units of *X* at $10 per unit, its total revenue is $1,000. In the next chapter, we will begin our discussion of the firm's total revenue. In this chapter, we discuss

---
[3]. Ibid.

the side of the firm that deals with total cost. Of course, the total cost that a firm incurs does not simply fall out of the sky: It is related to the production of the firm. Produce nothing, incur no costs; produce something, incur costs. So, this chapter is focused on production and costs.

21-2a More on Total Cost

A disagreement sometimes arises as to what total cost should include. To illustrate, suppose Jill currently works as an attorney earning $80,000 a year. One day, dissatisfied with her career, Jill quits her job as an attorney and opens a pizzeria. After one year of operating the pizzeria, Jill sits down to compute her profit. She finds that she sold 20,000 pizzas at a price of $10 per pizza, so her total revenue (for the year) was $200,000. Jill computes her total costs by adding the dollar amounts she spent for everything she bought or rented to run the pizzeria. She spent $2,000 on plates, $3,000 on cheese, $4,000 on soda, $20,000 for rent in the mall where the pizzeria is located, $2,000 for electricity, and so on. The dollar payments Jill made for everything she bought or rented are called her *explicit costs*. An **explicit cost** is a cost that is incurred when an actual (monetary) payment is made. So Jill sums her explicit costs, which turn out to be $90,000. Then she computes her profit by subtracting $90,000 from $200,000, giving her a profit of $110,000.

A few days pass before Jill tells her friend Mariah that she earned a $110,000 profit her first year of running the pizzeria. Mariah asks, "Are you sure your profit is $110,000?" Jill assures her that it is. "Did you count the salary you earned as an attorney as a cost?" Mariah asks. Jill tells Mariah that she did not count the $80,000 salary as a cost of running the pizzeria because the $80,000 is not something she paid out to run the pizzeria. "I wrote a check to my suppliers for the pizza ingredients, soda, dishes, and so on," Jill says, "but I didn't write a check to anyone for the $80,000."

Mariah says that, although Jill did not pay out $80,000 in salary to run the pizzeria, still she forfeited $80,000 to run it. "What you could have earned but didn't is a cost to you of running the pizzeria," says Mariah.

Jill's $80,000 salary is what economists call an *implicit cost*. An **implicit cost** is a cost that represents the value of resources used in production for which no actual (monetary) payment is made. It is a cost incurred as a result of a firm's using resources that it owns or that the owners of the firm contribute to it.

If total cost is computed as explicit costs plus implicit costs, then Jill's total cost of running the pizzeria is $90,000 plus $80,000, or $170,000. Subtracting $170,000 from a total revenue of $200,000 leaves a profit of $30,000.

Explicit Cost
A cost incurred when an actual (monetary) payment is made.

Implicit Cost
A cost that represents the value of resources used in production for which no actual (monetary) payment is made.

> **Thinking Like an Economist**
>
> **What Does the Person "Give Up"?** The economist wants to know what a person gives up when she goes into business for herself. What she gives up isn't only the money she pays for resources (to run the business), but also the job she would have had (and the income she would have earned) had she not gone into business for herself.

21-2b Accounting Profit Versus Economic Profit

Economists refer to the first profit that Jill calculated ($110,000) as *accounting profit*. **Accounting profit** is the difference between total revenue and total cost, where total cost equals explicit costs [see Exhibit 1(a)]:

Accounting profit
The difference between total revenue and explicit costs.

Accounting profit = Total revenue − Total cost (Explicit costs)

EXHIBIT 1

Accounting Profit and Economic Profit

Accounting profit equals total revenue minus explicit costs. Economic profit equals total revenue minus the sum of explicit and implicit costs.

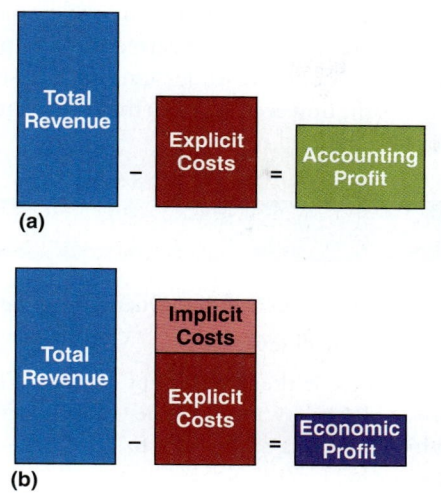

Economists refer to the second profit calculated ($30,000) as *economic profit*. **Economic profit** is the difference between total revenue and total cost, where total cost equals the sum of explicit and implicit costs [see Exhibit 1(b)]:

Economic profit = Total revenue − Total cost (Explicit costs + Implicit costs)

Economic Profit
The difference between total revenue and total cost, including both explicit and implicit costs.

To illustrate the difference between explicit and implicit costs, suppose a person has $100,000 in the bank, earning an interest rate of 5 percent a year. This amounts to $5,000 in interest a year. Now suppose the person takes the $100,000 out of the bank to start a business. The $5,000 in *lost interest* is included in the implicit costs of owning and operating the firm. To see why, let's change the example somewhat. Suppose the person does not use her $100,000 in the bank to start a business but leaves it in the bank and instead takes out a $100,000 loan at an interest rate of 5 percent. Then the interest she has to pay on the loan—$5,000 a year—certainly would be an explicit cost and would take away from her overall profit. It just makes sense, then, to count the $5,000 interest that the owner doesn't earn if she uses her own $100,000 to start the business (instead of taking out a loan) as a cost, albeit implicit.

21-2c Zero Economic Profit Is Not as Bad as It Sounds

Economic profit is usually lower (never higher) than accounting profit. Whereas economic profit is the difference between total revenue and total cost (where total cost is the sum of explicit and implicit costs), accounting profit is the difference between total revenue and only explicit costs. Thus, a firm could earn both a positive accounting profit and a zero economic profit. In economics, a firm that makes a zero economic profit is said to be earning a **normal profit**:

Normal profit = Zero economic profit

However, the owner of a firm should not be worried about making zero economic profit for the year just ending. A zero economic profit—as bad as it may sound—means that the owner has generated total revenue sufficient to cover total cost—that is, *both explicit and implicit costs*.

Normal Profit
Zero economic profit, the level of profit necessary to keep resources employed in a firm. A firm that earns normal profit is earning revenue equal to its total costs (explicit plus implicit costs).

If, for example, the owner's implicit cost is a (forfeited) $100,000 salary working for someone else, then earning a zero economic profit means that he has done as well as he could have done in his next-best (alternative) line of employment.

When we realize that zero economic profit (or normal profit) means doing as well as could have been done, we understand that it isn't bad to make zero economic profit. Zero accounting profit, however, is altogether different: It implies that some part of total cost has not been covered by total revenue.

(Answers to Self-Test questions are in Answers to Self-Test Questions at the back of the book.)

1. Will individuals form teams or firms in all settings?
2. Suppose everything about two people is the same except that currently one person earns a high salary and the other person earns a low salary. Which person is more likely to start his or her own business and why?
3. Is accounting profit or economic profit larger? Why?
4. When can a business owner be earning a profit but not covering costs?

21-3 Production

Production is a transformation of resources or inputs into goods and services. You may think of production as you might think of making a cake. It takes certain ingredients to make a cake: sugar, flour, and so on. Similarly, it takes certain resources, or inputs, to produce a computer, a haircut, a piece of furniture, or a house.

Economists often talk about two types of inputs in the production process: fixed and variable. A **fixed input** is an input whose quantity cannot be changed as output changes. To illustrate, suppose the Alvarez and Ayers Bookshelf Company has rented a factory under a six-month lease: Alvarez and Ayers, the owners of the company, have contracted to pay the $16,000 monthly rent for six months, no matter what. Whether Alvarez and Ayers produce one bookshelf or 7,000, the $16,000 rent for the factory must be paid. The factory is a fixed input in the production process of bookshelves.

A **variable input** is an input whose quantity can be changed as output changes. Examples of variable inputs for the Alvarez and Ayers Bookshelf Company include wood, paint, nails, and so on. These inputs can (and most likely will) change as the production of bookshelves changes. As they produce more bookshelves, Alvarez and Ayers purchase more of these inputs; as they produce fewer bookshelves, they purchase fewer of these inputs. Labor might also be a variable input for Alvarez and Ayers. As they produce more bookshelves, they might hire more employees; as they produce fewer bookshelves, they might lay off some.

If any of the inputs of a firm are fixed inputs, then it is said to be producing in the *short run*. In other words, the **short run** is a period during which some inputs are fixed.

If none of the inputs of a firm is a fixed input—if all inputs are variable—then the firm is said to be producing in the *long run*. In other words, the **long run** is a period during which all inputs can be varied. (No inputs are fixed.)

When firms produce goods and services and then sell them, they necessarily incur costs. In this section, we discuss the production activities of the firm in the short run, leading to the law of diminishing marginal returns. In the next section, we tie the production of the firm to all the costs of production in the short run. We then turn to an analysis of production in the long run.

Fixed Input
An input whose quantity cannot be changed as output changes.

Variable Input
An input whose quantity can be changed as output changes.

Short Run
A period during which some inputs in the production process are fixed.

Long Run
A period during which all inputs in the production process can be varied. (No inputs are fixed.)

21-3a Common Misconception About the Short Run and Long Run

Individuals naturally think that the long run is a longer period than the short run. For example, if the short run is six months, then the long run is, say, 10 months. But this perspective is not the right way to differentiate the short run from the long run. Think of each as a period during which some condition exists. The short run is the period during which at least one input is fixed, and it could be a period of six months, two years, and so on. The long run is not necessarily longer in months and years than the short run; it is simply the period during which all inputs are variable (i.e., no input is fixed). In terms of days, weeks, and months, the short run could be a longer period than the long run.

21-3b Production in the Short Run

Suppose two inputs (or resources)—labor (L) and capital (C)—are used to produce some good. Furthermore, suppose one of those inputs—capital—is fixed. Obviously, because an input is fixed, the firm is producing in the short run.

In Exhibit 2, column 1 shows the units of the fixed input, capital (fixed at 1 unit). Column 2 shows different units of the variable input, labor. Notice that we go from 0 (no workers) through 10 units (10 workers). Column 3 shows the quantities of output produced with 1 unit of capital and different amounts of labor. (The quantity of output is sometimes referred to as the *total physical product*, or *TPP*.) For example, 1 unit of capital and 0 units of labor produce 0 output; 1 unit of capital and 1 unit of labor produce 18 units of output; 1 unit of capital and 2 units of labor produce 37 units of output; 1 unit of capital and 3 units of labor produce 57 units of output; and so on.

EXHIBIT 2

Production in the Short Run and the Law of Diminishing Marginal Returns

In the short run, as additional units of a variable input are added to a fixed input, the marginal physical product of the variable input may increase at first. Eventually, the marginal physical product of the variable input decreases. The point at which marginal physical product decreases is the point at which diminishing marginal returns have set in.

(1) Capital (C), fixed input (units)	(2) Labor (L), variable input (number of workers)	(3) Quantity of Output, Q (units)	(4) Marginal Physical Product (MPP) of Labor, MPP of labor = $\Delta Q/\Delta L$, $\Delta(3)/\Delta(2)$ (units)
1	0	0	
1	1	18	18
1	2	37	19
1	3	57	20
1	4	76	19
1	5	94	18
1	6	111	17
1	7	127	16
1	8	137	10
1	9	133	−4
1	10	125	−8

Marginal Physical Product (MPP)
The change in output that results from changing the variable input by one unit, with all other inputs held fixed.

Column 4 shows the marginal physical product of the variable input. The **marginal physical product (MPP)** of a variable input is equal to the change in output that results from changing the variable input by one unit while *holding all other inputs fixed*. Because, in our example, the variable input is labor, we are talking about the *MPP* of labor. Specifically, the *MPP* of labor is equal to the change in output Q that results from changing labor L by one unit while *holding all other inputs fixed*:

$$\text{MPP of labor} = \Delta Q / \Delta L$$

Notice that the marginal physical product of labor first rises (from 18 to 19 to 20), then falls (from 20 to 19 to 18 to 17 to 16 to 10), and then becomes negative (−4 and −8). When the *MPP* is rising, we say that there is increasing *MPP*; when it is falling, there is diminishing *MPP*; and when it is negative, there is negative *MPP*.

Now, focus on the point at which the *MPP* first begins to decline, namely, with the addition of the fourth worker. The point at which the *MPP* of labor first declines is the point at which diminishing marginal returns are said to have set in. Diminishing marginal returns are common in production—so common, in fact, that economists refer to the law of diminishing marginal returns (or the law of diminishing marginal product). The **law of diminishing marginal returns** states that *as ever larger amounts of a variable input are combined with fixed inputs, the marginal physical product of the variable input eventually will decline*.

Law of Diminishing Marginal Returns
As ever larger amounts of a variable input are combined with fixed inputs, the marginal physical product of the variable input eventually will decline.

The question is, Why does the *MPP* of the variable input eventually decline? To answer this question, think of adding agricultural workers (variable input) to 10 acres of land (fixed input). The workers must clear the land, plant the crop, and then harvest the crop. In the early stages of adding labor to the land, perhaps the *MPP* rises or remains constant. But eventually, as we continue to add more workers to the land, it becomes overcrowded with workers. Workers are stepping around each other, stepping on the crops, and so on. Because of these problems, output growth begins to slow.

It may seem strange that the firm in Exhibit 2 would ever hire beyond the third worker. After all, the *MPP* of labor is at its highest (20) with the third worker. Why hire the fourth worker if the *MPP* of labor is going to fall to 19? The firm may hire the fourth worker because the worker adds output. It would be one thing if the quantity of output were 57 units with three workers and fell to 55 units with the addition of the fourth worker, but this isn't the case. With the addition of the fourth worker, output rises from 57 units to 76 units. The firm has to ask and answer two questions: (1) What can the additional 19 units of output be sold for? (2) What does it cost to hire the fourth worker? Suppose the additional 19 units can be sold for $100, and it costs the firm $70 to hire the fourth worker. In that case, hiring the fourth worker makes sense.

21-3c Whose Marginal Productivity Are We Talking About?

Look back at Exhibit 2, and note the data that follows the fourth worker. When the fourth worker is added, the quantity of output rises from 57 units to 76 units. Also, marginal productivity is 19 units. It is easy to fall into the trap of believing that 19 units is the marginal productivity of the fourth worker, but this is a misreading of the data. It's not as though the fourth worker walks through the door and we attach the number "19" to him. Instead, 19 is the marginal productivity of labor when there are four workers working with the one (fixed) unit of capital. The number can be as easily attached to the first, second, or third worker as it can be to the fourth worker.

Chapter 21 Production and Costs

> **Thinking Like an Economist**
>
> **Comparing One Thing with Another** In economics, when making decisions, you usually compare one alternative with another. To illustrate, suppose you need to decide how much time to devote to studying. Would you consider just the additional *benefits* of spending more time studying, or would you consider the additional *costs* of spending more time studying too? You would want to consider both.
>
> Similarly, when a firm has to decide how many workers to hire, it wouldn't consider only the additional benefits of hiring more workers (as measured by their additional output times the price the additional output could be sold for). Instead, it would consider the additional benefits against the additional costs of hiring more workers.

21-3d Marginal Physical Product and Marginal Cost

A firm's costs are tied to its production. Specifically, the *marginal cost* (*MC*) of producing a good is a reflection of the *MPP* of the variable input. Our objective in this section is to prove that this statement is true. Before doing so, however, we need to define and discuss some economic cost concepts.

Some Economic Cost Concepts Certainly, a cost is incurred whenever a fixed input or variable input is employed in the production process. The costs associated with fixed inputs are called **fixed costs**. The costs associated with variable inputs are called **variable costs**.

Because the quantity of a fixed input does not change as output changes, neither do fixed costs change with output. Payments for such things as fire insurance (the same amount every month), liability insurance, and the rental of a factory and machinery are usually considered fixed costs. Whether the business produces 1, 10, 100, or 1,000 units of output, the rent for its factory is not likely to change. The rent is whatever amount was agreed to with the owner of the factory for the duration of the rental agreement.

Because the quantity of a variable input changes with output, so do variable costs. For example, it takes labor, wood, and glue to produce wooden bookshelves. The quantity of all these inputs (labor, wood, and glue) changes as the number of wooden bookshelves produced changes.

The sum of fixed costs and variable costs is **total cost (TC)**. If total fixed costs (*TFC*) are $100 and total variable costs (*TVC*) are $300, then total cost (*TC*) is $400:

$$TC = TFC + TVC$$

Given total cost, we can formally define marginal cost. **Marginal cost (MC)** is the change in total cost *TC* that results from a change in quantity of output *Q*:

$$MC = \frac{\Delta TC}{\Delta Q}$$

The Link Between *MPP* and *MC* In Exhibit 3, we establish the link between the *MPP* of a variable input and *MC*. The first four columns present much of the same data first presented in Exhibit 2. Column 3 shows the different quantities of output produced by 1 unit of capital (fixed input) and various amounts of labor (variable input), and column 4 shows the *MPP* of

Fixed Costs
Costs that do not vary with output; the costs associated with fixed inputs.

Variable Costs
Costs that vary with output; the costs associated with variable inputs.

Total Cost (TC)
The sum of fixed costs and variable costs.

Marginal Cost (MC)
The change in total cost that results from a change in quantity of output: $MC = \Delta TC/\Delta Q$.

EXHIBIT 3

Marginal Physical Product and Marginal Cost

(a) The marginal-physical-product-of-labor curve. The curve is derived by plotting the data from columns 2 and 4 in the table. (b) The marginal cost curve. The curve is derived by plotting the data from columns 3 and 8 in the table. Notice that as the MPP curve rises, the MC curve falls; and as the MPP curve falls, the MC curve rises.

(1) Capital (C), fixed input (units)	(2) Labor (L), variable input (workers)	(3) Quantity of Output, Q (units)	(4) Marginal Physical Product (MPP) of Labor, MPP of labor = $\Delta Q/\Delta L$ = $\Delta(3)/\Delta(2)$ (units)	(5) Total Fixed Cost (TFC)	(6) Total Variable Cost (TVC)	(7) Total Cost (TC), (5)+(6)	(8) Marginal Cost (MC), $\Delta TC/\Delta Q$, $\Delta(7)/\Delta(3)$
1	0	0		$40	$0	$40	
1	1	18	18	40	20	60	$1.11
1	2	37	19	40	40	80	$1.05
1	3	57	20	40	60	100	$1.00
1	4	76	19	40	80	120	$1.05
1	5	94	18	40	100	140	$1.11
1	6	111	17	40	120	160	$1.17
1	7	127	16	40	140	180	$1.25

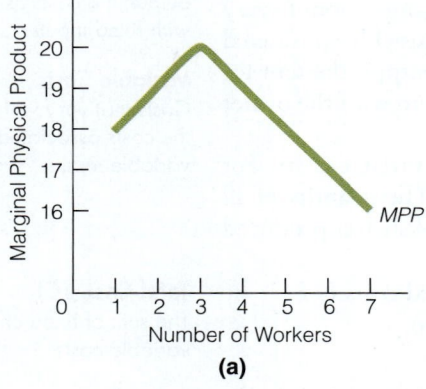

(a)

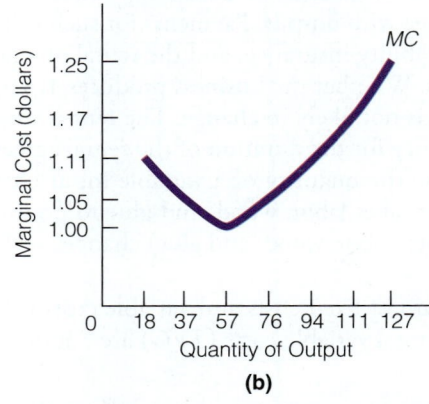

(b)

labor. Exhibit 3(a) shows the MPP curve, which is based on the data in column 4. Notice that the MPP curve first rises and then falls.

In column 5, we have identified the total fixed cost (TFC) of production as $40. (Recall that fixed costs do not change as output changes.) For column 6, we have assumed that each worker is hired for $20; so, when there is only 1 worker, total variable cost (TVC) is $20; when there are 2 workers, total variable cost is $40; and so on. Column 7 shows total cost at various output levels; the figures in this column are simply the sum of the fixed costs in column 5 and the variable costs in column 6. Finally, in column 8, we compute marginal cost. Exhibit 3(b) shows the MC curve, which is based on the data in column 8.

Chapter 21 Production and Costs

Columns 4 and 8 show *MPP* and *MC*, respectively. Notice that when *MPP* is rising (from 18 to 19 to 20), *MC* is decreasing (from $1.11 to $1.05 to $1.00), and when *MPP* is falling (from 20 to 19, etc.), *MC* is increasing (from $1.00 to $1.05, etc.). In other words, *MPP* and *MC* move in opposite directions. You can also see this relationship by comparing the *MPP* curve with the *MC* curve. When the *MPP* curve is going up, the *MC* curve is moving down, and when the *MPP* curve is going down, the *MC* curve is going up. Of course, all this is common sense: As *MPP* rises—or, to put it differently, as the productivity of the variable input rises—we would expect costs to decline; and as the productivity of the variable input declines, we would expect costs to rise.

In conclusion, then, what the *MC* curve looks like depends on what the *MPP* curve looks like. Recall that the *MPP* curve must have a declining portion because of the law of diminishing marginal returns. So, if the *MPP* curve first rises and then (when diminishing marginal returns set in) falls, the *MC* curve must first fall and then rise.

Another Way to Look at the Relationship Between *MPP* and *MC* An easy way to see that *MPP* and *MC* move in opposite directions is to reexamine the definition of *MC* (the change in total cost divided by the change in output). The change in total cost is the additional cost of an additional unit of the variable input. (See Exhibit 3.) The change in output is the *MPP* of the variable input. Thus, *MC* is equal to the additional cost of an additional unit of the variable input, divided by the input's *MPP*. In Exhibit 3, the variable input is labor, so $MC = W/MPP$, where *MC* = marginal cost, *W* = wage, and *MPP* = marginal physical product of labor.

The following table reproduces column 4 from Exhibit 3, notes the wage and uses the equation $MC = W/MPP$ to compute *MC*:

MPP	Variable Cost (W)	W/MPP = MC
18 units	$20	$20/18 = $1.11
19	20	20/19 = 1.05
20	20	20/20 = 1.00
19	20	20/19 = 1.05
18	20	20/18 = 1.11
17	20	20/17 = 1.17
16	20	20/16 = 1.25

Now compare the marginal cost figures in the last column in the table with the marginal cost figures in column 8 of Exhibit 3. Whether marginal cost is defined as equal to $\Delta TC/\Delta Q$ or as equal to *W/MPP*, the result is the same. The latter way of defining marginal cost, however, shows explicitly that as *MPP* rises, *MC* falls, and that as *MPP* falls, *MC* rises:

$$\frac{W}{MPP \uparrow} = MC \downarrow$$

$$\frac{W}{MPP \downarrow} = MC \uparrow$$

21-3e Average Productivity

When the press or noneconomists use the word *productivity*, they are usually referring to *average physical product* instead of *marginal physical product*. To illustrate the difference, suppose 1 worker can produce 10 units of output a day and 2 workers can produce 18 units of output a day. Then *MPP* is 8 units (*MPP* of labor = $\Delta Q/\Delta L$). In contrast, average physical product, which is quantity of output divided by quantity of labor, is equal to 9 units.

$$AP \text{ of labor} = \frac{Q}{L}$$

Usually, when the term *labor productivity* is used in the newspaper and in government documents, it refers to the average hourly (physical) productivity of labor. By computing the average productivity of labor for different countries and noting the annual percentage changes, we can compare labor productivity between and within countries. Government statisticians have chosen 2012 as a benchmark year (a year against which we measure other years). They have also set a productivity index (a measure of productivity) of 100 for the year 2012. By computing a productivity index for other years and noting whether it is above, below, or equal to 100, the statisticians know whether productivity is rising, falling, or remaining constant, respectively. Finally, by computing the percentage change in productivity indexes from one year to the next, they know the rate at which productivity is changing.

Suppose the productivity index for the United States is 120 in year 1 and 125 in year 2. Because the productivity index is higher in year 2 than in year 1, labor productivity increased over the year; that is, output produced increased per hour of labor expended.

Economics 24/7

Is Labor Being Misallocated Across U.S. Cities?[4]

The median house price in San Francisco in April 2018 was $1.61 million. At the same time, the median house price in the United States was $312,400. What do house prices have to do with labor being misallocated across U.S. cities?

Our story begins with labor productivity (the marginal product of labor). Labor productivity is not the same across all American cities. In some cities, it is higher than in other cities. For example, in recent years, it has been particularly high in cities such as New York Metropolitan Area and the San Francisco Bay Area.

When labor productivity is high in some cities and low in others, what we would expect to see is labor moving from the low-productivity areas to the high-productivity areas. To illustrate, suppose in city 1, labor can produce 2*X* per hour and in city 2 labor

ATOSAN/SHUTTERSTOCK.COM

can produce 5*X* per hour. We would expect to see that labor moves from city 1 to city 2. A major reason the labor is expected to move from city 1 to city 2 is because where labor productivity is high, the demand for labor is high, and wages follow. Labor is chasing the higher wages.

As a result of labor moving from low- to high-productivity cities, output is expected to rise. After all, if we can move labor from a place where it produces 2*X* per day to a place where it can produce 5*X* a day, we get an increase of 3*X* per day.

Summarizing, if labor productivity differs between cities, then a movement of labor from low- to high-productivity cities will lead to (1) an increase in the wages of those persons moving and (2) greater output.

---

[4] This piece is based on "Housing Constraints and Spatial Misallocation," by Chang-Tai Hsieh and Enrico Moretti, NBER Working Paper 21154 at www.nber.org/papers/w21154.pdf, and "More Permissive Zoning Codes Could Make U.S. Workers Richer," by Benjamin Somogyi, *The Regulatory Review*, June 14, 2018.

But what could limit or restrict labor moving from low- to high-productivity areas and from low- to high-wage areas is the price of housing in those areas. We can now return to the San Francisco Bay Area, where house prices are some of the highest in the country. Some people will resist moving from low- to high-productivity areas (where they can gain higher wages) because the housing prices are just too high for them to pay. A person might say, "Sure, I can earn a higher income in San Francisco than in Birmingham, New York, but even with the higher income, I still won't be able to buy a house."

One major reason for high house prices in the San Francisco Bay Area is land-use or zoning restrictions, which restrict such things as where apartments, condominiums, and houses can be built; how high up apartment and condo buildings can be built; the percentage of a given lot size those buildings can occupy; and so on. In other words, the land-use restrictions dampened the supply of housing and, thus, caused high house prices. The high housing prices, in turn, limited the free flow of labor from low- to high-productivity areas and, therefore, prevented many workers from receiving higher wages and from output rising (as much as it would have risen had labor not been misallocated between low- and high-productivity areas).

In an NBER Working Paper by economists Chang-Tai Hsieh and Enrico Moretti, the authors concluded that stringent restrictions in new housing supply across 220 metropolitan areas resulted in limiting the number of workers who had access to high productivity areas, and lowered "aggregate US growth by 36 percent from 1964 to 2009."[5]

[5.] Chang-Tai Hsieh and Enrico Moretti, *Housing Constraints and Spatial Misallocation*, https://eml.berkeley.edu/~moretti/growth.pdf.

---

1. If the short run is six months, does it follow that the long run is longer than six months? Explain your answer.
2. "As we add more capital to more labor, the law of diminishing marginal returns eventually will set in." What is wrong with this statement?
3. Suppose an *MC* curve falls when output is in the range from 1 unit to 10 units. Then it flattens out and remains constant over an output range from 10 units to 20 units, after which it rises over a range from 20 units to 30 units. What does the curve's behavior have to say about the *MPP* of the variable input?

21-4 Costs of Production: Total, Average, Marginal

As we continue our discussion of the costs of production, the easiest way to see the relationships among the various costs is with the example in Exhibit 4.

Column 1 of Exhibit 4 shows the various quantities of output, ranging from 0 units to 10 units. Column 2 shows the total fixed costs of production (*TFC*), set at $100. Recall that fixed costs do not change as output changes. Therefore, *TFC* is $100 when output is 0 units, 1 unit, 2 units, and so on. Because *TFC* does not change as *Q* changes, the *TFC* curve in the exhibit is a horizontal line at $100.

In column 3, we have computed **average fixed cost (AFC)**, which is total fixed cost divided by quantity of output:

$$AFC = \frac{TFC}{Q}$$

Average Fixed Cost (AFC)
Total fixed cost divided by quantity of output:
$AFC = TFC/Q$.

For example, look at the fourth entry in column 3. To get a dollar amount of $33.33, we simply took *TFC* at 3 units of output, or $100, and divided by 3. Notice that the *AFC* curve in the exhibit continually declines.

EXHIBIT 4

Total, Average, and Marginal Costs

TFC equals $100 (column 2 in the table) and TVC is as noted in column 4. From the data, we calculate AFC, AVC, TC, ATC, and MC. The curves associated with TFC, AFC, TVC, AVC, TC, ATC, and MC are shown in diagrams at the bottom of the corresponding columns. (*Note:* Scale is not the same for all diagrams.)

(1) Quantity of Output, Q (units)	(2) Total Fixed Cost (TFC)	(3) Average Fixed Cost (AFC) AFC = TFC/Q = (2)/(1)	(4) Total Variable Cost (TVC)	(5) Average Variable Cost (AVC) AVC = TVC/Q = (4)/(1)
0	$100	—	$0	—
1	100	$100.00	50	$50.00
2	100	50.00	80	40.00
3	100	33.33	100	33.33
4	100	25.00	110	27.50
5	100	20.00	130	26.00
6	100	16.67	160	26.67
7	100	14.28	200	28.57
8	100	12.50	250	31.25
9	100	11.11	310	34.44
10	100	10.00	380	38.00

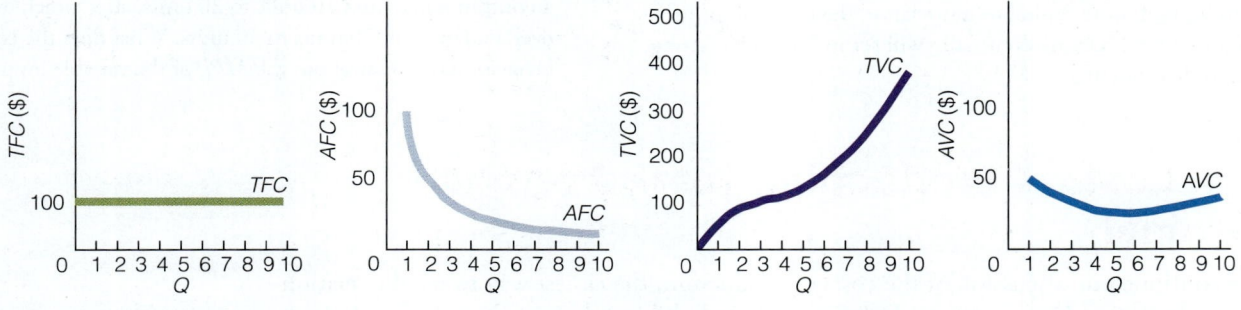

In column 4, we have simply entered some hypothetical data for total variable cost (*TVC*). The *TVC* curve in the exhibit rises because variable costs are likely to increase as output increases.

In column 5, we have computed **average variable cost (AVC)**, which is total variable cost divided by quantity of output:

$$AVC = \frac{TVC}{Q}$$

For example, look at the third entry in column 5. To get a dollar amount of $40.00, we simply took *TVC* at 2 units of output, or $80, and divided by 2. Notice that the *AVC* curve declines and then rises.

Average Variable Cost (AVC)
Total variable cost divided by quantity of output: AVC = TVC/Q.

Chapter 21 Production and Costs

EXHIBIT 4

Continued

(6) Total Cost (TC) TC = TFC + TVC = (2) + (4)	(7) Average Total Cost (ATC) ATC = TC/Q = (6)/(1)	(8) Marginal Cost (MC) MC = ΔTC/ΔQ = Δ(6)/Δ(1)
$100.00	—	—
150.00	$150.00	$50.00
180.00	90.00	30.00
200.00	66.67	20.00
210.00	52.50	10.00
230.00	46.00	20.00
260.00	43.33	30.00
300.00	42.86	40.00
350.00	43.75	50.00
410.00	45.56	60.00
480.00	48.00	70.00

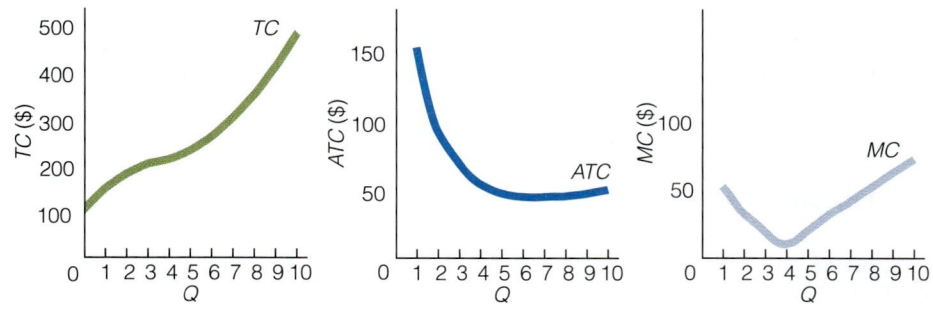

Column 6 shows total cost (*TC*). Total cost is the sum of total variable cost and total fixed cost. Notice that the *TC* curve does not start at zero because, even when output is zero, there are some fixed costs. In this example, total fixed cost (*TFC*) at zero output is $100, so the total cost (*TC*) curve must start at $100 instead of at $0.

Column 7 shows **average total cost (ATC)**, which is total cost divided by quantity of output:

$$ATC = \frac{TC}{Q}$$

Average total cost is sometimes called *unit cost*.

Average Total Cost (ATC)
Total cost divided by quantity of output: ATC = TC/Q

Alternatively, we can say that *ATC* equals the sum of *AFC* and *AVC*:

$$ATC = AFC + AVC$$

To understand why this alternative formulation makes sense, remember that $TC = TFC + TVC$. Thus, if we divide all total magnitudes by quantity of output (Q), we necessarily get $ATC = AFC + AVC$. Notice that the *ATC* curve falls and then rises.

Column 8 shows marginal cost (*MC*), which is the change in total cost divided by the change in quantity of output:

$$MC = \frac{\Delta TC}{\Delta Q}$$

The *MC* curve has a declining portion and a rising portion. When *MC* is declining, *MPP* is rising. When *MC* is rising, the *MPP* of the variable input is falling. Obviously, the low point on the *MC* curve is when diminishing marginal returns set in.

Exhibit 5 brings together much of the material we have discussed relating to short-run production and costs.

21-4a The *AVC* and *ATC* Curves in Relation to the *MC* Curve

What do the average total and average variable cost curves look like in relation to the *MC* curve? To explain, we need to discuss the **average–marginal rule**, which is best defined with an example.

Suppose that 20 persons are in a room and that each person weighs 170 pounds. Your task is to calculate the average weight per person. The calculation is accomplished by adding the individual weights and dividing by 20. Obviously, this average weight will be 170 pounds. Now an additional person enters the room. We will refer to this additional person as the marginal (additional) person, and we will call the additional weight he brings into the room the marginal weight.

Let's suppose the weight of the marginal person is 275 pounds. Then, based on the 21 persons now in the room, the average weight per person is 175 pounds. The new average weight is greater than the old average weight because the average weight was pulled up by the weight of the additional person. In short, *when the marginal magnitude is above the average magnitude, the average magnitude rises*. This is one part of the average–marginal rule.

Now suppose the weight of the marginal person is *less than* the average weight of 170 pounds, such as 65 pounds. Then the new average is 165 pounds. In this case, the average weight was pulled *down* by the weight of the additional person. Thus, *when the marginal magnitude is below the average magnitude, the average magnitude falls*. This is the other part of the average–marginal rule. Putting the two parts together, we have

$$\text{Marginal} < \text{Average} \rightarrow \text{Average} \downarrow$$

$$\text{Marginal} > \text{Average} \rightarrow \text{Average} \uparrow$$

We can apply the average–marginal rule to find out what the *ATC* and *AVC* curves look like in relation to the *MC* curve. The following analysis holds for both the *ATC* curve and the *AVC* curve: We reason that

1. if marginal cost is below (less than) average variable cost, then average variable cost is falling; and
2. if marginal cost is above (greater than) average variable cost, then average variable cost is rising.

average–marginal rule
When the marginal magnitude is above the average magnitude, the average magnitude rises; when the marginal magnitude is below the average magnitude, the average magnitude falls.

EXHIBIT 5

A Review of Production and Costs in the Short Run

Concept	Explanation	Example	Other Information (if relevant)
Production in the Short Run	Firm is producing with at least one input that is fixed.	Firm produces with capital and labor, where capital is the fixed input and labor is the variable input.	
Marginal Physical Product (MPP)	$MPP = \Delta Q/\Delta \text{Variable Input}$	If $\Delta Q = 40$ units, and ΔVariable Input $= 1$, then $MPP = 40$ units.	
Law of Diminishing Marginal Returns	The law of diminishing marginal returns states that, as ever-larger amounts of a variable input are combined with a fixed input, the MPP of the variable input eventually declines.	See Exhibit 2. Diminishing marginal returns "kick in" with the addition of the fourth worker.	The law of diminishing marginal returns holds only in the short run, when at least one input is fixed.
Total Cost (TC)	$TC = TFC + TVC$	Let $TFC = \$10$, and $TVC = \$40$; it follows that $TC = \$50$.	
Total Fixed Cost (TFC)	$TFC = AFC \times Q$	Let $AFC = \$4$ and $Q = 40$ units; it follows that $TFC = \$160$.	TFC is constant over quantity of output. For example, TFC is, say, $100 when quantity of output is 10 units and also when quantity of output is 20 units.
Total Variable Cost (TVC)	$TVC = AVC \times Q$	Let $AVC = \$6$ and $Q = 40$ units; it follows that $TVC = \$240$.	TVC changes as quantity of output changes.
Average Fixed Cost (AFC)	$AFC = TFC/Q$	Let $TFC = \$50$ and $Q = 10$; it follows that $AFC = \$5$.	AFC declines as quantity of output rises.
Average Variable Cost (AVC)	$AVC = TVC/Q$	Let $TVC = \$120$ and $Q = 20$; it follows that $AVC = \$6$.	
Average Total Cost (ATC)	(1) $ATC = TC/Q$ (2) $ATC = AFC + AVC$	(1) Let $TC = \$50$ and $Q = \$5$; it follows that $ATC = \$10$. (2) Let $AFC = \$4$ and $AVC = \$1$; it follows that $ATC = \$5$.	ATC is the same as *unit cost*. Also, notice that ATC can be computed two ways, as we show in the Explanation column.
Marginal Cost (MC)	$MC = \Delta TC/\Delta Q$	Suppose that TC increases from $40 to $45 as quantity of output rises from 101 to 102 units. It follows that MC, which is the change in total cost divided by the change in quantity of output, is $5.	There is a second way of computing MC when the variable input is labor: $MC = W/MPP$, where $W =$ wage rate and $MPP =$ marginal physical product of labor.

This reasoning implies that the relationship between the *AVC* curve and the *MC* curve must look like that in Exhibit 6(a). In region 1, marginal cost is below average variable cost, and average variable cost is falling. In region 2, marginal cost is above average variable cost, and average variable cost is rising. In sum, the relationship between the *AVC* curve and the *MC* curve, as shown in Exhibit 6(a), is consistent with the average–marginal rule.

EXHIBIT 6

Average and Marginal Cost Curves
(a) The relationship between AVC and MC.
(b) The relationship between ATC and MC.

The MC curve intersects both the AVC and ATC curves at their respective low points (L). This behavior is consistent with the average–marginal rule. (c) The AFC curve declines continuously.

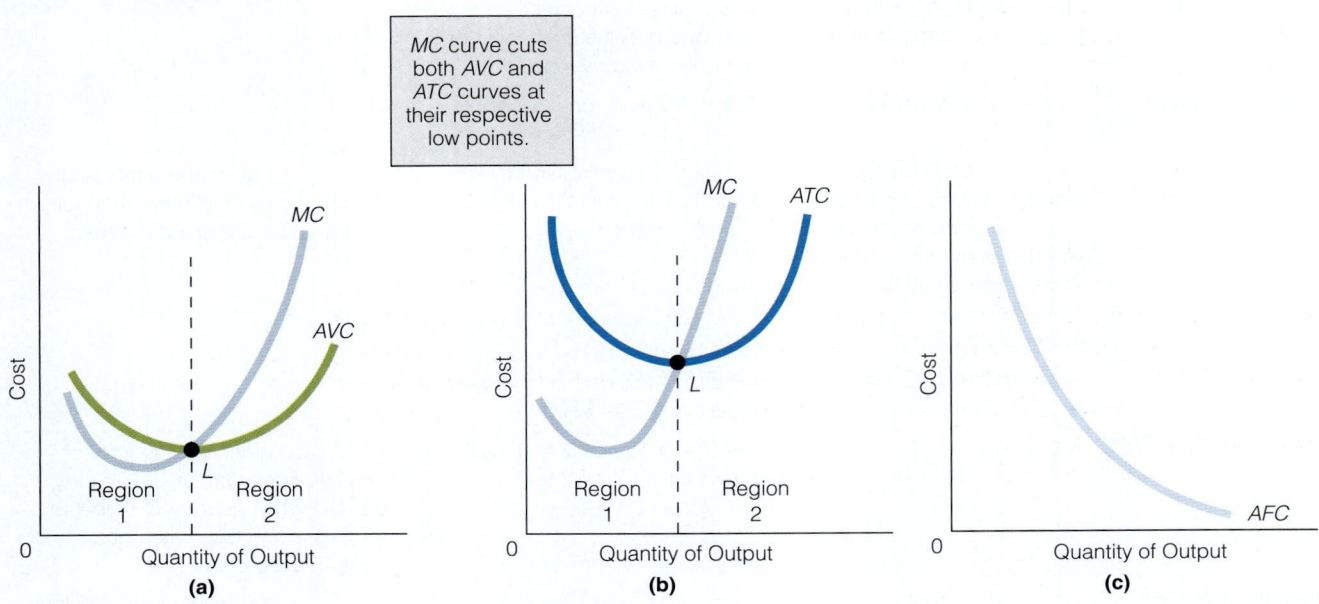

In addition, because average variable cost is pulled down when marginal cost is below it and pulled up when marginal cost is above it, the MC curve must intersect the AVC curve at the latter's lowest point. This lowest point is point L in Exhibit 6(a).

The same relationship that exists between the MC and AVC curves also exists between the MC and ATC curves, as shown in Exhibit 6(b). In region 1, marginal cost is below average total cost, and, consistent with the average–marginal rule, average total cost is falling. In region 2, marginal cost is above average total cost, and average total cost is rising. The MC curve must therefore intersect the ATC curve at the latter's lowest point.

There is no relationship between the average fixed cost curve and the MC curve. We can indirectly see why by recalling that average fixed cost is simply total fixed cost (which is constant over output) divided by output ($AFC = TFC/Q$). As output (Q) increases and total fixed cost (TFC) remains constant, average fixed cost (TFC/Q) must decrease continuously. [See Exhibit 6(c).]

Finding Economics

Why Doesn't Oliver Cheat? Oliver is sitting in class taking a test, and his teacher is out of the class. He could easily look over at his neighbor's paper (which is uncovered) to see what the answer to question 25 is, but he doesn't. Why doesn't he cheat? Does it have anything to do with the average–marginal rule?

There may be a guilt cost to Oliver cheating, but let's ignore that reason for a moment. Even without a guilt cost and without the chance of being caught, Oliver may still not cheat, for a reason that could have something to do with the average–marginal rule. People usually cheat by copying the work of someone who they believe is smarter than they are. Suppose Oliver believes that his grade on the test will be 65 and that Ian (who is sitting next to him) will receive a grade of 60. Oliver's grade of 65 can be viewed as the average grade and Ian's as the marginal grade. Because the marginal grade is less than the average grade, the marginal will pull down the average. There's no need to cheat if copying someone else's work only lowers Oliver's grade. Oliver is more likely to cheat if he thinks that cheating will raise his grade, but that can occur only if he cheats off a person whose grade is likely to be higher than his (if he doesn't cheat).

21-4b Tying Short-Run Production to Costs

To see how costs are tied to production, let's summarize some of our earlier discussions. (See Exhibit 7.) We assume that production takes place in the short run, so there is at least one fixed input. Suppose we initially add units of a variable input to the fixed input and the *MPP* of the variable input (e.g., labor) rises. Then, as a result of *MPP* rising, MC falls. From the average–marginal rule, we know that, when *MC* has fallen enough to be below *AVC*, *AVC* will begin to decline. Also, when *MC* has fallen enough to be below *ATC*, *ATC* will begin to decline.

Eventually, though, the law of diminishing marginal returns will set in. When it does, the *MPP* of the variable input declines. As a result, *MC* rises. When *MC* has risen enough to be above *AVC*, *AVC* will rise. Also, when *MC* has risen enough to be above *ATC*, *ATC* will rise.

So what happens in terms of production (rising or falling *MPP*) affects *MC*, which in turn eventually affects *AVC* and *ATC*. In short, the cost of a good is tied to its production.

21-4c Seeing How Things Came to Be

In economics, learning what comes before an event is important. To illustrate, suppose *ATC* is rising. Can you see the process that brought this event (*ATC* rising) at this particular moment?

Let's take one step back at a time. *ATC* is rising because (one step back) *MC* rose to a level above *ATC*. But why did *MC* rise to a level above *ATC*? Or, for that matter, why is *MC* rising

EXHIBIT 7

Tying Production to Costs

What happens in terms of production (*MPP* rising or falling) affects *MC*, which in turn eventually affects *AVC* and *ATC*.

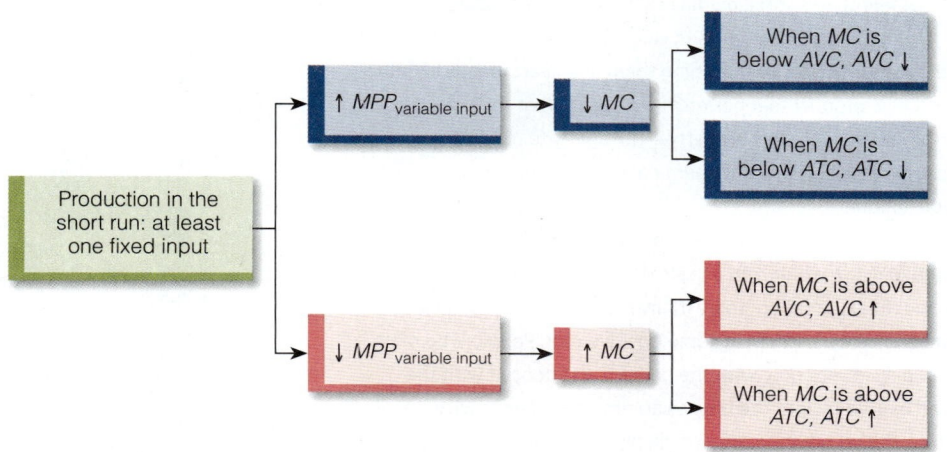

at all? *MC* is rising because *MPP* (one step back) is declining. But why is *MPP* declining? *MPP* is declining because (one step back) the law of diminishing marginal returns sets in.

Looking at a tree, you see its branches and leaves. If you look back, though, you can see the seed that was planted and that grew into the tree. You can do the same in economics. When looking at rising *ATC*, most of us simply see rising *ATC*. But if you look far enough back, you can see the law of diminishing marginal returns growing into rising *ATC*.

21-4d One More Cost Concept: Sunk Cost

Sunk cost
A cost incurred in the past that cannot be changed by current decisions and therefore cannot be recovered.

Sunk cost is a cost incurred in the past that cannot be changed by current decisions and therefore cannot be recovered. For example, suppose that a firm must purchase a $10,000 government license before it can legally produce and sell lamp poles and that the government will not buy back the license or allow it to be resold. The $10,000 the firm spends to purchase the license is a sunk cost. It is a cost that, after it has been incurred (after the $10,000 was spent), cannot be changed by a current decision (the firm cannot go back into the past and undo what was done) and cannot be recovered (the government will neither buy back the license nor allow it to be resold).

Let's consider another example of a sunk cost. Suppose Koji buys a movie ticket, walks into the theater, and settles down to watch the movie. Thirty minutes into the movie, he realizes that he hates it. The money he paid for the ticket is a sunk cost. The cost was incurred in the past, it cannot be changed, and it cannot be recovered. (We are assuming that movie theaters do not give your money back if you dislike the movie.)

Economics 24/7

Social Media and Marginal Cost

A key property of social media sites is that they allow someone to interact with a very large group of people across thousands of miles and various time zones *at essentially zero marginal cost*. Zero marginal cost: that is what is special about social media, and it is what differentiates social media in a big way from traditional media.

Using social media, a person can, for instance, send out a tweet to thousands of people, informing them of an earthquake in China or of a new product that performs well, or of what the person did in Hawaii on vacation. This property—the ability to reach large groups of people at very low, if any, marginal cost—is what makes social media unique.

Now, if talking, communicating, and interacting has become so cheap, what would you expect the consequences to be? First, you would expect there to be many more interactions between people at zero cost than at some positive cost. People who once could play games only with the person next door or with the friend invited over to the house can now play games with people all over the world. It is commonplace to find someone in, say,

Charleston, South Carolina, playing a video game with someone in Changsha, China. In other words, social media caused people who never would interact to interact, simply by lowering the cost of interacting with people over thousands of miles and various time zones.

By lowering the costs of interacting, social media sites have enabled some groups to form that otherwise could not and, therefore, would not have been formed. For example, think of the persons that come together on Yelp, a website that offers rating and review services.

By lowering the costs of "saying or writing something," social media has greatly increased the amount of things that are said and written. At one time, the only way the average person could comment on a political issue and have that comment reach large numbers of people was to write a letter to the editor of a newspaper. That is no longer the case. Today, anyone with a personal computer, tablet, or smartphone can read a news article online and then post a comment at almost zero cost. We would expect that, at such low cost, there would be many more comments than when costs are higher. And with a greater number of comments, we would expect the average quality of a comment to decline—and some argue that it has. One can find all manner of comments online today, from the insightful to the ordinary to the insubstantial.

Economists' Advice: Ignore Sunk Costs Economists advise individuals to ignore sunk costs. To illustrate, for Koji, who bought the movie ticket but dislikes the movie, the movie ticket is a sunk cost. Now, suppose Koji says the following to himself as he is watching the movie:

I paid to watch this movie, but I really hate it. Should I get up and walk out, or should I stay and watch the movie? I think I'll stay and watch the movie because, if I leave, I'll lose the money I paid for the ticket.

The error that Koji is making is believing that, if he walks out of the theater, he will lose the money he paid for the ticket. But he has already lost the money for the ticket. Whether he stays and watches the movie or leaves, the money is gone forever. It is a sunk cost.

An economist would advise Koji to ignore what has happened in the past and what can't be undone. In other words, ignore sunk costs. The question is not, "What have I already lost?" Nothing can be done about what has been lost. Instead, Koji should ask and answer these questions: What do I gain (what are my benefits) if I stay and watch the movie? What do I lose (what are my costs) if I stay and watch the movie? If what Koji expects to gain by staying and watching the movie is greater than what he expects to lose, he should stay and watch the movie. However, if what he expects to lose by staying and watching the movie is greater than what he expects to gain, he should leave.

To see this point more clearly, let's say that Koji has decided to stay and watch the movie because he doesn't want to lose the price of the movie ticket. Two minutes after he makes this decision, you walk up to him and offer him $200 to leave the theater. Do you think Koji will say, "I can't leave the movie theater, because, if I do, I will lose the price of the movie ticket?" Or do you think that he is more likely to take the money and leave? Most people will say that Koji will take the $200 and leave the movie theater simply because, if he doesn't leave, he loses the opportunity to receive $200.

However, wouldn't he have forfeited something—albeit not $200—if no one offered him $200 to leave? He might have given up at least $1 in benefits doing something else. In short, he must have had some opportunity cost of staying at the movie theater before the $200 was offered. The problem is that, somehow, by letting sunk cost influence his decision, Koji was willing to ignore this opportunity cost of staying at the theater. The $200 offer only made that cost obvious.

Consider another situation. Alicia purchases a pair of shoes on sale (no refunds), wears them for a few days, and then realizes that they are uncomfortable. An economist would recommend that Alicia simply not wear the shoes. To an economist, the cost of the shoes is a sunk cost because it (1) was incurred in the past, (2) cannot be changed by a current decision, and (3) cannot be recovered. An economist would advise Alicia not to base her current decision as to whether to wear the shoes on what has happened and what cannot be changed. If Alicia lets what she has done and can't undo influence her present decision, she runs the risk of compounding her mistake.

To illustrate, if Alicia decides to wear the uncomfortable shoes because she thinks that it is a waste of money not to, she may end up with an even bigger loss: certainly less comfort and possibly a trip to the podiatrist. The relevant question she must ask herself is not, "What did I give up by buying the shoes?" The right question is, "What will I give up by wearing the uncomfortable shoes?"

The message is that a present decision can affect only the future, never the past. Bygones are bygones; sunk costs are sunk costs.

Economics 24/7

Producing a Grade in a College Course

One way to think of your taking a college course is as a consumer. To illustrate, you might think of an economics lecture in the same way you would a movie. You sit in the classroom and watch the lecturer lecture. You sit in a theater and watch the movie on the screen.

Another (and perhaps "more nearly accurate") way to think of your taking a college course is as a producer. But if, by taking a course, you are a producer, what is it exactly that you are producing? The immediate answer is a grade. You work at producing an A, or a B, or a C, and so on.

If we dig below the surface of the grade, though, what you really are producing is knowledge for yourself. The grade is simply a reflection of the knowledge, in the sense that a higher grade reflects more knowledge produced by you for you and a lower grade reflects less knowledge produced by you for you.

Now, one of the ways to understand what production and costs are about is to think through your actions as a producer. With this idea in mind, let's consider your producing a grade in a college course.

In your production of a grade, there are both fixed and variable costs. Your paper and pen (that you use to take notes) are largely fixed inputs. The cost of these items constitutes your fixed cost. No matter what grade you produce or how much knowledge you acquire, the cost of your paper and pen is not going to change.

It is the same whether you end up producing an A, a B, or a C in the course.

Your variable costs relate to how carefully you listen, how carefully you take notes, and how many course assignments you complete. We would expect that the variable costs will rise as you listen more carefully, take more careful notes, and work on and turn in more assignments.

If we add your pen-and paper-costs (fixed costs) to your listening and note-taking costs (variable costs), we have the total cost of producing the grade.

Now consider marginal cost. Marginal cost is the change in total cost given a change in quantity of output. The "quantity of output" term here can be misleading, because rarely does a student sitting in class think of his or her producing so many units of a good in the way a computer firm produces computers or a furniture firm produces furniture. Still, the student produces something, and that something can be roughly described as "units of knowledge." The more units of knowledge produced (by you for you), the higher the grade is likely to be. So is there a positive marginal cost of producing a higher grade?

We expect that there would be, and you probably would agree if you have ever made a mental note of the "extra work" it takes you to move your current course grade up from an 89 (B+) to a 92 (A–). In other words, the marginal cost (to you) of producing a higher grade in the course, or acquiring more knowledge from the course, is positive and not zero. [As an aside, it could very well be that different students incur different marginal costs of moving their grade up from an 89 to a 92. In other words, it might be less costly (or easier) for some students to raise their grade 3 points than it is for other students.]

Let's compare the marginal cost of raising *your grade* in two courses, X and Y. The marginal cost of raising your grade by 3 points is $100 of extra effort in course X and $300 of extra effort in course Y. Many students may express the difference here by saying, "Course Y is a tougher course than course X." ("Econ 302 is a lot tougher than Sociology 270.") Will the difference in marginal cost in the two courses affect your behavior? Will it be the determining factor in which of the two courses you decide to enroll in (assuming that you don't have to take both courses)? It could be, if the benefits of taking the two courses are the same. All other things being equal, you will probably prefer to take course X than course Y.

Finally, do sunk costs exist in a college course? Suppose you took a midterm last week and received a low grade. Are the costs associated with taking the midterm a sunk cost? Well, a cost is sunk if it was (1) incurred in the past, (2) cannot be changed by current decisions, and, therefore, (3) cannot be recovered. The costs associated with taking the midterm (1) were incurred last week, (2) cannot be changed by a current decision (we are assuming that your professor will not let you retake the midterm, and, therefore, (3) cannot be recovered. Hence, the costs associated with taking the midterm are sunk costs.

Behavioral Economics and Sunk Cost In a real-life experiment, two researchers randomly distributed discounts to buyers of subscriptions to Ohio University's 1982–1983 theater season.[6] One group of ticket buyers paid the normal ticket price of $15 per ticket, a second group received $2 off per ticket, and a third group received $7 off per ticket. In short, some buyers paid lower ticket prices than others.

The researchers found that people who paid more for their tickets attended the theater performances more often than those who paid less. Some people argue that the reason is that people who paid more for their tickets somehow wanted to attend the theater more than those who paid less. But this explanation isn't likely, because the discounts to buyers were distributed randomly. Instead, it seems to be that the more someone paid for the ticket (everyone paid for the ticket before the night of the performance), the greater was the sunk cost. And the greater the sunk cost, the more likely individuals were to attend the theater performance. In other words, at least some people were not ignoring sunk cost.

Viewing Sunk Cost as a Constraint or Not Microeconomics emphasizes that all economic actors deal with objectives, constraints, and choices. Let's focus briefly on constraints. All economic actors would prefer to have fewer rather than more constraints and to have constraints that offer more rather than less latitude. For example, a firm would probably prefer to be constrained in having to buy its resources from five suppliers rather than from only one supplier. A consumer would rather have a budget constraint of $4,000 a month instead of $2,000 a month.

---

[6] Arkes and Catherine Blumer, "The Psychology of Sunk Cost," *Organizational Behavior and Human Decision Processes* 124 (1985).

Now, suppose person *A* considers sunk cost when she makes a decision and person *B* ignores it when he makes a decision. Does one person face fewer constraints, *ceteris paribus*? The person who ignores sunk cost, person *B*, faces fewer constraints. Person *A* acts as if a constraint is there—the constraint of sunk cost, the constraint of having to rectify a past decision—when it really exists only in her mind.

In this sense, the fabricated constraint of sunk cost is very different from the real constraint of, say, scarcity. Whether a person believes it or not, scarcity exists. People are constrained by scarcity, just as they are by the force of gravity, whether they know it or not. But people are not constrained by sunk cost if they choose not to be. If you let bygones be bygones, if you realize that sunk cost is a cost that has been incurred and can't be changed, then it cannot constrain you when you are making a current decision.

Economists look at things this way: There are enough constraints in the world; you are not made better off by behaving as if there is one more than there actually is.

Self-Test

1. Identify two ways to compute average total cost (*ATC*).
2. Would a business ever sell its product for less than cost? Explain your answer.
3. What happens to unit costs as marginal costs rise? Explain your answer.
4. Do changes in *MPP* influence unit costs? Explain your answer.

21-5 Production and Costs in the Long Run

This section discusses long-run production and costs. As noted earlier, there are no fixed inputs and no fixed costs in the long run. Consequently, the firm has *greater flexibility* in the long run than in the short run. (Because we discuss both short-run and long-run average total cost curves, we distinguish between them with prefixes: *SR* for short run and *LR* for long run.)

21-5a Long-Run Average Total Cost Curve

In the short run, because there are fixed costs and variable costs, total cost is the sum of the two. But in the long run, there are no fixed costs, so variable costs *are* total costs. This section focuses on (1) the long-run average total cost (*LRATC*) curve and (2) what it looks like.

Consider the manager of a firm that produces bedroom furniture. When all inputs are variable, the manager must decide what the situation of the firm should be in the upcoming short-run period. For example, he might need to determine the size of the plant: small, medium, or large. Once this decision is made, the firm is locked into a specific plant size for the short run. Associated with each of the three different plant sizes is a short-run average total cost (*SRATC*) curve, as illustrated in Exhibit 8(a).

Suppose the manager of the firm wants to produce output level Q_1. Then, obviously, he will choose the plant size represented by $SRATC_1$. This size gives a lower unit cost of producing Q_1 than the plant size represented by $SRATC_2$, a size that has a higher unit cost of producing Q_1 ($6 as opposed to $5).

However, if the manager chooses to produce Q_2, he will choose the plant size represented by $SRATC_3$, because the unit cost of producing Q_2 is lower with that plant size than it is with the plant size represented by $SRATC_2$.

Chapter 21 Production and Costs

EXHIBIT 8

Long-Run Average Total Cost Curve (LRATC)

(a) There are three short-run average total cost curves for three different plant sizes. If these are the only plant sizes, then the long-run average total cost curve is the heavily shaded, blue scalloped curve. (b) The long-run average total cost curve is the heavily shaded, blue smooth curve. The LRATC curve in (b) is not scalloped because it is assumed that there are so many plant sizes that the LRATC curve touches each SRATC curve at only one point.

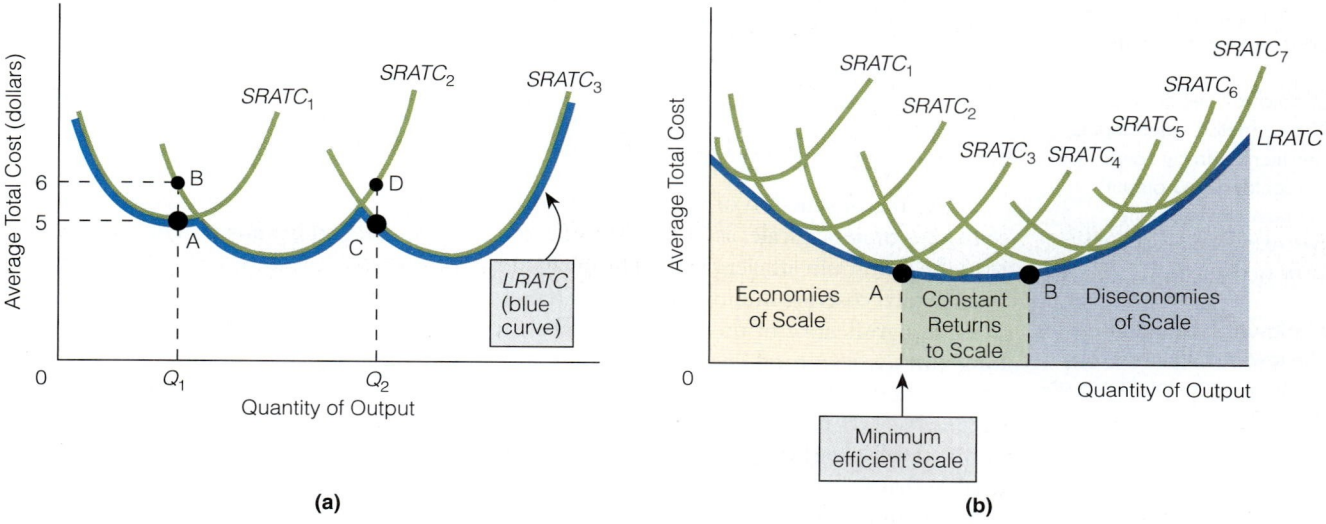

(a)   (b)

If we were to ask the same question for every (possible) output level, we would derive the **long-run average total cost (LRATC) curve**. The LRATC curve shows the lowest unit cost at which the firm can produce any given level of output. In Exhibit 8(a), the LRATC curve consists of the portions of the three SRATC curves that are tangential to the blue curve; it is the scalloped blue curve.

Exhibit 8(b) shows a host of SRATC curves and one LRATC curve. In this case, the LRATC curve is not scalloped, as it was in part (a). The LRATC curve is smooth in part (b) because we assume that there are many plant sizes in addition to the three represented in (a). In other words, although they have not been drawn, short-run average total cost curves representing different plant sizes exist in (b) between $SRATC_1$ and $SRATC_2$, between $SRATC_2$ and $SRATC_3$, and so on. In this case, the LRATC curve is smooth and touches each SRATC curve at one point.

Long-Run Average Total Cost (LRATC) Curve
A curve that shows the lowest (unit) cost at which a firm can produce any given level of output.

21-5b Economies of Scale, Diseconomies of Scale, and Constant Returns to Scale

Suppose two inputs—labor and capital—are used together to produce a good. If inputs are increased by some percentage (say, 100 percent) and if output increases by a greater percentage (more than 100 percent), then unit costs fall, and **economies of scale** are said to exist.

For example, suppose that good X is made with two inputs, Y and Z, and it takes 20 Y and 10 Z to produce 5 units of X. Suppose also that the cost of each unit of input Y is $1 and the cost of each unit of input Z is $1. Thus, a total cost of $30 is required to produce 5 units of X. The unit cost (average total cost) of good X is $6 ($ATC = TC/Q$). Now, consider a doubling of inputs Y and Z, to 40 Y and 20 Z, and a more than doubling in output, say, to 15 units

Economies of Scale
Economies that exist when inputs are increased by some percentage and output increases by a greater percentage, causing unit costs to fall.

Constant Returns to Scale
The condition when inputs are increased by some percentage and output increases by an equal percentage, causing unit costs to remain constant.

Diseconomies of Scale
The condition when inputs are increased by some percentage and output increases by a smaller percentage, causing unit costs to rise.

Minimum Efficient Scale
The lowest output level at which average total costs are minimized.

of X. Then a total cost of $60 is required to produce 15 units of X, and the unit cost (average total cost) of good X is $4.

An increase in inputs can have two other results. If inputs are increased by some percentage and output increases by an *equal* percentage, then unit costs remain constant, and **constant returns to scale** are said to exist. If inputs are increased by some percentage and output increases by a *smaller* percentage, then unit costs rise, and **diseconomies of scale** are said to exist.

The three conditions can easily be seen in the LRATC curve in Exhibit 8(b): If economies of scale are present, the LRATC curve is falling; if constant returns to scale are present, the curve is flat; if diseconomies of scale are present, the curve is rising. In sum,

Economies of scale → LRATC is falling
Constant returns to scale → LRATC is constant
Diseconomies of scale → LRATC is rising

If, in the production of a good, economies of scale give way to constant returns to scale or to diseconomies of scale, as in Exhibit 8(b), the point at which this transition occurs is referred to as the minimum efficient scale. The **minimum efficient scale** is the lowest output level at which average total costs are minimized. Point A represents the minimum efficient scale in Exhibit 8(b).

The significance of the minimum efficient scale of output can be seen by looking at the long-run average total cost curve between points A and B in Exhibit 8(b). Between these points, there are constant returns to scale: The average total cost is the same over the various output levels between the two points. This means that larger firms (firms producing greater output levels) within the range from point A to point B do not have a cost advantage over smaller firms that operate at the minimum efficient scale.

Keep in mind that economies of scale, diseconomies of scale, and constant returns to scale are relevant only in the long run. Implicit in the definition of these terms, and explicit in our examples, all inputs necessary to the production of a good are changeable (not fixed). Because no input is fixed, economies of scale, diseconomies of scale, and constant returns to scale are relevant only in the long run.

Exhibit 9 reviews some of the material we have discussed about long-run production and costs.

EXHIBIT 9

A Review of Production and Costs in the Long Run

Concept	Explanation	Example	Other Information (if relevant)
Production in the long run	There are no fixed inputs in the production process. All inputs are variable.	Firms use two inputs—capital (C) and labor (L)—and both are variable.	
Economies of scale	Percentage increase in output is greater than percentage increase in inputs.	Inputs increase by, say, 5 percent, and quantity of output increases by, say, 9 percent.	When the firm experiences economies of scale, its LRATC (long-run average total cost) curve declines.
Diseconomies of scale	Percentage increase in output is less than percentage increase in inputs.	Inputs increase by, say, 5 percent, and quantity of output increases by, say, 2 percent.	When the firm experiences diseconomies of scale, its LRATC (long-run average total cost) curve rises.
Constant returns to scale	Percentage increase in output is equal to percentage increase in inputs.	Inputs increase by, say, 5 percent, and quantity of output increases by 5 percent.	When the firm experiences constant returns to scale, its LRATC curve is constant.

21-5c Why Economies of Scale?

Up to a certain point, long-run unit costs of production fall as a firm grows, for two main reasons: (1) Growing firms offer greater opportunities for employees to specialize. Individual workers can become highly proficient at narrowly defined tasks, often producing more output at lower unit costs. (2) Growing firms (especially, large growing firms) can take advantage of highly efficient mass production techniques and equipment that ordinarily require large setup costs and thus are economical only if they can be spread over a large number of units. For example, assembly-line techniques are usually relatively cheap when millions of units of a good are produced but are expensive when only a few thousand units are produced.

21-5d Why Diseconomies of Scale?

Diseconomies of scale usually arise at the point where a firm's size causes coordination, communication, and monitoring problems. In very large firms, managers often find it difficult to coordinate work activities, communicate their directives to the right persons in a timely way, and monitor personnel effectively. The business operation simply gets too big. There is, of course, a monetary incentive not to pass the point of operation at which diseconomies of scale exist, and firms usually find ways to do so, including reorganizing, dividing operations, hiring new managers, and more.

21-5e Minimum Efficient Scale and Number of Firms in an Industry

Some industries are composed of a smaller number of firms than other industries. Or we can say that there is a different degree of concentration in different industries.

The minimum efficient scale (*MES*) as a percentage of U.S. consumption or total sales is not the same for all industries. For example, in industry X, *MES* as a percentage of total sales might be 6.6, and in industry Y, it might be 2.3. In other words, firms in industry X reach the minimum efficient scale of plant and thus exhaust economies of scale at an output level of 6.6 percent of total industry sales, whereas firms in industry Y experience economies of scale only up to an output level of 2.3 percent of total industry sales.

Clearly, we would expect to find fewer firms in industry X. By dividing the *MES* as a percentage of total sales into 100, we can estimate the number of efficient firms it takes to satisfy total consumption for a particular product. For the product produced by industry X, it takes 15 firms ($100/6.6 = 15$). For the product produced by industry Y, it takes 43 firms.

21-6 Shifts in Cost Curves

In discussing the shape of short- and long-run cost curves, we assumed that certain factors remained constant. We discuss a few of these factors now and describe how changes in them can shift cost curves.

21-6a Taxes

Consider a tax on each unit of a good produced. Suppose, for example, that a company has to pay a tax of $3 for each unit of X it produces. What effects will this tax have on the firm's cost curves? Well, the tax won't affect the firm's fixed costs, because the tax is paid only when output is produced—and fixed costs are present even if output is zero. (If the tax were a lump-sum tax—that is, if the company pays a lump sum no matter how many units of X it produces—then the tax *would* affect fixed costs.) So, given that the tax is not a lump-sum tax, we conclude that the tax does not affect fixed costs and therefore cannot affect average fixed cost.

The tax, however, will affect variable costs. As a consequence of the tax, the firm has to pay more for each unit of X it produces. Because variable costs rise, so does total cost. This relationship means that average variable cost and average total cost rise and that the representative cost curves shift upward. Finally, because marginal cost is the change in total cost divided by the change in output, marginal cost rises, and the marginal cost curve shifts upward.

21-6b Input Prices

A rise or fall in variable input prices causes a corresponding change in the firm's average total, average variable, and marginal cost curves. For example, if the price of steel rises, the variable costs of building skyscrapers rise, and so must average variable cost, average total cost, and marginal cost. The cost curves shift upward. If the price of steel falls, the opposite effects occur.

21-6c Technology

Technological changes often bring either (1) the capability of using fewer inputs to produce a good (e.g., the introduction of the personal computer reduced the hours necessary to key and edit a manuscript) or (2) lower input prices (e.g., technological improvements in transistors led to price reductions in the transistor components of calculators). In either case, technological changes of this variety lower variable costs and consequently lower average variable cost, average total cost, and marginal cost. The cost curves shift downward.

---

1. Give an arithmetical example to illustrate economies of scale.
2. What would the *LRATC* curve look like if there were always constant returns to scale? Explain your answer.
3. Firm *A* charged $4 per unit when it produced 100 units of good *X*, and it charged $3 per unit when it produced 200 units. Furthermore, the firm earned the same profit per unit in both cases. How can this happen?

Office Hours

"What Is the Difference Between the Law of Diminishing Marginal Returns and Diseconomies of Scale?"

Student: I'm not sure I understand the difference between the law of diminishing marginal returns and diseconomies of scale. They sound similar to me.

Instructor: The law of diminishing marginal returns holds in the short run when at least one input is fixed. In our example in class, we held capital constant (at one unit) and changed the units of labor. Diseconomies of scale are relevant to the long run, which is a period when all inputs are variable. In other words, no input is fixed.

Student: But don't both the law of diminishing marginal returns and diseconomies of scale have something to do with less output per unit of input?

Instructor: Let's define each and see. The law of diminishing marginal returns says that, as we add additional units of a variable input (such as labor) to a fixed input (such as capital), we get to a point where the *MPP* of the variable input (the *MPP* of labor) declines.

This decline has to do with less output per unit of input. Specifically, as we add additional units of the variable input to the fixed input, our output might rise, but it rises at a decreasing rate. To illustrate, adding the fourth worker to the production process might raise output from 100 units to 120 units (an increase of 20 units), but adding the fifth worker raises output from 120 units to 135 units (an increase of 15 units).

Student: Okay, then, how is the law of diseconomies of scale different?

Instructor: Here is an example of diseconomies of scale: The firm increases each of its inputs by, say, 10 percent, but its output rises by only 3 percent. In other words, its output rises less than the increase in its inputs. Also, notice that we don't hold any input fixed. We have assumed that there are two inputs the firm uses—labor and capital—and that it increases its usage of each input by 10 percent.

Student: Are we getting less output per unit of input, as we did with respect to the law of diminishing marginal returns?

Instructor: Yes and no. We are getting less output per unit of input if we compare diseconomies of scale with, say, economies of scale. To illustrate, with economies of scale, we might increase each input by 10 percent and end up with 20 percent more output. With diseconomies of scale, we increase each input by 10 percent and end up with, say, only 3 percent more output. Obviously, when diseconomies of scale exist, we get less output for each percentage increase in inputs than we do when economies of scale exist.

Points to Remember

1. The law of diminishing marginal returns holds in the short run when at least one input is fixed.
2. Diseconomies of scale are relevant to the long run, which is a period when all inputs are variable.

Chapter Summary

The Firm

- Armen Alchian and Harold Demsetz argue that firms are formed when individuals derive benefits from working as a team—specifically, when the sum of what individuals can produce as a team is greater than the sum of what individuals can produce alone: Sum of team production > Sum of individual production.

- Team production has its advantages and disadvantages. The chief advantage (in many cases) is the positive difference between the output produced by the team and the sum of the output produced by individuals working alone. The chief disadvantage is the increased shirking that happens on teams. The role of the monitor (manager) in the firm is to preserve the increased output and to reduce or eliminate the increased shirking. The monitors have a monetary incentive not to shirk their monitoring duties when they are residual claimants.

- Ronald Coase argued that firms exist to reduce the "costs of negotiating and concluding a separate contract for each exchange transaction which takes place on a market." In short, firms exist to reduce transaction costs.

Explicit Cost and Implicit Cost

- An explicit cost is incurred when an actual (monetary) payment is made. An implicit cost represents the value of resources used in production for which no actual (monetary) payment is made.

Economic Profit and Accounting Profit

- Economic profit is the difference between total revenue and total cost, including both explicit and implicit costs. Accounting profit is the difference between total revenue and explicit costs. Economic profit is usually lower (never higher) than accounting profit. Economic profit (not accounting profit) motivates economic behavior.

Production and Costs in the Short Run

- The short run is a period in which some inputs are fixed. The long run is a period in which all inputs can be varied. The costs associated with fixed and variable inputs are referred to as fixed costs and variable costs, respectively.

- Marginal cost is the change in total cost that results from a change in quantity of output.
- The law of diminishing marginal returns states that, as ever larger amounts of a variable input are combined with fixed inputs, the marginal physical product of the variable input eventually will decline. When this decline happens, marginal cost rises.
- The average–marginal rule states that, if the marginal magnitude is above (below) the average magnitude, then the average magnitude rises (falls).
- The marginal cost curve intersects the average variable cost curve at its lowest point. The marginal cost curve intersects the average total cost curve at its lowest point. There is no relationship between marginal cost and average fixed cost.

Production and Costs in the Long Run

- In the long run, because there are no fixed costs, variable costs equals total costs.
- The long-run average total cost curve is the envelope of the short-run average total cost curves. It shows the lowest unit cost at which a firm can produce a given level of output.
- If inputs are increased by some percentage and output increases by a greater percentage, then unit costs fall and economies of scale exist. If inputs are increased by some percentage and output increases by an equal percentage, then unit costs remain constant and constant returns to scale exist. If inputs are increased by some percentage and output increases by a smaller percentage, then unit costs rise and diseconomies of scale exist.
- The minimum efficient scale is the lowest output level at which average total costs are minimized.

Sunk Cost

- Sunk cost is a cost incurred in the past that cannot be changed by current decisions and therefore cannot be recovered. A person or firm that wants to minimize losses will hold sunk costs to be irrelevant to present decisions.

Shifts in Cost Curves

- A firm's cost curves will shift if there is a change in taxes, input prices, or technology.

Key Terms and Concepts

Business Firm
Market Coordination
Managerial Coordination
Shirking
Monitor
Residual Claimant
Profit
Explicit Cost
Implicit Cost
Accounting Profit
Economic Profit
Normal Profit
Fixed Input
Variable Input
Short Run
Long Run
Marginal Physical Product (*MPP*)
Law of Diminishing Marginal Returns
Fixed Costs
Variable Costs
Total Cost (*TC*)
Marginal Cost (*MC*)
Average Fixed Cost (*AFC*)
Average Variable Cost (*AVC*)
Average Total Cost (*ATC*), or Unit Cost
Average–Marginal Rule
Sunk Cost
Long-Run Average Total Cost (*LRATC*) Curve
Economies of Scale
Constant Returns to Scale
Diseconomies of Scale
Minimum Efficient Scale

Questions and Problems

1. Explain the difference between managerial coordination and market coordination.
2. Is the managerial coordination that goes on within a business firm independent of market forces? Explain your answer.
3. Explain why even conscientious workers will shirk more when the cost of shirking falls.
4. Illustrate the average–marginal rule in a noncost setting.
5. "A firm that earns only normal profit is not covering all its costs." Do you agree or disagree? Explain your answer.
6. The average variable cost curve and the average total cost curve get closer to each other as output increases. What explains this convergence?

Chapter 21 Production and Costs

7. Explain why earning zero economic profit is not as bad as it sounds.
8. Why does the *AFC* curve continually decline (and get closer and closer to the quantity axis)?
9. What is the difference between diseconomies of scale and the law of diminishing marginal returns?
10. When would total costs equal fixed costs?
11. Is studying for an economics exam subject to the law of diminishing marginal returns? If so, what is the fixed input? What is the variable input?
12. Some individuals decry the decline of the small family farm and its replacement with the huge corporate megafarm. Discuss the possibility that this shift is a consequence of economies of scale.
13. We know that there is a link between productivity and costs. For example, recall the link between the marginal physical product of the variable input and marginal cost. With this link in mind, what link might there be between productivity and prices?
14. Some people's everyday behavior suggests that they do not hold sunk costs irrelevant to present decisions. Give some examples different from those presented in this chapter.
15. Explain why a firm might want to produce its good even after diminishing marginal returns have set in and marginal cost is rising.
16. People often believe that large firms in an industry have cost advantages over small firms in the same industry. For example, they might think that a big oil company has a cost advantage over a small oil company. For this to be true, however, what condition must exist? Explain your answer.
17. The government says that firm *X* must pay $1,000 in taxes simply because it is in the business of producing a good. What cost curves, if any, does this tax affect?
18. On the basis of your answer to question 17, does *MC* change if *TC* changes?
19. Under what condition would a billionaire producer be rich yet earn zero economic profit?

Working with Numbers and Graphs

1. For each lettered space in the following table, determine the appropriate dollar amount:

(1) Quantity of Output, Q (units)	(2) Total Fixed Cost ($)	(3) Average Fixed Cost (AFC)	(4) Total Variable Cost (TVC)	(5) Average Variable Cost (AVC)	(6) Total Cost (TC)	(7) Average Total Cost (ATC)	(8) Marginal Cost (MC)
0	$200	A	$0		V		
1	200	B	30	L	W	GG	QQ
2	200	C	50	M	X	HH	RR
3	200	D	60	N	Y	II	SS
4	200	E	65	O	Z	JJ	TT
5	200	F	75	P	AA	KK	UU
6	200	G	95	Q	BB	LL	VV
7	200	H	125	R	CC	MM	WW
8	200	I	165	S	DD	NN	XX
9	200	J	215	T	EE	OO	YY
10	200	K	275	U	FF	PP	ZZ

2. Give a numerical example to show that as marginal physical product (*MPP*) rises, marginal cost (*MC*) falls.
3. Price = $20, quantity = 400 units, unit cost = $15, and implicit costs = $4,000. What does economic profit equal?
4. If economic profit equals accounting profit, what do implicit costs equal?
5. If accounting profit is $400,000 greater than economic profit, what do implicit costs equal?
6. If marginal physical product is continually declining, what does marginal cost look like? Explain your answer.
7. If the *ATC* curve is continually declining, what does this imply about the *MC* curve? Explain your answer.
8. When will total cost equal total variable cost?
9. Answer the following:
    a. If *TVC* = $80 and AVC = 4, then what does quantity (Q) equal?
    b. If total cost is $40 when $Q = 2$ and total cost is $45 when $Q = 3$, then what does marginal cost equal?
    c. What does average fixed cost equal at $Q = 2$ if total variable cost is $15 at $Q = 2$?
    d. Why does the *AFC* curve get continually closer to the horizontal axis in Exhibit 6(c) as quantity of output increases?

Perfect Competition

CHAPTER 22

Introduction

Every firm shares two things with all other firms. First, every firm has to answer certain questions: (1) What price should the firm charge for the good it produces and sells? (2) How many units of the good should the firm produce? (3) How much of the resources that the firm needs to produce its good should it buy? Regardless of whether a firm sells shirts or cars, whether it is large or small, whether it is located in Georgia or Maine, it must answer all three of these questions. Period.

Second, every firm finds itself operating in a certain market structure. A **market structure** is a firm's environment or setting whose characteristics influence the firm's pricing and output decisions. This chapter focuses on a particular market structure: perfect competition.

22-1 The Theory of Perfect Competition

The theory of **perfect competition** is built on four assumptions:

1. *There are many sellers and many buyers, none of which is large in relation to total sales or purchases.* This assumption speaks to both demand (the number of buyers) and supply (the number of sellers). Given many buyers and sellers, each buyer and each seller may act independently of other buyers and sellers, respectively, and each is such a small part of the market as to have no influence on price.

2. *Each firm produces and sells a homogeneous product.* Each firm sells a product that is indistinguishable from all other firms' products in a given industry. (For example, a buyer of wheat cannot distinguish between one farmer's wheat and another farmer's wheat.) As a consequence, buyers are indifferent to the sellers.

3. *Buyers and sellers have all relevant information about prices, product quality, sources of supply, and so forth.* Buyers and sellers know who is selling what, at what prices, at what quality, and on what terms. In short, they know everything that relates to buying, producing, and selling the product.

Market Structure
The environment whose characteristics influence a firm's pricing and output decisions.

Perfect Competition
A theory of market structure based on four assumptions: (1) There are many sellers and buyers; (2) the sellers sell a homogeneous good; (3) buyers and sellers have all relevant information; (4) entry into, and exit from, the market is easy.

521

4. *Firms have easy entry and exit.* New firms can enter the market easily, and existing firms can exit the market easily. There are no barriers to entry or exit.

Before discussing the perfectly competitive firm in the short and long run, we discuss some of the characteristics of the perfectly competitive firm that logically follow from these four assumptions.

22-1a A Perfectly Competitive Firm Is a Price Taker

A perfectly competitive firm is a **price taker**, which is a seller that does not have the ability to control the price of its product; in other words, such a firm "takes" the price determined in the market. For example, if Farmer Stone is a price taker, he can increase or decrease his output without significantly affecting the price of his product.

Why is a perfectly competitive firm a price taker? A firm is restrained from being anything but a price taker if it finds itself one among many firms whose supply is small relative to the total market supply (assumption 1 in the theory of perfect competition) and if it sells a homogeneous product (assumption 2) in an environment where buyers and sellers have all relevant information (assumption 3).

Some people suggest that the assumptions of the theory of perfect competition give economists what they want. In other words, economists want the perfectly competitive firm to be a price taker, so they choose the assumptions that make it so. But this isn't the case. Instead, economists start out with certain assumptions and then logically conclude that the firm for which these assumptions hold, or that behaves as if these assumptions hold, is a price taker; that is, it has no control over price. Afterward, economists test the theory by observing whether it accurately predicts and explains the real-world behavior of some firms. Then, until a counterexample is found, economists have good reason to believe what the theory states.

22-1b The Demand Curve for a Perfectly Competitive Firm Is Horizontal

The perfectly competitive setting has many sellers and many buyers. Together, all buyers make up the market demand curve; together, all sellers make up the market supply curve. An equilibrium price is established at the intersection of the market demand and market supply curves [Exhibit 1(a)].

When the equilibrium price has been established, a single perfectly competitive firm faces a horizontal (flat, perfectly elastic) demand curve at the equilibrium price [Exhibit 1(b)]. In short, the firm takes the equilibrium price as given—hence, the firm is a price taker—and sells all quantities of output at this price.[1]

Why Does a Perfectly Competitive Firm Sell at the Equilibrium Price? If a perfectly competitive firm tries to charge a price higher than the market-established equilibrium price, it won't sell any of its product. The reasons are that the firm sells a homogeneous product, its supply is small relative to the total market supply, and all buyers are informed about where they can obtain the product at the lower price.

If the firm wants to maximize profits, it does not offer to sell its good at a lower price than the equilibrium price. Why should it? It can sell all it wants at the market-established equilibrium price. The equilibrium price is the only relevant price for the perfectly competitive firm.

Price Taker
A seller that does not have the ability to control the price of the product it sells; the seller "takes" the price determined in the market.

---

[1] The horizontal demand curve means not that the firm can sell an infinite amount at the equilibrium price, but that price will be virtually unaffected by the variations in output that the firm may find it practicable to make.

EXHIBIT 1

The Market Demand Curve and Firm Demand Curve in Perfect Competition

(a) The market, composed of all buyers and sellers, establishes the equilibrium price. (b) A single perfectly competitive firm then faces a horizontal (flat, perfectly elastic) demand curve. We conclude that the firm is a price taker: it takes the equilibrium price established by the market and sells any and all quantities of output at this price. (The capital D represents the market demand curve; the lowercase d represents the single firm's demand curve.)

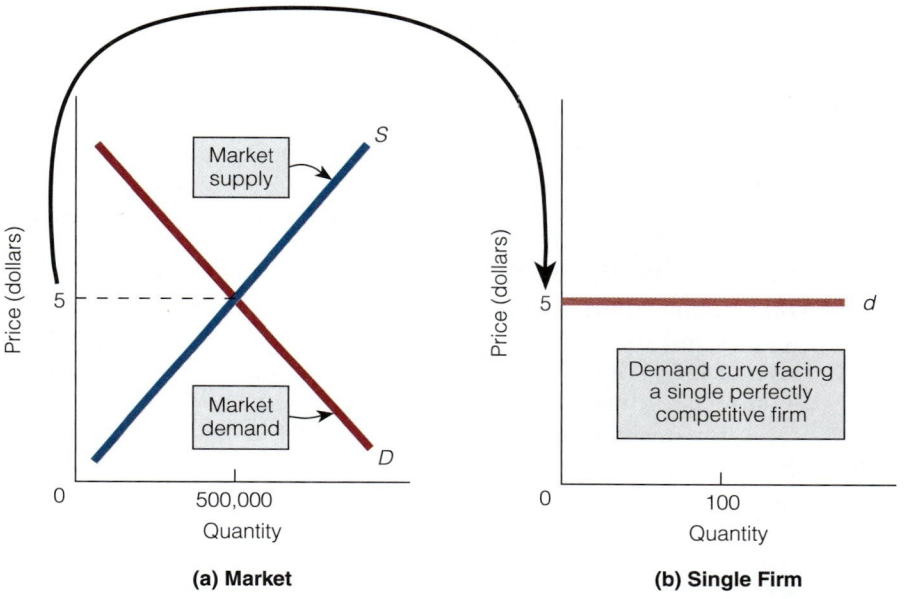

(a) Market

(b) Single Firm

Finding Economics

When Selling Shares of Stock Roberta wakes up in the morning and turns on her computer. She checks the prices of the stocks she owns. The price of stock X is selling at $35 per share. She had bought 200 shares of the stock when the price was only $11, and now she decides to sell. She places a sell order with her online broker, and in a matter of minutes, she has sold her 200 shares of stock. Where is the economics? Does Roberta's sale of stock have anything to do with operating in a perfectly competitive market?

If Roberta wants to sell her shares of stock X, she must sell at the current market price. Roberta, as a seller of stock, is a price taker. She cannot sell her shares of stock at $2 over the current price, and she will not sell below the market price. Why should she sell her shares of stock at $33 when she can sell them at the current market price of $35?

22-1c Common Misconceptions About Demand Curves

The law of demand posits an inverse relationship between price and quantity demanded. So it follows that, if a demand curve is to represent the law of demand graphically, it must be downward sloping. A common misconception, though, is to think that *all* demand curves have to be downward sloping. Why this is not true can be explained by distinguishing the market demand curve from the demand curve faced by a single firm.

In Exhibit 1(a), the market demand curve is downward sloping, implying an inverse relationship between price and quantity demanded, *ceteris paribus*. The *single* perfectly competitive firm's demand curve does not contradict this relationship; the curve simply represents the pricing situation in which the *single* perfectly competitive firm finds itself. Recall from an earlier chapter that the more substitutes a good has, the higher the price elasticity of demand will be. In the perfectly competitive market setting, there are many substitutes for the firm's product—so many, in fact, that the firm's demand curve is perfectly elastic.

Intuitively, a single perfectly competitive firm's supply is such a *small percentage* of the total market supply that the firm cannot perceptibly influence price by changing its quantity of output. To put it differently, the firm's supply is so small, compared with the total market supply, that the inverse relationship between price and quantity demanded, although present, cannot be observed on the firm's level, although it is observable on the market level.

22-1d The Marginal Revenue Curve of a Perfectly Competitive Firm Is the Same as Its Demand Curve

Total revenue is the price of a good multiplied by the quantity sold. If the equilibrium price is $5, as in Exhibit 2(a), and the perfectly competitive firm sells 3 units of its good, its total revenue is $15. If the firm sells an additional unit, bringing the total number of units sold to 4, its total revenue is $20.

A firm's **marginal revenue (MR)** is the change in total revenue (*TR*) that results from selling one additional unit of output (*Q*):

$$MR = \frac{\Delta TR}{\Delta Q}$$

Marginal Revenue (MR)
The change in total revenue (*TR*) that results from selling one additional unit of output (*Q*).

EXHIBIT 2

The Demand Curve and the Marginal Revenue Curve for a Perfectly Competitive Firm

(a) By computing marginal revenue, we find that it is equal to price. (b) By plotting columns 1 and 2, we obtain the firm's demand curve; by plotting columns 2 and 4, we obtain the firm's marginal revenue curve. The two curves are the same.

(1) Price	(2) Quantity	(3) Total Revenue = (1) × (2)	(4) Marginal Revenue = $\Delta TR/\Delta Q$ = $\Delta(3)/\Delta(2)$
$5	1	$5	$5
5	2	10	5
5	3	15	5
5	4	20	5

(a)

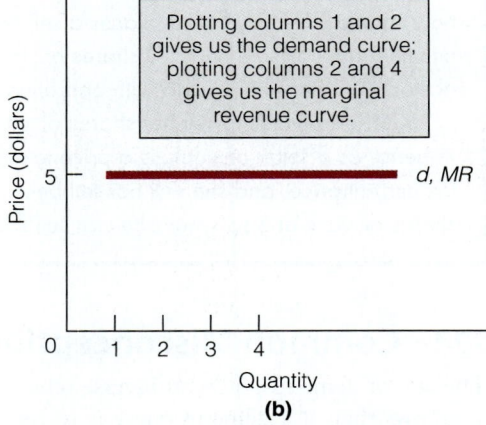

Plotting columns 1 and 2 gives us the demand curve; plotting columns 2 and 4 gives us the marginal revenue curve.

(b)

Column 4 in Exhibit 2(a) shows that the firm's marginal revenue ($5) at any output level is always equal to the equilibrium price ($5). For a perfectly competitive firm, therefore, price (P) is equal to marginal revenue:

For a perfectly competitive firm, $P = MR$

But if price is equal to marginal revenue, then *the marginal revenue curve for the perfectly competitive firm is the same as its demand curve.*

A demand curve plots price against quantity, whereas a marginal revenue curve plots marginal revenue against quantity. If price equals marginal revenue, then the demand curve and marginal revenue curve are the same [Exhibit 2(b)]:

For a perfectly competitive firm, Demand curve = Marginal revenue curve

22-1e Theory and Real-World Markets

The theory of perfect competition describes how firms act in a market structure in which (1) there are many buyers and sellers, none of whom is large in relation to total sales or purchases; (2) sellers sell a homogeneous product; (3) buyers and sellers have all relevant information; and (4) market entry and exit are easy. These assumptions are closely met in some real-world markets, such as some agricultural markets and a small subset of the retail trade. The stock market, with its hundreds of thousands of buyers and sellers of stock, is also sometimes cited as an example of perfect competition.

The four assumptions of the theory of perfect competition are also *approximated* in some real-world markets. In such markets, the number of sellers may not be large enough for every firm to be a price taker, but the firm's control over price may be negligible. The amount of control may be so negligible, in fact, that the firm acts *as if* it were a perfectly competitive firm.

Similarly, buyers may not have all relevant information concerning price and quality. However, they may still have a great deal of information, and the information they do not have may not matter. The products that the firms in the industry sell may not be homogeneous, but the differences may be inconsequential.

In short, a market that does not *exactly* meet the assumptions of perfect competition may nonetheless *approximate* the assumptions to a degree that it behaves *as if* it were a perfectly competitive market. If so, then the theory of perfect competition can be used to predict that market's behavior.

(Answers to Self-Test questions are in Answers to Self-Test Questions at the back of the book.)

1. "If a firm is a price taker, it does not have the ability to control the price of the product it sells." What does this statement mean?
2. Why is a perfectly competitive firm a price taker?
3. The horizontal demand curve for the perfectly competitive firm signifies that it cannot sell any of its product for a price higher than the market equilibrium price. Why not?
4. Suppose the firms in a real-world market do not sell a homogeneous product. Does it necessarily follow that the market is not perfectly competitive?

22-2 Perfect Competition in the Short Run

For the perfectly competitive firm, a price taker, price is equal to marginal revenue ($P = MR$), and, therefore, the firm's demand curve is the same as its marginal revenue curve. This section discusses the amount of output the firm will produce in the short run.

22-2a What Level of Output Does the Profit-Maximizing Firm Produce?

In Exhibit 3, the perfectly competitive firm's demand curve (d) and marginal revenue curve (MR, which is the same as d) are drawn at the equilibrium price of $5. The firm's marginal cost curve (MC) is also shown. On the basis of these curves, the firm will continue to increase its quantity of output as long as marginal revenue is greater than marginal cost. It will not produce units of output for which marginal revenue is less than marginal cost. Therefore, the firm will stop increasing its quantity of output when marginal revenue and marginal cost are equal. The **profit maximization rule** for a firm says *produce the quantity of output at which $MR = MC$.*[2] In Exhibit 3, $MR = MC$ at 125 units of output.

For the perfectly competitive firm, the profit maximization rule can be written as $P = MC$ because, for that firm, $P = MR$. In other words, in perfect competition, profit is maximized when

$$P = MR = MC$$

Profit Maximization Rule
Profit is maximized by producing the quantity of output at which $MR = MC$.

EXHIBIT 3

The Quantity of Output That the Perfectly Competitive Firm Will Produce

The firm's demand curve is horizontal at the equilibrium price. Its demand curve is its marginal revenue curve. The firm produces that quantity of output at which $MR = MC$.

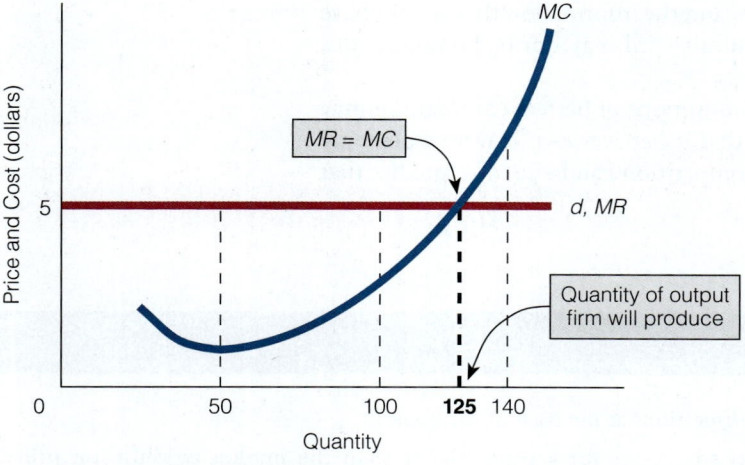

22-2b The Perfectly Competitive Firm and Resource Allocative Efficiency

Resources (or inputs) are used to produce goods and services; for example, wood may be used to produce a chair. To the buyers of a good, the resources used in its production have an exchange value that is approximated by the price that people pay for the good. For example, when buying a chair for $100, Lavaughn values the resources used to produce the chair as worth at least $100. Wood that is used to produce chairs cannot be used to produce desks. Hence, the opportunity cost of producing chairs is best measured by the marginal cost of producing the chairs.

Now, suppose that 100 chairs are produced and that, at this quantity, the price is greater than marginal cost; for example, suppose the price is $100 and the marginal cost is $75. Then, obviously, buyers place a higher value on wood when it is used to produce chairs than when it is used to produce an alternative good.

[2.] The profit maximization rule is the same as the loss minimization rule because maximizing profits is impossible without minimizing losses. The profit maximization rule holds for *all firms*, not just for perfectly competitive firms.

Producing a good—any good—until price equals marginal cost ensures that all units of the good are produced that are of greater value to buyers than the alternative goods that might have been produced. In other words, a firm that produces the quantity of output at which price equals marginal cost ($P = MC$) is said to exhibit **resource allocative efficiency**.

Does the perfectly competitive firm exhibit resource allocative efficiency? We know two things about this type of firm: First, the perfectly competitive firm produces the quantity of output at which $MR = MC$. Second, for such a firm, $P = MR$. If the perfectly competitive firm produces the output at which $MR = MC$ and if, for this firm, $P = MR$, then the firm produces the output at which $P = MC$. In short, the perfectly competitive firm *is* resource allocative efficient.

Also, for a perfectly competitive firm, profit maximization and resource allocative efficiency are not at odds. (Whether they might be for other market structures is discussed in the next two chapters.) The perfectly competitive firm seeks to maximize profit by producing the quantity of output at which $MR = MC$. Because, for that firm, $P = MR$, it automatically accomplishes resource allocative efficiency ($P = MC$) when it maximizes profit ($MR = MC$).

Resource Allocative Efficiency
The situation in which firms produce the quantity of output at which price equals marginal cost: $P = MC$.

Thinking Like an Economist

Profit Maximization Can Be Consistent with Consumer Welfare With good X, as with all goods, there is a right and a wrong quantity to produce. From the perspective of consumers, the right quantity is the efficient quantity. The consumer says to the manufacturers of X, "keep producing X as long as its price is greater than its marginal cost. Stop when $P = MC$. Let's say that $P = MC$ when the quantity of X is 10,000 a month.

The question now is whether the manufacturers of X want to produce 10,000 units of X a month. For manufacturers, the right quantity of X is the quantity at which $MR = MC$. In other words, manufacturers will continue making units of X as long as MR is greater than MC and they will stop when $MR = MC$.

For a perfectly competitive firm, we know that $P = MR$, so what consumers want (produce until $P = MC$) is really the same thing that manufacturers want (produce until $MR = MC$). Simply put, when manufacturers do what is in their best interest—produce until $MR = MC$—they are automatically producing the efficient amount of the good—an amount that, in fact, consumers want. Who would have thought it?

22-2c To Produce or Not to Produce: That Is the Question

The cases described next illustrate three applications of the profit maximization (loss minimization) rule by a perfectly competitive firm.

Case 1: Price Is Above Average Total Cost Exhibit 4(a) illustrates the perfectly competitive firm's demand and marginal revenue curves. If the firm follows the profit maximization rule and produces the quantity of output at which marginal revenue equals marginal cost, it will produce 100 units of output—the profit-maximizing quantity of output. At this quantity

EXHIBIT 4

Profit Maximization and Loss Minimization for the Perfectly Competitive Firm: Three Cases

(a) In case 1, $TR > TC$, and the firm earns profits. It continues to produce in the short run. (b) In case 2, $TR < TC$, and the firm takes a loss. It shuts down in the short run because it minimizes its losses by doing so; it is better to lose $400 in fixed costs than to take a loss of $450. (c) In case 3, $TR < TC$, and the firm takes a loss. It continues to produce in the short run because it minimizes its losses by doing so; it is better to lose $80 by producing than to lose $400 in fixed costs.

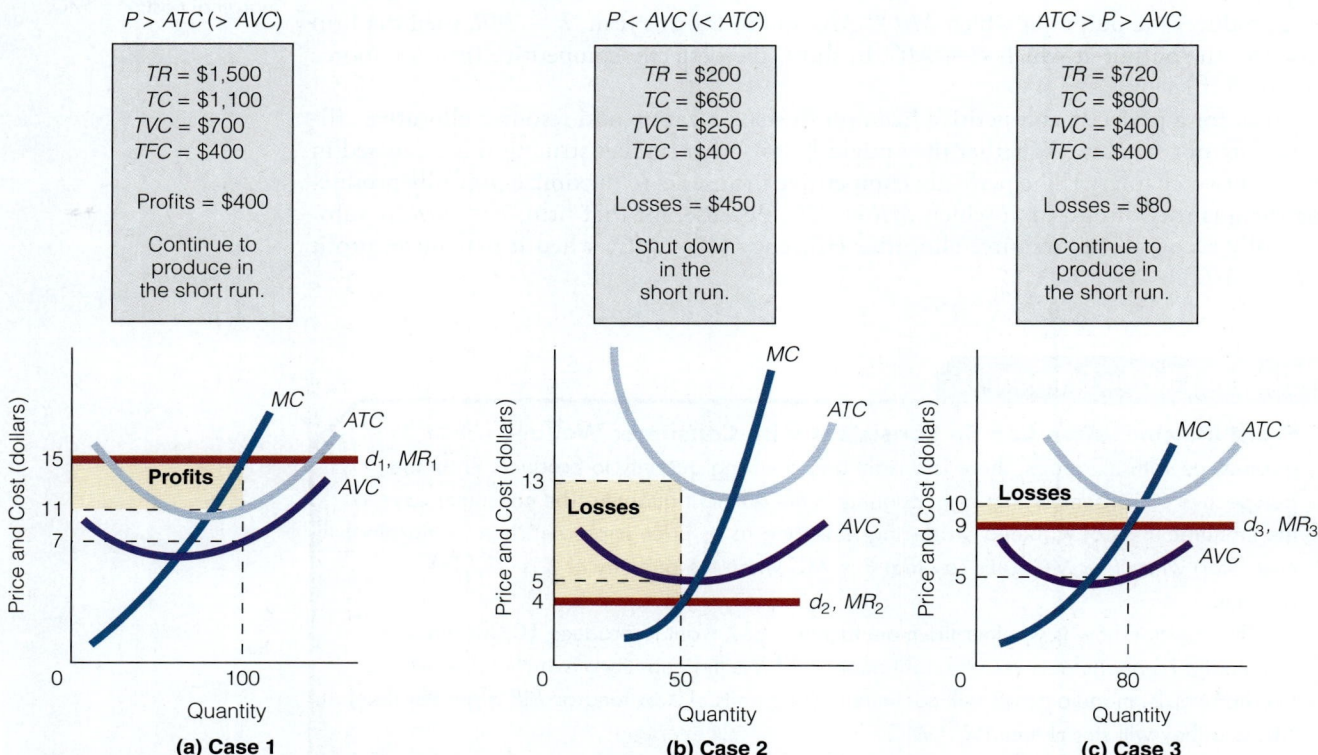

of output, price is above average total cost. Using the information in the exhibit, we can make the following calculations:

Case 1	
Equilibrium price (P)	= $15
Quantity of output produced (Q)	= 100 units
Total revenue (P × Q = $15 × 100)	= $1,500
Total cost (ATC × Q = $11 × 100)	= $1,100
Total variable cost (AVC × Q = $7 × 100)	= $700
Total fixed cost (TC − TVC = $1,100 − $700)	= $400
Profits (TR − TC = $1,500 − $1,100)	= $400

Therefore, for the perfectly competitive firm, if price is above the average total cost, the firm maximizes profits by producing the quantity of output at which $MR = MC$.

Case 2: Price Is Below Average Variable Cost Exhibit 4(b) illustrates the case in which price is below the average variable cost. The equilibrium price at which the perfectly competitive firm sells its good is $4. At this price, total revenue is less than both total cost and total variable cost, as the following calculations indicate:

Case 2	
Equilibrium price (P)	= $4
Quantity of output produced (Q)	= 50 units
Total revenue (P × Q = $4 × 50)	= $200
Total cost (ATC × Q = $13 × 50)	= $650
Total variable cost (AVC × Q = $5 × 50)	= $250
Total fixed cost (TC − TVC = $650 − $250)	= $400
Profits (TR − TC = $200 − $650)	= −$450

So, if the firm produces in the short run, it will take a loss of $450. If, however, it shuts down, its loss will be less, namely, its fixed costs, which amount to the difference between total cost and variable cost ($TFC + TVC = TC$, so $TC - TVC = TFC$). This difference is $400 ($650 − $250). Thus, between the two options of producing in the short run or shutting down, the firm will minimize its losses by shutting down ($Q = 0$). It will lose $400 by shutting down, whereas it will lose $450 by producing in the short run. Therefore, to minimize its loss, the firm should shut down.

In general, then, if price is below average variable cost, the perfectly competitive firm minimizes losses by choosing to shut down—that is, by not producing.

Case 3: Price Is Below Average Total Cost but Above Average Variable Cost
Exhibit 4(c) illustrates the case in which price is below average total cost but above average variable cost. The equilibrium price at which the perfectly competitive firm sells its good is $9. If the firm follows the profit maximization rule, it will produce 80 units of output. At this price and quantity of output, total revenue is less than total cost (hence, the firm will incur a loss), but total revenue is greater than total variable cost. The calculations are as follows:

Case 3	
Equilibrium price (P)	= $9
Quantity of output produced (Q)	= 80 units
Total revenue (P × Q = $9 × 80)	= $720
Total cost (ATC × Q = $10 × 80)	= $800
Total variable cost (AVC × Q = $5 × 80)	= $400
Total fixed cost (TC − TVC = $800 − $400)	= $400
Profits (TR − TC = $720 − $800)	= −$80

If the firm decides to produce in the short run, it will take a loss of $80. If it shuts down, it will lose its fixed costs, which, in this case, are $400 ($TC - TVC = \$800 - \$400$). Therefore, continuing to produce in the short run is better than shutting down. Losses are minimized by producing.

In general, then, if price is below average total cost but above average variable cost, the perfectly competitive firm minimizes its losses by continuing to produce in the short run instead of shutting down.

22-2d Common Misconceptions Over the Shutdown Decision

Asked when a business firm should shut down (stop producing), the noneconomist is likely to say when the firm is no longer earning a profit. In economics, that is when price is lower than average total cost ($P < ATC$). But that could be the wrong way to go, as we have just shown. Even if price is below average total cost and a loss is being incurred, a firm should not necessarily shut down. The shutdown decision depends, in the short run, on whether the firm loses more by shutting down than by not shutting down. Even though price is below average total cost, it could still be above average variable cost, and if it is, the firm minimizes its losses (in the short run) by continuing to produce than by shutting down.

Summary of Cases 1–3 *A perfectly competitive firm produces in the short run as long as price is above average variable cost (cases 1 and 3):*

$$P > AVC \rightarrow \text{Firm produces}$$

A perfectly competitive firm shuts down in the short run if price is less than average variable cost (case 2):

$$P < AVC \rightarrow \text{Firm shuts down}$$

We can summarize the same information in terms of total revenue and total variable costs. *A perfectly competitive firm produces in the short run as long as total revenue is greater than total variable costs (cases 1 and 3):*

$$TR > TVC \rightarrow \text{Firm produces}$$

A perfectly competitive firm shuts down in the short run if total revenue is less than total variable costs (case 2):

$$TR < TVC \rightarrow \text{Firm shuts down}$$

Exhibit 5 reviews some of the material discussed in the previous section. Exhibit 6 reviews, in a question-and-answer format, some of the material discussed in the last few sections.

EXHIBIT 5

What Should a Perfectly Competitive Firm Do in the Short Run?

The firm should produce in the short run as long as price (P) is above average variable cost (AVC). It should shut down in the short run if price is below average variable cost.

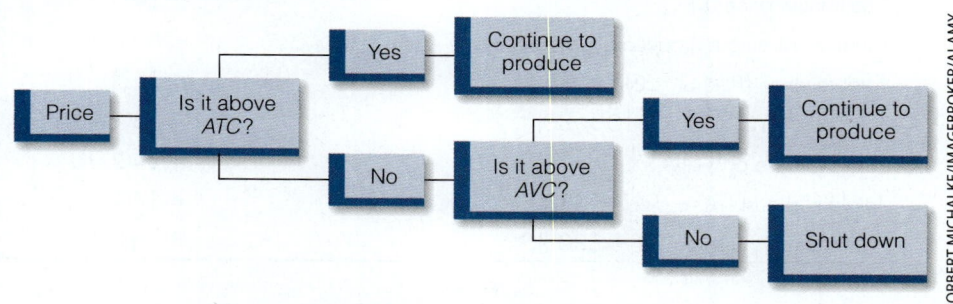

EXHIBIT 6

Q&A About Perfect Competition

Question	Answer
What four assumptions is the theory of perfect competition built on?	1. There are many buyers and many sellers. 2. Each firm produces and sells a homogeneous good. 3. Buyers and sellers have all relevant information about prices, product quality, sources of supply, and so forth. 4. Firms have easy entry into the market and easy exit out of the market.
What does it mean to say the perfectly competitive firm is a price taker?	The perfectly competitive firm *takes* the market-determined equilibrium price as the price at which it sells its product. The firm has no ability to control the price of the product it sells.
At what price does the perfectly competitive firm sell its product?	It sells at the price determined by the market. In other words, market demand and market supply determine the price of the good—say, $10—and then the firm takes this price as the price at which it will sell its product.
What quantity does the single perfectly competitive firm produce?	The quantity at which $MR = MC$.
How do we know if the perfectly competitive firm is earning profit or incurring a loss?	If $P > ATC$ for the firm, then it is earning profit. If $P < ATC$ for the firm, then it is incurring a loss.
What is resource allocative efficiency, and is the perfectly competitive firm resource allocative efficient?	Resource allocative efficiency exists if firms produce the quantity of output at which $P = MC$. The perfectly competitive firm is resource allocative efficient. Proof: (1) The firm produces the quantity of output at which $MR = MC$. (2) In perfect competition, $P = MR$. (3) Because $P = MR$ and the firm produces the quantity at which $MR = MC$, it follows that $P = MC$. Hence, the firm is resource allocative efficient.

Economics 24/7

Restaurant Shut Downs and the Coronavirus

In early 2020, the World Health Organization identified SARS-CoV-2 as a new type of coronavirus. This followed a December 2019 outbreak of the coronavirus in China. Covid-19 is the disease caused by SARS-CoV-2.

It wasn't long before the new coronavirus had come to the United States. Fear of the rampant transmission of the new coronavirus made it such that in March 2020, lockdowns and stay-at-home orders were being issued in the United States. Certain businesses were ordered to close—such as restaurants, bars, gyms, and hair salons—and people were ordered to stay at home unless they had to purchase groceries, go to the doctor, or satisfy certain other necessities.

In time, the lockdowns caused by the outbreak of the coronavirus caused some restaurants to close their doors for good.

We have learned that a business can take a loss and still continue to operate if its total revenue is greater than its total variable cost ($TR > TVC$). For example, consider the following case (all dollar amounts are on a monthly basis):

$$TR = \$50,000$$
$$TC = \$55,000$$
$$TVC = \$25,000$$
$$TFC = \$30,000$$
$$Losses = \$5,000$$

In this case, losses are $5,000. Still, even with losses, the restaurant would continue to produce in the *short run* because if it shuts down, it will lose its fixed costs of $30,000, and taking a loss of $30,000 is worse than taking a loss of $5,000. We state again that if total revenue is greater than total variable cost, a firm—even if it is taking a loss—will continue to produce in the short run. It will not shut down in the short run.

Now what the coronavirus and lockdowns did was to essentially lower the total revenue for many restaurants to a point that it fell below its total variable cost. (In time, some restaurants were allowed to open up if they could serve customers outside and at a certain distance from each other.) Now, with no, or fewer, customers at a restaurant, we would expect total revenue for the restaurant to fall. For example, if the average price of a meal is $50, and 1,000 meals a month are served, total revenue is $50,000. But with zero meals served, total revenue is $0; or with, say, 300 meals served, total revenue is $15,000.

We would expect that with lockdowns (complete or partial) total variable cost would fall too. If the restaurant is serving many fewer customers, it needs to purchase less food, hire fewer servers, and so on. With total revenue and total variable costs falling, whether or not the restaurant shuts down in the short run depends up how much each declines relative to the other. Suppose our new dollar amounts are:

$$TR = \$15,000$$
$$TC = \$40,000$$
$$TVC = \$10,000$$
$$TFC = \$30,000$$
$$Losses = \$25,000$$

In this case, total revenue and total variable cost have both declined, but total revenue is still greater than total variable cost. If the restaurant continues to operate, it incurs a loss of $25,000. If it shuts down, it loses its fixed costs of $30,000. It is better to take

a loss of $25,000 than to take one of $30,000. It will continue to operate in the short run.

But suppose the dollar amounts had been the following:

$$TR = \$15,000$$
$$TC = \$47,000$$
$$TVC = \$17,000$$
$$TFC = \$30,000$$
$$Losses = \$32,000$$

Again, like in the previous case, both total revenue and total variable cost have declined, but this time total revenue is less than total variable cost. If the restaurant continues to operate, it takes a loss of $32,000, and if it shuts down, it loses its fixed costs of $30,000. It is better to take a loss of $30,000 than to take one of $32,000. The restaurant will shut down.

A summary: What the coronavirus and lockdowns did was to lower both total revenue and total variable cost for restaurants. For some restaurants, it lowered total revenue by enough to fall below total variable cost. Those restaurants ended up shutting down.

22-2e The Perfectly Competitive Firm's Short-Run Supply Curve

Short-Run (Firm) Supply Curve
The portion of the firm's marginal cost curve that lies above the average variable cost curve.

The perfectly competitive firm produces (supplies output) in the short run if price is above average variable cost. It shuts down (does not supply output) if price is below average variable cost. Therefore, the **short-run (firm) supply curve** is the portion of the firm's marginal cost curve that lies above the average variable cost curve. Only a price above average variable cost will induce the firm to supply output. The short-run supply curve of the perfectly competitive firm is illustrated in Exhibit 7.

22-2f From Firm Supply Curve to Market (Industry) Supply Curve

If the perfectly competitive firm's short-run supply curve is the part of its marginal cost curve above its average variable cost curve, then deriving the **short-run market (industry) supply curve** is a simple matter:[3] We horizontally add the short-run supply curves for all firms in the perfectly competitive market or industry.

Consider, for simplicity, an industry made up of three firms: A, B, and C. [See Exhibit 8(a).] At a price P_1, firm A supplies 10 units, firm B supplies 8 units, and firm C supplies 18 units. One point on the market supply curve thus corresponds to P_1 on the price axis and 36 units (10 + 8 + 18 = 36) on the quantity axis.[4] If we follow this procedure for all prices, we have the short-run market supply curve. This curve, shown in the market setting in part (b) of the exhibit, is used along with the market demand curve (derived in Chapter 3) to determine equilibrium price and quantity.

EXHIBIT 7

The Perfectly Competitive Firm's Short-Run Supply Curve

The short-run supply curve is that portion of the firm's marginal cost curve that lies above the average variable cost curve.

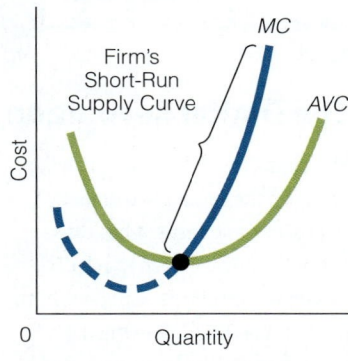

Short-Run Market (Industry) Supply Curve
The horizontal sum of all existing firms' short-run supply curves.

EXHIBIT 8

Deriving the Market (Industry) Supply Curve for a Perfectly Competitive Market

In (a), we add (horizontally) the quantity supplied by each firm to derive the market supply curve. The market supply curve and the market demand curve are shown in (b). Together, they determine equilibrium price and quantity.

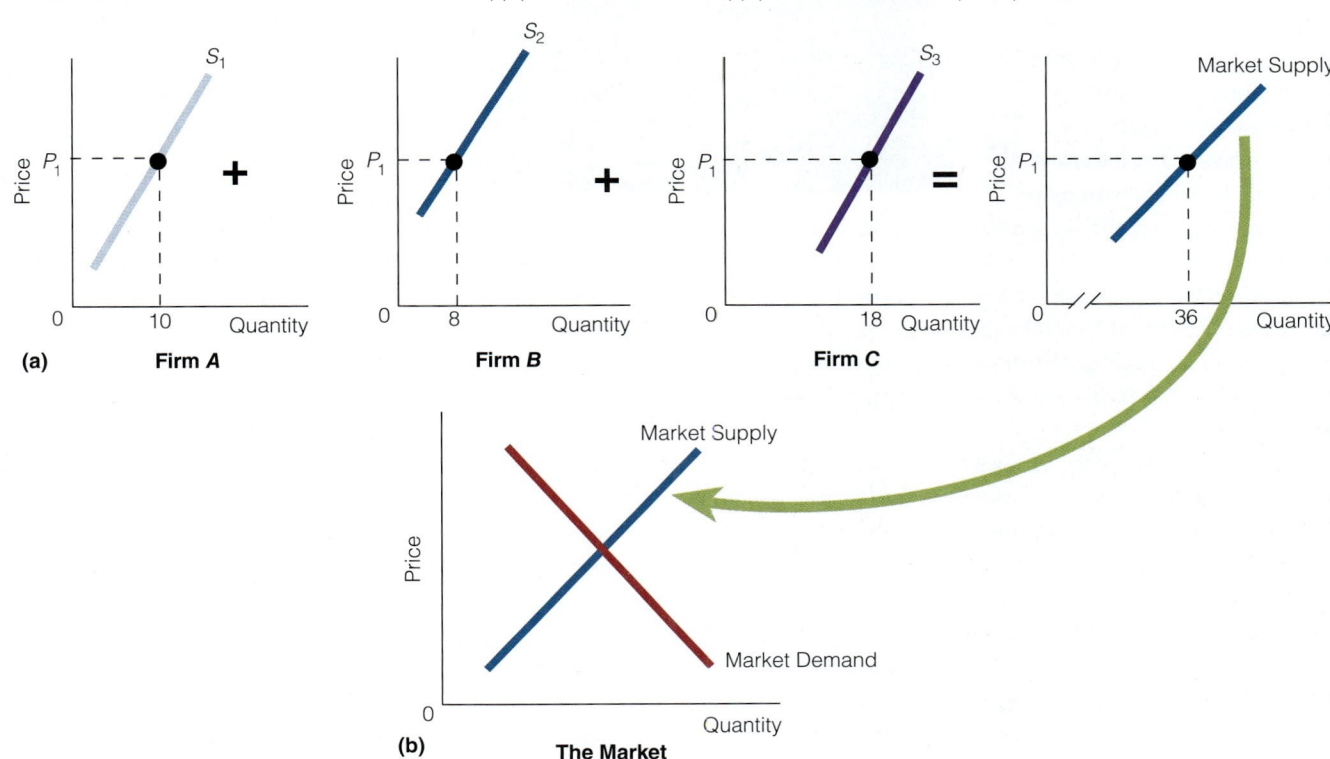

[3.] In discussing market structures, the words "industry" and "market" are often used interchangeably when a single-product industry is under consideration, which is the case here.

[4.] We add one qualification: Each firm's supply curve is drawn on the assumption that the prices of the variable inputs are constant.

Economics 24/7

The Digital Revolution, Price, and Marginal Cost

The digital revolution has had a big effect on the dollar price of many goods. In some cases, it has caused the dollar price to drop to zero. For example, consider newspapers, both print and online. Before the digital revolution, only printed newspapers existed. What did one have to give up to read a newspaper? First, there was the dollar price of the newspaper—say, $1—and whatever one could be doing, but wasn't, while one was reading the newspaper. Today, many newspapers are free (zero price) online. So what does a person today who reads the newspaper online (that she once read in its printed version) give up? No longer is there the $1 price, so one simply gives up whatever one could be doing, but isn't, while reading the online newspaper. In short, when it comes to reading newspapers, the digital revolution has caused the dollar price to drop to zero.

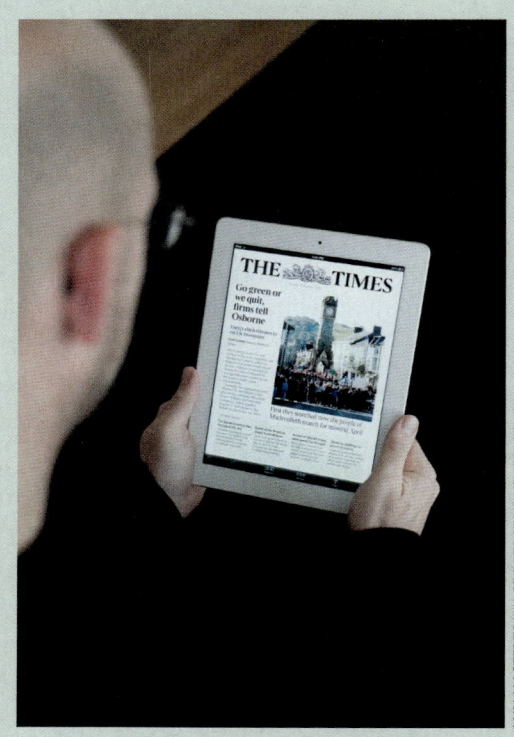

But why is that? Think back to our model of perfect competition. In that model, the price the customer paid for a good or service was equal to the marginal cost of producing the product ($P = MC$). So, if marginal cost was $4, then price was $4.

Now ask yourself what the marginal cost is for a newspaper company that wants an additional reader for its newspaper. Well, if it's a printed newspaper, there is the positive additional cost of producing an additional copy of the newspaper. But if it's an online newspaper, the marginal cost is zero. The newspaper has already been uploaded to the company website, and if, say, 10,000 people are reading the newspaper online, then there is really no additional cost incurred (by the newspaper publishing company) if one more person reads the newspaper online. In other words, the marginal cost here is zero, and in this case, the price (of the online newspaper) tends to gravitate toward zero.

But, then, we notice that not all online newspapers come at zero price. Some online publications, such as *The Wall Street Journal* or *The Economist*, charge a fee if a reader chooses to read more than a small number of articles. For example, with some publications, two or three articles a week might be free, but if a person wants to read more, a subscription to the publication is required. Why do *The Wall Street Journal* and *The Economist* require readers (beyond a certain limit) to become subscribers while many other publications do not? It has to do with how many close or perfect substitutes there are for the publications.

Think of hundreds of local newspapers across the country. For the most part, they are close to identical (homogeneous): they often report the same sports stories, national news stories, weather across the country, and so on. What is different among local newspapers is, of course, the local news. In other words, only the local newspaper in Savannah, Georgia, has the local Savannah news, and only the local newspaper in Topeka, Kansas, has the local Topeka news. But isn't the local news in each town newspaper enough to make local newspapers dissimilar? Not so much if people can easily get the local news by searching on the Internet.

In the end, the reason that *The Wall Street Journal* and *The Economist* can charge for their online publications, and that it is so much harder for the local newspaper in Anytown, USA, to do so, is that *The Wall Street Journal* and *The Economist* are more nearly unique products. For example, some readers think that, when it comes to economic and financial news and analysis, there really is no close substitute for *The Wall Street Journal*. And when it comes to economic and political reporting and analysis, there is no close substitute for *The Economist*.

22-2g Why Is the Market Supply Curve Upward Sloping?

When the demand and supply curves were introduced in Chapter 3, the supply curve was drawn upward sloping. To understand why, consider the following questions and answers:

- *Question 1:* Why do we draw market supply curves upward sloping?

- *Answer:* Because market supply curves are the horizontal sum of firms' supply curves and firms' supply curves are upward sloping.

- *Question 2:* But why are firms' supply curves upward sloping?

- *Answer:* Because the supply curve for each firm is the portion of its marginal cost (MC) curve that is *above* its average variable cost (AVC) curve—and this portion of the MC curve is upward sloping.

- *Question 3:* But why do MC curves have an upward-sloping portion?

- *Answer:* According to the law of diminishing marginal returns, the marginal physical product (MPP) of a variable input eventually declines. When that happens, the MC curve begins to rise.

Conclusion: Because of the law of diminishing marginal returns, MC curves are upward sloping, and because MC curves are upward sloping, so are market supply curves.

---

1. If a firm produces the quantity of output at which $MR = MC$, does it necessarily earn profits?
2. In the short run, if a firm finds that its price (P) is less than its average total cost (ATC), should it shut down its operation?
3. The noneconomist says that a firm maximizes profits when total revenue (TR) minus total cost (TC) is as large as possible and positive. The economist says that a firm maximizes profits when it produces the level of output at which $MR = MC$. Explain how the two ways of looking at profit maximization are consistent.
4. Why are market supply curves upward sloping?

22-3 Perfect Competition in the Long Run

The number of firms in a perfectly competitive market may not be the same in the short run as in the long run. For example, if the typical firm is making economic profits in the short run, new firms will be attracted to the industry, and the number of firms will increase. If the typical firm is sustaining losses, some existing firms will exit the industry, and the number of firms will decrease. The two processes are explained in greater detail later in this section. For now, we begin by outlining the conditions of long-run competitive equilibrium.

22-3a The Conditions of Long-Run Competitive Equilibrium

The following conditions characterize **long-run competitive equilibrium**:

1. *Economic profit is zero; that is, price (P) is equal to short-run average total cost (SRATC):*

$$P = SRATC$$

The logic of this condition is clear when we analyze what will happen if price is above or below short-run average total cost. If it is above short-run average total cost, positive economic profits will attract firms to the industry in order to obtain the profits. If price

Long-Run Competitive Equilibrium
The condition in which $P = MC = SRATC = LRATC$. Economic profit is zero, firms are producing the quantity of output at which price is equal to marginal cost, and no firm has an incentive to change its plant size.

is below short-run average total cost, losses will result, and some firms will want to exit the industry. Long-run competitive equilibrium cannot exist if firms have an incentive to enter or exit the industry in response to positive economic profits or losses. For long-run equilibrium to exist, there can be no incentive for firms to enter or exit. This condition is brought about by zero economic profit (normal profit), which is a consequence of the equilibrium price being equal to short-run average total cost.

2. *Firms are producing the quantity of output at which price (P) is equal to marginal cost (MC):*

$$P = MC$$

Perfectly competitive firms naturally move toward the output level at which marginal revenue (or price, because, for a perfectly competitive firm, $MR = P$) equals marginal cost.

3. *No firm has an incentive to change its plant size to produce its current output; that is, at the quantity of output at which $P = MC$, the following condition holds:*

$$SRATC = LRATC$$

To understand this condition, suppose $SRATC > LRATC$ at the quantity of output established in condition 2. Then the firm has an incentive to change its plant size in the long run because it wants to produce its product with the plant size that will give it the lowest average total cost (unit cost). It will have no incentive to change its plant size when it is producing the quantity of output at which price equals marginal cost and $SRATC$ equals $LRATC$.

The three conditions necessary for long-run competitive equilibrium can be stated as shown in Exhibit 9: Long-run competitive equilibrium exists when $P = MC = SRATC = LRATC$.

In conclusion, long-run competitive equilibrium exists when firms have no incentive to make any changes—that is, when there is no incentive for firms to do any of the following:

1. Enter or exit the industry
2. Produce more or less output
3. Change their plant size

EXHIBIT 9

Long-Run Competitive Equilibrium

(a) Equilibrium in the market.
(b) Equilibrium for the firm. In (b), $P = MC$ (the firm has no incentive to move away from the quantity q_1 of output at which this equality occurs), $P = SRATC$ (there is no incentive for firms to enter or exit the industry), and $SRATC = LRATC$ (there is no incentive for the firm to change its plant size).

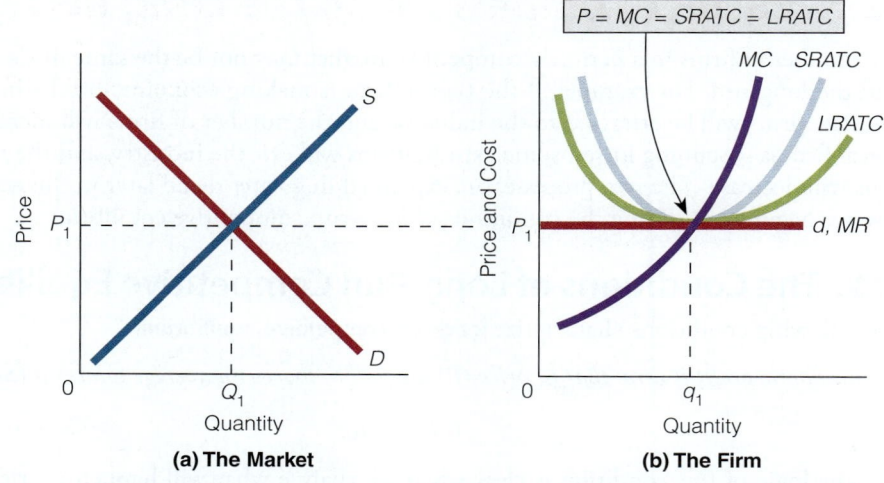

(a) The Market

(b) The Firm

Thinking Like an Economist

Equilibrium Is Where Things Are Headed The concept of equilibrium is important in economics because equilibrium is where things are headed; in a way, it is the destination point. Suppose that firms in a perfectly competitive market are currently earning positive economic profit. At this point, say, 100 firms are in the market. But things are not likely to stay that way, and the number of firms is not likely to remain at 100. Firms are earning positive profits, so firms that are not currently in the market will join the market, pushing the number of participants upward from 100. Only when all firms are earning normal profit (zero economic profit) will the number of firms remain where it is. Only then will the market be in equilibrium.[5]

When you get on a plane in, say, Los Angeles that is headed for New York City, you are fairly sure that the trip is not over until you reach New York City. However, knowing when the trip is over in economics is not as easily determined. Theoretically, we know that the trip is over when equilibrium has been reached. But what conditions indicate that equilibrium has been reached?

22-3b The Perfectly Competitive Firm and Productive Efficiency

A firm that produces its output at the lowest-possible per-unit cost (lowest ATC) is said to exhibit **productive efficiency**. The perfectly competitive firm is productively efficient in long-run equilibrium, as shown in Exhibit 9. Productive efficiency is desirable from society's standpoint because perfectly competitive firms are economizing on society's scarce resources and therefore not wasting them.

To illustrate, suppose the lowest unit cost at which good X can be produced is $3, the minimum ATC. If a firm produces 1,000 units of good X at this unit cost, then its total cost is $3,000. Now suppose the firm produces good X not at its lowest unit cost of $3, but at a slightly higher unit cost of $3.50. Then total cost now equals $3,500, and resources worth $500 were employed producing good X that could have been used to produce other goods had the firm exhibited productive efficiency. In other words, society could have been richer in goods and services, but because of the firm's decision to produce at $3.50, it isn't.

Productive Efficiency
The situation in which a firm produces its output at the lowest-possible per-unit cost (lowest ATC).

22-3c Industry Adjustment to an Increase in Demand

An increase in market demand for a product can throw an industry out of long-run competitive equilibrium. Exhibit 10 describes the process, numbered in the exhibit as follows:

1. We start at long-run competitive equilibrium, where $P = MC = SRATC = LRATC$.
2. Then, market demand rises for the product produced by the firms in the industry, and the equilibrium price rises.
3. As a consequence, the demand curve faced by an individual firm (the firm's marginal revenue curve) shifts upward.

---

[5] We are assuming that our other long-run equilibrium conditions hold, such as that no firms want to change their plant size and that there is no incentive for any firm to produce any more or any less output.

4. Next, *existing firms* in the industry increase the quantity of output because marginal revenue now intersects marginal cost at a higher quantity of output.

5. In the long run, new firms begin to enter the industry because price is currently above average total cost and there are positive economic profits.

6. As new firms enter the industry, the market (industry) supply curve shifts rightward.

7–8. As a consequence, equilibrium price falls until long-run competitive equilibrium is reestablished—that is, until economic profit is zero once again.

EXHIBIT 10

The Process of Moving from One Long-Run Competitive Equilibrium Position to Another

This exhibit describes what happens on both the market level and the firm level when demand rises and throws an industry out of long-run competitive equilibrium.

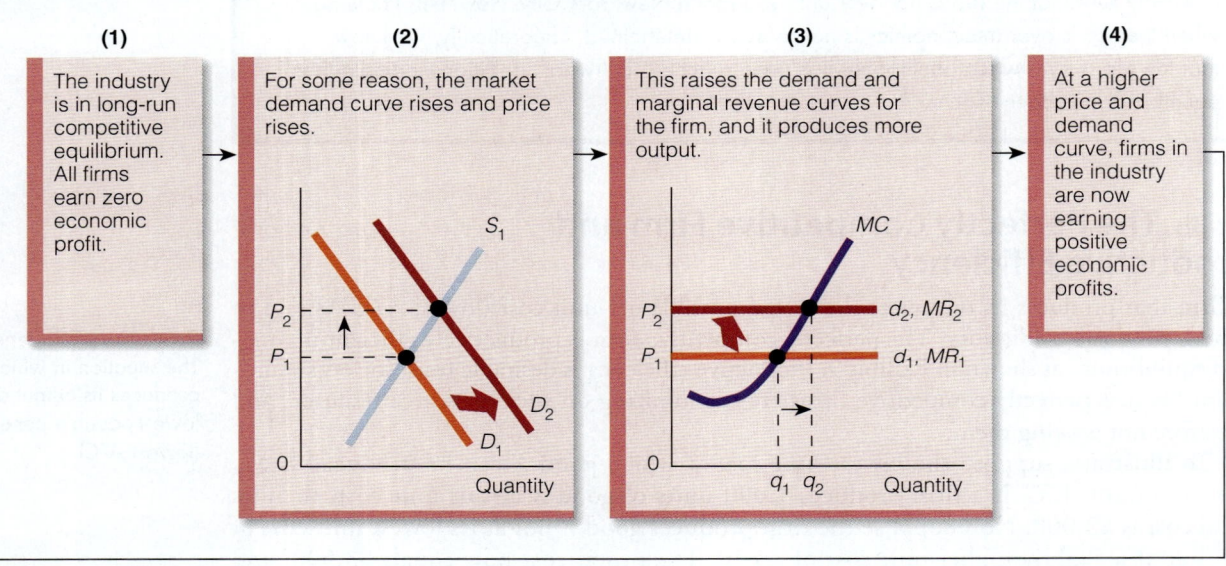

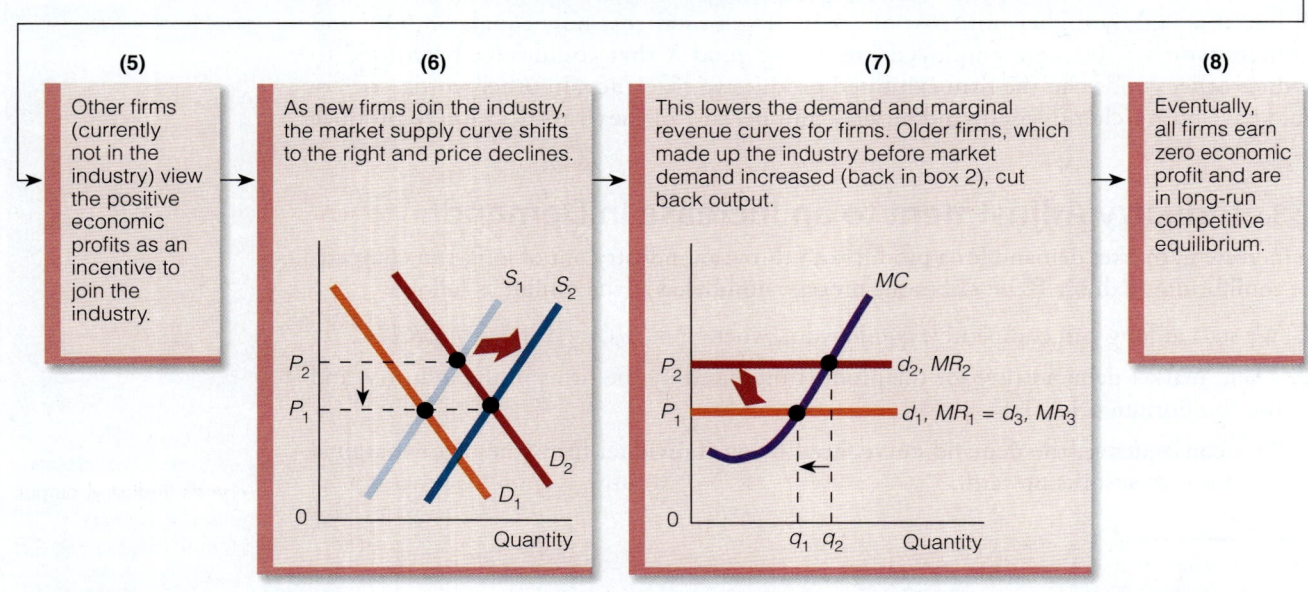

Now look at the process again, from the initial increase in market demand to the reestablishment of long-run competitive equilibrium: Price increased in the short run (owing to the increase in demand) and then decreased in the long run (owing to the increase in supply). Also, profits increased (owing to the increase in demand and consequent increase in price) and then decreased (owing to the increase in supply and consequent decrease in price). They went from zero to some positive amount and then back to zero.

The *up-and-down* movements in both price and profits in response to an increase in demand are important. Too often, people see only the primary upward movements in both price and profits, and they ignore or forget the secondary downward movements. However, the secondary effects in price and profits are as important as the primary effects.

The adjustment to an increase in demand brings up an important question: If price first rises owing to an increase in market demand and later falls owing to an increase in market supply, will the new equilibrium price be greater than, less than, or equal to the *original* equilibrium price? (In Exhibit 10, the new equilibrium price is shown as equal to the original equilibrium price, but this need not be the case.)

For example, if the equilibrium price is $10 before the increase in market demand, will the new equilibrium price (after market and firm adjustments) be greater than, less than, or equal to $10? The answer depends on whether cost is remaining constant, increasing, or decreasing in the industry.

Constant-Cost Industry In a constant-cost industry, average total costs (unit costs) do not change as output increases or decreases when firms enter or exit the industry. If market demand increases for a good produced by firms in a constant-cost industry, price will initially rise and then will finally fall to its original level, as shown in Exhibit 11(a). Point 1 represents long-run competitive equilibrium, at which economic profits are zero. Then demand increases, and price rises from P_1 to P_2. At P_2, there are positive economic profits, which cause the firms currently in the industry to increase output, so we move up the supply curve, S_1, from point 1 to point 2. Next, new firms, drawn by the profits, enter the industry, causing the supply curve to shift rightward (S_2).

For a constant-cost industry, output is increased without a change in the price of inputs. Because of this situation, the firms' cost curves do not shift. But if costs do not rise to reduce the profits in the industry, then price must fall. (Profits can be reduced in two ways: through a rise in costs or a fall in price.) Price must fall to its original level P_1 before profits can be zero, implying that the supply curve shifts rightward by the same amount that the demand curve shifts rightward. In the exhibit, this shift is from S_1 to S_2. The two long-run equilibrium points (1 and 3), at which economic profits are zero, define the **long-run (industry) supply (LRS) curve**. A **constant-cost industry** is thus characterized by a horizontal long-run supply curve.

Increasing-Cost Industry In an increasing-cost industry, average total costs (unit costs) increase as firms enter the industry and output increases; average total costs decrease as firms exit the industry and output decreases. If market demand increases for a good produced by firms in an increasing-cost industry, price will initially rise and then finally fall to a level above its original level.

In Exhibit 11(b), as before, point 1 represents long-run competitive equilibrium. Demand increases, and price rises from P_1 to P_2. This shift brings about positive economic profits, which cause firms in the industry to increase output and new firms to enter the industry. So far, the process is the same as that for a constant-cost industry. However, in an increasing-cost industry, as firms purchase more inputs to produce more output, some input prices rise and cost curves shift. In short, as industry output increases, profits are caught in a two-way squeeze: price is

Long-Run (Industry) Supply (LRS) Curve
A graphic representation of the quantities of output that an industry is prepared to supply at different prices after the entry and exit of firms are completed.

Constant-Cost Industry
An industry in which average total costs do not change as (industry) output increases or decreases when firms enter or exit the industry, respectively.

EXHIBIT 11

Long-Run Industry Supply Curves

LRS = Long-run industry supply. Each part illustrates the same scenario but with different results, depending on whether the industry has (a) constant costs, (b) increasing costs, or (c) decreasing costs. In each part, we start at long-run competitive equilibrium (point 1). Demand then increases, price rises from P_1 to P_2, and there are positive economic profits. Consequently, existing firms increase output and new firms are attracted to the industry. In (a), input costs remain constant as output increases, so the firms' cost curves do not shift. Profits fall to zero through a decline in price. This scenario implies that, in a constant-cost industry, the supply curve shifts rightward by the same amount as the demand curve shifts rightward. In (b), input costs increase as output increases. Profits are squeezed by a combination of rising costs and falling prices. The new equilibrium price P_3 for an increasing-cost industry is higher than the old equilibrium price P_1. In (c), input costs decrease as output increases. The new equilibrium price P_3 for a decreasing-cost industry is lower than the old equilibrium price P_1.

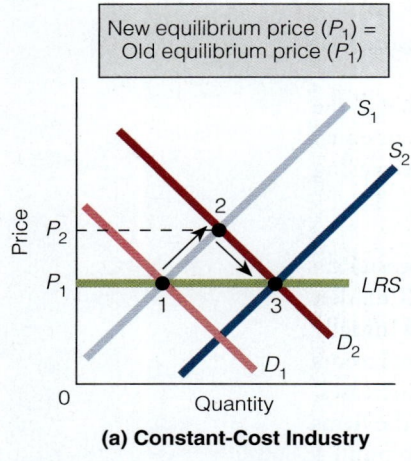
(a) Constant-Cost Industry

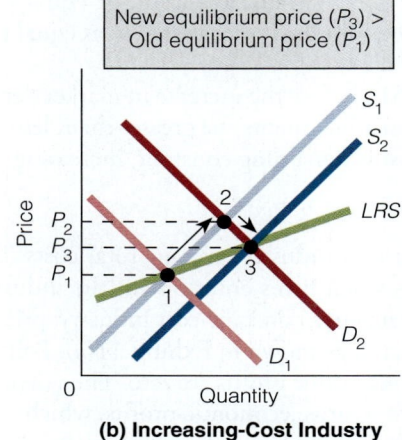
(b) Increasing-Cost Industry

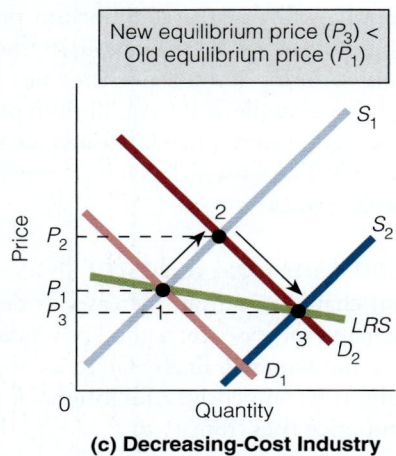
(c) Decreasing-Cost Industry

---

coming down, and costs are rising. If costs are rising as price is falling, then price will not have to fall to its original level before zero economic profits rule once again. Thus, in an increasing-cost industry, price will not have to fall as far to restore long-run competitive equilibrium as it will in a constant-cost industry. We would expect, then, that, when an increasing-cost industry experiences an increase in demand, the new equilibrium price will be higher than the old equilibrium price. Accordingly, the supply curve shifts rightward by less than the demand curve shifts rightward. An **increasing-cost industry** is characterized by an upward-sloping long-run supply curve.

Decreasing-Cost Industry In a decreasing-cost industry, average total costs (unit costs) decrease as firms enter the industry and output increases; average total costs increase as firms exit the industry and output decreases. If market demand increases for a good produced by firms in a decreasing-cost industry, then price will initially rise and then finally fall to a level below its original level. In Exhibit 11(c), price moves from P_1 to P_2 and then to P_3. In such an industry, average total costs decrease as new firms enter the industry, so price must fall below its original level to eliminate profits. A **decreasing-cost industry** is characterized by a downward-sloping long-run supply curve.

Common Misconceptions About Profits The noneconomist often views profits in much the same way as the English teacher views a period. Profits come at the end of a

Increasing-Cost Industry An industry in which average total costs increase as output increases and decrease as output decreases when firms enter and exit the industry, respectively.

Decreasing-Cost Industry An industry in which average total costs decrease as output increases and increase as output decreases when firms enter and exit the industry, respectively.

production process, and a period comes at the end of a sentence. In reality, profit is more like a comma, in that something comes after it. Profit is more like an ongoing process, as just explained: Demand rises, causing price to rise, causing profits to rise. But things don't stop there: The higher profits encourage new firms to enter the market, causing the supply curve in the market to shift rightward, in turn causing price and profits to fall.

Think of how not knowing about the up-and-down movements in price and profits can lead to some unintended effects. The demand for a good rises, and with it, both price and profits rise. Big profits are reported in the news, and politicians start talking about taxing those so-called high profits. However, might taxing those high profits stop the price–profits story from continuing? Without the profits, new firms don't enter the market. Without the new firms, supply doesn't increase. In other words, taxing the profits might have the unintended effect of reducing the supply of goods from what it would be if the profits weren't taxed.

22-3d Profit from Two Perspectives

From one perspective, profit serves as an *incentive* for individuals to produce. From another perspective, it serves as a *signal*.

Profit serves as an incentive by prompting or encouraging certain behavior. John produces furniture to sell because he hopes to earn a profit; Jackie opens up a hair salon because she hopes to earn a profit.

As a signal, profit acts a little like a neon sign, identifying where resources are most welcome. To illustrate, suppose company A produces good A' and company B produces good B'. Suppose also that, currently, company A is earning profits producing good A' and company B is incurring a loss producing good B'. To those viewing the profits and losses from the outside, it is as if the profits are signaling, "If you are thinking of producing either good A' or good B', choose A'. That is where the profit can be found." Stated differently, it is as if profit tells others where resources are best allocated: Allocate them toward producing good A'.

Thinking Like an Economist

Easy Entry Into a Market Matters Once again, demand rises, price rises, and profits go from zero to positive. Yet, as explained, the increase in profits is not the end of the story, as long as new firms can enter the market. But suppose they can't. If something prevents firms from entering the market, the end of the story will not be the same, with price moving down and profit returning to zero. The different ending points out how important easy entry into the market is to the story. Without easy entry, the story is a different one altogether: Prices are more likely to stay high, and profits are more likely to stay positive.

22-3e Industry Adjustment to a Decrease in Demand

Demand can decrease as well as increase. Suppose that, starting at long-run competitive equilibrium, market demand decreases. As a consequence, in the short run, the equilibrium price falls, effectively shifting the firm's demand curve (marginal revenue curve) downward. Some firms in the industry then decrease production because marginal revenue intersects marginal cost at a lower level of output, and other firms shut down.

In the long run, some firms will leave the industry because price is below average total cost, and they are suffering ongoing losses. As firms leave the industry, the market supply curve shifts leftward. As a consequence, the equilibrium price rises and continues to rise until long-run competitive equilibrium is reestablished—that is, until there are, once again, zero economic profits (instead of negative economic profits). Whether the new equilibrium price is greater than, less than, or equal to the original equilibrium price depends on whether cost is decreasing, increasing, or remaining constant, respectively, in the industry.

22-3f Differences in Costs, Differences in Profits: Now You See It, Now You Don't

Two farmers, Hancock and Cordero, produce wheat. Farmer Cordero grows his wheat on fertile land; farmer Hancock grows her wheat in poor soil. Both farmers sell their wheat for the same price, but because of the difference in the quality of their land, Cordero has lower average total costs than Hancock, as shown in Exhibit 12. Given the initial situations of the two farmers ATC_1, we notice that Cordero is earning profits and Hancock is not. Cordero is earning profits because he pays lower average total costs than Hancock as a consequence of farming higher-quality land.

But Cordero is not likely to continue earning profits. Individuals will bid up the price of the fertile land that Cordero farms vis-à-vis the poor-quality land that Hancock farms. In other words, if Cordero is renting his farmland, the rent he pays will increase to reflect the superior quality of the land. The rent will increase by an amount equal to the profits earned per period—that is, an amount equal to the shaded portion in Exhibit 12(b). If Cordero owns the land, the superior quality of the land will have a higher implicit cost.

In Exhibit 12(b), ATC_2 reflects either the higher rent Cordero must pay for the superior land or the full implicit cost he incurs by farming the land he owns. In either case, when the average total cost curve reflects all costs, Cordero will be in the same situation as Hancock: he, too, will be earning zero economic profits.

The profit has gone as payment for the higher-quality, more productive resource responsible for the lower average total costs in the first place. Consequently, average total costs are no longer relatively lower for the person or firm that employs the higher-quality, more productive resource or input.

EXHIBIT 12

Differences in Costs, Differences in Profits: Now You See It, Then It's Gone

At ATC_1 for both farmers, Cordero earns profits and Hancock does not. Cordero earns profits because the land he farms is of higher quality (is more productive) than Hancock's land. Eventually, this fact is taken into account, by Cordero either paying higher rent for the land or incurring implicit costs for it. Either way, Cordero's ATC curve moves upward to the same level as Hancock's and Cordero earns zero economic profits. The profits have gone as payment (implicit or explicit) for the higher-quality, more productive land.

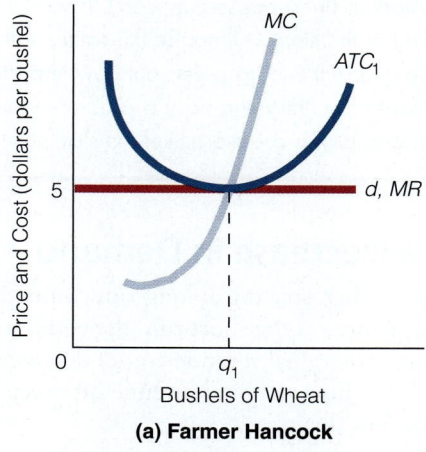
(a) Farmer Hancock

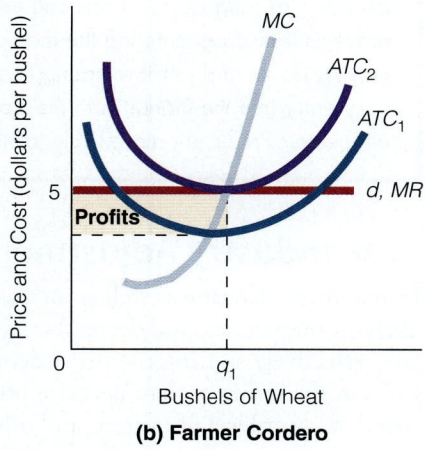
(b) Farmer Cordero

Economics 24/7

How Is High-Quality Land Like a Genius Software Engineer?

In the example of two farmers who produce wheat, Cordero was earning profits and Hancock was not, because Cordero farmed higher-quality land. In time, though, Cordero's higher profits ended up going into higher rent for the higher-quality land. The profit therefore went as payment for the higher-quality, more productive resource responsible for the lower average total costs in the first place.

In the field of designing and developing computer software applications, suppose there are two companies, *A* and *B*. Software engineers work at both companies, but one of company *A*'s software engineers is considered a genius within the software industry. Currently, the genius earns the same salary as other software engineers in the software industry.

Because the genius works for company *A*, company *A* comes up with better software applications than other companies. As a result, company *A* not only sells more software applications but also can charge higher prices for the software it sells. Thus, largely as a result of having hired the genius software engineer, company *A* currently earns higher profits than company *B* does.

If company *A*'s higher profits are attributable to the genius software engineer, then other software companies will soon compete to hire him. He will find his salary being bid up. To keep the software genius, company *A* will have to turn over some of its profits to him in the form of salary. Profits on Wednesday turn into the genius's salary on Thursday.

High-quality land is like a genius software engineer in that both are the source of profits, and those profits eventually get transformed into something else. In the farming example, high profits get turned into higher rent for the higher-quality land. In the software engineer example, high profits (for company *A*) get turned into a higher salary for our genius software engineer. Stated differently, the higher-quality land in our first example "is" the genius software engineer in the second.

22-3g Profit and Discrimination

A firm's discriminatory behavior can affect its profits in the context of the model of perfect competition. Suppose that, under the conditions of long-run competitive equilibrium, at which firms are earning zero economic profits, the owner of a firm chooses not to hire an excellent (i.e., above average) worker simply because of that worker's race, religion, or gender. What happens to the owner of the firm who discriminates in any way? If he chooses not to employ high-quality employees because of their race, religion, or gender, then his costs will rise above those of competitors who hire the best employees irrespective of race, religion, or gender. Because he is initially earning zero profit ($TR = TC$), the act of discrimination will raise TC and push the firm into taking economic losses. If the owner in the example is a manager, he may lose his job because the firm's owners may decide to replace managers earning subnormal profits. Thus, profit maximization by shareholders works to reduce discrimination.

1. If firms in a perfectly competitive market are earning positive economic profits, what will happen?
2. If firms in a perfectly competitive market want to produce more output, is the market in long-run equilibrium?
3. If a perfectly competitive market in long-run equilibrium witnesses an increase in demand, what will happen to price?
4. Two firms produce computer software. Firm A employs a software genius at the same salary that firm B employs a mediocre software engineer. Will the firm that employs the software genius earn higher profits than the other firm, *ceteris paribus*?

22-4 Topics for Analysis in the Theory of Perfect Competition

This section briefly analyzes three topics in the theory of perfect competition: higher costs and higher prices, advertising, and setting prices.

22-4a Do Higher Costs Mean Higher Prices?

Suppose that 600 firms are in an industry and that each firm sells the same product at the same price. Then one of these firms experiences a rise in its marginal costs of production. Someone immediately comments, "Higher costs for the firm today, higher prices for the consumer tomorrow," the assumption being that firms experiencing a rise in costs simply pass the higher costs on to consumers in the form of higher prices.

Passing along costs, however, cannot occur in a perfectly competitive market. In that kind of market, each firm in the industry is a price taker; furthermore, only one firm has experienced a rise in marginal costs. Because this firm supplies only a tiny percentage of the total market supply, the market supply curve is unlikely to undergo more than a negligible change. And if the market supply curve does not change, neither will the equilibrium price. In short, a rise in costs incurred by one of many firms does not mean that consumers will pay higher prices. Of course, if many of the firms in the industry experience a rise in costs, the market supply curve will be affected, along with price.

22-4b Will the Perfectly Competitive Firm Advertise?

Individual farmers don't advertise. You've never seen an advertisement for, say, farmer Johnson's milk, for a couple of reasons. First, farmer Johnson sells a homogeneous product, so advertising his milk is the same as advertising every dairy farmer's milk. Second, farmer Johnson is in a perfectly competitive market, so he can sell all the milk he wants at the going price. Why should he advertise? From his viewpoint, advertising has all cost and no benefits.

However, a perfectly competitive industry might advertise. For example, if farmer Johnson won't advertise his milk, the milk industry might advertise milk in general in the hope of shifting the market demand curve for milk to the right.

22-4c Supplier-Set Price Versus Market-Determined Price: Collusion or Competition?

Suppose the only thing you know about an industry is that all the firms in it sell their products at the same price. To explain this unanimity, some people argue that the firms are colluding—that is, they come together, pick a price, and stick to it. Collusion, of course, is one way for all firms to arrive at the same price for their products, but it is not the only way. Another way, as described in this chapter, is that all firms are price takers; that is, the firms are in a perfectly competitive market structure. In that case, there is no collusion.

1. In a perfectly competitive market, do higher costs mean higher prices?

2. If you see a product advertised on television, does it follow that the product cannot be produced in a perfectly competitive market?

Office Hours

"Do You Have to Know the MR = MC Condition in Order to Be Successful in Business?"

Student: Something seems odd to me. Some people are successful in business without knowing any of the material in this chapter. Isn't it possible for a person to be successful in business without knowing the $MR = MC$ condition or the shutdown decision (shut down when P is less than AVC), and so on?

Instructor: Yes, but keep in mind that someone doesn't have to know the $MR = MC$ condition to try to put it into operation. Most people don't know the physics behind the operation of a car, but they drive a car as if they do know the physics.

Student: Are you saying that we can know and not know something at the same time? That sounds odd to me.

Instructor: That's not exactly what I am saying. You can do something you don't know you're doing. Let me give you an example. Suppose Jack owns and operates his own business producing shoe boxes. He has never taken an economics course in his life, and he doesn't know the first thing about marginal revenue, marginal cost, average total cost, and so on. Not knowing these things doesn't mean that he doesn't have to figure out how many shoe boxes to produce. So how does he do it without a knowledge of marginal revenue and marginal cost? All Jack has to know is that it is a good idea to keep producing shoe boxes when more money is coming in the front door (in additional revenue) than is going out the back door (in additional costs). That's it. That basic, very elemental idea is behind the $MR = MC$ condition.

Student: Does the same hold for things like knowing when to continue producing a good and knowing when to shut down?

Instructor: Yes. The economist advises a business owner to shut down when $P < AVC$, but this is just a slightly more sophisticated way of expressing the idea that a firm should shut down when it would lose more from not shutting down. Consider Yvonne, who, like Jack, owns her own business. She is currently wondering whether she should stop producing a good. She may not know the first thing about the relationship between price and average variable cost, but she certainly can put some numbers down on paper and figure out how much money she loses if she shuts down and how much money she loses if she doesn't shut down.

Student: I think I see what you are getting at. The economist seems only to be formalizing what people do if they are trying to maximize their profits or minimize their losses. The average businessperson simply continues producing additional units of a good as long as more money comes into the firm by selling the additional unit than is going out by producing it. Then the economist simply says, "Produce as long as *MR* is greater than *MC*." Am I right?

Instructor: Yes, you're right.

Student: Looking at things that way makes the material in this chapter seem a little easier and a little more grounded in reality.

Instructor: That's good to hear.

Points to Remember

1. Not knowing the $MR = MC$ condition doesn't mean that a real-world businessperson doesn't abide by it.
2. Many of the rules or conditions in this chapter (e.g., produce until $MR = MC$, shut down when $P < AVC$) are simply formalized ways of expressing what individuals in business settings do when they seek to maximize profits or minimize losses.

Chapter Summary

The Theory of Perfect Competition

- The theory of perfect competition is built on four assumptions: (1) There are many sellers and many buyers, none of whom is large in relation to total sales or purchases. (2) Each firm produces and sells a homogeneous product. (3) Buyers and sellers have all relevant information with respect to prices, product quality, sources of supply, and so on. (4) Entry into, and exit from, the industry is easy.
- The theory of perfect competition predicts the following: (1) Economic profits will be squeezed out of the industry in the long run by the entry of new firms; that is, zero economic profit exists in the long run. (2) In equilibrium, firms produce the quantity of output at which price equals marginal cost. (3) In the short run, firms will stay in business as long as price covers average variable costs. (4) In the long run, firms will stay in business as long as price covers average total costs. (5) In the short run, an increase in demand will lead to a rise in price; whether the price in the long run will be higher than, lower than, or equal to the original price depends on whether the firm is in an increasing-, decreasing-, or constant-cost industry.

The Perfectly Competitive Firm

- The perfectly competitive firm is a price taker. It sells its product only at the market-established equilibrium price.
- The perfectly competitive firm faces a horizontal (flat, perfectly elastic) demand curve. Its demand curve and its marginal revenue curve are the same.
- The perfectly competitive firm (as well as all other firms) maximizes profits (or minimizes losses) by producing the quantity of output at which $MR = MC$.

- For the perfectly competitive firm, price equals marginal revenue.
- The perfectly competitive firm is resource allocative efficient because it produces the quantity of output at which $P = MC$.

Production in the Short Run

- If $P > ATC \, (> AVC)$, the firm earns economic profits and will continue to operate in the short run.
- If $P < AVC \, (< ATC)$, the firm takes losses. It will shut down because the alternative (continuing to produce) increases the losses.
- If $ATC > P > AVC$, the firm takes losses. Nevertheless, it will continue to operate in the short run because the alternative (shutting down) increases the losses.
- The firm produces in the short run only when price is greater than average variable cost. Therefore, the portion of its marginal cost curve that lies above the average variable cost curve is the firm's short-run supply curve.

Conditions of Long-Run Competitive Equilibrium

- Long-run competitive equilibrium exists when there is no incentive for firms (1) to enter or exit the industry, (2) to produce more or less output, and (3) to change their plant size. We formalize these conditions as follows: (1) Economic profits are zero. Firms have no incentive to enter or exit the industry. (2) Firms are producing the quantity of output at which price is equal to marginal cost. (Firms have no incentive to produce more or less output. After all, when $P = MC$, it follows that $MR = MC$ for the perfectly competitive firm, and, thus, the firm is maximizing profits.) (3) $SRATC = LRATC$ at the

quantity of output at which $P = MC$. Firms do not have an incentive to change their plant size.)
- A perfectly competitive firm exhibits productive efficiency because, in the long run, it produces its output at the lowest possible per-unit cost (lowest ATC).

Industry Adjustment to a Change in Demand

- In a constant-cost industry, an increase in demand will result in a new equilibrium price equal to the original equilibrium price (before demand increased). In an increasing-cost industry, an increase in demand will result in a new equilibrium price higher than the original one. In a decreasing-cost industry, an increase in demand will result in a new equilibrium price lower than the original one.
- The long-run supply curve for a constant-cost industry is horizontal (flat, perfectly elastic). The long-run supply curve for an increasing-cost industry is upward sloping. The long-run supply curve for a decreasing-cost industry is downward sloping.

Key Terms and Concepts

Market Structure
Perfect Competition
Price Taker
Marginal Revenue (MR)
Profit Maximization Rule

Resource Allocative Efficiency
Short-Run (Firm) Supply Curve

Short-Run Market (Industry) Supply Curve
Long-Run Competitive Equilibrium
Productive Efficiency

Long-Run (Industry) Supply (LRS) Curve
Constant-Cost Industry
Increasing-Cost Industry
Decreasing-Cost Industry

Questions and Problems

1. "The firm's entire marginal cost curve is its short-run supply curve." Is the preceding statement true or false? Explain your answer.
2. In a perfectly competitive market, firms always operate at the lowest per-unit cost." Is the preceding statement true or false? Explain your answer.
3. "Firm A, one firm in a competitive industry, faces higher costs of production. As a result, consumers end up paying higher prices." Discuss.
4. Suppose all firms in a perfectly competitive market structure are in long-run equilibrium. Then demand for the firms' product increases. Initially, price and economic profits rise. Soon afterward, the government decides to tax most (but not all) of the economic profits, arguing that the firms in the industry did not earn the profits. Rather, the profits were simply the result of an increase in demand. What effect, if any, will the tax have on market adjustment?
5. Explain why one firm sometimes appears to be earning higher profits than another but, in reality, is not.
6. For a perfectly competitive firm, profit maximization does not conflict with resource allocative efficiency. Do you agree? Explain your answer.
7. The perfectly competitive firm does not increase its quantity of output without limit, even though it can sell all it wants at the going price. Why not?
8. You read in a business magazine that computer firms are reaping high profits. With the theory of perfect competition in mind, what do you expect to happen over time to each of the following?
   a. Computer prices
   b. The profits of computer firms
   c. The number of computers on the market
   d. The number of computer firms
9. In your own words, explain resource allocative efficiency.
10. The term "price taker" can apply to buyers as well as to sellers. A price-taking buyer is a buyer who cannot influence price by changing the amount she buys. What goods do you buy for which you are a price taker? What goods do you buy for which you are not a price taker?
11. Why study the theory of perfect competition if no real-world market completely satisfies all of the theory's assumptions?
12. Explain why a perfectly competitive firm will shut down in the short run if price is lower than average variable cost but will continue to produce if price is below average total cost but above average variable cost.
13. In long-run competitive equilibrium, $P = MC = SRATC = LRATC$. Because $P = MR$, we can write the preceding condition as $P = MR = MC = SRATC = LRATC$. The condition thus consists of four parts: (a) $P = MR$, (b) $MR = MC$,

(c) $P = SRATC$, and (d) $SRATC = LRATC$. Part (b)—$MR = MC$—is true because the perfectly competitive firm attempts to maximize profits, and that equation represents how it does so. What are the explanations for parts (a), (c), and (d)?

14. Suppose the government imposes the following production tax on one perfectly competitive firm in an industry: For each unit the firm produces, it must pay $1 to the government. Will consumers in this market end up paying higher prices because of the tax? Why or why not?

15. Why is the marginal revenue curve for a perfectly competitive firm the same as its demand curve?

16. Many plumbers charge the same price for coming to your house to fix a kitchen sink. Is this because plumbers are colluding?

17. Do firms in a perfectly competitive market exhibit productive efficiency? Why or why not?

18. Profit serves as both an incentive and a signal. Explain.

Working with Numbers and Graphs

1. Given the following information, state whether the perfectly competitive firm should shut down or continue to operate in the short run:
   a. $Q = 100$; $P = \$10$; $AFC = \$3$; $AVC = \$4$.
   b. $Q = 70$; $P = \$5$; $AFC = \$2$; $AVC = \$7$.
   c. $Q = 150$; $P = \$7$; $AFC = \$5$; $AVC = \$6$.

2. If total revenue increases at a constant rate, what does this condition imply about marginal revenue?

3. According to the accompanying table, what quantity of output should the firm produce? Explain your answer.

Q	TR	TC
0	$0	$0
1	100	50
2	200	110
3	300	180
4	400	260
5	500	360
6	600	480

4. Is the firm in question 3 a perfectly competitive firm? Explain your answer.

5. Explain how a market supply curve is derived.

6. Draw the relevant curves and the areas within them that show the following:
   a. A perfectly competitive firm that earns profits
   b. A perfectly competitive firm that incurs losses but that will continue operating in the short run
   c. A perfectly competitive firm that incurs losses and that will shut down in the short run

7. Why is the perfectly competitive firm's supply curve the portion of its marginal cost curve that is above its average variable cost curve?

8. In the accompanying figure, what area(s) represent(s) the following at Q_1?
   a. Total cost
   b. Total variable cost
   c. Total revenue
   d. Loss (negative profit)

9. Why does the MC curve cut the ATC curve at the latter's lowest point?

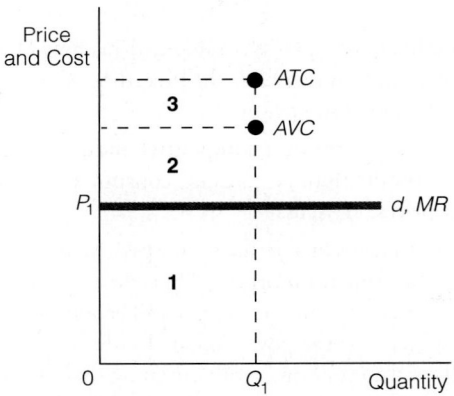

10. Suppose all firms in a perfectly competitive market are in long-run equilibrium. Illustrate what a perfectly competitive firm will do if market demand rises.

Monopoly

CHAPTER 23

Introduction

Monopoly is at the opposite end of the market structure spectrum from perfect competition. We begin our discussion of monopoly by outlining the assumptions on which the theory of monopoly is built. We then move on to talk about the quantity of output the monopolist wants to produce and the price (per unit) at which it sells that output. Much of this chapter focuses on the differences between the perfectly competitive firm and the monopoly firm.

23-1 The Theory of Monopoly

The theory of **monopoly** is built on three assumptions:

1. *There is one seller.* In effect, the firm is the industry. Contrast this situation with perfect competition, where many firms make up the industry.
2. *The single seller sells a product that has no close substitutes.* Because there are no close substitutes for its product, the single seller—the monopolist or monopoly firm—faces little, if any, competition.
3. *The barriers to entry are extremely high.* In the theory of perfect competition, a firm can enter the industry easily. In the theory of monopoly, entering the industry is very hard (if not impossible). Extremely high barriers keep out new firms.

Examples of monopoly include many public utilities (local public utilities such as electricity, water, and gas companies) and the U.S. Postal Service (in the delivery of first-class mail).

Monopoly
A theory of market structure based on three assumptions: There is one seller, it sells a product that has no close substitutes, and the barriers to entry are extremely high.

23-1a Barriers to Entry: A Key to Understanding Monopoly

If a firm is a single seller of a product, why don't other firms enter the market and produce the same product? The answer is that legal barriers, economies of scale, or one firm's exclusive ownership of a scarce resource may make it difficult or impossible for new firms to enter the market.

Legal Barriers Legal barriers include public franchises, patents, and government licenses. A **public franchise** is a right that government grants to a firm and that permits the firm to provide a particular good or service and excludes all others from doing so (thus eliminating potential competition by law). For example, the U.S. Postal Service has been granted the exclusive franchise to deliver first-class mail. Many public utilities operate under state and local franchises, as do food and gas suppliers along many state turnpikes.

In the United States, patents are granted to inventors of a product or process for a period of 20 years. During that time, the patent holder is shielded from competitors: No one else can legally produce and sell the patented product or process. The rationale behind patents is that they encourage innovation in an economy. Few people will waste their time and money trying to invent a new product if their competitors can immediately copy and sell it.

Entry into some industries and occupations requires a government-granted license. For example, radio and television stations cannot operate without a license from the Federal Communications Commission (FCC). In most states, a person needs to be licensed to join the ranks of physicians, dentists, architects, nurses, embalmers, barbers, veterinarians, and lawyers, among others.

Economies of Scale In some industries, low average total costs (low unit costs) are obtained only through large-scale production. Thus, if new entrants are to compete in the industry, they must enter it on a large scale. But having to produce on this scale is risky and costly, and it therefore acts as a barrier to entry. If economies of scale are so pronounced that only one firm can survive in the industry, the firm is called a **natural monopoly**. Often-cited examples of natural monopoly include public utilities that provide gas, water, and electricity. A later chapter discusses government regulation of a natural monopoly.

Exclusive Ownership of a Necessary Resource Existing firms may be protected from the entry of new firms by the exclusive or nearly exclusive ownership of a resource needed to enter the industry. The classic example is the Aluminum Company of America (Alcoa), which, for a time, controlled almost all the sources of bauxite in the United States. Alcoa was the sole producer of aluminum in the country from the late nineteenth century until the 1940s.

23-1b What Is the Difference Between a Government Monopoly and a Market Monopoly?

Sometimes high barriers to entry exist because competition is legally prohibited, and sometimes barriers exist independently. When high barriers take the form of public franchises, patents, or government licenses, competition is *legally* prohibited. When high barriers take the form of economies of scale or exclusive ownership of a resource, competition is not legally prohibited. In the latter cases, nothing legally prohibits rival firms from entering the market and competing, even though they may choose not to do so; there is no sign on the industry entrance that reads, "No competition allowed."

Public Franchise
A firm's government-granted right that permits the firm to provide a particular good or service and that excludes all others from doing so.

Natural Monopoly
The condition in which economies of scale are so pronounced that only one firm can survive.

Some economists use the term "government monopoly" to refer to a monopoly that is legally protected from competition and the term "market monopoly" to refer to a monopoly that is not legally protected from competition. But these terms do not imply that one type is better or worse than the other.

Economics 24/7

Monopoly and the Boston Tea Party

The original meaning of the word "monopoly" was "an exclusive right to sell something." At one time, kings and queens granted monopolies to people whom they favored. The monopoly entitled the person to be the sole producer or seller of a particular good. If anyone dared to compete, the crown could have the offender fined or imprisoned.

The issue of monopoly came up in the early history of the America. In 1767, the British Parliament passed the Townshend Acts, which imposed taxes (or duties) on various products imported into the American colonies. The taxes were so hated in the colonies that they prompted protest and noncompliance, and they were repealed in 1770, except for one: the tax on tea. Some historians state that the British Parliament left the tax on tea to show the colonists that it had the right to raise tax revenue without seeking colonial approval. To get around the tax, the colonists started to buy tea from Dutch traders.

Then, in 1773, the British East India Company was in financial trouble. To help solve its financial problems, it sought a special privilege—a monopoly—from the British Parliament. In response, Parliament passed the Tea Act, which granted the company the sole right to export tea to the colonies—a monopoly. The combination of the tax and the monopoly right given to the British East India Company angered the colonists and is said to have led to the Boston Tea Party on December 16, 1773. The colonists who took part in the Boston Tea Party threw overboard 342 chests of tea owned by the monopoly-wielding British East India Company.

(Answers to Self-Test questions are in Answers to Self-Test Questions at the back of the book.)

1. "There are always some close substitutes for the product any firm sells; therefore, the theory of monopoly (which assumes no close substitutes) cannot be useful." Comment.
2. How do economies of scale act as a barrier to entry?
3. How is a movie superstar like a monopolist?

23-2 Monopoly Pricing and Output Decisions

A monopolist is a **price searcher**—that is, a seller with the ability to control, to some degree, the price of the product it sells. In contrast to a price taker, a price searcher can raise its price and still sell its product—although it will not sell as many units as it would at the lower price. The pricing and output decisions of the monopolist are discussed in this section.

Price Searcher
A seller that has the ability to control, to some degree, the price of the product it sells.

23-2a The Monopolist's Demand and Marginal Revenue

In the theory of monopoly, the monopoly firm is the industry, and the industry is the monopoly firm; they are one and the same. Thus, the demand curve for the monopoly firm *is* the market demand curve, which is downward sloping. Because a downward-sloping demand curve posits an inverse relationship between price and quantity demanded, more is sold at lower prices than at higher prices, *ceteris paribus*. Unlike the perfectly competitive firm, the monopolist can raise its price and still sell its product (though not as much).

Because it faces a downward-sloping demand curve, to sell an additional unit of its product, the monopolist must necessarily lower its price for the product. For example, suppose the monopoly seller originally planned to sell 2 units of *X* a day at $10 each and now wishes to sell 3 units a day. To sell more units, it must lower the price to, say, $9.75, and it sells the 3 units at $9.75 each.[1]

So, to sell an additional unit, a monopoly firm must lower its price on all previous units. Note that the terms "previous" and "additional" do not refer to an actual sequence of events. A firm doesn't sell 100 units of a good and then decide to sell one more unit. The firm is in an either–or situation: Either the firm sells 100 units over some length of time, or it sells 101 units over the same length of time. If the firm wants to sell 101 units, the price per unit must be lower than if it wants to sell 100 units.

A monopoly seller both gains and loses by lowering the price of its product. As Exhibit 1 shows, the monopolist in our example gains $9.75, the price of the additional unit sold, because the price was lowered. It loses 50¢: 25¢ on the first unit it used to sell at $10, plus 25¢ on the second unit it used to sell at $10.

Gains are greater than losses; the monopolist's net gain from selling the additional unit of output is $9.25 ($9.75 − $0.50 = $9.25). This is the monopolist's *marginal revenue*,

EXHIBIT 1

The Dual Effects of a Price Reduction on Total Revenue

To sell an additional unit of its good, a monopolist needs to lower the price of the good. This price reduction both gains revenue and loses revenue for the monopolist. In the exhibit, the revenue gained and revenue lost are shaded and labeled. Marginal revenue is equal to the revenue gained (tan) minus the revenue lost (green).

(1) P	(2) Q	(3) TR	(4) MR
$10.00	2	$20.00	—
9.75	3	29.25	$9.25

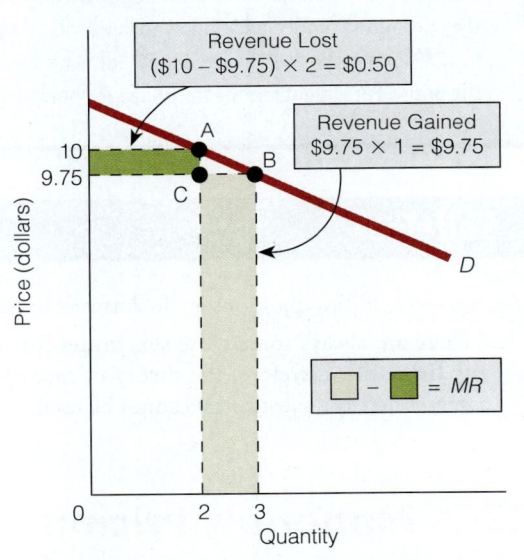

---

[1] This discussion is of the behavior of a single-price monopolist, which is a monopolist that sells all units of its product for the same price. Later, we discuss a price-discriminating monopolist.

the change in total revenue that results from selling one additional unit of output. (Total revenue is $20 when 2 units are sold at $10 each and $29.25 when 3 units are sold at $9.75 each. The change in total revenue that results from selling one additional unit of output is $9.25.)

Notice that the price of the good ($9.75) is greater than the marginal revenue ($9.25): $P > MR$. This is the case for a monopoly seller or any price searcher (recall that, for the firm in perfect competition, $P = MR$):

$$\text{For a monopolist, } P > MR$$

23-2b The Monopolist's Demand Curve and Marginal Revenue Curve Are Not the Same

In perfect competition, the firm's demand curve *is* the same as its marginal revenue curve. In monopoly, the firm's demand curve is not the same as its marginal revenue curve but rather lies *above* its marginal revenue curve.

The relationship between a monopolist's demand curve and marginal revenue curve is illustrated in Exhibit 2. The demand curve (D) plots price and quantity; the marginal revenue curve (MR) plots marginal revenue and quantity. Because price is greater than marginal revenue for a monopolist, its demand curve necessarily lies *above* its marginal revenue curve. (Note that price and marginal revenue are the same for the first unit of output, so the demand curve and the marginal revenue curve will share one point in common.)

23-2c Price and Output for a Profit-Maximizing Monopolist

The monopolist that seeks to maximize profit produces the quantity of output at which $MR = MC$ (as did the profit-maximizing perfectly competitive firm) and *charges the highest price per unit at which this quantity of output can be sold.*

In Exhibit 3, the highest price at which Q_1, the quantity at which $MR = MC$, can be sold is P_1. At Q_1, the monopolist charges a price that is greater than its marginal cost ($P > MC$). Therefore, the monopolist is *not* resource allocative efficient.

EXHIBIT 2

Demand Curve and Marginal Revenue Curve

The demand curve plots price against quantity. The marginal revenue curve plots marginal revenue against quantity. For a monopolist, $P > MR$, so the marginal revenue curve must lie below the demand curve. (Note that, when a demand curve is a straight line, the marginal revenue curve bisects the horizontal axis halfway between the origin and the point where the demand curve intersects the horizontal axis.)

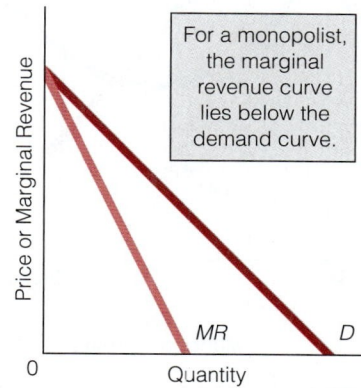

For a monopolist, the marginal revenue curve lies below the demand curve.

EXHIBIT 3

The Monopolist's Profit-Maximizing Price and Quantity of Output

The monopolist produces the quantity of output (Q_1) at which $MR = MC$ and charges the highest price per unit (P_1) at which this quantity of output can be sold. Notice that, at the profit-maximizing quantity of output, price is greater than marginal cost ($P > MC$).

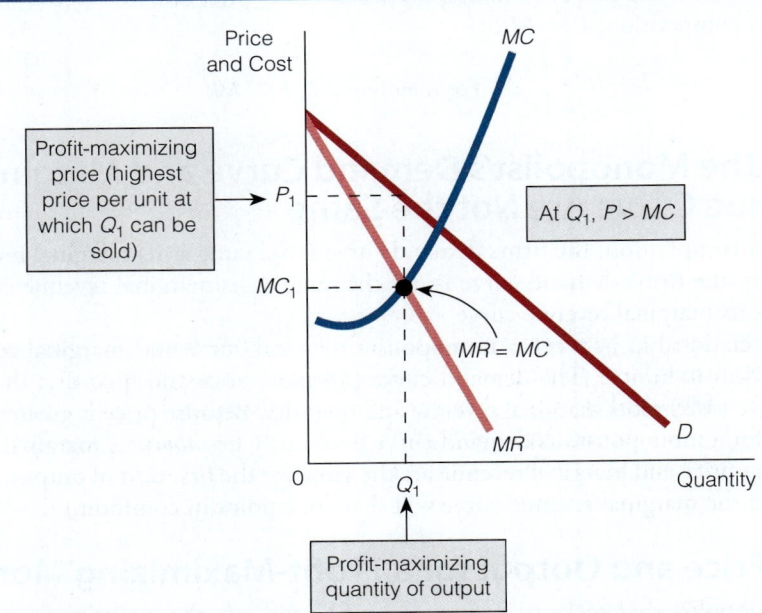

EXHIBIT 4

Monopoly Profits and Losses

A monopoly seller is not guaranteed any profits. In (a), price is above average total cost at Q_1, the quantity of output at which $MR = MC$. Therefore, TR (the area OP_1BQ_1) is greater than TC (the area $OCAQ_1$), and profits equal the area CP_1BA. In (b), price is below average total cost at Q_1. Therefore, TR (the area OP_1AQ_1) is less than TC (the area $OCBQ_1$), and losses equal the area P_1CBA.

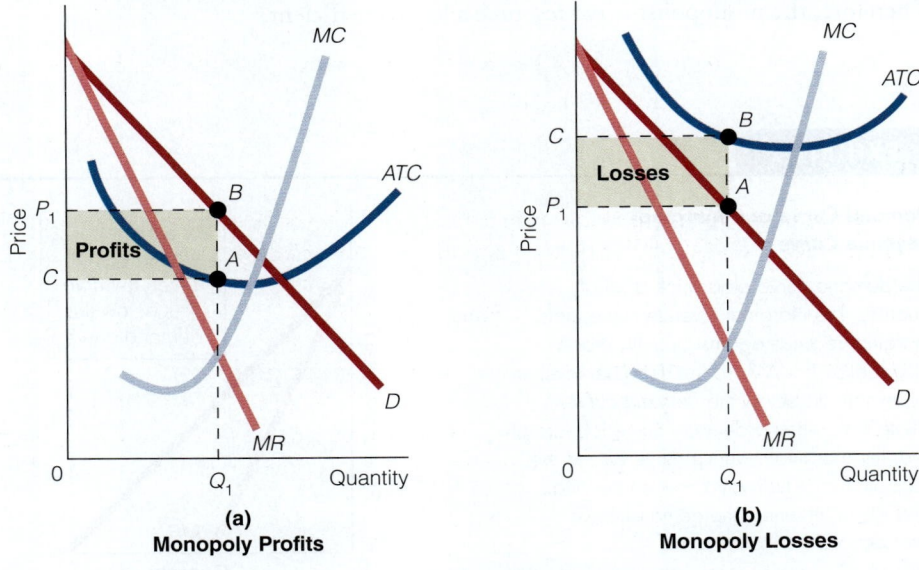

Whether profits are earned depends on whether P_1 is greater or less than average total cost at Q_1. In short, the profit-maximizing price may be the loss-minimizing price. Monopoly profits and monopoly losses are illustrated in Exhibit 4.

Some people argue that suggesting that a monopolist can take a loss is unrealistic. If the monopolist is the only seller in the industry, they maintain, it is guaranteed a profit. But even when a firm is the only seller of a product, it may not earn a profit. A monopolist cannot charge any price it wants for its good—only the highest price that the demand curve allows it to charge. In some instances, the highest price may be lower than the firm's average total costs (unit costs). If so, the monopolist incurs a loss, as shown in Exhibit 4(b).

23-2d Comparing the Demand Curve in Perfect Competition with the Demand Curve in Monopoly

The perfectly competitive firm is a *price taker*; it has no control over the price of the product it sells. The monopoly firm is a *price searcher*; it has some control over the price of the product it sells. Essentially, what determines whether a firm is a price taker or a price searcher is the demand curve that it faces. The perfectly competitive firm faces a horizontal demand curve. The monopoly firm faces a downward-sloping demand curve. If a firm faces a horizontal (or flat) demand curve, then it is a price taker. If a firm faces a downward-sloping demand curve, then it is a price searcher. Let's remind ourselves what each demand curve implies about the firm's ability to control price. A horizontal (or flat) demand curve implies that the firm can sell its good at only *one price*: the price determined by the market. In other words, if the market-determined price is $10, then the perfectly competitive firm's demand curve is a horizontal line at $10. In contrast, a downward-sloping demand curve implies that the firm can sell its good at *different prices*. For example, it might sell 100 units at $12 per unit and 150 units at $11 per unit. In short, it "searches" for the best price among the many possible prices.

23-2e If a Firm Maximizes Revenue, Does It Automatically Maximize Profit Too?

Profit is the difference of total revenue (TR) and total cost (TC):

$$\text{Profit} = TR - TC$$

Because TC is the sum of total fixed costs (TFC) and total variable costs (TVC), we can rewrite our profit equation as

$$\text{Profit} = TR - (TFC + TVC)$$

Maximizing profit is the same as maximizing total revenue under one condition: $TVC = 0$. When $TVC = 0$, TVC falls out of our profit equation, and we are left with

$$\text{Profit} = TR - TFC$$

Because TFC is constant as output increases, a rise in TR will automatically increase profit by the same amount. To illustrate, if $TR = \$100$ and $TFC = \$40$, then profit is $60. If TR rises by $10 to $110, and TFC remains constant at $40, then profit rises to $70. The rise in TR is equal to the rise in profit: $10. Therefore, to maximize total revenue is to maximize profit.

Now change things a bit. Suppose TVC is not zero. We return to our profit equation:

$$\text{Profit} = TR - (TFC + TVC)$$

Again, let $TR = \$100$ and $TFC = \$40$. But this time, $TVC = \$20$. It follows that profit is $40. Now, if TR rises to $110, will profit again rise by $10, as it did in the previous example? Perhaps not, because what happens to profit depends on what happens not only to TR, but to TVC too. Suppose TVC rises to $37 as TR rises by $110. Now profit is $33. In other words, total revenue increased (from $100 to $110), but profit decreased (from $40 to $33).

Therefore, profit maximization is the same as revenue maximization only when there are no variable costs (i.e., when $TVC = \$0$).

23-3 Perfect Competition and Monopoly

Because perfect competition and monopoly are at opposite ends of the market structure spectrum, there are major differences between them. In this section, we discuss those differences.

23-3a Price, Marginal Revenue, and Marginal Cost

Here are two key differences between perfect competition and monopoly:

1. For the perfectly competitive firm, $P = MR$; for the monopolist, $P > MR$. The perfectly competitive firm's demand curve *is* its marginal revenue curve; the monopolist's demand curve lies *above* its marginal revenue curve.

2. The perfectly competitive firm charges a price equal to its marginal cost; the monopolist charges a price greater than its marginal cost. That is,

$$\text{Perfect competition: } P = MR \text{ and } P = MC$$
$$\text{Monopoly: } P > MR \text{ and } P > MC$$

23-3b Monopoly, Perfect Competition, and Consumers' Surplus

A monopoly firm differs from a perfectly competitive firm in terms of how much consumers' surplus buyers receive. To illustrate, Exhibit 5 shows a downward-sloping market demand curve D, a downward-sloping marginal revenue curve MR, and a horizontal marginal cost curve MC. Although you are used to seeing upward-sloping marginal cost curves, nothing prevents marginal cost from being constant over some range of output. A horizontal MC curve simply means that marginal cost is constant. Now, if the market in Exhibit 5 is perfectly competitive, the demand curve *is* the marginal revenue curve. Therefore, the profit-maximizing output is Q_{PC} and the buyer will pay P_{PC} per unit of the good. Recall that consumers' surplus is the area under the demand curve and above the price. For the perfectly competitive firm, consumers' surplus is the triangular area $Q_{PC}AB$.[2]

In a monopoly market, the demand curve and the marginal revenue curve are different. The profit-maximizing output is where the MR curve intersects the MC curve; thus, the profit-maximizing output is Q_M, and the price the buyer pays is P_M. In the case of monopoly, consumers' surplus is the area $P_M AC$.

Obviously, consumers' surplus is greater in the perfectly competitive case than in the monopoly case by the area $P_{PC}P_M CB$. This area is the loss in consumers' surplus due to monopolization.

---

[2] The demand curve is downward sloping because we are looking at the market demand curve, not the firm's demand curve. All market demand curves are downward sloping.

EXHIBIT 5

Monopoly, Perfect Competition, and Consumers' Surplus

If the market in the exhibit is perfectly competitive, the demand curve is the marginal revenue curve. The profit-maximizing output is Q_{PC}, and price is P_{PC}. Consumers' surplus is the area $P_{PC}AB$. If the market is a monopoly market, the profit-maximizing output is Q_M, and price is P_M. In this case, consumers' surplus is the area P_MAC. Consumers' surplus is greater by the area $P_{PC}P_MCB$ in perfect competition than in monopoly.

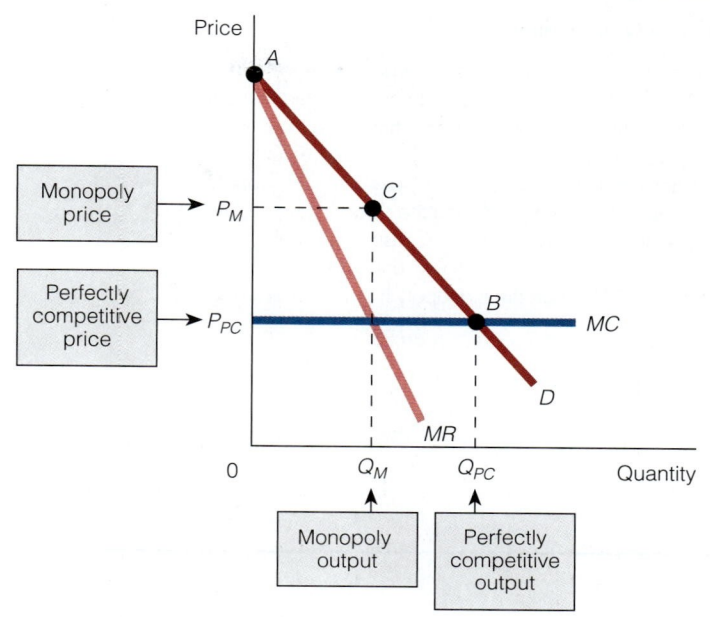

23-3c Monopoly or Nothing?

Suppose you could push one of two buttons to determine the conditions under which a particular good is produced. If you push the first button, the good is produced under the conditions of perfect competition. If you push the second button, the good is produced under the conditions of monopoly. Which button would you push?

From a consumer's perspective, perfect competition would seem to be the better choice because it provides more output and a lower price than monopoly does. In short, there is more consumers' surplus. Perfect competition would therefore seem to be superior to monopoly. But life doesn't always present a choice between perfect competition and monopoly. Sometimes it presents a choice between monopoly and nothing.

Exhibit 6 shows the demand curve (D) for a good, along with the relevant marginal revenue curve (MR) and two sets of MC and ATC curves. Assume that MC_1 and ATC_1 are the relevant cost curves. Because the MC_1 curve is so far above the MR curve, the two do not intersect. In other words, there is no profit-maximizing quantity of output for a firm to produce. Although there is demand for the particular good, the costs of producing it are so high that no firm will produce it. Consumers therefore receive no consumers' surplus from the purchase and consumption of the good.

But suppose a firm—a single firm—is able to lower costs to MC_2 and ATC_2. Now marginal cost is low enough for the firm to produce the good. The firm produces a quantity Q_M and charges a price P_M. The area P_MAB is equal to consumers' surplus.

No doubt, the firm producing this good and charging a price P_M is a monopoly firm. However, consumers are better off having a monopoly firm produce the good than having no firm produce it: If no firm produces the good because costs are too high, consumers' surplus is zero, but when the monopoly firm produces the good, consumers' surplus is positive.

EXHIBIT 6

Monopoly or Nothing?

We start with the demand and marginal revenue curves and with $MC_1 = ATC_1$. Because cost is "so high," no firm produces the good. Later, a single firm figures out how to lower cost to $MC_2 = ATC_2$. This firm produces Q_M and charges the monopoly price of P_M per unit. Is monopoly preferable to no firm producing the good? From a consumer's perspective, the answer is yes. Consumers' surplus is zero when no firm produces the good, and consumers' surplus is the area $P_M AB$ when the monopoly firm produces the good.

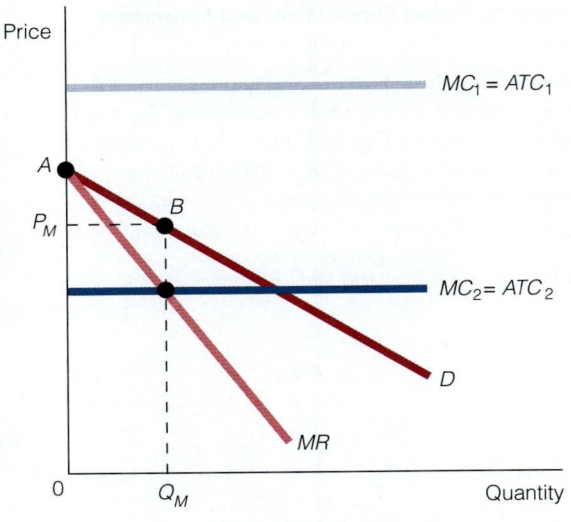

So, under certain conditions, a monopoly may be created in a market because a firm figures out a way to lower the cost of producing a good enough to make producing it worthwhile. Of course, once the monopoly firm exists, consumers would prefer that the good be produced under perfect competition than under monopoly conditions. But that is not always the relevant choice. Sometimes, the choice is between monopoly and nothing, and when that is the choice, the consumers' surplus is greater with monopoly than it is with nothing.

Economics 24/7

Google, Facebook, Monopoly, and Property Rights

Our definition of a monopolist is of a firm that is a single seller of a good or service. When compared to a perfectly competitive firm, a monopolist produces less output and charges a higher price. Now consider both Google and Facebook. First, neither Google nor Facebook seem to be trying to restrict their service to customers; they are not trying to reduce their customer base. If anything, they seem to want to do the opposite; they want as many people as possible using their services. Second, instead of charging a higher price than a perfectly competitive firm, both Google and Facebook charge zero price. So, we need to ask, Can firms that do not restrict their user (customer) base and do not charge a positive price be monopolists? The answer would seem to be no.

Yet there is often some hesitation accepting this conclusion. After all, some say, both Google and Facebook are very large companies that service a large percentage of their respective markets. Google's market share of the worldwide search engine market in October 2020 was estimated to be 88 percent; its share of the U.S. search engine market was 82 percent. Facebook's market share of the U.S. social media market in October 2020 was is 61 percent. Together, Facebook and Google received near 60 percent of the U.S. digital advertising revenue in 2020. Most of this revenue comes from both Facebook's and Google's selling targeted ads based on the data they collect from their user base.

Implicit in our standard definition of monopoly (single seller of a good) is the idea that the monopoly is a producer of a good or service and that it is selling that good or service to buyers. And, of course, it is typical of a producer to charge a price for its good or service. But Google and Facebook do not charge a price. So, are they producers, and is the user base really the consumers?

Some have argued that if you are not paying for the product, then you are the product. Let's try to reframe the Google/Facebook user base scenario the following way: Both Google and Facebook are not charging you to use their platform services because what they want is your data so that they can sell targeted ads to advertisers. In other words, in one respect, you are the consumer, and Google and Facebook are the producers—you consume search engines and social media, and Google and Facebook provide these; but in another respect, you are the producer and Google and Facebook are the consumers—you produce your data, and Google and Facebook consume it. No wonder, some say, that Google and Facebook do not charge us; in fact, they should be paying us for the data we produce for them to sell what they really want to sell—ads. In conclusion, some economists have argued that the definition of what constitutes a monopoly might need to be adjusted given the rise of Google and Facebook and the less-than-clear delineation between who is consumer and who is producer.

One proposal that has been made to interject greater competition in the search engine and social media markets is to allow for data portability. This constitutes

allowing users to take all the digital connections they create on a platform like Facebook to another rival platform. It would work similarly to telephone number portability now: Individuals can take their cell phone numbers with them when moving from, say, Verizon to AT&T. Both telephone and data portability raise a property rights issue. In the telephone portability setting, it has been determined that you own the telephone number; the company that first gave it to you does not. With data portability, the issue is, say, with Facebook: Who owns the data and digital connections—you or Facebook?

Moving forward, you can expect to hear debates over the issues we have introduced here—that of whether or not Google and Facebook are monopolists, what is the right way to define a monopolist, and who owns the data that users produce when they consume such things as search engines and social media. (In a later chapter on antitrust and regulation, we discuss the lawsuits brought by the Department of Justice and the Federal Trade Commission in 2020 against Google and Facebook.) If you would like to hear an economist who advances data portability and greater competition for Google and Facebook, you can listen and see economist Luigi Zingales on YouTube at www.youtube.com/watch?v=O4yONaEK4G0.

1. Why does the monopolist's demand curve lie above its marginal revenue curve?
2. Is a monopolist guaranteed to earn profits?
3. Is a monopolist resource allocative efficient? Why or why not?
4. Why do you think a monopolist is called a price searcher? What is it searching for?

23-4 The Case Against Monopoly

Monopoly is often said to be inefficient in comparison with perfect competition. This section examines some of the shortcomings of monopoly.

23-4a The Deadweight Loss of Monopoly

Exhibit 7 shows demand, marginal revenue, marginal cost, and average total cost curves. For simplicity's sake, assume that the product is produced under constant cost conditions so that marginal cost equals long-run average total cost. If the product is produced under perfect competition, then output Q_{PC} is produced and is sold at price P_{PC}. At the competitive equilibrium output level, $P = MC$. If the product is produced under monopoly, output Q_M is produced and is sold at price P_M. At the monopoly equilibrium, $P > MC$.

As the exhibit shows, greater output is produced under perfect competition than under monopoly. The net value of the difference in these two output levels is said to be the **deadweight loss of monopoly**. In Exhibit 7, the value to buyers of increasing output from Q_M to Q_{PC} is equal to the maximum amount they would pay for this increase in output, designated by the trapezoidal area $Q_M CBQ_{PC}$. The costs that would have to be incurred to produce the additional output are designated by the rectangular area $Q_M DBQ_{PC}$. The difference between the two is the triangle DCB, *the amount buyers value the additional output over and above the costs of producing the additional output*. This triangular area is the loss attached to not producing the competitive quantity of output. The triangle DCB is referred to as the *deadweight loss triangle*.

Therefore, monopoly produces a quantity of output that is too small in comparison to the quantity of output produced in perfect competition. This difference in output results in a welfare loss to society.

Arnold Harberger was the first economist who tried to determine the actual size of the deadweight loss cost of monopoly in the manufacturing sector of the U.S. economy. He estimated the loss to be a small percentage of the economy's total output. Additional empirical work by other economists puts the figure at approximately 1 percent of total output.

Deadweight Loss of Monopoly
The net value (the value to buyers over and above the costs to suppliers) of the difference between the competitive quantity of output (where $P = MC$) and the monopoly quantity of output (where $P > MC$); the loss due to not producing the competitive quantity of output.

EXHIBIT 7

Deadweight Loss and Rent Seeking as Costs of Monopoly

The monopolist produces Q_M, and the perfectly competitive firm produces the higher output level Q_{PC}. The deadweight loss of monopoly is the triangle (DCB) between these two levels of output. Rent-seeking activity is directed to obtaining the monopoly profits, represented by the area $P_{PC} P_M CD$. Rent seeking is a socially wasteful activity because resources are expended to transfer income rather than to produce goods and services.

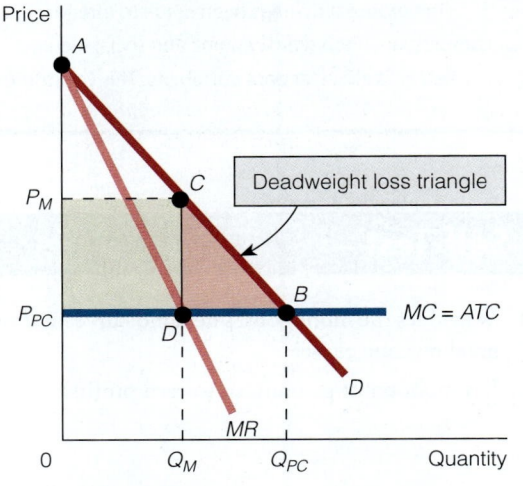

23-4b Does It Matter to You if There Is a Deadweight Loss Triangle?

Look at Exhibit 7. There you will see a triangle (*DCB*) that represents the deadweight loss of monopoly. Does that deadweight loss of monopoly matter to you?

To get the answer, consider that with a monopoly an output of Q_M is produced and offered for sale, whereas, with perfect competition, an output of Q_{PC} is produced and offered for sale (see Exhibit 7). Let's suppose that Q_{PC} equals 100 units, and Q_M represents 55 units. This means that, under a monopoly, 45 fewer units are produced than would be produced under perfect competition.

Producing and selling 45 fewer units is a loss if people value those 45 units more than it costs to produce those 45 units. And this is the case, as we can see in Exhibit 7. We know that the value of those 45 units to buyers is greater than the costs to producers of producing those 45 units because we can see that the demand curve, which represents the value to buyers, lies above the *MC* curve, which represents the costs to producers, between the quantities of Q_{PC} and Q_M. The deadweight loss triangle represents how much, in terms of net benefits, is lost when 55 units (Q_M) is produced instead of 100 units (Q_{PC}).

Now suppose you wanted to buy an additional 45 units under monopoly conditions (as opposed to perfectly competitive conditions). You wouldn't be able to because they wouldn't exist. The manifestation of this loss is the deadweight loss triangle.

23-4c Rent Seeking

Sometimes, individuals and groups try to influence public policy in the hope of redistributing (transferring) income from others to themselves. In Exhibit 7, the market produces Q_{PC} output and charges a price P_{PC}. Suppose, however, that one of the, say, 100 firms currently producing some of Q_{PC} asks the government to grant it a monopoly; that is, firm *A* asks the government to prevent the 99 other firms from competing with it. Consider the benefit for firm *A* of becoming a monopolist (a single seller). Currently, it is earning zero economic profit because it is selling at a price that equals *ATC*. If it becomes a monopolist, though, it will earn profits equal to the area $P_{PC}P_M CD$ in Exhibit 7.

These profits are the result of a *transfer* from buyers to the monopolist. To see why, consider what happens to consumers' surplus. If the market in Exhibit 7 is perfectly competitive, consumers' surplus is equal to the triangular area $P_{PC}AB$; if the market is monopolized, consumers' surplus is equal to the smaller triangular area $P_M AC$. The difference is the area $P_{PC}P_M CB$, the area that represents the loss in consumers' surplus if the market is monopolized. Part of this area—the rectangular area $P_{PC}P_M CD$—is transferred to the monopolist in terms of profits. *In other words, if the market is monopolized, part of the consumers' surplus that is lost to buyers becomes profits for the monopolist.* (The other part is the deadweight loss of monopoly, identified by the deadweight loss triangle *DCB*.)

If firm *A* tries to get the government to transfer income in the form of consumers' surplus from buyers to itself, it is undertaking a *transfer-seeking activity*. In economics, such activities are usually called **rent seeking**. In other words, firm *A* is *rent seeking*.[3]

Economist Gordon Tullock has made the point that rent-seeking behavior is individually rational but socially wasteful. To see why, suppose the profits in Exhibit 7 (the area $P_{PC}P_M CD$) are equal to $10 million. Firm *A* wants the $10 million in profits, so it asks the government for

Rent Seeking
Actions of individuals and groups that spend resources to influence public policy in the hope of redistributing (transferring) income to themselves from others.

---

[3] The word "rent" (used in this context) often confuses people. In everyday life, "rent" refers to the payment for an apartment. In economics, rent—or, more formally, economic rent—is a payment in excess of opportunity cost. The term "rent seeking" was introduced by economist Anne Krueger in her article "The Political Economy of the Rent-Seeking Society," *American Economic Review* 64 (June 1974): 291–303.

a monopoly because it wants the government to prevent the 99 other firms from competing with it.

Firm *A* will not get its monopoly privilege simply by asking for it. The firm will have to spend money and time to convince government officials that it should give the firm this monopoly privilege. It will have to hire lobbyists, take politicians and other government officials to dinner, and perhaps make donations to some of them. Firm *A* will have to spend resources to get what it wants, and all the resources firm *A* uses to try to bring about a transfer from buyers to itself, says Tullock, are wasted. Those resources cannot be used to produce shoes, computers, television sets, and many other things that people would like to buy. The resources are instead used to try to transfer income from one party to another, not to produce more goods and services.

Society would be very different if no one produced anything but instead invested time and money in rent seeking. For example, Jones would try to get what is Matsui's, Matsui would try to get what is Kahn's, and Kahn would try to get what is Patel's. No one would produce anything; everyone would simply spend time and money trying to get what currently belongs to someone else. In such a world, no one would produce the food, the computers, and the cars that people would like to buy.

Tullock makes the point that the resource cost of rent seeking should be added to the deadweight loss of monopoly. This addition, according to Tullock, makes the overall cost of monopoly to society higher than anyone initially thought.

23-4d X-Inefficiency

Economist Harvey Leibenstein maintains that the monopolist is not under pressure to produce its good at the lowest-possible cost; it can produce its good above the lowest-possible unit cost and still survive. Certainly, the monopolist benefits if it can and does lower its costs, but it doesn't have to in order to survive (with the proviso that average total costs cannot be higher than price). Leibenstein refers to the organizational slack that is directly tied to the monopolist operating at a cost that is higher than the lowest possible as **X-inefficiency**.

Obtaining accurate estimates of X-inefficiency is difficult, but whatever its magnitude, forces are at work to mitigate it. For example, if a market monopoly is being run inefficiently, other people, realizing this situation, may attempt to buy the monopoly and to lower costs in order to make higher profits.

X-Inefficiency
The increase in costs, due to the organizational slack in a monopoly, resulting from the absence of competitive pressure to push costs down to their lowest-possible level.

Economics 24/7

Religion and Monopoly

Suppose a government were to prohibit certain firms from competing in a particular market—say, the personal computer market. As a consumer, you might think that this government-imposed restraint on competition would probably end up harming you. After all, if only firms *A*, *B*, and *C* could produce and sell personal computers, and firms *D*, *E*, and *F* were prohibited from doing so, you might expect to pay higher prices for personal computers of lower quality than would be the case if all firms were permitted to compete for your personal computer dollar.

> Now suppose a government were to prohibit certain religions from competing in the religion market. For example, suppose that a particular government (in a particular country) permitted only religion A to exist. Other existing religions, as well as any new religions that might arise in the future, would be prohibited. If anyone were to practice a religion other than A, that person would be subject to fines and punishment and perhaps certain types of discrimination too.
>
> Here, then, we would have a religion—religion A—that held a monopoly position in society. Religion A would be the only legal provider of religion in our hypothetical country. Moreover, the barriers to entry in the religion market would be extremely high, in that the government decreed that no other religions could compete with religion A.
>
> If religions are analogous to firms, we would expect that the customers of religion (just like the customers of firms) would do better in an open, competitive religion market (with free entry and exit) than in a closed, monopolistic religion market (with high barriers to entry). Is there any empirical evidence that they do, in fact, do better?
>
> Laurence Iannaccone is an economist at Chapman University and a pioneer in the field of the economics of religion. He has argued that, across countries in which a free and open market in religion exists, a larger percentage of the population considers themselves religious, attends religious worship, and generally exhibits a greater degree of religiosity than in countries where religion is heavily regulated or where the state prohibits competition in religion. He states,
>
> > Weekly church attendance rates range from 40 percent of the total population of the United States (where the Constitution guarantees religious competition), to less than 10 percent in Scandinavian countries (where a single, state-run Lutheran church dominates the market, runs on tax dollars, and pays its clergy as civil servants). Indeed, every available measure of piety, including frequency of prayer, belief in God, and confidence in religion, is greater in countries with numerous competing churches than in countries dominated by a single established church, and these relationships remain strong even after controlling for income, education or urbanization.[4]
>
> ---
> [4] Laurence R. Iannaccone, "Introduction to the Economics of Religion," *Journal of Economic Literature*, September 1998, p. 1486.

23-5 Price Discrimination

The monopoly seller may sell all units of its product for the same price; that is, it may be a single-price monopolist. However, under certain conditions, a monopolist could practice **price discrimination**, which occurs when the seller charges different prices for the product it sells and the price differences do not reflect cost differences.

23-5a Types of Price Discrimination

There are three types of price discrimination:

- *Perfect price discrimination:* Suppose a monopolist produces and sells 1,000 units of good X. It sells each unit separately, charging the highest price that each consumer would be willing to pay for the product rather than go without it. This practice is **perfect price discrimination**, sometimes called *discrimination among units*.

- *Second-degree price discrimination:* If a monopolist charges a uniform price per unit for one specific quantity, a lower price for an additional quantity, and so on, then it is practicing **second-degree price discrimination**, sometimes called *discrimination among quantities*. For example, the monopolist might sell the first 10 units for $10 each, the next 20 units for $9 each, and so on.

Price Discrimination
A price structure in which the seller charges different prices for the product it sells and the price differences do not reflect cost differences.

Perfect Price Discrimination
A price structure in which the seller charges the highest price that each consumer is willing to pay for the product rather than go without it.

Second-Degree Price Discrimination
A price structure in which the seller charges a uniform price per unit for one specific quantity, a lower price for an additional quantity, and so on.

- *Third-degree price discrimination:* If a monopolist charges different prices in various markets or charges different prices to various segments of the buying population, then the monopolist is practicing **third-degree price discrimination**, sometimes called *discrimination among buyers*. For example, if your local pharmacy charges senior citizens lower prices for medicine than it charges non-senior citizens, then it is practicing *third-degree price discrimination*.

Third-Degree Price Discrimination
A price structure in which the seller charges different prices in different markets or charges different prices to various segments of the buying population.

23-5b Why a Monopolist Wants to Price-Discriminate

Suppose the following units of a product can be sold at varying maximum prices: first unit, $10; second unit, $9; third unit, $8; fourth unit, $7. If the monopolist wants to sell 4 units, and it charges the same price for each unit (suppose it is a single-price monopolist), its total revenue is $28 ($7 × 4). If the monopolist practices perfect price discrimination, it charges $10 for the first unit, $9 for the second unit, $8 for the third unit, and $7 for the fourth unit. Its total revenue is then $34 ($10 + $9 + $8 + $7). A comparison of total revenues with and without price discrimination explains why the monopolist would want to price-discriminate. A perfectly price-discriminating monopolist receives the maximum price for each unit of the good it sells; a single-price monopolist does not.

For the monopolist who practices perfect price discrimination, price equals marginal revenue ($P = MR$). To illustrate, when the monopolist sells its second unit for $9 (having sold the first unit for $10), its total revenue is $19—or its marginal revenue is $9, which is equal to the price of the second unit.

23-5c Conditions of Price Discrimination

Why the monopolist would *want* to price-discriminate is obvious. However, for it actually to price-discriminate, the following conditions must hold:

1. *The seller must exercise some control over price; that is, it must be a price searcher.* If the seller is not a price searcher (if it is a price taker), it has no control over price and therefore cannot sell a good at different prices to different buyers.

2. *The seller must be able to distinguish among buyers who are willing to pay different prices.* Unless the seller can distinguish among buyers who would pay different prices, it cannot price-discriminate. After all, how would it know whom to charge the higher or lower prices?

3. *Reselling the good to other buyers must be impossible or too costly.* **Arbitrage**, or buying low and selling high, must not be possible. If a buyer can resell the good, price discrimination is not possible because buyers of the good at a lower price will simply resell it to other buyers for a price lower than the original seller's higher price. In time, no one will pay the higher price.

Arbitrage
Buying a good at a low price and selling it for a higher price.

23-5d Moving to $P = MC$ Through Price Discrimination

We know that the perfectly competitive firm exhibits resource allocative efficiency; it produces the quantity of output at which $P = MC$. We also know that the single-price monopolist produces the quantity of output at which $P > MC$; that is, it produces an inefficient level of output. But does the perfectly price-discriminating monopolist also produce an inefficient level of output?

Economics 24/7

One for $40 or Two for $70

Sellers sometimes advertise one unit of their good for $X, but two units of the same good for less than $2X. For example, a clothing store might advertise one pair of men's trousers for $40 but two pairs for $70 (which is $10 less than double $40). At first sight, this might appear to be quite a deal. Whether it is or is not is a personal judgment. What it is for certain, however, is an act of price discrimination.

Look at the situation in terms of an individual's demand curve for trousers. For example, an individual's demand curve might tell us that he is willing to buy one pair of trousers at $40 a pair but that he will buy two pairs if the price is $30 a pair. In other words, one point on the demand curve represents $40 and one pair of trousers, and a second point on the demand curve (lower down) represents $30 and two pairs of trousers.

Now, suppose the store wishes to sell this person two pairs of trousers. How might it go about doing that? Well, it could price trousers at $30 a pair, and then the person would buy two pairs. Under this pricing scheme, total revenue for the store is $60. Or it could price the first pair at $40 and the second pair at $30, for a total of $70 for two. ("Buy one

pair at full price and get the second pair for $10 off.") Will the individual be willing to pay $40 for the first pair and $30 for the second pair? From the person's demand curve, we realize that he would, because, as we stated earlier, one point on the person's demand curve represents $40 and one pair of trousers and another point represents $30 and two pairs of trousers.

The answer is no. For a perfectly price-discriminating monopolist, $P = MR$ (as is the case for the perfectly competitive firm). It follows that, when the perfectly price-discriminating monopolist produces the quantity of output at which $MR = MC$, it automatically produces the quantity at which $P = MC$. In short, the perfectly price-discriminating monopolist and the perfectly competitive firm both exhibit resource allocative efficiency.

In part (a) of Exhibit 8, the perfectly competitive firm produces where $P = MC$. In part (b), the single-price monopolist produces where $P > MC$. In part (c), the perfectly price-discriminating monopolist produces where $P = MC$.

There is one important difference between the perfectly competitive firm and the perfectly price-discriminating monopolist. Although both produce where $P = MC$, the perfectly competitive firm charges the same price for each unit of the good it sells whereas the perfectly price-discriminating monopolist charges a different price for each unit it sells.

EXHIBIT 8

Comparison of a Perfectly Competitive Firm, a Single-Price Monopolist, and a Perfectly Price-Discriminating Monopolist

For both the perfectly competitive firm (a) and the perfectly price-discriminating monopolist (c), $P = MR$ and the demand curve is the marginal revenue curve. Both produce where $P = MC$. The single-price monopolist (b), however, produces where $P > MC$, because for such a firm, $P > MR$ and its demand curve lies above its marginal revenue curve. One difference between the perfectly competitive firm and the perfectly price-discriminating monopolist is that the former charges the same price for each unit of the good that it sells whereas the latter charges a different price for each unit of the good that it sells.

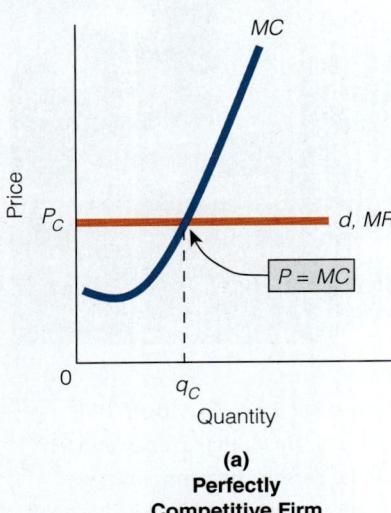
(a) Perfectly Competitive Firm

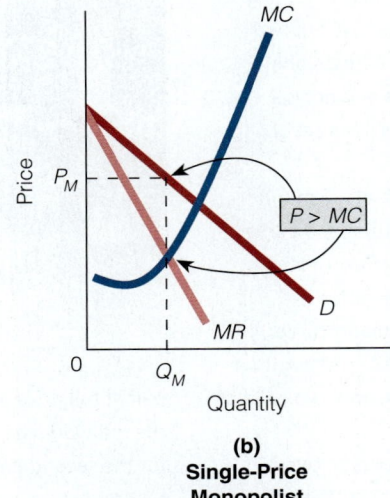
(b) Single-Price Monopolist

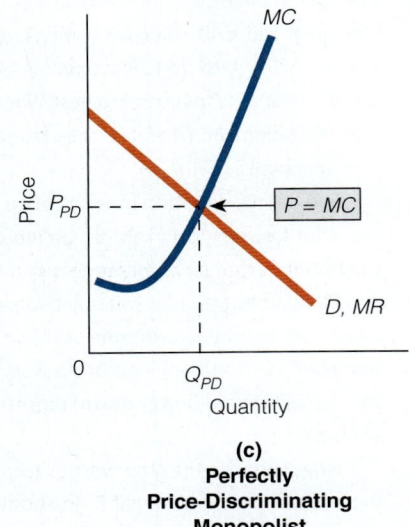
(c) Perfectly Price-Discriminating Monopolist

Economics 24/7

Do Colleges and Universities Price-Discriminate?

Many colleges and universities practice price discrimination. For example, consider the university that gives out student or financial aid. The student aid is nothing more than a reduction in the tuition a student pays. As an example, University X states that it will give a low-income student, if admitted, $10,000 in student aid. So, if the tuition at the university is, say, $15,000, the student ends up paying only $5,000. The student with a high income does not get the student aid and therefore pays $15,000 upon admission. Even though the cost to the university to educate each student is the same, the students pay different tuition prices.

Another example is the university that offers a scholarship to an academic high achiever or to a star athlete (just coming out of high school). To either or both, the university offers a scholarship, which lowers the tuition the person pays.

If the universities price-discriminate, they must meet all the conditions necessary for price discrimination:

- *The seller must be a price searcher.* First, universities are price searchers; they exercise some control over the tuition they charge. In other words, universities can lower tuition and sell more or raise tuition and sell less.

- *The seller must be able to distinguish among buyers who would be willing to pay different prices.* Universities can distinguish among students (customers) who would be willing to pay different prices. For example, the student with few universities seeking him would probably be willing to pay more than the student with many options.
- *Reselling the good to other buyers must be impossible or too costly.* The service the university sells cannot be resold to someone else. For example, reselling an economics lecture is difficult. You could, of course, tell someone what was covered in the lecture, perhaps for a small payment or a promise to do the same for you at a later date. But this is like telling someone about a movie. Reselling something that is consumed on the premises is often difficult or impossible.

Universities meet all three requirements.

23-5e Coupons and Price Discrimination

Third-degree price discrimination, or discrimination among buyers, is sometimes employed by means of cents-off coupons. (Third-degree price discrimination exists if a seller sells the same product at different prices to different segments of the population.)

One of the conditions of price discrimination is that the seller has to be able to distinguish among customers who are willing to pay different prices. For example, some sellers think that people who value their time highly are willing to pay a higher price for a product than people who do not. These sellers argue that people who place a high value on their time want to economize on the shopping time connected with the purchase. If sellers want to price-discriminate between these two types of customers—charging more to customers who value time more and charging less to customers who value time less—they must determine the category into which each of their customers falls.

If you were a seller, how would you go about finding out this information? Many real-world sellers place cents-off coupons in newspapers and magazines. They hypothesize that people who place a relatively low value on their time are willing to spend it clipping and sorting coupons. People who place a relatively high value on their time are not. In effect, price discrimination works much like the following scenario in, say, a grocery store:

1. The posted price for all products is the same for all customers.
2. Both Alejandra and Axel put product X in their shopping carts.
3. When Alejandra gets to the checkout counter, the clerk asks, "Do you have any coupons today?" Alejandra says no. She is therefore charged the posted price for all products, including X.
4. When Axel gets to the checkout counter, the clerk asks, "Do you have any coupons today?" Axel says yes and gives the clerk a coupon for product X. Axel pays a lower price for it than Alejandra pays.

Thus, one of the uses of the cents-off coupon is to enable the seller to charge a higher price to one group of customers than to another group. (We say *one* of the uses because cents-off coupons are also used to induce customers to try a product.)

> **Thinking Like an Economist**
>
> A seller price discriminates and charges customer A $100 for the same good for which customer B pays $80. Someone concludes that A is subsidizing B: A pays the higher price so that B can pay the lower price. For example, the adult pays $15 for admission to the movie theater so the child can pay $6. The restaurant charges the 30-year-old customer $40 for the meal that it charges the 65-year-old customer $33.
>
> This is contrary to the way the economist thinks. The economist asks: Why would a seller charge a lower price to B ($80) just because A paid a higher price ($100)? Instead, sellers would prefer to charge the highest price to each customer that the customer would pay. If the seller could have charged a higher price than $80 to customer B (say, the same $100 it charged to A) then the seller would have done just that.

1. What are some of the costs, or shortcomings, of monopoly?
2. What is the deadweight loss of monopoly?
3. Why must a seller be a price searcher (among other things) before he can price-discriminate?

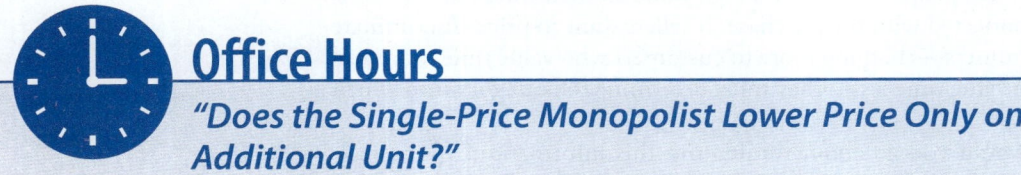

Office Hours

"Does the Single-Price Monopolist Lower Price Only on the Additional Unit?"

Student: You said that a single-price monopolist has to lower its price to sell an additional unit of the good it produces. Does this statement mean that it can sell the first unit of a good for, say, $20, but that if it wants to sell a second unit, it has to lower the price to, say, $19?

Instructor: I would say things a little differently. If the monopoly firm wants to sell one unit, it charges $20, but if it wants to sell two units, it must charge $19 for each of the two units.

Student: How is what you said different from what I said?

Instructor: I spoke of two units instead of the second unit.

Student: I don't see the critical difference.

Instructor: Your statement made it sound as though the monopolist earned $20 on the first unit and $19 on the second unit, but this is not how things work for a single-price monopolist. A single-price monopolist has to charge the same price for *every unit* of the good it sells. In other words, if it sells 100 units, it sells each of the 100 units for the same price. It doesn't sell the first unit for $20, the second unit for $19, and so on.

Student: But I'm still confused. We know that a monopoly firm has to lower its price to sell an additional unit, so why can't we just say that it has to lower its price to sell the *second* unit?

Instructor: Because it has to lower the price on the previous (the first) unit, too, if it wants to sell two units. To illustrate, suppose the price of a good is $20, and at this price, the quantity demanded is 1 unit. At a price of $19, the quantity demanded rises to 2 units. What you said implied that the firm would sell the first unit for $20. Then, with that transaction done, it considers whether it wants to sell an additional unit (the second unit). If it does, it charges $19 for it. That's not the way things happen. The firm—from the beginning, before any units of the good have been sold—has to decide whether it wants to sell 1 unit or 2. If it wants to sell only 1 unit, it charges $20. If it wants to sell 2 units, it sells each unit for $19.

Student: I think I understand now. That's what you must have meant in class when you said that the word "additional" doesn't refer to a sequence of events, as in "sell the first unit, then sell the additional unit (the second unit), and so on." Instead, the story is, "sell 1 unit at $4, *or* sell two units at $3 each, *or* sell three units at $2 each, and so on."

Instructor: Yes, that's correct.

Points to Remember

1. A single-price monopolist must lower its price to sell an additional unit of the good it produces.
2. The lower price (necessary to sell an additional unit) applies to the additional unit and *to all units that preceded it*.

Chapter Summary

The Theory of Monopoly

- The theory of monopoly is built on three assumptions: (1) There is one seller. (2) The single seller sells a product for which there are no close substitutes. (3) The barriers to entry into the industry are extremely high.
- High barriers to entry may take the form of legal barriers (public franchises, patents, government licenses), economies of scale, or exclusive ownership of a scarce resource.

Monopoly Pricing and Output

- The profit-maximizing monopolist produces the quantity of output at which $MR = MC$ and charges the highest price per unit at which this quantity of output can be sold.
- For the single-price monopolist, $P > MR$; therefore, its demand curve lies above its marginal revenue curve.
- The single-price monopolist sells its output at a price higher than its marginal cost ($P > MC$) and therefore is *not* resource allocative efficient.
- Consider a perfectly competitive market and a monopoly market, each with the same demand and marginal cost curves. Consumers' surplus is greater in the perfectly competitive market.

Rent Seeking

- Activity directed at competing for and obtaining transfers is referred to as rent seeking. From society's perspective, rent seeking is a socially wasteful activity. People use resources to bring about a transfer of income from others to themselves instead of producing goods and services.

Price Discrimination

- Price discrimination occurs when a seller charges different prices for its product and the price differences are not due to cost differences.
- Before a seller can price-discriminate, certain conditions must hold: (1) The seller must be a price searcher. (2) The seller must be able to distinguish among customers who are willing to pay different prices. (3) Reselling the good to others must be impossible or too costly for a buyer.
- A seller that practices perfect price discrimination (charges the maximum price for each unit of product sold) sells the quantity of output at which $P = MC$. This kind of seller exhibits resource allocative efficiency.
- The single-price monopolist is said to produce too little output because it produces less than would be produced under perfect competition. This is not the case for a perfectly price-discriminating monopolist.

Key Terms and Concepts

Monopoly
Public Franchise
Natural Monopoly
Price Searcher
Deadweight Loss of Monopoly
Rent Seeking
X-Inefficiency
Price Discrimination
Perfect Price Discrimination
Second-Degree Price Discrimination
Third-Degree Price Discrimination
Arbitrage

Questions and Problems

1. The perfectly competitive firm exhibits resource allocative efficiency ($P = MC$), but the single-price monopolist does not. What is the reason for this difference?
2. Because the monopolist is a single seller of a product with no close substitutes, can it obtain any price for its good that it wants? Why or why not?
3. When a single-price monopolist maximizes profits, price is greater than marginal cost. In other words, buyers are willing to pay more for additional units of output than the units cost to produce. Given this situation, why doesn't the monopolist produce more?
4. Is there a deadweight loss if a firm produces the quantity of output at which price equals marginal cost? Explain.
5. Under what condition will a monopoly firm incur losses?
6. A perfectly competitive firm will produce more output and charge a lower (per-unit) price than a single-price monopoly firm. Do you agree or disagree with this statement? Explain your answer.
7. Rent seeking is individually rational but socially wasteful. Explain.
8. Occasionally, students accuse their instructors, rightly or wrongly, of practicing grade discrimination. These students claim that the instructor "charges" some students a higher price for a given grade than he or she charges other students (by requiring some students to do more or better work). Unlike price discrimination, grade discrimination involves no money. Discuss the similarities and differences between the two types of discrimination. Which do you prefer less or perhaps dislike more? Why?
9. Make a list of real-world price discrimination practices. Do they meet the conditions posited for price discrimination?
10. Make a list of market monopolies and a list of government monopolies. Which list is longer? Why do you think this is so?
11. Fast-food stores often charge higher prices for their products in high-crime areas than they charge in low-crime areas. Is this an act of price discrimination? Why or why not?
12. Coupons tend to be more common on small-ticket items than on big-ticket items. Explain why.
13. A firm maximizes its total revenue. Does it automatically maximize its profit too? Why or why not?

Working with Numbers and Graphs

1. Draw a graph that shows a monopoly firm incurring losses.
2. A monopoly firm is currently earning positive economic profit, and the owner decides to sell it. He asks for a price that takes into account the economic profit. Explain and diagrammatically show what a price that takes into account economic profit does to the average total cost (ATC) curve of the firm.
3. Suppose a single-price monopolist sells its output Q_1 at P_1. Then it raises its price to P_2, and its output falls to Q_2. In terms of Ps and Qs, what does this monopolist's marginal revenue equal?

Use the accompanying figure to answer questions 4–6:

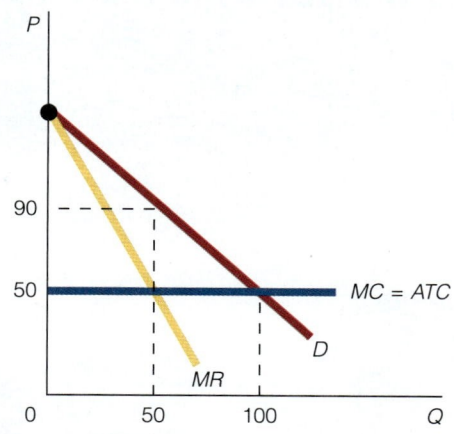

4. If the market is perfectly competitive, how much does profit equal?
5. If the market is a monopoly market, how much does profit equal?
6. Redraw the figure and label consumers' surplus when the market is perfectly competitive and when it is monopolized.

CHAPTER 24
Monopolistic Competition, Oligopoly, and Game Theory

Introduction

How do firms in a market act toward one another? Are they fiercely competitive, much like runners in a race to the finish line, where only one can be the winner? Or do firms act like people strolling in a park on a warm spring day, without a care in the world and certainly without competition on their minds? As you read this chapter, keep these two images in mind. Also, keep two words in mind: *competition* and *collusion*. This chapter is about both.

24-1 The Theory of Monopolistic Competition

Monopolistic Competition
A theory of market structure based on three assumptions: many sellers and buyers, firms producing and selling slightly differentiated products, and easy entry and exit.

The theory of **monopolistic competition** is built on three assumptions:

1. *There are many sellers and buyers.* This assumption holds for perfect competition too. For that reason, you might think that the monopolistic competitor should be a price taker, but it is a price searcher, basically because of the next assumption.

2. *Each firm (in the industry) produces and sells a slightly differentiated product.* Differences among the products may be due to brand names, packaging, location, credit terms connected with the sale of the product, the friendliness of the salespeople, and so forth. Product differentiation may be real or imagined. For example, aspirin may be aspirin, but if some people view a name-brand aspirin (such as Bayer®) as better than a generic brand, product differentiation exists.

3. *Entry and exit are easy.* Monopolistic competition resembles perfect competition in this respect. There are no barriers to entry and exit, legal or otherwise. Examples of industries with monopolistic competition include retail clothing, computer software, restaurants, and service stations.

24-1a The Monopolistic Competitor's Demand Curve

The perfectly competitive firm has many rivals, all producing the same good, so the good that it produces has an endless number of substitutes. Accordingly, the elasticity of demand for its product is extremely high—so high, in fact, that the demand curve it faces is horizontal (for all practical purposes).

The monopoly firm has practically no rivals, and it produces a good that has no substitutes. The elasticity of demand for its product is low, as partly reflected by its downward-sloping demand curve.

The monopolistic competitor, like the perfectly competitive firm, has many rivals. But unlike the rivals of the perfectly competitive firm, the monopolistic competitor's rivals do not sell exactly the same product that the monopolistic competitor sells. Because its product has substitutes, but not perfect ones, the elasticity of demand for the monopolistic competitor's product is not as great as that of the perfectly competitive firm. Nor does its demand curve look like the one faced by the perfectly competitive firm. The monopolistic competitor's demand curve is not horizontal; it is downward sloping.

24-1b The Relationship Between Price and Marginal Revenue for a Monopolistic Competitor

Because a monopolistic competitor faces a downward-sloping demand curve, it has to lower its price to sell an additional unit of the good it produces. (It is a price searcher.) For example, let's say that it can sell 3 units at $10 each but that it has to lower its price to $9 to sell 4 units. Its marginal revenue is therefore $6 (total revenue at 3 units is $30, and total revenue at 4 units is $36), which is below its price of $9. Thus, for the monopolistic competitor $P > MR$.

24-1c Output, Price, and Marginal Cost for the Monopolistic Competitor

The monopolistically competitive firm is the same as both the perfectly competitive firm and the monopoly firm in one regard: It produces the quantity of output at which $MR = MC$. In Exhibit 1, the firm produces q_1. For this quantity, the monopolistic competitor charges the highest price it can charge: P_1 in the exhibit.

For the monopolistic competitor, $P > MR$. Because the monopolistic competitor produces the quantity of output at which $MR = MC$, it must produce a level of output at which price is greater than marginal cost ($P > MC$), as is obvious in Exhibit 1.

24-1d Will There Be Profits in the Long Run?

If the firms in a monopolistically competitive market are currently earning profits, as is the firm in Exhibit 1, they most likely will not continue to earn profits in the long run. The assumption of easy entry and exit precludes this possibility. If firms in the industry are

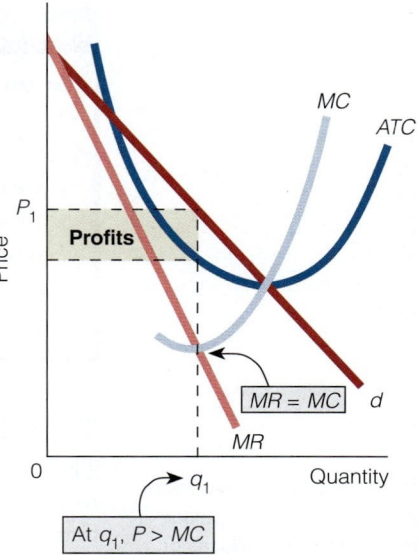

EXHIBIT 1

The Monopolistically Competitive Firm's Output and Price

The monopolistic competitor produces that quantity of output for which $MR = MC$. This quantity is q_1 in the exhibit. The monopolistic competitor charges the highest price consistent with q_1, namely, P_1.

At q_1, $P > MC$

EXHIBIT 2

Monopolistic Competition in the Long Run

Because of easy entry into the industry, there are likely to be zero economic profits in the long run for a monopolistic competitor. In other words, P = ATC.

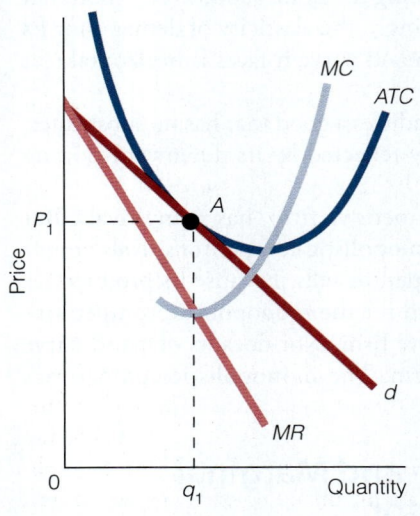

earning profits, new firms will enter the industry and reduce the demand that each firm faces. In other words, the demand curve for each firm may shift to the left. Eventually, in the long run, competition will reduce economic profits to zero, as is shown for the monopolistically competitive firm in Exhibit 2.

Note, however, that the answer to the question of whether firms will continue to earn profits in the long run was they "most likely" won't, instead of no. In monopolistic competition, new firms usually produce a *close substitute* for the product made by existing firms, not an *identical* one. In some instances, this difference may be enough to upset the zero economic profit condition in the long run. An existing firm may be able to differentiate its product sufficiently in the minds of buyers such that it continues to earn profits, even though new firms enter the industry and compete with it.

Firms that try to differentiate their products from those of other sellers in ways other than price are said to be engaged in *nonprice competition*. This type of competition may take the form of advertising or of trying to establish a well-respected brand name, among other efforts. For example, soft-drink companies' advertising often tries to stress the uniqueness of their product. In the past, Dr. Pepper has been advertised as "the unusual one" and 7-Up as "the uncola." In a similar vein, Wheaties has been promoted as the "breakfast of champions," and Budweiser as the "king of beers." Apple has a well-respected name in personal computers, Bayer in aspirin, and Marriott in hotels. Such well-respected names sometimes differentiate products sufficiently in the minds of buyers so that short-run profits are not easily or not completely eliminated by the entry of new firms into the industry.

Finding Economics

In an Online Radio Service Abbie just found an online radio station that plays the songs and artists she wants to hear. She keys in the title of the song or the name of the artist she would like to hear, and the service creates a virtual radio station just for her. Where is the economics?

Firms can compete in terms of price (price competition) or in areas other than price (nonprice competition). With respect to free radio (radio you do not pay to hear), radio stations cannot compete on price, so they must turn to nonprice competition. Customizing a radio station for a listener is a nonprice way of competing for listeners.

24-1e Excess Capacity: What Is It, and Is It "Good" or "Bad"?

The theory of monopolistic competition makes a major prediction, which is generally referred to as the **excess capacity theorem**: A monopolistic competitor will produce an output smaller than the one that would minimize its unit costs of production.

At point A in Exhibit 3(a), the monopolistic competitor is in long-run equilibrium because profits are zero ($P = ATC$). Point A is *not* the lowest point on the average total cost curve; the lowest point is point L. Therefore, in long-run equilibrium, when the monopolistic competitor

Excess Capacity Theorem
A monopolistic competitor in equilibrium produces an output smaller than the one that would minimize its costs of production.

earns zero economic profits, it is not producing the quantity of output at which average total costs (unit costs) are minimized, given the scale of the plant. Exhibit 3 contrasts the perfectly competitive firm and the monopolistic competitor in long-run equilibrium. In part (b), the perfectly competitive firm is earning zero economic profits, and price (P_{C_1}) equals average total cost (ATC). Furthermore, the point at which price equals average total cost (point L) is the lowest point on the ATC curve. In long-run equilibrium, the perfectly competitive firm produces the quantity of output at which unit costs are minimized.

Now look back at part (a). The monopolistic competitor is earning zero economic profits, and price (P_{MC_1}) equals average total cost. If the monopolistic competitor produced the quantity of output at which unit costs were minimized, it would produce q_{MC_2}. For this reason, it has been argued that the monopolistic competitor produces too little output (q_{MC_1} instead of q_{MC_2}) and charges too high a price (P_{MC_1} instead of P_{MC_2}). With respect to output, too little translates into the monopolistic competitor's underutilizing its present plant size; it is said to have *excess capacity*. In part (a), the excess capacity is equal to the difference of q_{MC_2} and q_{MC_1}.

Some have argued that the monopolistic competitor operates at excess capacity because it faces a downward-sloping demand curve. In Exhibit 3(a), the only way the firm would not operate at excess capacity is if its demand curve were tangent to the ATC curve at point L—the lowest point on the ATC curve. But for tangency at L to occur, the demand curve *would have to be horizontal*, a condition that would require homogeneous products. A downward-sloping demand curve *cannot* be tangent to the ATC curve at point L.

In short, *the monopolistic competitor operates at excess capacity as a consequence of its downward-sloping demand curve*, and its downward-sloping demand curve is a consequence of differentiated products. A question that many economists ask, but not all answer in the same way, is this: *If excess capacity is the price we pay for differentiated products (more choice), is it too high a price?*

EXHIBIT 3

A Comparison of Perfect Competition and Monopolistic Competition: The Issue of Excess Capacity

The perfectly competitive firm produces a quantity of output consistent with lowest unit costs. The monopolistic competitor does not. If it did, it would produce q_{MC_2} instead of q_{MC_1}. The monopolistic competitor is said to underutilize its plant size or to have excess capacity.

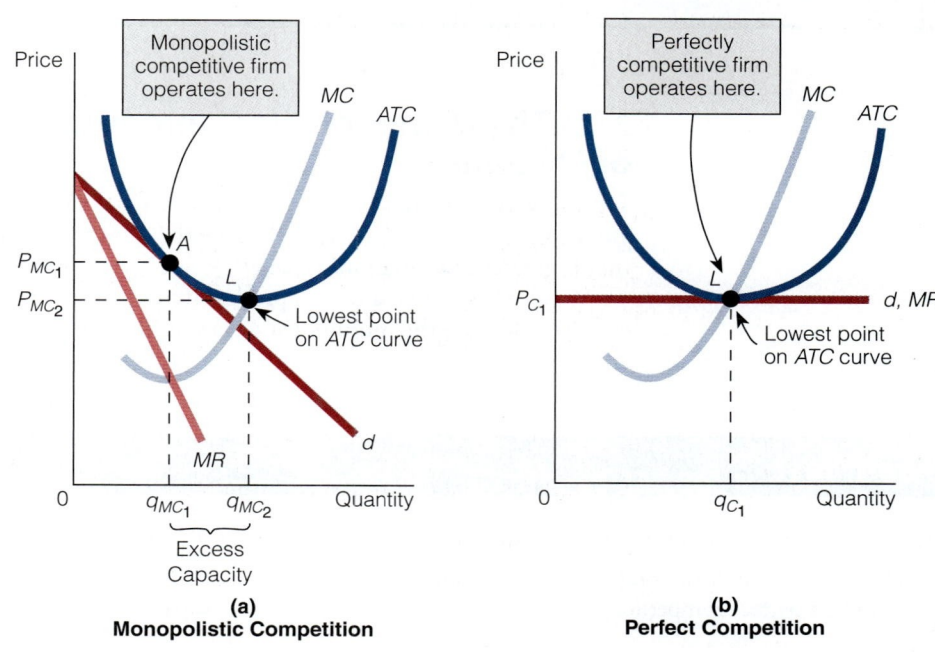

(a) Monopolistic Competition

(b) Perfect Competition

Economics 24/7

The People Wear Prada

Suppose you own a business that is considered a monopolistically competitive firm. Your business is one of many sellers, you sell a product slightly differentiated from the products of your competitors, and entry into and exit from the industry are easy. Would you rather your business were a monopoly firm? Wouldn't it be better for you to be the *only* seller of a product than to be one of many? Most business owners would answer yes, so we consider how monopolistic competitors may try to become monopolists.

One possibility is through a designer label. If a monopolistic competitor can, through the use of a designer label, persuade the buying public that her product is more than just slightly differentiated from those of her competitors, she stands a better chance of becoming a monopolist. (Remember that a monopolist produces a good that has *no* close substitutes.)

For example, many firms produce women's jeans, and, to many people, the jeans all look very much alike. To differentiate its product from the pack, a firm could add a designer label to the jeans to suggest uniqueness—that they are the only Calvin Klein jeans, for example. For added impact, it could try to persuade the buying public through advertising that its jeans are "the" jeans worn by the most famous, best-looking people.

Think of a list of firms that have employed a designer label to try to outcompete their competitors: Gucci, Tommy Hilfiger, Perry Ellis, Liz Claiborne, Armani, Versace, Dolce & Gabbana, Prada, Valentino, Chanel, L. L. Bean, and many others.

24-1f The Monopolistic Competitor and Two Types of Efficiency

We know that a firm is resource allocative efficient if it charges a price that is equal to its marginal cost—that is, if $P = MC$. Because the monopolistically competitive firm charges a price that is greater than marginal cost ($P > MC$), it is not resource allocative efficient.

We also know that a firm is productive efficient if it charges a price that is equal to its lowest ATC. Because the monopolistic competitor operates at excess capacity, it is not productive efficient.

(Answers to Self-Test questions are in Answers to Self-Test Questions at the back of the book.)

1. How is a monopolistic competitor like a monopolist? How is it like a perfect competitor?
2. Why do monopolistic competitors operate at excess capacity?

24-2 Oligopoly: Assumptions and Real-World Behavior

Unlike perfect competition, monopoly, and monopolistic competition, there is no one accepted theory of **oligopoly**. However, the different theories of oligopoly have the following common assumptions:

1. *There are few sellers and many buyers.* The assumption is usually that the few firms of an oligopoly are interdependent; each one is aware that its actions influence the others and that the actions of the other firms affect it. This interdependence among firms is a key characteristic of oligopoly.
2. *Firms produce and sell either homogeneous or differentiated products.* Aluminum is a homogeneous product produced in an oligopolistic market; cars are a differentiated product produced in an oligopolistic market.
3. *The barriers to entry are significant.* Economies of scale constitute perhaps the most significant barrier to entry in an oligopoly, but patent rights, exclusive control of an essential resource, and legal obstacles also act as barriers to entry.

The oligopolist is a price searcher. Like all other firms, it produces the quantity of output at which $MR = MC$.

> **Oligopoly**
> A theory of market structure based on three assumptions: few sellers and many buyers, firms producing either homogeneous or differentiated products, and significant barriers to entry.

24-2a The Concentration Ratio

Which industries today are dominated by a small number of firms—that is, are oligopolistic? Economists have developed the *concentration ratio* to help answer this question. The **concentration ratio** is the percentage of industry sales (or assets, output, labor force, or some other factor) accounted for by x number of firms in the industry. The x in the definition is usually four or eight, but it can be any number (although it is usually small):

> **Concentration Ratio**
> The percentage of industry sales (or assets, output, labor force, or some other factor) accounted for by x number of firms in the industry.

Four-firm concentration ratio: CR_4 = Percentage of industry sales accounted for by four largest firms

Eight-firm concentration ratio: CR_8 = Percentage of industry sales accounted for by eight largest firms

A high concentration ratio implies that few sellers make up the industry; a low concentration ratio implies that more than a few sellers make up the industry.

As an example, let's calculate a four-firm concentration ratio for industry Z. Suppose total industry sales for a given year are $5 million and the four largest firms in the industry account for $4.5 million in sales. The four-firm concentration ratio is 0.90, or 90 percent ($5 million $\times$ 0.90 = $4.5 million). Industries with high four- and eight-firm concentration ratios in recent years are cigarettes, cars, tires, cereal breakfast foods, farm machinery, and soap and other detergents, to name a few.

Although concentration ratios are often used to determine the extent (or degree) of oligopoly, they are not perfect guides to industry concentration. Most important, they do not take into account foreign competition and competition from substitute domestic goods. For example, the U.S. automobile industry is concentrated, but it still faces stiff competition from abroad. A more relevant concentration ratio for this particular industry might be one computed on a worldwide basis.

24-3 Price and Output Under The Cartel Theory

In this section we discuss why oligopoly firms might want to form a cartel and some of the problems they encounter in doing so.

24-3a The Cartel Theory

Cartel Theory
A theory of oligopoly in which oligopolistic firms act as if there were only one firm in the industry.

Cartel
An organization of firms that reduces output and increases price in an effort to increase joint profits.

The key behavioral assumption of the **cartel theory** is that, within a given industry, oligopolists act as if there were only one firm. In short, they form a cartel to capture the benefits that would exist for a monopolist. A **cartel** is an organization of firms that reduces output and increases price in an effort to increase joint profits.

Forming and maintaining a cartel has its benefits. Exhibit 4 shows an industry in long-run competitive equilibrium. Price is P_1, and quantity of output is Q_1. The industry is producing the output at which price equals marginal cost, and economic profits are zero. Now, suppose the firms making up the industry form a cartel and reduce output to Q_C. Then the new price is P_C (the cartel price), and profits, which are equal to the area CP_CAB, can be shared among the members of the cartel. With no cartel, there are no profits; with a cartel, profits are earned. Thus, the firms have an incentive to form a cartel and to behave cooperatively rather than competitively.

However, firms may not be able to form a cartel, even though they have a profit incentive to do so. Also, even if they are able to form the cartel, the firms may not be able to maintain it. Firms that wish to form and maintain a cartel will encounter several problems, two of which are that legislation prohibits certain types of cartels in the United States and organizing and forming a cartel involves costs as well as benefits.[1]

EXHIBIT 4

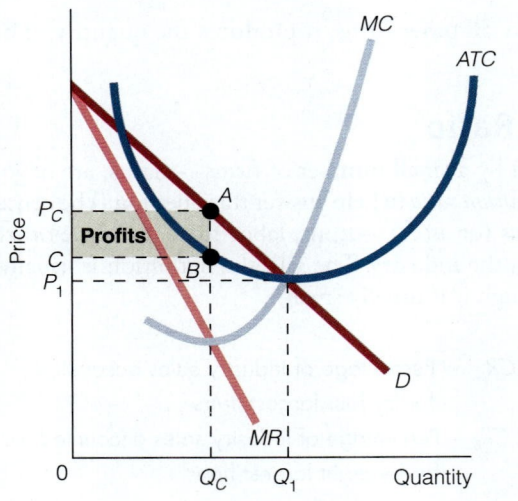

The Benefits of a Cartel (to Cartel Members)

We assume that the industry is in long-run competitive equilibrium, producing Q_1 and charging P_1. There are no profits. A reduction in output to Q_C through the formation of a cartel raises prices to P_C and brings profits of CP_CAB. (*Note*: In an earlier chapter, a horizontal demand curve faces the *firm*. Here a downward-sloping demand curve faces the *industry*. Don't be misled by this difference. No matter what type of demand curve we use, long-run competitive equilibrium is where $P = MC = SRATC = LRATC$.)

The Problem of Forming the Cartel Even if it were legal, getting the sellers of an industry together to form a cartel can be costly, even when the number of sellers is small. Each potential cartel member may resist incurring the costs of forming the cartel because it stands to benefit more if other firms do the work. In other words, each potential member has an incentive to be a free rider—to stand by and take a free ride on the actions of others.

The Problem of Formulating Cartel Policy Even if prospective firms form a cartel, the problem of formulating policy arises. For example, firm *A* might propose that each cartel member reduce output by 10 percent, and firm *B* might advocate that all bigger cartel members

---

[1] Sometimes, economists discuss the benefits and costs of organizing a cartel without specifying the market structure. We have followed suit here by broadening our discussion of cartel theory to include market structures other than oligopoly. This broadening of the discussion will be noticeable in places. For example, even though there are few sellers in oligopoly, we discuss cartel theory in the context of both few and many sellers.

reduce output by 15 percent and all smaller members reduce output by 5 percent. In fact, there may be as many policy proposals as there are cartel members, and reaching agreement may be difficult. Such disagreements become harder to resolve as the differences among cartel members in costs, size, and so forth, grow.

The Problem of Entry into the Industry Even if the cartel members manage to agree on a policy that generates high profits, those high profits will provide an incentive for firms outside the industry to join the industry. If current cartel members cannot keep new suppliers from entering, the cartel is likely to break up.

The Problem of Cheating As paradoxical as it first appears, after the cartel agreement is made, members have an incentive to cheat on it. Exhibit 5 shows three situations for a *representative firm* of the cartel: (1) the situation before the cartel is formed, (2) the situation after the cartel is formed when all members adhere to the cartel price, and (3) the situation if the firm cheats on the cartel agreement but the other cartel members do not.

Before the cartel is formed, the firm in the exhibit is in long-run competitive equilibrium; it produces output q_1, charges price P_1, and earns zero economic profits. After the cartel is formed, the firm reduces its output to q_C, as directed by the cartel (the cartel has set a quota for each member), and it charges the cartel price of P_C. Now the firm earns profits equal to the area CP_CAB.

What happens if the firm cheats on the cartel agreement and produces q_{CC} instead of the stipulated q_C? As long as other firms do not cheat, this firm views its demand curve as

EXHIBIT 5

The Benefits of Cheating on the Cartel Agreement

In the exhibit, we see the situation for a representative firm of a cartel. In long-run competitive equilibrium, the firm produces q_1 and charges P_1, earning zero economic profits. As a consequence of the cartel agreement, it reduces its output to q_C and charges P_C. Its profits are the area CP_CAB. If the firm cheats on the cartel agreement and others do not, it will increase output to q_{CC} and reap profits of FP_CDE. Note, however, that if this firm can cheat on the cartel agreement, so can others. Given the monetary benefits gained by cheating, it is likely that the cartel will exist for only a short time.

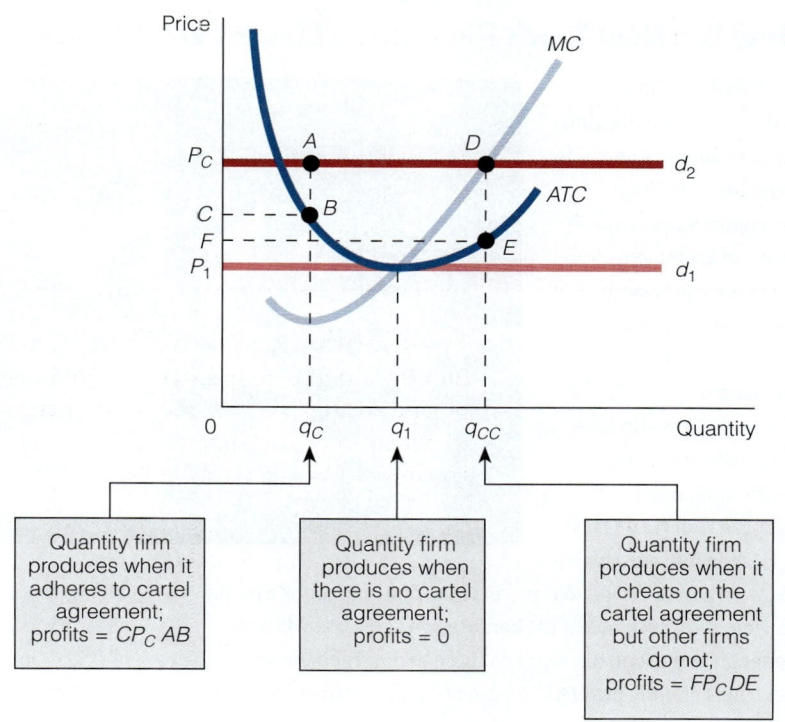

Quantity firm produces when it adheres to cartel agreement; profits = $CP_C AB$

Quantity firm produces when there is no cartel agreement; profits = 0

Quantity firm produces when it cheats on the cartel agreement but other firms do not; profits = $FP_C DE$

horizontal at the cartel price (P_C). The reason is simple: Because it is one of a number of firms, our hypothetical representative firm cannot affect price by changing output. Therefore, it can produce and sell additional units of output without lowering its price. So, if the firm cheats on the cartel agreement and other firms do not, then the cheating firm can increase its profits from the smaller amount CP_CAB to the larger amount FP_CDE. Of course, if all the firms cheat, the cartel members are back where they started—with no cartel agreement and at price P_1.

This analysis illustrates a major theme of cartels: firms have an incentive to form a cartel, but once it is formed, they have an incentive to cheat. As a result of this flaw, some economists have concluded that, even if cartels are formed successfully, they are not likely to be effective for long.

1. "Firms have an incentive to form a cartel, but once it is formed, they have an incentive to cheat." What is the specific incentive to form the cartel? What is the incentive to cheat on the cartel?

2. Is an oligopolistic firm a price taker or a price searcher? Explain your answer.

Economics 24/7

How Is a New Year's Resolution Like a Cartel Agreement?

In a cartel, one firm makes an agreement with another firm or other firms. In a New Year's resolution, you essentially make an agreement with yourself. So both cases—the cartel and the resolution—involve an agreement.

Both cases also raise the possibility of cheating on the agreement. Suppose your New Year's resolution is to exercise more, take better notes in class, and read one good book a month. You might set such objectives because you know you will be better off in the long run if you do these things. Then the short run enters into the picture. You have to decide between exercising today or plopping down in your favorite chair and watching television. You have to decide between starting to read *Moby Dick* or catching up on the latest entertainment news in *People* magazine. The part of you that wants to hold to the resolution is at odds with the part of you that wants to watch television or read *People*. Often, the television-watching, *People*-reading part wins out. Breaking a New Year's resolution—as you probably already know—is just too easy.

So is breaking a cartel agreement. For the firm that has entered into the agreement, the lure of higher profits is often too strong to resist. In addition, the firm is concerned that, if it doesn't break the agreement (and cheat), some other firm might, and then it will have lost out completely.

In short, both resolutions and cartel agreements take a lot of willpower to hold them together. Willpower, however, seems to be in particularly short supply, and something is needed to take its place. Both a resolution and a cartel agreement need something if they are to endure: Something or someone has to exact a penalty from the party who breaks the resolution or cartel agreement. Government sometimes plays this role for firms. Family members and friends occasionally play the role for individuals by reminding or reprimanding them if they fail to live up to their resolutions. (Usually, though, family members and friends are not successful.)

So we draw the following conclusions:

- First, an agreement is at the heart of both a New Year's resolution and a cartel.
- Second, both the resolution and the cartel are subject to cheating behavior.
- Third, if the resolution and the cartel are to have a long life, they often need someone or something to prevent each party from breaking the agreement.

24-4 Game Theory, Oligopoly, and Contestable Markets

Of the four market structures (perfect competition, monopoly, monopolistic competition, and oligopoly), oligopoly is often described as the most difficult to analyze. Analysis is difficult because of the interdependence among firms in such a market. Economists often use game theory to get a workable understanding of the interdependence of oligopoly firms. **Game theory** is a mathematical technique used to analyze the behavior of decision makers who (1) try to reach an optimal position through game playing or the use of strategic behavior, (2) are fully aware of the interactive nature of the process at hand, and (3) anticipate the moves of other decision makers.

In this section, we describe a famous game and then use it to discuss oligopoly behavior. We also discuss the issue of contestable markets.

Game Theory
A mathematical technique used to analyze the behavior of decision makers who try to reach an optimal position for themselves through game playing or the use of strategic behavior, who are fully aware of the interactive nature of the process at hand, and who anticipate the moves of other decision makers.

24-4a Prisoner's Dilemma

A well-known game in game theory, the prisoner's dilemma, illustrates a case in which individually rational behavior leads to a jointly inefficient outcome. The lesson of the game has been described this way: "You do what is best for you, I'll do what is best for me, and somehow we end up in a situation that is not best for either of us." Here is how the game is played.

The Facts Two men, Bob and Nathan, are arrested and charged with jointly committing a crime. They are put into separate cells so that they cannot communicate with each other. The district attorney (DA) goes to each man separately and says the following:

- If you confess to the crime and agree to turn state's evidence and if your accomplice does not confess, I will let you off with a $500 fine.
- If your accomplice confesses to the crime and agrees to turn state's evidence and if you do not confess, I will fine you $5,000.
- If both you and your accomplice remain silent and refuse to confess to the crime, I will charge you with a lesser crime, which I can prove you committed, and you and your accomplice will pay fines of $2,000 each.
- If both you and your accomplice confess, I will fine each of you $3,000.

EXHIBIT 6

Prisoner's Dilemma

Nathan and Bob each have two choices: confess or not confess. No matter what Bob does, it is always better for Nathan to confess. No matter what Nathan does, it is always better for Bob to confess. Both Nathan and Bob confess and end up in box 4, with each paying a $3,000 fine. Both men would have been better off had they not confessed. That way they would have ended up in box 1, paying a $2,000 fine.

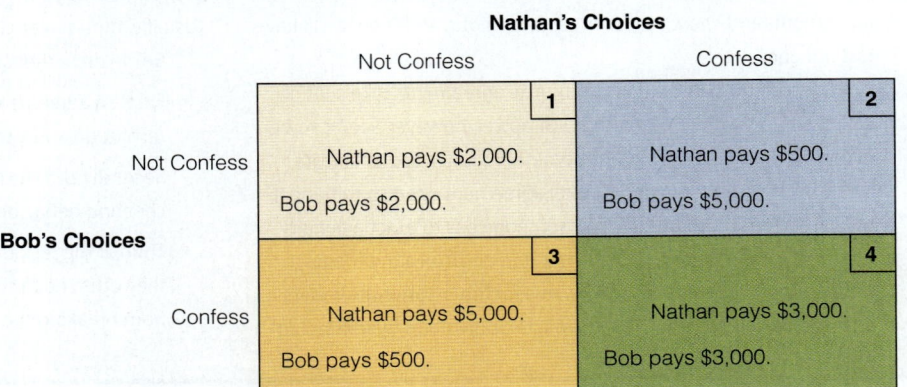

The Options and Consequences Each man has two choices: confess or not confess, as shown in the grid in Exhibit 6. The grid shows the following possibilities laid out by the district attorney:

- *Box 1*. If both men do not confess, each pays a fine of $2,000.
- *Box 2*. If Nathan confesses and Bob does not, then Nathan gets off with the light fine of $500 and Bob pays the stiff penalty of $5,000.
- *Box 3*. If Nathan does not confess and Bob confesses, then Nathan pays the stiff penalty of $5,000 and Bob pays the light fine of $500.
- *Box 4*. Finally, if both men confess, each pays $3,000.

What Nathan Thinks Nathan considers his choices and their possible outcomes. He reasons to himself, "I have two options, confess or not confess, and Bob has the same two options. Let me ask myself two questions:

- "*If Bob chooses not to confess, what is the best thing for me to do?* The answer is to confess, because, if I do not confess, I will end up in box 1, paying $2,000, but if I confess, I will end up in box 2, paying only $500. No doubt about it: If Bob chooses not to confess, I should confess."
- "*If Bob chooses to confess, what is the best thing for me to do?* The answer is also to confess, because, if I do not confess, I will end up in box 3, paying $5,000, but if I confess, I will pay $3,000. No doubt about it: If Bob chooses to confess, I should confess."

Nathan's Conclusion Nathan concludes that, no matter what Bob chooses to do—not confess or confess—he (Nathan) is always better off if he confesses. Therefore, Nathan decides to confess to the crime.

The Situation Is the Same for Bob Bob goes through the same mental process that Nathan does. Asking himself the same two questions Nathan asked himself, Bob gets the same answers and draws the same conclusion. Therefore, Bob decides to confess to the crime.

The Outcome
The DA goes to each man and asks him what he has decided. Both Nathan and Bob say, "I confess." The outcome is shown in box 4, with each man paying a fine of $3,000.

Now Look Where They Could Be
Another outcome represented by one of the four boxes is better for both Nathan and Bob than the one whereby each pays $3,000: In box 1, both Nathan and Bob pay $2,000. To get to box 1, all the two men had to do was keep silent and not confess.

Changing the Game
What would happen if the DA gave Nathan and Bob another chance? Suppose she tells them that she will not accept their confessions. Instead, she wants them to talk it over together for 10 minutes, after which time she will come back, place each man in a separate room, and ask for his decision. The second time, she will accept each man's decision, no matter what.

Will a second chance change the outcome? Most people will say yes, arguing that Nathan and Bob will now see that their best choice is to remain silent so that each ends up with a $2,000 fine instead of a $3,000 fine. Let's assume that they do see this and Nathan and Bob enter into an agreement to remain silent.

Nathan's Thoughts on the Way to His Room
The DA returns and takes Nathan to a separate room. On the way, Nathan thinks to himself, "I'm not sure I can trust Bob. Suppose he goes back on our agreement and confesses. If I hold to the agreement and he doesn't, he'll end up with a $500 fine and I'll end up paying $5,000. Of course, if I break the agreement and confess and he holds to the agreement, then I'll reduce my fine to $500. Maybe the best thing for me to do is break the agreement and confess, hoping that he doesn't, and I'll pay only $500. If I'm not so lucky, at least I'll protect myself from paying $5,000."

Once in the room, the DA asks Nathan what his decision is. He says, "I confess."

The Situation Is the Same for Bob
Bob sees the situation in the same way that Nathan does and again chooses to confess.

The Outcome Again
Both men end up confessing a second time. Each pays $3,000, realizing that if they had been silent and kept to their agreement, their fine would be only $2,000 each.

24-4b Oligopoly Firms' Cartels and the Prisoner's Dilemma

When oligopoly firms enter into a cartel agreement, do they create a prisoner's dilemma? Most economists answer yes. To illustrate, suppose two firms, *A* and *B*, produce and sell the same product and are in stiff competition with each other. In fact, the competition is so stiff that each firm earns only $10,000 in profits. Soon the two firms decide to enter into a cartel agreement in which each agrees to raise prices and, after prices are raised, not to undercut the other. If they hold to the agreement, each firm will earn profits of $50,000. But if one firm holds to the cartel agreement and the other does not, the one that does not will earn profits of $100,000, and the one that does will earn $5,000 in profits. Of course, if neither holds to the agreement, then both will be back where they started, earning $10,000 in profits. The choices for the two firms and the possible outcomes are outlined in Exhibit 7.

Each firm is likely to behave as the two prisoners did in the prisoner's dilemma game. Each firm will see the chance to earn $100,000 by breaking the agreement (instead of $50,000 by

EXHIBIT 7

Cartels and the Prisoner's Dilemma

Many economists suggest that firms trying to form a cartel are in a prisoner's dilemma situation. Both firms A and B earn higher profits holding to a (cartel) agreement than not, but each will earn even higher profits if it breaks the agreement while the other firm holds to it. We predict that, if cartel formation is a prisoner's dilemma situation, then cartels will be short lived.

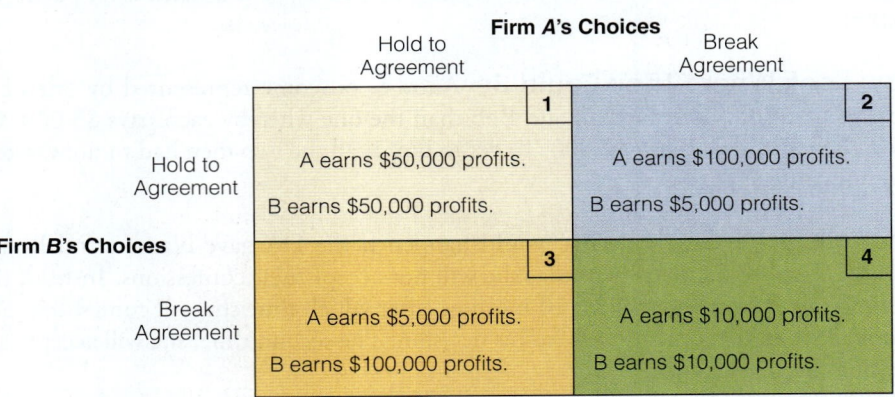

---

holding to it); each will also realize that if it does not break the agreement and the other firm does, it will be in a worse situation than it was before entering into the cartel. Most economists predict that the two firms will end up in box 4 in Exhibit 7, earning the profits they did before they entered into the agreement. In sum, they will cheat on the cartel agreement and again be in competition—the very situation they wanted to escape.

The only way out of the prisoner's dilemma for the two firms is to have some entity enforce the cartel agreement so that the two firms do not cheat. As odd as it may sound, sometimes government has played this role. Normally, we think of government as trying to break up cartel agreements because, after all, such agreements are illegal. Nevertheless, sometimes government acts as the enforcer, not the eliminator, of cartel agreements.

For example, the Civil Aeronautics Board (CAB) was created in the days of airline regulation to protect the airlines from so-called cutthroat competition. The CAB had the power to set airfares, allocate air routes, and prevent the entry of new carriers into the airline industry. In the days before deregulation, the federal government's General Accounting Office estimated that airline fares would have been, on average, as much as 52 percent lower if the CAB had not been regulating them. Clearly, the CAB was doing for the airlines what an airline cartel would have done: preventing price competition, allocating routes, and preventing new entries into the industry.

In a similar vein, Judge Richard Posner has observed that "the railroads supported the enactment of the first Interstate Commerce Act, which was designed to prevent railroads from price discrimination, because discrimination was undermining the railroad's cartels."[2]

24-4c Are Markets Contestable?

Market structures, from perfect competition to oligopoly, have been traditionally defined in terms of the *number of sellers*. In perfect competition, there are many sellers; in monopoly, there is only one; in monopolistic competition, there are many; in oligopoly, there are few. The message is that the number of sellers in a market influences their behavior. For example, the monopoly seller is more likely to restrict output and charge higher prices than is the perfect competitor.

---

[2] Richard A. Posner, "Theories of Regulation," *Bell Journal of Economics and Management Science* 5 (Autumn): 337.

Some economists have shifted the emphasis from the number of sellers in a market to the issue of *entry into and exit from an industry*. This shift brings us to a discussion of contestable markets. A **contestable market** is a market in which the following conditions are met:

1. *Entry into the market is easy, and exit from it is costless.*
2. *New firms entering the market can produce the product at the same cost that current firms produce it.*
3. *Firms exiting the market can easily dispose of their fixed assets by selling them elsewhere.* In other words, except for depreciation, fixed costs are not sunk but recoverable.

> **Contestable Market**
> A market in which entry is easy and exit is costless, new firms can produce the product at the same cost as current firms, and exiting firms can easily dispose of their fixed assets by selling them.

Suppose that eight firms are in an industry and that all of them are earning profits. Then, firms outside the industry notice the situation and decide to enter the industry. (By condition 1, nothing prevents their entry.) They acquire the necessary equipment and produce the product at the same cost that current producers do. Time passes, and the firms that entered the industry decide to exit it. They can either switch their machinery into another line of production or sell their equipment for what they paid for it, less depreciation.

Perhaps the most important element of a contestable market is so-called hit-and-run entry and exit. New entrants can enter (hit), produce the product, take profits from current firms, and then exit costlessly (run).

The theory of contestable markets has been criticized because of its assumptions—in particular, the assumption that entry into the industry is free and exit is costless. However, even though this theory, like most theories, does not describe the real world perfectly, it has its usefulness.

At a minimum, the contestable markets theory has rattled orthodox market structure theory. Here are a few of its conclusions:

1. Even if an industry is composed of a small number of firms—or even just one firm—the firms do not necessarily perform in a noncompetitive way. They might be extremely competitive if the market they are in is contestable.
2. Profits can be zero in an industry even if the number of sellers in the industry is small.
3. If a market is contestable, inefficient producers cannot survive. Cost inefficiencies invite lower-cost producers into the market, driving price down to the minimum average total cost and forcing inefficient firms to change their ways or exit the industry.
4. If, as the previous conclusion suggests, a contestable market encourages firms to produce at their lowest-possible average total cost and charge a price equal to average total cost, then they also will sell at a price equal to marginal cost. (The marginal cost curve intersects the average total cost curve at its minimum point.)

The theory of contestable markets has also led to a shift in policy perspectives. To some (but certainly not all) economists, the theory suggests a new way to encourage firms to act as perfect competitors. Rather than direct interference in the behavioral patterns of firms, efforts should perhaps be directed at lowering entry and exit costs.

24-4d Necessary and Sufficient Conditions and Efficiency

In the last few chapters, we have discussed various market structures. We started by discussing perfect competition, then moved on to discuss monopoly, and finally, in this chapter, we discussed monopolistic competition and oligopoly.

The only market structure (out of the four we discussed) that we labeled as resource allocative efficient was perfect competition. Recall that a firm is resource allocative efficient if it produces the level of output at which price equals marginal cost ($P = MC$). This condition holds for a perfectly competitive firm.

Also, when discussing a perfectly competitive firm, we said that in the long run it is productive efficient; that is, it produces its output at the lowest per-unit cost, or average total cost ($P = ATC$).

For the first-time student of economics, there is almost no way of coming away from a discussion of the four market structures without thinking that perfect competition is far and away the superior market structure because of its efficiency properties. But keep one thing in mind: the conditions that we specified for the theory of perfect competition (such as many sellers and many buyers, a homogeneous product, buyers having all relevant information, and easy entry and exit) are sufficient—not necessary—conditions for achieving efficiency. What this statement means is that, if these conditions hold, they are enough to give us the result of efficiency. It is similar to saying that, if A exists, then X will follow. In other words, A is sufficient to get X to follow.

But these (perfectly competitive) conditions are not *necessary* to achieve efficiency. That is, even if A does not exist, but C exists instead, X could follow. In terms of achieving efficiency, even if there is a market that does not satisfy all the conditions of perfect competition, efficiency can still be achieved.

With this idea of necessary and sufficient conditions in mind, think again of contestable markets. Just because a given contestable market does not satisfy all the conditions of a perfectly competitive market, it does not necessarily follow that the given contestable market will not achieve efficiency (resource allocative or productive). In fact, in laboratory experiments, the economist Vernon Smith, a founder of experimental economics, has found that participants who have significant price-setting power (which does not exist in perfect competition) and little or no information about their counterparts consistently produce efficient results, given certain trading institutions.

24-5 A Review of Market Structures

Exhibit 8 reviews some of the characteristics and consequences of the four different market structures: perfect competition, monopoly, monopolistic competition, and oligopoly. The first four columns of the exhibit summarize the characteristics. The last column notes the long-run

EXHIBIT 8

Characteristics and Consequences of Market Structures

Market Structure	Number of Sellers	Type of Product	Barriers to Entry	Long-Run Market Tendency of Price and *ATC*
Perfect competition	Many	Homogeneous	No	$P = ATC$ (zero economic profits)
Monopoly	One	Unique	Yes	$P > ATC$ (positive economic profits)[a,c]
Monopolistic competition	Many	Slightly differentiated	No	$P = ATC$ (zero economic profits)[b]
Oligopoly	Few	Homogeneous or differentiated	Yes	$P > ATC$ (positive economic profits)[a,c]

[a.] It is possible for positive profits to turn into zero profits through the capitalization of profits or rent-seeking activities.
[b.] It is possible for the firm to earn positive profits in the long run if it can differentiate its product sufficiently in the minds of the buying public.
[c.] It is possible for positive profits to turn into zero profits if the market is contestable.

market tendencies of price and average total cost. The relationship between price and ATC indicates whether long-run profits are possible. In the exhibit, three of the four market structures (monopoly, monopolistic competition, and oligopoly) have superscript letters beside the possible profits. These letters refer to notes that describe alternative market tendencies given different conditions. For example, the market tendency in oligopoly is for $P > ATC$ and for profits to exist in the long run. Because oligopoly has significant barriers to entry, short-run profits cannot be reduced by competition from new firms entering the industry. However, the market tendency of price and average total cost may be different if the particular oligopolistic market is contestable.

24-6 Applications of Game Theory

Game theory, especially the prisoner's dilemma, is applicable to a number of real-world situations. In this section, we discuss a few of these applications.

24-6a Grades and Partying

Suppose your economics professor announces in class one day that on the next test she will give the top 10 percent of the students in the class As, the next 15 percent Bs, and so on. Because studying to get, say, a 60 takes less time than studying to get a 90 on the test, you hope that everyone studies only a little. If so, you can study only a little and earn a high letter grade. But, of course, everyone in the class is thinking the same thing.

Envision yourself entering into an agreement with your fellow students. You say the following to them one day:

> There are 30 students in our class. Each of us can choose to study either two hours or four hours for the test. Our relative standing in the class will be the same whether we all study for two hours or all study for four hours. So why don't we all agree to study for only two hours. That way, we have two extra hours to do other things. I'd rather receive my B by studying for only two hours than studying for four.

Everyone agrees with the logic of the argument and agrees to study only two hours. Of course, once all the students have agreed to do this, they have an incentive to cheat on the agreement and study more. If everyone else in your class agrees to study two hours and you study four, you increase your relative standing in the class. You go from, say, a B to an A.

You and the other students in your class are in a prisoner's dilemma. Exhibit 9 shows the payoffs for you and for Jill, a representative other student. If both you and Jill study four hours, you each receive an 85, which is a B (box 4). With your professor's new relative grading plan, if you study two hours and Jill studies two hours, the grade for each of you falls to 65, but now 65 is a B (box 1). In other words, in comparison with box 4, box 1 is better because you receive the same letter grade (B) in both cases but spend less time studying.

Of course, once you and Jill agree to lower your study time from four hours to two, each of you has an incentive to cheat on the agreement. If you study four hours and Jill studies two, then you raise your grade to an 85, which is now an A, whereas Jill's grade is 65, which now becomes a C (box 2). Of course, if Jill studies four hours and you study two, then Jill raises her grade to an 85, which is now an A, and your grade is 65, which is now a C (box 3).

No matter what you think Jill is going to do, the best thing for you to do is study four hours.[3] The same holds for Jill with respect to whatever you choose to do. The outcome, then, is box 4, where both of you study four hours.

---

[3] We are assuming that the cost of studying two additional hours is lower than the benefits you receive by raising your grade one letter.

EXHIBIT 9

Studying and Grades

Suppose your letter grade in class depends on how well you do relative to others. In this setting, you and the other students are in a prisoner's dilemma, which is shown here. If you and Jill (a representative other student) each study 4 hours, each of you earns a point grade of 85, which is a B (box 4). If each of you studies 2 hours, each of you earns a point grade of 65, which is a B (box 1). Box 1 is preferred over box 4 because you get the same letter grade in each box, but you study less in box 1 than in box 4.

If you study 4 hours while Jill studies 2 hours, your point grade rises to 85 and Jill's point grade remains at 65. In this case, 85 is an A, and 65 is a C (box 2). You are better off and Jill is worse off.

If you study 2 hours while Jill studies 4 hours, Jill's point grade rises to 85 and your point grade remains at 65. Jill earns a letter grade of A, and you earn a letter grade of C.

No matter what Jill decides to do—study 2 or 4 hours—it is always better for you to study 4 hours (assuming that the costs of studying additional hours are less than the benefits of studying additional hours). The same holds for Jill. Our outcome, then, is box 4, where both you and Jill study 4 hours.

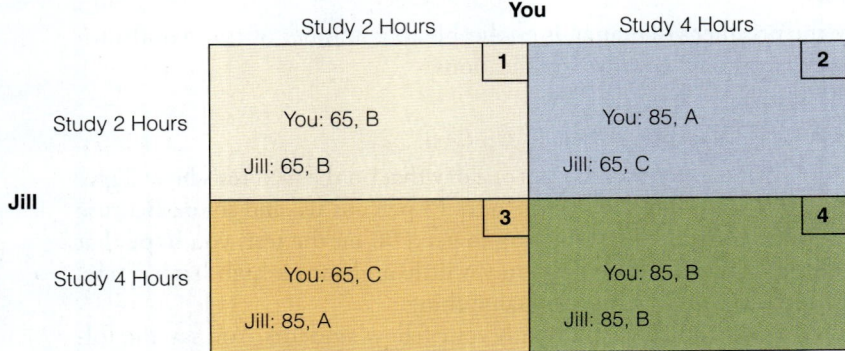

Ideally, what you and Jill need is a way to enforce your agreement not to study more than two hours. How might students do this? One way is to party. (That's right, party.) If you can get all the students in your class together and party, you can be fairly sure that no one is studying. In general, students in the same class understand (1) that some professors set aside some percentage of As for the top students in the class (no matter how low the top is) and (2) that the students in the class are all in a prisoner's dilemma. They realize that it would be better for them to cooperate and study less than to compete and study more. Instead of actually entering into an agreement to study less (sign on the dotted line), they think up ways to keep the studying time down. One way to keep the studying time down—one way to enforce the implicit and unspoken agreement not to study too much—is to do things with others that do not entail studying. One such institution that satisfies all requirements is partying: everyone is together, not studying.

24-6b The Arms Race

During much of the Cold War, the United States and the Soviet Union engaged in an arms race. Each country was producing armaments directed at the other. Occasionally, representatives of the two countries would meet and try to slow down the race. The United States would agree to cut armaments production if the Soviet Union did, and vice versa. Many arms analysts generally agreed that the arms agreements between the United States and the Soviet Union were unsuccessful. In other words, representatives of the two countries would meet and enter into an agreement not to compete so heavily on arms production, but then the countries would just keep competing.

The two countries were in a prisoner's dilemma. When both the United States and the Soviet Union were competing on arms production, they were in box 4 of Exhibit 10, each receiving a utility level of 7. Their collective objective was to move from box 4 to box 1, with each cooperating with the other and reducing its production of armaments. In box 1, each country received a utility level of 10. The arms agreements that the United States and the Soviet Union entered into were attempts to get to box 1.

Of course, after the agreement was signed, each country had an incentive to cheat. Certainly, the United States would be better off if it increased its armaments production while the Soviet Union cut back its production. Then the United States could establish clear military superiority over the Soviet Union. The same held for the Soviet Union with respect to the United States.

The payoff matrix in Exhibit 10 makes it easy to see that the best strategy for both the United States and the Soviet Union was to compete. So the two countries ended up in box 4, racing to outproduce the other in arms.

24-6c Speed Limit Laws

Envision a world with no law against speeding. In such a world, you and everyone else speeds. With everyone speeding, a good number of accidents occur each day, some of which may involve you. In time, everyone decides that something has to be done about the speeding. It is just too dangerous, everyone admits, to let it continue.

Someone offers a proposal: "Let's agree that we will post signs on the road that state the maximum speed. Furthermore, let's agree here and now that we will all obey the speed limits." The proposal sounds like a good one, and everyone agrees to it.

Of course, as we know by now, once the agreement not to speed is made, we have a prisoner's dilemma. Each person will be better off if he (and he alone) speeds while everyone

EXHIBIT 10

An Arms Race

In the days of the Cold War, the United States and the Soviet Union were said to be in an arms race. Actually, the arms race was a result of the two countries being in a prisoner's dilemma. Start with each country racing to produce more military goods than the other country; that is, each country is in box 4. In their attempt to move to box 1, they enter into an arms agreement (to reduce the rate at which they produce arms). But no matter what the Soviet Union does (hold to the arms agreement or break it), it is always better for the United States to break the agreement. The same holds for the Soviet Union with respect to the United States. The two countries end up in box 4. (*Note*: In the exhibit, the higher the number, the better the position is for the country.)

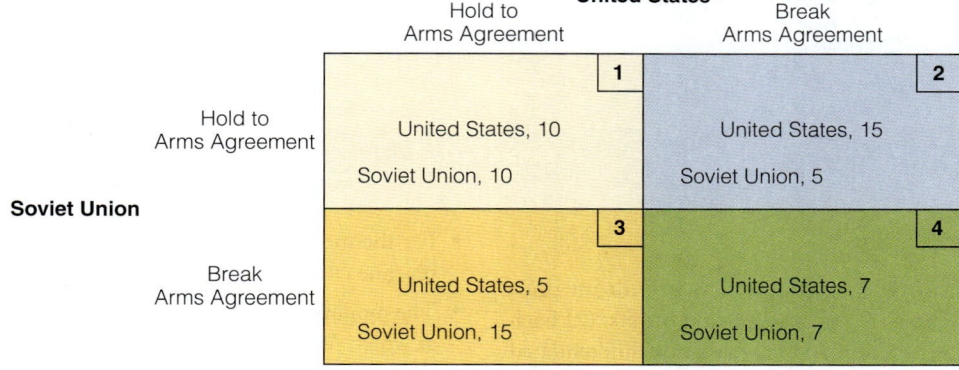

else obeys the speed limit. In the beginning, everyone agrees to the speed limit; in the end, however, everyone breaks it.

What is missing, of course, is an effective enforcement mechanism. To move the speeders out of the classic prisoner's dilemma box (box 4 in our earlier examples) to box 1, someone or something has to punish people who do not cooperate. A law against speeding—backed up by the police and the court system—solves the prisoner's dilemma. The law, the police, and the court system change the payoff for cheating on the agreement.

Office Hours

"Are Firms (as Sellers) Either Price Takers or Price Searchers?"

Student: Now that I have studied four different market structures, I want to see whether I have some things correct. First, am I correct that all firms—no matter the market structure—will seek to produce that quantity of output at which $MR = MC$?

Instructor: Yes, that's correct.

Student: And is it correct that a firm either faces a horizontal demand curve and is a price taker or faces a downward-sloping demand curve and is a price searcher? In other words, is it true that a firm is either one of two things: a price taker or a price searcher? To put it differently: (1) Perfectly competitive firms are price takers; and (2) monopoly, monopolistically competitive, and oligopolistic firms are price searchers.

Instructor: Yes, that's correct. To be more specific, if a firm is a price taker, it does not have to lower its price to sell additional units of a good. It can sell 100 units at $4 per unit, and it can sell 200 units at $4 a unit. But for a price searcher, the only way it can sell additional units of a good is by lowering its price. In other words, it can sell 100 units at $4 per unit, but if it wants to sell 101 units, it has to charge less than $4 per unit.

Student: As for the issue of resource allocative efficiency ($P = MC$), am I right that a price taker is resource allocative efficient but a price searcher is not, unless it can and does practice perfect price discrimination?

Instructor: Yes, that's correct.

Points to Remember

1. All firms seek to produce the quantity of output at which $MR = MC$.
2. A firm faces either a horizontal demand curve or a downward-sloping demand curve; that is, a firm is either a price taker or a price searcher, respectively.
3. Perfectly competitive firms are price takers, and monopoly, monopolistically competitive, and oligopolistic firms are price searchers.
4. A price taker is resource allocative efficient, and a price searcher is not, unless it can and does practice perfect price discrimination.

Chapter Summary

Monopolistic Competition

- The theory of monopolistic competition is built on three assumptions: (1) There are many sellers and buyers. (2) Each firm in the industry produces and sells a slightly differentiated product. (3) Entry and exit are easy.
- The monopolistic competitor is a price searcher.
- For the monopolistic competitor, $P > MR$ and the marginal revenue curve lies below the demand curve.
- The monopolistic competitor produces the quantity of output at which $MR = MC$. It charges the highest price per unit for this output.

- Unlike the perfectly competitive firm, the monopolistic competitor does not exhibit resource allocative efficiency.
- The monopolistically competitive firm does not earn profits in the long run (because of easy entry into the industry), unless it can successfully differentiate its product (e.g., by brand name) in the minds of buyers.

Excess Capacity Theorem

- The excess capacity theorem states that a monopolistic competitor will, in equilibrium, produce an output smaller than that at which average total costs (unit costs) are minimized. Thus, the monopolistic competitor is not productive efficient.

Oligopoly Assumptions

- All of the many different oligopoly theories are built on the following assumptions: (1) There are few sellers and many buyers. (2) Firms produce and sell either homogeneous or differentiated products. (3) The barriers to entry are significant.
- One of the key characteristics of oligopolistic firms is their interdependence.

Cartel Theory

- The cartel theory assumes that firms in an oligopolistic industry act in a manner consistent with there being only one firm in the industry.
- Four problems are associated with cartels: (1) the problem of forming the cartel, (2) the problem of formulating policy, (3) the problem of entry into the industry, and (4) the problem of cheating.
- Firms that enter into a cartel agreement are in a prisoner's dilemma situation, where individually rational behavior leads to a jointly inefficient outcome.

The Theory of Contestable Markets

- The conditions for a contestable market are as follows: (1) Entry into the market is easy, and exit from it is costless. (2) New firms entering the market can produce the product at the same cost as current firms. (3) Firms exiting the market can easily dispose of their fixed assets by selling them elsewhere (less depreciation).
- Compared with orthodox market structure theories, the theory of contestable markets places more emphasis on the issue of entry into and exit from an industry and less emphasis on the number of sellers in an industry.

Game Theory

- Game theory is a mathematical technique used to analyze the behavior of decision makers (1) who try to reach an optimal position through game playing or the use of strategic behavior, (2) who are fully aware of the interactive nature of the process at hand, and (3) who anticipate the moves of other decision makers.
- The prisoner's dilemma game illustrates individually rational behavior leading to a jointly inefficient outcome.

Key Terms and Concepts

Monopolistic Competition
Excess Capacity Theorem
Oligopoly
Concentration Ratio
Cartel Theory
Cartel
Game Theory
Contestable Market

Questions and Problems

1. What, if anything, do all firms in all four market structures have in common?
2. "Excess capacity is the price we pay for product differentiation." Evaluate this statement in terms of monopolistic competition.
3. Why might a producer use a designer label to differentiate her product from that of another producer?
4. Will there be profits in the long run in a monopolistically competitive market? Explain your answer.
5. Would you expect cartel formation to be more likely in industries composed of a few firms or in those which include many firms? Explain your answer.
6. Does the theory of contestable markets shed any light on oligopoly pricing theories? Explain your answer.

7. There are 60 types or varieties of product X on the market. Is product X made in a monopolistically competitive market? Explain your answer.

8. Why does the interdependence of firms play a major role in oligopoly but not in perfect competition or monopolistic competition?

9. Concentration ratios have often been used to note the tightness of an oligopoly market. A high concentration ratio indicates a tight oligopoly market, and a low concentration ratio indicates a loose oligopoly market. Would you expect firms in tight markets to reap higher profits, on average, than firms in loose markets? Would it matter if the markets were contestable? Explain your answers.

10. Market theories are said to have the happy consequence of getting individuals to think in more focused and analytical ways. Is this effect true for you? Give examples to illustrate.

11. Give an example of a prisoner's dilemma situation other than the ones mentioned in this chapter.

12. How are oligopoly and monopolistic competition alike? How are they different?

Working with Numbers and Graphs

1. Diagrammatically identify the quantity of output a monopolistic competitor produces and the price it charges.

2. Diagrammatically identify a monopolistic competitor that is incurring losses.

3. Total industry sales are $105 million. The top four firms account for sales of $10 million, $9 million, $8 million, and $5 million, respectively. What is the four-firm concentration ratio?

4. Refer to the accompanying figure. Because of a cartel agreement, a firm has been assigned a production quota of q_2 units. The cartel price is P_2. What do the firm's profits equal if it adheres to the cartel agreement? What do the firm's profits equal if it breaks the cartel agreement and produces q_3?

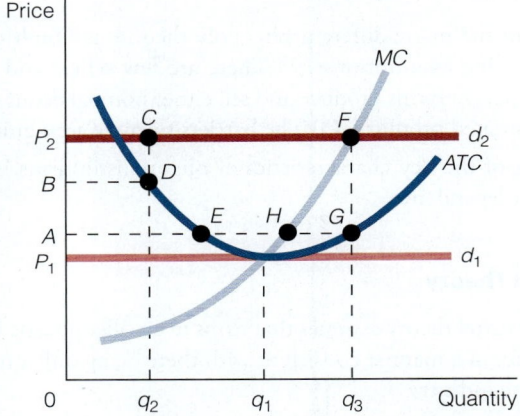

CHAPTER 25
Government and Product Markets: Antitrust and Regulation

Introduction
In Washington, D.C., you may see the building that houses the Department of Justice. One of the many duties of the Justice Department is the enforcement of the country's antitrust laws, whose stated purpose is to control monopoly and to preserve and promote competition. Does it matter to your life whether the Justice Department does a good, bad, or mediocre job of controlling monopoly and preserving and promoting competition? It matters in more ways than you can imagine.

25-1 Antitrust

A monopoly (1) produces a smaller output than is produced by a perfectly competitive firm with the same revenue and cost considerations, (2) charges a higher price, and (3) causes a deadweight loss. Some economists argue that, on the basis of these facts, government should place restrictions on monopolies. In addition, government should restrict the activities of cartels because the objective of a cartel is to behave as if it were a monopoly.

Other economists argue that monopolies do not have as much market power as some people think: Witness the competition some monopolies face from broadly defined substitutes and imports. As for cartels, they usually contain the seeds of their own destruction, so it is only a matter of (a usually short) time before they fall apart naturally.

We are concerned not with the debate about whether to restrict monopoly power but, rather, with how government deals with it—specifically, through antitrust laws and regulation. We examine antitrust law in this section and regulation in the next. **Antitrust law** is legislation passed for the stated purpose of controlling monopoly power and preserving and promoting competition. Let's look at the uses and effects of a few of the major antitrust acts.

Antitrust Law
Legislation passed for the stated purpose of controlling monopoly power and preserving and promoting competition.

25-1a Antitrust Acts

The following are a few key acts whose provisions constitute U.S. antitrust policy:

- Sherman Act (1890)
- Clayton Act (1914)
- Federal Trade Commission Act (1914)
- Robinson–Patman Act (1936)
- Wheeler–Lea Act (1938)
- Celler–Kefauver Antimerger Act (1950)

Sherman Act (1890) The Sherman Act was passed to deal with mergers of companies. (A *merger* occurs when two companies combine under single ownership of control.) At that time, the organization that companies formed by combining was called a **trust**, a term that gave us the word *antitrust*.

The Sherman Act contains two major provisions:

1. "Every contract, combination in the form of trust or otherwise, or conspiracy, in restraint of trade or commerce among the several states, or with foreign nations, is hereby declared to be illegal."
2. "Every person who shall monopolize, or attempt to monopolize, or combine or conspire with any other person or persons to monopolize any part of the trade or commerce . . . shall be guilty of a misdemeanor."

Some people have argued that the provisions of the Sherman Act are vague. For example, the act never explains which specific acts constitute a restraint of trade, although it declares such acts illegal.

Clayton Act (1914) The Clayton Act makes the following business practices illegal when their effects "may be to substantially lessen competition or tend to create a monopoly":

1. *Price discrimination.* An example is charging different customers different prices for the same product when the price differences are not related to cost differences.
2. *Exclusive dealing.* This is selling to a retailer on the condition that the retailer not carry any rival products.
3. *Tying contracts.* Arrangements made whereby the sale of one product is dependent on the purchase of some other product or products.
4. *The acquisition of competing companies' stock if the acquisition reduces competition.* Some say a major loophole of the act is that it does not ban the acquisition of competing companies' physical assets and therefore does not prevent anticompetitive mergers from doing what they are intended to do.

The Clayton Act also makes the following arrangement illegal at all times, not just when its effects "may be to substantially lessen competition":

5. *Interlocking directorates.* In this type of arrangement, the directors of one company sit on the board of another company in the same industry.

Trust
A combination of firms that come together to act as a monopolist.

Federal Trade Commission Act (1914) The Federal Trade Commission Act contains the broadest and most general language of any antitrust act. It declares illegal "unfair methods of competition in commerce." In essence, it declares illegal acts that are judged to be "too aggressive" in competition. The problem is how to decide what is fair and what is unfair, what is aggressive but not too aggressive. This act also set up the Federal Trade Commission (FTC) to deal with "unfair methods of competition."

Robinson–Patman Act (1936) The Robinson–Patman Act was passed in an attempt to decrease the failure rate of small businesses by protecting them from the competition of large and growing chain stores. The large chain stores were receiving price discounts from suppliers and, in turn, passing the discounts on to their customers. As a result, small businesses had a difficult time competing, and many of them failed. The Robinson–Patman Act prohibits suppliers from offering special discounts to large chain stores unless they also offer the discounts to everyone else. Many economists believe that, rather than preserving and strengthening competition, the Robinson–Patman Act limits it. The act seems to be more concerned about a certain group of competitors than about the process of competition and the buying public as a whole.

Wheeler–Lea Act (1938) The Wheeler–Lea Act empowers the Federal Trade Commission to deal with false and deceptive acts or practices. Major moves in this area have been against advertising that the FTC has deemed false and deceptive.

Celler–Kefauver Antimerger Act (1950) The Celler–Kefauver Act was designed to close the merger loophole in the Clayton Act. (See point 4 in the earlier list discussing the Clayton Act.) The Celler–Kefauver Act bans anticompetitive mergers that occur as a result of one company's acquiring the physical assets of another company.

Economics 24/7

The DOJ, FTC, Google, and Facebook

In 2020, the Department of Justice (DOJ) sued Google, and the Federal Trade Commission (FTC) sued Facebook. On October 20, 2020, the DOJ, along with 11 State Attorneys General, filed a civil antitrust lawsuit against Google. The suit claims that Google has a monopoly position in both the search and search advertising markets and that it uses anticompetitive and exclusionary practices to maintain its monopoly positions, in defiance of the Sherman Act.

Here are some of anticompetitive and exclusionary practices the DOJ claims Google practices:

- Google enters into exclusivity agreements with firms to preinstall Google Search on their devices and forbid the installation of competing search services.

(Continued)

- It enters into tying contracts and other arrangements that force preinstallation of its search applications in prime locations on mobile devices and makes them undeletable, regardless of consumer preference.
- It entered into a long-term agreement with Apple that required Google to be the default and de facto exclusive general search engine on Apple's Safari browser and other Apple search tools.
- It generally uses its monopoly profits to buy preferential treatment for its search engine on devices, web browsers, and other search access points.[1]

On December 9, 2020, the Federal Trade Commission (FTC) and 46 states sued Facebook. The FTC alleges that Facebook "is illegally maintaining its personal social networking monopoly through a years-long course of anticompetitive conduct."[2] According to the FTC, Facebook's acquisitions of its rivals Instagram (in 2012) and WhatsApp (in 2014), along with its imposition of certain anticompetitive conditions on software developers, are all part of a systematic strategy to eliminate threats to its monopoly position in social networking.

With respect to Instagram, the FTC claims that Facebook saw Instagram as a rapidly growing start-up company that emerged at a critical time in personal social networking competition when consumers were embracing photo sharing. The FTC complaint goes on to allege that "Facebook executives, including CEO Mark Zuckerberg, quickly recognized that Instagram was a vibrant and innovative personal social network and an existential threat to Facebook's monopoly power."[3] So what did Facebook do in the face of this "existential threat"? The FTC complaint alleges that Facebook initially "tried to compete with Instagram by improving its own offerings, but ultimately chose to buy Instagram rather than compete with it."[4]

The FTC complaint also alleges that Facebook, over many years, "has imposed anticompetitive conditions on third-party software developers' access to valuable interconnections to its platform, such as the application programming interfaces (APIs) that allow developers' apps to interface with Facebook. In particular, Facebook allegedly has made key APIs available to third-party applications *only* on the condition that they refrain from developing competing functionalities, and from connecting with or promoting other social networking services."[5]

As of this writing, we don't know what the outcome of these suits will be. Google and Facebook strongly deny the charges made by both the DOJ and FTC and plan to challenge them in court. It's likely that it will take years before a final decision in these cases is rendered.

[1.] DOJ Press Release, October 20, 2020, *Justice Department Sues Monopolist Google for Violating Antitrust Laws*
[2.] FTC Press Release, December 9, 2020, *FTC Sues Facebook for Illegal Monopolization*.
[3.] Ibid.
[4.] Ibid.
[5.] Ibid.

25-1b Unsettled Points in Antitrust Policy

Where the lines should be drawn in implementing antitrust policy is not always clear. Which firms should be allowed to enter into a merger and which should be prohibited? What constitutes restraint of trade? Which firms should be treated as monopolists and broken into smaller firms? Which firms should be left alone?

As you might guess, not everyone answers these questions the same way. In short, some points of antitrust policy are still unsettled.

Does the Definition of the Market Matter? How a market is defined—broadly or narrowly—helps determine whether a firm is considered a monopoly. For example, in an important antitrust suit in 1945, a court ruled that Alcoa (Aluminum Company of America) was a monopoly because it had 90 percent of the virgin aluminum ingot market. If Alcoa's market had been broadened to include stainless steel, copper, tin, nickel, and zinc (some of the goods competing with aluminum), it is unlikely that Alcoa would have been ruled a monopoly.

Later court rulings have tended to define markets broadly rather than narrowly. For instance, in the DuPont case in 1956, the market relevant to DuPont was ruled to be the flexible wrapping materials market rather than the narrower cellophane market.

Concentration Ratios

Concentration ratios have often been used to gauge the amount of competition in an industry, but their use presents two major problems. First, concentration ratios do not address the issue of foreign competition. For example, the four-firm concentration ratio in an industry may be very high, but the four firms that make up the concentration ratio may still face stiff competition from abroad. Second, a four-firm concentration ratio can remain stable over time despite competition among the four major firms in the industry.

In 1982, the Justice Department replaced the four- and eight-firm concentration ratios with the Herfindahl index, although it, too, is subject to some of the same criticisms as the concentration ratios. The **Herfindahl index**, which measures the degree of concentration in an industry, is equal to the sum of the squares of the market shares of each firm in the industry. That is,

$$\text{Herfindahl index} = (S_1)^2 + (S_2)^2 + \cdots + (S_n)^2$$

where S_1 through S_n are the respective market shares of firms 1 through n. For example, if 10 firms are in an industry and if each firm has a 10 percent market share, then the Herfindahl index is 1,000 ($10^2 + 10^2 + 10^2 + 10^2 + 10^2 + 10^2 + 10^2 + 10^2 + 10^2 + 10^2 = 1,000$).

Exhibit 1 compares the Herfindahl index with the four-firm concentration ratio. When the four-firm concentration ratio is used, the top four firms (A–D) have a 48 percent market share, which generally is thought to describe a concentrated industry. A merger between any of the top four firms and any other firm (e.g., between firm B and firm G in Exhibit 1) would give the newly merged firm a greater market share than any existing firm and usually incur frowns at the Justice Department.

The Herfindahl index for the industry is 932, however, and the Justice Department generally considers any number less than 1,000 representative of an *un*concentrated (or competitive) industry. An index between 1,500 and 2,500 is considered representative of a moderately concentrated industry, and an index greater than 2,500 is representative of a highly concentrated industry.

When is the Justice Department likely to take antitrust actions? Primarily when transactions increase the HHI [the Herfindahl-Hirschman Index, another name for the Herfindahl Index]

Herfindahl Index
An index that measures the degree of concentration in an industry, equal to the sum of the squares of the market shares of each firm in the industry.

EXHIBIT 1

A Comparison of the Four-Firm Concentration Ratio and the Herfindahl Index

According to the old method (in this case, the four-firm concentration ratio), the top four firms in the industry shown have a 48 percent market share. The Justice Department would therefore likely frown on a proposed merger between any of the top four firms and any other firm (including another one of the top four firms). However, the Herfindahl index of 932 is representative of an unconcentrated industry.

Firms	Market Share (%)
A	15
B	12
C	11
D	10
E	8
F	7
G	7
H	6
I	6
J	6
K	6
L	6

Old Method: Four-Firm Concentration Ratio

15% + 12% + 11% + 10% = 48%

New Method: Herfindahl Index

Square the market share of each firm and then add:

$(15)^2 + (12)^2 + (11)^2 + (10)^2 + (8)^2 + (7)^2 + (7)^2 + (6)^2 + (6)^2 + (6)^2 + (6)^2 + (6)^2 = 932$

by more than 200 points in highly concentrated markets [markets with an index greater than 2,500].

To illustrate, suppose seven firms are in an industry. Two of the firms, A and B, want to merge. The market share of firm A is 35 percent, and the market share of firm B is 34 percent. The market shares for the other five firms in the industry are 10 percent, 10 percent, 5 percent, 5 percent, and 1 percent, respectively. Then the Herfindahl index for this industry is 2,632 ($35^2 + 34^2 + 10^2 + 10^2 + 5^2 + 5^2 + 1^2$).

If the merger is approved, there will be 6, not 7, firms in the industry. Moreover, the market share of the merged firm (when A and B form one firm) will be 69 percent. The Herfindahl index after the merger will be 5,012. In other words, the increase will be 2,380 points if the firms merge. With this substantial increase in the index, the proposed merger is likely to be blocked.

Innovation and Concentration Ratios Because innovation and technical change are so important to our economic well-being, some economists argue that concentration ratios should not play so large a role in determining a merger's approval. The merger's effect on innovation should also be taken into account. There is some evidence that antitrust authorities accept this line of thinking.

In the past, small firms in highly competitive markets with many rivals were thought to have a stronger incentive to innovate than firms in markets where only a few firms existed and where each firm had sizable market power. Increasingly, however, these small competitive firms seem often to face a greater risk of innovation than firms with substantial market power, and therefore they tend to innovate less.

To illustrate, consider a market with 100 firms, each of which supplies one-hundredth of the market. Suppose one of these firms invests heavily in research and develops a new product or process. It has to worry about any of its 99 rivals soon developing a similar innovation and therefore reducing the value of its innovation. In contrast, if a firm is one of four firms and has substantial market power, it doesn't face as much so-called innovative risk. It has only three, not 99, rivals to worry about. And, of course, the less likely it is that competitors can render one's own innovations less valuable, the higher the expected return from innovating will be.

Today, antitrust authorities say that they consider the benefits of both competition and innovation when ruling on proposed mergers. On the one hand, increased competition lowers prices for consumers. On the other hand, monopoly power may yield more innovation. If it does, then the lower prices brought about through increased competition have to be weighed against the increased innovation that may come about through greater market concentration and monopoly power.

Economics 24/7

Thomas Edison and Hollywood

Thomas Alva Edison was born in 1847 and died in 1931. In his 84 years of life, Edison was granted 1,093 patents. Almost everyone knows the role Edison played in the development of electric light and power, but not everyone knows the role he played in indirectly and unwittingly making Hollywood the film capital of the world.

Our story begins with an Edison invention, a machine called the kinetophonograph, which showed a moving picture that was synchronized with a phonograph record. Later, Edison invented the kinetoscope, a device that allowed users to deposit a coin and watch a short motion picture through a small hole.

After inventing the kinetophonograph and kinetoscope, Edison went on to construct the first building that was used solely to make movies. A hole in the ceiling of the building allowed the sun to shine through and illuminate the stage. The entire building was placed on a set of tracks so that it could be moved around to follow the sun. The first film that Edison produced was a 15-minute movie called *The Great Train Robbery*. Over the years, he produced more than 2,000 short films.

There is some evidence that Edison and a few other people tried to gain complete control over the movie industry in its early days. Edison played a critical role in putting together the Movie Trust, sometimes called the Edison Trust, a group of 10 film producers and distributors. The Movie Trust reportedly tried to eliminate its competition. First, it entered into an exclusive contract with Eastman Kodak Company, which manufactured film, to sell film only to it. Second, it refused to lease or sell equipment to certain filmmakers and theater owners. One of the independent movie producers whom the Movie Trust tried to run out of the industry was Carl Laemmle. Laemmle and some other movie producers decided to leave the East Coast, where the Movie Trust had the

greatest control over the industry, and went to the West Coast, specifically to southern California. Others soon followed. The rush of independent filmmakers to southern California set the stage for the development of Hollywood as the film capital of the world. In 1917, the Movie Trust was dissolved by court order, but by then, the movie industry had a new home. Laemmle, for example, founded Universal Studios in Hollywood in 1912.

Whether Hollywood would be the film capital of the world had it not been for the Movie Trust is doubtful. Without the exclusionary and anticompetitive tactics of the Movie Trust, the film capital of the world would probably be on the East Coast of the United States, very likely in or near New York City.

25-1c Antitrust and Mergers

There are three basic types of mergers:

1. A **horizontal merger** is a merger between firms that are selling similar products in the same market. For example, suppose both companies A and B produce cars. If the two companies combine under single ownership of control, then the merger is horizontal.

2. A **vertical merger** is a merger between companies in the same industry but at different stages of the production process. A vertical merger occurs between companies, one of which buys (or sells) something from (or to) the other. For example, suppose company C, which produces cars, buys tires from company D. If the two companies combine under single ownership of control, then the merger is vertical.

3. A **conglomerate merger** is a merger between companies in different industries. For example, if company E, in the car industry, and company F, in the pharmaceutical industry, combine under single ownership of control, then the result is a conglomerate.

Of the three types of mergers—vertical, horizontal, and conglomerate—the federal government looks most carefully at proposed horizontal mergers. These mergers are the most likely to change the degree of concentration, or competition, in an industry. For example, if General

Horizontal Merger
A merger between firms that are selling similar products in the same market.

Vertical Merger
A merger between companies in the same industry but at different stages of the production process.

Conglomerate Merger
A merger between companies in different industries.

Motors (manufacturer of cars) and Ford Motor Company (cars) were to merge horizontally, then competition in the car industry would be likely to decrease by more than if General Motors (cars) and BF Goodrich (tires) were to merge vertically. In the latter case, the competition among car companies and among tire companies is likely to be the same after the merger as it was before. (However, that is not necessarily the case, so the government does not always approve vertical mergers.)

25-1d Common Misconceptions About Antitrust Policy

Some people believe that all the big issues in antitrust policy have been settled. This belief is simply not true. For example, predatory pricing practices—such as selling a good for a low price in order to eliminate competitors—are deemed illegal. But difficult questions arise: How low must a price be before it is deemed predatory? How long must the low price persist before it is deemed predatory?

Also, in a monopoly case, the relevant market is not always obvious. For example, is the relevant market for carbonated soft drinks the carbonated soft-drink market? Or is it the much larger beverage market (which includes carbonated soft drinks, water, juices, etc.)?

Finally, mergers and tying arrangements are deemed illegal if they "substantially reduce competition," but how much competition has to be reduced before it is "substantial"?

25-1e Network Monopolies

A network connects things. A telephone network connects telephones; the Internet (which is a network of networks) connects computers; and a bank network connects, among other things, automated teller machines (ATMs).

A **network good** is a good whose value increases as the expected number of units sold increases. A telephone is a network good. You buy a telephone to network with other people. It has little value to you if you expect only 100 people to buy telephones, but its value increases for you if you expect thousands or millions of people to buy telephones. Software is also a network good, in the sense that if persons *A* and *B* both buy software *X*, they can then easily exchange documents. As new buyers buy a network good, the present owners of the good receive greater benefits because the network connects them to more people. For example, if persons *C* and *D* also buy software *X*, persons *A* and *B* benefit more because they can exchange documents with two more people.

The production and sale of a network good can lead to monopoly. Suppose three companies (*A*, *B*, and *C*) make some version of network good *X*. Company *A* makes the most popular version, so its good is said to have the greatest network value. Consequently, people who are thinking of buying good *X* buy it from company *A*. As more people purchase good *X* from company *A*, the network value increases, prompting even more people to buy good *X* from company *A* rather than from the other two companies. Eventually, the customers of companies *B* and *C* may switch to company *A*, and at some point, almost everyone buys good *X* from company *A*. Company *A* is then a network monopoly.

Antitrust Policy for Network Monopolies Currently, the antitrust authorities move against a network monopoly on the basis of how it behaves, not because of what it is. For example, the authorities would not issue a complaint against company *A* in our example unless it undertook predatory or exclusionary practices to *maintain* its monopoly position.

Innovation and Network Monopolies Recall that economists are undecided as to whether market share helps or hinders innovation. For example, one firm among four firms

---

Network Good
A good whose value increases as the expected number of units sold increases.

may have less innovative risk than one firm among 100. Therefore, the firm with a larger market share would innovate more, *ceteris paribus*. Presumably, a network monopoly will have a large market share and therefore should be a major innovator.

Actually, the situation may be different for network monopolies because high switching costs sometimes accompany a network monopoly. To illustrate, suppose firm A produces network good A. Suppose further that network good A begins to sell quite well, and because it is a network good, its robust sales increase its value to potential customers. Then potential customers soon turn into actual customers, and before long, good A has set the market, or industry, standard.

Because network good A is now the industry standard and because network goods (especially those related to the high-tech industries) are sometimes difficult to learn, good A may have a lock on the market. Specifically, a **lock-in effect** increases the costs of switching from good A to another good. Because of the relatively high switching costs, good A has some staying power in the market. Firm A, the producer of good A, thus has staying power too, possibly causing firm A to rest on its laurels. Instead of innovating—instead of trying to outcompete its existing and future rivals with better production processes or better products—it may do very little. Firm A will realize that the high switching costs keep customers from changing to a different network good. Some economists suggest that, in this environment, the network monopoly may have little reason to innovate.

Lock-In Effect
The situation in which a product or technology becomes the standard and is difficult or impossible to dislodge from that role.

Economics 24/7

High-Priced Ink Cartridges and Expensive Minibars

Shopping for a printer for your computer, you see one priced at $169. "That's a good price," you think, so you buy it. Later, you learn that you have to pay $43 for an ink cartridge. The printer wasn't so well priced after all.

You spend the night at a hotel. Once in your room, you look in the minibar and decide to eat a small bag of almonds. You learn later, after looking at your bill, that the small bag of almonds came with a price tag of $6.

You sign up with a cell phone company, decide on a plan, and get a free cell phone. Later, you learn that for every minute you go over your allotted monthly number of minutes, you pay 33¢.

Because of such everyday occurrences, some economists today are talking about the hidden-fee economy—an economy

in which many main items for sale (a printer, a hotel room, cell phone service) come with high hidden fees that you did not expect when you purchased the main item.

According to two economists, David Laibson and Xavier Gabaix, firms reap certain benefits through hidden fees. (There are certain costs, too, but sometimes the benefits are greater than the costs.) For example,[1] suppose that hotel X rents its rooms for $80 a night and has some hidden fees: $12 for parking, $6 for a small bag of almonds from the minibar, and $3 for a local call. Suppose also that

---
[1] The source of the material in this feature (and the source of the example) is Christopher Shea, "The Hidden Economy," *The Boston Globe*, June 27, 2006.

hotel Y rents its rooms for $95 a night and has no high hidden fees. It does not charge for parking or for a local call, and the small bag of almonds comes at the price that it sells for at a grocery store. What are the major differences between the two hotels? On the basis of just the price of a room, hotel X is cheaper than hotel Y. Add in hidden and unexpectedly high fees, however, and hotel X is a culprit while hotel Y is not.

The natural question to ask is, Why doesn't hotel Y simply advertise the fact that its competitor, hotel X, is trying to dupe its customers by charging high hidden fees? (The ad might read, "Sure, hotel X has cheaper rooms, but what about all the hidden fees?") According to Laibson and Gabaix, that strategy could backfire because of one of the two types of customers who frequent hotel X. One type of customer is unaware of the hidden fees and initially responds to the lower room rate of hotel X. With this customer, the strategy of pointing out the hidden fees of hotel X will be successful. Another type of customer is sophisticated when it comes to sellers' tactics. This customer realizes that, if she doesn't park at hotel X, doesn't eat anything from the minibar, and makes calls on her cell phone instead of on the hotel telephone, she can then get a lower priced room at hotel X. The ad by hotel Y simply notifies the sophisticated customer that she can get a good deal at the hotel with the hidden fees, as long as she doesn't purchase the goods or services that come with the high hidden fees.

So hotel Y both gains and loses with its ad pointing out the high hidden fees of hotel X. It gains the clueless customers ("Thanks for telling me about those hidden fees!"), but it may lose some sophisticated customers ("Thanks for telling me about the lower priced rooms your competitor is offering!"). If hotel Y thinks that it will lose more sophisticated customers than it will gain clueless ones, it will not run the ad. Instead, it may simply join the ranks of hotels like hotel X and lower its room rate and increase the use of high hidden fees.

But consider something else. Barry Nalebuff, a professor of business strategy, has noted that a firm that charges hidden fees incurs a cost and that cost comes in the form of customers getting angry at the hidden fees. Angry customers, Nalebuff says, often turn their backs on sellers they are angry with. In other words, they seek out other (perhaps more up-front and straightforward) sellers to buy from.

In the end, it becomes a matter of a seller having to consider both the benefits and the costs of a hidden-fees strategy. Perhaps the benefits initially outweigh the costs, but there is no guarantee that, in time, the costs won't rise above the benefits.

(Answers to Self-Test questions are in Answers to Self-Test Questions at the back of the book.)

1. Why does it matter whether a market is defined broadly or narrowly for purposes of antitrust policy?
2. Suppose that 20 firms are in an industry and that each firm has a 5 percent market share. What is the four-firm concentration ratio for this industry? What is the Herfindahl index?
3. What is the advantage of the Herfindahl index over the four- and eight-firm concentration ratios? Explain your answer.

25-2 Regulation

This section examines the various types of regulation, theories of regulation, the stated objectives of regulatory agencies, and the effects of regulation on natural and other monopolies.

25-2a The Case of Natural Monopoly

We know that if economies of scale are so pronounced or so large in an industry that only one firm can survive, that firm is a *natural monopoly*. Firms that supply local electricity, gas, and water service are usually considered natural monopolies.

In Exhibit 2, the market consists of one firm, which produces Q_1 units of output at an average total cost of ATC_1. (Q_1 is the output at which $MR = MC$; to simplify the diagram, the MR curve is not shown.) At Q_1, the allocation of resources is inefficient. Resource allocative efficiency exists when the marginal benefit to demanders of the resources used in the goods they buy equals the marginal cost to suppliers of the resources used in the production of the goods they sell. In Exhibit 2, resource allocative efficiency exists at Q_2, corresponding to the point where the demand curve intersects the MC curve.

There are two ways to reach the higher, efficient quantity of output, Q_2: (1) The firm currently producing Q_1 could increase its output to Q_2. (2) Another firm could enter the market and produce Q_3—the difference between Q_2 and Q_1. Each way has its associated costs. If the firm currently in the market increases its production to Q_2, it incurs average total costs of ATC_2. If, instead, a new firm enters the market and produces Q_3, it incurs an average total cost of ATC_3. In this way, both firms together produce Q_2, but the new firm incurs average total costs of ATC_3 whereas the existing firm incurs average total costs of ATC_1.

As long as the objective is to increase output to the level of resource allocative efficiency, it is cheaper (total costs are lower) to have the firm currently in the market increase its output to Q_2 than to have two firms together produce Q_2. So the situation in Exhibit 2 is a natural monopoly situation. A natural monopoly exists when one firm can supply the entire output demanded at lower cost than two or more firms can. A natural monopoly will evolve over time as the low-cost producer undercuts its competitors.

Some economists say that the natural monopolist will charge the monopoly price. In Exhibit 3, the natural monopoly firm produces quantity Q_1, at which marginal revenue equals marginal cost, and charges price P_1, which is the highest price per unit consistent with the output it produces. Because it charges the monopoly price, some people argue that the natural monopoly firm should be regulated. The form that the regulation should take is a question addressed in the next section.

EXHIBIT 2

The Natural Monopoly Situation

The only existing firm produces Q_1 at an average total cost of ATC_1. (Q_1 is the output at which $MR = MC$; to simplify the diagram, the MR curve is not shown.) Resource allocative efficiency exists at Q_2. There are two ways to obtain this output level: (1) The only existing firm can increase its production to Q_2, or (2) a new firm can enter the market and produce Q_3, which is the difference between Q_2 and Q_1. The first way minimizes total cost; the second way does not. The graph shown, then, represents a natural monopoly situation: One firm can supply the entire output that is demanded at a lower cost than two or more firms can.

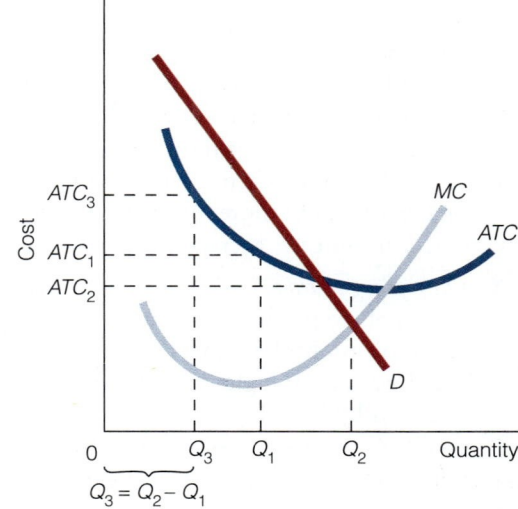

EXHIBIT 3

The Profit-Maximizing Natural Monopoly

The natural monopoly that seeks to maximize profits will produce the quantity of output at which $MR = MC$ and charge the (monopoly) price P_1.

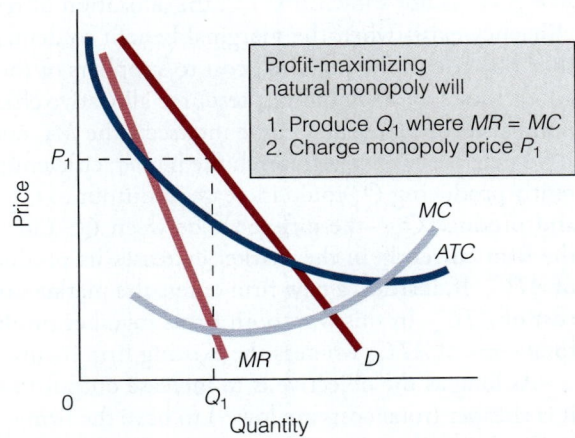

Profit-maximizing natural monopoly will
1. Produce Q_1 where $MR = MC$
2. Charge monopoly price P_1

25-2b Regulating the Natural Monopoly

The natural monopoly may be regulated through price, profit, or output regulation:

1. *Price regulation.* Marginal cost pricing is one form of price regulation. The objective is to set a price for the natural monopoly firm that equals its marginal cost at the quantity of output at which demand intersects marginal cost. In Exhibit 4, this price is P_1. At that price, the natural monopoly takes a loss: At Q_1, average total cost is greater than price and thus total cost is greater than total revenue. Obviously, the natural monopoly would rather go out of business than be subject to this type of regulation, unless it receives a subsidy for its operation.

2. *Profit regulation.* Government may want the natural monopoly to earn only zero economic profits. If so, government will require the natural monopoly to charge price P_2 (because $P_2 = ATC$) and to supply the quantity demanded at that price (Q_2). This form of regulation is often called *average cost pricing*. Theoretically, it may seem like a good way to proceed, but in practice, it often turns out differently. The problem is that, if the natural monopoly is always held to zero economic profits—and is not allowed to fall below or rise above this level—then it has an incentive to let costs rise. Higher costs—in the form of higher salaries or more luxurious offices—simply mean higher prices to cover the higher costs. In this case, average cost pricing is not likely to be an efficient way to proceed.

3. *Output regulation.* Government can mandate a quantity of output it wants the natural monopoly to produce. Suppose that quantity is Q_3 in Exhibit 4 so that there are positive economic profits because price is above average total cost. However, the natural monopoly could want even higher profits, and at a fixed quantity of output, higher profits can be obtained by lowering costs. The natural monopolist might lower costs by reducing the quality of the good or service it sells, knowing that it faces no direct competition and that it is protected (by government) from competitors.

Government regulation of a natural monopoly does not always turn out the way it was intended. Regulation—whether it takes the form of price, profit, or output regulation—can distort the incentives of those who operate the natural monopoly. For example, if profit is

EXHIBIT 4

Regulating a Natural Monopoly

The government can regulate a natural monopoly through (1) price regulation, (2) profit regulation, or (3) output regulation. Price regulation usually means marginal cost pricing, and profit regulation usually means average cost pricing.

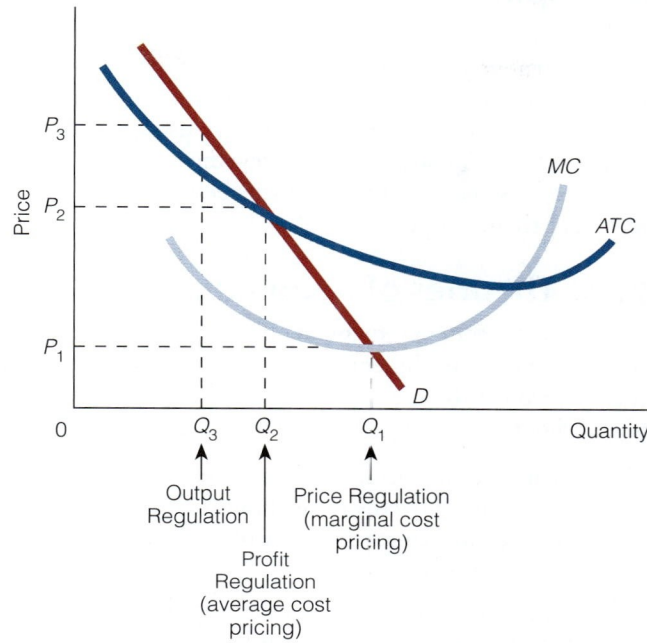

regulated to the extent that zero economic profits are guaranteed, then the natural monopoly has little incentive to hold costs down. Furthermore, the owners of the natural monopoly have an incentive to try to influence the government officials or other persons who are regulating the firm.

In addition, each of the three types of regulation requires information. For example, if the government wishes to set price equal to marginal cost or average total cost for the natural monopoly, it must know the cost conditions of the firm.

Three problems arise in gathering information: (1) The cost information is not easy to determine, even for the natural monopoly itself. (2) The cost information can be rigged (to a degree) by the natural monopoly, and therefore, the regulators will not get a true picture of the firm. (3) The regulators have little incentive to obtain accurate information because they are likely to keep their jobs and prestige even if they work with less-than-accurate information. (This problem raises another question: Who will ensure that the regulators do a good job?)

Finally, the issue of *regulatory lag* is indirectly related to information. **Regulatory lag** is the period between the time a natural monopoly's costs change and the time the regulatory agency adjusts prices to account for the change. For example, suppose the local gas company rates are regulated. Subsequently, the gas company's costs rise, and it seeks a rate hike through the local regulatory body. The rate hike is not likely to be approved quickly. The gas company will probably have to submit an application for a rate hike, document its case, have a date set for a hearing, argue its case at the hearing, and then wait for the regulatory agency to decide on the merits of the application. Many months may pass between the beginning of the process and the end. During that time, the regulated firm will be operating in ways and under conditions that both the firm and the regulatory body might not have desired.

Regulatory Lag
The period between the time a natural monopoly's costs change and the time the regulatory agency adjusts prices to account for the change.

25-2c Regulating Industries That Are Not Natural Monopolies

Some firms are regulated even though they are not natural monopolies. For instance, in the past, government has regulated both the airline and trucking industries. In the trucking industry, the Interstate Commerce Commission (ICC) fixed routes, set minimum freight rates, and erected barriers to entry. In the airline industry, the Civil Aeronautics Board (CAB) did much the same thing. Some economists view the regulation of competitive industries as unnecessary. They see it as evidence that the firms being regulated are, in turn, controlling the regulation to reduce their competition.

25-2d Theories of Regulation

The **capture theory of regulation** holds that, no matter what the motive is for the initial regulation and the establishment of the regulatory agency, the agency eventually will be captured (i.e., controlled) by the special interests of the industry being regulated. The following are a few of the interrelated points that have been put forth to support this theory:

1. In many cases, persons who have been in the industry are asked to regulate the industry because they know the most about it. Such regulators are likely to feel a bond with people in the industry, to see their side of the story more often than not, and, thus, to be inclined to cater to them.

2. At regulatory hearings, members of the industry attend in greater force than do taxpayers and consumers. The industry turns out in force because the regulatory hearing can affect it substantially and directly. In contrast, the effect on individual taxpayers and consumers is usually small and indirect. (The effect is spread over millions of people.) Thus, regulators are much more likely to hear and respond to the industry's side of the story.

3. Members of the regulated industry make a point of getting to know the members of the regulatory agency. They may talk frequently about business matters; perhaps they socialize. The bond between the two groups grows stronger over time, possibly having an impact on regulatory measures.

4. After they either retire or quit their jobs, regulators often go to work for the industries they once regulated.

The capture theory is markedly different from what has come to be called the **public interest theory of regulation**. This theory holds that regulators are seeking to do—and will do through regulation—what is in the best interest of the public or society at large.

An alternative to both theories is the **public choice theory of regulation**. This theory suggests that, to understand the decisions of regulatory bodies, we must first understand how the decisions affect the regulators themselves. For example, a regulation that increases the power, size, and budget of the regulatory agency should not be viewed in the same way as a regulation that decreases the agency's power and size. The theory predicts that the outcomes of the regulatory process will tend to favor the regulators instead of either business interests or the public.

These are three interesting, different, and, at first sight, believable theories of regulation, and economists have directed much effort to testing them. There is no clear consensus yet, but in the area of business regulation, the adherents of the capture and public choice theories have been increasing.

Capture Theory of Regulation
A theory holding that, no matter what the motive is for the initial regulation and the establishment of the regulatory agency, the agency eventually will be captured (controlled) by the special interests of the industry being regulated.

Public Interest Theory of Regulation
A theory holding that regulators are seeking to do—and will do through regulation—what is in the best interest of the public or society at large.

Public Choice Theory of Regulation
A theory holding that regulators are seeking to do—and will do through regulation—what is in their best interest (specifically, to enhance their power and the size and budget of their regulatory agencies).

25-2e The Costs and Benefits of Regulation

Suppose a business firm is polluting the air with smoke from its factories. The government then passes an environmental regulation requiring such firms to purchase antipollution devices that reduce the smoke emitted into the air.

Among the benefits of this kind of regulation is the obvious one of cleaner air, but cleaner air can lead to other benefits. For example, people may have fewer medical problems in the future. In some parts of the country, pollution from cars and factories causes people to cough, feel tired, and experience eye discomfort. More important, some people have chronic medical problems from constantly breathing dirty air. Government regulation that reduces the amount of pollution in the air clearly helps these people.

However, regulation usually comes with costs as well as with benefits. For example, when a business firm incurs the cost of antipollution devices, its overall costs of production rise. Simply put, making its product is costlier for the firm after the regulation is imposed. As a result, the business firm may produce fewer units of the product, raising its product price and causing some workers to lose their jobs.

If you are a worker who loses your job, you may view the government's insistence on antipollution devices differently than if, say, you are someone suffering from chronic lung disease. If you have asthma, less pollution may be the difference between feeling well and feeling sick. If you are a worker for the business firm, less pollution may cost you your job. Ideally, you prefer a little less pollution in your neighborhood, but perhaps not at the cost of losing your job.

Economists are neither for nor against such government regulation. The job of the economist is to make the point that regulation involves both benefits and costs. To the person who sees only the costs, the economist asks, what about the benefits? To the person who sees only the benefits, the economist asks, what about the costs? Then the economist goes on to identify the benefits and the costs as best as possible.

1. State one criticism of average cost pricing.
2. State the essence of the capture theory of regulation.
3. What is the difference between the capture theory and the public choice theory of regulation?
4. Are economists for or against regulation?

Office Hours

"What Is the Advantage of the Herfindahl Index?"

Student: In the last chapter, we learned about the four- and eight-firm concentration ratios. These ratios were used to compute the percentage of sales accounted for by the largest four and eight firms in an industry, respectively. In other words, the ratios were used to measure concentration in an industry. In this chapter, we learned about the Herfindahl index, which also measures concentration in an industry. Is the Herfindahl index better at measuring concentration than the other two ratios?

Instructor: Many economists think so. The Herfindahl index provides some information that the four- and eight-firm concentration ratios don't. To illustrate, consider two settings: (1) Four firms together have a 50 percent market share, and there are only five other firms in the industry; (2) four firms together have a 50 percent market share, and there are 50 other firms in the industry. The four-firm concentration ratio is the same in both settings, but the Herfindahl index is not.

Student: In other words, the four-firm concentration ratio is 50 percent in both settings, but the Herfindahl index in the first setting would be different from the Herfindahl index in the second setting because of how it is calculated. Is that correct?

Instructor: Yes, that's correct.

Student: This has me thinking. Something about the concentration ratios and Herfindahl index makes me a little uneasy. In the past, I haven't been able to figure out what it is, but now I think I can. There seems to be a little too much emphasis and importance on a single number. Is a high number for the Herfindahl index (say, above 2,500) always bad? It just seems to me that a high number doesn't always have to signify the same thing.

Instructor: Others have made that very point. In fact, both the four- and eight-firm concentration ratios, as well as the Herfindahl index, have been criticized for implicitly arguing from firm size and industry concentration to market power. Both assume that firms with large market shares have market power—which they are likely to be abusing, but perhaps they're not. Size could be a function of efficiency, and a firm with a large market share could be serving the buying public well.

Student: Yes, that is what I was getting at. It seems to me that the process of how a firm got to be big matters.

Instructor: I should say that the terms "process" and "behavior" have come to mean more in recent years, particularly with economists and with the Antitrust Division of the U.S. Justice Department. With respect to behavior, these days, more emphasis is placed on how the firm behaves—no matter its size and market power. To illustrate, two firms of equal size relative to other firms in their respective industries could behave differently. One firm may reduce output and charge higher prices, while the other firm may increase output and charge lower prices.

Points to Remember

1. In the two settings (four firms have 50 percent market share, but the number of other firms in the industry is different), the four-firm concentration ratio is the same, but the Herfindahl index is not. The Herfindahl index supplies more information, specifically about the dispersion of firm size in an industry, than either the four- or eight-firm concentration ratio does.
2. In recent years, process (how did the firm get to be big?) and behavior (how does the firm act?) have come to mean more when firms are evaluated.

Chapter Summary

Dealing with Monopoly Power

- A monopoly produces less than a perfectly competitive firm produces (assuming the same revenue and cost conditions), charges a higher price, and causes a deadweight loss. These factors represent the monopoly power problem, and solving it is usually put forth as a reason for antitrust laws and/or government regulatory actions. Some economists note, though, that government antitrust and regulatory actions do not always have their intended effect. In addition, such actions are sometimes implemented when there is no monopoly power problem to solve.

Antitrust Laws

- Two major criticisms have been directed at the antitrust acts. First, some argue that the language in the laws is vague; for example, even though the words "restraint of trade" are used in the Sherman Act, the act does not clearly explain what actions constitute a restraint of trade. Second, it has been argued that some antitrust acts appear to hinder, rather than promote, competition; an example is the Robinson–Patman Act.
- Antitrust policy has a few unsettled points. One centers on the proper definition of a market—specifically, whether it should be defined narrowly or broadly. How this question is answered

has an impact on which firms are considered monopolies. In addition, the use of concentration ratios for identifying monopolies or deciding whether to allow two firms to enter into a merger has been called into question. Recently, for purposes of implementing antitrust policy, concentration ratios have been largely replaced with the Herfindahl index, which is subject to some of the same criticisms as the concentration ratios. Antitrust authorities are also beginning to consider the benefits of innovation in ruling on proposed mergers.

Regulation

- Even if we assume that the intent of regulation is to serve the public interest, we may not assume that it will in fact do so. To work as desired, regulation (1) must be based on complete information (e.g., the regulatory body must know the cost conditions of the regulated firm) and (2) must not distort incentives (e.g., to keep costs down). Many economists are quick to point out that neither condition is likely to be fully met.

- Government uses three basic types of regulation to regulate natural monopolies: price, profit, and output regulation. Price regulation usually means marginal cost price regulation—that is, setting $P = MC$. Profit regulation usually means zero economic profits. Output regulation specifies a particular quantity of output that the natural monopoly must produce.

- The capture theory of regulation holds that, no matter what the motive is for the initial regulation and the establishment of the regulatory agency, the agency eventually will be captured (controlled) by the special interests of the industry being regulated. The public interest theory holds that regulators are seeking to do—and will do through regulation—what is in the best interest of the public or society at large. The public choice theory holds that regulators are seeking to do—and will do through regulation—what is in their best interest (specifically, enhance their own power, size, and budget).

Key Terms and Concepts

Antitrust Law
Trust
Herfindahl Index
Horizontal Merger
Vertical Merger
Conglomerate Merger
Network Good
Lock-In Effect
Regulatory Lag
Capture Theory of Regulation
Public Interest Theory of Regulation
Public Choice Theory of Regulation

Questions and Problems

1. Why was the Robinson–Patman Act passed? The Wheeler–Lea Act? The Celler–Kefauver Antimerger Act?
2. Explain why defining a market narrowly or broadly can make a difference in how antitrust policy is implemented.
3. What is one difference between the four-firm concentration ratio and the Herfindahl index?
4. How does a vertical merger differ from a horizontal merger? Why would the government look more carefully at one than at the other?
5. What is the implication of saying that regulation is likely to affect incentives?
6. Explain price regulation, profit regulation, and output regulation.
7. Why might profit regulation lead to rising costs for the regulated firm?
8. What is the major difference between the capture theory of regulation and the public interest theory of regulation?
9. George Stigler and Claire Friedland studied both unregulated and regulated electric utilities and found no difference in the rates they charged. One could draw the conclusion that regulation is ineffective when it comes to utility rates. What ideas or hypotheses presented in this chapter might have predicted this result?
10. The courts have ruled that it is a reasonable restraint of trade (and therefore permissible) for the owner of a business to sell his business and sign a contract with the new owner saying that he will not compete with her within a vicinity of, say, 100 miles, for a period of, say, 5 years. If this type of contract is a reasonable restraint of trade, can you give an example of what you would consider an unreasonable

restraint of trade? Explain how you decide what is a reasonable restraint of trade and what isn't.

11. In your opinion, what is the best way to deal with the monopoly power problem? Do you advocate antitrust laws, regulation, or something not discussed in the chapter? Give reasons for your answer.

12. It is usually asserted that public utilities such as electric companies and gas companies are natural monopolies, but an assertion is not proof. How would you go about trying to prove (or disprove) that electric companies and the like are (or are not) natural monopolies? (*Hint:* Consider comparing the average total cost of a public utility that serves many customers with the average total cost of a public utility that serves relatively few customers.)

13. Discuss the advantages and disadvantages of regulation (as you see it).

14. Explain how the lock-in effect might make it less likely for a firm that benefits from it to innovate.

Working with Numbers and Graphs

1. Calculate the Herfindahl index and the four-firm concentration ratio for the following industry:

Firms	Market Share (%)
A	17
B	15
C	14
D	14
E	12
F	10
G	9
H	9

Use the accompanying figure to answer questions 2–4.

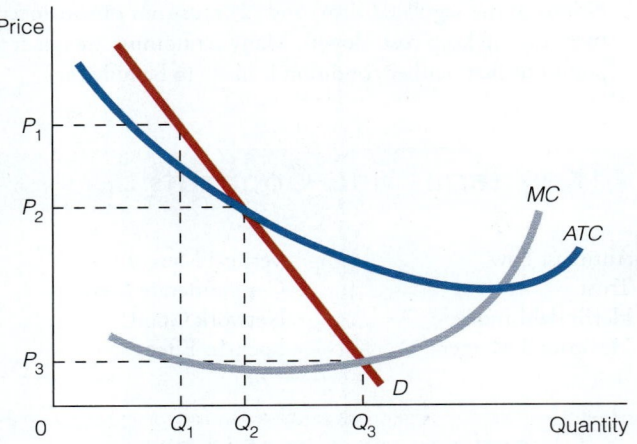

2. Is the firm in the figure a natural monopoly? Explain your answer.

3. Will the firm in the figure earn profits if it produces Q_3 and charges P_3? Explain your answer.

4. Which quantity in the figure is consistent with profit regulation? With price regulation? Explain your answers.

Introduction

Employees want to know why their salaries can't be higher: They would like to have more income for spending and saving. Employees might wonder, "Why am I not getting paid $10,000 more? Why not $20,000 more?" Of course, employers look at salaries differently: They would like to pay lower salaries. Employers may look at a salary and wonder, "Why couldn't I have paid $10,000 less? Why not $20,000 less?" Salaries are determined by economic forces. This chapter identifies the factors and the process affecting your pay. Without a doubt, this chapter is relevant to you.

26-1 Factor Markets

Just as there is a demand for and a supply of a product, there is a demand for and a supply of a factor, or resource, such as labor.

26-1a The Demand for a Factor

All firms—perfectly competitive firms, oligopolistic firms, or whatever—purchase factors in order to make products to sell. For example, farmers buy tractors and fertilizer in order to produce crops to sell. Car companies buy steel in order to build cars to sell.

The demand for factors is a **derived demand**; that is, it is derived from, and directly related to, the demand for the product that the resources go to produce. If the demand for the product rises, so does the demand for the factors that go into the making of the product. If the demand for the product falls, so does the demand for the factors. For example, if the demand for a university education falls, so does the demand for university professors. If the demand for computers rises, so does the demand for skilled computer workers.

When the demand for a seller's product rises, the seller needs to decide how much more of a factor to buy. Marginal revenue product and marginal factor cost are relevant to this decision.

Derived Demand
Demand that is the result of some other demand. For example, factor demand is derived from the demand for the products that the factors go to produce.

26-1b Marginal Revenue Product: Two Ways to Calculate It

Marginal Revenue Product (MRP)
The additional revenue generated by employing an additional factor unit.

Marginal revenue product (**MRP**) is the additional revenue generated by employing an additional factor unit, such as one more unit of labor. For example, if a firm employs one more unit of a factor and its total revenue rises by $20, the *MRP* of the factor equals $20. Marginal revenue product can be calculated in two ways, either as

$$MRP = \frac{\Delta TR}{\Delta \text{Quantity of the factor}}$$

or as

$$MRP = MR \times MPP$$

where TR = total revenue, MR = marginal revenue, and MPP = marginal physical product. Exhibit 1 shows the two methods for calculating *MRP* for a hypothetical firm.

EXHIBIT 1

Calculating Marginal Revenue Product (MRP)

There are two methods of calculating *MRP*. Part (a) shows one method ($MRP = \Delta TR/\Delta$Quantity of the factor), and part (b) shows the other ($MRP = MR \times MPP$).

(1) Quantity of Factor X	(2) Quantity of Output, Q	(3) Product Price, Marginal Revenue (P = MR)	(4) Total Revenue TR = P × Q = (3) × (2)	(5) Marginal Revenue Product of Factor X: MRP = ΔTR/ΔQuantity of Factor X = Δ(4)/Δ(1)
0	10*	$5	$50	—
1	19	5	95	$45
2	27	5	135	40
3	34	5	170	35
4	40	5	200	30
5	45	5	225	25

(a)

(1) Quantity of Factor X	(2) Quantity of Output, Q	(3) Marginal Physical Product MPP = Δ(2)/Δ(1)	(4) Product Price, Marginal Revenue (P = MR)	(5) Marginal Revenue Product of Factor X: MRP = MR × MPP = (4) × (3)
0	10*	—	$5	—
1	19	9	5	$45
2	27	8	5	40
3	34	7	5	35
4	40	6	5	30
5	45	5	5	25

(b)

*Because the quantity of output is 10 at 0 units of factor X, other factors (not shown in the exhibit) must also be used to produce the good.

Method 1: $MRP = \Delta TR/\Delta \text{Quantity of the Factor}$ Look at Exhibit 1(a):

- Column 1 shows the different quantities of factor X.
- Column 2 shows the quantity of output produced at the different quantities of factor X.
- Column 3 lists the price and the marginal revenue of the product that the factor goes to produce. We have assumed that the product's price (P) equals the product's marginal revenue (MR). So the seller in Exhibit 1 is a perfectly competitive firm, for which $P = MR$.
- In column 4, we calculate the total revenue, or price multiplied by quantity.
- In column 5, we calculate the marginal revenue product (MRP) by dividing the change in total revenue (from column 4) by the change in the quantity of the factor.

Method 2: $MRP = MR \times MPP$ Now look at Exhibit 1(b). Columns 1 and 2 are the same as in Exhibit 1(a), and the other columns show the corresponding calculations.

26-1c The *MRP* Curve Is the Firm's Factor Demand Curve

Look again at column 5 in part (a) of Exhibit 1. Column 5 shows the *MRP* for factor X. By plotting the data in column 5 against the quantity of the factor (in column 1), we derive the *MRP* curve for factor X. This curve is the same as the firm's demand curve for factor X (or, simply, the firm's factor demand curve; see Exhibit 2):

MRP curve = Factor demand curve

The *MRP* curve in Exhibit 2 is downward sloping. You can understand why when you recall that *MRP* can be calculated as $MRP = MR \times MPP$. With regard to *MPP*, the marginal physical product of a factor, you know that, according to the law of diminishing marginal returns, the *MPP* of a factor will eventually diminish. Because *MRP* is equal to $MR \times MPP$ and because *MPP* will eventually decline, *MRP* will eventually decline too.

26-1d Value Marginal Product

Value marginal product (*VMP*) is equal to the price of the product multiplied by the marginal physical product of the factor:

$$VMP = P \times MPP$$

EXHIBIT 2

The *MRP* Curve Is the Firm's Factor Demand Curve

The data in columns (1) and (5) in Exhibit 1 are plotted to derive the *MRP* curve. The curve shows the various quantities of the factor the firm is willing to buy at different prices, which is what a demand curve shows. The *MRP* curve is the firm's factor demand curve.

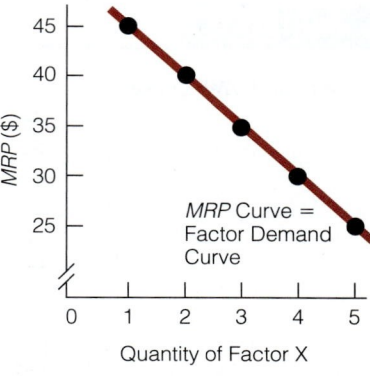

For example, if $P = \$10$ and $MPP = 9$ units, then $VMP = \$90$. Think of *VMP* as a measure of the value that each factor unit adds to the firm's product or simply as *MPP* measured in dollars.

A firm wants to know the *VMP* of a factor because it helps in deciding how many units of the factor to hire. To illustrate, put yourself in the shoes of the owner of a firm that produces computers. One of the factors you need to produce computers is labor, and you currently are thinking of hiring an additional worker. Whether you actually hire the additional worker will depend on (1) how much better off you are—in dollars and cents—with the additional worker and (2) what you have to pay the new hire. Simply put,

Value Marginal Product (*VMP*)
The price of a good multiplied by the marginal physical product of the factor: $VMP = P \times MPP$.

you want to know what the worker will do for you and what you will have to pay the worker. The *VMP* of a factor is a dollar measure of how much an additional unit of the factor will do for you.

26-1e An Important Question: Is *MRP* = *VMP*?

In the computations of *MRP* in Exhibit 1, price (P) was equal to marginal revenue (MR) because we assumed that the firm was perfectly competitive. Then, because $P = MR$ for a perfectly competitive firm, $MRP = VMP$ for a perfectly competitive firm. Given that

$$MRP = MR \times MPP$$

and

$$VMP = P \times MPP$$

it follows that

$$MRP = VMP \text{ for a perfectly competition firm}$$

because $P = MR$ for a perfectly competitive firm. [See Exhibit 3(a).]

Although $MRP = VMP$ for perfectly competitive firms, this is not the case for firms that are price searchers (monopolist, monopolistically competitive, and oligopolistic firms). All these firms face downward-sloping demand curves for their products. For all of these

---

EXHIBIT 3

MRP and VMP Curves

$MRP = MR \times MPP$ and $VMP = P \times MPP$. (a) The *MRP* (factor demand) curve and the *VMP* curve. These are the same for a price taker, or perfectly competitive firm, because $P = MR$. (b) The *MRP* (factor demand) curve and the *VMP* curve for a firm that is a price searcher (monopolist, monopolistic competitor, oligopolist). The *MRP* curve lies below the *VMP* curve because, for these firms, $P > MR$.

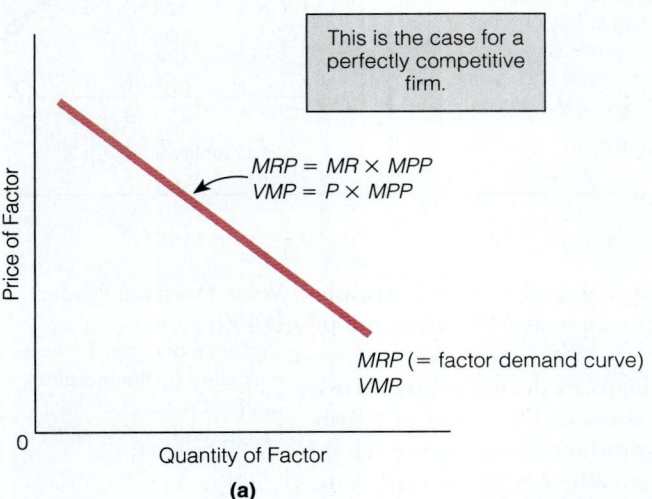
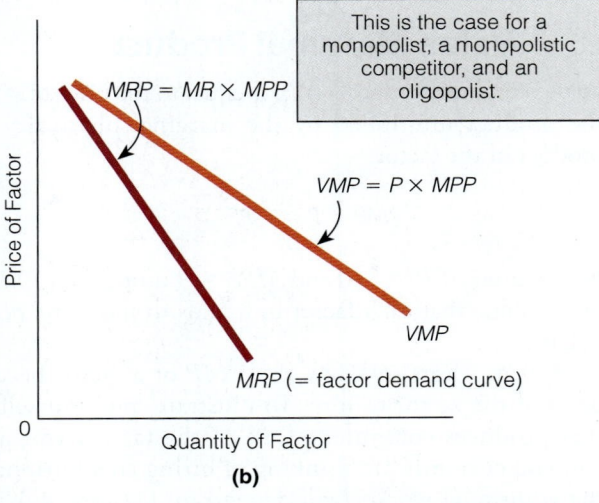

firms, $P > MR$, so VMP (which is $P \times MPP$) is greater than MRP (which is $MR \times MPP$).[1] That is,

VMP > MRP for monopolists, monopolistic competitors, and oligopolists

[See Exhibit 3(b).]

26-1f Marginal Factor Cost: The Firm's Factor Supply Curve

Marginal factor cost (MFC) is the additional cost incurred by employing an additional factor unit. It is calculated as

$$MFC = \frac{\Delta TC}{\Delta \text{Quantity of the factor}}$$

where TC = total costs.

Let's suppose a firm is a **factor price taker**: It can buy all it wants of a factor at the equilibrium price. For example, suppose the equilibrium price for factor X is $5. If a firm is a factor price taker, it can buy any quantity of factor X at $5 per factor unit. [See Exhibit 4(a).] For this kind of firm, the marginal factor cost (MFC) curve (the firm's factor supply curve) would be horizontal (flat, or perfectly elastic), as shown in Exhibit 4(b).[2]

Marginal Factor Cost (MFC)
The additional cost incurred by employing an additional factor unit.

Factor Price Taker
A firm that can buy all of a factor it wants at the equilibrium price. Such a firm faces a horizontal (flat, perfectly elastic) supply curve of factors.

EXHIBIT 4

Calculating MFC and Deriving the MFC Curve (the Firm's Factor Supply Curve)

In (a), MFC is calculated in column 4. Notice that the firm is a factor price taker because it can buy any quantity of factor X at a given price per factor unit ($5, as shown in column 2). In (b), the data from columns (1) and (4) are plotted to derive the MFC curve, which is the firm's factor supply curve.

(1) Quantity of Factor X	(2) Price of Factor X	(3) Total Cost TC = (2) × (1)	(4) MFC = ΔTC/ΔQuantity of the factor = Δ(3)/Δ(1)
0	$5	$0	—
1	5	5	$5
2	5	10	5
3	5	15	5
4	5	20	5
5	5	25	5
6	5	30	5

(a)

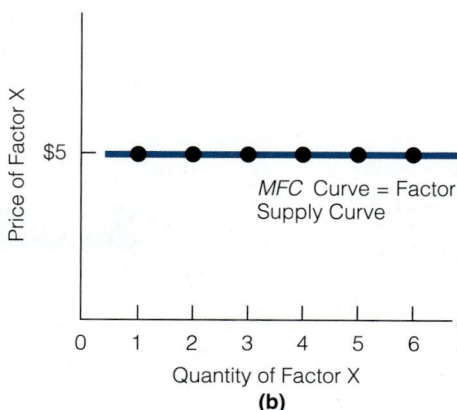

(b)

---

[1] An exception is the perfectly price-discriminating monopoly firm, for which $P = MR$.
[2] Although the MFC (factor supply curve) for the single-factor price taker is horizontal, the market supply curve is upward sloping. This situation is similar to the one for the perfectly competitive firm, where the firm's demand curve is horizontal but the market (or industry) demand curve is downward sloping. In factor markets, we are simply talking about the supply side of the market instead of the demand side. The firm's supply curve is flat because it can buy additional factor units without driving up the price of the factor; it buys a relatively small portion of the factor. For the industry, however, higher factor prices must be offered to entice factors (e.g., workers) from other industries. The difference in the two supply curves—the firm's and the industry's—is basically a reflection of the different sizes of each.

26-1g How Many Units of a Factor Should a Firm Buy?

Suppose you graduate with a BA in economics and go to work for a business firm. The first day on the job, you are involved in a discussion about factor X. Your employer asks you, "How many units of this factor should we buy?" What would you say?

Your response is based on marginal analysis. "Continue buying additional units of the factor," you say, "until the additional revenue generated by employing an additional factor unit is equal to the additional cost incurred by employing an additional factor unit." Simply stated, keep buying additional units of the factor until $MRP = MFC$. In Exhibit 5, MRP equals MFC at a factor quantity of Q_1.

> **Thinking Like an Economist**
>
> **Different Markets, Same Principles** In the product market, a firm produces that quantity of output at which marginal revenue equals marginal cost ($MR = MC$). In the factor market, a firm buys the factor quantity at which marginal revenue product equals marginal factor cost ($MRP = MFC$). The economic principle of equating additional benefits with additional costs holds in both markets.

26-1h When There Is More Than One Factor, How Much of Each Factor Should the Firm Buy?

Until now, we have discussed the purchase of only one factor. Suppose, however, that a firm requires two factors, labor (L) and capital (K), to produce its product. How does it combine these two factors to minimize costs? Does it combine, say, 20 units of labor with 5 units of capital or perhaps 15 units of labor with 8 units of capital?

The answer is that the firm purchases the two factors until the ratio of MPP to price for one factor equals the ratio of MPP to price for the other factor—in other words,

$$\frac{MPP_L}{P_L} = \frac{MPP_K}{P_K}$$

EXHIBIT 5

Equating *MRP* and *MFC*

The firm continues to purchase a factor as long as the factor's *MRP* exceeds its *MFC*. In the exhibit, the firm purchases Q_1.

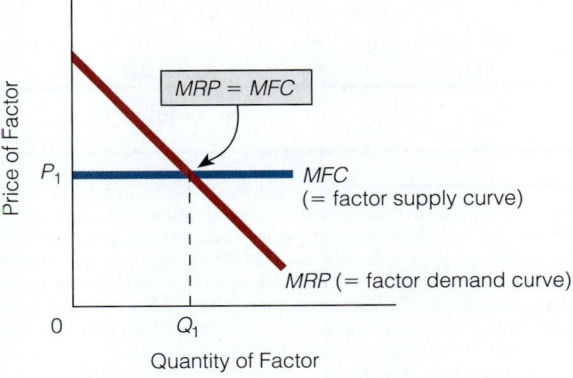

This is the **least-cost rule**. To understand its logic, consider an example. Suppose that, for a firm, (1) the price of labor is $5, (2) the price of capital is $10, (3) an extra unit of labor results in an increase in output of 25 units, and (4) an extra unit of capital results in an increase in output of 25 units. Notice that MPP_L/P_L is greater than MPP_K/P_K: $25/\$5 > 25/\$10$. Thus, for this firm, $1 spent on labor is more effective at raising output than $1 spent on capital. In fact, it is twice as effective.

Now, suppose the firm currently spends an extra $5 on labor and an extra $10 on capital. With this purchase of the two factors, the firm *is not* minimizing costs. It spends an additional $15 and produces 50 additional units of output. If, instead, it spent an additional $10 on labor and $0 on capital, it could still have produced the 50 additional units of output and saved $5.

To minimize costs, the firm will rearrange its purchases of factors until the least-cost rule is met. To illustrate, if $MPP_L/P_L > MPP_K/P_K$, then the firm buys more labor and less capital. As a result, the *MPP* of labor falls and the *MPP* of capital rises, bringing the two ratios closer in line. The firm continues to buy more of the factor whose *MPP*-to-price ratio is larger. It stops when the two ratios are equal.

Least-Cost Rule
Rule that specifies the combination of factors that minimizes costs and so requires that the following condition be met: $MPP_1/P_1 = MPP_2/P_2 = \ldots = MPP_N/P_N$ where the subscript numbers stand for the different factors.

> ### Thinking Like an Economist
>
> **Two Different Settings, Same Principles** We can compare a firm's least-cost rule with how buyers allocate their consumption dollars. A buyer of goods in the product market chooses combinations of goods so that the marginal utility of good A divided by the price of good A is equal to the marginal utility of good B divided by the price of good B—that is, $MU_A/P_A = MU_B/P_B$.
>
> A firm buying factors in the factor market chooses combinations of factors so that the marginal physical product of, say, labor, divided by the price of labor (the wage rate), is equal to the marginal physical product of capital, divided by the price of capital—that is, $MPP_L/P_L = MPP_K/P_K$.
>
> Thus, consumers buy goods in the same way that firms buy factors. This similarity points out something that you may already have sensed: Although economic principles are few, they sometimes seem numerous because we find them in so many different settings.
>
> The same economic principle lies behind equating the *MU/P* ratios for different goods in the product market and equating the *MPP/P* ratios for different resources in the resource market. In short, only one economic principle is at work in the two markets, not two different ones. That principle simply says that, in their attempt to meet their objectives, economic actors will arrange their purchases in such a way that they receive equal additional benefits per dollar of expenditure.
>
> Seeing how a few economic principles operate in many different settings is part of the economic way of thinking.

(Answers to Self-Test questions are in Answers to Self-Test Questions at the back of the book.)

1. When a perfectly competitive firm employs one worker, it produces 20 units of output, and when it employs two workers, it produces 39 units of output. The firm sells its product for $10 per unit. What is the marginal revenue product connected with hiring the second worker?
2. What is the difference between marginal revenue product (*MRP*) and value marginal product (*VMP*)?
3. What is the distinguishing characteristic of a factor price taker?
4. How much labor should a firm purchase?

26-2 The Labor Market

Labor is a factor of special interest because, at one time or another, most people find themselves in the labor market. This section discusses, first, the demand for labor; then, the supply of labor; and, finally, the two together. The section focuses on a firm that is a price taker both in the product market (i.e., a perfectly competitive firm) and in the factor market.[3] In this setting, the demand for and supply of labor determine wage rates.

26-2a Shifts in a Firm's *MRP*, or Factor Demand, Curve

As explained earlier, a firm's *MRP* curve is its factor demand curve, and marginal revenue product equals marginal revenue multiplied by marginal physical product:

$$MRP = MR \times MPP \quad (1)$$

For a perfectly competitive firm, for which $P = MR$, we can write equation (1) as

$$MRP = P \times MPP \quad (2)$$

Now consider the demand for a specific factor input: labor. What will happen to the factor demand (*MRP*) curve for labor as the price of the product that the labor produces changes? In Exhibit 6, the initial product price is $10, and the initial factor demand curve is MRP_1. At wage rate W_1, the firm hires Q_1 labor. Suppose the product price rises to $12. As we can see from equation (2), *MRP* also rises. At each wage rate, the firm wants to hire more labor. For example, at W_1, it wants to hire Q_2 labor instead of Q_1. In short, a rise in product price shifts the firm's *MRP*, or factor demand, curve rightward. If product price falls from $10 to $8, then *MRP* falls. At each wage rate, the firm wants to hire less labor. For example, at W_1, it wants to hire Q_3 labor instead of Q_1. In short, a fall in product price shifts the firm's *MRP*, or factor demand, curve leftward.

EXHIBIT 6

Shifts in the Firm's *MRP*, or Factor Demand, Curve

It is always the case that $MRP = MR \times MPP$. For a perfectly competitive firm, for which $P = MR$, it follows that $MRP = P \times MPP$. If *P* changes, *MRP* will change. For example, if the product price rises, then *MRP* rises, and the firm's *MRP* curve (factor demand curve) shifts rightward. If the product price falls, then *MRP* falls, and the firm's *MRP* curve (factor demand curve) shifts leftward. If *MPP* rises (reflected in a shift in the *MPP* curve), then *MRP* rises, and the firm's *MRP* curve shifts rightward. If *MPP* falls, then *MRP* falls, and the firm's *MRP* curve shifts leftward.

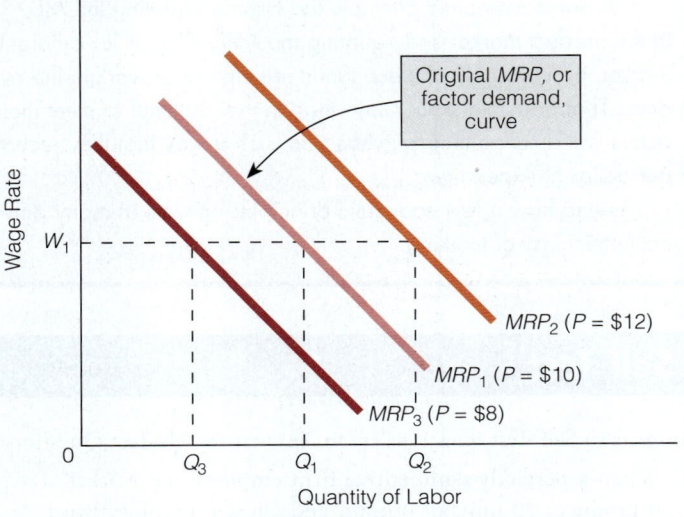

---

[3] Keep in mind that, in the labor market here, neither buyers nor sellers have any control over wage rates. Consequently, supply and demand are our analytical tools. In the next chapter, we modify this analysis.

Changes in the *MPP* of the factor—reflected in a shift in the *MPP* curve—also change the firm's *MRP* curve. As we can see from equation (2), an increase in, say, the *MPP* of labor will increase *MRP* and shift the *MRP*, or factor demand, curve rightward. A decrease in *MPP* will decrease *MRP* and shift the *MRP*, or factor demand, curve leftward.[4]

Economics 24/7

Why Jobs Don't Always Move to a Low-Wage Country

Some people think that tariffs are needed to protect U.S. workers. They argue that, without tariffs, U.S. companies will relocate to countries where wages are lower. They will produce their products there and then transport the products to the United States to sell them. Tariffs will make this scenario less likely because the gains the companies receive in lower wages will be offset by the tariffs imposed on their goods.

What this argument overlooks is that U.S. companies are interested not only in what they pay workers but also in the marginal productivity of the workers. For example, suppose a U.S. worker earns $10 an hour and a Mexican worker earns $4 an hour. Say the marginal physical product (*MPP*) of the U.S. worker is 10 units of good *X* and the *MPP* of the Mexican worker is 2 units. Thus, we have lower wages in Mexico and higher productivity in the United States. Where will the company produce?

To answer this question, compare the output produced per $1 of cost in the two countries:

$$\text{Output produced per \$1 of cost} = \frac{\text{MPP of the factor}}{\text{Cost of the factor}}$$

In the United States, at an *MPP* of 10 units of good *X* and a wage rate of $10, workers produce 1 unit of good *X* for every $1 they are paid:

$$\frac{\text{MPP of U.S. labor}}{\text{Wage rate of U.S. labor}} = \frac{10 \text{ units of good } X}{\$10}$$
$$= 1 \text{ unit of good } X \text{ per \$1}$$

In Mexico, at an *MPP* of 2 units and a wage rate of $4, workers produce half a unit of good *X* for every $1 they are paid:

$$\frac{\text{MPP of Mexican labor}}{\text{Wage rate of Mexican labor}} = \frac{2 \text{ units of good } X}{\$4}$$
$$= 1/2 \text{ unit of good } X \text{ per \$1}$$

Thus, the company gets more output per $1 of cost by using U.S. labor and will produce good *X* in the United States. It is cheaper to produce the good in the United States than it is in Mexico, even though wages are lower in Mexico.

In other words, U.S. companies look at the following ratios:

$$\begin{array}{cc} (1) & (2) \\ \dfrac{\text{MPP of labor in U.S.}}{\text{Wage rate in U.S.}} & \dfrac{\text{MPP of labor in country } X}{\text{Wage rate in country } X} \end{array}$$

If ratio (1) is greater than ratio (2), U.S. companies will hire labor in the United States. As they do so, the *MPP* of labor in the United States will decline (according to the law of diminishing marginal returns). Companies will continue to hire labor in the United States until ratio (1) is equal to ratio (2).

[4.] We are talking about a change in *MPP* that is reflected in a shift in the *MPP* curve, not a movement along a given *MPP* curve.

EXHIBIT 7

The Derivation of the Market Demand Curve for Labor Units

Two firms, A and B, make up the buying side of the market for labor. At a wage rate of W_1, firm A purchases 100 units of labor and firm B purchases 150 units. Together, they purchase 250 units, as illustrated in (c). Then the wage rate rises to W_2, and the amount of labor purchased by both firms initially falls to 180 units, as shown in (c). Higher wage rates translate into higher costs, a fall in product supply, and a rise in product price from P_1 to P_2. Finally, an increased price raises MRP, and each firm has a new MRP curve. The horizontal addition of the new MRP curves shows that the two firms together purchase 210 units of labor. Connecting the units of labor purchased by both firms at W_1 and W_2 gives the market demand curve.

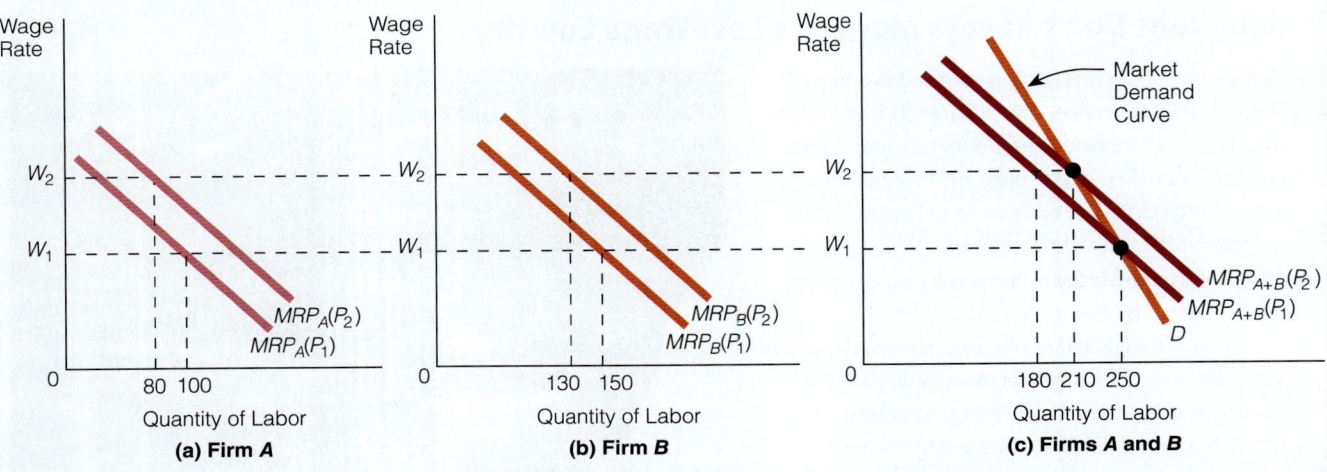

26-2b Market Demand for Labor

We would expect the market demand curve for labor to be the horizontal addition of the firm's demand curves (*MRP* curves) for labor. However, this expectation is not met, as Exhibit 7 illustrates. Two firms, A and B, make up the buying side of the factor market, and the product price for both firms is P_1. Parts (a) and (b) in the exhibit show the *MRP* curves for the two firms, based on this product price.

At a wage rate of W_1, firm A purchases 100 units of labor, the amount of labor at which its marginal revenue product equals marginal factor cost (or the wage). At this same wage rate, firm B purchases 150 units of labor. If we add the *MRP* curves of firms A and B horizontally, we get the curve $MRP_{A+B}(P_1)$ in part (c), in which the two firms together purchase 250 units of labor at W_1.

Now assume that the wage rate increases to W_2. In part (c), firms A and B move up the given MRP_{A+B} curve and purchase 180 units of labor. The process may seem to end here, but, of course, it does not, because a higher wage rate increases each firm's costs and thus shifts its supply curve leftward. This shift, in turn, leads to an increase in product price, to P_2.

Recall that the firm's marginal revenue product is equal to marginal revenue (or price if the firm is perfectly competitive) times marginal physical product: $MRP = MR \times MPP = P \times MPP$. So, if price rises (which it did), so does *MRP*, and, therefore, each firm faces a new *MRP* curve at the wage rate W_2. Parts (a) and (b) in Exhibit 7 illustrate these new *MRP* curves for firms A and B, and part (c) shows the horizontal addition of the *new MRP* curves. Now the firms together purchase 210 units of labor at W_2.

After all adjustments have been made, connecting the units of labor purchased by both firms at W_1 and W_2 gives the market demand curve in part (c).

26-2c The Elasticity of Demand for Labor

If the wage rate rises, firms will cut back on the labor they hire. How much they cut back depends on the **elasticity of demand for labor**, which is the percentage change in the quantity demanded of labor divided by the percentage change in the price of labor (the wage rate). That is,

$$E_L = \frac{\text{Percentage change in quantity demanded of labor}}{\text{Percentage change in wage rate}}$$

where E_L = coefficient of elasticity of demand for labor or, simply, the elasticity coefficient.

For example, when the wage rate changes by 20 percent, the quantity demanded of a particular type of labor changes by 40 percent. The elasticity of demand for this type of labor is, then, 2 (40 percent ÷ 20 percent), and the demand between the old wage rate and the new wage rate is elastic. There are three main determinants of elasticity of demand for labor:

- The elasticity of demand for the product that labor produces
- The ratio of labor costs to total costs
- The number of substitute factors

Elasticity of Demand for Labor
The percentage change in the quantity demanded of labor divided by the percentage change in the wage rate.

Elasticity of Demand for the Product That Labor Produces

If the demand for the product that labor produces is highly elastic, a small percentage increase in price (e.g., owing to a wage increase that shifts the supply curve for the product leftward) will decrease the quantity demanded of the product by a relatively large percentage. In turn, this will greatly reduce the quantity of labor needed to produce the product, implying that the demand for labor is highly elastic too.

The relationship between the elasticity of demand for the product and the elasticity of demand for labor is as follows:

- The higher the elasticity of demand for the product, the higher is the elasticity of demand for the labor that produces the product.
- The lower the elasticity of demand for the product, the lower is the elasticity of demand for the labor that produces the product.

Ratio of Labor Costs to Total Costs

Labor costs are a part of total costs. Consider two situations: in one, labor costs are 90 percent of total costs; in the other, labor costs are only 5 percent of total costs. Suppose wages increase by $2 per hour. Then total costs are affected more when labor costs are 90 percent of total costs (the $2-per-hour wage increase is being applied to 90 percent of all costs) than when labor costs are only 5 percent of total costs. Thus, price rises more when labor costs are a larger percentage of total costs. And, of course, the more price rises, the more the quantity demanded of the product falls. Therefore, labor, being a derived demand, is affected more. In short, for a $2-per-hour wage increase, the decline in the quantity demanded of labor is greater when labor costs are 90 percent of total costs than when labor costs are 5 percent of total costs.

The relationship between the ratio of labor cost to total cost and the elasticity of demand for labor is as follows:

- The higher the ratio of labor cost to total cost, the higher is the elasticity of demand for labor (i.e., the greater is the cutback in labor for any given wage increase).
- The lower the ratio of labor cost to total cost, the lower is the elasticity of demand for labor (i.e., the less is the cutback in labor for any given wage increase).

Number of Substitute Factors The more substitutes labor has, the more sensitive buyers of labor will be to a change in its price. This principle was established in the discussion of price elasticity of demand. The more factors that can be substituted for labor, the more likely it is that firms will cut back on their use of labor if its price rises. In sum,

- The more substitutes there are for labor, the higher will be the elasticity of demand for labor.
- The fewer substitutes there are for labor, the lower will be the elasticity of demand for labor.

26-2d Market Supply of Labor

As the wage rate rises, the quantity supplied of labor rises, *ceteris paribus*. The upward-sloping labor supply curve in Exhibit 8 illustrates this relationship. At a wage rate of W_1, individuals are willing to supply 100 labor units. At the higher wage rate of W_2, individuals are willing to supply 200 labor units. Some individuals who were not willing to work at a wage rate of W_1 are willing to work at a wage rate of W_2, and some individuals who were working at W_1 will be willing to supply more labor units at W_2. At the even higher wage rate of W_3, individuals are willing to supply 280 labor units.

26-2e An Individual's Supply of Labor

Exhibit 8 shows an upward-sloping *market* supply curve of labor. Let's consider an *individual's* supply curve of labor—specifically, whether Dion's supply curve of labor is upward sloping. The answer depends on the relative strengths of the substitution and income effects.

Suppose Dion currently earns $10 an hour and works 40 hours a week. If Dion's wage rate rises to, say, $15 an hour, he will feel two effects, pulling him in opposite directions:

1. *Substitution effect.* As his wage rate rises, Dion recognizes that his monetary reward from working has increased. As a result, Dion will want to work more—say, 45 hours a week instead of 40 hours (an additional 5 hours).

2. *Income effect.* As his wage rate rises, Dion knows that he can earn $600 a week (40 hours at $15 an hour) instead of $400 a week (40 hours at $10 an hour). If leisure is a normal good (the demand for which increases as income increases), then Dion will want to consume more leisure as his income rises. But the only way to consume more leisure is to work fewer hours. Consequently, Dion might want to decrease his work hours per week from 40 to 37 (3 fewer hours).

Clearly, then, the substitution effect pulls Dion in one direction (toward working 5 more hours), and the income effect pulls him in the opposite direction (toward working 3 fewer hours). Which effect is stronger? In our numerical example, the substitution effect is stronger, so, on net, Dion wants to work 2 more hours a week as his wage rate rises. This means that Dion's supply curve of labor is upward sloping between a wage rate of $10 and $15 per hour.

EXHIBIT 8

The Market Supply of Labor

A direct relationship exists between the wage rate and the quantity of labor supplied.

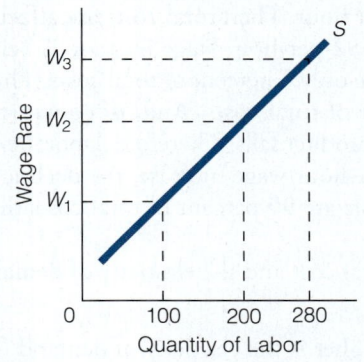

Finding Economics

In the Number of Hours a Person Works Bilal works at a job where it is easy to get overtime. He has been earning $20 an hour for the last year, and most weeks, he works 45 hours. He recently got a raise to $23 an hour. Since getting his $3-an-hour raise, he has been working about 40 hours a week. Where is the economics?

The economics can be found in the substitution and income effects. As a result of the higher wage, part of Bilal wants to work more; this is the substitution effect at work. But part of Bilal wants to work less; this is the income effect at work. In the end, Bilal works fewer hours (40 instead of 45), showing that his income effect was stronger than his substitution effect.

Economics 24/7

Artificial Intelligence, Robotics, and the Future of Jobs and Wages[1]

The term *artificial intelligence* (AI) was first used by computer scientist John McCarthy in 1956. AI is a collection of advanced technologies that allow machines (and robots) to sense, comprehend, act, and learn. Today, AI and robotics are following in the path of automation technologies in the past—namely, replacing human labor with machines to perform various tasks and processes.

What will advancements in AI and robotics mean for the future of jobs and wages? Will AI lead to some workers losing their jobs? Will wages decline? Will the income distribution become more unequal? Will workers who lose their jobs be able to find new jobs?

In "Artificial Intelligence, Automation and Work," economists Acemoglu and Restrepo address some of these questions. They argue that the net effect on employment and wages of advancing AI depends upon three effects: the displacement effect and two countervailing effects, the productivity effect and the reinstatement effect.

The Displacement Effect. When workers lose their jobs to machines, to AI, or to AI and robotics, they are said to be displaced. For example, in the past, farm workers were displaced by harvesters and plows. In recent years, travel agents and tax preparers have been displaced by software. In the future, truck drivers may be displaced by self-driving or autonomous trucks. In all three cases, a machine, AI, or AI and robotics provides a substitute for human labor, and substituting for labor leads to a decline in the demand for labor and in wages.

A Countervailing Force: The Productivity Effect. Often, when labor becomes too expensive relative to capital, firms substitute capital for labor to reduce costs. These lower costs in producing goods and services can lead to lower prices, thus increasing the purchasing power and monetary wealth of consumers. Consumers with more wealth will likely increase their demand for

---

[1] This feature is based on "Artificial Intelligence, Automation and Work," by Daron Acemoglu and Pascual Restrepo in *Economics of Artificial Intelligence: An Agenda*, edited by Ajay Agrawal, Avi Goldfarb and Joshua Gans. The paper can be found at http://www.nber.org/chapters/c14027.pdf.

(Continued)

goods and services, some of which may not be produced with AI and robotics. So this higher demand for goods and services leads to a higher demand for labor, causing wages to rise. A historical example can be found in agriculture, where machinery led to lower costs of production, reduced prices, and wealthier consumers who increased their demand for many nonagricultural goods, thereby indirectly increasing the demand for the labor that produced those nonagricultural goods.

A Countervailing Force: The Reinstatement Effect. In the past, new technologies (steam, electricity, the Internet) all led to new kinds of jobs. It is likely to be no different with advancing AI and robotics. Think of new job tasks and titles that exist today that did not exist shortly ago, such as virtual assistant, well-being coach, social media manager, app developer, web analyst, data scientist, UX designer, and so on.

So, as AI and robotics advance, the big question is what AI and robotics will mean for employment and wages. How will the three effects of displacement, productivity, and reinstatement play out? If the displacement effect is stronger than the two countervailing effects, we can expect jobs and wages to decline. If the displacement effect is perfectly balanced by the two countervailing effects, or if it is weaker than the two countervailing effects, then jobs and wages will not decline. In the past, technological advancements have not led to high unemployment and declining wages, but will this be the case in the future? That is the question that has always been up for debate, and it is no different now.

26-2f Shifts in the Labor Supply Curve

Changes in the wage rate change the quantity supplied of labor units; that is, they cause a *movement* along a given supply curve. Two factors of major importance, however, can *shift* the entire labor supply curve: wage rates in other labor markets and the nonmoney, or nonpecuniary, aspects of a job.

Wage Rates in Other Labor Markets Suppose Ana works as a technician in a television-manufacturing plant, but she has skills suitable for a number of jobs. One day, she learns that the computer-manufacturing plant on the other side of town is offering 33 percent more pay per hour. Ana is also trained to work as a computer operator, so she decides to leave her current job and apply for work at the computer-manufacturing plant. In short, the wage rate offered in other labor markets can bring about a shift of the supply curve in a particular labor market.

Nonmoney, or Nonpecuniary, Aspects of a Job Other things held constant, people prefer to avoid dirty, heavy, dangerous work in cold climates. An increase in the overall unpleasantness of a job (e.g., an increased probability of contracting lung cancer by working in a coal mine) will cause a decrease in the supply of labor to the associated firm or industry and a leftward shift in its labor supply curve. An increase in the overall pleasantness of a job (e.g., employees are now entitled to a longer lunch break and use of the company gym) will cause an increase in the supply of labor to the associated firm or industry and a rightward shift in its labor supply curve.

26-2g Putting Supply and Demand Together

Exhibit 9 illustrates a labor market. The equilibrium wage rate and quantity of labor are established by the forces of supply and demand. At a wage rate of W_2, there is a surplus of labor. Some people who want to work at this wage rate will not be able to find jobs and will begin to offer their services for a lower wage rate. The wage rate will move down until it reaches W_1.

At a wage rate of W_3, there is a shortage of labor. Some demanders of labor will begin to bid up the wage rate until it reaches W_1. At the equilibrium wage rate, W_1, the quantity supplied of labor equals the quantity demanded of labor.

EXHIBIT 9

Equilibrium in a Particular Labor Market

The forces of supply and demand bring about the equilibrium wage rate and quantity of labor. At the equilibrium wage rate, the quantity demanded of labor equals the quantity supplied. At any other wage rate, there is either a surplus or a shortage of labor.

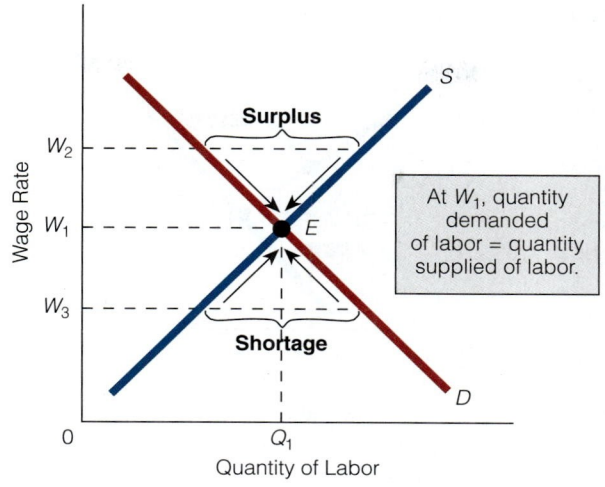

26-2h Why Do Wage Rates Differ?

To discover why wage rates differ, we must determine what conditions are necessary for everyone to receive the same pay. Assume the following conditions:

1. The demand for every type of labor is the same. (Throughout our analysis, any wage differentials caused by demand are short-run phenomena.)
2. The jobs have no special nonpecuniary aspects.
3. All labor is ultimately homogeneous, and laborers can be trained at no cost (costlessly) for different types of employment.
4. All labor is mobile at zero cost.

Given these conditions, there would be no difference in wage rates in the long run. Exhibit 10 shows two labor markets, A and B. Initially, the supply conditions are different, with a greater supply of workers in labor market B (S_B) than in labor market A (S_A). Because of the different supply conditions, more labor is employed in labor market B (Q_B) than in labor market A (Q_A) and the equilibrium wage rate in labor market B ($10) is lower than it is in labor market A ($30).

The differences in the wage rates between the two labor markets will not last. We have assumed that (1) labor can move costlessly from one labor market to another (so labor moves from the lower paying job to the higher paying job); (2) the jobs have no special nonpecuniary aspects (there are no nonpecuniary reasons for not moving); (3) labor is ultimately homogeneous (workers who work in labor market B can work in labor market A); and (4) if workers need training to move from one labor market to another, they not only are capable of being trained but also can acquire the training costlessly.

As a result, some workers in labor market B will relocate to labor market A, decreasing the supply of workers to the level S'_B in labor market B and increasing the supply to the level S'_A in market A. The relocation of workers ends when the equilibrium wage rate in both markets is the same, at $20. Therefore, wage rates will not differ in the long run if our four conditions hold.

EXHIBIT 10

Wage Rate Equalization Across Labor Markets

Given the four necessary conditions (noted in the text), there will be no wage rate differences across labor markets. We start with a wage rate of $30 in labor market A and a wage rate of $10 in labor market B. Soon, some individuals in B relocate to A. This shift increases the supply in one market (A), driving down the wage rate, and decreases the supply in the other market (B), driving up the wage rate. Equilibrium comes when the same wage rate is paid in both labor markets. This outcome critically depends on the necessary conditions holding.

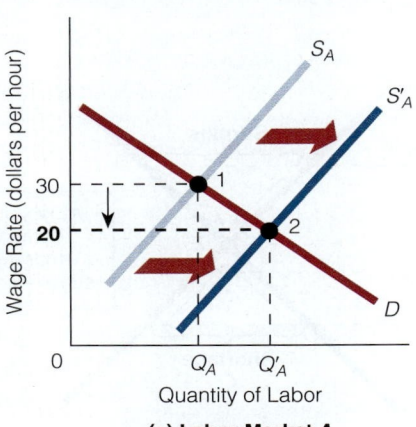

(a) Labor Market A

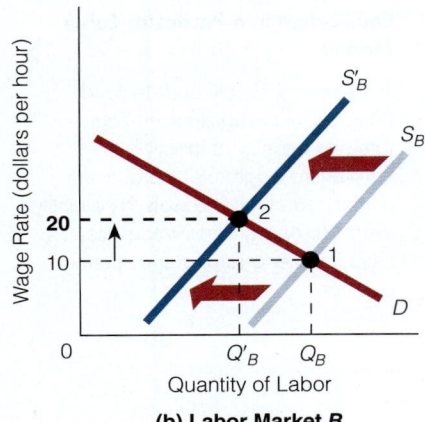

(b) Labor Market B

Given the conditions under which wage rates will not differ, we now know why wage rates do differ. Obviously, they differ because demand conditions are not the same in all labor markets (a factor that explains only short-run wage differentials) and because supply conditions are not the same in all markets. Jobs *do have* nonpecuniary aspects, labor is *not* homogeneous, labor *cannot* be retrained without cost, and labor is *not* costlessly mobile.

26-2i Why Demand and Supply Differ Among Labor Markets

If wage rates differ because demand and supply conditions differ from one market to another, the next question is why. Let's consider the factors that affect the demand for, and the supply of, labor.

Demand for Labor The market demand curve for labor is based on the *MRP* curves for labor of the individual firms in the market. So we need to look at what affects the components of *MRP*, namely, *MR* and *MPP*.

Marginal revenue, *MR*, is indirectly affected by product supply and demand conditions because these conditions determine price ($MR = \Delta TR/\Delta Q$ and $TR = P \times Q$). Thus, product demand and supply conditions affect factor demand. In short, because the supply and demand conditions in product markets are different, the demand for labor in labor markets will be different too.

The second factor, the marginal physical product of labor, is affected by individual workers' *own abilities and skills* (both innate and learned), the *degree of effort* they put forth on the job, and the *other factors of production* available to them. (American workers are more productive than workers in many other countries because they work with many more capital goods and much more technical know-how.) If all individuals had the same innate and learned skills and abilities, applied the same degree of effort on the job, and worked with the same amount and quality of other factors of production, wages would differ less than they currently do.

Supply of Labor As noted, the supply conditions in labor markets are different. First, jobs have *different nonpecuniary qualities*. Working as a coal miner in West Virginia is not as attractive a job as working as a tour guide at a lush resort in Hawaii. We would expect this difference to be reflected in the supply of coal miners and tour guides.

Second, supply is also a reflection of the *number of persons who can actually do a job*. Williamson may want to be a nuclear physicist but may not have the ability in science and mathematics to become one. Johnson may want to be a basketball player but may not have the ability to become one.

Third, even if individuals have the ability to work at a certain job, they may perceive the *training costs as too high* (relative to the perceived benefits) to train for it. For example, Tyler may have the ability to be a brain surgeon but views the years of schooling required to be too high a price to pay.

Fourth, sometimes the supply in different labor markets reflects a difference in the *cost of moving* across markets. Thus, wage rates might be higher in Alaska than in Alabama for comparable labor because the workers in Alabama find the cost of relocating to Alaska too high relative to the benefits of receiving a higher wage.

In conclusion, because the wage rate is determined by supply-and-demand forces, the factors that affect these forces indirectly affect wage rates. Exhibit 11 summarizes these factors.

EXHIBIT 11

The Wage Rate

A step-by-step framework that describes the factors that affect the wage rate.

> What factors affect the wage rate in a single competitive labor market?
> The supply of and demand for labor.
> But what factors affect labor supply and demand? Many factors. We categorize them accordingly.

Demand for Labor
> Because the *MRP* curve is the factor demand curve, we need to look at what affects the components of *MRP*, namely, *MR* (or *P*, if the firm is a product price taker) and *MPP* of labor.

Supply of Labor
> Wage rates in other labor markets
> Nonpecuniary aspects of the job
> Number of persons who can do the job
> Training costs
> Moving costs

MR
> Product supply and demand conditions determine price and therefore indirectly affect marginal revenue. ($MR = \Delta TR/\Delta Q$ and $TR = P \times Q$, so we can see the link between *P* and *MR*.)

MPP of Labor
> Own abilities and skills
> Degree of effort on the job
> Other factors of production available to labor

26-2j Why Did You Choose Your Major?

What happens in the labor market sometimes influences our lives. Consider a college student who is trying to decide whether to major in accounting or literature. The student believes that literature is more fun and interesting but that accounting, on average, will earn her enough additional income to compensate for the lack of fun in accounting. Specifically, at a $90,000 annual salary for accounting and a $56,000 annual salary for teaching literature, the student is indifferent between accounting and literature. But at a $95,000 annual salary for accounting and a $56,000 annual salary for teaching English, accounting moves ahead.

Of course, what accounting pays is determined by the demand for and supply of accountants. Given that fact, we see that other people influenced the student's decision to become an accountant. To illustrate, suppose Congress passes more intricate tax laws that require more accountants to figure them out. The change in the law increases the demand for accountants, which in turn raises the wage rate for them. And an increase in the wage rate for accountants increases the probability that more people—perhaps you—will major in accounting, not in literature, philosophy, or history.

As you can see, economics—in which markets play a major role—helps explain why part of your life is the way it is.

26-2k Marginal Productivity Theory

An analysis of some of the things we know from this chapter leads us to the following conclusions:

1. If a firm is a factor price taker, then its marginal factor cost is constant and equal to its factor price ($MFC = P$). If the factor price taker hires labor, then, for the firm, $MFC = W$, where W is the wage rate.
2. Firms hire the factor quantity at which $MRP = MFC$.
3. Given points 1 and 2 together, a factor price taker pays labor a wage equal to its marginal revenue product: $W = MRP$. Because $MFC = W$ (point 1) and $MRP = MFC$ (point 2), it follows that $W = MRP$.
4. If a firm is perfectly competitive, then $MRP = VMP$.
5. If a firm is both perfectly competitive (a product price taker) and a factor price taker, it pays labor a wage equal to its value marginal product: $W = VMP$. Because $W = MRP$ (point 3) and $MRP = VMP$ (point 4), it follows that $W = VMP$.

Marginal Productivity Theory
Marginal productivity theory states that firms in competitive or perfect product and factor markets pay their factors their marginal revenue products.

These four points constitute the **marginal productivity theory**, which states that, if a firm sells its product and purchases its factors in competitive or perfect markets (i.e., it is a perfectly competitive firm and a factor price taker), then it pays its factors their MRP or VMP. (The two are equal for a product price taker.)

The theory holds that, under the competitive conditions specified, if a factor unit is withdrawn from the productive process and the amount of all other factors remains the same, then the decrease in the value of the product produced equals the factor payment received by the factor unit. To illustrate, suppose Sean works for a perfectly competitive firm (firm X) producing good X. One day, he quits his job (but nothing else relevant to the firm changes). Then, as a result, the total revenue of the firm falls by $100. If Sean was paid $100, then he received his MRP. He was paid a wage equal to his contribution to the productive process.[5]

---

[5] Recall that MRP can be calculated in two ways: $MRP = \Delta TR/\Delta$ Quantity of the factor and $MRP = MR \times MPP$. In this example, we use the first method. When Sean quits his job, the change in the denominator is 1 factor unit. If, as a result, TR falls by $100, then the change in the numerator must be $100.

1. The demand for labor is a derived demand. What could cause a firm's demand curve for labor to shift rightward?
2. Suppose the coefficient of elasticity of demand for labor is 3. What does this mean?
3. Why are wage rates higher in one competitive labor market than in another? In short, why do wage rates differ?
4. Workers in labor market X do the same work as workers in labor market Y, but they earn $10 less per hour. Why?

Economics 24/7

Who Pays the Social Security Tax?

When Congress established the Social Security system, it instituted Social Security taxes and split the tax between the employer and the employee. By doing so, it intended to split the cost of the system. But economists know that taxes *placed* on one group of persons can be actually *paid* for by another group. To a large extent, that is so with the Social Security tax: Although half of the tax is placed on the employer and half is placed on the employee, the employee ends up paying almost all of the tax.

Exhibit 12 shows an approximation of this statement. We say "approximation" because most economists believe that the supply curve for labor *in the aggregate is extremely inelastic*. For simplicity, the supply curve is drawn as perfectly inelastic.

When no Social Security tax is placed on the employer, D_1 is the relevant demand curve for labor. The equilibrium wage rate is $19; that is, employers are willing to pay a maximum of $19 per hour (per worker) for Q_1 workers.

EXHIBIT 12

Who Pays the Social Security Tax?

With no Social Security tax, the equilibrium wage rate is $19 per hour; that is, employers are willing to pay a maximum of $19 per hour (per worker) for Q_1 workers. With the Social Security tax fully placed on the employer and computed on an hourly basis, employers are willing to pay $19 per hour *minus* the hourly computed tax for Q_1 workers. Because we have assumed that the hourly tax is $1 per employee and that the supply curve for labor is perfectly inelastic in the aggregate, the new equilibrium wage rate is $18. Under the conditions stated, the employee ends up paying the full Social Security tax in the form of lower wages.

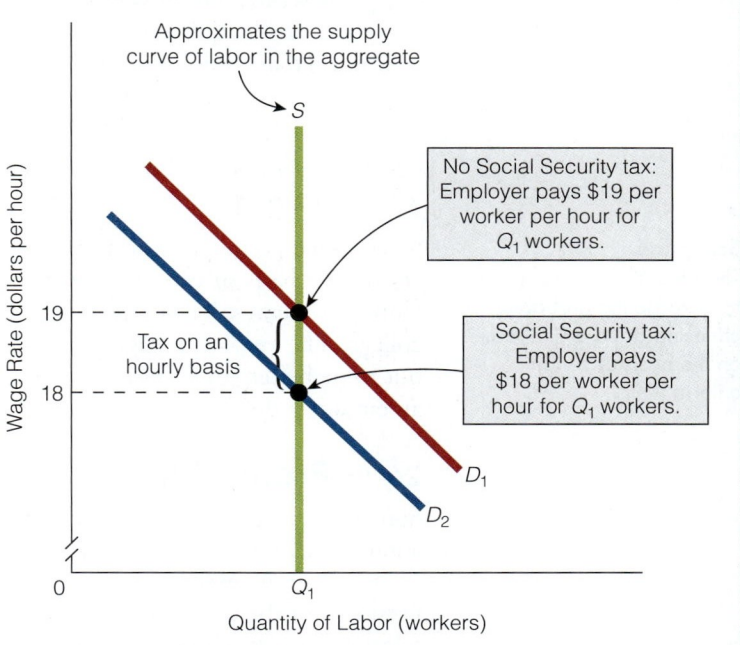

(Continued)

Now, instead of placing half the Social Security tax on the employer and half on the employee, let's take an extreme position and place the *entire tax on the employer*. Suppose employers calculate the Social Security tax on an hourly basis and find that they have to pay $1 per hour for every employee they hire. If $19 was the equilibrium wage rate *before the tax*, then employers are not willing to pay any more for the same number of workers *after the tax*. Employers are willing to pay labor only $19 per hour *minus* the hourly computed tax. In short, from the employer's perspective, the demand curve for labor falls by $1 for each alternative quantity of labor. In other words, the demand curve shifts leftward and down from D_1 to D_2. Given our vertical supply curve of labor, the new equilibrium wage rate is now $18 per worker for Q_1 workers.

So, if the supply curve is perfectly inelastic, and if the Social Security tax is *placed* wholly on employers, employees will end up *paying* the full tax in the form of lower wages.

26-3 Labor Markets And Information

This section looks at job hiring, employment practices, and employment discrimination, as well as how information or the lack of it affects these considerations.

26-3a Screening Potential Employees

Employers typically do not know exactly how productive a prospective employee will be. What the employer wants, but lacks, is complete information about the employee's future job performance. This need raises two questions:

1. *Why would an employer want complete information about a potential employee's future job performance?* The answer is obvious: Employers have a strong monetary incentive to hire good, stable, quick-learning, responsible, hardworking, punctual employees. One study found that corporate spending on training employees reached $40 billion annually. Obviously, corporations want to see the highest return possible for their training expenditures, so they try to hire employees who will make the training worthwhile.

2. *What does the employer do in the absence of such complete information?* This is where screening comes in.

Screening is the process employers use to increase the probability of choosing good employees on the basis of certain criteria. For example, as a step in the screening mechanism, an employer might ask a young college graduate searching for a job what his or her GPA was in college. The employer might know from past experience that persons with high GPAs turn out to be better employees, on average, than persons with low GPAs. Screening is one thing an employer does in the absence of complete information.

Screening
The process employers use to increase the probability of choosing good employees on the basis of certain criteria.

26-3b Promoting from Within

Sometimes employers promote from within the company because they have more information about present employees than about prospective employees.

Suppose the executive vice president in charge of sales is retiring from Company X. The president of the company could hire an outsider to replace the vice president but will often select an insider whom she knows well. What may look like discrimination to outsiders may simply be a reflection of the difference in costs to the employer of acquiring relevant information about employees inside and outside the company.

26-3c Discrimination or an Information Problem?

Suppose the world is made up of just two kinds of people: those with characteristic X and those with characteristic Y, or X people and Y people. Over time, it so happens that most employers are X people and that they tend to hire and promote proportionally more X than Y people. Are the Y people being discriminated against?

They could be. Nothing said so far rules out this possibility. But another explanation is that, over time, X employers have learned that Y people, on average, do not perform as well as X people. So, in this example, we simply state that X people are not discriminating against Y people. Instead, Y people are not being hired and promoted as often as X people because, for whatever reason, Y people, on average, are not as productive.

Suppose that, in this environment, an extremely productive Y person applies for a job with an X employer. The problem is that the X employer does not know—that is, lacks complete information about—the full abilities of the Y person. Furthermore, acquiring complete information is costly. The employer bases her decision to reject the Y person's job application on what she knows about Y people, which is that, on average, they are not as productive as X people. She makes this decision not because she has something against Y people but because acquiring complete information on every potential employee—X or Y—is simply too costly.

Legislation mandating equal employment opportunities requires employers to absorb some information costs to open the labor markets to all. All but the smallest of firms are required to search for qualified Y persons who can perform the job even if the employer believes that the average Y person cannot. Requiring employers to forgo the use of a screening mechanism typically increases firm costs and raises prices to consumers, but the premise of the legislation is that the social benefits of having more Y persons in the mainstream of society more than outweigh such costs.

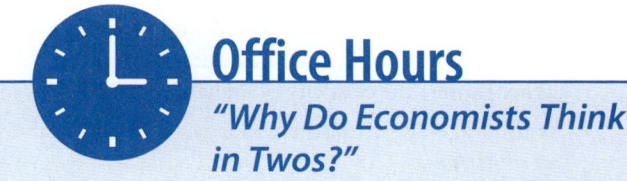

Office Hours
"Why Do Economists Think in Twos?"

Student: Before I read this chapter, I had thought that U.S. firms would rather pay low wages in other countries than pay high wages in the United States. Now I realize that wages aren't the only thing that matters to a firm: The productivity of labor matters too.

Instructor: Does this ring a bell?

Student: What do you mean?

Instructor: Well, one of the things emphasized in the "Thinking Like an Economist" feature in various chapters is that economists often compare one thing with another when trying to determine what economic actors will do. To illustrate, when a firm decides where to hire labor, it compares wage rates against productivity in various countries. The firm compares marginal revenue with marginal cost when it decides how much of a good to produce. Marginal revenue product is compared with marginal factor cost when a firm decides how much of a factor to hire or buy. A consumer who decides to buy more or less of various goods compares marginal utility with price.

Student: So what's the lesson? Why do economists seem to think in twos?

Instructor: The lesson goes back to something explained in Chapter 1: Usually, our activities have costs and benefits. Producing goods in the United States has a cost (paying high wages) and a benefit too (high productivity). Producing an additional unit of a good has a cost (*MC*) but an additional benefit too (*MR*). Hiring an additional unit of labor comes with a cost (the wage rate) but with a benefit too (higher *VMP* or *MRP*). In the end, what matters is not the costs alone, or the benefits alone, but the benefits relative to the costs.

Points to Remember

1. When firms are trying to decide where to hire workers (the United States or Mexico), wages are not the only factor that matters. Productivity matters too.
2. Economists often think in twos. They often compare the benefits and costs of doing X, where X can stand for various actions (e.g., hiring workers in various countries, producing an additional unit of a good, and so on).

Chapter Summary

Derived Demand

- The demand for a factor is derived; hence, it is called a *derived demand*. Specifically, it is derived from, and directly related to, the demand for the product that the factor goes to produce; for example, the demand for auto workers is derived from the demand for autos.

MRP, MFC, VMP

- Marginal revenue product (MRP) is the additional revenue generated by employing an additional factor unit. Marginal factor cost (MFC) is the additional cost incurred by employing an additional factor unit. The profit-maximizing firm buys the factor quantity at which $MRP = MFC$.
- The MRP curve is the firm's factor demand curve; it shows how much of a given factor the firm buys at different prices.
- Value marginal product (VMP) is a measure of the value that each factor unit adds to the firm's product. Whereas $MRP = MR \times MPP$, $VMP = P \times MPP$. For a perfectly competitive firm, $P = MR$, so $MRP = VMP$. For a monopolist, a monopolistic competitor, or an oligopolist, $P > MR$, so $VMP > MRP$.

The Least-Cost Rule

- A firm minimizes costs by buying factors in the combination at which the MPP-to-price ratio for each factor is the same. For example, for two factors, labor (L) and capital (K), the least-cost rule is $MPP_L/P_L = MPP_K/P_K$.

Labor and Wages

- A change in the price of the product that labor produces or a change in the marginal physical product of labor (reflected in a shift in the MPP curve) will shift the demand curve for labor.
- The higher (lower) the elasticity of demand is for the product that labor produces, the higher (lower) the elasticity of demand is for labor. The higher (lower) the ratio is of labor cost to total cost, the higher (lower) the elasticity of demand is for labor. The more (fewer) substitutes there are for labor, the higher (lower) the elasticity of demand is for labor.
- As the wage rate rises, the quantity supplied of labor rises, *ceteris paribus*.
- At the equilibrium wage rate, the quantity supplied of labor equals the quantity demanded of labor.

Demand for and Supply of Labor

- The demand for labor is affected by (1) marginal revenue and (2) marginal physical product. The supply of labor is affected by (1) wage rates in other labor markets, (2) the nonpecuniary aspects of the job, (3) the number of persons who can do the job, (4) training costs, and (5) moving costs.

Key Terms and Concepts

Derived Demand
Marginal Revenue Product (MRP)
Value Marginal Product (VMP)
Marginal Factor Cost (MFC)
Factor Price Taker
Least-Cost Rule
Elasticity of Demand for Labor
Marginal Productivity Theory
Screening

Questions and Problems

1. What does it mean to say that the demand for a factor is a derived demand?
2. Why is the *MRP* curve a firm's factor demand curve?
3. "*VMP = MRP* for a price taker but not for a price searcher." Do you agree or disagree with this statement? Explain your answer.
4. Compare the firm's least-cost rule with how buyers allocate their consumption dollars.
5. The supply curve is horizontal for a factor price taker; however, the industry supply curve is upward sloping. Explain why this occurs.
6. What forces and factors determine the wage rate for a particular type of labor?
7. What is the relationship between labor productivity and wage rates?
8. What might be one effect of government legislating wage rates?
9. Using the theory developed in this chapter, explain the following:
   a. Why a worker in Ethiopia is likely to earn much less than a worker in Japan
   b. Why the army expects recruitment to rise during economic recessions
   c. Why basketball stars earn relatively large incomes
   d. Why jobs that carry a health risk offer higher pay than jobs that do not, *ceteris paribus*
10. Discuss the factors that might prevent the equalization of wage rates for identical or comparable jobs across labor markets.
11. Prepare a list of questions that an interviewer is likely to ask an interviewee in a job interview. Try to identify which of the questions are part of the interviewer's screening process.
12. Explain why the market demand curve for labor is not simply the horizontal addition of the firms' demand curves for labor.
13. Discuss the firm's objective, its constraints, and how it makes choices in its role as a buyer of resources.
14. Explain the relationship between each of the following pairs of concepts:
    a. The elasticity of demand for a product and the elasticity of demand for the labor that produces the product
    b. The ratio of labor cost to total cost and the elasticity of demand for labor
    c. The number of substitutes for labor and the elasticity of demand for labor
15. How might you go about determining whether a person is worth the salary he or she is paid?
16. What do substitution and income effects have to do with the supply curve of labor?

Working with Numbers and Graphs

1. Determine the appropriate numbers for the lettered spaces:

(1) Units of Factor X	(2) Quantity of Output	(3) Marginal Physical Product of X (MPP_x)	(4) Product Price, Marginal Revenue (P = MR)	(5) Total Revenue	(6) Marginal Revenue Product of X (MRP_x)
0	15	0	$8	F	L
1	24	A	8	G	M
2	32	B	8	H	N
3	39	C	8	I	O
4	45	D	8	J	P
5	50	E	8	K	Q

2. On the basis of the preceding table, if the price of a factor is constant at $48, how many units of the factor will the firm buy?
3. In one diagram, draw the *VMP* curve and the *MRP* curve for an oligopolist. Explain why the curves look the way you drew them.
4. Explain why the factor supply curve is horizontal for a factor price taker.
5. Look at the two factor demand curves in the accompanying figure. Is the price of the product that labor goes to produce higher for MRP_2 than for MRP_1? Explain your answer.

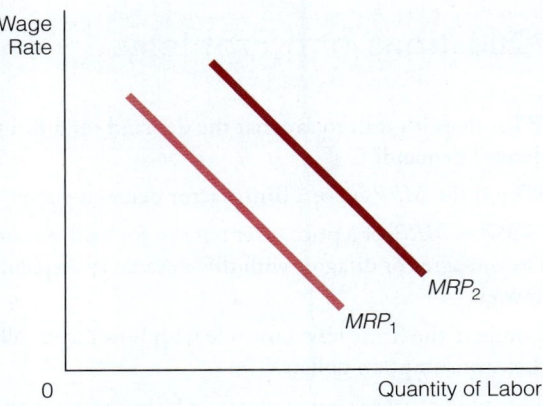

Wages, Unions, and Labor

CHAPTER 27

Introduction

Certain organizations seem to engender controversy. Labor unions are such organizations. Some people are strongly prounion; others are strongly antiunion. Moreover, many millions of people between these extremes don't have a strong opinion on labor unions. In this chapter, we discuss the objectives, practices, and effects of unions.

27-1 Objectives of Labor Unions

Labor unions usually seek at least one of three objectives:

- to employ all their members,
- to maximize the total wage bill, or
- to maximize income for a limited number of union members.

27-1a Employment for All Members

Suppose the demand curve in Exhibit 1 represents the demand for labor in a given union, and the total membership of the union is Q_1. If the objective of the union is to have its total membership employed, then the wage rate that must exist in the market is W_1. At W_1, firms want to hire the total union membership.

EXHIBIT 1

Labor Union Objectives

If total membership in the union is Q_1 and the union's objective is employment for all of its members, it chooses W_1. If the objective is to maximize the total wage bill, it chooses W_2, the wage at which the elasticity of demand for labor equals 1. If the union's objective is to maximize the income of a limited number of union workers (represented by Q_3), it chooses W_3.

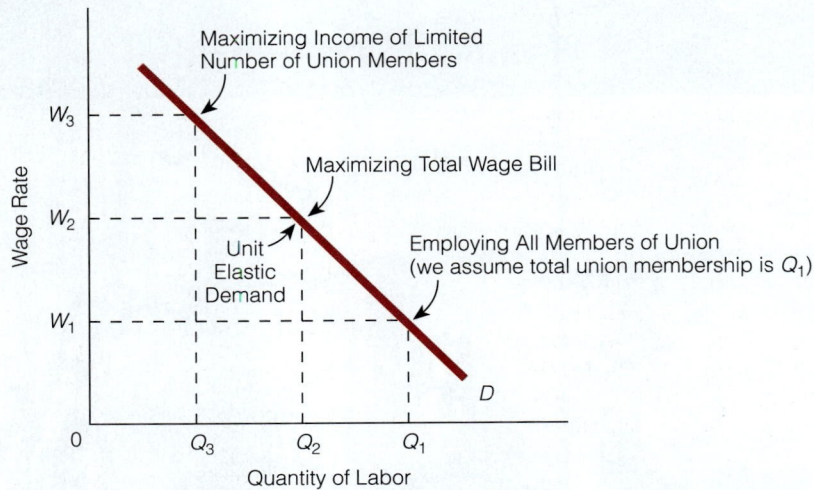

27-1b Maximizing the Total Wage Bill

The total wage bill paid to the membership of a union is equal to the wage rate multiplied by the number of labor hours worked. One objective of a labor union is to maximize this dollar amount—that is, to maximize the number of dollars coming *from* the employer *to* union members.

In Exhibit 1, the wage rate that maximizes the total wage bill is W_2. At W_2, the quantity of labor is Q_2 and the elasticity of demand for labor is equal to 1. Recall that total revenue (or total expenditure) is maximized when the price elasticity of demand is equal to 1—in other words, when demand has unit elasticity. So the total wage bill is maximized at that point where the demand for labor is unit elastic. However, less union labor is working at W_2 than at W_1, indicating that there is a trade-off between higher wages and the employment of union members.

27-1c Maximizing Income for a Limited Number of Union Members

Some economists have suggested that a labor union might want neither total employment of its membership nor maximization of the total wage bill. Instead, it might prefer to maximize income for a *limited number* of union members, perhaps those with the most influence or seniority in the union. Suppose this group is represented by Q_3 in Exhibit 1. The highest wage at which this group can be employed is W_3; thus, the union might seek this wage rate instead of any lower rate.

27-1d Wage–Employment Trade-Off

Exhibit 1 suggests that a union can get higher wage rates, but some of the union members will lose their jobs in the process. Hence, the wage–employment trade-off depends on the *elasticity of demand for labor*.

To illustrate, consider the demand for labor in two unions, *A* and *B*, shown in Exhibit 2. Suppose both unions bargain for a wage increase from W_1 to W_2. Then the quantity of labor drops much more in union *B*, where the demand for labor is elastic between the two wage

EXHIBIT 2

The Wage–Employment Trade-Off: Two Cases

For union A, which has an inelastic demand for its labor between W_1 and W_2, a higher wage rate brings about a smaller cutback in the quantity of labor than for union B, which has an elastic demand for its labor between W_1 and W_2. Accordingly, we predict that union B will be less likely to push for higher wages than union A because its wage–employment trade-off is more pronounced.

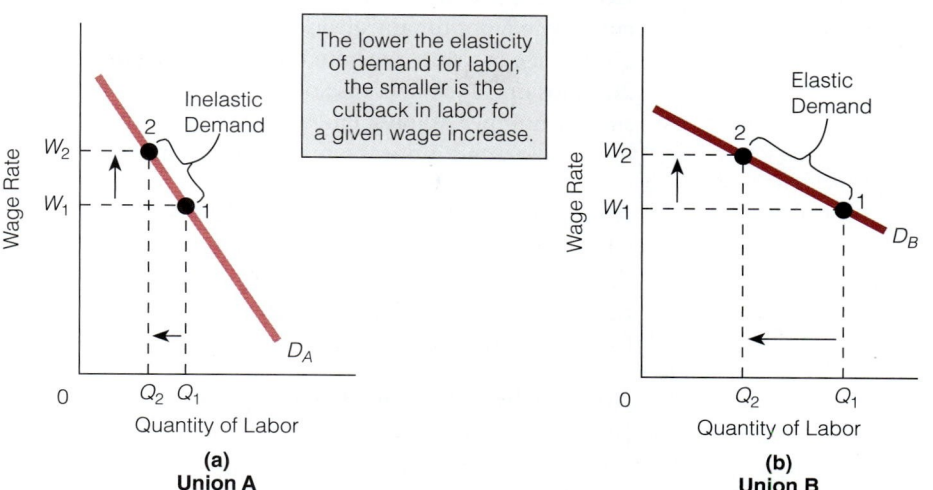

The lower the elasticity of demand for labor, the smaller is the cutback in labor for a given wage increase.

(a) Union A

(b) Union B

rates, than in union A, where the demand for labor is inelastic between the two wage rates. Thus, union B is less likely than union A to push for higher wages, *ceteris paribus*. The reason is that the wage–employment trade-off is more pronounced for union B than for union A. Pushing for higher wages is simply costlier (in terms of union members' jobs) for union B than it is for union A.

Finding Economics

In a Union Roundtable Discussion The leaders of a union are sitting around the table, discussing what to do in the upcoming negotiations with management. One person argues for a 7 percent wage increase. Another person argues for a 10 percent wage increase, saying, "I don't think a 10 percent wage increase will lose us many jobs—if any." Where is the economics?

The economics is in the statement about the 10 percent wage increase. Believing that few, if any, jobs will be lost tells us that the person believes either that the wage–employment trade-off is small or that the demand for union labor is highly inelastic (maybe even perfectly inelastic if there will be no loss of jobs).

27-2 Practices of Labor Unions

This section explains how labor unions try to meet their objectives by influencing one or more of the following factors:

- The elasticity of demand for labor
- The demand for labor
- The supply of labor

We also discuss how unions can directly affect wages.

27-2a Affecting the Elasticity of Demand for Union Labor

Exhibit 2 shows that the lower the elasticity of demand is for labor, the smaller will be the cutback in labor for any given wage increase. Obviously, the smaller the cutback in labor for a given wage increase, the better it is for the labor union. Given a choice between losing either 200 jobs or 50 jobs because of a wage rate increase of $2, the labor union prefers to lose the smaller number of jobs. Thus, a labor union looks for ways to lower the elasticity of demand for its labor, and it does so mainly by attempting to reduce the availability of substitutes.

Availability of Substitute Products Consider the United Automobile Workers union, whose members produce American automobiles. We know that the lower the elasticity of demand is for American automobiles, the lower the elasticity of demand will be for the labor that produces automobiles. So unions might attempt to reduce the availability of substitutes for the products they produce by such means as restrictions on imports.

Availability of Substitute Factors The fewer the substitute factors there are for union labor, the lower the elasticity of demand will be for union labor. Union labor has two general substitutes: nonunion labor and certain types of machines. For example, a musical synthesizer (which can sound like many different instruments) is a substitute for a group of musicians playing different instruments. Labor unions have often attempted to reduce the availability of substitute factors—both nonunion and nonhuman. Thus, labor unions sometimes oppose the relaxation of immigration laws, they generally are in favor of a high minimum wage (which increases the relative price of nonunion labor vis-à-vis union labor), and they usually oppose machines that can be substituted for their labor. In addition, in the area of construction, unions usually specify that certain jobs are done by, say, electricians only (thus prohibiting substitute factors from being employed on those jobs).

27-2b Affecting the Demand for Union Labor

Labor unions can try to meet their objectives by increasing the demand for union labor. All other things held constant, this approach leads to higher wage rates and more union labor employed. Labor unions can increase the demand for their labor in a number of ways.

Increasing Product Demand Unions occasionally urge the buying public to buy the products produced by union labor. Union advertisements urge people to "look for the union label" or to look for the label that reads "Made in the U.S.A." As mentioned, unions sometimes also support legislation that either keeps out imports altogether or makes them more expensive.

Increasing Substitute Factor Prices If union action leads to a rise in the relative price of factors that are substitutes for union labor, the demand for union labor rises. For this reason, unions have often lobbied for an increase in the minimum wage—the wage received mostly by unskilled labor, which is a substitute for skilled union labor. The first minimum-wage legislation was passed in 1938, when many companies were moving from the unionized North to the nonunionized South. The minimum wage made the nonunionized, relatively unskilled labor in the South more expensive and is said to have slowed the movement of companies to the South.

Increasing Marginal Physical Product If unions can increase the productivity of their members, the demand for their labor will rise. With this idea in mind, unions prefer to add skilled labor to their ranks, and they sometimes undertake training programs for new entrants.

27-2c Affecting the Supply of Union Labor

Labor unions also try to meet their objectives by decreasing the supply of labor, because a decreased supply translates into higher wage rates. One way to lower the supply below what it might be if the union did not exist is to control the supply of labor in a market.

Craft unions, in particular, have been moderately successful in getting employers to hire only union labor. In the past, they were successful at turning some businesses into closed shops. A **closed shop** is an organization in which an employee must belong to the union before being able to work. (In contrast, in an *open shop*, an employer may hire union or nonunion workers.) When unions can determine, or at least control in some way, the supply of labor in a given market, they can decrease it from what it would be otherwise. They can do this by restricting membership, by requiring long apprenticeships, or by imposing rigid certification requirements. In 1947, the Taft–Hartley Act prohibited the closed shop.

The **union shop**, however, is legal in many states today. A union shop is an organization that does not require individuals to be union members to be hired but does require them to join the union within a certain time after becoming employed.

Today, unions typically argue for union shops, against open shops, and against the prohibition of closed shops. They also typically argue against state right-to-work laws (which some, but not all, states have), which make it illegal to require union membership for purposes of employment. (The Taft–Hartley Act allowed states to pass right-to-work laws and thus to override federal legislation that legalized union shops.) In short, the union shop is illegal in right-to-work states.

Closed Shop
An organization in which an employee must belong to the union before he or she can be hired.

Union Shop
An organization in which a worker is not required to be a member of the union in order to be hired but must become a member within a certain time after being employed.

Collective Bargaining
The process whereby wage rates and other issues are determined by a union bargaining with management on behalf of all union members.

Strike
The union employees' refusal to work at a certain wage or under certain conditions.

27-2d Affecting Wages Directly: Collective Bargaining

Besides increasing wage rates indirectly by influencing the demand for and supply of their labor, unions can directly affect wage rates through collective bargaining. **Collective bargaining** is the process whereby unions bargain with management on behalf of union members to determine wage rates. In collective bargaining, union members act together as a single unit to increase their bargaining power with management. On the other side of the market, employers of labor may also band together and act as one unit, with the same objective: to increase *their* bargaining power.

From the viewpoint of the labor union, collective bargaining is unlikely to be successful unless the union can strike. A **strike** occurs when unionized employees refuse to work at a certain wage or under certain conditions.

Exhibit 3 illustrates the effects of successful union collective bargaining. Suppose the initial wage rate that exists in the labor market is the competitive wage rate W_1. This is the wage rate that would exist if each employee were to bargain separately with management. The equilibrium quantity of labor is Q_1.

EXHIBIT 3

Successful Collective Bargaining by the Union

We start at a wage rate of W_1. The union's objective is to increase the wage rate to W_2. Such a wage rate means that the union holds that the new supply curve of labor is $S'S$—the heavy supply curve. To convince management that the new supply curve looks as the union says it does, the union will have to either threaten a strike or call one. We assume that the union is successful at raising the wage rate to W_2. As a consequence, the quantity of labor employed is less than it would have been at W_1.

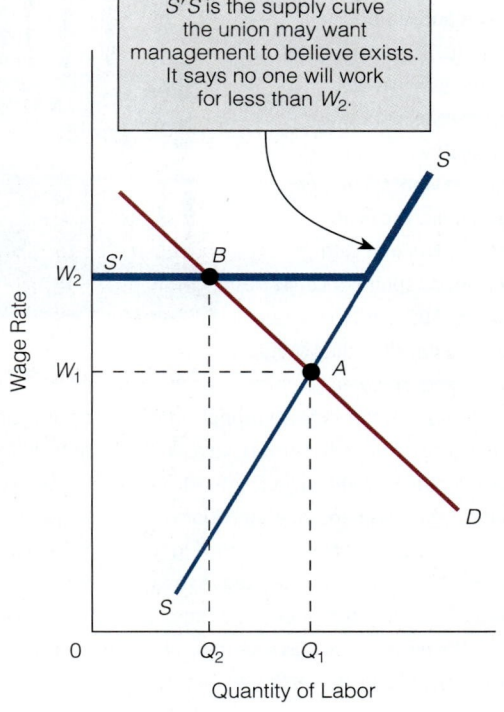

$S'S$ is the supply curve the union may want management to believe exists. It says no one will work for less than W_2.

Management and the union now sit down at a collective-bargaining session. The union specifies that it wants a wage rate of W_2 and says that *none of its members will work at a lower wage rate*. Thus, the union holds that the new supply curve is $S'S$—the heavy supply curve in Exhibit 3. In effect, the union is telling management that it cannot hire anyone for a wage rate lower than W_2.

Whether the union can bring about this higher wage rate (W_2) depends on whether it can prevent labor from working at less than that wage. That is, if management does not initially agree to W_2, the union will have to call a strike and show management that it cannot hire any labor for a wage rate lower than W_2. It has to convince management that the new supply curve looks the way the union says it looks. (We assume that the strike threat, or actual strike, is successful for the union and that management agrees to the higher wage rate of W_2.) As a result, the quantity of labor employed, Q_2, is less than it would have been at W_1. The new equilibrium is at point B instead of point A.

Economics 24/7

Technology, the Price of Competing Factors, and Displaced Workers[1]

For most of the eighteenth century in England, spinners and weavers worked on hand-operated spinning wheels and looms. Then, in the 1770s, a mechanical spinner was invented that required steam or water power, so yarn-spinning factories were set up near water mills. The factory workers, working with mechanical spinners, could produce 100 times more yarn in a day than they could using hand-operated spinners.

Because of the increased supply of yarn, the price fell, and the quantity demanded of yarn increased substantially. In turn, the heightened demand increased the demand for weavers who continued to use hand-operated looms. As a result, weavers' wages increased. In reaction to the higher wages for weavers, entrepreneurs and inventors began to experiment with different kinds of weaving machines. Their experiments began to pay off: in 1787, the power loom was invented, although it was not perfected until the 1820s. By the 1830s, two workers using a power loom could produce in one day 20 times what a weaver could produce on a hand-operated loom.

Soon, the weavers who used hand-operated looms found themselves without jobs, displaced by the power loom. Some of the displaced workers showed their frustration and anger at their predicament by burning power looms and factories.

The story of spinners and weavers in eighteenth-century England helps us realize two important points about technology. First, as long as technology advances, some workers will be temporarily displaced. Second, an advance in technology often has an identifiable cause; it doesn't simply fall out of the sky. If it had not been for the higher weavers' wages, the power loom might not have been invented.

---

[1]. This feature is based on Elizabeth Hoffman, "How Can Displaced Workers Find Better Jobs?" in *Second Thoughts: Myths and Morals of U.S. Economic History*, ed. by Donald McCloskey (Oxford: Oxford University Press, 1993).

27-2e Strikes

The purpose of a strike is to convince management that the supply curve is what the union says it is. Often, success depends on the ability of striking union employees to prevent nonstriking and nonunion employees from working for management at a lower wage rate than the union is seeking through collective bargaining. For example, if management can easily hire individuals at a wage rate lower than W_2 in Exhibit 3, it will not be convinced that the heavy supply curve is the relevant supply curve.

(Answers to Self-Test questions are in Answers to Self-Test Questions at the back of the book.)

1. What will lower the demand for union labor?
2. What is the difference between a closed shop and a union shop?
3. What is the objective of a strike?

27-3 Effects of Labor Unions

This section addresses two questions:

- What are the effects of labor unions on wage rates?
- Are the effects the same in all labor markets?

27-3a The Case of Monopsony

A single buyer in a factor market is known as a **monopsony**. Some economists refer to a monopsony as a buyer's monopoly; that is, whereas a monopoly is a single *seller* of a product, a monopsony is a single *buyer*.

For example, if a firm in a small town is the only buyer of labor because there are no other firms for miles around, the firm is a monopsony. Because it is a monopsony, it cannot buy additional units of a factor without increasing the price it pays for it (in much the same way that a monopolist in the product market cannot sell an additional unit of its good without lowering the price.) The reason is that the supply of labor the monopsonist faces is the market supply of labor.

Marginal factor cost *(MFC)* increases as the monopsonist buys additional units of a factor, and the supply curve of the factor *is not the same* as the firm's *MFC* curve. [For a price taker in the factor market, *MFC* is constant, and the *MFC* curve is the same as the supply curve for the factor. A monopsonist is not a price taker in the factor market: *MFC* rises as the monopsonist buys additional units of a factor, and its *MFC* curve and supply curve (for the factor) are not the same.]

As shown in Exhibit 4, *MFC* increases as additional units of the factor are purchased. Notice in part (a) that, as workers are added, the wage rate rises. For example, for the monopsonist to employ two workers, the wage rate must rise from $16.00 per hour to $16.05. To employ three workers, the monopsonist must offer to pay $16.10. Comparing column 2 with column 4, we notice that the *MFC* for a monopsonist is greater than the wage rate (in the same way that for a monopolist in a product market, price is greater than marginal revenue). Plotting columns 1 and 2 gives the supply curve for the monopsonist [see Exhibit 4(b)]; plotting columns 1 and 4 gives the monopsonist's *MFC* curve. Because *MFC* is greater than the wage rate, the supply curve lies below the *MFC* curve.

Monopsony
A single buyer in a factor market.

EXHIBIT 4

The Labor Union and the Monopsonist

(a) For the monopsonist, MFC > wage rate. This relationship implies that the supply curve the monopsonist faces lies below its MFC curve. (b) The monopsonist purchases quantity Q_1 of labor and pays a wage rate W_1, which is less than MRP. (In other words, labor is being paid less than its MRP.) (c) If the labor union succeeds in increasing the wage rate from W_1 to W_2 through collective bargaining, then the firm will also hire more labor (Q_2 instead of Q_1). We conclude that, in the case of monopsony, higher wage rates (over a given range) do not imply fewer persons working.

(1) Workers	(2) Wage Rate	(3) Total Labor Cost (1) × (2)	(4) Marginal Factor Cost $\frac{\Delta(3)}{\Delta(1)}$
0	—	—	—
1	$16.00	$16.00	$16.00
2	16.05	32.10	16.10
3	16.10	48.30	16.20
4	16.15	64.60	16.30
5	16.20	81.00	16.40

(a)

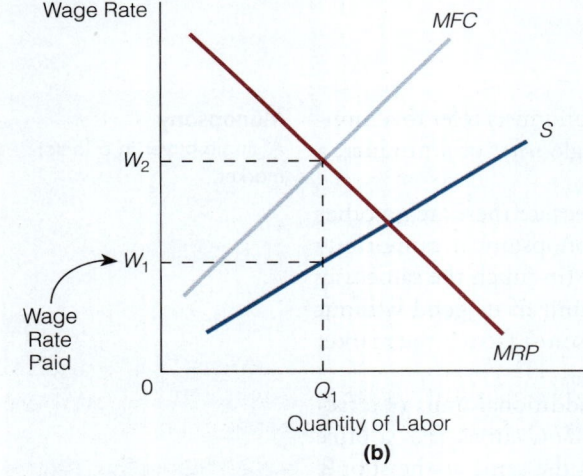

(b)

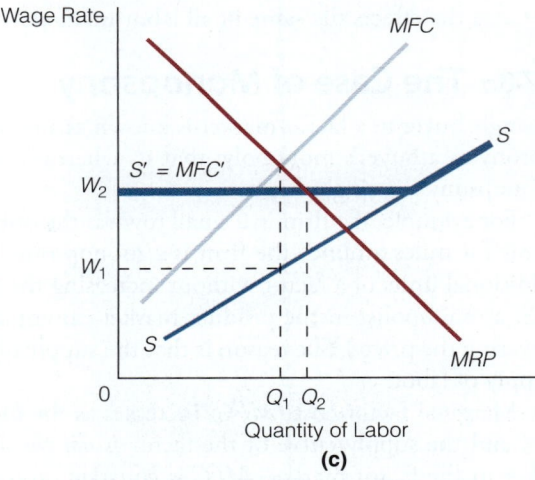

(c)

Exhibit 4(b) shows that the monopsonist chooses to purchase Q_1 units of labor (where MRP = MFC) and that it pays a wage rate of W_1 (the wage rate necessary to get Q_1 workers to offer their services).

If the monopsonist were to pay workers what their services were worth to it (as represented by the MRP curve), it would pay a higher wage. Some persons contend that labor unions and collective bargaining are necessary when labor is paid less than its marginal revenue product. Furthermore, they argue that successful collective bargaining on the part of the labor union in this setting is not subject to the wage–employment trade-off it encounters in other settings, as illustrated in Exhibit 4(c).

In Exhibit 4(c), successful collective bargaining by the labor union moves the wage rate from W_1 to W_2. The labor union is essentially saying to the monopsonist that it cannot hire any labor below W_2. If the labor union is right, then the monopsonist's MFC curve changes from MFC to MFC′, which corresponds to the new supply curve the monopsonist faces, $S'S$. The monopsonist once again purchases the quantity of labor at which marginal revenue product equals MFC. But now, because the MFC curve is MFC′, equality is at Q_2 workers and a wage rate of W_2. Therefore, over a range, there is no wage–employment trade-off for the labor union when it faces a monopsonist. It can raise both the wage rate and the number of workers employed.

27-3b Unions' Effects on Wages

Most studies show that some unions have increased their members' wages substantially whereas other unions have not done so at all. Work by H. Gregg Lewis concludes that, during the period 1920–1979, the average wage of union members was 10–15 percent higher than that of comparable nonunion labor. (Keep in mind, though, that the union–nonunion wage differential can differ quite a bit in different years and among industries; for data on this subject, see Exhibit 5.)

The Union–Nonunion Wage Gap Exhibit 6 illustrates the theoretical basis of the observation that higher union wages lead to lower nonunion wages (a union–nonunion wage gap). Two sectors of the labor market are shown: the unionized sector in part (a) and the nonunionized sector in part (b). Assume that labor is homogeneous and that the wage rate is $25 an hour in both sectors.

EXHIBIT 5

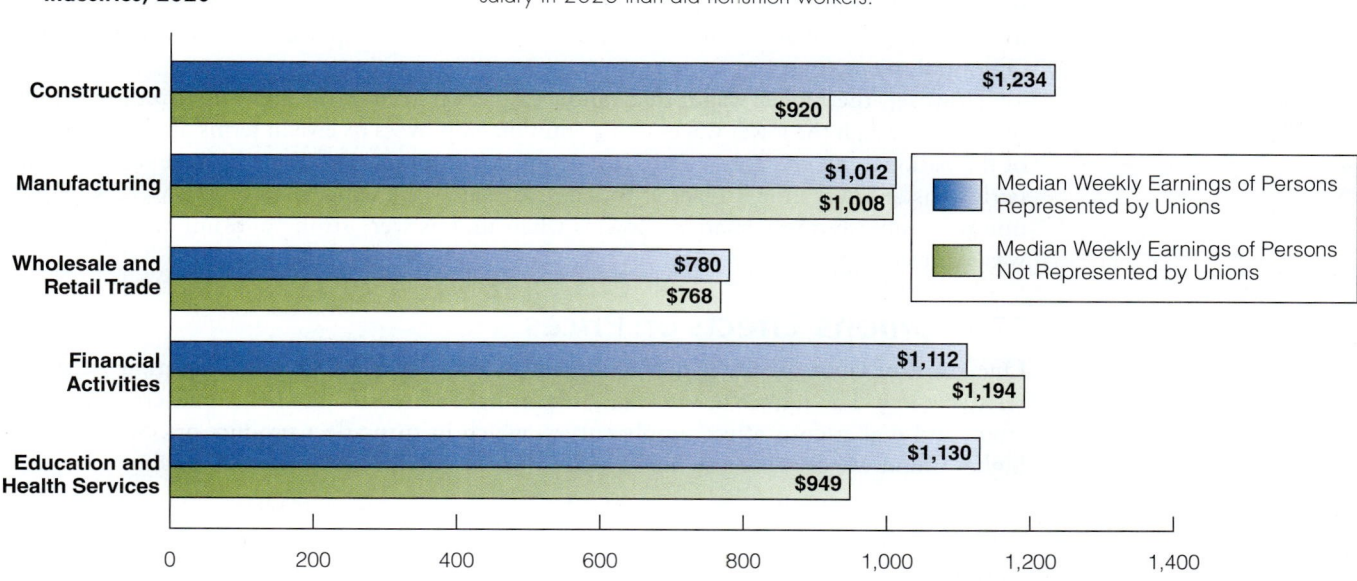

Median Weekly Earnings in the Union and Nonunion Sectors, Selected Industries, 2020

In four of the five (selected) industries shown, union workers earned a higher weekly salary in 2020 than did nonunion workers.

Source: Bureau of Labor Statistics

EXHIBIT 6

The Effect of Labor Unions on Union and Nonunion Wages

We begin at a wage rate of $25 in both the unionized sector (a), and the nonunionized sector (b). Next, the union manages to increase its wage rate to $28, either through collective bargaining or by decreasing the supply of labor in the unionized sector (shown). Fewer persons now work in the unionized sector, and we assume that those persons who lose their jobs move to the nonunionized sector. Consequently, the supply of labor in the nonunionized sector rises, and the wage rate falls.

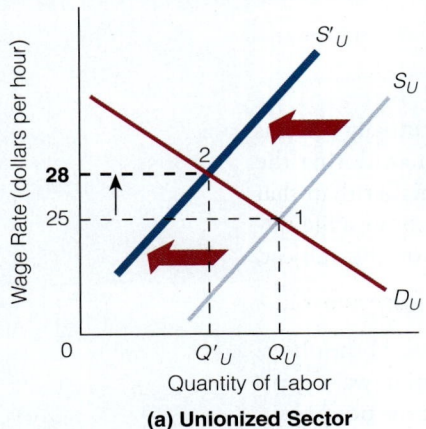

(a) Unionized Sector

Changes in supply conditions and wage rates in the unionized sector can cause changes in supply conditions and wage rates in the nonunionized sector.

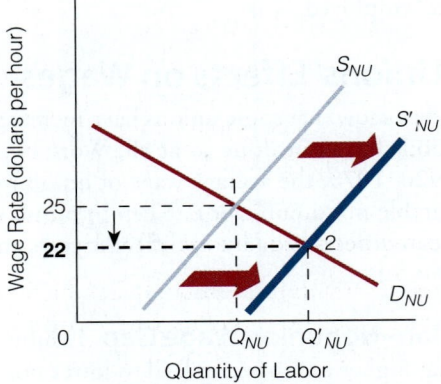

(b) Nonunionized Sector

The labor union either collectively bargains to a higher wage rate of, say, $28 an hour or manages to reduce supply so that the higher wage rate comes about. (The exhibit shows a decrease in supply.) As a consequence, less labor is employed in the unionized sector. If those now not working in the unionized sector can work in the nonunionized sector, then the supply of labor in the nonunionized sector increases from S_{NU} to S'_{NU} and the wage rate in the nonunionized sector falls to $22 an hour. Therefore, there are theoretical and empirical reasons for believing that labor unions increase the wages of union employees and decrease the wages of nonunion employees.

However, the higher wages that union employees receive through unionization do not seem to outweigh the lower wages that nonunion employees receive in terms of the percentage of the national income that goes to labor (union plus nonunion), a percentage that has been fairly constant over time. In fact, it was approximately the same when unions were weak and union membership was relatively low as when unions were strong and union membership was relatively high.

27-3c Unions' Effects on Prices

One effect of labor unions is that union wages are relatively high and nonunion wages are relatively low. The higher union wages mean higher costs for the firms that employ union labor, and higher costs affect supply curves, which in turn affect product prices. Therefore, higher union wages will cause higher prices for the products that the union labor produces.

Conversely, lower nonunion wages mean lower costs for the firms that employ nonunion labor and, thus, lower prices for the products produced by nonunion labor.

27-3d Unions' Effects on Productivity and Efficiency: Two Views

There are two major views of the effects that labor unions have on productivity and efficiency.

The Traditional (or Orthodox) View The traditional view holds that labor unions have a negative impact on productivity and efficiency. Its proponents make the following arguments:

- Labor unions often have unnecessary staffing requirements and insist that only certain persons be allowed to do certain jobs. Because of these considerations, the economy operates below its potential—that is, inefficiently.
- Strikes disrupt production and prevent the economy from realizing its productive potential.
- Labor unions drive an artificial wedge between the wages of comparable labor in the union and nonunion sectors of the labor market.

This last point warrants elaboration. In Exhibit 6, labor is homogeneous, and the wage rate is initially the same in both sectors of the labor market. Union efforts then increase the wage rate in the union sector and decrease the wage rate in the nonunion sector. At this point, the marginal revenue product of persons who work in the union sector is higher than the marginal revenue product of individuals who work in the nonunion sector. [We are farther up the factor demand (MRP) curve in the union than in the nonunion sector.] If labor could move from the nonunionized sector to the unionized sector, it would be moving from where it is worth less to where it is worth more, but it cannot do so because of the supply-restraining efforts of the union. Economists call this state of affairs a misallocation of labor: Not all labor is employed where it is the most valuable.

The Labor Union as a Collective Voice There is evidence that, in some industries, union firms have a higher rate of productivity than nonunion firms. Some economists believe that this effect is a result of the labor union's role as a collective voice mechanism for its members. Without a labor union, workers who are disgruntled with their jobs, who feel taken advantage of by their employers, or who feel unsafe in their work will leave their jobs and seek work elsewhere. Job exiting comes at a cost: It raises the turnover rate, results in lengthy job searches during which individuals are not producing goods and services, and raises training costs. Such costs can be reduced, it is argued, when a labor union acts as a collective voice for its members. Instead of individual employees having personally to discuss ticklish matters with their employer, the labor union does so for them. Overall, the labor union makes employees feel more confident, less intimidated, and more secure in their work. Such positive feelings usually mean happier, more productive employees. Some proponents of this view also hold that employees are less likely to quit their jobs. In fact, there is evidence that unionism does indeed reduce job quits.

Critics have contended, though, that the reduced job quits are less a function of the labor union's collective voice than of the labor union's institutional capability of increasing its members' wages. Also, the productivity-increasing aspects of the labor union, which are linked to its role as a collective voice mechanism, are independent of the productivity-decreasing aspects of the labor union in its role as a monopolizer of labor.

Economics 24/7

Unions, Profits, and Prices

Sometimes, the effects of an action are different in the short run than in the long run. With this in mind, consider the layperson's view of labor unions, which is that labor unions obtain higher wages for their members at the expense of the owners of the firm and not at the expense of other workers. But this view may be built upon only the short-run effect of higher wages and not the long-run effect.

To explain, consider that, in the theory of perfect competition, if short-run profits exist, new firms will enter the industry, the industry supply curve will shift rightward, prices will decrease, and profits are competed away. Conversely, given short-run losses, firms exit the industry; the industry supply curve shifts leftward, prices increase, and losses finally disappear. So, in the long run, there is zero economic profit in the perfectly competitive market.

Now in this market structure, consider a labor union that manages to obtain higher wages for its members. In the short run, these higher wages can diminish profits, as any cost increase would diminish profits, *ceteris paribus*. But in the long run, adjustments are made as firms exit the industry, supply curves shift, less is produced, some people may lose their jobs, and prices rise. In the long run, zero economic profit will exist. Therfore, in the short run, higher wages may come out of profits, but in the long run they probably do not.

Does this matter to you? It very well might if you are the union worker who got a higher wage in the short run, only to lose your job in the long run.

Thinking Like an Economist

Primary and Secondary Effects Economists make the important distinction between primary and secondary effects—that is, between what happens in the short run and what happens in the long run. For example, higher wages for union workers may initially come at the expense of profits, but as time passes, this may not continue to be the case.

1. What is a major difference between a monopsonist and a factor price taker?
2. Under what conditions will the minimum wage increase the number of people working?
3. How could a collectively bargained higher wage rate in the unionized sector of the economy lead to a lower wage rate in the nonunionized sector of the economy?

Office Hours

"Don't Higher Wages Reduce Profits?"

Student: I'm beginning to find that many things in economics are counterintuitive. Things I expect to be true turn out to be false, and things that I think are false turn out to be true.

Instructor: Are you thinking of something in particular?

Student: I had thought that labor unions obtained higher wages at the expense of the firm owners by reducing the owners' profits. Now I know that this is not necessarily true in the long run, especially in a perfectly competitive market.

Instructor: Any thoughts on why economics is full of the counterintuitive?

Student: I'm not sure.

Instructor: Well, part of the answer might have to do with how far we take the analysis. To illustrate, consider your example dealing with the labor union and profits. You had thought that the labor union obtained higher wages at the expense of the firm owners. That can be true in the short run. In other words, your intuition was correct for the short run. But when we extended the analysis beyond the immediate effects of higher wages, things began to turn out differently than you thought.

Student: So, is there a lesson here?

Instructor: Don't stop analyzing things too soon. The problem, though, is that we don't always know that we're stopping too soon.

Student: In other words, I saw the story this way: Wages for members of labor unions rise, causing profits to fall for owners of firms. But I should have seen it this way: Wages for members of labor unions rise, profits fall for owners of firms, some firms leave the industry, the market supply curve shifts leftward, and price rises.

Of course, my problem, as you imply, was that I didn't know that I should have gone beyond steps 1 and 2. I didn't know steps 3 through 5 were there. So I guess my question now is, how do you get to those steps if you don't know they exist?

Instructor: That's a good question. What you need is a device to use that can propel you onward. That device comes in the form of the question, is there anything else? To illustrate, go back to the way you initially saw the story: Wages for members of labor unions rise, causing profits to fall for owners of firms.

Now, instead of putting a period at the end of that, ask a question: If profits fall for the owners of firms, what, if anything, do falling profits lead to? This question—a form of the question "Is there anything else?"—propels you forward and reduces the probability that you will stop before you have tried to figure out the full story.

Points to Remember

1. Do higher wages lead to lower profits—end of story? Our answer depends on how far we take the analysis.
2. To propel our analysis forward, we often need to ask whether there is anything else.

Chapter Summary

Objectives of a Union

- Objectives of a union include (1) employment for all its members, (2) maximization of the total wage bill, and (3) maximization of the income for a limited number of union members. A labor union faces a wage–employment trade-off: Higher wage rates mean lower labor union employment. An exception is when a labor union faces a monopsonist; then the union can raise both wage rates and employment of its members (over a given range). Exhibit 4(c) illustrates this possibility.

Practices of a Labor Union

- To soften the wage-employment trade-off, a labor union seeks to lower the elasticity of demand for its labor. Ways of doing this are (1) reducing the availability of substitute products and (2) reducing the availability of substitute factors for labor.
- Union wage rates can be increased indirectly by increasing the demand for union labor or by reducing the supply of union labor, or they can be increased directly by collective bargaining. To increase demand for its labor, a union might try to (1) increase demand for the good it produces, (2) substitute factor prices, or (3) increase its marginal physical product. To decrease the supply of its labor, a union might argue for closed and union shops and against right-to-work laws.
- In a way, successful collective bargaining by a labor union changes the supply curve of labor that the employer faces. The labor union is successful if, through its collective-bargaining efforts, it can prevent the employer from hiring labor at a wage rate below a union-determined level. In this case, the supply curve of labor becomes horizontal at the union-determined wage rate. (see Exhibit 3).

Monopsony

- For a monopsonist, MFC rises as it buys additional units of a factor. Also, the monopsonist's supply curve lies below its MFC curve. The monopsonist buys the factor quantity at which $MRP = MFC$. The price of the factor is less than the monopsonist's MFC, so the monopsonist pays the factor less than its marginal revenue product.

Effects of Unions

- There is evidence that labor unions generally have the effect of increasing their members' wage rates (over what they would be without the union) and of lowering the wage rates of nonunion labor.
- The traditional view of labor unions holds that unions negatively affect productivity and efficiency by (1) arguing for, and often obtaining, unnecessary staffing requirements, (2) calling strikes that disrupt production, and (3) driving an artificial wedge between the wages of comparable labor in the union and nonunion sectors.
- The new view of labor unions holds that labor unions act as a collective voice mechanism for individual union employees and cause them to feel more confident in their jobs and less intimidated by their employers. This effort leads to more productive employees, who are less likely to quit.

Key Terms and Concepts

Closed Shop
Union Shop
Collective Bargaining
Strike
Monopsony

Questions and Problems

1. Will a union behave differently if it wants to get all of its members employed instead of maximizing the total wage bill? Explain your answer.
2. What does the elasticity of demand for labor have to do with the wage–employment trade-off?
3. Identify one practice of labor unions that is consistent with the following:
    a. Affecting the elasticity of demand for union labor
    b. Increasing the demand for union labor
    c. Decreasing the supply of labor union workers

4. What view is a labor union likely to hold on each of the following issues?
   a. A quota on imported products
   b. Free trade
   c. A decrease in the minimum wage
5. Most actions or practices of labor unions are attempts to affect one of three factors. What are they?
6. Explain why the monopsonist pays a wage rate less than labor's marginal revenue product.
7. Organizing labor unions may be easier in some industries than in others. What industry characteristics make unionization easier?
8. What is the effect of labor unions on nonunion wage rates?
9. Some persons argue that a monopsony firm exploits its workers if it pays them less than their marginal revenue products. Others disagree. They say that, as long as the firm pays the workers their opportunity costs (which must be the case, or else the workers would not stay with the firm), the workers are not being exploited. This view suggests that there are two definitions of exploitation:
   a. Paying workers below their marginal revenue products (even if wages equal the workers' opportunity costs)
   b. Paying workers below their opportunity costs

   Keeping in mind that your answer may be a subjective judgment, which definition of exploitation do you think is more descriptive of the process and why?
10. A discussion of labor unions usually evokes strong feelings. Some people argue vigorously against labor unions; others argue with equal vigor for them. Some people see labor unions as the reason the workers in this country enjoy as high a standard of living as they do; others see labor unions as the reason the country is not so well off economically as it might be. Speculate on why the topic of labor unions generates such strong feelings and emotions—often with little analysis.
11. What forces may lead to the breakup of an employer (monopsony) cartel?
12. Unions can affect (a) a firm's profits, (b) the price consumers pay for a good, and (c) the wages received by nonunion workers. Do you agree or disagree? Explain your answer.
13. Contrast the traditional (or orthodox) and new views of labor unions.

Working with Numbers and Graphs

1. Determine the appropriate numbers for the lettered spaces:

(1) Workers	(2) Wage Rate	(3) Total Labor Cost	(4) Marginal Factor Cost
1	A	$12.00	$12.00
2	$12.10	24.20	E
3	12.20	C	F
4	B	D	12.60

2. Which demand curve for labor in the accompanying figure exhibits the most pronounced wage–employment trade-off? Explain your answer.

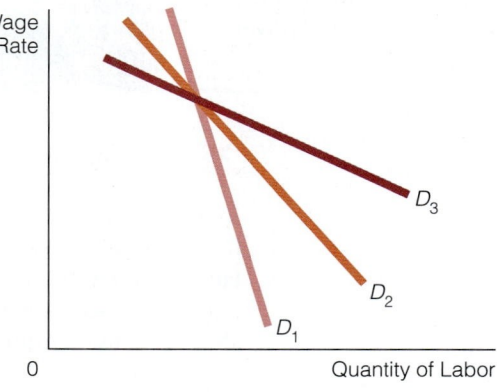

3. Diagrammatically explain how changes in supply conditions and wage rates in the unionized sector can cause changes in supply conditions and wage rates in the nonunionized sector.

CHAPTER 28
The Distribution of Income and Poverty

Introduction

A random sample of people from the general population will have various incomes. Some people will be in the top 20 percent of income earners, some in the lowest 20 percent, and many others between these two extremes. In other words, some people earn high incomes, some earn low incomes, and many earn middle incomes. What factors influence the amount of income a person earns? Why are some people more likely than others to be poor? Why are some people more likely to be rich? You'll find the answers to these questions and to many other questions about the distribution of income and poverty in this chapter.

28-1 Some Facts About Income Distribution

In discussing public policy issues, people sometimes talk about a single fact when they should talk about a collection of facts. A single fact is usually not as informative as a collection of facts, in much the same way that a single snapshot does not tell as much of a story as a moving picture—a succession of snapshots—does. This section presents a collection of a few facts about the distribution of income in the United States.

28-1a Who Are the Rich and How Rich Are They?

By many interpretations, the lowest fifth (the lowest quintile) of households in the United States is considered poor, the top fifth is considered rich, and the middle three-fifths are considered middle income.[1]

In 2019, the lowest fifth (the poor) in the United States received 3.1 percent of the total money income, the second fifth received 8.3 percent, the third fifth received 14.1 percent, the fourth fifth received 22.7 percent, and the top fifth (the rich) received 51.9 percent

---
[1] A household consists of all people who occupy a housing unit. It includes the related family members and all unrelated people living in the unit.

(see Exhibit 1).[2] The average income in 2019 for those persons in the lowest fifth was $15,286; $40,652 for those in the second fifth; $68,938 for those in the third fifth; $111,112 for those in the fourth fifth; and $254,449 for those in the highest fifth.

Has the income distribution become more or less equal over time? Exhibit 2 shows the income shares of households in 1967 and 2019. In 1967, the highest fifth (top) of households accounted for 43.8 percent of all income; in 2019, the percentage had risen to 51.9 percent. Exhibit 3 shows how mean quintile household income has changed for different quintiles during the period 1967–2019.

At the other end of the income spectrum, in 1967 the lowest fifth received 4.0 percent of all income; in 2019, the percentage had fallen to 3.1 percent. The middle groups—the three-fifths of income recipients between the lowest fifth and the highest fifth—accounted for 52.3 percent of all income in 1967 and 45.1 percent in 2019.

Many people implicitly assume that the quintiles (the fifths) in the income distribution contain an equal number of persons, but they do not. Instead, each quintile contains an equal percentage (20 percent) of households. But a household can contain any number of people. For example, in the United States, high-income households tend to be married couples with many members and earners. Low-income households tend to be single persons with little or no earnings. For example, in 2019, the average household in the top quintile consisted of 3.2 persons while the average household in the bottom quintile comprised 1.8 persons.

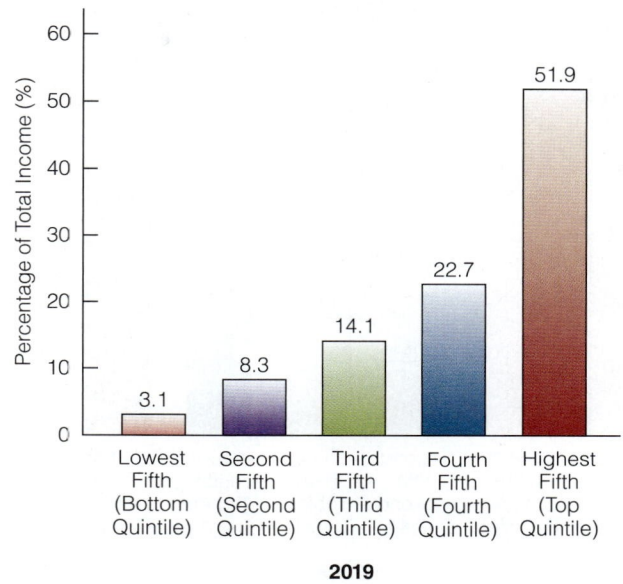

EXHIBIT 1

Distribution of Household Income Shares, 2019

The annual income shares for different quintiles of households is shown here.

Source: U.S. Bureau of the Census.

28-1b The Effect of Age on the Income Distribution

In analyzing the income distribution, we have to distinguish between people who are poor for long periods (sometimes their entire lives) and people who are poor temporarily. Consider Shandra, who attends college and works part time as a server at a nearby restaurant. Currently, her income is so low that she falls into the lowest quintile of income earners, but she isn't likely always to be in this quintile. After she graduates from college, Shandra's income will probably rise. If she is like most people, her income will rise during her twenties, thirties, and forties. In her late forties or early fifties, her income will take a slight downturn and then level off.

Possibly—in fact, very likely—people in their late twenties, thirties, or forties will have a higher income than people in their early twenties or people in their sixties, even though their total lifetime incomes will be identical. If we view each person over time, income equality is greater than if we view each person at a particular point in time (say, when one person is 58 years old and another is 68).

Exhibit 4 shows the incomes of John and Stephanie over a span of years. In 2000, John is 18 years old and earning $10,000 per year and Stephanie is 28 years old and earning $30,000

---

[2] Because of rounding, percentages in this chapter do not always sum to 100 percent.

EXHIBIT 2

Income Distribution, 1967 and 2019

Note that income shares have not been adjusted for such things as taxes and in-kind transfer payments, which are transfer payments made in terms of a specific good or service rather than in cash.

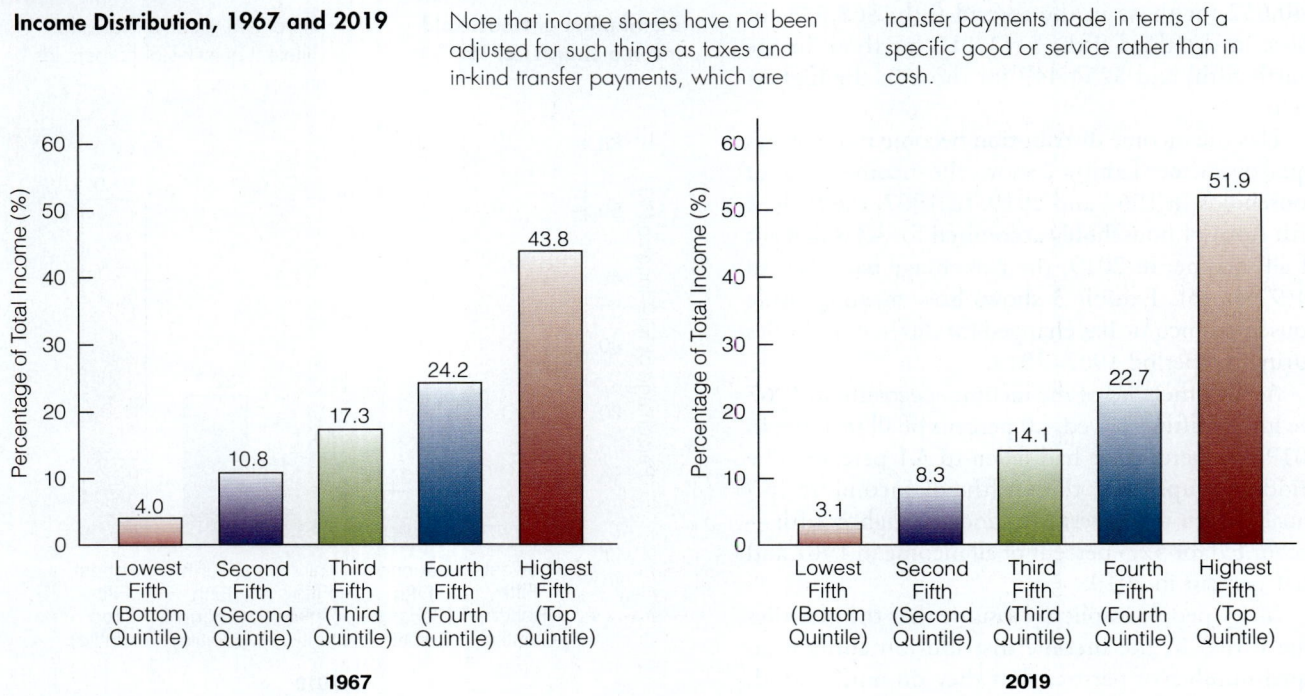

a year. The income distribution between John and Stephanie is unequal in 2000. Ten years later, the income distribution is still unequal, with Stephanie earning $45,000 and John earning $35,000. In fact, the income distribution is unequal in every year shown in the exhibit. However, the total income earned by each person is $419,000, giving a perfectly equal income distribution over time.

In the United States, people seem to experience quite a bit of upward income mobility over time. The University of Michigan's Panel Survey on Dynamics tracked 50,000 Americans for 17 years. Of the people in the lowest fifth of the income distribution in 1975, only 5.1 percent were still there in 1991—and 29 percent of them had reached the highest fifth!

In-Kind Transfer Payments
Transfer payments, such as medical assistance and subsidized housing, that are made in a specific good or service rather than in cash.

Thinking Like an Economist

Why Poor? Many people believe that poor is poor, but not the economist, who wants to know why the person is poor. Is he poor because he is young and just starting out in life? Would he be considered poor if we were to take into account the **in-kind transfer payments** or in-kind benefits he receives? Some people argue that when someone is poor, you do not ask questions; you simply try to help. But the economist knows that not everyone is in the same situation for the same reason and that the reason may determine whether you proceed with help and, if you do proceed, how to do so. Both the elderly person with a disability and the young, smart college student may earn the same low income, but you may feel more obliged to help the elderly person with a disability.

Chapter 28 The Distribution of Income and Poverty

EXHIBIT 3

Mean Quintile Household Income, 1967–2019

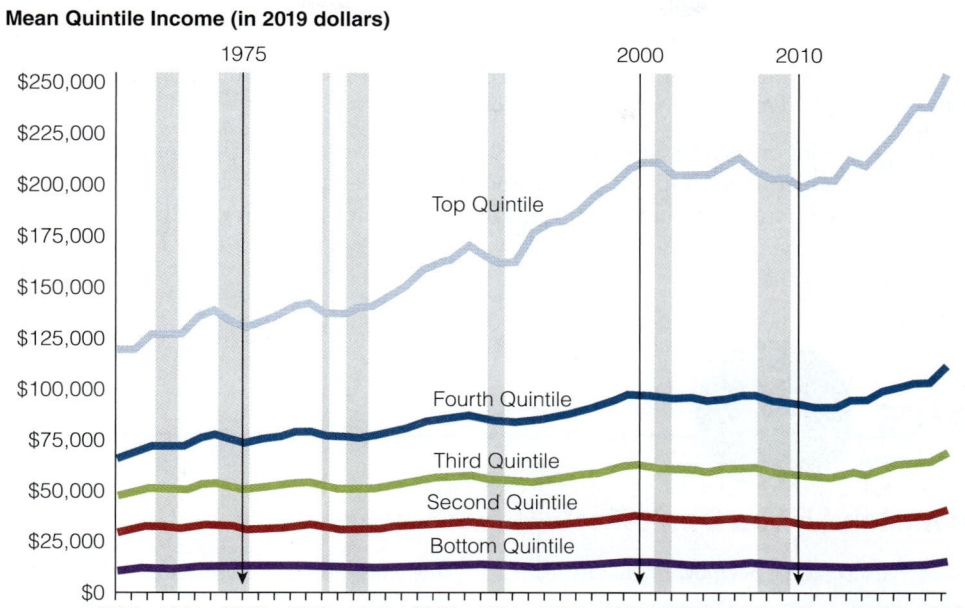

Source: Figure created by the Congressional Research Service based on data from U.S. Census Current Population Survey.

EXHIBIT 4

Income Distribution at One Point in Time and Over Time

In each year, the income distribution between John and Stephanie is unequal, with Stephanie earning more than John in 2000, 2010, 2020, and 2030 and John earning more than Stephanie in 2040. In the five years specified, however, both John and Stephanie earned the same total income of $419,000, giving a perfectly equal income distribution over time.

Year	John's Age (years)	John's Income	Stephanie's Age (years)	Stephanie's Income
2000	18	$10,000	28	$30,000
2010	28	35,000	38	45,000
2020	38	72,000	48	90,000
2030	48	132,000	58	185,000
2040	58	170,000	68	69,000
Total		$419,000		$419,000

28-1c A Simple Equation

The following simple equation combines four of the factors that determine a person's income:

$$\text{Individual income} = \text{Labor income} + \text{Asset income} + \text{Transfer payments} - \text{Taxes}$$

- *Labor income* is equal to the wage rate an individual receives, multiplied by the number of hours worked.

- *Asset income* consists of such things as the return to saving, the return to capital investment, and the return to land.

- *Transfer payments* are payments to persons that are not made in return for goods and services currently supplied (e.g., Social Security payments and cash welfare assistance are government transfer payments).

- Finally, from the sum of labor income, asset income, and **transfer payments**, we subtract *taxes* to see what an individual is left with (i.e., individual income).

The preceding equation provides a quick way of focusing on the direct and indirect factors affecting an individual's income and on the degree of income inequality in society. The next section examines the conventional ways that income inequality is measured.

Transfer Payments
Payments to persons that are not made in return for goods and services currently supplied.

Economics 24/7

Statistics Can Mislead if You Don't Know How They Are Made

If you read that U.S. household income has not grown in the last 20 years, would you conclude that incomes in the United States are stagnant? Many people might think so, but it may not be true. A household consists of all the people who occupy a housing unit. Individual incomes can rise while household incomes remain unchanged if households become smaller over time.

To illustrate, suppose 10 households have four persons in each. Each person in each household earns $30,000 a year. So each household earns an income of $120,000 a year. Some years pass, each person's income in each household rises to $60,000, but two of every four persons in each household leave to set up a new household. In other words, we now have 20 households with two persons in each, and the total income of each of the 20 households is still $120,000. On an individual basis, certainly all 40 persons are better off earning $60,000 each than earning $30,000 each. But on the basis of household income, we get a very different picture. *Lesson*: Individual income can rise while household income remains unchanged because households could be getting smaller as individual incomes rise.

Consider another assertion: "The middle class in this country is getting smaller and smaller." On the surface, this statement sounds fairly ominous. Where is the middle class going? Is it disappearing because it is becoming poorer or because it is becoming richer?

The problem is that, if we have a fixed definition of the middle class—say, persons who earn between $40,000 and $50,000 a year—then a changing income distribution can cause the number of persons in that (middle-class) income range to fall. Suppose that, of 10 people, the lowest-earning person earns $10,000 a year, the next-lowest-earning person earns $20,000 a year, and so on, up to the highest-earning person, who earns $100,000 a year.

Incomes for various persons ($000)
10, 20, 30, 40, 50, 60, 70, 80, 90, 100

Let's say that the middle class consists of persons in the middle of the income distribution: those who earn between $40,000 and $70,000 a year. In other words, the middle class consists of four persons. These four persons' incomes are enclosed in brackets in the following sequence:

10, 20, 30, [40, 50, 60, 70], 80, 90, 100

Years pass, and now everyone earns $50,000 more than before. So, now the lowest-earning person earns $60,000 a year and the highest-earning person earns $150,000:

Incomes for various persons ($000)
60, 70, 80, 90, 100, 110, 120, 130, 140, 150

The income distribution has become skewed toward higher incomes. The middle class has been cut in half if we continue to define it as persons earning between $40,000 and $70,000 a year. Now only two persons fall within this category: the person who once earned $10,000 and now earns $60,000 and the person who once earned $20,000 and now earns $70,000.

Lesson: As individual incomes rise, the middle class can get smaller (and disappear altogether) if it is defined by a fixed-dollar income range. Contrary to what some people believe, a disappearing middle class does not necessarily connote a world of only the rich and the poor.

Economics 24/7

Education and Income

Does the level of your educational attainment matter to you? Does it matter if you if you have only a high school education as opposed to a college education? There are data that show that one's weekly income and chances of becoming unemployed do depend upon one's level of educational attainment.

To illustrate, in 2019, the median (usual) weekly earnings for a person with less than a high school diploma was $592, and the unemployment rate for persons with less than a high school diploma was 5.4 percent. In contrast, the median weekly earnings for a person with a high school diploma was $746, and the unemployment rate was 3.7 percent.[3]

Let's go even higher on the educational attainment scale. If a person had some college but no degree, median weekly earnings rose to $833, and the unemployment rate fell to 3.3 percent.

Going even higher, if a person had a bachelor's degree, the median weekly earnings rose to $1,248, and the unemployment rate fell to 2.2 percent. And moving even higher, to a person with a master's degree, the median weekly earnings increased to $1,497, and the unemployment rate fell to 2.0 percent.

Does it matter what your educational attainment level is? It seems to matter when it comes to both one's weekly earnings (the higher one's educational attainment, the higher one's weekly earnings) and the chances of one becoming unemployed (the higher one's educational attainment level, the less likely one is to be unemployed).

---

[3] The source for all data is the Bureau of Labor Statistics and the Current Population Survey.

(Answers to Self-Test questions are in Answers to Self-Test Questions at the back of the book.)

1. How can government change the distribution of income?
2. "Income inequality at one point in time is sometimes consistent with income equality over time." Comment.
3. Martha and Lazaro have the same income this year: $40,000. Does it follow that their income came from the same sources? Explain your answer.

28-2 Measuring Income Equality

Two commonly used measures of income inequality are the Lorenz curve and the Gini coefficient.

28-2a The Lorenz Curve

Lorenz Curve
A graph of the income distribution that expresses the relationship between the cumulative percentage of households and the cumulative percentage of income.

The **Lorenz curve** represents the distribution of income; it expresses the relationship between the cumulative percentage of households and the cumulative percentage of income.

Exhibit 5 shows a hypothetical Lorenz curve. The data in part (a) are used to plot the Lorenz curve in part (b). According to (a), the lowest fifth of households has an income share of 10 percent, the second fifth has an income share of 15 percent, and so on. The Lorenz curve in (b) is derived by plotting five points:

- Point A represents the cumulative income share of the lowest fifth of households (10 percent of income goes to the lowest fifth of households).

- Point B represents the cumulative income share of the lowest fifth plus the second fifth (25 percent of income goes to two-fifths, or 40 percent, of the income recipients).

- Point C represents the cumulative income share of the lowest fifth, plus the second fifth, plus the third fifth (45 percent of income goes to three-fifths, or 60 percent, of the income recipients).

Points D and E are calculated in the same way as points A, B, and C.

Connecting the five points gives the Lorenz curve that represents the data in (a); the Lorenz curve is another way of depicting the income distribution in (a).

What would the Lorenz curve look like if there were perfect income equality among all households? It would be the line of perfect income equality illustrated in Exhibit 5(b). At any

EXHIBIT 5

A Hypothetical Lorenz Curve

The data in (a) were used to derive the Lorenz curve in (b). The bowed Lorenz curve shows an unequal distribution of income. The more bowed the Lorenz curve, the more unequal is the distribution of income.

Quintile	Income Share (%)	Cumulative Income Share (%)
Lowest fifth	10	10
Second fifth	15	25
Third fifth	20	45
Fourth fifth	25	70
Highest fifth	30	100

(a)

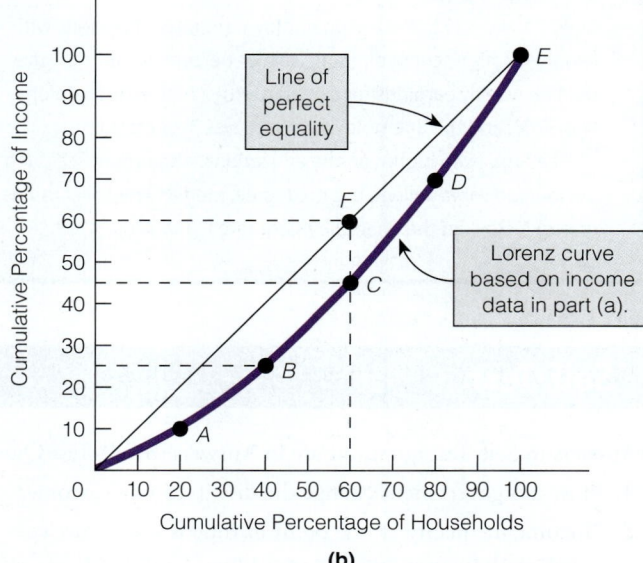

(b)

point on this 45-degree line, the cumulative percentage of income (on the vertical axis) equals the cumulative percentage of households (on the horizontal axis). For example, at point F, 60 percent of the households receive 60 percent of the total income.

28-2b The Gini Coefficient

The **Gini coefficient**, a measure of the degree of inequality in the income distribution, is used in conjunction with the Lorenz curve. It is equal to the area between the line of perfect income equality (or the 45-degree line) and the actual Lorenz curve, divided by the entire triangular area under the line of perfect income equality:

Gini Coefficient
A measure of the degree of inequality in the income distribution.

$$\text{Gini coefficient} = \frac{\text{Area between the line of perfect income equality and actual Lorenz curve}}{\text{Entire triangular area under the line of perfect income equality}}$$

Exhibit 6 illustrates both the line of perfect income equality and an actual Lorenz curve. The Gini coefficient is computed by dividing the shaded area (the area between the line of perfect income equality and the actual Lorenz curve) by the area $0AB$ (the entire triangular area under the line of perfect income equality).

The Gini coefficient is a number between 0 and 1. At one extreme, the Gini coefficient equals 0 if the numerator in the equation is 0, meaning that there is no area between the line of perfect income equality and the actual Lorenz curve. In that case, the lines are the same. Thus, a Gini coefficient of 0 means perfect income equality.

At the other extreme, the Gini coefficient equals 1 if the numerator in the equation is equal to the denominator. If this is the case, the actual Lorenz curve is as far away from the line of perfect income equality as is possible. Thus, a Gini coefficient of 1 means complete income inequality. (In this situation, in terms of the actual Lorenz curve, one person would have all the income there is, and no one else would have any. In Exhibit 6, a Lorenz curve representing complete income inequality would lie along the horizontal axis from 0 to A and then move from A to B.)

EXHIBIT 6

The Gini Coefficient

The Gini coefficient is a measure of the degree of income inequality. It is equal to the area between the line of perfect income equality and the actual Lorenz curve, divided by the entire triangular area under the line of perfect income equality. In the diagram, the area representing the Gini coefficient is equal to the shaded portion divided by the triangular area $0AB$. A Gini coefficient of 0 means perfect income equality; a Gini coefficient of 1 means complete income inequality. The larger the Gini coefficient, the greater is the income inequality; the smaller the Gini coefficient, the lower is the income inequality

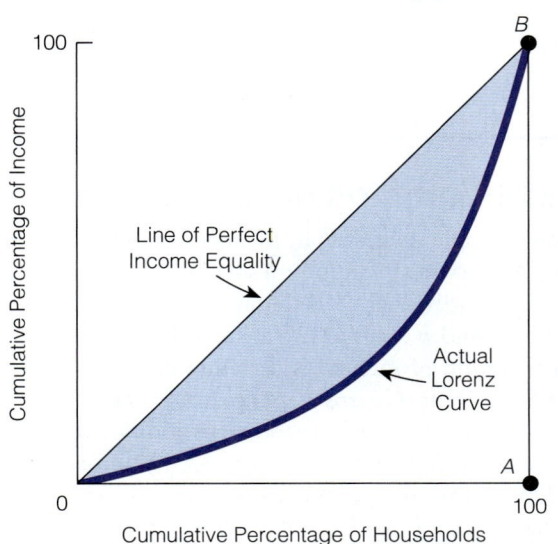

If a Gini coefficient of 0 represents perfect income equality and a Gini coefficient of 1 represents complete income inequality, then the larger the Gini coefficient is, the higher the degree of income inequality will be. Conversely, the smaller the Gini coefficient is, the lower the degree of income inequality. In 2020, the Gini coefficient in the United States was 0.465. By way of comparison, here were the Gini coefficients in 2020 for some other countries: Brazil, 0.524; Russia, 0.353; Norway, 0.285; Mexico, 0.427; Greece, 0.364; South Korea, 0.324.

28-2c A Limitation of the Gini Coefficient

Although the Gini coefficient indicates a lot about the degree of inequality in income distribution, we have to be careful not to misinterpret it. For example, if the Gini coefficient is 0.33 in country 1 and 0.25 in country 2, we know that the income distribution is more nearly equal in country 2 than in country 1. But in which country does the lowest fifth of households receive the larger percentage of income? The natural inclination is to answer, "in the country with the more nearly equal income distribution: country 2."

However, this answer may not be true. Exhibit 7 shows two Lorenz curves. Overall, Lorenz curve 2 is closer to the line of perfect income equality than Lorenz curve 1 is; thus, the Gini coefficient is smaller for Lorenz curve 2 than for Lorenz curve 1. But the lowest 20 percent of households has a smaller percentage of total income with Lorenz curve 2 than with Lorenz curve 1.

Therefore, the Gini coefficient cannot tell us what is happening in different quintiles. If the Gini coefficient is lower in country 2 than in country 1, it does not necessarily follow that the lowest fifth of households has a greater percentage of total income in country 2 compared with country 1.

EXHIBIT 7

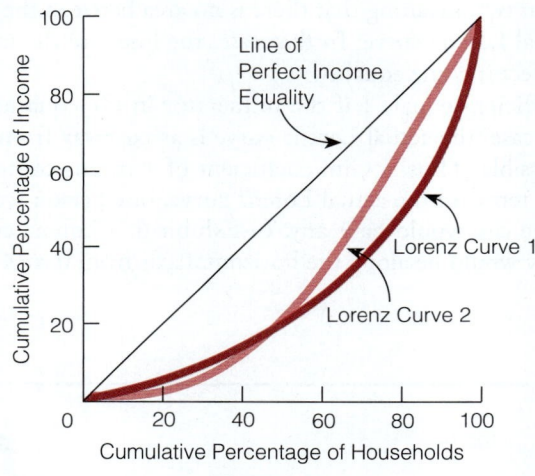

Limitation of the Gini Coefficient

By itself, the Gini coefficient cannot tell us anything about the income share of a particular quintile. Although there is a tendency to believe that the bottom quintile receives a larger percentage of total income the lower the Gini coefficient, that need not be the case. In the diagram, the Gini coefficient for Lorenz curve 2 is lower than the Gini coefficient for Lorenz curve 1 but the bottom 20 percent of households obtains a smaller percentage of total income in the case of Lorenz curve 2, the curve with a lower Gini coefficient.

28-2d Common Misconceptions about Income Inequality

Some people suggest that, in a country where income inequality is rising, individuals cannot become better off. Suppose a society is made up of five individuals, A–E. Let the yearly income for each individual be as follows: A earns $20,000, B earns $10,000, C earns $5,000, D earns $2,500, and E earns $1,250. Then the total yearly income in this society is $38,750, and the distribution of income is certainly unequal: A earns 51.61 percent of the income, B earns 25.81 percent, C earns 12.90 percent, D earns 6.45 percent, and E earns only 3.23 percent.

Now suppose each person earns additional real income. A earns $10,000 more real income, for a total of $30,000; B earns $3,000 more real income, for a total of $13,000; C earns $2,000 more real income, for a total of $7,000; D earns $1,000 more real income, for a total of $3,500; and E earns $200 more real income, for a total of $1,450. In terms of real income, each of the five persons is better off, but the income distribution has become even more unequal. For example, A (at the top fifth of income earners) now receives 54.60 percent of all income instead of 51.61 percent, and E (at the bottom fifth of income earners) now receives 2.64 percent instead of 3.23 percent. A newspaper headline might read, "The rich get richer as the poor get poorer." People reading this headline might naturally think that the poor in society are worse off. But we know that they are not worse off in terms of the goods and services they can purchase. They have more real income than they had when the income distribution was less unequal. In short, everyone can be better off even if the income distribution becomes more unequal.

1. Starting with the top fifth of income earners and proceeding to the lowest fifth, suppose the income share of each group is 40 percent, 30 percent, 20 percent, 10 percent, and 5 percent. Can these percentages be right?

2. Country A has a Gini coefficient of 0.45. What does that statement mean?

28-3 Why Income Inequality Exists

The question of why income inequality exists can be answered by focusing on our earlier simple equation:

$$\text{Individual income} = \text{Labor income} + \text{Asset income} + \text{Transfer payments} - \text{Taxes}$$

Generally, income inequality exists because people do not receive the same labor income, asset income, and transfer payments, and/or because they do not pay the same taxes. By focusing on factors that often contribute to differences, this section discusses some of the specific reasons that people don't receive, say, the same labor income and asset income.

28-3a Factors Contributing to Income Inequality

In this section, we discuss some of the factors that economists argue contribute to income inequality.

Innate Abilities and Attributes Individuals are not all born with the same innate abilities and attributes. People vary in their degrees of intelligence, in their appearance, and in their levels of creativity. Some individuals have more marketable innate abilities and attributes than others. For example, the natural athlete or the person who is musically gifted or mathematically adept is more likely to earn a higher income than someone with lesser abilities or attributes.

Work and Leisure There is a trade-off between work and leisure: more work means less leisure, and less work means more leisure. Some individuals will choose to work more hours (or take a second job) and thus have less leisure, and this choice will be reflected in their labor income: They will earn a larger income than persons who choose not to work more, *ceteris paribus*.

Education and Other Training Economists usually refer to schooling and other types of training as an investment in human capital. To buy or to invest in a capital good, a person has to give up present consumption and does so in the hope that the capital good will increase future consumption.

Human Capital
Education, development of skills, and anything else that is particular to the individual and that increases personal productivity.

Schooling can be looked on as capital. First, one must give up present consumption to obtain it. Second, by providing individuals with certain skills and knowledge, schooling can increase their future consumption over what it would be without schooling. Schooling, then, is human capital. In general, **human capital** includes education, the development of skills, and any other improvements that are particular to the individual and that increase productivity.

Contrast a person who has obtained an education with a person who has not. The educated person is likely to have certain skills, abilities, and knowledge that the uneducated person lacks. Consequently, the educated person is likely to be worth more to an employer. Most college students know this truth; it is one of the reasons they attend college.

Risk Taking Individuals have different attitudes toward risk. Some individuals are more willing to take on risk than others. Some of the individuals who are willing to take on risk will do well and rise to the top of the income distribution, and others will fall to the bottom. Individuals who prefer to play it safe aren't as likely to reach the top of the income distribution or to hit bottom.

Institutional Factors: Minimum Wage Fluctuations and Declining Unionization
In his work, economist David S. Lee showed that some of the growing wage inequality (especially at the lower income levels of the income distribution) in the United States in the 1980s was due to the "erosion of the real value of the federal minimum wage rate during the 1980s."[4] In other words, the minimum wage at the time was not keeping pace with inflation, leading to greater wage inequality. Specifically, the declining value of the minimum wage in the 1980s contributed to the growing wage inequality between workers at the bottom of the income distribution and those at the middle of the distribution, particularly for women. Additionally, economist David Card found that declining unionization rates, especially for low-skill males, contributed to an increase in wage inequality for male workers.[5]

Skill-Biased Technological Change Some economists have argued that technological change can lower the demand for certain low- and middle-wage workers while at the same time increasing the demand for high-skilled, high-wage workers. Essentially, "new technology raises the productivity—and their value to employers—of highly skilled workers who perform complex, non-routine tasks (e.g., physicians, managers). Productivity rises because technology *complements* the work performed by these groups of workers; it replaces time-consuming routine tasks (e.g., data processing, information organization), streamlines processes, and increases the precision of work performed by highly skilled workers."[6] This leads to productivity improvements for one group of workers, which increases the demand and, thus, wages for these workers but reduces the demand for certain middle- and low-skilled workers who initially performed the routine tasks.

Wage Discrimination
The situation in which individuals of equal ability and productivity (as measured by their contribution to output) are paid different wage rates.

Wage Discrimination **Wage discrimination** exists when an employer pays different wages to individuals of equal ability and productivity, as measured by their marginal revenue products. For example, in 2020, females working full time earned approximately 83 percent of the male median income. In the same year, African Americans had a median income

---

[4.] *Wage Inequality in the United States During the 1980s: Rising Dispersion or Falling Minimum Wage,* by David S. Lee, The Quarterly Journal of Economics, Vol. 114, No.3 (August 1999).

[5.] *The Effects of Unions on Wage Inequality in the U.S. Labor Market,* by David Card, Industrial and Labor Relations Review, Vol. 54, No. 2 (January 2001).

[6.] *The U.S. Income Distribution: Trends and Issues,* January 13, 2021, Congressional Research Service.

EXHIBIT 8

Real Median Household Income by Race and Hispanic Origin: 1967 to 2019

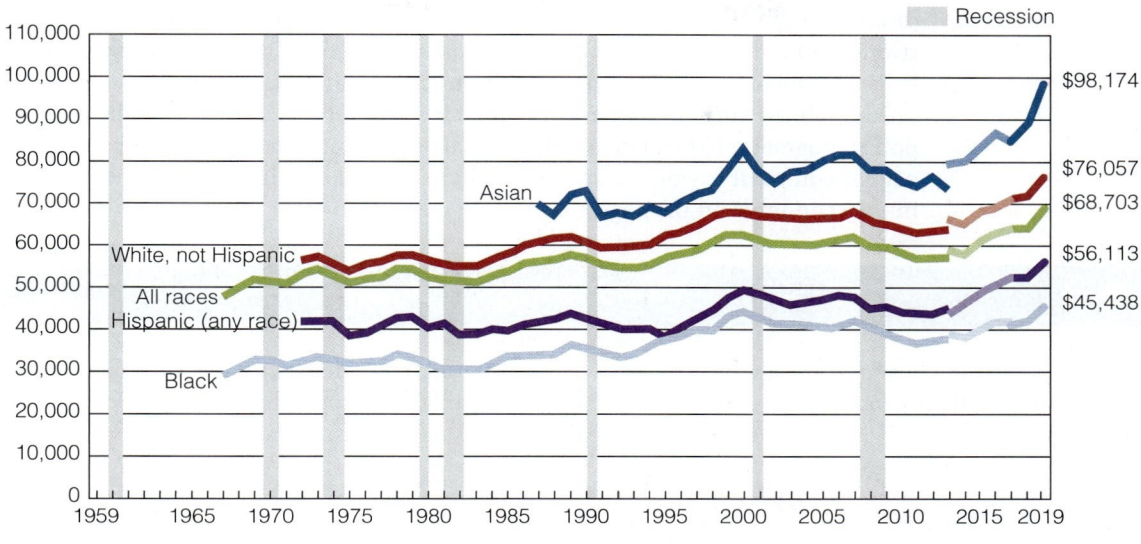

Source: U.S. Census Bureau, Current Population Survey, 1968 to 2020 Annual Social and Economic Supplements (CPS ASEC).

approximately 78 percent that of whites. These differences between white and black incomes and between male and female incomes are not due wholly to discrimination. Most empirical studies show that approximately half the differences are due to variations in education, productivity, and job training (although one may ask whether discrimination has anything to do with the education, productivity, and job training differences). The remainder of the wage differential is due to other factors, one of which is hypothesized to be discrimination. Exhibit 8 shows the real median household income by race and Hispanic origin, 1967–2019.

28-3b Income Differences: Some Are Voluntary; Some Are Not

Even in a world with no discrimination, differences in income would exist because of other factors. Some individuals would have more marketable skills than others, some individuals would decide to work harder and longer hours than others, some individuals would take on more risk than others, and some individuals would undertake more schooling and training than others. Thus, some degree of income inequality occurs because individuals are innately different and make different choices. However, some degree of income inequality is also due to factors unrelated to innate ability or choices—such as discrimination or luck.

In an ongoing and interesting debate on the topic of discrimination-based income inequality, the opposing sides weight various factors differently. Some people argue that wage discrimination would be reduced if markets were allowed to be more competitive, more open, and freer. They believe that, in an open and competitive market with few barriers to entry and with no government protection of privileged groups, discrimination would have a high price. Firms that didn't hire the best and the brightest—regardless of race, religion, or gender—would suffer. They would ultimately pay for their act of discrimination by having higher labor costs and lower profits. Individuals holding this view usually propose that government deregulate markets, reduce legal barriers to entry, and, in general, not interfere with the workings of the free-market mechanism.

Others contend that, even if the government were to follow this script, much wage discrimination would still exist. They think that government should play an active legislative role in reducing both wage discrimination and other types of discrimination that they believe ultimately result in wage discrimination, such as discrimination in education and in on-the-job training. Proponents of an active role for government usually believe that such policy programs as affirmative action, equal pay for equal work, and comparable worth (equal pay for comparable work) are beneficial in reducing both the amount of wage discrimination in the economy and the degree of income inequality.

1. Jack and Harry work for the same company, but Jack earns more than Harry. Is this evidence of wage discrimination? Explain your answer.

2. A person decides to assume a lot of risk in earning an income. How could this decision affect her income?

28-4 Poverty

This section presents some facts about poverty and examines its causes.

28-4a What Is Poverty?

There are principally two views on poverty:

- *Poverty should be defined in absolute terms.* In absolute terms, poverty might be defined as follows: Poverty exists when the income of a family of four is less than $10,000 per year.

- *Poverty should be defined in relative terms.* In relative terms, poverty might be defined as follows: Poverty exists when the income of a family of four places it in the lowest 10 percent of income recipients.

Viewing poverty in relative terms means that poverty will always exist—unless, of course, income equality is absolute. Given any unequal income distribution, some individuals will always occupy the bottom rung of the income ladder; thus, there will always be poverty. This assertion holds no matter how high the absolute standard of living is of the members of the society. For example, in a society of 10 persons in which 9 earn $1 million per year and 1 earns $400,000 per year, the person earning $400,000 per year is in the bottom 10 percent of the income distribution. If poverty is defined in relative terms, this person is considered to be living in poverty.

The U.S. government defines poverty in absolute terms. The absolute poverty measure was developed in 1964 by the Social Security Administration on the basis of findings of the Department of Agriculture. Called the **poverty income threshold** or **poverty line**, this measure refers to the income below which people are considered to be living in poverty. Individuals or families with incomes below the poverty income threshold, or poverty line, are considered poor.

The poverty threshold is updated yearly to reflect changes in the consumer price index. In 2019, the poverty income threshold was $26,172 for a family of four and $13,300 for an individual (under 65 years old). In 2019, 34 million people, or 10.5 percent of the U.S. population, were living below the poverty line.

Poverty Income Threshold (Poverty Line)
The income level below which people are considered to be living in poverty.

28-4b Limitations of the Official Poverty Income Statistics

The official poverty income statistics have certain limitations and shortcomings:

- Poverty figures are based solely on money incomes. Many money-poor persons receive in-kind benefits. For example, a family of four with a money income of $26,172 in 2019 was defined as poor, although it might have received in-kind benefits worth, say, $4,000. If the poverty figures are adjusted for in-kind benefits, the percentage of persons living in poverty drops.

- Poverty figures are not adjusted for unreported income, leading to an overestimate of poverty.

- Poverty figures are not adjusted for regional differences in the cost of living, leading to both overestimates and underestimates of poverty.

- Government counters are unable to find some poor persons—such as some of the homeless—a circumstance that leads to an underestimate of poverty.

28-4c Who Are the Poor?

Although the poor are persons of all religions, colors, genders, ages, and ethnic backgrounds, some groups are represented much more prominently in the poverty figures than others. For example, in 2019, the poverty rate for non-Hispanic Whites was 7.3 percent; for Blacks, it was 18.8 percent; and for Hispanics (any race), it was 15.7 percent. In terms of actual numbers of persons in poverty, 14.2 million were non-Hispanic Whites, 8.1 million were Black, and 9.5 million were Hispanic.

In that same year, the poverty rate for males (9.4 percent) was lower than for females (11.5 percent). Foreign-born non-citizens had a higher poverty rate (16.3 percent) than native born persons (10.1 percent), and the unemployment rate among the poor in the South was higher (12.0 percent) than it was in the Northeast (9.4 percent), the Midwest (9.7 percent) and the West (9.5 percent). The poverty rate for those persons without a high school diploma in 2019 was 23.7 percent and for those with a bachelor's degree or higher it was 3.9 percent.

28-4d What Is the Justification for Government Redistributing Income?

Some individuals say that there is no justification for government welfare assistance—that is, redistributing income. In their view, playing Robin Hood is not a proper role of government. Persons who make this argument say they are not against helping the poor (e.g., they are usually in favor of private charitable organizations), but they are against government using its powers to take from some to give to others.

Those who believe in government welfare assistance usually present the *public good–free rider* justification or the *social-insurance* justification. Proponents of the public good–free rider position make the following arguments: Most individuals in society would feel better if there were little or no poverty. Witnessing the signs of poverty—such as slums, hungry and poorly clothed people, and the homeless—is distressing. Therefore, there is a demand for reducing or eliminating poverty.

The reduction or elimination of poverty is a *nonexcludable public good*—a good that, if consumed by one person, can be consumed by other persons to the same degree and the consumption of which cannot be denied to anyone. That is, when poverty is reduced or eliminated, everyone will benefit from no longer viewing the upsetting sights of poverty, and no one can be excluded from such benefits. If no one can be excluded from experiencing the benefits of a reduction in, or the elimination of, poverty, then individuals will not have any incentive to pay for what they can get for free. Thus, they will become free riders. Economist Milton Friedman sums up the force of the argument this way:

> I am distressed by the sight of poverty. I am benefited by its alleviation; but I am benefited equally whether I or someone else pays for its alleviation; the benefits of other people's charity therefore partly accrue to me. To put it differently, we might all of us be willing to contribute to the relief of poverty, provided everyone else did it. We might not be willing to contribute the same amount without such assurance.[7]

Accepting the public good–free rider argument means that government is justified in taxing all persons to pay for the welfare assistance of some.

The social-insurance justification is a different type of justification for government welfare assistance. It holds that individuals not currently receiving welfare think that they might one day need it and thus are willing to take out a form of insurance for themselves by supporting welfare programs with their tax dollars and votes.

Self-Test

1. "Poor people will always exist." Comment.

2. What percentage of the U.S. population was living in poverty in 2019?

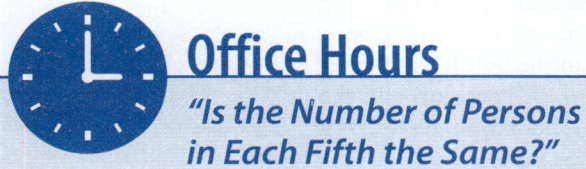

Office Hours

"Is the Number of Persons in Each Fifth the Same?"

Student: Earlier you said that, in 2019, the lowest fifth of household income earners in the United States received 3.1 percent of the total money income, the second fifth received 8.3 percent, the third fifth received 14.1 percent, the fourth fifth received 22.7 percent, and the top fifth received 51.9 percent. Am I right that each fifth contains the same number of individuals? In other words, if there are 100 individuals in the lowest fifth, it follows that there are 100 individuals in the top fifth too.

Instructor: No, you're not right. The quintiles (the fifths) are unequal in size because they are based on a count of households rather than persons and not every household has the same number of persons in it. For example, one household can have two persons in it, and another has four.

Student: Well, then, are more persons in the top fifth of income earners than in the lowest fifth of income earners?

Instructor: Yes. For example, in 2002, the top fifth contained 24.6 percent of the population whereas the lowest fifth contained 14.3 percent of the population. Stated differently, the top fifth contained 69.4 million persons, and the lowest fifth contained 40.3 million persons.

Student: What happens to the income distribution if we adjust each fifth so that it contains an equal number of persons? In other words, what happens if we adjust every fifth so that it contains 20 percent of the population?

Instructor: The income distribution becomes less unequal. To illustrate, if you look at the data for 2002 and deal with households instead of persons, you'd conclude that the lowest fifth received 3.5 percent of the total money income and the top fifth received 49.7 percent. Now, if you adjust the fifths so that each has 20 percent of the population, then you'll find that the lowest fifth received 9.4 percent (instead

---

[7.] Milton Friedman, *Capitalism and Freedom* (Chicago: University of Chicago Press, 1962), p. 91.

of 3.5 percent) of the total money income and the top fifth received 39.6 percent (instead of 49.7 percent).[8]

Student: Can income distribution be adjusted for other things?

Instructor: Yes. For one thing, persons in each fifth do not all work the same number of hours. For example, in 2002, individuals in the lowest fifth performed 4.3 percent of all work in the U.S. economy, and those in the highest fifth performed 33.9 percent. To be fair, though, the low levels of paid employment in the lowest fifth reflect the low numbers of working-age people in this group. In 2002, the lowest fifth contained only 11.2 percent of all working-age adults whereas the highest fifth contained 27.6 percent. However, when we compare working-age adults in the lowest fifth with working-age adults in the highest fifth, we learn that the average working-age adult in the lowest fifth worked about half as many hours a year as the working-age adult in the highest fifth.

Now, if we adjust the income distribution to show us what it would be like if the average working-age adult in the lowest fifth worked as many hours as the average working-age adult in the top fifth, the income distribution becomes less unequal. In 2002, the lowest fifth would have received 12.3 percent (instead of 3.5 percent) of the total money income, and the top fifth would have received 35.8 percent (instead of 49.7 percent).

Student: The income distribution seems as though it can be portrayed in different ways. We can choose to adjust for taxes and transfer payments or choose not to; we can choose to adjust for the number of persons or choose not to; we can choose to adjust for the number of hours worked or choose not to.

Instructor: You're right about that. And that is part of the reason for such heated debate over income distribution. Person A might think it's better to view the income distribution after having adjusted for something (such as taxes, transfer payments, the number of persons, and the like), and Person B might think it better to view the income distribution before adjusting.

Points to Remember

1. The bottom fifth of household income earners does not contain the same number of persons as the top fifth of household income earners. For example, in 2002, the top fifth contained 69.4 million persons whereas the lowest fifth contained 40.3 million persons.

2. The income distribution (or distribution of income) can be adjusted for various factors. Such adjustments often change the degree of income equality or inequality of the income distribution.

---

[8] The adjusted income distributions in this feature come from Census Bureau data and a publication by Robert Rector and Rea Hederman, Jr., *Two Americas: One Rich, One Poor? Understanding Income Inequality in the United States* (August 24, 2004), http://www.heritage.org/Research/Taxes/bg1791.cfm

Chapter Summary

The Distribution of Income

- In 2019, the lowest fifth of households received 3.1 percent of the total money income, the second fifth received 8.3 percent, the third fifth received 14.1 percent, the fourth fifth received 22.7 percent, and the top fifth received 51.9 percent.

- The government can change the distribution of income through taxes and transfer payments. Individual income = Labor income + Asset income + Transfer payments − Taxes. Government directly affects transfer payments and taxes.

- The Lorenz curve represents the income distribution. The Gini coefficient is a measure of the degree of inequality in the distribution of income. A Gini coefficient of 0 means perfect income equality; a Gini coefficient of 1 means complete income inequality.

Poverty

- The income poverty threshold, or poverty line, is the income level below which a family or person is considered poor and living in poverty.

- Poverty income statistics have their limitations. The statistics are usually not adjusted for (1) in-kind benefits, (2) unreported and illegal income, and (3) regional differences in the cost of living. Furthermore, the statistics do not count the poor who exist but who are out of sight, such as some of the homeless.

- People who believe government should redistribute income from the rich to the poor usually base their argument on the public good–free rider justification or the social-insurance justification. The public good–free rider justification holds that many people are in favor of redistributing income from the rich to the poor and that the elimination of poverty is a public good. Unfortunately, individuals cannot create a public good because of the incentive that everyone has to free ride on the contributions of others. Consequently, government is justified in taxing all persons to pay for the welfare assistance of some. The social-insurance justification holds that individuals not currently receiving redistributed monies may one day find themselves in a position where they will need to, so they are willing to take out a form of insurance. In essence, they are willing to support redistribution programs today so that the programs exist if they should need them in the future.

Key Terms and Concepts

In-Kind Transfer Payments
Transfer Payments
Lorenz Curve
Gini Coefficient
Human Capital
Wage Discrimination
Poverty Income Threshold (Poverty Line)

Questions and Problems

1. What percentage of total money income did the lowest fifth of households receive in 2019? The fourth fifth?
2. "The Gini coefficient for country A is 0.35, and for country, B it is 0.22. Therefore, the bottom 10 percent of income recipients in country B has a greater percentage of the total income than the bottom 10 percent of the income recipients in country A." Do you agree or disagree? Why?
3. Would you expect greater income inequality in country A, where there is a large disparity in age, or in country B, where there is a small disparity in age? Explain your answer.
4. Compare the U.S. income distribution in 1967 with the income distribution in 2019. Has the U.S. income inequality increased or decreased? What percentage of total money income did the top fifth of U.S. households receive in 2019?
5. What role might each of the following play in contributing to income inequality?
   a. Risk taking
   b. Education
   c. Innate abilities and attributes
6. Welfare recipients would rather receive cash benefits than in-kind benefits, but much of the welfare system provides in-kind benefits. Is there any reason for not giving recipients their welfare benefits the way they want to receive them? Would it be better to move to a welfare system that provides benefits only in cash?
7. What is the effect of age on the income distribution?
8. Can more people live in poverty at the same time that a smaller percentage of people live in poverty? Explain your answer.
9. How would you determine whether the wage difference between two individuals is due to wage discrimination?
10. Define each of the following:
    a. In-kind transfer payment
    b. Lorenz curve
    c. Wage discrimination

Working with Numbers and Graphs

1. The lowest fifth of income earners has a 10 percent income share; the second fifth, a 17 percent income share; the third fifth, a 22 percent income share; the fourth fifth, a 24 percent income share; and the highest fifth, a 27 percent income share. Draw the Lorenz curve.
2. In Exhibit 7, using Lorenz curve 2, calculate the approximate percentage of income that goes to the second-highest 20 percent of households.
3. Is it possible for everyone's real income to rise even though the income distribution in a society has become more unequal? Prove your answer with a numerical example.

Interest, Rent, and Profit

CHAPTER 29

Introduction

The time between when individuals decide to start a business and the day they open their door for the first time can seem like forever. Starting up a business involves decisions and payments. Most likely, the entrepreneurs will need to obtain a loan, on which they will pay interest. They will need to find a suitable location and may need to pay rent on a piece of land. Finally, the grand-opening day arrives, and the new owners can look forward to earning a profit.

Interest, rent, and profit are the payments to capital, land, and entrepreneurship, respectively. A knowledge of these three payments is critical to understanding how markets operate and how economies function.

29-1 Interest

The word "interest" is used in two ways in economics. Sometimes, it refers to the price for credit, or **loanable funds**. For example, Nelson borrows $100 from Sarah and pays her back $110 a year later. The interest, obviously, is $10. "Interest" can also refer to the return that capital earns as an input in the production process. A person who buys a machine (a capital good) for $1,000 and earns $100 a year by using the productive services of the machine is said to earn $100 interest, or a 10 percent interest rate, on the capital.

Economists refer to both the price for loanable funds and the return on capital goods as interest because the two tend to become equal, as discussed later in this section.

Loanable Funds
Funds that someone borrows and another person lends, for which the borrower pays an interest rate to the lender.

29-1a Loanable Funds: Demand and Supply

The equilibrium interest rate, or the price for loanable funds (or credit), is determined by the demand for and supply of loanable funds (or credit). The demand for loanable funds is composed of the demand for consumption loans, the demand for investment loans, and government's demand for loanable funds. [The U.S. Treasury may need to finance budget deficits by borrowing (demanding) loanable funds in the loanable funds market.] This chapter focuses on the demand for consumption loans and the demand for investment loans. The supply of loanable funds comes from people's savings and from newly created money. The chapter discusses only people's savings.

So, in this chapter, the demand for loanable funds is taken to be composed of the demand for (1) consumption loans and (2) investment loans. The supply of loanable funds is taken to be composed entirely of people's savings.

The Supply of Loanable Funds Savers are people who consume less than their current income. Without savers, there would be no supply of loanable funds. Savers receive an interest rate for the use of their funds, and the amount of funds saved and loaned is directly related to the interest rate.[1] Specifically, the supply curve of loanable funds is upward sloping: The higher the interest rate is, the greater the quantity supplied of loanable funds will be; the lower the interest rate, the less the quantity supplied of loanable funds will be.

Positive Rate of Time Preference
A preference for earlier over later availability of goods.

The Demand for Loanable Funds: Consumption Loans Consumers demand loanable funds because they have a **positive rate of time preference**; that is, consumers prefer earlier availability of goods to later availability. For example, most people would prefer to have a car today than to have one five years from today.

There is nothing irrational about a positive rate of time preference; most, if not all, people have it. People differ, though, as to the *degree* of their preference for earlier availability. Some people have a high rate of time preference, signifying that they greatly prefer present to future consumption. ("I *must* have that new car today.") Other people have a low rate, signifying that they prefer present to future consumption only slightly. People with a high rate of time preference are less likely to postpone consumption than people with a low rate. People with a high rate of time preference feel that they need to have things now.

Consumers' positive rate of time preference is the reason for a demand for consumption loans. Consumers borrow today to buy today; they will pay back the borrowed amount plus interest tomorrow. The interest payment is the price consumers pay for the earlier availability of goods.

Roundabout Method of Production
The production of capital goods that enhance productive capabilities.

The Demand for Loanable Funds: Investment Loans Investors (or firms) demand loanable funds (or credit) so that they can invest in capital goods and finance roundabout methods of production. A firm using a **roundabout method of production** first produces capital goods and then uses those goods to produce consumer goods.

Compare the direct method and the roundabout method for catching fish. In the direct method, a person uses his hands to catch fish. In the roundabout method, the person weaves a net (which is a capital good) and then uses the net to catch fish. Using the direct method, Ruben can catch 4 fish per day. Using the roundabout method, he can catch 10 fish per day. Suppose Ruben takes 10 days to weave a net. If Ruben does not weave a net and instead catches fish by hand, he can catch 1,460 fish per year (4 fish per day times 365 days). If, however, Ruben spends 10 days weaving a net (during which time he catches no fish), he can catch 3,550 fish the first year (10 fish per day times 355 days). Thus, the capital-intensive roundabout method of production is highly productive.

Because roundabout methods of production are so productive, investors are willing to borrow funds to finance them. For example, Ruben might reason, "I'm more productive if I use

---

[1] Because a higher interest rate may have both a substitution effect and an income effect, many economists argue that a higher interest rate can lead to either more saving or less saving, depending on which effect is stronger. We ignore these complications at this level of analysis and hold that the supply curve of loanable funds (from savers) is upward sloping.

a fishing net, but I'll need to take 10 days off from catching fish and devote all my energies to weaving a net. What will I eat during the 10 days? Perhaps I can borrow some fish from my neighbor. I'll need to borrow 40 fish for the next 10 days. But I must make it worthwhile for my neighbor to enter into this arrangement, so I will promise to pay her back 50 fish at the end of the year. Thus, my neighbor will lend me 40 fish today in exchange for 50 fish at the end of the year. I realize I'm paying an interest rate of 25 percent [the interest payment of 10 fish is 25 percent of the number of fish borrowed, 40], but it will be worth it." The highly productive nature of the capital-intensive roundabout method of production is what makes the loan worthwhile.

The reasoning in the fish example is repeated whenever a firm makes a capital investment. Producing computers on an assembly line is a roundabout method of production compared with producing them one by one by hand. Making copies on a copying machine is a roundabout method of production compared with copying by hand. In both cases, firms are willing to borrow now, use the borrowed funds to invest in capital goods in order to finance roundabout methods of production, and pay back the loan with interest later. If roundabout methods of production were not productive, firms would not be willing to borrow.

The Loanable Funds Market The sum of the demand for consumption loans and the demand for investment loans is the total demand for loanable funds. The demand curve for loanable funds is downward sloping: As interest rates rise, consumers' cost of earlier availability of goods rises, and they curtail their borrowing. Also, as interest rates rise, some investment projects that would be profitable at a lower interest rate will no longer be profitable. Therefore, the interest rate and the quantity demanded of loanable funds are inversely related.

Exhibit 1 illustrates the demand for and supply of loanable funds. The equilibrium interest rate occurs where the quantity demanded of loanable funds equals the quantity supplied of loanable funds.

29-1b The Price for Loanable Funds and the Return on Capital Goods Tend to Equality

As already explained, both the price for loanable funds and the return on capital are referred to as interest because they tend to become equal. To illustrate, suppose the return on capital is 10 percent and the price for loanable funds is 8 percent. Then, in this setting, firms will borrow in the loanable funds market and invest in capital goods. As they do so, the quantity of capital increases, and its return falls (capital is subject to diminishing marginal returns). In short, the return on capital and the price for loanable funds begin to approach each other.

Now suppose instead that the percentages are reversed: The price for loanable funds is 10 percent, and the return on capital is 8 percent. In this situation, no one will borrow loanable funds at 10 percent to invest at 8 percent. Over time, the capital stock will decrease (capital depreciates over time; it doesn't last forever), its marginal physical product will rise, and the return on capital and the price for loanable funds will eventually equal each other.

EXHIBIT 1

Loanable Funds Market

The demand curve shows the different quantities of loanable funds demanded at different interest rates. The supply curve shows the different quantities of loanable funds supplied at different interest rates. Through the forces of supply and demand, the equilibrium interest rate and the quantity of loanable funds at that rate are established as i_1 and Q_1, respectively.

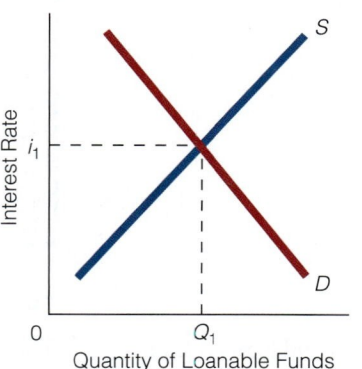

29-1c Why Do Interest Rates Differ?

The supply-and-demand analysis in Exhibit 1 suggests that the economy has only one interest rate. In reality, it has many. For example, a major business is not likely to pay the same interest rate for an investment loan to purchase new machinery as the person next door pays for a consumption loan to buy a car. Some of the factors that affect interest rates are discussed next. In each case, the *ceteris paribus* condition holds.

Risk Any time a lender makes a loan, there is a possibility that the borrower will not repay it. Some borrowers are better credit risks than others. A major corporation with a long and established history is probably a better credit risk than a person who has been unemployed three times in the last seven years. The more risk associated with a loan, the higher the interest rate will be; the less risk associated with a loan, the lower the interest rate will be.

Term of the Loan In general, the longer the term of the loan is, the higher the interest rate will be; the shorter the term of the loan, the lower the interest rate will be. Borrowers are usually more willing to pay higher interest rates for long-term loans because the longer term gives them greater flexibility. Lenders require higher interest rates to part with their funds for extended periods.

Cost of Making the Loan A loan for $1,000 and a loan for $100,000 may require the same amount of record keeping, making the larger loan cheaper (per dollar) to process than the smaller loan. In addition, some loans require frequent payments (e.g., payments for a car loan), whereas others do not. This difference is likely to be reflected in higher administrative costs for loans with more frequent payments. Therefore, loans that cost more to process and administer will have higher interest rates than loans that cost less to process and administer.

> **Thinking Like an Economist**
>
> **Tending to Equality** In economics, factors typically converge. For example, in supply-and-demand analysis, the quantity demanded and the quantity supplied of a good tend to equality (through the equilibrating process). In consumer theory, the marginal utility–price ratios for different goods tend to equality. And, as just discussed, the price of loanable funds and the return on capital tend to equality (become equal).
>
> In economics, many things tend to equality because equality is often representative of equilibrium. When quantity demanded equals quantity supplied, a market is said to be in equilibrium. When the marginal utility–price ratio for all goods is the same, the consumer is said to be in equilibrium. *In*equality therefore often signifies *dis*equilibrium. When the price of loanable funds is greater than the return on capital, there is disequilibrium.
>
> The economist, knowing that equality often signifies equilibrium, looks for inequalities and then asks, "So what happens now?"

29-1d Nominal and Real Interest Rates

The **nominal interest rate** is the interest rate determined by the forces of supply and demand in the loanable funds market; it is the interest rate in current dollars. The nominal interest rate will change if the demand for or supply of loanable funds changes.

Individuals' expectations of inflation are one of the factors that can change both the demand for and supply of loanable funds. (Inflation occurs when the money prices of goods, on average, increase over time.) Exhibit 2 shows how inflation can affect the nominal interest

---

Nominal Interest Rate
The interest rate determined by the forces of supply and demand in the loanable funds market.

rate. The current interest rate shown is 8 percent, and the actual and expected inflation rates are zero (Actual inflation rate = Expected inflation rate = 0 percent). Later, both the demanders and suppliers of loanable funds expect a 4 percent inflation rate. In anticipation of this expected rise in the inflation rate, borrowers (demanders of loanable funds) are willing to pay 4 percent more interest for their loans because they expect to be paying back the loans with dollars that have 4 percent less buying power than the dollars

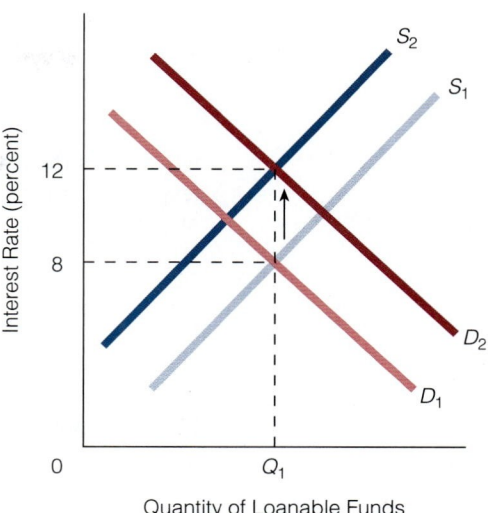

EXHIBIT 2

Expected Inflation and Interest Rates

We start at an 8 percent interest rate and an actual and expected inflation rate of 0 percent. Later, both borrowers and lenders expect an inflation rate of 4 percent. Borrowers are willing to pay a higher interest rate because they will be paying off their loans with cheaper dollars. Lenders require a higher interest rate because they will be paid back in cheaper dollars. The demand and supply curves shift such that, at Q_1, borrowers are willing to pay, and lenders require, a 4 percent higher interest rate. The nominal interest rate is now 12 percent. The real interest rate is 8 percent. (Real interest rate = Nominal interest rate − Expected inflation rate)

they are being lent. In other words, if they wait to buy the goods, the prices will have risen by 4 percent. To beat the price increase, they are willing to pay up to 4 percent more to borrow funds in order to purchase the goods now. In effect, the demand curve for loanable funds shifts rightward so that, at Q_1, borrowers are willing to pay a 4 percent higher interest rate.

At the same time, the lenders (the suppliers of loanable funds) require a 4 percent higher interest rate (i.e., 12 percent) to compensate them for the 4 percent less valuable dollars in which the loan will be repaid. In effect, the supply curve of loanable funds shifts leftward so that, at Q_1, lenders will receive an interest rate of 12 percent.

Thus, an expected inflation rate of 4 percent increases the demand for loanable funds and decreases their supply so that the interest rate is 4 percent higher than it was when the inflation rate was expected to be zero. In this example, 12 percent is the nominal interest rate—the interest rate in current dollars—and it includes the expected inflation rate.

If we adjust for the expected inflation rate, we have the **real interest rate**: the nominal interest rate minus the expected inflation rate (Real interest rate = Nominal interest rate − Expected inflation rate). In our example, the real interest rate is 8 percent (12 percent − 4 percent).

The real interest rate, not the nominal interest rate, matters to borrowers and lenders. Consider a lender who grants a $1,000 loan to a borrower at a 20 percent nominal interest rate at a time when the actual inflation rate is 15 percent. The amount repaid to the lender is $1,200, but $1,200 with a 15 percent inflation rate does not have the buying power that $1,200 with a zero inflation rate has. The 15 percent inflation rate wipes out much of the gain, and the lender's real return on the loan is not 20 percent, but only 5 percent. Thus, the rate lenders receive and borrowers pay (and, therefore, the rate they care about) is the real interest rate.

Real Interest Rate
The nominal interest rate adjusted for expected inflation; that is, the nominal interest rate minus the expected inflation rate.

29-1e Present Value: What Is Something Tomorrow Worth Today?

Because of people's positive rate of time preference, $100 today is worth more than $100 a year from now. (Wouldn't you prefer to have $100 today to having $100 in a year?) Thus, $100 a year from now must be worth less than $100 today. The question is *how much* $100 a year from now is worth today. This question involves the concept of **present value**, which is

Present Value
The current worth of some future dollar amount of income or receipts.

the current worth of some future dollar amount (of receipts or income). In our example, "present value" refers to what $100 a year from now is worth today.

Present value (*PV*) is computed with the formula

$$PV = \frac{A_n}{(1+i)^n}$$

where A_n is the actual amount of income or receipts in some future year, i is the interest rate (expressed as a decimal), and n is the number of years in the future. Thus, the present value of $100 one year in the future at a 10 percent interest rate is $90.91:

$$PV = \frac{\$100}{(1+0.10)^1}$$
$$= \$90.91$$

That is, the right to receive $100 a year from now is worth $90.91 today. In other words, if $90.91 is put into a savings account paying a 10 percent interest rate, it would equal $100 in a year.

Suppose we wanted to know what a future income stream, instead of a future dollar amount, is worth today. The general formula is

$$PV = \sum_{i=0}^{n} \frac{A_n}{(1+i)^n}$$

where the Greek letter Σ stands for "sum of."

To see how the formula works, suppose a firm buys a machine that will earn $100 a year for the next three years. What is this future income stream, at $100 per year for three years, worth today? That is, what is the present value of that future income stream? At a 10 percent interest rate, it has a present value of $248.68:

$$PV = \frac{A_1}{(1+0.10)^1} + \frac{A_2}{(1+0.10)^2} + \frac{A_3}{(1+0.10)^3}$$
$$= \frac{\$100}{1.10} + \frac{\$100}{1.21} + \frac{\$100}{1.331}$$
$$= \$90.91 + \$82.64 + \$75.13 = \$248.68$$

Finding Economics

In Living Longer Suppose that, because of an advancement in medical science, people start living longer. Can living longer affect the price of antique cars, famous paintings, and fine jewelry? Where is the economics?

The economics can be found in the concept of present value. Suppose that you are considering the purchase of a painting and that you would receive $2,000 worth of benefits a year from owning and viewing the painting. The dollar price you would be willing to pay for the painting is based partly on the present value of the benefits you would receive over the number of years you plan to enjoy the painting. The number of years could be higher because you expect to live longer. At a given interest rate, the longer you expect to live, the greater will be the present value of the benefits you receive from the painting, and the more you would be willing to pay for the painting.

Economics 24/7

Investment, Present Value, and Interest Rates

Firms will often increase their level of investment (e.g., purchase more capital goods) as interest rates fall. Suppose a firm is thinking of purchasing a capital good that costs $1,000. The firm expects that the capital good will add to its revenue in each of two years. In year 1, the capital good is expected to add $600, and in year 2, $500. Should the firm purchase the capital good?

One way to decide whether to purchase the capital good is to compare its cost ($1,000) against the additional revenue it is expected to generate ($1,100). Because the additional revenue is greater than the cost, the inclination to say that the firm should buy the capital good is strong. But not all the additional revenue is generated in the first year of the life of the good: Some of that additional revenue—$500—comes in year 2.

So we need to compute the present value of a stream of revenue to be realized over two years. Here is the calculation:

$$PV = \frac{\$600}{(1+i)^1} + \frac{\$500}{(1+i)^2}$$

What the present value (*PV*) turns out to be depends, of course, on the interest rate. At the assumed interest rate of 10 percent, the present value is $958.67. Now we see that, because the cost of the capital good ($1,000) is greater than the present value of the additional revenue generated by its use, the capital good is not worth purchasing.

But suppose the interest rate falls to 5 percent. Now the present value is $1,024.93. At the lower interest rate, the capital good is worth purchasing, because the present value of the additional revenue generated by its use (or $1,024.93) is greater than its purchase price.

The point is simple: Lower interest rates raise present values, and higher present values that are connected with the purchase of capital goods lead firms to buy more capital goods (i.e., increase their investing).

Economics 24/7

Is the Car Worth Buying?

Business firms often compute present values in deciding whether to buy capital goods. Should consumers do the same when they are thinking about buying a durable good (i.e., a good that will last for a few years), such as a car?

Suppose you're thinking about buying a car. The market price of the car is $35,000, and you anticipate that you will receive

$5,000 worth of services from the car each year for the next 10 years, after which time the car will have to be scrapped and will have no salvage value.

Now ask yourself the same type of question that the business firm asks when it considers buying a capital good: Is the present value of the car more than, less than, or equal to the present market price of the car?

(Continued)

> To answer this question, you need to calculate the present value of the car. A car that yields $5,000 worth of benefits each year for 10 years at a 4 percent interest rate has a present value of approximately $40,554:
>
> $$PV = \frac{\$5,000}{(1+0.04)^1} + \frac{\$5,000}{(1+0.04)^2} + \ldots + \frac{\$5,000}{(1+0.04)^{10}}$$
> $$= \$40,554 \text{ (approximately)}$$
>
> The market price of the car ($35,000) is less than its present value ($40,554), so purchasing the car is worthwhile.
>
> You should also be attentive to the interest rate. All other things remaining constant, an increase in the interest rate will lower the present value of the car. For example, at an 8 percent interest rate, the present value of the car is approximately $33,550. Now the market price of the car ($35,000) is *greater than* the present value of the car ($33,550), so the purchase is not worthwhile.
>
> Thus, we would expect fewer cars to be sold when the interest rate rises and more cars to be sold when the interest rate falls, because a change in the interest rate changes the present value of cars.

(Answers to Self-Test questions are in Answers to Self-Test Questions at the back of the book.)

1. Why does the price for loanable funds tend to equal the return on capital goods?
2. Why does the real interest rate, not the nominal interest rate, matter to borrowers and lenders?
3. What is the present value of $1,000 two years from today if the interest rate is 5 percent?
4. A business firm is thinking of buying a capital good, which will earn $2,000 a year for the next four years and cost $7,000. The interest rate is 8 percent. Should the firm buy the capital good? Explain your answer.

29-2 Rent

Mention the word "rent," and people naturally think of someone living in an apartment and making monthly payments to a landlord. That is not the type of rent discussed in this chapter. To an economist, rent means **economic rent**—that is, a payment in excess of opportunity costs (as discussed in an earlier chapter). A subset of economic rent, called **pure economic rent**, is a payment in excess of opportunity costs when opportunity costs are zero. Historically, the term "pure economic rent" was first used to describe the payment to the factor land, which is perfectly inelastic in supply.

In Exhibit 3, the total supply of land is fixed at Q_1 acres; there can be no more and no less than this amount of land. The payment for land (R_1) is determined by the forces of supply and demand. R_1 is more than sufficient to bring Q_1 acres into supply. In fact, by reason of the fixed supply of land (the supply curve is perfectly inelastic), the Q_1 acres would have been forthcoming at a payment of $0. In short, this land has zero opportunity costs. Therefore, the full payment—all of R_1—is referred to as pure economic rent.

Economic Rent
Payment in excess of opportunity costs.

Pure Economic Rent
A category of economic rent such that the payment is to a factor that is in fixed supply, implying that the factor has zero opportunity costs.

29-2a David Ricardo, the Price of Grain, and Land Rent

In nineteenth-century England, people were concerned about the rising price of grains, which were a staple in many English diets. Some argued that grain prices were rising because land rents were going up rapidly. People began pointing fingers at the landowners, maintaining that the high rents the landowners received for their land made it more and more costly for farmers to raise grains. These higher costs, in turn, were passed on to consumers in the form of higher prices. According to this argument, the solution was to lower rents, which would lead to lower costs for farmers and, eventually, to lower prices for consumers.

English economist David Ricardo thought that this line of argument stood logic on its head. He contended that it wasn't that grain prices were high because rents were high (as most individuals thought) but, conversely, that rents were high because grain prices were high. In current economic terminology, his argument was as follows: Land is a factor of production; therefore, the demand for it is derived. Land is also in fixed supply; therefore, the only thing that will change the payment made to land is a change in the demand for it. (The supply curve isn't going to shift, and thus, the only thing that can change price is a shift in the demand curve.) Landowners have no control over the demand for land, which comes from other persons who want to use it.

In nineteenth-century England, the demand came from farmers who were raising grains and other foodstuffs. Landowners could not have pushed up land rents, because they had no control over the demand for their land. Therefore, rents were high because the demand for land was high, and the demand for land was high because grain prices were high. Economists put it this way: *Land rents are price determined, not price determining.*

EXHIBIT 3

Pure Economic Rent and the Total Supply of Land

The total supply of land is fixed at Q_1. The payment for the services of this land is determined by the forces of supply and demand. Because the payment is for a factor in fixed supply, the payment is referred to as pure economic rent.

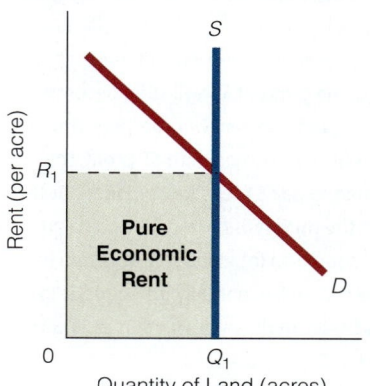

Economics 24/7

Grain Prices and Land Rent

David Ricardo argued that high grain prices cause high land rents. For example, suppose that there are three grades of land: excellent, good, and poor. Suppose also that grain can be produced on each grade of land. The excellent land can produce 10 bushels of grain, the good land can produce 5 bushels of grain, and the poor land can produce 2 bushels of grain. Further, it costs $10 to farm each grade of land, and the price of grain is currently $1.50 a bushel.

Under these circumstances, not all three grades of land will be farmed. Only the excellent grade of

land will be farmed, because it can produce 10 bushels of grain, which can then be sold at $1.50 a bushel for a total revenue of $15. At a cost of $10 to farm this land, the farmer is then left with a $5 profit.

No one will farm the good or the poor land, though, because neither grade of land will earn the farmer any profit. The good land will cost $10 to farm but will generate only 5 bushels of grain, for a total revenue of $7.50. The poor land will cost $10 to farm but will generate only 2 bushels of grain, for a total revenue of $3.

(Continued)

So the excellent land is the only grade that will be farmed if the price of grain is $1.50 a bushel, because that land earns the farmer $5 in profit. But the $5 profit may not last. If the farmer leases the land, the profit of $5 will soon become $5 in land rent for the owner of the land. Farmers will compete among themselves to lease the land from its owner. With $5 profit, the first farmer says that he is willing to pay $1 rent for the land, but the second farmer says $2, and the third farmer says $3, and so on. So the profit on the land will soon turn into land rent received by the owner of the land. The land rent will eventually go up to $5. In other words, the excellent land—given the price of grain at $1.50 a bushel—will fetch a rent of $5.

Now suppose the price of grain rises from $1.50 a bushel to $2.10 a bushel. Two things will happen at this higher price. First, the good land, which wasn't farmed when the price of grain was $1.50, will now be farmed. The good land generates 5 bushels of grain that, when sold at $2.10 a bushel, will generate $10.50 in revenue. Because the cost of farming the land is $10, this sale leaves the farmer with a profit of 50¢. Farming the good land is now profitable.

Second, the land rent on the excellent land will rise from $5. At a grain price of $2.10 a bushel, the excellent land now generates $21 in revenue. Given a cost of $10 for farming the excellent land, this amount of revenue generates $11 in profit, or only $6 in profit if we assume that the farmer is paying the owner of the excellent land $5 in land rent. Either way, we can expect land rent to rise soon, as farmers compete for the land that is generating the additional profits. We expect the land rent ultimately to rise to $11.

So higher grain prices initially increase the profit on farming high-quality, or excellent, land. But higher profit ends up as higher land rent as farmers compete for the land. In short, high grain prices cause high land rents, and rising grain prices cause rising rents.

29-2b The Supply Curve of Land Can Be Upward Sloping

Exhibit 3 depicts the supply of land as fixed—the case when the total supply of land is in question. For example, this country has only so many acres of land, and that amount is not likely to change.

Most subparcels of land, however, have competing uses. Consider 25 acres of land on the periphery of a major city. That parcel can be used for farmland, a shopping mall, or a road. If a parcel of land (as opposed to all land, or the total supply of land) has competing uses (the land can be used one way or another), then it has opportunity costs. Land that is used for farming could be used for a shopping mall. To reflect the opportunity cost of that land, the supply curve is upward sloping. The upward slope implies that if individuals want more land for a specific purpose—say, for a shopping mall—they must bid high enough to attract existing land away from other uses (e.g., farming). Exhibit 4 illustrates this phenomenon, in which the equilibrium payment to land is R_1. The shaded area indicates the economic rent.

EXHIBIT 4

Economic Rent and the Supply of Land (Competing Uses)

A particular parcel of land, as opposed to the total supply of land, has competing uses, or positive opportunity costs. For example, to obtain land to build a shopping mall, the developers must bid high enough to attract existing land away from competing uses. The supply curve is upward sloping. At a payment of R_1, economic rent is identified as the payment in excess of (positive) opportunity costs.

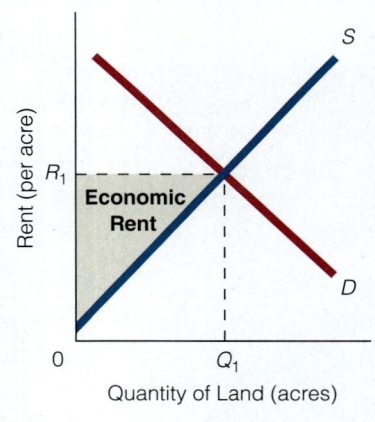

29-2c Economic Rent and Other Factors of Production

The concept of economic rent applies to economic factors besides land. For example, it applies to labor. Suppose Hanson works for company X and is paid $90,000 a year. Suppose further that in his next-best alternative job, he would be earning $67,000. Then Hanson is receiving economic rent by working for company X, in that he is receiving a payment in excess of his opportunity costs. That excess is his economic rent.

Or consider the local McDonald's that hires teenagers. It pays all its beginning employees the same wage, but not all beginning employees have the same opportunity cost. Suppose two teenagers, Emily and Pablo, sign on to work at McDonald's for $15.00 an hour. Emily's next-best alternative wage is $15.00 an hour, working for her mother's business, and Paul's is $13.00 an hour, working in another store. Then Emily receives no economic rent in her McDonald's job, but Pablo receives $2.00 an hour economic rent in that same job.

Over time, teenagers and other beginning employees usually find that their opportunity costs rise (owing to continued schooling and job experience) and that the McDonald's wage no longer covers their opportunity costs. When this happens, they quit.

29-2d Economic Rent and Baseball Players: Perspective Matters

Economic rent varies with the perspective from which the factor is viewed. If a baseball star who earns $1 million a year playing baseball weren't playing the sport, he would be a coach at a high school. Therefore, the difference between what he is currently paid ($1 million a year) and what he would earn as a coach (say, $70,000 a year) is economic rent in the amount of $930,000. Thus, in this case, economic rent is determined by identifying the alternative to the baseball star's playing major league ball.

However, a different alternative would be identified by asking what the alternative is to the baseball star's playing baseball *for his present team*. The answer is that he probably can play for another team. For example, if he weren't playing for the Boston Red Sox, he might be playing for the Pittsburgh Pirates, earning $950,000 a year. His economic rent in this instance is only $50,000. So the player's economic rent as *a player for the Boston Red Sox* is $50,000 a year, and his next-best alternative is earning $950,000 a year playing for the Pittsburgh Pirates. But his economic rent as *a baseball player* is $930,000, and his next-best alternative is being a high school coach earning $70,000 a year.

29-2e Competing for Artificial and Real Rents

Individuals and firms compete for both *artificial rents* and *real rents*. An artificial rent is an economic rent that is artificially contrived by government; that is, it would not exist without government. Suppose government decides to award a monopoly right to one firm to produce good X. In so doing, it legally prohibits all other firms from producing good X. If the firm with the monopoly right receives a price for good X in excess of its opportunity costs, it receives a rent or monopoly profit because of government's restraint on supply.

Firms that compete for the monopoly right to produce good X expend resources in a socially wasteful manner. They use resources to lobby politicians in the hope of getting the monopoly, and those resources (from society's perspective) could be better used to produce goods and services.

Competing for real rents is different, however. If the rent is real (not artificially created) and if there are no barriers to competing for it, resources are used in a way that is socially productive. For example, suppose firm Z currently receives economic rent in the production of good Z. Suppose also that government does not prohibit other firms from competing with firm Z, so some do. Then the other firms also produce good Z, thus increasing its supply and lowering its price. The lower price reduces the rent firm Z receives in its production of good Z. In the end, firm Z has less rent and society has more of good Z and pays a lower price for it.

Self-Test

1. Give an example to illustrate that economic rent varies with the perspective from which a factor is viewed.
2. Nick's salary is pure economic rent. What does this statement imply about Nick's next-best alternative salary?
3. What are the social consequences of firms competing for artificial rents, as opposed to competing for real rents (in an environment in which there are no barriers to competing for real rents)?

29-3 Profit

The profits that appear in newspaper headlines are *accounting profits*, not economic profits. Economic profit is the difference between total revenue and total cost, and both explicit and implicit costs are included in total cost. Economists emphasize economic profit over accounting profit because economic profit determines entry into and exit from an industry. For the most part, all this is how economic profit figured in the discussion of market structures in previous chapters.

In this section, we discuss profit as the payment to a resource. Recall the four resources, or factors of production: land, labor, capital, and entrepreneurship. Firms make payments to each of these resources: wages are the payment to labor, interest is the payment to capital, rent is the payment to land, and profit is the payment to entrepreneurship. Understanding the source of profits enables us to find out why economic profit exists.

29-3a Theories of Profit

Several different theories address the question of where profit comes from—that is, the source of profit. One theory holds that profit would not exist in a world of certainty; hence, uncertainty is the source of profit. Another theory is that profit is the return for alertness to broadly defined arbitrage opportunities. A third theory posits that profit is the return to the entrepreneur for innovation.

Profit and Uncertainty Uncertainty exists when the probability of something occurring is so unpredictable that it cannot be estimated. (For example, what is the probability that the United States will enter a world war in 2030?) Risk, which many people mistake for uncertainty, exists when the probability of a given event can be estimated. (For example, a coin toss has a 50–50 chance of coming up heads.) Therefore, risks can be insured against, but uncertainties cannot.

Anything that can be insured against can be treated as just another cost of doing business, and thus, insurance coverage is an input in the production process. Only uncertain events can cause a firm's revenues to diverge from costs (including insurance costs). The investor/decision maker who is adept at making business decisions under conditions of uncertainty earns a profit. For example, on the basis of experience and some insights, an entrepreneur may believe that 55 percent of all college students will buy laptops next year. This assessment, followed by investing in a chain of retail computer stores near college campuses, will ultimately prove to be right or wrong. The essential point is that the entrepreneur's judgment cannot be insured against. If it is correct, the entrepreneur will earn a profit; if it is incorrect, the entrepreneur will suffer a loss.

Profit and Arbitrage Opportunities The way to make a profit, the advice goes, is to buy low and sell high (usually the same item). For example, someone might buy good X in New York for $10 and sell good X in London for $11. We might say that the person is alert to where she can buy low and sell high, and thereby earn a profit. She is alert to what is called an *arbitrage opportunity*.

Sometimes, "buying low and selling high" does not refer to the same item. The phrase can refer to buying factors in one set of markets at the lowest-possible prices, combining the factors into a finished product, and then selling the product in another market for the highest-possible price. An example is buying oranges and sugar (in the orange and sugar markets, respectively), combining the two factors, and selling an orange soft drink (in the soft-drink market). If doing so results in profit, the person who undertook the act is considered alert to an (broadly defined) arbitrage opportunity. He saw that oranges and sugar together, in the form of an orange soft drink, would fetch more than the sum of oranges and sugar separately.

Profit and Innovation In this theory, profit is the return to the entrepreneur as innovator—the person who creates new profit opportunities by devising a new product, production process, or marketing strategy. Viewed in this way, profit is the return to innovative genius. People such as Thomas Edison, Henry Ford, Richard Sears, and Steve Jobs are said to have had innovative genius.

29-3b Profit and Loss as Signals

Although profit and loss are often viewed in terms of the benefit or harm they bring to persons, they also signal how a market may be changing. On the one hand, when a firm earns a profit, entrepreneurs in other industries view the profit as a signal that the firm is producing and selling a good that buyers value more than the factors that go into making the good. (The firm would not earn a profit unless its product had more value than the total of the payments to the other three factors of production.) The profit causes entrepreneurs to move resources into the production of the profit-linked good. In short, resources follow profit.

On the other hand, if a firm is taking a loss, the loss is a signal to the entrepreneur that the firm is producing and selling a good that buyers value less than the factors that go into making the good. The loss causes resources to move out of the production of the loss-linked good. Resources turn away from losses.

29-4 The Entrepreneur

Back in Chapter 1, we identified four resources, or factors of production: land, labor, capital, and entrepreneurship. We know that land, labor, capital, and entrepreneurship go together to produce goods and services. When you think of land (natural resources), labor, and capital, it is fairly easy to envision someone taking these resources and putting them together to produce, say, a house or a car. Entrepreneurship, however, leaves us wondering. What is it exactly that entrepreneurship entails? We know what labor and capital look like, and we know what oil as a resource looks like, but what does entrepreneurship look like? How will we know it if we see it? What specifically is it that the entrepreneur does? In this section, we answer that question.

29-4a A Market

The role of the entrepreneur is closely tied to what happens in a market. A market is a place where individuals come together to exchange or trade: I will trade you $50 for a shirt; I will trade you $100 for a pair of shoes. We know that individuals will agree to a trade only if they expect to be made better off through the trade. In other words, Stephanie trades her $100 for the shoes, and the shoe salesman trades the shoes for the $100, only if each expects to be made better off by the trade.

Entrepreneurs operate within markets. Specifically, their actions are directed toward increasing the number of trades. Think of the situation strictly in numerical terms. Suppose 1,000 individuals are making 500 trades a week (among themselves). The entrepreneur will try to figure out a way to increase that number to 600 trades. What does the entrepreneur do? The entrepreneur devises ways to increase trade.

29-4b How Can the Entrepreneur Increase Trade?

There are two major ways of increasing trade. The first is to produce a good or service that satisfies an unmet demand. Think of Steve Jobs, the cofounder of Apple, Inc. Jobs was instrumental in the development of such products as the personal computer, the iPad, the iPhone, and the iPod. Focus for a minute on the iPod. Here is a product, small in size, that allows a person to compile and then listen to a large number of songs. Certainly, there was a time before the iPod existed. If we go back to that time—say, 1986—and ask the question whether people have a demand for a product that is easy to carry and that can hold thousands of songs that people want to listen to, what do you think would be the answer? Our guess is that the answer would be yes. But back in 1986, that demand would have been unmet. It was a demand for a good that simply did not exist yet.

What Steve Jobs did was satisfy that unmet demand. In that he did, he increased trade. After the introduction of the iPod, people were willing to trade dollars for iPods. Both the people who traded those dollars for iPods and the people who traded iPods for dollars were made better off through the trades.

So, in virtue of the fact that Steve Jobs came out with a good that increased trade by satisfying an unmet demand (for that good), he was an entrepreneur.

Now let's turn to the second major way of increasing trade: by reducing the transaction costs of making trades. With this idea in mind, consider the people behind the creation of eBay. Go back to a time before eBay, and consider two people, on opposite sides of the world, who might want to trade with each other. More specifically, consider a person living in London who wants to sell an old Beatles album. Suppose someone in Topeka, Kansas, wants to buy an old Beatles album. The problem here is that the two people—buyer and seller of the Beatles album—can't find each other. The transaction costs of their getting together and consummating a trade are just too high for them to overcome. Enter eBay, which lowers those transaction costs. What eBay essentially does is tell everyone in the world the following: If you have something you want to sell, come to us, and we will introduce you to a buyer; if you have something you want to buy, come to us, and we will introduce you to a seller. In other words, what eBay has done is make it easier for buyers and sellers to find each other. The easier it became, the more likely a trade would occur.

By lowering the transaction costs of making certain kinds of trades, the people behind eBay increased the number of trades. Inasmuch as they increased the number of trades, they were acting as entrepreneurs.

29-4c Turning Potential Trades into Actual Trades

One way to describe entrepreneurs is to say that they turn potential trades into actual trades. That is exactly what both Steve Jobs and eBay did. Jobs took an unmet demand and satisfied it; eBay took trades that couldn't be realized because of high transaction costs, lowered the transaction costs, and thus turned potential trades into actual trades.

29-4d A Necessary Condition: Turn Potential Trades Into Actual Trades in a Way Acceptable to Consumers

The way the entrepreneur turns a potential trade into an actual trade is important. Not all roads the entrepreneur may travel down to accomplish the feat will meet with success. For example, suppose there were 15 different ways to develop, produce, and sell the iPod. The most expensive way would give us a $100,000 price tag. Would the iPod then have been a product consumers would have run to the stores to purchase? Probably not. The point is that while entrepreneurs turn potential trades into actual trades, they have to do so in a way that is acceptable to consumers.

29-4e Can Increasing Trades in One Area Reduce Trades in Another?

So far, we have talked about the entrepreneur as a person who promotes trade. In the example of Steve Jobs, the entrepreneur produced a good that satisfied a (theretofore) unmet demand. In the example of eBay, the entrepreneur lowered transaction costs and promoted trade. In the arbitrage example, the entrepreneur bought in one location and sold in another. But couldn't it very well be that in all these three cases, while trade blossomed in one place, it declined in another?

Could it be that, because of the iPod, there are now fewer trades for radios, or tape recorders, or stereos? In other words, didn't the iPod displace some products that consumers earlier had traded money for? Didn't the personal computer displace the typewriter? Didn't the car displace the horse?

Or consider the eBay in which the person in London sold the old Beatles album to the person in Topeka, Kansas. Mightn't it have been the case that, if there were no eBay, the person in London could have put an ad in the newspaper and eventually found a person who would buy his old Beatles album?

There are cases in which the entrepreneur actually does increase the number of trades. In other words, trades may rise from 500 to 600. There are also cases in which the entrepreneur does *not* increase the number of trades, but instead changes the nature of the trade (500 trades of dollars for X instead of 500 trades of dollars for Y). Finally, there are cases in which entrepreneurs do a little of both: They increase the number *and* nature of trades (600 trades of dollars for X instead of 500 trades of dollars for Y).

29-4f Uncertainty and the Entrepreneur

All entrepreneurs do something in the present that they hope will turn out well for them in the future. But no one knows exactly what the future will hold. It follows, then, that all entrepreneurs bear some degree of uncertainty. They operate with a cloud of uncertainty hanging over them.

Steve Jobs didn't know for sure if the iPod would be a success. He only thought it could be. The people who created eBay didn't know for sure if their company would be a success. They only thought it could be.

All entrepreneurs look for the $10 bill on the sidewalk, so to speak. But they can't be sure that the $10 bill is not a counterfeit bill or play money—so to speak. All entrepreneurs might think that they have discovered an economic opportunity that others remain blind to, but they can't be sure how things will turn out for them if they seize it. The landscape is littered with entrepreneurs who tried and failed.

Self-Test

1. What is the difference between risk and uncertainty?
2. Why does profit exist?
3. "Profit is not simply a dollar amount; it is a signal." Comment.
4. What are two majors ways of increasing trade?

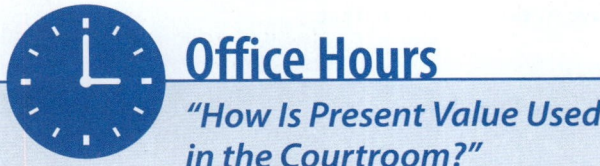

Office Hours
"How Is Present Value Used in the Courtroom?"

Student: I've heard that present value is sometimes used in law cases. Is this true? And if so, how?

Instructor: Yes, it's true. It could be used in a divorce case. For example, suppose Anya and Noah are getting a divorce. Anya worked during the time Noah went to medical school. In the divorce, Anya and Noah agree to split the assets they own together: the house, the paintings, the jewelry, the cars, and so on. Anya claims that Noah's medical degree is an asset that she should have part of. "After all," she says, "I helped pay for Noah's medical education."

Student: So is the objective now to find out what the medical degree is worth?

Instructor: Yes. And this is where present value comes in. Suppose Noah will earn $100,000 more each year for the next 25 years because he went to medical school. Anya's attorney needs to find the present value of this dollar amount, which turns out to be approximately $1.57 million.

Now the court has to decide whether the medical degree is an asset whose proceeds should be divided between Anya and Noah.

Student: Does present value come up in any other cases?

Instructor: Yes. Present value is sometimes used in injury cases. For example, suppose Jackie gets hit by a drunk driver and can't work any longer. She might ask to be compensated for the injury plus the loss in her earning power. Her lawyer will need to find the present value of her lost earnings (over, say, the next 10 years).

Points to Remember

1. Present value can be used to determine today's worth of a medical education.
2. Present value can be used to determine today's worth of a loss in earning power.

Chapter Summary

Interest

- Interest is (1) the price paid by borrowers for loanable funds and (2) the return on capital in the production process. These two things tend to become equal.
- The equilibrium interest rate (in terms of the price for loanable funds) is determined by the demand for and supply of loanable funds. The supply of loanable funds comes from savers, people who consume less than their current incomes. The demand for loanable funds comes from the demand for consumption loans and the demand for investment loans.
- Consumers demand loanable funds because they have a positive rate of time preference: They prefer earlier, rather than later, availability of goods. Investors (or firms) demand loanable funds so that they can finance roundabout methods of production.
- The nominal interest rate is the interest rate determined by the forces of supply and demand in the loanable funds market;

it is the interest rate in current dollars. The real interest rate is the nominal interest rate adjusted for expected inflation. Specifically, Real interest rate = Nominal interest rate − Expected inflation rate (or Nominal interest rate = Real interest rate + Expected inflation rate).

Rent

- Economic rent is a payment in excess of opportunity costs. A subset of economic rent is pure economic rent, which is a payment in excess of opportunity costs when opportunity costs are zero. Historically, the term *pure economic rent* was used to describe the payment to the factor land, because land (in total) was assumed to be fixed in supply (perfectly inelastic). Today, the terms "economic rent" and "pure economic rent" are also used in speaking about economic factors other than land.

- David Ricardo argued that high land rents were an effect of high grain prices, not a cause of them (in contrast to many of his contemporaries who thought high rents caused the high grain prices). In other words, land rents are price determined, not price determining.

- The amount of economic rent that a factor receives depends on the perspective from which the factor is viewed. For example, a university librarian earning $80,000 a year receives $2,000 in economic rent if his next-best alternative income at another university is $78,000. His economic rent is $10,000 if his next-best alternative is in a nonuniversity (nonlibrarian) position that pays $70,000.

Profit

- Several theories address the question of the source of profit. One theory holds that profit would not exist in a world of certainty; hence, uncertainty is the source of profit. Another theory holds that profit is the return for alertness to arbitrage opportunities. A third theory states that profit is the return to the entrepreneur for innovation.

The Entrepreneur

- Entrepreneurs operate within markets; specifically, their actions are directed toward increasing the number of trades.
- There are two major ways of increasing trade. The first is to produce a good or service that satisfies an unmet demand. The second is to reduce the transaction costs of making trades.

Key Terms and Concepts

Loanable Funds
Positive Rate of Time Preference
Roundabout Method of Production
Nominal Interest Rate
Real Interest Rate
Present Value
Economic Rent
Pure Economic Rent

Questions and Problems

1. What does it mean to say that an individual has a positive rate of time preference?
2. What does having a positive rate of time preference have to do with positive interest rates?
3. How would the interest rate change as a result of the following?
   a. A rise in the demand for consumption loans
   b. A decline in the supply of loanable funds
   c. A rise in the demand for investment loans
4. The interest rate on loan X is higher than the interest rate on loan Y. What might explain the difference in interest rates between the two loans?
5. The real interest rate can remain unchanged as the nominal interest rate rises. Do you agree or disagree with this statement? Explain your answer.
6. What type of person is most willing to pay high interest rates?
7. Some people have argued that, in a moneyless (or barter) economy, interest would not exist. Would it? Explain your answer.
8. In what ways are a baseball star who can do nothing but play baseball and a parcel of land similar?
9. What does it mean to say that land rent is price determined, not price determining?

10. What is the link between profit and uncertainty?
11. What is the overall economic function of profits?
12. "The more economic rent a person receives in his job, the less likely he is to leave the job and the more content he will be on the job." Do you agree or disagree? Explain your answer.
13. It has been said that a society with a high savings rate is a society with a high standard of living. What is the link (if any) between saving and a relatively high standard of living?
14. Make an attempt to calculate the present value of your future income.
15. Describe the effect of each of the following events on individuals' rate of time preference and thus on interest rates:
    a. A technological advance that increases longevity
    b. An increased threat of war
    c. Growing older
16. "As the interest rate falls, firms are more inclined to buy capital goods." Do you agree or disagree? Explain your answer.
17. What is it that the entrepreneur does?

Working with Numbers and Graphs

1. Compute the following:
   a. The present value of $25,000 each year for 4 years at a 7 percent interest rate
   b. The present value of $152,000 each year for 5 years at a 6 percent interest rate
   c. The present value of $60,000 each year for 10 years at a 6.5 percent interest rate
2. Rodrigo is a baseball player who earns $1 million a year playing for team X. If he weren't playing baseball for team X, he would be playing baseball for team Y and earning $800,000 a year. If he weren't playing baseball at all, he would be working as an accountant earning $120,000 a year. What is his economic rent as a baseball player playing for team X? What is his economic rent as a baseball player?
3. Diagrammatically represent pure economic rent.

Health Economics: Experiments, Disparities, and Prices

CHAPTER 30

Introduction

Everyone pays for health care, even those who rarely visit a doctor, clinic, or hospital. Nearly one out of every five dollars spent in the United States is spent on health care. Health care is one input in determining one's health. Along with health care (visits to doctors and hospitals, prescription drugs), other factors—such as one's income, level of education, race, and occupation—are also important in determining one's health. This chapter introduces you to some of the fascinating and diverse questions that health economists spend their days trying to answer.

30-1 Why Health Economics?

Why health economics and not the economics of video games or the economics of cryptocurrencies? As interesting as these alternatives may be, you can get through life fine without knowing much about the economics of video games and cryptocurrencies. Health is different; everyone gets sick at some time in their lives, and everyone pays for health in one way or another. Health care spending is a large part of the U.S. economy. To give one example, Medicare and Medicaid (which are tax-supported public insurance programs for elderly and low-income Americans, respectively) account for a quarter of all U.S. federal spending each year. If you pay taxes, you pay for health care.

When it comes to a person's health care, two things stand out as important considerations: one's health and one's wallet. Health care's impact on one's wallet hasn't always been what it is today. In 1960, $1 out of every $20 spent in the United States was spent on health care, compared to $1 out of every $5 today.

Health care spending is greater per capita in the United States than in many countries in the world. For example, health care spending is $10,000 per person in the United States and $5,000 per person in Canada. What explains this difference? Do people in the United States care twice as much about health care as people in Canada? Do Americans have more chronic health conditions, or are they in need of more heart, lung, or hip surgeries than Canadians? Probably not. So, what explains the per capita health care spending gap? In this chapter, we'll explore what economists have done to try to answer this question.

30-1a What Makes Health Care Different?

Economists discuss and study a lot of different markets: the markets for cars, food, computers, clothing, and so on. They also discuss and study health care markets. In fact, health care markets receive special treatment from economists because they have certain factors that are not present in many other markets. Three such factors are uncertainty, insurance, and externalities. We explain each of these factors in what follows.

Uncertainty How much money do you need to budget next month for rent, for groceries, or for gasoline for your car? You probably can come close to knowing the exact amount. But how much do you need to budget for a hip replacement? Because you likely don't know the probability of your needing a hip replacement, that question is more difficult to answer. Of course, if the price of a hip replacement were $30, you wouldn't worry about it very much. But given the median price of a hip replacement in the United States today is $30,000, this bill would adversely affect most people. What a negative income shock it would be for most people—as if their income immediately dropped by $30,000.

Being uncertain of what medical problem you may have in the future and knowing that any possible medical problem could cost you a lot of money motivates you to buy health insurance. Simply stated, uncertainty and potentially large negative income shocks explain much of the demand for health insurance.

Insurance The widespread use of insurance in health care markets distinguishes it from many other markets. We now know that uncertainty and the potential for negative income shocks motivate the demand for health insurance. However, once people obtain health insurance, they may act differently than they would if they didn't have health insurance; in short, having health insurance can affect your behavior.

To illustrate, consider two scenarios, *A* and *B*. In *A*, you do not have health insurance; in *B*, you do. In which setting are you more likely to reflect on the prices for various medical procedures—such as a general checkup at your doctor's office, a knee surgery, or a procedure to remove a skin tag from your arm? Put another way, are you more likely to ask your doctor the cost of a particular procedure when you have insurance or when you don't have insurance? You are probably more likely to ask when you have to pay the entire price for the procedure than when you only pay a copayment and the insurance company pays the rest.

The point is that, in health care markets, where health insurance predominates, patients aren't as likely to consider the price of various medical procedures because they won't be paying the entire cost of the procedures. The cost is split between the patient and the insurance company, and the insurance company pays the bulk of the payment.

Back to the important question—how are health care markets different than many other markets? There are usually three entities that exist in any health care exchange: the patient, the hospital or doctor, and the insurance company. Meanwhile, in many other markets, there are only two such entities—for instance, you and the car seller when you want to buy a car, you and the seller of the laptop when you want to buy a laptop. But when you want to "buy" a knee surgery, there are three: you (the patient), the surgeon, and the insurance company.

Externalities Much of what people do does not negatively or positively affect others. Suppose Kenny is sitting on the couch in his living room watching a Lakers game on TV. His action doesn't affect you either positively or negatively. But the same cannot be said when it comes to something like COVID-19. If a person with COVID-19 was near another person, then that other person could get COVID-19 too. In this case, one person's behavior adversely affects another person; this is an example of a **negative externality**.

Negative externalities can often present themselves in health care markets. When they do, there needs to be some way of dealing with them. In the COVID-19 example, government placed rules and regulations on individuals and businesses, mandating social distancing, wearing a mask, getting the vaccine for the coronavirus which causes COVID-19, and so on.

Negative Externality
The condition in which a person's or group's actions impose a cost (an adverse side effect) on others.

(Answers to the Self-Test are in the Answers to Self-Test Questions at the back of the book.)
1. What makes health care markets different from other markets?
2. How does the high price of health care make uncertainty particularly problematic?
3. What's an example of a negative externality present in health care markets, other than the example of COVID-19, discussed in this section?

30-2 The Demand for Health Care

Is the demand for health care inelastic or elastic? If demand is elastic, it means that the percentage change in quantity demanded is greater than the percentage change in price. For example, the price rises by 10 percent, and quantity demanded falls by 20 percent. If demand is inelastic, it means that the percentage change in quantity demanded is less than the percentage change in price—for example, if the price rises by 10 percent, and the quantity demanded falls by 1 percent.

Now suppose that the demand for health care were perfectly inelastic. This would mean that if price were to change, quantity demanded wouldn't change at all. In this unusual case, if price were to rise for, say, hip replacement surgery, the number of hip replacements wouldn't go down or up—it would stay the same as before the price went up. In this case, then, the consumption of health care by patients would be totally insensitive to changes in price.

We don't live in a world of perfectly inelastic demand for health care. There is sufficient evidence that people do respond to the price of health care, but not everyone responds to the same degree. Factors such as a person's income, insurance, and preferences influence the degree to which one responds.

Dr. Robinson, an orthopedic surgeon who commonly performs hip replacement surgeries, wants to know what the demand is for hip replacement surgery. She wants to know if patients will "buy" 10 hip replacements a month if the price is $10,000 and only eight hip replacements a month if the price is $15,000.

To try to discern the demand for hip replacement (performed by Dr. Robinson), the doctor asks her assistant to call up former patients who have had hip replacements and ask them if they would not have gotten the hip replacement if the price had been $5,000 higher. The assistant does this and reports back that every single patient that was called said they would still have gotten the hip replacement from Dr. Robinson even if the price had been $5,000 higher. In addition, each patient praises Dr. Robinson for the absolutely great work she did on their hips.

From the survey results, Dr. Robinson knows the demand for her performing hip replacements is perfectly inelastic between the price of $10,000 and $15,000. But might Dr. Robinson's former patients be biased in favor of her? After all, this group of individuals don't really constitute a random sample of people. They are all persons who know Dr. Robinson and have had hip replacement surgery performed by her, which makes one wonder if the true demand for hip replacement really is perfectly inelastic between the price of $10,000 and $15,000. In order to determine this, a survey could be given to a sample of people from the general population—not just Dr. Robinson's patients.

So, let's consider such a sample taken from the general population. Suppose a random sample of 1,000 people are chosen to survey (from a general population of 120,000 people) in the vicinity of Dr. Robinson's office. Suppose we ask this question to all 1,000 people: Would you get a hip replacement if the price were $10,000? Would you get a hip replacement if the price were $15,000? But now a problem presents itself. If two people both say yes to both questions, we still can't be sure that we are locating a particular point on a demand curve, because although both persons are quoted the price of $10,000 and $15,000, it may not be the case that both persons actually pay $10,000 and $15,000.

There is a difference between the price the surgeon quotes for hip replacement and the price that the patient pays. We'll call the first price the "doctor price," and we'll call the second price the "out-of-pocket price." To see how these two prices can differ for two different people, consider patients A and B, both of whom are considering hip replacement. Both are quoted the same doctor price of $15,000. But person A has health insurance that requires a copay of $500 for the hip replacement, and person B has health insurance that requires a copay of $3,000 for the hip replacement. So, when both persons are quoted the doctor price of $15,000, person A thinks $500, and person B thinks $3,000.

To complicate things even further, person A, who thinks $500, may have purchased health insurance knowing a hip replacement was in his future. Person B may have purchased health insurance figuring the chance of a hip replacement being in his future was small.

The people in the world like person A are planning for hip replacements and buying generous health insurance before the need for a health replacement arises. When quoted a price for a hip replacement (the doctor price), they lower this price substantially in their minds. They are the ones who will pay the $500. On the other hand, the people like person B are not planning for hip replacements, and so when they are quoted a price for a hip replacement (the doctor price), they don't lower the price as much as person A did. They are the ones who will end up paying $3,000.

Based on these different out-of-pocket prices, they answer the surveyor's question as to what they will buy at different doctors' prices differently.

All this leaves our Dr. Robinson, who simply wanted to know the demand for hip replacements performed by her, a little befuddled. She is not sure what to conclude from the survey results. After all, not everyone will be paying the same price for a hip replacement, and, therefore, we find it hard to trace out a demand curve for hip replacements in the same way that one might trace out a demand curve for laptops, shirts, books, or many other goods. In these cases, everyone faces the same price, which is not the case for hip replacements.

30-2a The RAND Health Insurance Experiment

Randomized Controlled Trial (RCT)
A study in which individuals are assigned to different groups (treatment group versus placebo or control group) at random.

The RAND Health Insurance Experiment, or simply RAND HIE, is one of the best-known and widely cited experiments in health care. One of the reasons this experiment appears so frequently in the literature has to do with the methodology used in the experiment. The RAND HIE was a **randomized controlled trial (RCT)**, meaning that individuals were assigned to different treatment groups at random. The chief characteristic of an RCT is that participants in different groups of an experiment are similar in characteristics to those in other groups.

To illustrate, suppose a pharmaceutical company wants to test a new drug. To conduct an RCT, the company chooses people at random and then gives half the people the drug and the other half a placebo (the group that receives the drug is called the *treatment group*, and the group that does not receive the drug is called the *placebo* or *control* group), and the company does not tell individuals in which group they were placed. In other words, individuals do not know if they had been given the drug or a placebo. The pharmaceutical company reports the findings of both groups. If, for example, the group that received the drug ended up with lower blood pressure than the group that didn't receive the drug, the company concludes that the drug lowers blood pressure.

In the RAND HIE, participants were assigned randomly to four different health insurance plans that differed in the percentage a patient had to pay for medical treatment. Specifically, the four plans had cost-sharing arrangements of 0 percent, 25 percent, 50 percent, and 95 percent. In each case, the percentage stated was the percentage that participants would have to pay for their health care. For example, individuals assigned to the 0 percent group had to pay 0 percent of their health care (the insurance company would pay the entire bill); individuals assigned to the 95 percent group had to pay 95 percent of their health care, and the insurance company would pay 5 percent of the bill.

Picture a downward-sloping demand curve for health care. If the price of health care is zero, you would expect the quantity demanded of health care would be much larger than if the price of health care were 95 percent of every dollar. Of course, if the demand curve were perfectly inelastic (vertical), you would expect that the quantity demanded of health care would be the same at zero price and at 95 cents for every dollar.

The RAND HIE found that the demand curve for health care is downward sloping. People on the 0 percent plan had more visits to the doctor and hospital than people on the other plans. Moreover, the less one had to pay for health care, the more visits one made.

Before you assume that the people in the 0 percent group had more visits to the doctor and hospital than others because they were naturally a sicker group, or initially had more health problems than persons in other groups, remember that the experiment here was an RCT. The individuals in each group were assigned at random. The researchers didn't assign people with more health problems to be in the 0 percent group and those persons with fewer health problems to be in the 95 percent group. For all practical purposes, individuals in every one of the four groups shared the same characteristics. They were essentially—but not literally—"the same" people.

Take a look at Exhibit 1. Column 2 lists the average annual number of outpatient visits for persons in each group. An outpatient visit constitutes a visit to a doctor for, perhaps, the problem of a nagging cough, or the flu, or running a fever. Column 3 lists the average annual number of inpatient visits. An inpatient visit constitutes being admitted to a hospital. In column 4, you will find the probability of emergency room use.

Notice that as the percentage a person has to pay for their health care rises, the average annual number of inpatient and outpatient visits decreases. In addition, one's probability of emergency room use decreases too.

So, does the price one has to pay for their own health care matter to how much health care one is likely to consume? The answer from the RAND HIE is yes: When it comes to buying health care, price matters.

Note an important difference between the numbers in columns 2 and 3. You'll notice that the difference between the numbers in column 2 are larger than the difference between the numbers in column 3. Specifically, going from 2.99 to 1.90 in column 2 is a 36 percent decrease, but going from 0.133 to 0.098 in the column 3 is a smaller, 26 percent decrease.

EXHIBIT 1

Use of Health Care as Estimated by the RAND HIE

The RAND HIE showed that consumers reduce their use of health care services when faced with higher prices.

Demand for outpatient care is more sensitive to price than demand for inpatient care.

(1) Cost-Sharing Arrangement	(2) Average Number of Annual Outpatient Episodes	(3) Average Number of Annual Inpatient Visits	(4) Probability of Emergency Room Use
0% (free)	2.99	0.133	22%
25%	2.32	0.109	19%
50%	2.11	0.099	20%
95%	1.90	0.098	15%

Source: Bhattacharya, Jay, Timothy Hyde, and Peter Tu. *Health Economics*. Macmillan International Higher Education, 2013.

What are we to make of the larger differences in column 2 compared with the smaller differences in column 3? Column 2 has to do with outpatient episodes (visits to the doctor), and column 3 has to do with inpatient visits (visits to the hospital). When one goes to the doctor's office, it is because one is experiencing symptoms ranging from very mild to severe, from a mild cough to the symptoms of what could turn out to be cancer or another serious disease. But when one is going in for an inpatient visit (when one has to go to the hospital for surgery, for example), the issue is almost always serious.

The larger and smaller differences between columns 2 and 3 tell us that people are more sensitive to price for outpatient care than for inpatient care. For example, price is more likely to be a consideration when one is going to the doctor for a mild cough than when one is going to the hospital for surgery. Let's use the extreme to highlight the difference. It's like people saying, "I'm not going to the doctor if I have to pay 95 percent of the bill to find out I just have a mild cough that will go away in a week, but I will go to the hospital, and have the surgeon perform surgery on me, if I have lung cancer—even if I do have to pay 95 percent of the bill."

The RAND HIE and Mortality The people in the 0 percent group, we know, had less expensive health care than people in the other groups, and they also had more inpatient and outpatient visits. In other words, they consumed more health care than the other groups. Did this greater consumption of health care cause them to live longer? We invite you to take a guess. Do you think that people who consume more health care end up living longer than those who do not?

The answer from the RAND HIE experiment is yes and no.

Look at column 2 in Exhibit 2, which lists the relative mortality rate when all participates in the experiment are considered. The relative mortality rate for the groups that had to make a copay for their health insurance—that is, the individuals in the 25 percent, 50 percent, and 95 percent groups—is 1. The relative mortality rate of the people in the copay group serves as our point of comparison. A relative mortality rate greater than 1 means that the group had a higher likelihood of dying during the experiment than people in the copay group; a number less than 1 means the group was less likely to die during the experiment than the people in the copay group.

Notice that the number in the 0 percent group is 0.99. This means that people in the 0 percent group—the group of people who received free health care—were 99 percent as likely

EXHIBIT 2

Health Care Outcomes as Estimated by the RAND HIE

The RAND HIE compared mortality across patients assigned to the four different health insurance plans. The mortality rate for copay patients is normalized to 1 in the exhibit. The 0.99 in the exhibit means people in the free care plan were 99 percent as likely to die during the experiment as people in the copay plans, which means access to free health care had essentially no impact on the likelihood of someone dying during the study period. However, there was a significant mortality difference between the high-risk participants in the free and copay plans (see column 3).

(1) Cost-Sharing Arrangement	(2) Relative Mortality Rate (All Participants)	(3) Relative Mortality Rate (High-Risk Participants)
Free (0%)	0.99	1.90
Copay (25%, 50%, 95%)	1	2.10

Source: Bhattacharya, Jay, Timothy Hyde, and Peter Tu. Health Economics. Macmillan International Higher Education, 2013.

to die during the 15 years of the health insurance experiment as were people in the other groups. So, did free health care increase one's mortality? The answer is no; and that is a startling finding for many.

Now look at column 3 in Exhibit 2. Here we see the relative mortality rate for high-risk participants in the experiment. Patients were classified at the beginning of the experiment as high-risk based on their smoking status, cholesterol level, and blood pressure. These people were considered to have a higher probability of dying than the general population, which is why the numbers in the column 3 are greater than 1.

The difference between the numbers in column 3 are greater than the difference between the numbers in column 2. That tells us that free health care (the 0 percent group) matters more when it comes to high-risk individuals than when it comes to all participants. But how much does it matter? The difference between the mortality rates of the free and copay high-risk individuals was 0.20 (2.10 − 1.90). This means the high-risk participants on the free insurance plan were about 10 percent (0.20/2.10) less likely to die than the high-risk participants on the copay plans. Does free health care matter when it comes to high-risk individuals? Yes.

The RAND HIE and Other Considerations The RAND HIE study completed 23 health comparisons between individuals in the four groups. The study found statistically significant differences between the groups when it came to three measures: blood pressure, near-sightedness, and far-sightedness. The study found that more affordable health care (in other words, the lower the percentage of the total medical bill that one has to pay) does not significantly improve health for the general population, but it does for high-risk individuals. This finding has been supported by other studies, too—most notably, the Oregon Medicaid Experiment.

Finding Economics

In Oregon Another health insurance experiment that receives a lot of attention is the Oregon Medicaid Experiment. In 2008, Oregon held a lottery to determine whether low-income adult Oregonians would receive Medicaid. This lottery randomly assigned low-income Oregonians to two groups: one that faced lower out-of-pocket health care costs

(Continued)

> due to being covered by Medicaid and another that had higher out-of-pocket costs due to lack of insurance. Because people were randomly assigned to the two groups, researchers had a perfect opportunity to answer similar questions to those the RAND HIE sought to address. Like the RAND HIE, the Oregon Medicaid Experiment showed that the people that faced lower out-of-pocket costs (i.e., the lottery winners) used more health care services than the group of people that faced higher out-of-pocket costs (i.e., the lottery losers). Similar to the RAND HIE's findings, the Oregon Medicaid Experiment also found essentially no difference in the mortality rates between the two groups.

What Are We to Conclude from the RAND HIE Experiment? Here are some things that have been concluded from the RAND HIE Experiment:

1. On average, the less people pay for their health care, the more inpatient and outpatient visits they make.
2. From #1, we conclude that price does matter to people when it comes to health care. The demand for health care is not perfectly inelastic.
3. People are more sensitive to price when it comes to outpatient visits (visits to the doctor for anything from mild to possibly serious issues) than when it comes to inpatient visits (visits to the hospital).
4. In the general population, mortality does not seem to be affected by one's consumption of health care. People with greater health care (as evidenced by more inpatient and outpatient visits) aren't less likely to die than others with less health care. However, when it comes to high-risk individuals, greater health care does impact relative mortality rates.
5. In the general population, greater consumption of health care (because of its greater affordability) doesn't seem to improve health, but for high-risk individuals, it does make a difference.

1. Does the price of health care affect the purchase of health care services?
2. Does the price of health care affect health?
3. Is the demand for outpatient care or inpatient care more price sensitive?

30-3 Social Determinants of Health

Health economics is a broader field than health care economics. In fact, health care economics is a subset of health economics in much the same way that international economics or microeconomics is a subset of economics. Up until this point, we have discussed health care exclusively. Health care relates to health measures provided by doctors, hospitals, clinics, and pharmaceutical companies.

However, while health care can improve health, it alone cannot make someone healthy. Other factors—such as one's diet, physical activity level, and genetic makeup—matter too.

Do other measures—such as one's income, education, sex, or race—impact health? Do these things matter to health? It turns out they do, and they are jointly referred to as the

social determinants of health. In this section, we discuss differences in health across social factors, which are often referred to as **health disparities**.

30-3a Health Disparities

One commonly used measure to study health disparities is life expectancy (see Exhibit 3). Life expectancy varies across sex. For example, in 2018, life expectancy at birth was five years longer for females (at 81.2 years) than for males (at 76.2 years). Life expectancy also varies among races and ethnicities. In 2018, life expectancy for Black individuals was 74.9 years, 78.7 years for White individuals, and 81.8 years for Hispanic individuals.

Often the health disparities by sex, race, and ethnicity get the most attention from the public, but disparities also exist when it comes to education, income, disability status, geographic location (urban versus rural), sexual identity and orientation, as well as access to health care and safe and decent housing. We will discuss a few of these disparities in this chapter, starting with education.

In Exhibit 4, you will find the expected age at death for different groups of persons. The first group is Black men. Notice that in this group, one is expected to die at any earlier age if one's highest level of education is high school than if one has attended some college. Also, within the same group, one is expected to die at an earlier age if one has only completed some college education than if one has obtained a four-year college degree or higher.

EXHIBIT 3

U.S. Life Expectancy at Birth by Sex and Race/Ethnicity, 2018

The exhibit shows disparities in life expectancy at birth by sex and race. The life expectancy for women is five years higher than that of men. The life expectancy of Hispanics is three years higher than that of Whites—which is, in turn, four years higher than that of Blacks.

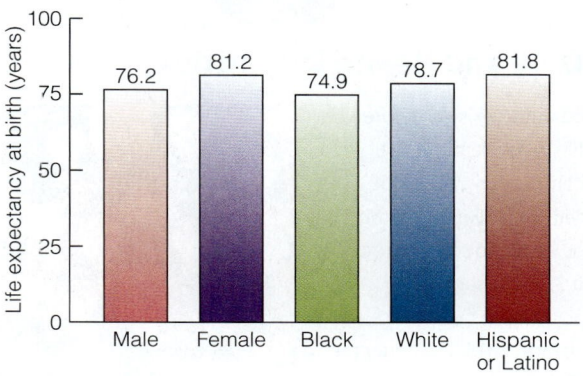

Source: CDC, Table 1, https://www.cdc.gov/nchs/data/hestat/life-expectancy/life-expectancy-2018.htm (sex) and CDC, Table I-21 (p. 76) https://www.cdc.gov/nchs/data/nvsr/nvsr69/nvsr69-13-tables-508.pdf (race/ethnicity).

Social Determinants of Health
Social and economic conditions that impact one's health.

Health Disparities
Differences in health outcomes across levels of socioeconomic status.

EXHIBIT 4

Expected Age at Death by Race, Sex, and Education, 2017

The exhibit shows disparities in life expectancy at birth by race, sex, and education. Life expectancy increases with education within each race-sex combination. The number of additional years of life expectancy that highly educated people attain differs across the groups. For Black men, the average life expectancy of college graduates is nine years higher than high school graduates. For Black women, the difference is only 5 years.

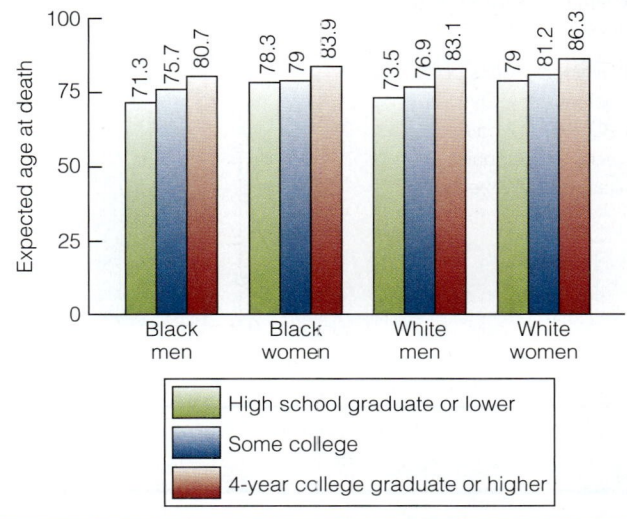

Source: Sasson & Hayward, JAMA 2019, Table 1, https://jamanetwork.com/journals/jama/fullarticle/2748794.

What we find for Black men also holds for Black women, White men, and White women when it comes to education and expected age at death. On average, the more education one has, the greater one's expected age at death.

Economics 24/7

COVID-19 and Health Disparities

Health disparities existed before the COVID-19 pandemic in the United States in early 2020. But the pandemic made many of the disparities worse. To see this, return to Exhibit 3, which shows life expectancy at birth by sex, race, and ethnicity in 2018. The larger the height difference between the bars, the greater the disparity.

Now look at Exhibit 5. This exhibit shows the life expectancy by race and ethnicity pre-COVID-19 (2019) and during the pandemic (2020). The approximately one-year drop in life expectancy at birth by race and ethnicity is clear across all three races and ethnicities. This drop alone is staggering.

If we were to track the race and ethnicity life expectancy measures shown back in Exhibit 3 over the last decade or so, we'd see life expectancy at birth either increased slightly or remained the same. In other words, before COVID-19, life expectancy at birth was either improving or staying the same, but COVID-19 caused it to decline 1.9 years for Hispanics, 0.8 year for non-Hispanic Whites, and 2.7 years for non-Hispanic Blacks. Therefore, the life expectancy disparity between non-Hispanic Whites and non-Hispanic Blacks grew from 4.1 years in 2019 (78.8 years versus 74.7 years) to 6.0 years in 2020 (78 years versus 72 years.)

EXHIBIT 5

Life Expectancy at Birth by Race/Ethnicity Before and After the Start of COVID-19

Life expectancy was greater for all three groups of persons (shown here) in 2019 (before the COVID-19 pandemic) than during (2020). COVID-19 caused life expectancy to decline 1.9 years for Hispanics, 0.8 years for non-Hispanic Whites, and 2.7 years for non-Hispanic Blacks.

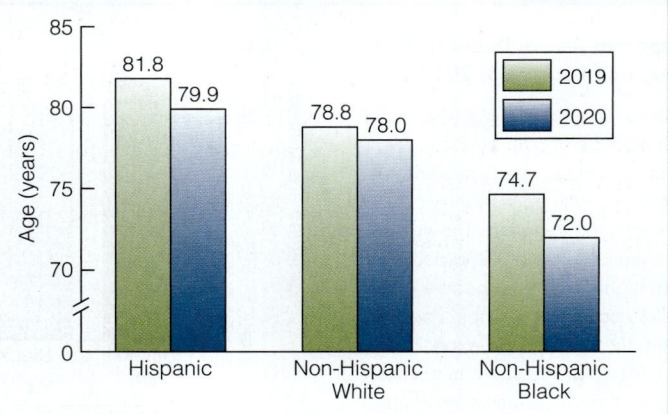

Source: CDC, Figure 2 https://www.cdc.gov/nchs/data/vsrr/VSRR10-508.pdf

Increases in disparities across other measures of health show the same general pattern—the pandemic exacerbated health disparities that were already present. How so? It's been suggested that it is likely due to a combination of differences in the medical conditions that are most common among certain groups, exposure from living in densely populated cities, and the difference in the jobs that could be done virtually. Software engineers who can code equally well from home as they can in an office were likely better off than grocery store workers who didn't have the option of working from home.

The exhibit shows life expectancy at birth before and after the start of COVID-19. Life expectancy at birth decreased across all races as a result of COVID-19, with the Black population experiencing the largest decrease in life expectancy.

30-3b Causes of Health Disparities

What causes the health disparities shown in Exhibit 4? Why do people with more education have a higher expected age at death than people with less education? Before we jump to the conclusion that more education *causes* better health (as evidenced in life expectancy), remember that *correlation is not causation*. More education may be correlated with greater life expectancy (they both move up and down together), but it doesn't follow that more education causes greater life expectancy.

In health economics, trying to identify the *causes* of health disparities is one of the most active research areas. So far, no single theory has been able to explain all the health disparities, and maybe no single theory ever will. But several theories proposed successfully explain various disparities to varying degrees.

The Efficient-Producer Hypothesis Researchers have theorized that more education does, in fact, cause better health. This is the essence of the **efficient-producer hypothesis**. In a nutshell, the hypothesis states that individuals with more education are more efficient producers of health than individuals with less education. Here "efficiency" essentially means that more highly educated groups understand their doctors better, make better use of medical technology, make better health-related choices, and so on.

Now stop and consider the reverse of this hypothesis. Suppose someone hypothesizes that it is not more education that leads to better health, but it is better health than leads to more education. Healthier people not only get more education than sick people, but it is the better health that causes them to get more education.

To add weight to the argument, consider children in poor health. A number of studies have shown that children born with low or very low birth weight (an indicator of poor health later in life) obtain less schooling than those born with higher birth weight. This turns out to be true even among twins.

Also consider that children who are sick or malnourished are more likely to miss school, are less likely to learn while in school, and ultimately end up going to school fewer years than those children without these conditions.

If you were a health researcher, you would definitely want to know the direction cause and effect moves. Is it more education that causes better health, or is it better health that causes more education? Knowing which it is may matter enormously for policy purposes. If better health causes more schooling, then policymakers want to focus on reducing the incidences of low-birth-weight and sick and malnourished children, knowing that if this can be done, more education will follow. Alternatively, if it is more education that leads to better health, then policymakers might want to find ways to encourage children to stay in school longer, knowing that better health outcomes will follow.

Efficient-Producer Hypothesis
Hypothesizes that individuals with more education are more efficient producers of health than individuals with less education.

The empirical evidence is growing that more education causes better health. Several reasons have been given for this. First, it could be that better-educated people receive more directly useful information on how to take care of their health. For example, most high school students in the United States are required to take nutrition classes. Also, education can endow individuals with both certain information and traits that benefit health and an enhanced ability to understand the directions of complex medical treatment regimens. Finally, education strongly correlates to the type of job one has. Highly educated people often have more indoor, less physical jobs than people with less education. Having jobs that are indoors, are in safe environments, and do not put one at risk for health problems can help people stay healthy.

Early Childhood Does early childhood matter to health disparities found in later life? One theory suggests that health disparities in later life are the result of deprivation in the womb or in early childhood. To illustrate, suppose a young child experiences famine. That child's genes then instruct the body to hoard fat in order to deal with the initial deprivation caused by the famine. Such gene instructions and subsequent body changes may make children better adapted to deal with famine, but those adaptations are no longer necessary if famine no longer exists. The child is then left with added body weight as an adult that could bring on certain health problems. For example, body mass index has a strong relationship to diabetes and insulin resistance.

During World War II, a German blockade caused parts of Holland to face a terrible famine. This tragic event created two groups of infants in Holland: those who had been in womb during the famine and those conceived immediately after the famine ended. The two groups of infants were similar in most ways other than one group experienced nutritional deprivation in the womb and the other did not. When comparing the two groups of children as adults, researchers found that the nutritionally deprived children experienced much worse overall health as adults than did the adults who were not nutritionally deprived as children.[1]

Income People with high incomes can afford to purchase more things than people with low incomes, and one of the things they can buy more of is health care. In addition to being able to buy more health care, they are also able to afford gym memberships and homes in unpolluted neighborhoods, both of which can promote health.

A 2005 study of Swedish lottery participants found that winning the lottery had a significant positive effect on health. The study found that lottery wins that increased one's income by at least 10 percent reduced the five-year mortality rate by 2 percentage points, from 6 percent to 4 percent.[2]

Stress Sustained periods of stress have been shown to negatively impact health. People cite such things as taking exams, negative working relations with one's boss, not having enough money to pay the rent, struggling to put food on the table, and so on, as leading to stress. One theory is that people in the lowest income tax bracket face more stressful events than others. An oft-cited 2010 review of the link between stress and health reported these five major findings: (1) Stress has a damaging effect on both mental and physical health; (2) differential exposure to stressful events is the primary way that physical and mental health inequalities are

---

[1] Roseboom, Tessa J., Jan HP Van Der Meulen, Anita C. J. Ravelli, Clive Osmond, David J. P. Barker, and Otto P. Bleker. Effects of Prenatal Exposure to the Dutch Famine on Adult Disease in Later Life: An Overview. *Twin Research and Human Genetics* 4, no. 5 (2001): 293–298.

[2] Lindahl, Mikael. "Estimating the effect of income on health and mortality using lottery prizes as an exogenous source of variation in income." *Journal of Human resources* 40, no. 1 (2005): 144–168.

produced; (3) the health of minorities is harmed by stress due to discrimination; (4) stressful events exist over one's entire life and across generations; (5) positive self-esteem and/or social support help to reduce the negative impact of stressful events.[3]

1. How large is the gap between males' and females' life expectancy at birth? Among Blacks, Whites, and Hispanics?
2. How did COVID-19 affect health disparities?
3. What are some of the potential causes of health disparities?

30-4 Health Care

30-4a Prices

Suppose you want to know how much you have spent on apples this month. How would you determine this amount? You would multiply the price of an apple by the number of apples you purchased. The same process is used to determine health care spending. One would multiply the quantity of health care services by the prices of those services. The result is total spending on health care services.

If we break down health care spending into prices and quantities, it is obvious why the United States spends so much more on health care than most other countries do. One highly cited article in the journal *Health Affairs* (2003) provides the reasons in its title: "It's the Prices, Stupid: Why the United States Is So Different from Other Countries."

The authors followed up the original 2003 article with another article in 2019, entitled "It's Still the Prices, Stupid: Why the U.S. Spends So Much on Health Care, and a Tribute to Uwe Reinhardt." (Uwe Reinhardt was a professor of political economy at Princeton University and a prominent scholar in health care economics who passed away in 2017.)

Both articles applied essentially the same methodology, and in both articles, the authors reported that health care services in the United States are utilized to about the same extent as health care services in other countries. So, if the quantity of health care is the same in other countries, but total spending is very different, then differences in prices explain the differences in total spending. The higher prices of health care in the United States explain the higher total health care spending in the United States relative to most other countries.

Let's pause to examine the price differences among countries. Exhibit 6 shows the price for select health care services (hip replacements, knee replacements, normal delivery, etc.) in eight countries: the United States, the United Kingdom, Switzerland, Holland, Australia, New Zealand, South Africa, and the United Arab Emirates. The prices for the seven countries other than the United States indicate what percentage below or above its price for a particular service is in relation to the U.S. price. For example, you can see that when it comes to a hip replacement, the price in Holland is about 20 percent of the price in the United States.

Notice that all the dots in the exhibit lie to the left of the red dots for the United States, except for one. That means for all the health care services (except for one), all countries have lower prices than in the United States. The only country with a higher price for a health care service is New Zealand, for cataract surgery.

---

[3] Thoits, Peggy A. "Stress and health: Major findings and policy implications." *Journal of health and social behavior* 51, no. 1_suppl (2010): S41–S53.

EXHIBIT 6

U.S. Health Care Prices Compared to Other Countries, 2017

The exhibit shows the prices of common health care services across eight countries, including the United States. The prices for the non-U.S. countries are shown as a percentage of the U.S. price. U.S. health care prices are significantly higher than those in other countries.

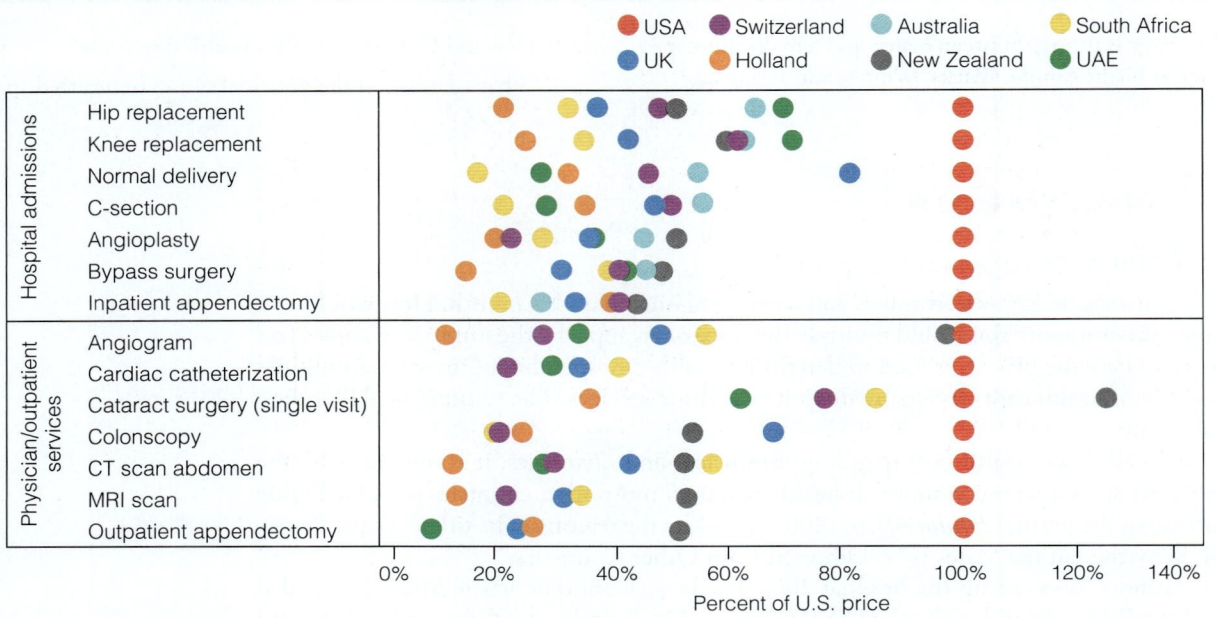

Source: Health Care Cost Institute, Figure 1 https://healthcostinstitute.org/hcci-research/international-comparisons-of-health-care-prices-2017-ifhp-survey.

Not only are health care prices higher in the United States than most other countries, but they are rising quickly too. Many researchers have explained this by pointing to U.S. high labor costs, along with increasingly high-quality care, the power of monopoly exercised by U.S. hospitals, medical malpractice laws, and waste.

A 2012 study by the Institute of Medicine estimated that 30 cents of every dollar spent on health care in the United States is wasted. U.S. health spending in 2019 alone was $3.8 trillion. The study found that of this amount, $1.1 trillion was wasted—that is an awful lot of waste. In the same year, there were only 16 countries in the world that had a gross domestic product (GDP) greater than $1.1 trillion. That means that the U.S. health care system wastes more in health care spending than what all but 16 countries in the world produce.

The study identified six categories of waste (ranked according to most dollars wasted): administrative complexity, overtreatment, fraud and abuse, pricing failures, care delivery failures, and care coordination failures.

If you've heard of doctors complaining that they have too much paperwork to complete, that's administrative complexity at work. If doctors didn't have to deal with so many different forms from so many different insurers, they could spend more time on direct patient health care. Overtreatment refers to people receiving unnecessary or duplicative health care services. Antibiotics are of no use to ending a cold or flu, but sometimes people receive antibiotic prescriptions to treat them.

An example of health care fraud and abuse is hospitals and physicians improperly billing patients, claiming that a service was more complicated and time consuming than it was in order to obtain a greater reimbursement. Price failures refer to the price of health care services being substantially higher than cost, which implies that health care providers might have significant market power.

30-4b Access

The median cost of a childbirth delivery without complications was $11,200 in the United States in 2017. For most Americans, paying that price out-of-pocket, in one lump sum, is not feasible. That is one of the major reasons that most Americans have health insurance. With health insurance, the bulk of that $11,200 is paid for by the insurer.

In this context, when people say that someone doesn't have "access to health care," what they are really talking about is having access to health insurance. For most people, without access to health insurance, one's access to health care is greatly limited.

In many countries, access to health insurance is not a concern. In a number of countries—Australia, France, Germany, Italy, Spain, Sweden, and the United Kingdom, to name a few—universal health care exists so that *all* citizens (and sometimes residents who are not citizens) have access to health care. This is not currently true—and never has been true—in the United States. In the United States, 29 million people (or 11 percent of the population younger than 65 years of age) did not have health insurance in 2019. This group consists of people under 65 years of age who primarily have moderate-to-high income but do not work for an employer that offers health insurance.

30-4c Insurance

The U.S. health care system is often categorized according to the type of health insurance Americans have. The three main types of health insurance are commercial, Medicare, and Medicaid. Commercial insurance is privately provided; both Medicare and Medicaid are government-run programs that cover specific segments of the population. **Medicare** covers older adults (one becomes eligible for Medicare at age 65), and **Medicaid** covers low-income individuals. In 2019, Medicare covered 14 percent of the population, and Medicaid covered 20 percent.

These three types of insurance collectively covered 90 percent of the U.S. population in 2019. Of the remaining 10 percent of the population, 9 percent are uninsured, and about 1 percent are covered by the military or the Veterans Administration.

Commercial insurance covers 56 percent of the U.S. population, more than any other type of insurance. Employer-sponsored insurance accounts for 89 percent of the commercial insurance market while non-group insurance (insurance purchased directly from an insurance company as opposed to through an employer) accounts for the remaining 11 percent. The origin of employer-sponsored insurance—the insurance that employees get through their employers—can be traced back to World War II. At the time, the war created a large labor shortage in the United States as people were sent off to war. With fewer workers left in the United States, businesses had to compete for these workers by offering higher wages; in turn, these higher wages led to higher prices. President Franklin Roosevelt's solution to this brewing problem was to freeze wages through an executive order.

As a result, businesses were prohibited from offering higher wages to compete for workers. So, instead, they competed by offering health insurance benefits; businesses would pay for much of the health insurance their employees received. In 1943, the Internal Revenue Service (IRS) effectively encouraged the relationship between employers and employer-based health

Medicare
The U.S. government-run health insurance program for adults ages 65 and older.

Medicaid
The U.S. government-run health insurance program for low-income individuals.

Commercial Insurance
Insurance provided by private insurance companies, typically through one's employer.

insurance by making the insurance benefits tax exempt. This made it more affordable to obtain health insurance through an employer than to obtain it any other way.

Today, commercial health insurance is managed by private health insurance companies such as UnitedHealth, Anthem, Centene, and Humana. Employers can choose to be either self-insured or fully insured. To be self-insured means the employer accepts the risks that come with covering their employees with health insurance. To be fully insured means the employer pays a premium to an insurance company and the insurance company takes on the risk of insuring the employees.

Health insurance companies in the commercial insurance market negotiate with medical providers (e.g., hospitals and physicians) on prices and reimbursements for services rendered. Hospitals and physicians want to be paid more, insurers want to pay out less. The bargaining power that medical providers have relative to insurers is important in determining reimbursement rates. Hospital X, which is the only hospital within 100 miles, is likely to obtain higher reimbursement rates than hospital Y, which is one of four hospitals within 100 miles. Similarly, an insurer that is only one of two choices available is likely to have more bargaining power than an insurer that is one of 10 options.

Among the three major types of insurance—commercial, Medicare, and Medicaid—it is in the commercial market where prices are negotiated. Both Medicare and Medicaid prices are administratively set by government. This difference leads to higher prices in the commercial market than the prices set by Medicare and Medicaid. A recent study found that average commercial hospital prices were almost double those set by Medicare and Medicaid. In a similar vein, commercial physician prices were 60 percent higher than Medicare prices.[4] Medicaid prices are generally even lower than Medicare prices.

30-4d Health Care Reform

Affordable Care Act (ACA)
The most recent major health care reform in the United States that was signed into law in 2010.

A discussion of health care reform is never far from the surface. Rarely is there a presidential election debate where health care reform is not discussed and argued over. Often, the debate focuses on cost, access, and quality. The **Affordable Care Act (ACA)**, colloquially referred to as Obamacare, passed into law in 2010, was the last major health care reform in the United States. While it was unequivocally successful at increasing access to health care, its impact on cost and quality has been hotly debated.

The ACA did two major things to reduce the number of uninsured in the United States. The first was to give states the option to expand Medicaid, the government-run program that covers the low-income population. Before the ACA, states used a combination of income, household size, disability status, and a few other factors to determine Medicaid eligibility. The ACA made it possible for states to extend Medicare eligibility from a select group of people with low incomes to everyone with income less than 133 percent of the federal poverty line. States that exercised this option found that the ranks of the Medicaid-eligible persons increased. The federal government tried to provide an incentive to the states to exercise this option; specifically, it agreed to pay a significant portion of the added costs of covering more people.

The second thing the ACA did to increase access was to open ACA Marketplaces. These are where people who don't currently receive insurance from their employers, are too young for

---

[4.] Chernew, M. E., Hicks, A.L., and Shah, S. A.. Wide State-Level Variation In Commercial Health Care Prices Suggests Uneven Impact of Price Regulation: An Examination of State-Level Price Variation in the Commercial Market, Relative to Medicare, for a Broader Set of States and a Wider Set of Services Than Had Been Previously Examined. *Health Affairs.* 2020 May 1;39(5):791–799.

Medicare, or who earn too much to qualify for Medicaid can obtain health insurance coverage. The government subsidized the cost of the ACA Marketplace plans for individuals and families with incomes of less than 400 percent of the federal poverty level in order to encourage more people to get insured. Increased eligibility for Medicaid, together with the ACA Marketplaces (with cost-sharing subsidies), has led to a significant decline in the percentage of the U.S. population without health insurance: It was 18 percent in 2010 (before the ACA was passed into law), and it was 11 percent in 2019.

Today's debate on health care reform often focuses on the costs and benefits of universal health insurance. With universal health insurance, no one is without health insurance. Sometimes people speak of "Medicare for All." In its purest form, this type of plan would simply place everyone in the country on Medicare. In other words, people would not have to wait until age 65 to become Medicare eligible; all ages would be eligible for Medicare.

No doubt, this would significantly increase the role of government in the U.S. health care system. Because of this, there are both strong proponents of, and opponents to, Medicare for All.

Some have suggested that a better route to health care reform would be to add a "public option" onto the existing ACA. A public option would be a government-run plan that would compete with private insurance plans. Individuals would be free to choose the public option if they wanted to, but they would not be required to do so.

1. Which country has the highest medical prices across a range of common services? How might the high prices be explained?

2. What group of people in the United States is most likely to be uninsured?

3. What are some of the health care reform discussions you might hear about in the years to come?

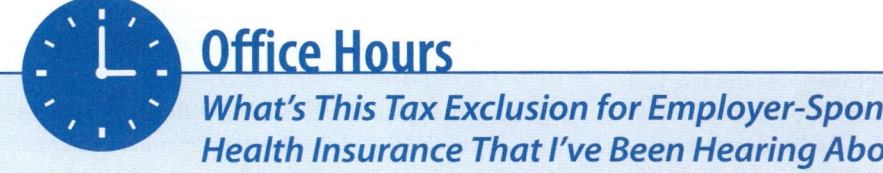

Office Hours

What's This Tax Exclusion for Employer-Sponsored Health Insurance That I've Been Hearing About?"

Student: This chapter mentioned that part of the reason for the United States being tied to a system of employer-provided health insurance is that the IRS decided to exempt employer-based health insurance from taxation. Why would that decision tie the United States to employer-provided health insurance?

Instructor: Good question. Excluding employer-based health insurance from taxation means it costs less to get health insurance through an employer than to purchase it on your own, which means people are likely to continue purchasing health insurance through their employers.

Student: I don't see how a tax exclusion makes it cheaper to buy health insurance through an employer.

Instructor: Maybe some numbers would help. Let's say your employer offers to purchase a health insurance plan on your behalf for $5,000 or give you $5,000 in cash.

Student: Oh, but if I take the cash that's going to get taxed, right? So it will end up being something like $4,000. The exact amount will depend on my tax rate, but that's an estimate.

Instructor: That's exactly right. If your employer offered $5,000 in cash, you'll have $4,000 after taxes with which to go shopping for health insurance. It's unlikely you'll be able to find a health insurance plan for $4,000 that was as generous as the $5,000 plan you turned down from your employer.

Student: Does the tax exclusion incentivize employers to provide more generous health insurance than they would otherwise?

Instructor: Yes, and this is one of the complaints that many economists have about the tax exclusion for employer-sponsored health insurance. It incentivizes overly generous health insurance. For instance, an employer can offer an employee $5,000 of health insurance or $5,000 of cash; it makes no difference to the employer. But to the employee, that $5,000 in cash will turn out to be $4,000 in cash (after taxes). And if you're a particularly high earner, the $5,000 could turn into something closer to $3,000 than $4,000. It seems plausible many people will prefer $5,000 in health insurance benefits over $3,000 cash or $10,000 in health insurance benefits over $6,000. That is, people will prefer more generous health insurance than they would have absent the tax exclusion. The more expensive the health insurance package, the larger the difference between the price of the insurance you receive and the after-tax income you'd receive as an alternative.

Points to Remember

1. The tax exclusion for employer-sponsored health insurance makes obtaining insurance through your employer cheaper than obtaining it on your own.
2. The tax exclusion incentivizes more generous health insurance and leaves the federal government with less tax revenue than it would have without it.

Chapter Summary

Why Health Economics?

- Everyone gets sick, and everyone—even those who are young, healthy, and rarely visit a doctor—pays for health care. Nearly $1 out of every $5 spent in the United States is spent on health care.
- U.S. health care costs have rapidly grown over the last half century from $1 in every $20 being spent on health care in 1960 to nearly $1 in $5 being spent on health care today.
- Health care is only one input into affecting someone's health. A number of other factors, including socioeconomic status, play a large part in determining health.
- Uncertainty, insurance, and externalities make the analysis of health care markets different than other markets discussed thus far in the book.

The Demand for Health Care

- The purchase of health care responds to price; people do not agree to doctor-recommended tests, procedures, and medications without some consideration of price.
- More affordable health care doesn't significantly improve health for the general population, but it can improve health for high-risk groups.

Social Determinants of Health

- Health disparities have been identified across several dimensions including race/ethnicity, sex, education, income, sexual identity and orientation, access to health insurance, access to decent and safe housing, disability status, and geographic location (urban versus rural).
- Some of the possible causes of these disparities include education, early childhood deprivation, income, and stress.

U.S. Health Care

- Prices for common medical services and procedures are significantly higher in the United States than in other high-income countries.
- Proposed health care reforms often target increasing access to health insurance.
- Commercial, Medicare, and Medicaid are the three major health insurance types in the United States; among them, they cover 90 percent of the U.S. population.

Key Terms and Concepts

Negative Externality
Randomized Controlled Trial (RCT)
Social Determinants of Health
Health Disparities
Efficient-Producer Hypothesis
Medicare
Medicaid
Commercial Insurance
Affordable Care Act

Questions and Problems

1. Explain what makes health care markets different from other markets.
2. Between 1960 and today, U.S. health care shifted from accounting for $1 out of every $20 spent to $1 out of every $5 spent. List some of the reasons why this happened.
3. What are some of the dimensions along which health disparities exist?
4. What are some of the causes that have been identified to explain health disparities?
5. Explain the way in which differences in education can cause differences in health. Also explain why it's not immediately obvious that this causal pathway runs from education to health instead of from health to education.
6. Why are the prices commercial insurers pay medical providers higher than those paid by Medicare or Medicaid?
7. Did COVID-19 exacerbate or lessen health disparities? What do you think caused the change?
8. How does the tax exclusion of employer-sponsored health insurance make it cheaper for you to obtain health insurance through your employer than by yourself?
9. How much of U.S. health spending is estimated to be wasted spending? List the categories of waste mentioned in the chapter.
10. What was the last major health care reform in the United States, and what were the most significant changes it made to the U.S. health care system?
11. What's the history behind why U.S health insurance is largely employer-based? What does the history tell you about possible unintended consequences of restricting certain practices?
12. In this chapter, what were some of the problems that Dr. Robinson ran into while trying to determine the demand for her surgical services?
13. Is it the difference in the prices or the difference in quantities of health care services in the United States that explain why its health care spending per capita is higher than other countries' health care spending?
14. What's the evidence for income differences being a cause of health differences?

CHAPTER 31

Market Failure: Externalities, Public Goods, and Asymmetric Information

Introduction

Markets are a major topic in this book. We have analyzed how markets work, beginning with the simple supply-and-demand model, as well as various market structures: perfect competition, monopoly, and others. Goods and services are produced in markets. For example, cars are produced in car markets, houses are produced in housing markets, and computers are produced in computer markets. We now ask: Do these markets produce the right amount (the optimal or ideal amount) of these various goods? What are the right amounts? For example, what is the ideal or optimal amount of houses to produce, and does the housing market actually produce that amount?

When a market produces more or less than the ideal or optimal amount of a particular good, economists say there is **market failure**. Economists want to know under what conditions market failure may occur. This chapter presents three topics in which market failure is a prominent part of the discussion: externalities, public goods, and asymmetric information.

31-1 Externalities

Sometimes, when goods are produced and consumed, side effects (spillover or third-party effects) are felt by people who are not directly involved in the market exchanges. In general, these side effects are called **externalities**, because the costs or benefits are external to the persons who caused them. In this section, we discuss the various costs and benefits of activities and describe how and when activities cause externalities. We then explain graphically how externalities can result in market failure.

31-1a Costs and Benefits of Activities

Most activities in life have both costs and benefits. For example, when Jim sits down to read a book, reading has some benefits for Jim and some costs. These benefits and costs are private to him—they affect only him; hence, we call them *private benefits* and *private costs*.

Jim can also undertake an activity that has benefits and costs not only for him but also for others. Suppose he decides to smoke a cigarette in the general vicinity of Angelica. For Jim, smoking the cigarette has both benefits and costs—his private benefits and costs. But Jim's

Market Failure
A situation in which the market does not provide the ideal or optimal amount of a good.

Externality
A side effect of an action that affects the well-being of third parties.

smoking might also affect Angelica: for example, she may react to cigarette smoke by coughing. In this case, Jim's smoking might impose a cost on Angelica. Because the cost Jim imposes on her is external to him, we call it an *external cost*. Jim's activity imposes a *negative externality* on Angelica, for which she incurs an external cost. A **negative externality** exists when a person's or group's actions impose a cost (or adverse side effect) on others.

In another example, suppose Jim lives across the street from Melanie and beautifies his front yard (which Melanie can clearly see from her house) by planting trees, flowers, and a new lawn. Obviously, Jim receives some benefits and costs by beautifying his yard, but Melanie enjoys some benefits too: Not only does she have a pretty yard to look at (in much the same way that someone might benefit by gazing at a beautiful painting), but Jim's beautification efforts may also raise the market value of Melanie's property.

Because the benefit that Jim generates for Melanie is external to him, it is an *external benefit*. Jim's activity generates a *positive externality* for Melanie, for which she receives an external benefit. A **positive externality** exists when a person's or group's actions create a benefit (or beneficial side effect) for others.

> **Negative Externality**
> The condition in which a person's or group's actions impose a cost (an adverse side effect) on others.

> **Positive Externality**
> The condition in which a person's or group's actions create a benefit (a beneficial side effect) for others.

Finding Economics

In Students Talking in Class Blake sits near the back of the room in his biology class. Two students who sit near Blake often talk to each other while the class is in session. They usually whisper, but still, their talking disturbs Blake. Where is the economics?

As far as Blake is concerned, the two talking students are doing something (talking during the class) that adversely affects him. For Blake, their talking is a negative externality.

31-1b Marginal Costs and Benefits of Activities

When considering activities that have different degrees or amounts of costs and benefits (smoking one or two cigarettes an hour, planting three trees or four), economists speak in terms of marginal benefits and costs. More specifically, for Jim, various activities have marginal private benefits (*MPB*) and marginal private costs (*MPC*). If Jim's activities generate external benefits or costs for others, then it makes sense to speak in terms of marginal external benefits (*MEB*) and marginal external costs (*MEC*).

To analyze the effects of an activity, we need to know the total marginal costs and benefits, so we sum them. The sum of marginal private costs (*MPC*) and marginal external costs (*MEC*) is referred to as **marginal social costs (*MSC*)**:

$$MSC = MPC + MEC$$

In our example, Jim's smoking a cigarette imposed an external cost on Angelica. Suppose Jim's *MPC* of smoking a cigarette is $1 and Angelica's *MEC* of Jim's smoking a cigarette is $2. Therefore, the *MSC* of Jim smoking a cigarette (taking into account both Jim's private costs and Angelica's external costs) is $3.

The sum of marginal private benefits (*MPB*) and marginal external benefits (*MEB*) is called **marginal social benefits (*MSB*)**:

$$MSB = MPB + MEB$$

Jim's beautifying his yard created an external benefit for Melanie. Suppose Jim's *MPB* of beautifying his yard is $5 and Melanie's *MEB* is $3. Then the *MSB* of Jim's beautifying his yard (at a given level of beautification) is $8.

> **Marginal Social Costs (*MSC*)**
> The sum of marginal private costs (*MPC*) and marginal external costs (*MEC*): $MSC = MPC + MEC$.

> **Marginal Social Benefits (*MSB*)**
> The sum of marginal private benefits (*MPB*) and marginal external benefits (*MEB*): $MSB = MPB + MEB$.

31-1c Social Optimality, or Efficiency, Conditions

For an economist, there is always a right amount of something. There is a right amount of time to study for a test, a right amount of exercise, and a right number of cars to be produced. The right amount, for an economist, is the **socially optimal amount (output)**, or the efficient amount (output): the amount at which $MSB = MSC$. In other words, the right amount of anything is the amount at which the MSB (of that thing) equals the MSC (of that thing). Later in this section, we illustrate this condition graphically.

> **Socially Optimal Amount (Output)**
> An amount that takes into account and adjusts for all benefits (external and private) and all costs (external and private); the amount at which $MSB = MSC$. Sometimes referred to as the efficient amount.

31-1d Three Categories of Activities

For the person who engages in an activity (whether it is producing a computer or studying for an exam), the activity almost always brings benefits and costs. It is hard to think of any activities in life in which private benefits and private costs do not exist.

Not so hard, however, is thinking of activities in life in which external benefits and external costs do not exist. For example, when reading a book, a person incurs benefits and costs, but probably no one else does. We can characterize this effect in the following way: $MPB > 0$, $MPC > 0$, $MEB = 0$, $MEC = 0$. Marginal private benefits and costs are both positive (greater than zero), but there are no marginal external benefits or costs. In other words, the activity has no positive or negative externalities.

Therefore, activities may be categorized according to whether negative or positive externalities exist, as shown in the following table[1]:

Category	Definition	Meaning in Terms of Marginal Benefits and Costs
1	No negative or positive externality	$MEC = 0$ and $MEB = 0$; it follows that $MSC = MPC$ and $MSB = MPB$.
2	Negative externality but no positive externality	$MEC > 0$ and $MEB = 0$; it follows that $MSC > MPC$ and $MSB = MPB$.
3	Positive externality but no negative externality	$MEB > 0$ and $MEC = 0$; it follows that $MSB > MPB$ and $MSC = MPC$.

31-1e Externalities in Consumption and in Production

Externalities can arise because someone *consumes* something that has an external benefit or cost for others or because someone *produces* something that has an external benefit or cost for others. Consider two examples of negative externalities. Marisella plays the radio in her car loudly, adversely affecting drivers around her at the stoplight. In this situation, Marisella is consuming music and creating a negative externality for others. Company X produces cars in its factory. As a result of the production process, company X emits pollution into the air that adversely affects some people who live downwind from the factory. In this situation, the negative externality is the result of company X producing a good.

31-1f Diagram of a Negative Externality

Exhibit 1 shows the downward-sloping demand curve, D, for some good. Because the demand curve represents the marginal private benefits received by the buyers of the good, it is the same as the MPB curve. Because there are no positive externalities in this case, $MPB = MSB$, so

---

[1] Theoretically, there is a fourth category—in which both a positive externality and a negative externality exist—but one would reasonably assume that this category has little, if any, practical relevance. For example, suppose Jim smokes a cigarette and cigarette smoke is a negative externality for Angelica but a positive externality for Bobby. It is possible that what is a bad for Angelica is a good for Bobby, but little is added to the discussion (at this time) by considering such cases.

the demand curve is also the *MSB* curve. The supply curve, *S*, represents the marginal private costs (*MPC*) of the producers of the good. Equilibrium in this market setting is at E_1; Q_1 is the output—specifically, the market output.

Assume that negative externalities arise as a result of the production of the good. For example, suppose the good happens to be cars, whose production in a factory causes the emission of some air pollution. Because of the negative externalities, external costs associated with the production of the good exist; these costs are not taken into account at the market output. Still, by adding them (as best we can) to the marginal private costs, we can take into account the marginal external costs linked to the negative externalities. The result is the marginal social cost (*MSC*) curve shown in Exhibit 1. If all costs (both external and private) are taken into account, then equilibrium becomes E_2, where $MSB = MSC$. The quantity Q_2 produced at E_2 is the socially optimal, or efficient, output.

When negative externalities exist, the market output (Q_1) is greater than the socially optimal output (Q_2). The market is said to fail (hence the term "market failure") because it *overproduces* the good connected with the negative externality. The shaded triangle in Exhibit 1 is the visible manifestation of the market failure. It represents the net social cost of producing the market output (Q_1) instead of the socially optimal output (Q_2) or of moving from the socially optimal output to the market output.

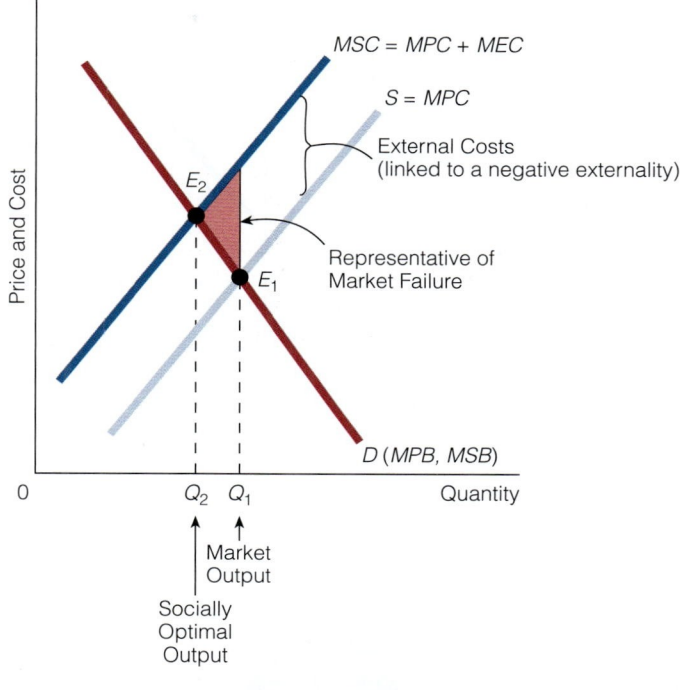

EXHIBIT 1

The Negative Externality Case

Because of a negative externality, marginal social costs (*MSC*) are greater than marginal private costs (*MPC*), and the market output is greater than the socially optimal output. The market is said to fail in that it overproduces the good.

To understand exactly how the triangle in Exhibit 1 represents the net social cost of moving from the socially optimal output to the market output, look at Exhibit 2, in which, as in Exhibit 1, Q_2 is the socially optimal output and Q_1 is the market output. If society moves from Q_2 to Q_1, who specifically benefits and how do we represent the benefits? Buyers benefit (they are a part of society) because they will be able to buy more output at prices they are willing to pay. Thus, the area under the demand curve between Q_2 and Q_1 represents the benefits to society of moving from Q_2 to Q_1. (See the shaded area in window 1 of Exhibit 2.)

Next, if society moves from Q_2 to Q_1, both sellers and third parties incur costs. Sellers incur private costs, and third parties incur external costs. The area under *S* (the *MPC* curve) between Q_2 and Q_1 takes into account only part of society—sellers—and ignores third parties. The area under the *MSC* curve between Q_2 and Q_1 represents the full costs to society of moving from Q_2 to Q_1. (See the shaded area in window 2.)

The shaded area in window 2 is larger than the one in window 1, so the costs to sellers and third parties of moving from Q_2 to Q_1 outweigh the benefits to buyers of moving from Q_2 to Q_1. The difference between the shaded areas is the triangle shown in the main diagram. Thus, the costs to society outweigh the benefits to society by the area of the triangle. In short, the triangle in this example represents the net social cost of moving from Q_2 to Q_1, or of producing Q_1 instead of Q_2.

EXHIBIT 2

The Triangle

Q_2 is the socially optimal output; Q_1 is the market output. If society moves from Q_2 to Q_1, buyers benefit by an amount represented by the shaded area in window 1, but sellers and third parties together incur greater costs, represented by the shaded area in window 2. The triangle (the difference between the two shaded areas) represents the net social cost to society of moving from Q_2 to Q_1, or of producing Q_1 instead of Q_2.

(Note: On the vertical axis in windows 1 and 2, P = price and C = cost.)

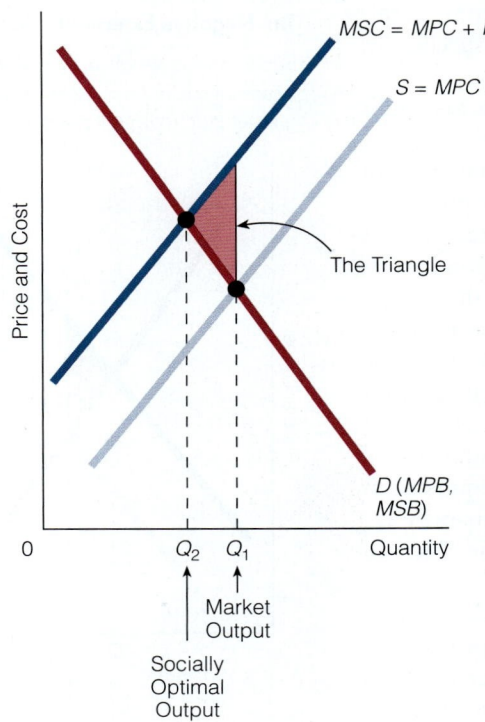

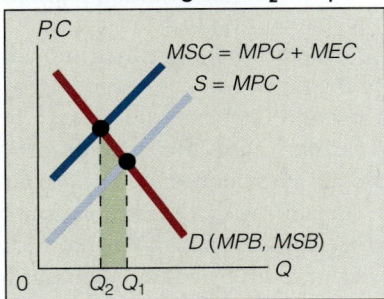

Window 1
Benefits of moving from Q_2 to Q_1

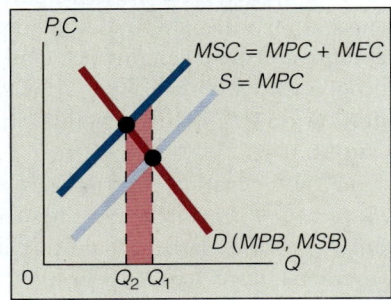

Window 2
Costs of moving from Q_2 to Q_1

Economics 24/7

An Unintended Effect of Texting

A negative externality exists when a person's or group's actions impose a cost (an adverse side effect) on others. Are there any negative externalities connected with texting? Suppose Rob is in his car driving home. Before he reaches his destination, he hears the "ping" on his cell phone, letting him know that a text message has arrived. He looks at the cars around him and concludes that it is safe for him to look down at his phone and read the message. He does so. No problem. Then, he decides to continue to drive while he responds to the text message. As he is texting, his eyes aren't on the road or the cars and pedestrians around him. He ends up running into the back of the car in front of him, and that car then pushes the car ahead of it into the crosswalk where people are walking. Two pedestrians are struck and hurt. As far as it goes for the driver of the car two cars in front of Rob (and maybe of the driver of the car in front of him) and the two pedestrians, Rob has undertaken an action—texting while driving—that has adversely affected them. Rob's direct action of texting created an unintended and negative effect on some others.

31-1g Diagram of a Positive Externality

Exhibit 3 shows the downward-sloping demand curve, D, for some good. This curve represents the marginal private benefits received by the buyers of the good, so it is the same as the MPB curve. The supply curve, S, represents the marginal private costs (MPC) of the producers of the good. The marginal social costs (MSC) are the same as the marginal private costs—$MPC = MSC$—because there are no negative externalities in this case. Equilibrium in this market setting is at E_1; Q_1 is the output—specifically, the market output.

EXHIBIT 3

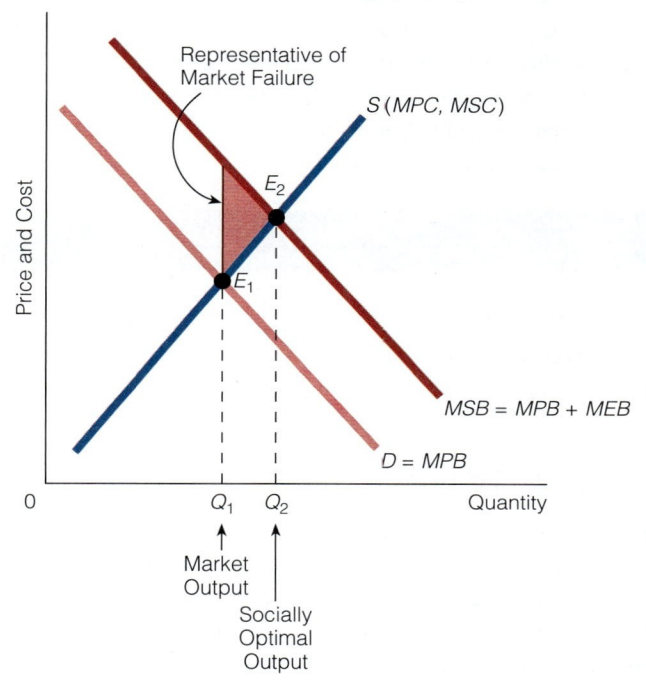

The Positive Externality Case

Because of a positive externality, marginal social benefits (MSB) are greater than marginal private benefits (MPB), and the market output is less than the socially optimal output. The market is said to fail in that it underproduces the good.

Assume that positive externalities arise as a result of the production of the good. For example, suppose Erica is a beekeeper who produces honey. The hives are near an apple orchard, and her bees occasionally fly over to the orchard and pollinate the blossoms, in the process making the orchard more productive. The orchard owner thus benefits from Erica's bees.

Because positive externalities exist, the production of the good has external benefits; these benefits are not taken into account at the market output. Still, by adding them (as best we can) to the marginal private benefits, we can take into account the marginal external benefits linked to the positive externalities. The result is the marginal social benefit (MSB) curve shown in Exhibit 3. If all benefits (both external and private) are taken into account, then equilibrium becomes E_2, where $MSB = MSC$. The quantity Q_2 produced at E_2 is the socially optimal (or efficient) output.

The market output (Q_1) is less than the socially optimal output (Q_2) when positive externalities exist (just the opposite of when negative externalities exist). The market is said to fail (hence the term "market failure") because it *underproduces* the good connected with the positive externality. The shaded triangle in Exhibit 3 is the visible manifestation of the market failure. It represents the net social benefit *that is lost* by producing the market output (Q_1)

instead of the socially optimal output (Q_2). Stated differently, at the socially optimal output (Q_2), society realizes greater benefits than at the market output (Q_1). So, by being at Q_1, society loses out on some net benefits that it could obtain if it were at Q_2.

> **Thinking Like an Economist**
>
> **The Benefits and the Costs of Making the Move** An economist may seem to prefer the socially optimal output (according to which all benefits and costs are taken into account) to the market output (in which only private benefits and costs are taken into account), but not necessarily. An economist prefers the socially optimal output to the market output (assuming that they are different) only when the benefits of moving from the market output to the socially optimal output are greater than the costs. To illustrate, suppose $400 in benefits exists if we move from the market output to the socially optimal output, but the costs of making the move are $1,000. According to an economist, trying to make the adjustment would not be worthwhile.

(Answers to Self-Test questions are in Answers to Self-Test Questions at the back of the book.)

1. What is the major difference between the market output and the socially optimal output?
2. For an economist, is the socially optimal output always preferred to the market output?

31-2 Internalizing Externalities

Internalizing Externalities
An externality is internalized if the persons or group that generated the externality incorporate into their own private or internal cost–benefit calculations the external benefits (in the case of a positive externality) or the external costs (in the case of a negative externality).

An externality is **internalized** if the persons or group generating the externality incorporate into their own private, or *internal*, cost–benefit calculations the external benefits (in the case of a positive externality) or the external costs (in the case of a negative externality). Simply put, internalizing externalities is the same as adjusting for externalities. An externality has been internalized, or adjusted for, *completely* if, as a result, the socially optimal or efficient output emerges. A few of the numerous ways to adjust for, or internalize, externalities are presented in this section.

31-2a Persuasion

Many negative externalities arise partly because persons or groups do not consider other individuals when they decide to undertake an action. An example is the person who plays music loudly at 3 o'clock in the morning. Perhaps if he considered the external cost of his action to his neighbors, he either would not play the music at all or would turn it down.

Trying to persuade those who impose external costs on us to take these costs into account is one way to make the imposers adjust for—or internalize—externalities. In today's world, such slogans as "Don't Drink and Drive" and "Don't Litter" are attempts to persuade individuals to consider the effects of their actions on others. The golden rule of ethical conduct, in one form or another—for example, "Do unto others as you would have them do unto you"—makes the same point.

31-2b Taxes and Subsidies

Taxes and subsidies are sometimes used as corrective devices for a market failure. A tax adjusts for a negative externality; a subsidy adjusts for a positive externality.

Consider the negative externality case in Exhibit 1. The objective of a corrective tax would be to move the supply curve S to the MSC curve (recall that a tax can shift a supply curve) and therefore move from the market-determined output, Q_1, to the socially optimal output, Q_2.

In the case of a positive externality, illustrated in Exhibit 3, the objective would be to subsidize the demand side of the market so that the demand curve D moves to the MSB curve and output moves from Q_1 to the socially optimal output, Q_2.

However, taxes and subsidies also involve costs and consequences. For example, suppose, as illustrated in Exhibit 4, that government misjudges the external costs when it imposes a tax on the supplier of a good. Then, instead of the supply S_1 moving to S_2 (the MSC curve), it moves to S_3. As a result, the output level will be farther away from the socially optimal output than it was before the "corrective" tax was applied.

EXHIBIT 4

A Corrective Tax Gone Wrong

Government may miscalculate external costs and impose a tax that moves the supply curve from S_1 to S_3 instead of from S_1 to S_2. As a result, the output level will be farther away from the socially optimal output than before the "corrective" tax was applied. (Q_3 is farther away from Q_2 than Q_1 is from Q_2.) For a corrective tax to bring about the socially optimal output, the tax would have to be set such that the S_1 curve shifts leftward to S_2.

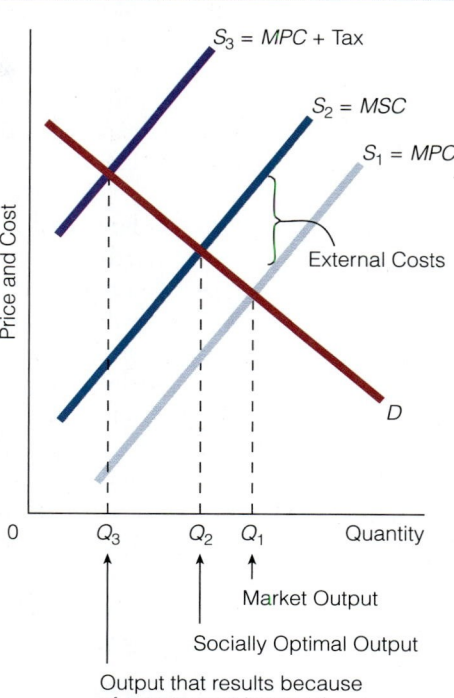

31-2c Assigning Property Rights

Consider the idea that air pollution and ocean pollution—both of which are examples of negative externalities—are the result of the air and oceans being unowned. No one owns the air, and no one owns the oceans. Because no one does, many individuals feel free to emit wastes into them. If private property, or ownership, rights in air and oceans could be established, the negative externalities would likely decrease. If someone owns a resource, then actions that damage it have a price, namely, the damages that the resource owner can sue for.

For example, in the early West, when grazing lands were open and unowned (common property), many cattle ranchers allowed their herds to overgraze. The reason was simple: No one owned the land, so no one could stop the overgrazing to preserve the value of the land. Even if one rancher decided not to allow his herd to graze, all he did was leave more grazing land for other ranchers. As a consequence of overgrazing, a future generation inherited barren, wasted land. From the point of view of future generations, the cattle ranchers who allowed their herds to overgraze were generating negative externalities.

If the Western lands had been privately owned, overgrazing would not have occurred because the monetary interests of the landowner would not have permitted it. The landowner would have charged ranchers a fee to graze their cattle, and more grazing would have entailed additional fees. There would have been less grazing at a positive fee than at a zero fee (the case when the lands were open and unowned). In other words, the externalities would have been internalized.

31-2d Voluntary Agreements

Externalities can sometimes be internalized through individual voluntary agreements. Suppose Pete and Sean live alone on a tiny island. They have agreed, between themselves, that Pete owns the northern part of the island and Sean owns the southern part. Pete occasionally plays his drums in the morning, and the sound awakens Sean, causing a negative externality problem. Pete wants to be free to play his drums in the morning, and Sean would like to sleep.

Suppose Sean values his sleep in the morning by a maximum of six oranges; that is, he would give up six oranges to be able to sleep without Pete playing his drums. On the other hand, Pete values drum playing in the morning by three oranges. He would give up a maximum of three oranges to be able to play his drums in the morning. Because Sean values his sleep by more than Pete values playing his drums, they have an opportunity to strike a deal. Sean can offer Pete some number of oranges greater than three, but fewer than six, to refrain from playing his drums in the morning. The deal will make both Pete and Sean better off.

In this example, the negative externality problem is successfully addressed through the individuals' voluntarily entering into an agreement. The condition for this output is that the *transaction costs*, or costs associated with making and reaching the agreement, must be low relative to the expected benefits of the agreement.

31-2e Combining Property Rights Assignments and Voluntary Agreements

The last two ways of internalizing externalities—property rights assignments and voluntary agreements—can be combined, as in the following example[2]: Suppose a rancher's cattle occasionally stray onto the adjacent farm and damage or eat some of the farmer's crops. The court assigns liability to the cattle rancher and orders him to prevent his cattle from straying; thus, a property rights assignment solves the externality problem. As a result, the rancher puts up a strong fence to prevent his cattle from damaging his neighbor's crops.

But the court's property rights assignment may be undone by the farmer and the cattle rancher if they find that doing so is in their mutual interest. Suppose the rancher is willing to pay $100 a month to the farmer for permission to allow his cattle to stray onto the farmer's land, and the farmer is willing to give permission for $70 a month. Then, if the transaction costs are trivial or zero, the farmer and the rancher will undo the court's property rights assignment. For a payment of $70 or more a month, the farmer will allow the rancher's cattle to stray onto his land.

Coase Theorem Suppose, in our example, that instead of assigning liability to the cattle rancher, the court had given him the property right to allow his cattle to stray. What would the resource allocative outcome have been in this case? With the opposite property rights assignment, the cattle would have been allowed to stray (exactly the outcome of the previous property rights assignment after the cattle rancher and farmer voluntarily agreed to undo the court's decision).

The **Coase theorem** can be expressed in various ways, two of which are as follows: (1) In the case of trivial or zero transaction costs, a property rights assignment will be undone

Coase Theorem
The proposition that private negotiations between people will lead to an efficient resolution of externalities, as long as property rights are well defined and transaction costs are trivial or zero.

---

[2] See Ronald Coase, "The Problem of Social Cost," *Journal of Law and Economics* 3 (October 1960): 1–44.

(exchanged) if it benefits the relevant parties to undo it. (2) In the case of trivial or zero transaction costs, the resource allocative outcome will be efficient.

The Coase theorem is significant for two reasons: (1) It shows that, under certain conditions, the market can internalize externalities. (2) It provides a benchmark for analyzing externality problems; that is, it shows what will happen if transaction costs are trivial or zero.

Pigou Versus Coase The first editor of the *Journal of Law and Economics* was Aaron Director. In 1959, Director published an article by Ronald Coase entitled "The Federal Communications Commission." In the article, Coase took issue with economist A. C. Pigou, a trailblazer in the area of externalities and market failure, who had argued that government should use taxes and subsidies to adjust for negative and positive externalities, respectively. Coase argued that, in the case of negative externalities, whether the state should tax the person imposing the negative externality is not clear. First, Coase stressed the reciprocal nature of externalities, pointing out that it takes two to make a negative externality. (Who is harming whom is not always clear.) Second, Coase proposed a market solution to externality problems that was not implicit in Pigou's work.

Director and others believed that Coase was wrong and Pigou was right. Coase, who was teaching at the University of Virginia at the time, was invited to discuss his thesis with Director and a handful of well-known economists. The group included Martin Bailey, Milton Friedman, Arnold Harberger, Reuben Kessel, Gregg Lewis, John McGee, Lloyd Mints, George Stigler, and, of course, Director.

The group met at Director's house one night. Before Coase began to outline his thesis, the group took a vote and found that everyone (with the exception of Coase) sided with Pigou. Then the sparks began to fly, and Friedman, it is reported, opened fire on Coase. Coase answered the intellectual attacks of his colleagues, and, at the end of the debate, another vote was taken. This time, everyone sided with Coase against Pigou. It is reported that, as the members of the group left Director's home that night, they said to one another that they had witnessed history in the making. The Coase theorem had taken hold in economics.

31-2f Beyond Internalizing: Setting Regulations

One way to deal with externalities—in particular, with negative externalities—is for government to apply regulations directly to the activities that generate the externalities. For example, factories producing goods also produce smoke, which is often seen as a negative externality. Government may decide that the factory must install pollution-reducing equipment, that it can emit only a certain amount of smoke into the air per day, or that it must be moved to a less populated area.

Critics of this approach often note that regulations, once instituted, are difficult to remove, even if conditions warrant their removal. Also, regulations are often applied across the board when individual circumstances dictate otherwise. For example, factories in relatively pollution-free cities might be required to install the same pollution control equipment as factories in smoggy, pollution-ridden cities.

Finally, regulation entails costs. If government imposes regulations, it needs regulators (whose salaries must be paid), offices (to house the regulators), word processors (to produce the regulations), and more. As noted earlier, dealing with externalities successfully may offer benefits, but the costs need to be considered as well.

Economics 24/7

Tribes, Transaction Costs, and Social Media

At one time in human history, it was common for humans to be members of tribes. Which tribe was dictated by where a person lived. If the only mode of transportation is walking by foot, it would make sense that people would stay near the group into which they were born. So, if you were born into group X in location X, you spent much of your life in group X. Group X was your tribe, so to speak. It was also common, long ago, for the individuals within a group or tribe to share a race or ethnicity. In short, we can speak of an ethnic or racial tribe.

As methods of transportation improved (from walking, to riding a horse, to driving a car, to flying in an airplane), the locale in which one was born became less of a constraint to movement. And because it became easier for people to travel, it would naturally become easier for individuals who were born into one tribe to travel outside their particular tribe. It also became easier for individuals who perhaps shared the same race as others within their tribe to find other tribes with whose members they had more in common than simply race and with whom they had common interests.

Think of the idea of tribes and social media today. What social media has largely done is make it more likely that people will form social tribes, no matter what race or ethnicity they may be. To illustrate, Meetup is an online social networking portal that helps facilitate off-line group meetings in different localities. Group members share a common interest, such as health, pets, hobbies, politics, and books. Essentially, Meetup lowers the transaction costs of forming groups. Picking a city at random reveals just a few of the many groups identified on Meetup that were getting together: active singles; cheap-movie-night group; French-speaking group; mountain/trail and road biking group; sailing group; geek girls group; corgi Meetup group; baby playgroup; yoga group; book divas; and drink, dives, and darts group.

Think of how individuals living 100,000 years ago, stuck in their tribe identified by race or ethnicity, might have reacted if, magically, they could get together with those in other tribes with whom they shared a nonethnic or nonracial attribute. There might have been the "counting-stars group," or the "run-among-the-trees group."

What the social networking portal Meetup has allowed people to do—perhaps more than anything else—is allow people who didn't have a "group" (because there were not enough people in the

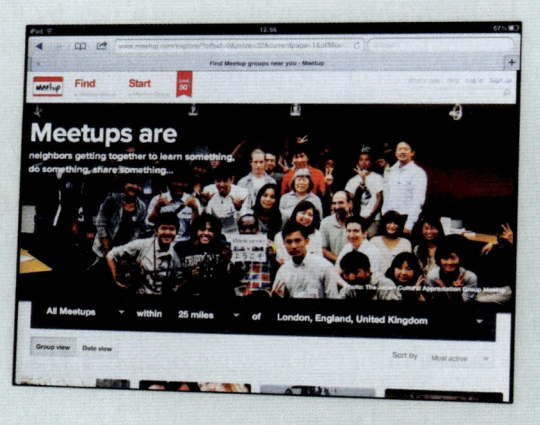

group in which they lived and worked who shared their interests) to find each other. To illustrate, if your home and work group, or "tribe," consists of no one who seems to enjoy reading books by author Neil Gaiman, and that is a passion for you, then you might feel somewhat left out. Everyone wants to talk football, you think, but I can't find anyone who wants to talk about Neil Gaiman books.

So what were some of the first groups to sign up on Meetup when it came into existence? They weren't Episcopalian groups, because Episcopalians already have a place where they meet up. Here were some of the topics of interest that were most often identified for groups on Meetup: witches, Slashdot, Xena, pagans, ex-Jehovah's Witness, *Star Trek*, and vampires.[3]

It could very well be that people have always preferred to organize or group themselves in terms of their interests than in terms of their race or ethnicity, but that it was just so hard to do before transportation and communication became easy and cheap. What a social medium like Meetup does is make it very easy and cheap for individuals to group themselves in terms of what is of great importance to their personal and social lives. As an aside, there are over 225,000 groups listed on Meetup!

---

[3] See Clay Shirky, *Here Comes Everybody: The Power of Organizing Without Organizations* (New York: Penguin Press, 2008).

1. What does it mean to internalize an externality?
2. Are the transaction costs of buying a house higher or lower than those of buying a hamburger at a fast-food restaurant? Explain your answer.
3. Does the property rights assignment a court makes matter to the resource-allocative outcome?
4. What condition must be satisfied for a tax to adjust correctly for a negative externality?

31-3 Environmental Policy

In an earlier section, we discussed how the presence of (negative or positive) externalities can lead us away from social optimality or efficiency. In this section, we consider different approaches to dealing with negative environmental externalities, which we will address under the general term of "pollution." We discuss the specifics of three types of policies: (1) government regulation, or command and control; (2) emission taxes; and (3) tradable pollution permits (also known as cap and trade).

31-3a Method 1: Government Regulation, or Command and Control

Suppose that 10 tons of pollution (say, from factories) are emitted into the air over a given area during a certain period. One command-and-control policy that government might enact is to specify a certain type of pollution control technology to be used by factory owners. In other words, government mandates that factory owners must use technology X instead of technology Y because technology X causes less pollution to be emitted into the air than technology Y. As a result, pollution emission might fall, say, from 10 tons of pollution to 7 tons.

Another possible command-and-control policy might be to simply set a quantitative goal that is applied to the factories emitting pollution. In other words, simply specify that no factory can emit more than, say, 2 tons of pollution into the air over some time frame.

Generally, economists do not favor command-and-control policies as a means of reducing pollution. One reason is that mandating certain technologies to be used reduces the incentive to discover new, sometimes lower cost methods of reducing pollution. Also, mandating that all factories must eliminate, say, 3 tons of pollution fails to take into account that it is less costly for some factories to eliminate pollution than for others to do so. To illustrate, consider Exhibit 5, which shows the cost to each of three firms of eliminating various amounts of pollution.

Suppose that, currently, each firm is emitting 3 tons of pollution, for a total of 9 tons emitted. Suppose also that the government wants to reduce pollution by 6 tons (and thus bring the overall pollution level down from 9 tons to 3 tons). Thus, the government mandates that

EXHIBIT 5

The Cost of Reducing Pollution for Three Firms

These are hypothetical data showing the cost of reducing pollution for firms X, Y, and Z:

Cost of Eliminating:	Firm X	Firm Y	Firm Z
First ton of pollution	$50	$70	$500
Second ton of pollution	75	85	1,000
Third ton of pollution	100	200	2,000

each firm must eliminate 2 tons of pollution. The cost to firm X of eliminating its first 2 tons of pollution is $125 ($50 + $75 = $125); the cost to firm Y of eliminating its first 2 tons is $155; and the cost to firm Z of eliminating its first 2 tons of pollution is $1,500. The total cost of eliminating 6 tons of pollution is $1,780 ($125 + $155 + $1,500 = $1,780). Is there a cheaper way of eliminating 6 tons of pollution? Yes, firms X and Y could have eliminated 3 tons of pollution each, for a total cost of $580 ($50 + $75 + $100 + $70 + $85 + $200 = $580).

31-3b Method 2: Emission Taxes

As we discussed earlier, a tax can be used to deal with a negative externality, and the ideal corrective tax is equal to the marginal external cost associated with the negative externality. Economists generally prefer a corrective tax to command and control because such a tax can achieve the same reduction in pollution as a command-and-control policy, but in an efficient manner. The reason is that a tax effectively places a price on the right to pollute. The firm then has to weigh its cost of eliminating pollution against the tax it would pay if it didn't eliminate pollution. For example, suppose there is a $40 emission tax for each ton of pollution emitted. Then a firm that is emitting pollution would have to consider how much it would have to pay to eliminate a given amount of pollution and how much of a tax it would have to pay if it didn't.

Let's return to Exhibit 5 to see how a tax might work at eliminating 6 tons of pollution (the same quantity of pollution eliminated through the command-and-control policy). Suppose the tax were set at $330 per ton of pollution. Under this tax, firms X and Y would each reduce all 3 tons of their pollution, for a total of 6 tons of pollution eliminated. Firm Z would not eliminate any of its pollution, because, for each ton of pollution it emits, the cost of eliminating that amount of pollution is greater than the tax. The total cost to firms X and Y of eliminating their pollution would be $580, which again is much less than the total cost of $1,780 under the command-and-control system whereby each firm was mandated to eliminate 3 tons of pollution. Also, under an emission tax, firms have an incentive to find cleaner (less polluting) ways of producing their goods, because a cleaner way of producing goods means less pollution and a lower tax bill for polluting.

31-3c Method 3: Tradable Pollution Permits (Cap and Trade)

Under a system of tradable pollution permits, or cap and trade, a "cap," or ceiling, is placed on how much pollution can be emitted. Permits to pollute are then allocated to polluters (or auctioned off to the highest bidder), after which the polluters can trade (buy and sell) the permits. With this idea in mind, turn again to Exhibit 5. As before, the objective of the government is to eliminate 6 tons of pollution so that the total amount of pollution will fall from 9 tons to 3 tons. Toward that end, the government issues three pollution permits, one to each of the three firms. A single pollution permit allows the holder (of the permit) to emit 1 ton of pollution.

Currently, firm X has one pollution permit in its possession, so it can emit 1 ton of pollution and must eliminate the other 2. But firm X does not have to keep its pollution permit. It can sell its permit and then take measures to eliminate all 3 tons of its pollution. Might firm X be better off selling the permit and eliminating all 3 tons of pollution? We can ask the same question about firms Y and Z too? The answer for all of the firms depends on the price of a pollution permit.

A market for pollution permits emerges. The owners of the three firms get together, and the owner of firm Z says to the owners of the other two firms that he has to pay $500 to eliminate the first ton of pollution, so if anyone would be willing to sell him a permit for less than $500, he will buy it. Firms X and Y sell their permits because, for each of them, the cost of eliminating its third ton of pollution is less than $500. Suppose that, in the end, a price of $330 is agreed to as the price for a permit. As a result, firms X and Y each sell their permits to firm Z for $330 a permit. Then firms X and Y eliminate 3 tons of pollution each, for a total of 6 tons eliminated, and firm Z, now holding 3 pollution permits, eliminates no pollution.

What is the cost of using tradable permits to eliminate pollution? Again, it is $580, which is the cost to firm X of eliminating all three units of pollution ($225) plus the cost to firm Y of eliminating all three units of pollution ($355).

You may wonder why we are not counting the cost to firm Z of buying the permits from firms X and Y. After all, firm Z paid $660 to buy two pollution permits. Although the $660 is a real cost of doing business for firm Z, it is not a cost to society of eliminating pollution. The $660 was not actually used to eliminate pollution; it was simply a transfer from firm Z to firms X and Y. The distinction is between a resource cost, which signifies an expenditure of resources, and a transfer, which does not.

Finally, instead of simply handing out pollution permits to firms, the government could auction off the permits. Under an auction, the government collects the revenue from the permits instead of letting it go to private firms.

31-3d Similarities and Differences Between Emission Taxes and Tradable Pollution Permits

One similarity between emission taxes and tradable permits is that both place a price on pollution. In both cases, one has *to pay* to pollute. With emission taxes, firms have to pay a tax to the government; with tradable permits, either firms have to pay each other to pollute (firm Z has to buy the permit from firm X) or they have to pay government at the permit auction. With auctioned permits, the government gets revenue in the same way that it gets revenue from an emission tax.

One way to clearly see the similarity between emission taxes and tradable pollution permits is in terms of Exhibit 6. Panels (a) and (b) each show the demand to pollute. In both

EXHIBIT 6

Emission Taxes and Tradable Pollution Permits

In panel (a), the emission tax is $50, and the quantity demanded of pollution is 100 units. In panel (b), the government supplies 100 pollution permits (thus allowing 100 tons of pollution), and then supply and demand end up determining the price of a pollution permit at $50. Here, we have a case where the price to pollute (in the form of a tax or the price of a pollution permit) and the quantity of pollution are the same in both cases.

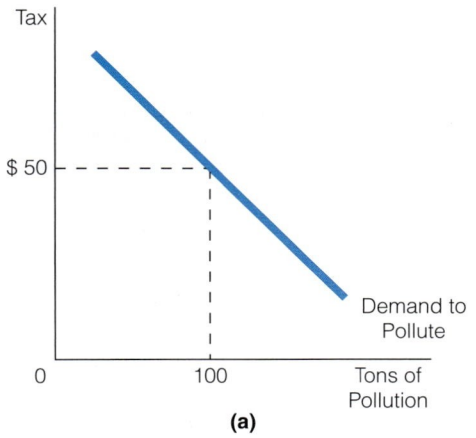

(a)

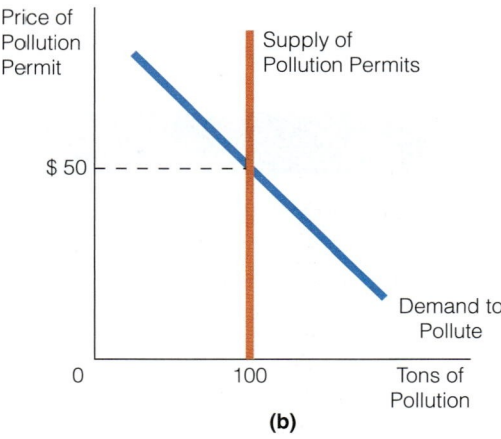

(b)

panels, the demand is the same. In panel (a), an excise (corrective) tax is set at $50. At this tax, the quantity demanded of pollution (how much pollution polluters are willing to purchase) is 100 tons.

In panel (b), under a system of tradable pollution permits, government sets 100 tons of pollution as the permissible amount of pollution. In effect, it sets the supply curve of pollution permits at 100 tons. Then this supply, combined with the demand to pollute, determines the price of a pollution permit as $50.

Under our scenario, the emission tax equals the price of the pollution permit. That's because we used the quantity demanded of 100 units of pollution in panel (a) as the permissible amount of pollution in panel (b). If we had, for example, set the permissible amount of pollution in panel (b) as 200 units, the price of the pollution permit would have been lower than the emission tax.

Under an emission tax, a price (a tax) is set, and then the quantity of pollution is determined. Under a tradable pollution permits system, the quantity of permissible pollution is set, and then the price of the pollution permit is determined. Under the specific conditions we specified (the quantity of pollution is the same in both cases), the emission tax equals the price of the pollution permit.

One of the things that government can't know with an emission tax is what the quantity demanded of pollution will be, given any specific tax. For example, if government sets the emission tax at $50, it can't be sure whether the quantity demanded of pollution at that tax will be 100 tons, more than 100 tons, or less than 100 tons. That's because it can't be sure what the demand is for pollution. So, if government sets as its objective to have only 100 tons of pollution, it can't be sure what emission tax will generate 100 tons as the quantity demanded of pollution.

This problem does not exist under a system of tradable permits. If government wants to permit only 100 tons of pollution, it will allocate only 100 permits. The equilibrium price of a pollution permit will then end up being a price that equates quantity demanded with the quantity supplied of 100.

Simply put, emission taxes and tradable pollution permits end up creating different kinds of uncertainty. Under an emission tax, polluters know what price they have to pay to pollute, but government doesn't know how much pollution will be generated. Under a tradable pollution permits system (cap and trade), government knows the amount of pollution, but polluters don't immediately know what the price to pollute will be. These uncertainties can be important, but they don't change the fundamental similarities between emission taxes and tradable permit systems.

1. Why is it likely that tradable pollution permits will eliminate a given level of pollution at lower cost than a command-and-control system, which mandates that each polluter eliminate the same amount of pollution?

2. Emission taxes and tradable pollution permits create different kinds of uncertainty. Explain.

3. Under both emission taxes and tradable pollution permits, polluters must pay to pollute. Explain.

31-4 Public Goods: Excludable and Nonexcludable

Many economists maintain that the market fails to produce nonexcludable public goods. In this section, we discuss public goods in general and nonexcludable public goods in particular.

31-4a Goods

Economists talk about two kinds of goods: private and public. A *private good* is a good whose consumption by one person reduces its consumption for another person. For example, a sweater, an apple, and a computer are all private goods. If one person is wearing a sweater, another person cannot wear (consume) it. If one person takes a bite of an apple, there is less apple for someone else to consume. If someone is using a computer, someone else can't use it. A private good is said to be **rivalrous in consumption**.

A **public good**, in contrast, is a good whose consumption by one person does not reduce its consumption by another. For example, a movie in a movie theater is a public good. If there are 200 seats in the theater, then 200 people can see the movie at the same time, and no one person's viewing of it detracts from another's. An economics lecture is also a public good. If there are 30 seats in the classroom, then 30 people can consume the economics lecture at the same time, and one person's consumption does not detract from any other's. The chief characteristic of a public good is that it is **nonrivalrous in consumption**, which means that its consumption by one person does not reduce its consumption by others.

All public goods are nonrivalrous in consumption, but they are not all the same. Some public goods are **excludable**, and some are nonexcludable. A public good is excludable if it is possible, or not prohibitively costly, to exclude someone from obtaining the benefits of it after it has been produced. For example, a movie in a movie theater is excludable in that persons who do not pay for admission can be excluded from seeing it. The same holds for an economics lecture. Someone who does not pay the tuition to attend the lecture can be excluded from consuming it. So both movies in movie theaters and economics lectures in classrooms are *excludable public goods*.

A public good is **nonexcludable** if it is impossible, or prohibitively costly, to exclude someone from obtaining the benefits of the good after it has been produced. National defense is a public good in that it is nonrivalrous in consumption. For example, if the U.S. national defense system is protecting people in New Jersey from incoming missiles, then it is automatically protecting people in New York as well. And just as important, protecting people in New Jersey does not reduce the degree of protection for the people in New York. Second, once national defense has been produced, excluding someone from consuming its services is impossible (or prohibitively costly). Thus, national defense is a *nonexcludable public good*. The same holds for flood control or large-scale pest control. After the dam has been built or the pest spray has been sprayed, excluding persons from benefiting from it is impossible.

31-4b The Free Rider

When a (private or public) good is excludable, individuals can obtain the benefits of it only if they pay for it. For example, no one can consume an apple (a private good) or a movie in a movie theater (a public good) without first paying for it. This is not the case with a nonexcludable public good, though. Individuals *can* obtain the benefits of a nonexcludable public good without paying for it. Persons who do so are referred to as **free riders**. Because of the so-called *free-rider problem*, most economists hold that the market will fail to produce nonexcludable public goods or at least fail to produce them at a desired level.

Rivalrous in Consumption
Said of a good whose consumption by one person reduces its consumption by others.

Public Good
A good whose consumption by one person does not reduce its consumption by another person—that is, it is nonrivalrous in consumption.

Nonrivalrous in Consumption
Said of a good whose consumption by one person does not reduce its consumption by others.

Excludable
A characteristic of a good whereby it is possible or not prohibitively costly to exclude someone from receiving the benefits of the good after it has been produced.

Nonexcludable
A characteristic of a good whereby it is impossible or prohibitively costly to exclude someone from receiving the benefits of the good after it has been produced.

Free Riders
Anyone who receives the benefits of a good without paying for it.

To illustrate, consider someone contemplating the production of nonexcludable public good X, which—because it is a public good—is also nonrivalrous in consumption. After good X has been produced and provided to one person, others have no incentive to pay for it (even if they demand it), because they can receive all of its benefits without paying. No one is likely to supply a good that people can consume without paying for it. The market, it is argued, will not produce nonexcludable public goods. The door is then opened to government involvement in the production of nonexcludable public goods. Many argue that, if the market will not produce nonexcludable public goods, even though they are demanded, then the government must.

The free-rider argument is the basis for accepting government's (the public's, or taxpayers') provision of nonexcludable public goods. However, a nonexcludable public good is not the same as a government-provided good. A nonexcludable public good is a good that is nonrivalrous in consumption and nonexcludable. A government-provided good is self-defined: a good that government provides. In some instances, a government-provided good is a nonexcludable public good, such as national defense. However, it need not be: The government furnishes mail delivery and education, two goods that are also provided privately but are excludable and thus not subject to free riding.

Economics 24/7

Will Nonexcludable Public Goods Be Provided by the Market Under a Certain Condition?

When Google was founded in September 1998, it answered 10,000 search queries per day. One year later, it answered 3.5 million search queries per day. Today, Google answers, on average, 90,000 search queries each second—or more than 3.5 billion search queries per day. Obviously, Google provides a worthwhile service that billions of people use.

Now notice something important about the service that Google provides. First, that service is nonrivalrous: One person's use of Google does not take away from another person's use of Google. Second, Google's service is nonexcludable. As long as individuals have access to the Internet, they are not prohibited from using Google. As discussed in this chapter, nonrivalry combined with nonexcludability are two features of a nonexcludable public good. Therefore, Google's search engine is a nonexcludable public good.

Google is not a government entity; it is a private firm that operates in the private sector. Elsewhere in this chapter we discussed that private firms in the private sector (market entities) aren't normally the firms that provide nonexcludable public goods. Typically, market entities do not produce and provide nonexcludable public goods because they cannot figure out how to get paid. But Google has certainly figured out a way to get paid: It collects user data, analyzes it, and then sells targeted ads. In 2019,

Google's ad revenue was $135 billion.[4] In this sense, Google's business is not so much the search engine business as much as it is the ad-selling business.

To sum it up, under nonexcludable public goods can be provided by market entities under the condition that the private firms that produce and provide the nonexcludable public goods can figure out some way to get paid.

---

[4] See Statista at www.statista.com/statistics/266249/advertising-revenue-of-google/.

31-4c Nonexcludable Versus Nonrivalrous

The reason the market fails to produce a demanded good only when the good is nonexcludable is that the free-rider problem arises only if the good is nonexcludable. The rivalry-versus-nonrivalry issue is not relevant to the issue of market failure; that is, a good can be rivalrous or nonrivalrous in consumption and still be produced by the market. For example, a movie may be nonrivalrous in consumption but excludable too. And the market has no problem producing movies and movie theaters. The free-rider problem occurs only with goods that are nonexcludable.

The lighthouse makes for a good metaphor. For a long time, a lighthouse was thought to have the two characteristics of a nonexcludable public good: (1) It is nonrivalrous in consumption; any ship can use the light from the lighthouse, and one ship's use of it does not detract from another's. (2) It is nonexcludable; excluding any nonpaying ships from using the light is difficult. The lighthouse seemed to be a perfect good for government provision.

However, economist Ronald Coase found that, in the eighteenth and early nineteenth centuries, many lighthouses were privately owned; the market had not failed to provide lighthouses. Economists were left to conclude either that the market could provide nonexcludable public goods or that the lighthouse was not a nonexcludable public good, as had been thought. Closer examination showed that, although the lighthouse was nonrivalrous in consumption (it was a public good), the costs of excluding others from using it were fairly low (so it was an excludable public good). Lighthouse owners knew that usually only one ship was near the lighthouse at a time and that they could turn off the light if a ship did not fly the flag of a paying vessel.

Economics 24/7

Culture as a Public Good

Pizza is a private good, and national defense is a nonexcludable public good. Pizza isn't a contentious issue. No matter what kind of pizza you like, you can buy it. Others don't have to eat the pizza you order if they don't want to. They can order their own.

But the same doesn't hold for national defense. Once the United States has a particular quality and quantity of national defense, everyone in the United States "consumes" the same national defense—the same "national defense pizza." No wonder people argue over national defense: One size and quality does not fit everyone's tastes.

Given that difference, consider culture. Is culture more like pizza or national defense? A dictionary definition of *culture* is "the totality of socially transmitted behavior patterns, arts, beliefs, institutions, and all other products of human work and thought." Apparently, a lot of different things—institutions, behavior patterns, beliefs—constitute a culture.

Not all people have the same culture. The culture of one group, or nation, of people, might be different from the culture of another. The American culture is different from the Brazilian culture, and so on. Differences are perhaps the most noticeable when people move to a place where the culture is very different from their own.

The culture of a place or a people is usually strong enough to be easily recognized and noticed. In the sense that it is easily recognizable and ever present, culture can be considered a nonexcludable public good. All public goods (whether excludable or nonexcludable) are nonrivalrous in consumption; that is, one person's consumption does not detract from another person's consumption. Culture has this same characteristic, and any given culture is also nonexcludable, in that people can neither be excluded from it by others nor very easily exclude themselves from it—unless, of course, one chooses to become a hermit. For better or worse, a specific culture is what it is, and it is a nonexcludable public good.

Cultures sometimes change. For example, many people say that the culture of the United States in the 1950s was different from today's U.S. culture. When people make this statement, they often specify some way in which the culture today is different. They may speak about social mores, family relationships, music, politics, and so on.

Now, think of cultures as you would think of items on a restaurant menu. Just as you can choose chicken, pasta, fish, or steak from a menu, suppose you could pick cultures from a menu. What would your preferred culture look like? What would it consist of? If you have a preferred culture, it tells you something about yourself and others. Maybe everyone has a preferred culture—in which some things are spoken of and others things are not, some things are acceptable and other things are not, and so on.

Many political arguments today are actually about culture. Think about immigration; abortion; liberal and conservative movements; arguments over capitalism and socialism; and the kind, level, and scope of taxes and of federal spending. In what way does culture impact the arguments about these topics?

What's not clear is how to specify the production function for a culture (what are the inputs?), how cultures get produced, or how and why they sometimes change. Still, in that a given culture is a nonexcludable public good, it is easy to understand why people would disagree over its makeup. After all, it's not pizza.

Economics 24/7

"They Paved Paradise and Put Up a Parking Lot"

Suppose Yuri owns 5 acres of land in the middle of a large city. One day, he is contacted by a man who wants to buy the land for $5 million. Yuri asks the person what he plans to do with the land; the man says he represents a company that wants to "put up a parking lot." Yuri is seriously thinking about selling the land to the man.

In time, the people who live and work in the area find out that Yuri is contemplating selling the land to someone who wants to put up a parking lot. They urge Yuri not to sell. They say that they like looking at Yuri's land the way it is: natural and green. They tell Yuri that his land is a green space in the city and that thousands of people enjoy passing by it every day. Yuri tells the people that he is happy about that, but that he needs to pay his bills, so he has to sell the land. Yuri tells the people that they can buy the land themselves if they want to—assuming that they are willing and able to pay $5 million for it.

So, of two groups of people, the first is represented by the man who wants to buy the land to put up a parking lot. This group includes the buyer, the company he represents, and all the people who would like to park their cars at the parking lot. Yuri's land has a certain value to these people. Call these people "group P" (for "parking lot").

The second group consists of the people who benefit from the land in its natural state. These might be the people who live or work by Yuri's land or who pass by it regularly. They like seeing the land in its natural state, especially because so few green places are left in the city. We'll call these people "group G" (for "green").

Which group, P or G, values the land more? There are three possibilities: (1) Group P values the land more than group G, (2) group G values the land more than group P, and (3) each group values the land as much as the other.

So far, we know that group P values the land at (at least) $5 million, because this price is what the group has agreed to pay for it. Suppose that group G values the land at $8 million. The members of group G, however, are probably not as able to express how much they value the land as the members of group P are.

The members of group G face high transaction costs to find out how much each values the land and would be willing to pay to keep the land in its natural state. In contrast, the company that wants to put up a parking lot on the land can figure out relatively easily what persons are likely to pay for parking in the city. Other parking lots in the city are already charging x dollars per hour for parking.

Also, the land in its natural state is a nonexcludable public good. Everyone in the area around the land can see it, enjoy it, walk near it, and so on. If these people are asked to donate money to buy it so that it can stay in its natural state, many are likely to assume the role of free riders.

So the combination of high transaction costs and the likelihood of free riders is a difficult problem to overcome. In other words, the $8 million value that group G places on the land might never be realized. And if isn't realized, then group G is not going to be able to bid for the land against group P.

Of course, things could be different. Maybe group P values the land much more than group G does, but that isn't the point. *Even if* group G values the land more than group P, the members of group G might find it harder to express their greater value

for the land than the members of group P do. The "$8 million value of the land" is never heard, but the "$5 million value" is heard loud and clear in the form of a specific dollar offer to purchase. Not hearing the $8 million bid then leads Yuri to believe that the high bid is $5 million. In this case, putting up a parking lot is really not the most valuable thing to do with the land.

1. Why does the market fail to produce nonexcludable public goods?
2. Identify each of the following goods as a nonexcludable public good, an excludable public good, or a private good:
   a. A composition notebook used for writing
   b. A Shakespearean play performed in a summer theater
   c. An apple
   d. A telephone in service
   e. Sunshine
3. Give an example, other than a movie in a movie theater or a play in a theater, of a good that is nonrivalrous and excludable.

31-5 Asymmetric Information

In market failure, the market does not provide the efficient or optimal amount of a good. This chapter has shown that both externalities and nonexcludable public goods can lead to market failure. Specifically, in the presence of externalities, the market output is different from the socially optimal output. (In the case of negative externalities, the market produces too much; in the case of positive externalities, the market produces too little.) In the case of nonexcludable public goods, some economists maintain that the market produces zero output. Assuming that there is a demand for the nonexcludable public good, zero output is definitely too little.

This section looks at another possible cause of market failure: asymmetric information. **Asymmetric information** is information that either the buyer or the seller in a market exchange has and that the other does not have. In other words, some information is hidden. For example, the seller of a house may have information about the house that the buyer does not have, such as that the roof leaks during heavy rainfall.

Asymmetric Information
Information that either the buyer or the seller in a market exchange has and that the other does not have.

EXHIBIT 7

Asymmetric Information in a Product Market

Initially, the seller has some information that the buyer does not have; there is asymmetric information. As a result, D_1 represents the demand for the good, and Q_1 is the equilibrium quantity. Then the buyer acquires the information that she did not have earlier, and there is symmetric information. The information causes the buyer to lower her demand for the good, so D_2 is now the relevant demand curve, and Q_2 is the equilibrium quantity. Conclusion: Fewer units of the good are bought and sold when there is symmetric information than when there is asymmetric information.

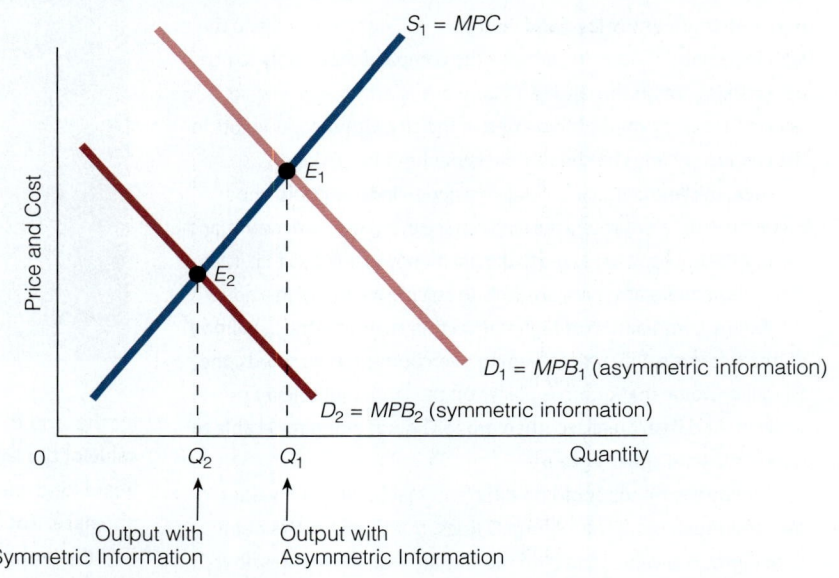

Analyzing the effects of asymmetric information is similar to analyzing externalities—with one important difference: Externalities involve buyers, sellers, and third parties. The discussion that follows considers only buyers and sellers.

31-5a Asymmetric Information in a Product Market

In the discussion of externalities, the demand for a good represents marginal private benefits and the supply of a good represents marginal private costs. This is also the case for the asymmetric information situation shown in Exhibit 7; that is, the demand curve D_1 represents marginal private benefits (*MPB*), and the supply curve, S_1, represents marginal private costs (*MPC*). In the exhibit, D_1 and S_1 are the relevant curves when the seller has some information that the buyer does not have. Therefore, Q_1 is the market output when there is asymmetric information.

Suppose the buyer acquires the information that she previously did not have (but that the seller did have). With the new information, the buyer concludes that purchasing this particular good does not seem as appealing. The information she has acquired causes the buyer to lower her demand for the good. The relevant demand curve is now D_2. With symmetric information, the market output will be Q_2, which is less than Q_1.

As an example, the suppliers of cigarettes know that cigarette consumption can cause cancer but do not release that information to potential buyers. Under this condition, suppliers of cigarettes have certain information about cigarettes that buyers don't have; there is asymmetric information. If buyers do not have this information, the demand for cigarettes may be higher than it would be if buyers had it. In Exhibit 7, demand is D_1 instead of D_2. So more cigarettes will be purchased and consumed (Q_1) when there is asymmetric information than when there is symmetric information (Q_2).

EXHIBIT 8

Asymmetric Information in a Factor Market

Initially, the buyer (of the factor labor), or the firm, has some information that the seller (of the factor) does not have; there is asymmetric information. Consequently, S_1 is the relevant supply curve, W_1 is the equilibrium wage, and Q_1 is the equilibrium quantity of labor. Then sellers acquire information that they did not have earlier, and there is symmetric information. The information causes the sellers to reduce their supply of the factor, and now S_2 is the relevant supply curve, W_2 is the equilibrium wage, and Q_2 is the equilibrium quantity of labor. Conclusion: Fewer factor units are bought and sold, and wages are higher when there is symmetric information than when there is asymmetric information.

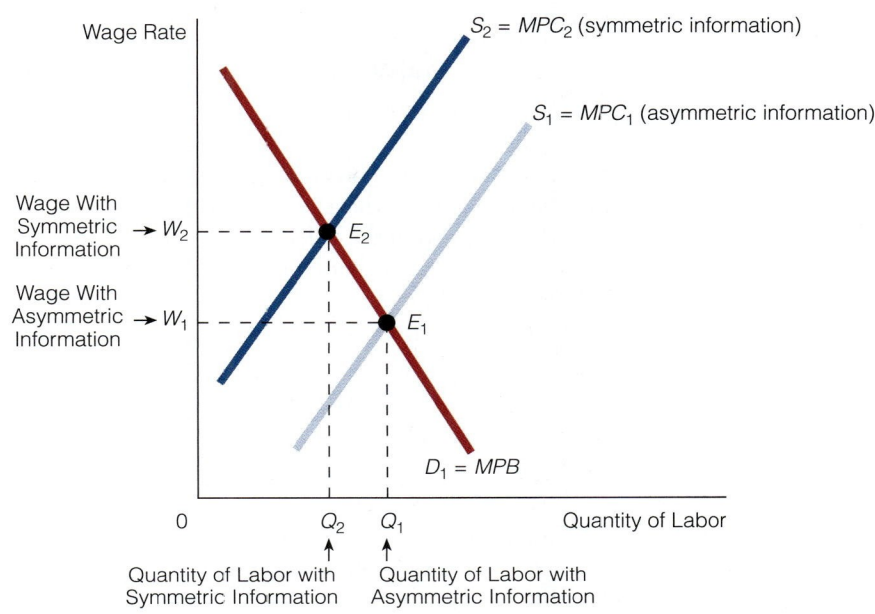

31-5b Asymmetric Information in a Factor Market

Suppose that, in a resource or factor market, such as the labor market shown in Exhibit 8, the buyer has information that the seller does not have. The employing firm knows that its workers will be using a possibly toxic substance that may cause health problems in 20–30 years. Further, the company does not release this information to workers but hides it from them. Without this information, the supply curve of labor is represented by S_1 and the quantity of labor will be Q_1 at a wage rate of W_1. With the information, though, not as many people will be willing to work at the firm at the current wage. The supply curve of labor will shift left to S_2. The new equilibrium position shows that the quantity of labor falls to Q_2, and the wage rate rises to W_2.

31-5c Is There Market Failure?

Does asymmetric information cause markets to fail? In other words, does it create a situation in which the market does not provide the optimal output of a particular good? Certainly, in our examples, the output level of a good and the quantity of labor were lower with symmetric information than with asymmetric information. Stated differently, asymmetric information seemingly resulted in too much or too many of something—either too much of a good being consumed or too many workers employed at a particular firm.

Some people argue that asymmetric information exists in nearly all exchanges. Rarely do buyers and sellers have the same information; each usually knows something the other doesn't. However, this argument misses the point, which is whether the asymmetric information fundamentally changes the outcome from what it would be if there were symmetric information. For example, the argument goes, a seller may know something that a buyer doesn't know, but even if the buyer knew what the seller knows, the outcome would be the same.

To illustrate, suppose a person buys a medication to relieve a severe headache. The person does not know that one side effect of the medication is sleepiness. In this case, asymmetric information may not matter. Possibly, the buyer would not have changed her behavior even if she had known that the medication caused sleepiness. So there is asymmetric information, but it may not change the outcome.

In another setting, however, the result may be different. Suppose the seller of a used car knows that the car is a lemon but the buyer doesn't know. The person buys the car because he doesn't have the information the seller has. Asymmetric information matters here in that the buyer would not have bought the car—or would not have bought the car at a given price—had he known what the seller knew. In this setting, asymmetric information changes the outcome.

Therefore, although the presence of asymmetric information does not guarantee that the market fails, if the asymmetric information brings about a different outcome than if there were symmetric information, then the case for market failure can be made.

31-5d Adverse Selection

Some economists argue that, under certain conditions, information problems can eliminate markets (i.e., create *missing markets*) or change the composition of markets (i.e., bring about *incomplete markets*). In the used-car market of our previous example,[5] sellers know more than buyers about the cars they are offering to sell; there is asymmetric information. For example, a seller knows whether the car requires a lot of maintenance. Because most buyers find it difficult to tell the difference between good used cars and lemons, suppose that a single used-car price that reflects both lemons and good cars emerges for a given model, make, and year of car.

Suppose this price is $10,000. Then, on the one hand, an owner of a lemon will think that that is a good price because she will receive an average price for a below-average car that she is selling. But on the other hand, a person who owns an above-average car will find that price too low; he won't want to sell his car for an average price. So, as a result of lemon owners' liking the price and good car owners' not liking it, lemon owners will offer their cars for sale (the price is great), and the owners of good used cars will not (the price is too low).

This situation is called the problem of adverse selection. **Adverse selection** exists when the parties on one side of the market have information not known to others and self-select in a way that adversely affects the parties on the other side of the market. In the example presented, the owners of lemons offer their cars for sale; they select to sell their cars because they know (and only they know) that the average price they are being offered for their below-average cars is a good deal.

Through adverse selection, the supply of lemons on the market will rise, and the supply of high-quality, or good, used cars will fall. The relatively greater number of lemons will lower the average quality of a used car. As a result, for a given make, model, and year of used car, a new average price will emerge that is lower than it was before.

Let's say the new price is $8,000. The process then repeats itself: People with above-average cars will think that the average price of $8,000 is too low, and people with below-average cars will think that it is a good price. The people with above-average cars will drop out of the used car market, leaving only those with below-average used cars. Again, this will lead to a decline in the average quality of a used car, and eventually the average price of a used car will drop once more.

Adverse Selection
A phenomenon in which the parties on one side of the market have information not known to others and self-select in a way that adversely affects the parties on the other side of the market.

[5.] The material that follows is based on the classic article by George Akerlof, "The Market for Lemons," *Quarterly Journal of Economics* (August 1970): 488–500.

Thus, asymmetric information leads to adverse selection, which—in the example of the used-car market—brings about a steady decline in the quality of used cars offered for sale. Theoretically, the adverse selection problem could lead to the total elimination of the good used-car market. In other words, the lemons will drive all the good cars out of the market.

Still, this type of ultimate adverse selection would not happen in the used-car market for several possible reasons. For example, a buyer could hire his own mechanic to check the car he is thinking about buying. By doing so, he would acquire almost as much, if not as much, information about the car as the seller has. Thus, there would no longer be asymmetric information. Or the seller of a high-quality used car could offer a warranty on her car. Essentially, she could offer to fix any problems with the used car for a certain length of time after she sells it. The warranty offer would likely increase both the demand for the car and its price. (Owners of lemons would not be likely to offer warranties, so their cars would sell for less than cars with warranties.)

In some cases, government has played a role in dealing with adverse selection problems. State governments can pass, and in some situations have passed, lemon laws, stating that car dealers must take back any defective cars. In addition, many states now require car dealers to openly state whether a used car is offered with a warranty or as is.

31-5e Moral Hazard

In the preceding used-car example illustrating adverse selection, asymmetric information existed *prior* to an exchange. Before dollars changed hands, the seller of the used car had information about the car that the potential buyer did not have.

Asymmetric information can also exist *after* a transaction has been made. If it does, it can cause a moral hazard problem. **Moral hazard** occurs when one party to a transaction changes his behavior in a way that is hidden from, and costly to, the other party. For example, suppose Alexis buys a health insurance policy. After she has the insurance, she may be less careful to maintain good health because the cost to her of future health problems is not as high as it would have been without the insurance. Alexis does not set out to make herself ill so that she can collect on the insurance, but her incentive to be as careful about her health and physical well-being is not as strong as it once was. As another example, a person with automobile collision insurance may be more likely to drive on an icy road in December in Minneapolis than if he didn't have the insurance. Or a person who has earthquake insurance may be more likely to forget to do a few things that will minimize damage during an earthquake, such as attaching bookcases to the walls. In these examples, the moral hazard problem causes people to take too few precautionary actions.

Insurance companies try to control for moral hazard in different ways. One way is by specifying certain precautions that an insured person must take. For example, a company that insures your house from fire may require you to have smoke detectors and a fire extinguisher. The insurance company may also set a deductible so that you pay part of the loss in case of a fire, thereby increasing your cost in the event of a fire and providing you with an added incentive to be careful.

Moral Hazard
A condition that exists when one party to a transaction changes his or her behavior in a way that is hidden from and costly to the other party.

---

1. Give an example that illustrates how asymmetric information can lead to more of a good being consumed than if there is symmetric information.

2. Adverse selection has the potential to eliminate some markets. How so?

3. Give an example of moral hazard that is not used in the text.

Office Hours

"Doesn't It Seem Wrong to Let Some Business Firms Pay to Pollute?"

Student: In our discussion, I know that pollution permits proved to be less costly at reducing pollution than setting pollution standards, but letting a business firm get away with polluting if it can pay enough money seems wrong. It seems as if it is paying to do something wrong.

Instructor: There's a different way to look at things. The firm is not paying to pollute; instead, it is paying to have some other business firm reduce *its* pollution. Suppose firm A can eliminate its pollution at a lower cost than firm B can. Firm B now pays firm A to eliminate its own (firm A's) pollution. Instead of saying that firm B is "paying to pollute," why not say that "firm B is paying firm A not to pollute"?

Student: Putting it that way makes firm B sound like the good guy—the firm that pays other firms not to pollute.

Instructor: My point is that you cast firm B as the bad guy—the firm that pays to pollute. What I did was simply bring out another aspect of what is happening. Firm B pays firm A *not to pollute* (that is my part of the story) so that, in turn, *it can pollute* (that is your part of the story). Also, keep in mind that, at the end of the process, pollution is reduced, not increased. Instead of having the pollution from firms A and B, we have less (or no) pollution from firm A and perhaps the same amount of pollution from firm B.

Student: I see your point, but wouldn't it still be fairer if no money changed hands and both firms A and B were told that they had to eliminate x amount of pollution? In other words, wouldn't it be fairer to treat each firm the same way?

Instructor: Let's divide the world up into the two firms, A and B, and everyone else. Now, as far as A and B are concerned, each of these two firms would prefer a system of pollution permits to a system of standards. We know this because a pollution permits program can always be turned into a command-and-control program if doing so is preferable to buying and selling permits. To illustrate, suppose firms A and B are each emitting 3 units of pollution. Government now gives each firm 1 pollution permit, allowing it to emit 1 unit of pollution. If neither firm buys or sells its 1 permit, then what we essentially have is a standards system for eliminating (some) pollution. Each firm reduces its pollution from 3 units to 1 unit. End of story. But if the two firms start trading permits for money, we can conclude that each firm is better off with a pollution permits system than with a standards system. And this is what we usually see: firms buying and selling permits.

Student: So the point is that firms A and B prefer a pollution permits system to a standards system?

Instructor: Yes. But now we are left with what we call an "everyone else": Is everyone else better off with a pollution permits system than with a standards system? The answer is yes, because it is less costly to eliminate a given amount of pollution with a pollution permits system than with standards. "Less costly" here means "fewer resources used." If fewer resources are used to eliminate pollution, then more resources are left over for other things. As a member of the "everyone else" group, I am better off with more resources left over, than with fewer resources, to produce things that I want to buy.

So let's now return to your original question: Wouldn't it be fairer if no money changed hands and both firms A and B were told that they had to eliminate x amount of pollution? To whom would that be fairer? It's not fairer to firms A and B, because they prefer pollution permits to standards. And it's not really fairer to everyone else, because we suspect that everyone else prefers to have more instead of fewer resources left over after x amount of pollution has been emitted.

Points to Remember

1. Saying that "firms are paying to pollute" leaves out some of what is happening with a pollution permits system. Some firms are paying other firms not to pollute so that they can pollute. Firm B is paying firm A to not pollute so that it (firm B) can pollute.
2. Pollution permits (that can be bought and sold) can eliminate a given amount of pollution with a lower resource cost than can a command-and-control system.

Chapter Summary

Externalities

- An externality is a side effect of an action that affects the well-being of third parties. There are two types of externalities: negative and positive. A negative externality exists when an individual's or group's actions impose a cost (an adverse side effect) on others. A positive externality exists when an individual's or group's actions cause a benefit (a beneficial side effect) for others.

- When either negative or positive externalities exist, the market output is different from the socially optimal output. In the case of a negative externality, the market is said to overproduce the good connected with the negative externality. (The socially optimal output is less than the market output; see Exhibit 1.) In the case of a positive externality, the market is said to underproduce the good connected with the positive externality. (The socially optimal output is greater than the market output; see Exhibit 3.)

- Negative and positive externalities can be internalized, or adjusted for, in a number of different ways, including persuasion, the assignment of property rights, voluntary agreements, and taxes and subsidies. Also, regulations may be used to adjust for externalities directly.

The Coase Theorem

- The Coase theorem is the proposition that private negotiations between people will lead to an efficient resolution of externalities, as long as property rights are well defined and transaction costs are trivial or zero. The Coase theorem is significant for two reasons: (1) It shows that, under certain conditions, the market can internalize externalities. (2) It provides a benchmark for analyzing externality problems; that is, it shows what would happen if transaction costs are trivial or zero.

The Environment

- Under government regulation, or command-and-control, government might specify a certain type of pollution control technology to be utilized by polluters or simply set a quantitative goal that is applied to polluters with respect to emitting pollution.

- Generally, economists do not favor command-and-control policies as a means of reducing pollution. One reason is that mandating certain technologies to be used reduces the incentive to discover new, lower-cost methods of reducing pollution. Another reason is that it is often costlier to eliminate a given quantity of pollution by mandating that each polluter eliminate the same amount of pollution than by implementing emission taxes or tradable pollution permits.

- Under an emission tax, the tax is set, and then the quantity demanded of pollution is determined by the demand for pollution.

- Under tradable pollution permits, government sets the quantity of pollution that is permissible and then issues or auctions off pollution permits that can be bought and sold.

- Emission taxes and tradable pollution permits end up creating different kinds of uncertainty. Under an emission tax, polluters know what price they have to pay to pollute, but government doesn't know how much pollution will be generated. Under a tradable pollution permits system (cap and trade), government knows the amount of pollution, but polluters don't immediately know what the price to pollute will be.

Public Goods

- A public good is a good characterized by nonrivalry in consumption.

- A public good can be excludable or nonexcludable. Excludable public goods are goods that, while nonrivalrous in consumption, can be denied to people if they do not pay for them. Nonexcludable public goods are goods that are nonrivalrous in consumption and cannot be denied to people who do not pay for them.

- The market is said to fail in the provision of nonexcludable public goods because of the free-rider problem; that is, a supplier of the good is not able to extract payment for the good because its benefits can be received without payment.

Asymmetric Information

- Asymmetric information exists when either the buyer or the seller in a market exchange has some information that the other does not have. Outcomes based on asymmetric information may be different from outcomes based on symmetric information.

- Adverse selection exists when the parties on one side of the market have information not known to others and self-select in a way that adversely affects the parties on the other side of the market. Adverse selection can lead to missing or incomplete markets.

- Moral hazard occurs when one party to a transaction changes his or her behavior in a way that is hidden from, and costly to, the other party.

Key Terms and Concepts

Market Failure
Externality
Negative Externality
Positive Externality
Marginal Social Costs (MSC)
Marginal Social Benefits (MSB)
Socially Optimal Amount (Output)
Internalizing Externalities
Coase Theorem
Rivalrous in Consumption
Public Good
Nonrivalrous in Consumption
Excludable
Nonexcludable
Free Rider
Asymmetric Information
Adverse Selection
Moral Hazard

Questions and Problems

1. Under what condition will $MSC = MPC$? When will $MSB = MPB$?

2. Suppose there is a negative externality. If a tax is used to correct for the negative externality, what condition must be satisfied? What must the tax equal?

3. Explain why the shaded triangle in Exhibit 3 is representative of a market failure.

4. When will asymmetric information in a product market not cause market failure?

5. Give an example that illustrates the difference between private costs and social costs.

6. Consider two types of divorce laws. Law A allows either the husband or the wife to obtain a divorce without the other person's consent. Law B permits a divorce only if both parties agree to it. Will there be more divorces under law A or law B, or will there be the same number of divorces under both laws? Why?

7. People have a demand for sweaters, and the market provides sweaters. There is evidence that people also have a demand for national defense, but the market does not provide it. Why doesn't the market provide national defense? Is it because government is providing national defense, and, therefore, there is no need for the market to do so? Or is it because the market can't provide it?

8. Identify three activities that generate negative externalities and three activities that generate positive externalities. Explain why each activity you identified generates the type of externality you specified.

9. Give an example of each of the following:
   a. A good that is rivalrous in consumption and is excludable.
   b. A good that is nonrivalrous in consumption and is excludable.
   c. A good that is rivalrous in consumption and is nonexcludable.
   d. A good that is nonrivalrous in consumption and is nonexcludable.

10. Some individuals argue that, with increased population growth, negative externalities will become more common and there will be more instances of market failure, and more need for government to solve externality problems. Other individuals believe that, as time passes, technological advances will be used to solve negative externality problems, and there will be fewer instances of market failure and less need for government to deal with externality problems. What do you believe will happen? Give reasons to support your position.

11. Name at least five government-provided goods that are excludable public goods.

12. There is a view that life is one big externality: Just about everything someone does affects someone else either positively or negatively. To permit government to deal with externality problems is to permit government to tamper with everything in life. No clear line divides externalities in which government should become involved from those it should not. Do you support this position? Why or why not?

13. Economists sometimes shock noneconomists by stating that they do not favor the complete elimination of pollution. Explain the rationale for this position.
14. Explain how both an emission tax and a tradable pollution permits system can reduce pollution.
15. Identify each of the following as an adverse selection or a moral hazard problem:
    a. A person with car insurance fails to lock his car doors when he shops at a mall.
    b. A person with a family history of cancer purchases the most complete health coverage available.
    c. A person with health insurance takes more risks on the ski slopes of Aspen than he would without health insurance.
    d. A college professor receives tenure (assurance of permanent employment) from her employer.
    e. A patient pays his surgeon before she performs the surgery.

Working with Numbers and Graphs

1. Graphically portray the following:
   a. A negative externality
   b. A positive externality
2. Graphically represent the following:
   a. A corrective tax that achieves the socially optimal output
   b. A corrective tax that moves the market output farther away from the socially optimal output than was the case before the tax was applied
3. Using the following data, prove that pollution permits that can be bought and sold can reduce pollution from 12 tons to 6 tons at a lower cost than a regulation that specifies that each of the three firms must cut its pollution in half.

	Firm X	Firm Y	Firm Z
Cost of eliminating:			
First ton of pollution	$200	$500	$1,000
Second ton of pollution	300	700	2,000
Third ton of pollution	400	800	2,900
Fourth ton of pollution	500	900	3,400

CHAPTER 32
Public Choice and Special-Interest Group Politics

Introduction

Economics is a powerful analytical tool. As you have seen, it can be used to analyze how markets and the economy work. In this chapter, we use economics to analyze the behavior of politicians, voters, and members of special-interest groups. Specifically, we analyze **public choice**, the branch of economics in which economic principles and tools are applied to public sector decision making. Public choice is, in a sense, economics applied to politics.

Public Choice
The branch of economics in which economic principles and tools are applied to public sector decision making.

32-1 Public Choice Theory

Public choice theorists reject the notion that people are like Dr. Jekyll and Mr. Hyde—that is, that they exhibit greed and selfishness in their transactions in the private (market) sector and altruism and public spirit in their actions in the public sector. The same people who are the employers, employees, and consumers in the market sector are the politicians, bureaucrats, members of special-interest groups, and voters in the public sector. According to public choice theorists, people in the market sector and people in the public sector behave differently not because they have different motives (or are different types of people) but because the two sectors have different institutional arrangements.

As a simple example, Catalina works for a private, profit-seeking firm that makes electronic components. Catalina is cost conscious, does her work on time, and generally works hard. She knows that she must exhibit this type of work behavior if she wants to keep her job, get a raise, and be promoted. Suppose now that Catalina leaves her job at the electronic components company and takes a job with the Department of Health and Human Services (HHS) in Washington, D.C. Public choice theorists maintain that Catalina is the same person (with different motives), whether working for HHS or for the electronic components company.

However, even though Catalina is the same person in and out of government, she will not necessarily exhibit the same work behavior. The costs and benefits of certain actions may be substantially different at HHS than at the electronic components company. For example, perhaps the cost of being late for work is less in Catalina's new job at HHS than it was at her old job. In her former job, she had to work overtime if she came in late; in her new job, her boss doesn't say anything. Catalina is therefore more likely to be late in her new job than she was in her old one. She is simply responding to costs and benefits as they exist in her new work environment.

32-2 The Political Market

Economists who practice positive economics want to understand their world. They want to understand not only the production and pricing of goods, unemployment, inflation, and the firm, but also political outcomes and political behavior. This section is an introduction to the political market.

32-2a Moving Toward the Middle: The Median Voter Model[1]

In Exhibit 1, parts (a), (b), and (c) all show a normal distribution of voters in which the political spectrum goes from the far left to the far right. In this normal distribution of voters, few voters hold positions in either of the two extreme wings. Assuming, then, that voters will vote

EXHIBIT 1

The Move Toward the Middle

Given the voter distribution shown here, political candidates tend to move toward the middle of the political spectrum. Starting with (a), the Republican receives more votes than the Democrat and would win the election if it were held today. To offset this advantage, as shown in (b), the Democrat moves inward toward the middle of the political spectrum. The Republican tries to offset the Democrat's movement inward by also moving inward. As a result, both candidates move toward the political middle, getting closer to each other over time, as shown in (c).

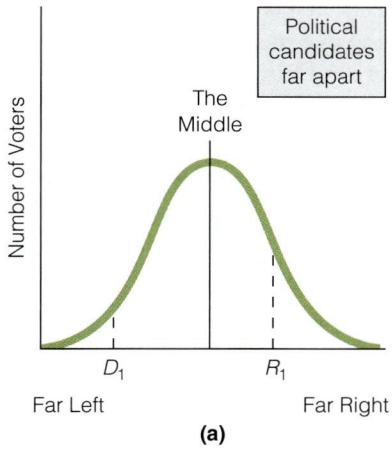
(a)

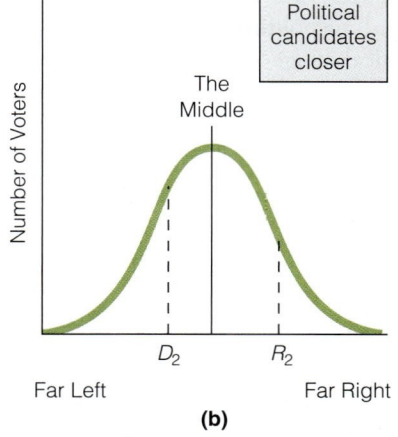
(b)

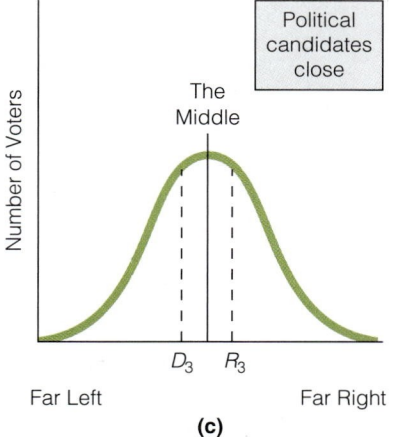
(c)

---

[1] In our example to illustrate the median voter model, we assume a normal voter distribution, a two-person race, and that voters always vote for the candidate that comes closer to matching their political views. In reality, there are other voter distributions besides the normal voter distribution. For example, a voter distribution could be bimodal with one mode at the far left of the political spectrum and one at the far right. Some have argued that the voter distribution in the United States today is more likely to be bimodal than normal. Still, we have elected to present the model in its earliest and most basic form: normal voter distribution, the median voter occupies the middle of the political spectrum, there are no voter dropouts at either end of the political spectrum, and a two-person race.

for the candidate who comes closest to matching their ideological or political views, people whose views are in the far left of the political spectrum will vote for the candidate closest to the far left, and so on.

Our election process begins with two candidates, a Democrat and a Republican, occupying the positions D_1 and R_1, respectively, in part (a) of Exhibit 1. The Republican would receive all the votes of the voters who position themselves to the right of R_1, the Democrat would receive all the votes of the voters who position themselves to the left of D_1, and the voters between R_1 and D_1 would divide their votes between the two candidates. Thus, as shown, the Republican would receive more votes than the Democrat if the election were held today.

If, however, the election were not held today, the Democrat would likely notice (through polls and other sources) that her opponent was doing better than she was. To offset this advantage, she would move toward the center, or middle, of the political spectrum to pick up some votes. Part (b) in Exhibit 1 illustrates this move by the Democrat. Now voters to the left of D_2 would vote for the Democrat, voters to the right of R_2 would vote for the Republican, and the voters between the two positions would divide their votes between the two candidates. If the election were held at this time, the Democrat would win.

In part (c), each candidate, in an attempt to get more votes than his or her opponent, has moved closer to the middle. Thus, at election time, the two candidates are likely to be positioned side by side at the political center, or middle (D_3 and R_3).

The tendency of political candidates to move toward the center of the voter distribution—captured in the **median voter model**—is what causes many voters to complain (specifically when dealing with a normal voter distribution) that there is not much difference between candidates.

Median Voter Model
A model suggesting that candidates in a two-person political race will attempt to match the preferences of the median voter.

32-2b What Does the Theory Predict?

Here are a few of the predictions of the median voter model:

1. *Candidates will label their opponent as being either too far to the right or too far to the left.* The candidates know that whoever is closer to the middle of the political spectrum (in a two-person race) will win more votes and thus the election. Therefore, to win, they will move toward the political middle, at the same time saying that their opponent is a member of the political fringe (i.e., a person far from the center). A Democrat may argue that his Republican opponent is too conservative; a Republican may argue that her Democratic opponent is too liberal.

2. *Candidates will call themselves middle-of-the-roaders, not right- or left-wingers.* In their move toward the political middle, candidates will try to portray themselves as moderates. In their speeches, they will assert that they represent the majority of voters and that they are practical, not ideological. They will not be likely to refer to themselves as ultraliberal or ultraconservative or as right- or left-wingers because to do so would send a self-defeating message to the voters.

3. *Candidates will take polls, and, if they are not doing well in the polls and their opponents are, they will modify their positions to become more like their opponents.* Polls tell candidates who the likely winner of the election will be. A candidate who finds that she will lose the election (she is "down in the polls") is not likely to sit back and do nothing. The candidate will change her positions. Often, she will become more like the winner of the poll—that is, more like her political opponent.

4. *Candidates will speak in general, instead of specific, terms.* Voters agree more on ends than on the means of accomplishing those ends. For example, voters of the left, right, and middle believe that a strong economy is better than a weak economy. However, they

do not all agree on the best way to make the economy strong. The person on the right might advocate less government intervention as one way, whereas the person on the left might advocate more government intervention. Most political candidates soon learn that addressing the issues specifically requires them to discuss means and that doing so increases the probability of their having an extreme-wing label attached to them. For example, a candidate who advocates more government intervention in the economy is more likely to be labeled "too far left" than a candidate who simply calls for a stronger national economy without discussing any specific means. In the candidate's desire to be perceived as a middle-of-the-roader, he is much more likely to talk about ends, on which voters agree, than about means, on which voters disagree.

Economics 24/7

A Simple-Majority Voting Rule: The Case of the Statue in the Public Square

Public questions are often decided by the simple-majority decision rule. Although most people think that this is the fair and democratic way to do things, in certain instances, a simple majority vote leads to undertaking a project whose costs are greater than its benefits.

Consider a community of 10 people, whose names are listed in column 1 of Exhibit 2. The community is considering whether to purchase a statue to put in the center of the public square. The cost of the statue is $1,000, and the community has previously

EXHIBIT 2

Simple-Majority Voting and Inefficiency

The simple-majority decision rule sometimes generates inefficient results. Here, a statue is purchased even though the total dollar value of the benefits of the statue is less than the total dollar costs.

(1) Individuals	(2) Dollar Value of Benefits to Individual	(3) Tax Levied on Individual	(4) Net Benefit or Net Cost	(5) Vote for or Against
Applebaum	$150	$100	+$50	For
Borges	140	100	+40	For
Calabrese	130	100	+30	For
Davidson	110	100	+10	For
Emerson	101	100	+1	For
Fang	101	100	+1	For
Guerra	50	100	−50	Against
Halabi	10	100	−90	Against
Isley	10	100	−90	Against
Janowitz	10	100	−90	Against
Total	$812	$1,000		

(Continued)

agreed that if the statue is purchased, the 10 individuals will share the cost equally; that is, each will pay $100 in taxes (see column 3).

Column 2 shows the dollar value of the benefits that each individual will receive from the statue. For example, Applebaum places a dollar value of $150 on the statue, Borges places a dollar value of $140 on the statue, and so on. Column 4 notes the net benefit or net cost of the statue to each individual. A net benefit occurs if the dollar value an individual places on the statue is greater than the tax (cost) incurred. A net cost results if the reverse is true. Finally, column 5 indicates how each member of the community would vote. An individual who believes that the statue has a net benefit will vote for it, and an individual who believes that the statue has a net cost will vote against it. Thus, six individuals vote for the statue, and four individuals vote against it. The majority rules, and the statue is purchased and placed in the center of the public square.

However, the total dollar value of benefits to the community ($812) is less than the total tax cost to the community ($1,000). Accordingly, using the simple-majority decision rule has resulted in the purchase of the statue even though the benefits of the statue to the community are less than its costs.

This outcome is not surprising when you understand that the simple-majority decision rule does not take into account the intensity of individuals' preferences. No matter how strongly a person feels about an issue, he or she registers only one vote. For example, even though Emerson places a net benefit of $1 on the statue and Halabi places a net cost of $90 on the statue, each individual has only one vote. Halabi has no way to register the fact that he does not want the statue more than Emerson wants it.

Economics 24/7

The Median Voter Model and the U.S. Supreme Court in 2018

In the median voter model presented in this chapter, we explained that two candidates running for the same elected office have an incentive to move toward the middle of the voter distribution. Given the voter distribution we used (a normal curve), that means that the two candidates running for the same elected office have an incentive to move toward (or capture the vote of) the median voter—the voter who has an equal number of voters to the left as to the right of her. As it turns out, the median voter model can be applied to more than just candidates running for the same elected office: It also can be applied to the U.S. Supreme Court.

The U.S. Supreme Court is composed of nine Supreme Court justices. In early 2018, those justices were John Roberts, Clarence Thomas, Ruth Bader Ginsburg, Stephen Breyer, Samuel Alito, Sonia Sotomayor, Elena Kagan, Neil Gorsuch, and Anthony Kennedy. Roberts, Gorsuch, Thomas, and Alito were sometimes referred to as the four conservative justices; Breyer, Ginsburg, Sotomayor, and Kagan were sometimes referred to as the four liberal justices. Oftentimes, the conservative justices would

> vote as a block, as would the liberal justices. That left Anthony Kennedy as the median justice, or the deciding justice. Just as the median voter decides who wins the election, Justice Anthony Kennedy would sometimes decide the ruling of the Supreme Court on a particular case.
>
> So, if you were back in 2018 and arguing a case before the Supreme Court, who would you most direct your arguments to, assuming you wanted to win the case? You would probably choose the median justice, and that is what many Supreme Court lawyers did. They would focus much of their legal briefs and oral arguments on persuading Justice Kennedy, as they felt certain that four of the remaining eight justices would vote one way and the other four of the eight justices would vote the opposite way. Justice Kennedy was the deciding vote, the median justice who would decide the Court's ruling. Here is a short YouTube video on Justice Kennedy as the median justice: https://www.youtube.com/watch?v=ye7tditqM_Q.
>
> On June 27, 2018, Justice Kennedy reported that he would retire from the Supreme Court. Kennedy would therefore no longer be the median justice. At the time, most people thought John Roberts, the Chief Justice of the Supreme Court, would end up taking Kennedy's place.
>
> Things are a little different at the time of this writing, in late 2021. Today, the nine justices of the Supreme Court consist of John Roberts, Clarence Thomas, Stephen Breyer, Samuel Alito, Sonia Sotomayor, Elena Kagan, Neil Gorsuch, Brett Kavanaugh, and Amy Coney Barrett. Gone is the breakdown between four liberal and four conservative justices. Most would say that today the conservative–liberal split is either 6–3 or 5–4, in favor of conservative justices.

32-3 Voters and Rational Ignorance

The preceding section explains something about the behavior of politicians, especially near or at election time. We turn now to voters.

32-3a The Costs and Benefits of Voting

Political commentators often remark that the voter turnout for this or that election was low: "Only 54 percent of registered voters actually voted." Are voter turnouts low because Americans are apathetic? Are they uninterested in political issues?

Public choice economists often explain low voter turnouts in terms of the costs and benefits of voting. As an example, Mark is thinking about voting in a presidential election. Mark may receive many benefits from voting: He may feel more involved in public affairs or think that he has met his civic responsibility. He may see himself as patriotic, or he may believe he has a greater right to criticize government if he takes an active part in it. In short, he may benefit by seeing himself as a doer instead of a talker. Ultimately, however, he will weigh these positive benefits against the costs of voting, which include driving to the polls, standing in line, and so on. If, in the end, Mark perceives the benefits of voting as greater than the costs, he will vote.

But suppose Mark believes that he receives only one benefit from voting: determining the outcome of the election. His benefits-of-voting equation may look like this:

$$\text{Mark's benefits of voting} = \text{Probability of Mark's vote determining the election outcome} \times \text{Additional benefits Mark receives if his candidate wins}$$

Now, suppose two candidates, A and B, are running for office. If Mark votes, he will vote for A because he estimates that he benefits by $100 if A is elected but only by $40 if B is elected. The difference, $60, represents the additional benefits Mark receives if his candidate wins.

However, the probability that Mark's vote will determine the outcome is minuscule. With many potential voters, such as there are in a presidential election, the probability that one person's vote will determine the outcome is close to zero. To recognize this fact on an intuitive level, suppose A and B are the two major candidates in a presidential campaign. If you, as an individual voter, vote for A, the outcome of the election is likely to be the same as if you had voted for B or not voted at all. In other words, whether you vote at all, vote for A, or vote for B, the outcome is likely to be the same. In Mark's benefits-of-voting equation, $60 is multiplied by a probability so small that it might as well be 0. So, $60 times 0 is 0. In short, Mark receives no benefits from voting.

But Mark may face certain costs. His costs-of-voting equation may look like this:

Mark's cost of voting = Cost of driving to the polls
+ Cost of standing in line
+ Cost of filling out the ballot

Obviously, Mark faces some positive costs of voting. Because his benefits of voting are 0 and his costs of voting are positive, Mark makes the rational choice if he decides not to vote.

Clearly, not everyone behaves this way—that is, chooses not to vote. Many people do vote in elections. What separates the Marks in the world from the people who vote is probably that the voters receive some benefits that Mark does not. They might receive benefits simply by being part of the excitement of election day, by doing what they perceive as their civic duty, or for some other reason.

The point public choice economists make is that, if many individual voters will vote only if they perceive their vote as making a difference, then they probably will not vote, because their vote is unlikely to make a difference. Thus, the low turnouts that appear to be a result of voter apathy may instead be a result of cost–benefit calculations.

32-3b Rational Ignorance

How often have you heard an opinion like this one? "Democracy would be better served if voters would take more of an interest in, and become better informed about, politics and government. Voters don't know much about the issues."

The problem, however, is not that voters are too stupid to learn about the issues. Many citizens who know little about politics and government are quite capable of learning about both, but they choose not to make the effort. The reason is perhaps predictable: The costs of becoming informed often outweigh the benefits. In short, many persons believe that becoming informed is simply not worth the effort. Hence, on an individual basis, it makes sense to be uninformed about politics and government—that is, to be in a state of **rational ignorance**.

As an example, Shonia has many things she can do with her leisure time. She could read a good novel, watch a television program, go out with friends, or become better informed about the candidates and the issues in the upcoming U.S. Senate race. Becoming informed, however, has costs. If Shonia stays home and reads about the issues, she can't go out with her friends. If she stays up late to watch a news program, she might be too tired to work efficiently the next day. These costs have to be weighed against the benefits of becoming better informed about the candidates and the issues. For Shonia, as for many people, the benefits are unlikely to be greater than the costs.

Many people see little personal benefit in becoming more knowledgeable about political candidates and issues. As with voting, the decision to remain uninformed may be linked to the small impact that any single individual can have in a large-numbers setting.

Rational Ignorance
The state of not acquiring information because the costs of acquiring it are greater than the benefits.

Economics 24/7

Economic Illiteracy and Democracy

Citizens can vote even if they have no idea what they are doing. If enough voters fit that description, democratic governments are bound to make foolish decisions.

—Bryan Caplan, *Straight Talk About Economic Literacy*

Economist Bryan Caplan argues that a large percentage of the American public is economically illiterate. The result is that a lot of foolishness gets turned into national economic policy.[2]

Although determining whether someone is illiterate may be easy, ascertaining whether someone is economically illiterate is not so easy. To determine illiteracy, you can just ask people to read or write something. If they can read and write, they are not illiterate. If they can't read or write, they are illiterate.

Unfortunately, there is no such simple test to determine economic illiteracy. Instead, Caplan points to a survey that compared the responses of 1,510 average Americans with those of 250 professional economists to the same set of questions concerning economics and the economy. Here is one question from the survey: "Which do you think is more responsible for the recent increase in gasoline prices: the normal law of supply and demand, oil companies are trying to increase profits, both, or neither?" Although only 8 percent of economists said that recent increases in gas prices were due to oil companies trying to increase profits, 78 percent of the noneconomists polled explained high gas prices in that way. The explanation for high gas prices chosen by 83 percent of economists was supply and demand.

Indirectly, Caplan uses the economists' overwhelming response to the question as a benchmark by which to measure the economic illiteracy of the public. The closer the public's responses are to the economists' responses, the less economically illiterate the public is; the farther away the public's responses are from the economists' responses, the more economically illiterate the public is.

According to Caplan, who looked at responses to numerous questions, the American public is largely economically illiterate. Caplan argues that such a great degree of economic illiteracy has to do with the price one pays for it. In fact, the price is rather low, and when the price is low, you would expect a higher degree of economic illiteracy than when the price is high. In other words, false beliefs about economics are cheap. As Caplan says, if you underestimate the costs of excessive drinking, you can ruin your life, but if you underestimate the economic benefits of, say, free international trade, nothing really bad happens to you. Whatever happens to you is what would have happened if you didn't underestimate the economic benefits of free international trade. In other words, when being wrong really has no cost, a lot of people will be wrong—especially if one receives a personal psychological lift from holding an erroneous belief or position. Caplan puts it succinctly: "In a sense, then, there is a method to the average voter's madness. Even when his views are completely wrong, he gets the psychological benefit of emotionally appealing political beliefs at a bargain price. No wonder he buys in bulk."[3] In other words, x might be the wrong answer to the question, but if x

---

[2] Bryan Caplan, *The Myth of the Rational Voter: Why Democracies Choose Bad Policies* (Princeton, NJ: Princeton University Press, 2007).

[3] Bryan Caplan, "The Myth of the Rational Voter," *Cato Unbound*, November 6, 2006, http://www.cato-unbound.org/2006/11/06/bryan-caplan/the-myth-of-the-rational-voter.

(Continued)

is emotionally appealing to the respondent and if having the wrong answer doesn't adversely affect the respondent, then the respondent will choose x.

But if many people choose x, then x may get turned into policy at a national level. In other words, if the majority of voting Americans believe that placing tariffs on foreign imports is desirable (when economists largely disagree), then, in a political system in which politicians compete for votes, the public's erroneous belief is likely to find its way into international trade policy.

If one person's erroneous belief adversely affects only him, that is one thing. But it is quite another thing, Caplan argues, when the erroneous beliefs of many people adversely affect those who do not hold that belief. Yet this outcome is what we often get in a representative democracy. Economically erroneous beliefs, chosen on an individual level because they are cheap to choose, often add up to democracies' choosing bad economic policies.

(Answers to Self-Test questions are in Answers to Self-Test Questions at the back of the book.)

1. If a politician running for office does not speak in general terms, does not try to move to the middle of the political spectrum, and does not take polls, is the median voter model therefore wrong?
2. Voters often criticize politicians running for office who do not speak in specific terms (i.e., do not specify which spending programs will be cut, whose taxes will be raised, etc.). If voters want politicians running for office to speak in specific terms, why don't politicians do so?
3. Would bad weather be something that could affect voter turnout? Explain your answer.

32-4 More About Voting

Voting is often the method used to make decisions in the public sector. In this section, we discuss two examples that describe some of the effects (some might say problems) of voting as a decision-making method.

32-4a Example 1: Voting for a Nonexcludable Public Good

Suppose a community of seven persons, A–G, wants to produce or purchase nonexcludable public good X. Each person in the community wants a different number of units of X, as shown in the following table:

Person	Number of Units of X Desired
A	1
B	2
C	3
D	4
E	5
F	6
G	7

If the community of seven persons holds a simple majority vote, then all seven will vote to produce or purchase at least 1 unit of X. Six people (B–G) will vote for at least 2 units; five people (C–G), for at least 3 units; four people (D–G), for at least 4 units; three people (E–G), for at least 5 units; and two people (F–G), for at least 6 units. Only one person (G) will vote for 7 units.

The largest number of units that receives a simple majority vote (half the total number of voters plus 1, or 4 votes) is 4 units. In other words, the community will vote to produce or purchase 4 units of X. Interestingly, 4 units is the most preferred outcome of only one of the seven members of the community, person D, who is the median voter. Half the voters (A, B, and C) prefer fewer than 4 units, and half the voters (E, F, and G) prefer more. Thus, our voting process has resulted in only the median voter obtaining his most preferred outcome.

The outcome would have been the same even if the numbers had looked as they do in the following table:

Person	Number of Units of X Desired
A	0
B	0
C	0
D	4
E	7
F	7
G	7

In this case, four people (D–G) would have voted for at least 4 units, and only three people would have voted for anything less than 4 units. Again, 4 units would have been the outcome of the vote, and only the median voter would have obtained his most preferred outcome.

32-4b Example 2: Voting and Efficiency

Suppose three individuals have the marginal private benefits (MPB) shown in the following table for various units of the nonexcludable public good Y:

Person	MPB of First Unit of Y	MPB of Second Unit of Y	MPB of Third Unit of Y
A	$400	$380	$190
B	150	110	90
C	100	90	80

If the cost of providing a unit of good Y is $360, what is the socially optimal, or efficient, amount of good Y? To answer this question, recall a few of the relationships from the last chapter:

1. The socially optimal, or efficient, amount of anything is the amount at which the marginal social benefits (MSB) equal the marginal social costs (MSC).

2. The sum of the marginal private benefits (MPB) and the marginal external benefits (MEB) equals the marginal social benefits (MSB): $MPB + MEB = MSB$.

3. The sum of the marginal private costs (MPC) and the marginal external costs (MEC) equals the marginal social costs (MSC): $MPC + MEC = MSC$.

In our example, the MSC for each unit of Y is given as $360. We calculate the MSB for each unit by summing the MPBs shown in the relevant column of the table. For the first unit, the MSB is $650 ($400 + $150 + $100); for the second unit, it is $580; and for the third unit, it is $360. The socially optimal, or efficient, amount of good Y is 3 units because, at that amount, MSB = MSC.

Whether voting will give us efficiency depends largely on what tax each person, A–C, expects to pay. Suppose each person must pay an equal share of the price of a unit of good Y. In other words, the tax for each person is $120 ($360 per unit ÷ 3 persons = $120 per person per unit).

Person A will vote for 3 units because his MPB for each unit is greater than his tax of $120 per unit. Person B will vote for only 1 unit because his MPB for the first unit is greater than his tax of $120 per unit, but his MPB is not greater for the second or third unit. Person C will not vote for any units because his MPB for each unit is less than his tax of $120 per unit. Thus, the outcome from using a simple-majority vote is only 1 unit, and a process of voting in which each voter pays an equal tax results in an inefficient outcome.

Now suppose that, instead of paying an equal tax (of $120), each person pays a tax equal to his MPB at the socially optimal, or efficient, outcome. The socially optimal, or efficient, outcome is 3 units of good Y, so person A would pay a tax of $190 (his MPB for the third unit is $190), person B would pay a tax of $90, and person C would pay a tax of $80. (The sum of the taxes paid is equal to the cost of the unit, or $360.)

With this different tax structure, will voting generate efficiency? If each person casts a truthful vote, the answer is yes: Each person will vote for 3 units.[4] In other words, if everyone casts a truthful vote and everyone pays a tax equal to his or her MPB at the efficient outcome, then voting will generate efficiency.

Comparing the two tax structures—one in which each person pays an equal tax and one in which each person pays a tax equal to his MPB—we see that the tax structure makes the difference. In the case of equal tax shares, voting did not lead to efficiency; in the case of unequal tax shares, it did.

1. If the MSC in Example 2 had been $580 instead of $360, what would the socially optimal, or efficient, outcome have been?

2. In Example 2, with equal taxes, did the outcome of the vote make anyone worse off? If so, whom and by how much?

32-5 Special-Interest Groups

Special-Interest Groups
Subsets of the general population that hold (usually) intense preferences for or against a particular government service, activity, or policy and that often gain from public policies that may not be in accord with the interests of the general public.

Special-interest groups are subsets of the general population that hold (usually) intense preferences for or against a particular government service, activity, or policy. Often, special-interest groups gain from public policies that may not be in accord with the interests of the general public. In recent decades, they have played a major role in government.

---

[4] Look at the situation for person A: His MPB for the first unit is $400, and his tax is $190, so he votes for the first unit. His MPB for the second unit is $380, and his tax is $190, so he votes for the second unit. His MPB for the third unit is $190, and his tax is $190, so he votes for the third unit. With respect to the last unit for person A, we are assuming that if his MPB is equal to the tax, he will vote in favor of the unit. The same holds for the analysis of voting for persons B and C.

32-5a Information and Lobbying

Whereas the general voter is usually uninformed about issues, members of a special-interest group are very well informed, at least about the issues they are interested in. For example, teachers are likely to know a lot about government education policies, farmers about government agriculture policies, and union members about government union policies. The reason for their greater awareness is simple: The more directly and intensely issues affect them, the greater the incentive is for individuals to become informed about them.

Given an electorate composed of uninformed general voters and informed members of special-interest groups, the groups are often able to sway politicians in their favor. This effect occurs even when the general public is made worse off by such actions (which, of course, is not always the case).

Suppose special-interest group A, composed of 5,000 individuals, favors a policy that will result in the redistribution of $50 million from 100 million general taxpayers to the group. Then the dollar benefit for each member of the special-interest group is $10,000. Given the substantial dollar amount involved, members of the special-interest group are likely to (1) sponsor or propose legislation to redistribute the money and (2) lobby the politicians who will decide the issue.

Further, the politicians will probably not hear from the general voter (i.e., the general taxpayer). The general voters–taxpayers will be less informed about the legislation than the members of the special-interest group, and anyway, even if they were adequately informed, each person would have to calculate the benefits and the costs of lobbying against the proposed legislation. If the legislation passes, the average taxpayer will pay approximately 50¢, and the benefits of lobbying against the legislation are probably not greater than 50¢. Therefore, even if they are informed about the legislation, the general taxpayers would not be likely to argue against it. The benefits just wouldn't be worth the time and effort. Special-interest bills therefore have a good chance of being passed in our legislatures.

32-5b Congressional Districts as Special-Interest Groups

Most people do not ordinarily think of congressional districts as special-interest groups. Instead, special-interest groups are commonly thought to include the ranks of public school teachers, steel manufacturers, automobile manufacturers, farmers, environmentalists, bankers, truck drivers, doctors, and the like. On some issues, however, a congressional district may be a special-interest group.

Suppose an air force base is located in a Texas congressional district. In this scenario, a Pentagon study determines that the base is not needed and that Congress should shut it down. The Pentagon study demonstrates that the cost to the taxpayers of keeping the base open is greater than the benefits to the country of maintaining it. But closing the air force base will hurt the pocketbooks of the people in the congressional district housing the base. Their congressional representative knows this, and also that if she can't keep the base open, she isn't as likely to be reelected to office.

Therefore, she speaks to other members of Congress about the proposed closing. In a way, she acts as a lobbyist for her congressional district. Most members of Congress are probably willing to go along with the Texas representative, even though they know that their constituents will be paying more in taxes, according to the Pentagon, than is necessary to ensure the national security of the country. If they don't go along with her, when they need a vote on one of their own special-interest projects (sometimes the term "pork barrel" is used), the representative from Texas may not be so cooperative. In short, members of Congress sometimes trade votes: my

Logrolling
The exchange of votes to gain support for legislation.

vote on your air force base for your vote on subsidies to dairy farmers in my district. This type of vote trading—the exchange of votes to gain support for legislation—is commonly referred to as **logrolling**.

32-5c Public-Interest Talk, Special-Interest Legislation

Special-interest groups lobbying for special-interest legislation usually don't use the term *special-interest legislation*, but, rather, something like "legislation in the best interest of the general public." Here are a couple of examples, past and present.

In the early nineteenth century, the British Parliament passed the Factory Acts, which put restrictions on women and children working. Those who lobbied for the restrictions said they did so for humanitarian reasons: to protect young children and women from difficult and hazardous work in the cotton mills. There is evidence, however, that the men working in the factories were the main lobbyists for the Factory Acts and that a reduced supply of women and children directly benefited them by raising their wages. The male factory workers appealed to individuals' higher sensibilities instead of letting it be known that they would benefit at the expense of others.

Today, people calling for, say, economic protection from foreign competitors or greater federal subsidies rarely explain that they favor the measure because the legislation will make them better off while someone else pays the bill. Instead, they usually voice the public-interest argument. They say economic protectionism isn't necessary to protect industry *X*, but it is necessary to protect American jobs and the domestic economy. The special-interest message often is, "Help yourself by helping us."

Sometimes this message is sincere, but other times, it is not. In either case, it is likely to be as forcefully voiced.

32-5d Rent Seeking

Rent Seeking
Actions of individuals and groups who spend resources to influence public policy in the hope of redistributing (transferring) income to themselves from others.

Rent seeking consists of the actions of individuals and groups who spend resources to influence public policy in the hope of redistributing (transferring) income to themselves from others. To illustrate, suppose Corbin is one of many producers of shoes, and suppose he realizes that he would be better off if he were the only one who produces shoes. With less competition from other shoe producers, the supply of shoes would fall, and the price would rise. Corbin would then end up selling shoes at $200 a pair instead of $80 a pair.

In pursuit of his aim, suppose Corbin hires a law firm that specializes in lobbying government for its clients. Members of the law firm go to members of Congress and ask them to pass a law prohibiting all companies other than the Corbin Shoe Company from producing shoes. The attorneys representing Corbin promise to donate money to the political campaigns of the congressional members with whom they speak. They also promise that Corbin of Corbin Shoe Company will try to persuade his workers that their work interests are best served by voting for specific members of Congress.

In this scenario, Corbin is using resources to effect a transfer. Corbin has spent money to influence Congress to give him a special privilege: the right to be the only producer of shoes. In essence, Corbin is trying to bring about a transfer from shoe consumers to himself. He wants consumers to end up paying more for shoes so that he earns more from producing them. He is spending money to try to bring about this transfer from others to him. Corbin is a *rent seeker*: he is using resources (the money he spends goes for resources) in order to bring about a transfer from others to him.

Let's say that Corbin spends a total of $100,000 to bring about the transfer. This is the cost of his rent seeking. From Corbin's perspective, the decision to spend $100,000 to bring about a transfer of, say, $1 million is rational. But from society's perspective, all the resources that Corbin uses to effect a transfer are wasted. The $100,000 is wasted because money spent trying to effect a transfer cannot be used to produce goods and services.

To see the negative effects rent seeking has on society even more clearly, consider an extreme example. Let's say that today 1,000 individuals are all producing goods and services. Together, they produce about $2 million worth of output a day. Tomorrow, all 1,000 individuals decide to spend their time and money trying to bring about a transfer. In other words, instead of producing, they spend their time rent seeking. At the end of the day, the cost to society of these 1,000 individuals' rent seeking instead of producing is $2 million worth of output. Society is poorer by $2 million because the 1,000 individuals turned away from producing and toward rent seeking. In short, rent seeking is a socially wasteful activity.

32-5e Bringing About Transfers

In Exhibit 3, the market equilibrium price of a certain good is P_1. At this price, identifying both consumers' surplus and producers' surplus is easy. Consumers' surplus is the area under the demand curve and above the equilibrium price, out to the equilibrium quantity, Q_1: the triangular area $A + B + C$. Producers' surplus is the area under the equilibrium price and above the supply curve, out to the equilibrium quantity, Q_1: the triangular area $D + E$.

Now, suppose the producers of the good lobby government for a price floor, P_1. If government grants this floor, then the new price in the market is P_2, and consumers' surplus ends up being only area A. Consumers lose area $B + C$ in consumers' surplus. At the new price P_2, producers lose area E in producers' surplus, and they gain area B. As long as area E (what they lose) is smaller than area B (what they gain), producers are better off selling at price P_2 than P_1. In Exhibit 3, area E is clearly smaller than B, so producers are better off.

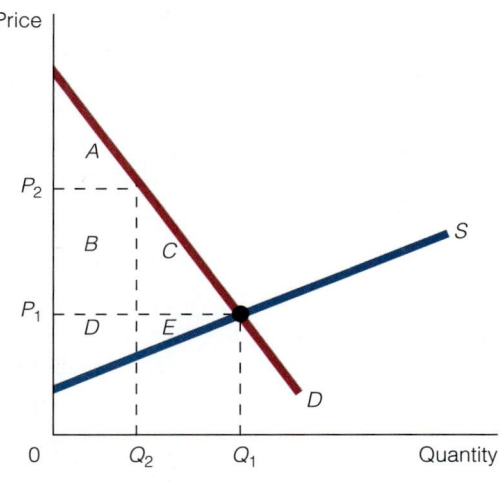

EXHIBIT 3

A Price Floor and a Transfer from Consumers to Producers

The market equilibrium price of the good is P_1. Consumers' surplus is the area $A + B + C$. Producers' surplus is the area $D + E$. If producers of the good lobby for and receive a price floor of P_2, then consumers' surplus ends up being only area A. Consumers lose areas $B + C$ in consumers' surplus, and producers gain area B in producers' surplus. By obtaining the price floor through government, producers of the good were able to take some consumers' surplus away from consumers and turn it into producers' surplus for themselves.

The price floor has thus created a transfer. Area B, which was once consumers' surplus, is now producers' surplus. By getting the price floor, the producers of the good were able to take some consumers' surplus away from consumers and turn it into producers' surplus. If area B is equivalent to, say, $1,000, then producers have been able to transfer $1,000 from consumers to themselves. All the resources that the producers expended to get that transfer of $1,000 are referred to as the *rent-seeking costs*—that is, the costs of trying to bring about the transfer. Again, from society's perspective, the resources expended to effect the transfer are wasted in that they cannot be used to produce goods and services. Society as a whole is just a little bit poorer because of the rent-seeking behavior of the producers.

32-5f Information, Rational Ignorance, and Seeking Transfers

Will rent seekers tell the truth about their rent-seeking efforts (assuming that they know the truth)? Suppose Corbin knows that his rent seeking will lead to greater producers' surplus for him and less consumers' surplus and that the losses to consumers will be greater than his gains. (If you look back at Exhibit 3, you will notice that the losses to consumers from the price floor—areas $B + C$—are greater than the gain of area B to the producer.) Will he advertise this information? Will he, for instance, lobby government by saying, "I would like a price floor for what I sell. I know that this will end up hurting consumers more than it benefits me, but so be it. As long as I am made better off, I don't really care how much consumers are made worse off. Can I have the transfer?"

He is unlikely to say this. For one thing, making such a barefaced request draws attention to the fact that he gains at consumers' expense and that his gain is smaller than what consumers lose. Corbin wouldn't draw attention to this fact. Instead, he might try to argue that what is good for him is good (not bad) for others.

Can such rent-seeking efforts be successful? Won't the politicians turn Corbin down because moving from an equilibrium price to a price floor hurts consumers more than it helps producers? (Yet there are price floors in the real world.) Won't consumers rally against Corbin because they know that they are being hurt by his actions? Moreover, aren't consumers greater in number than Corbin (who is only one), and don't politicians care about votes (which means that they must then care about the number of voters)?

First, consumers may not rally against Corbin, because they may not even know that he is lobbying government for a price floor. Recall the issue of rational ignorance—that is, not acquiring information because the costs of acquiring it are greater than the benefits.

Most individuals are rationally ignorant of many issues. If you know less about French literature than you could know, then you are rationally ignorant of the subject. If you know less about computers than you could know, then you are rationally ignorant of computers.

Similarly, many people are rationally ignorant of politics and government; that is, they know less than they could know—and that is largely because the marginal benefits of acquiring this kind of information are so low. And the benefits are low because an individual's one vote matters so little in the determination of an election, as we discussed earlier. In other words, the probability that your one vote will break a tie and decide who wins and who loses in an election—especially when millions of people are eligible to vote—is infinitesimally small.

So, if your vote is not going to determine the outcome of an election, what does it matter how much or how little information you have about the candidates, the issues, and the events? The answer to that question is perhaps best framed in terms of your options. Let's say two major candidates, *A* and *B*, are running for U.S. senator from your state. Then you have the following options:

- *Option 1:* Be fully informed (on the Senate election issues) and vote for *A*.
- *Option 2:* Be fully informed and vote for *B*.
- *Option 3:* Be rationally ignorant and vote for *A*.
- *Option 4:* Be rationally ignorant and vote for *B*.
- *Option 5:* Be fully informed and not vote.
- *Option 6:* Be rationally ignorant and not vote.

No matter which option you choose, the outcome of the election will be what it will be. Your vote will likely not break a tie; your vote will not determine the outcome of the election. Therefore, the least costliest option is obviously option 6, to be rationally ignorant and not vote.

Of course, not everyone chooses this option. In the last presidential election, approximately 159 million persons voted, although millions of other eligible voters chose not to vote. Of the approximately 159 million who did vote, probably very many were rationally ignorant. Being otherwise would have been just too costly for them, especially given the fact that very few of them were under the delusion that their single vote would determine outcome of the election.

So, if producers seek a transfer that ends up hurting consumers, consumers are not likely to know about it if they are rationally ignorant, and the incentive for them to be rationally ignorant is huge. Thus, when a producer lobbies members of Congress for a price floor that helps him and hurts consumers, the consumers may not even know about the rent seeking. And even if they do, do they also know that a price floor leads to a greater loss in consumers' surplus than an increase in producers' surplus, especially when the producer has an incentive not to state the details of the transfer? Instead, the producer will probably wrap his special-interest legislation in "public-interest talk." Perhaps he will argue that, without a price floor for his good, few producers will produce it and that if few producers produce the good, people will lose their jobs, communities will lose tax revenue, and so forth. None of this is necessarily true, of course, but trying to figure out whether it might be true may be too costly an effort for most individuals to undertake.

But suppose that rational ignorance does not exist: Everyone knows everything about everything. Then, when the producer lobbies government for a price floor, consumers immediately know about his activities; furthermore, they know that the loss of consumers' surplus (as a result of the price floor) will be greater than the gain in producers' surplus. Even so, consumers may still not fight the producers because, simply put, the loss to each individual consumer might be so small that it is not worth fighting to stop the price floor.

As an example, suppose 100 producers will receive a total benefit of $10 million if the price floor replaces the equilibrium price in the market. That amount is an average of $100,000 per producer. But suppose consumers will lose $15 million as a result of the price floor. If there are 100 million consumers, the average consumer loses only 15¢. A consumer will probably not spend $1 to fight a policy that costs him or her only 15¢.

The key in seeking transfers is to spread the loss from the transfer over as many people as possible so that, on a per-person basis, the loss is very small. The loss should be small enough that the individual will have little reason to argue against the policy that inflicts the loss.

32-6 Constitutional Economics

Most of economics deals with behavior within a certain set of constraints. For example, consider that your decisions as to what and how much to buy take place within income and price constraints. If your income is $1,000 a month and the price of all goods is $1, then you can purchase only 1,000 units of various goods a month.

Sometimes the constraints within which we choose are given, as in the example presented in the previous paragraph. But sometimes we *choose* to place ourselves within certain constraints. Consider a person who has decided that he wants to lose 15 pounds. To help himself lose the weight, he never keeps any snacks (potato chips, ice cream, or cookies) in his house. By this action, he has deliberately chosen to constrain himself (from eating snacks late at night when he knows that he is generally inclined to).

On a collective level, think of a group of people choosing to constrain their driving behavior by opting for speed limit laws. Each person reasons that, without such laws, he can drive as fast he wants to—but then, so can everyone else. But if all drivers can drive as fast as they want, there may be more accidents (and deaths) than if everyone had to obey a speed limit. Each person then opts to constrain his and everyone else's behavior by opting for speed limit laws.

In this chapter, we have discussed behavior within a political or government context. That behavior occurred within certain constraints. For example, voters could not vote more than once, elections were held every two or four years, and so on.

Might individuals living within a particular political setting seek to constrain themselves or others in some way in order to obtain better results than could be obtained in an environment without constraints or with different constraints? For example, at the current moment, there is no constraint as to how much the federal government can spend. Some people argue that, as a result of this absence of a limit, the federal government is likely to spend too much—as is manifest by the nation's large budget deficits. Suppose the federal government were to opt for a constraint on itself? Suppose the Congress were to pass a law that stated that it could not spend more in any given year than the projected tax revenues in that year. For example, if projected tax revenues were $3.2 trillion, then spending had to be $3.2 trillion or less. Passing such a law would constrain the Congress; it would place a ceiling on how much the Congress could spend in a given year.

There is a branch of economics called constitutional economics or constitutional political economy in which economists study the types of constraints that individuals might place upon themselves in order to achieve some objective that doesn't seem achievable in an environment that lacks constraints.

In fact, constitutional economists sometimes argue that better outcomes are more readily forthcoming out of government by changing institutions, constraints, laws, and rules than by changing people. In other words, within a given set of institutions, constraints, laws, and rules, outcomes might be the same no matter who is elected to office. For example, whether Republicans or Democrats are overwhelmingly elected to political office, big budget deficits might be the order of the day unless there is some constraint placed on government against running a budget deficit.

1. The average farmer is likely to be better informed about federal agricultural policy than the average food consumer is. Why?
2. Consider special-interest legislation that will transfer $40 million from group A to group B, a group with 10,000 persons. Is this legislation more likely to pass when group A consists of (a) 10,000 persons or (b) 10 million persons? Explain your answer.
3. Give an example of public-interest talk spoken by a special-interest group.
4. Why is rent-seeking activity socially wasteful?

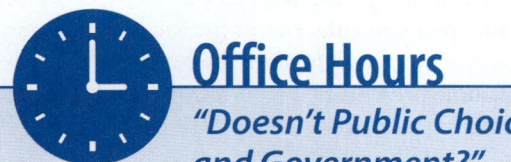

Office Hours

"Doesn't Public Choice Paint a Bleak Picture of Politics and Government?"

Student: In a way, public choice paints a rather bleak picture of politics and government.

Instructor: How so?

Student: Politicians don't seem to care about what is right or wrong. They just move to the middle of the voter distribution. People don't always vote, because voting is sometimes too costly. People aren't always well informed on issues, because accessing the information is too costly. And to top it off, special interests are engaged in rent seeking. Doesn't all this sound dismal to you?

Instructor: It sounds as if you want things to work differently. Well, unfortunately, as the Rolling Stones told us, "You can't always get what you want."

Student: I have to confess that I would like it if things worked differently. I want politicians to do the right thing, and I want people to be informed on issues and to cast intelligent votes.

Instructor: Many people probably want the same thing. My guess is that public choice economists want the same thing, but we can't let what we want color how we see the world.

Student: But who is to say that public choice economists analyze the world in the right way? Maybe they are an overly cynical bunch of economists.

Instructor: What they are doesn't matter. What matters is what they say and what they predict. We don't judge an economic theory by how it sounds to us or by how we feel about it; we judge it by how well it explains and predicts what we see in the world. If politicians move to the center of the voter distribution, if people are rationally ignorant, and if special interests sometimes engage in rent seeking, then that's the way things are, whether we like it or not.

Student: But aren't economists supposed to be trying to make the world better?

Instructor: Let's assume that they are. Then isn't a good understanding of the world critical to doing this? For example, if the world is X, and I think it is Y, then I might make mistakes when I try to make the world a better place. Basing what I do on how things are has to be better than basing them on how I might want them to be.

Student: I see your point. It's sort of like a doctor who wants to know your true condition before she prescribes any therapy. She may not like the fact that you have a particular disease, but it's important that she know about it so that she can prescribe the right medicine.

Instructor: I think that captures the spirit of what I'm talking about.

Student: Does it follow, then, that everything in public choice theory is right?

Instructor: No, it doesn't follow. Public choice theory—just like any theory in economics—has to be judged on how well it explains and predicts.

Points to Remember

1. Theories should be judged on how well they explain and predict (not on how they sound or feel).
2. Good economics seeks to know what exists, no matter how pleasant or unpleasant that is.

Chapter Summary

Politicians and the Middle: The Median Voter Model

- In a two-person race, candidates for the same office will gravitate toward the median voter. If a candidate does not do so and her opponent does, the opponent will win the election.
- Candidates usually pick labels for themselves that represent the middle of the political spectrum, they speak in general terms, and they take polls and adjust their positions accordingly.

Voting and Rational Ignorance

- Voting has both costs and benefits. Many potential voters will not vote because the costs of voting—in terms of time spent going to the polls and so on—outweigh the benefits of voting, measured as the probability of their single vote determining the election outcome.
- Being unable to learn certain information is different from choosing not to learn it. Many voters choose not to be informed about political and government issues because the costs of becoming informed outweigh the benefits of becoming informed. They choose to be rationally ignorant.

More About Voting

- In a simple-majority vote, given several options to choose from, the voting outcome is the same as the most preferred outcome of the median voter.
- Simple-majority voting together with equal tax shares can generate a different result from simple-majority voting together with unequal tax shares.

Special-Interest Groups

- Special-interest groups are usually well informed about their issues because individuals have a greater incentive to become informed about issues that directly and intensely affect them.
- Legislation that concentrates benefits on a few and disperses costs over many is likely to pass because the beneficiaries will have an incentive to lobby for it, whereas those who pay the bill will not lobby against it because each of them pays such a small part of the bill.
- Special-interest groups often engage in rent seeking, which is the expenditure of scarce resources to capture a pure transfer. Rent seeking is a socially wasteful activity because the resources used to effect transfers are not used to produce goods and services.

Constitutional Economics

- The subject matter of constitutional economics is choosing rules or constraints within which collective choices are made.
- Constitutional economists often argue that governmental outcomes will be more readily forthcoming by changing institutions, constraints, laws, and rules than by changing people. In other words, within a given set of institutions, constraints, laws, and rules, outcomes might be the same no matter who is elected to office.

Key Terms and Concepts

Public Choice
Median Voter Model
Rational Ignorance
Special-Interest Groups
Logrolling
Rent Seeking

Questions and Problems

1. Some observers maintain that not all politicians move toward the middle of the political spectrum in order to obtain votes. They often cite Barry Goldwater in the 1964 presidential election and George McGovern in the 1972 presidential election as examples. Goldwater was viewed as occupying the right end of the political spectrum and McGovern as occupying the left end. Would these two examples necessarily be evidence that does not support the median voter model? Are they exceptions to the theory explained in this chapter?

2. The economist James Buchanan said, "If men should cease and desist from their talk about and their search for evil men and commence to look instead at the institutions manned by ordinary people, wide avenues for genuine social reform might appear." What did he mean?

3. Would voters have a greater incentive to vote in an election involving only a few registered voters or in one that has many? Why? Why might a Republican label her opponent too far left and a Democrat label his opponent too far right?

4. Many individuals learn more about the car they are thinking of buying than about the candidates running for president of the United States. Explain why.

5. If the model of politics and government presented in this chapter is true, what are some of the things we would expect to see?

6. It has often been said that Democratic candidates are more liberal in Democratic primaries and Republican candidates are more conservative in Republican primaries than either is in the general election. Explain why.

7. What are some ways of reducing the cost of voting to voters?

8. Provide a numerical example that shows that simple-majority voting may be consistent with efficiency. Next, provide a numerical example that shows that simple-majority voting may be inconsistent with efficiency.

9. John chooses not to vote in the presidential election. Does it follow that he is apathetic when it comes to presidential politics? Explain your answer.

10. Some individuals see national defense spending as benefiting special interests—in particular, the defense industry. Others see it as directly benefiting not only the defense industry but the general public as well. Does this same difference between viewpoints apply to issues other than national defense? Name a few.

Chapter 32 Public Choice and Special-Interest Group Politics

11. Evaluate each of the following proposals for reform in terms of the material discussed in this chapter:
    a. Linking all spending programs to visible tax hikes
    b. A balanced-budget amendment stipulating that Congress cannot spend more than total tax revenues
    c. A budgetary referendum process whereby the voters actually vote on the distribution of federal dollars to the different categories of spending (x percentage to agriculture, y percentage to national defense, etc.) instead of letting elected representatives decide.

12. "Rent seeking may be rational from the individual's perspective, but it is not rational from society's perspective." Do you agree or disagree? Explain your answer.

Working with Numbers and Graphs

1. Suppose that three major candidates—A, B, and C—are running for president of the United States and that the distribution of voters is that shown in Exhibit 1. Two of the candidates—A and B—are currently viewed as right of the median voter, and C is viewed as left of the median voter. Is it possible to predict which candidate is the most likely to win?

2. Look back at Exhibit 2. Suppose that the net benefits and net costs for each person are known a week before election day and that it is legal to buy and sell votes. Furthermore, suppose that neither buying nor selling votes has any conscience cost (i.e., one does not feel guilty buying or selling votes). Would the outcome of the election be the same? Explain your answer.

3. In part (a) of the accompanying figure, the distribution of voters is skewed to the left; in part (b), the distribution is skewed neither left nor right; and in part (c), it is skewed right. Assuming a two-person race for each distribution, will the candidate who wins the election in (a) hold different positions from the candidates who win the elections in (b) and (c)? Explain your answer.

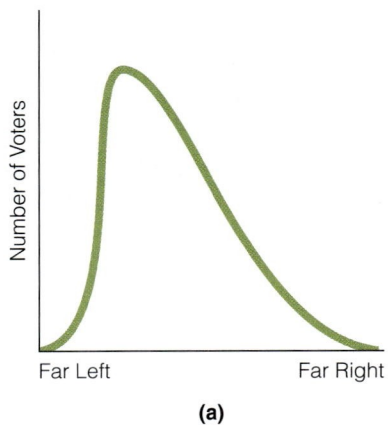

(a)

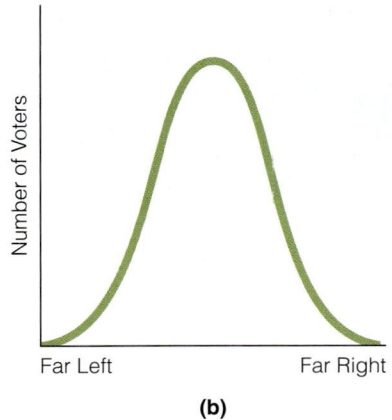

(b)

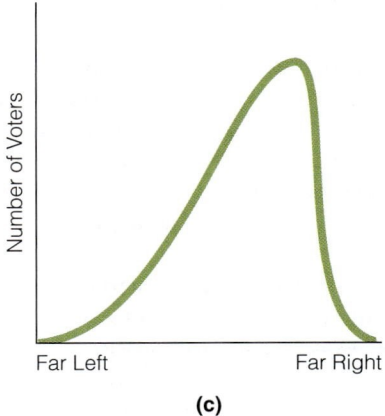

(c)

CHAPTER 33

New Frontiers in Economic Research: Causal Inference and Machine Learning

Introduction

Economics gives us a set of conceptual tools to understand the world. In the past, economic reasoning alone guided these tools, but now, we can use data to refute or validate theories. Each year, the amount of data available to us is increasing exponentially, and economics is a field of study that is being guided by data to a larger and larger extent.

In this chapter, we discuss new frontiers in economic research and, in particular, the role data play in economics today. We examine how economists have borrowed from the natural sciences, using natural experiments to find answers to important economic questions. We then take a look at a more recent innovation, the use of big data and machine learning techniques to make both predictions and policy recommendations.

33-1 Causal Inference

In any science—whether it be physics, chemistry, biology, or economics—a key objective is to figure out what causes observable phenomena to happen, but it isn't always easy to identify the cause.

When there are many things going on at the same time, scientists have to figure out a way to infer cause. This process of "figuring out" is called causal inference. In our case, the scientists are economists; in this section, we discuss how economists infer the causes of economic phenomena.

The main topic of our discussion is *natural experiments*. In what follows, we discuss three main ways economists exploit natural experiments: difference-in-differences, instrumental variables, and regression discontinuity. To provide a background of all three methods, let's explore the difference between correlation and causation.

33-1a Correlation and Causation

Did you know that European countries that have more storks tend to have higher (human) birth rates? Exhibit 1 plots the number of births in a country versus the number of breeding pairs of storks. As can be seen, countries with more storks tend to have more human births. Does this mean the myth that storks deliver babies is actually true? No. While there is a **correlation** between storks and birth rates, there is no causal effect of storks on birth rates. The fact that the two appear to be related in our data is just due to chance.

This is an example of a spurious correlation. **Spurious correlations** are everywhere in the world; if two things tend to move together, we say they are correlated. But economists are not generally interested in whether two things are simply correlated, but they are interested in whether they are *causally* related. Next, we consider an example of a causal question in economics and discuss how we might begin to answer it.

But before we get to that, here are some other instances of fairly strong correlations, but probably not causal relationships: global average temperature and the number of pirates (1820–2000), low-rated M. Night Shyamalan movies and newspaper sales (1999–2010), Mexican lemon imports into the United States and highway deaths (1996–2000), Facebook users and the yield on 10-year Greek bonds (2005–2011), and obesity and the total credit market debt as a percentage of gross domestic product (1962–2010).

Correlation
Any mutual relationship between two things, either causally or by chance. For example, professional basketball players tend to be taller than average, so basketball ability is correlated with height.

Spurious Correlations
When two things appear related, but the fact that they appear related is just due to random chance.

EXHIBIT 1

Do More Storks Cause Higher Birth Rates?

In the exhibit, we see that, generally, the greater the number of stork breeding pairs (horizontal axis), the higher the human birth rate (vertical axis). For example, Turkey has a greater number of stork breeding pairs than Greece does, and the birth rate is higher in Turkey than in Germany.

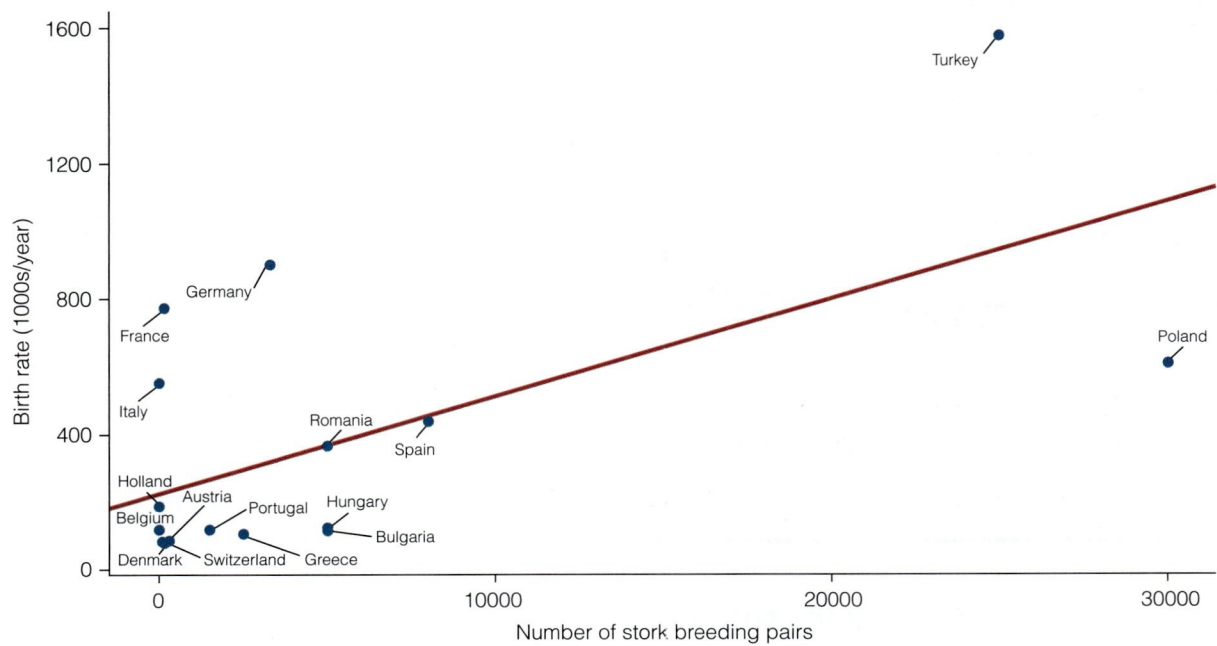

Source: Storks Deliver Babies (p = 0.008). *Teaching Statistics*, Volume 22, Issue 2, 2000, page 36.

Economics 24/7

Spurious Correlations

Look at Exhibit 2(a). There you see a red line and blue line. Notice that the two lines tend to move up and down together. The red line represents something, and the blue line represents something else.

Let's say that the red line represents X, and the blue line represents Y. Does it appear that X and Y are causally related? Many people might think so, and maybe, at first glance, you do too. But, in actuality, the red line represents the total revenue generated by arcades during the period 2000–2009, and the blue line represents the number of computer science doctorates awarded in the United States during the same period. See Exhibit 2(b), which is simply Exhibit 2(a), but with the arcade revenue and number of computer science degrees awarded identified. Is there a causal relationship between arcade revenue and number of computer science doctorates awarded? Probably not.

EXHIBIT 2(A)

33-1b Does the Minimum Wage Increase Unemployment?

In an earlier chapter, we discussed how the minimum wage impacts the quantity demanded of labor: An increase in the minimum wage increases the price of labor. When the price of labor goes up, the quantity demanded of labor declines, resulting in lower employment levels for unskilled workers.

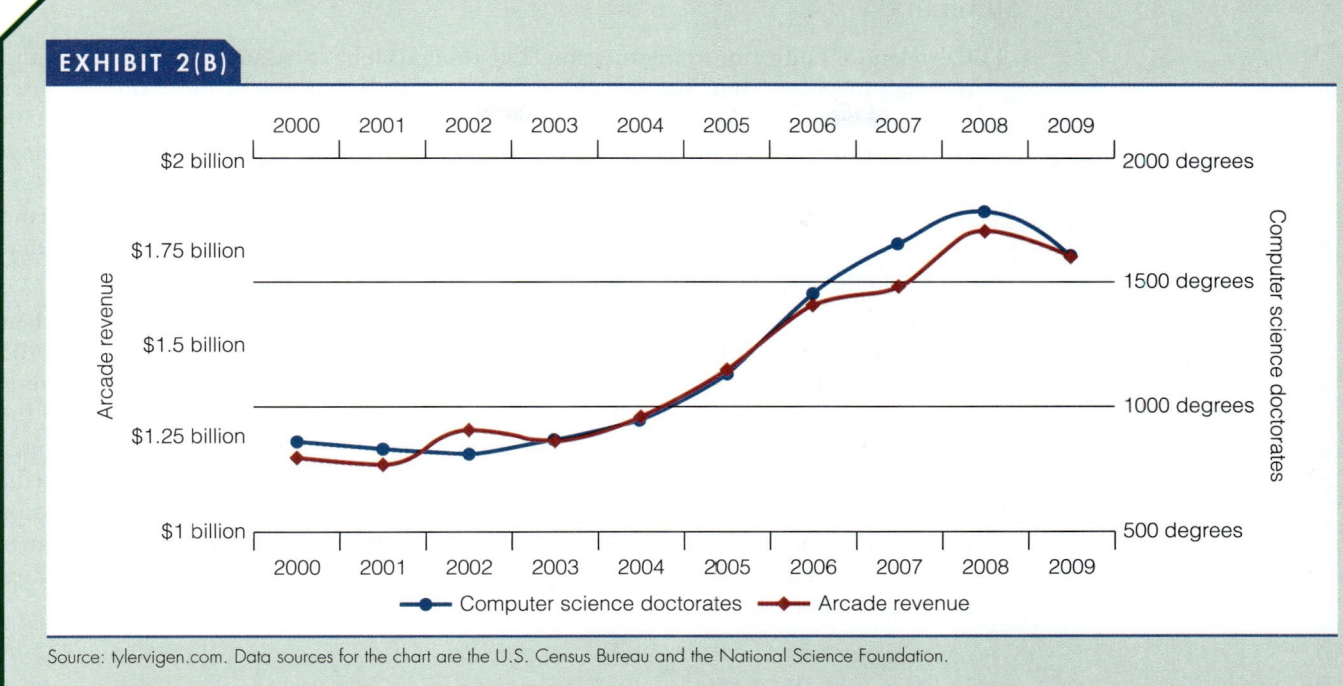

Source: tylervigen.com. Data sources for the chart are the U.S. Census Bureau and the National Science Foundation.

One naïve approach to estimate the effect of a minimum wage on employment is to look at variation across states. In the United States, there is a federally mandated minimum wage, and, in addition, some states set state-level minimum wage rates. For example, whereas the federally mandated minimum wage might be $7.25, a state could set its state-level minimum wage rate at $10.00, which supersedes the federally mandated minimum wage. State-level policies create variation in minimum wage rates from state to state.

Can we simply compare a high-minimum-wage state to a low-minimum-wage state to find out how much the minimum wage impacts employment? In other words, if state 1 has a high minimum wage rate and high unemployment among unskilled labor and state 2 has a low minimum wage rate and low unemployment among unskilled labor, does it then follow that a high minimum wage rate *causes* increased unemployment?

Before you answer, let's consider two real states, one with a higher minimum wage rate than the other. At the time of this writing, the State of Washington had set its minimum wage rate at $13.50 per hour. Nearby Idaho, on the other hand, had set its minimum wage rate at $7.50 per hour, which was equal to the federal minimum wage rate.

If we compare unemployment rates in Washington to unemployment rates in Idaho, does it seem reasonable that we will identify the causal effect of minimum wages? At first glance, you might think the answer is yes, but that would be assuming that everything in the two states is the same, except that one has a higher minimum wage rate than the other. The truth is that Washington and Idaho are different in more ways than simply one having a higher minimum wage rate than the other.

For example, on average, it costs much less to live in Idaho than in Washington, and the cost of living could impact unemployment rates. This is only a single difference between our two states; there are many more. Therefore, when we compare unemployment rates in Idaho and Washington, we are not truly estimating the causal effect of the minimum wage because it is just as likely that some other difference between the states—and not necessarily the difference in the minimum wage rate—is causing differences in unemployment rates.

Summary

1. Correlation is different from causation. Two things can be correlated—they increase and decrease together—but that fact alone does not mean that one of those things causes the other. For example, there are more dogs in the United States today than in 1950. There is also more obesity in the United States today than in 1950. But it doesn't follow that the increased number of dogs in the United States caused higher rates of obesity. While it is easy to see that correlation is not causation when we present an extreme example like this, the problem is that for many correlations, it is not so apparent that they are not causations.

2. Suppose we found that between two states one had a higher minimum wage rate than the other. In the higher-minimum-wage state the unemployment rate (among the unskilled) is higher than in the lower-minimum-wage state. In other words, there is a correlation between the minimum wage rate and unemployment. Do we know for certain that a higher minimum wage rate is the cause of the higher unemployment rate? No, there could be other factors at work in the two states that explain the difference in unemployment rates. In short, not everything is the same between the two states except for the difference in the minimum wage; consequently, we cannot rightly assume that it is the minimum wage rate that explains the difference in the unemployment rates between the two states.

33-1c Controlled Experiments

In our example considering the minimum wage and unemployment rates in Washington and Idaho, we couldn't be sure that the different minimum wage rates in the two states explain the different unemployment rates because there were so many factors that are different between the two states, not just the minimum wage rate.

Controlled Experiment
An experiment in which all factors between two groups except for one are the same. A randomized controlled trial (RCT) is often synonymous with a controlled experiment. In a randomized controlled trial, experimental subjects are randomly split into treatment and control groups.

In other sciences, such as medicine, there is a method to determining answers to causal questions: **controlled experiments**. For example, in a clinical trial for a pharmaceutical drug, who receives the drug and who receives a placebo (the group that receives the placebo is called the *placebo* or *control* group while the group that receives the drug is called the *treatment* group) are randomized. This type of experiment is often referred to as a randomized controlled trial (RCT).

Therefore, any difference in health outcomes between the treatment and the control groups must be due to the drug—as everything else between the two groups is the same. To illustrate, suppose two groups of people are chosen at random. Because the selection of groups is randomized, we can be fairly sure that the two groups have similar characteristics. In other words, they come very close to having "everything the same between them."

Then we introduce a difference between the two groups. We give one group a drug and we give the other group a placebo, and individuals in neither group know whether they received the drug or the placebo.

Now we wait to see if individuals in the two groups react differently to the drug than to the placebo. If individuals in the treatment group develop a cough and a rash but individuals in the control group (placebo) do not, then we can be fairly sure that it is the drug that caused the cough and the rash. In this case, we determine that the drug causes some harm. On the other hand, if individuals in the treatment group find their blood pressure has decreased and the members of the control group do not, then we can be fairly sure that the drug lowers blood pressure.

33-1d Natural Experiments

Economists unfortunately cannot perform controlled experiments in the way medical researchers can, but sometimes they can come close to a controlled experiment with what is called a **natural experiment**. In these instances, "nature" presents economists with what comes close to being a controlled experiment. Economists seek natural experiments that mimic controlled experiments. This enables economists to understand whether a relationship between two things is causation or merely correlation. Natural experiments have allowed economists to make progress on a wide range of issues.

Let's return to the earlier minimum wage discussion. Is there a natural experiment that can be undertaken to determine if there is a cause-and-effect relationship between changes in the minimum wage and employment? Fortunately, yes. In 1994, David Card and Alan Krueger identified such a natural experiment that convincingly allowed them to identify the effect of the minimum wage on employment.[1]

In 1992, New Jersey increased the state-level minimum wage from $4.25 to $5.05 per hour. Neighboring Pennsylvania, however, made no change to its minimum wage. Card and Krueger realized that eastern Pennsylvania is very similar to western New Jersey. They border each other and have very similar local economies. (This is different from our Washington–Idaho example, where there were likely to be big differences between the two states.)

Knowing that towns in New Jersey and eastern Pennsylvania tend to be similar, Card and Krueger hypothesized that restaurants in eastern Pennsylvania that continued to pay the unchanged minimum wage rate would be a good control group for restaurants in New Jersey that had to pay the recently increased minimum wage rate.

To see if a difference in minimum wage rates causes a difference in employment, we can compare the change in employment in western New Jersey to the change in employment in Pennsylvania—both before and after the minimum wage rate in New Jersey increased.

Let's consider a hypothetical example in which we have two restaurants: one in New Jersey and one in Pennsylvania. In 1991 (before the minimum wage rate increases in New Jersey), the New Jersey restaurant employs 20 workers. The Pennsylvania restaurant also employs 20 workers. These numbers are displayed on the vertical axis in Exhibit 3(a), and the year is displayed on the horizontal axis.

In 1992, the minimum wage rate was increased in New Jersey. Due to the higher labor costs, we see employment in the New Jersey restaurant drop by 5 workers, to 15 workers. On the other hand, we see employment in the Pennsylvania restaurant remains constant, at 20 workers. See Exhibit 3(a). Therefore, it appears that an *increase* in the minimum wage *decreases* employment by 5 workers.

Keep in mind that in this example we focused on the *change* in employment in the two restaurants. In the New Jersey restaurant, there was a change (a decrease) of 5 workers. In the Pennsylvania restaurant, there was no change, so the change in workers was 0.

But *what if* there had been a change in both restaurants? Suppose we had found that the number of workers in the New Jersey restaurant fell from 20 to 15 (a change of 5), and the number of workers in the Pennsylvania restaurant fell from 20 to 15 (a change of 5). See Exhibit 3(b). Would that finding have changed our estimate of the causal effect of the minimum wage? Yes. In that case, we could not unequivocally conclude that the minimum wage rate increase in New Jersey caused the decline in employment in New Jersey.

> **Natural Experiment**
> A study in which groups of individuals or places are exposed to a treatment by chance. For example, in 1992, New Jersey passed a law that increased the minimum wage. Therefore, workers in fast-food restaurants in New Jersey were exposed to the treatment (a higher minimum wage), while fast-food workers in nearby Pennsylvania were not.

[1.] See *Minimum Wages and Employment: A Case Study of the New Jersey and Pennsylvania Fast Food Industries* in The American Economic Review, Volume 85, 1994, page 772.

EXHIBIT 3

How to Estimate the Effect of a Minimum Wage Increase

In part (a), we consider a hypothetical case of two restaurants—one in New Jersey and one in Pennsylvania. Before the minimum wage change (which occurs in 1992), both restaurants have 20 employees. After the minimum wage increase, the number of employees in the New Jersey restaurant decreases to 15 while the number in the Pennsylvania restaurant remains stable at 20. Therefore, in this case, we estimate that the minimum wage corresponds to a decrease in employment by 5 workers. In part (b), we again consider a hypothetical case of two restaurants, one in New Jersey and one in Pennsylvania. Before the minimum wage change (in 1992), both restaurants have 20 employees. After the minimum wage change, the number of employees in the New Jersey restaurant and Pennsylvania restaurant both decrease to 15. Because there is no change in the minimum wage in Pennsylvania, the decline in employment in Pennsylvania must be due to some other factor that may also be impacting employment in New Jersey (such as an economic downturn in the region). Therefore, in this case, we estimate that the minimum wage has no effect on employment, because employment in Pennsylvania and New Jersey changed by the exact same amount.

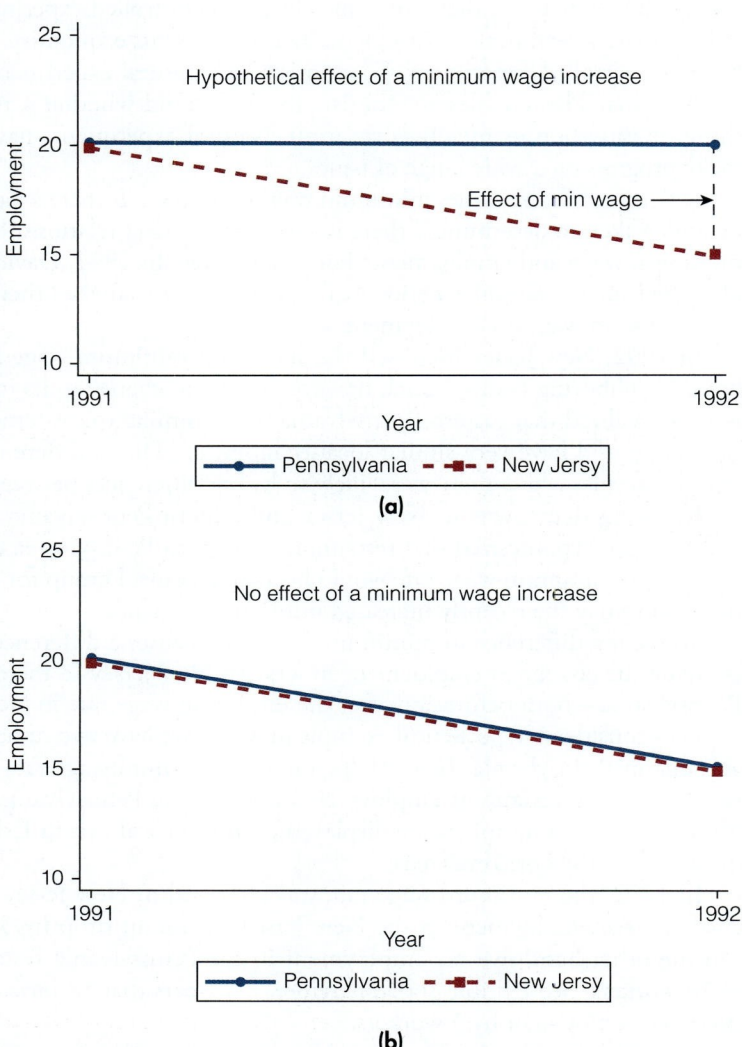

Difference-in-Differences A method to infer causality that compares differences between two groups (a treated group and a control group) over time.

In this case, since employment in both states declined—and since there was no change in the minimum wage rate in Pennsylvania, but there was an increase in the minimum wage in New Jersey—how could we be sure that whatever non-minimum wage factor caused the employment decline in Pennsylvania didn't also cause the employment decline in New Jersey? Maybe it was factor X in Pennsylvania that caused restaurant workers to go from 20 to 15 and caused the restaurant workers in New Jersey to go from 20 to 15, too. In other words, it wasn't the increase in the minimum wage rate that caused the decline in New Jersey; it was factor X.

Because we are comparing the *change* in New Jersey to the *change* in Pennsylvania, this is known as **difference-in-differences**. In short, we estimate the effect of the minimum wage change by computing the difference between employment changes in New Jersey and Pennsylvania. Hence, the name *difference-in-differences*.

What Card and Krueger (1994) did was survey fast food restaurants in both New Jersey and Pennsylvania and identified the number of restaurant workers in both states *before* and *after* the wage increase in New Jersey. They found that the levels of employment in New Jersey were relatively stable across time, even after the minimum wage increased.

Before we conclude that raising the minimum wage rate had *no effect* on employment in New Jersey, let's investigate what happened in Pennsylvania. Maybe this was a period in which the local economy (in eastern Pennsylvania and New Jersey) was expanding, and it was this "expansion" that offset the otherwise negative effects on employment of the minimum wage hike in New Jersey.

Card and Krueger also found relatively stable employment levels in the fast-food restaurants in Pennsylvania (actually, there was a small decline). Therefore, economic expansion was not a mitigating factor. Card and Krueger concluded that the increase in the minimum wage in New Jersey *did not decrease employment* in New Jersey.

But before we conclude that an increase in minimum wage never causes a decline in employment, remember that this is a natural experiment that "nature" presented to Card and Krueger in which the minimum wage rate was raised from $4.25 to $5.05. And based on what "nature" presented to them, they developed a natural experiment for which they concluded specifically that the minimum wage hike from $4.25 to $5.05 between 1991 and 1992 did not cause a decline in employment in New Jersey.

But suppose New Jersey had instead doubled its minimum wage rate from $4.25 to $8.50. Could we make the assumption that this relatively large increase in the minimum wage rate would have the same results? No. It may be that small increases in the minimum wage rate do not cause a decline in employment but that large increases do. It is important to remember that the results of a natural experiment cannot necessarily be generalized to hypothetical changes that have not occurred.

Summary

1. Sometimes "nature" presents us with a natural experiment that mimics the gold standard of experiments designed to identify causal relationships: the controlled experiment.

2. The essence of a natural experiment is that there is random selection of two groups, and one of the two groups can be used as the control group, and the other group can be used as the treatment group.

3. Card and Krueger's work in the New Jersey–Pennsylvania case was a natural experiment. There were strong similarities between the towns on the border of the two states. New Jersey increased its minimum wage rate, whereas Pennsylvania did not. This presented a key difference between the two states. Card and Krueger then examined whether this difference between the two states actually affected employment.

4. Results from natural experiments are only relevant for the specific natural experiment that is conducted. A given natural experiment is not necessarily applicable to hypothetical changes that have not occurred.

33-1e Natural Experiments in Macroeconomics

In macroeconomics, it is often more difficult to find such clear natural experiments. For example, when the Federal Reserve increases the money supply, this impacts the entire United States, not just some states and not others. Comparing across countries is often problematic, as there are often many differences between countries. In our previous example, while New Jersey and eastern Pennsylvania may be similar in terms of economic conditions, the same is not likely true when comparing the United States to other countries.

However, there are occasionally natural experiments that allow us to test macroeconomic theory. For example, a classic question in macroeconomics is whether increased lending to distressed banks during a bank run can quicken economic recovery. During the Great Depression, many banks began to fail; they did not have enough deposits on hand to pay their customers who came looking for their money. Households became fearful that their savings would disappear overnight, and so they rushed to their banks to withdraw their money from their accounts. This is called a *bank run*.

At the time, there were basically two schools of thought concerning how a central bank should respond to a bank run in order to promote economic recovery. The first school of thought promoted increased lending to distressed banks in order to provide the banks with enough liquidity to meet their customer withdrawals. This enables a bank to stay afloat during the downturn; in the long run, the bank will recover.

The second school of thought is to not increase lending. If the banks are failing because of an economic downturn, then artificially keeping them afloat will not lead to a recovery. It could instead waste resources and result in a slower economic recovery overall.

In the United States, there are 12 regional Federal Reserve District banks, and these banks do not always agree in terms of what particular policy should be implemented at a given time. For example, during the Great Depression, the Atlanta Federal Reserve District Bank decided to increase lending to distressed commercial banks that were experiencing bank runs. Meanwhile, the St. Louis Federal Reserve District Bank made the opposite decision. It feared that the banks would go out of business no matter what they did and therefore decided not to increase lending to them.

Interestingly, northern Mississippi falls under the St. Louis Fed's jurisdiction whereas southern Mississippi falls under Atlanta's jurisdiction. Therefore, some of the banks in Mississippi saw increased lending, while others did not. This gives us a clean natural experiment by which we can study the effects of different monetary (or lending) practices. In this case, we can simply compare the economy of northern Mississippi to that of southern Mississippi as the Great Depression progressed.

Economists Richardson and Troost (2009) compared bank survival rates in northern Mississippi and southern Mississippi.[2] They found that banks were more likely to survive in the region in which the Federal Reserve District bank increased lending. This led to a quicker economic recovery for the entire region. Therefore, in this setting, we have a very clear answer to the question of whether increased lending to distressed banks during a bank run can help in an economic recovery: The answer is yes. Increased lending can be a successful tool to prevent bank failures and quicken economic recovery.

(Answers to Self-Test questions are in Answers to Self-Test Questions at the back of the book.)

1. Between 2000 and 2009, the divorce rate in Maine and the per capita consumption of margarine both increased and decreased together. Does it follow that increases and decreases in the per capita consumption of margarine caused the increases and decreases in the divorce rate in Maine? Explain your answer.

2. In a controlled experiment, what does the control group refer to? What does the treatment group refer to?

3. What made the Card–Krueger study of the minimum wage rate in two states a natural experiment?

4. What was the finding of economists Richardson and Troost in their study of banks in northern Mississippi and southern Mississippi?

---

[2] See *Monetary Intervention Mitigated Banking Panics During the Great Depression: Quasi-experimental Evidence from a Federal Reserve District Border, 1929–1933* in Journal of Political Economy – Volume 117, Issue 6 – 2009, page 1031.

33-2 Lotteries: An Introduction to Instrumental Variables

So far, we have discussed how to use variation in policies across locations as natural experiments to identify causal relationships. However, this is not the only way to identify causal relationships from natural experiments. Next, we discuss another method—the use of *instrumental variables*. An **instrumental variable** is a variable that creates random variation among individuals. We focus on one type of instrumental variable you are probably familiar with: lotteries.

33-2a The Vietnam War Draft Lottery

When you mention the word *lottery*, people often think of gambling. "I bought a lottery ticket today; the payout is up to $325 million right now."

But lotteries don't always imply gambling. There are many instances of lotteries that have nothing to do with gambling. One example is the Vietnam War Draft lottery. On December 1, 1969, the United States conducted a lottery of persons within a certain age range to determine the order of call to military service in the Vietnam War. The way the lottery worked was that all 366 days of the year (including February 29) were printed on a slip of paper. The pieces of paper were then placed in plastic capsules and scrambled, and then the capsules were drawn one at a time.

The first date drawn was September 14. Individuals that were eligible for the draft and were born on September 14 would be the first to be called to active military service. The draw continued until every day of the 366 days had been drawn. If an individual had a birthday that was drawn early in the lottery, then there was a good chance that person would be drafted into military service. Later dates, however, weren't likely to be drafted.

The Vietnam War lottery design generated random variation in who served in the military. For example, individuals who were born on September 14 were drafted, as this was the first date drawn. However, individuals whose birthday was September 24 were not, as this was the last date drawn. The only difference between the two groups is that they were born 10 days apart. In other words, the individuals whose birthday was September 14 were really no different than the individuals whose birthday was September 24. It wasn't that the individuals whose birthday was September 14 were tall, smart, and athletic and the individuals whose birthday was September 24 were different in each case. Again, even though the persons born on September 14 were in the drafted group and the September 24 individuals were not, the individuals in both groups were still similar.

Economist Joshua Angrist used the Vietnam War Draft lottery to study the impact of military service on earnings.[3] One argument posed was that serving in the military can give an individual skills valued by the civilian sector, enabling veterans to obtain high-paying jobs after their military service. Another argument was that serving in the military displaces other activities that increase earnings—such as receiving education—and therefore leads to lower long-run earnings.

Without a draft—with a voluntary military service instead—comparing the earnings for veterans and non-veterans would not answer the causal question of whether military service

> **Instrumental Variable**
> A variable that creates random variation in a treatment. For example, if the treatment is "serving in the military," then we can use the outcome of the Vietnam War Draft lottery as an instrumental variable because being drafted (and therefore going on to serve in the military) was determined by chance.

---

[3] See *Lifetime Earnings and the Vietnam Era Draft Lottery: Evidence from Social Security Administrative Records* in The American Economic Review – Volume 80 – 1990, page 313.

Self-Select
Choosing for oneself to participate in something. For example, individuals who volunteer for military service self-select into the military. Individuals who are drafted do not self-select into the military.

increases one's earnings. That's because, with voluntary military service, individuals **self-select** into the military; they decide for themselves whether or not they want to join the military. And the individuals who select to go into the military could be very different than those who select not to enlist.

But a military draft doesn't have this *self-selection problem*. Again, with the Vietnam War Draft lottery, the people whose birthdays were picked early in the lottery were essentially the same as people whose birthdays were picked late in the lottery. It is the "randomness" that ensures that the two groups of individuals—those with birthdays picked early in the lottery and those whose birthdays were picked late in the lottery—are much the same people.

Angrist (1990) found that veteran status due to being drafted into the Vietnam War decreased earnings for White veterans by about 15 percent, both right after they left the military service and long after their service ended. In other words, their short-run and long-run earnings suffered. Results for minorities were more mixed, with some evidence that earnings were lower for minority veterans soon after they left military service but then higher in the long run.

Because the variation here (between those who served in the military and those who did not) was due to a draft lottery, Angrist was able to establish a causal relationship between military service and earnings.

33-2b School Lotteries

In some cities—such as Boston, Chicago, New Orleans, and New York—school assignments are partially randomized through a lottery. For example, if a school has more students who want to enroll in the school than places available, the available places are allocated by lottery. The school lottery then provides us with a way to find the causal effects of school quality.

For example, in Cullen, Jacob, and Levitt (2006), the authors use lotteries in the Chicago public school system to estimate the effect of randomly being assigned to a higher-quality school.[4] Students who win lotteries in this system have access to more and better resources. Contrary to expectations, however, the authors found no evidence that being randomly assigned to a higher-quality school improved student academic performance.

33-2c Judge Lotteries

In the United States, judges make numerous decisions. For example, in many criminal cases, the judge decides the incarceration length for the defendant. Some judges take a "tough on crime" approach and assign long incarceration lengths. One popular rationale for this stance is that longer prison sentences act as a deterrent to future crime. If the punishment is harsh, then defendants are supposedly deterred from committing future crimes once they are released.

Other judges, however, assign short incarceration lengths, with the rationale that longer prison sentences impose a high burden on individuals. Being in prison longer means that individuals will be out of the labor force for a long time, which may make it harder for them to find a job once released. And without a means to support one's self, they may actually be more likely to commit future crimes.

So how do we figure out whether longer incarceration lengths lead to more or less future crime? A naïve approach would be to compare outcomes for defendants that have long

---

[4] See *The Effect of School Choice on Participants: Evidence from Randomized Lotteries* in Econometrica, Volume 74, Issue 5, 2006, page 1191.

incarceration lengths to those who have short incarceration lengths, but this is not likely to identify what we want to identify, as individuals with longer sentences have likely committed more serious crimes. Therefore, it may not be surprising if individuals who are incarcerated longer for more serious crimes are actually more likely to reoffend after release than individuals who are incarcerated for shorter durations for less serious crimes.

What we need is a source of random variation. In this setting, we can consider the judge a defendant is assigned to (within a certain location) as essentially random. Therefore, one defendant may win the "judge lottery" by being assigned to a lenient judge. Another defendant charged with having *committed the same crime* and with the *same criminal history* may lose the "judge lottery" by being assigned to a strict judge.

Economist Michael Mueller-Smith uses this type of variation to study the effects of incarceration length on defendants in Texas.[5] He finds that defendants who "win the lottery" and receive shorter sentences are less likely to commit crimes after they are released than individuals who are incarcerated for longer. Additionally, he finds those with shorter sentences have higher quarterly earnings than those with longer sentences, indicating that longer incarceration lengths have negative impacts on an individual's earnings.

33-2d Lotteries, Randomness, and Instrumental Variables

The essence of all our lottery examples is that lotteries generate randomness, and randomness is what is needed so that we can be sure that people who are divided into two groups—such as those who were drafted into the Vietnam War and those who were not, those who went to the high-quality school and those who did not, and those with shorter prison sentences and those with longer prison sentences—are essentially the same people.

With both groups of people being essentially the same, we can determine whether a specific factor that differs between the two groups causes different results. Does being drafted into military service affect earnings? Does attending the high-quality school affect student performance? Does serving a longer prison sentence increase the probability an individual participates in crime after being released from prison?

There is a name for something, like a lottery, that can be used to identify whether a given factor can generate a difference or variation in effect between otherwise similar individuals: it is called an **instrumental variable**. The lottery, in all our examples, is an instrumental variable. Economists are always looking for new instrumental variables because instrumental variables create random variation across individuals. Just like experimenters create variation between the treatment and control groups in controlled experiments, instrumental variables create differences in natural experiments.

Summary

1. Lotteries are not just for gambling. We have discussed three other types of lotteries: the draft lottery, the school lottery, and the judge lottery. Lotteries are consistent with randomness and randomness is the setting in which causal relationships can often be identified.

2. An instrumental variable is any variable that creates random variation across individuals. The lottery, in all our examples, was an instrumental variable.

[5.] See *The Criminal and Labor Market Impacts of Incarceration* – Working Paper.

1. A person wants to find out if military service has an impact on earnings. Would it be better to study the earnings of individuals who were drafted by lottery into the military or individuals who joined the military voluntarily? Explain your answer.

2. In the discussion of the draft lottery, the lottery itself was considered an instrumental variable. In this context, what is an instrumental variable?

33-2e Regression Discontinuity Design

In our methods to infer causality so far, the key has been to identify situations in which individuals are randomly split into two groups: those who receive the treatment and those who do not. In our next method, this will still be the key, but we will utilize a particular type of variation—variation due to cutoff rules.

To understand this next method, let's focus on the word *discontinuity* in the term **regression discontinuity design**. Many policies involve discontinuities. For example, in some countries, college admissions are based solely on test scores. When a university is making admission decisions, it chooses a **cutoff rule**; it then accepts applicants with a score above or equal to the cutoff and rejects applicants with a score below the cutoff. This cutoff rule therefore creates a discontinuity in admissions decisions at the threshold for acceptance.

Why is this helpful in our pursuit of identifying causal relationships? To answer this question, let's expand on our university admission example. Imagine that we want to identify the causal effect of attending highly ranked University X on the earnings of its students. If we think of students attending highly ranked University X as the treatment group, we need a proper control group—a group that is similar but that does not attend University X.

Is the general population of students a good control group? Probably not. Individuals that attend highly ranked University X are probably different than those chosen from the general population in a variety of dimensions. For example, on average, individuals attending highly ranked University X probably have much higher test scores than the general population.

So how can we identify the causal effect of attending University X? One possibility is to compare students who are *barely accepted* to the university to those who are *barely rejected*. For example, imagine University X bases its admission decisions on a single test score and decides to reject students with a score less than 90, and accept all students with a score greater than or equal to 90.

Individuals who receive a score of 89 are probably just as smart as individuals who receive a score of 90. The only difference is a single point on the exam, which could reasonably be due to luck. Maybe the person who received the 90 happened to guess better that day than the individual who received an 89. Even though these two students have similar overall ability, the student with a 90 is accepted to University X, while the student who received an 89 is rejected.

This basic insight gives us a way to construct a control and treatment group by exploiting the *discontinuity* in admissions. Individuals who are just *barely accepted* are probably quite similar to individuals who are just *barely rejected*. By using the students around the discontinuity (i.e., the cutoff rule for admissions) we are able to mimic a controlled experiment. We can simply compare earnings for the students who just barely pass the threshold for admission (the treatment group) to students who just barely fall below the threshold for admission (the control group) to identify the causal effect of attending highly ranked University X on earnings.

The key to using a regression discontinuity design (to identify causal effects) is to look for settings with cutoff rules. Another example of using a cutoff rule are elections. Because this may not be immediately obvious, let's consider a very specific type of election: labor union

---

Regression Discontinuity Design
A method to identify causal effects by using a cutoff rule. For example, if admissions to a university were determined solely by a test score, then those who fall just below the threshold for admission are probably quite similar to those who fall at or just above the threshold. Therefore, we can compare their outcomes (such as earnings) over time to identify the causal effect of attending the university.

Cutoff Rule
Any decision that is made that is determined by a threshold.

elections. In the United States, when a workforce seeks to unionize, they will generally hold an election. If more than 50 percent of the workers vote to unionize, then the workforce will become unionized. If less than 50 percent of the workers vote to unionize, the workforce will remain without a union.

A classic question in labor economics is what the cost of unionization is to firms. For example, one argument is that unions increase the cost of labor, which may make firms less profitable and lead to the firms going out of business. While it seems simple to compare survival rates for firms in which the workforce is unionized to firms in which the workforce is not unionized, this will not identify the causal effect of unions on firms in general. For example, maybe unions only form in very large and productive firms. Therefore, if we compare unionized firms to nonunionized firms, we might find that unionized firms survive longer. But this may simply be due to the fact that unionized firms are formed in larger and more productive firms.

What we need is a way to construct a control group for unionized firms. We can apply a similar intuition as in the university admissions example. In that example, students who score just below the cutoff for admissions are rejected and students who score equal to or just above the cutoff are accepted. Therefore, we could construct our treated group as students who are barely accepted and our control group as students who are barely rejected.

Similarly, firms in which the vote share to unionize is 50 percent or just above 50 percent are probably similar to firms in which the vote share to unionize is just below 50 percent. The only difference is a few votes. Therefore, in this example, our treatment firms are firms that just barely have enough votes to unionize, while our control firms have just barely too few votes to unionize.

Dinardo and Lee (2004)[6] use this insight to compare outcomes for firms in which a union barely won an election to firms in which a union barely lost an election. Given how close these election outcomes are in practice, whether or not a firm is unionized is due mostly to random chance in this setting,

Dinardo and Lee found very small impacts on employment levels and firm survival rates from unionization. It is often argued that unionization will lower total employment by making labor more expensive. However, this did not seem to be true in this setting. Firms that barely unionized have the same number of workers as firms that barely did not unionize. Therefore, it does not seem to be true that unionizing lowers the total number of workers in a firm.

Summary

1. In some settings, treatment and control groups are determined by a cutoff rule. Individuals just above the cutoff will receive treatment. Individuals just below will not. The individuals near the cutoff will tend to be quite similar, so by comparing individuals near the cutoff on either side, we can mimic a controlled experiment.

2. One example of a regression discontinuity design is college admissions. In some countries, admissions are entirely determined by a test score. Students scoring just below a cutoff for admissions are rejected, and students scoring equal to or just above the cutoff are accepted. Therefore, we can compare earnings for students who are barely rejected to students who are barely accepted to identify whether there is a causal effect of attending the university on earnings.

[6.] See *Economic Impacts of New Unionization on Private Sector Employers: 1984–2001* in The Quarterly Journal of Economics, Volume 119, Issue 4, page 1383.

33-2f Summary of Causal Inference

We started this investigation of causal inference with an explanation of the difference between correlation and causation. Just because X and Y are correlated, it doesn't follow that X causes Y or that Y causes X. Correlation is never—we repeat, *never*—enough to establish causation.

In their research, economists are interested in identifying the cause of certain effects. They set out to scientifically establish true cause–effect relationships when it comes to economic phenomena. It would be helpful if economists could conduct controlled experiments, but they often can't. So they are left with having to *infer* causality. They infer causality by finding situations in the real world that mimic controlled experiments—situations in which nature has provided a treatment group and a control group. The key to finding such settings is to search for random variation.

33-3 Big Data and Machine Learning

In our discussion of causal inference, data played a large role. Data was used to infer causal relationships. Data continues to play a large part in our upcoming discussion, but here, rather than being used to infer causal relationships, data is used to make accurate predictions. In this section, we look at relatively new fields in economics: big data and machine learning.

33-3a The Goal of Big Data and Machine Learning

Big data and machine learning have already revolutionized some industries. In business, the often-immediate objective is to predict something. For example, if you run a business, you might want to predict which individuals are most likely to buy your product.

In order to accurately predict who will buy your product, you need to collect data. For example, you might find that persons with a college education are more likely than persons without a college education to buy your product. Knowing this, you can target your ads to individuals who have a college education, because they are likely to become your customer base.

Here you are not so much concerned with a causal relationship—you are not trying to figure out what *causes* people with a higher education to buy your product; you are simply trying to predict *which* people are most likely to buy your product.

Increasingly, predictions are made through the use of **machine learning**. While machine learning sounds complex, for most purposes, it can be thought of as a way to use characteristics (often referred to as *features*) to predict an outcome.

To illustrate, suppose a company has a long list of consumer characteristics. This list has information on consumer age, household location, educational level, credit scores, and so on. How can the company determine which characteristics are the most important in making accurate predictions about who, when, and where consumers will buy the company's product? How can the company determine whether or not consumer age—or location, or highest level of education—is important?

Machine learning gives us a way to select the most important and relevant variables and then use these variables to make accurate predictions. The specific way in which the variables are chosen and used to form predictions varies across different **algorithms**. Algorithms are the specific sets of steps that a computer takes in order to learn what variables are important for prediction. An enormous number of algorithms have already been developed for various purposes. While not all machine-learning algorithms are alike, they do share a set of common features, which we discuss next.

Machine Learning
Computer algorithms that discover how to perform a task without explicitly being programmed to do so.

Algorithm
An algorithm is a sequence of operations used to perform some task, often by a computer.

Economics 24/7

Netflix and Big Data

You are scrolling through Netflix, and you see Netflix's "Top Picks" for you. You look through the selection and find yourself nodding in agreement with Netflix's choices. Netflix knows you so well! But how did it figure out what you would like to watch?

The answer is that Netflix uses machine learning. In 2006, Netflix held an open competition for programmers, academics, and hobbyists to build an algorithm that can recommend movies to customers better than Netflix's own algorithm, Cinematch. The prize was one million dollars.

It took three years, but in 2009, a team called BellKor's Pragmatic Chaos built an algorithm that beat Netflix's algorithm and claimed the million-dollar prize. As required by the competition, the winners published the algorithm used to win the competition. It was complicated, to say the least.

KOBLIZEEK / ALAMY STOCK PHOTO

Instead of a single algorithm, BellKor's Pragmatic Chaos used hundreds of algorithms, with their final recommendations being an average of the hundreds of different algorithms. This is called an *ensemble method* and works much like averaging. If you ask 100 people to guess how many jelly beans are in a jar, some might guess too many, others too few, but on average, they will probably get close to the right answer. In the same way, one algorithm might determine a given movie is a bad recommendation, and another one might determine that the movie is a good recommendation. On average, the many algorithms will tend to recommend the right movies.

33-3b Regularization

One question any machine-learning algorithm must answer is which variables should be included when making a particular prediction. Should one's age, educational level, and family background be used in predicting one's income, and should one's consumption of pizza, shoe size, and handwriting ability not be used? When trying to make accurate predictions, it is tempting to consider as many variables as possible. Surely more data is better, right? It turns out that is not always true.

For example, imagine a university wants to target online ads for a specific academic program (say, the MBA program) to certain individuals. The university may have access to a wealth of data on individuals, including birth date, gender, hobbies, current education, and so on. Does the university want to use every variable available to predict whether a given individual is likely to apply to the program that it is advertising? Not necessarily.

To see why, consider the following. Suppose the university identifies the characteristics of the students who are currently in the program it is thinking of advertising. It finds that they tend to be between 18 and 25 years of age. Thus, it seems reasonable to target the advertisement to individuals in this age group.

But, then, the university notices that more of their current students were born on Monday than any other day of the week. Should "born on Monday" be added to the algorithm? Probably not. That's because within every sample of students, there are likely to be some variables that seem important simply due to random chance. The fact that more of the current students were born on Monday than any other day of the week is almost certainly due to random chance. It is hard to imagine why the day of the week one was born on would have anything to do with one's educational decisions.

So how do we go about identifying which variables (among potentially thousands of variables) are truly important for our prediction? **Regularization** refers to the process of eliminating variables that are only weakly related to our target of interest. To make better predictions, we should exclude these variables. In our example, "born on a Monday" clearly should be excluded, but in other cases, it will not be so obvious which variables should be eliminated. Is there a data-driven way to separate the valuable variables from the worthless ones? The answer is the topic of the next section.

33-3c Cross-Validation

Consider again the example of the university trying to predict who will likely be interested in a particular academic program. How do we determine *definitively* that "born on a Monday" should not be included in the university's predictive algorithm?

One answer is *cross-validation*. Imagine instead of having data on just one year of students enrolled in the program, we now have data on two years of students. In the first year of students, we find that students are more likely to be born on a Monday. We think this is probably due to a spurious correlation, but how can we be sure?

One simple way is to check to see if this is true in the second year of enrolled students. If we look at the second year of students and find that they are not more likely to be born on Monday, then this is good evidence that our finding in the first year was just a fluke. Given that it was just a fluke, it is probably not a good idea for the university to target its ad to individuals who were born on Monday.

Cross-Validation
A technique used to assess whether a set of results will generalize to a different setting or dataset.

This is a simplified version of **cross-validation**. The basic idea of cross-validation is that if a variable is strongly predictive, then it will likely be predictive no matter how the data is "sliced." For example, if we split the data into two equal parts, then for a variable to be strongly predictive, it should predict accurately in both splits of the data. If it is only predictive in one split of the data, then it was probably just a fluke. In our university example, if "born on Monday" is truly a good predictor of individuals who will be interested in the academic program, then it should have shown up in both years of student data. If we had had data on three years, it should have shown up in all three years. But if it didn't, then it probably is not a valuable variable to consider when trying to make accurate predictions.

33-3d Machine Learning and Public Policy

In addition to its usefulness in making predictions on consumer purchases, machine learning can also be used to make public policy decisions. For example, pretrial detention (being placed in jail before a trial date) is a setting in which prediction plays a key role in policy.

In the United States, when individuals are arrested for a crime, they often have a bail hearing before being either detained or released. At the bail hearing, the judge looks over the characteristics of the defendant—including criminal history if there is one, the current charge against the defendant, and so on—and makes a bail decision. Often, the judge releases the individual with no conditions—known as "release on recognizance." In other words, there is no need to post bail; the individual can go now and return for trial.

At other times, the judge assigns a bail amount that the defendant must pay before being released. In some cases, this will be a relatively low amount; in other cases, the bail can be quite substantial. If the individuals are unable to pay bail, they are detained (in jail) until their trial date. Additionally, if the judge determines defendants are too high risk to be released, the judge can order them to be detained until the trial.

In making the decision, the judge has a *prediction problem*. Judges must use observable characteristics (age, criminal history, etc.) to predict defendants' future behavior. Will this defendant commit further crimes while out on bail? Will this defendant show up in court?

What many judges rely on in making their predictions is their expertise and experience. The judge might reason: *I have seen this type of defendant before and usually this type of defendant, given this type of crime, doesn't show up for trial.* In some sense, over time, judges develop a mental algorithm that assists them in making predictions. But this is not the only way one can proceed?

Another option is to use a machine-learning algorithm to predict whether a defendant will fail to appear at a future court date or will participate in further crime if released. In Kleinberg et al. (2018), the authors explored the potential gains from using such an algorithm.[7] They found that replacing judges with a machine-learning algorithm could simultaneously (1) release more defendants before trial and (2) decrease failure-to-appear rates. It can achieve both goals simultaneously by only assigning bail to those defendants with the highest probability of missing future court dates.

33-3e Algorithmic Fears

While machine-learning algorithms provide a potential improvement over judicial decision making, some fear that this gives too much power to an algorithm. Why might we be afraid of this? There are a few reasons.

One concern is that machine-learning algorithms might overlook important considerations when making a decision. For example, imagine a judge who faces two defendants. The machine-learning algorithm finds that one defendant is high risk and therefore recommends no bail with immediate detention or, instead, an extremely high bail amount. The other defendant is found to be low risk, and the recommendation is release on recognizance.

Why might the judge decide to overrule the machine-learning algorithm? One reason is that the judge may think it important to weigh many different factors (not just one) when making a decision. For example, the high-risk individual may be unemployed, and the judge may fear that assigning a high bail amount might place an undue burden on the individual. In this case, the judge and algorithm disagree because the algorithm only considers whether a given defendant is expected to appear at a future court date. It does not care about other factors. Some believe that by focusing on only one factor, we may miss other important and relevant considerations.

Another worry is that an algorithm may discriminate against minorities. To understand how this might arise, suppose that income in the lowest income bracket is highly predictive of a defendant failing to appear on trial date. If minority defendants have lower incomes on average, then the algorithm will automatically tag minority defendants as higher risk. Therefore, on average, minority defendants will be more likely to be assigned monetary bail before trial than nonminority defendants.

Given the potential for **algorithmic discrimination**, Kleinberg et al. (2018) consider how a machine-learning algorithm's decision would directly compare to the current status quo. Contrary to potential fears, they find that a machine-learning algorithm actually increases release rates for minority defendants relative to other defendants.

Algorithmic Discrimination
In some cases, algorithms may unfairly treat one group favorably relative to another group. For example, an algorithm that is more likely to recommend a male job applicant relative to an equally qualified female applicant would exhibit algorithmic discrimination against women.

[7.] See *Human Decisions and Machine Predictions? Quarterly Journal of Economics*, Volume 133, Issue 1, 2018, page 237.

33-3f Summary of Big Data and Machine Learning

We started with a problem. We want to predict something, and we have a potentially huge number of variables, but how do we decide which ones to use, and how do we use the variables to form predictions? One potential answer is to use the recent progress that has been made in machine learning. This subset of statistics provides powerful tools to make the most accurate predictions possible.

While machine learning has traditionally been used in businesses, it is starting to have an impact in the social sciences. Many policy problems can be thought of as prediction problems. Who should have to pay bail before being released after an arrest? What areas are most likely to experience gun violence? Where should public services be allocated to make the greatest impact in terms of, say, employment or health?

33-4 The Importance of Data

In both our topics in this chapter—causal inference and machine learning— the key factor is data. Each year, data is becoming a more important component of economic research. We need data in order to answer questions and test economic theories. Recently, researchers have classified whether an economics paper is empirical (indicating data is being used) or theoretical (indicating no data is used) for more than 100,000 economic articles.[8] In Exhibit 4, the authors of this work plot the fraction of empirical papers (the vertical axis) over time (the horizontal axis) across many fields of economics. Across all fields, there has been a steady rise in the fraction of papers that use data. Given the massive increase in data availability and computing power in recent years, this is a trend that will likely continue in the future.

EXHIBIT 4

Economics Is Becoming More Data Driven Each Year

In this exhibit, which appears in a research article titled "Economics Research Evolves: Fields and Styles," the authors classified articles as empirical or theoretical. An empirical paper uses some sort of data analysis. On the vertical axis, we see the fraction of all papers that are classified as empirical, and the horizontal axis plots the year. As can be seen in the exhibit, across many different fields of economics, the fraction of papers that uses data has been steadily increasing year after year.

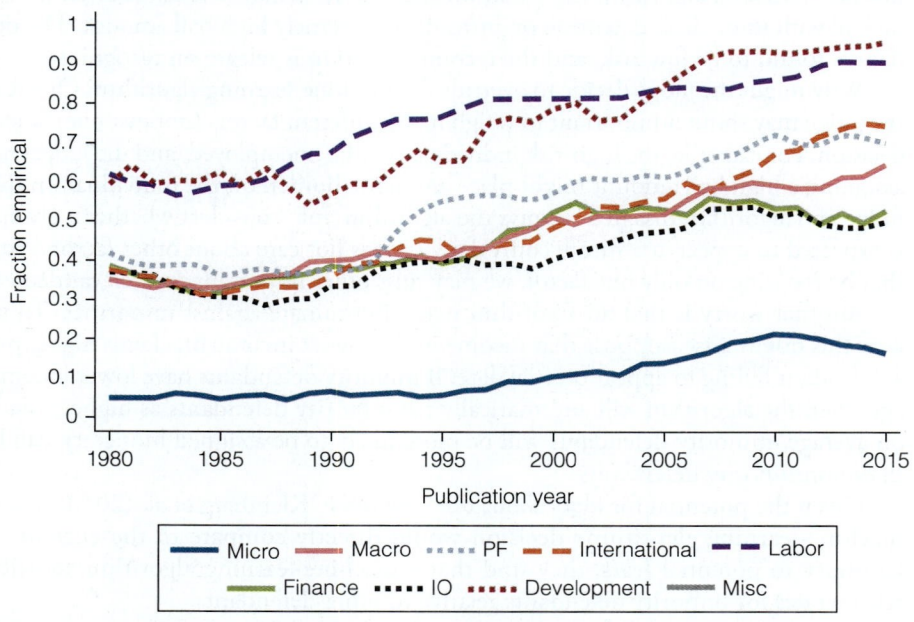

[8]. See *Economics Research Evolves: Fields and Styles* in American Economic Review: Papers and Proceedings – Volume 107, Issue 5 – 2017, page 293.

1. What does regularization refer to?
2. What was the conclusion of the Kleinberg et al. (2018) study on judicial decision making and a machine-learning algorithm when it comes to predicting failure to appear for trial?

Office Hours

"I've Got a Question on Each of the Three Topics: Natural Experiments, Instrumental Variables, and Algorithms?"

Student: How do researchers know when they have a good natural experiment? Are there such things as bad natural experiments?

Instructor: The good, or most effective, natural experiments are those that mimic as closely as possible a controlled experiment, in which there are two groups—a control group and a treatment group—of similar characteristics. Moreover, one of the two groups—the treatment group—is exposed to some condition or some factor that the control group is not. A bad "natural experiment" wouldn't be a natural experiment at all because it wouldn't have a clear-cut control and treatment group.

Student: Going back to the Card–Krueger study of the minimum wage, then, the two groups would be the group in eastern Pennsylvania and the group in New Jersey. And the group in eastern Pennsylvania was the control group while the group in New Jersey was the treatment group.

Instructor: That's right. And the New Jersey group was the treatment group because that group was exposed to the increase in the minimum wage in the state.

Student: Now let me ask you a question about *instrumental variables*. When I read the term "instrumental variable," I think of a single variable. For example, one's income might be a variable, or one's height, or one's weight. But in the text, it seems to say that a "lottery" is an instrumental variable. But a lottery isn't something singular like one's income, or one's height, and so on. The dictionary definition of a lottery is this: "a process or thing whose success or outcome is governed by chance." I guess my question is how can a variable, as in instrumental variable, be a process? Variable seems to connote one singular factor. But a process is a method of doing something.

Instructor: When a lottery is undertaken, there are those that win the lottery and those that lose the lottery. Therefore, you can think of the instrumental variable as the *outcome* of the lottery. In other words, just like we can describe an individual's income and height as variables, we can also include a variable that indicates whether an individual won or lost a given lottery.

Student: I hear a lot of talk these days about algorithms. Do data specialists actually write computer code for algorithms? Is that how things are done? In other words, an algorithm is really just a set of instructions that specifies what to do. For example, someone might come up with an algorithm to simply go through all the data that is available and pick up any statement in which the word "money" appears. Next, those statements in which the word "money" are gathered and sorted according to whether they also contain the word "steal" too. All of the statements that have both "money" and "steal" in them are identified. Is this an algorithm?

Instructor: An algorithm is any set of rules or steps. Often the set of rules or steps is written in computer code and evaluated by the computer in order to perform some specific task. For example, if the goal of the programmer is to collect all statements with the word "money" and "steal," the programmer can tell the computer (using code) to start at the beginning of the document and scan for these words. The programmer instructs the computer to proceed to the next sentence if the words are not in the sentence and to copy the sentence if the words are in the statement. This is a clear list of operations that a computer can perform. Therefore, it is an algorithm.

Points to Remember

1. A good natural experiment creates random variation across individuals or locations. This allows us to construct a treatment and control group that are more or less identical on all dimensions, with the only difference being the treatment of interest.
2. Computer algorithms are simply sets of steps that are used to perform an action. Computer programmers can build algorithms using computer code.

Chapter Summary

Causation Is Not Correlation

- A correlation is when two things tend move together. But sometimes two things moving together might just be due to random chance. What economists often care about is whether two things are *causally* linked—that is, whether *X causes Y* or whether *Y causes X*.

How to Identify Causal Effects

- Medical scientists have a clear and convincing way to identify causal effects. They run controlled experiments. For example, to test the effectiveness of a pharmaceutical drug, one group (the treatment group) is given the drug, while another group (the control group) is given a placebo. Who is selected for the treatment and control group is entirely random; therefore, any differences in health between the treatment and control group must be due to the drug.
- In economics, it is generally difficult (if not impossible) to conduct controlled experiments. However, economists can find situations in the real world in which individuals or places are sorted into a treatment group and control group in a somewhat random manner. Therefore, they can use these situations to identify causal effects.

Natural Experiments

- Natural experiments are situations in the real world in which some places or people receive a treatment while others don't. For example, a minimum wage change can be used as a natural experiment. The key in an effective natural experiment is to make sure the treatment and control group are as similar as possible. For example, in Card and Krueger (1994), the authors use New Jersey (a state that experienced a minimum wage increase) as the treatment group and nearby Pennsylvania (a state that did not experience a minimum wage increase) as the control group in order to identify the effect of a minimum wage hike on employment in restaurants.

Instrumental Variables

- Instrumental variables are variables that create random variation in a treatment across individuals. For example, lotteries are one type of instrumental variable. In the Vietnam War draft, one group of persons was drafted and served in the military; another group was not drafted and did not serve in the military. Because persons in the two groups were only determined by the birth date of the individual, this lottery generated random variation as to who ended up serving in the military. Therefore, it was possible to compare the earnings of individuals in the two groups to identify the causal effect of serving in the military on earnings.

Regression Discontinuity Design

- Regression discontinuity design refers to situations that involve a cutoff rule. For example, in some countries, admissions to universities are determined by a cutoff on a test. Individuals who score just below the cutoff on a test are rejected, and individuals who score at or just above the cutoff are accepted. If we are interested in estimating the effect of attending a given university on earnings of its students, we can compare earnings for students that are barely accepted to students that are barely rejected. The students that are accepted are the treatment group, and the students that are rejected are the control group. The intuition for this approach is that small differences in test scores are probably mostly driven by chance. For example, a marginally accepted student may have made slightly better guesses than a marginally rejected student, but the two probably have similar levels of ability overall.

Big Data and Machine Learning

- When it comes to big data and machine learning, we are no longer interested in causal effects; instead, we are interested in prediction. In order to make accurate predictions, we must find a way to deal with potentially huge datasets. Machine learning offers a set of tools to accomplish this. It enables us to find the most important variables for prediction. While this has been traditionally applied in business settings (e.g., to predict who will buy a product), it is becoming increasingly used in policy decisions. In order to inform good policy, we often need good predictions.

Key Terms and Concepts

Correlation
Spurious Correlation
Controlled Experiment
Natural Experiment

Difference-in-Differences
Instrumental Variable
Self-Select

Regression Discontinuity Design
Cutoff Rule
Machine Learning

Algorithm
Cross-Validation
Algorithmic Discrimination

Questions and Problems

1. What does casual inference refer to?
2. What does it mean if someone says that "correlation is not causation"?
3. The fact that European countries with more storks also tend to have higher human birth rates is an example of what type of correlation?
4. What is a controlled experiment?
5. In the Card–Krueger study discussed in the chapter, we referred to it as a natural experiment. Why was it a natural experiment instead of a controlled experiment?
6. Card and Krueger found that the increased minimum wage rate in New Jersey did not cause a decline in employment in New Jersey. Does it follow that increases in the minimum wage would therefore never and in no place cause a decline in employment? Explain your answer.
7. What are the details of economist Joshua Angrist's study of the Vietnam War Draft lottery?
8. What does it mean for a defendant to "win the judge lottery"?
9. What is the essence or key characteristic of a regression discontinuity?
10. Dinardo and Lee (2004) study the effect of unions on firm employment with a regression discontinuity. What is the discontinuity in their setting?
11. How is the goal of big data and machine learning different from the goal of causal inference?
12. Economists use data to accomplish various goals or objectives. What are these goals or objectives?
13. In machine learning, what does the concept of "regularization" refer to?

CHAPTER 34
International Trade

> **Introduction**
>
> Economics is about trade, and trade crosses boundaries. People trade not only with people who live in their city, state, or country, but also with people in other countries. Many of the goods you consume are undoubtedly produced in other countries. This chapter examines international trade and the prohibitions sometimes placed on it.

34-1 International Trade Theory

International trade takes place for the same reasons that trade at any level and anywhere exists. Individuals trade to make themselves better off. Jacob and Isabella, both of whom live in Cincinnati, Ohio, trade because they both value something the other has more than they value some of their own possessions. On an international scale, Elaine in the United States trades with Li Jun in China because Li Jun has something that Elaine wants and Elaine has something that Li Jun wants.

Obviously, the countries of the world have different terrains, climates, resources, worker skills, and so on. Therefore, some countries will be able to produce goods that other countries cannot produce or can produce only at extremely high costs. For example, Hong Kong has no oil, and Saudi Arabia has a large supply of it. Bananas do not grow easily in the United States, but they flourish in Honduras. Americans could grow bananas if they used hothouses, but it is cheaper for Americans to buy bananas from Hondurans than to produce bananas themselves.

Major U.S. exports include automobiles, computers, aircraft, corn, wheat, soybeans, scientific instruments, coal, and plastic materials. Major imports include petroleum, automobiles, clothing, iron and steel, office machines, footwear, fish, coffee, and diamonds. Some of the major exporting countries of the world are the United States, China, Germany, Japan,

34-1a How Countries Know What to Trade

Recall the economic concept of **comparative advantage**, a concept discussed in Chapter 2. In this section, we discuss comparative advantage in terms of countries rather than in terms of individuals.

Comparative Advantage
The advantage a country has when it can produce a good at lower opportunity cost than another country can.

Comparative Advantage Assume a two-country, two-good world. Suppose the countries are the United States and Japan, and the goods are food and clothing. Both countries can produce the two goods in the four different combinations listed in Exhibit 1. For example, the United States can produce 90 units of food and 0 units of clothing, 60 units of food and 10 units of clothing, or either of the other two combinations shown. Japan can produce 15 units of food and 0 units of clothing, 10 units of food and 5 units of clothing, or two other combinations.

Now, suppose the United States is producing and consuming the two goods in the combination represented by point B on its production possibilities frontier (PPF), and Japan is producing and consuming the combination of the two goods represented by point F on its PPF. In this case, neither of the two countries is specializing in the production of one of the two goods, nor are the two countries trading with each other. We call this situation the *no-specialization–no-trade (NS–NT) case* (column 1 of Exhibit 2).

EXHIBIT 1

Production Possibilities in Two Countries

The United States and Japan can produce the two goods in the combinations shown. Initially, the United States is at point B on its PPF, and Japan is at point F on its PPF. Both countries can be made better off by specializing in and trading the good in which each has a comparative advantage.

United States			Japan		
Points on Production Possibilities Frontier	Food	Clothing	Points on Production Possibilities Frontier	Food	Clothing
A	90	0	E	15	0
B	60	10	F	10	5
C	30	20	G	5	10
D	0	30	H	0	15

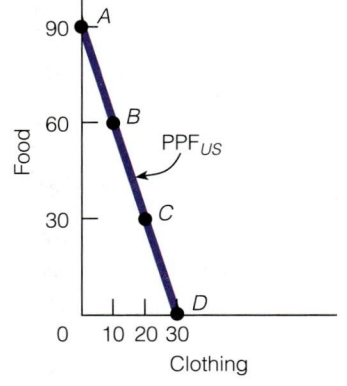
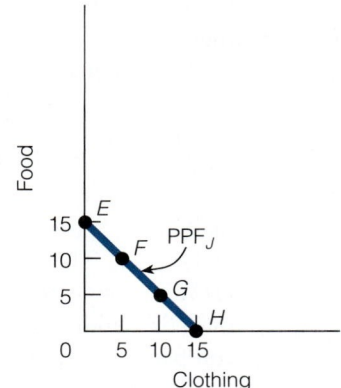

EXHIBIT 2

Both Countries Gain from Specialization and Trade

Column 1: Both the United States and Japan operate independently of each other. The United States produces and consumes 60 units of food and 10 units of clothing. Japan produces and consumes 10 units of food and 5 units of clothing.

Column 2: The United States specializes in the production of food; Japan specializes in the production of clothing. **Column 3:** The United States and Japan agree to terms of trade of 2 units of food for 1 unit of clothing. They go on to trade 20 units of food for 10 units of clothing. **Column 4:** Overall, the United States consumes 70 units of food and 10 units of clothing; Japan consumes 20 units of food and 5 units of clothing. **Column 5:** Consumption levels are higher for both the United States and Japan in the S–T case than in the NS–NT case.

	No-Specialization–No-Trade (NS–NT) Case		Specialization–Trade (S–T) Case				
Country	(1) Production and Consumption in the NS–NT Case		(2) Production in the S–T Case		(3) Exports (−) Imports (+) Terms of Trade Are 2F = 1C	(4) Consumption in the S–T Case (2) + (3)	(5) Gains from Specialization and Trade (4) − (1)
United States							
Food	60 }	Point B in	90 }	Point A in	−20	70	10
Clothing	10	Exhibit 1	0	Exhibit 1	+10	10	0
Japan							
Food	10 }	Point F in	0 }	Point H in	+20	20	10
Clothing	5	Exhibit 1	15	Exhibit 1	−10	5	0

Suppose further that the United States and Japan decide to specialize in the production of a specific good and to trade with each other. We call this situation the *specialization–trade (S–T) case*. Whether the two countries will be better off through specialization and trade is best explained by means of a numerical example, but first we need to find the answers to two other questions: What good should the United States specialize in producing? And what good should Japan specialize in producing? The general answer to both questions is the same: *Countries specialize in the production of the good in which they have a comparative advantage*. A country has a comparative advantage with respect to another country in the production of a good when the one country can produce the good at a lower opportunity cost than the other country can.

For instance, in our hypothetical example, the opportunity cost to the United States of producing 1 unit of clothing (C) is 3 units of food (F): For every 10 units of clothing the United States produces, it forfeits 30 units of food. Thus, the opportunity cost of producing 1 unit of food is 1/3 unit of clothing. In Japan, the opportunity cost of producing 1 unit of clothing is 1 unit of food. (For every 5 units of clothing Japan produces, it forfeits 5 units of food.) So, in the United States, the situation is $1C = 3F$, or $1F = 1/3C$; in Japan, the situation is $1C = 1F$, or $1F = 1C$. The United States can produce food at a lower opportunity cost than Japan can ($1/3C$, as opposed to $1C$), whereas Japan can produce clothing at a lower opportunity cost than the United States can ($1F$, as opposed to $3F$). In other words, the United States has a comparative advantage in food, and Japan has a comparative advantage in clothing.

Finally, suppose that the two countries specialize in the production of the goods in which they have a comparative advantage. The United States specializes in the production of food (producing 90 units), and Japan specializes in the production of clothing (producing 15 units).

In Exhibit 1, the United States locates at point *A* on its PPF, and Japan locates at point H on its PPF. (The two points are listed in column 2 of Exhibit 2.)

Settling on the Terms of Trade After they have determined which goods they will specialize in producing, the two countries must settle on the terms of trade—that is, how much food to trade for how much clothing. The United States faces the following situation: For every 30 units of food it does not produce, it can produce 10 units of clothing, as shown in Exhibit 1. Thus, 3 units of food have an opportunity cost of 1 unit of clothing ($3F = 1C$), or 1 unit of food has a cost of 1/3 unit of clothing ($1F = \frac{1}{3}C$). Japan faces the following situation: For every 5 units of food it does not produce, it can produce 5 units of clothing. Thus, 1 unit of food has an opportunity cost of 1 unit of clothing ($1F = 1C$). For the United States, $3F = 1C$, and for Japan, $1F = 1C$.

With these cost ratios, both countries should be able to agree on terms of trade that specify that $2F = 1C$. The United States would benefit by giving up 2 units of food, instead of 3 units, for 1 unit of clothing, whereas Japan would benefit by getting 2 units of food, instead of only 1 unit, for 1 unit of clothing. So, if the two countries agree to the terms of trade $2F = 1C$, and if they do trade—in absolute amounts, 20 units of food for 10 units of clothing (column 3 of Exhibit 2)—will they make themselves better off? We'll soon see that they will.

Results of the Specialization–Trade (S–T) Case Now the United States produces 90 units of food and trades 20 units to Japan, receiving 10 units of clothing in exchange. The United States consumes 70 units of food and 10 units of clothing. Japan produces 15 units of clothing and trades 10 units to the United States, receiving 20 units of food in exchange. Japan consumes 5 units of clothing and 20 units of food. (The two sets of numbers are shown in column 4 of Exhibit 2.)

Column 5 of Exhibit 2 shows both countries' gains from specialization and trade: The United States and Japan each consume 10 more units of food and no less clothing in the specialization–trade case than in the no-specialization-no-trade case. Apparently, then, a country gains by specializing in producing and trading the good in which it has a comparative advantage.

34-1b A Common Misconception About How Much We Can Consume

No country can consume beyond its PPF if it doesn't specialize and trade with other countries. But, as we have just seen, it can do so when there is specialization and trade. Look at the PPF for the United States in Exhibit 1. In the NS–NT case, the United States consumes 60 units of food and 10 units of clothing; that is, the United States consumes at point *B* on its PPF. In the S–T case, however, it consumes 70 units of food and 10 units of clothing. A point that represents this combination of the two goods is beyond the country's PPF.

34-1c How Countries Know When They Have a Comparative Advantage

Government officials of a country do not analyze pages of cost data to determine what their country should specialize in producing and then trade. Bureaucrats do not plot production possibilities frontiers on graph paper or calculate opportunity costs. Instead, the individual's desire to earn a dollar, a peso, or a euro determines the pattern of international trade. The desire to earn a profit determines what a country specializes in and trades.

To illustrate, suppose Jules, an enterprising Frenchman, visits the United States and observes that beef is relatively cheap (compared to the price in France) and that perfume is relatively expensive. Noticing the price differences for beef and perfume between his country and the United States, he decides to buy some perfume in France, bring it to the United States, and sell it there for the relatively higher U.S. price. With his profits from the perfume transaction, he buys beef in the United States, ships it to France, and sells it there for the relatively higher French price. Obviously, Jules is buying low and selling high. He buys a good in the country where it is cheap and sells it in the country where it is expensive.

Jules's activities have a couple of consequences. First, he is earning a profit. The larger the price differences are between the two countries and the more he shuffles goods between countries, the more profit Jules earns.

Second, Jules's activities are moving each country toward its comparative advantage. The United States ends up exporting beef to France, and France ends up exporting perfume to the United States. Just as the pure theory predicts, individuals in the two countries specialize in and trade the good in which they have a comparative advantage. The outcome is brought about spontaneously through the actions of individuals trying to make themselves better off; they are simply trying to gain through trade.

> **Thinking Like an Economist**
>
> **The Benefits of Searching for Profit** Is the desire to earn profit useful to society at large? Jules's desire for profit moved both the United States and France toward specializing in and trading the good in which each had a comparative advantage. And when countries specialize and trade, they are better off than when they do neither.

34-1d Why Does the United States Both Export and Import Cars? Why Not Just One or the Other?

After learning about comparative advantage and international trade, one would think that countries would specialize in producing certain goods and services and then exporting them. For example, one country might specialize in producing and exporting cars, and another country would specialize in producing and exporting computers. But, then, if this is true, why does the United States both export and import cars instead of only exporting cars or only importing cars? The same can be asked about Japan: It exports and imports cars, but why doesn't it just do one or the other?

When countries trade goods within the same industry, it is called **intra-industry trade**. Cars produced in the United States and cars produced in Japan are in the same industry (the car industry). Because the United States and Japan both export cars to each other and import cars from each other, the two countries are engaged in international intra-industry trade.

But before we discuss the possible causes of intra-industry trade, let's consider that the definition of an industry and, therefore, of intra-industry trade can be vague and problematic. The degree of intra-industry trade depends upon how broadly or narrowly an industry is defined—for example, the transportation industry versus the car industry.

To illustrate, suppose country 1 exports buses to and imports cars from country 2. Country 2, in turn, exports cars to and imports buses from country 1. If the industry is the transportation industry—which includes both cars and buses—then it follows that both countries are engaging in intra-industry trade. However, if the industry is considered to be the car industry or the bus industry, they are not engaging in intra-industry trade. In this case,, buses are in the bus industry, and cars are in the car industry; therefore, the two countries are not trading within the same industry.

Intra-industry Trade
Intra-industry trade exists when countries trade goods within the same industry. For example, the United States and Japan both export cars to each other and import cars from each other.

Now let's assume that both countries are exporting cars to and importing cars from each other, but suppose country 1 is exporting large SUVs to country 2 and is importing small cars from Country 2. Both countries are engaged in trading cars, so if the relevant industry is defined as the car industry, they are engaged in intra-industry trade. But if the relevant industries are the SUV industry and the small-car industry, they are not.

Beside the issue with determining the relevant industry, we are still left with the question of why countries might engage in intra-industry trade. As some economists have suggested, this might have to do with product differentiation and preferences.

With respect to product differentiation, countries are rarely exporting and importing the identical good. Yes, the United States exports and imports cars, but it exports Fords and Chevrolets and imports Volvos (from Sweden) and BMWs (from Germany). Fords, Chevrolets, Volvos, and BMWs are all cars, but they are not identical cars. This instance of product differentiation may be consistent with peoples' preferences. Some car customers in the United States prefer to buy Volvos over Fords; some car customers in Germany prefer to buy Fords over BMWs. Wine is produced in both the United States and in France, and both countries engage in intra-industry trade when it comes to wine, as some people in the United States prefer French wines to American wines.

Finally, consider the issue of **economies of scale** and intra-industry trade. Economies of scale are said to exist when inputs are increased by some percentage and output increases by a greater percentage, causing unit costs to fall. The important point here is that sometimes, as firms grow larger, their unit costs decline. As a result of their declining costs, they can outcompete other firms in the industry by charging lower prices while still earning a profit.

Suppose, then, that two car firms in country 1 have economies of scale in the production of small cars and two car countries in country 2 have economies of scale in the production of large cars. Each of the two car companies with economies of scale, in each of the two countries, can outcompete all other car companies in their respective countries. But without international trade, the residents of each country would be missing out on the ability to choose to buy their cars from a wide selection of cars—both small and large. If people in both countries want a variety of cars to choose from, then international trade—in this case, intra-industry trade—accomplishes two goals at the same time: The economies of scale give customers lower prices, and the international trade gives them the choice they desire.

Economies of Scale
Economies that exist when inputs are increased by some percentage and output increases by a greater percentage, causing unit costs to fall.

(Answers to Self-Test questions are in Answers to Self-Test Questions at the back of the book.)

1. Suppose the United States can produce 120 units of X at an opportunity cost of 20 units of Y, and the United Kingdom can produce 40 units of X at an opportunity cost of 80 units of Y. Identify favorable terms of trade for the two countries.

2. If a country can produce more of all of its goods than any other country can, would it benefit from specializing and trading? Explain your answer.

3. Do government officials analyze data to determine what their country can produce at a comparative advantage?

34-2 Trade Restrictions

International trade theory holds that countries gain from free international trade—that is, from specializing in the production of the goods in which they have a comparative advantage and trading them for other goods. In the real world, however, numerous types of trade restrictions imposed by many countries give rise to the following question: If countries gain from international trade, why are there trade restrictions? The answer requires an analysis of costs and benefits; specifically, we need to determine who benefits and who loses when trade is restricted. First, we need to explain some pertinent background information.

34-2a The Distributional Effects of International Trade

The previous section explained that specialization and international trade benefit individuals in different countries, but the benefit is a *net* benefit. Not every individual person may gain.

To illustrate, suppose Niesha lives and works in the United States and makes clock radios. She produces and sells 12,000 clock radios per year at a price of $40 each. Currently, clock radios are not traded internationally. Individuals in other countries who make clock radios do not sell them in the United States.

Then, one day, the U.S. market is opened to clock radios from China. Chinese manufacturers seem to have a comparative advantage in the production of clock radios because they sell theirs in the United States for $25 each. Niesha realizes that she cannot compete at this price. Her sales drop to such a degree that she goes out of business. Thus, the introduction of international trade in this instance has harmed Niesha personally.

34-2b Consumers' and Producers' Surpluses

The preceding example raises the issue of the distributional effects of free trade. The benefits of international trade are not equally distributed to all individuals in the population. Therefore, the topics of consumers' and producers' surpluses (Chapter 3) are relevant to our discussion of international trade.

Recall that *consumers' surplus* is the difference between the maximum price a buyer is willing and able to pay for a good or service and the price actually paid for the good or service:

Consumers' surplus = Maximum buying price − Price paid

Consumers' surplus is a dollar measure of the benefit gained by being able to purchase a unit of a good for less than one is willing to pay for it. For example, if Yakov would have paid $18 to see the movie at the Cinemax but paid only $12, his consumers' surplus is $6. Consumers' surplus is the consumers' net gain from trade.

Producers' surplus (or sellers' surplus) is the difference between the price sellers receive for a good and the minimum or lowest price for which they would have sold the good:

Producers' surplus = Price received − Minimum selling price

Producers' surplus is a dollar measure of the benefit gained by being able to sell a unit of output for more than one is willing to sell it. For example, if Farah sold her knit sweaters for $24 each but would have sold them for as low as (but no lower than) $14 each, her producer surplus is $10 per sweater. Producers' surplus is the producers' net gain from trade.

Both consumers' and producers' surplus are represented in Exhibit 3. In part (a), the shaded triangle represents consumers' surplus. This triangle comprises the area under the demand curve and above the equilibrium price. In part (b), the shaded triangle represents producers' surplus. This triangle comprises the area above the supply curve and under the equilibrium price.

34-2c The Benefits and Costs of Trade Restrictions

Of the numerous ways to restrict international trade, tariffs and quotas are two of the more common. We use the tools of supply and demand to discuss these two methods, concentrating on two groups: U.S. consumers and U.S. producers.

EXHIBIT 3

Consumers' and Producers' Surplus

(a) Consumers' surplus. As the shaded area indicates, the difference between the maximum or highest amount consumers would be willing to pay and the price they actually pay is consumers' surplus. (b) Producers' surplus. As the shaded area indicates, the difference between the price sellers receive for the good and the minimum or lowest price they would be willing to sell the good for is producers' surplus.

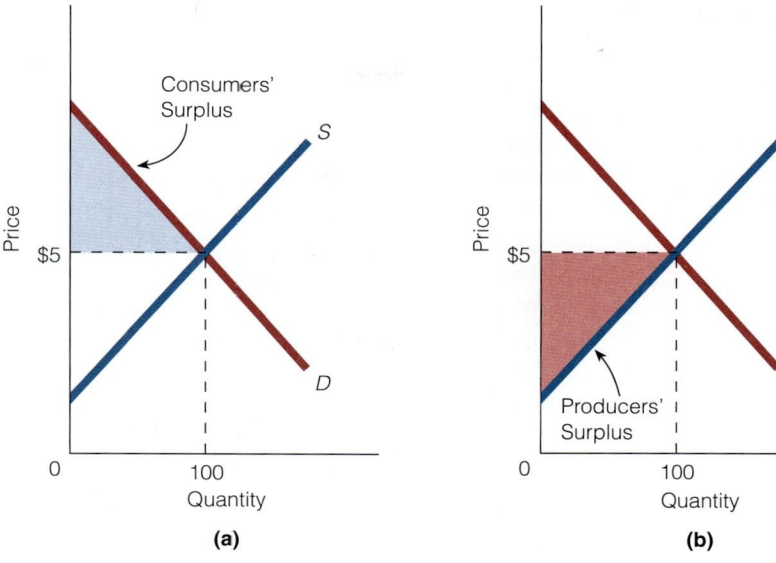

Tariffs A **tariff** is a tax on imports. The primary effect of a tariff is to raise the price of the imported good for the domestic consumer. Exhibit 4 illustrates the effects of a tariff on cars imported into the United States. The world price for cars is P_W, as shown in part (a). At this price in the domestic U.S. market, U.S. consumers buy Q_2 cars, as shown in part (b). They buy Q_1 cars from U.S. producers and $Q_2 - Q_1$ (the difference of Q_2 and Q_1) cars from foreign producers. In other words, U.S. imports at P_W are $Q_2 - Q_1$.

In this situation, consumers' surplus is the area under the demand curve and above the world price, P_W: the sum of the areas 1, 2, 3, 4, 5, and 6 in part (b). Producers' surplus is the area above the supply curve and below the world price, P_W: area 7.

Now, suppose a tariff is imposed, and so the price for imported cars in the U.S. market rises to $P_W + T$ (the world price plus the tariff). At this price, U.S. consumers buy Q_4 cars: Q_3 from U.S. producers and $Q_4 - Q_3$ from foreign producers. U.S. imports are thus $Q_4 - Q_3$, a smaller number of imports than at the pretariff price. An effect of tariffs, then, is to reduce imports. After the tariff has been imposed, at price $P_W + T$, consumers' surplus consists of areas 1 and 2, and producers' surplus consists of areas 3 and 7.

Clearly, consumers receive more consumers' surplus when tariffs do not exist and less when they do exist. In our example, consumers received areas 1 through 6 in consumers' surplus when the tariff did not exist, but they receive only areas 1 and 2 when the tariff exists. Because of the tariff, consumers' surplus was reduced by an amount equal to areas 3, 4, 5, and 6.

Producers, though, receive less producers' surplus when tariffs do not exist and more when they do exist. In our example, producers received producers' surplus equal to area 7 when the tariff did not exist, but they receive producers' surplus equal to areas 3 and 7 with the tariff. Because of the tariff, producers' surplus increased by an amount equal to area 3.

The government collects tariff revenue equal to area 5. This area is obtained by multiplying the number of imports ($Q_4 - Q_3$) by the tariff, which is the difference between $P_W + T$ and P_W.[1]

Tariff
A tax on imports.

---

[1] For example, if the tariff is $100 and the number of imports is 50,000, then the tariff is $5 million.

EXHIBIT 4

The Effects of a Tariff

A tariff raises the price of cars from P_W to $P_W + T$, decreases consumers' surplus, increases producers' surplus, and generates tariff revenue. Because consumers lose more than producers and government gain, there is a net loss due to the tariff.

	Consumers' Surplus	Producers' Surplus	Government Tariff Revenue
Free trade (No tariff)	1 + 2 + 3 + 4 + 5 + 6	7	None
Tariff	1 + 2	3 + 7	5
Loss or gain	− (3 + 4 + 5 + 6)	+3	+5
Result of tariff	= Loss to consumers + Gain to producers + Tariff revenue		
	= − (3 + 4 + 5 + 6)	+ 3	+ 5
	= − (4 + 6)		

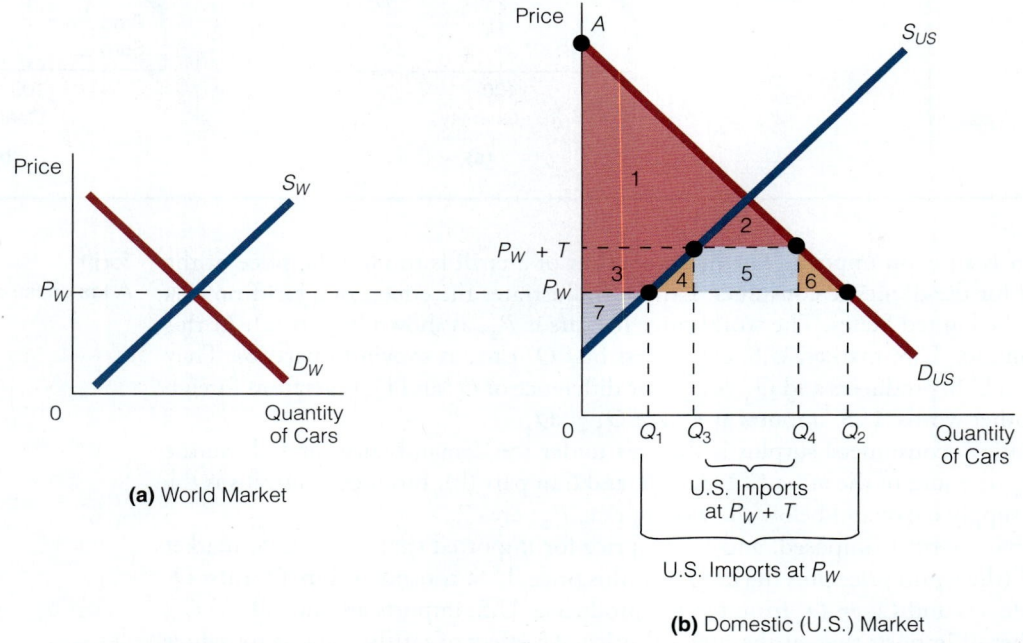

(a) World Market

(b) Domestic (U.S.) Market

In conclusion, the effects of a tariff are a decrease in consumers' surplus, an increase in producers' surplus, and tariff revenue for government. Because the loss to consumers (areas 3, 4, 5, and 6) is greater than the gain to producers (area 3) plus the gain to government (area 5), *a tariff results in a net loss*. The net loss is areas 4 and 6.

Quota
A legal limit imposed on the amount of a good that may be imported.

Quotas A **quota** is a legal limit imposed on the amount of a good that may be imported. For example, the government may decide to allow no more than 100,000 foreign cars or no more than 30,000 Japanese television sets to be imported. A quota reduces the supply of a good and raises the price of imported goods for domestic consumers.

Once again, we consider the situation in the U.S. car market. (See Exhibit 5.) At a price of P_W [established in the world market for cars—see part (a)], U.S. consumers buy Q_1 cars

EXHIBIT 5

The Effects of a Quota

A quota that sets the legal limit of imports at $Q_4 - Q_3$ causes the price of cars to increase from P_W to P_Q. A quota raises the price, decreases consumers' surplus, increases producers' surplus, and provides a gain to importers. Because consumers lose more than producers and importers gain, there is a net loss due to the quota.

	Consumers' Surplus	Producers' Surplus	Gain to Importers
Free trade (No quota)	1 + 2 + 3 + 4 + 5 + 6	7	—
Quota	1 + 2	3 + 7	5
Loss or gain	− (3 + 4 + 5 + 6)	+3	+5

Result of quota = Loss to consumers + Gain to producers + Gain to importers
= − (3 + 4 + 5 + 6)   +3   +5
= − (4 + 6)

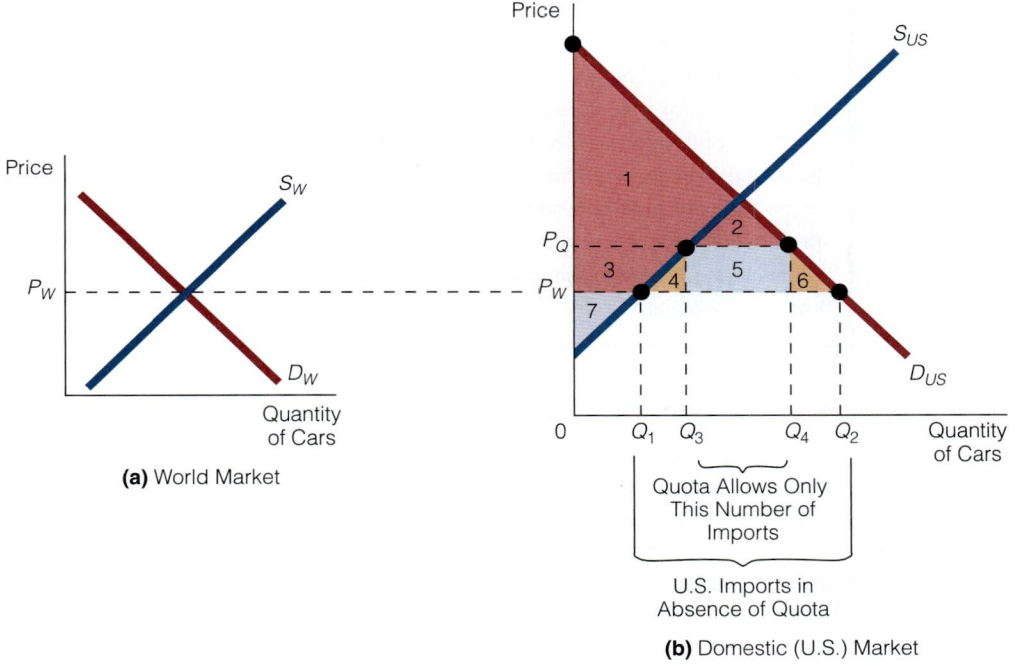

(a) World Market

(b) Domestic (U.S.) Market

from U.S. producers and $Q_2 - Q_1$ cars from foreign producers. [See part (b).] Consumers' surplus is equal to the sum of areas 1, 2, 3, 4, 5, and 6. Producers' surplus is equal to area 7.

Suppose now that the U.S. government sets a quota equal to $Q_4 - Q_3$. Because this quantity is the number of foreign cars U.S. consumers imported when the tariff was imposed (Exhibit 4), the price of cars rises to P_Q in Exhibit 5 (a price equal to $P_W + T$ in Exhibit 4). At P_Q, consumers' surplus is equal to areas 1 and 2, and producers' surplus consists of areas 3 and 7. The decrease in consumers' surplus due to the quota is equal to areas 3, 4, 5, and 6; the increase in producers' surplus is equal to area 3.

However, area 5 is not transferred to government, as was the case when a tariff was imposed. Rather, it represents a gain earned by the importers (and sellers) of $Q_4 - Q_3$ foreign-made cars.

Before the quota, importers were importing $Q_2 - Q_1$ cars, but only part $(Q_4 - Q_3)$ of that total quantity is relevant because $Q_4 - Q_3$ number of cars is the quantity of imports now that the quota has been established. Before the quota was established, the dollar amount that the importers received for $Q_4 - Q_3$ cars was $P_W \times (Q_4 - Q_3)$. Because of the quota, the price rises to P_Q, and they now receive $P_Q \times (Q_4 - Q_3)$. The gain is area 5.

In conclusion, the effects of a quota are a decrease in consumers' surplus, an increase in producers' surplus, and a gain for importers. Because the loss to consumers (areas 3, 4, 5, and 6) is greater than the increase in producers' surplus (area 3) plus the gain to importers (area 5), there is a *net loss as a result of the quota*. The net loss is equal to areas 4 and 6.

> **Finding Economics**
>
> **In a Policy Debate** There is a debate tonight at the college Irina attends, with four people on each side of the issue: Should the United States practice free trade? Irina attends the debate and comes away thinking that both sides made good points. The side opposing free trade argued that, because other countries do not always practice free trade, neither should the United States. The side in favor of free trade argued that free trade leads to lower prices for U.S. consumers. Where is the economics?
>
> Most of the debate, we believe, will fit into our discussion of Exhibits 4 and 5. These two exhibits show what happens to consumers and producers, and to society as a whole, as the result of both free and prohibited trade. The diagrams show (1) the benefits of prohibited free trade to domestic producers; (2) the costs of prohibited trade to domestic consumers; (3) tariff revenue to government, if such revenue exists; and (4) the overall net costs to prohibited trade.

34-2d Why Nations Sometimes Restrict Trade

If free trade results in net gain, why do nations sometimes restrict trade? The case for free trade (no tariffs or quotas) so far in this chapter appears to be a strong one. It has not gone unchallenged, however. Some persons maintain that, at certain times, free trade should be restricted or suspended. In almost all cases, they argue that doing so is in the best interest of the public or country as a whole. In other words, they advance a public-interest argument. Other persons contend that the public-interest argument is only superficial: down deep, they say, it is a special-interest argument clothed in idealistic words. As you might guess, the debate between the two groups is often heated.

The sections that follow describe some arguments that have been advanced for trade restrictions.

The National Defense Argument Certain industries—such as aircraft, petroleum, chemicals, and weapons—are necessary to the national defense. Suppose the United States has a comparative advantage in the production of wheat and country X has a comparative advantage in the production of weapons. Many Americans feel that the United States should not specialize in the production of wheat and then trade wheat to country X in exchange for weapons. Leaving weapons production to another country, they maintain, is too dangerous.

The national defense argument may have some validity, but even valid arguments may be abused. Industries that are not really necessary to the national defense may maintain otherwise. In the past, the national defense argument has been used by some firms in the following industries: pens, pottery, peanuts, papers, candles, thumbtacks, tuna fishing, and pencils.

The Infant Industry Argument Alexander Hamilton, the first U.S. Secretary of the Treasury, argued that so-called infant, or new, industries often need protection from older, established foreign competitors until they are mature enough to compete on an equal basis. Today, some persons voice the same argument. The infant industry argument is clearly an argument for temporary protection. However, critics charge that after an industry is protected from foreign competition, removing the protection is almost impossible: The once-infant industry will continue to maintain that it isn't old enough to go it alone. Critics of the infant industry argument say that political realities make it unlikely that a benefit, once bestowed, will be removed.

Finally, the infant industry argument, like the national defense argument, may be abused. All new industries, whether or not they could currently compete successfully with foreign producers, would argue for protection on infant industry grounds.

The Antidumping Argument *Dumping* is the sale of goods abroad at a price below their cost and below the price charged in the domestic market. If a French firm sells wine in the United States for a price below the cost of producing the wine and below the price charged in France, it is dumping wine in the United States. Critics of dumping maintain that it is an unfair trade practice that puts domestic producers of substitute goods at a disadvantage.

In addition, critics charge that dumpers seek only to penetrate a market and drive out domestic competitors, after which they raise prices. However, some economists point to the infeasibility of this strategy. After the dumpers have driven out their competition and raised prices, their competition is likely to return. For their efforts, the dumpers, in turn, would have incurred only a string of losses (owing to their selling below cost). Opponents of the antidumping argument also point out that domestic consumers benefit from dumping because they pay lower prices.

Dumping
The sale of goods abroad at a price below their cost and below the price charged in the domestic market.

Economics 24/7

Offshore Outsourcing, or Offshoring

Outsourcing is the term used to describe work done for a company by another company or by people other than the originating company's employees. Outsourcing entails purchasing a product or process from an outside supplier rather than producing it in-house. To illustrate,

suppose company X has, in the past, hired employees for personnel, accounting, and payroll services, but now a company in another state performs these duties. In this case, company X has outsourced those work activities.

When a company outsources certain work activities to individuals in another country, it is said to be engaged in offshore outsourcing, or offshoring. Consider a few examples:

(Continued)

A New York securities firm replaces 800 software engineering employees with a team of software engineers in India. A computer company replaces 200 on-call technicians in its headquarters in Texas with 150 on-call technicians in India.

The benefits of offshoring for a U.S. firm are obvious: It pays lower wages to individuals in other countries for the same work that U.S. employees do for higher wages. Benefits also flow to the employees hired in the foreign countries. The costs of offshoring are said to fall on persons who lose their jobs as a result, such as the software engineer in New York or the on-call computer technician in Texas. Some have argued that offshoring is a major political issue and that it could bring with it a wave of protectionism.

Offshoring will undoubtedly have both proponents and opponents. On a net basis, however, are there more benefits than costs or more costs than benefits? Consider a U.S. company that currently employs Kathleen as a software engineer, paying her $x a year. Then, one day, the company tells Kathleen that it has to let her go; it is replacing her with a software engineer in India who will work for $z a year (and, yes, $z < x$).

Why doesn't Kathleen simply agree to work for $z, the same wage as that was agreed to by the Indian software engineer? That's because Kathleen can work elsewhere for some wage between $x and $z. Assume that this wage is $y. So, even though offshoring has moved Kathleen from earning $x to earning $y, $y is still more than $z.

In short, the U.S. company is able to lower its costs from $x to $z, and Kathleen's income falls from $x to $y. The U.S. company lowers its costs more than Kathleen's income falls because the difference between $x and $z is greater than the difference between $x and $y.

If the U.S. company operates in a competitive environment, its lower costs will shift its supply curve to the right and lower prices. In other words, offshoring can reduce prices for U.S. consumers. The political fallout from offshoring might, in the end, depend on how visible to the average American the employment effects of offshoring are relative to the resulting price reduction.

The Foreign Export Subsidies Argument Some governments subsidize firms that export goods. It is often argued that if a country offers a below-market (interest rate) loan to a company, the government subsidizes the production of the good the firm produces. If, in turn, the firm exports the good to a foreign country, that country's producers of substitute goods call foul. They complain that the foreign firm has been given an unfair advantage that they should be protected against.[2]

Others say that consumers should not turn their backs on a gift (in the form of lower prices). If foreign governments want to subsidize their exports and thus give a gift to foreign consumers at the expense of their own taxpayers, then the recipients should not complain. Of course, the recipients are usually not the ones who are complaining. Rather, the complainers are the domestic producers who can't sell their goods at as high a price because of the so-called gift that domestic consumers are receiving from foreign governments.

The Low Foreign Wages Argument Some argue that American producers can't compete with foreign producers because American producers have to pay high wages to their workers, and foreign producers pay low wages. The American producers insist that international trade must be restricted or they will be ruined. However, the argument overlooks why American wages are high and why foreign wages are low in the first place: productivity. High productivity and high wages are usually linked, as are low productivity and low wages. If an American worker, who receives $20 per hour, can produce (on average) 100 units of good X per hour, working with numerous capital goods, then the cost per unit may be lower than when a foreign worker, who receives $2 per hour, produces (on average) 5 units of X per hour,

---

[2.] Words are important in this debate. For example, domestic producers who claim that foreign governments have subsidized foreign firms say that they are not asking for economic protectionism but only retaliation, reciprocity, or, simply, tit for tat—words that have less negative connotation than those their opponents use.

working by hand. In short, a country's high-wage disadvantage may be offset by its productivity advantage, and a country's low-wage advantage may be offset by its productivity disadvantage. High wages do not necessarily mean high costs when productivity and the costs of nonlabor resources are included.

The Saving Domestic Jobs Argument Sometimes, the argument against completely free trade is made in terms of saving domestic jobs. Actually, this argument has cropped up before in its different guises. For example, the low foreign wages argument is one form of it: If domestic producers cannot compete with foreign producers because foreign producers pay low wages and domestic producers pay high wages, domestic producers will go out of business, and domestic jobs will be lost. The foreign export subsidies argument is another version: If foreign government subsidies give a competitive edge to foreign producers, not only will domestic producers fail, but as a result of their failure, domestic jobs also will be lost.

Critics of the saving domestic jobs argument (in all its guises) counterargue as follows: If a domestic producer is being outcompeted by foreign producers and if domestic jobs in an industry are being lost as a result, the world market is signaling that those labor resources could be put to better use in an industry in which the country holds a comparative advantage.

Thinking Like an Economist

Economics Versus Politics International trade often becomes a battleground between economics and politics. The simple tools of supply and demand and of consumers' and producers' surpluses show that free trade leads to net gains. On the whole, tariffs and quotas make living standards lower than they would be if free trade were permitted. On the other side, though, are the realities of business and politics. Domestic producers may advocate quotas and tariffs to make themselves better off, giving little thought to the negative effects on foreign producers or domestic consumers.

Perhaps the battle over international trade comes down to this: Policies are advocated, argued, and lobbied for largely on the basis of their distributional effects, as opposed to their aggregate or overall effects. On an aggregate level, free trade produces a net gain for society, whereas restricted trade produces a net loss. But economists understand that, even if free trade in the aggregate produces a net gain, not every single person will benefit more from free trade than from restricted trade. An example in this chapter showed how a subset of the population (producers) gains more, in a particular instance, from restricted trade than from free trade. In short, economists realize that the crucial question in determining real-world policies is more often, "How does it affect me?" than "How does it affect us?"

1. Who benefits and who loses from tariffs? Explain your answer.
2. Identify the directional change in consumers' surplus and producers' surplus when we move from free trade to tariffs. Is the change in consumers' surplus greater than, less than, or equal to the change in producers' surplus?
3. What is a major difference between the effects of a quota and the effects of a tariff?
4. Outline the details of the infant industry argument for trade restriction.

Office Hours

"Should We Impose Tariffs If They Impose Tariffs?"

Student: Here is a problem I have with our discussion of free trade and prohibited trade. Essentially, I am in favor of free international trade, but I think the United States should have free trade with countries that practice free trade with us. In other words, if country X practices free trade with the United States, then the United States should practice free trade with it. But if country Y places tariffs on U.S. goods that enter country Y, then the United States ought to place tariffs on country Y's goods that enter our country.

Instructor: Many people feel the same way you do, but this opinion overlooks something that we showed in Exhibits 4 and 5: The losses of moving from free trade to prohibited trade (where either tariffs or quotas exist) are greater than the gains. Remember? There is a net loss to society in that move.

Student: I just think it is only fair that other countries get what they give. If they give free trade to us, then we ought to give free trade back to them. If they place tariffs and quotas on our goods, then we ought to do the same to their goods.

Instructor: You need to keep in mind the price the United States has to pay for this policy of tit for tat.

Student: What do you mean? What price does the United States have to pay?

Instructor: It has to incur the net loss illustrated in Exhibits 4 and 5. If you look back at Exhibit 4, for example, you'll notice that moving from free trade to prohibited trade (1) decreases consumers' surplus, (2) increases producers' surplus, and (3) raises tariff revenue. But when we count up all the gains of prohibited trade and compare them with all the losses, we conclude that the losses are greater than the gains. In other words, prohibited trade leads to a net loss.

Student: But suppose our practicing tit for tat (giving free trade for free trade and prohibited trade for prohibited trade) forces other countries to move away from prohibited trade. In other words, we need to look at this issue of free versus prohibited trade over time. Maybe the United States has to practice prohibited trade today (with those countries that impose tariffs or quotas on the United States) in order to force those countries to practice free trade tomorrow. Couldn't it work out that way?

Instructor: It could work out that way, or things could escalate toward greater prohibited trade. In other words, country A imposes tariffs and quotas on country B, then country B raises its tariffs and quotas even higher on country A, so country A retaliates and raises its tariffs and quotas on country B, and so on.

Student: So, is your point that free trade is the best policy to practice, no matter what other countries do?

Instructor: That is what many economists would say, but that is not the point I am making here. I am making two points with respect to the discussion. First, in response to your position that the United States ought to practice tit for tat (give free trade for free trade, tariffs for tariffs, quotas for quotas), I am simply drawing your attention to the net loss Americans incur if they practice prohibited trade—no matter what other countries are doing. In other words, there is a net loss for Americans, regardless of whether other countries are practicing free or prohibited trade. Second, with respect to your second point about prohibited trade today leading to free trade tomorrow, I am saying that we can't be sure that prohibited trade today won't lead to greater prohibitions on trade tomorrow. This is not to say that you can't be right: It is possible for prohibited trade today to lead to less prohibited trade tomorrow.

Points to Remember

1. A country that imposes tariffs or quotas on imported goods incurs a net loss, no matter what another country is doing—whether it is practicing free or prohibited trade.
2. We cannot easily predict the outcome of the United States' practicing tit for tat in international trade.

Chapter Summary

Specialization and Trade

- A country has a comparative advantage in the production of a good if it can produce the good at a lower opportunity cost than another country can.

- Individuals in countries that specialize and trade have a higher standard of living than they would if their countries did not specialize and trade.

- Government officials do not analyze cost data to determine what their country should specialize in and trade. Instead, the desire to earn a dollar, peso, or euro guides individuals' actions and produces the unintended consequence that countries specialize in and trade the good(s) in which they have a comparative advantage. However, trade restrictions can change this outcome.

Tariffs and Quotas

- A tariff is a tax on imports. A quota is a legal limit on the amount of a good that may be imported.
- Both tariffs and quotas raise the price of imports.
- Tariffs lead to a decrease in consumers' surplus, an increase in producers' surplus, and tariff revenue for the government. Consumers lose more through tariffs than producers and government (together) gain.
- Quotas lead to a decrease in consumers' surplus, an increase in producers' surplus, and additional revenue for the importers who sell the amount specified by the quota. Consumers lose more through quotas than producers and importers (together) gain.

Arguments for Trade Restrictions

- The national defense argument states that certain goods—such as aircraft, petroleum, chemicals, and weapons—are necessary to the national defense and should be produced domestically whether the country has a comparative advantage in their production or not.
- The infant industry argument states that infant, or new, industries should be protected from free (foreign) trade so that they have time to develop and compete on an equal basis with older, more established foreign industries.
- The antidumping argument states that domestic producers should not have to compete (on an unequal basis) with foreign producers that sell products below cost and below the prices they charge in their domestic markets.
- The foreign export subsidies argument states that domestic producers should not have to compete (on an unequal basis) with foreign producers that have been subsidized by their governments.
- The low foreign wages argument states that domestic producers cannot compete with foreign producers that pay low wages to their employees when domestic producers pay high wages to their employees. For high-paying domestic firms to survive, limits on free trade are proposed.
- The saving domestic jobs argument states that foreign producers will be able to outcompete domestic producers through low foreign wages or government subsidies (or dumping and similar practices) and that, therefore, domestic jobs will be lost. For domestic firms to survive and domestic jobs not to be lost, limits on free trade are proposed.
- Not everyone accepts the arguments for trade restrictions as valid. Critics often maintain that the arguments can be and are abused and that, in most cases, they are motivated by self-interest.

Key Terms and Concepts

Comparative Advantage
Intra-industry Trade
Economies of Scale
Tariff
Quota
Dumping

Questions and Problems

1. Although a production possibilities frontier is usually drawn for a country, one could be drawn for the world. Picture the world's production possibilities frontier. Is the world positioned at a point on the PPF or below it? Give a reason for your answer.
2. If country A is better than country B at producing all goods, will country A still be made better off by specializing and trading? Explain your answer. (*Hint*: Look at Exhibit 1.)
3. The desire for profit can end up pushing countries toward producing goods in which they have a comparative advantage. Do you agree or disagree? Explain your answer.
4. Whatever can be done by a tariff can be done by a quota. Discuss.
5. Neither free trade nor prohibited trade comes with benefits only. Both come with benefits and costs. Therefore, free trade is no better or worse than prohibited trade. Comment.

6. Consider two groups of domestic producers: those that compete with imports and those that export goods. Suppose the domestic producers that compete with imports convince the legislature to impose a high tariff on imports—so high, in fact, that almost all imports are eliminated. Does this policy in any way adversely affect domestic producers that export goods? If so, how?

7. Suppose the U.S. government wants to curtail imports. Would it be more likely to favor a tariff or a quota to accomplish its objective? Why?

8. Suppose the landmass known to you as the United States of America had been composed of separate countries instead of separate states since the nation's founding. Would you expect the standard of living of the people who inhabit this landmass to be higher, lower, or equal to what it is today? Why?

9. Even though Jeremy is a better gardener and novelist than Bill, Jeremy still hires Bill as his gardener. Why?

10. Suppose that a constitutional convention is called tomorrow and that you are chosen as one of the delegates from your state. You and the other delegates must decide whether it will be constitutional or unconstitutional for the federal government to impose tariffs and quotas or to restrict international trade in any way. What would be your position?

11. Some economists have argued that, because domestic consumers gain more from free trade than domestic producers gain from (import) tariffs and quotas, consumers should buy out domestic producers and rid themselves of costly tariffs and quotas. For example, if consumers save $400 million from free trade (through paying lower prices) and producers gain $100 million from tariffs and quotas, consumers can pay producers something more than $100 million but less than $400 million and get producers to favor free trade too. Assuming that this scheme were feasible, what do you think are either the positive and/or negative aspects of it?

12. If there is a net loss to society from tariffs, why do tariffs exist?

Working with Numbers and Graphs

1. Using the data in the accompanying table, answer the following questions:

   a. For which good does Canada have a comparative advantage?
   b. For which good does Italy have a comparative advantage?
   c. What might be a set of favorable terms of trade for the two countries?
   d. Prove that both countries would be better off in the specialization–trade case than in the no-specialization–no-trade case.

2. In the accompanying figure, P_W is the world price and $P_W + T$ is the world price plus a tariff. Identify the following:

   a. The level of imports at P_W
   b. The level of imports at $P_W + T$
   c. The loss in consumers' surplus as a result of a tariff
   d. The gain in producers' surplus as a result of a tariff
   e. The revenue received as a result of a tariff
   f. The net loss to society as a result of a tariff
   g. The net benefit to society of moving from a tariff to no tariff

Points on Production Possibilities Frontier	Canada		Italy	
	Good X	Good Y	Good X	Good Y
A	150	0	90	0
B	100	25	60	60
C	50	50	30	120
D	0	75	0	180

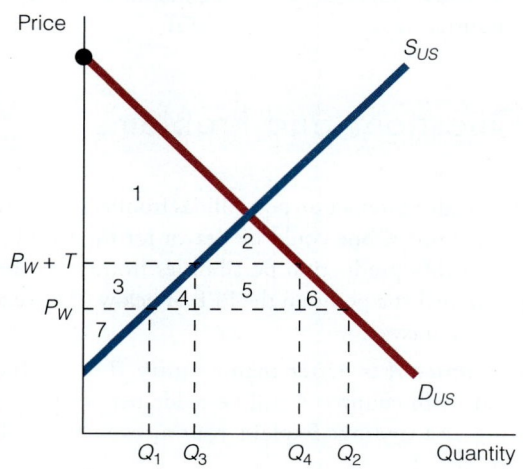

CHAPTER 35

International Finance

Introduction

When people travel to a foreign country, they buy goods and services in the country, and prices are quoted in yen, pounds, euros, pesos, or some other currency. For example, a U.S. tourist in Germany might want to buy a good priced in euros and, therefore, would want to know what the good costs in dollars and cents. The cost in U.S. dollars depends on the current exchange rate between the dollar and the euro, but what determines the exchange rate? That is just one of the many questions answered in this chapter.

35-1 The Foreign Exchange Market

The United States imports and exports goods and services. The difference between the value of its exports and the value of its imports is called *net exports*. Net exports are sometimes referred to as the **trade balance** (or balance of trade). If the value of exports is greater than the value of imports, a country is said to be running a **trade surplus**; if the value of imports is greater than the value of exports, the country is running a **trade deficit**.

One thing that can affect a country's trade balance is the value of its currency in relation to other currencies. Currencies of different countries are exchanged (bought and sold for a price) in the **foreign exchange market**. The price that currencies are bought and sold for is called the **exchange rate**. For instance, it might take $1.20 to buy a euro and 6 cents to buy a Mexican peso.

In this section, we explain why currencies are demanded and supplied in the foreign exchange market. Then we discuss how the exchange rate expresses the relationship between the demand for and the supply of currencies.

Trade Balance
The value of a country's exports minus the value of its imports; sometimes referred to as net exports.

Trade Surplus
The condition that exists when the value of a country's exports is greater than the value of its imports.

Trade Deficit
The condition that exists when the value of a country's imports is greater than the value of its exports.

791

Foreign Exchange Market
The market in which currencies of different countries are exchanged.

Exchange Rate
The price of one currency in terms of another currency.

35-1a The Demand for Goods

To simplify our analysis, we assume that there are only two countries in the world: the United States and Mexico. Thus, there are only two currencies in the world: the U.S. dollar (USD) and the Mexican peso (MXN). We want to answer the following two questions:

1. What creates the demand for and the supply of dollars on the foreign exchange market?
2. What creates the demand for and the supply of pesos on the foreign exchange market?

Suppose an American wants to buy a couch from a Mexican producer. Before he can purchase the couch, the American must buy Mexican pesos; hence, Mexican pesos are demanded. The American buys Mexican pesos with U.S. dollars; that is, he supplies U.S. dollars to the foreign exchange market and demands Mexican pesos. Therefore, *the U.S. demand for Mexican goods leads to (1) a demand for Mexican pesos and (2) a supply of U.S. dollars on the foreign exchange market.* [See Exhibit 1(a).] In other words, the demand for pesos and the supply of dollars are linked:

Demand for pesos ↔ Supply of dollars

The result is similar for a Mexican who wants to buy a computer from a U.S. producer. Before she can purchase the computer, the Mexican must buy U.S. dollars; hence, U.S. dollars are demanded. The Mexican buys the U.S. dollars with Mexican pesos. Therefore, *the Mexican demand for U.S. goods leads to (1) a demand for U.S. dollars and (2) a supply of Mexican pesos on the foreign exchange market.* [See Exhibit 1(b).] In other words, the demand for dollars and the supply of pesos are linked:

Demand for dollars ↔ Supply of pesos

35-1b The Demand for and Supply of Currencies

Exhibit 2 shows the market for pesos. The quantity of pesos is on the horizontal axis, and the exchange rate—stated in terms of the *dollar price per peso*—is on the vertical axis. In Exhibit 2(a), the demand curve for pesos is downward sloping, indicating that, as the dollar price per peso declines, the quantity of pesos demanded (by Americans) rises. To illustrate,

---

EXHIBIT 1

The Demand for Goods and the Supply of Currencies

EXHIBIT 2

The Demand for and Supply of Pesos on the Foreign Exchange Market (a) The demand for pesos. As the dollar price of a peso falls, the quantity demanded of pesos rises. (b) The supply of pesos. As the dollar price of a peso rises, the quantity supplied of pesos rises.

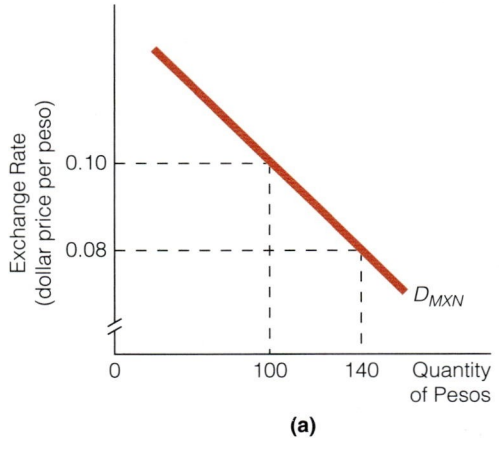
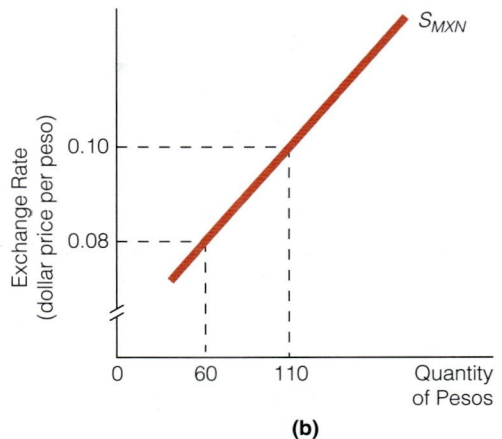

if Americans have to pay 10 cents to buy a peso, they might offer to buy 100 pesos, but if Americans have to pay 8 cents to buy a peso, they might offer to buy 140 pesos.

The supply curve for pesos in Exhibit 2(b) is upward sloping, indicating that, as the dollar price of a peso rises—that is, as Mexicans receive more for a peso—the quantity of pesos supplied (by Mexicans) rises. To illustrate, at 8 cents for a peso, Mexicans might offer to sell 60 pesos, but at 10 cents for a peso, they might offer to sell 110 pesos.

35-2 Flexible Exchange Rates

In this section, we discuss how exchange rates are determined in the foreign exchange market when the forces of supply and demand are allowed to rule. Economists refer to this dynamic as a **flexible exchange rate system**. In the next section, we discuss how exchange rates are determined under a fixed exchange rate system.

35-2a The Equilibrium Exchange Rate

In a completely flexible exchange rate system, the forces of supply and demand determine the exchange rate. In our two-country–two-currency world, suppose the equilibrium exchange rate (dollar price per peso) is 0.10 USD = 1 MXN, as shown in Exhibit 3. At this dollar price per peso, the quantity demanded of pesos equals the quantity supplied. There are no shortages or surpluses of pesos. At any other exchange rate, however, either an excess demand for pesos or an excess supply of pesos exists.

At the exchange rate of 0.12 USD = 1 MXN, a surplus of pesos exists. As a result, downward pressure will be placed on the dollar price of a peso (just as downward pressure would be placed on the dollar price of an apple if there were a surplus of apples). At the exchange rate of 0.08 USD = 1 MXN, there is a shortage of pesos, and upward pressure will be placed on the dollar price of a peso.

Flexible Exchange Rate System
A system whereby exchange rates are determined by the forces of supply and demand for a currency.

EXHIBIT 3

A Flexible Exchange Rate System

At 0.12 USD = 1 MXN, there is a surplus of pesos, placing downward pressure on the exchange rate. At 0.08 USD = 1 MXN, there is a shortage of pesos, placing upward pressure on the exchange rate. At the equilibrium exchange rate, 0.10 USD = 1 MXN, the quantity demanded of pesos equals the quantity supplied of pesos.

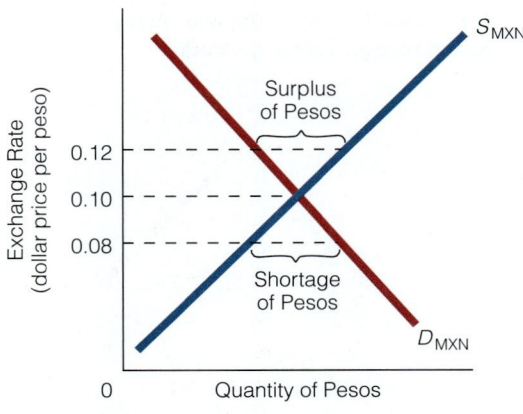

35-2b Changes in the Equilibrium Exchange Rate

A change in the demand for pesos, in the supply of pesos, or in both will change the equilibrium dollar price per peso. If the equilibrium dollar price per peso rises—say, from 0.10 USD = 1 MXN to 0.12 USD = 1 MXN—the peso is said to have **appreciated** and the dollar to have **depreciated**. A currency has appreciated in value if it takes more of a foreign currency to buy it. A currency has depreciated in value if it takes more of it to buy a foreign currency.

For example, a movement in the equilibrium exchange rate from 0.10 USD = 1 MXN to 0.12 USD = 1 MXN means that it now takes 12 cents instead of 10 cents to buy a peso, so the dollar has depreciated. The other side of the coin, so to speak, is that it takes fewer pesos to buy a dollar, so the peso has appreciated. That is, at an exchange rate of 0.10 USD = 1 MXN, it takes 10 pesos (1.00/0.10 = 10) to buy $1, but at an exchange rate of 0.12 USD = 1 MXN, it takes only 8.33 pesos (1.00/0.12 = 8.33) to buy $1.

Appreciated
An increase in the value of one currency relative to other currencies.

Depreciated
A decrease in the value of one currency relative to other currencies.

Economics 24/7

Does It Matter to You If the Dollar Depreciates?

On Monday, February 8, 2021, one British pound could be purchased for $1.37 and one euro could be purchased for $1.20. This means if you were an American in London on February 8, 2021, and wanted to buy a British-made sweater priced at £60, you would need to pay $82.20. Or if you were an American in Paris on February 8, 2021, and wanted to buy a French-made shirt priced at €30, you would need to pay $36.

Does it matter to you if the dollar depreciates? We know that if the dollar depreciates, it will take more dollars and cents to buy one British pound and one euro. Let's suppose the dollar depreciates such that it takes $1.50 to buy a pound. What would the British-made sweater priced at £60 now cost you in terms of dollars and cents? The answer is $1.50 times 60, or $90. What once cost $82.20 now costs $90. Does dollar depreciation matter to you if you are buying a good in London? It does. It means that you will end up paying more (in dollars and cents) for everything you buy in London.

Now, let's change things. Suppose that, instead of going to London and buying different goods and services, you simply have a savings account in a British bank, and the balance of the savings account is £5,000. If you want to close that savings account and covert pounds to dollars, you will get $6,850 from that savings account if one pound trades for $1.37. But if one pound trades for $1.50, you will get $7,500 from that savings account. Since you had a savings account denominated in pounds, and because the dollar depreciated in value, the pound appreciated. Your pound-denominated savings account fetches more dollars and cents at $1.50 a pound than $1.37 a pound.

We return to our question: Does it matter to you if the dollar depreciates? If you are an American in London buying goods and services, the dollar depreciation makes those goods and services more expensive. If you are an American with a pound-denominated savings account in London, then you are going to get more dollars and cents for each pound you have in that savings account.

35-2c Factors That Affect the Equilibrium Exchange Rate

If the equilibrium exchange rate can change owing to a change in the demand for and supply of a currency, then understanding what factors can change demand and supply is important. This section presents three such factors.

A Difference In Income Growth Rates An increase in a country's income will usually cause the nation's residents to buy more of both domestic and foreign goods. The increased demand for imports will result in an increased demand for foreign currency.

Suppose U.S. residents experience an increase in income, but Mexican residents do not. As a result, Americans want to buy more Mexican goods, so the demand curve for pesos shifts rightward, as illustrated in Exhibit 4. This shift causes the equilibrium exchange rate to rise from 0.10 USD = 1 MXN to 0.12 USD = 1 MXN. Because Americans must now pay 12 cents instead of 10 cents to buy a peso, the dollar has depreciated, and the peso has appreciated.

Differences in Relative Inflation Rates Suppose the U.S. price level rises 10 percent at a time when Mexico experiences stable prices. Then an increase in the U.S. price level (in the face of a stable price level in Mexico) will make Mexican goods relatively less expensive for Americans and U.S. goods relatively more expensive for Mexicans. As a result, the U.S. demand for Mexican goods will increase, and the Mexican demand for U.S. goods will decrease.

EXHIBIT 4

The Growth Rate of Income and the Exchange Rate

If U.S. residents experience a growth in income but Mexican residents do not, U.S. demand for Mexican goods will increase, and with it, the demand for pesos. As a result, the exchange rate will change: The dollar price of pesos will rise, meaning that the dollar depreciates and the peso appreciates.

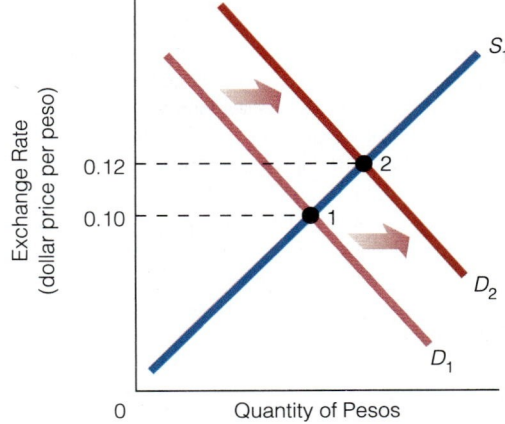

As a result of the rising U.S. demand for Mexican goods, the demand for pesos rises, as shown in Exhibit 5. As a result of the falling Mexican demand for U.S. goods, the demand for dollars decreases, and, therefore, the supply of pesos decreases too. Exhibit 5 also shows the supply of and the decline in pesos. [Remember that the Mexican demand for U.S. goods is tied to the Mexican demand for U.S. dollars, and, in turn, the Mexican demand for U.S. dollars is tied to the Mexican supply of pesos—see Exhibit 1(b).]

As Exhibit 5 shows, the result of an increase in the demand for Mexican pesos and a decrease in their supply constitutes an *appreciation* of the peso and a *depreciation* of the dollar. It now takes 11 cents, instead of 10 cents, to buy 1 peso (depreciation of the dollar); it now takes 9.09 pesos, instead of 10 pesos, to buy $1 (appreciation of the peso).

An important question is how much will the U.S. dollar depreciate as a result of the rise in the U.S. price level? (Mexico's price level does not change.) The **purchasing power parity (PPP) theory** predicts that the U.S. dollar will depreciate by 10 percent as a result of the 10 percent rise in the U.S. price level. This prediction requires the dollar price of a peso to rise to 11 cents (0.10 × 10 cents = 1 cent, 10 cents + 1 cent = 11 cents). A 10 percent depreciation of the dollar restores the *original relative prices of American goods to Mexican customers*.

To illustrate, consider a U.S. car with a price tag of $20,000. If the exchange rate is 0.10 USD = 1 MXN, a Mexican buyer of the car will pay 200,000 pesos. If the car price increases by 10 percent, to $22,000, and the dollar depreciates 10 percent (to 0.11 USD = 1 MXN), the Mexican buyer of the car will still pay only 200,000 pesos:

Purchasing Power Parity (PPP) Theory
Theory stating that exchange rates between any two currencies will adjust to reflect changes in the relative price levels of the two countries.

Exchange Rate	Dollar Price	Peso Price
0.10 USD = 1 MXN	20,000 USD	200,000 MXN [(20,000 ÷ 0.10) MXN]
0.11 USD = 1 MXN	22,000 USD	200,000 MXN [(22,000 ÷ 0.11) MXN]

In short, the PPP theory predicts that *changes in the relative price levels of two countries will affect the exchange rate in such a way that 1 unit of a country's currency will continue to buy the same amount of foreign goods as it did before the change in the relative price levels*. In our example,

EXHIBIT 5

Inflation, Exchange Rates, and Purchasing Power Parity (PPP)

If the price level in the United States increases by 10 percent while the price level in Mexico remains constant, then Mexican goods become cheaper for Americans, and U.S. goods become more expensive for Mexicans. Thus, the demand for pesos rises, and the supply of pesos declines. As a result, the exchange rate will change: The dollar price of pesos will rise, meaning that the dollar depreciates and the peso appreciates. PPP theory predicts that the dollar will depreciate in the foreign exchange market until the original price (in pesos) of American goods to Mexican customers is restored. In this example, the dollar is required to depreciate 10 percent.

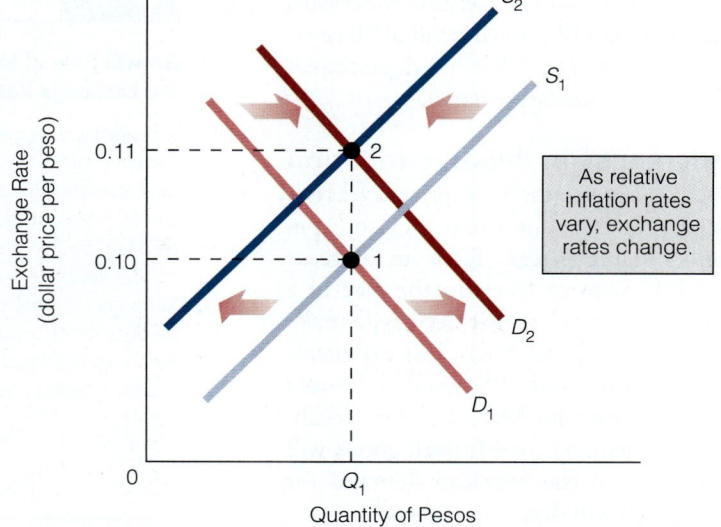

the higher U.S. inflation rate causes a change in the equilibrium exchange rate and leads to a depreciated dollar, but 1 peso continues to have the same purchasing power it previously did.

The PPP theory of exchange rates has made some accurate predictions and some not-so-accurate ones. Many economists suggest that the theory's predictions are not always accurate because the demand for and the supply of a currency are affected *by more than the difference in inflation rates between countries*. For example, as noted, different income growth rates affect the demand for a currency and, therefore, the exchange rate. In the *long run*, however, and particularly when the *difference in inflation rates between countries is large*, the PPP theory does predict exchange rates accurately.

Changes in Real Interest Rates
More than goods flow between countries. Financial capital also moves between countries. The flow of financial capital depends on different countries' *real interest rates*—interest rates adjusted for inflation.

To illustrate, suppose that the real interest rate is 3 percent in both the United States and Mexico. Suppose further that the real interest rate in the United States then increases to 4.5 percent. As a result, Mexicans will want to purchase financial assets in the United States that pay a higher real interest rate than do financial assets in Mexico. The Mexican demand for dollars will increase, and, therefore, Mexicans will supply more pesos. As the supply of pesos increases on the foreign exchange market, the exchange rate (the dollar price per peso) will change: Fewer dollars will be needed to buy pesos. In short, the dollar will appreciate, and the peso will depreciate.

Finding Economics

In the President Speaking to an Economic Advisor The president of the United States is speaking to an economic advisor. The president asks, "What are the effects of the rather large budget deficits?" In response, the advisor might say that large budget deficits can affect interest rates, the value of the dollar, exports and imports, and the trade balance. "How so?" the president asks. Big deficits, the advisor answers, mean that the federal government will have to borrow funds, and the borrowing will increase the demand for credit, in turn, pushing up the interest rate. Then, as the U.S. interest rate rises relative to interest rates in other countries, foreigners will want to purchase financial assets in the United States that pay a higher return. This desire will increase the demand for dollars, the dollar will appreciate, and foreign currencies will depreciate—in turn, affecting both import and export spending.

Economics 24/7

The U.S. Dollar as the Primary Reserve Currency

Today, the U.S. dollar is the primary (i.e., the main) reserve currency. A *reserve currency* is a currency that central banks and major financial institutions hold in significant quantities as part of their foreign exchange reserves. For example, in 2021 the U.S. dollar accounted for 61 percent of foreign exchange reserves held by central banks, whereas the euro accounted for 21 percent. Also, major products bought and sold in the world market are usually denominated in the primary reserve currency.

(Continued)

In other words, the U.S. dollar serves as the so-called unit of account of major global products. For this reason, and because governments and major financial institutions are willing to hold U.S. dollars, the demand for dollars on foreign exchange markets is higher than it would be if dollars weren't the major global reserve currency.

So what would happen to the value of the U.S. dollar on foreign exchange markets if it were no longer the primary reserve currency? The demand for dollars would decline, and subsequently, so would the exchange rate value of the dollar.

One of the advantages to a country whose currency is the primary reserve currency is that it can borrow at lower interest rates than other countries can. For example, in August 2011, China held approximately $3.2 trillion of its foreign exchange reserves in dollars. Most of these dollar holdings were in the form of U.S. government bonds. In effect, because of the dollar's primary reserve currency status, China was more willing than it would have been had the dollar not been the primary reserve currency to buy dollar-denominated U.S. government bonds. But, of course, heightened demand for U.S. government bonds means that the U.S. government can fetch a higher price when selling those bonds and therefore pay a lower interest rate on them.[1]

Economists debate whether the U.S. dollar will remain as the primary reserve currency over the next decade. Some argue that the dollar will likely remain the primary reserve currency; others think that either the euro or renminbi (the official currency of the People's Republic of China) will displace it.

---

[1] To see that the price of bonds and the interest rate on the bond are inversely related, take a bond with the face value of $10,000 that is sold for $9,000 and matures in one year. The interest rate on this bond is found by solving for i in the following equation: $9,000 = $10,000/(1 + i)^1. Solving for i gives us an interest rate of 11.11 percent. Now, if the price of the bond had been higher, at, say, $9,500, we would change the price of the bond in the earlier equation accordingly and again solve for i. This result would give us an interest rate of 5.2 percent. In other words, the price of the bond and the interest rate are inversely related: As the price of the bond rises, the interest rate declines.

(Answers to Self-Test questions are in Answers to Self-Test Questions at the back of the book.)

1. In the foreign exchange market, how is the demand for dollars linked to the supply of pesos?
2. What could cause the U.S. dollar to appreciate against the Mexican peso on the foreign exchange market?
3. Suppose that the U.S. economy grows and that the Swiss economy does not. How will this difference affect the exchange rate between the dollar and the Swiss franc? Why?
4. What does the purchasing power parity theory say? Give an example to illustrate your answer.

Fixed Exchange Rate System
A system whereby a nation's currency is set at a fixed rate relative to all other currencies, and central banks intervene in the foreign exchange market to maintain the fixed rate.

35-3 Fixed Exchange Rates

The major alternative to the flexible exchange rate system is the **fixed exchange rate system**, which works the way it sounds: Exchange rates are fixed; they are not allowed to fluctuate freely in response to the forces of supply and demand. Central banks buy and sell currencies to maintain agreed-on exchange rates. The workings of the fixed exchange rate system are described in this section.

35-3a Fixed Exchange Rates and Overvalued or Undervalued Currency

Once again, we assume a two-country–two-currency world, but this time the United States and Mexico agree to fix the exchange rate of their currencies: Instead of letting the dollar depreciate or appreciate relative to the peso, the two countries agree to set the price of 1 peso at $0.12; that is, they agree to the exchange rate of 0.12 USD = 1 MXN. Generally, we call this the fixed exchange rate, or the *official price*, of a peso.[2] Because we will include more than one official price in our discussion, 0.12 USD = 1 MXN is official price 1 (Exhibit 6).

If the dollar price of pesos is above its equilibrium level (as it is at official price 1), then a surplus of pesos exists, and the peso is said to be **overvalued**. In other words, the peso is fetching more dollars than it would at equilibrium. For example, if 1 peso trades for $0.10 at equilibrium, but 1 peso trades for $0.12 at the official exchange rate, then the peso is said to be overvalued.

If the peso is overvalued, then the dollar is undervalued; that is, it is fetching fewer pesos than it would at equilibrium. For example, if $1 trades for 10 pesos at equilibrium, but $1 trades for 8.33 pesos at the official exchange rate, then the dollar is **undervalued**.

Overvalued
A currency is overvalued if its price in terms of other currencies is above the equilibrium price.

Undervalued
A currency is undervalued if its price in terms of other currencies is below the equilibrium price.

EXHIBIT 6

A Fixed Exchange Rate System

In a fixed exchange rate system, the exchange rate is fixed, and it may not be fixed at the equilibrium exchange rate. The exhibit shows two cases: (1) If the exchange rate is fixed at official price 1, the peso is overvalued, the dollar is undervalued, and a surplus of pesos exists. (2) If the exchange rate is fixed at official price 2, the peso is undervalued, the dollar is overvalued, and a shortage of pesos exists.

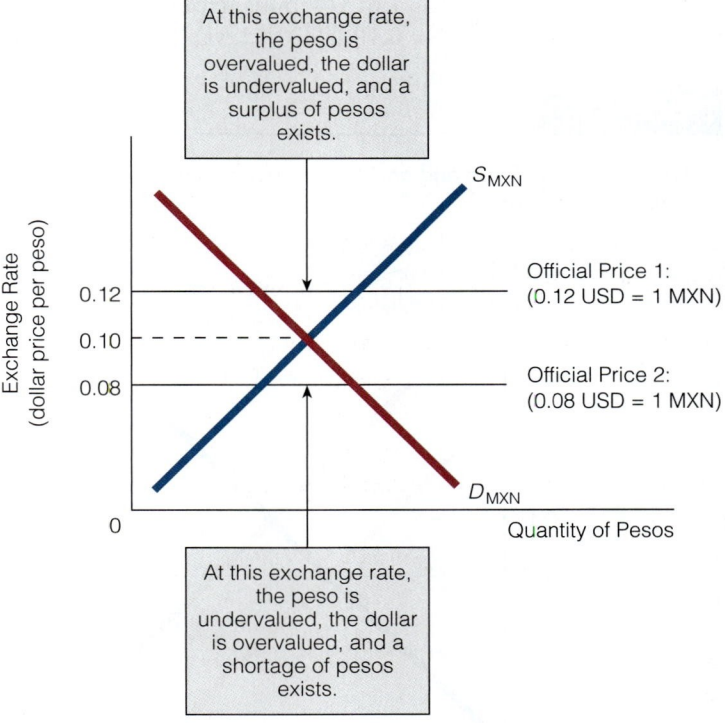

[2.] If the price of 1 peso is $0.12, then the price of $1 is approximately 8.33 pesos. Thus, setting the official price of a peso in terms of dollars automatically sets the official price of a dollar in terms of pesos.

Similarly, if the dollar price of pesos is below its equilibrium level (as it is at official price 2 in Exhibit 6), then a shortage of pesos exists and the peso is undervalued; that is, the peso is not fetching as many dollars as it would at equilibrium. If the peso is undervalued, then the dollar must be overvalued. In sum,

Overvalued peso ↔ Undervalued dollar

Undervalued peso ↔ Overvalued dollar

35-3b What Is So Bad About an Overvalued Dollar?

You read in the newspaper that the dollar is overvalued and that economists are concerned about the overvalued dollar. They are concerned because the exchange rate, and hence the value of the dollar in terms of other currencies, affects the amount of U.S. exports and imports.

To illustrate, suppose the demand for pesos and the supply of pesos are represented by D_1 and S_1, respectively, in Exhibit 7. With this demand curve and supply curve, the equilibrium exchange rate is 0.10 USD = 1 MXN. Let's also suppose that the exchange rate is fixed at this equilibrium exchange rate. In other words, the equilibrium exchange rate and the fixed exchange rate are initially the same.

Time passes, and the demand curve for pesos eventually shifts to the right, from D_1 to D_2. Under a flexible exchange rate system, the exchange rate would rise to 0.12 USD = 1 MXN. But a fixed exchange rate, not a flexible one, is in effect, so the exchange rate stays at 0.10 USD = 1 MXN. Thus, the fixed exchange rate (0.10 USD = 1 MXN) is below the new equilibrium exchange rate (0.12 USD = 1 MXN)

Recall that, when the dollar price per peso is below its equilibrium level (as it is now), the peso is undervalued, and the dollar is overvalued. To illustrate, at equilibrium (point 2 in Exhibit 7), 1 peso would trade for 0.12 dollars, but at its fixed rate (point 1), it trades for only 0.10 dollars, so the peso is undervalued. At equilibrium (point 2), $1 would trade for 8.33 pesos, but at its fixed rate (point 1), it trades for 10 pesos, so the dollar is overvalued.

What is bad about an overvalued dollar is that it makes U.S. goods more expensive for foreigners to buy, possibly affecting U.S. exports. For example, suppose a U.S. good costs $100. At the equilibrium exchange rate (0.12 USD = 1 MXN), a Mexican would pay 833 pesos for the good, but at the fixed exchange rate (0.10 USD = 1 MXN), he will pay 1,000 pesos:

EXHIBIT 7

Fixed Exchange Rates and an Overvalued Dollar

Initially, the demand for and supply of pesos are represented by D_1 and S_1, respectively. The equilibrium exchange rate is 0.10 USD = 1 MXN, which also happens to be the official (fixed) exchange rate. In time, the demand for pesos rises to D_2, and the equilibrium exchange rate rises to 0.12 USD = 1 MXN. The official exchange rate is fixed, however, so the dollar will be overvalued.

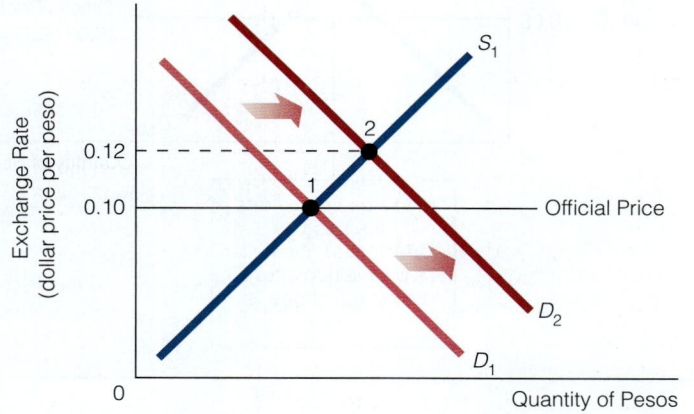

Exchange Rate	Dollar Price	Peso Price
0.12 USD = 1 MXN (equilibrium)	100 USD	833 MXN [(100 ÷ 0.12) MXN]
0.10 USD = 1 MXN (fixed)	100 USD	1,000 MXN [(100 ÷ 0.10) MXN]

The higher the prices are of U.S. goods (exports), the fewer of those goods Mexicans will buy, and, as just discussed, an overvalued dollar makes U.S. export goods higher in price.

35-3c Government Involvement in a Fixed Exchange Rate System

Suppose the governments of Mexico and the United States agree to fix the exchange rate at 0.12 USD = 1 MXN, as shown in Exhibit 6. At this exchange rate, a surplus of pesos exists. To maintain the exchange rate at 0.12 USD = 1 MXN, the Federal Reserve System (the Fed) could buy the surplus of pesos with dollars. As a result, the demand for pesos will increase, and the demand curve will shift to the right, ideally by enough to raise the equilibrium rate to the current fixed exchange rate.

Alternatively, instead of the Fed's buying pesos (to "mop up" the excess supply of pesos), the Banco de México (the central bank of Mexico) could buy pesos with some of its reserve dollars. (It doesn't buy pesos with pesos, because using pesos would not reduce the surplus of pesos on the market.) This action by the Banco de México would also increase the demand for pesos and raise the equilibrium rate.

Finally, the two actions could be combined; that is, both the Fed and the Banco de México could buy pesos.

35-3d Options Under a Fixed Exchange Rate System

Suppose there is a surplus of pesos in the foreign exchange market, indicating that the peso is overvalued and the dollar is undervalued. Also suppose that, although the Fed and the Banco de México each attempt to rectify this situation by buying pesos, their combined action is not successful: The surplus of pesos persists for weeks, along with an overvalued peso and an undervalued dollar. In this case, a few options are still available.

Devaluation and Revaluation Mexico and the United States could agree to reset the official price of the dollar and the peso. Doing so entails *devaluation* and *revaluation*. A **devaluation** occurs when the official price of a currency is lowered. A **revaluation** occurs when the official price of a currency is raised.

For example, suppose the first official price of a peso is 0.10 USD = 1 MXN, or 1 USD = 10 MXN. Then, Mexico and the United States agree to change the official price of their currencies. The second official price is 0.12 USD = 1 MXN, or 1 USD = 8.33 MXN.

Moving from the first official price to the second means that the peso has been revalued, because it takes *more dollars to buy a peso* (12 cents instead of 10 cents). Of course, moving from the first official price to the second also means that the dollar has been devalued, because it takes *fewer pesos to buy a dollar* (8.33 pesos instead of 10 pesos).

One country might want to devalue its currency, but another country might not want to revalue its currency. For example, if Mexico wants to devalue its currency relative to the U.S. dollar, U.S. authorities might not always willingly comply because, if they do, the United States

Devaluation
A government action that changes the exchange rate by lowering the official price of a currency.

Revaluation
A government action that changes the exchange rate by raising the official price of a currency.

will not sell as many goods to Mexico. As explained earlier, revaluing the dollar means that Mexicans have to pay more for it; instead of paying, say, 8.33 pesos for $1, Mexicans might have to pay 10 pesos. At a revalued dollar (a higher peso price for a dollar), Mexicans will find U.S. goods more expensive and will not want to buy as many. Americans who produce goods to sell to Mexico may see that a revalued dollar will hurt their pocketbooks, so they will argue against it.

Protectionist Trade Policy (Quotas and Tariffs) To deal with, say, an overvalued dollar (and, say, an undervalued Chinese renminbi), the United States can impose quotas and tariffs on Chinese goods in order to reduce U.S. consumption of them. (An earlier chapter explains how both tariffs and quotas meet this objective.) A drop in U.S. consumption of Chinese goods goes hand in hand with a decrease in the demand for the Chinese renminbi. In turn, a decline in the demand for the Chinese renminbi can affect the value of the U.S. dollar. In this case, it can eliminate an overvalued dollar.

However, economists are quick to point out that overvalued currencies are sometimes used as an excuse to promote trade restrictions, many of which simply benefit special interests (e.g., U.S. producers that compete for sales with foreign producers in the U.S. market).

Changes in Monetary Policy Sometimes, a country can use monetary policy to support the exchange rate or the official price of its currency. Suppose the United States is continually importing more than it exports. To remedy this imbalance, the United States might enact a tight monetary policy to retard inflation and drive up interest rates (at least in the short run). The tight monetary policy will reduce the U.S. rate of inflation and thereby lower U.S. prices relative to prices in other nations. This effect will make U.S. goods relatively cheaper than they were before (assuming that other nations don't also enact a tight monetary policy), thereby promoting U.S. exports and discouraging foreign imports. It will also generate a flow of investment funds into the United States in search of higher real interest rates.

Some economists argue against fixed exchange rates because they think it unwise for a nation to adopt a particular monetary policy simply to maintain an international exchange rate. Instead, they believe that domestic monetary policies should be used to meet domestic economic goals, such as price stability, low unemployment, low and stable interest rates, and so forth.

1. Under a fixed exchange rate system, if one currency is overvalued, then another currency must be undervalued. Explain why this statement is true.
2. How does an overvalued dollar affect U.S. exports and imports?
3. In each of the following cases, identify whether the U.S. dollar is overvalued or undervalued:
    a. The fixed exchange rate is $2 = £1, and the equilibrium exchange rate is $3 = £1.
    b. The fixed exchange rate is $1.25 = €1, and the equilibrium exchange rate is $1.10 = €1.
    c. The fixed exchange rate is $1 = 10 pesos, and the equilibrium exchange rate is $1 = 14 pesos.
4. Under a fixed exchange rate system, why might the United States want to devalue its currency?

35-4 Fixed Exchange Rates versus Flexible Exchange Rates

As in many economic situations, any exchange rate system has both its costs and its benefits. This section discusses some of the arguments and issues surrounding fixed exchange rates and flexible exchange rates.

35-4a Promoting International Trade

Which are better at promoting international trade, fixed or flexible exchange rates? This section presents the case for each.

The Case for Fixed Exchange Rates Proponents of a fixed exchange rate system often argue that fixed exchange rates promote international trade whereas flexible exchange rates stifle it. A major advantage of fixed exchange rates is certainty. Individuals in different countries know from day to day the value of their nation's currency. With flexible exchange rates, individuals are less likely to engage in international trade because of the added risk of not knowing from one day to the next how many dollars, euros, or yen they will have to trade for other currencies. Certainty is a necessary ingredient in international trade; flexible exchange rates promote uncertainty, which hampers international trade.

Economist Charles Kindleberger, a proponent of fixed exchange rates, stated that having fixed exchange rates is analogous to having a single currency for the entire United States instead of having a different currency for each of the 50 states. One currency in the United States promotes trade, whereas 50 different currencies would hamper it. In Kindleberger's view,

> *The main case against flexible exchange rates is that they break up the world market.... Imagine trying to conduct interstate trade in the USA if there were fifty different state monies, none of which was dominant. This is akin to barter, the inefficiency of which is explained time and again by textbooks.*[3]

The Case for Flexible Exchange Rates As noted, advocates of flexible exchange rates maintain that it is better for a nation to adopt policies to meet domestic economic goals than to sacrifice domestic economic goals in order to maintain an exchange rate. Also, the chance is too great that the fixed exchange rate will diverge greatly from the equilibrium exchange rate, creating persistent trade problems for some countries (with import spending continually greater than export spending) and thus leading them to impose trade restrictions (tariffs and quotas) that hinder international trade.

The Current System Today's international monetary system is described as a managed flexible exchange rate system, sometimes referred to more casually as a **managed float**. In a way, this system is a rough compromise between the fixed and flexible exchange rate systems. The current system operates under flexible exchange rates, but not completely: Now and then, nations intervene to adjust their official reserve holdings to moderate major swings in exchange rates.

Managed Float
A managed flexible exchange rate system under which nations intervene now and then to adjust their official reserve holdings in order to moderate major swings in exchange rates.

---

[3] Charles Kindleberger, *International Money* (London: Allen and Unwin, 1981), p. 174.

35-4b Optimal Currency Areas

An **optimal currency area** is a geographic area in which exchange rates can be fixed or a *common currency* can be used without sacrificing domestic economic goals, such as low unemployment. The concept of an optimal currency area originated in the debate over whether fixed or flexible exchange rates are better. Most of the pioneering work on optimal currency areas was done by Robert Mundell, winner of the 1999 Nobel Prize in Economics.

Before discussing an optimal currency area, we need to look at the relationships among labor mobility, trade, and exchange rates. *Labor mobility* means that the residents of one country can move easily to another country.

Optimal Currency Area
A geographic area in which exchange rates can be fixed or a common currency used without sacrificing domestic economic goals, such as low unemployment.

Trade and Labor Mobility Suppose there are only two countries: the United States and Canada. The United States produces calculators and soft drinks, and Canada produces bread and muffins. Currently, the two countries trade with each other, and there is complete labor mobility between them.

One day, the residents of both countries reduce their demand for bread and muffins and increase their demand for calculators and soft drinks. In other words, relative demand changes: Demand increases for U.S. goods and falls for Canadian goods. Business firms in Canada lay off employees because their sales have plummeted. Incomes in Canada begin to fall, and the unemployment rate begins to rise. In the United States, prices initially rise because of the increased demand for calculators and soft drinks. In response to the higher demand for their products, U.S. business firms begin to hire more workers and increase their production. Their efforts to hire more workers drive wages up and reduce the unemployment rate.

Because labor is mobile, some of the newly unemployed Canadian workers move to the United States to find work, easing the economic situation in both countries. The movement of labor will reduce some of the unemployment problems in Canada, and, with more workers in the United States, more output will be produced, thus dampening upward price pressures on calculators and soft drinks. Clearly, then, changes in relative demand pose no major economic problems for either country if labor is mobile.

Trade and Labor Immobility Now let's suppose that relative demand has changed but that labor is *not* mobile between the United States and Canada, perhaps because of political or cultural barriers. If people cannot move, then what happens in the economies of the two countries depends largely on whether exchange rates are fixed or flexible.

If exchange rates are flexible, the value of the U.S. currency will change vis-à-vis the Canadian currency. If Canadians want to buy more U.S. goods, they will have to exchange their domestic currency for U.S. currency. The demand for U.S. currency on the foreign exchange market will increase at the same time that the supply of Canadian currency increases. Consequently, U.S. currency will appreciate, and Canadian currency will depreciate. In this case, because Canadian currency depreciates, U.S. goods become relatively more expensive for Canadians, so they buy fewer of them. And because U.S. currency appreciates, Canadian goods become relatively cheaper for Americans, so they buy more Canadian goods. As a result, Canadian business firms begin to sell more goods, so they hire more workers, the unemployment rate drops, and the bad economic times in Canada begin to disappear.

If exchange rates are fixed, however, U.S. goods will not become relatively more expensive for Canadians, and Canadian goods will not become relatively cheaper for Americans. Consequently, the bad economic times in Canada (high unemployment) might last for a long time, indeed, instead of beginning to reverse. Thus, if labor is immobile, changes in relative demand may pose major economic problems when exchange rates are fixed but not when they are flexible.

Costs, Benefits, and Optimal Currency Areas In addition to benefits, flexible exchange rates have costs. Exchanging one currency for another (say, U.S. dollars for Canadian dollars or U.S. dollars for Japanese yen) incurs a charge, and the risk of not knowing what the value of one's currency will be on the foreign exchange market on any given day is greater. For many countries, the benefits outweigh the costs, so they have flexible exchange rate systems.

Suppose some of the costs of flexible exchange rates could be eliminated while maintaining the benefits, so that if labor is mobile between the two countries, they could have a fixed exchange rate or adopt a common currency and retain the benefits of flexible exchange rates. In that case, they do not have to have separate currencies that float against each other because resources (labor) can move easily and quickly in response to changes in relative demand. The two countries can either fix exchange rates or adopt the same currency.

When labor in countries within a geographic area is mobile enough to move easily and quickly in response to changes in relative demand, the countries are said to constitute an *optimal currency area*. Countries in such an area can either fix their currencies or adopt the same currency and thus keep all the benefits of flexible exchange rates without incurring any of the costs.

The states of the United States are commonly said to constitute an optimal currency area. Labor can move easily and quickly between, say, North Carolina and South Carolina in response to relative changes in demand. Some economists have argued that the countries that compose the European Union make up an optimal currency area and, therefore, adopting a common currency—the euro—benefits these countries. Other economists disagree, arguing that, although labor is somewhat more mobile in Europe today than in the past, given language and cultural differences, labor mobility is less than sufficient to produce a true optimal currency area.

Office Hours

"Why Is the Depreciation of One Currency Tied to the Appreciation of Another?"

Student: I know that when the dollar depreciates, some other currency appreciates. Is this just the way it is? For example, if $1 dollar equals €1 euro, and then $1.25 equals €1, the arithmetic of exchange rates tells me that now $1 will fetch only €0.8. Is that all there is to it?

Instructor: Not exactly. You're focusing on the arithmetic of exchange rates to the exclusion of the economics. There is an economic reason that dollar depreciation is linked to euro appreciation.

Student: What is that economic reason?

Instructor: Think of what can lead to the dollar's depreciating. Suppose you want to travel to Germany, where the euro is used. You take your dollars and buy euros with them. In other words, you do two things: You (1) buy euros by (2) supplying dollars. Now think of how you are affecting the market for euros and the market for dollars. You are increasing the demand for euros in the market for euros, and you are increasing the supply of dollars in the market for dollars. In other words, your demand for euros is linked to your supply of dollars. Therefore, if you increase the demand for euros, you are automatically increasing the supply of dollars.

Student: I'm used to thinking that my buying something affects only one market. For instance, when I buy more books, the purchase affects only the market for books. You seem to be telling me that this is not the case when I buy a currency, such as the euro. To buy euros is to supply dollars.

Instructor: That's right. So when you increase the demand for euros, you automatically increase the supply of dollars. And then we have to ask ourselves what happens in each of the two markets: the market for euros and the market for dollars.

Student: Well, if I increase the demand for euros, the price of a euro in terms of dollars will rise. Also, if I increase the supply of dollars, the price of a dollar in terms of euros will fall.

Instructor: And what do you call it when the price of a euro has risen in terms of dollars?

Student: We say the dollar has depreciated, because it now takes more dollars and cents to buy a euro.

Instructor: And what do you call it when the price of a dollar has fallen in terms of euros?

Student: We say the euro has appreciated, because it now takes fewer euros to buy a dollar.

Instructor: So let's go back to your original query. You wondered whether the dollar's depreciating and the euro's appreciating were just matters of arithmetic. Now we know that they aren't. They are curves shifting in different markets.

Points to Remember

1. To buy a currency is to affect two markets, not just one. If you buy euros, you affect the euro market. But by selling dollars to buy euros, you also affect the dollar market.
2. The fact that when one currency depreciates, another appreciates is a matter of curves shifting in two currency markets.

Chapter Summary

The Foreign Exchange Market

- The market in which currencies of different countries are exchanged is called the foreign exchange market. In this market, currencies are bought and sold for a price: the exchange rate.
- When the residents of a nation demand a foreign currency, they must supply their own currency. For example, if Americans demand Mexican goods, they also demand Mexican pesos and supply U.S. dollars. If Mexicans demand American goods, they also demand U.S. dollars and supply Mexican pesos.

Flexible Exchange Rates

- Under flexible exchange rates, the foreign exchange market will equilibrate at the exchange rate for which the quantity demanded of a currency equals the quantity supplied of the currency; for example, the foreign exchange market equilibrates when the quantity demanded of U.S. dollars equals the quantity supplied of U.S. dollars.
- If the price of a nation's currency increases relative to a foreign currency, the nation's currency is said to have appreciated. For example, if the price of a peso rises from 0.10 USD = 1 MXN to 0.15 USD = 1 MXN, then the peso has appreciated. If the price of a nation's currency decreases relative to a foreign currency, the nation's currency is said to have depreciated. For example, if the price of a dollar falls from 10 MXN = 1 USD to 8 MXN = 1 USD, then the dollar has depreciated.
- Under a flexible exchange rate system, the equilibrium exchange rate is affected by a difference in income growth rates between countries, a difference in inflation rates between countries, and a change in (real) interest rates between countries.

Fixed Exchange Rates

Under a fixed exchange rate system, countries agree to fix the price of their currencies. The central banks of the countries must then buy and sell currencies to maintain the exchange rate that was agreed on.

The Current International Monetary System

Today's international monetary system is described as a managed flexible exchange rate system, or managed float. For the most part, the exchange rate system is flexible, although nations periodically intervene in the foreign exchange market in order to adjust rates.

Key Terms and Concepts

Trade Balance
Trade Surplus
Trade Deficit
Foreign Exchange Market
Exchange Rate
Flexible Exchange Rate System
Appreciation
Depreciation
Purchasing Power Parity (PPP) Theory
Fixed Exchange Rate System
Overvalued
Undervalued
Devaluation
Revaluation
Managed Float
Optimal Currency Area

Questions and Problems

1. Explain the link between the Mexican demand for U.S. goods and the supply of pesos. Next, explain the link between the U.S. demand for Mexican goods and the supply of dollars.
2. The lower the dollar price of a peso, the higher is the quantity demanded of pesos and the lower is the quantity supplied of pesos. Do you agree or disagree? Explain.
3. What does it mean to say that the U.S. dollar has depreciated in value in relation to the Mexican peso? What does it mean to say that the Mexican peso has appreciated in value relative to the U.S. dollar?
4. Suppose the United States and Japan have a flexible exchange rate system. Explain whether each of the following events will lead to an appreciation or depreciation of the U.S. dollar and Japanese yen:
    a. U.S. real interest rates rise above Japanese real interest rates.
    b. The Japanese inflation rate rises relative to the U.S. inflation rate.
    c. An increase in U.S. income combines with no change in Japanese income.
5. Give an example of how a change in the exchange rate alters the relative price of domestic goods in terms of foreign goods.
6. What are the strong and weak points of the flexible exchange rate system? What are the strong and weak points of the fixed exchange rate system?
7. Explain the details of the purchasing power parity (PPP) theory.
8. A country whose currency is the primary reserve currency can likely borrow at lower interest rates than it could if its currency were not the primary reserve currency. Do you agree or disagree? Explain.
9. What does it mean to say that a currency is overvalued? undervalued?
10. Under a flexible exchange rate system, if the equilibrium exchange rate is 0.10 USD = 1 MXN and the current exchange rate is 0.12 = 1 MXN, will the U.S. dollar appreciate or depreciate? Explain.
11. Under a fixed exchange rate system, setting the official price of a peso in terms of dollars automatically sets the official price of a dollar in terms of pesos. Do you agree or disagree? Explain.
12. Country X wants to lower the value of its currency on the foreign exchange market. Under a flexible exchange rate system, how can it do that?
13. What is an optimal currency area?
14. Country 1 produces good X, and country 2 produces good Y. People in both countries begin to demand more of good X and less of good Y. Assume that there is no labor mobility between the two countries and that a flexible exchange rate system exists. What will happen to the unemployment rate in country 2? Explain.
15. How important is labor mobility in determining whether an area is an optimal currency area?
16. If everyone in the world spoke the same language, would the world be closer to or further from being an optimal currency area? Explain.

Working with Numbers and Graphs

1. On Thursday, one Russian ruble equaled $0.013, and on Friday it equaled $0.014. On Thursday, one U.S. dollar equaled 5.369 Brazilian real, and on Friday, one U.S. dollar equaled 5.245 Brazilian real. Between Thursday and Friday, did the dollar appreciate or depreciate against the Russian ruble? Between Thursday and Friday did the dollar appreciate or depreciate against the Brazilian real?

2. If $1 equals ¥0.0093, what does ¥1 equal?
3. If $1 equals 7.7 krone (Danish), what does 1 krone equal?
4. If $1 equals 31 rubles, what does 1 ruble equal?
5. If the exchange rate is $0.08 = 1 MXN, what is the cost in dollars of a Mexican table priced at 500 pesos?

Self-Test Appendix

Chapter 1

Chapter 1, Page 4

1. False. It takes two things for scarcity to exist: finite resources and infinite wants. If people's wants were equal to or less than the finite resources available to satisfy their wants, scarcity would not exist. Scarcity exists only because people's wants are greater than the resources available to satisfy their wants. Scarcity is the condition resulting from infinite wants clashing with finite resources.

2. Because of scarcity, there is a need for a rationing device. People will compete for the rationing device. For example, if dollar price is the rationing device, people will compete for dollars.

3. Because our unlimited wants are greater than our limited resources—that is, because scarcity exists—some wants must go unsatisfied. We must choose which wants we will satisfy and which we will not.

Chapter 1, Page 15

1. Every time a student is late to history class, the instructor subtracts 1/10 of a point from the person's final grade. Economists predict that, if the instructor raises the opportunity cost of being late to class by subtracting one point from the final grade, then fewer students will be late to class. In sum, the higher the opportunity cost is for being late to class, the less likely it is that people will be late to class.

2. Yes. To illustrate, suppose the marginal benefits and marginal costs (in dollars) are as follows for various hours of studying:

Hour	Marginal Benefits	Marginal Costs
First Hour	$20.00	$10.00
Second Hour	$14.00	$11.00
Third Hour	$13.00	$12.00
Fourth Hour	$12.10	$12.09
Fifth Hour	$11.00	$13.00

Clearly, you will study the first hour, because the marginal benefits are greater than the marginal costs. Stated differently, studying the first hour has a net benefit of $10 (the difference between the marginal benefits of $20 and the marginal costs of $10). If you stop studying after the first hour and do not proceed to the second hour, then you forfeit the net benefit of $3 for the second hour. To maximize your net benefits of studying, you must proceed until the marginal benefits and the marginal costs are as close to equal as possible. They never actually reach equality—in the language of calculus, they approach each other asymptotically—however, economists speak of the equality of the two for convenience. In this case, you should study through the fourth hour. You would not study the fifth hour because it is not worth it: The marginal benefits of studying the fifth hour are less than the marginal costs, and, therefore, have a net cost.

3. You might be sleepy the next day, less alert while driving, and so on.

Chapter 1, Page 18

1. The purpose of building a theory is to explain something that is not obvious. For example, the reason for changes in the unemployment rate is not obvious, so the economist would build a theory to explain this.

2. A theory of the economy seeks to explain why certain things in the economy happen. For example, a theory of the economy might try to explain why prices rise or why output falls. A description of the economy is simply a statement of what exists in the economy. For example, we could say that the economy is growing or contracting or that more jobs are available this month than last month. A description doesn't answer questions; it simply tells us what is. A theory tries to answer a question, such as, "Why are more jobs available this month than last month?"

3. If you do not test a theory, you will never know whether you have accomplished your objective in building the theory in the first place. In other words, you will not know whether you have explained something accurately. We do not simply accept a theory just because it sounds right because what sounds right may actually be wrong. For example, during the time of Columbus, the theory that the Earth was flat might have sounded right to many people, and the theory that the Earth was round might have sounded ridiculous. However, what sounded right turned out to be wrong—the Earth is round.

4. Unless stated otherwise, when economics instructors identify the relationship between two variables, they implicitly make the *ceteris paribus* assumption. In other words, the instructor is really saying, "If the price of going to the movies goes down, people will go to the movies more often—assuming that nothing else changes, such as the quality of movies, and so on." Instructors don't always state *"ceteris paribus,"* because if they did, they would be using the term every minute of a lecture. So the instructor is right; although a student who is new to economics might not know what the instructor is assuming but not saying.

Chapter 2

Chapter 2, Page 49

1. A straight-line PPF represents the constant opportunity costs between two goods. For example, for every unit of X produced, one unit of Y is forfeited. A bowed-outward PPF represents increasing opportunity costs. For example, we may have to forfeit 1 unit of X to produce the 11th unit of Y, but we have to forfeit 2 units of X to produce the 100th unit of Y.

2. A bowed-outward PPF is representative of increasing costs, because the PPF would not be bowed otherwise. To prove this statement, look back at Exhibits 1 and 2. In Exhibit 1, costs are constant (not increasing), and the PPF is a straight line. In Exhibit 2, costs are increasing, and the PPF is bowed outward.

3. The first condition is that the economy is currently operating *below* its PPF. It is possible to move from a point below the PPF to a point on the PPF and get more goods. The second condition is that the economy's PPF shifts outward.

4. False. Take a look at Exhibit 5. All of the numerous productive efficient points lie on the PPF.

Chapter 3

Chapter 3, Page 68

1. Popcorn is a normal good for Sandi, and prepaid telephone cards are an inferior good for Mark.

2. Asking why demand curves are downward sloping is the same as asking why price and quantity demanded are inversely related (as one rises, the other falls). Two reasons for this inverse relationship are mentioned in this section: (1) As price rises, people substitute lower-priced goods for higher-priced goods. (2) Because individuals receive less utility from an additional unit of a good they consume, they are only willing to pay less for the additional unit, which is a reflection of the law of diminishing marginal utility.

3. Suppose only two people, Bob and Alice, have a demand for good X. At a price of $7, Bob buys 10 units and Alice buys 3 units; at a price of $6, Bob buys 12 units and Alice buys 5 units. One point on the market demand curve represents a price of $7 and a quantity demanded of 13 units; another point represents $6 and 17 units. A market demand curve is derived by adding the quantities demanded at each price.

4. A change in income, preferences, prices of related goods, the number of buyers, and expectations of future price can change demand. A change in the price of the good changes the quantity demanded of it. For example, a change in *income* can change the *demand* for oranges, but only a change in the *price* of oranges can directly change the *quantity demanded* of oranges.

Chapter 3, Page 74

1. Increasing the quantity supplied of houses over the next 10 hours would be difficult, so the supply curve in (a) is vertical, as in Exhibit 7. Increasing the quantity supplied of houses over the next 3 months is possible, so the supply curve in (b) is upward sloping.

2. a. The supply curve shifts to the left.
   b. The supply curve shifts to the left.
   c. The supply curve shifts to the right.

3. False. If the price of apples rises, then the *quantity supplied* of apples will rise—not the *supply*. We are talking about a *movement* from one point on a supply curve to a point higher up on the supply curve, not a shift in the supply curve.

Chapter 3, Page 87

1. Disagree. In the text, we plainly saw how supply and demand worked at an auction. Supply and demand are at work in the grocery store too, even though no auctioneer is present. The essence of the auction example is that the auctioneer raises the price when there is a shortage and lowers the price when there is a surplus. The same thing happens at the grocery store. For example, given a surplus of cornflakes, the manager of the store is likely to run a sale (lower prices) on them. Many markets without auctioneers act *as if* auctioneers were raising and lowering prices in response to shortages and surpluses.

2. No. It could be the result of a higher supply of computers. Either a decrease in demand or an increase in supply will lower price.

3. a. Lower price and lower quantity.
   b. Lower price and higher quantity.
   c. Higher price and lower quantity.
   d. Lower price and lower quantity.

4. At the equilibrium quantity, the maximum buying price and the minimum selling price are the same. For example, in Exhibit 15, both prices are $40 at the equilibrium quantity of 4. The equilibrium quantity is the only quantity at which the maximum buying price and the minimum selling price are the same.

5. $44; $34.

Chapter 4

Chapter 4, Page 95

1. A rationing device is necessary because scarcity exists. If scarcity did not exist, a rationing device would not be needed.

2. If (dollar) price is the rationing device used, then individuals have an incentive to produce goods and services, sell them for money (for the dollar price), and then use the money to buy what they want. If another rationing device were used (say, first come, first served or "need"), then the incentive to produce would be dramatically dampened. Why produce a good if the only way you can "sell" it (i.e., ration the good) is by way of first come, first served?

3. Price conveys information about the relative scarcity of a good. In the orange juice example, a rise in the price of orange juice transmitted information relating to the increased relative scarcity of orange juice due to a cold spell in Florida.

Chapter 4, Page 105

1. Yes, if nothing else changes—that is, yes, *ceteris paribus*. However, if other things change, they may not. For example, if the government imposes an effective price ceiling on gasoline, Jamie may pay lower gas prices at the pump but have to wait in line to buy the gas (because of first-come, first-served rationing of the shortage). Whether Jamie is better off paying a higher price and not waiting in line or paying a lower price and waiting in line is not clear. The point, however, is that buyers don't necessarily prefer lower prices to higher prices unless everything else (quality, wait, service, etc.) stays the same.

2. Disagree. Both long-lasting shortages and long lines are caused by price ceilings. First, the price ceiling is imposed, creating the shortage; then the rationing device of first come, first served emerges because price isn't permitted to fully ration the good. Every day, shortages occur that don't cause long lines to form. Instead, buyers bid up the price so that output and price move to equilibrium, and there is no shortage.

3. Buyers might argue for price ceilings on the goods they buy, especially if they don't know that price ceilings have some effects they may not like (e.g., fewer exchanges, first-come, first-served rationing devices). Sellers might argue for price floors on the goods they sell, especially if they expect their profits to rise. Employees might argue for a wage floor on the labor services they sell, especially if they don't know that they may lose their jobs or have their hours cut back as a result.

Chapter 4, Page 108

1. $1A = \frac{2}{3}B$ and $1B = 1.5A$

2. The statement is correct in the sense that good X has a higher money price than it used to have. It is misleading because a higher money price doesn't necessarily mean a higher relative price. For example, if the absolute (money) price of good X is $10 and the absolute price of good Y is $20, then the relative price of X is ½ unit of Y. Now, suppose the absolute price of X rises to $15 while the absolute price of Y rises to $60. Then the new relative price of X is ¼ unit of Y. In other words, the absolute price of X rises (from $10 to $15), while its relative price falls (from ½ Y to ¼ Y). Thus, good X can become more expensive in money terms as it becomes cheaper in terms of other goods.

Chapter 5

Chapter 5, Page 112

1. Yes, we would expect that the demand for a U-Haul in Texas (going to California) would be less than the demand for a U-Haul in California (going to Texas). Therefore, all things remaining constant, we would expect the U-Haul rate going from California to Texas to be higher than the U-Haul rate going from Texas to California.

2. The demand for and supply of houses are not the same in all cities, and as a result, house prices are not likely to be the same in all cities.

Chapter 5, Pages 114

1. No. In Exhibit 1, the two demand curves are parallel because the subsidy is always $1 and the vertical distance between the two curves is $1. With a different subsidy for different units of good X (a larger subsidy for the first unit than for the second and so on), the vertical distance between the two demand curves (the one with the subsidy and the one without the subsidy) is not always going to be the same. Therefore, the two demand curves will not be parallel.
2. The subsidy will cause the demand for solar panels to rise, and as a result, the price of solar panels will likely rise.

Chapter 5, Page 115

1. Answers will vary. Students sometimes say that it is fairer if everyone is charged the same price. Is it unfair, then, that moviegoers pay less if they go to the 2 p.m. movie than if they go to the 8 p.m. movie?
2. We learned about price ceilings in the previous chapter. Specifically, we learned that a price ceiling creates a shortage. In the application dealing with the 10 a.m. class, the university charged a below-equilibrium price for the 10 a.m. class, leading to a shortage of such classes.

Chapter 5, Page 117

1. If supply and tuition are constant and demand rises, the shortage of openings at the university will become greater. The university will continue to use its nonprice-rationing devices (GPA, SAT scores, and ACT scores) but will have to raise the standards of admission. Instead of requiring a GPA of, say, 3.5 for admission, it may raise the requirement to 3.8.
2. Not likely. A university that didn't make admission easier in the face of a surplus of openings might not be around much longer. When tuition cannot be adjusted directly—in other words, when the rationing device (price) cannot be adjusted—it is likely that the nonprice-rationing device (standards) will be.

Chapter 5, Page 119

1. The price of food will rise along with the premium for food insurance.
2. The new demand curve would be between D_1 and D_2.

Chapter 5, Page 120

1. A possible answer: Of two cities, one has clean air, and the other has dirty air. The demand to live in the city that has clean air is higher than the demand to live in the city that has dirty air. As a result, housing prices are higher in the city that has clean air.
2. Ultimately, the person who owns the land in the city with good weather receives the payment. Look at it this way: People have a higher demand for houses in cities that have good weather than they have for houses in cities that have bad weather. As a result, house builders receive higher prices for houses built and sold in cities that have good weather. Because of the higher house prices, builders have a higher demand for land in cities that have good weather. In the end, higher demand for land translates into higher land prices or land rents for landowners.

Chapter 5, Page 122

1. The airline company will likely use the rationing device of first come, first served. The people who book their reservations early get their pick of seats; those who do not book early have to take the leftover seats.
2. The equilibrium price of the window seat is less than the equilibrium price of the aisle seat; the equilibrium price of the middle seat is less than the equilibrium price of the window seat. For example, if the equilibrium price of the aisle seat is $300, then the equilibrium price of the window seat might be $280, with the equilibrium price of the middle seat even lower at $250.

Chapter 5, Page 124

1. Yes. For example, suppose a 30 percent down payment, instead of a 10 percent down payment, was needed to obtain a mortgage loan. Due to the increase in the down payment requirement, fewer individuals would be able to obtain a loan to buy a house, which would lower the demand for houses and drive down house prices.
2. Yes. Reducing one's taxes because one has purchased a house makes buying a house more attractive, which would lead to a higher demand for houses. The higher demand for houses raises the equilibrium price of houses.

Chapter 5, Page 126

1. A speculator seeks to buy low and sell high. If she does so, she benefits. But by buying low and selling high, a speculator can reallocate supply and change prices in a way that benefits consumers. To illustrate, suppose a tornado threatens to reduce the wheat crop in the Midwest. Speculators translate this possibility into a future decrease in the supply of, and rise in the

price of, wheat. So they buy wheat today (before the tornado strikes and when it is relatively cheap) and sell it later (after the tornado has struck and the price is relatively expensive). In the process, they reallocate some of the supply of wheat from today to the future, and as supply changes, so does price. As for the buyers of wheat and wheat products, they may prefer to spread out the price-related pain of the tornado by paying a higher price for wheat today and a lower price for wheat in the future. For example, without the speculators reallocating some wheat, wheat prices might be $4 a bushel before the tornado and $9 after. But with the speculators, wheat prices might be $6 before the tornado and $7 after the tornado.

2. Without speculation, the price of good X is $40 on Monday through Thursday and $50 on Friday through Sunday. In this instance, good X can be moved. Suppose that speculators buy some of good X on Monday through Thursday at the lower price and sell it on Friday through Sunday at the higher price. This difference in price should last only a short while because in their attempts to buy low and sell high, speculators are reallocating some of the supply of good X from Monday through Thursday to Friday through Sunday. The lower supply on Monday through Thursday will raise the price of good X on these days, and the higher supply on Friday through Sunday will lower the price of good X on these days. In the end, it is likely that the same price for good X will exist Monday through Sunday.

Chapter 5, Page 127

1. Any price greater than 70¢.
2. Assuming that tolls are not used, freeway congestion will worsen. An increase in driving population simply shifts the demand curve for driving to the right.

Chapter 5, Page 129

1. Moving from a system in which patients cannot sue their HMOs to one in which they can gives patients something they didn't have before (the right to sue) at a higher price (higher charges for health-care coverage). The "free lunch"—the right to sue—isn't free after all.
2. If the students get the extra week and nothing else changes, then the students will probably say that they were better off. But if, as a result, the professor grades their papers harder than she would have otherwise, then some or all of the students might say that they weren't made better off by the extra week.

Chapter 6
Chapter 6, Page 140

1. The CPI is calculated as follows: (1) Define a market basket; (2) determine how much it would cost to purchase the market basket in the current year and in the base year; (3) divide the dollar cost of purchasing the market basket in the current year by the dollar cost of purchasing the market basket in the base year; (4) multiply the quotient by 100. (For a review of this process, see Exhibit 1.)
2. It is a year that is used for comparison purposes with other years.
3. Annual nominal income has risen by 13.85 percent, and prices have risen by 4.94 percent. We conclude that because nominal income has risen more than prices, real income has increased. Alternatively, you can look at the situation this way: Real income in year 1 was $31,337, and real income in year 2 was $33,996.

Chapter 6, Page 147

1. The frictionally unemployed person has readily transferable skills, and the structurally unemployed person does not.
2. It implies that the (actual, measured) unemployment rate in the economy is greater than the natural unemployment rate. For example, if the unemployment rate is 8 percent and the natural unemployment rate is 6 percent, the cyclical unemployment rate is 2 percent.

Chapter 7
Chapter 7, Page 156

1. GDP is a measure of production in a country. When stocks are purchased and sold, no production occurs. A stock purchase and sale simply represents the trading of existing assets. Specifically, if person A owns 100 shares of stock X and then sells the shares to person B, all that has happened is that person B owns something that person A once owned. No more goods and services have been produced.
2. No. GDP doesn't account for all productive activity (e.g., it omits the production of nonmarket goods and services). A GDP of $0 doesn't necessarily mean that there was no production in the country.

Chapter 7, Page 160

1. In the expenditure approach, GDP is computed by finding the sum of consumption, investment, government purchases, and net exports. (Net exports are equal to exports minus imports.)

2. Yes. To illustrate, suppose consumption is $200, investment is $80, and government purchases are $70. The sum of these three spending components of GDP is $350. Now, suppose that exports are $0 but imports are $100, in which case net exports are –$100. Because GDP = $C + I + G + (EX - IM)$, GDP is $250.

3. No. Each individual would have $40,000 worth of goods and services only if the entire GDP were equally distributed across the country. There is no indication, however, that this is the case. The $40,000 (per-capita GDP) says that the average person in the country has access to $40,000 worth of goods and services, but in reality, the average person may not exist. For example, in a two-person universe, if Smith earns $10,000 and Jones earns $20,000, then the average would be $15,000. Since neither Smith nor Jones earned the average, the average person in this scenario does not exist.

Chapter 7, Page 168

1. We can't know for sure. We can only say what might have caused the rise in GDP. It could be (a) a rise in prices with no change in output, (b) a rise in output with no change in prices, (c) rises in both prices and output, or (d) a percentage increase in prices that is greater than the percentage decrease in output, or even some other situation.

2. More output was produced in year 2 than in year 1.

3. Yes. Business cycles—ups and downs in Real GDP—don't prevent Real GDP from growing over time. Exhibit 6 shows Real GDP higher at the second peak than at the first, even though there is a business cycle between the peaks.

Chapter 8

Chapter 8, Page 189

1. In the real balance effect, a rise in the price level causes purchasing power to fall (and vice versa), thereby decreasing or increasing a person's monetary wealth. As people become more or less wealthy, the quantity demanded of Real GDP rises or falls, respectively.

2. If the dollar appreciates, it takes more foreign currency to buy a dollar and fewer dollars to buy foreign currency. U.S. goods (denominated in dollars) become more expensive for foreigners, and foreign goods become cheaper for Americans. In turn, foreigners buy fewer U.S. exports, and Americans buy more foreign imports. As exports fall and imports rise, net exports fall. If net exports fall, total expenditures fall, *ceteris paribus*. As total expenditures fall, the *AD* curve shifts to the left.

3. Total spending is the product of the money supply and velocity. Let the money supply be $400 and velocity be 3. Then total spending is $1,200. Now, suppose that the money supply rises to $500 but velocity declines to 2. Then total spending has fallen to $1,000, even though the money supply has increased. So, yes, the money supply can rise while total spending declines.

Chapter 8, Page 193

1. As wage rates decline, the cost per unit of production falls. In the short run (assuming that prices are constant), profit per unit rises. Higher profit causes producers to produce more units of their goods and services. In short, the *SRAS* curve shifts to the right.

2. Last year, 10 workers produced 100 units of good *X* in 1 hour. This year, 10 workers produced 120 units of good *X* in 1 hour.

3. Workers initially misperceive the change in their real wage as being due to a change in the price level. For example, if the nominal wage is $30, and the price level is 1.50, the real wage is $20. If the nominal wage falls to $25, and the price level falls to 1.10, the real wage is now $22.72. But suppose workers misperceive the decline in the price level and mistakenly believe that it has fallen to 1.40. They would perceive their real wage as $17.85 ($25 ÷ 1.40). In other words, they will misperceive their real wage as falling when it has actually increased. How will workers react if they believe that their real wage has fallen? They will cut back on the quantity supplied of labor, reducing output (or Real GDP). This process is consistent with an upward-sloping *SRAS* curve: A decline in the price level leads to a reduction in output.

Chapter 8, Page 200

1. In long-run equilibrium, the economy is producing Natural Real GDP. In short-run equilibrium, the economy is not producing Natural Real GDP, although the quantity demanded of Real GDP equals the quantity supplied of Real GDP.

2. The diagram should show the price level in the economy at P_1 and Real GDP at Q_1, but the intersection of the *AD* curve and the *SRAS* curve is at some point other than P_1, Q_1. In addition, the *LRAS* curve should not be at Q_1 or at the intersection of the *AD* and *SRAS* curves.

Chapter 9

Chapter 9, Page 210

1. Say's law states that supply creates its own demand. In a barter economy, Jones supplies good X so that she can use it to demand some other good (e.g., good Y). The act of supplying is motivated by the desire to demand. Supply and demand are opposite sides of the same coin.

2. No, total spending will not decrease. For classical economists, an increase in saving (reflected in a decrease in consumption) will lower the interest rate and stimulate investment spending. As one spending component (consumption) goes down, another (investment) goes up. Moreover, according to classical economists, the decrease in one spending component will be completely offset by an increase in another spending component, so that overall spending does not change.

3. Prices and wages are flexible; they move up and down in response to market conditions.

Chapter 9, Page 215

1. A recessionary gap exists if the economy is producing a Real GDP level that is less than Natural Real GDP. An inflationary gap exists if the economy is producing a Real GDP level that is more than Natural Real GDP.

2. When the economy is in a recessionary gap, the labor market has a surplus. When the economy is in an inflationary gap, the labor market has a shortage.

3. The economy is somewhere above the institutional PPF and below the physical PPF.

Chapter 9, Page 224

1. In a recessionary gap, the existing unemployment rate is greater than the natural unemployment rate, implying that unemployment is relatively high. As wage contracts expire, business firms negotiate new ones that pay workers lower wage rates. As a result, the SRAS curve shifts rightward. At the same time, the price level begins to fall. The economy moves down the AD curve—eventually intersecting the LRAS curve. At this point, the economy is in long-run equilibrium.

2. In an inflationary gap, the existing unemployment rate is less than the natural unemployment rate, implying that unemployment is relatively low. As wage contracts expire, business firms negotiate contracts that pay workers higher wage rates. As a result, the SRAS curve shifts leftward. At the same time, the price level begins to rise. The economy moves up the AD curve—eventually to the point where it intersects the LRAS curve. At this point, the economy is in long-run equilibrium.

3. In the long run, changes in aggregate demand affect only the price level, not the Real GDP level or the unemployment rate. Stated differently, changes in AD in an economy have no long-run effect on the Real GDP that a country produces or on its unemployment rate; in the long run, changes in AD change only the price level.

Chapter 10

Chapter 10, Page 238

1. They mean that an economy might not self-regulate at Natural Real GDP (Q_N). Instead, an economy can get stuck in a recessionary gap.

2. To say that the economy is self-regulating is the same as saying that prices and wages are flexible and adjust quickly. They are just two ways of describing the same thing.

3. Aggregate demand might be too low mainly because Say's law may not hold in a money economy. This statement raises the question: Why *doesn't* Say's law hold in a money economy? Keynes argued that an increase in saving, which leads to a decline in demand, does not necessarily bring about an equal amount of additional investment, which would lead to an increase in demand, because neither saving nor investment is exclusively affected by changes in the interest rate. (See Exhibit 1 for the way Keynes might have used numbers to explain his position.)

Chapter 10, Page 243

1. Autonomous consumption is one of the components of overall consumption. To illustrate, look at the consumption function: $C = C_0 + (MPC \times Y_d)$. The part of overall consumption (C) that is autonomous is C_0, and this part does not depend on disposable income. The part of consumption that does depend on disposable income (i.e., that changes as disposable income changes) is ($MPC \times Y_d$). For example, assume that $MPC = 0.80$. If Y_d rises by $1,000, then consumption goes up by $800.

2. $\dfrac{1}{1 - 0.70} = \dfrac{1}{0.30} = 3.33$

3. The multiplier falls. For example, if $MPC = 0.80$, then the multiplier is 5, but if $MPC = 0.20$, then the multiplier is 1.25.

Chapter 10, Page 248

1. Keynes believed that the economy might not always self-regulate at Natural Real GDP. In other words, households and businesses (the private sector of the economy) are not always capable of generating enough aggregate demand in the economy for the economy to equilibrate at Natural Real GDP.

2. The increase in autonomous spending will lead to a greater increase in total spending and to a rightward shift in the AD curve. If the economy is operating in the horizontal section of the Keynesian AS curve, Real GDP will rise and there will be no change in prices.

3. Agree. The economist who believes that the economy is inherently unstable sees a role for government, which is supposed to stabilize the economy at Natural Real GDP. The economist who believes that the economy is self-regulating (capable of moving itself to Natural Real GDP) sees little, if any, role for government in the economy because the economy is already doing the job government would supposedly do.

Chapter 10, Page 255

1. When $TP > TE$, firms are producing and offering for sale more units of goods and services than consumers want to buy. As a result, business inventories rise above optimal levels. In reaction, firms cut back on their production of goods and services. The cutback in production leads to a decline in Real GDP. Real GDP stops falling when $TP = TE$.

2. When $TE > TP$, consumers want to buy more than firms are producing and offering for sale. As a result, business inventories fall below optimal levels. In reaction, firms increase the production of goods and services. The increase in production leads to a rise in Real GDP. Real GDP stops rising when $TP = TE$.

Chapter 11

Chapter 11, Page 267

1. With a proportional income tax, the tax rate is constant as one's income rises. With a progressive income tax, the tax rate rises as one's income rises (up to some point). With a regressive income tax, the tax rate falls as one's income rises.

2. In 2017, the top 5 percent of income earners received 36.53 percent of all income and paid 59.14 percent of all income taxes.

3. Individual income tax, corporate income tax, Social Security taxes, and Medicare taxes.

4. The cyclical budget deficit is the part of the budget deficit that is the result of a downturn in economic activity.

Chapter 11, Page 276

1. If crowding out does not occur, expansionary fiscal policy is predicted to increase aggregate demand and, if the economy is in a recessionary gap, either reduce or eliminate the gap. However, if the crowding out is complete, then expansionary fiscal policy will not meet its objective. For example, suppose government purchases rise by $100 million and private spending decreases by $100 million. Then there is no net effect on aggregate demand.

2. Suppose the economy is currently in a recessionary gap in period 1. Expansionary fiscal policy is needed to remove the economy from its recessionary gap, but the fiscal policy lags (data lag, wait-and-see lag, etc.) may be so long that, by the time the fiscal policy is implemented, the economy has moved itself out of the recessionary gap, making the expansionary fiscal policy not only unnecessary but potentially capable of moving the economy into an inflationary gap. (Exhibit 5 depicts this scenario.)

3. Suppose the federal government spends more on a particular program. As a result, the budget deficit grows and the federal government increases its demand for loanable funds (or credit) to finance the larger deficit. Because of the heightened demand for loanable funds, the interest rate rises; then, in response to the higher interest rate, business firms cut back on investment. Thus, an increase in government spending has indirectly led to a decline in investment spending.

Chapter 11, Page 280

1. Suppose that a person's taxable income rises by $1,000 to $45,000 a year and that person's taxes rise from $10,000 to $10,390 as a result. Then her marginal tax rate—the percentage of additional taxable income she pays in taxes—is 39 percent. Her average tax rate—the percentage of her (total) income that she pays in taxes—is 23 percent.

2. Not necessarily. A rise in revenues depends on whether the percentage rise in tax rates is greater than or less than the percentage fall in the tax base. Here's a simple example: Suppose the average tax rate is 10 percent and the tax base is $100. Then tax revenues equal $10. If the

tax rate rises to 12 percent (a 20 percent rise) and the tax base falls to $90 (a 10 percent fall), then tax revenues rise to $10.80. In other words, if the tax rate rises by a greater percentage than the tax base falls, tax revenues rise. Now suppose that the tax base falls to $70 (a 30 percent fall) instead of to $90, then tax revenues would be $8.40. In other words, if the tax rate rises by a smaller percentage than the tax base falls, tax revenues fall.

Chapter 12

Chapter 12, Page 290

1. Money evolved because individuals wanted to make trading easier (less time consuming). This desire motivated individuals to accept the good (in a barter economy) that had greater acceptability than all other goods. In time, the effect snowballed, and finally the good that initially had greater acceptability became widely accepted for purposes of exchange. At this point, the good became money.

2. No, since demand deposits and money market deposit accounts are both included in M1, the M1 money supply does not change.

3. In a barter (moneyless) economy, a double coincidence of wants will not occur for every transaction. When it does not occur, the cost of the transaction increases because more time must be spent to complete the trade. In a money economy, money is acceptable for every transaction. All buyers offer money for what they want to buy, and all sellers accept money for what they want to sell.

Chapter 12, Page 293

1. When money consisted of gold, goldsmiths took in other people's gold and stored it for them. To acknowledge that they held deposited gold, goldsmiths issued receipts, called *warehouse receipts*, to their customers. Warehouse receipts were fully backed by gold; they simply represented gold in storage. Goldsmiths later began to recognize that, on an average day, few people redeemed their receipts for gold. Many individuals traded the receipts for goods and seldom requested the gold itself. In short, the receipts had become money, widely accepted for purposes of exchange. Sensing opportunity, goldsmiths began to lend some of the stored gold, realizing that they could earn interest on the loans without defaulting on their pledge to redeem the warehouse receipts when presented.

2. A banking arrangement that allows banks to hold reserves equal to only a fraction of their deposit liabilities.

Chapter 12, Page 296

1. It is a moral hazard problem. A moral hazard problem exists when one party to a transaction changes his or her behavior in a way that is hidden from, and costly to, the other party. By promising to pay Ana's expenses over $1,000, Esteban provides Ana with an incentive to push her expenses beyond $1,000, especially if she thinks that her expenses will be close to $1,000. Simply put, Ana has an incentive to act in a way that is hidden from, and potentially costly to, Esteban. How might Esteban lessen the moral hazard problem? Perhaps he could promise to pay a certain percentage of each dollar of Ana's expenses over $1,000 instead of promising to pay every dollar of them.

2. A bank's capital, or net worth, is equal to the difference of its assets and liabilities. As bank A's assets decline in value (because some loans are not being repaid), the difference of its assets and liabilities diminishes, so its bank capital diminishes. If assets fall below liabilities, the bank will end up with negative bank capital (i.e., negative net worth).

3. Financial intermediaries bring lenders and borrowers together. For example, Smith wants to lend $100 and Jones wants to borrow $100, but neither Smith nor Jones is in contact with the other. Instead of dealing with each other directly, both Smith and Jones go to a bank. Smith deposits $100 into the bank, and then the bank lends some or all of the $100 to Jones.

Chapter 13

Chapter 13, Page 309

1. a. Money supply falls.
   b. Money supply rises.
   c. Money supply falls.

2. The federal funds rate is the interest rate one bank charges another bank for a loan. The discount rate is the interest rate the Fed charges a bank for a loan.

3. Reserves in bank A rise; reserves in the banking system remain the same (bank B loses the reserves that bank A borrowed).

4. Reserves in bank A rise; reserves in the banking system rise because there is no offset in reserves for any other bank.

Chapter 13, Page 314

1. No, the Fed does not use open market operations to change the federal funds rate today. What is uses instead are the IOR rate and the ON-RRP rate. The Fed did, however, use open market operations to change the federal funds rate in the past.

2. It sets a federal funds rate target range that is lower than the current federal funds rate. To illustrate, suppose the current federal funds rate is 3 percent, and the Fed wants to lower the federal funds rate to somewhere between 1.00 percent and 1.25 percent. It will set the target range at 1.00 to 1.25 percent. The ON-RRP rate is set at the bottom of the range, and the IOR rate is set at the top of the range.

3. The primary tool is the IOR rate, which is the interest rate the Fed pays to banks on reserves. The secondary tool is the ON-RRP rate, which is the interest rate a nonbank financial institution earns on an overnight RRP agreement. An ON-RRP is a security the Fed sells to a nonbank financial institution that it agrees to buy back the next day.

Chapter 14
Chapter 14, Page 325

1. If $M \times V$ increases, total expenditures increase. In other words, people spend more. For example, instead of spending $3 billion on goods and services, they spend $4 billion. But more spending (greater total expenditures) means that there must be greater total sales. $P \times Q$ represents this total dollar value of sales.

2. The equation of exchange is a truism, or tautology: MV necessarily equals PQ. This is similar to saying that $2 + 2$ necessarily equals 4. It cannot be otherwise. The simple quantity theory of money, which is built on the equation of exchange, can be tested against real-world events. The simple quantity theory of money assumes that both velocity and Real GDP are constant and then, on the basis of these assumptions, predicts that changes in the money supply will be strictly proportional to changes in the price level. This prediction can be measured against real-world data, so the simple quantity theory of money may offer insights into how the economy works. The equation of exchange does not do this.

3. a. The AD curve shifts rightward.
   b. The AD curve shifts leftward.
   c. The AD curve shifts rightward.
   d. The AD curve shifts leftward.

Chapter 14, Page 329

1. a. As velocity rises, the AD curve shifts to the right. In the short run, P rises and Q rises. In the long run, Q will return to its original level, and P will be higher than it was in the short run.

   b. As velocity falls, the AD curve shifts to the left. In the short run, P falls and Q falls. In the long run, Q will return to its original level and P will be lower than it was in the short run.

   c. As the money supply rises, the AD curve shifts to the right. In the short run, P rises and Q rises. In the long run, Q will return to its original level, and P will be higher than it was in the short run.

   d. As the money supply falls, the AD curve shifts to the left. In the short run, P falls and Q falls. In the long run, Q will return to its original level, and P will be lower than it was in the short run.

2. Yes, a change in velocity can offset a change in the money supply and have no effect on aggregate demand. Suppose that the money supply rises and velocity falls. A rise in the money supply shifts the AD curve to the right, and a fall in velocity shifts the AD curve to the left. If the strength of each change is the same, AD does not change.

Chapter 14, Page 337

1. This question cannot be answered on the basis of the information given. We know only that three prices have gone up; we don't know whether other prices (in the economy) have gone up, whether other prices have gone down, or whether some have gone up and others have gone down. To determine whether inflation has occurred, we have to know what has happened to the price level, not simply to three prices.

2. No. For continued inflation (continued increases in the price level) to be the result of continued decreases in $SRAS$, workers would have to continually ask for and receive higher wages while output was dropping and the unemployment rate was rising. This combination of circumstances is not likely.

3. Continued inflation.

Chapter 14, Page 343

1. 3 percent.

2. Yes, it is possible. It would occur if the expectations effect immediately set in and outweighed the liquidity effect.

3. Certainly, the Fed can directly affect the supply of loanable funds and the interest rate. But it also works as a catalyst to indirectly affect the loanable funds market and the interest rate via the changes in Real GDP, the price level, and the expected inflation rate. We can say this: The Fed directly affects the interest rate via the liquidity effect, and

Chapter 15

Chapter 15, Page 355

1. Smith buys a bond for a face value of $10,000 that promises to pay a 10 percent interest rate each year for 10 years. In 1 year, though, bonds are offered for a face value of $10,000 that pay an 11 percent interest rate each year for 10 years. If Smith wants to sell his bond, he won't be able to sell it for $10,000. No one today will pay $10,000 for a bond that pays a 10 percent interest rate when a new $10,000 bond pays an 11 percent interest rate. Smith will have to lower the price of his bond if he wants to sell it. Thus, as interest rates rise, the prices of old or existing bonds decrease.

2. We disagree for two reasons. First, if the money market is in the liquidity trap, a rise in the money supply will not affect interest rates and, therefore, will not affect investment or the goods-and-services market. Second, even if the money market is not in the liquidity trap, a rise in the money supply affects the goods-and-services market indirectly: The rise in the money supply lowers the interest rate, causing investment to rise (assuming that investment is not interest insensitive). As investment rises, the *AD* curve shifts rightward, affecting the goods-and-services market. In the Keynesian transmission mechanism, an important, intermediate market lies between the money market and the goods-and-services market. Thus, the money market can only indirectly affect the goods-and-services market.

3. A rise in the money supply brings about an excess supply of money in the money market. This surplus of money flows to the goods-and-services market, stimulating aggregate demand.

Chapter 15, Page 367

1. This is an open-ended question whose answer depends on many factors. First, what does the rule specify? Not all rules are alike. Second, the answer depends on the stability and predictability of velocity. For example, suppose the rule specifies that each year the money supply will rise by the average annual growth rate in Real GDP. If velocity is constant, this trend will produce price stability. But if velocity is extremely volatile, changes in velocity might offset changes in the money supply, leading to deflation instead of price stability. For example, suppose Real GDP rises by 3 percent and the money supply increases by 3 percent, but velocity decreases by 3 percent. Then the change in velocity offsets the change in the money supply, leaving a net effect of a 3 percent rise in Real GDP. The increase in Real GDP would then lead to a 3 percent decline in the price level.

2. Here is the Taylor rule specification: Federal funds rate target = 1.5(4 percent) + 0.5(5 percent) + 1 = 9.5 percent.

3. The monetary policy prescription of the market monetarists is to change the money supply in a direction and by a magnitude sufficient to hit the Nominal GDP target. For example, if the target is to have Nominal GDP grow by 5 percent annually, then adjust the money supply growth so that the target of 5 percent is hit.

Chapter 16

Chapter 16, Page 381

1. A given Phillips curve identifies different combinations of inflation and unemployment, for example, a 4 percent inflation with 5 percent unemployment and a 2 percent inflation with 7 percent unemployment. For these combinations of inflation and unemployment to be permanent, there must only be one (downward-sloping) Phillips curve that never changes.

2. Sometimes there is and sometimes there isn't. Look at Exhibit 3. Unemployment is higher and inflation is lower in 1964 than in 1965, so there is a trade-off between these two years. But both unemployment and inflation are higher in 1980 than in 1979, so between those two years, there was no trade-off between inflation and unemployment.

3. Workers are fooled into thinking that the inflation rate is lower than it is. In other words, they underestimate the inflation rate and, therefore, overestimate the purchasing power of their wages.

Chapter 16, Page 393

1. No. The PIP says that, under certain conditions, neither expansionary fiscal policy nor expansionary monetary policy will be able to increase Real GDP and lower the unemployment rate in the short run. The conditions are that the policy change is anticipated correctly, that individuals form their expectations rationally, and that wages and prices are flexible.

2. None. Given an unanticipated increase in aggregate demand, the economy moves from point 1 to point 2 (in Exhibit 10) in the short run and then to point 3. This behavior occurs whether people are holding rational or adaptive expectations.

3. In the short run, the price level rises and Real GDP declines. In the long run, the price level rises and Real GDP is constant.

Chapter 16, Page 396

1. Both. The relevant question is whether the decline in the money supply was caused by a change on the supply side of the economy. If the answer is no, then the decline in the money supply is consistent with a demand-induced business cycle. If the answer is yes, then it is consistent with a supply-induced (real) business cycle.

2. New Keynesians believe that prices and wages are somewhat inflexible; new classical economists believe that prices and wages are flexible.

Chapter 17
Chapter 17, Page 413

1. Such a shift is shown in Exhibit 4(a). A decline in taxes shifts the labor supply curve to the right, increasing the equilibrium level of labor in the labor market. More labor generates more output (Real GDP), as shown in Exhibit 4(b). More Real GDP is consistent with the *LRAS* curve shifting to the right [Exhibit 4(c)].

2. Physical capital consists of the goods that are produced and used as inputs for further production. Examples of such goods are factories, machinery, tools, computers, and buildings. Human capital refers to the knowledge and skills individuals acquire through education, training, and experience.

3. In neoclassical growth theory, technology was, in a sense, just there. Technological advances just happened, but how these advances happened was not fully understood. Technology was something that was exogenous—outside the economic system and outside of our control. In new growth theory, technology is said to be endogenous. It can be increased or decreased by the amount of resources devoted to it. Also, technology is viewed as being related to ideas.

4. Labor is the movement factor, and both capital and the technology coefficient are shift factors.

Chapter 18
Chapter 18, Page 421

1. New technologies, new kinds of products, and new methods of production are being created while old technologies, old kinds of products, and old methods of production are being destroyed or are becoming obsolete.

2. The productivity effect occurs when the cost of producing automated tasks declines, causing the economy to expand and increase the demand for labor in non-automated tasks.

3. The displacement effect occurs when workers lose jobs because of creative destruction. Think of farm workers being displaced by harvesters and plows.

Chapter 18, Page 428

1. Rent seeking consists of the actions of individuals and groups that spend resources to influence public policy in the hope of redistributing or transferring income to themselves from others.

2. Tullock realized that in the process of seeking rents, rent seekers not only made expenditures that ended up reducing some of the gains to the beneficiaries of rent seeking, but also—and this is the key insight—wasted resources.

3. A firm hires lobbyists to seek a special privilege from Congress—say, the right to be the sole producer of a particular good. Resources are wasted because the resources that were used to seek the special privilege could have been used to produce goods.

Chapter 19
Chapter 19, Page 442

1. $E_d = 1.44$.

2. If there is a change in price, the quantity demanded will change (in the opposite direction) by 0.39 times the percentage change in price. For example, if the price rises 10 percent, then the quantity demanded will fall 3.9 percent. If the price rises 20 percent, then the quantity demanded will fall 7.8 percent.

3. a. Total revenue falls.
   b. Total revenue falls.
   c. Total revenue remains constant.
   d. Total revenue rises.
   e. Total revenue rises.

4. Alexi is implicitly assuming that demand is inelastic. If, however, she is wrong and demand is elastic, then a rise in price will actually lower total revenue.

Chapter 19, Page 446

1. No. Moving from seven to nine substitutes doesn't necessarily change demand from being inelastic to elastic. It simply leads to a rise in price elasticity of demand, *ceteris*

paribus. For example, if price elasticity of demand is 0.45 when good X has seven substitutes, it will be higher when there are nine substitutes, *ceteris paribus*. Higher could be an elasticity of 0.67. If this is the case, demand is still inelastic (but less so than before).

2. a. Dell computers
   b. Heinz ketchup
   c. Perrier water

   In all three cases, the good with the higher price elasticity of demand is the more specific of the two goods; therefore, it has more substitutes.

Chapter 19, Page 456

1. An income elasticity of demand of 1.33 means that the good in question is a normal good, and that it is income elastic; that is, as income rises, the quantity demanded rises by a greater percentage. In this case, quantity demanded rises by 1.33 times the percentage change in income. Thus, if income rises by 10 percent, the quantity demanded of the good will rise by 13.3 percent.

2. A change in price does not change the quantity supplied.

3. Tax revenue is equal to the tax times the quantity sold. If demand is inelastic, then the higher price brought about by the tax will result in a smaller cutback in quantity sold.

4. Under the condition that the demand for computers is perfectly inelastic or that the supply of computers is perfectly elastic.

Chapter 20

Chapter 20, Page 464

1. The paradox is that water, which is essential to life, is cheap, and diamonds, which are not essential to life, are expensive. The solution to the paradox depends on knowing the difference between total and marginal utility and the law of diminishing marginal utility. By saying that water is essential to life and diamonds are not essential to life, we signify that water gives us high total utility relative to diamonds. However, price is not a reflection of total utility, it is a reflection of marginal utility. The marginal utility of water is less than that of diamonds. How can the total utility of water be greater than that of diamonds, but the marginal utility of water be less than that of diamonds? According to the law of diminishing marginal utility, there is so much more water relative to diamonds that the next (additional) unit of water gives us less utility (lower marginal utility) than the next unit of diamonds.

2. If total utility declines, marginal utility must be negative. For example, if total utility is 30 utils when Lydia consumes 3 apples and 25 utils when she consumes 4 apples, then the fourth apple must have a marginal utility of –5 utils. Chapter 1 explains that something that takes utility away from us (or gives us disutility) is called a *bad*. For Lydia, the fourth apple is a bad, not a good.

3. The total and marginal utilities of a good are the same for the first unit of the good consumed. For example, before Tomás eats his first apple, he receives no utility or disutility from apples. Eating the first apple, he receives 15 utils. So the total utility (TU) for 1 apple is 15 utils, and the marginal utility (MU) for the first apple is 15 utils. Exhibit 1 shows that TU and MU are the same for the first unit of good X.

Chapter 20, Page 469

1. Alessandro is not in the consumer equilibrium, because the marginal utility per dollar of X is 16 utils and the marginal utility per dollar of Y is 13.14 utils. To be in equilibrium, a consumer has to receive the same marginal utility per dollar for each good consumed.

2. It means that the marginal utility–price ratio for one of the goods is higher than the ratio for the other good.

Chapter 20, Page 476

1. Yes, Bijan is compartmentalizing. He is treating the $100 that comes from his grandmother differently from the $100 that comes from his father.

2. The endowment effect relates to individuals valuing X more highly when they possess it than when they don't but are thinking of acquiring it. Friedman argues that, if we were to go back in time to a hunter–gatherer society, when there were no well-established property rights (no rules as to what is mine and what is yours), we would find individuals who would fight hard to keep what they possessed but would not fight as hard to acquire what they did not possess. These individuals would have a higher probability of surviving than those who would fight hard in both cases and, therefore, put themselves at greater risk. Those who would fight hard only to keep what they possessed and, therefore, put themselves at less risk, would have a higher probability of reproductive success. The characteristic of holding onto what you have has been passed down from generation to generation, and, although it may not be as important today as it was in a hunter–gatherer society, it still influences behavior.

Chapter 21

Chapter 21, Page 494

1. No. Individuals will form teams or firms only when the sum of what they can produce as a team or firm is greater than the sum of what they can produce working alone.

2. The person earning the low salary has lower implicit costs and so is more likely to start a business. She gives up less to start a business.

3. Accounting profit is larger. Only explicit costs are subtracted from total revenue in computing accounting profit, but both explicit and implicit costs are subtracted from total revenue in computing economic profit. If implicit costs are zero, then accounting profit and economic profit are the same. Economic profit is never greater than accounting profit.

4. A business owner can be earning a profit but not covering costs when he is earning (positive) accounting profit but his total revenue does not cover the sum of his explicit and implicit costs. For example, suppose Brad earns a total revenue of $100,000, and has explicit costs of $40,000 and implicit costs of $70,000. His accounting profit is $60,000, but his total revenue of $100,000 is not large enough to cover the sum of his explicit and implicit costs ($110,000). Brad's economic profit is a negative $10,000. In other words, although Brad earns an accounting profit, he takes an economic loss.

Chapter 21, Page 501

1. No. The short run and the long run are not lengths of time. The short run is that period during which some inputs are fixed, and therefore, the firm has fixed costs. The long run is any period during which no inputs are fixed (i.e., all inputs are variable), and thus, all costs are variable costs. The period during which there are no fixed inputs can be shorter than the period during which there are fixed inputs.

2. The law of diminishing marginal returns holds only when we add more of one input to a given (fixed) quantity of another input. The statement does not identify one input as fixed (it says that both increase), so the law of diminishing marginal returns is not relevant in this situation.

3. When MC is declining, MPP is rising; when MC is constant, MPP is constant; and when MC is rising, MPP is falling.

Chapter 21, Page 512

1. $ATC = TC/Q$ and $ATC = AFC + AVC$.

2. Yes. Suppose a business incurs a cost of $10 to make a product. However, before it can sell the product, the demand for it falls and moves the market price from $15 to $6. Does the owner of the business say, "I can't sell the product for $6 because I'd be taking a loss"? If she does, she chooses to let a sunk cost affect her current decision. Instead, she should ask herself: Will the market price of the product rise, or will it fall further? If she thinks that it will fall further, she should sell the product today for $6.

3. Unit costs are another name for average total costs (ATC), so the question is, "what happens to ATC as MC rises?" You might be inclined to say that, as MC rises, so does ATC, but this is not necessarily so. (See region 1 in Exhibit 6(b).) What matters is whether MC is greater than ATC. If it is, then ATC will rise. If it is not, then ATC will decline. This is a trick question of sorts. There is a tendency to misinterpret the average-marginal rule and to believe that, as marginal cost rises, average total cost rises and that, as marginal cost falls, average total cost falls. But the average-marginal rule actually says that when MC is above ATC, ATC rises, and when MC is below ATC, ATC falls.

4. Yes. As marginal physical product (MPP) rises, marginal cost (MC) falls. If MC falls enough to move below unit cost, which is the same as average total cost, then unit cost declines. Similarly, as MPP falls, MC rises. If MC rises enough to move above unit cost, then unit cost rises.

Chapter 21, Page 516

1. Suppose it currently takes 10 units of X and 10 units of Y to produce 50 units of good Z. Let both X and Y double to 20 units each. As a result, the output of Z more than doubles to 150 units. When inputs are increased by some percentage and output increases by a greater percentage, economies of scale are said to exist. When economies of scale exist, unit costs fall, and another name for unit costs is average total costs.

2. The $LRATC$ curve would be horizontal. When there are constant returns to scale, output doubles if inputs double. But unit costs stay constant, so the LRATC curve is horizontal.

3. Unit costs must have been lower when the firm produced 200 units than when it produced 100 units. That is,

there were economies of scale between 100 units and 200 units. To explain further, profit per unit is the difference of price per unit and cost per unit (or unit costs): Profit per unit = Price per unit − Cost per unit. Suppose the unit cost is $3 when the price is $4, giving a profit per unit of $1. There are economies of scale as the firm raises output from 100 units to 200 units. Unit costs must fall—say, to $2 per unit. If the price is $3, then there is still a profit of $1 per unit.

Chapter 22

Chapter 22, Page 525

1. It means that the firm cannot change the price of the product it sells by its actions. For example, if firm A cuts back on the supply of what it produces and the price of its product does not change, then firm A cannot control the price of the product it sells. In other words, if price is independent of a firm's actions, that firm does not have any control over price.

2. The easy, and incomplete, answer is that a perfectly competitive firm is a price taker because it is in a market in which it cannot control the price of the product it sells. But why not? The complete answer is that the firm is in a market in which (1) its supply is small relative to the total market supply; (2) it sells a homogeneous good; and (3) all buyers and sellers have all relevant information about prices, product quality, sources of supply, and so forth.

3. If a perfectly competitive firm tries to charge a price higher than the equilibrium price, all buyers will know that it is trying to do so (assumption 3). These buyers will then simply buy from another firm that sells the same (homogeneous) product (assumption 2).

4. No. A market doesn't have to perfectly match all assumptions of the theory of perfect competition for it to be labeled a perfectly competitive market. What is important is whether the market acts as if it is perfectly competitive. "If it walks like a duck and it quacks like a duck, it's a duck." If it acts like a perfectly competitive market, it's a perfectly competitive market.

Chapter 22, Page 535

1. No. Whether a firm earns profits depends on the relationship between price (P) and average total cost (ATC). If $P > ATC$, then the firm earns profits. To understand this relationship, remember that profits exist when total revenue (TR) minus total cost (TC) is a positive number. Total revenue is simply price times quantity ($TR = P \times Q$), and total cost is average total cost times quantity ($TC = ATC \times Q$). Because quantity (Q) is common to both TR and TC, if $P > ATC$, then $TR > TC$ and the firm earns profits.

2. In the short run, whether a firm should shut down depends on the relationship between price and average variable cost (AVC), not between price and ATC. It depends on whether price is greater or less than average variable cost. If $P > AVC$, the firm should continue to produce; if $P < AVC$, it should shut down.

3. As long as $MR > MC$—for example, $MR = \$6$ and $MC = \$4$—the firm should produce and sell additional units of a good because doing so adds more to TR ($6) than it does to TC ($4). Whenever you add more to TR than you do to TC, the gap between the two becomes larger.

4. We start with the upward-sloping market supply curve and work backward. First, market supply curves are upward sloping because they are the "addition" of individual firms' supply curves, which are upward sloping. Second, individual firms' supply curves are upward sloping because they are the portion of their marginal cost curves above their average variable cost curves, and this portion of the MC curve is upward sloping. Third, marginal cost curves have upward-sloping portions because of the law of diminishing marginal returns. Therefore, market supply curves are upward sloping because of the law of diminishing marginal returns.

Chapter 22, Page 544

1. According to the theory of perfect competition, the profits will draw new firms into the market. As these new firms enter the market, the market supply curve will shift to the right. As a result of a larger supply, price will fall. As price declines, profit will decline until firms in the market are earning (only) normal (or zero economic) profit. When there is zero economic profit, firms no longer have an incentive to enter the market.

2. No. The market is in long-run competitive equilibrium only when firms have no incentive to (1) enter or exit the industry, (2) produce more or less output, or (3) change their plant size. If any of these conditions is not met, then the market is not in long-run equilibrium.

3. Initially, price will rise. Recall from Chapter 3 that, when demand increases, *ceteris paribus*, price rises. In time, though, price will drop because new firms will

enter the industry because of the positive economic profits generated by the higher price. How far the price drops depends on whether the firms are in a constant-cost, increasing-cost, or decreasing-cost industry. In a constant-cost industry, price will return to its original level; in an increasing-cost industry, price will return to a level above its original level; and in a decreasing-cost industry, price will return to a level below its original level.

4. Maybe initially, but probably not after certain adjustments are made. If firm A really has a genius on its payroll and, as a result, earns higher profits than firm B, then firm B might try to hire the genius away from firm A by offering him or her a higher income. To keep the genius, firm A will have to match the offer. As a result, the costs of firm A will rise, and if nothing else changes, its profits will decline.

Chapter 22, Page 545

1. It depends on how many firms in the market witness higher costs. If it is only one, then the market supply curve is not likely to shift enough to bring about a higher price. If, however, many firms in the market witness higher costs, then the market supply curve will shift left and price will rise.

2. No. Perfectly competitive firms that sell homogeneous products will not advertise individually, but the industry might advertise in the hope of pushing the market (industry) demand curve (for their product) to the right.

Chapter 23
Chapter 23, Page 551

1. Let's assume that any product a firm sells has some close substitutes. The question, however, is how close the substitute has to be before the theory of monopoly is not useful. For example, a "slightly close" substitute for a seller's product may not be close enough to matter. The theory of monopoly may still be useful in predicting a firm's behavior.

2. Economies of scale exist when a firm doubles inputs and its output more than doubles, lowering its unit costs (average total costs) in the process. If economies of scale exist only when a firm produces a large quantity of output and one firm is already producing this output, then new firms (that start off producing less output) will have higher unit costs than those of the established firm. Some economists argue that these higher unit costs will make the new firms uncompetitive compared with the established firm. In other words, economies of scale will act as a barrier to entry, effectively preventing firms from entering the industry and competing with the established firm.

3. In a monopoly, there is a single seller of a good that has no close substitutes, and the barriers to entry are extremely high. If a movie superstar has so much talent that the moviegoing public puts her in a class by herself, she might be considered a monopolist. Anyone can try to compete with her, but she may have such great talent (relative to everyone else) that no one will be able to compete. Her immense talent acts as a barrier to entry in the sense that, even if others try to compete with her, they won't be a close enough substitute for her.

Chapter 23, Page 559

1. The single-price monopolist has to lower price in order to sell an additional unit of its good. (This condition is what a downward-sloping demand curve necessitates.) As long as it has to lower price to sell an additional unit, its marginal revenue will be below its price. A demand curve plots price (P) and quantity (Q), and a marginal revenue curve plots marginal revenue (MR) and quantity (Q). Because $P > MR$ for a monopolist, its the demand curve will lie above its the marginal revenue curve.

2. No. Profit depends on whether price is greater than average total cost. A monopolist could produce the quantity of output at which $MR = MC$, charge the highest price per unit possible for the output, and still have its unit costs (ATC) greater than the price. In this case, the monopolist incurs losses and does not earn profits.

3. No. The last chapter explains that a firm is resource allocative efficient when it charges a price equal to its marginal cost ($P = MC$). The monopolist does not do this but, rather, charges a price above marginal cost. Profit maximization ($MR = MC$) does not lead to resource allocative efficiency ($P = MC$) because, for the monopolist, $P > MR$. This is not the case for the perfectly competitive firm, for which $P = MR$.

4. A monopolist is searching for the highest price at which to sell a product. In contrast, the perfectly competitive firm doesn't have to search; it simply takes the equilibrium price established in the market. For example,

suppose Nancy is a wheat farmer. She gets up one morning and wants to know the price at which she should sell her wheat. She simply turns on the radio, listens to the farm report, and finds out that the equilibrium price per bushel of wheat is $5. Being a price taker, she knows that she can't sell her wheat for a penny more than $5 (the highest price), and she won't want to sell her wheat for a penny less either. The monopoly firm doesn't know what the highest price is for the product it sells. It has to search for it and experiment with different prices before it finds the highest price.

Chapter 23, Page 568

1. Monopoly has at least the following three costs, or shortcomings:

   a. A monopoly firm produces too little output relative to the output of a perfectly competitive firm; this difference causes the deadweight loss of monopoly.

   b. The profits of the monopoly are sometimes subject to rent-seeking behavior. Rent seeking, while rational for an individual firm, wastes society's resources. Society receives no benefit if one firm expends resources to take over the monopoly position of another firm. Resources that could have been used to produce goods (e.g., computers, software, shoes, and houses) are used to transfer profits from one firm to another instead.

   c. A monopolist might not produce products at the lowest possible cost. Again, failure to do so wastes society's resources.

2. An example helps to illustrate this concept. Suppose a perfectly competitive firm produces 100 units of good X, but a monopoly firm produces only 70 units, which is a difference of 30 units. Buyers value these 30 units by more than it would cost the monopoly firm to produce them, yet the monopoly firm chooses not to produce the units. The net benefit (benefits to buyers minus costs to the monopolist) of producing these 30 units is said to be the deadweight loss of monopoly. It represents how much buyers lose because the monopolist chooses to produce less than the perfectly competitive firm would.

3. If a seller is not a price searcher, then it is a price taker. A price taker can sell its product at only one price: the market equilibrium price.

Chapter 24

Chapter 24, Page 576

1. A monopolistic competitor is like a monopolist in that (1) it faces a downward-sloping demand curve, (2) it is a price searcher ($P > MR$), and (3) it is not resource allocative efficient. It is like a perfect competitor in that (1) it sells to many buyers and competes with many sellers, and (2) entry into and exit from the market are easy.

2. Essentially, they face downward-sloping demand curves. Because the demand curve is downward sloping, it cannot be tangent to the lowest point on a U-shaped ATC curve. (See Exhibit 3.)

Chapter 24, Page 580

1. The incentive in both cases is the same: to increase their profits. After the cartel is formed, however, each firm has an incentive to break the cartel to increase its profits even further. (See Exhibit 5.) If there is no cartel agreement, the firm is earning zero profits by producing quantity q_1. After the cartel is formed, it earns CP_CAB in profits by producing quantity q_C. But it can earn even higher profits (FP_CDE) by cheating on the cartel and producing quantity q_{CC}.

2. An oligopolistic firm is a price searcher. A price searcher faces a downward-sloping demand curve. Also, an oligopolistic firm has some control over the price it charges. Such control is the hallmark of a price searcher.

Chapter 25

Chapter 25, Page 602

1. How a market is defined will help determine whether a firm is considered a monopoly. If a market is defined broadly, it will include more substitute goods, so the firm is less likely to be considered a monopoly. If a market is defined narrowly, it will include fewer substitute goods, so the firm is more likely to be considered a monopoly.

2. The four-firm concentration ratio is 20 percent; the Herfindahl index is 500. The formulas in Exhibit 1 show how each is computed.

3. The Herfindahl index provides information about the dispersion of firm size in an industry. For example, suppose the top four firms in an industry have 15 percent, 10 percent, 9 percent, and 8 percent market shares, respectively. The four-firm concentration ratio will be the same for an

industry with 15 firms as it is for an industry with 150 firms. The Herfindahl index will be different in the two situations.

Chapter 25, Page 607

1. Average cost pricing is the same as profit regulation. The regulators state that the natural monopolist must charge a price equal to its average total cost ($P = ATC$). Under this pricing policy, there is no incentive for the natural monopolist to keep costs down. In fact, there may be an incentive to deliberately push costs up. Higher costs—in the form of higher salaries or more luxurious offices—simply mean higher prices to cover the higher costs.

2. No matter the motive for initially regulating an industry, the regulating agency will eventually be captured by the special interests (the firms) in the industry. In the end, the regulatory body will not so much regulate the industry as serve the interests of the firms in it.

3. According to the capture theory, the outcomes of the regulatory process will favor the regulated firms. According to the public choice theory, the outcomes of the regulatory process will favor the regulators.

4. Sometimes they favor regulation, and at other times they do not. Economists make the point that regulation involves both costs and benefits, and whether a particular regulation is worthwhile depends on whether the costs are greater than or less than the benefits.

Chapter 26

Chapter 26, Page 617

1. $MRP = MR \times MPP$. For a perfectly competitive firm, $MR = P$, so MR is $10. MPP in this case is 19 units. It follows that $MRP = 190.

2. There is no difference between MRP and VMP if the firm is perfectly competitive. In this situation, $P = MR$, and because $MRP = MR \times MPP$ and $VMP = P \times MPP$, the two are the same. If the firm is a price searcher—a monopolist, a monopolistic competitor, or an oligopolist—$P > MR$; therefore, $VMP > MRP$.

3. A factor price taker can buy all that is wanted of a factor at the equilibrium price, and will not cause the factor price to rise. For example, if firm X is a factor price taker in the labor market, it can buy all the labor it wants at the equilibrium wage, and it will not cause this wage to rise.

4. It should buy the quantity at which the MRP of labor equals the MFC of labor.

Chapter 26, Page 629

1. The MRP curve is the firm's factor demand curve. $MRP = P \times MPP$ for a perfectly competitive firm; so, if either the price of the product that labor produces rises or the MPP of labor rises (reflected in a shift in the MPP curve), the factor demand curve shifts rightward.

2. It means that, for every 1 percent change in the wage rate, the quantity demanded of labor changes inversely by three times this percentage. For example, if wage rates rise 10 percent, then the quantity demanded of labor falls 30 percent.

3. The short answer is because supply-and-demand conditions differ among markets. The question of why supply-and-demand conditions differ is answered in Exhibit 11.

4. We can't answer this question specifically without more information. We know that, under the following four conditions, wage rates would not differ: (1) The demand for every type of labor is the same; (2) the jobs have no special nonpecuniary aspects; (3) all labor is ultimately homogeneous and can costlessly be trained for different types of employment; and (4) all labor is mobile at zero cost. Wage rates differ when one or more of these conditions are not met. For example, perhaps labor is not mobile at zero cost.

Chapter 27

Chapter 27, Page 641

1. The demand for union labor is lowered by a decline in (a) the demand for the product that union labor produces, (b) the price of substitute factors, and (c) the marginal physical product of union labor.

2. A closed shop requires an employee to be a member of the union before being hired; a union shop does not. The union shop requires employees to join the union within a certain period after becoming employed.

3. The purpose of a strike is to prove to management that union members will not work for a wage rate that is lower than the rate specified by the union. In terms of Exhibit 3, it is to prove that union members will not work for less than W_2.

Chapter 27, Page 646

1. A monopsonist cannot buy additional units of a factor without increasing the price it pays for the factor. A factor price taker can.

2. The minimum wage can increase the number of people working under the following conditions: (1) The firm hiring the labor is a monopsonist, and (2) the minimum wage is above the wage it is already paying and below the

wage that corresponds to the point where $MFC = MRP$. In Exhibit 4(c), suppose the firm is currently purchasing Q_1 quantity of labor and paying wage W_1. Then W_2 becomes the minimum wage the monopsonist can pay to workers. Now it hires Q_2 workers. Notice, however, that if the monopsonist had to pay a wage higher than the wage that equates MFC and MRP, it would employ fewer workers than Q_1.

3. If the higher wage rate reduces the number of people working in the unionized sector and the people who lose their jobs in the unionized sector move to the nonunionized sector, then the supply of labor will increase in the nonunionized sector and wage rates will fall. (See Exhibit 6.)

Chapter 28

Chapter 28, Page 655

1. Government can change the distribution of income through transfer payments and taxes. Look at this equation: Individual income = Labor income + Asset income + Transfer payments − Taxes. By increasing one person's taxes and increasing another person's transfer payments, government can change people's incomes.

2. The statement is true. For example, two people can have unequal incomes at any one point in time and still earn the same total incomes over time. For example, suppose that, in year 1, Patrick earns $40,000 and Francine earns $20,000. Then, in year 2, Francine earns $40,000 and Patrick earns $20,000. In each year, there is income inequality, but over the two years, Patrick and Francine earn the same income ($60,000).

3. No. Individual income = Labor income + Asset income + Transfer payments − Taxes. Martha's income could come entirely from labor income, and Lazaro's income could come entirely from asset income. The same dollar income does not necessarily come from the same source.

Chapter 28, Page 659

1. No. The income shares total 105 percent.

2. A Gini coefficient of 0 represents perfect income equality, and a Gini coefficient of 1 represents complete income inequality. Thus, we are sure that country A has neither perfect income equality nor complete income inequality. Saying anything further is difficult. Usually, the Gini coefficient is used as a comparative measure. For example, if country A's Gini coefficient is 0.45 and country B's is 0.60, we could say that country A has a more equal (less unequal) distribution of income than country B.

Chapter 28, Page 662

1. The simple fact that Jack earns more than Harry is not evidence of wage discrimination. We do not know whether wage discrimination exists. For example, we do not know whether Jack and Harry work the same job, how productive each is, and so on.

2. It could affect it negatively or positively. The probability of both higher and lower incomes is greater if a person assumes a lot of risk than if a person plays it safe. Suppose Nancy has decided that she wants to be an actress, although her parents want her to be an accountant. The chances of her being successful in acting are small, but if she is successful, she will earn a much higher income than if she had been an accountant. (A top actress earns more than a top accountant.) Of course, if she isn't successful, she will earn less income as an actress than she would have as an accountant. (The average actress earns less than the average accountant.)

Chapter 28, Page 664

1. Whether poor people always exist depends on how we define poverty. If we define it in relative terms and we assume no absolute income equality, then some people must fall into, say, the lowest 10 percent of income earners. We could refer to these persons as poor. Remember, though, that these persons are relatively poor—they earn less than a large percentage of the income earners in the country—but we do not know anything about their absolute incomes. In a world of multimillion-dollar income earners, a person who earns $100,000 might be considered poor.

2. 10.5 percent.

Chapter 29

Chapter 29, Page 674

1. Because there is a monetary incentive for them to be equal. Suppose the return on capital is 12 percent, and the price for loanable funds is 10 percent. In this case, a person could borrow loanable funds at 10 percent and invest in capital goods to earn the 12 percent return. In the meantime, though, the amount of capital increases and its return falls. If the interest rates are reversed and the return on capital is lower than the price for a loanable fund, no one will borrow to invest in capital goods. Over time, then, the stock of capital will diminish, and its return will rise.

2. Because the real interest rate is the rate paid by borrowers and received by lenders. For example, a person who borrows funds at a 12 percent interest rate when the inflation rate is 4 percent will be paying only an 8 percent (real) interest rate

to the lender. Stated differently, the lender has 8 percent, not 12 percent, more buying power by making the loan.

3. $907.03. The formula is $PV = \$1,000/(1 + 0.05)^2$.

4. No. The present value of $2,000 a year for four years at an 8 percent interest rate is $6,624.25. [$PV = \$2,000/(1 + 0.08)^1 + \$2,000/(1 + 0.08)^2 + \$2,000/(1 + 0.08)^3 + + \$2,000/(1 + 0.08)^4$]. The present value is less than the cost of the capital good, so the purchase is not worth-while.

Chapter 29, Page 678

1. Jones earns $2 million a year as a news anchor for KNBC. His next-best alternative in the news industry is earning $1.9 million a year as a news anchor for KABC. If Jones were not working in the news industry, his next-best alternative would be as a journalism professor earning $100,000 a year. Within the news industry, Jones earns $100,000 economic rent (the difference between $2 million and $1.9 million). Outside the news industry, Jones earns $1.9 million in economic rent (the difference between $2 million and $100,000).

2. It is $0.

3. When a firm competes for artificial rents, it expends resources to transfer economic rent from another firm to itself. In other words, resources are used to bring about a transfer. No additional goods or services are produced as a part of the process. But when a firm competes for real rents, resources are used to produce additional goods and services.

Chapter 29, Page 682

1. A probability cannot be assigned to uncertainty; a probability can be assigned to risk.

2. Many theories purport to explain profit. One theory states that profit exists because uncertainty exists—no uncertainty, no profit. Another states that profit exists because of arbitrage opportunities (the opportunities to buy low and sell high) to which some people are alert. Still another theory states that profit exists because some people (entrepreneurs) are capable of creating profit opportunities by devising a new product, production process, or marketing strategy.

3. Profit can be a signal, especially if it is earned in a competitive market. Specifically, profit signals that buyers value a good (as evidenced by the price they are willing and able to pay for the good) more than the factors that go into making the good.

4. (1) Produce a good or service that satisfies an unmet demand. (2) Reduce the transaction costs of making trades.

Chapter 30

Chapter 30, Page 687

1. Uncertainty, insurance, and externalities create unique problems for health care markets.

2. Health care services are both uncertain and expensive. If they were uncertain but cheap, there wouldn't be much of a problem. If Sophia misjudges her need for stamps, she just goes out and buys more stamps; her bank account barely feels the stamp purchase. If Sophia misjudges her need for a hip replacement, her bank account will certainly feel the impact of her error in judgment. Uncertainty, in combination with potentially large negative income shocks, is what makes this factor particularly problematic for health care markets.

3. Colds, flus, and smoking are a few of the many possible examples.

Chapter 30, Page 692

1. Yes, the RAND HIE provides convincing evidence that when it comes to buying health care, price matters.

2. Yes, but more affordable health care only seems to benefit high-risk groups in any measurable way. For the general population, the impact of the price of health care on health appears minimal.

3. Outpatient care is more price sensitive because it covers minor as well as serious medical problems. Inpatient care is generally reserved for serious medical conditions. People are less likely to forgo medical services for serious conditions than for minor conditions as the price for services increases.

Chapter 30, Page 697

1. There is a five-year difference between the life expectancy of American men and women (76.2 years and 81.2 years, respectively). In 2018, the life expectancy for Black Americans was reported as 74.9 years, whereas life expectancy for White and Hispanic Americans was reported as 78.7 years and 81.8 years, respectively.

2. The current evidence suggests COVID-19 exacerbated health disparities by race/ethnicity.

3. Education, early childhood deprivation, income, and stress are some of the potential causes of health disparities.

Chapter 30, Page 701

1. The United States has the highest medical prices for most common services. A number of theories as to why health

care prices are rising so quickly have been proposed, including high labor costs, improving health care quality, hospitals exercising monopoly power, medical malpractice laws, and waste.

2. Those who are too young to qualify for Medicare, have too much income to qualify for Medicaid, and aren't offered health insurance through their employer are the most likely to be uninsured.

3. It seems likely that extending the Affordable Care Act in certain directions will be discussed. More dramatic health care system overhauls, such as Medicare for All, will still be discussed but face substantial political hurdles.

Chapter 31

Chapter 31, Page 710

1. The market output does not reflect or adjust for either external costs (in the case of a negative externality) or external benefits (in the case of a positive externality). The socially optimal output does.

2. Certainly, if no costs are incurred by moving from the market output to the socially optimal output, the answer is yes. But this isn't likely to be the case. The economist considers whether the benefits of moving to the socially optimal output are greater than or less than the costs of moving to the socially optimal output. If the benefits are greater than the costs, then yes; if the benefits are less than the costs, then no.

Chapter 31, Page 715

1. Internalizing an externality means adjusting the private cost by the external cost. To illustrate, suppose that someone's private cost is $10 and the external cost is $2. If the person internalizes the externality, the external cost becomes his or her cost, which is now $12.

2. Transaction costs are associated with the time and effort needed to search out, negotiate, and consummate an exchange. These costs are higher for buying a house than for buying a hamburger. It takes more time and effort to search out a house to buy, negotiate a price, and consummate the deal than it takes to search out and buy a hamburger.

3. Under certain conditions, no. Specifically, if transaction costs are zero or trivial, the property rights assignment that a court makes is irrelevant to the resource-allocative outcome. Of course, if transaction costs are not zero or trivial, then the property rights assignment a court makes does matter.

4. Given a negative externality, there is a marginal external cost. The marginal external cost (MEC) plus the marginal private cost (MPC) equals the marginal social cost (MSC): $MSC = MPC + MEC$. If a tax (t) is to adjust correctly for the marginal external cost associated with the negative externality, it must be equal to the marginal external cost; in other words, tax $= MEC$. With this condition fulfilled, $MPC + \text{tax} = MSC = MPC + MEC$.

Chapter 31, Page 718

1. Under a system in which each polluter eliminates the same amount of pollution, both the polluters that have a high cost of eliminating pollution and the polluters that have a lost cost of eliminating pollution have to eliminate the same amount of pollution. Under a tradable pollution permits system, it is primarily the low-cost polluters that end up eliminating most of the pollution.

2. Under an emissions tax, polluters know what price they have to pay to pollute but the government doesn't know how much pollution will be generated. Under a tradable pollution permits system (cap and trade), the government knows the amount of pollution but polluters don't immediately know what the price to pollute will be.

3. Under an emission tax, the price to pollute is the tax; under a tradable pollution permits system, the price to pollute is the price of the pollution permit.

Chapter 31, Page 723

1. After a nonexcludable public good is produced, the individual or firm that produced it wouldn't be able to collect payment for it. When a nonexcludable public good is provided to one person, it is provided to everyone. Because an individual can consume the good without paying for it, he is likely to take a free ride. Another way of answering this question is simply to say, "The market fails to produce nonexcludable public goods because of the free-rider problem."

2. (a) A composition notebook is a private good. It is rivalrous in consumption: If one person is using it, someone else cannot. (b) A Shakespearean play performed in a summer theater is an excludable public good. It is nonrivalrous in consumption (everyone in the theater can see the play) but excludable (a person must pay to get into the theater). (c) An apple is a private good. It is rivalrous in consumption: If one person eats it, someone else cannot. (d) A telephone in service is a private good. One person using the phone (e.g., in your house) prevents someone

else from using it. (e) Sunshine is a nonexcludable public good. It is nonrivalrous in consumption (one person's consumption of it doesn't reduce its consumption by others) and nonexcludable (people cannot be excluded from consuming the sunshine).

3. A concert is an example. If one person consumes the concert, others can still consume it to the same degree. However, people can be excluded from consuming it.

Chapter 31, Page 727

1. The sellers of a fictional product X know that the good could, under certain conditions, cause health problems, but they do not release this information to the buyers. Consequently, the demand for good X is likely to be greater than it would be if there was symmetric information. The quantity consumed of good X is likely to be higher when there is asymmetric information than when there is symmetric information.

2. In the used-car market discussed in the text, if there is asymmetric information for two types of used cars—good used cars and lemons—the market price for a used car may understate the value of a good used car and overstate the value of a lemon. This discrepancy will induce sellers of lemons to enter the market and sellers of good cars to leave it. (The owners of good used cars will not want to sell their cars for less than their cars are worth.) In theory, the used-car market may eventually consist of nothing but lemons. In other words, a used-car market for good cars no longer will exist.

3. A college professor tells her students that she does not believe in giving grades of D or F. As a result, her students do not take as many precautionary measures to guard against receiving low grades. Does your example have the characteristic of this example—namely, one person's assurance affecting another person's incentive?

Chapter 32

Chapter 32, Page 740

1. No. The model doesn't say every politician has to do these things; it simply predicts that politicians who do these things have an increased chance of winning the election in a two-person race.

2. Voters may want more information from politicians, but supplying that information is not always in the best interests of political candidates. When they speak in specific terms, politicians are often labeled as being at one end or the other of the political spectrum. But, generally, this is not how elections are won.

3. Yes. In the cost equation of voting, we included (1) the cost of driving to the polls, (2) the cost of standing in line, and (3) the cost of filling out the ballot. Bad weather (heavy rain, snow, and ice) would likely raise the cost of driving to the polls and standing in line, thereby raising the cost of voting. The higher the cost of voting is, the less likely it is that people will vote, *ceteris paribus*.

Chapter 32, Page 742

1. Two units.

2. In Example 2 with equal taxes, one unit received a simple majority of the votes. Person C was made worse off by $20 because his *MPB* for the first unit of good Y was $100 but he ended up paying a tax of $120.

Chapter 32, Page 748

1. Both farmers and consumers are affected by federal agricultural policy, but not in the same way and not to the same degree. Federal agricultural policy directly affects farmers' incomes, usually by a large amount. It indirectly affects consumers' costs, but not as much as it affects farmers' incomes. Therefore, farmers have more at stake than consumers when it comes to federal agricultural policy. People tend to be better informed about matters that mean more to them.

2. The legislation is more likely to pass when group A includes 10 million persons because the wider the dispersal of the costs of the legislation, the greater the likelihood of passage. When costs are widely dispersed, the cost to any one individual is so small that she or he is unlikely to lobby against the legislation.

3. Examples include teachers saying that more money for education will help the country compete in the global marketplace, domestic car manufacturers saying that tariffs on foreign imports will save American jobs and domestic manufacturing, and farmers saying that subsidies to farmers will preserve the American farm and a way of life that Americans cherish. Whether any of these groups is right or wrong is not the point. The point is that special-interest groups are likely to advance their arguments (good or bad) with public-interest talk.

4. Rent seeking is socially wasteful because the resources that are used to seek rent could be used to produce goods and services instead.

Chapter 33

Chapter 33, Page 760

1. What is shown here between the divorce rate in Maine and per capita consumption of margarine is correlation, not causation. Two things can move together, but it does not necessarily follow that a change in one of those things causes the change in the other.

2. The control group consists of those persons resembling the treatment group in all ways other than the fact that they do not receive the factor under study, and therefore, they serve as a comparison group when treatment results are evaluated. The treatment group consists of those persons resembling the control group in all ways other than the fact that they do receive the factor under study. For example, consider a control group and a treatment group when it comes to trying to figure out the effects of a new pharmaceutical drug. The control group does not receive the drug, and the treatment group does.

3. It was the fact that the towns in the two states were very similar in many ways. The demographics and characteristics of the people on the New Jersey side of the New Jersey–Pennsylvania border were very much like the people on the eastern Pennsylvania side of the border. Then, with similar groups of people in the two states, it just so happened that New Jersey increased its minimum wage rate, whereas Pennsylvania did not.

4. Richardson and Troost noticed that banks in northern Mississippi were under the St. Louis Fed's jurisdiction and that banks in southern Mississippi were under the Atlanta Fed's jurisdiction. They also noticed that the two Federal Reserve District banks had different policies for lending to banks in trouble in the Great Depression. While the Atlanta Fed decided to increase lending to failing banks, the St. Louis Fed did not. Richardson and Troost found that banks were more likely to survive in the region in which the Federal Reserve District bank increased lending and that there was quicker economic recovery in that region.

Chapter 33, Page 764

1. It would be better to study the earnings of those who were drafted by lottery into the military because if people join the military voluntarily, there is a self-selection problem. That is, people who self-select to join the military could have characteristics different from those who choose not to join the military. What is needed to establish causal relationships is two groups of persons that are similar, after which some factor is introduced that holds for one group but not the other.

2. It is a variable that creates random variation across individuals. The draft lottery guaranteed that the people who were drafted into the military were much the same as the people who were not drafted. In this sense, the lottery is creating random variation in military service across individuals.

Chapter 33, Page 771

1. Regularization refers to the process of eliminating variables that are only weakly related to our target of interest.

2. The authors found that replacing judges with a machine-learning algorithm could (1) release more defendants before trial while (2) decreasing failure-to-appear rates. It can achieve both goals simultaneously by assigning bail only to those defendants with the highest probability of missing future court dates.

Chapter 34

Chapter 34, Page 779

1. For the United States, $1X = \frac{1}{6}Y$, or $1Y = 6X$. For the United Kingdom, $1X = 2Y$ or $1Y = \frac{1}{2}X$. Let's focus on the opportunity cost of $1X$ in each country: In the United States, $1X = \frac{1}{6}$; and in the United Kingdom, $1X = 2Y$. Terms of trade that are between these two end points would be favorable for the two countries. For example, suppose we choose $1X = 1Y$. This choice is good for the United States, which would prefer to give up $1X$ and get $1Y$ in trade than to give up $1X$ and get only $\frac{1}{6}Y$ without trade. Similarly, the United Kingdom would prefer to give up $1Y$ and get $1X$ in trade than to give up $1Y$ and get only $\frac{1}{2}X$ without trade. Any terms of trade between $1X = \frac{1}{6}Y$ and $1X = 2Y$ will be favorable to the two countries.

2. Yes. The theory of comparative advantage demonstrates this idea. Exhibit 1 shows that the United States could produce more food and clothing than Japan. Still, the United States benefits from specialization and trade, as shown in Exhibit 2. In column 5 of this exhibit, the United States can consume 10 more units of food by specializing and trading than it could consume without specialization and trade.

3. No. It is the desire to buy low and sell high (earn a profit) that pushes countries into producing and trading at a comparative advantage. Government officials do not collect cost data and then issue orders to firms in the country

to produce X, Y, or Z. We have not drawn the PPFs in this chapter and identified the cost differences between countries to show what countries actually do in the real world. Instead, we described things simply to show how countries benefit from specialization and trade.

Chapter 34, Page 787

1. Domestic producers benefit because producers' surplus rises; domestic consumers lose because consumers' surplus falls. Also, the government benefits in that it receives the tariff revenue. Moreover, consumers lose more than the producers and government gains, so tariffs result in a net loss.

2. The consumers' surplus falls by more than the producers' surplus rises.

3. With a tariff, the government receives tariff revenue. With a quota, it does not. In the latter case, the revenue that would have gone to the government goes to the importers who get to satisfy the quota instead.

4. Infant or new domestic industries need to be protected from older, more established competitors until they are mature enough to compete on an equal basis. Tariffs and quotas provide these infant industries the time they need.

Chapter 35

Chapter 35, Page 798

1. As the demand for dollars increases, the supply of pesos increases. For example, suppose someone in Mexico wants to buy something produced in the United States. The American wants to be paid in dollars, but the Mexican has pesos, not dollars. So she has to buy dollars with pesos; in other words, she has to supply pesos to buy dollars. Thus, as she demands more dollars, she will have to supply more pesos.

2. The dollar is said to have appreciated against the peso when it takes more pesos to buy a dollar and fewer dollars to buy a peso. In order for this eventuality to occur, either the demand for dollars must increase, which means that the supply of pesos increases, or the supply of dollars must decrease, which means that the demand for pesos decreases.

3. *Ceteris paribus*, the dollar will depreciate relative to the franc. As incomes for Americans rise, the demand for Swiss goods rises. Rising demand for Swiss goods increases the demand for francs and the supply of dollars on the foreign exchange market. In turn, the dollar depreciates and the franc appreciates.

4. The theory states that the exchange rate between any two currencies will adjust to reflect changes in the relative price levels of the two countries. For example, suppose the U.S. price level rises 5 percent and Mexico's price level remains constant. According to the PPP theory, the U.S. dollar will depreciate 5 percent relative to the Mexican peso.

Chapter 35, Page 802

1. The terms *overvalued* and *undervalued* refer to the equilibrium exchange rate: The exchange rate at which the quantity demanded and the quantity supplied of a currency are the same in the foreign exchange market. Let's suppose the equilibrium exchange rate were 0.10 USD = 1 MXN. This is the same as saying that 10 pesos = \$1. If the exchange rate were fixed at 0.12 USD = 1 MXN, which is the same as 8.33 pesos = \$1, the peso would be overvalued and the dollar would be undervalued. Specifically, a currency is overvalued if one unit of it fetches more of another currency than it would in equilibrium; a currency is undervalued if 1 unit of it fetches less of another currency than it would in equilibrium. In equilibrium, one peso would fetch \$0.10, and at the current exchange rate it fetches \$0.12, so the peso is overvalued. In equilibrium, \$1 would fetch 10 pesos, and at the current exchange rate, it fetches only 8.33 pesos, so the dollar is undervalued.

2. An overvalued dollar means that some other currency—let's say the Japanese yen—is undervalued. On the one hand, an overvalued dollar makes U.S. goods more expensive for the Japanese, so they buy fewer U.S. goods and the United States exports less. On the other hand, an undervalued yen makes Japanese goods cheaper for Americans, so they buy more Japanese goods and the United States imports more. Thus, an overvalued dollar reduces U.S. exports and raises U.S. imports.

3. a. Dollar is overvalued.
   b. Dollar is undervalued.
   c. Dollar is undervalued.

4. When a country devalues its currency, it makes it cheaper for foreigners to buy its products.

Glossary

A

absolute (money) price The price of a good in money terms.

absolute real economic growth An increase in Real GDP from one period to the next.

abstract The process (used in building a theory) of focusing on a limited number of variables to explain or predict an event.

accounting profit The difference between total revenue and explicit costs.

activists Persons who argue that monetary and fiscal policies should be deliberately used to smooth out the business cycle.

adaptive expectations Expectations that individuals form from past experience and modify slowly as the present and the future become the past (i.e., as time passes).

adverse selection A phenomenon that occurs when parties on one side of the market who have information not known to others self-select in a way that adversely affects parties on the other side of the market.

Affordable Care Act (ACA) The most recent major health care reform in the United States that was signed into law in 2010.

aggregate demand The quantity demanded of all goods and services (Real GDP) at different price levels, *ceteris paribus*.

Aggregate Demand (AD) curve A curve that shows the quantity demanded of all goods and services (Real GDP) at different price levels, *ceteris paribus*.

aggregate supply The quantity supplied of all goods and services (Real GDP) at different price levels, *ceteris paribus*.

algorithm An algorithm is a sequence of operations used to perform some task, often by a computer.

algorithmic discrimination In some cases, algorithms may unfairly treat one group favorably relative to another group. For example, an algorithm that is more likely to recommend a male job applicant relative to an equally qualified female applicant would exhibit algorithmic discrimination against women.

antitrust law Legislation passed for the stated purpose of controlling monopoly power and preserving and promoting competition.

appreciated An increase in the value of one currency relative to other currencies.

arbitrage Buying a good at a low price and selling it for a higher price.

asset Anything of value that is owned or that one has claim to.

asymmetric information A situation in which an economic agent on one side of a transaction has information that an economic agent on the other side of the transaction does not have.

automatic fiscal policy Changes in government expenditures and/or taxes that occur automatically without (additional) congressional action.

autonomous consumption The part of consumption that is independent of disposable income.

Average Fixed Cost (AFC) Total fixed cost divided by quantity of output: $AFC = TFC/Q$.

average inflation targeting The policy of trying to keep the average inflation rate over a specific time period at a certain target rate (say, 2 percent).

Average Total Cost (ATC) Total cost divided by quantity of output: $ATC = TC/Q$

Average Variable Cost (AVC) Total variable cost divided by quantity of output: $AVC = TVC/Q$.

average–marginal rule When the marginal magnitude is above the average magnitude, the average magnitude rises; when the marginal magnitude is below the average magnitude, the average magnitude falls.

B

bad Anything from which individuals receive disutility or dissatisfaction.

balance sheet A record of the assets and liabilities of a bank.

balanced budget Government expenditures equal to tax revenues.

barter Exchanging goods and services for other goods and services without the use of money.

base year The year chosen as a point of reference or basis of comparison for prices in other years; a benchmark year.

board of governors The governing body of the Federal Reserve System.

budget constraint All the combinations, or bundles, of two goods a person can purchase, given a certain money income and prices for the two goods.

budget deficit Government expenditures greater than tax revenues.

budget surplus Tax revenues greater than government expenditures.

business cycle Recurrent swings (up and down) in Real GDP.

business firm An entity that employs factors of production (resources) to produce goods and services to be sold to consumers, other firms, or the government.

C

capital Produced goods—such as factories, machinery, tools, computers, and buildings—that can be used as inputs for further production.

capital consumption allowance (depreciation) The estimated amount of capital goods used up in production through natural wear, obsolescence, and accidental destruction.

capture theory of regulation A theory holding that, no matter what the motive is for the initial regulation and the establishment of the regulatory agency, the agency eventually will be captured (controlled) by the special interests of the industry being regulated.

cartel An organization of firms that reduces output and increases price in an effort to increase joint profits.

cartel theory A theory of oligopoly in which oligopolistic firms act as if there were only one firm in the industry.

cash leakage Occurs when funds are held as currency instead of deposited into a checking account.

ceteris paribus A Latin term meaning *all other things constant* or *nothing else changes*.

closed shop An organization in which an employee must belong to the union before he or she can be hired.

Coase Theorem The proposition that private negotiations between people will lead to an efficient resolution of externalities, as long as property rights are well defined and transaction costs are trivial or zero.

collective bargaining The process whereby wage rates and other issues are determined by a union bargaining with management on behalf of all union members.

commercial insurance Insurance provided by private insurance companies, typically through one's employer.

comparative advantage The situation in which someone can produce a good at lower opportunity cost than someone else can.

complements Two goods that are used jointly in consumption.

complete crowding out A decrease in one or more components of private spending that completely offsets the increase in government spending.

concentration ratio The percentage of industry sales (or assets, output, labor force, or some other factor) accounted for by x number of firms in the industry.

conglomerate merger A merger between companies in different industries.

constant returns to scale The condition when inputs are increased by some percentage and output increases by an equal percentage, causing unit costs to remain constant.

constant-cost industry An industry in which average total costs do not change as (industry) output increases or decreases when firms enter or exit the industry, respectively.

consumer equilibrium The equilibrium that occurs when the consumer has spent all of his or her income and the marginal utilities per dollar spent on each good purchased *are* equal: $MU_A/P_A = MU_B/P_B = \cdots = MU_Z/P_Z$, where the letters A–Z represent all the goods a person buys.

Consumer Price Index (CPI) The weighted average of prices of a specific set of goods and services purchased by a typical household; a widely cited index number for the price level.

Consumers' Surplus (CS) The difference between the maximum price a buyer is willing and able to pay for a good or service and the price actually paid. (CS = Maximum buying price − Price paid.)

consumption The sum of spending on durable goods, nondurable goods, and services.

consumption function The relationship between consumption and disposable income. In the consumption function used in this text, consumption is directly related to disposable income and is positive even at zero disposable income: $C = C_0 + (MPC)(Y_d)$.

contestable market A market in which entry is easy and exit is costless, new firms can produce the product at the same cost as current firms, and exiting firms can easily dispose of their fixed assets by selling them.

continued inflation A continued increase in the price level.

contractionary fiscal policy Decreases in government expenditures and/or increases in taxes in order to achieve economic goals.

contractionary monetary policy The policy by which the Fed decreases the money supply and increases (short-term) interest rates; the policy is often undertaken to reduce aggregate demand.

controlled experiment An experiment in which all factors between two groups except for one are the same. A randomized controlled trial (RCT) is often synonymous with a controlled experiment. In a randomized controlled trial, experimental subjects are randomly split into treatment and control groups.

correlation Any mutual relationship between two things, either causally or by chance. For example, professional basketball players tend to be taller than average, so basketball ability is correlated with height.

cross elasticity of demand A measure of the responsiveness in quantity demanded of one good to changes in the price of another good.

cross-validation A technique used to assess whether a set of results will generalize to a different setting or dataset.

crowding out The decrease in private expenditures that occurs as a consequence of increased government spending or the need to finance a budget deficit.

currency Coins and paper money.

cutoff rule Any decision that is made that is determined by a threshold.

cyclical deficit The part of the budget deficit that is a result of a downturn in economic activity.

cyclical unemployment rate The difference between the unemployment rate and the natural unemployment rate.

D

deadweight loss The loss to society of not producing the competitive, or supply-and-demand-determined, level of output.

deadweight loss of monopoly The net value (the value to buyers over and above the costs to suppliers) of the difference between the competitive quantity of output (where $P = MC$) and the monopoly quantity of output (where $P > MC$); the loss due to not producing the competitive quantity of output.

decisions at the margin Decision making characterized by weighing the additional (marginal) benefits of a change against the additional (marginal) costs of a change with respect to current conditions.

decreasing-cost industry An industry in which average total costs decrease as output increases and increase as output decreases when firms enter and exit the industry, respectively.

Glossary

demand The willingness and ability of buyers to purchase different quantities of a good at different prices during a specific period.

demand curve The graphical representation of the law of demand.

demand for money (balances) The inverse relationship between the quantity demanded of money (balances) and the price of holding money (balances).

demand schedule The numerical tabulation of the quantity demanded of a good at different prices. A demand schedule is the numerical representation of the law of demand.

depreciated A decrease in the value of one currency relative to other currencies.

derived demand Demand that is the result of some other demand. For example, factor demand is derived from the demand for the products that the factors go to produce.

devaluation A government action that changes the exchange rate by lowering the official price of a currency.

diamond–water paradox The observation that things with the greatest value in use sometimes have little value in exchange, and things with little value in use sometimes have the greatest value in exchange.

difference-in-differences A method to infer causality that compares differences between two groups (a treated group and a control group) over time.

direct finance A method of transferring money whereby borrowers and lenders come together in a market setting, such as the bond market.

directly related Two variables are directly related if they change in the same way.

discount loan A loan the Fed makes to a commercial bank.

discount rate The interest rate the Fed charges depository institutions that borrow reserves from it; the interest rate charged on a discount loan.

discretionary fiscal policy Deliberate changes in government expenditures and/or taxes in order to achieve economic goals.

diseconomies of scale The condition when inputs are increased by some percentage and output increases by a smaller percentage, causing unit costs to rise.

disequilibrium A state of either surplus or shortage in a market.

disequilibrium price A price other than the equilibrium price. A price at which the quantity demanded does not equal the quantity supplied.

disposable income The portion of personal income that can be used for consumption or saving. It is equal to personal income minus personal taxes (especially income taxes).

disutility The dissatisfaction one receives from a bad.

double coincidence of wants In a barter economy, a requirement that must be met before a trade can be made. The term specifies that a trader must find another trader who at the same time is willing to trade what the first trader wants and wants what the first trader has.

double counting Counting a good more than once when computing GDP.

dumping The sale of goods abroad at a price below their cost and below the price charged in the domestic market.

E

economic growth Increases in Real GDP.

economic profit The difference between total revenue and total cost, including both explicit and implicit costs.

economic rent Payment in excess of opportunity costs.

economics The science of scarcity; the science of how individuals and societies deal with the fact that wants are greater than the limited resources available to satisfy those wants.

economies of scale Economies that exist when inputs are increased by some percentage and output increases by a greater percentage, causing unit costs to fall.

efficiency Exists when marginal benefits equal marginal costs.

efficiency wage models These models hold that it is sometimes in the best interest of business firms to pay their employees wage rates that are higher than the equilibrium wage rate.

efficient-producer hypothesis Hypothesizes that individuals with more education are more efficient producers of health than individuals with less education.

elastic demand The demand that occurs when the percentage change in quantity demanded is greater than the percentage change in price. Quantity demanded changes proportionately more than price changes.

elasticity of demand for labor The percentage change in the quantity demanded of labor divided by the percentage change in the wage rate.

employment rate The percentage of the civilian noninstitutional population that is employed: Employment rate = Number of employed persons ÷ Civilian noninstitutional population.

entrepreneurship The talent that some people have for organizing the resources of land, labor, and capital to produce goods, seek new business opportunities, and develop new ways of doing things.

equation of exchange An identity stating that the money supply (M) times velocity (V) must be equal to the price level (P) times Real GDP (Q): $MV \equiv PQ$.

equilibrium Equilibrium means "at rest." Equilibrium in a market is the price–quantity combination from which buyers or sellers do not tend to move away. Graphically, equilibrium is the intersection point of the supply and demand curves.

equilibrium price (market-clearing price) The price at which the quantity demanded of a good equals the quantity supplied.

equilibrium quantity The quantity that corresponds to the equilibrium price. The quantity at which the amount of the good that buyers are willing and able to buy equals the amount that sellers are willing and able to sell, and both equal the amount actually bought and sold.

excess capacity theorem A monopolistic competitor in equilibrium produces an output smaller than the one that would minimize its costs of production.

excess reserves Any reserves held beyond the required amount; the difference between (total) reserves and required reserves.

exchange (trade) The giving up of one thing for something else.

exchange rate The price of one currency in terms of another currency.

excludable A characteristic of a good whereby it is possible or not prohibitively costly to exclude someone from receiving the benefits of the good after it has been produced.

expansionary fiscal policy Increases in government expenditures and/or decreases in taxes in order to achieve particular economic goals.

expansionary monetary policy The policy by which the Fed increases the money supply and decreases (short-term) interest rates; the policy is often undertaken to increase aggregate demand.

expectations effect The change in the interest rate due to a change in the expected inflation rate.

explicit cost A cost incurred when an actual (monetary) payment is made.

exports Total foreign spending on domestic (U.S.) goods.

externality A side effect of an action that affects the well-being of third parties.

F

factor price taker A firm that can buy all of a factor it wants at the equilibrium price. Such a firm faces a horizontal (flat, perfectly elastic) supply curve of factors.

federal funds market A market in which banks lend reserves to one another, usually for short periods.

federal funds rate The interest rate in the federal funds market; the interest rate banks charge one another to borrow reserves.

federal funds rate target The interest rate that the Fed wants the federal funds rate to be.

Federal Open Market Committee (FOMC) The Fed's 12-member policy-making group that reviews economic and financial conditions and determines the appropriate stance of monetary policy.

Federal Reserve System (the Fed) The central bank of the United States.

final good A good in the hands of its final user.

financial intermediary An institution that transfers funds from those who want to lend funds to those who want to borrow them.

fine-tuning The (usually frequent) use of monetary and fiscal policies to counteract even small undesirable movements in economic activity.

fiscal policy Changes in government expenditures and/or taxes aimed at achieving economic goals, such as low unemployment, stable prices, and economic growth.

fixed costs Costs that do not vary with output; the costs associated with fixed inputs.

fixed exchange rate system A system whereby a nation's currency is set at a fixed rate relative to all other currencies, and central banks intervene in the foreign exchange market to maintain the fixed rate.

fixed input An input whose quantity cannot be changed as output changes.

fixed investment Business purchases of capital goods, such as machinery and factories, and purchases of new residential housing.

flexible exchange rate system A system whereby exchange rates are determined by the forces of supply and demand for a currency.

foreign exchange market The market in which currencies of different countries are exchanged.

fractional reserve banking A banking arrangement that allows banks to hold reserves equal to only a fraction of their deposit liabilities.

free riders Anyone who receives the benefits of a good without paying for it.

frictional unemployment Unemployment that is due to the natural so-called frictions in the economy and that is caused by changing market conditions and represented by qualified individuals with transferable skills who change jobs.

Friedman natural rate theory Within the Phillips curve framework, the idea that, in the long run, unemployment is at its natural rate and that there is a long-run Phillips curve, which is vertical at the natural rate of unemployment.

full employment The condition that exists when the unemployment rate is equal to the natural unemployment rate.

G

game theory A mathematical technique used to analyze the behavior of decision makers who try to reach an optimal position for themselves through game playing or the use of strategic behavior, who are fully aware of the interactive nature of the process at hand, and who anticipate the moves of other decision makers.

gini coefficient A measure of the degree of inequality in the income distribution.

good Anything from which individuals receive utility or satisfaction.

government purchases Federal, state, and local government purchases of goods and services, and gross investment in highways, bridges, and so on.

government transfer payments Payments to persons that are not made in return for currently supplied goods and services.

Gross Domestic Product (GDP) The total market value of all final goods and services produced annually within a country's borders.

H

health disparities Differences in health outcomes across levels of socioeconomic status.

Herfindahl index An index that measures the degree of concentration in an industry, equal to the sum of the squares of the market shares of each firm in the industry.

horizontal merger A merger between firms that are selling similar products in the same market.

human capital The knowledge and skills a person acquires through education, training, and experience.

human capital Education, development of skills, and anything else that is particular to the individual and that increases personal productivity.

I

implicit cost A cost that represents the value of resources used in production for which no actual (monetary) payment is made.

imports Total domestic (U.S.) spending on foreign goods.

incentive Something that encourages or motivates a person to undertake an action.

income effect The change in the interest rate due to a change in Real GDP.

income elastic The condition that exists when the percentage change in quantity demanded of a good is greater than the percentage change in income.

income elasticity of demand A measure of the responsiveness of quantity demanded to changes in income.

income inelastic The condition that exists when the percentage change in quantity demanded of a good is less than the percentage change in income.

income unit elastic The condition that exists when the percentage change in quantity demanded of a good is equal to the percentage change in income.

incomplete crowding out A decrease in one or more components of private spending that only partially offsets the increase in government spending.

increasing-cost industry An industry in which average total costs increase as output increases and decrease as output decreases when firms enter and exit the industry, respectively.

independent Two variables are independent if, as one changes, the other does not.

indifference curve The curve that represents an indifference set and that shows all the bundles of two goods giving an individual equal total utility.

indifference curve map A map that represents a number of indifference curves for a given individual with reference to two goods.

indifference set A group of bundles of two goods that give an individual equal total utility.

indirect finance A method of transferring money whereby funds are loaned and borrowed through a financial intermediary.

inelastic demand The demand that occurs when the percentage change in quantity demanded is less than the percentage change in price. Quantity demanded changes proportionately less than price changes.

inferior good A good for which demand falls (rises) as income rises (falls).

inflation An increase in the price level.

inflationary gap The condition in which the Real GDP that the economy is producing is greater than the Natural Real GDP and the unemployment rate is less than the natural unemployment rate.

in-kind transfer payments Transfer payments, such as medical assistance and subsidized housing, that are made in a specific good or service rather than in cash.

insolvency A condition in which one's liabilities are greater than one's assets.

institution The rules of the game in a society or, more formally, the humanly devised constraints that shape human interaction; the rules and regulations, laws, customs, and business practices of a country.

instrumental variable A variable that creates random variation in a treatment. For example, if the treatment is "serving in the military," then we can use the outcome of the Vietnam War Draft lottery as an instrumental variable because being drafted (and therefore going on to serve in the military) was determined by chance.

Interest on Reserves Rate (IOR rate) The interest rate the Fed pays on reserves. Today, it is the primary tool the Fed uses to indirectly change the federal funds rate and conduct monetary policy.

interest rate effect The changes in household and business buying as the interest rate changes (in turn, a reflection of a change in the demand for or supply of credit brought on by price level changes).

intermediate good A good that is an input to the production of a final good.

internalizing externalities An externality is internalized if the persons or group that generated the externality incorporate into their own private or internal cost–benefit calculations the external benefits (in the case of a positive externality) or the external costs (in the case of a negative externality).

international trade effect The change in foreign sector spending as the price level changes.

interpersonal utility comparison Comparing the utility one person receives from a good, service, or activity with the utility another person receives from the same good, service, or activity.

intra-industry trade Intra-industry trade exists when countries trade goods within the same industry. For example, the United States and Japan both export cars to each other and import cars from each other.

inventory investment Changes in the stock of unsold goods.

inversely related Two variables are inversely related if they change in opposite ways.

investment The sum of all purchases of newly produced capital goods, changes in business inventories, and purchases of new residential housing.

L

labor The work brought about by the physical and mental talents that people contribute to the production process.

Labor Force Participation Rate (LFPR) The percentage of the civilian noninstitutional population that is in the civilian labor force: Labor force participation rate = Civilian labor force ÷ Civilian noninstitutional population.

Laffer curve The curve, named after economist Arthur Laffer, that shows the relationship between tax rates and tax revenues. According to the Laffer curve, as tax rates rise from zero, tax revenues rise, reach a maximum at some point, and then fall with further increases in tax rates.

laissez-faire A public policy of not interfering with market activities in the economy.

land All natural resources, such as minerals, forests, water, and unimproved land.

law of demand As the price of a good rises, the quantity demanded of the good falls, and as the price of a good falls, the quantity demanded of the good rises, *ceteris paribus*.

law of diminishing marginal returns As ever larger amounts of a variable input are combined with fixed inputs, the marginal physical product of the variable input eventually will decline.

law of diminishing marginal utility Over a given period, the marginal (or additional) utility or satisfaction gained by consuming equal successive units of a good will decline as the amount consumed increases.

law of increasing opportunity costs As more of a good is produced, the opportunity costs of producing that good increase.

law of supply As the price of a good rises, the quantity supplied of the good rises, and as the price of a good falls, the quantity supplied of the good falls, *ceteris paribus*.

least-cost rule Rule that specifies the combination of factors that minimizes costs and so requires that the following condition be met: $MPP_1/P_1 = MPP_2/P_2 = \ldots = MPP_N/P_N$ where the subscript numbers stand for the different factors.

liability Anything that is owed to someone else.

liquidity effect The change in the interest rate due to a change in the supply of loanable funds.

liquidity trap The horizontal portion of the demand curve for money.

loanable funds Funds that someone borrows and another person lends, for which the borrower pays an interest rate to the lender.

lock-in effect The situation in which a product or technology becomes the standard and is difficult or impossible to dislodge from that role.

logrolling The exchange of votes to gain support for legislation.

long run A period during which all inputs in the production process can be varied. (No inputs are fixed.)

Long-Run (Industry) Supply (*LRS*) Curve A graphic representation of the quantities of output that an industry is prepared to supply at different prices after the entry and exit of firms are completed.

Long-Run Aggregate Supply (*LRAS*) Curve A curve that represents the output the economy produces when wages and prices have adjusted to their final equilibrium levels and when workers do not have any relevant misperceptions. The *LRAS* curve is a vertical line at the level of Natural Real GDP.

Long-Run Average Total Cost (*LRATC*) Curve A curve that shows the lowest (unit) cost at which a firm can produce any given level of output.

long-run competitive equilibrium The condition in which $P = MC = SRATC = LRATC$. Economic profit is zero, firms are producing the quantity of output at which price is equal to marginal cost, and no firm has an incentive to change its plant size.

long-run equilibrium The condition that exists in the economy when wages and prices have adjusted to their (final) equilibrium levels and when workers do not have any relevant misperceptions. Graphically, long-run equilibrium occurs at the intersection of the *AD* and *LRAS* curves.

Lorenz curve A graph of the income distribution that expresses the relationship between the cumulative percentage of households and the cumulative percentage of income.

M

machine learning Computer algorithms that discover how to perform a task without explicitly being programmed to do so.

macroeconomics The branch of economics that deals with human behavior and choices as they relate to highly aggregate markets (e.g., the market for goods and services) or the entire economy.

managed float A managed flexible exchange rate system under which nations intervene now and then to adjust their official reserve holdings in order to moderate major swings in exchange rates.

managerial coordination The process in which managers direct employees to perform certain tasks.

marginal (income) tax rate The change in a person's tax payment divided by the change in taxable income: ΔTax payment ÷ ΔTaxable income.

Marginal Benefits (*MB*) Additional benefits; the benefits connected with consuming an additional unit of a good or undertaking one more unit of an activity.

Marginal Cost (*MC*) The change in total cost that results from a change in quantity of output: $MC = \Delta TC/\Delta Q$.

Marginal Factor Cost (*MFC*) The additional cost incurred by employing an additional factor unit.

Marginal Physical Product (*MPP*) The change in output that results from changing the variable input by one unit, with all other inputs held fixed.

marginal productivity theory Marginal productivity theory states that firms in competitive or perfect product and factor markets pay their factors their marginal revenue products.

marginal propensity to consume The ratio of the change in consumption to the change in disposable income: $MPC = \Delta C/\Delta Y_d$.

Marginal Propensity to Save (*MPS*) The ratio of the change in saving to the change in disposable income: $MPS = \Delta S/\Delta Y_d$.

marginal rate of substitution The amount of one good that an individual is willing to give up to obtain an additional unit of another good and maintain equal total utility.

Marginal Revenue (*MR*) The change in total revenue (*TR*) that results from selling one additional unit of output (*Q*).

Marginal Revenue Product (*MRP*) The additional revenue generated by employing an additional factor unit.

Marginal Social Benefits (*MSB*) The sum of marginal private benefits (*MPB*) and marginal external benefits (*MEB*): $MSB = MPB + MEB$.

Marginal Social Costs (*MSC*) The sum of marginal private costs (*MPC*) and marginal external costs (*MEC*): $MSC = MPC + MEC$.

marginal utility The additional utility a person receives from consuming an additional unit of a good.

market Any place people come together to trade.

market coordination The process in which individuals perform tasks, such as producing certain quantities of goods, on the basis of changes in market forces, such as supply, demand, and price.

market failure A situation in which the market does not provide the ideal or optimal amount of a good.

market structure The environment whose characteristics influence a firm's pricing and output decisions.

median voter model A model suggesting that candidates in a two-person political race will attempt to match the preferences of the median voter.

Medicaid The U.S. government-run health insurance program for low-income individuals.

Medicare The U.S. government-run health insurance program for adults ages 65 and older.

medium of exchange Anything that is generally acceptable in exchange for goods and services; a function of money.

microeconomics The branch of economics that deals with human behavior and choices as they relate to relatively small units: an individual, a firm, an industry, a single market.

minimum efficient scale The lowest output level at which average total costs are minimized.

monetary policy Changes in the money supply and interest rates by the Fed in order to meet certain goals such as maximum employment and stable prices.

monetary wealth The value of a person's monetary assets. Wealth, as distinguished from monetary wealth, refers to the value of all assets owned, both monetary and nonmonetary. In short, a person's wealth equals his or her monetary wealth (e.g., $1,000 cash) plus nonmonetary wealth (e.g., a car or a house).

money Any good that is widely accepted for purposes of exchange and the repayment of debt.

Money Market Deposit Account (MMDA) An interest-earning account at a bank or thrift institution, for which a minimum balance is usually required and most of which offer limited check-writing privileges.

Money Market Mutual Fund (MMMF) An interest-earning account at a mutual fund company, for which a minimum balance is usually required and most of which offer limited check-writing privileges.

monitor A person in a business firm who coordinates team production and reduces shirking.

monopolistic competition A theory of market structure based on three assumptions: many sellers and buyers, firms producing and selling slightly differentiated products, and easy entry and exit.

monopoly A theory of market structure based on three assumptions: There is one seller, it sells a product that has no close substitutes, and the barriers to entry are extremely high.

monopsony A single buyer in a factor market.

moral hazard A condition that exists when one party to a transaction changes his or her behavior in a way that is hidden from and costly to the other party.

multiplier The number that is multiplied by the change in autonomous spending to obtain the change in total spending. The multiplier (m) is equal to $1 \div (1 - MPC)$. If the economy is operating below Natural Real GDP, then the multiplier is the number that is multiplied by the change in autonomous spending to obtain the change in Real GDP.

N

national income Total income earned by U.S. citizens and businesses, no matter where they reside or are located. National income is the sum of the payments to resources (land, labor, capital, and entrepreneurship): National income = Compensation of employees + Proprietors' income + Corporate profits + Rental income of persons + Net interest.

natural experiment A study in which groups of individuals or places are exposed to a treatment by chance. For example, in 1992, New Jersey passed a law that increased the minimum wage. Therefore, workers in fast-food restaurants in New Jersey were exposed to the treatment (a higher minimum wage), while fast-food workers in nearby Pennsylvania were not.

natural monopoly The condition in which economies of scale are so pronounced that only one firm can survive.

Natural Real GDP The Real GDP that is produced at the natural unemployment rate. Also, the Real GDP that is produced when the economy is in long-run equilibrium.

natural unemployment Unemployment caused by frictional and structural factors in the economy: Natural unemployment rate = Frictional unemployment rate + Structural unemployment rate.

negative externality The condition in which a person's or group's actions impose a cost (an adverse side effect) on others.

net domestic product GDP minus the capital consumption allowance.

net exports Exports minus imports.

network good A good whose value increases as the expected number of units sold increases.

neutral good A good for which demand does not change as income rises or falls.

nominal income The current dollar amount of a person's income.

nominal interest rate The interest rate actually charged (or paid) in the market; the market interest rate: Nominal interest rate = Real interest rate + Expected inflation rate.

nominal interest rate The interest rate determined by the forces of supply and demand in the loanable funds market.

nonactivists Persons who argue against the deliberate use of discretionary fiscal and monetary policies to smooth out the business cycle. They believe in a permanent, stable, rule-oriented monetary and fiscal framework.

nonexcludable A characteristic of a good whereby it is impossible or prohibitively costly to exclude someone from receiving the benefits of the good after it has been produced.

nonrivalrous in consumption Said of a good whose consumption by one person does not reduce its consumption by others.

normal good A good for which demand rises (falls) as income rises (falls).

normal profit Zero economic profit, the level of profit necessary to keep resources employed in a firm. A firm that earns normal profit is earning revenue equal to its total costs (explicit plus implicit costs).

normative economics The study of *what should be* in economics.

O

oligopoly A theory of market structure based on three assumptions: few sellers and many buyers, firms producing either homogeneous or differentiated products, and significant barriers to entry.

ON-RRP rate The interest rate a nonbank financial institution earns on an overnight RRP.

one-shot inflation A one-time increase in the price level; an increase in the price level that does not continue.

open market operation Consists of open market purchases and open market sales. Open market purchases consist of the buying of government securities by the Fed. Open market sales consist of the selling of government securities by the Fed.

open market purchase The buying of government securities by the Fed.

open market sale The selling of government securities by the Fed.

opportunity cost The most highly valued opportunity or alternative forfeited when a choice is made.

optimal currency area A geographic area in which exchange rates can be fixed or a common currency used without sacrificing domestic economic goals, such as low unemployment.

overvalued A currency is overvalued if its price in terms of other currencies is above the equilibrium price.

own price The price of a good. For example, if the price of oranges is $1, this is its own price.

P

per-capita real economic growth An increase from one period to the next in per-capita Real GDP, which is Real GDP divided by population.

perfect competition A theory of market structure based on four assumptions: (1) There are many sellers and buyers; (2) the sellers sell a homogeneous good; (3) buyers and sellers have all relevant information; (4) entry into, and exit from, the market is easy.

perfect price discrimination A price structure in which the seller charges the highest price that each consumer is willing to pay for the product rather than go without it.

perfectly elastic demand The demand that exists when a small percentage change in price causes an extremely large percentage change in quantity demanded (from buying all to buying nothing).

perfectly inelastic demand The demand that exists when quantity demanded does not change as price changes.

personal income The amount of income that individuals actually receive. It is equal to national income minus undistributed corporate profits, social insurance taxes, and corporate profits taxes, plus transfer payments.

Phillips curve A curve that originally showed the relationship between wage inflation and unemployment and that now more often shows the relationship between price inflation and unemployment.

Policy Ineffectiveness Proposition (PIP) If (1) a policy change is correctly anticipated, (2) individuals form their expectations rationally, and (3) wages and prices are flexible, then neither fiscal policy nor monetary policy is effective at meeting macroeconomic goals.

positive economics The study of *what is* in economics.

positive externality The condition in which a person's or group's actions create a benefit (a beneficial side effect) for others.

positive rate of time preference A preference for earlier over later availability of goods.

poverty income threshold (poverty line) The income level below which people are considered to be living in poverty.

present value The current worth of some future dollar amount of income or receipts.

price ceiling A government-mandated maximum price above which legal trades cannot be made.

price discrimination A price structure in which the seller charges different prices for the product it sells and the price differences do not reflect cost differences.

price elasticity of demand A measure of the responsiveness of quantity demanded to changes in price.

price elasticity of supply A measure of the responsiveness of quantity supplied to changes in price.

price floor A government-mandated minimum price below which legal trades cannot be made.

price index A measure of the price level.

price level A weighted average of the prices of all goods and services.

price searcher A seller that has the ability to control, to some degree, the price of the product it sells.

price taker A seller that does not have the ability to control the price of the product it sells; the seller "takes" the price determined in the market.

price-level effect The change in the interest rate due to a change in the price level.

Producers' (Sellers') Surplus (PS) The difference between the price sellers receive for a good and the minimum or lowest price for which they would have sold the good. (PS = Price received − Minimum selling price.)

production function A function that specifies the relation between technology and the quantity of factor inputs to output, or Real GDP.

Production Possibilities Frontier (PPF) The possible combinations of two goods that can be produced during a certain span of time under the conditions of a given state of technology and fully employed resources.

productive efficiency The situation in which a firm produces its output at the lowest-possible per-unit cost (lowest *ATC*).

productive efficient The condition in which the maximum output is produced with the given resources and technology.

productive inefficient The condition in which less than the maximum output is produced with the given resources and technology. Productive inefficiency implies that more of one good can be produced without any less of another being produced.

profit The difference between total revenue and total cost.

profit maximization rule Profit is maximized by producing the quantity of output at which $MR = MC$.

progressive income tax An income tax system in which one's tax rate rises as taxable income rises (up to some point).

proportional income tax An income tax system in which a person's tax rate is the same regardless of taxable income.

public choice The branch of economics in which economic principles and tools are applied to public sector decision making.

public choice theory of regulation A theory holding that regulators are seeking to do—and will do through regulation—what is in their best interest (specifically, to enhance their power and the size and budget of their regulatory agencies).

public debt The total amount that the federal government owes its creditors.

public franchise A firm's government-granted right that permits the firm to provide a particular good or service and that excludes all others from doing so.

public good A good whose consumption by one person does not reduce its consumption by another person—that is, it is nonrivalrous in consumption.

public interest theory of regulation A theory holding that regulators are seeking to do—and will do through regulation—what is in the best interest of the public or society at large.

purchasing power The quantity of goods and services that can be purchased with a unit of money. Purchasing power and the price level are inversely related: As the price level goes up (down), purchasing power goes down (up).

Purchasing Power Parity (PPP) Theory Theory stating that exchange rates between any two currencies will adjust to reflect changes in the relative price levels of the two countries.

pure economic rent A category of economic rent such that the payment is to a factor that is in fixed supply, implying that the factor has zero opportunity costs.

Q

quota A legal limit imposed on the amount of a good that may be imported.

R

Randomized Controlled Trial (RCT) A study in which individuals are assigned to different groups (treatment group versus placebo or control group) at random.

rational expectations Expectations that individuals form on the basis of past experience and their predictions about the effects of present and future policy actions and events.

rational ignorance The state of not acquiring information because the costs of acquiring it are greater than the benefits.

rationing device A means for deciding who gets what of available resources and goods.

real balance effect The change in the purchasing power of dollar-denominated assets that results from a change in the price level.

Real GDP The value of the entire output produced annually within a country's borders, adjusted for price changes.

real income Nominal income adjusted for price changes.

real interest rate The nominal interest rate minus the expected inflation rate. When the expected inflation rate is zero, the real interest rate equals the nominal interest rate.

real interest rate The nominal interest rate adjusted for expected inflation; that is, the nominal interest rate minus the expected inflation rate.

recessionary gap The condition in which the Real GDP that the economy is producing is less than the Natural Real GDP and the unemployment rate is greater than the natural unemployment rate.

regression discontinuity design A method to identify causal effects by using a cutoff rule. For example, if admissions to a university were determined solely by a test score, then those who fall just below the threshold for admission are probably quite similar to those who fall at or just above the threshold. Therefore, we can compare their outcomes (such as earnings) over time to identify the causal effect of attending the university.

regressive income tax An income tax system in which a person's tax rate declines as his or her taxable income rises.

regulatory lag The period between the time a natural monopoly's costs change and the time the regulatory agency adjusts prices to account for the change.

relative price The price of a good in terms of another good

rent seeking Actions of individuals and groups who spend resources to influence public policy in the hope of redistributing (transferring) income to themselves from others.

required reserve ratio (r) A percentage of each dollar deposited that must be held in reserve form (specifically, as bank deposits at the Fed or vault cash).

required reserves The minimum dollar amount of reserves a bank must hold against its checkable deposits, as mandated by the Fed.

reserve deficient The situation that exists when a bank holds fewer reserves than specified by the required reserve ratio.

reserve requirement The Fed rule that specifies the amount of reserves a bank must hold to back up deposits.

reserves The sum of bank deposits at the Fed and vault cash.

residual claimant Persons who share in the profits of a business firm.

resource allocative efficiency The situation in which firms produce the quantity of output at which price equals marginal cost: $P = MC$.

revaluation A government action that changes the exchange rate by raising the official price of a currency.

rivalrous in consumption Said of a good whose consumption by one person reduces its consumption by others.

roundabout method of production The production of capital goods that enhance productive capabilities.

S

savings deposit An interest-earning account at a commercial bank or thrift institution.

Say's law Supply creates its own demand. Production creates enough demand to purchase all the goods and services the economy produces.

scarcity The condition in which our wants are greater than the limited resources available to satisfy those wants.

screening The process employers use to increase the probability of choosing good employees on the basis of certain criteria.

second-degree price discrimination A price structure in which the seller charges a uniform price per unit for one specific quantity, a lower price for an additional quantity, and so on.

self-select Choosing for oneself to participate in something. For example, individuals who volunteer for military service self-select into the military. Individuals who are drafted do not self-select into the military.

shirking The behavior of a worker who is putting forth less than the agreed-to effort.

short run A period during which some inputs in the production process are fixed.

short-run (firm) supply curve The portion of the firm's marginal cost curve that lies above the average variable cost curve.

Short-Run Aggregate Supply (SRAS) curve A curve that shows the quantity supplied of all goods and services (Real GDP) at different price levels, *ceteris paribus*.

short-run equilibrium The condition in the economy when the quantity demanded of Real GDP equals the (short-run) quantity supplied of Real GDP. This condition is met where the aggregate demand curve intersects the short-run aggregate supply curve.

short-run market (industry) supply curve The horizontal sum of all existing firms' short-run supply curves.

shortage (excess demand) A condition in which the quantity demanded is greater than the quantity supplied. Shortages occur only at prices below the equilibrium price.

simple deposit multiplier The reciprocal of the required reserve ratio r: $1/r$.

simple quantity theory of money The theory which assumes that velocity (V) and Real GDP (Q) are constant and predicts that changes in the money supply (M) lead to strictly proportional changes in the price level (P).

slope The ratio of the change in the variable on the vertical axis to the change in the variable on the horizontal axis.

social determinants of health Social and economic conditions that impact one's health.

socially optimal amount (output) An amount that takes into account and adjusts for all benefits (external and private) and all costs (external and private); the amount at which $MSB = MSC$. Sometimes referred to as the efficient amount.

special-interest groups Subsets of the general population that hold (usually) intense preferences for or against a particular government service, activity, or policy and that often gain from public policies that may not be in accord with the interests of the general public.

spontaneous order The spontaneous and unintended emergence of order out of the self-interested actions of individuals; an unintended consequence of human action, with emphasis placed on the word "unintended."

spurious correlations When two things appear related, but the fact that they appear related is just due to random chance.

stagflation The simultaneous occurrence of high rates of inflation and unemployment.

store of value The ability of an item to hold value over time; a function of money.

strike The union employees' refusal to work at a certain wage or under certain conditions.

structural deficit The part of the budget deficit that would exist even if the economy was operating at full employment.

structural unemployment Unemployment due to structural changes in the economy that eliminate some jobs and create others for which the unemployed are unqualified.

subsidies A monetary payment by government to a producer of a good or service.

substitutes Two goods that satisfy similar needs or desires.

sunk cost A cost incurred in the past that cannot be changed by current decisions and therefore cannot be recovered.

supply The willingness and ability of sellers to produce and offer to sell different quantities of a good at different prices during a specific period.

supply schedule The numerical tabulation of the quantity supplied of a good at different prices. A supply schedule is the numerical representation of the law of supply.

surplus (excess supply) A condition in which the quantity supplied is greater than the quantity demanded. Surpluses occur only at prices above the equilibrium price.

T

tariff A tax on imports.

tax base In terms of income taxes, the total amount of taxable income. Tax revenues = Tax base × (average) Tax rate

technology The body of skills and knowledge involved in the use of resources in production. An advance in technology commonly increases the ability to produce more output with a fixed amount of resources or the ability to produce the same output with fewer resources.

theory An abstract representation of the real world designed with the intent to better understand it.

third-degree price discrimination A price structure in which the seller charges different prices in different markets or charges different prices to various segments of the buying population.

tie-in sale A sale whereby one good can be purchased only if another good is also purchased.

time deposit An interest-earning deposit with *a specified maturity date*. Time deposits are subject to penalties for early withdrawal—that is, withdrawal before the maturity date. Small-denomination time deposits are deposits of less than $100,000.

Total Cost (*TC*) The sum of fixed costs and variable costs.

Total Revenue (*TR*) Price times quantity sold.

Total Surplus (*TS*) The sum of consumers' surplus and producers' surplus. ($TS = CS + PS$.)

Glossary

total utility The total satisfaction a person receives from consuming a particular quantity of a good.

trade balance The value of a country's exports minus the value of its imports; sometimes referred to as net exports.

trade deficit The condition that exists when the value of a country's imports is greater than the value of its exports.

trade surplus The condition that exists when the value of a country's exports is greater than the value of its imports.

transfer payments Payments to persons that are not made in return for goods and services currently supplied.

transitivity The principle whereby, if A is preferred to B and B is preferred to C, then A is preferred to C.

transmission mechanism The routes, or channels, traveled by the ripple effects that the money market creates and that affect the goods-and-services market. (The goods-and-services market is represented by the aggregate demand and aggregate supply curves in the AD–AS framework.)

trust A combination of firms that come together to act as a monopolist.

U

undervalued A currency is undervalued if its price in terms of other currencies is below the equilibrium price.

unemployment rate The percentage of the civilian force that is unemployed: Unemployment rate = Number of unemployed persons ÷ Civilian labor force.

union shop An organization in which a worker is not required to be a member of the union in order to be hired but must become a member within a certain time after being employed.

unit elastic demand The demand that occurs when the percentage change in quantity demanded is equal to the percentage change in price. Quantity demanded changes proportionately to price changes.

unit of account A common measure in which relative values are expressed; a function of money.

(Upward-Sloping) Supply Curve The graphical representation of the law of supply.

utility A measure of the satisfaction, happiness, or benefit that results from the consumption of a good.

utils An artificial construct used to measure utility.

V

Value Marginal Product (VMP) The price of a good multiplied by the marginal physical product of the factor: $VMP = P \times MPP$.

variable costs Costs that vary with output; the costs associated with variable inputs.

variable input An input whose quantity can be changed as output changes.

velocity The average number of times a dollar is spent to buy final goods and services in a year.

vertical merger A merger between companies in the same industry but at different stages of the production process.

W

wage discrimination The situation in which individuals of equal ability and productivity (as measured by their contribution to output) are paid different wage rates.

wealth The value of all assets owned, both monetary and nonmonetary.

X

x-inefficiency The increase in costs, due to the organizational slack in a monopoly, resulting from the absence of competitive pressure to push costs down to their lowest-possible level.

Index

A

Absolute (money) price, 105–106, 109
Absolute real economic growth, 400, 401, 414
Abstraction, 17
Accounting profits, 492–493, 517, 678
Activist monetary policy. *See* Discretionary monetary policy
Activities
  benefits and costs of, 704–705
  categories of, 706
Activists, 358
Actual price level, 384–385
Actual trades, 680–681
Administered rates, 315
Adaptive expectations, 380–381
Adelman, Irma, 36
Adverse selection, 293–294, 726–727
Adverse supply shocks, 192
Advertising, in perfect competition, 544
Affordable Care Act (ACA), 700
Age, and income distribution, 651–653
Aggregate demand (*AD*), 174–188, 201–202
  factors affecting, 182–186, 201
  in monetarism, 326–328
  and money supply, 186–187
  and net exports, 181–182
  price level, 195, 196
  vs. quantity demanded, change in, 179–180
  Real GDP, 195, 196
  and short-run equilibrium, 193–197
  in simple quantity theory of money, 323
  and spending, 181–182
Aggregate demand–aggregate supply (*AD–AS*)
  framework, 175, 200–201
  monetarism in, 326–328
  simple Keynesian model in, 244–248, 257
  simple quantity theory of money in, 323
Aggregate demand (*AD*) curve, 175–188
  as downward sloping, 176–178
  and fiscal policy, 268

and job prospects, 198–199
  shift factors for, 180–181
  in simple Keynesian model, 244–248
  in simple quantity theory of money, 322–323
Aggregate supply (*AS*), 189–202. *See also* Long-run aggregate supply; Short-run aggregate supply
  and marginal tax rates, 276–277
  and short-run equilibrium, 193–197
  in simple quantity theory of money, 323
Aggregate supply (*AS*) curve
  in simple Keynesian model, 244–248
  in simple quantity theory of money, 323
Air travel
  aisle seat, 121–122, 131
  cartels in, 583–584
  overbooking, 87
  ticket prices, 60
Alchian, Armen A., 489
Algorithm, 766
Algorithmic discrimination, 769
Aluminum Company of America (Alcoa), 550, 596
American Economic Review (journal), 375, 376
Angrist, Joshua, 761, 762
Antidumping argument for trade restrictions, 785
Antitrust law, 593–602, 608–609
  common misconceptions about, 600
  and mergers, 599–600
  and network monopolies, 600–601
  overview of specific laws, 594–595
  unsettled points in, 596–598
Apple, Inc., 680
Appreciation, currency, 185, 794, 805–806
Arbitrage, 564, 678–679
Arbitrage opportunities, 678–679
Arkwright, Robert, 418
Arms race, 588–589
Artificial intelligence (AI), 623–624
Artificial rents, 677
Asset(s), 294
Asset income, 653–654, 659
Asymmetric information, 293–294, 723–727, 729–730

Athletes, college, 123
Auctions, 74–75
Automatic fiscal policy, 267
Autonomous consumption, 239–240
Autor, David, 419, 420
Average cost pricing, 604
Average fixed costs (*AFC*) of production, 501–504
Average inflation targeting, 363
Average–marginal rule, 504–506
Average physical product, 499
Average productivity, 499–500
Average total costs (*ATC*) of production, 504–506
Average variable costs (*AVC*) of production, 504–506

B

Bads, 2, 20, 153
Bailey, Martin, 713
Bailouts, government, 425
Balanced budgets, 262
Balances (demand for money), 348–349
Balance sheets, 294–295, 297
Banking
  balance sheets in, 294–295, 297
  development of, 291–292
Bank insolvency, 295–296
Bank run, 760
Bar graphs, 28–29
Barter, 285
Barter economies, 205, 285–287
Baseball players, 677
Base year, 135
Bastiat, Frédéric, 426
Baum, L. Frank, 292
Beatles, The, 139
Beauty, 94
Becker, Gary, 35
Behavioral economics, 469–478
Behavior and opportunity cost, 6–7
Beneficial supply shocks, 192
Benefits, 1, 7, 21
  marginal, 7, 9–10, 19–20, 705
  net, 1, 10
  private, 704–705
Big data and machine learning
  algorithmic discrimination, 769–770
  algorithms, 766, 771

cross-validation, 768
  goal, 766
  Netflix, 767
  public policy, 768–769
  regularization, 767–768
Billionaires, 3
Birthrates, 65
Black Reconstruction (DuBois), 35
Board of Governors, 299
Bonds
  conventional, 344
  prices of, and interest rates, 353–354, 368, 371–373
Books, buying, 4
Boston Tea Party, 551
British East India Company, 424, 551
Brute force, 94
Bryan, William Jennings, 292
Buchanan, James, 274–276
Budget (federal), 260–266
  balanced, 262
  income tax structures, 261–262
  surpluses in, 262, 281–282
Budget (federal) deficit, 262, 266, 281–282
  and democracy, 273–276
Budget (personal), 445–446
  constraints on, 480–486
Bureau of Economic Analysis (BEA), 29
Burnham, Terence, 474
Business cycle(s), 167–168, 171
Business-cycle macroeconomics, 223–224, 226, 413
Business cycle theory, real, 394–395, 397–398
Business firms, 488–494, 516–517
  monopolistic (*See* Monopolies)
  number per industry, 515
  reasons for existence of, 488–491, 516–517
  in theory of perfect competition, 521–525, 546
  two sides of, 491–494
Business taxes
  indirect, 164
  and investments, 184
  and production costs, 515–516
Buyers, number of, 65
Buying low and selling high, 679

845

C

Calabresi, Steven G., 423
California gold rush, 324
Candlemaker's Petition, 426
Cap and trade (tradable pollution permits), 716–717, 728
Capital, 2
  human, 408
  and production function, 659–660
  return on, 669
Capital consumption allowance, 164. *See also* Depreciation
Caplan, Bryan, 739
Capture theory of regulation, 606
Car buying, 673–674
Card, David, 757, 759, 772
Cartels, 578–581, 583–584, 591
Cartel theory, 578
Cartwright, Edmund, 418
Cash leakage, 305
Causal inference
  controlled experiments, 756
  defined, 752
  difference-in-differences, 758
  macroeconomics, 759–760
  minimum wage impacts, 754–756
  natural experiment, 757–759
  spurious correlations, 753–754
Celler–Kefauver Antimerger Act (1950), 595
Central Bank Digital Currency (CBDC), 301
Ceteris paribus, 15–16, 21, 325
Cheating
  and average-marginal rule, 506–507
  in cartels, 579–580
Checkable deposits, 288
Chess, 382
Choices, 3
  menu of, 376
Choice theory, public, 606, 732–733, 748–749
Civil Aeronautics Board (CAB), 87, 584, 606
Civilian labor force, 140
Civilian noninstitutional population, 140
  10 A.M. classes in college, 114–115, 131
  equilibrium price, 114
  quantity demanded, seats, 114, 115
  remembering price, 115
Classical economics, 205–206
  critique of, 229–238
  vs. Keynes, 237–238
  new, 386–390, 396, 397

  on self-regulating economies, 221
Clayton Act (1914), 594
Closed economies, 238
Closed shops, 639
Coase, Ronald, 490–491, 713, 729
Coase theorem, 713, 729
Cocaine, 439
Coffee mugs, 471–472
Cold War, 588, 589
Coefficient of price elasticity of demand, 433
Collective bargaining, 639–640
Colleges
  admissions, 5
  10 A.M. classes in, 114–115, 131
  campus parking, 104
  costs, 8
  rational expectations, 385
  superathletes, 122–123, 131
  tuition, 445–446
Colleges admissions
  financial aid, 566–567
  majors, 33–39
  price discrimination, 566–567
Command-and-control policy, 715–716
Commercial insurance, 699
Common currency, 804–805
Comparative advantage, 51, 775–779
Compartmentalization, 470–471
Competing factors, 640
Competition. *See also* Perfect competition
  monopolistic, 572–576, 590–591
  nonprice, 574
  scarcity and, 3
Competitive equilibrium, long-run, 535–537, 546–547
Complements, 65
Complete crowding out, 269–271
Concentration ratios, 577, 597–598, 607
Conglomerate mergers, 599–600
Congressional districts, 743–744
Constant-cost industry, 539, 540
Constant-money-growth-rate rule, 362
Constant opportunity costs, 40–41, 55
Constant returns to scale, 513–514
Constitutional economics, 747–748, 750
Consumer equilibrium, 465–468
Consumer Price Index (CPI), 134–136
Consumers' surplus (*CS*), 80–82, 89
  equilibrium in terms of, 80–82
  and international trade, 780, 781
  in monopolies, 556–557
  and price floors, 103–104

Consumption, 157
  and aggregate demand, 181
  autonomous, 239
  externalities in, 706
  factors affecting, 183–184
  in GDP, 157
  induced, 239–240
  in simple Keynesian model, 239–241, 257
Consumption function, 239–240, 257
Consumption loans, 668
Contestable markets, 584–585, 591
Continued inflation, 334–336, 345
Contractionary fiscal policy, 267
Contractionary monetary policy, 355
Contraction, in business cycle, 167–168
Controlled experiment, 756
Conventional bonds, 344
Coronavirus. *See* COVID-19 pandemic
Corporations. *See also* Business firms; Perfect competition
  profits of, in national income, 161
Correlation, 753
Cost(s), 1, 7, 21. *See also specific types*
  in perfect competition, 542, 544
  of production, 501–515, 517–518
  zero, 6
Cost curves, shifts in, 515–516, 518
Cross-validation of dataset, 768
Coupons, 567–568
Courtney, Cliff, 424
Courtney, Jim, 424
COVID-19 pandemic
  CBO projections, 263
  health disparities, 694–695
  negative externality, 687
  PPF, 48–49
  restaurant shut downs, 531–532
Creative destruction
  automation, 419–420
  capitalism, 417–418
  competition, 417
  defined, 416
  effects, 430
  examples, 418, 430
  government assistance, 420
  measure, 417–418, 430
  parts, 420–421
  worries, 418–419, 430
Credit cards, 290
Crime, 439
Crony capitalism
  consumers' surplus, 422
  defined, 421
  examples, 423–425, 430
  firm, 428
  lobbyist, 426–428

  producers' surplus, 422
  rent seeking, 421–422, 430
  wastes resources, 429
Cross elasticity of demand, 447–448, 457
Crowding out, 269–271, 273
Cullen, Julie Berry, 762
Currencies, 288. *See also* Dollar; Exchange rates
  appreciation of, 185, 794, 805–806
  common, 804, 805
  demand for and supply of, 792–793
  depreciation of, 185, 794, 805–806
  overvalued, 799–801
  undervalued, 799–800
Currency areas, optimal, 804–805
Cutoff rule, 764
Cyclical deficits, 262
Cyclical unemployment rate, 145–147

D

Data lag, 272
Deadweight losses, 103–104
Deadweight loss of monopoly, 560
Deadweight loss triangle, 561
Decisions at the margin, 7–8, 21
Decreasing-cost industries, 540
Deficits trade, 791
Demand, 58–68, 89. *See also specific types*
  change in, 62–66
  10 A.M. classes in college, 114–114, 131
  college superathletes, 122–123, 131
  and consumer equilibrium, 465–467
  derived, 611, 632
  elasticity of (*See* Elasticity)
  on a freeway, 126–127, 132
  industry adjustment to change in, 537–541, 547
  language of, 75
  law of, 59, 466, 478
  vs. quantity demanded, 59
  and supply, 74–87
  and U-Haul rates, 111–112, 131
Demand curves, 59–60. *See also* Aggregate demand curve
  change in, 63–66
  common misconceptions about, 523–524
  as downward-sloping, 59
  indifference curves, 486
  individual *vs.* market, 61–62

inflation and unemployment, 380
in monopolies, 552–555
monopolistic competition, 573
movement factors and shift factors for, 67–68
in perfect competition theory, 522–523, 555
Demand for money (balances), 348–349
Demand schedules, 59–60
Demand-side fiscal policy, 268–276, 281
Democracy
and budget deficits, 273–276
economic illiteracy, 739–740
Democracy in Deficit (Buchanan and Wagner), 274–276
Demsetz, Harold, 489
Department of Justice (DOJ), 595–596
Deposits, 288
Depreciation
currency, 185
in GDP, 164
Depreciation currency, 794, 805–806
Depressions, economic, 292
Derived demand, 611, 632
Designer labels, 576
Devaluation, 801–802
Diagrams, 24–32
Diamond–water paradox, 460, 463–464, 477–478
Difference-in-differences, 758
Digital revolution, 534
Diminishing marginal returns, law of, 70, 494, 507–508, 516–518, 535
Diminishing marginal utility, law of, 60–61, 461–465, 477
Dinardo, John, 765
Direct finance, 293
Direction, *vs.* magnitude, 101
Directly related variables, 24
Director, Aaron, 713
Discount loans, 308
Discount rates, 308, 316
Discouraged workers, 142–143, 144–145, 148–149
Discovery process, 409
Discretionary fiscal policy, 267
Discretionary (activist) monetary policy, 358–359, 368
Discrimination. *See also* Price discrimination
vs. information problem, 631
and profit, 543–544
types of, 563–564
wage, 660–661

Diseconomies of scale, 513–514, 516–517
Disequilibrium, 75, 199–200, 251–253
Disequilibrium price, 75
Displaced workers, 640
Disposable income, 164
Distributional effects of international trade, 780
Disutility, 2
Dollar
overvalued, 800–801
as primary reserve currency, 797–798
Dollar price, 3, 94
Dollar, U.S.
appreciation of, 185
change in value over time, 138
depreciation of, 185–186
vs. euro, exchange rate for, 188
and gold standard, 365–367
Double coincidence of wants, 286
Double counting, 152
Downward-sloping demand curve. *See* Demand curves
Doyle, Arthur Conan, 45
Drug busts, 439
DuBois, W.E.B., 35
Dumping, 785
DuPont, 596
Durable goods, 157, 170

E

Easterlin paradox, 154–156
Easterlin, Richard, 154
eBay, 680–681
Economics. *See also specific policies and schools*
"bread and butter," 58
categories of, 18–19, 21
definition of, 2
majoring in, 33–38
myths about, 34–36
process of, 780–781
Economica (journal), 286, 374
Economic freedom, 412
Economic growth, 400–413
absolute real, 400, 401
basics about, 400–401
definition of, 47, 167
per-capita real, 400
in PPF framework, 47–48
and production function, 402–412, 414
rates of, 400–401
and Real GDP, 167, 171
Economic-growth macroeconomics, 223–224

Economic illiteracy, 739–740
Economic policies, growth-promoting *vs.* transfer-promoting, 438–439. *See also specific types*
Economic profits, 492–494, 517, 678
Economic rent, 674–677
Economic states, 1, 210, 215, 225–226
in labor market, 211–213
and PPF, 213–215, 226
in self-regulating economies, 215–219
in *TE–TP* framework, 251–253
three types of, 202, 210, 211, 225
Economies of scale, 513–514, 550, 779
Economy, monetarist view of, 329
Economy, U.S., changes over time to size of, 167
Edison, Thomas Alva, 598–599
Education, and income inequality, 659
Effectiveness lag, 272
Efficiency, 9–10, 21
labor unions' effects on, 645
productive, 47, 537–538
resource allocative, 526–527
and voting, 740–742
Efficiency wage models, 233
Efficient-producer hypothesis, 695–696
Elastic demand, 435, 438–440
Elasticity, 432–458
of demand, 432–434 (*See also* Price elasticity of demand)
of demand for labor, 621–622, 638
of supply, 449–452, 457
and taxes, 468, 452–457
Elements of Economics, The (Tarshis), 238
Emission taxes, 716
Empirical evidence, 696
Employed persons, 140–141
Employee compensation, 161
Employee screening, 630
Employment, full, 144
Employment rate, 141
common misconceptions about, 142
Encouraging carpooling, 127
Endowment effect, 471–472
Entrepreneurship, 2, 679–683
Entry into industries
barriers to, 550
in contestable markets, 584–585
Environmental externalities, 715–718

Environmental policy, 715–718
Environmental regulation, 607, 715
Equality, tending to, 670
Equation of exchange, 318–319, 344–345
Equilibrium, 75–85
consumer, 465–467, 478, 485
in labor market, 211–213
long-run, 197–199
long-run competitive, 535–536, 546
in money market, 349
moving to, 75–78
and predictions, 79–80
short-run, 193–196
in simple Keynesian model, 244–245, 247
Equilibrium exchange rate, 793–797
Equilibrium price, 75, 82–85
Equilibrium quantity, 75, 82–85
Equilibrium wage rate, 624–625, 628
Euro, 188
Excess capacity theorem, 574–576, 591
Excess demand. *See* Shortages
Excess reserves, 303, 315
Excess supply. *See* Surplus
Exchange. *See* Trade
Exchange rates, 793–807
current system of, 803, 806
definition of, 185, 791–792
for dollar *vs.* euro, 188
fixed, 798–803, 831–840
flexible, 793–798, 803–806
and net exports, 185–186
Excludable public goods, 719
Expansionary fiscal policy, 267, 269–271
Expansionary monetary policy, 355
Expansion, in business cycle, 167
Expectations, 381–386
adaptive, 381
and fiscal policy, 279
for income, 183
for inflation rate, 339–341, 344, 381
in new classical economics, 386–391
for policy, 382–383, 386–391
for price, 65, 72, 182
for price level, 193, 383–384, 411
rational, 381–394
for sales, 184
for tax rates, 279
Expectations effect, 341
Expenditure approach to GDP, 156–160, 169–170
Expenditures. *See* Spending
Explicit costs, 492, 493, 517

Exports 158. *See also* Net exports
Externalities, 704–718, 729. *See also* Negative externality
  in environmental policy, 715
  internalizing, 710–714
  positive, 705

F

Facebook, 558–559, 595–596
Factor markets, 611–617. *See also* Labor markets
  asymmetric information in, 725
  demand in, 611–613
  supply in, 615–616
Factor price takers, 615–616
Factors of production. *See* Goods; Input(s); Resources
Factory Acts, 744
False information, 97–98
Federal budget. *See* Budget
"Federal Communications Commission, The" (Coase), 713
Federal debt. *See* Public debt
Federal funds market, 308
Federal funds rate, 308, 309
Federal funds rate target, 309
Federal Open Market Committee (FOMC), 300
Federal Reserve Act (1913), 299
Federal Reserve Bank, 299
Federal Reserve Districts, 299, 300
Federal Reserve notes, 301
Federal Reserve System (the Fed), 288, 299–315
  common misconceptions about, 213–215
  Central Bank Digital Currency (CBDC), 301
  history of, 300–302
  monetary policy, 300, 313 (*See also* Interest on Reserves (IOR))
  in money supply, 300, 303–309
  recent actions by, 363
  in reserves, 302–309, 310
  structure of, 299–300
  tools and policy of, 300–301
Federal Trade Commission (FTC), 595–596
Fed watchers, 382
Final goods, 152
Financial aid, 566
Financial crisis of 2007–2009
  Great Recession in, 364
  housing prices in, 234–235
  and market monetarism, 363
Financial intermediaries, 293, 296

Financial system, 293–296, 297
Financial transactions, 153
Fine-tuning, 358
Firms. *See* Business firms
First-come, first-served (FCFS) basis, 94, 96
Fiscal policy, 267–276, 281
  contractionary, 267
  demand-side, 268–276, 281
  expansionary, 267, 269–673
  supply-side, 276–280
Fisher effect, 341
Fisher, Irving, 320, 341
Fixed costs, 497
Fixed exchange rates, 798–806
Fixed inputs, 494
Fixed investment, 157
Flat tax, 261
Flexible exchange rates, 793–798, 803
Foreign exchange market, 791–793
Foreign export subsidies argument for trade restrictions, 786–787
Foreign real national income (foreign Real GDP), 185
45-degree line, 26–28
Fractional reserve banking, 291
Framing, 474–476
Free lunch, 4
Free riders, 664, 719–721
  problem, 721
Frey, Carl Benedikt, 419
Frictional unemployment, 143
Friedman, David, 472–473
Friedman fooling theory, 378
Friedman, Milton, 324, 376–379, 397, 664, 713
Friedman natural rate theory, 378–379, 397
Full employment, 144
Future, expectations for. *See* Expectations

G

Gabaix, Xavier, 601
Game theory, 581
  applications of, 587–590
  and oligopolies, 581–585
Gasoline shortages, 98
General Theory of Employment, Interest and Money, The (Keynes), 229, 237
George, Henry, 679
Gini coefficient, 657–658
Gold, 291–292
Gold rush, 324
Goldsmiths, 291

Gold standard, 292, 365
Goods, 2. *See also specific types*
Google, 82, 558–559, 595–596, 720
Government. *See also specific agencies and policies*
  assistance from, 663
  in fixed exchange rate system, 801–802
  housing prices, 124, 131
  income inequality, 661–662
  loans, 124, 131
  macroeconomic debates, 443–457
  in simple Keynesian model, 247, 254
  taxation by (*See* Tax)
Government monopolies, 550–551
Government purchases, 157
  and aggregate demand, 181
  factors affecting, 182–183
  in GDP, 157
  vs. government spending, 260
Government regulation, 602–609
  benefits and costs of, 607
  of externalities, 713, 716
  natural monopolies, 602–605
  and supply, 73
  theories of, 606–607
Government spending (expenditures), 260–261, 281
Government transfer payments, 153, 157
Grade point averages (GPAs), 115–116, 131–132
Grades
  and game theory, 587–588
  inflation of, 333, 625–626
  production of, 510–511
  and time spent studying, 50
Grain prices, 674–676
Great Recession, 364–365. *See also* Financial crisis of 2007–2009
Great Train Robbery, The (movie), 599
Gross Domestic Product (GDP), 28, 151–173
  common misconceptions about, 159
  expenditure approach to computing, 156–160, 169–170
  final *vs.* intermediate goods in, 152
  income approach to computing, 161–165
  per-capita, 153–156, 163
  price level, 196
  Real (*See* Real GDP)
  subtract imports, 159
Gross family product (GFP), 154
Group projects, 490

Growth-promoting policies, 411–412
Gym memberships, 464–465

H

Hamilton, Alexander, 785
Happiness economics, 154–156
Harberger, Arnold, 560, 713
Hargreaves, James, 418
Health care
  access, 699
  cost of, 467
  insurance, 699–700
  and price elasticity of demand, 446
  prices, 697–699
  reform, 700–701
Health disparities, 693–695
  causes, 695–697
  COVID-19 pandemic, 694–695
  measure, 693
Health economics
  COVID-19, 687
  demand, 687–688
  factors, 686–687
  health disparities, 693–695
  negative externality, 687
  RAND Health Insurance Experiment, 689–692
  social determinants, 693
Health maintenance organizations (HMOs), 129
Herfindahl Index, 597–598, 607–608
Hidden fees, 601
Holiday, J.S., 324
Hollywood, 598–599
Horizontal mergers, 599–600
Hours worked, 623
Household income, 654
Housing bust, 234–235
Housing market, 1
Housing prices, 120, 124
  and aggregate demand, 184
  and elasticity of supply, 451
  in financial crisis of 2007–2009, 234–235
  labor productivity, 500–501
  and weather, 468
Human capital, 408, 660

I

Iannaccone, Laurence, 563
Ideas, 408–409
Identifying rationing devices, 116
Idle resources, 242

Index

Illiteracy, economic, 739–740
Implicit costs, 492, 493, 517
Imports, 158
Incentives, 11–12, 21
    movie studios *vs.* Netflix, 11–12
    profit as, 541
    tax, 279
Income. *See also specific types*
    calculating, 653
    and demand, 64
    elastic, 448
    and exchange rates, 795
    expectations of future, 183
    groups pay, 261–262
    inelastic, 448
    and labor unions, 636
    poverty-level, 662–664
    unit elastic, 448
Income approach to GDP, 159–164
Income distribution, 650–658, 665
    common misconceptions about, 658–659
    facts about, 650–654
    measurement of inequality in, 655–659
    quintiles in measurement of, 650–651, 664–665
Income effect, 339, 622
Income elasticity, 449
Income elasticity of demand, 448–449, 457
Income growth rates, 795
Income inelasticity, 449
Income inequality, 655–662
    common misconceptions about, 658–659
    measurement of, 655–659
    reasons for existence of, 659–662
Income redistribution, 663–664
Income taxes
    and consumption, 184
    marginal, 276
    structures for, 261–263
Income unit elasticity, 449
Incomplete crowding out, 269–271
Incomplete markets, 725
Increasing-cost industries, 539–541
Increasing opportunity costs, 41–44, 55
Independent variables, 25
Indifference curve(s), 480–486
Indifference curve maps, 484–486
Indifference sets, 482
Indirect business taxes, 163
Indirect finance, 293
Individual demand curves, 61
Individual income, 653–654
Induced consumption, 239–240
Inefficiency productive, 47

X-inefficiency, 562, 597
Inelastic demand, 435, 440
Infant industry argument for trade restrictions, 784
Inferior goods, 64, 447
Inflation, 330–336, 345
    continued, 334–336, 345
    and CPI, 136–137
    defined, 136
    and exchange rates, 795–797
    expected rate of, 338–340, 344, 380
    grade, 332–333
    one-shot, 333, 345
    in Phillips curve, 374–380
    and price controls, 336
    stagflation, 375, 376
Inflationary gaps, 210–213
    and monetary policy, 354–357
    self-regulating economies in, 218
Inflation-indexed treasury bonds, 344
Inflation targeting, 363
Information
    asymmetric, 293–294, 724–727
    and labor markets, 630
    and special-interest groups, 742–743, 745–747
    transmission of, through price, 94–95
Ink cartridge prices, 601–602
In-kind transfer payments, 652
Innate abilities and attributes, 659
Innovation
    and antitrust law, 597–598, 601
    and profit, 679
Input(s), 494
Input prices, 515
Insolvency, bank, 295
Institutions, 410–412
Instrumental variable (Lotteries)
    definition, 763
    judge, 762–763
    randomness, 763
    regression discontinuity design, 764–765
    school, 762
    Vietnam War Draft Lottery, 761–762
Insurance company medical care, 117, 119
Interest, 667–674, 679, 683. *See also specific types*
Interest-insensitive investments, 351–352
Interest rate(s), 670–674
    and bond prices, 353–354, 368, 371–372
    and consumption, 183–184
    and exchange rates, 797

flexibility of, and classical economics, 206–208
    and investment, 184
    and liquidity trap, 353–354
    and money supply, 336–343, 345
    nominal, 343, 345
    real, 343, 345, 670–671, 797
    reasons for differences in, 670
Interest rate effect, 177, 178
Interest on Reserves (IOR)
    federal funds rate, 312
    interest rates, 310, 312, 315
    negative interest rates, 314
    ON-RRP rate, 311
Intermediate goods, 152
Internalizing externalities, 710–714
International finance, 791–808
International trade, 774–790
    and exchange rates, 803
    restrictions on, 779–789
    theory of, 774–779
International trade effect, 177, 178
Interpersonal utility comparisons, 463
Interstate Commerce Commission (ICC), 606
Intra-industry trade, 778
Inventory investment, 157, 159
Inventory, optimum, 251
Inversely related variables, 25
Investment, 157
    and aggregate demand, 181
    factors affecting, 182, 184–185
    in GDP, 158
    and interest rates, 673–674
Investment loans, 668–669
Invisible hand of market, 488–489
iPod, 680–682

J

Jacob, Brian, 762
Job leavers, 142
Job losers, 142
Jobs, Steve, 680–681
Journal of Economic Education, 37
Journal of Law and Economics, 712
Judge lotteries, 762–763
Justice Department, U.S., 597–598

K

Kahn, Alfred, 87
Kahneman, Daniel, 474
Kapital, Das (Marx), 237
Kessel, Reuben, 713

Keynesian model, simple, 238–255, 257
    in *AD–AS* framework, 244–248, 257
    assumptions in, 238
    consumption in, 238–241, 257
    fiscal policy in, 268–269, 281
    multiplier in, 241–243, 257
    saving in, 240–241
    in *TE–TP* framework, 248–257
    theme of, 246–248, 254–257
Keynesian transmission mechanism, 348–354
Keynes, John Maynard, 229–238
Keynes, John Neville, 237
Kindleberger, Charles, 803
Kleinberg, Jon, 769
Kling, Arnold, 356–357
Krueger, Alan, 757, 759, 772

L

Labor, 2
Labor costs, 621
Labor, division of, 623
Labor force, civilian, 140
Labor force participation rate (LFPR), 141
Labor income, 653
Labor markets, 618–629
    demand in, 618–621, 624–625, 631, 632
    and economic states, 211–212
    and information, 631
    and production function, 405–407
    supply in, 622–630
Labor mobility, 804
Labor productivity, 191, 500
Labor unions, 635–649
    effects of, 641–646, 648
    objectives of, 635–637, 647
    practices of, 637–641, 647
Laemmle, Carl, 599
Laffer, Arthur, 277–279
Laffer curve, 277
Lags
    in fiscal policy, 271–273
    regulatory, 605
Laibson, David, 602
Laissez-faire, 219
Land, 2
    quality of, 541, 543
    supply of, 674–676
Land rent, 674–675
Late
    arriving to class, 6, 104–105

Laws. *See specific laws*
  of demand, 59
  of diminishing marginal utility, 60
  of increasing opportunity costs, 44
  of supply, 68
Law, apartment rent and, 128
Law School Admission Test (LSAT), 37
Least-cost rule, 617, 632
Lee, David S., 765
Legal systems, 411
Legislative lag, 272
Leibenstein, Harvey, 562
Leisure, 153, 287, 659
Levitt, Steven, 762
Lewis, Gregg, 713
Liabilities, 294–295
Life expectancy, 672
Line graphs, 30–31
Line, slope of, 25–26
Liquidity effect, 338
Liquidity trap, 353–354
List, John, 472
Literacy, economic, 739–740
Loan(s). *See specific types*
  cost of, 670
  terms of, 670
Loanable funds, 337–342
  demand for, 668–669
  price for, 669
  supply of, 668
Lobbying, 741–742
Lock-in effect, 600
Logrolling, 742
Long run
  changes to self-regulating economies in, 219–220
  perfect competition in, 526–544, 547
  production in, 495, 512–516, 518
Long-run aggregate supply (*LRAS*), 175, 188–192, 197–202
Long-run aggregate supply (*LRAS*) curve, 197–198
Long-run average total cost (*LRATC*) curve, 512–513
Long-run competitive equilibrium, 535–544
Long-run equilibrium, 197–200, 202, 211–213
Long-run Phillips curve, 376–379
Long-run (industry) supply (*LRS*) curves, 540
Lopokova, Lydia, 237
Lorenz curve, 656–658
Loss, as signal, 679–680
Loss minimization rule. *See* Profit maximization rule
Low foreign wages argument for trade restrictions, 786
Lucas, Robert, 381
Luxuries, 444

M

M1, 288
M2, 288
Machine learning, 766
Macroeconomics, 19
  business-cycle, 223–224, 226, 413
  economic-growth, 223–224, 226, 413
  underpinnings, 321–322
Magnitude, *vs.* direction, 101
Majoring in economics, 33–39
  and labor markets, 626–627
Majority voting rule, 266, 735–736
Managed flexible exchange rate, 803, 806
Managed float, 803, 806
Managerial coordination, 489
Marginal benefits, 7, 9, 19, 705
Marginal costs, 7, 9, 19, 497
  and digital revolution, 534
  and marginal physical product, 497–500
  in monopolies, 556
  monopolistic competition, 573
  private *vs.* social, 705
Marginal factor cost (*MFC*), 615–616, 632
Marginal income tax rates, 276
Marginal physical product (*MPP*), 496–499, 619, 638
Marginal productivity, 496
Marginal productivity theory, 628–629
Marginal propensity to consume (*MPC*), 239
Marginal propensity to save (*MPS*), 241–242
Marginal rate of substitution, 483–484
Marginal revenue (*MR*), 524–525
  in monopolies, 552–553, 556
  in monopolistic competition, 573
Marginal revenue product (*MRP*), 612–615, 618–619, 631
Marginal social benefits (*MSB*), 705
Marginal social costs (*MSC*), 705
Marginal utilities, 461–463, 477
  equating, 465–466
  law of diminishing, 461–465, 477–478
Market(s). *See also specific types*
  adjustments in, 232–235
  and business firms, 488–489, 491
  definition of, 58, 596
  entrepreneurs in, 679
  invisible hand of, 488–489
  nonexcludable public goods, 720
  supply and demand in, 74–89
Market basket, 134–135

Market-clearing price (equilibrium price), 75, 83–85
Market coordination, 489
Market demand curves, 61–62
Market-determined price, 545
Market failures, 704–731. *See also specific types*
Market interest rate. *See* Nominal interest rates
Market monetarism, 363
Market monopolies, 550–551
Market structures, 521, 585–586. *See also specific types*
Market supply curves, 70–71
  short run, 532–533
  upward sloping, 535
Marshall, Alfred, 237, 320
Marshall, James, 324
Marx, Karl, 237
Maximum prices, 78–79
McGee, John, 713
Median voter model, 733–737, 749
Medicaid, 699
Medical care. *See* Health care
  insurance company, 117, 119, 699
  prices, 117–119, 131
  quantity demanded, 118, 119
  X-rays, 118, 119
Medium of exchange, 285
Meetup, 714–715
Meltzer, Allan, 35
Menu of choices, 376
Mergers, 599–600
Meta-ideas, 410
Microeconomics, 19
Midpoint formula, 433
Millionaires, 463
Minibar prices, 601–602
Minimum efficient scale (*MES*), 514–516
Minimum prices, 78–79
Minimum wage, 100–101, 660
Mints, Lloyd, 713
Missing markets, 726
Mitchell, Matthew, 425
Models. *See* Theories
Monetarism, 326–329, 345
  in *AD–AS* framework, 326–328
  four positions in, 326
  market, 363
  monetary policy in, 353–354, 368
  views on economy in, 329–330
Monetary History of the United States, A (Friedman and Schwartz), 324
Monetary policy, 348–369
  contractionary, 355, 357
  debates in, 358–361, 367, 368
  definition of, 300
  discretionary (activist), 358, 368
  expansionary, 355, 357

in fixed exchange rate system, 802
  and inflationary and recessionary gaps, 355–358
  Keynesian, 348–354, 368
  monetarist, 354–355, 368
  rules-based (nonactivist), 359–367, 369
  transmission mechanisms in, 348–355
Monetary wealth, 176
Money, 284–287, 297
  cashless society, 289
  currency, 289–290
  demand for, 348–349
  functions of, 285
  M-Pesa, 290–291
  origins of, 285–287
  and price level, 318–325
  simple quantity theory of, 320–323
  subjective well-being, 154–156
Money economies, 230–231, 285–287
MoneyIllusion, The (Sumner), 364
Money market
  and bond market, 371–372
  equilibrium in, 349–350
  in Keynesian transmission mechanism, 348–350
Money market deposit accounts (MMDAs), 288
Money market mutual funds (MMMFs), 288
Money price, 105–106, 109
Money supply, 287–289, 297
  and aggregate demand, 186
  contraction process for, 306–307
  definitions of, 287–289
  expansion process for, 303–306
  and expectations, 392
  the Fed's role in, 300, 303–306, 316, 361
  and interest rates, 337–343, 345
  and price level, 318–325, 337–342
  and velocity, 187–189
Monitors (managers), 489–490
Monopolies, 549–571
  and antitrust law, 600–601, 608
  case against, 560–563
  definition of, 558–559
  government *vs.* market, 550–551
  natural, 550, 602–606
  network, 600–601
  vs. perfect competition, 555
  price discrimination in, 563–568, 569
  pricing and output in, 551–556, 569
  regulation of, 602–606
  theory of, 549–550, 569

Monopolistic competition, 572–577, 590
Monopsony, 641–643, 648
Moral hazards, 294, 727–728
Mortgage loans, financial crisis of 2007–2009, 234–235
Movement factors, 67–68, 180
Movie industry, 599
Movie Trust, 599
M-Pesa, 290
Mueller-Smith, Michael, 763
Multiplier, 241–243, 257
Mundell, Robert, 804

N

Nalebuff, Barry, 602
National Bureau of Economic Research (NBER), 168
National Collegiate Athletic Association (NCAA), 122, 123
National debt. *See* Public debt
National defense, 784
Natural experiment, 757
National income, 161–164
    foreign real, 185
Natural monopolies, 550
    regulation of, 602–606
Natural Real GDP, 198
    in economic states, 210–214
Natural resources, 2, 408
Natural unemployment, 144
Natural unemployment rate, 144, 224
    common misconceptions about, 213–215
Necessary conditions, 585
Necessities, 444, 467
Negative externality, 687, 705
    diagram of, 706–708
    environmental, 715–718
    internalizing, 710–715
Negative interest rates, 314
Negative visualization, 83
Neoclassical growth theory, 409
Net benefits, 1, 10
Net domestic product (NDP), 164
Net exports, 158, 791
    and aggregate demand, 181
    factors affecting, 182, 185–186
    in GDP, 158
Netflix, 767
Net interest, 162
Net losses. *See* Deadweight losses
Net public debt, 263
Network goods, 600, 601
Network monopolies, 600–601
Neuroeconomics, 476
Neutral goods, 65
New classical economics, 386–390, 396, 397

New entrants, 142
New growth theory, 409, 414
New Keynesian rational expectation theory, 393–394, 397
Newspapers, 534
New Year's resolutions, 580
Nominal GDP targeting, 363–364
Nominal income, 136–137
Nominal interest rates, 343, 345, 670–671
Nominal wages, 189–190
Nonactivist monetary policy. *See* Rules-based monetary policy
Nonactivists, 358
Nondurable goods, 157
Nonexcludable public goods, 663, 719–720, 740–741
Nonlabor inputs, prices of, 191
Nonmarket goods and services, 152
Nonpecuniary aspects of jobs, 624, 626
Nonprice competition, 574
Nonprice-rationing devices, 96, 131
Nonrivalrous in consumption, 719–720
Nonunion wages, 643–644
Normal goods, 64, 448
Normal profit, 493
Normative economics, 18
North, Douglass, 410
No-specialization-no-trade (*NS-NT*) case, 775

O

Obesity, and soda tax, 107
Occupational Outlook Handbook, 39
Offshoring, 785–786
Okun, Arthur, 277
Oligopolies, 577–586, 590
    assumptions about, 577, 591
    cartels as, 578–581, 583–584, 591
    and game theory, 581–586
Olson, Mancur, 411
One-shot inflation, 330–333, 345
Open economies, 238
Open market operations, 304, 315
Open market purchase, 304
Open market sale, 307
Opportunity costs, 1, 4–7, 21
    constant, 40–41, 55
    increasing, 41–44, 55
    in international trade, 775–777
Optimal currency areas, 804–805
Optimum inventory, 251
Osborne, Michael A., 419
Oswald, Andrew, 469
Output
    in cartel theory, 578–580
    in money *vs.* barter economies, 287
    in monopolies, 551–556, 569

    in monopolistic competition, 573
    in perfect competition, 526
    regulation of, 604
Outsourcing, 785
Overbooking of flights, 87
Overnight loans, 308
Overnight Reverse RePurchase (ON-RRP) rate, 311
Overvalued currency, 799–801
Own price, 62

P

Pandemic. *See* COVID-19 pandemic
Parking, 104–105, 722–723
Patents, 550
Patterns of sustainable specialization and trade (PSST), 357–358
Peak, in business cycle, 167
Per-capita GDP, 153, 156
Per-capita real economic growth, 400
Perceptions of reality, 379
Perfect competition, 521–548
    efficiency in, 526–527, 585–586
    in long-run, 535–544, 547
    monopolies, 555–558
    vs. real-world markets, 525
    in short run, 526–535, 546
    topics for analysis in, 544–545
Perfectly elastic demand, 436–437
Perfectly inelastic demand, 436–437
Perfect price discrimination, 563–568, 569
Personal consumption expenditure (PCE) index, 137–138
Personal income, 165
Persuasion, 710
Phillips, A.W., 374, 397
Phillips curve, 374–381, 397
Pie charts, 28
Pigou, A.C., 713
Placebo or control group, 689
Plosser, Charles, 35
Policy. *See also specific types*
    expectations for, 381–383, 384–386
Policy ineffectiveness proposition (PIP), 387
Political market, 733–749
Politics, 733–749. *See also* Voting
    interest groups in, 742–747, 749–750
    of international trade, 787
    median voter model in, 733–735, 749
Pollution
    environmental policy on, 607, 715–718, 728
    regulation of, 715
Positive economics, 18

Positive externalities, 705
    diagram of, 709–710
    internalizing, 710–711
Positive rate of time preference, 668
Posner, Richard, 584
Post-college jobs, 198–199
Potential trades, 680
Poverty, 662–666
    kind transfer payments, 652
    and welfare assistance, 663–664
Poverty income threshold (poverty line), 662
Predetermined-money-growth-rate rule, 362
Predictions and equilibrium, 79–80
Preferences, and demand, 65
Prelec, Drazen, 471
Present value, 671–673, 682
Price, Larissa, 423
Price(s), 93–110. *See also specific types*
    aisle seat, 121–122, 131
    in American Airlines, 121
    in cartel theory, 578–580
    classical economics on, 209, 225
    colleges admission, 116–117, 131
    and demand, 64–65
    and digital revolution, 534
    easier-to-obtain loans, 124, 131
    expectations of future, 65, 72, 183
    gas, 139–140
    good schools, 120
    for good weather, 119–120, 131
    hamburger, 85
    higher housing, 120, 124, 131
    house, 119, 139–140
    Keynes on, 235–238, 257
    labor unions' effects on, 644
    medical care, 117–119, 131
    in monopolies, 551–556, 569
    in monopolistic competition, 573
    and patterns, 125, 131
    in perfect competition, 544–545
    vs. price level, 134
    and quantity demanded, 60–61
    as rationing device, 93–94
    regulation of, 604–605
    remembering, 115
    renters better off, 128–129, 132
    and speculators, 125, 131
    substitutes and complements, 66–67
    and supply, 72
    and surplus or shortage, 75
    as transmitter of information, 94–95
    variability, 125, 131
    X-rays, 118, 119
    zero, 6
Price ceilings, 95–99, 108, 109
Price controls, 95–105, 336
Price discrimination, 563–567, 569

Index

Price elasticity of demand, 432–434, 457
  along straight-line demand curve, 443
  determinants of, 444–445, 457
  and total revenue, 437–440, 456, 457
Price elasticity of supply, 449, 457
Price floors, 99–105, 109
Price index, 134, 148. *See also* Consumer Price Index
Price inflation rates, 375
Price level(s), 134–140, 148
  actual, 384
  change in, and aggregate demand curve, 176–177
  expectations for, 193, 383–384, 386
  measurement of, 134–140
  and money supply, 318–325, 337–342
  vs. price, 134
  in recessionary gaps, 223
Price-level effect, 341–342
Price searchers, 551, 555, 590–591
Price takers, 522, 555, 590
  factor, 615–616
Primary reserve currency, 797–798
Prisoner of war (POW) camps, 286
Prisoner's dilemma, 581–584, 587–589
Private costs and benefits, 704–705
Private goods, 719
Private property rights, 711
Producers' (or sellers') surplus, 80–82, 89
  equilibrium in terms of, 80–82
  and international trade, 780–781
  and price floors, 103–104
Product demand, and labor unions, 638
Production, 494–499
  costs of, 501–515, 518
  externalities in, 706
  in long run, 495, 512–515, 518
  in short run, 495–496, 507, 517–518
Production function, 402–403, 414
  and capital, 408
  graphical representation of, 402–403
  and institutions, 410–411
  and labor, 406–407
  and *LRAS* curve, 404–405
Production possibilities frontier (PPF), 40–57
  bowed-outward, 41–44
  COVID-19 pandemic, 48–49
  economic concepts in, 45–49, 55
  and economic states, 213–215, 226

  model of, 51–52
  and opportunity costs, 40–44, 55
  purpose, 54
  and specialization and trade, 51–52, 55
  straight-line, 40–41
Productive efficiency, 47, 537–538
Productive inefficiency, 47
Productivity
  and aggregate supply, 191
  average, 499–500
  labor, 192, 500
  labor unions' effects on, 644–645
  marginal, 496
Productivity index, 499
Product markets, asymmetric information in, 723–724
Profit(s), 491, 678–679, 683
  accounting *vs.* economic, 492–493, 517, 678
  common misconceptions about, 540
  differences in, 542–543
  and discrimination, 543–544
  incentive *vs.* signal, 679
  as incentive *vs.* signal, 541
  labor unions' effects on, 647
  in monopolies, 553–556
  monopolistic competition, 573–574
  regulation of, 604–605
  theories of, 678–679
Profit maximization rule, 526–530, 545
  in monopolies, 553–556
Progressive income tax, 261–262
Prohibited prices, 97
Promoting from within, 630
Property rights
  and externalities, 711–713
  structures for, 410–411
Proportional income tax, 261–263
Proprietors' income, 161
Protectionist trade policy, 802
Public choice theory, 606, 732–737, 748–749
Public debt, 263
Public franchises, 550
Public goods, 718–723, 729
  culture, 721–722
  excludable, 719
  nonexcludable, 663, 719–723, 740–741
Public good-free rider justification, 663
Public-interest talk, 744
Public interest theory of regulation, 606
Purchasing power, 176

Purchasing power parity (PPP) theory, 796
Pure economic rent, 674–675

Q

Quantity demanded, 59, 115–116
  change in, 62–64, 179–180
  vs. demand, 59
  medical care, 118, 119
  and price, 60–61
Quantity supplied, 73
Quotas, 782–784, 789, 802

R

Radford, R.A., 286
Randomized Controlled Trial (RCT), 688
Rational expectations, 381–394
Rational ignorance, 737–740, 746–747
Rationing devices, 3, 5
  nonprice, 96
  price as, 94–95
Real balance effect, 176–178
Real business cycle theory, 394–396, 397, 764
Real GDP, 165–171
  AD/SRAS, 195, 196
  and business cycles, 167–168, 171
  change in quantity demanded of, 179–180
  changes over time, 168
  computing, 166
  and economic growth, 167, 407
  in economic states, 210–213
  general equation for, 166
  and loanable funds, 338
  Natural, 198, 210–213
  in simple quantity theory of money, 320–323
  tax revenues, 407
  usefulness of, 165
Real income, 136–137
Real interest rates, 343, 345, 670–671, 797
Reality, perceptions of, 379
Real rents, 677
Real wages, 189–190, 383
Recession, 168
Recessionary gaps, 210–213
  and monetary policy, 355–358
  self-regulating economies in, 216, 221–222, 225
  in simple Keynesian model, 246–247, 254
Recovery, in business cycle, 168
Reentrants, 142

Regressive income tax, 261–262
Regulation. *See* Government regulation
Regulatory lag, 605
Related goods, prices of, 65, 72
"Relation Between Unemployment and the Rate of Change of Money Wages in the United Kingdom, The" (Phillips), 374
Relative price, 105–110
  and monetary policy, 361
  and taxes, 106–108
Relative rank and status, 469
Religion, and monopoly, 562
Rent, 674–678, 683
Rental income, 161
Rent seeking
  in monopolies, 560–562, 569
  in special-interest groups, 744–747
Rent-seeking costs, 745
Required reserves, 302–303, 315
Required reserve ratio, 303, 315, 308, 316
Reserve(s), 302–303, 315
  in balance sheets, 294
  the Fed's role in, 300, 363
  market for, 308
Reserve currency, 797–798
Reserve deficient, 307
Reserve requirement, 302, 315
Residual claimants, 490
Resource allocative efficiency, 526–527, 564, 576
Resources, 2, 20
  prices of, and supply, 71
  unemployed, 47
Restraint of trade, 608
Retained earnings, 161
Return on capital goods, 669
Revaluation, 801
Revenue. *See specific types*
Ricardo, David, 423, 674, 675
Richardson, Gary, 760
Rise and Decline of Nations, The (Olson), 411
Risk, and interest rates, 670
Risk taking, and income inequality, 659
Rivalrous in consumption, 719
Rivlin, Alice, 35
Robinson-Patman Act (1936), 595
Robotics, 623–624
Romeo and Juliet (Shakespeare), 287
Romer, Paul, 409–410
Roundabout methods of production, 668–669
Rules-based (nonactivist) monetary policy, 359–367, 369
Rule of 70, 401

Index

S

Sales tax, 265
Samuelson, Paul, 374–375
SARS-CoV-2, 531. *See also* COVID-19 pandemic
Saving(s) in simple Keynesian model, 241
Saving domestic jobs argument for trade restrictions, 787
Savings deposits, 288
Say's law, 205–206, 208, 225, 230–231
Scarcity, 1–4, 21
    effects of, 3–4, 6
    in PPF framework, 45–47
School lotteries, 762
Schumpeter, Joseph A., 416–417, 429
Schwartz, Anna, 324
Science of exchange, 13
Scope and Method of Political Economy, The (Keynes), 237
Screening of potential employees, 630
Second-degree price discrimination, 563
Self-regulating economies, 215–224, 226
    changes in short and long run to, 219–221
    classical economics on, 221
    critique of, 229–238
    in inflationary gaps, 217
    in monetarism, 326
    policy implications of, 219
    in recessionary gaps, 216
Self-select, 762
Sellers, number of, 72, 584
Sellers' surplus. *See* Producers' surplus
Services, 157
Shake Shack, 85
Shakespeare, William, 287
Sherman Act (1890), 594
Shift factors, 67–68, 180
    for aggregate demand curves, 180–187
    for demand curves, 67–68
    for short-run aggregate supply curves, 191–192
    for supply curves, 71–73
Shirking, 489–490
Shortages (excess demand), 75
    in labor market, 211–213
    and price, 75–78
    and price ceilings, 96
Short run
    changes to self-regulating economies in, 219–221
    perfect competition in, 526–535, 546
    production in, 494–496, 507–508, 517
Short-run aggregate supply (*SRAS*), 181–182, 189–193, 195, 196, 202
Short-run aggregate supply (*SRAS*) curve, 189–193
    and job prospects, 198–199
    in monetarism, 326
    and price-level expectations, 383–384
    shift factors in, 191–193
    as upward sloping, 189–190
Short-run average total cost (*SRATC*) curve, 512
Short-run equilibrium, 193–197, 199–200, 202
Short-run market (industry) supply curve, 532–533
Short-run Phillips curve, 376–377
Short-run (firm) supply curve, 532–533
Shutdown decision, 530
Signal, profit as, 541, 679
Simester, Duncan, 471
Simon, Julian, 87
Simple deposit multiplier, 306
Simple-majority voting, 266, 735–736
Simple quantity theory of money, 320–323
Single-price monopolists, 598, 564, 568
Slope, 25
    of budget constraint, 480
    of curve, 26–27
    of line, 25–26
    vs. price electricity of demand, 434
Smith, Adam, 237, 401, 488
Smith, Vernon, 35
Social determinants of health, 693
Social-insurance justification, 663
Socially optimal amount (output), 706, 710
Social media
    and marginal costs, 508
    negative externalities of, 708
    and social tribes, 714–715
Social Security, 629–630
Social Security taxes, 629–630
Soda taxes, 107
Solow, Robert, 35, 374
Special-interest groups, 411–412, 414, 742–747, 750
Specialization
    and international trade, 775–776
    and patterns of sustainable trade, 357–358
    and trade, in PPF framework, 51–52, 55
Specialization-trade (*S-T*) case, 776–777
Speed limit laws, 589
Spending. *See* Government spending
    and aggregate demand, 181–182
    in computing of GDP, 156–160, 169–170
    money supply and velocity in, 186–188
    total, 182
    types of, 157
Spontaneous order, 86
Spring break, 243
Spurious correlation, 753
Stagflation, 375, 376
Starr, Ringo, 139
State of the economy, 1
Statistics discrepancies in, 164
    misleading, 654–655
Stein, Gertrude, 285
Stevenson, Betsey, 154–155
Sticky wages, 189–190
Stigler, George, 713
Store of value, 285
Straight Talk About Economic Literacy (Caplan), 739–740
Strikes, union, 641
Structural deficits, 262
Structural unemployment, 143
Studying
    and grades, 587–588
    and PPF, 50
Subsidies, 72, 112–114, 131
    and externalities, 711
    vs. tax deductions, 265
Substitutes
    and demand, 64–66
    and labor market, 622
    and labor unions, 637, 638
    in price elasticity of demand, 444
Substitution effect, 622
Sufficient conditions, 585
Sumner, Scott, 364
Sunk costs, 508–512, 518
Supermajority voting rule, 266
Supplier-set price, 545
Supply, 69–74, 89. *See also specific types*
    change in, 71–73
    definition of, 58, 68
    and demand, 74–88
    elasticity of, 449–452, 457
    language of, 75
    law of, 68–70
    vs. quantity supplied, 73
Supply curves, 69–73. *See also* Aggregate supply curve
    market, 71
    shift factors for, 71–73
    short-run (firm), 532–533
    short-run market (industry), 532–533
    as upward sloping, 70–71
    upward sloping market, 535
Supply schedules, 70
Supply shocks, 192
Supply-side fiscal policy, 276–280, 282
Surplus (excess supply), 75, 89
    budget, 262, 281
    in labor market, 211–213
    negative visualization, 83
    and price, 75
    and price floor, 99
    trade, 791
Sustainable specialization and trade, patterns of, 357–358
Sutter, John, 324

T

Taft-Hartley Act, 639
Tariffs, 781–782, 788
    benefits and costs of, 780–782
    in fixed exchange rate system, 802
    reciprocity in, 788
Tarshis, Lorie, 238
Tax(es), 281. *See also specific types*
    and elasticity, 441, 452–458
    expectations of future rates, 279
    and externalities, 711
    in income calculation, 653
    in Laffer curve, 277–279
    placement *vs.* payment of, 452–453
    and production costs, 515
    and supply, 72
    and taxes, 106–108
Tax base, 278–279
Tax deductions, 265
Tax revenues, 261
    and degree of elasticity, 455–456
    in Laffer curve, 277–279
Taylor, John, 363
Taylor rule, 363
Tea Act, 551
Teams, 489–490
Technology, 47
    digital revolution in, 534
    and economic growth, 408–409
    in PPF framework, 47–48
    and production costs, 516
    and supply, 72
    workers displaced by, 640
Technology coefficient, 408–409
Terms of loans, 670

Theories, 16, 21. *See also specific theories*
Third-degree price discrimination, 564, 567
Third party, 117
Thurow, Lester, 36
Ticket prices
  airline, 60
  concert, 139, 442
Tie-in sales, 97
Time
  and price elasticity of demand, 445
  and price elasticity of supply, 449–451
Time deposits, 288
Time preference, positive rate of, 668
Tolls, 126, 127
Total costs, 491–492, 497, 621
Total expenditures, 251
Total expenditures curve, 250–251
Total expenditures–total production framework, 248–257
Total fixed costs, production, 501–503
Total physical product, 495
Total production, 251
Total revenue (TR)
  of business firms, 491
  defined, 437
  and price elasticity of demand, 437, 456, 457
Total spending, 182
Total surplus, 80
Total utility, 460–461, 466
Total variable costs of production, 502
Total wage bill, 636
Townshend Acts, 551
Tradable pollution permits (cap and trade), 716–718, 729
Trade (exchange), 13, 21. *See also* International trade
  entrepreneurs' effects on, 680–681
  medium of exchange in, 285
  and price ceilings, 96
  and price floors, 99
  restraint of, 594
  and specialization, 51–52, 55
Trade balance, 791
Trade deficits, 791
Trade restrictions, 779–788
  arguments for implementing, 784–785
  benefits and costs of, 780–784
  protectionist, 802

Trade surplus, 791
Training, and income inequality, 659–660
Transaction costs, 285–286, 680
Transactions money, 288
Transfer payments, 153, 157, 654
Transfer-promoting policies, 411–412
Transitivity, 484–485
Transmission lag, 272
Transmission mechanisms, 348–355
Treatment group, 689
Tribes, 714
Troost, William, 760
Trough, of business cycle, 168
Trusts, 594
Tuition, 445–446
Tullock, Gordon, 422, 423, 561
Tversky, Amos, 474

U

Uber and Airbnb, case of, 14
U-HAUL rates and demand, 111–112, 131
Ultimatum game, 474
Uncertainty, 678, 681–682
Underemployed workers, 145
Underground economy, 153
Undervalued currency, 799–800
Undistributed profits, 161
Unemployed persons, 140–141, 144–146
Unemployed resources, 47
Unemployment, 140–149
  reasons for, 142
  types of, 143–144
Unemployment rate, 141–149
  common misconceptions about, 142, 213–215
  cyclical, 145–147
  definition of, 141
  natural, 144, 213–215, 224
  in Phillips curve, 374–381
  reasons for decline in, 148
Unintended effects, 12–13, 98
Union-nonunion wage gap, 643–644
Unions. *See* Labor unions
Union shops, 639
Unit cost (average total cost), 503
Unit elastic demand, 435, 440
Unit of account, 285
Universities. *See* Colleges
Upward-sloping market supply curves, 535

Upward-sloping supply curve. *See* Supply curves
Used goods, 153
U.S. Supreme Court, 123
Util(s), 460
Utility, 1, 2, 460–469
  marginal, 461–463, 477–478
  maximizing, 466
  total, 460–461, 466
Utility theory, 460–463

V

Value-added tax (VAT), 263–265
Value marginal product, 613, 632
Variable costs, 497
Variable inputs, 494
Vault cash, 302
Velocity
  and equation of exchange, 319
  in monetarism, 326
  and money supply, 186–187
  in simple quantity theory of money, 320–323
Vertical mergers, 598
Vietnam War Draft Lottery, 761–762
Voluntary agreements, 712–713
Voting, 733–749
  efficiency, 740–742
  median voter model of, 733–735, 749
  nonexcludable public goods, 740–741
  and rational ignorance, 737–740, 749
  and special-interest groups, 742–747, 750
Voting rules, 266, 735

W

Wage(s)
  classical economics on, 209, 225
  flexibility of, 256
  Keynes on, 231–232, 236–238, 257
  labor unions' effects on, 643–644, 647
  minimum, 100–101
  nominal, 189–190
  real, 189–190, 383
  sticky, 189–190
Wage discrimination, 660–661
Wage-employment trade-off, 636–637

Wage inflation, 374–375
Wage rates
  changes in, 191–192
  equilibrium, 624–626
  Keynes on, 231–232, 257
  and labor markets, 625–626, 631, 632
  labor unions' effects on, 636–637, 639–640, 643–644
Wagner, Richard, 274–275
Wait-and-see lag, 272
Wants, double coincidence of, 286
Warehouse receipts, 290–291
Wealth, 183
  and consumption, 183
  and happiness, 154–156
  monetary, 176
Wealth of Nations (Smith), 237, 401, 612
Weather, and housing prices, 468–469
Weidenbaum, Murray, 35
Welfare assistance, 663–664
Well-being, subjective, 155
Wheeler-Lea Act (1938), 595
Williams, Walter, 35
Wolfers, Justin, 155
Wonderful Wizard of Oz, The (Baum), 292
Worker misperceptions, 190
Work-leisure tradeoffs, 659
World Rushed In, The (Holiday), 324
W-X-Y-Z explanation, 186

X

X-inefficiency, 562

Y

Yale University, 5
Yellow Brick Road, 292

Z

Zero crowding out, 269–271
Zero economic profit, 493
Zero marginal cost, 508
Zero price *vs.* zero cost, 6
Zizzo, Daniel, 469
Zywicki, Todd, 421